Telecommunication Laws in Europe

Sixth Edition

Telecommunication Laws in Europe

Law and Regulation of Electronic Communications in Europe

Sixth Edition

Edited by
Joachim Scherer
Baker & McKenzie
Frankfurt

BAKER & McKENZIE   Bloomsbury Professional

Bloomsbury Professional Limited,
Maxwelton House,
41–43 Boltro Road,
Haywards Heath,
West Sussex RH16 1BJ

A CIP Catalogue record for this book is available from the British Library.

ISBN: 978 1 84766 885 1

Typeset by Columns Design XML Ltd, Reading
Printed and bound in Great Britain by CPI Group (UK) Ltd, Croydon, CR0 4YY

Foreword

EU regulation has delivered for the European citizen, and the European economy. Starting with the liberalisation of telecommunications services in the 1990s, the 1998 Regulatory Package was heavily revised in 2002 and 2009. All this together has delivered competition, choice, and lower prices.

Any regulatory framework needs to adapt, taking into account both market and technology developments. That includes in particular technological convergence and the dramatic increase in Internet usage, including the move to 'superfast' broadband networks that power so many new high-speed services. More and more people and businesses are taking those services for granted, and they could underpin the European economy of tomorrow.

The digital revolution has transformed many areas of our life: economic, social, cultural, educational and governmental. It is stimulating innovation in almost every economic sector, with new services and products dreamed up daily. No wonder the digital economy is growing seven times faster than overall economic growth.

This development has been driven by interplay at three levels: communications networks, content and technology. Major factors have been:

- better access to communications networks, for suppliers as well as users of services. They are more available, more affordable, higher quality and with greater choice, not least thanks to the liberalisation that resulted in increased competition and new innovative services;
- technological advances that brought increased capacity (bandwidth); and
- an explosion of content, including user-generated content.

These three factors interact and stimulate each other. And we face the latest in a series of waves of innovation, as there is a growing use of new apps including social networking, as cloud computing entering the mainstream, and as people increasingly use tablets and mobiles to go online.

The liberalisation of communications networks and services has meant greater freedom both for providers and users of networks, services and content – unleashing great creativity and innovation. However, this greater freedom and choice in the market place doesn't mean the absence of regulations: sometimes, the opposite. In fact, boosting competition often calls for a degree of sector-specific regulation to guarantee a level playing field, such as regarding access to bandwidth. In addition, regulation remains important, for instance, to ensure users can do business and conclude agreements online just as they might offline, or to make the online world a safer, securer place that users can trust.

The digital environment doesn't see national borders: but different legal and regulatory standards can create artificial barriers, even within the EU's single market. In the EU, our shared attitude and unity of purpose have made it possible in a relatively short time to adopt a coherent and effective set of laws – though there is still more to be done.

The Digital Agenda for Europe was adopted in 2010, as an integral part of the Europe 2020 strategy, to stimulate the digital economy and address societal challenges through information and communication technologies. The Digital Agenda announced a total of 101 actions, including 16 key actions, spread over 7 areas:

- a vibrant digital single market;
- interoperability and standards;
- trust and security;
- fast and ultrafast internet access;
- research and innovation;
- enhancing digital literacy; and
- ICT-enabled benefits for EU society.

The Digital Agenda has met many of its targets and is on track to meet many others. Regular Internet usage is rising steadily, especially among disadvantaged groups. The number of citizens who have never used the Internet is decreasing. Similarly, online buying continues to increase although the pace of growth in cross-border e-Commerce is too slow. High-speed broadband shows the first signs of taking off, including ultra-fast connections above 100 Mbps. However, significant differences remain among different Member States in terms of network coverage, speeds and uptake rates. European policy action is needed to minimise and eliminate to achieve a true Digital Single Market.

Although in many areas developments are very promising, we cannot afford to rest on our laurels, or be complacent. The digital economy is still held back by a patchy policy framework across Europe. So I will be proposing new initiatives to re-focus the Digital Agenda, increase investment in broadband and maximise the digital sector's contribution to European economic recovery. For example, we will seek to make deploying high speed electronic communications infrastructure more efficient and less costly, and put forward measures in the areas of broadband use, net neutrality, wireless roll-out and spectrum use, and cybersecurity.

The digital economy is a vibrant and growing part of our world. But it does not exist in a legal vacuum. The transposition of the EU regulatory framework for electronic communications by all Member States was completed at the end of 2012. Joachim Scherer has done a remarkable job in bringing together the analysis of this regulatory framework, as well as the relevant laws in EU Member States and non-EU countries. I hope this stands as an important reference for legislators, law professionals, businessmen, students and citizens.

Neelie Kroes
Vice President, European Commission
Responsible for the Digital Agenda

Preface

Telecommunications networks and services are the backbone of the information society. Their development, operation and constant innovation requires a legal and regulatory framework which ensures fair and effective competition and consumer protection and safeguards public interest objectives, such as confidentiality of communications and the protection of privacy.

More than 25 years ago, the European Community embarked on an ambitious course: to liberalise the telecommunications markets in the Member States and to harmonise the conditions for market entry and competition with a view to creating a single European market for telecommunication networks and services. On 1 January 1998, the telecommunication markets in the European Union were fully liberalised. Ten years later, in November 2009, the EU adopted its 2009 Regulatory Package of legislative measures for the electronic communications sector. The 2009 Regulatory Package substantially amends the rules that were adopted in 2002 – it is now the third generation of EU law which has been put in place since the European Commission's initial liberalisation and harmonisation measures.

The 2009 Regulatory Package introduces changes to the previous set of rules with a view to improving the independence of the national regulatory authorities, enhancing regulatory consistency between Member States (by establishing a complex system of regulatory governance), promoting investment in next generation access networks, protecting consumer rights, securing 'net neutrality' and enhancing data protection.

The Regulatory Package should have been transposed into national law by the end of May 2011, but it has taken several Member States much longer to take the necessary steps. Meanwhile, many European States which are not – or not yet – members of the European Union, have adapted their national legislation and their regulatory approaches to the EU Framework.

The objective of this book – as of the previous editions – is to provide an overview of both the emerging pan-European legislative framework for electronic communications and its application at national level in the 27 EU Member States and seven non-EU Member States, including one acceding and several candidate countries. Thirty-four country chapters, all of which follow the EU Regulatory Framework's structure and use its legal categories as a frame of reference and analysis, highlight the common characteristics of national laws and regulation of electronic communications, as well as the differences which remain, despite the EU's ongoing harmonisation efforts.

The analyses of the European Framework and the various country chapters are complemented by chapters on EU Competition Law and on EU Data Protection and Privacy as they relate to the telecommunications sector, an analysis of the international legal framework for telecommunications under the ITU and WTO rules, and a chapter on compliance and risk management. Establishing effective compliance programmes for companies, including telecommunications companies, has never been more important. The chapter 'Compliance and Risk Management', which is included in this book for the first time, addresses two areas of particular relevance for the electronic communications sector: compliance with anti-bribery and corruption rules, and compliance with export controls and trade sanctions.

The contributions to the sixth edition of this book have again been prepared by members of Baker & McKenzie's European IT/Communications Law Practice Group and by telecommunication law experts from correspondent law firms in Bulgaria, Croatia, Cyprus, Denmark, Estonia, Finland, Greece, Ireland, Latvia, Lithuania, Macedonia, Malta, Norway, Portugal, Romania, the Slovak Republic and Slovenia.

The editor gratefully acknowledges the invaluable editorial assistance of Caroline Heinickel.

The law is as at 15 January 2013, save as otherwise stated.

Joachim Scherer, Frankfurt am Main

1 February 2013

Contents

Part 2
International Regulatory Framework

Part 4
Telecommunication Laws in Non-EU Member States

List of Contributors

AUSTRIA

Franz-Josef Arztmann and Gregor Klammer
Baker & McKenzie – Diwok Hermann Petsche Rechtsanwälte GmbH
Schottenring 25
1010 Vienna
Austria

BELGIUM

Daniel Fesler and Elisabeth Dehareng
Baker & McKenzie CVBA/SCRL
Louizalaan 149 Avenue Louise
Eleventh Floor
Brussels 1050
Belgium

BULGARIA

Violetta Kunze and Lilia Kisseva
Djingov, Gouginski, Kyutchukov & Velichkov
10 Tsar Osvoboditel Blvd.
Sofia 1000
Bulgaria

COMPLIANCE AND RISK MANAGEMENT

Sunny Mann, Laura Philippou and Mayuko Roald
Baker & McKenzie LLP
100 New Bridge Street
London EC4V 6JA
United Kingdom

CROATIA

Iskra Bubaš and Igor Mucalo
Veršić Marušić Law Office
Trg N. Š. Zrinskog 9
HR-10000 Zagreb
Croatia

CYPRUS

Adamos K Adamides
Scordis, Papapetrou & Co LLC
(incorporating by way of merger Adamos K Adamides & Co),
Advocates & Legal Consultants
1st floor, 35, Thekla Lyssiotis Street,
Eagle Star House
Limassol 3030
Cyprus

CZECH REPUBLIC

Tomas Skoumal, Petra Ledvinkova and Patrik Kastner
Baker & McKenzie, v.o.s., advokátní kancelář
Klimentská 46
110 02 Prague 1
Czech Republic

DATA PROTECTION AND PRIVACY

Holger Lutz and Caroline Heinickel
Baker & McKenzie
Partnerschaft von Rechtsanwälten, Wirtschaftsprüfern, Steuerberatern und Solicitors
Bethmannstrasse 50–54
60311 Frankfurt/Main
Germany

DENMARK

Henning Hansen and Niels M Andersen
Bech-Bruun law firm
Langelinie Allé 35
2100 Copenhagen
Denmark

ESTONIA

**Pirkko-Liis Harkmaa, Katri
Paas-Mohando and Martin-Kaspar Sild**
LAWIN
Niguliste 4
Tallinn, 10130
Estonia

EU COMPETITION LAW IN THE
TELECOMMUNICATIONS
SECTOR

Keith Jones
Baker & McKenzie LLP
100 New Bridge Street
London EC4V 6JA
United Kingdom

EU ELECTRONIC
COMMUNICATIONS LAW
AND POLICY

Joachim Scherer
Baker & McKenzie
Partnerschaft von Rechtsanwälten,
Wirtschaftsprüfern, Steuerberatern und
Solicitors
Bethmannstrasse 50–54
60311 Frankfurt/Main
Germany

FINLAND

**Henriikka Piekkala and Markus von
Schrowe**
Attorneys at Law Borenius Ltd
Yrjönkatu 13 A
FI-00120 Helsinki
Finland

FRANCE

Christian Blomet and Magalie Dansac
Baker & McKenzie SCP
1 rue Paul Baudry
75008 Paris
France

GERMANY

Joachim Scherer and Caroline Heinickel
Baker & McKenzie
Partnerschaft von Rechtsanwälten,
Wirtschaftsprüfern, Steuerberatern und
Solicitors
Bethmannstrasse 50–54
60311 Frankfurt/Main
Germany

GREECE

Alkistis Christofilou
Rokas
I.K. Rokas & Partners Law Firm
25 & 25A Boukourestiou Str.
106 71 Athens
Greece

HUNGARY

**Tamás Kaibinger, Emese Szitási, and
Péter Vörös, with Ines Radmilovic**
Kajtár Takács Hegymegi-Barakonyi
Baker & McKenzie Ügyvédi Iroda
Dorottya utca 6.
1051 Budapest
Hungary

IRELAND

Claire Waterson
William Fry Solicitors
Fitzwilton House
Wilton Place
Dublin 2
Ireland

John Handoll
Amarchand Mangaldas
Amarchand Towers
216 Okhla Industrial Estate, Phase III
New Delhi 110020
India

ITALY

Raffaele Giarda and Andrea Mezzetti
Baker & McKenzie
Viale di Villa Massimo, 57
Rome 00161
Italy

ITU/WTO

Joachim Scherer
Baker & McKenzie
Partnerschaft von Rechtsanwälten,
Wirtschaftsprüfern, Steuerberatern und
Solicitors
Bethmannstrasse 50–54
60311 Frankfurt/Main
Germany

Serge Pannatier
Baker & McKenzie Geneva
Rue Pedro-Meylan 5
Geneva 1208
Switzerland

LATVIA
Sarmis Spilbergs
LAWIN
Elizabetes 15
Riga LV-1010
Latvia

LITHUANIA
Jaunius Gumbis and Tomas Kamblevicius
LAWIN Lideika, Petrauskas, Valiūnas ir partneriai
Jogailos 9
LT-01116 Vilnius
Lithuania

LUXEMBOURG
Audrey Rustichelli and Raphaël Collin
Baker & McKenzie
10 – 12 Boulevard Roosevelt
2450 Luxembourg
Luxembourg

MACEDONIA
Metodija Velkov
Polenak Law Firm
98 Orce Nikolov
1000 Skopje
Macedonia

MALTA
Paul Micallef Grimaud
Ganado Advocates
171 & 176, Old Bakery Street
Valletta VLT 1455
Malta

NETHERLANDS
Robert Boekhorst and Kevin van 't Klooster
Baker & McKenzie
Claude Debussylaan 54
1082 MD Amsterdam
The Netherlands

NORWAY
Espen Sandvik and Nicolai Stenersen
Arntzen de Besche Advokatfirma AS
Bygdøy allé 2
P.O. Box 2734 Solli
0204 Oslo
Norway

POLAND
Justyna Michalak-Królicka and Natalia Marczuk
Baker & McKenzie Krzyzowski i Wspólnicy Spólka Komandytowa
Rondo ONZ 1
Warsaw 00–124
Poland

PORTUGAL
António de Mendonça Raimundo and Miriam Brice
Albuquerque & Associados
Sociedade de Advogados RL
Calçada Bento Rocha Cabral, 1
1250–047 Lisboa
Portugal

ROMANIA
Horatiu Dumitru and Bogdan-Petru Mihai
Musat & Asociatii
43 Aviatorilor Blvd, 1st District
Code 011853, Bucharest
Romania

RUSSIA
Edward Bekeschenko
Baker & McKenzie – CIS, Limited
Sadovaya Plaza, 12th Floor
7 Dolgorukovskaya Street
Moscow 127006
Russia

SLOVAK REPUBLIC
Lubomir Marek
Marek & Partners
Advokati/Attorneys-at-Law
Palisady 36
811 06 Bratislava
Slovak Republic

SLOVENIA
Jure Levovnik and Mitja Podpečan
Jadek & Pensa
Tavčarjeva 6,
1000 Ljubljana
Slovenija

SPAIN
Raul Rubio
Baker & McKenzie Madrid SLP
Paseo de la Castellana, 92
Madrid 28046
Spain

SWEDEN
Stefan Brand and Filip Skoglund
Baker & McKenzie Advokatbyrå KB
PO Box 180
Vasagatan 7, Floor 8
Stockholm SE-101 23
Sweden

SWITZERLAND
Markus Berni and Kathleen Weislehner
Baker & McKenzie
Holbeinstrasse 30
Zurich 8034
Switzerland

TURKEY
Birturk Aydin and Hakki Can Yildiz
Esin Attorney Partnership, Istanbul,
Member Firm of Baker & McKenzie
International, a Swiss Verein
Levent Cad. Yeni Sulun Sok No 1
34330 1 Levent – Besiktas
Istanbul
Turkey

UKRAINE
Vyacheslav Yakymchuk and Olena Kuchynska
Baker & McKenzie
Renaissance Business Center
24 Vorovskoho Street
Kyiv 01054
Ukraine

UNITED KINGDOM
Peter Strivens, Richard Pike, Ben Slinn and Keith Jones
Baker & McKenzie LLP
100 New Bridge Street
London EC4V 6JA
United Kingdom

Key EU Directives

DIRECTIVE	FULL TITLE	OJ REFERENCE
Access Directive	Directive 2002/19/EC of the European Parliament and of the Council of 7 March 2002 on access to, and interconnection of, electronic communications networks and associated facilities	[2002] OJ L108/7
Authorisation Directive	Directive 2002/20/EC of the European Parliament and of the Council of 7 March 2002 on the authorisation of electronic communications networks and services	[2002] OJ L108/21
Framework Directive	Directive 2002/21/EC of the European Parliament and of the Council of 7 March 2002 on a common regulatory framework for electronic communications networks and services;	[2002] OJ L108/33
Universal Service Directive	Directive 2002/22/EC of the European Parliament and of the Council of 7 March 2002 on universal service and users' rights relating to electronic communications networks and services	[2002] OJ L108/51
E-Privacy Directive	Directive 2002/58/EC of the European Parliament and of the Council of 12 July 2002 concerning the processing of personal data and the protection of privacy in the electronic communications sector	[2002] OJ L201/37
Data Protection Directive	Directive 95/46/EC of the European Parliament and of the Council of 24 October 1995 on the protection of individuals with regard to the processing of personal data and on the free movement of such data	[1995] OJ L281/31

DIRECTIVE	FULL TITLE	OJ REFERENCE
Electronic Communications Competition Directive	Commission Directive 2002/77/EC of 16 September 2002 on competition in the markets for electronic communications networks and services	[2002] OJ L249/21
Data Retention Directive	Directive 2006/24/EC of the European Parliament and of the Council of 15 March 2006 on the retention of data generated or processed in connection with the provision of publicly available electronic communications services or of public communications networks and amending Directive 2002/58/EC	[2006] OJ L105/54
Audiovisual Media Services Directive	Directive 2010/13/EU of the European Parliament and of the Council of 10 March 2010 on the coordination of certain provisions laid down by law, regulation or administrative action in Member States concerning the provision of audiovisual media services	[2010] OJ L95/1
Citizens' Rights Directive	Directive 2009/136/EC of the European Parliament and the Council of 25 November 2009 amending Directive 2002/22/EC on universal service and users' rights relating to electronic communications networks and services, Directive 2002/58/EC concerning the processing of personal data and the protection of privacy in the electronic communications sector and Regulation (EC) No 2006/2004 on cooperation between national authorities responsible for the enforcement of consumer protection law	[2009] OJ L337/11

DIRECTIVE	FULL TITLE	OJ REFERENCE
Better Regulation Directive	Directive 2009/140/EC of the European Parliament and of the Council of 25 November 2009 amending Directives 2002/21/EC on a common regulatory framework for electronic communications networks and services, 2002/19/EC on access to, and interconnection of, electronic communications networks and associated facilities, and 2002/20/EC on the authorisation of electronic communications networks and services	[2009] OJ L337/37

Key EU Regulations, Decisions and Recommendations

REGULATION, DECISION OR RECOMMENDATION	FULL TITLE	OJ REFERENCE
Roaming Regulation	Regulation (EU) No 513/2012 of the European Parliament and of the Council of 13 June 2012 on roaming on public mobile communications networks within the Union (recast)	[2012] OJ L172/10
BEREC Regulation	Regulation (EC) No 1211/2009 of the European Parliament and of the Council of 25 November 2009 establishing the Body of European Regulators for Electronic Communications (BEREC) and the Office	[2009] OJ L337/1
Merger Regulation	Council Regulation No 139/2004 on the control of concentrations between undertakings	[2004] OJ L24/1
Dual Use Regulation	Council Regulation (EC) No 428/2009 of 5 May 2009 setting up a Community regime for the control of exports, transfer, brokering and transit of dual-use items (as amended)	[2009] OJ L134/1

REGULATION, DECISION OR RECOMMENDATION	FULL TITLE	OJ REFERENCE
Block Exemption Regulations	Commission Regulation No 772/2004 on the application of Article 81(3) of the Treaty to categories of technology transfer agreements	[2004] OJ L123/11
	Commission Regulation No 2790/1999 on the application of Article 81(3) of the Treaty to categories of vertical agreements and concerted practices	[1999] OJ L336/21
	Commission Regulation No 2659/2000 on the application of Article 81(3) to categories of research and development agreements	[2000] OJ L304/07
	Commission Regulation No 2658/2000 on the application of Article 81(3) to categories of specialisation agreements	[2000] OJ L304/03
Market Recommendation	Commission Recommendation 2007/879/EC of 17 December 2007 on relevant product and service markets within the electronic communications sector susceptible to ex ante regulation in accordance with Directive 2002/21/EC of the European Parliament and of the Council on a common regulatory framework for electronic communications networks and services	[2007] OJ L344/65
NGA Recommendation	Commission Recommendation 2010/572/EU of 20 September 2010 on regulated access to Next Generation Access Networks (NGA)	[2010] OJ L251/35
Termination Rate Recommendation	Commission Recommendation of 7 May 2009 on the Regulatory Treatment of Fixed and Mobile Termination Rates in the EU	[2009] OJ L124/67
Accounting Recommendation	Commission Recommendation of 19 September 2005 on accounting separation and cost accounting systems under the regulatory framework for electronic communications	[2005] OJ L266/64

REGULATION, DECISION OR RECOMMENDATION	FULL TITLE	OJ REFERENCE
Decision 2002/622/EC	Commission Decision No. 2002/622/EC of 26 July 2002 establishing a Radio Spectrum Policy Group	[2002] OJ L198/49
Radio Spectrum Decision	Decision No 676/2002/EC of the European Parliament and of the Council of 7 March 2002 on a regulatory framework for radio spectrum policy in the European Community (Radio Spectrum Decision)	[2002] OJ L108/1
Radio Spectrum Policy Programme Decision	Decision No 243/2012/EU of the European Parliament and of the Council of 14 March 2012 establishing a multi-annual radio spectrum policy programme	[2012] OJ L81/7

Part I
Telecommunication Law and Policy of the European Union

Electronic Communication Law and Policy of the European Union[1]

Joachim Scherer
Baker & McKenzie, Frankfurt

INTRODUCTION

1.1   In the 21st century, electronic communication plays a key role in creating and exchanging information and knowledge, speeding up economic recovery from the financial and economic crises of the recent past and laying the foundations for a sustainable future. Electronic communications networks are the backbone of the 'information society'. The European Commission's ('the Commission') 'Digital Agenda for Europe'[2] is one of the political initiatives of the Europe 2020 strategy[3] and defines the key enabling role that the use of information and communication technologies (ICT) play for the European Union's overarching objectives of 'smart, sustainable and inclusive growth'.[4] The 'Digital Agenda for Europe' is composed of seven 'pillars': 'Digital Single Market',[5] 'Interoperability & Standards',[6] 'Trust & Security',[7] 'Fast and ultra-fast Internet access',[8] 'Research and Innovation',[9] 'Enhancing digital literacy, skills and inclusion',[10] and 'ICT enabled benefits for EU

---

1   Editing of this chapter closed on 28 December 2012. The author would like to thank Caroline Heinickel for her valuable contribution in drafting this chapter.
2   See the Digital Agenda's website https://ec.europa.eu/digital-agenda/ (accessed on 30 November 2012).
3   Communication from the Commission, 'Europe 2020 A strategy for smart, sustainable and inclusive growth', COM(2010) 2020 final, 3 March 2010.
4   See Communication from the Commission, 'Europe 2020 A strategy for smart, sustainable and inclusive growth', COM(2010) 2020 final, 3 March,2011.
5   Pillar I aims at supporting the music download business, facilitating online payments by establishing a 'single area' and enhancing the protection of consumers in cyberspace through an update to the EU market rules for the 'digital area'.
6   Pillar II aims at improving the setting of standards and increasing interoperability for ICT equipment and services.
7   Pillar III aims at enhancing online security and at furthering data protection.
8   Pillar IV aims at introducing Internet download rates of 30 mbps for all EU citizens and at achieving a subscription rate of at least 50 per cent of EU households to Internet connections above 500 mbps by 2020 through stimulating investments and radio spectrum regulation measures.
9   Pillar V aims at coordinating and furthering ICT research and development and at enhancing private funding.
10   Pillar VI aims at eliminating the 'Digital Divide' still present in the EU to ensure that all EU citizens can fully participate in an ICT-based society.

society'.[11] It covers EU as well as international dimensions of these 'pillars' such as, eg the promotion of the internationalisation of Internet governance.

1.2   In the early 1980s, the telecommunication sector in Europe was still characterised by exclusive rights of national telecommunication organisations ('TOs') in almost all Member States of the European Union to provide telecommunication networks and services. In 1987, the Commission issued its Green Paper on the development of the common market for telecommunication services and equipment, and started a Europe-wide debate on the liberalisation and harmonisation of the telecommunication regulatory environment, with the objective of adapting it to the requirements of a single Community-wide market.

One of the first landmarks in liberalising the telecommunication markets was the abolition of the TOs' national monopolies for terminal equipment on the basis of the Commission Directive on competition in the markets for telecommunication terminal equipment ('Terminal Equipment Directive'),[12] which was repealed in 2008 by the Commission Directive on competition in the markets in telecommunications terminal equipment, once liberalisation had been achieved.[13] The Services Directive of 28 June 1990 which required Member States to remove 'all special or exclusive rights' that had been granted to TOs 'for the supply of telecommunication services other than voice telephony' (Article 2(1)),[14] was a further step in the liberalisation process. It was subsequently amended to include the abolishment of exclusive rights for the provision of satellite services,[15] to open cable television networks for use for the provision of 'already liberalized' telecommunications services[16] and, in 1996, to oblige Member States to lift all restrictions on operators of mobile and personal communications systems with regard to the establishment of their own infrastructure, the use of infrastructures provided by third parties, and the sharing of infrastructure, other facilities and sites.[17]

The liberalisation process culminated with the Full Competition Directive,[18] which implemented the full liberalisation of telecommunication networks and services with effect from 1 January 1998. The Full Competition Directive required Member States to take the necessary steps to ensure that markets were fully open by

---

11   Pillar VII incorporates social and public goals such as the use of ICT reduce energy consumption (e.g. through smart grid technology) or furthering e-health access.

12   Directive 88/301/EEC [1988] OJ L131/73: for further details see fifth edition of this publication, para 1.16.

13   Commission Directive 2008/63/EC of 20 June 2008 on competition in the markets in telecommunications terminal equipment [2008] OJ L162/20.

14   Commission Directive 90/388/EEC of 28 June 1990 on competition in the markets for telecommunications services [1990] OJ L192/10: for further details see fourth edition of this book, paras 1.19 et seq.

15   Commission Directive 94/46/EC of 13 October 1994 amending Directive 88/301/EEC and Directive 90/388/EEC in particular with regard to satellite communications [1994] OJ L268/15, see fourth edition of this book, para 1.23.

16   Commission Directive 95/51/EC of 18 October 1995 amending Directive 90/388/EEC with regard to the abolition of the restrictions on the use of cable television networks for the provision of already liberalised telecommunications services [1995] OJ L256/49: for further details see fourth edition of this book, paras 1.24 et seq.

17   Commission Directive 96/2/EC of 16 January 1996 amending Directive 90/388/EEC with regard to mobile and personal communications [1996] OJ L20/59: for further details see fourth edition of this book, paras 1.27 et seq.

18   Commission Directive 96/19/EC of 13 March 1996 amending Directive 90/388/EEC with regard to the implementation of full competition in telecommunications markets [1996] OJ L74/13: for further details see fourth edition of this book, paras 1.30 et seq.

1 January 1998.[19] Besides these liberalisation-related provisions, the Directive established basic principles and procedural requirements for licensing new entrants to both the voice telephony and the telecommunication infrastructure ('network') markets[20] and introduced basic rules on interconnection.[21]

1.3   The liberalisation process was complemented by the Council's harmonisation directives which aimed at enabling and facilitating the provision of pan-European telecommunications services. These include: the ONP Framework Directive (1990),[22] which was intended to facilitate access by private companies to public telecommunication networks and to certain public telecommunication services; the Leased Lines Directive (1992),[23] which aimed at ensuring the EU-wide availability of a minimum set of leased lines with harmonised technical characteristics; and the Voice Telephony Directive (1995),[24] which was replaced, in 1998, by the Directive of the European Parliament and of the Council 'on the application of open network provision (ONP) to voice telephony and on universal service for telecommunication in a competitive environment.[25] It continued to pursue the twofold aim of the preceding Directive – to ensure the availability of good quality fixed telephony services throughout the EU and to define the set of services to which all users should have access in the context of universal service.

In July 1997, the ONP Framework Directive (1990) and the Leased Lines Directive (1992) were adapted to the 'competitive environment in telecommunications'. Different from the ONP Framework Directive (1990), the ONP Framework Directive (1997)[26] applied not only to the TOs but to all organisations providing public telecommunication networks or services, taking into account an organisation's position in the relevant market. The Directive followed three main approaches for the safeguarding of effective competition in the internal market: it set out the harmonised basic principles to be followed by ONP conditions, it encouraged technical harmonisation by market players on a voluntary basis by providing for the Commission to publish a list of technical European standards drawn up as a basis for harmonised technical interfaces or service features for ONP;[27] and it ensured the

---

19   With the possibility of transitional periods of up to two years (for Member States with less developed networks) or up to five years (for Member States with very small networks).
20   For details see fourth edition of this book, paras 1.31 et seq.
21   For details see fourth edition of this book, para 1.33.
22   Council Directive 90/387/EEC of 28 June 1990 on the establishment of the internal market for telecommunications services through the implementation of open network provision [1990] OJ L192/1: for further details see fourth edition of this book, paras 1.37 et seq.
23   Council Directive 92/44/EEC of 5 June 1992 on the application of open network provision to leased lines [1992] OJ L165/27: for further details see 4th edition, paras 1.42 et seq.
24   Directive 95/62/EC of the European Parliament and of the Council of 13 December 1995 on the application of open network provision (ONP) to voice telephony [1995] OJ L321/6: for further details see fourth edition of this book, paras 1.44 et seq..
25   Directive 98/10/EC of the European Parliament and of the Council of 26 February 1998 on the application of open network provision (ONP) to voice telephony and on universal service for telecommunications in a competitive environment ('ONP Voice Telephony Directive (1998)') [1998] OJ L101/24: for further details see fifth edition of this book, para 1.25.
26   Directive 97/51/EC of the European Parliament and of the Council of 6 October 1997 amending Council Directives 90/387/EEC and 92/44/EEC for the purpose of adaptation to a competitive environment in telecommunications ('ONP Framework Directive (1997)') [1997] OJ L295/23: for further details see fifth edition of this book, paras 1.26 et seq.
27   However, Commission or Council were entitled to make the implementation of such standards or specifications compulsory if the voluntary approach had failed.

effective structural separation of the NRAs from activities that were associated with ownership or control of telecommunication networks, services or equipment.[28]

1.4   In June 1997 the European Parliament and the Council adopted the Directive on interconnection in telecommunication ('Interconnection Directive').[29] The Directive established obligations to grant and rights to obtain interconnection[30] and provided for regulatory measures and dispute resolution procedures at the national level.[31] It promoted a high degree of standardisation and transparency of interconnection terms and prices.[32] It imposed additional obligations on TOs providing public telecommunication networks and systems which have significant market power, in particular with regard to interconnection charges.[33]

To ensure a Community-wide, harmonised framework for licensing and authorisations regimes which do not impose undue burdens on operators, the Community, in 1997, adopted the Licensing Directive[34] setting out principles which the Member States had to observe if they made the provision of a telecommunication service subject to authorisation.

Data protection issues in the old regulatory framework were addressed by the 1995 Directive on the protection of individuals with regard to the processing of personal data and on the free movement of such data,[35] covering all kinds of data processing and by a sector-specific Directive, issued in 1997, dealing with data protection in the telecommunication sector.[36]

1.5   Only four years after the liberalisation and the re-regulation of the European telecommunications markets that came with it,[37] the European Union adopted a

---

28   For further details see fifth edition of this book, para 1.26.
29   Directive 97/33/EC of the European Parliament and of the Council of 30 June 1997 on interconnection in telecommunications with regard to ensuring universal service and interoperability through application of the principles of Open Network Provision (ONP) [1997] OJ L199/32: for further details see fourth edition of this book, paras 1.93 et seq.
30   For details see fourth edition of this book, paras 1.98 et seq.
31   For details see fourth edition of this book, paras 1.100 et seq.
32   For details see fourth edition of this book, para 1.105.
33   For details see fourth edition of this book, paras 1.106 et seq.
34   Directive 97/13/EC of the European Parliament and the Council of 10 April 1997 on a common framework for general authorisations and individual licenses in the field of telecommunications services [1997] OJ L117/15.
35   Council Directive 95/46/EC [1995] OJ L281/31; Directive 97/66/EC of the European Parliament and of the Council concerning the processing of personal data and the protection of privacy in the telecommunications sector [1998] OJ L24/1.
36   Directive 97/66/EC of the European Parliament and of the Council concerning the processing of personal data and the protection of privacy in the telecommunications sector [1998] OJ L24/1.
37   The most important legal instruments of re-regulation include: Directive 97/51/EC of the European Parliament and of the Council of 6 October 1997 amending Council Directives 90/387/EEC and 92/44/EEC for the purpose of adaptation to a competitive environment in telecommunications [1997] OJ L295/23; Directive 97/13/EC of the European Parliament and of the Council of 10 April 1997 on a common framework for general authorisations and individual licenses in the field of telecommunications services [1997] OJ L117/15; Directive 97/33/EC of the European Parliament and of the Council of 30 June 1997 on interconnection in telecommunications with regard to ensuring universal service and interoperability through application of the principles of Open Network Provision ('ONP') [1997] OJ L199/32; Directive 98/10/EC of the European Parliament and of the Council of 26 February 1998 on

package of six Directives[38] and one Decision[39] constituting a legal framework for electronic communications (the '2002 Regulatory Package').[40]

In response to the conclusions from both the Convergence Green Paper and the 1999 Review,[41] the Commission, in July 2000, proposed five Draft Directives[42] and one draft Decision[43] for a new regulatory framework for electronic communications networks and services. Except for the E-Privacy Directive, all Directives and the Decision were adopted in the European Parliament's second reading in February 2002.[44] They were published on 24 April 2002 in the *Official Journal*, and entered

---

the application of open network provision (ONP) to voice telephony and on universal service for telecommunications in a competitive environment [1998] OJ L 101/24; see also at paras 1.3 and 1.4.

38   Directive 2002/21/EC of the European Parliament and of the Council of 7 March 2002 on a common regulatory framework for electronic communications networks and services ('Framework Directive') [2002] OJ L108/33; Directive 2002/19/EC of the European Parliament and of the Council of 7 March 2002 on access to, and interconnection of, electronic communications networks and associated facilities ('Access Directive') [2002] OJ L108/7; Directive 2002/20/EC of the European Parliament and of the Council of 7 March 2002 on the authorisation of electronic communications networks and services ('Authorisation Directive') [2002] OJ L108/21; Directive 2002/22/EC of the European Parliament and of the Council of 7 March 2002 on universal service and users' rights relating to electronic communications networks and services ('Universal Service Directive') [2002] OJ L108/51; Directive 2002/58/EC of the European Parliament and of the Council of 12 July 2002 concerning the processing of personal data and the protection of privacy in the electronic communications sector ('E-Privacy Directive') [2002] OJ L 201/37; Commission Directive 2002/77/EC of 16 September 2002 on competition in the markets for electronic communications networks and services [2002] OJ L 249/21.

39   Commission Decision (2002/622/EC) of 26 July 2002 establishing a Radio Spectrum Policy Group [2002] OJ L198/49.

40   See Bondroit, Cheffert et al, 'Vers un nouveau cadre réglementaire européen des réseaux et services de communications électroniques: Réflexions à mi-chemin' (2001) La Revue Ubiquité 41; Nikolinakos, 'The new European regulatory regime for electronic communications networks and associated services' [2001] 22(3) ECLR 93; Scherer, 'Die Umgestaltung des europäischen und deutschen Telekommunikationsrechts durch das EU-Richtlinienpaket' (2002) Kommunikation und Recht 273 et seq, 329 et seq, 385 et seq; Sinclair, 'A new European communications services regulatory package: an overview' (2001) 7(6) CTLR 156.

41   See para 1.11 below.

42   Proposal for a Directive of the European Parliament and of the Council on a common regulatory framework for electronic communications networks and services, COM(2000) 393 final, 12 July 2000; Proposal for a Directive of the European Parliament and of the Council on the authorisation of electronic communications networks and services, COM(2000) 386 final, 12 July 2000; Proposal for a Directive of the European Parliament and of the Council on access to, and interconnection of, electronic communications networks and associated facilities, COM(2000) 384 final, 12 July 2000; Proposal for a Directive of the European Parliament and of the Council on universal service and users' rights relating to electronic communications networks and services, COM(2000) 392 final, 12 July 2000.

43   Proposal for a Decision of the European Parliament and of the Council on a regulatory framework for radio spectrum policy in the European Community, COM(2000) 407 final, 12 July 2000.

44   Framework Directive, European Parliament Decision (second reading) of 12 December 2001 [2002] OJ C177E/142; Access Directie, European Parliament Decision (second reading) of 12 December 2001 [2002] OJ C 177E/152; Authorisation Directive, European Parliament Decision (second reading) of 12 December 2001 [2002] OJ C177E/155; Universal Service Directive, European Parliament Decision (second reading) of 12 December 2001 [2002] OJ C177E/157; Radio Spectrum Decision, European Parliament Decision (second reading) of 12 December 2001 [2002] OJC177 E/164.

into force the day following publication. Due to far-reaching amendments by the European Parliament, the adoption and publication of the E-Privacy Directive was delayed until July 2002.[45] In addition, the Commission proposed a Regulation for unbundled access to the local loop,[46] which was adopted in December 2000[47] and entered into force on 2 January 2001. Moreover, the Commission adopted a Directive on competition in the markets for electronic communications services,[48] consolidating all relevant provisions of Directive 90/388 (and the sector-specific amendments) and replacing all existing 'liberalisation Directives'[49] in the telecommunications sector.

1.6 In 2006, the Commission launched a comprehensive review of the 2002 Regulatory Package[50] concluding that its main objectives, the promotion of competition, the completion of the single market and the promotion of the EU citizens' interests had not been achieved.[51] The review found that the single market for telecommunications has not yet been established[52] mainly due to a lack of coherent application and enforcement of the rules set forth in the EU framework.[53] The Commission found that these shortcomings were caused in particular by:

- a lack of enforcement competencies on the part of the Commission to ensure a consistent regulatory practice on the national level, in particular with respect to the imposition of ex ante obligations on undertakings found to have significant market power;[54]

- a lack of independence of the national regulatory authorities from commercial and political influence and the failure of some of the EU Member States to furnish the regulatory authorities with sufficient means to perform their regulatory responsibilities;[55] and

---

45   European Parliament Decision (second reading) of 30 May 2002 [2003] OJ C187E/103; Directive 2002/58/EC of the European Parliament and of the Council of 12 July 2002 concerning the processing of personal data and the protection of privacy in the electronic communications sector (Directive on privacy and electronic communications) [2002] OJ L201/37.

46   Proposal for a Regulation of the European Parliament and of the Council on unbundled access to the local loop, COM(2000) 394 final, 12 July 2000.

47   [2000] OJ L336/4.

48   Commission Directive 2002/77/EC of 16 September 2002 on competition in the markets for electronic communications networks and services [2002] OJ L249/21.

49   See para 1.2 above.

50   Communication from the Commission to the European Parliament, the Council, the European and Social Committee and the Committee of the Regions, on the Review of the EU Regulatory Framework for electronic communications networks and services, COM(2006) 334 final, 29 June 2006; Commission Staff Working Document to the Communication from the Commission to the European Parliament, the Council, the European and Social Committee and the Committee of the Regions, on the Review of the EU Regulatory Framework for electronic communications networks and services, COM(2006) 334 final, 29 June 2006, SEC(2006) 816, 28 June 2006.

51   Communication from the Commission to the European Parliament, the Council, the European and Social Committee and the Committee of the Regions, report on the outcome of the Review of the EU regulatory framework for electronic networks and services in accordance with Directive 2002/21/EC and Summary of the 2007 Reform Proposals, COM(2007) 696 final, 13 November 2007, p 13.

52   COM(2006) 334 final, 29 June 2006, p 8.

53   COM(2007) 696 final, 13 November 2007, p 3.

54   SEC(2006) 816, 28 June 2006, p 18; COM(2007) 696 final, 13 November 2007, pp 8 et seq.

55   Commission Staff Working Document, Impact Assessment, 13 November 2007, SEC(2007)1472 final, 13 November 2007, p 68; Communication from the Commission to the

- an overly long duration of appeal procedures as well as the practice by the national courts to regularly suspend regulatory decisions.[56]

Furthermore, the review identified a need for significant improvement of spectrum management.[57]

In November 2007 the Commission submitted to the European Parliament and the Council for adoption in the co-decision procedure its proposals to reform the 2002 Regulatory Package. The proposals' key objectives were to 'address the institutional, procedural and normative deficiencies of the decentralized enforcement system put in place by the 2002 Regulatory Package that has purportedly seriously hindered the achievement of a borderless internal market for electronic communications networks and services'[58] and, thus, consolidate the single market[59] and to improve spectrum management.[60] Furthermore, the proposals sought to strengthen consumers' and users' rights and to ensure that consumers could fully benefit from the single market for electronic communications.[61]

Following controversial and extended negotiations, in April 2009, the European Parliament and the Council found a compromise on the telecommunications reform package. On 6 May 2009, however, the European Parliament, rather than endorsing the entire amended reform package, rejected the intended rules concerning the barring of end users from accessing the Internet in cases of copyright infringements. Instead, the European Parliament voted to adopt the so-called 'amendment 138' which the Parliament had supported in its first reading and which the Council had subsequently rejected. The controversy between Parliament and Council involved the amendment to Article 8(1) of the Framework Directive intended to secure the judicial protection of the Internet users' fundamental rights in national proceedings on alleged breaches of copyright laws that may lead to measures blocking Internet access.[62] Following a conciliation procedure, the Council in November 2009 adopted the amended regulatory package (the '2009 Regulatory Package').

The 2009 Regulatory Package comprises two directives, the 'Better Regulation Directive'[63] (amending the Framework Directive, the Access Directive and the Authorization Directive), as well as the 'Citizens' Rights Directive',[64] which amends

---

European Parliament, the Council, the European Economic and Social Committee and the Committee of the Regions, European Electronic Communications Regulation and Markets 2006 (12th report), COM(2007) 155 final, 29 March 2007, p 14.

56 COM(2006) 334 final, 29 June 2009, p 9; SEC(2006) 816 28 June 2006, p 33.

57 COM(2006) 334 final. 29 June 2006, p 7; SEC(2006) 816, 28 June 2006, pp 11 et seq; COM(2007) 696 final, 13 November 2007, pp 6 et seq.

58 F Rizzuto, 'Reforming the "constitutional fundamentals" of the European Union telecommunications regulatory framework' [2010] 16(2) CTLR 44.

59 COM(2006) 334 final, 29 June 2006, p 7.

60 COM(2007) 696 final, 13 November 2007, pp 6 et seq.

61 COM(2007) 696 final, 13 November 2007, p 10.

62 For further details on the provisions regarding 'Internet freedom', see paras 1.36 et seq below.

63 Directive 2009/140/EC of the European Parliament and of the Council of 25 November 2009 amending Directives 2002/21/EC on a common regulatory framework for electronic communications networks and services, 2002/19/EC on access to, and interconnection of, electronic communications networks and associated facilities, and 2002/20/EC on the authorisation of electronic communications networks and services [2009] OJ L337/37.

64 Directive 2009/136/EC of the European Parliament and the Council of 25 November 2009 amending Directive 2002/22/EC on universal service and users' rights relating to electronic communications networks and services, Directive 2002/58/EC concerning the processing of

in particular the Universal Services Directive and the e-Privacy Directive. Further-more, the telecoms reform package comprises a Regulation establishing a European electronic communications market authority, which is called the Body of European Regulators for Electronic Communications ('BEREC').[65]

The Better Regulation Directive and the Citizens' Rights Directive entered into force on 19 December 2009. The EU Member States were obligated to transpose them into national law by 25 May 2011.

1.7 The convergence of the telecommunications, media and information tech-nology sectors has created challenges for the EU regulatory framework. The borders between these once separate sectors are blurred, and market players are confronted with multiple layers of legislation addressing different aspects of the converging communications systems and services. The 2002 EU Regulatory Pack-age' met the challenge of convergence (ie 'the technological improvements by which a number of networks arise with enhanced capabilities to provide multiple services' where one service may be provided over a number of different networks)[66] by providing a single legal framework not only for 'telecommunication networks' but for all 'electronic communication networks' including mobile networks, cable TV networks and even electricity cable systems (if used for the conveyance of signals).[67] Electronic communication (ie the conveyance of signals over electronic communi-cations networks) is, however, only one aspect of the entire phenomenon of the 'information society'. In addition to the 'transmission'-related rules governing electronic communications networks and services, the policy and law of the EU have addressed and continue to address 'content'-related issues such as the regu-lation of audio-visual media[68]and the regulatory challenges presented by the Internet (eg the question of responsibility for content on the Internet,[69] domain names[70] and copyright protection).[71] Moreover, as new services, such as cloud computing services[72] and machine to machine ('M2M') services,[73] which may combine elements of electronic communications as well as content services, are

---

personal data and the protection of privacy in the electronic communications sector and Regulation (EC) No 2006/2004 on cooperation between national authorities responsible for the enforcement of consumer protection law [2009] OJ L337/11.

65   Regulation (EC) No 1211/2009 of the European Parliament and of the Council of 25 Novem-ber 2009 establishing the Body of European Regulators for Electronic Communications (BEREC) and the Office [2009] OJ L337/1.

66   BEREC report on convergent services (BoR (10) 65) (December 2010), p 2.

67   See Framework Directive, Recital 5.

68   Directive 2010/13/EU of the European Parliament and of the Council of 10 March 2010 on the coordination of certain provisions laid down by law, regulation or administrative action in Member States concerning the provision of audiovisual media services (Audiovisual Media Services Directive) [2010] OJ L95/1.

69   Decision No 276/1999/EC of the European Parliament and of the Council of 25 January 1999 adopting a multi-annual Community action plan on promoting safer use of the Internet by combating illegal and harmful content on global networks [1999] OJ L33/1, amended by Regulation (EC) No 1882/2003 of the European Parliament and of the Council of 29 Septem-ber 2003 [2003] OJ L284/1, and by Decision No 787/2004/EC of the European Parliament and of the Council of 21 April 2004 [2004] OJ L138/12; Council Decision of 29 May 2000 to combat child pornography on the Internet [2000] OJ L138/1.

70   Eg Council Resolution of 3 October 2000 on the organisation and management of the Internet [2000] OJ C293/3.

71   Directive 2001/29/EC of the European Parliament and of the Council of 22 May 2001 on the harmonisation of certain aspects of copyright and related rights in the information society [2001] OJ L167/10.

72   Cloud Computing describes infrastructure, platforms, software and services provided over an

offered over convergent networks, the borders between electronic communication services and content services begin to blur.

This chapter deals mainly with the 'core' regulatory aspects of electronic communication in the EU, addressing only in a non-exhaustive way the related areas of media and content regulation. Chapter 2 addresses the application of the competition rules to electronic communications.

FUNDAMENTALS OF EU TELECOMMUNICATIONS LAW

Legislative Powers of the European Union in the Field of Telecommunications

1.8 The EU has legislative powers only in those fields for which the Treaty on the Functioning of the European Union ('TFEU') specifically establishes such powers. Legislative activities in the field of telecommunications can be based either on Article 114 (ex Article 95 of the EC Treaty ('ECT')), aimed at creating a genuine internal market for the free movement of people, goods and services in the EU, or on Article 106 (ex Article 86 of the ECT), providing for the abolition of special or exclusive rights granted to undertakings. In 1993, the Maastricht Treaty introduced explicit telecommunication policy goals which are still relevant today: according to Articles170 to 172 of the EC Treaty (ex Articles154 to 156 ECT) the EU shall contribute to the establishment and development of trans-European networks.[74] Moreover, Article 173 of the TFEU (ex Article 57 of the ECT) calls for action by the EU and the Member States to create a favourable and competitive environment for the Community's industry.

1.9 The EU has, since 1987, pursued a dual regulatory approach of liberalising the telecommunications sector and harmonising market conditions.[75] This approach is a consequence of the distribution of the main regulatory powers between Commission and Council. The Commission is empowered by Article 106 of the TFEU (ex Article 86(3) of the ECT) to dismantle monopoly rights, while the Council is entitled to adopt measures aimed at establishing the internal market under Article 114 of the TFEU (ex Article 95 ECT).[76] On completion of market liberalisation in the EU, this 'duality' of liberalisation and harmonisation powers and the underlying tension between the Commission and the Member States has

---

external network where the services are deployed as a kind of outsourcing: see BEREC report on convergent services (BoR (10) 65) (December 2010), p 6.

73   M2M describes the 'exchange of information in data format between two remote machines, through a mobile or fixed network, without human intervention', see BEREC report on convergent services (BoR (10) 65) (December 2010), p 6. The BEREC, in its Draft Work Programme 2013 (BoR(12)92) (September 2012), p 17, recognises the increasing importance of M2M services, stating that 'Machine-to-Machine' is a rapidly developing market' and that 'conservative predictions raise the number of M2M devices to more than 1 billion by 2020'.

74   See Decision No 1376/2002/EC of the European Parliament and of the Council of 12 July 2002 amending Decision No 1336/97/EC on a series of guidelines for trans-European telecommunications networks [2002] OJ L200/1. On 19 October 2011 the Commission issued a proposal for a Regulation on guidelines for trans-European telecommunications networks which is to replace Decision No 1336/97/EC: see Commission Proposal for a Regulation of the European Parliament and of the Council on guidelines for trans-European telecommunications networks and repealing Decision No 1336/97/EC, COM(2011) 657, final.

75   See paras 1.2 to 1.5 above.

76   See para 1.4 above.

been replaced by a political controversy over 'community-centric' versus 'state-centric' regulation and enforcement: Member States tend to consider national regulatory competence and control in the telecommunications sector an important factor to secure the achievement of economic and social policy objectives. Therefore, the EU Member States were reluctant to transfer direct regulatory powers to a 'European Regulator' and favoured a 'state-centric' regulatory model. As a result, the Commission received only limited powers to have the NRAs adopt the Commission's views on appropriate measures to counter distortions to competition resulting from the presence of significant market power on national markets.[77]

Following its review of the 2002 Regulatory Package, where the Commission had concluded that single market integration was severely hampered by an inconsistent application of regulatory remedies on a national level,[78] the Commission's initial reform proposals sought to implement a far more 'community-centric' regulatory and enforcement regime by introducing an EU regulatory body with legal enforcement powers[79] and expanding the Commission's competencies to include veto powers with regard to remedies imposed by the NRAs following market decision and analysis,[80] as well as afford it the possibility to pass Decisions requiring NRAs to replace intended remedies by remedies of the Commission's choosing.[81] These proposals have mostly been rejected in the course of the review process: the proposed 'European Electronic Communications Market Authority' has been replaced by BEREC, which has no legal enforcement powers and which is controlled by the Members States.[82] Furthermore, the Commission has not been given competency to issue binding Decisions with regard to remedies chosen by the NRAs; rather, the Commission may issue Recommendations only, which the Member States can reject as they have retained the power to ultimately decide which remedies are to be imposed to counter market failures.[83]

In sum, the 'state-centric' regulatory enforcement system introduced by the 2002 Regulatory Package has been replaced by a highly complicated system of negotiations and co-regulation which is still largely controlled by the Member States where it concerns the actual choosing and implementing of measures designed to counter identified market failure. It remains to be seen whether this approach can serve to counter the inconsistent application of regulatory remedies on a national level[84] and to help consolidate the single market for electronic telecommunications.

Shaping EU Telecommunications Law: Basic Policy Decisions

1.10   The major policy decisions on the path towards full liberalisation of the European telecommunication markets and a harmonised regulatory framework have been brought about by a series of policy papers and resolutions. The policy

---

77   See at para 1.58 below.
78   See para 1.6 above.
79   See Proposal for a Regulation of the European Parliament and of the Council establishing the European Electronic Communications Market Authority, COM(2007) 699, final, 13 November 2007.
80   For details on market analysis and definition as well as the imposition of remedies, see paras 1.62 to 1.77 below.
81   See the Commission Proposal COM(2007) 697, final, 13 November 2007, proposed Art 7, paras 4 and 5 of the Framework Directive.
82   See below, at 1.18.
83   Art 7a(4) et seq of the Framework Directive as amended.
84   See para 1.6 above.

papers,[85] prepared and published by the Commission, are consultative documents setting out basic policy goals for public debate. On that basis, the Council of Telecommunications Ministers and, in some cases, the European Parliament generally adopt resolutions (ie legally non-binding political decisions, establishing action plans and timetables for future legislative and other measures).

1.11   The liberalisation and re-regulation of the telecommunications markets was introduced through several Commission 'Green Papers'.[86]

In 1997 the Commission began to prepare for the transition to the 2002 Regulatory Framework by analysing the implications of convergence in the 'Convergence Green Paper'.[87] In June 2000 the Commission published its '1999 Review', exploring regulatory options for the new legal framework.[88]

1.12   In 2006 the Commission began its review of the 2002 Regulatory Package by issuing its paper COM (2006) 334, final which identified two main areas for change under the 2002 regulatory package, the application to electronic communications of the Commission's policy approach on spectrum management,[89] and the reduction of the regulatory burdens in connection with ex-ante regulation[90] as well as additional changes necessary to consolidate the single market, further the interests of consumers and users, improve security and remove outdated provisions from the regulatory framework.[91] The review process ended with the implementation of the 2009 Regulatory Package.

1.13   Further recent policy initiatives include the European Commission's 'Digital Agenda for Europe'[92] as one of the initiatives of the Europe 2020 strategy[93] issued by the Commission in 2010. The Digital Agenda paper defines the key enabling role that the use of information and communication technologies (ICT) have to play in the European Union's overarching objectives of 'smart, sustainable and inclusive

---

85   See, eg COM(2007) 696 final, 13 November 2007, p 3, and also para 1.2 above.

86   See the Commission's 1987 Green Paper on the development of the common market for telecommunication services and equipment proposed the introduction of more competition in the telecommunication market combined with a higher degree of harmonisation which resulted in the liberalisation and re-regulation of the telecommunications markets: see at paras 1.2 et seq above. Further Commission Green Papers included the Green Paper on a common approach to mobile and personal communications in the European Union ('Mobile Green Paper'), 27 April 1994, COM(94) 145 final and the 1994/1995 Green Paper on the liberalisation of telecommunications infrastructure and cable television networks ('Infrastructure Green Paper'), 25 October 1004 COM(94) 440.final: Part One and 25 January 1995, COM(94) 682 final: Part Two. In 1995 the Commission adopted a Green Paper on a numbering policy for telecommunication services in Europe Towards an European numbering environment ('Green Paper on a numbering policy for telecommunications'), COM(1996) 590 final, 20 November 1996.

87   Green Paper on the convergence of the telecommunications, media and information technology sectors, and the implications for Regulation – Towards an information society approach, COM(1997) 623 final, 03 December 1998.

88   COM(1999) 539 final, 10 November 1999; for an analysis see Scherer, 'The 1999 Review – Towards a new regulatory framework', (2000) info, Vol 2 Iss 3, 313.

89   COM(2005) 411, 6 September 2005.

90   COM (2006) 334 final, 29 June 2006, p 6.

91   COM (2006) 334 final, 29 June 2006, p 7.

92   See the Digital Agenda's website https://ec.europa.eu/digital-agenda/ (accessed on 30 November 2012).

93   Communication from the Commission, Europe 2020 A strategy for smart, sustainable and inclusive growth, COM(2010) 2020 final, 3 March 2010.

growth'.[94] Furthermore, Commission policy papers also play an important role in the development of the EU's frequency management policy.[95]

The Regulatory Instruments

1.14   The most important and most frequently utilised legislative instruments setting a regulatory framework for the telecommunication sector are Directives. In addition, the EU also utilises Decisions[96] and Regulations.[97] The electronic communications regulatory framework also provides for the use of legally non-binding sector-specific measures, such as guidelines,[98] Recommendations[99] and working papers.[100] These 'soft law' regulatory tools can be more easily and quickly agreed on than Directives or Regulations and can be adopted to changing technological and market conditions, allowing for a high degree of responsiveness to changing

---

94   See Communication from the Commission, Europe 2020 A strategy for smart, sustainable and inclusive growth, COM(2010) 2020 final, 3 March 2010, p 11; for details see above at para 1.1.

95   See para 1.101 et seq below.

96   Eg Commission Decision 2007/176/EC of 11 December 2006 establishing a list of standards and/or specifications for electronic communications networks, services and associated facilities and services and replacing all previous versions [2007] OJ L86/11, amended by Commission Decision 2008/286/EC [2008] OJ L93/24; Commission Decision 2007/116/EC of 15 February 2007 on reserving the national numbering range beginning with '116' for harmonised numbers for harmonised services of social value [2007] OJ L49/30, amended by Commission Decision 2007/698/EC [2007] OJ L284/31, and Commission Decision 2009/884/EC [2009] OJ L317/46; Decision No 676/2002/EC of the European Parliament and of the Council of 7 March 2002 on a regulatory framework for radio spectrum policy in the European Community (Radio Spectrum Decision) [2002] OJ L108/1, 24 April 2002.

97   Regulation (EC) No 1211/2009 of the European Parliament and of the Council of 25 November 2009 establishing the Body of European Regulators for Electronic Communications (BEREC) and the Office [2009] OJ L337/1; Regulation (EU) No 531/2012 on roaming on public mobile communications networks within the Union (recast) ('Roaming Regulation') [2012] OJ L172/10; Regulation (EC) No 2887/2000 of the European Parliament and of the Council of 18 December 2000 on unbundled access to the local loop [2000] OJ L336/4 has been repealed by Art 4 of the Better Regulation Directive.

98   Eg Commission Guidelines on market analysis and the assessment of significant market power under the Community regulatory framework for electronic communications networks and services [2002] OJ C165/6 ('Commission Guidelines on market analysis').

99   Eg Commission Recommendation 2010/572/EU of 20 September 2010 on regulated access to Next Generation Access Networks (NGA) [2010] OJ L251/35; Commission Recommendation of 7 May 2009 on the Regulatory Treatment of Fixed and Mobile Termination Rates in the EU [2009] OJ L124/67; Commission Recommendation of 15 October 2008 on notifications, time limits and consultations provided for in Article 7 of Directive 2002/21/EC of the European Parliament and of the Council on a common regulatory framework for electronic communications networks and services, C(2008) 5925, final; Commission Recommendation 2007/879/EC of 17 December 2007 on relevant product and service markets within the electronic communications sector susceptible to ex ante regulation in accordance with Directive 2002/21/EC of the European Parliament and of the Council on a common regulatory framework for electronic communications networks and services [2007] OJ L344/65; Commission Recommendation 2005/698/EC of 19 September 2005 on accounting separation and cost accounting systems under the regulatory framework for electronic communications [2005] OJ L266/64.

100   Eg Commission Staff Working Document, Communication from the Commission to the Council, the European Parliament, the European Economic and Social Committee and the Committee of the Regions on the Review of the EU Regulatory Framework for electronic communications networks and services, SEC(2006) 816, 28 June 2006; Commission Staff Working Paper on the Review of the Scope of Universal Service in accordance with Article 15

regulatory needs.[101] The 'cost' of such increased regulatory flexibility, however, is a loss of legal certainty.

1.15   Directives are addressed to, and binding upon, the Member States and require implementation by national laws (Article 288(3) of the TFEU (ex Article 249(3) of the ECT)). Regulations are directly applicable in all Member States and do not need implementation (Article 288(2) of the TFEU (ex Article 249(2) of the ECT)). Directives can be issued by the Council together with the European Parliament, by the Council alone, or by the Commission, depending on the relevant provision of the TFEU on which the Regulations and Directives are based. Directives and Regulations in the telecommunication sector are primarily based either on Article 114 of the TFEU (ex Article 95 of the ECT) or on Article 106 of the TFEU (ex Article 86 of the ECT).[102] The implications of these two legal bases are different: Article 114 of the TFEU provides for the adoption of measures for the approximation of national laws in order to establish the Single European Market. Its predecessor provision, Article 95 of the ECT, has served as the basis of various Council Directives.[103] Directives based on Article 114 of the TFEU are adopted in the ordinary legislative procedure under the co-decision procedure introduced by the Maastricht Treaty, today specified in Article 294 of the TFEU. This procedure strengthens the legislative powers of the European Parliament to the extent that the Parliament may prevent the entry into force of such a Directive. By contrast, the procedure under Article 106(3) of the TFEU (ex Article 86(3) ECT) does not provide for the involvement of the Council or the European Parliament.

1.16   In contrast to Regulations and Directives, Decisions are specifically addressed to natural persons, legal persons, or Member States; they apply solely to their addressees (Article 288(4) of the TFEU (ex Article 294(4) of the ECT)). The Commission's power to issue Decisions can either be derived directly from Treaty provisions (see Article 106(3) of the TFEU (ex Article 86(3) of the ECT)) or from powers conferred by the legislative bodies (Article 17(1) of the TFEU (ex Article 211, 4th indent of the ECT)).[104]

Regulatory Authorities at European Level

1.17   The principal institutional actors at the Community level in regulating the telecommunication sector are the Commission, the Council and, to a lesser extent, the European Parliament. Within the Commission, the Directorate General for Communications Networks, Content and Technology (DG CONNECT) is responsible for telecommunication policy, replacing, from 1 July 2012, the Information Society and Media ('INFSOC') Directorate General.. The main goal of DG CONNECT is to 'manage the Digital Agenda'.[105] This is to be achieved by supporting research and innovation in the ICT environment, promote sharing of knowledge and use of and access to digital goods and services, enhancing digital

---

of Directive 2002/22/EC, SEC(2005)660, 25 April 2004; Commission Staff Working Document on the treatment of Voice over Internet Protocol ('VoIP') under the EU Regulatory Framework, 14 June 2004.

101   COM(1999) 539, final, 10 November 1999, p 18; see J Scherer, 'The 1999 Review – towards a new regulatory framework', info (2000) Vol 2 Iss 3, pp 313, 320.

102   See para 1.9 above.

103   Eg the Directives of the '2002 Regulatory Package' with the exception of the Commission Directive on competition in the markets for electronic communications networks and services.

104   See Art 18(3) of the Universal Service Directive.

105   See para 1.1 above.

security, and supporting an open Internet. The Directorate General for Competition, which played a major role in the liberalisation of the electronic communications sector, is responsible for the application of the general EU competition law rules set forth in Articles 101 and 102 of the TFEU (ex Articles 81 and 82 of the ECT). Furthermore, the Directorate General for Competition applies the EU rules on state aids set forth in Article 107 of the TFEU (ex Article 87 ECT).

1.18   There is still no central authority responsible for telecommunication issues at the EU level. Several proposals on the establishment and structure of such an authority have been discussed[106] in the 1990s and again in the course of the 2006 review of the 2002 Regulatory Package.[107] But the proposal to implement a centralised pan-European regulatory authority was rejected once again.[108]

However, the 2002 Regulatory Package, in lieu of a centralised European regulatory agency, established a network of organisational entities with a view to advising the Commission on regulatory measures at the EU level, to ensure cooperation among NRAs and between NRAs and the Commission, and to develop best regulatory practices at the EU level and, beyond the boundaries of the European Union, at a pan-European level: the Communications Committee ('CoCom') and the Radio Spectrum Committee have been established on the basis of Article 22 of the Framework Directive and Article 3 of the Radio Spectrum Decision,[109] respectively. These committees have both advisory and decision-making functions in line with the Council's (new) comitology rules.[110]

Similarly, the Commission has established an advisory group on radio spectrum policy, the Radio Spectrum Policy Group, which is composed of one high-level government expert from each Member State and a high-level representative from the Commission.[111] The purpose of this Group is to assist and advise the Commission on radio spectrum policy, on coordination of policy approaches and, where appropriate, on harmonised conditions with regard to the availability and efficient use of radio spectrum necessary for the establishment and functioning of the internal market.

---

106 For a more recent contribution see Ewan Sutherland, 'A Single European Regulatory Authority', International Telecommunications Society, Biennial Conference Montreal, 24–27 June 2008, available at www.imaginar.org/its2008/43.pdf (last accessed 28 December 2012).

107 See Proposal for a Regulation of the European Parliament and of the Council establishing the European Electronic Communications Market Authority, COM(2007) 699, final, 13 November 2007, see also speech of Commissioner V Reding, SPEECH/06/422 (27 June 2006).

108 Commission Staff Working Document, Impact Assessment, SEC(2006) 817, 29 June 2006, p 21.

109 Commission Decision 2009/884/EC [2009] OJ L317/46; Decision No 676/2002/EC of the European Parliament and of the Council of 7 March 2002 on a regulatory framework for radio spectrum policy in the European Community (Radio Spectrum Decision) [2002] OJ L108/1.

110 Regulation (EU) No 182/2011 of the European Parliament and of the Council of 16 February 2011 laying down the rules and general principles concerning mechanisms for control by Member States of the Commission's exercise of implementing powers, [2011] OJ L65/13, repealing Regulation No 1999/468/EC [1999] OJ L184/23.

111 Cf Arts 1 and 3 of Commission Decision (2002/622/EC) of 26 July 2002 establishing a Radio Spectrum Policy Group [2002] OJ L198/49, amended by Commission Decision 2009/978/EU of 16 December 2009 [2009] OJ L336/50.

The European Regulators Group for Electronic Communications Networks and Services (ERG), which had been established as an advisory body of the Commission,[112] has been transformed into the Body of European Regulators for Electronic Communication (BEREC) following the 2006 review of the 2002 Regulatory Package.[113]

The main objectives of BEREC are to 'contribute to the development and better functioning of the internal market for electronic communications networks and services, by aiming to ensure a consistent application of the EU regulatory framework for electronic communications',[114] to 'promote cooperation between NRAs, and between NRAs and the Commission',[115] and to 'advise the Commission, and upon request, the European Parliament and the Council.'[116] In this capacity, BEREC inter alia delivers opinions on the NRAs' draft decisions on market definition and analysis as well as the imposition of remedies in the consolidation procedure under Article 7 of the Framework Directive,[117] supports the Commission when issuing Market Recommendations,[118] and, upon request, provides assistance to the NRAs in market analysis proceedings.[119] Furthermore, BEREC monitors and reports on the electronic communications sector and publishes an annual report[120] on developments in the sector.[121]

The NRAs and the Commission must take 'the utmost account' of any opinion, recommendation, guidelines, advice, and regulatory best practice adopted by BEREC.[122]

1.19   At a pan-European level – and without the involvement of the Commission – the NRAs, in 1997, established the Independent Regulators Group (IRG) which currently consists of representatives from 34 NRAs.[123] The purpose of this group is to share experience and viewpoints among its members on issues of common interest and to develop 'principles of implementation and best practice' ('PIBs') on regulatory matters.

---

112 Commission Decision (2002/627/EC) of 29 July 2002 establishing the European Regulators Group for Electronic Communications Networks and Services [2002] OJ L200/38.

113 Regulation (EC) No 1211/2009 of the European Parliament and of the Council of 25 November 2009 establishing the Body of European Regulators for Electronic Communications (BEREC) and the Office [2009] OJ L337/1. BEREC consists of the 'Board' and is assisted by the 'Office'. The Board is composed of the heads of the 27 NRAs. The Office is a Community Body which is managed by the 'Management Committee' where the 27 NRAs and the Commission are represented.

114 Art 1, para 3, Regulation (EC) No 1211/2009.

115 Art 1, para 4, Regulation (EC) No 1211/2009.

116 Art 1, para 4, Regulation (EC) No 1211/2009.

117 Art 3, para 1, lit a, Regulation (EC) No 1211/2009.

118 Art 3, para 1, lit c, Regulation (EC) No 1211/2009.

119 Art 3, para 1, lit d, Regulation (EC) No 1211/2009.

120 See Body of European Regulators for Electronic Communications, Annual Report 2010 (BoR (11) 19) (May 2011), providing an overview on BEREC's activities which had, in 2010 a particular focus on roaming and next generation network access and on identifying 'emerging challenges' such as, e g those resulting from convergence.

121 Art 3, para 1, lit n, Regulation (EC) No 1211/2009.

122 Art 3, para 3, Regulation (EC) No 1211/2009.

123 Corresponding to 27 EU Member States, four EFTA members and three candidate countries to the EU.

THE EU REGULATORY FRAMEWORK

Introduction

1.20   With its 2002 Regulatory Package, the European legislator pursued four main regulatory objectives, namely: simplifying and consolidating the current legislation;[124] adapting the regulatory framework to deal with convergence,[125] providing for more flexible regulation[126] and implementing a more harmonised application of the regulatory framework throughout the Community.[127]

In its 2006/2007 review of the 2002 Regulatory Package, the Commission found that these goals had not been fully met and identified shortcomings of the existing system[128] which were addressed in the 2009 Regulatory package consisting of two Directives amending the Directives of the 2002 Regulatory Package and one Regulation establishing the BEREC.[129]

Regulatory Objectives

1.21   The 2009 Regulatory Package introduced changes in the key areas 'better regulation for competitive electronic communications', 'the single market for electronic communications' and 'connecting with citizens'.[130] These changes sought to:

- further secure the independence of the NRAs;[131]
- further the consistency of regulation through establishing the BEREC[132] and provide for a right of the Commission to issue Recommendations with respect to remedies notified by NRAs in the course of market regulation[133] and Decisions where regulatory inconsistencies persist long-term across the EU;[134]
- introduce functional separation as a 'last-resort' remedy;[135]
- introduce measures to accelerate broadband roll-out, particularly in rural areas,[136] and to promote competition and investment in next generation access networks ('NGAs');[137]
- protect consumer and user interests by granting consumers the right to change their communications provider in one working day while keeping their

---

124   Communications Review, COM(1999) 539 final, 10 November 1999, p 19; for further details on convergence, see para 1.7 above
125   Recital 5 of the Framework Directive.
126   See Recitals 25 and 27 of the' Framework Directive; see also Communications Review, COM(1999) 539, final, 10 November 1999, pp 7, 14, 57–59.
127   See Art 1(1) and (2) of the Framework Directive, and Recital 16 of theFramework Directive.
128   For details on the identified shortcomings of the 2002 Regulatory Package, see para 1.6 above.
129   See para 1.6 above.
130   See COM(2007) 696 final, 13 November 2007.
131   Arts 3(3), 3a of the Framework Directive, see also Recital 13 of the Better Regulation Directive.
132   Regulation EC/1211/2009 (BEREC Regulation).
133   Art 7a of the Framework Directive.
134   Art 19(1) of the Framework Directive.
135   Art 13a of the Framework Directive.
136   See in particular Arts 8(5)(d) and 12 of the Framework Directive and Art 12(2)(c) of the Access Directive.
137   See in particular Arts 13(1) of the Access Directive and Recital 57 of the Better Regulation Directive.

number[138] and by expanding the information to be provided in consumer contracts;[139]

- introduce an 'Internet freedom provision' to secure the EU citizens' right to Internet access;[140]
- secure 'Internet neutrality';[141]
- enhance the protection of the EU citizen's privacy and strengthening the existing data protection rules;[142] and
- improve access to emergency services.[143]

1.22 The 2009 Regulatory Package has still not fully achieved the objective of simplifying and consolidating the European regulatory framework: the Framework Directive and the specific Directives continue to be characterised by a multitude of cross-references and contain numerous provisions allowing for the adoption of guidelines, Recommendations and Decisions,[144] which have developed into a 'regulatory jungle' comparable to the previous regulatory framework.

In addition, the Member States still retain competency in certain areas such as numbering regulations.

Furthermore, the transposition of the regulatory framework into the national laws of the Member States is not fully coherent. In particular, the treatment of electronic communications services for business customers vary to a large extent across the EU. Depending on the national transposition of the 2009 Regulatory Package's measures to protect user interests, the difficulties faced by providers of business services may become even more pronounced. It is therefore doubtful that the measures implemented by the 2009 Regulatory Package will lessen the obstacles for pan-European (business) services caused by the highly complex regulatory framework which is inconsistently implemented at the Member State level.

1.23 The 2009 Regulatory Package has maintained the formalised procedure of market definition and analysis as the basis for the NRAs' decision on which remedies foreseen by the Access Directive and the Universal Service Directive are imposed on an undertaking found to have significant market power ('SMP'). The NRAs have broad discretion in the selection of these regulatory remedies.[145] This broad discretion has resulted in the inconsistent application of remedies by the NRAs which, in turn, has hindered the establishment of the single market for electronic communications.[146] The 2009 Regulatory Package seeks to secure a more consistent regulation at the Member State level through the establishment of BEREC[147] and by enabling the Commission to issue recommendations with regard to remedies notified by NRAs in the course of market regulation.[148]

---

138 Art 30(4) of the Universal Services Directive.
139 Art 20 of the Universal Services Directive.
140 Art 1(3a) of the Framework Directive.
141 Art 8(4)(g) of the Framework Directive, and Arts 21 and 22(3) of the Universal Services Directive.
142 See, e g Arts 4(3) and 5(3) of the e-Privacy Directive.
143 Art 26 of the Universal Services Directive.
144 See para 1.14 above.
145 See Art 8(2) of the Access Directive and the discretionary powers of the NRAs under Arts 9–13 of the Access Directive.
146 SEC(2006) 816, 28 June 2006, p 18; COM(2007) 696 final, 13 November 2007, p 8 et seq.
147 See para 1.18 above.
148 See para 1.58 below.

The EU Regulatory Framework: Overview

1.24   The Framework Directive[149] defines the scope of applicability of the EU Regulatory Framework and its most important legal terms. It requires the Member States to guarantee the independence of the NRAs and the effective structural separation of their regulatory functions from activities associated with ownership or control of undertakings providing electronic communications networks or services (Article 3(2) of the Framework Directive) and to ensure that NRAs exercise their powers impartially, transparently and in a timely manner and have sufficient financial and human resources to perform the responsibilities conferred to them (Article 3(3) of the Framework Directive). It further establishes policy objectives and regulatory principles for the NRAs' regulatory tasks (Article 8 of the Framework Directive) and provides for a consolidation procedure under which the NRAs must 'contribute to the development of the internal market by cooperating with each other and the Commission in a transparent manner to ensure the consistent application, in all Member States', of the Regulatory Framework (Article 7(2) of the Framework Directive) and a procedure for the consistent application of remedies which provides for extensive cooperation by BEREC, the NRAs and the Commission (Article 7a of the Framework Directive). Furthermore, the Framework Directive establishes rules on the management of scarce resources, eg radio frequencies, numbering, naming and addressing (Articles 9, 9a, 9b and 10 of the Framework Directive). The Directive also establishes an obligation on the Member States to cooperate with each other and the Commission in the strategic planning, coordination and harmonisation of radio spectrum use in the EU (Article 8a of the Framework Directive) and provides for the granting of rights of way (Article 11 of the Framework Directive), co-location and facility sharing (Article 12 of the Framework Directive).

With respect to the activities of undertakings providing public communications networks or publicly available electronic communications services which have special or exclusive rights for the provision of services in other sectors in the same or another Member State, the Directive requires Member States to ensure accounting separation and 'structural separation' for the activities associated with the provision of electronic communications networks and services (Article 13 of the Framework Directive).

The 2009 Regulatory Package also introduced new provisions aimed at securing network and services security and integrity including an obligation of undertakings to inform their NRA of breaches of network security or integrity which have had a significant impact on the integrity on the operation of networks or services (Articles 13a and 13b of the Framework Directive). At the core of the Framework Directive are rules regarding the determination of significant market power (Article 14 of the Framework Directive) on the basis of a market definition procedure (Article 15 of the Framework Directive) and a market analysis procedure (Article 16 of the Framework Directive) to be initiated and conducted by the respective NRA in accordance with Community law.

1.25   The Authorisation Directive[150] seeks to simplify and harmonize the authorisation rules and conditions for all electronic communications networks and services (Article 1(1) of the Authorisation Directive). The provision of electronic communications networks or services may, in principle, only be subject to a general

---

149   Further details below, para 1.32 et seq.
150   Further details below, para 1.90 et seq. See also Nihoul and Rodford, *EU Electronic Communications Law* (Oxford University Press, 2011), Chap 2.

authorisation (Article 3(2) of the Authorisation Directive). Individual rights of use may only be granted where necessary for the use of radio frequencies or numbers (Article 5(1) of the Authorisation Directive). As a rule, individual rights for the use of frequencies and numbers are to be granted only on the basis of open, objective, transparent, non-discriminatory and proportionate procedures (Article 5(2) of the Authorisation Directive). The Authorisation Directive establishes the rights and obligations of the addressees of the general authorisations, of the users of radio frequencies and numbers (Articles 4 and 6 of the Authorisation Directive) and establishes far-reaching rights of the Member States to impose 'administrative charges' on undertakings providing a service or a network under the general authorisation or exercising a right of use (Article 12 of the Authorisation Directive).

1.26   The Access Directive[151] harmonises the way in which Member States regulate, at the wholesale level, access to, and interconnection of electronic communications networks and associated facilities (Article 1(1) of the Access Directive). The Directive creates a framework for the relationships between suppliers of networks and services, based on the principle of priority of commercial negotiations, while allowing for regulatory intervention by the NRAs at their own initiative or, in the absence of agreement between undertakings, at the request of either of the parties involved (Article 5 of the Access Directive). The Directive establishes far-reaching regulatory powers of the NRAs with respect to undertakings designated as having SMP (Article 8 of the Access Directive). If an NRA finds that an undertaking has SMP on an electronic communications market, it must impose at least one remedy to counter the lack of effective competition found on that market (Article 8(2) of the Access Directive). These remedies include obligations relating to transparency (Article 9 of the Access Directive), non-discrimination (Article 10 of the Access Directive), accounting separation (Article 11 of the Access Directive), obligations of access to, and use of specific network facilities (Article 12 of the Access Directive), price control and cost accounting obligations including cost orientation of prices (Article 13 of the Access Directive).

The 2009 Regulatory Package has introduced 'functional separation' as an exceptional measure that the NRAs can impose on vertically integrated undertakings following authorisation by the Commission of such measure (Article 13a of the Access Directive). The Access Directive further establishes a number of regulatory powers, to be exercised regardless of the existence of significant market power, with a view to ensure adequate access and interconnection and interoperability of services 'in a way that promotes efficiency, sustainable competition, and gives the maximum benefit to end-users' (Article 5 of the Access Directive).

1.27   Whereas the Access Directive establishes a framework for the regulation of wholesale markets, the Universal Service Directive governs the provision of electronic communications networks and services to end users (Article 1(1) of the Universal Service Directive).[152] The Directive aims at ensuring the availability throughout the Community of good quality services publicly available through effective competition and deals with circumstances in which the needs of end users are not satisfactorily met by the markets. To this end, the Directive establishes a minimum set of services of a specified quality to which all end users must have

---

151   Further details below, para 1.130 et seq. See also Nihoul and Rodford, *EU Electronic Communications Law* (Oxford University Press, 2011), Chap 3.
152   Further details below, para 1.172 et seq. See also Nihoul and Rodford, *EU Electronic Communications Law* (Oxford University Press, 2011), Chap 4

access at an affordable price in the light of specific national conditions (Articles 4 to 7, and 9 of the Universal Service Directive). The Universal Service Directive allows Member States to designate one or more undertakings to guarantee the provision of these universal services (Article 8 of the Universal Service Directive) and to establish mechanisms for the financing of universal service obligations (Article 13 of the Universal Service Directive). In addition, the Universal Service Directive establishes rules for the regulation of services provided by undertakings designated as having SMP to end users, including the regulation of retail tariffs (Article 17 of the Universal Service Directive), sector-specific consumer protection rules (Article 20 et seq of the Universal Service Directive), which were significantly extended by the 2009 Regulatory Package in particular with respect to information and transparency duties (Articles 20 and 21 of the Universal Service Directive), and obligations towards disabled end users (Article 23a of the Universal Service Directive). The Universal Service Directive further includes provisions regarding European emergency call numbers and telephone access codes (Article 26 et seq of the Universal Service Directive), dispute resolution (Article 34 of the Universal Service Directive), and provisions facilitating changes of the provider of electronic communications services including number portability (Article 30 of the Universal Service Directive) which the 2009 Regulatory Package significantly amended to the benefit of the end users.

1.28   The Directive concerning the processing of personal data and the protection of privacy in the electronic communications sector (the Privacy Directive)[153] harmonises the national provisions required to ensure an adequate level of protection of fundamental rights and freedoms, in particular the right to privacy and confidentiality with respect to the processing of personal data in the electronic communications sector (Article 1(1) of the Privacy Directive). The Privacy Directive contains provisions regarding the processing of personal data (Article 4 of the Privacy Directive) including a requirement for providers to inform their subscribers of personal data breaches (Article 4(3) of the Privacy Directive) which was introduced by the 2009 Regulatory Package, and provisions on the confidentiality of communications (Article 5 of the Privacy Directive), the processing of traffic data (Article 6 of the Privacy Directive), the protection of location data (Article 9 of the Privacy Directive), and the protection from unsolicited communications (Article 13 of the Privacy Directive). Furthermore, the Privacy Directive provides for a right of end users to receive non-itemised bills (Article 7 of the Privacy Directive), to stop automatic call forwarding (Article 11 of the Privacy Directive), and to refuse inclusion of their data in public directories (Article 12 of the Privacy Directive).

1.29   The Directive on Competition in the Markets for Electronic Communications Services[154] has simplified and consolidated the provisions of the former liberalisation Directives[155] in one single piece of legislation. Apart from the

---

153   See Chapter 3, 'Data Protection and Privacy'.
154   Directive 2002/77/EC [2002] OJ L249/21.
155   Commission Directive 90/388/EEC of 28 June 1990 on competition in the markets for telecommunications services [1990] OJ L192/10, as amended by Commission Directive 94/46/EC of 13 October 1994 amending Directive 88/301/EEC and Directive 90/388/EEC in particular with regard to satellite communications [1994] OJ L268/15; Commission Directive 95/51/EC of 18 October 1995 amending Directive 90/388/EEC with regard to the abolition of the restrictions on the use of cable television networks for the provision of already liberalised telecommunications services [1995] OJ L256/49; Commission Directive 96/2/EC of 16 January 1996 amending Directive 90/388/EEC with regard to mobile and personal communications

clarification of certain provisions and terminological adjustments (eg 'telecommunications services', 'telecommunications networks') to the terms used in the other Directives of the EU Regulatory Framework, the main provisions remain unaltered.

1.30 The Regulation on roaming on public mobile communications networks within the Community ('Roaming Regulation')[156] aims at ensuring that users of public mobile communications networks do not pay excessive prices for regulated roaming calls,[157] regulated roaming SMS messages,[158] and regulated data roaming services[159] when travelling in the EU (Article 1(1), sub-para 1 of the Roaming Regulation). The Roaming Regulation imposes maximum prices for regulated roaming services both on the wholesale level (Articles 7 and 9 of the Roaming Regulation), and the retail level (the 'euro tariff', Articles 8 and 10 of the Roaming Regulation). Furthermore, the Roaming Regulation imposes transparency and safeguard mechanisms for regulated data roaming services including an obligation to provide information on charges incurred and a monthly 'default financial limit' to the charges due for regulated data roaming services (Article 15 of the Roaming Regulation). Transparency requirements also apply with respect to the retail charges for regulated SMS services (Article 14 of the Roaming Regulation).

In addition to these obligations which were already included in the previous version of the Roaming Regulation,[160] the current Roaming Regulation most notably includes an obligation on mobile network operators to offer access to roaming services at the wholesale level (Article 3(1) of the Roaming Regulation), both in the

[1996] OJ L20/59; Commission Directive 96/19/EC of 28 February 1996 amending Directive 90/388/EEC regarding the implementation of full competition in telecommunications markets [1996] OJ L74/13; Commission Directive 1999/64/EC of 23 June 1999 amending Directive 90/388/EEC in order to ensure that telecommunications networks and cable TV networks owned by a single operator are separate legal entities [1999] OJ L175/39.

156 Regulation (EU) No 513/2012 of the European Parliament and of the Council of 13 June 2012 on roaming on public mobile communications networks within the Union (recast) [2012] OJ L172/10. The ECJ has confirmed the validity of the previous version of the Roaming Regulation in its judgment of 8 June 2010, *Vodafone and Others* (C-58/08) [2010] ECR I-4999. For a critical view see Brennecke, 'The EU Roaming Regulation and its non-compliance with Article 95 EC', Beiträge zum Transnationalen Wirtschaftsrecht, October 2008, pp 45 et seq.

157 A regulated roaming call is 'a mobile voice telephony call made by a roaming customer, originating on a visited network and terminating on a public communications network within the Union or received by a roaming customer, originating on a public communications network within the Union and terminating on a visited network' (Art 2, lit h of the Roaming Regulation).

158 A regulated roaming SMS message is 'an SMS message sent by a roaming customer, originating on a visited network and terminating on a public communications network within the Union or received by a roaming customer, originating on a public communications network within the Union and terminating on a visited network' (Art 2, lit k of the Roaming Regulation).

159 A regulated data roaming service is 'a roaming service enabling the use of packet switched data communications by a roaming customer by means of his mobile device while it is connected to a visited network. A regulated data roaming service does not include the transmission or receipt of regulated roaming calls or SMS messages, but does include the transmission and receipt of MMS messages' (Art 2, lit m of the Roaming Regulation).

160 Regulation (EC) No 717/2007 of the European Parliament and of the Council of 27 June 2007 on roaming on public mobile communications networks within the Community ('Roaming Regulation') [2007] OJ L171/ 32, amended by Regulation (EC) No 544/2009 [2009] OJ L167/12.

form of direct wholesale roaming access[161] and wholesale roaming resale access.[162] The mobile network operators are required to publish a reference offer (Article 3(5) of the Roaming Regulation) in accordance with the guidelines on wholesale roaming access prepared by BEREC (Article 3(8) of the Roaming Regulation).[163] Requests for wholesale roaming access can only be refused 'on the basis of objective criteria'[164] (Article 3(2) of the Roaming Regulation).

1.31   The Radio Spectrum Decision[165] establishes a procedure which allows the EU to pursue, largely independently of, but in co-ordination with, the European Conference of Postal and Telecommunications Administrations ('CEPT'), a Community radio spectrum policy. The Decision establishes a consultative body, the Radio Spectrum Committee, which assists the Commission in coordinating policy approaches and, where appropriate, developing harmonised conditions regarding the availability and efficient use of the radio spectrum (Article 1 of the Radio Spectrum Decision).

Regulatory Principles: the Framework Directive

Scope of regulation

1.32   The European legislator has reacted to the technical convergence of mobile and satellite communications with the fixed network, cable television and telecommunications networks and power lines, and communications services on the basis of the Internet protocol by creating a single legal framework for all transmission networks and electronic communication services provided over those networks.[166] To achieve this, the scope of applicability of the traditional European telecommunications law has been expanded by replacing the terms 'public telecommunications network' and 'telecommunications services'[167] with the new, broader terms 'electronic communications network' and 'electronic communications service', and including the – albeit not fully mandatory – requirement of a technology neutral regulation as a regulatory principle of the EU Regulatory Framework (Article 8(1) of the Framework Directive). The 2009 Regulatory Package has confirmed and broadened this approach by requiring radio spectrum management that is both technology neutral (Article 9(3) of the Framework Directive) and service neutral (Article 9(4) of the Framework Directive).[168]

---

161   Direct wholesale roaming access is 'making available of facilities and/or services by a mobile network operator to another undertaking, under defined conditions, for the purpose of that other undertaking providing regulated roaming services to roaming customers' (Art 2, lit p of the Roaming Regulation).

162   Wholesale Roaming Resale Access is 'the provision of roaming services on a wholesale basis by a mobile network operator different from the visited network operator to another undertaking for the purpose of that other undertaking providing regulated roaming services to roaming customers' (Art 2, lit q of the Roaming Regulation).

163   BEREC Guidelines on the application of Article 3 of the Roaming Regulation – Wholesale Roaming Access (BoR(12)105) (27 September 2012), p 3.

164   For further details see BEREC Guidelines on the application of Article 3 of the Roaming Regulation – Wholesale Roaming Access (BoR(12)105) (27 September 2012), p 2.

165   Further details below, para 1.103 et seq.

166   See para 1.7 above.

167   See statutory definitions in Art 1(1) of the Services Directive and in Art 2(3) and (4) of the ONP Framework Directive 1990.

168   See para 1.101 below.

1.33 The term 'electronic communications network', as defined in Article 2(a) of the Framework Directive, means:

'transmission systems and, where applicable, switching or routing equipment and other resources including network elements which are not active which permit the conveyance of signals by wire, by radio, by optical or by other electromagnetic means'.

The reference to 'network elements which are not active' has been included to meet the 2009 Regulatory Package's objective that 'certain definitions should be clarified or changed to take account of market and technological developments and to eliminate ambiguities identified in implementing the regulatory framework'.[169]

By way of example, the Directive mentions satellite networks, fixed (circuit- and packet- switched, including Internet) and mobile terrestrial networks, electricity cable systems, to the extent that they are used for the purpose of transmitting signals,[170] networks used for radio and television broadcasting, and cable television networks, regardless of the type of information conveyed. This non-inclusive enumeration leaves room for technological developments, such as Voice over Internet Protocol ('VoIP') services[171] which have started to gradually replace 'traditional' voice telephony services over the Public Switched Telephony Network ('PSTN') in the recent past.[172]

1.34 'Electronic communications service' is defined in Article 2(c) of the Framework Directive as:

'a service normally provided for remuneration which consists wholly or mainly in the conveyance of signals on electronic communications networks'.

This definition clarifies that electronic communication services comprise, but are not limited to, telecommunications services and transmission services and networks used for broadcasting, but that they exclude services 'providing, or exercising

---

169 Better Regulation Directive, Recital 12.
170 Cf Commission Recommendation 2005/292/EC on broadband communication through power lines [2005] OJ L93/42..
171 VoIP is a generic term for the conveyance of voice, fax and related services partially or wholly over packet-switched IP-based networks, cf European Regulators Group, 'ERG Common Position on VoIP' (ERG (07) 56rev2) (December 2007), at 1. The ERG Common Position included a comprehensive analysis of ex-ante regulation applied to VoIP services and set out recommended approaches on 15 separate points including access to emergency services, numbering and number portability, and the regulatory qualification of different VoIP services in order to further a harmonised regulatory treatment of VoIP services in the EU. VoIP is a catch-all term for a variety of services which range from mere PC-to-PC communication over the public Internet to full replacements of traditional PSTN-telephony which allow for the receiving of calls using local or nomadic telephone numbers and affording the subscribers the ability to place calls to any national or international number by way of a PSTN-breakout. For a categorisation of various classes of VoIP offerings and a description of their treatment under the Member States' regulatory frameworks for electronic communications, see also Elximann and Wernick, 'The Regulation of Voice over IP (VoIP) in Europe' (2008), a study prepared on behalf of the EU Commission. In 2009 the ERG issued the ERG, VoIP-Action Plan to achieve conformity with ERG Common Position, ERG (09) 19 which provides a comprehensive overview on the measures taken by the NRAs to meet the common positions set forth in ERG's 2007 common position on VoIP.
172 ERG, Common Position on VoIP (ERG (07) 56rev2,) (December 2007), p 4.

editorial control over, content transmitted using electronic communications networks and services' as well as 'information society services',[173] which do not consist
wholly or mainly in the conveyance of signals on electronic communications
networks.

Ultimately, none of these boundary lines allow for a clear-cut separation of the
scope of applicability of the various legislative measures. Rather, in the regulatory
practice, NRAs are constantly required to decide whether or not a given service is
an 'electronic communications service' or a 'content'-related service, particularly
with respect to services which include features of both content and transmission
services, such as, for example, complex VoIP services, cloud computing services, and
unified communications services.

Furthermore, there are undoubtedly legal interfaces between 'transmission infrastructures' and 'content' if and when regulatory decisions regarding the transmission infrastructure have a direct or indirect effect on 'content'. The 'regulation of
transmission infrastructures' and the 'regulation of content' are explicitly inter-
twined in Article 8(1), para 3 of the Framework Directive which allows the NRAs
to 'contribute within their competencies to ensuring the implementation of policies
aimed at the promotion of cultural and linguistic diversity, as well as media
pluralism'.[174] It may become necessary to further refine the existing definition of
'electronic communications services' in order to secure a consistent treatment of
complex services that include features of both electronic communications and
content services, and where it is difficult, if not impossible, to determine whether
such services consist 'wholly or mainly' in the transmission of signals.

1.35   The scope of applicability of the directives and, in turn, the regulatory
powers of the NRAs (see Article 8(2) of the Access Directive) is expanded by the
inclusion of 'associated facilities' and 'associated services'. Associated facilities are:

> 'associated services, physical infrastructures and other facilities or elements
> associated with an electronic communications network and/or an electronic
> communications service which enable and/or support the provision of services
> via that network and/or service or have the potential to do so' and include,
> inter alia, buildings or entries to buildings, antennae, ducts, wires and towers'
> (Article 2(e) of the Framework Directive).

Associated services are 'those services associated with an electronic communications network and/or an electronic communications service which enable and/or
support the provision of services via that network and/or service or have the
potential to do so' and include, among other things, conditional access systems,
electronic programme guides as well as identity, location and presence services'
(Article 2(ea) of the Framework Directive).

'Internet freedom'

1.36   The 2009 Regulatory Framework introduced, in Article 1(3a) of the Framework Directive, a provision adopting limitations to 'measures taken by Member

---

173 See statutory definition in Art 1 of Directive 98/34/EC as amended by Directive 98/48/EC of
      the European Parliament and the Council of 20 July 1998 [1998] OJ L217/18: 'any service
      normally provided for remuneration, at a distance, by electronic means and at the individual
      request of a recipient of services'.
174 Other content-related provisions can be found in Art 5(1), sub-para 2(b) of the Access
      Directive and Art 31 of the Universal Service Directive.

States regarding end-users' access to, or use of, services and applications through electronic communications networks' (the 'Internet Freedom Provision'). Such measures must respect the fundamental rights and freedoms of natural persons guaranteed by the European Convention for the Protection of Human Rights[175] and the Fundamental Freedoms and general principles of Community law.[176] Furthermore, the Internet Freedom Provision contains procedures which Member States must follow when taking such measures.

1.37   To fully understand the Internet Freedom Provision's purpose and meaning, one must consider its legislative history.

Prior to passage of this provision, there was an understanding that the prosecution of non-commercial infringement of intellectual property rights, in particular by means of criminal law, was within the jurisdiction and responsibility of the Member States; while there were EU legislative acts on the enforcement of intellectual property rights for cases of commercial infringements,[177] the fundamental allocation of the responsibility for the prosecution of non-commercial IP rights infringements had not been challenged.[178] This national legislation was criticised for enabling the executive to restrict users' Internet access without judicial review and for putting the burden of proof on the subscriber.[179]

In particular, the French government had initiated a national legislative initiative to combat online infringements of copyright, allowing the French administration, inter alia, to restrict French citizens accused of online copyright infringements from accessing the Internet.[180] In short, the French opposition made use of the reform process debated in the European Parliament to counteract, at the EU level, the French legislation by promoting the inclusion of the Internet Freedom Provision in the 2009 Regulatory Package.[181] The protracted negotiations on the Internet Freedom Provision delayed the adoption of the 2009 Regulatory Package significantly. The inclusion of the Internet Freedom Provision in the EU Regulatory

---

175   These include Arts 6 (Right to a fair trial) and 10 (Freedom of expression) of the European Convention on Human Rights (ECHR).

176   These include Arts 11 (Freedom of expression and information), 47 (Right to an effective remedy and to a fair trial) and 48 (Presumption of innocence and right of defence) of the Charter of Fundamental Rights of the European Union.

177   Directive 2004/48 of 29 April 2004 on the enforcement of intellectual property rights [2004] OJ L195/16.

178   F Rizzuto, 'European Union Telecommunications Law Reform and Combatting Online Non-Commercial Infringements of Copyright: Seeing Through the Legal Fog' [2011] 17(3) CTLR 75.

179   This, among other things, is why the French Constitutional court found the (first) HADOPI law to be partly unconstitutional. (HADOPI refers to Haute autorité pour la diffusion des oeuvres et la protection des droits sur Internet.) It was held that nowadays, Art 11 (freedom of speech) of the French Declaration of the Rights of Man and the Citizen of 1789 also implies the freedom to access online services. Conseil constitutionnel [CC], Decision no 2009–580 DC, 22 June 2009, *Journal Officiel de la Republique Francaise* [JO – Official Gazette of France] 13 June 2009, 9675, para 12. The decision is available in English at http://www.conseil-constitutionnel.fr/conseil-constitutionnel/root/bank_mm/anglais/2009_580dc.pdf   (accessed 3 December 2012). For a detailed analysis see Lucchi 'Access to Network Services and Protection of Constitutional Rights: Recognizing the Essential Role of Internet Access for the Freedom of Expression' (2011) 19 Cardozo J Int'l & Comp L 645.

180   Known as the HADOPI law, implementing the so called 'Three-Strikes-Out'-approach; see E Bonadio, 'File sharing, copyright and freedom of speech' [2011] 33 EIPR 619.

181   Rizzuto, 'European Union Telecommunications Law Reform and Combatting Online Non-Commercial Infringements of Copyright: Seeing Through the Legal Fog' [2011] 17(3) CTLR 75.

Framework also raised significant concerns with respect to a possible lack of the EU's power to regulate this issue.[182]

1.38   The Internet Freedom Provision (Article 1(3a) of the Framework Directive) in its final form contains two key elements.

The first key element is the creation of a right to access the Internet, which derives mainly from the fundamental right of freedom of expression and information.[183] While it remains unclear whether the Internet Freedom Provision implies that Internet access would constitute a new autonomous fundamental right,[184] the provision, in any case, regards Internet access as a prerequisite for exercising the fundamental rights of free speech, free reception and impartation of information[185] and provides that taking into account this relevance, such access may not be freely restricted on the national level.[186]

The second key element of the 'Internet Freedom' provision therefore consists of detailed procedural guidelines for the national prosecution of non-commercial online copyright infringement: measures restricting end-users' access to or use of 'services and applications through electronic communications networks' have to be 'appropriate, proportionate and necessary', and national prosecution procedures must follow specific standards of due process, which include 'due respect for the principle of the presumption of innocence and the right to privacy', a right to be heard as well as a right to effective and timely judicial review. These provisions must be seen in the context of the above mentioned French HADOPI law, as this law, inter alia, contained a significant shift of the burden of proof, requiring the Internet subscribers accused of copyright infringement to prove that they had properly secured their Internet access, or that a third party was in fact responsible for the alleged infringement.[187]

The question that remains, however, is how will national legislators transpose the 'Internet Freedom' provision, including its procedural requirements, and whether substantive amendments to existing national laws will become inevitable. Furthermore, there seems to be room for clarification by way of ECJ rulings with respect to the full scope of the procedural rules as well as the possible lack of EU powers to regulate 'Internet Freedom' issues.

---

182   Report of the EP delegation to the Conciliation Committee (A7–0070/2009) (16 November 2009) p 7; for an in-depth analysis of the Internet Freedom Provision and its genesis see Rizzuto, 'European Union Telecommunications Law Reform and Combatting Online Non-Commercial Infringements of Copyright: Seeing Through the Legal Fog' [2011] 17(3) CTLR 75.

183   Articles 10 (Freedom of expression) ECHR and 11 (Freedom of expression and information) of the Charter of Fundamental Rights of the European Union (CFREU).

184   See D Dods, P Brisby et al, 'Reform of European electronic communications law: a special briefing on the radical changes of 2009', [2010] 16(4) CTLR 102.

185   See, on the importance of 'Internet Freedom' to the exercising of fundamental rights, Commissioner N Kroes, 'Internet Freedom' (SPEECH/12/326) (4 May 2009).

186   The Commission stated that the amendment is an important restatement of key legal principles inherent in the legal order of the European Union, especially of citizens' fundamental rights, MEMO/08/681, 7 November 2008.

187   See E Bonadio, 'File sharing, copyright and freedom of speech' [2011] 33 EIPR 619.

National regulatory authorities: organisation, regulatory objectives, competencies and procedural rules

1.39   Some Member States still retain (partial) ownership or control of undertakings providing electronic communications networks or services. In order to secure the independence of their national regulatory authorities, the Member States must ensure that their NRAs 'are legally distinct from and functionally independent of all organisations providing electronic communications networks, equipment or services' (Article 3(2) of the Framework Directive) and there is in place effective structural separation of the regulatory function from activities associated with ownership and control. The Member States also must ensure that NRAs exercise their powers 'impartially and transparently' and that they have sufficient financial and human resources to perform the tasks assigned to them (Article 3(3) of the Framework Directive). The requirement for independence of the NRAs has been further specified by the 2009 Regulatory Package: when performing their tasks under the national rules transposing the EU Regulatory Framework, the NRAs must act independently and may not seek or take instructions from any other body. These requirements are, however, not intended to prevent 'supervision in accordance with national constitutional law' (Article 3(3a) of the Framework Directive). The possibility to provide for supervision of the NRA's actions where this is required by the Member States' constitutions has been included in the course of the review process in order to avoid conflicts between the constitutional demands for control of executive bodies through democratically legitimised bodies[188] and the demands of the EU Regulatory Framework in respect of the NRA's independence.[189] To further secure the independence of the NRAs, only appeal bodies established in accordance with Article 4 of the Framework Directive[190] may suspend or overturn the NRAs' decisions (Article 3(3a) of the Framework Directive).

1.40   Article 8 of the Framework Directive requires the Member States to ensure that the NRAs pursue certain policy objectives and abide by the regulatory principles established by Community law. The NRAs must take all 'reasonable' measures which are aimed at achieving a number of regulatory objectives which are set out in three categories: promotion of competition, development of the internal market, and promotion of the interests of the citizens of the European Union. Each of these overarching, primary regulatory objectives is specified by a broad variety of non-exhaustive secondary objectives. In taking regulatory measures, the NRAs must adhere to the principle of proportionality (Article 8(1), para 1 of the Framework Directive).

Article 8 of the Framework Directive sets forth three primary policy objectives:

- to promote competition and the provision of electronic communications networks and services;

---

188   Such conflicts might, for example, have arisen under German constitutional law, which requires effective supervision of the executive bodies' actions by a ministry that is accountable to Parliament.

189   See also ECJ judgment of 9 March 2010, *Commission v Germany* (C-518/07) [2010] ECR I-01885, holding that Germany had failed to ensure 'complete independence', ie 'independence of any external influence' of the data protection supervision authorities by providing for administrative surveillance; however, the Framework Directive explicitly provides for a supervision of the NRAs where required by the Member State's constitution.

190   See paras 1.50 and 1.51 below.

- to contribute to the development of the internal market; and
- to promote the interests of EU citizens.

1.41   The primary policy objective to promote competition and the provision of electronic communications networks and services means, among other things, that the national regulatory authorities must:

- ensure that all users 'derive maximum benefit in terms of choice, price and quality';
- ensure that 'there is no distortion or restriction of competition in the electronic communications sector, including the transmission of content'; and
- encourage 'efficient use' and ensure 'the effective management of radio frequencies and numbering resources' (Article 8(2) of the Framework Directive).

The ECJ has interpreted Article 8 of the Framework Directive to include a duty for Member States to ensure that the NRAs:

> 'take all reasonable measures aimed at promoting competition in the provision of electronic communication services, ensuring that there is no distortion or restriction of competition in the electronic communications sector and removing obstacles to the provision of those services on the European level'.[191]

1.42   The primary policy objective to contribute to the development of the internal market, means, among other things, that the NRAs must:

- remove 'remaining obstacles to the provision of electronic communications networks, associated facilities and services and electronic communications services at the EU level';
- encourage 'the establishment and development of trans-European networks and the inter-operability of trans-European services, and end-to-end connectivity'; and
- cooperate with each other, with the Commission and with BEREC to ensure 'the development of a consistent regulatory practice' and the consistent application of the EU Regulatory Framework (Article 8(3) of the Framework Directive).

1.43   The primary policy objective to promote the interests of the EU citizens means, among other things, that the NRAs must:

- ensure that all EU citizens have access to the Universal Service;
- ensure a high level of consumer protection;
- contribute to ensure a 'high level of protection of personal data and privacy';
- promote the provision of 'clear information' to users;
- address the 'needs of specific social groups, in particular disabled users, elderly users and users with specific social needs';
- ensure public network integrity and security; and
- promote 'the ability of end-users to access and distribute information or run applications and services of their choice' (Article 8(4) of the Framework Directive).[192]

---

191   ECJ judgment of 12 November 2009 *Telia Sonera Finland Oyi* (C-192/08) [2009] ECR I-10717, at [49–62].

192   This refers to 'net neutrality': see para 1.198 et seq below.

1.44 The 2009 Regulatory Package has further specified that in pursuit of these primary policy objectives the NRAs are to apply 'objective, transparent, non-discriminatory and proportionate regulatory principles'. This means that the NRA must among other things:

- promote the predictability of regulation through a consistent regulatory approach;
- ensure the non-discriminatory treatment of undertakings providing electronic communications networks and services;
- safeguard competition and promote infrastructure-based competition, where appropriate;
- promote 'efficient investment and innovation in new and enhanced infrastructures' and, in this context, ensure that ex-ante obligations take sufficient account of investment risks and permit cooperative arrangements to diversify the risks of investment while securing competition and preserving the principle of non-discrimination;
- take account of geographic varieties relating to competition and consumers within a Member State; and
- impose ex-ante regulatory obligations 'only where there is no effective and sustainable competition and relaxing or lifting such obligations as soon as that condition is fulfilled'.

1.45 The colourful patchwork of the three primary policy objectives is complemented by the regulatory objectives established in the Specific Directives.[193] When balancing the various regulatory objectives, the NRAs will need to consider their relative importance, which is expressed, to a certain extent, by subtle differences in wording ('ensure', 'encourage', 'promote', 'contribute', 'address').

An additional, albeit not mandatory, requirement for the NRAs' regulatory decisions is that they should be technologically neutral: Member States are obliged to ensure that NRAs 'take the utmost account of the desirability of making regulations technologically neutral'.

The obligation of NRAs to contribute to the achievement of content-related regulatory objectives is even weaker, which is hardly surprising given the 'content neutrality' of the 2002 Regulatory Package.[194] However, the access to such content by means of electronic communications has been safeguarded through the introduction of an Internet Freedom Provision in Art 1(3a) of the Framework Directive.[195]

1.46 Article 5(1) of the Framework Directive requires the Member States to ensure that NRAs are able to request, from undertakings providing electronic communications networks and services, all the information, including financial information, that is necessary to ensure conformity with the provisions of the Framework Directive and the Specific Directives. The 2009 Regulatory Package has amended this obligation to include 'information concerning future network or service developments that could have an impact on the wholesale services that [network and service providers] make available to competitors' while undertakings with SMP on wholesale markets may be asked to provide accounting data on the retail markets that are associated with the wholesale markets they have SMP on. The information must be provided 'promptly on request and to the time scales and level of detail required by the national regulatory authority'. The information

---

193 Article 1(1) and (2) of the Access Directive, Art 1(1) and (2) of the Universal Service Directive, Art 1(1) of the Authorisation Directive.
194 See Art 1(3) of the Framework Directive.
195 See para 1.36 et seq above.

request needs to comply with the principle of proportionality and the NRA must provide the reasons justifying the request for information.

1.47   The Framework Directive establishes a number of procedural rules which pertain, in part, to the regulatory procedures of the NRAs and, in part, to the cooperation between NRAs and Commission. These procedural rules include:

- obligations to publish information;[196]
- obligations to conduct public hearings or consultations;[197] and
- obligations to cooperate.[198]

1.48   Regarding the obligations to conduct public hearings or consultations, the consultation procedure under Article 6 of the Framework Directive is of particular importance. This article requires that Member States ensure that a consultation procedure is conducted where NRAs intend to take measures in accordance with the Framework Directive or the Specific Directives or where they intend to impose restrictions to the use of radio frequencies for electronic communication services according to Article 9(3) and (4) of the Framework Directive 'which have a significant impact on the relevant market'.[199] The Directive does not specify how 'a significant impact on the relevant market' is to be assessed. The Directive also fails to provide detailed guidance for conducting the consultation procedure: the NRAs must 'give interested parties the opportunity to comment on the draft measure within a reasonable period'. This leaves open the question as to who is to be included among the 'interested parties'.[200] It would seem, from the wording of other provisions of secondary Community law, that 'interested parties' are 'third parties whose interests may be affected'; this means that the consultation procedure is not open to any party, but only to parties who can show a sufficient interest in the decision at hand.[201]

More generally, Article 3(4) of the Framework Directive requires the Member States to ensure 'consultation and cooperation' between the NRAs of the various Member States and between the NRAs and national authorities entrusted with the implementation of competition law and consumer law 'on matters of common interest'. This general cooperation obligation is further specified in Article 3(5) of

---

196   Article 5(4) of the Framework Directive: obligation to publish such information as would contribute to an open and competitive market; Art 10(3) of the Framework Directive: obligation to publish the national numbering plans; Art 24(1) of the Framework Directive: obligation to publish up-to-date information pertaining to the application of the Directives.

197   Article 6 of the Framework Directive: see para 1.48 below; Art 12(2) of the Framework Directive: obligation to hold a public consultation with all 'interested parties' prior to imposing the sharing of facilities or property.

198   Articles 7 and 7(a) of the Framework Directive, See para 1.53 et seq below.

199   See Arts 7(9), 20 and 21 of the Framework Directive for exceptions.

200   See N Nikolinakos, 'The new European regulatory regime for electronic communications networks and associated services: the proposed Framework and Access/Interconnection Directives' [2001] 22(3) ECLR 93.

201   Cf Recital 32, Art 17(1), sub-para 3, Art 27(4) and Art 33(2) of Council Regulation (EC) No 1/2003 of 16 December 2002 on the implementation of the rules on competition laid down in Articles 81 and 82 of the Treaty [2003] OJ L1/1; for a clear distinction between parties showing 'a sufficient interest' and 'other third parties' see also Recital 6, and in particular Art 9 of Commission Regulation (EC) No 2842/98 of 22 December 1998 on the hearing of parties in certain proceedings under Articles 85 and 86 of the EC Treaty [1998] OJ L354/18; see also M Szydlo, 'The promotion of investments in new markets in electronic communications and the role of national regulatory authorities after Commission v Germany' [2011] 60(2) ICLQ 533.

the Framework Directive, which requires NRAs and national competition authorities to provide each other 'with the information necessary for the application of the
provisions of [the Framework Directive] and the Specific Directives'.

1.49   Article 20 of the Framework Directive sets out the Community law framework for the establishment of dispute resolution procedures to be conducted by the
NRAs for speedy, non-judicial resolution of controversies between undertakings in
a given Member State. Under this provision, the NRA must, at the request of one
of the parties to a controversy, issue a binding decision on any dispute:

> 'arising in connection with obligations arising under [the Framework Direc-
> tive] or the Specific Directives between undertakings providing electronic
> communications networks or services in a Member State or between such
> undertakings and other undertakings in the Member State benefiting from
> obligations of access and/or interconnection under [the Framework Directive]
> or the Specific Directives'.

This binding decision must be rendered 'in the shortest possible time frame'.[202] By
way of example, the recitals of the Framework Directive[203] mention disputes
'relating to obligations for access and interconnection or to the means of transferring subscriber lines'. The dispute resolution procedure does not preclude either
party from bringing an action before the national courts (Article 20(5) of the
Framework Directive).

With respect to cross-border disputes arising under the Framework Directive or the
Specific Directives between parties in different Member States where the dispute lies
within the competence of NRAs of more than one Member State, the Framework
Directive provides for a co-ordinated dispute resolution procedure at the request of
one of the parties. The competent NRAs coordinate their efforts and have a right to
approach BEREC and request an opinion as to the actions to be taken in
accordance with the Framework Directive and/or the Specific Directives to resolve
the cross-border dispute (Article 21(2) of the Framework Directive). The Member
States may make provision to enable the competent NRAs jointly to decline to
resolve a dispute 'where other mechanisms, including mediation, exist and would
better contribute to resolution of the dispute in a timely manner' (Article 21(3),
para 1 of the Framework Directive). If, however, after four months the dispute is
not resolved, if the dispute has not been brought before the court by the parties
seeking regress, and if either party requests it, the NRAs must 'coordinate their
efforts in order to bring about the resolution of the dispute' while 'taking the
utmost account of any opinion adopted by BEREC' (Article 21(3) of the Framework Directive). As with dispute resolution procedures for disputes within a
Member State, the dispute resolution procedure for cross-border disputes does not
preclude either party from bringing an action before the courts (Article 21(4) of the
Framework Directive).

Right of appeal against NRA's decisions

1.50   Article 4(1), sentence 1 of the Framework Directive provides that 'effective
measures' must exist at a national level, under which any user or undertaking
providing electronic communications networks or services 'who is affected' by a
decision of an NRA has the right of appeal against the decision to an 'appeal body'

---

202 Within four months, except in exceptional circumstances.
203 Recital 32 of the Framework Directive.

that is independent of the parties involved. In this context, the right of appeal against the decision of a national regulatory authority must be 'based on an effective appeal mechanism which permits the merits of the case duly to be taken into account'.[204] The independent appeal body may, but is not required to be a court (Article 4(1), sentence 2 of the Framework Directive). Pending the outcome of any appeal, the decision of the NRA shall stand 'unless the appeal body decides otherwise' (Article 4(1), sentence 3 of the Framework Directive).

1.51   Article 4(1), sentence 1 of the Framework Directive does not limit the right of appeal to the addressees which are subject to an NRA's decision.[205] Rather, it establishes an obligation of national legislators, under EU law, to provide a right of appeal to a user or undertaking providing electronic networks or services who or which may derive rights from the EU legal order (in particular from the electronic communications Directives) and whose rights are affected by an NRA's decision.[206] In this context it is sufficient that the party's rights are 'potentially' affected by the NRA's decision.[207] National legislators are not prevented, by Article 4(1) of the Framework Directive, from extending the right of appeal to other third parties that have an interest in the outcome of the controversy.

The Commission's powers of control and harmonisation

1.52   The European legislator has delegated broad regulatory powers to the NRAs and has strengthened the NRAs' discretion to select the appropriate regulatory remedies;[208] these regulatory powers at the national level are counterbalanced, however, by requirements for co-ordination of NRAs' decisions and positions at the EU level in order to secure a coordinated and coherent application of the EU Regulatory Framework by the Member States.[209] This co-ordination is achieved in the first instance by requiring the NRAs to cooperate and to consult with each other, the Commission and BEREC[210] (Articles 7(2) and (3), and 7a(2) to (6) of the Framework Directive).[211] Furthermore, powers of control and harmonisation have been granted to the Commission, including a right to veto certain decisions of the NRAs.

---

204   ECJ Judgment of 13 July 2006, *Mobistar SA* (C-438/04) [2006] ECR I-06675 at [38].
205   Such narrow scope of the right of appeal set forth in Art 4(1) of the Framework Directive might be assumed, considering Recital 12 which states that 'any party who *is the subject of a decision* by a national regulatory authority should have the right to appeal to a body that is independent of the parties involved' [emphasis added].
206   ECJ Judgment of 21 February 2008 *Tele 2 Telecommunication* (C-426/05) [2008] ECR I-00685 at [32], confirming a right of appeal against an NRA's decision in the context of market analysis for the competitors of the regulated undertaking whose rights were adversely affected by the decision; see also ECJ Judgment of 24 April 2008 *Arcor v Bundesrepublik Deutschland* (C-55/06) [2008] ECR I-02931 at [176].
207   ECJ Judgment of 21 February 2008 *Tele 2 Telecommunication* (C-426/05) [2008] ECR I-00685 at [39]; see also ECJ Judgment of 24 April 2008 *Arcor v Bundesrepublik Deutschland* (C-55/06) [2008] ECR I-02931 at [176]
208   See para 1.23 above and paras 1.75 1.122 and 1.142 below.
209   SEC(2006) 816, 28 June 2006, p 18; COM(2007) 696 final, 13 November 2007, p 8 et seq.
210   See paras 1.18 and 1.24 above.
211   See para 1.53 et seq.

The consolidation procedure

1.53   Under the heading 'Consolidating the internal market for electronic communications', the Framework Directive, in Article 7, establishes a co-operation obligation under which the NRAs must co-operate with each other, the Commission and
BEREC 'in a transparent manner' in order to ensure 'the consistent application, in
all Member States, of the [Framework] Directive and the Specific Directives'
(Article 7(2) of the Framework Directive). The provision further establishes a
two-tiered 'consolidation procedure' (Article 7(3)–(5) of the Framework Directive).

1.54   The NRAs are required to notify the Commission and the NRAs in other
Member States and to conduct a consultation procedure (Article 7(3)) before taking
a measure which:

- falls within the scope of Articles 15 or 16 of the Framework Directive[212] or
  Articles 5 or 8 of the Access Directive;[213] and
- would affect trade between Member States.

The Commission has adopted detailed rules for the notification process in a
Recommendation[214] and may according to the newly adopted Article 7a of the
Framework Directive issue further Recommendations or guidelines regarding the
co-ordination procedure which define the form, content and level of detail for
notifications under Article 7(3) of the Framework Directive, the circumstances in
which a notification will not be required, and the calculation of time-limits. The
NRA must make its draft measure available to the Commission, BEREC and
the other national regulatory authorities, together with the reasons on which the
measure is based. The NRAs in other Member States, BEREC and the Commission
then have one month to comment on the draft measure; this time limit may not be
extended.[215]

Once the comment period has ended, the NRA may adopt draft measures that are
not subject to the veto-procedure,[216] taking 'the utmost account of comments of
other national regulatory authorities, BEREC and the Commission' (Article 7(7) of
the Framework Directive); this means that the measure may be adopted despite
objections raised by other NRAs and/or the Commission.

1.55   When a measure that an NRA intends to take aims to define a relevant
market which differs from those defined in the Commission's Recommendation on
relevant product and service markets, [217] or decide whether or not to designate an
undertaking as having, either individually or jointly with others, significant market
power,[218] the one-month consultation period is followed by the veto procedure

---

212 Measures of the NRA in the context of the market definition procedure or the market
     analysis procedure – see para 1.62 et seq. below.
213 Measures concerning access and interconnection (Art 5 of the Access Directive) and measures
     concerning undertakings designated to have SMP (Art 8 of the Access Directive); see
     paras 1.141 et seq and 1.145 et seq below.
214 Commission Recommendation of 23 July 2003 on notifications, time limits and consultations
     provided for in Art 7 of Directive 2002/21/EC of the European Parliament and of the Council
     on a common regulatory framework for electronic communications networks and services
     [2003] OJ L190/13.
215 Article 7(3), sentence 3 of the Framework Directive.
216 See para 1.55 below.
217 See para 1.73 et seq below.
218 See paras 1.71 et seq and 1.75 below.

under Article 7(4) of the Framework Directive[219] if the measure would affect trade between the Member States and the Commission has indicated to the NRA that:

- it considers that the draft measure would create a barrier to the single market; or
- it has serious doubts as to its compatibility with Community law and, in particular, the objectives referred to in Article 8 of the Framework Directive.

In this case, the NRA is prevented from adopting the measure for a further two months; this period may not be extended.

During this two-month period, the Commission may issue a decision requiring the NRA concerned to withdraw the draft measure (Article 7(5)(a) of the Framework Directive) or take back its reservations concerning the draft measure (Article 7(5)(a) of the Framework Directive), taking utmost account of the opinion of BEREC before issuing its decision. This decision must be accompanied by a detailed and objective analysis of why the Commission considers that the draft measure should not be adopted, together with specific proposals for amending the draft measure (Article 7(5) of the Framework Directive).[220]

Following the Commission's decision requiring the NRA to withdraw a measure, the NRA concerned must amend or withdraw the measure within a period of six months following the Commission's decision; the Commission does not have a right to replace the proposed measure of the NRA with a measure of its own. The NRA's amended measure is subject to public consultation and re-notification (Article 7(6) of the Framework Directive).

1.56   An assessment as to whether a proposed measure 'would affect trade between Member States' is based on the same standard as the comparable assessment under Articles 101(1) and 102 sentence 2 of the TFEU (ex Articles 81(1) and 82, sentence 2 of the ECT). This means that it must be possible to foresee with a sufficient degree of probability on the basis of a set of objective factors of law or of fact that the measure in question 'may have an influence, direct or indirect, actual or potential, on the pattern of trade between Member States'.[221] The same applies to the prognosis that a proposed measure of an NRA 'would create a barrier to the single market'. The alternatively existing threshold of 'serious doubts as to [the draft measure's] compatibility with Community law' appears to be more difficult to overcome, whereas the further requirement of 'serious doubts as to its compatibility with ... the objectives referred to in article 8' can be more easily met, given both the vagueness and the multitude of the objectives set out in Article 8 of the Framework Directive. [222] In its veto decisions, to date, the Commission has held, inter alia, that a draft measure designating or not designating an undertaking with SMP and the regulatory obligations that may or may not be imposed in one Member State with respect to the provision of a given service 'may have an influence, direct or indirect,

---

219   NRAs may in exceptional circumstances derogate from the consolidation procedure and adopt provisional measures (Art 7(6) of theFramework Directive); see para 1.57 below.

220   See Commission Recommendation of 23 July 2003 on notifications, time limits and consultations provided for in Art 7 of Directive 2002/21/EC of the European Parliament and of the Council on a common regulatory framework for electronic communications networks and services [2003] OJ L190/13.

221   ECJ Judgment of 30 June 1966, Case 56–65, *Société Technique Minière v Maschinenbau Ulm GmbH* [1966] ECR 282.

222   See para 1.40 et seq above.

actual or potential, on the ability of undertakings established in other Member States to provide such electronic communications services'.[223]

1.57   The consultation procedure as well as, in particular, the veto procedure can lead to significant delays of the regulatory procedures at national level. The NRAs can aim at avoiding the veto procedure, however, by taking the Commission's objections into account during the consultation procedure.

The veto procedure is the quid pro quo for the flexible and procedure-oriented regulatory approach provided for in the EU Regulatory Package, under which ex-ante obligations can only be imposed on undertakings which have been designated, in the course of a complex, multi-tiered market definition and market analysis procedure, as undertakings with significant market power.[224]

As of April 2010, the Commission had taken six veto decisions, which covered nine cases.[225] In these veto decisions the Commission held, among other things, that:

- the Polish regulator had not provided sufficient reasons for its decision to regulate the markets for Internet traffic exchange services (IP-Peering and IP-Transit) and to support its finding of SMP on these markets;[226]
- the Polish regulator did not sufficiently justify its intent to regulate broadband access services in addition to regulating retail narrowband access;[227]
- the Finnish regulator had failed to provide sufficient evidence to support its finding of the absence of SMP in the markets for (retail) publicly available international telephone services provided at fixed locations for residential customers and for non-residential customers;[228]
- the Finnish regulator had failed to provide sufficient evidence to support its finding of the existence of SMP in the market for access and call origination on public mobile telephone networks;[229]
- the Austrian regulator had failed to provide sufficient evidence to support its finding of the absence of SMP on the market for transit services in the fixed public telephone network;[230] and
- the German regulator had failed to provide sufficient evidence to support its finding that the alternative fixed telephone network operators in Germany, despite having a market share of 100 per cent with respect to their respective networks, did not have SMP in the market for call termination on individual public telephone networks at a fixed location.[231]

While emphasising that the NRAs are accorded discretionary powers corresponding to the complex character of the economic, factual and legal situations that must be assessed, the Commission has included, in its veto decisions, detailed 'proposals' for amending the draft measures. However, the actual number of veto

---

223   Cf Commission Decision of 20 February 2004, C(2004)527 final, para 14.
224   See para 1.63 et seq below.
225   Cf S Krueger, 'A consistent and effective implementation of the new regulatory framework: the triangle formed by the European Commission, BEREC and National Regulators' (presentation at the CMT-Conference on The New Regulatory Framework for Telecommunications in Europe, Barcelona, 26 April 2010), p 6, available on: http://www.cmt.es/es/publicaciones/anexos/EC,_BEREC_and_National_Regulators.pdf (accessed on 4 December 2012).
226   Commission Decision of 4 March 2010 in Cases PL/2009/1019 and PL/2009/1020.
227   Commission Decision in Cases PL/2009/518 and PL/2006/24.
228   Commission Decision of 20 February 2004, C (2004) 527 final, para 15 et seq.
229   Commission Decision of 05 October 2004, C (2004) 3682 final, para 11 et seq.
230   Commission Decision of 20 October 2004, C (2004) 4070 final, para 15 et seq.
231   Commission Decision of 17 May 2005, C (2005) 1442 final, para 17 et seq.

decisions is very small compared to the number of notified measures. This indicates that the Commission has refrained from micro-managing the NRAs' market analyses and has limited itself to monitoring misuses of the NRAs' discretion instead.

An NRA may only 'in exceptional circumstances' adopt provisional measures by way of derogation from the consultation and veto procedures where it considers that there is an urgent need to act in order to safeguard competition and protect the interests of users. In this case, the NRA must, without delay, communicate its provisional measures, with full reasons, to the Commission, BEREC and the other NRAs (Article 7(9) of the Framework Directive).

The co-regulation procedure

1.58   The 2009 Regulatory Framework introduced in Article 7a of the Framework Directive a 'co-regulation' procedure intended to secure 'the consistent application of remedies' throughout the EU.

If the Commission is of the opinion that a notified[232] draft measure which seeks to impose, amend or withdraw a remedy imposed on an SMP undertaking or an undertaking controlling access to end users would create a barrier to the single market or in the case of serious doubts as to its compatibility with EU law, the Commission may, within a period of one month, inform the relevant NRA concerned and BEREC of its opinion, including the reasons for its opinion. The NRA concerned may not adopt the intended measure for a further three months following (Article 7a(1), sub-para 1 of the Framework Directive). In the event that no such notification is given, the NRA concerned may adopt the draft measure, taking utmost account of any comments made by the Commission, BEREC and any other NRA (Article 7a(1), sub-para 2 of the Framework Directive).

During the three-month period following such notification of the Commission of its serious doubts under Article 7a(1), sub-para 1 of the Framework Directive, BEREC and the NRA concerned are required to 'co-operate closely' with the objective of identifying the most appropriate and effective measure in the light of the objectives laid down in Article 8 of the Framework Directive and taking into due account the 'need to ensure the development of consistent regulatory practice' and the views of market participants (Article 7a(2) of the Framework Directive).

Within six weeks from the beginning of the three-month period, BEREC must deliver a reasoned opinion on the Commission's notification, indicating whether it believes that the draft measure should be amended or withdrawn, and including specific proposals to that end where appropriate (Article 7a(3) of the Framework Directive).

If BEREC, in its opinion, agrees with the serious doubts of the Commission, it co-operates with the relevant NRA with the aim to identify the most appropriate and effective measure. In this event the NRA may either amend or withdraw its draft measure (Article 7a(4)(a) of the Framework Directive) or make use of its competence to maintain its draft measure as originally notified (Article 7a(4)(b) of the Framework Directive).

If the NRA amends or maintains its draft measure, or if BEREC does not share the serious doubts of the Commission or does not issue an opinion pursuant to

---

232   Article 7(3) of the Framework Directive: see para 1.53 above.

Article 7a(3) of the Framework Directive, the Commission may, within one month following the end of the three-month period following its notification of serious doubts, either issue a recommendation requiring the NRA concerned to amend or withdraw the draft measure or take a decision to lift its reservations to the draft measure while, in both cases, taking utmost account of any opinion issued by BEREC (Article 7a(5) of the Framework Directive). The NRA may either follow the recommendation of the Commission or adopt the measure despite recommendations to the contrary and has to inform the Commission and BEREC of its final decision (Article 7(6) of the Framework Directive). If the Commission has recommended amendment or withdrawal of the draft measure, the NRA has to provide a reasoned justification if it decides not to amend or withdraw its measure (Article 7a(7) of the Framework Directive).

While the Commission has, under the co-regulation mechanism, a larger say regarding the implementation of remedies by the NRAs, it still lacks veto powers or other binding legal means to set-aside or influence the NRAs' decisions with respect to the application of remedies. It remains to be seen whether the complex co-regulation procedure will contribute to a consistent application of remedies throughout the EU as intended or whether further and more stringent measures will have to be taken to ensure a harmonised approach.

The Commission's power to stipulate standards and specifications

1.59   The Commission's powers to ensure the harmonised application of the EU Regulatory Framework include the publication of non-compulsory standards and specifications to promote the harmonised provision of electronic communications networks and services, the initiation of standardisation procedures, and the power to make technical standards or specifications compulsory if the non-compulsory standards or specifications have not been adequately implemented so that interoperability of services in one or more Member States cannot be ensured (Article 17(3) of the Framework Directive). If the Commission intends to make technical standards compulsory, it will issue a 'notice' and invites comments through a public consultation; the implementation of the relevant standards is made compulsory by referring to them as compulsory standards in the list of standards or specifications published in the *Official Journal*[233] (Article 17(4) of the Framework Directive).

The Commission's power to issue recommendations

1.60   In addition to the recommendations[234] and guidelines[235] which seek to harmonise the market definition and market analysis procedures, the Commission has the power, under Article 19 of the Framework Directive, to issue:

'[a] recommendation or a decision on the harmonised application of the provisions in this [Framework] Directive and the Specific Directives in order to further the achievement of the objectives set out in article 8 [Framework Directive]'.

---

233   See Commission Decision (2007/176/EC) of 11 December 2006 establishing a list of standards and/or specifications for electronic communications networks, services and associated facilities and services and replacing all previous versions [2007] OJ L86/11, as amended by Commission Decision 2008/286/EC of 17 March 2008 [2008] OJ L93/24.

234   Article 15(1) of the Framework Directive; see para 1.66 et seq below.

235   Article 15(2) of the Framework Directive; see para 1.63 below.

These recommendations are issued on the basis of the advisory procedure (Article 22(2) of the Framework Directive) and need to take utmost account of' the opinion of BEREC. The – legally non-binding – recommendations (Article 288(5) of the TFEU (Article 249(5) of the EC Treaty)) have a specific 'soft law' quality: Member States must ensure that the NRAs 'take the utmost account of those recommendations in carrying out their tasks' (Article 19(2), sentence 1 of the Framework Directive). Where a national regulatory authority chooses not to follow a recommendation, it must inform the Commission, giving the reasons for its position (Article 19(2), sentence 2 of the Framework Directive).

Safeguarding the Commission's powers of control and harmonisation

1.61 In order to contribute to the development of the single market in the most effective manner, the NRAs need to cooperate closely with each other, the Commission and BEREC (Article 7(2) of the Framework Directive). Moreover, the Commission needs to receive, from Member States and NRAs, all information necessary for the exercise of its harmonisation and control duties. To this end, Article 5(2) of the Framework Directive establishes a right of the Commission to obtain from NRAs all information 'necessary for it to carry out its tasks under the Treaty'. In addition, the EU Regulatory Framework establishes a number of specific information and cooperation obligations, which are set out in the table below.

Provision	Obligation
Article 3(3c) Framework Directive	Obligation of NRAs to take utmost account of BEREC's opinions and common positions when adopting their own decisions for the national markets.
Article 4(3) Framework Directive	Obligation of the Member States to provide the Commission and BEREC with information on the general subject, the number and the duration of appeal proceedings against decisions of NRAs, as well as on the number of decisions to grant interim measures.
Article 7a Framework Directive	Obligation of NRAs, BEREC and the Commission to co-operate with each other with regard to the imposition of remedies.
Article 8a(2) Framework Directive	Duty of the Member States to co-operate with each other and with the Commission, to promote the co-ordination and harmonisation of radio spectrum policy approaches in the EU.
Article 13a(3) Framework Directive	Obligation of NRAs to inform NRAs in other Member States and the European Network and Information Security Agency (ENISA) of breaches of security or loss of integrity that have had a significant impact on the operation of networks or services.
Articles 15(2), 16(1) Framework Directive	Obligation of NRAs to take utmost account of the Commission's Market Recommendation and the Guidelines on market analysis when they define and analyse relevant markets.

Provision	Obligation
Article19(1) Framework Directive	Obligation of Member States to take utmost account of the Commission's Recommendations on the harmonised application of the Directives.
Article24(2) Framework Directive	Obligation of Member States to provide the Commission with up-to-date information pertaining to the application of the Directives.
Article8(5) Access Directive	Obligation of NRAs to notify the Commission of decisions to impose, amend or withdraw obligations on market players not designated as having SMP in order to comply with international commitments.
Article13a(2) and (3) Access Directive	Obligation of NRAs to submit a detailed and reasoned proposal to the Commission when the NRAs intend to impose an obligation for functional separation.
Article15(2) Access Directive	Obligation of Member States to provide to the Commission information on the specific obligations imposed on undertakings under the Access Directive.
Article16 sentence 2 Authorisation Directive	Obligation of Member States to supply at the Commission's request information on the functioning of the national authorisation systems.
Article22(3) Universal Service Directive	Obligation of NRAs to provide the Commission and the BEREC with a summary of the grounds for action, the envisaged requirements and the proposed course of action before setting minimum quality of service requirements on undertakings providing public communications networks.
Article36(1) and (2) Universal Service Directive	Obligation of NRAs to notify the Commission of the names of undertakings designated as having universal service obligations under Article8(1) of the Universal Service Directive as well as of the universal service obligations imposed on such undertakings.

'Significant Market Power' as fundamental prerequisite of regulation

1.62 The Framework Directive and the Specific Directives establish a number of regulatory powers of the NRAs with respect to providers of electronic communications networks and services.[236] The majority of these regulatory powers are aimed at undertakings designated as having significant market power ('SMP').[237] In order to achieve public interest objectives other than the promotion of competition, e g cultural and linguistic diversity, media pluralism, and including the objectives of

---

236 Cf Revised ERG Common Position on the approach to Appropriate remedies in the ECNS regulatory framework (ERG (06)33) (May 2006); see also ERG Common Position on Best Practices in Remedies Imposed as a Consequence of a Position of Significant Market Power in the Relevant Markets for Wholesale Leased Lines (ERG (07) 54 final).

237 See para 1.64 et seq below.

interoperability and of 'end-to-end' communications, the Directives also provide for regulatory powers regardless of the regulated enterprise's market position.[238]

The following regulatory measures apply exclusively to undertakings designated as having significant market power:

- transparency obligations in conjunction with access and interconnection (Article 9 of the Access Directive);
- obligation of non-discrimination regarding access and interconnection (Article 10 of the Access Directive);
- obligation of accounting separation (Article 11 of the Access Directive);
- obligations of access to, and use of, specific network facilities (Article 12 of the Access Directive);
- price control and cost accounting obligations (Article 13 of the Access Directive, Article 18(1), sentence 2 in conjunction with No 2 Annex II of the Universal Service Directive);
- functional separation (Article 13a of the Access Directive); and
- regulatory controls on retail services (Article 17 of the Universal Service Directive).

THE CONCEPT OF SIGNIFICANT MARKET POWER IN THE EU REGULATORY FRAMEWORK

1.63   Under the EU Regulatory Framework, the definition of SMP set forth in the Framework Directive is equivalent to the competition law concept of 'dominant market power'. By using this concept, the legislator has taken an important step toward the intended replacement of sector-specific regulation by competition law.[239] The former greater predictability of regulatory measures which had been ensured by the 25 per cent threshold under the previous regulatory framework[240] has been replaced by a 'more flexible' threshold for regulatory measures; this flexibility, however, is limited by the procedural rules of the Framework Directive governing the determination of SMP undertakings and by the Commission Guidelines on market analysis and the assessment of significant market power under the Community regulatory framework for electronic communications networks and services[241] ('Commission Guidelines on Market Analysis').

SIGNIFICANT MARKET POWER – ASSESSMENT CRITERIA

1.64   The Framework Directive replaces the rebuttable presumption which had been set out in several Directives of the previous regulatory framework, under which significant market power was presumed to exist if an organisation had 'a share of more than 25 per cent of a particular telecommunications market in the

---

238   Eg Arts 5 and 6 of the Access Directive, Art 12(2) of the Framework Directive, Arts 29, 30 and 31 of the Universal Service Directive.

239   The aim of the EU Regulatory Framework is to progressively reduce ex-ante sector specific rules as competition in the markets develops and, ultimately, for electronic communications to be governed by competition law only: see Recital 5 of the Better Regulation Directive.

240   Article 4(3) of Directive 97/33/EC [1997] OJ L199/32, as amended by Directive 98/61/EC [1998] OJ L268/37.

241   Commission Guidelines on market analysis and the assessment of significant market power under the Community regulatory framework for electronic communications networks and services [2002] OJ C165/6.

geographical area in a Member State within which it is authorised to operate,[242] with a new definition of significant market power, following closely the definition established, in the case law of the European Court of Justice, for a 'dominant market position'.[243] According to Article 14(2) of the Framework Directive, an undertaking:

> 'shall be deemed to have significant market power if, either individually or jointly with others, it enjoys a position equivalent to dominance, that is to say a position of economic strength affording it the power to behave to an appreciable extent independently of competitors, customers and ultimately consumers'.

The Directive adopts the concept of collective dominance, which has been clarified and developed through jurisprudence of the European Courts in recent years.[244] In particular, the existence of structural links among the undertakings concerned is not a prerequisite for a finding of collective dominance.[245] In ECJ case law, three cumulative criteria must be fulfilled to conclude that undertakings are jointly dominant on a market:

(i)   sufficient market transparency which allows the oligopolistic undertakings to detect defection from the tacitly collusive behaviour;

(ii) deterrent mechanisms to secure sustainability of the coordination; and

(iii) a lack of power of customers and existing and future competitors to jeopardise the results expected from the coordination.[246]

However, these criteria must not be applied 'mechanically' but rather assessed taking into account the 'overall economic mechanism of a hypothetical tacit collusion'.[247] Annex II to the Framework Directive provides an 'indicative' and 'not exhaustive' list of market characteristics which are relevant when assessing joint dominance in the context of electronic communications. These include:

● low elasticity of demand;
● similar market shares;
● high legal or economic barriers to entry;
● vertical integration with collective refusal to supply;
● lack of countervailing buyer power; and
● lack of potential competition.

---

242   Article 4(3) of the Interconnection Directive (as amended by Directive 98/61/EC); see also Art 2(3) of the Leased Lines Directive (as amended by ONP Framework Directive (1997)); Art 2(2)(i) of the Voice Telephony Directive (1998) and Art 7(1)(d) in conjunction with Art 2(2) of the Directive 97/13/EC.

243   See the ECJ's definition as provided in ECJ Judgment of 14 February 1978, *United Brands v Commission* (27/76) [1978] ECR I-207, at 286.

244   See ECJ Judgment of 10 July 2008, *Impala* [2008] (413/06) ECR-I 4591; Judgment of the Court of First Instance 28 June 2005, *Airtours* (T-342/99 DEP) [2004] ECR-II 1785; see also ECJ Judgment of 16 March 2000, *Compagnie Maritime Belge et al v Commission* (C-395/96 P and C- 396/96 P) [2000] ECR-I 1365, 1387 et seq, and Judgment of the Court of First Instance, *Gencor v Commission* (T-102/96) [1999] ECR-II 753, 815 et seq; for details see also Commission Guidelines on market analysis, para 86 et seq and European Regulators Group, Working paper on the SMP concept for the new regulatory framework, (ERG(93) 09rev3)(September 2005), p 9 et seq.

245   Commission Guidelines on Market Analysis, paras 87 and 90–94.

246   ECJ Judgment of 10 July 2008, *Impala* (C-413/06) [2008] ECR-I 4591; see also European Regulators Group, Working paper on the SMP concept for the new regulatory framework, (ERG(93) 09rev3) (September 2005), p 9 et seq.

247   ECJ Judgment of 10 July 2008, *Impala* (C-413/06) [2008] ECR-I 4591.

1.65   Article 14(3) of the Framework Directive facilitates the regulation of verti-cally integrated providers of networks and services. Specifically, this article provides that, where an undertaking has SMP 'on a specific market (the first market), it may also be designated as having significant market power on a closely related market (the second market), where the links between the two markets are such as to allow the market power held in the first market to be leveraged into the second market, thereby strengthening the market power of the undertaking'.[248] Article 14(3), sentence 2 of the Framework Directive which allows the imposition of remedies on such undertakings regarding the second market, was introduced by the 2009 Regulatory Package in order 'to clarify that remedies such as non-discrimination, transparency, accounting separation and prohibitions on anti-competitive bundling, etc may be applied "cross market" to address leverage problems' without a require-ment for the NRAs to find 'double dominance' both on the first and second market.[249] However, if an undertaking has been designated as having SMP on an upstream wholesale or access market, the NRAs will usually be in a position to prevent likely spill-over or leverage effects from the upstream market downstream into the retail or services market by imposing on that undertaking specific obliga-tions provided for in the Directives to avoid such effects.[250]

1.66   The concept of significant market power is further specified in the Commis-sion Guidelines on Market Analysis which were adopted on the basis of Art-icle 15(2) of the Framework Directive.[251] The assessment of significant market power is based on a two-step approach. As a first step, the relevant market must be defined because whether or not there is significant market power present on a market can only be determined by reference to the relevant market in question.[252] As a second step, it must be assessed whether the undertaking or undertakings operating on that relevant market enjoy 'a position equivalent to dominance' (Article 15(1) of the Framework Directive) or whether the market is effectively competitive.

1.67   The definition of the 'relevant' market includes determining which products and/or services belong to the respective market,[253] and identifying the geographical scope of the market in question, e g whether the market must be defined on a national or sub-national (e g a regional) level.[254]

---

248 See ECJ Judgment of 14 November 1996,*Tetra Pak v Commission* (C-333/94P) [1996] ECR-I 5951, 6008 et seq; ECJ Judgment of 3 October 1985, *Centre Belge d'Etudes de Marche SA v Compagnie Luxembourgeoise de Telediffusion SA* (311/84) [1985] ECR-I 3261 at 3278; ECJ Judgment of 13 December 1991, *Régie des Télégraphes et des Téléphones v GB-Inno-BM* (18/88) [1991] ECR-I, 5941, at 5979 et seq; see also Koenig, Kühlings and Braun, 'Die Interpendenz von Märkten in der Telekommunikation', (2001) Computer und Recht 745 at 825; S Polster and M Brandl, 'The new concept of market dominance in the proposed EU telecommunications framework', [2001] 7(8) CTLR 216 at 218.

249 European Parliament, 'Report on the on the proposal for a directive of the European Parliament and of the Council amending Directive 2002/21/EC on a common regulatory framework for electronic communications networks and services, Directive 2002/19/EC on access to, and interconnection of, electronic communications networks and associated facili-ties, and Directive 2002/20/EC on the authorisation of electronic communications networks and services' (A-0321/2008), 22 July 2008, p 65.

250 Commission Guidelines on Market Analysis, para 84.

251 [2002] OJ C165/6.

252 Commission Guidelines on Market Analysis, para 34.

253 Definition of the relevant product/service market, see para 1.68.

254 Definition of the relevant geographical market, see para 1.69.

1.68   Under the Commission Guidelines on Market Analysis, the main criteria for defining the relevant product/service market are demand-side substitutability and supply-side substitutability:[255]

(1)   Demand-side substitutability can be used to determine to what extent consumers are willing to substitute other services or products for the relevant product or service[256] in reaction to price increases. The concept of demand-side substitutability correlates with the competition law concept of 'sufficient interchangeability' as defined by ECJ case law[257]

(2)   Supply-side substitutability indicates whether suppliers which do not yet offer the products or services in question are willing to switch their line of production in the medium to short term or to offer the relevant product or services without having to face significant additional costs,[258] in reaction to price increases.

One way for the NRAs to assess the existence of demand- and supply-side substitutability is to apply the so-called 'SSNIP test'[259] or 'hypothetical monopolist test' which is commonly applied in proceedings under Article 101 of the TFEU (ex Article 81 of the EC Treaty) and Article 102 of the TFEU (ex Article of the 82 EC Treaty). Under this test, an NRA examines the effects of a small but significant lasting increase in the price of a given product or service, assuming the prices of all other products or services remain constant.[260] The Commission acknowledges that the significance of a price increase will depend on each individual case but expects that NRAs should normally examine the customers' (ie the consumers or undertakings concerned) reaction to a permanent price increase of between 5 and 10 per cent. Where prices are subject to regulation, the cost-based, regulated price, which should mirror the prices that would be set under competitive conditions, should generally serve as the starting point for the application of the hypothetical monopolist test.[261] The Commission believes that the responses by customers will aid the NRA's assessment as to whether substitutable products or services exist and, if they do, where the boundaries of the relevant product/service markets should be drawn.[262] The Commission also believes that substitutability between different electronic communications services will increase through convergence.[263]

1.69   With respect to the definition of the geographic market, the Commission Guidelines on Market Analysis refer to the well-established case law of the ECJ pursuant to which the relevant geographic market comprises:

---

255   Commission Recommendation 2007/879/EC of 17 December 2007 on relevant product and service markets within the electronic communications sector susceptible to ex ante regulation in accordance with Directive 2002/21/EC of the European Parliament and of the Council on a common regulatory framework for electronic communications networks and services [2007] OJ L344/65, Recital 4.

256   Commission Guidelines on Market Analysis, para 39.

257   'Demand-side substitutability' correlates with the competition law concept of 'sufficient interchangeability', see eg ECJ judgment of 13 December 1979, *Hoffmann-La Roche v Commission* (C-85/79) [1979] ECR I-00461 at [28]; ECJ judgment of 14 November 1996, (C-333/94 P) *Tetra Pack v Commission* (C-333/94 P) [1996] ECR I 5951 at [13].

258   Commission Guidelines on Market Analysis, para 39.

259   The term 'SSNIP' refers to a 'Small but Significant Non-transitory Increase in Price'.

260   Commission Guidelines on Market Analysis, para 40.

261   Commission Guidelines on Market Analysis, para 42.

262   Commission Guidelines on Market Analysis, para 40.

263   Commission Guidelines on Market Analysis, para 47; see also draft BEREC Report on Impact of Fixed Mobile Substitution on Market Definition (BoR (11) 54) (8 December 2011).

'an area in which the undertakings concerned are involved in the supply and demand of the relevant products and services, in which area the conditions of competition are similar or sufficiently homogenous and which can be distinguished from neighbouring areas in which the prevailing conditions of competition are appreciably different'.[264]

Recently, the concept of 'regional regulation', based on the definition of markets for electronic communications which do not cover the entire territory of a Member State, has become increasingly relevant.[265] This is a consequence of the existence of competitive electronic communications infrastructures predominantly in urban areas of several Member States so that the competitive conditions may vary on a sub-national level.[266]

1.70   The Commission emphasises that market definition is not a mechanical or abstract process but rather 'requires an analysis of any available evidence of past market behaviour and an overall understanding of the mechanics of a given sector'. Therefore, taking into account in particular the characteristics of the fast changing and steadily developing electronic communications sector, 'a dynamic rather than a static approach is required when engaging in a prospective, or forward-looking, market analysis'.[267]

1.71   In assessing whether or not an undertaking has significant market power on the relevant market, ie 'a position of economic strength affording [the undertaking] the power to behave, to an appreciable extent, independently of competitors, customers, and, ultimately consumers' (Article 14(2) of the Framework Directive), the NRAs have to ensure that their decisions are in accordance with the Commission's practice and the relevant jurisprudence of the ECJ and the General Court.[268] Although the Framework Directive has aligned the definition of SMP with the courts' definition of dominance within the meaning of Article 102 of the TFEU (ex Article 82 of the EC Treaty), the application of the EU Regulatory Framework's definition of SMP by the NRAs requires 'certain methodological adjustments ...

---

264 Commission Guidelines on Market Analysis, para 56, see also ECJ judgment of 14 February 1978, *United Brands v Commission* (27/76) [1978] ECR I-207, at 284.

265 See, e g Commission Staff Working Document, Explanatory Note Accompanying document to the Commission Recommendation on Relevant Product and Service Markets within the electronic communications sector susceptible to ex ante regulation in accordance with Directive 2002/21/EC of the European Parliament and of the Council on a common regulatory framework for electronic communications networks and services (second edition) (SEC(2007) 1483/2) (13 November 2007), at 2.4 and ERG Common Position on Geographic Aspects of Market Analysis (definition and remedies) (ERG(08) 20 final) (October 2008). See also OECD (2010), 'Geographically Segmented Regulation for Telecommunications', *OECD Digital Economy Papers*, No 173, (OECD Publishing, 22 June 2010), available at http://dx.doi.org/10.1787/5km4k7mggw7f-en (accessed on 6 December 2012).

266 SEC(2007) 1483/2 (13 November 2007), at 2.4, ERG(08) 20 final, p 2 et seq. See also Communication from the Commission to the European Parliament, the Council, the European and Social Committee and the Committee of the Regions, on market reviews under the EU Regulatory Framework (3rd report) Further steps towards the consolidation of the internal market for electronic communications, COM(2010) 271 final, 1 June 2010, p 4 and Commission Recommendation 2010/572/EU of 20 September 2010 on regulated access to Next Generation Access Networks (NGA) [2010] OJ L251/35, Recital 9 and para 9.

267 Commission Guidelines on Market Analysis, para 35; see also SEC(2007) 1483/2, 13 November 2007, at 2.2.

268 Commission Guidelines on Market Analysis, para 70. The General Court was named 'Court of First Instance' until 30 November 2012.

regarding the way market power is assessed'.[269] These necessary adjustments result from the fact that competition authorities apply Article 102 of the TFEU ex post, whereas the NRAs must apply the definition of SMP ex ante on a 'forward-looking' basis and are therefore required to base their market analysis on a prognostic assessment which must take into account the expected or foreseeable developments at a technological and economic level over a period of time 'linked to the timing of the next market review'. [270]

The ex-ante assessment of SMP is, in essence, measured by reference to the power of the undertaking concerned to raise prices by restricting output without incurring a significant loss of sales or revenues.[271] In addition to the market share of an undertaking, the criteria upon which the forward-looking market analysis can be based include amongst others:

- the overall size of the undertaking;
- control of infrastructure not easy to duplicate;
- technological advantages or superiority;
- the absence of or low countervailing buying power;
- easy or privileged access to capital markets/financial resources;
- product/services diversification (eg bundled products or services);
- the existence of economies of scale or economies of scope;
- vertical integration;
- a highly developed distribution and sales network;
- the absence of potential competition; and
- barriers to extension.[272]

A dominant position can derive from a combination of these and other criteria, which become more relevant as indicators of significant market power where an undertaking's market share is lower than 50%.

Following established case law, very large market shares (in excess of 50 per cent) are as such, save in exceptional circumstances, evidence of the existence of a dominant position;[273] undertakings with market shares of between 25 and 50 per cent are likely to enjoy a dominant position if additional criteria confirm that the undertaking can behave to an appreciable extent independently of its competitors, customers and consumers.

Undertakings with market shares of no more than 25 per cent are not likely to enjoy a dominant position in their market.[274] In general, the development of market shares will be more meaningful than a snapshot picture of market shares at a given time: The persistence of high market shares over time may indicate significant market power, while declining shares might be a sign of increasing competition;

---

269 Commission Guidelines on Market Analysis, para 70.
270 SEC(2007) 1483/2, 13 November 2007, at 2.1.
271 Commission Guidelines on Market Analysis, para 73.
272 Commission Guidelines on Market Analysis, para 78; for further criteria see also European Regulators Group, Working paper on the SMP concept for the new regulatory framework (September 2005), ERG(03) 09rev3, p 3 et seq (single dominance) and p 9 et seq (collective dominance).
273 Commission Guidelines on Market Analysis, para 75; see also Commission Decision of 20 February 2004, C(2004) 527 final, paras 16 et seq; Decision of 17 May 2005, C(2005) 14442 final, para 17 et seq.
274 Commission Guidelines on Market Analysis, para 75.

fluctuating market shares over time may also be indicative of an absence of significant market power in the relevant market.[275]

SIGNIFICANT MARKET POWER – PROCEDURES

1.72   The NRAs decide whether the relevant market is effectively competitive (Article 16(3) of the Framework Directive) or not effectively competitive but dominated by an undertaking which, either individually or jointly with others, enjoys significant market power (Article 16(4) of the Framework Directive).

This decision is prepared in the course of two distinct procedures: the market definition procedure (Article 15 of the Framework Directive); and the market analysis procedure (Article 16 of the Framework Directive). Both of these procedures require the involvement of the Commission, BEREC and the NRAs.

1.73   The market definition procedure is initiated at the European level: The Commission has adopted a recommendation on relevant product and service markets ('Market Recommendation') which identifies those product and service markets within the electronic communication sector, the characteristics of which 'may be such as to justify the imposition of regulatory obligations'.[276] The Market Recommendation seeks to achieve a higher degree of harmonisation and consistency in the application of the EU Regulatory Framework by ensuring that 'the same product and services markets will be subject to Market Analysis in all Member States'.[277]

While the initial Recommendation on relevant product and service markets[278] had defined 18 markets 'in which ex ante regulation may be warranted',[279] which included seven retail-level markets[280] and 11 wholesale-level markets,[281] the current Market Recommendation defines only one market at retail level, the market for 'access to the public telephone network at a fixed location for residential and non-residential customers' and six markets at the wholesale-level. At a wholesale-level the current Market Recommendation retained the markets for 'call origination

---

275   Commission Guidelines on Market Analysis, para 75.
276   Commission Recommendation 2007/879/EC of 17 December 2007 on relevant product and service markets within the electronic communications sector susceptible to ex ante regulation in accordance with Directive 2002/21/EC of the European Parliament and of the Council on a common regulatory framework for electronic communications networks and services [2007] OJ L344/65.
277   SEC(2007) 1483/2, 13 November 2007, p 4.
278   See Krüger, ‚Marktabgrenzung im Telekommunikationssektor und die Definition von beträchtlicher Marktmacht (SMP)', Kommunikation & Recht-Beilage 1/2003, p 9.
279   Commission Recommendation on relevant markets, para 2.
280   These included the markets for network access, markets for local and/or national telephone services, and markets for international telephone services and distinguish between residential and non-residential customers (markets Nos 1 to 6).
281   These included the markets for 'call origination on the public telephone network provided at a fixed location' (market No 8), call termination on individual public telephone networks provided at a fixed location (market No 9), 'transit services in the fixed public telephone network' (market No 10), 'wholesale unbundled access (including shared access) to metallic loops and sub-loops' (Market No 11), 'wholesale broadband access' (market No 12), 'wholesale terminating segments of leased lines' (market No 13) and 'wholesale trunk segments of leased lines' (market No 14), as well as three mobile communications markets, the market for 'access and call origination on public mobile telephone networks' (market No 15), the market for 'voice call termination on individual mobile networks' (market No 16), and the 'wholesale national market for international roaming on public networks' (market No 17).

on the public telephone network provided at a fixed location' (market No 2, ex market No 8), the market for 'call termination on individual public telephone networks provided at a fixed location' (market No 3, ex market No 9), the market for 'wholesale (physical) network infrastructure access (including shared or fully unbundled access) at a fixed location' (Market No 4, ex market No 11), the market for 'wholesale broadband access' (market No 5, ex market No 12), the market for 'wholesale terminating segments of leased lines' (market No 6, ex market no. 13) and one mobile market, the market for 'voice call termination on individual mobile networks' (market No 7, ex market No 16). On 16 October 2012 the Commission launched a public consultation on the revision of the Market Recommendation.[282]

Recently, doubts have been raised as to whether the Market Recommendation is suited to provide a basis for the consistent application of the EU Regulatory Framework as it may be too inflexible to accommodate national differences in the competitive conditions in the telecommunications sector across the Member States.[283] This is because the Market Recommendation is seen to be based on 'European average conditions'[284] while in reality there are some significant differences in the competitive conditions on the markets for electronic communications between the Member States[285] which may require the NRAs to deviate from the product and service markets listed in the Market Recommendation[286] as Article 15(3) of the Framework Directive states that the NRAs are to define relevant markets 'appropriate to national circumstances'. However, the current Market Recommendation provides for a possibility for NRAs to deviate from the markets set forth in the Market Recommendation while, at the same time, prescribing the 'three-criteria' test as a – harmonised – methodical basis for such deviation. The Market Recommendation therefore attempts to provide a middle ground between the need for harmonisation and consistency and the requirement to allow for an application of ex ante-regulation that is suited to the specific competitive conditions in the national relevant markets.[287]

1.74 The market definition procedure continues at the national level: the NRAs must define relevant markets 'appropriate to national circumstances'. In defining

---

282 The consultation documents can be accessed at http://ec.europa.eu/digital-agenda/en/news/public-consultation-revision-recommendation-relevant-markets-2007879ec#%5Fen.htm (last accessed on 6 December 2012); the consultation closed on 8 January 2013.

283 See Ulrich Stumpf, ,Regulierungsinstrumente und Befugnisse bei der Regulierung marktbeherrschender Unternehmen am Beispiel des Telekommunikationssektors', in Gramlich and Manger-Nestler, *Europäisierte Regulierungsstrukturen und -netzwerke*, (Nomos, 2011), p 76.

284 See Ulrich Stumpf, ,Regulierungsinstrumente und Befugnisse bei der Regulierung marktbeherrschender Unternehmen am Beispiel des Telekommunikationssektors', in Gramlich and Manger-Nestler, *Europäisierte Regulierungsstrukturen und -netzwerke*, (Nomos, 2011), pp 68 et seq.

285 These differences relate in particular to the differences in the deployment of TV cable-networks as alternative infrastructure and the status of Next Generation Access Network roll-out: see Wolfgang Kiesewetter, 'Die Empfehlungspraxis der EU-Kommission im Lichte einer zunehmenden Differenzierung nationaler Besonderheiten in den Wettbewerbsbedingungen unter besonderer Berücksichtigung der Relevante-Märkte-Empfehlung', WIK Diskussionsbeitrag Nr 363, December 2011 ('WIK-Diskussionsbeitrag Nr 363'), p 3 et seq.

286 Cases where an NRA has deviated from the Market Recommendation include Cases PL/2009/1019 and PL/2009/1020 where the Polish regulator intended to regulate the markets for Internet traffic exchange services (IP-Peering and IP-Transit); the Commission has vetoed the Polish regulator's draft measure.

287 Cf Wolfgang Kiesewetter, WIK Diskussionsbeitrag Nr. 363, p 26 and para 1.74 for details on the 'three criteria test'.

the relevant markets, the NRAs are not only bound by 'the principles of competition law' but also must take 'the utmost account of the recommendation and the guidelines' (Article 15(3) of the Framework Directive). Although this alters neither the non-binding nature of the recommendation nor of the guidelines, (Article 288(5) of the TFEU (ex Article 249(5) of the ECT)), it does require that NRAs justify their market definitions.

Market definition at the national level requires the application of the 'three-criteria test' where an NRA assesses markets not defined in the Market Recommendation.[288] The NRA must assess whether the following three criteria are met cumulatively:

(i)   the presence of structural, legal or regulatory high and non-transitory barriers to entry;
(ii) a market structure which does not tend towards effective competition within the relevant time horizon,[289] taking into account the competitive conditions behind the entry barriers; and
(iii) the insufficiency of general competition law to adequately address the identified market failures.[290]

Where these three criteria are not met for a market defined in the Market Recommendation, the NRAs may opt not to conduct a market analysis for the market in question.[291]

The need to justify national market definitions is further strengthened by procedural rules: if an NRA intends to deviate from the relevant markets defined in the Market Recommendation, it must give interested parties the opportunity to comment (Article 6) and, in addition, must follow the consultation procedure under Article 7 (Article 15(3), sentence 2 Framework Directive). If the Commission believes that the definition of a relevant market which differs from those set out in the Market Recommendation would affect trade between Member States or if it has serious doubts as to its compatibility with Community law, the Commission can issue a decision requiring the relevant NRA to withdraw its proposed market definition in accordance with Article 7(4) of the Framework Directive.[292] The Commission may define trans-national markets after consultation with the NRAs in accordance with the procedure set out in Article 22(3) of the Framework Directive.

1.75   The market definition procedure is followed by a market analysis procedure, which seeks to determine whether a relevant market is 'effectively competitive' (Article 16(3) of the Framework Directive). In the course of the market analysis, the NRAs must again take 'the utmost account of the [Commission's] Guidelines' (Article 16(1), sentence 1 of the Framework Directive). The Framework Directive specifically distinguishes three procedural alternatives:

•   *Alternative 1:* The NRA concludes that the relevant market is 'effectively competitive'. In this case, it shall not impose or maintain any specific regulatory obligations and, in cases where sector-specific regulatory obligations already exist, such obligations placed on undertakings in that relevant

---

288   Market Recommendation, at 2;
289   As regards the temporal aspect of market analysis, see para 1.71 above.
290   Market Recommendation, at 2; for further details on the assessment criteria, see Market Recommendation, Recital 5 et seq.
291   Market Recommendation, Recital 17.
292   See para 1.55 et seq above; see also Commission Decision of 4 March 2010 in Cases PL/2009/1019 and PL/2009/1020.

market shall be withdrawn. The 'parties affected', which will include the competitors on the relevant market, shall be given 'an appropriate period of notice' prior to the withdrawal of the obligations (Article 16(3) of the Framework Directive).

- *Alternative 2:* The NRA determines that a relevant market is not effectively competitive. In this case it has to identify undertakings with significant market power[293] on that market, and impose on such undertakings 'appropriate specific regulatory obligations' in accordance with Article 16(2) of the Framework Directive to maintain or amend such obligations where they already exist (Article 16(4) of the Framework Directive).
- It should be noted that neither alternative 1 nor alternative 2 allows for any discretion of the NRA in deciding whether to impose sector-specific obligations ('remedies'). If the market is 'effectively competitive', the NRA cannot impose sector-specific regulatory obligations (unless certain exceptions apply[294]); if, however, a relevant market is not effectively competitive, the NRA is obliged to impose 'appropriate specific regulatory obligations' upon the undertakings designated as having SMP, which means that at a minimum one remedy must be imposed. The NRA's discretion therefore relates (only) to the selection of the appropriate remedy.
- *Alternative 3:* In the case of trans-national markets which have been identified by a Commission Decision (Article 15(4) of the Framework Directive), the NRAs concerned must jointly conduct the market analysis 'taking the utmost account of the guidelines' and decide 'in a concerted fashion' on any imposition, maintenance, amendment or withdrawal of regulatory obligations (article 16(5) Framework Directive).

1.76 All three procedural alternatives are subject to the provisions regarding the consultation procedure (Article 6 of the Framework Directive) and the consolidation procedure (Article 7 of the Framework Directive). As a consequence, all 'interested parties' must be given the opportunity to comment on draft measures to impose, maintain, amend or withdraw SMP obligations. Furthermore, the NRAs of other Member States, BEREC, and the Commission must be consulted. In all three procedural alternatives, the Commission has a right of veto if it believes that an intended decision, by the NRA, to designate or not to designate an undertaking as having SMP would affect trade between Member States, and provided that the Commission has indicated to the NRA that it believes that the proposed decision 'would create a barrier to the single market or that it has serious doubts as to the proposed decision's compatibility with Community law' and, in particular, the regulatory objectives referred to in article 8 Framework Directive (article 7(4) Framework Directive).[295]

1.77 The 2009 Regulatory Package has introduced mandatory time limits for the NRA's market analysis procedures (both with regard to new procedures and the review of existing measures) with a goal to provide market players with regulatory certainty (Article 16(6) of the Framework Directive)[296]: As a rule, the NRAs have to perform a market analysis and to notify, to the Commission, the draft measure within three years from the adoption of the previous measures relating to the relevant market. As an exception, this three-year review period may be extended for up to three additional years if an NRA has notified a proposed extension to the

---

293 See para 1.64 et seq above.
294 See para 1.143 et seq below.
295 See para 1.40 et seq above.
296 See Recital 47 of the Framework Directive.

Commission including the reasons for such extension and if the Commission does not object within one month of this notification (Article 15(6), lit a of the Framework Directive).

Where a revised recommendation on relevant markets is adopted and markets are concerned which have not previously been notified to the Commission, the NRAs must perform a market analysis and notify the draft measure to the Commission within two years (Article 15(6), lit b of the Framework Directive). NRAs from Member States which have newly joined the EU must perform market analyses and notify their draft measures within two years from the respective Member States' accession (Article 15(6), of the lit c Framework Directive).

Where an NRA has not completed its analysis of a relevant market identified in the relevant market recommendation within these time limits it may approach BEREC for assistance with the market analysis and identification of the remedies to be imposed (Article 15(7) of the Framework Directive).

RULES ON RADIO FREQUENCY SPECTRUM MANAGEMENT

1.78   The 2009 Regulatory Package introduced substantial changes to allow for strategic planning and EU-wide co-ordination of spectrum policy and to further liberalise and harmonise both the management of radio frequencies and the granting of rights of use for radio frequencies. Whereas the Framework Directive sets out the general principles and procedures of strategic planning and management of spectrum[297] as well as the related competencies of the Commission, the Member States and the NRAs, the Authorisation Directive addresses rights of use for radio frequencies and their allocation.[298] Furthermore, the EU Regulatory Framework provides for specific exceptions to the frequency management rules where broadcasting services are concerned: Broadcasting services are exempted from the revised, more flexible frequency management procedures; measures that require an electronic communications service to be provided in a specific frequency band can be justified when necessary to ensure the fulfilment of a general interest objective, such as, among other things, the provision of broadcasting services (Article 9(4) of the Framework Directive). In addition, frequency trading or transfer[299] is not applicable with respect to frequencies which are used for broadcasting (Article 9b of the Framework Directive).

Further duties of the NRAs

1.79   The NRAs' regulatory duties under the Framework Directive further include the management of national numbering resources and rights of way as well as the regulation of the shared use of network infrastructure and facilities by providers of electronic communications networks.

MANAGEMENT OF NATIONAL NUMBERING RESOURCES

1.80   The EU Regulatory Framework, in the Framework Directive (Article 10) and in the Authorisation Directive (Articles 5–6 and 10–15), contains rules relating to numbering, naming and addressing. Whereas the Framework Directive defines

---

297   See para 101 et seq below
298   See para 1.107 et seq below.
299   See para 1.111 below.

the duties of the NRAs with respect to the assignment of national numbering resources and the management of the national numbering plans (Article 10(1), sentence 1 of the Framework Directive), and the basic principles for the allocation of numbers, the Authorisation Directive defines the rights of use in relation to numbers and the corresponding obligations that the NRAs may impose upon providers of electronic communications networks and services.[300]

The duties of the NRAs include the allocation of numbering resources and the administration of the national numbering plans (Article 10(1), sentence 1 of the Framework Directive). The allocation of national numbering resources is governed by the principles of objectivity, transparency, and non-discrimination (Article 10(1), sentence 2 of the Framework Directive).

1.81   The principle of non-discrimination (equal treatment) is specified in Article 10(2), sentence 1 of the Framework Directive with respect to national numbering plans and procedures and also applies with respect to the relationship between the assignees of numbering resources and third parties. Member States must ensure that an undertaking which has been allocated a range of numbers does not discriminate against other providers of electronic communications services with respect to the number sequences used to give access to their services; this non-discrimination obligation applies regardless of the market position of the undertaking concerned (Article 10(2), sentence 2 of the Framework Directive). The transparency obligation (Article 10(1) of the Framework Directive) is further specified by an obligation to publish national numbering plans and all subsequent additions or amendments to these plans (Article 10(3) of the Framework Directive).

1.82   In order to ensure harmonisation of the use of numbering resources both within the Community and beyond the Community's borders, Article 10(4) and (5) of the Framework Directive establishes co-operation and co-ordination obligations. In order to harmonise numbering resources within the Community to support the functioning of the internal market and the development of pan-European services, the Commission may take appropriate 'technical implementing measures' on the basis of the regulatory procedure in accordance with Article 22(3) of the Framework Directive. Article 19(1) of the Framework Directive complements this harmonisation power and allows the Commission to take 'the appropriate technical implementing measures' if it finds that divergence at national level with respect to national provisions regarding the harmonisation of numbering resources creates a barrier to the single market.

RIGHTS OF WAY

1.83   Article 11 of the Framework Directive establishes principles for the granting of rights of way, ie of 'rights to install facilities on, over, or under public or private property' (Article 11(1), sentence 1 of the Framework Directive).

1.84   The Directive distinguishes between rights of way for undertakings 'authorised to provide public electronic communications networks' and 'undertakings authorised to provide electronic communications networks other than to the public', and allows Member States to establish differing procedures depending on whether the applicant is providing public communications networks or not (Article 11(1), sentence 2 of the Framework Directive). In either case, however, the procedures for the granting of rights to install the relevant facilities must be covered

---

300   See para 1.115 et seq below.

by the same administrative principles: the procedures must be simple, efficient, transparent, publicly available and apply without discrimination and without delay (Article 11(1), sentence 1, indent 3 of the Framework Directive).

Article 11(1), sentence 3 of the Framework Directive does not require the Member States to provide that undertakings which are authorised to provide electronic communications networks other than to the public are able to obtain, upon application, a right to install facilities on, over or under public property. Rather, the Directive merely provides that the administrative principles set out in Article 11(1), sentence 2 of the Framework Directive should apply only if national law allows for the granting of such rights. This interpretation of the requirements set forth in Article 11(1), sentence 3 of the Framework Directive is preferable since it reflects the principle of neutrality with regard to the rules of Member States governing the system of property ownership (Article 345 of the TFEU (ex Article 295 of the ECT)), which are specifically confirmed in Recital 22 of the Framework Directive. As the Directive is 'without prejudice to national provisions governing the expropriation or use of property', it cannot be assumed that the Directive intends to require the Member States to create new, extended rights of way.

1.85   Article 11(2) of the Framework Directive obliges Member States to ensure that, where public or local authorities retain ownership or control of undertakings operating public electronic communications networks or services, there is effective 'structural separation' of the function responsible for granting the rights of way from activities associated with ownership or control. In addition, Article 11(3) of the Framework Directive requires Member States to ensure that 'effective mechanisms exist to allow undertakings to appeal against decisions on the granting of rights of way to a body that is independent of the parties involved'.

CO-LOCATION AND SHARING OF NETWORK ELEMENTS AND ASSOCIATED FACILITIES FOR PROVIDERS OF ELECTRONIC COMMUNICATIONS NETWORKS

1.86   The NRAs should encourage the facility sharing on the basis of voluntary agreements.[301] One of the goals of the 2009 Regulatory Package is to strengthen the powers of Member States to ensure that the roll-out of new networks, in particular of next generation access networks ('NGA') could be implemented in a 'fair, efficient and environmentally responsible way'. In order to achieve this goal, the 2009 Regulatory Package strengthened and expanded the provisions regarding mandated facility and property sharing independently of access obligations imposed on undertakings having SMP.[302]

1.87   Article 12(1) of the Framework Directive provides for the power of the NRAs to impose the compulsory sharing of network elements and associated facilities on undertakings operating electronic communications networks which have been granted rights of way or which may take advantage of procedures for the expropriation or use of property. These measures may mandate the sharing of facilities and property such as buildings, entries to buildings, building wiring, masts, antennae, towers and other supporting constructions, ducts, conduits, manholes and cabinets (Article 12(1) of the Framework Directive) and may also be imposed as a requirement to grant physical co-location (Article 12(2), sentence 1 of the Framework Directive).

---

301   Cf Recital 23 of the Framework Directive.
302   Cf Recital 43 of the Better Regulation Directive.

These obligations may only be imposed 'taking full account of the principle of proportionality' (Article 12(1) of the Framework Directive) and after an 'appropriate period of public consultation' open to all interested parties (Article 12(2) of the Framework Directive).

1.88 Where a 'duplication of such infrastructure would be economically inefficient or physically impracticable', Member States have to provide for the NRAs' right to impose, on the owners of such wiring as well as on network operators having been granted rights of way or able to take advantage of procedures for the expropriation or use of property, 'obligations in relation to the sharing of wiring inside buildings or up to the first concentration or distribution point where this is located outside the building'. These sharing or coordination arrangements may include rules for the allocation of the costs of the sharing which may be adjusted for risk where appropriate (Article 12(3) of the Framework Directive). These measures may only be taken following public consultation (Article 12(3) of the Framework Directive) and must be objective, transparent and non-discriminatory (Article 12(5) of the Framework Directive).

By including the 'owners of wiring' within the potential addressees of sharing obligations, the Commission's goal of enhancing broadband coverage is furthered. 'Owners of wiring' incudes in particular the owners of cable TV wiring already present in a large number of households as addressees of potential obligations, thereby facilitating access to the homes of the end users without limiting such obligations to SMP-undertakings.

1.89 To further promote the efficient sharing of facilities and property, the 2009 Regulatory Package introduced a right for 'competent national authorities' to request information from undertakings 'in order for these authorities in conjunction with national regulatory authorities, to be able to establish a detailed inventory of the nature, availability and geographical location of the facilities' which may be the subject of mandated facility sharing (Article 12(4) of the Framework Directive).

Regulation of Market Entry: the Authorisation Directive

Objectives and scope of regulation

1.90 The Authorisation Directive seeks to harmonise and simplify the authorisation rules and conditions with the goal of implementing an internal market in electronic communications networks and services (Article 1(1) of the Authorisation Directive). The Directive requires the Member States to ensure the freedom to provide electronic communications networks and services (Article 3(1), sentence 1 of the Authorisation Directive). This freedom may only be limited by conditions specifically set out in the Authorisation Directive (Article 3(1), sentence 1 of the Authorisation Directive).

1.91 The Directive provides that the provision of electronic communications networks or services may, in principle, only be subject to a 'general authorisation' (Article 3(2), sentence 1 of the Authorisation Directive).[303] The priority of general authorisations over the granting of individual rights of use also applies with respect to use of frequencies (Article 5(1) of the Framework Directive). To ensure compliance with the conditions of the general authorisations or the usage rights, the Authorisation Directive establishes harmonised enforcement powers for the NRAs

---

303 See para 1.92 et seq below.

and provides for a harmonised application of 'administrative charges' which may be imposed on undertakings providing a service or a network under the general authorisations or exercising a right of use, as well as the fees for rights of use and rights to install facilities.[304] With respect to existing authorisations, the Directive establishes transitional rules, which have to be applied in conjunction with Article 9a of the Framework Directive (Article 17 of the Authorisation Directive).[305]

Establishing a regime of general authorisations

1.92   The Authorisation Directive seeks to prevent barriers to market entry and to secure the freedom to provide electronic communications networks and services by abolishing the licensing (or 'permit') requirement for the provision of electronic telecommunications networks and services under the former telecommunications regulatory regime[306] and providing for a priority of general authorisations for the use of radio spectrum resources over the granting of individual usage rights.

PROCEDURAL RULES

1.93   The Member States may make the provision of electronic communications networks or services subject to general authorisations (Article 3(1) of the Authorisation Directive), more specifically, subject to the conditions set out in the general authorisations (Articles 6(1) and 10 of the Authorisation Directive). In addition, Member States may establish a notification requirement for the provision of electronic communications networks and services. This notification may not, however:

> 'entail more than a declaration by a legal or natural person to the national regulatory authority of the intention to commence the provision of electronic communications networks or services and the submission of a minimum of information which is required to allow the NRA to keep a register of providers of electronic communications networks and services' (Article 3(3) of the Authorisation Directive).

The notification must not be combined with any form of 'explicit decision' or any other administrative act by the NRA before undertakings may begin providing electronic communications networks and services (Article 6(2), sentence 2 of the Authorisation Directive); rather, the undertaking concerned may begin its activity immediately upon notification (Article 3(2), sentence 3 of the Authorisation Directive), subject only to provisions regarding the rights of use for radio frequencies or numbers (Articles 5, 6 and 7 of the Authorisation Directive).

1.94   Under Article 9 of the Authorisation Directive, NRAs must, at the request of an undertaking, issue within one week a standardised declaration 'confirming, where applicable, that the undertaking has submitted a notification under Article 3(2) and detailing under what circumstances any undertaking providing electronic communications networks or services under the general authorisation has the right to 'apply for rights to install facilities, negotiate interconnection and/or obtain access or interconnection'. The purpose of this standardised declaration is to facilitate the exercise of those rights in relation to other governmental entities or other undertakings.

---

304   See para 1.126 et seq below.
305   See para 1.129 below.
306   See fourth edition of this book, para 1.144 et seq.

CONTENT OF GENERAL AUTHORISATIONS

1.95 The 'general authorisation' is 'a legal framework established by a Member State ensuring rights for the provision of electronic communications networks or services and laying down sector-specific obligations that may apply to all or to specific types of electronic communications networks and services' (Article 2(2) of the Authorisation Directive).

1.96 From the general authorisation, a 'minimum' number of rights, set out in Article 4 of the Authorisation Directive, is derived, namely:

- a right to provide electronic communications networks and services; and
- a right that applications for the necessary rights to install facilities are considered in accordance with the provisions with respect to rights of way[307] (Article 4(1)(a) and (b) of the Authorisation Directive),

and, in the case of undertakings providing electronic communications networks or services to the public

- the right to negotiate interconnection with and where applicable obtain access to or interconnection from other providers of publicly available communications networks and services covered by a general authorisation anywhere in the Community in accordance with the provisions of the Access Directive; and
- the right to be given an opportunity to be designated to provide different elements of an universal service and/or to cover different parts of the national territory in accordance with the Universal Service Directive (Article 4 (2)(a) and (b) of the Authorisation Directive).

1.97 The Directive does not define, in detail, the manner in which Member States must establish the 'legal framework', which constitutes 'general authorisations' (Article 2(2)(a) of the Authorisation Directive). In particular, the Directive leaves to Member States the decision as to whether general authorisations should be granted on the basis of governmental ordinances or in the form of 'class licences'.[308] The use of the term 'general authorisation' (in German *Allgemeingenehmigung*, in French *autorisation générale*, in Italian *autorizzazione generale*, in Spanish *autorización general*) would seem to indicate that the 'legal framework' is to be established by the executive branch of the national governments.

CONDITIONS ATTACHED TO GENERAL AUTHORISATIONS

1.98 The general authorisations for the provision of electronic communications networks or services may be subject only to those conditions that are listed in the Annex to the Authorisation Directive. Part A of the Annex establishes a 'maximum' list of conditions, which is considerably more precise than the conditions set out in the 1997 Licensing Directive.[309] The conditions may be attached to general authorisations, but only if they are objectively justified in relation to the network or service concerned, non-discriminatory, proportionate and transparent (Article 6(1), sentence 2 of the Authorisation Directive). The general authorisation shall only contain conditions which are 'specific for that sector ... and shall not duplicate

---

307 See para 1.83 et seq above.
308 See, on class licences, fourth edition of this book, para 16. 22 et seq
309 See Annex, paras 1–3.6 of the Licensing Directive.

conditions which are applicable to undertakings by virtue of other national legislation' (Article 6(3) of the Authorisation Directive).

1.99   The specific obligations which may be imposed on providers of electronic communications networks and services in the course of the ex-ante regulation of undertakings designated as having SMP on the basis of the Access Directive or on the basis of the Universal Service Directive[310] must be 'legally separate' from the rights and obligations under the general authorisation. In order to ensure regulatory transparency, the criteria and procedures for imposing such specific obligations on individual undertakings shall be set out in the general authorisation (Article 6(2) of the Authorisation Directive).

Rights of use for radio frequencies

1.100   The allocation of frequency bands and the assignment of rights of use for radio frequencies must take into account both general policy objectives provided for in the Framework Directive as well as the provisions of the Authorisation Directive which establish frequency assignment procedures and principles.

STRATEGIC PLANNING AND CO-ORDINATION OF SPECTRUM POLICY

1.101   The overall objective of spectrum policy in the European Union, as set out in the Framework Directive, is to ensure that radio frequencies which are 'a scarce public resource that has an important public and market value' are managed as effectively and efficiently as possible from an economic, social and environmental perspective, taking into account the important role of radio spectrum for electronic communications, the objectives of cultural diversity and media pluralism and social and territorial cohesion.[311] As EU spectrum management has not been able to keep up with the changes through 'rapid technological development and convergence'[312] a new system for spectrum management was introduced that 'permits different models of spectrum licensing (the traditional administrative, unlicensed and the new market-based approaches[313]) to co-exist so as to promote economic and technical efficiency' in the use of spectrum, provides for more flexibility in spectrum management and is based on the core principles of 'service neutrality' and 'technological neutrality'.[314]

1.102   To achieve the spectrum policy objectives, the Framework Directive has established a system for the Community's strategic planning, coordination and harmonisation of the use of radio spectrum in the EU. Traditionally, spectrum planning and allocation have been under the control of Member States' administrations, subject to international agreements including ITU regulations and co-ordination by CEPT.[315] The Framework Directive requires Member States to cooperate with each other and with the Commission in the strategic planning and

---

310   Obligations according to Arts 5(1) and (2), 6 and 8 of the Access Directive; art 17 of the Universal Service Directive.

311   Recital 24 of the Better Regulation Directive.

312   COM(2006) 334 final, 19 June 2006, p 7.

313   See Communication from the Commission to the Council, the European Parliament and the European Economic and Social Committee and the Committee of the Regions, A market-based approach to spectrum management in the European Union, COM(2005) 400 final, 14 September 2005.

314   COM(2006) 334 final, 19 June 2006, p 7.

315   The European Conference of Postal and Telecommunications Administrations (CEPT), an

coordination in the use of radio spectrum (Article 8a of the Framework Directive). The objective of this cooperation is:

'[to] promote the co-ordination of radio spectrum policy approaches in the European Community and, where appropriate, harmonized conditions with regard to the availability and efficient use of radio spectrum necessary for the establishment and functioning of the internal market in electronic communications' (Article 8a(2) of the Framework Directive).

The policy orientations and objectives for the strategic planning and harmonisation of the use of radio spectrum are set out in the European Community's 'multi-annual radio spectrum policy programmes' (Article 8a(3) of the Framework Directive).

These radio spectrum policy programmes ('RSPP') are Decisions adopted by the European Parliament and the Council.[316] On 14 March 2012, the first multi-annual RSPP ('RSPP 2012') was issued. The RSPP 2012 seeks, among other things, to encourage an efficient spectrum management and use, to ensure that sufficient spectrum is allocated to meet demand for wireless data services, to 'breach the digital dividend' by fostering the availability of broadband access and making available sufficient spectrum for broadband services, to maximise flexibility of spectrum use, to encourage 'passive infrastructure sharing',[317] to provide for a more efficient use of spectrum through increasing the use of general authorisations, to counter inefficient 'frequency hoarding', and to reduce the 'fragmentation ... of the internal market' through more coordinated and harmonised technical conditions for spectrum use (Article 3 of the RSPP 2012).

The RSPP 2012 further sets out 'general regulatory principles' which, among other things, confirm the priority of general authorisations over the granting of individual rights of use, the principles of 'technology and service neutrality', and the importance of harmonisation and enhanced flexibility of frequency use (Article 2 of the RSPP 2012).

The 'general regulatory principles' and 'policy objectives' are supported by provisions with respect to, inter alia, 'enhanced efficiency and flexibility' (Article 4 of the RSPP 2012), 'competition' (Article 5 of the RSPP 2012), and 'spectrum needs for wireless broadband communications' (Article 6 of the RSPP 2012) which set out co-operation requirements for the Member States and the Commission as well as promote certain actions to be taken by the Member States.

The RSPP 2012 sets up an 'inventory' to be administered by the Commission. This inventory will include data provided by the Member States and will support a coordinated strategic planning and spectrum management. It aims at allowing, among other things, the identification of frequency bands where the efficiency of frequency use can be improved (also by means of re-allocations) and at facilitating spectrum-sharing (Article 9 of the RSPP 2012).

---

organisation consisting of, at present, 48 countries which co-operate in the regulation of post, radio spectrum and communications networks.

316 See Decision No 243/2012/EU of the European Parliament and of the Council of 14 March 2012 establishing a multiannual radio spectrum policy programme [2012] OJ L81/7. See also Commission Proposal for a Decision of the European Parliament and of the Council establishing the first radio spectrum policy programme COM(2010) 471 final, 20 September 2010.

317 See para 1.87 et seq above.

Furthermore, the RSPP includes procedural rules to facilitate internal negotiations between the Commission and the Member States, between the Member States, and between Member States and countries neighbouring the EU as well as co-operation obligations (Article 10 et seq of the RSPP 2012).

The Member States must apply the 'policy orientations and objectives' set out in the RSPP 2012 by 1 July 2015 (Article 14 of the RSPP 2012)

1.103   The RSPPs are based on opinions of the radio spectrum policy group ('RSPG'), ie an advisory group which is composed of one high-level government expert from each Member State and a high-level representative from the Commission.[318]

The RSPG was established by the Commission's Radio Spectrum Decision, which was amended in 2009[319] and assists and advises the Commission on issues related to spectrum policy and in the coordination of spectrum policy approaches, with preparing the radio spectrum policy programmes, and, where appropriate on harmonising measures with regard to the availability and efficient use of radio spectrum necessary for the establishment and functioning of the internal market (Article 2(1) of the Radio Spectrum Decision). The RSPG also has to issue opinions or reports on matters related to electronic communications upon request by the European Parliament, the Council or the Commission (Article 4 of the Radio Spectrum Decision).

Based on the RSPG's opinions, which are legally non-binding, the Commission submits legislative proposals to the European Parliament and the Council, 'taking utmost account of the opinion of the Radio Spectrum Policy Group' (Article 8a(3) of the Framework Directive).

This complex planning process which attempts to strike an institutional balance among the Commission, the Member States and the European Parliament, was established as a reaction to the Commission's initial proposal to 'create an EU entity in charge of managing EU aspects of spectrum'.[320]

The institutional balance for international frequency policies is the same as for frequency policies at the EU level: based on opinions of the RSPG, the Commission may propose 'common policy objectives' to the European Parliament and the Council where this is necessary to ensure the effective co-ordination of the interests of the EU in international organisations, such as for example the ITU and CEPT (Article 8a(4) of the Framework Directive).[321]

1.104   The Radio Spectrum Decision further establishes a technology-neutral regulatory framework, allowing for the Community-wide harmonisation of frequency uses on the basis of a legally binding Community spectrum policy as well as a generally applicable procedure under which harmonisation measures are adopted

---

318   Cf Arts 1 and 3 of the Commission Decision of 26 July 2002 establishing a Radio Spectrum Policy Group [2002] OJ L198/49, amended by Commission Decision 2009/978/EU of 16 December 2009 [2009] OJ L336/50.

319   Decision No 676/2002/EC of the European Parliament and of the Council of 7 March 2002 on a regulatory framework for radio spectrum policy in the European Community (Radio Spectrum Decision) [2002] OJ L108/1, as amended by Commission Decision 2009/978/EU, [2009] OJ L336/50.

320   Proposal for a Regulation of the European Parliament and of the Council establishing the European Electronic Communications Market Authority, COM(2007) 699 final, 13 November 2007.

321   Cf Recital 30 of the Better Regulation Directive.

with a view to ensuring the effective implementation of a radio spectrum policy in the Community and to ensuring harmonised conditions for the availability and efficient use of radio spectrum (Article 1 of the Radio Spectrum Decision).

It is also aimed at the international representation of the Community, for example in the context of ITU World Radio Communication Conferences (Article 6 of the Radio Spectrum Decision). In this context, the RSPG supports the Commission in proposing common policy objectives to the Parliament and the Council where necessary to ensure an effective co-ordination of the EU's interests in international organisations 'competent in radio spectrum matters' (Article 2(2) of the Radio Spectrum Decision).

1.105 To date, the Commission has adopted numerous harmonisation Decisions on the basis of Article 4(3) of the Radio Spectrum Decision.[322] The procedures[323] for the adoption of technical implementing measures to ensure harmonised conditions for the availability and use of radio spectrum allow, on the one hand, for the continued co-operation between the Community and CEPT,[324] with a view to adopting harmonisation measures beyond the Community borders in all 48 member countries of CEPT while transforming those CEPT measures that comply with the Community's spectrum policy objectives, with the force of law. On the other hand, the Community retains the freedom to accelerate CEPT procedures, which have sometimes been exceedingly slow in the past, to reject measures proposed by CEPT, where necessary, and to adopt Community measures outside the remit of CEPT.

1.106 The availability of information regarding the national radio frequency allocation and information regarding the availability and use of radio spectrum in the Community is a precondition for the development of a Community radio spectrum policy. Article 5 of the Radio Spectrum Decision obliges Member States to publish this information in a user-friendly manner,[325] taking into account confidentiality requirements (Article 8 of the Radio Spectrum Decision).

---

322 See, eg Commission Decision 2009/766/EC of 16 October 2009 on the harmonisation of the 900 MHz and 1800 MHz frequency bands for terrestrial systems capable of providing pan-European electronic communications services in the Community [2009] OJ L274/32 as amended by Commission Implementing Decision 2011/251/EU of 18 April 2011 amending Decision 2009/766/EC on the harmonisation of the 900 MHz and 1800 MHz frequency bands for terrestrial systems capable of providing pan-European electronic communications services in the Community [2011] OJ L106/9; Commission Decision 2010/267/EU of 6 May 2010 on harmonised technical conditions of use in the 790–862 MHz frequency band for terrestrial systems capable of providing electronic communications services in the European Union [2010] OJ L117/95.

323 For details on the procedures established by the Radio Spectrum Decision see the fifth edition of this book, paras 1.195 et seq. In this context, note should be taken of the EU's changed rules applying to the Commission's exercise of implementing powers which are set out in Regulation (EU) No 182/2011 of the European Parliament and of the Council of 16 February 2011 laying down the rules and general principles concerning mechanisms for control by Member States of the Commission's exercise of implementing powers [2011] OJ L55/13 and which repeal Council Directive 1999/468/EC of 28 June 1999.

324 Cf Recital 13 of the Radio Spectrum Decision on the need for harmonising the use of radio spectrum, particularly at the Community's borders.

325 Cf Recital 14 of the Radio Spectrum Decision.

PRINCIPLES OF FREQUENCY ALLOCATION

1.107   To improve the consistency of spectrum allocation in the EU while ensuring a high degree of flexibility to take into account market needs and technological developments, the Framework Directive establishes three principles of frequency allocation that must be observed by Member States.

The principle of technology neutrality requires that all types of electronic communications technology may be used in the radio frequencies that are declared available for electronic communication services in the National Frequency Allocation Plans (Article 9(3), subpara 1 of the Framework Directive), subject to exceptions in limited cases (Article 9(3), subpara 2 of the Framework Directive).

The principle of service neutrality obligates Member States to ensure that all types of electronic communication services may be provided in those radio bands that have been allocated to electronic communications services. Exceptions are permissible only when they are justified in order to ensure the fulfilment of general interest objectives 'as defined by the Member States' (Article 9(4), subpara 2 of the Framework Directive).

The third principle governing Member States' frequency allocation plans is the principle of spectrum tradability: Member States shall ensure that undertakings may transfer or lease the rights of use of radio frequencies in commonly defined bands (Article 9b(1) of the Framework Directive).

The Framework Directive establishes a transitional phase of five years starting from 25 May 2011 for a reassessment of existing restrictions of the technology neutrality and the service neutrality of frequency uses (Article 9a(1) of the Framework Directive).

1.108   One example for the implementation of the principles of 'service neutrality' and 'technological neutrality' is the amendment of the 'GSM Directive[326] to allow for a more flexible usage of the 900 MHz frequency band.[327] While use of the 900 MHz spectrum had been reserved for 'a public pan-European cellular digital mobile communications service' to be provided based on the GSM standard,[328] the flexibilisation brought about in 2009 opens the 900 MHz spectrum for 'GSM and UMTS systems capable of providing electronic communications services that can coexist with the GSM system'.[329] Further, the amended GSM Directive provides for an obligation of the Member States to assess, prior to flexibilisation, whether the existing usage rights in the 900 MHz band must be re-allocated in order to prevent distortions to competition in the mobile markets concerned which may result from flexibilisation.[330] The Member States were obliged to implement the provisions of the amended GSM Directive by 9 May 2010. It is to be expected that the process of spectrum flexibilisation and, where necessary, refarming will be highly controversial at the Member State level.

---

326 Council Directive 87/372/EEC [1987] OJ L196/85.
327 Directive 2009/114/EC of the European Parliament and of the Council of 16 September 2009 amending Council Directive 87/372/EEC on the frequency bands to be reserved for the coordinated introduction of public pan-European cellular digital land-based mobile communications in the Community [2009] OJ L274/25.
328 Article 1 of the GSM Directive.
329 Article 1(1) of Council Directive 87/372/EEC as amended by Directive 2009/114/EC ('amended GSM Directive').
330 So-called 'refarming': see Art 1(2) of the amended GSM Directive.

1.109   The assignment of frequencies to particular users – which is referred to as 'granting of rights of use for radio frequencies' in the Authorisation Directive[331] – is governed by the principle that 'the least onerous authorization system possible should be used'.[332] With regard to rights of use of radio frequencies granted after 25 May 2011 and subject to transitional rules for frequencies assigned prior to 25 May 2011,[333] the principles of technology neutrality and service neutrality apply.

To facilitate access to radio frequency resources, the Authorisation Directive provides that conditions for the use of radio spectrum to provide electronic communication services should 'normally' be based on general authorisations.[334] The granting of individual rights of use is therefore the exception, rather than the rule. Member States may grant individual rights of use in a limited number of cases, mainly in order to avoid harmful interference and ensure technical quality of service, safeguard efficient use of spectrum or fulfil other objectives of general interest as defined by Member States in conformity with Community law (Article 5(1) of the Authorisation Directive). Where it is necessary to grant individual rights of use of radio frequencies, Member States are obliged to grant such rights, upon request, to any undertaking providing networks or services (Article 5(2) of the Authorisation Directive). Both the general authorisation as well as the individual granting of a right of use may be subject to conditions[335]

Procedural rules

1.110   The Directive provides that the procedures for the granting of frequency usage rights shall be open, objective, transparent, non-discriminatory and proportionate (Article 5(2), subpara 2 of the Authorisation Directive). The recitals clarify that Member States may, as part of the application procedure for granting rights to use a radio frequency, 'verify whether the applicant will be able to comply with the conditions attached to such rights'; if the applicant cannot prove this ability, the application for the right to use a radio frequency may be rejected.[336] An exception to the requirement of open procedures (but not to the principles of transparency, objectivity, proportionality and non-discrimination) may apply in cases where the granting of individual rights of use of radio frequencies to the providers of radio and television broadcast content services is necessary to achieve a general interest objective. Decisions on the vesting of rights of use must be taken 'as soon as possible after receipt of the complete application'; they must be communicated to the applicant and made public. In the case of radio frequencies that have been allocated for specific purposes within the national frequency plan, the decision must be taken within six weeks after receipt of the complete application (Article 5(3) of the Authorisation Directive).

Transferability and time limitations

1.111   As part of the EU's new approach to spectrum management, the Authorisation Directive seeks to enhance access to spectrum resources, innovation and

---

331   Cf Art 5(1) of the Authorisation Directive.
332   Recital 7 of the Authorisation Directive. See also Arti 2(a) of the RSPP 2012 (Decision No 243/2012/EU).
333   Cf Art 9a(1) of the Framework Directive.
334   Cf Recital 67 of the Better Regulation Directive; see also at para 1.92 et seq above
335   See para 1.112 below.
336   Recital 13 of the Authorisation Directive.

investment in new technologies by limiting the period of time for which frequency usage rights are granted and by allowing co-ordinated (ie governmentally controlled) spectrum trading.

When granting rights of use, Member States must specify whether those rights can be transferred by the holder of the rights, and under which conditions (Article 5(2), subpara 3 of the Authorisation Directive).

When Member States grant rights of use for a limited period of time, the duration must be 'appropriate for the services concerned' and allow for an appropriate period for investment amortisation. If individual rights to use radio frequencies are granted for 10 years or more and such rights may not be leased or transferred, the national authorities must conduct a review, including a public consultation, taking into account market coverage and technological development[337] in order to determine whether the individual right of use can be converted to a general authorisation or made transferable or leasable (Article 5(2), subpara 5 of the Authorisation Directive).

ADMISSIBLE CONDITIONS

1.112   The granting of frequency usage rights by general authorisation and by individual right of use may be subject only to the conditions specified in the Annex to the Authorisation Directive. Such conditions must be non-discriminatory, proportionate and transparent and must be in accordance with the principles of technology neutrality and service neutrality set out in Article 9 of the Framework Directive.[338] The Annex sets out a list of conditions which may be attached to a general authorisation and a list of conditions which may be attached to individual rights of use for radio frequencies. The latter include 'any commitments, which the undertaking obtaining the usage right has made in the course of a competitive or comparative selection procedure.' This may comprise network build-out obligations, obligations regarding geographical coverage as well as the obligation to pay fees for the right of use of the radio frequencies.[339]

LIMITATION OF THE NUMBER OF RIGHTS OF USE TO BE GRANTED

1.113   According to Article 5(5) of the Authorisation Directive, the number of rights of use for radio frequencies may be limited 'where this is necessary to ensure the efficient use of radio frequencies'. The substantive and procedural rules regarding such limitations are set out in Article 7: the decision to limit the number of rights of use to be granted for radio frequencies is to be prepared by giving all interested parties, including users and consumers, the opportunity to be heard. The decision must 'give due weight to the need to maximise benefits for users and to facilitate the development of competition' (Article 7(1)(a) of the Authorisation Directive). The decision, including its reasons, must be published and must be reviewed 'at reasonable intervals or at the reasonable request of affected undertakings' (Article 7(1)(e) of the Authorisation Directive). Where the granting of rights of use for radio frequencies has been limited, Member States may grant such rights on the basis of competitive or comparative selection procedures (Article 7(4) of the Authorisation Directive); the Directive does not grant preference to one of these two selection procedures.

---

337   Recital 69 of the Better Regulation Directive.
338   See para 1.107 above.
339   Annex, Part B, no 7.

HARMONISED ASSIGNMENT OF RADIO FREQUENCIES

1.114 Where the usage of radio frequencies has been harmonised, access conditions and procedures have been agreed on, and undertakings to which the radio frequencies shall be assigned have been selected in accordance with international agreements and Community rules, Member States are obliged to grant the right of use for such radio frequencies in accordance therewith and without imposing any further conditions, additional criteria or procedures which would restrict, alter or delay the correct implementation of the common assignment of such radio frequencies (Article 8 of the Authorisation Directive). In practice, the Commission bases spectrum harmonising measures predominantly on Article 4(3) of the Radio Spectrum Decision.[340]

Rights of use for numbers

GENERAL AUTHORISATIONS AND GRANTING OF INDIVIDUAL RIGHTS

1.115 The provisions in the Authorisation Directive with respect to rights of use for numbers follow broadly those regarding rights of use for radio frequencies. With respect to the granting of rights of use for numbers, the Directive provides, as in the case of radio frequencies, that rights of use shall be granted by Member States to any undertaking providing or using networks or services under a general authorisation upon request. It follows from Article 5(1) of the Authorisation Directive, which establishes the priority of general authorisations for the use of frequencies, that rights of use for numbers should be granted on an individual basis. The recitals indicate that rights to numbers may also be allocated from a European numbering plan.[341] Member States may, but are not required to, grant rights of use for numbers to undertakings other than providers of telecommunications networks or services.[342]

1.116 The assignment of rights of use for numbers must be based on open, objective, transparent, non-discriminatory and proportionate procedures (Article 5(2), sentence 2 of the Authorisation Directive). Decisions on rights of use for numbers shall be taken 'as soon as possible' after receipt of the complete application and must be communicated and published. In the case of numbers that have been allocated for specific purposes within the national numbering plan, allocation decisions shall be taken within three weeks (Article 5(3) of the Authorisation Directive). In the case of numbers of exceptional economic value that are to be assigned based on competitive or comparative selection procedures, allocation decisions shall be taken within a maximum period of six weeks (Article 5(4) of the Authorisation Directive).

ADMISSIBLE CONDITIONS

1.117 Rights of use for numbers may be granted for a limited period of time[343] provided that the duration is 'appropriate for the service concerned' (Article 5(4), sentence 4 of the Authorisation Directive). The regulatory approach regarding the conditions that may be attached to the rights of use for numbers is identical to the

---

340 See para 1.105 above.
341 See Recital 11 of the Authorisation Directive.
342 See Recital 14 of the Authorisation Directive.
343 See Annex, Part C, no 5 of the Authorisation Directive.

approach regarding radio frequencies: Part C of the Annex to the Authorisation Directive sets out an inclusive list of conditions which may be attached to rights of use for numbers. These include, inter alia, conditions for the effective and efficient use of numbers, the obligation to provide public directories subscriber information for the purposes of Articles 5 and 25 of the Universal Service Directive, and the obligation to pay usage fees in accordance with Article 13 of the Authorisation Directive.[344] Member States may determine whether or not rights of use for numbers can be transferred to other undertakings,[345] to the extent that number portability is not governed by Community law.[346]

LIMITATION OF THE NUMBER OF RIGHTS OF USE TO BE GRANTED

1.118   Member States may, after giving all interested parties the opportunity to comment, decide to grant rights of use for numbers of exceptional economic value through competitive or comparative selection procedures (Article 5(4) of the Authorisation Directive). The Directive does not, however, provide for detailed procedural rules as in the case of selection procedures regarding radio frequencies (Article 7 of the Authorisation Directive).

The NRAs' enforcement powers

1.119   In order to monitor whether undertakings comply with the conditions established in the general authorisations or with the conditions attached to rights of use granted to undertakings as well as to monitor the compliance with the 'specific obligations' which are imposed on providers of electronic communications networks and services designated as having SMP[347] (Article 10(1) of the Access Directive), NRAs need to obtain, from the undertakings, relevant information. To this end, the Authorisation Directive establishes far-reaching powers of the NRAs to obtain information (Article 10(1), sentence 2, and Article 11 of the Authorisation Directive).[348] The Directive also establishes both procedural and substantive rules to ensure compliance with the conditions of the general authorisations or rights of use and with respect to 'specific obligations' (Article 10, paras (2) to (7) of the Authorisation Directive).[349]

POWERS TO REQUEST INFORMATION

1.120   In exercising their powers to obtain information from undertakings operating under general authorisations, rights of use for frequencies or numbers or fulfilling 'specific obligations' which have been imposed on the basis of Article 6(2) of the Authorisation Directive,[350] the NRAs are bound by the principle of proportionality. They may only request information that is proportionate and objectively justified to achieve specific objectives (Article 11(1), sentence 1 of the Authorisation Directive) and are obliged to inform the undertakings of the specific purpose for

---

344   Annex, Part C, no 7 and Art 13 of the Authorisation Directive.
345   See Arts 9 and 9b of the Framework Directive for the transfer of rights of use for frequencies: see also para 1.111 above. See Art 5(2), sentence 5 for the transfer of rights of use for numbers.
346   See Art 30(1) of the Universal Service Directive.
347   Obligations according to Arts 5(1) and (2), 6 and 8 of the Access Directive; Art 17 of the Universal Service Directive.
348   See paras 1.120 et seq below.
349   See paras 1.122 et seq below.
350   See para 1.99 above.

which the information is to be used (Article 11(2) of the Authorisation Directive). The purposes for which information may be required by the NRAs include the 'systematic or case-by-case verification of compliance with' conditions attached to general authorisations regarding financial contributions to the funding of universal services (Annex, Part A, no 1) or administrative charges in accordance with Article 12 of the Authorisation Directive (Annex, Part A, no 2), and with conditions attached to rights of use for radio frequencies or numbers regarding the effective and efficient use of frequencies or numbers (Annex, Part B, No 2 and Annex, Part C, no 2) and regarding usage fees in accordance with Article 13 of the Authorisation Directive (Annex, Part B, No 6 and Annex, Part C, no 7). Moreover, NRAs may require information to verify compliance with obligations imposed on providers of electronic communications networks and services under Articles 5(1), 5(2), 6 and 8 of the Access Directive and Article 17 of the Universal Service Directive or with obligations imposed under the Universal Service Directive on undertakings designated to provide universal services. In addition, the NRA may engage in the case-by-case verification of compliance with any of the conditions set out in the Annex to the Authorisation Directive, where a complaint has been received or where the NRA has other reasons to believe that the condition is not being complied with or in the case of an investigation by the NRA upon its own initiative (Article 11(1)(b) of the Authorisation Directive). Furthermore, the NRA may require information for comparative overviews of quality and price of services and for market analysis[351] as well as to safeguard the effective management of radio frequencies and in order to evaluate further network developments which may have an impact on wholesale services made available for competitors.[352]

1.121 If an undertaking fails to provide information, inter alia, in conjunction with the verification of compliance with conditions of general authorisations within reasonable periods stipulated by the NRA, the NRA may impose financial penalties on the basis of national laws (Article 10(4) of the Authorisation Directive).

POWERS TO ENSURE COMPLIANCE WITH THE CONDITIONS OF THE AUTHORISATIONS

1.122 Article 10 of the Authorisation Directive establishes a tiered procedure for the enforcement of the conditions of the general authorisations, of rights of use, and of the 'specific obligations' of SMP undertakings, and sets out the measures that the NRAs may take: where an NRA finds that an undertaking is not complying with one or more of the conditions of the general authorisation, of rights of use or with the 'specific obligations' imposed on SMP undertakings, it shall notify the undertaking of those findings and give the undertaking a reasonable opportunity to state its view (Article 10(2) of the Authorisation Directive).

1.123 The NRAs may require the undertaking to cease the non-compliance or breach either immediately or within a reasonable period of time and shall take appropriate and proportionate action to ensure compliance; in this context, the Member States must grant to their NRAs the power to impose 'dissuasive financial penalties' which may have a retroactive effect and orders to cease or delay the provision of a service or a bundle thereof where continuation of service provision would lead to significant harm to competition until access obligations imposed

---

351 According to Arts 6(3), 7(3), 8(2) and 13(1) of the Access Directive or Arts 16(3), 17(1)(a), 18(1) and (2) and 19(2) of the Universal Service Directive.
352 Article 11(1) (g) and (h) of the Authorisation Directive which were introduced by the 2009 Regulatory Package.

following market analysis have been fulfilled (Article 10(3), sentences 1 and 2 of the Authorisation Directive). The measures taken by the NRAs must be communicated to the undertaking concerned together with the reasons for action and must afford the undertaking a reasonable period to comply with the measure (Article 10(3), sentence 3 of the Authorisation Directive).

1.124 NRAs may prevent an undertaking from continuing to provide electronic communications networks or services or suspend or withdraw rights of use only in cases of 'serious or repeated breaches' of relevant conditions or 'specific obligations', and where measures aimed at ensuring compliance have failed. Proportionate, effective and dissuasive sanctions and penalties may be imposed for such a breach, 'even if the breach has subsequently been rectified' (Article 10(5) of the Authorisation Directive).

1.125 Urgent interim measures are permissible if the relevant authority 'has evidence' of a breach of the conditions of the general authorisation, of rights of use or of 'specific obligations' of the SMP undertaking representing an 'immediate and serious threat to public safety, public security or public health' or likely to create serious economic or operational problems for other providers or users of electronic communications networks or services or other users of the frequency spectrum. Such interim measures may be valid for a maximum of three months and may be extended by a further three months where enforcement procedures have not been completed. (Article 10(6) of the Authorisation Directive). In transposing and applying the concepts of 'public safety', 'public security' and 'public health' into national laws and in applying these concepts, national legislators and regulators will have to be mindful of the jurisprudence of the ECJ in relation to the identical terms used in Article 30 of the ECT[353] which has been replaced by Articles 87 and 88 of the TFEU.

Administrative charges and fees for rights of use

ADMINISTRATIVE CHARGES

1.126 Article 12 of the Authorisation Directive introduces an important innovation to European telecommunications law: under this provision, Member States may impose on undertakings providing a service or a network under the general authorisation, or to whom a right of use has been granted, certain administrative charges. Despite the comforting wording that these administrative charges shall cover 'only' the administrative costs 'which will be incurred in the management, control and enforcement of the general authorisation scheme and of rights of use and of specific obligations as referred to in Article 6(2) (Article 12(1)(a) of the Authorisation Directive), it is clear that the administrative charges may cover the costs of the entirety of the NRAs' operations. Specifically, Article 12(1)(a) of the Authorisation Directive states in its second part that the administrative costs:

'may include costs for international cooperation, harmonisation and standardisation, market analysis, monitoring compliance and other market

---

353 See, with regard to 'public order', ECJ judgment of 23 November 1978, *Thompson* (7/78) [1978] ECR 2247 at 2275; ECJ judgment of 22 June 1994, *Deutsches Milchkonto* (C-426/92) [1994] ECR 2757 at 2782; ECJ judgment of 4 December 1974, *van Duyn v Home Office* (41/74) [1974] ECR 1337. For 'public safety', see ECJ judgment of 10 July 1984, *Campus Oil* (72/83) [1984] ECR 2727, 2751; ECJ judgment of 17 June 1987, *Commission v Italy* (154/85) [1987] ECR 2717. For 'health protection', see ECJ judgment of 8 July 1975, *Rewe* (4/75) [1975] ECR 843, 859; ECJ judgment of 12 March 1987, *Commission v Germany* (178/84) [1987] ECR 1227.

control, as well as regulatory work in all its preparation and enforcement of secondary legislation and administrative decisions, such as decisions on access and interconnection'.

On this basis, there will hardly be any administrative task of an NRA the cost of which the NRA may not defray by way of the administrative charge.

1.127 By way of limitation, Article 12(1)(b) of the Authorisation Directive provides that the administrative charges shall be imposed upon the individual undertakings providing a network or a service based on general authorisation or having been granted rights of use in an objective, transparent and proportionate manner which minimises additional administrative costs and attendant charges. The recitals mention, as an example of a fair, simple, and transparent alternative for these 'charge attribution criteria', a turnover-related distribution key.[354] The principle of proportionality is specified in the recitals by the caveat that the system for administrative charges should not distort competition or create barriers for entry into the market.[355]

As a procedural safeguard for the principle of proportionality, Article 12(2) of the Authorisation Directive provides that, where NRAs impose administrative charges, they shall publish a yearly overview of their administrative costs and of the total sum of the charges collected. Taking account of the difference between the total sum of the charges and the administrative costs, appropriate adjustments must be made (Article 12(2) of the Authorisation Directive).

It should be noted that the Directive does not establish an *obligation* on Member States to impose administrative charges and that the attribution basis for the charge does not need to include all of the administrative costs set out in Article 12(1)(a) of the Authorisation Directive.

FEES FOR RIGHTS OF USE

1.128 Notwithstanding the administrative charges and, as the recitals explicitly state, 'in addition' to them,[356] 'Member States may allow the relevant authority to impose fees for the rights of use for radio frequencies or numbers or rights to install facilities on, over or under public or private property'. These fees shall 'reflect the need to ensure the optimal use of the resources' (Article 13, sentence 1 of the Authorisation Directive).

Transitional regulations for existing authorisations

1.129 The Authorisation Directive contains transition provisions for those authorisations which were already in existence on 31 December 2009. These authorisations had to be brought into line with the provisions of the Directive by 19 December 2011 at the latest (Article 17(1) of the Authorisation Directive). Only where the application of this rule results in a reduction of the rights or in the extension of the obligations under an authorisation already in existence are Member States allowed to extend the validity of those rights and obligations until 30 September 2012, provided that the rights of other undertakings under EU law are not affected thereby (Article 17(2) of the Authorisation Directive).

---

354 Recital 31, sentence 4 of the Authorisation Directive.
355 Recital 31, sentence 1 of the Authorisation Directive.
356 Recital 32 of the Authorisation Directive.

Regulation of Network Access and Interconnection: the Access Directive

Objectives and scope of regulation

1.130   The Access Directive harmonises the way in which Member States regulate access to, and interconnection of, electronic communications networks and associated facilities and, therefore, concerns regulation at a wholesale level. The objective of the Directive is:

> '[to] establish a regulatory framework, in accordance with internal market principles, for the relationships between suppliers of networks and services that will result in sustainable competition, interoperability of electronic communications services and consumer benefits' (Article 1, sentence 2 of the Access Directive).

Ultimately, the EU Regulatory Framework aims at replacing the ex ante regulation of network access and interconnection by an ex post control under general competition law.[357]

1.131   The Directive defines the legal concepts of, and establishes the general principles for, access and interconnection, the rights and obligations of undertakings – in particular the principle that agreements on a commercial basis shall have priority over regulatory decisions – as well as powers and responsibilities of the NRAs.[358] With respect to these regulatory powers, the Directive sets out both regulatory powers which exist irrespective of the market position of undertakings[359] and regulatory powers which exist only with respect to SMP undertakings;[360] specific access obligations exist with respect to digital television and radio broadcasting services.[361]

1.132   The Access Directive applies to operators[362] of public communications networks[363] and to undertakings seeking interconnection or access to their networks or associated facilities. Non-public networks are not within the scope of the Directive, unless they benefit from access to public networks.[364] In accordance with the principle of content neutrality, which governs the entire EU Regulatory Framework,[365] the Access Directive does not apply to 'services providing content'.[366]

---

357 Recital 5 of the Better Regulation Directive.
358 See para 1.141 et seq below.
359 See para 1.143 et seq below.
360 See para 1.145 et seq below.
361 See para 1.167 et seq below.
362 An operator is 'an undertaking providing or authorized to provide a public communications network or associated facility' which may own the relevant infrastructure facilities or may rent some or all of them; cf Art 2(c) of the Access Directive and Recital 3, sentence 2.
363 See Art 2(c) of the Framework Directive for a statutory definition; see also Recital 1, sentence 3 of the Access Directive: 'The provisions of this Directive apply to those networks that are used for the provision of publicly available electronic communications services'.
364 Cf Recital 1 of the Access Directive.
365 Article 1(3) of the Framework Directive: see also paras 1.7 and 1.34 above.
366 Recital 2 specifically mentions, as an example of 'services providing content', the offer for sale of a package of sound or television broadcasting content.

Fundamental terms of regulation

1.133 The Access Directive, unlike its predecessors,[367] defines access broadly as:

> 'the making available of facilities and/or services, to another undertaking, on either an exclusive or non-exclusive basis, for the purpose of providing electronic communications services, including when they are used for the provision of information society services or broadcast content' (Article 2(a), sentence 1 of the Access Directive).

The latter part of the definition emphasises that the EU Regulatory Framework is a 'transmission-centric' regulatory framework.[368] This definition is further illustrated by a non-inclusive list of examples, according to which 'access' includes access to:

- network elements and associated facilities, which may involve the connection of equipment, by fixed or non-fixed means;[369]
- physical infrastructure including buildings, ducts and masts;
- relevant software systems including operational support systems;
- information systems and databases for pre-ordering, provisioning, ordering, maintaining and repair requests, and billing;
- number translation or systems offering equivalent functionality;
- fixed and mobile networks, in particular for roaming;
- conditional access systems for digital television services; and
- virtual network services (Article 2(a), sentence 2 of the Access Directive).

The Directive specifically excludes, from its scope of applicability, access by end users, which is governed by the Universal Service Directive.[370]

1.134 'Interconnection' is defined, in Article 2(b), sentence 2 of the Access Directive, as 'a specific type of access implemented between public network operators'. It is further described as:

> '[the] physical and logical linking of public communications networks used by the same or a different undertaking in order to allow the users of an undertaking to communicate with users of the same or another undertaking, or to access services provided by another undertaking' (Article 2(b), sentence 1 of the Access Directive).

Services of the (interconnected) public communications networks may be provided by the parties involved in the interconnection or by other parties who have access to the network.[371]

---

367 The previous telecommunications directives refrained from defining the term 'access' and addressed only the access to telecommunications networks, cf Art 4(2) of Directive 97/33/EC and Art 16(1) of Directive 98/10/EC.

368 See para 1.34 above.

369 This includes access to the local loop and to facilities and services that are necessary to provide services over the local loop; cf the definition of 'local loop' in Art 2(e) of the Access Directive as well as Annex II of the Access Directive.

370 Art 2(a) sentence 1 Access Directive; similarly art 2(1)(a) Directive 97/33/EC; cf fourth edition of this book, paras 1.96 et seq. Cf Art 1(2), sentence 3 of the Access Directive: see also para 1.185 et seq. below.

371 Article 2(b), sentence 1 Access Directive; similarly Art 2(1)(a) of the Directive 97/33/EC; cf fourth edition of this book, paras 1.96 et seq.

Regulatory principles

FREEDOM OF ACCESS

1.135   Member States must ensure that undertakings are not prevented from negotiating between themselves agreements on technical and commercial arrangements for access or interconnection either in the same Member States or in different Member States. In particular, undertakings requesting access or interconnection must not be required to obtain an authorisation to operate in the Member State where access or interconnection is requested.[372]

PRIORITY OF COMMERCIAL NEGOTIATIONS

1.136   The principle that commercial negotiation takes priority over regulatory intervention[373] follows from the regulatory approach of Articles 3 and 4 of the Access Directive on the one hand, and Article 5(1) and (3) of the Access Directive on the other hand. The principle of priority of commercial negotiations is also emphasised in the recitals which stipulate that 'undertakings which receive requests for access or interconnection should in principle conclude such agreements on a commercial basis, and negotiate in good faith'; NRAs should have the power to secure 'where commercial negotiation fails' adequate access and interconnection and interoperability of services in the interest of end-users.[374]

1.137   To that effect, Article 4(1), sentence 1 of the Access Directive establishes a right of operators of public communications networks 'to negotiate interconnection with each other'. At the request of another authorised undertaking, operators of public communications networks are obliged to negotiate, in good faith,[375] interconnection. The purpose of the right and obligation to negotiate is 'to ensure provision and interoperability of services throughout the Community'; this does not mean that the obligation to negotiate exists only in the case of cross-border interconnection. This follows both from the definition of 'interconnection' in Article 2(b) of the Access Directive, which is not limited to cross-border interconnection, and from the Directive's justification set out in a recital which explains that there should be no restrictions that prevent undertakings from negotiating access and interconnection arrangements between themselves, 'in particular', but not only, 'on cross-border agreements'.[376]

1.138   While the obligation to negotiate refers only to interconnection,[377] the obligation of operators to submit offers refers to both access and interconnection. This obligation to contract does not apply, however, to all operators of public communication networks, but only to those upon which the NRA has imposed

---

372   Art 3(1) of the Access Directive.
373   This principle was already enshrined in the previous regulatory framework, cf. Art 4(1) in conjunction with An Directive 97/33/EC.
374   Recital 5, sentence 2 and Recital 6 of the Access Directive; but see also art 5(4) Framework Directive on the authorisation of the NRA to take action ex-officio in reasonable cases.
375   ECJ judgment of 12 November 2009, *Telia Sonera Finland Oyi* (C-192/08)[2009] ERC I-10717 at [49–62]
376   Recital 5 of the Access Directive.
377   See ECJ judgment of 13 November 2008, *Commission v Poland* (C-227/07) [2008] ECR I – 8403 at [23], [35–47], [49]; ECJ judgment of 12 November 2009, *Telia Sonera Finland Oyi* (C-192/08) [2009] ERC I-10717 at [26–36], [40], [43–48].

specific 'obligations'.[378] Only those operators upon which the NRA has imposed obligations pursuant to Articles 5, 6 and 8 of the Access Directive are obliged to offer access and interconnection to other undertakings 'on terms and conditions consistent with' the obligations imposed.

1.139   Article 4(2) of the Access Directive establishes specific access obligations reflecting the Community's policy decision to introduce widescreen television services: Public electronic communications networks established for the distribution of digital television services must be capable of distributing widescreen television services and programs. Network operators that receive and re-distribute widescreen television services or programs are obliged to maintain the wide-screen format.[379]

1.140   Undertakings which acquire information from another undertaking 'before, during or after the process of negotiating access or interconnection arrangements' may use that information only for the purposes for which it was supplied. Member States are required to ensure the effectiveness of this confidentiality obligation which applies with respect to 'any other party', including 'other departments, subsidiaries or partners' of the undertaking (Article 4(3) of the Access Directive).

OVERVIEW OF THE NRAS' REGULATORY POWERS UNDER THE ACCESS DIRECTIVE

1.141   The Access Directive sets out general objectives to be pursued by the NRAs in exercising their responsibilities with respect to access and interconnection (Article 5(1), sub-para 1 of the Access Directive) and distinguishes between general regulatory powers (Article 5(1), sub-para 2 of the Access Directive) and those existing with respect to SMP undertakings (Article 8 of the Framework Directive), specifying the former (Article 5(1), sub-para 2 (a), (ab) and (b) of the Access Directive). In the exercise of all regulatory powers, the NRAs are bound by the principles of objectivity, transparency, proportionality and non-discrimination; all obligations and conditions imposed on the basis of Article 5 of the Access Directive are subject to the consultation procedure according to Article 6 of the Framework Directive and the consolidation procedure under Articles 7 and 7a of the Framework Directive (Article 5(2) of the Framework Directive).[380]

1.142   Article 5(1), sub-para 1 of the Access Directive establishes three specific tasks of the NRAs. They are required to encourage and, where appropriate, ensure:

- adequate access;
- adequate interconnection; and
- interoperability of services.

These specific obligations are to be fulfilled in pursuit of the more general objectives set out in Article 8 of the Framework Directive.[381] In exercising their responsibilities, the NRAs must promote efficiency, sustainable competition and provide the maximum benefit to end users. The multitude and variety of regulatory objectives contained in Article 5(1), sub-para 1 of the Access Directive allow for an

---

378   According to Art 5 (see para 1.143 et seq below), Art 6 (see para 1.167 et seq below) and Art 8 (see para 1.145 et seq below).

379   For an analysis of access obligations in connection with radio broadcasting services, see para 1.167 et seq below.

380   See paras 1.48 and 1.53 et seq above; on the corresponding requirements with respect to access related regulatory powers towards SMP undertakings, see Art 8(4) of the Access Directive.

381   See para 1.40 et seq above.

extraordinarily broad discretion of the NRAs in their selection of the appropriate regulatory measures, both when regulating undertakings regardless of their market position[382] and when regulating SMP undertakings.[383]

Regulatory powers applicable to all market participants

THE BASIC REGULATORY POWERS UNDER ARTICLE 5(1), SUB-PARA 2 (A), (AB)

1.143   Member States must grant their NRAs, regulatory powers with respect to operators regardless of their market position. Article 5 of the Access Directive specifies the purpose and the scope of these regulatory powers 'in particular' with respect to specific market segments,[384] which seems to indicate that additional, more far-reaching national regulation remains permissible. Under Article 5(1), sub-para 2(a) of the Access Directive, NRAs may 'to the extent that it is necessary to ensure end-to-end connectivity, [impose] obligations on undertakings that control access to end-users'. This provision is aimed at ensuring 'the end-to-end connectivity of the networks'.[385]

The 2009 Regulatory Package introduced further specific 'obligations' which NRAs may impose upon undertakings that control access to end users, regardless of their market position, in order to ensure end-to-end connectivity: Under Article 5(1), sub-para 2(ab) of the Access Directive, the NRAs may impose interoperability obligations on undertakings controlling access to end-users 'in justified cases'.

IMPOSING OTHER OBLIGATIONS

1.144   The obligations that the NRAs may impose on non-SMP undertakings controlling access to end-users are not exhaustively listed in Article 5(1) of the Access Directive.[386]

Rather, according to the cross-reference to Article 5(1) of the Access Directive contained in Article 8(3), first indent of the Access Directive, NRAs may not impose the obligations set out in Articles 9 to 13 of the Access Directive on operators that have not been designated as SMP undertakings, 'without prejudice' to Article 5(1) of the Access Directive. It follows, on the contrary, that the obligations set out in Articles 9 to 13 of the Access Directive may, under exceptional circumstances, be imposed upon operators that have not been designated as SMP undertakings 'to the extent that is necessary to ensure end-to-end connectivity', if and when such undertakings 'control access to end-users'. This includes the NRA's power to require a non-SMP undertaking which controls access to end-users to negotiate, in good faith, interconnection with other operators of public communications networks upon request.[387]

---

382   See para 1.143 et seq below.
383   See para 1.145 et seq below.
384   On regulatory powers with regard to the access to digital radio and television broadcasting services, see para 1.167 et seq below.
385   See Common Position (EC) No 36/2001 adopted by the Council of 17 September 2001 [2001] OJ C337/1, p 16.
386   ECJ judgment of 12 November 2009, *Telia Sonera Finland Oyi* (C-192/08) [2009] ECR I-10717 at [26–36], [40], [43–48].
387   ECJ judgment of 12 November 2009, *Telia Sonera Finland Oyi* (C-192/08) [2009] ECR I-10717 at [26–36], [40], [43–48].

Regulatory powers only applicable to market participants designated as having SMP

1.145 With respect to the regulation of access and interconnection for SMP undertakings, Article 8(1) of the Access Directive obliges the Member States to ensure that NRAs are empowered to impose the obligations set out in Articles 9 to 13a of the Access Directive. These obligations are:

- obligations of transparency (Article 9);
- obligations of non-discrimination (Article 10);
- obligations of accounting separation (Article 11);
- obligations of access to, and use of, specific network facilities (Article 12);
- obligations relating to price control and cost accounting (Article 13); and
- obligation relating to functional separation (Article 13a).

REGULATORY PRINCIPLES

1.146 If an undertaking has been designated as having significant market power on a specific market, the NRA is obliged to impose the obligations set out in the Access Directive 'as appropriate' (Article 8(1) of the Access Directive). This means that the NRA has discretion in the selection of the regulatory remedies to be imposed upon undertakings ('as appropriate'), but no discretion in deciding whether or not to impose remedies.[388] When selecting remedies, the NRAs are obliged to take into account 'the nature of the problem identified' and the objectives set out in Article 8 of the Framework Directive (Article 8(4) of the Access Directive). The Access Directive's reference to regulatory objectives set out in Article 8 of the Framework Directive broadens the NRAs' discretion. Limitations result, in particular, from the principle of proportionality, which is specifically mentioned in Article 8(4), sentence 1 of the Access Directive, and from the procedural requirement that obligations shall only be imposed following consultation in accordance with Articles 6 and 7 of the Framework Directive (Article 8(2), sentence 2 of the Access Directive).[389] It remains to be seen whether the further consultation procedure set forth in Article 7a of the Framework Directive[390] as well as the Commission's Recommendations[391] will serve their purpose to achieve a more consistent selection and application of remedies by the NRAs.[392]

---

388 Cf Art 8(2) of the Access Directive: '... the [NRA] shall impose the obligation ... as appropriate'. If SMP is found, the NRAs have to impose at least one remedy on the undertaking concerned.

389 See paras 1.48 and 1.53 et seq above.

390 See para 1.58 above.

391 See, e g Commission Recommendation 2010/572/EU of 20 September 2010 on regulated access to Next Generation Access Networks (NGA) [2010] OJ L251/35; Commission Recommendation 2009/396/EC of 7 May 2009 on the Regulatory Treatment of Fixed and Mobile Termination Rates in the EU [2009] OJ L124/67. The ERG, too, has issued guidance documents aimed at enhancing regulatory consistency in the application of remedies by the NRAs; these include ERG Common Position on best practice in remedies imposed as a consequence of a position of significant power in the relevant markets for wholesale leased lines (ERG (07) final 080331), and the more general Revised ERG Common Position on the approach to Appropriate remedies in the ECNS regulatory framework (ERG (06) 33) (May 2006).

392 In its third report on market reviews under the EU Regulatory Framework, the Commission has confirmed its findings from its 2006/2007 review that the NRA's practice regarding the

1.147   When an NRA intends to impose upon an operator with significant market power other obligations with respect to access or interconnection than those set out in Articles 9 to 13 of the Access Directive, specific procedural safeguards apply. In this case, the NRA has to submit its request to the Commission, which decides on it, taking utmost account of the opinion of BEREC following consultation with the Communications Committee.[393]

OBLIGATIONS OF TRANSPARENCY

1.148   According to Article 9(1) of the Access Directive, NRAs may impose, upon SMP undertakings, 'obligations for transparency in relation to interconnection and/or access'. These obligations serve, in particular, to speed up negotiation, avoid disputes and give confidence to market players that a service is not being provided on discriminatory terms.[394] The object of transparency obligations can be information in relation to access (Article 2(a) of the Access Directive) or interconnection of public communications networks (Article 2(b) of the Access Directive). The Directive mentions, in a non-exhaustive list ('such as'), accounting information, technical specifications, network characteristics, terms and conditions for supply and use including any conditions limiting access to and/or use of services and applications if such conditions are allowed under national law in conformity with EU law, and prices.[395]

1.149   The NRAs' discretion extends not only to the scope of the transparency obligation imposed, but also to the modalities of bringing about transparency. The NRAs may 'specify the precise information to be made available, the level of detail required and the manner of publication' (Article 9(3) of the Access Directive). This includes a determination as to whether or not the information has to be provided free of charge and whether such publication has to be made on paper or electronically.[396]

1.150   Specific means to ensure transparency are 'reference offers', the publication of which may be required by NRAs (Article 9(2) of the Access Directive). The NRAs' power to require the publication of a reference offer exists 'in particular', but not only, where an operator has obligations of non-discrimination.[397] The reference offers must comply with the unbundling obligation, which means that they must be sufficiently unbundled to ensure that undertakings are not required to pay for facilities which are not necessary for the service requested and must be broken down into components according to market needs and provide the associated terms and conditions including prices.

1.151   Specific transparency requirements apply with respect to operators with obligations to offer wholesale network infrastructure access, including shared or fully unbundled access to the local loop at a fixed location. Under Article 9(4) of the Access Directive, NRAs are obliged to ensure the publication of a reference

choice of remedies 'still varies across Europe, even where the underlying market problems are very similar': COM(2010) 271 final, 1 June 2010, p 4.

393   Art 8(3), sub-para 2 of the Access Directive in conjunction with Art 14(2) of the Framework Directive.
394   Cf Recital 16 of the Access Directive.
395   See also the Commission's Directive Proposal, COM(2000) 384 final, 12 July 2000, p 7, mentioning 'access, interconnection and interoperability conditions' as further examples.
396   Recital 16 of the Access Directive.
397   See para 1.152 below.

offer by such operators. The reference offer shall contain at least the elements set out in Annex II to the Access Directive, which corresponds in parts to the requirements formerly set out in Regulation 2887/2000.[398] This list has been amended and expanded by the 2009 Regulatory Package to not only cover local loop access but 'wholesale network infrastructure access' as such, of which local loop is only one, albeit an important, category and which, in reaction to the EU Regulatory Framework's goal to further NGA roll-out, now also explicitly covers, eg 'duct access enabling the roll-out of access networks' where necessary (Access Directive, Annex II, A.1(c)).

OBLIGATIONS OF NON-DISCRIMINATION

1.152 In order to ensure 'in particular' that SMP undertakings, specifically vertically integrated undertakings,[399] apply 'equivalent conditions in equivalent circumstances to other undertakings providing equivalent services and information to others under the same conditions and of the same quality as they provide for their own services, or those of their subsidiaries or partners', the NRAs may impose obligations of non-discrimination in relation to interconnection or access (Article 10(2) of the Access Directive).[400] The scope of applicability of these obligations is quite broad: the Directive merely requires that the non-discrimination obligations pertain to 'interconnection and/or access' and serve the objectives set out in Article 8 of the Access Directive.

1.153 The Commission has conducted a public consultation 'on the application of a non-discrimination obligation under Article 10 of the Access Directive' which closed on 28 November 2011, having identified the non-discrimination obligation as one of the key remedies 'to be imposed ex ante to resolve competition problems resulting from the existence of access bottlenecks'; the Commission found that the NRAs had, in their regulatory practice, mostly focussed on cases of price discrimination such as, for example, margin squeezes. In the Commission's opinion, however, discriminatory practices not related to pricing, such as quality discrimination, undue requirements or delaying tactics, can have even more severe results than price-based discrimination, a fact which has, to date, been recognised by some but not all NRAs. The Commission concluded that the non-discrimination obligation is not imposed consistently on a national level. This concerns, for example, obligations to 'provide strictly equivalent access conditions for wholesale products' and a trend for some NRAs to favour national companies to the disadvantage of foreign companies seeking access. A further area of concern is the conditions applied to the migration from 'old to new wholesale products', in particular the migration from legacy infrastructure to next generation access networks. Based on these considerations, the Commission has identified three 'main problems':

(i)   a lack of clarity as to the scope of the non-discrimination obligations which may cause regulation on a national level to be ineffective;

(ii) a 'too lenient approach' with regard to the imposition and enforcement of the obligation; and

---

398   Regulation (EC) No 2887/2000 of the European Parliament and the Council of 18 December 2000 on the unbundled access to local loops [2000] OJ L336/4, as repealed by Art 4 of the Better Regulation Directive.
399   Recital 17 of the Access Directive.
400   See also Arts 6 and 9 of Directive 97/33/EC.

(iii)   significant differences in the NRA's 'regulatory approaches across the EU' which hinders market integration and the provision of pan-European services.

To provide for a consistent application of the non-discrimination obligation, the Commission is working on a draft Recommendation on non-discrimination which is expected to be published by the end of 2012.[401]

SPECIFIC OBLIGATIONS OF ACCESS

1.154   While the obligations of transparency, non-discrimination and accounting separation seek to ensure fair access and interconnection, Article 12 of the Access Directive is aimed at the granting of access as such. Under this provision, the NRAs are empowered to impose obligations on SMP undertakings to meet reasonable requests for access to, and use of, specific network elements and associated facilities. In deciding on the imposition of access obligations, as in the case of the obligations under Articles 9 to 13 of the Access Directive, NRAs must take into account the regulatory objectives of Article 8 of the Framework Directive (cf Article 8(4) of the Access Directive). Obligations of access to, and use of, specific network facilities should be considered by NRAs in particular (but not only) in situations where the NRA considers that denial of access or unreasonable terms and conditions having a similar effect would hinder the emergence of a sustainable competitive market at the retail level, or would not be in the end users' interest (Article 12(1), sub-para 1 of the Access Directive).

1.155   Among the specific obligations which NRAs may impose upon SMP undertakings are the following:

- the obligation to 'give third parties access to specified network elements and/or facilities, including access to network elements which are not active and/or unbundled access to the local loop, to, inter alia, enable carrier selection, carrier pre-selection and/or subscriber line resale offers';
- the obligation to 'negotiate in good faith with undertakings requesting access';
- the obligation to 'provide specified services on a wholesale basis for resale by third parties';
- the obligation to 'grant open access to technical interfaces, protocols or other key technologies that are indispensable for the interoperability of services or virtual network services';
- the obligation to 'provide co-location or other forms of facility sharing';
- the obligation to 'interconnect networks or network facilities'; and
- the obligation to 'provide access to associated services such as identity, location or presence services'.

These and other specific obligations are set out in a non-exhaustive catalogue in Article 12(1), sub-para 2 of the Access Directive.

When imposing access obligations, the NRAs may attach conditions ensuring 'fairness, reasonableness and timeliness' (Article 12(1), sub-para 3 of the Access Directive).

1.156   Article 8(4) of the Access Directive repeats and Article 12(2) of the Access Directive reiterates that regulatory decisions regarding the imposition of access obligations shall be justified in the light of the objectives laid down in Article 8 of

---

the Framework Directive and must comply with the principle of proportionality (Article 8(1) of the Framework Directive)[402] which applies to all regulatory decisions. Article 12(2) of the Access Directive specifies the principle of proportionality by providing a non-exhaustive list of 'factors' which shall be taken into account when assessing whether access obligations would be proportionate to the objectives set out in Article 8 of the Framework Directive. These factors – many of which are based on the 'essential facilities' case law of the Commission and the ECJ[403] – have been amended by the 2009 Regulatory Package to support infrastructure investment, and include:

- the 'technical and economic viability of using or installing competing facilities, in the light of the rate of market development, taking into account the nature and type of interconnection and access involved';
- the 'feasibility of providing the access proposed, in relation to the capacity available';
- the 'initial investment by the facility owner, taking account of any public investment made and the risks involved in making the investment';
- the 'need to safeguard competition in the long term, with particular attention to economically efficient infrastructure-based competition'; and
- the 'provision of pan-European services'.

The recitals point out that mandating access to network infrastructures can be justified as 'a means of increasing competition', but that the imposition by NRAs of mandated access that increases competition in the short term should not reduce incentives for competitors to invest in alternative facilities that will secure more competition in the long term;[404] this aim has now been included in the factors listed in Article 12(2) of the Framework Directive. This emphasises the need to balance, in each individual case, the rights of an infrastructure owner to exploit its infrastructure for its own benefit, and the rights of other service providers to access facilities that are essential for the provision of competing services.[405]

PRICE CONTROL AND COST ACCOUNTING OBLIGATIONS

1.157   The obligations which NRAs may impose upon SMP undertakings include obligations relating to cost recovery and price controls, including obligations for cost orientation of prices in relation to the provision of specific types of interconnection and/or access (Article 13(1), sentence 1 of the Access Directive). These price control measures are predicated on indications, based on a market analysis under Article 16 of the Framework Directive, 'that the operator concerned might sustain prices at an excessively high level, or apply a price squeeze, to the detriment of end-users'. The Directive does not require proof of excessive prices or of price squeezing; rather, a mere 'indication' that a lack of effective competition might lead to these results is sufficient. In order to further infrastructure investments, in particular investments in NGA, Article 13(1), sentence 3 of the Access Directive provides for a duty of the NRAs:

---

402   See para 1.40 above.
403   Cf in particular European Commission: Decision (IV 34.174- *B& I Line PLC v Ceiling Harbours Ltd*) Bull EC No 6, 1992, para 1.3.30; Decision 94/19/EC of 21 December 1993 (IV/34.689 – *Sea Containers v Stena Sealink – Interim measures*) [1994] OJ L15/8; Decision 94/119/EC of 21 December 1993, *Port of Rødby* [1994] OJ L55/52. See also ECJ judgment of 6 April 1995, *Magill* (C-241/91 P and C-242/91) [1995] ECR I-743.
404   Recital 19 of the Access Directive.
405   Recital 57 of the Better Regulation Directive.

'[to] take into account the investments made by the operator and allow him a reasonable rate of return on adequate capital employed, taking into account any risks specific to a particular new investment network project'.[406]

1.158   Whereas the threshold for regulatory intervention by the NRAs is low, Article 13(1) of the Access Directive provides for a broad variety of regulatory measures, ranging, as the recitals specifically state,[407] from relatively light measures to relatively stringent measures, such as the obligation that the prices must be cost-oriented,[408] culminating in the ex-ante regulation of prices.

1.159   In determining cost-oriented prices, the NRAs have to take into account the investment made by the operator and allow him a 'reasonable rate of return on adequate capital employed, taking into account the risks involved' (Article 13(1), sentences 2 and 3 of the Access Directive). The burden of proof that 'charges are derived from costs including a reasonable rate of return on investment' lies with the regulated undertaking (Article 13(3), sentence 1 of the Access Directive); further- more, the undertaking must provide, at the NRAs' request, 'full justification' for its prices and, where necessary, adjust such prices (Article 13(3), sentence 3 of the Access Directive). The Directive specifically states that cost-orientation of prices means 'cost of efficient provision of services' and allows NRAs to use cost- accounting methods independent of those used by the undertaking in order to calculate the cost of efficient provision of services (Article 13(3), sentence 2 of the Access Directive).

1.160   When regulating cost recovery mechanisms or pricing methodologies, the NRAs are bound by the triple objectives of efficiency, promoting sustainable competition and maximising consumer benefits (Article 13(2), sentence 1 of the Access Directive). In pursuing these objectives, the NRAs may also 'take account' of prices available in comparable competitive markets (Article 13(2), sentence 2 of the Access Directive). This means that the NRAs may make use of national or international benchmarks which may be of relevance, particularly where the NRA has to determine whether an undertaking's prices are 'cost-orientated'

1.161   Under Article 13(1) of the Access Directive, the NRAs may also impose an obligation to implement specific cost-accounting systems. The obligation to imple- ment cost accounting systems serves to ensure that the regulated undertakings follow 'fair, objective and transparent criteria' when allocating their costs to their services where they are under an obligation for price controls or cost-orientated prices.[409] If an NRA mandates the implementation of a specific cost-accounting system in order to support price controls, the description of the cost-accounting system must be made publicly available, showing at a minimum the main categories under which costs are grouped and the rules used for cost allocation (Article 13(4), sentence 1 of the Access Directive). Compliance with the mandated cost accounting

---

406   Cf Commission Recommendation 2010/572/EU of 20 September 2010 on regulated access to Next Generation Access Networks (NGA) [2010] OJ L251/35, para 25.

407   See also Recital 20 of the Access Directive.

408   See, eg Commission Recommendation 2009/396/EC of 7 May 2009 on the Regulatory Treatment of Fixed and Mobile Termination Rates in the EU [2009] OJ L124/67, para 1 et seq.

409   Art 1, sub-para 2 of Commission Recommendation of 19 September 2005 on accounting separation and cost accounting systems under the regulatory framework for electronic communications [2005] OJ L 266/64 ('Accounting Recommendation'); further details on the scope of the obligation to implement cost accounting systems are set out in Arts 2 et seq of the Accounting Recommendation.

must be verified by a 'qualified independent body', which may either be the NRA or an independent third party;[410] the results of the review must be published.

OBLIGATION OF ACCOUNTING SEPARATION

1.162 The Access Directive establishes broad powers for NRAs to impose obligations for accounting separation 'in relation to specified activities related to interconnection and/or access' (Article 11(1), sub-para 1) and empowers NRAs to request, in particular, vertically integrated companies to make transparent their wholesale prices and their internal transfer prices (Article 11(1), sub-para 2). The main purpose of this specific accounting obligation is to ensure compliance with non-discrimination obligations under Article 10 of the Access Directive and to prevent unfair cross-subsidisation practices. The NRAs may specify the format and the accounting methodology to be used. The obligation to implement accounting separation is aimed at providing the NRA with more detailed information than available from the statutory financial statements of the regulated undertaking in order:

> 'to reflect as closely as possible the performance of parts of the notified operator's business as if they had operated as separate businesses, and in the case of vertically integrated undertakings, to prevent discrimination in favour of their own activities and to prevent unfair cross-subsidy'.[411]

1.163 In order to facilitate the verification of compliance with both transparency obligations and non-discrimination obligations, the NRAs may – above and beyond their information powers under Article 5 of the Framework Directive[412] – require that accounting records, including data on revenues received from third parties, are provided on request. This information may be published, subject to national and Community rules and commercial confidentiality, provided that the publication 'would contribute to an open and competitive market' (Article 11(2), sentence 2 of the Access Directive).[413]

OBLIGATION TO IMPLEMENT FUNCTIONAL SEPARATION

1.164 The 2009 Regulatory Package introduced 'functional separation' as a further remedy available to the NRAs in order to require the regulated undertaking to separate the entity which has control of the undertaking's access network from the undertaking's services entities operating on downstream markets.[414]

Where an NRA concludes that 'the appropriate obligations imposed under Articles 9 to 13 have failed to achieve effective competition and that there are important and persisting competition problems and/or market failures identified in relation to the wholesale provision of certain access product markets', the NRA may, as an exceptional measure, impose 'an obligation on vertically integrated undertakings to place activities related to the wholesale provision of relevant access products in an

---

410 See clarification in Recital 21 of the Access Directive.
411 Art 1, sub-para 3 of the Accounting Recommendation.
412 See para 1.46 above.
413 Details on the scope of the obligation to implement accounting separation are set out in Arts 2 et seq of the Accounting Recommendation.
414 Commission Questionnaire for the public consultation on the application of a non-discrimination obligation under Article 10 of the Access Directive (including functional separation under Article 13a), p 4.

independently operating business entity' (Article 13a(1), sub-para 1 of the Access Directive). The business entity of the vertically integrated undertaking has to provide access products and services to all undertakings, including to other business entities within the parent company on the same conditions and within the same timeframe (Article 13a(1), sub-para 2 of the Access Directive).[415]

1.165   Article 13a, paras (2)–(4) of the Access Directive sets out specific procedural rules for the imposition of functional separation. Where an NRA intends to impose functional separation on an undertaking it has to submit a reasoned proposal to the Commission, which includes:

- evidence justifying the NRA's conclusion that 'the appropriate obligations imposed under Articles 9 to 13 have failed to achieve effective competition' and that 'there are important and persisting competition problems and/or market failures' regarding the wholesale provision of the relevant access product market (Article 13a(2)(a) of the Access Directive);
- a reasoned assessment stating that there is little probability of 'effective and sustainable infrastructure-based competition within a reasonable timeframe' (Article 13a(2)(b) of the Access Directive);
- a detailed analysis of the impact of the functional separation on the NRA, on the regulated undertaking and the electronic communications sector as a whole, and on investments in the sector (Article 13a(2)(c) of the Access Directive); and
- an analysis of the reasons justifying the conclusion that functional separation will be the most efficient way to remedy the competition failures identified on the relevant market (Article 13a(2)(d) of the Access Directive).

The draft measure has to include:

- a description of the precise nature and level of the functional separation including details on the legal status of the separated business entity (Article 13a(3)(a) of the Access Directive);
- details on the assets of the separated business entity as well as on the products or services to be provided by the entity (Article 13a(3)(b) of the Access Directive); and
- details on documentation ensuring transparency and compliance with the obligation (Article 13a(3)(c)–(f) of the Access Directive).

The Commission then authorises or rejects the draft measure following the procedure under Article 8(3) of the Access Directive and taking utmost account of the opinion of BEREC (Article 13a(4) of the Access Directive).

Article 13a(5) of the Access Directive clarifies that the undertaking subject to functional separation may still be subject to the transparency, non-discrimination, accounting separation and other access-related obligations under Articles 9–13 of the Access Directive.

1.166   Article 13b of the Access Directive sets out an obligation for vertically integrated undertakings which have SMP on at least one relevant market to inform the NRA in advance of any voluntary separation of their local access networks or significant parts thereof; this obligation serves to allow the NRA to assess the impact of the planned transaction.

---

415   For further guidance on the concept of functional separation see BEREC Guidance on functional separation under Articles 13a and 13b of the revised Access Directive and national experiences February 2011, BOR (10) 44 Rev 1.

Access to digital radio and television broadcasting services

OBLIGATIONS TO PROVIDE ACCESS ON FAIR, REASONABLE AND NON-DISCRIMINATORY TERMS

1.167 The specific issues of access to digital radio and television broadcasting services[416] are governed by Article 5(1), sub-para 2(b) of the Access Directive. Under this provision, Member States may grant their NRAs the powers to impose, regardless of an undertaking's market position, fair, reasonable and non-discriminatory terms of access to Application Programming Interfaces (API)[417] and Electronic Programme Guides (EPG). This provision is to be read in conjunction with Article 6(1) and Part I of Annex I to the Access Directive, which transposed the provisions of the Television Standards Directive 95/47/EC on conditional access systems[418] into the EU Regulatory Framework.

OBLIGATIONS CONCERNING CONDITIONAL ACCESS SYSTEMS

1.168 Article 6(1) of the Access Directive provides that the conditions set out in Part 1 of Annex I to the Access Directive apply to conditional access to digital television and radio services broadcasts. According to these conditions, conditional access systems operated on the EU market are to have the necessary 'technical capability for cost-effective transcontrol allowing the possibility for full control by network operators at local or regional level of the services using such conditional access systems'.[419] Operators of conditional access services who provide access services to digital television and radio services and whose access is necessary for services broadcasters to reach any group of potential viewers or listeners are obliged to offer their services on fair, reasonable and non-discriminatory terms.[420] The owners of industrial property rights to conditional access products and systems shall not subject the granting of licences to conditions prohibiting, deterring or discouraging the inclusion in the same product of a common interface allowing connection with several other access systems.[421]

1.169 The obligations and conditions for access to digital television and radio services can be adapted to economic and technical developments under the regulatory procedure (Article 6(2) of the Access Directive).

1.170 Member States were afforded the possibility to allow their respective NRA to conduct a market analysis in accordance with Article 16(1) of the Framework Directive 'as soon as possible' after the entry into force of the 2002 Regulatory

---

416 The terminology of the Access Directive is inconsistent: Art 5(1)(b) mentions 'radio and television broadcasting services', Art 6 (3) sub-para 2(b)(i) mentions 'television and radio broadcasting services' while Art 31(1), sentence 1 of the Universal Service Directive mentions 'radio or television broadcast channels'.

417 According to Art 2(p) of the Framework Directive: 'Application programming interfaces (API)' means "the software interfaces between applications, made available by broadcasters or service providers, and the resources in the enhanced digital television equipment for digital television and radio services".'

418 Directive 95/47/EC of the European Parliament and the Council of 24 October 1995 on the use of standards for the transmission of television signals [1995] OJ L281/51; the Directive has been repealed by Art 26 of the Framework Directive.

419 Annex I, Part I(a) to the Access Directive.

420 Annex I, Part I(b) of the Access Directive.

421 Annex I, Part I(c) of the Access Directive.

Package in order to ascertain whether to maintain, amend or withdraw the conditions for access to digital television and radio services (Article 6(3) of the Access Directive). Where an NRA concluded, as a result of this market analysis, that one or more operators did not have significant market power on the relevant market, it could amend or withdraw the conditions imposed on the basis of Article 6 and Annex I. Whereas Article 16(3) of the Framework Directive provides that the NRA is obliged to withdraw obligations imposed on undertakings if the market is effectively competitive,[422] the Access Directive provides for the NRAs' discretion in the case of operators of access systems or services ('[NRA] may amend or withdraw'). If the NRA decides to amend or withdraw the access conditions, it is bound by the provisions of Article 6(3), sub-para 2(a) and (b) of the Access Directive: neither the accessibility for end-users to radio and television broadcasts and broadcasting channels and services specified in the 'must carry' provision under Article 31 of the Universal Service Directive, nor the prospects for effective competition in the markets for retail digital television and radio broadcasting services and for conditional access systems in other associated services, must be adversely affected by the amendment or withdrawal of access obligations.[423]

Obligations concerning the interoperability of digital interactive television services

1.171   In the interest of the speedy creation of 'open' APIs, Article 18(1) of the Framework Directive obliges the Member States to encourage providers of digital interactive television services and providers of enhanced digital television equipment to use and to comply with APIs.[424]

Regulation of Universal Services and Users' Rights: the Universal Service Directive

Objectives and scope of regulation

1.172   The Universal Service Directive seeks to ensure 'the availability throughout the Community of good quality, publicly available services through effective competition and choice'; in addition, it provides for regulatory measures in those cases of market failure 'in which the needs of end-users are not satisfactorily met by the market' and includes provisions aimed at facilitating access to electronic communications for disabled end users (Article 1(1) of the Universal Service Directive).

1.173   The EU Regulatory Framework contains provisions regarding the scope, imposition and financing of universal service obligations.[425] The Universal Service

---

422   See para 1.75 above.
423   Cf Art 6(3), sub-para 2(b)(i) and (ii) of the Access Directive.
424   For a list of standards regarding the interoperability of digital interactive television services see Commission Amendment of the List of standards and/or specifications for electronic communications networks, services and associated facilities and services [2006] OJ C71/04.
425   In essence, the current universal service provisions reflect the universal service regime of the previous EU framework, which was spread out over a number of Directives: see in particular Arts 3 and 4c of Directive 90/388/EEC of 28 June 1990 (in the version of Directive 96/19/EC of 13 March 1996 [1996] OJ L74/13) on competition in the markets for telecommunications services [1990] OJ L192/10; Art 5 of Directive 97/33/EC of 30 June 1997 (in the version of

Directive establishes a 'minimum set of services of specified quality to which all end users must have access, at an affordable price in the light of specific national conditions, without distorting competition' (Article 1(2) of the Universal Services Directive); the scope of services to be part of the universal service is a topic of continuous debate and controversy.[426] Furthermore, the Universal Service Directive provides, with reference to the Framework Directive,[427] for the regulation of SMP undertakings in retail markets, thereby complementing the Access Directive, which is aimed at wholesale markets[428] (article 17 Universal Services Directive).[429] Under the heading 'End-user interests and rights', the Directive establishes consumer rights, obligations of network operators and service providers and allows for regulatory measures in the interest of consumer and end-user protection (Articles 20–31 of the Universal Service Directive).[430]

Regulation of universal service obligations

SCOPE OF UNIVERSAL SERVICE OBLIGATIONS

1.174 The Member States are obliged to ensure that the services described in Articles 4–7 of the Universal Service Directive are made available to all end-users in their respective territory 'independently of geographical location, and, in the light of specific national conditions, at an affordable price' (Article 3(1) of the Universal Service Directive). The nature of the 'specific national conditions'[431] is neither defined in the provisions of the Universal Service Directive nor in its recitals. Recital 7 merely confirms what already follows from Article 3(1), namely that the 'specific national conditions' are relevant only for the determination of the 'affordable price'. In establishing the universal service obligation, the Universal Service Directive refers back to the definition set out in Article 2(j) of the Framework Directive which, in turn, refers to the Universal Service Directive for the definition of the 'minimum set of services' which comprise the 'universal service'. The Directive allows the Member States, to a large degree, to determine 'the most efficient and appropriate approach' to ensure the provision of universal services. They have to respect the principles of objectivity, transparency, non-discrimination and proportionality and are obliged to minimise market distortions, 'in particular the provision of services at prices or subject to other terms and conditions which depart from normal commercial conditions whilst safeguarding the public interest'.[432]

1.175 Despite an ongoing political controversy regarding the extension of the catalogue of universal services, in particular with a view to the inclusion of

---

Directive 98/61/EC of 24 September 1998 [1988] OJ L268/37) on interconnection in telecommunications with regards to ensuring universal service and the interoperability through application of the principles of Open Network Provision (ONP) [1997] OJ L199/23 and Art 4 of Directive 98/10/EC of 26 February 1998 on the application of open network provision (ONP) to voice telephony and on universal service for telecommunications in a competitive environment [1998] OJ L 101/24.

426 See para 1.175 below.
427 See para 1.62 et seq above.
428 See para 1.130 et seq above.
429 See para 1.185 et seq below.
430 See para 1.192 et seq below.
431 See also Art 3(1) of Directive 98/10/EC.
432 See also Art 3(1) of Directive 98/10/EC.

broadband Internet access services,[433] the EU legislators left the scope of universal service obligations essentially unchanged in the 2009 Regulatory Package[434] while, at the same time, adapting the list of obligations to the changes resulting from the move of electronic communications networks to IP networks and the increased importance of VoIP services[435] and strengthening the rights of disabled end users. The universal service obligations include in particular:

- the connection at a fixed location to the electronic communications network (Article 4(1) of the Universal Service Directive) and the availability of a publicly available telephone service over the network which allows for origi-nating and receiving national and international calls (Article 4(3) of the Universal Service Directive). The connection provided to the electronic communications networks has to be capable of supporting voice, facsimile and data communications at data rates which are sufficient to allow for 'functional Internet access',[436] taking into account technical feasibility as well as 'prevailing technology used by the majority of subscribers' (Article 4(2), sentence 1 of the Universal Service Directive);
- the provision of at least one comprehensive directory to be provided to end users either in printed or electronic form or both and to be updated at least once a year (Article 5(1)(a) of the Universal Service Directive);
- the provision of a comprehensive telephone directory enquiry service for end users (Article 5(1)(b) of the Universal Service Directive);[437] and
- the provision of public pay telephones 'or other public voice telephony access points' (Article 6(1)) including the possibility of making emergency calls from public pay telephones using the single European emergency call number and other national emergency numbers free of charge (Article 6(3)). The extension of the universal service obligation to include, as an alternative to public pay telephones ('or') the provision of 'other public voice telephony access points' has been implemented in reaction to the reduction of the number of public payphones and to ensure 'technology neutrality and continued access ... to voice telephony'.[438]

---

433 See, e g the contributions to the Commission's public consultation on universal service principles in e-communication (May 2010), available at http://ec.europa.eu/ information_society/policy/ecomm/library/public_consult/universal_service_2010/comments/ index_en.htm (accessed on 10 December 2012).

434 See Recital 5 of the Citizens' Rights Directive

435 Recital 15 of the Citizens Rights Directive states that: 'Member States should be able to separate universal service obligations concerning the connection to the public telecommunica-tions network at a fixed location from the provision of the publicly available telephone service' in reaction to the increasing move towards IP networks and an increased choice of consumers between a 'range of competing voice service providers'. As a result, the term 'connection to the public telephone network' has been replaced by the broader term 'connection to the public communications network' (see, e g Art 4(1) of the Universal Service Directive).

436 The term 'functional Internet access' provides the Member States with a degree of flexibility when defining the actual type of Internet access to be provided under the national universal service obligation; to date, three Member States (Finland, Spain and Malta) have opted to include broadband access: see Communication from the Commission to the European Parliament, the Council, the European Economic Committee and the Committee of the Regions, Universal service in e-communications: report on the outcome of the public consultation and the third periodic review of the scope in accordance with Article 15 of Directive 2002/22/EC, COM(2011) 795 final, 23 November 2011, p 3.

437 See para 1.202 below.

438 See Recital 11 of the Citizens' Rights Directive.

The rights of disabled users to 'equivalent access'[439] to the public telephone service and directory enquiry services, that are part of the universal service,[440] have been strengthened considerably by the 2009 Regulatory Package. Access of disabled end users 'should be 'functionally equivalent, such that disabled end-users benefit from the same usability of services as other end-users, but by different means'.[441] Such specific measures may include, for example, making available public telephones, public text telephones or equivalent measures for deaf or speech-impaired people, and providing services such as directory enquiry services or equivalent measures free of charge for blind or partially sighted people.[442] The Universal Service Directive has been changed to make the implementation of measures ensuring equivalent access for disabled end-users mandatory for the Member States ('Member States *shall* take specific measures').[443]

1.176   The list of universal services is exhaustive. The Directive provides that the Commission shall 'periodically' review the scope of the universal service every three years (Article 15(1) of the Universal Service Directive). In the course of this review, the Commission has to take into account social, economic and technological developments in accordance with Article 15(2) of the Universal Service Directive and the methodology which is set out in Annex V of the Universal Service Directive. The Directive provides that any change to the scope of universal services should be subject to the 'twin test' of services that become available to a substantial majority of the population, with a consequent risk of social exclusion for those who cannot afford them.[444] The 'twin test' is to be conducted at the EU level; consequently, Member States are not permitted to expand, on their own, the scope of universal service obligations or to impose on market players 'financial contributions which relate to measures which are not part of universal service obligations'.[445]

In its third periodic review of the scope of the universal service,[446] the Commission rejected, once more, demands to expand the universal service to include 'functional Internet access at broadband speeds' at EU level as it considered such inclusion 'premature'.[447]

1.177   Outside the scope of universal service obligations, Member States remain free to make publicly available further services and finance them in conformity with Community law, but not by means of contributions from market players (Article 32 of the Universal Service Directive).[448] This provision is aimed at opening, to

---

439   See also Art 23a of the Universal Service Directive which obligates the Member States to enable the NRAs to take measures to ensure 'equivalence in access and choice for disabled end-users'.

440   Arts 4(3) and 5 of the Universal Service Directive.

441   Recital 12 of the Citizens' Rights Directive.

442   See Recital 13 of the Universal Service Directive.

443   Prior to the 2009 Regulatory Package, Art 7(1) of the Universal Service Directive read: 'Member States *may* take specific measures ...'.

444   Recital 25 as well as Art 15 of the Universal Service Directive; on the criteria of review see Annex V of the Universal Service Directive.

445   Cf Recital 25 of the Universal Service Directive.

446   Communication from the Commission to the European Parliament, the Council, the European Economic Committee and the Committee of the Regions, Universal service in e-communications: report on the outcome of the public consultation and the third periodic review of the scope in accordance with Article 15 of Directive 2002/22/EC, COM(2011) 795 final, 23 November 2011.

447   COM(2011) 795 final, 23 November 2011, p 12 et seq.

448   Cf Recital 25 of the Universal Service Directive.

Member States, a broad spectrum of possible measures,[449] which are not, however, specified in the Universal Service Directive.

PROCEDURE FOR THE DESIGNATION OF UNDERTAKINGS OBLIGED TO PROVIDE
UNIVERSAL SERVICES

1.178   Member States are free in determining 'the most efficient and appropriate approach' to ensure the provision of universal services (Article 3(1) of the Universal Service Directive)[450] which may[451] include the 'designation' of one or more undertakings who have to provide different elements of universal service or have to cover different parts of the the Member State's territory. It follows from Article 8(2), sentence 2 of the Universal Service Directive that this 'designation' is a legally binding regulatory measure that is aimed to ensure, among other things, 'that universal service is provided in a cost-effective manner'. The designation procedure must be efficient, objective, transparent and non-discriminatory and may not exclude any undertaking a priori from being designated (Article 8(2), sentence 1 of the Universal Service Directive). Furthermore the procedure must adhere to the 'principle of minimal distortion to competition.' The ECJ has found that a designation procedure that excludes from the potential providers such undertakings that are unable to serve the entire territory of a Member State does not comply with the aforementioned criteria.[452]

Undertakings with a universal service obligation may use whatever technology is appropriate to meet their obligations as long as they comply with the quality requirements established under the Universal Service Directive and national legislation; this can for example include the use of VoIP technology.[453]

The 2009 Regulatory Package introduced obligations for undertakings which have been designated as universal service providers and which intend to transfer their local access network or a substantial part thereof to a separate legal entity under different ownership to inform the NRAs of their plans (Article 8(3) of the Universal Service Directive).

REGULATION OF RETAIL TARIFFS, USERS' EXPENDITURES AND QUALITY OF SERVICE

1.179   To ensure that the end user tariffs for the provision of universal services are affordable, Article 9(1) of the Universal Service Directive requires the NRAs to monitor the evolution and level of retail tariffs 'in particular in relation to national consumer prices and income'. The objective of this monitoring duty is to ensure that the services are provided 'at an affordable price' (Article 3(1) of the Universal Service Directive). It follows, from this objective as well as from the NRA's power to, inter alia, mandate 'special tariff options' or compliance with 'price caps' (Article 8(2) and (3) of the Universal Service Directive), that Member States are not only empowered to 'monitor' but also to regulate end user tariffs in order to achieve 'affordability'.

---

449   COM(2001) 503 final [2001] OJ C332 E/292, p 298.
450   ECJ judgment of 19 June 2008 *Commission v France* (C-220/07) [2008] ECR I-95 at [31–36].
451   Art 9(1) of the Universal Services Directive shows that there is no requirement for the Member States to designate a universal service provider, in particular, where the services concerned are 'available on the market'.
452   ECJ judgment of 19 June 2008 *Commission v France* (C-220/07) [2008] ECR I-95 at [31–36].
453   Cf Commission Staff Working Document on the treatment of Voice over Internet Protocol (VoIP) under the EU Regulatory Framework, 14 June 2004, p 11.

1.180   With respect to the regulation of end user tariffs, the Universal Service Directive provides for a number of regulatory options. Member States may:

- require that designated undertakings provide tariff options or packages to consumers that are different from the options offered under 'normal commercial conditions', for example to ensure that users with low incomes or with special social needs are not excluded from access to the electronic telecommunications network or from using the services that are part of the universal service (Article 9(2) of the Universal Service Directive);
- in addition to tariff regulation, ensure that consumers with low incomes or special social needs are given support (Article 9(3) of the Universal Service Directive); and
- require undertakings with universal service obligations to apply 'common tariffs, including geographical averaging, throughout the territory, in the light of national conditions or to comply with price caps' (Article 9(4) of the Universal Service Directive).

The NRAs have to ensure that, where a designated undertaking is obliged to provide special tariff options, common tariffs, including geographical averaging, or to comply with price caps, the conditions are fully transparent and are published and are applied in accordance with the principle of non-discrimination (Article 9(5) of the Universal Service Directive).

1.181   To allow subscribers to control their expenditures for universal services, the Universal Service Directive provides, on the one hand, that designated undertakings have to establish terms and conditions in a way that subscribers are not required to pay for facilities or services which are not necessary or not required for the service requested (Article 10(1) of the Universal Service Directive). On the other hand, Article 10(2) of the Universal Service Directive requires the Member States to ensure that the designated undertakings provide specific facilities and services specified in Part A of Annex I to the Universal Service Directive, allowing subscribers to monitor and control expenditure and avoid unwarranted disconnection of service. These facilities and services include, among others, itemised billing, selective call barring for outgoing calls or premium SMS or MMS (free of charge), and prepayment systems for the provision of access to the electronic communications network and the use of publicly available telephone services.[454] These broad obligations are limited by Article 10(3) of the Universal Service Directive which requires Member States to ensure that the relevant authority is able to waive the requirement to provide the facilities or services mentioned 'if it is satisfied that the facility is widely available'.

1.182   The Universal Service Directive establishes powers of the NRAs to establish quality standards and monitor compliance with performance targets in relation to universal services, which have been broadened by the 2009 Regulatory Package. Article 11 of the Universal Service Directive obliges NRAs to obtain information concerning the undertaking's performance in the provision of universal service according to the quality of service parameters set out in Annex III of the Universal Service Directive (Article 11(1) Universal Service Directive) and enables them to establish additional quality of service standards to assess the performance of undertakings in the provision of services to disabled users (Article 11(2) of the

---

454   The provision of these facilities and services according to Annex I, Part A of the Universal Service Directive is not a universal service obligation. This follows from the separation between Art 10(2) of the Universal Service Directive and the 'catalogue' of universal service obligations in Arts 4–7 of the Universal Service Directive.

Universal Service Directive). NRAs may set criteria for the content, form and manner of information to be published in order to ensure user-friendly access to such information for end users and consumers (Article 10(3) of the Universal Service Directive). In addition, NRAs are able to set performance targets Article 11(4) Universal Service Directive) and to monitor compliance with these targets by designated undertakings (Article 11(5) of the Universal Service Directive). If an undertaking persistently fails to meet the performance targets, the NRA may take 'specific measures' on the basis of the Authorisation Directive (Article 11(6), sentence 1 of the Universal Service Directive), which may include a prohibition to provide services (Article 10(5) of the Authorisation Directive). In order to ensure the accuracy and comparability of the data made available by undertakings with universal service obligations, NRAs may order independent audits or similar reviews of the performance data at the expense of the undertaking concerned (Article 11(6), sentence 2 of the Universal Service Directive).

COST CALCULATION AND FINANCING OF UNIVERSAL SERVICES

1.183   The Universal Service Directive requires Member States to ensure, upon request from a designated undertaking, the establishment of a financing mechanism if the undertaking is found to be 'subject to an unfair burden' (Article 13(1) of the Universal Service Directive). The Directive establishes rules for the determination of the net cost of the universal service provision: the NRAs may determine the net cost of the universal service obligation in accordance with Article 12(1) of the Universal Service Directive; in this case, they have to follow the calculation rules set out in Part A of Annex IV. Alternatively, the NRAs may base their calculation on the net costs of providing universal service identified by a 'designation mechanism' in accordance with Article 8(2) Universal Service Directive.

1.184   The compensation of the undertakings that have been designated for the provision of universal services can be based on a mechanism that ensures compensation of the net cost from public funds (Article 13(1)(a) of the Universal Service Directive)[455] and/or on a sharing of the net cost of universal service obligations between providers of electronic communications networks and services (Article 13(1)(b) of the Universal Service Directive). Contrary to the previous framework,[456] universal services cannot be financed by 'a supplementary charge added to the interconnection charge'.[457] The cost sharing (Article 13(1)(b) of the Universal Service Directive) has to be supervised by the NRA or 'another body independent from the beneficiaries under the NRA's supervision'; the sharing mechanism must comply with the principles of transparency, minimal market distortion, non-discrimination and proportionality (Article 13(3) in conjunction with Annex IV, Part B of the Universal Service Directive). The Member States have the right not to require contributions from undertakings whose national turnover is below a set threshold. An exemption applies to undertakings that are not providing services in the territory of the Member State that has established a sharing mechanism: These undertakings may not be subject to charges related to the sharing of the cost of universal service obligations (Article 13(4), sentence 2 of the Universal Service Directive).

---

455   The predecessor provision (Art 5 of Directive 97/33/EC) did not provide for this possibility.
456   See Art 5(2) of Directive 97/33/EC.
457   Art 5(2) of Directive 97/33/EC.

Regulation of retail markets

MARKET ANALYSIS

1.185   Regulation of retail services is based on a market analysis according to the rules set out in the Framework Directive.[458]

PREREQUISITES FOR THE REGULATION OF RETAIL MARKETS

1.186   On the basis of its market analysis, an NRA has to impose 'appropriate regulatory obligations on undertakings identified as having significant market power' on a relevant retail market (Article 17(1) of the Universal Service Directive). This obligation to regulate, which leaves no room for discretion, applies only if:

- the NRA has determined as a result of its market analysis[459] that a given retail market is not effectively competitive (Article 17(1)(a) of the Universal Service Directive); and
- the NRA has further concluded that obligations imposed under the Access Directive would not result in the achievement of the regulatory objectives set out in Article 8 of the Framework Directive[460] (Article 17(1)(b) of the Universal Service Directive).

Article 17(5) of the Universal Service Directive mirrors Article 17(1)(a) of the Universal Service Directive and clarifies that NRAs shall not apply retail control mechanisms to geographical or user markets where they are satisfied that there is effective competition.[461]

REGULATORY POWERS

1.187   If the NRA has determined that a given retail market is not effectively competitive and that regulation at the wholesale level would not achieve the regulatory objectives, it is obliged to 'impose appropriate regulatory obligations' on those undertakings that have been identified as having significant market power (Article 17(1) of the Universal Service Directive).

1.188   The NRAs' broad discretion in selecting regulatory remedies is somewhat mitigated by the regulatory objectives set out in Article 8 of the Framework Directive[462] and the principle of proportionality. The Universal Service Directive includes a non-exhaustive list of possible ex-ante obligations which NRAs may impose upon SMP undertakings. They include, but are not limited to, the requirements set out in Article 17(2), sentence 1 of the Universal Service Directive that the SMP undertakings do not:

- charge excessive prices;
- inhibit market entry or restrict competition by setting predatory prices;
- show undue preference to specific end-users; or
- unreasonably bundle services.

---

458   See para 1.64 et seq above.
459   See para 1.75 above and also Art 16(3) of the Framework Directive.
460   See para 1.40 et seq above; this requirement was included to prevent 'over-regulation', cf [2002] OJ C53E/195.
461   Measures of tariff regulation under Art 9(2) of the Universal Service Directive, requiring undertakings to provide special tariff options or tariff bundles, remain unaffected.
462   See paras 1.40 et seq above.

1.189   In order to protect the end-users' interests and to promote effective competition, NRAs may regulate end-user tariffs. Article 17(2), sentence 3 of the Universal Service Directive provides for three different types of tariff regulation. The NRAs:

(i)   may apply to SMP undertakings 'appropriate retail price cap measures';
(ii)   may take 'measures to control individual tariffs'; and
(iii)   can take measures 'to orient tariffs towards costs or prices on comparable markets'.

This list of possible regulatory measures, which may be taken 'as a last resort and after due consideration',[463] is non-exhaustive. The recitals specifically state that NRAs may use 'price cap regulation, geographical averaging *or similar instruments*' to achieve the twin objectives of promoting effective competition whilst pursuing public interest needs.[464]

The provisions allowing for end-user tariff regulation are complemented by mandatory rules regarding the implementation of cost accounting systems which further limit the NRAs' regulatory discretion. Where an SMP undertaking is subject to retail tariff regulation or other relevant retail controls, the NRAs are required to ensure that 'the necessary and appropriate cost accounting systems are implemented' (Article 17(4), sentence 1 of the Universal Service Directive) and may specify only format and accounting methodology to be used (Article 17(4), sentence 2 of the Universal Service Directive). Compliance with the cost accounting system is to be verified by a qualified independent body (Article 17(4), sentence 3 of the Universal Service Directive) which may also be the NRA itself.[465] The NRAs have to ensure that the statement concerning compliance with the cost accounting requirements is published annually (Article 17(4), sentence 4 of the Universal Service Directive).[466]

OBLIGATIONS CONCERNING THE PROVISION OF A MINIMUM SET OF LEASED LINES AND CARRIER (PRE-)SELECTION

1.190   The Citizens' Rights Directive repealed the requirement to provide a minimum set of leased lines at a retail level which was formerly included in Article 18 of the Universal Services Directive as it was found to be 'no longer necessary' due to market developments.[467]

1.191   Also repealed was Article 19 of the Universal Service Directive which provided for an obligation to provide access to the services of any interconnected provider of public telephone services, both on a call-by-call basis by dialling a carrier selection code and by means of pre-selection. It was concluded that an imposition of these obligations directly through EU legislation could 'hamper technological progress'[468]. Instead, NRAs may now impose these obligations as remedies under Article 12 of the Access Directive.[469]

---

463   Recital 26, sentence 8 of the Universal Service Directive.
464   Recital 26, sentence 8 of the Universal Service Directive (emphasis added).
465   Cf the clarification in Recital 27 of the Universal Service Directive.
466   See also Art 13(4), sentence 3 of the Access Directive.
467   Recital 19 of the Citizens' Rights Directive; for details on the obligation concerning the provision of a minimum set of leased lines see 5th edition of this book, para 1.176 et seq.
468   Recital 20 of the Citizens' Rights Directive.
469   See para 1.154 above.

End user rights

1.192   Chapter IV of the Universal Service Directive establishes under the heading 'end-user interests and rights' a number of rights of 'consumers' and 'end-users',[470] which correspond to the obligations of providers of specific communications networks and services.

CONTRACTS: OBLIGATION TO CONTRACT AND MINIMUM STANDARDS

1.193   Any consumer, ie any natural person who uses or requests the publicly available electronic communications service for purposes which are outside his or her trade, business or profession (Article 2(i) of the Framework Directive) and any other end-user[471] upon request has a right to enter into a contract with operators when subscribing to services providing connection to a public communications network or publicly available electronic communications services (Article 20(1), sentence 1 of the Universal Service Directive).

1.194   In the interests of 'transparency of information and legal security',[472] Article 20(1), sentence 2 of the Universal Service Directive establishes a number of minimum requirements for the contracts with undertakings providing connection or access to the public telephone network which have to be specified 'in a clear, comprehensive and easily accessible form'. These minimum requirements were considerably expanded by the 2009 Regulatory Package and include:

- the identity and address of the undertaking,
- details on the services provided, including, inter alia, information on the availability of access to emergency services and caller location information and any restriction to the provision of emergency services, the minimum quality of service levels offered (including compensation or refunds offered where these levels are not met), any measures implemented by the undertaking to manage traffic, types of maintenance and customer support services offered as well as on any restrictions imposed by the undertaking regarding the use of terminal equipment supplied (eg SIM-locks);
- details on prices and tariffs;
- information on the duration of the contract and the conditions for the renewal and the termination of the service;
- information on the means to initiate dispute settlement proceedings; and
- information on the actions that may be taken by the undertaking in case of 'security or integrity incidents or threats and vulnerabilities'.

1.195   Subscribers (including consumers and end users) have a right to withdraw from their contracts without penalty, upon notice of proposed modifications in the contractual conditions. They must be given adequate notice of such proposed modifications, which shall be not shorter than one month ahead of any modification (Article 20(4) of the Universal Service Directive).

---

470   See Art 2(i) and (n) of the Framework Directive. Consumer means 'any natural person who uses or requests a publicly available electronic communications service for purpose which are outside his or her trade, business or profession'; end-user means 'any user not providing public communications networks or publicly available electronic communications services'. The difference lies in the purpose of use.

471   This reference to 'other end-users' was included to serve in particular the interests of Small and Medium Enterprises ('SME'), cf Recital 21 of the Citizens' Rights Directive.

472   Cf Recital 30 of the Universal Service Directive.

TRANSPARENCY OBLIGATIONS

1.196   The NRAs have the power to require undertakings providing publicly available electronic communications networks or services to publish 'transparent, comparable, adequate and up-to-date information' on applicable prices, tariffs, on any charges due in connection with contract termination and on standard terms and conditions regarding access to and use of services provided to end-users and consumers; this includes, among other things, a description of the service and information regarding the scope of the service offered, information regarding standard tariffs, compensation and refund policies, the type of maintenance service offered, the standard contract conditions, including any minimum contractual period as well as information on contract termination and, where relevant, portability charges, and dispute settlement mechanisms (Article 21(1) of the Universal Service Directive). NRAs must encourage the provision of 'comparable information' to afford end-users and consumers the possibility to independently evaluate the costs of alternative usage patterns making use of interactive guides or similar means (Article 21(1) of the Universal Service Directive).

1.197   Furthermore, Member States must ensure under the amended and expanded Article 21(3) of the Universal Service Directive that NRAs are able to require undertakings that provide publicly available electronic communications networks or services to, inter alia:

- provide applicable tariff information to subscribers – the NRA may require that such information is made available 'immediately prior to connecting a call';
- inform subscribers of any changes to emergency call access and transmission of caller location data;
- provide information on measures implemented to manage traffic; and
- inform subscribers on their right to decide whether their information is included in a directory and about the type of personal data concerned.

Furthermore, the NRAs may require the undertakings concerned to 'distribute public interest information' which has been provided, in a standardised format, by the relevant public authorities, free of charge to existing and new subscribers; such information shall, inter alia, concern the most common uses of electronic communications services for unlawful activities or to distribute harmful content (eg copyright infringements) and the means of protection against privacy and data security risks (Article 21(4) of the Universal Service Directive).

QUALITY OF SERVICE: SECURING 'NET NEUTRALITY'

1.198   The EU Regulatory Framework does not contain provisions specifically targeted at securing 'net neutrality'. In a broad sense, 'net neutrality' is a concept related to the objective of an open Internet which is defined in Article 8(4)(g) of the Framework Directive as 'promoting the ability of end-users to access and distribute information or run applications and services of their choice'.[473] Instead, the EU Regulatory Framework has so far relied on transparency rules and provisions and

---

473   See para 1.43 above. See also BEREC, A framework for Quality of Service in the scope of Net Neutrality (BoR(11) 53) (8 December 2011), p 3. For an assessment of the need for EU legislation on 'net neutrality', see Dods, Brisby et al, 'Reform of European electronic communications law: a special briefing on the radical changes of 2009' (2010) 16(4) CTLR 102. For an analysis of 'net neutrality' from an economic perspective, see Kruse and

provided for a right of the NRAs to impose quality of service obligations to ensure 'net neutrality'.

1.199   The Member States have to ensure that the NRAs are able to require providers of public electronic communications networks and services to publish information on their quality of service levels (Article 22(1) of the Universal Service Directive) based on criteria established by the NRAs (Article 22(2) of the Universal Service Directive). Furthermore, the NRAs may impose minimum quality of service requirements on providers of public electronic communications networks and services in order to prevent a 'degradation of service' and a slowing of network traffic (Article 22(3), sentence 1 of the Universal Service Directive) after having provided the Commission and BEREC with a reasoned and detailed advanced notice of their intended action (Article 22(3), sentence 2 of the Universal Service Directive). The Commission may issue comments or Recommendations with regard to the intended quality of service requirements, which the NRAs have to take into utmost account in their decision on the imposition of those requirements (Article 22(3), sentence 3 and 4 of the Universal Service Directive).

1.200   This power of the NRAs to mandate minimum quality of service levels under Article 22(3) of the Universal Service Directive[474] is seen as one of the main regulatory instruments available to the NRAs to secure 'net neutrality'.[475]

In its 'Declaration on Net Neutrality', the EU Commission stated that it will:

> 'attach high importance to preserving the open and neutral character of the Internet, taking full account of the will of the co-legislators now to enshrine net neutrality as a policy objective and regulatory principle to be promoted by national regulatory authorities, alongside the strengthening of related transparency requirements and the creation of safeguard powers for national regulatory authorities to prevent the degradation of services and the hindering or slowing down of traffic over public networks. The implementation of these provisions and the impact of market and technological developments on "net freedoms" shall be monitored closely.'[476]

As part of its contribution to consultations launched by the Commission[477] on the topic of 'net neutrality', BEREC has identified two types of web services which were targeted by blocking or throttling measures:

- the throttling of video streaming and peer-to-peer filesharing, those web services typically require the transmission of large amounts of data; and
- the blocking of VoIP services on mobile networks, or charging extra for enabling VoIP services.

Berger-Kögler, 'Net Neutrality regulation on the Internet?', (2011) 2(1) Int J Management and Network Economics 3.

474   Supported by the amendments to Article 21 of the Universal Service Directive establishing transparency obligations of the providers with regard to traffic management measures: see para 1.197 above.

475   BEREC, A framework for Quality of Service in the scope of Net Neutrality (BoR (11) 53) (8 December 2011).

476   [2009] OJ C308/2.

477   Questionnaire for the public consultation on the open Internet and net neutrality in Europe, Publication date: 30 June 2010, available at: http://ec.europa.eu/information_society/policy/ecomm/library/public_consult/net_neutrality/index_en.htm (accessed on 10 December 2012); Commission Communication of April 19, 2011, The open Internet and net neutrality in Europe, COM (2011) 222 final.

BEREC concluded that those observed cases of blocking or throttling of traffic in the EU could be handled by the NRAs by applying the existing regulatory toolset[478] and has published a guidance document setting out a framework for establishing minimum quality of service parameters by the NRAs under Article 22(3) of the Universal Service Directive as well as on quality evaluation methods.[479] Furthermore, the amended transparency obligations (Article 21 of the Universal Service Directive) as well as the facilitated changes of providers (Article 30 of the Universal Service Directive)[480] are seen to play an important role in promoting net neutrality by ensuring that users obtain adequate information on possible limitations or any relevant traffic management measure in order to make informed choices.[481] The BEREC, having investigated traffic management measures used by operators, confirmed its previous findings that, to date, no regulation beyond the instruments of transparency and quality of service was necessary to promote net neutrality[482] even though it had found that traffic management measures contravening net neutrality could be observed.[483]

The Commission does not rule out that further regulatory measures may have to be taken should the existing regulatory toolset under the EU Regulatory Framework eventually turn out to be insufficient for handling threats to the free and open character of the Internet.[484] The Commission is expected to issue a Recommendation on net neutrality addressing, among other things, traffic management, transparency, switching, and IP interconnection.[485]

REGULATORY MEASURES CONCERNING THE AVAILABILITY OF SERVICES

1.201 The Member States must ensure the 'fullest possible availability' of publicly available telephone services provided over electronic communications networks in the event of catastrophic network breakdown or in cases of force majeure. To this end, undertakings providing publicly available telephone services at fixed locations must take all reasonable steps to ensure uninterrupted access to emergency services (Article 23 of the Universal Service Directive).

---

478 BEREC Response to the European Commission's consultation on the open Internet and net neutrality in Europe, (BoR (10) 42), p. 3.
479 A framework for Quality of Service in the scope of Net Neutrality (BoR (11) 53) (8 December 2011);BEREC has advised that it will issue a more in-depth BEREC guidance document in the course of 2012.
480 Commission Communication of 19 April 2011, The open Internet and net neutrality in Europe, COM (2011) 222 final, p 9, see also para 1.208 et seq below.
481 Commission Communication of 19 April 2011, The open Internet and net neutrality in Europe, COM (2011) 222 final, p 4 et seq; BEREC, A framework for Quality of Service in the scope of Net Neutrality (BoR (11) 53), p 53.
482 BEREC draft Guidelines for Quality of Service in the scope of Net Neutrality (BoR(12)32) (29 May 2012); BEREC has consulted two further documents in the context of Net Neutrality, the draft report on differentiation practices and related competition issues in the scope of Net Neutrality (BoR(12)31) (29 May 2012), and the draft report on an assessment of IP-interconnection in the context of Net Neutrality (BoR(12)33) (29 May 2012). The public consultation closed on 31 July 2012. For future activities of BEREC with respect to net neutrality see BEREC, Draft Working Programme 2013 (BoR(12)92) (September 2012), p 11 et seq.
483 BEREC, A view of traffic management and other practices resulting in restrictions to the open Internet in Europe (BoR(12)30) (29 May 2012).
484 Commission Communication of 19 April 19 2011, The open Internet and net neutrality in Europe (COM (2011) 222 final), p 8 et seq.
485 See BEREC, Draft Working Programme 2013 (BoR(12)92) (September 2012), p 10 et seq.

OPERATOR ASSISTANCE AND DIRECTORY ENQUIRY SERVICES

1.202   Subject to applicable data protection provisions,[486] subscribers[487] to publicly available telephone services have the right to have an entry in the publicly available directory and to have their information made available to providers of directory enquiry services and directories.[488] Undertakings which assign telephone numbers to subscribers must meet all reasonable requests to make available, for the purposes of the provision of publicly available directory enquiry services and directories, the relevant information in an agreed format on 'fair, objective, cost-oriented and non-discriminatory' terms.[489]

All end-users that are provided with a publicly available telephone service have a right to access directory enquiry services;[490] NRAs may impose obligations or conditions for the provision of directory enquiry services on undertakings controlling the access to end-users in accordance with Article 5 of the Access Directive.[491] Regulatory restrictions preventing end-users in one Member State from accessing directly the directory enquiry services in another Member State must be abolished.

EUROPEAN EMERGENCY CALL NUMBER

1.203   The rules regarding access to the single European emergency call number 112 are set out in Article 26 of the Universal Service Directive. All end-users provided with an electronic communications service for originating national calls to a number or numbers in the national numbering plan must be able to call the emergency services free of charge, making use of the European Emergency Call number 112 (Article 26(1) of the Universal Service Directive); the Member States must ensure equivalent access of disabled end-users to emergency services (Article 26(3), sentence 3 of the Universal Service Directive). Access to emergency services has to be provided by the undertakings providing electronic communications service for originating national calls to a number or numbers in the national numbering plan (Article 26(2) of the Universal Service Directive). Furthermore, the Directive establishes an obligation on 'the undertakings concerned' to make caller location information available to authorities handling emergency calls to the number 112. This obligation may be extended by the Member States to also cover calls to national emergency numbers (Article 26(5) of the Universal Service Directive). Article 26(6) of the Universal Service Directive requires Member States to ensure that citizens are 'adequately informed' about the existence and use of the single European emergency call number 112.

To provide for effective access to '112 services', the Commission may adopt technical implementing measures after consultation with BEREC (Article 26(7) of the Universal Service Directive).

---

486   See Art 25(5) of the Universal Service Directive, which refers particularly to Art 12 of the e-Privacy Directive.

487   The concept of 'subscriber' (Art 2(k) of the Framework Directive) is not limited to persons or legal entities who have entered into a 'written' contract with a provider of public electronic communications services: see ECJ judgment of 22 January 2009 *Commission v Poland* (C-492/07) [2009] ECR I-0008 at [22] and [26–30].

488   Art 25(1) of the Universal Service Directive in conjunction with Art 5(1)(a) of the Universal Service Directive.

489   Art 25(2) of the Universal Service Directive.

490   Art 25 (3), sentence 1 of the Universal Service Directive.

491   Art 25 (3), sentence 2 of the Universal Service Directive, see also para 1.143 above.

EUROPEAN TELEPHONE ACCESS CODES AND HARMONISED NUMBERS FOR HARMONISED
SERVICES OF SOCIAL VALUE

1.204   Member States must ensure that the '00' code is the standard international
access code; for calls between adjacent locations across borders between Member
States, special arrangements may be established or continued (Article 27(1) of the
Universal Service Directive). Article 26(2) of the Universal Service Directive
provides for the creation of a 'legal entity established within the Community' which
is to be designated by the Community for the management and promotion of the
European Telephony Numbering Space (Article 27(2) of the Universal Service
Directive). Undertakings providing public telephone networks must handle all calls
to the European telephone numbering space at rates that are 'similar to those
applied to calls to and from other Member States' (Article 27(3) of the Universal
Service Directive).

1.205   Article 27a of the Universal Service Directive requires Member States to
promote the harmonised numbers for harmonised services of social value under the
116 numbering range,[492] ensure that citizens are adequately informed of the
existence and use of these services and in addition to this, make 'every effort' to
ascertain that citizens have access to the missing children hotline available under the
number 116000; access to the hotline has not yet been implemented in all Member
States[493]

ACCESS TO NUMBERS AND SERVICES

1.206   End-users from one Member State must be able to access non-geographic
numbers (eg numbers for free phone or premium rate services) within the EU and
to all numbers provided in the EU where technically and economically feasible,
except where a called subscriber has chosen for commercial reasons to limit access
by calling parties located in specific geographical areas (Article 28(1) of the
Universal Service Directive). The recitals make it clear that tariffs charged to parties
calling from outside the Member State concerned need not be the same as for those
parties calling from inside that Member State.[494] Where justified due to misuse or
fraud, Member States must provide the relevant authorities with the means
to require providers of public electronic communications networks and services to
block access to services on a case-by-case basis or to withhold interconnection or
other service revenues (Article 28(1) of the Universal Service Directive)

---

492   Cf Commission Decision 2007/116/EC of 15 February 2007 on reserving the national
numbering range beginning with '116' for harmonised numbers for harmonised services of
social value [2007] OJ L49/30, amended by Commission Decision 2007/698/EC [2009]
OJ L284/31, and Commission Decision 2009/884/EC [2009] OJ L317/46.

493   For an overview on the implementation status see http://ec.europa.eu/justice/fundamental-
rights/rights-child/hotline/implementation/index_en.htm (accessed on 10 December 2012); see
also Communication from the Commission to the European Parliament, the Council, the
European Economic and Social Committee and the Committee of the Regions, Dial 116 000:
The European hotline for missing children (COM(2010) 674 final) (17 November 2010) which
is aimed at promoting the implementation of the hotline for missing children in the Member
States.

494   Art 28 of the Universal Service Directive and Recital 38.

OBLIGATIONS TO PROVIDE ADDITIONAL FACILITIES

1.207 Member States must ensure that NRAs are able to require all undertakings providing public telephone services or access to public communication networks to make available to end-users, subject to technical feasibility and economic viability, tone dialling, or dual tone multi-frequency operation and calling-line identification.[495] Member States are not required to impose obligations to provide these facilities: a Member State may waive the obligation for all or part of its territory if it considers, after public consultation, that there is already 'sufficient access' to these facilities (Article 29(2) of the Universal Service Directive).

Obligations facilitating change of provider

1.208 The ability to change one's provider is a key factor in securing competition on a retail level.[496] The European legislator considers number portability, ie the ability of end-users to retain their numbers independently of the undertaking providing the service, as 'a key facilitator of consumer choice and effective competition in a competitive telecommunications environment'[497] and has significantly expanded and strengthened the rights of subscribers to retain their numbers through the 2009 Regulatory Package. Furthermore, the ability to easily switch providers is seen as a factor promoting 'net neutrality'.[498]

1.209 Article 30(1) of the Universal Service Directive allows all subscribers, upon request, to retain their numbers independently of the undertaking providing the service. In the case of geographic numbers, the numbers can be retained at a specific location, whereas in the case of non- geographic numbers, they can be retained at any location; this does not apply to the porting of numbers between networks providing services at fixed locations and mobile networks.[499] While the Directive does not directly provide for the porting of numbers between networks providing services at fixed locations and mobile networks, the recitals state that Member States are free to allow for the transfer of numbers between fixed and mobile networks.[500] Number portability requirements also apply in relation to VoIP service providers which make available to their customers numbers from the national telephone numbering plan.[501]

The porting of the number and its activation after the porting process must be performed 'in the shortest possible time'; at the longest, customers having concluded a number porting agreement have to have their number activated with their new provider within one working day (Article 30(4), sub-para 1 of the Universal Service Directive).

The NRAs must ensure that the charges between operators related to the provision of number portability is cost oriented, and that direct charges to subscribers do not

---

495 Art 29(1) of the Universal Service Directive in conjunction with Annex I, Part B.
496 Recital 47 of the Citizens' Rights Directive.
497 See Recital 40 of the Universal Service Directive and Recital 47, sentence 3 of the Citizens' Rights Directive.
498 Commission Communication of 19 April 2011, The open Internet and net neutrality in Europe (COM (2011) 222 final), p 9: see also para 1.198 et seq above.
499 Annex I Part C of the Universal Service Directive.
500 Recital 40, sentence 3 of the Universal Service Directive.
501 This excludes, eg 'classical' peer-to-peer VoIP communications (such as 'Skype-to-Skype') which establishes Internet-based connections between the users' PCs without requiring the use of telephone numbers.

act as a disincentive for subscribers against changing their providers[502] (Article 30 of the Universal Service Directive).

1.210   Member States must ensure that contracts between consumers and providers of electronic communications services do not impose an initial contract term that exceeds 24 months and that undertakings enable users to enter into a contract with a maximum duration of 12 months; conditions and procedures for contract termination must not act as a disincentive against changing service provider (Article 30(5) and (6) of the Universal Service Directive).

1.211   Almost 25 years after the adoption of the first generation of EU Directives aimed at liberalising and harmonising the markets for telecommunications networks, services and equipment, the electronic communications markets remain subject to sector-specific regulation, which is based on principles of competition law and managed by a European network of regulatory governance.

This regulatory framework will continue to be adapted to changing market conditions, technological developments, and political circumstances – the next review is scheduled for 2014.

---

502 Cf on pricing rules for number portabilty which may include the ex ante setting of fixed maximum prices, ECJ judgment of 13 July 2006 *Mobistar SA* (C-438/04) [2006] ECR I-06675 at [20–30] and [32–37].

EU Competition Law in the Telecommunications Sector

Keith Jones
Baker & McKenzie LLP, London

INTRODUCTION

2.1   As discussed in Chapter 1, competition law is at the core of the EU legal framework for the telecommunications sector. The European Commission sees the telecommunications regulatory framework as a significant means to further liberalise the sector, with competition law concepts being a central component. As the former Competition Commissioner, Mario Monti, noted when the new framework was introduced:

> 'the aim of regulatory remedies should be to allow antitrust remedies to be the only ones needed in the long term. While for those parts of the industry which can be characterised as natural monopolies, this may be difficult to achieve, as technology develops regulatory intervention will increasingly play a smaller role'.[1]

At the same time, the Commission has increasingly used competition law to attack abusive practices in the telecommunications sector, in addition to reviewing strategic alliances and arrangements under the merger control rules and Article 101 of the TFEU (ex Article 81 EC). Recent examples of enforcement action by for the European Commission ('Commission') include fining Polish Telecom (TeleKomunikacja Polska[2]) €127 million in June 2011 and Téléfonica over €151 million in 2007[3] (contrast the amount with the fine on Deutsche Telekom of €12 million in 2003[4]) for abuse of dominance, a finding upheld by the General Court in March 2012. Deutsche Telekom (again) and its subsidiary Slovak Telekom are being investigated for abuse of dominance by way of margin squeeze in Slovakia[5]. There is an ongoing

---

1   See 'Remarks at the European Regulators Group Hearing on Remedies', 26 January 2004 (SPEECH/04/37).
2   COMP/39.525 *Telekomunikacja Polska*, 22 June 2011, summary decision [2011] OJ C324/7.
3   Case COMP/38.784 *Wanadoo España v Telefónica*, summary decision at [2008] OJ C83/5; on appeal, *Telefónica and Telefónica España v Commission* (T-336/07) judgment of 29 March 2012, not yet published.
4   Case COMP/37.451 *Deutsche Telekom AG*, 2003] OJ L263/9. On appeal, *Deutsche Telekom AG v Commission* (T-271/03) [2006] ECR II -477.
5   Case 39523 *Slovak Telekom*. See press release IP/12/462.

investigation into Téléfonica and Portugal Telecom regarding reciprocal non-compete clauses covering the Spanish and Portuguese markets,[6] with a statement of objections issued in October 2011. At the national level, Member States have also applied their competition law, with the Dutch Competition Authority imposing a fine on T-Mobile and others for a one-off exchange of price information.[7] It is clear, therefore, that an understanding of competition law and its underlying concepts is now of fundamental importance to the sector.

EU COMPETITION LAW – BASIC LEGISLATION AND NOTICES

2.2   There are three main components to EU competition law:[8] Article 101 of the TFEU (ex Article 81 EC), Article 102 of the TFEU (ex Article 82 EC) and the EU Merger Regulation ('EUMR').[9]

Article 101 – restrictive agreements[10]

2.3   Article 101 of the TFEU prohibits agreements and concerted practices between undertakings that have as their object or effect the prevention, restriction or distortion of competition. Intra-group agreements are generally not caught, as they are between entities that are part of the same 'undertaking'. Further, only agreements that give rise to an 'appreciable' restriction of competition are caught by Article 101(1) of the TFEU (a mere contractual restriction is not sufficient).[11] The Commission's 'de minimis notice' provides guidance on when an agreement will have an appreciable impact on competition.

2.4   Article 101 of the TFEU can apply to all commercial agreements and arrangements. If an agreement is found to violate Article 101(1) of the TFEU, it is void and unenforceable pursuant to Article 101(2) of the TFEU, unless the Article 101(3) TFEU criteria are satisfied. Article 101(3) of the TFEU is satisfied if the restrictive agreement:

- contributes to improving the production or distribution of goods or services and promotes technical or economic progress;

---

6   Case 39.839 *Telefónica and Portugal Telecom*. See press release IP/11/1241.
7   Cf *T-Mobile Netherlands* (C-8/08) [2009] ECR I-4529
8   A detailed analysis of the basic concepts underlying competition law, such as 'undertaking' and 'agreement' is outside the scope of this work. See Whish and Bailey *Competition Law* 7th ed (Oxford University Press, 2012), Chapters 3–5 for details.
9   Council Regulation No 139/2004 on the control of concentrations between undertakings, [2004] OJ L24/1.
10   The Commission's guidelines on the application of Article 101(3) (Commission Notice: Guidelines on the application of Article 81(3) of the Treaty [2004] OJ C101/97) contain a summary of how the Commission sees Art 101(1) (as well as 101(3)) as operating in practice. This deals with restrictions of competition 'by object' (those that by their very nature have the potential of restricting competition) and restrictions by effect. The Commission's 'Horizontal Guidelines' (Guidelines on the applicability of Art 101 of the Treaty on the Functioning of the European Union to horizontal co-operation agreements [2011] OJ C11/01) and the 'Vertical Guidelines' (Guidelines on Vertical Restraints [2000] OJ C291/01)) must also be taken into account.
11   Commission Notice on agreements of minor importance which do not appreciably restrict competition under Article [101](1) of the Treaty [2001] OJ C368/13. This notice is often (and naturally) confused with the legal concept of de minimis but the two are distinct. See Whish and Bailey *Competition Law* 7th ed, p 140 et seq and Bailey 'Restrictions of competition by object under Article 101 TFEU', (2012) 49 CMLR 559, pp 590–592.

- allows consumers a fair share of the resulting benefit;
- contains only indispensable restrictions; and
- does not afford the possibility of eliminating competition.

There are various 'block exemption' regulations that provide 'safe harbours' for particular types of agreements, including certain technology transfer agreements (e g licensing of IP rights, know-how, etc), vertical agreements, and various horizontal cooperation agreements (including research and development and specialisation).[12]

2.5   Certain practices such as price-fixing, market sharing and customer allocation between competitors will restrict competition 'by object'. Many such agreements, in particular cartels, will almost never be exempted under Article 101(3) of the TFEU. Agreements that restrict or inhibit the creation of a single market through preventing parallel imports are serious 'by object' infringements. The treatment of such restrictions is not sector specific.

2.6   Although Article 101 of the TFEU, as with Article 102 of the TFEU, only applies if there is an appreciable effect on trade between Member States, this is not likely to be significant given that relevant national competition law is aligned with EU competition law.[13]

Article 102 – the abuse of market power

2.7   Article 102 of the TFEU prohibits the abuse of a dominant position. Dominance' is defined in para 1.73 above. It is essentially the ability to act independently (to a certain degree) from competitors and customers on the market. In essence, this is the same as 'SMP' under the new regulatory framework.[14] While the text of Article 102 of the TFEU gives some examples of what constitutes an abuse of dominance, this is largely established through decisions of the Court of Justice of the European Union ('ECJ'). There are various types of abuse which can broadly be described as 'exploitative' or 'exclusionary' anti-competitive practices. Examples of exploitative anti-competitive practices include excessive pricing and tying (ie exploiting the dominant position by reaping the excess profit or by using it to gain an advantage in a related market). Exclusionary anti-competitive practices are largely focussed on protecting the dominant position or otherwise acting unfairly. Examples include predation (pricing below cost), loyalty rebates, margin (or price) squeezes, and refusals to deal. Other abuses include refusal to give access to an 'essential facility' and price discrimination.[15] Note also that delaying, or creating obstacles to, negotiations and dealings with competitors may be considered

---

12   Commission Regulation No 772/2004 on the application of Article 81(3) of the Treaty to categories of technology transfer agreements [2004] OJ L123/11; Commission Regulation No 2790/1999 on the application of Article 81(3) of the Treaty to categories of vertical agreements and concerted practices [1999] OJ L336/21; Commission Regulation No 2659/2000 on the application of Article 81(3) to categories of research and development agreements [2000] OJ L304/07; and Commission Regulation No 2658/2000 on the application of Article 81(3) to categories of specialisation agreements [2000] OJ L304/03.

13   The policy aim of creating a single market may be one possible difference. Note that it is possible to have stricter national competition law with respect to unilateral conduct, such as the concept of 'market strong' position ('*marktstark*') in Germany.

14   Regulation No 2887/2000 of the European Parliament and of the Council of 18 December 2000 on unbundled access to the local loop [2000] OJ L336/04.

15   For further information on abuse of dominance, see Whish and Bailey (above), Chapters 5, 17–18.

an abuse (whether there is an abuse will be a question of degree in any given case).[16] The application of Article 102 of the TFEU is particularly important in the telecommunications sector, given that the sector is generally characterised by former State monopolies/incumbents.

Fines and follow-on claims

2.8   There are significant consequences for breach of either Article 101 or Article 102. Fines can be imposed of up to 10 per cent of turnover and, while generally short of this, have been increasing in size. Further, in addition to relevant agreements or parts of agreements being void and unenforceable, third parties may claim damages to compensate for any loss suffered as a result of the infringement. Such claims are becoming increasingly common with various steps taken at national level to facilitate claims.

The EU Merger Regulation

2.9   The EU Merger Regulation provides the framework for assessing mergers and certain joint ventures that constitute 'concentrations' with a 'Community dimension', within the meaning of the EU Merger Regulation. If the EU Merger Regulation applies, national merger control does not, although there are various mechanisms for transferring cases to the 'best placed' authority. Fines can be imposed if parties implement a deal without having received prior clearance from the Commission.

Notices and Guidelines

2.10   The specific application of each of these aspects of competition law in the telecoms sector is described in more detail below.[17] The Commission has published numerous notices and guidelines which should also be considered.[18] Of particular importance are the EC Access Notice,[19] the Guidelines accompanying the block exemptions,[20] and the Guidelines on SMP.[21] Many of these changed due to the all-encompassing review of Article 101 of the TFEU, including several of the block exemptions. Further, a number of notices were issued to facilitate the modernisation

16   Case COMP 39.525 *TeleKomunikacja Polska*, 22 June 2012.
17   Article 86 of the TFEU. State aid and the public procurement rules are not within the scope of this chapter.
18   Relevant notices are found on the website of DG Competition: http://ec.europa.eu/competition/index_en.html.
19   Notice on the application of the competition rules to access agreements in the telecommunications sector – framework, relevant markets and principles [1998] OJ C265/2.
20   Commission Notice: Guidelines on Vertical Restraints [2000] OJ C291/01; and Commission Notice: Guidelines on the application of Article 81 of the EC Treaty to technology transfer agreements [2004] OJ C101/2. Commission Notice: Guidelines on the applicability of Article 81 of the EC Treaty to horizontal cooperation agreements [2003] OJ C3/2.
21   Guidelines on market analysis and the assessment of significant market power under the Community regulatory framework for electronic communications networks and services [2002] OJ C165/6.

of EU competition law enforcement (as discussed below). Similarly, the EU Merger Regulation was revised with new legislation and guidelines effective from 1 May 2004.[22]

MODERNISATION OF THE ENFORCEMENT OF EU COMPETITION LAW

2.11   With the enlargement of the EU, the Commission considered it necessary to modernise competition law enforcement. The EU adopted Regulation 1/2003[23] as a result, which took effect on 1 May 2004. This reformed the framework for enforcement throughout the EU. Detailed guidelines[24] dealing with the functioning of the rules were also issued.

2.12   Regulation 1/2003 brought about a number of fundamental changes to the previous system, including:

● *The abolition of the mandatory notification system under Article 101(3).* Prior to 1 May 2004 only the Commission could grant an exemption under Article 101(3). Now 'self-assessment' is key, ie firms undertake their own analysis.
● *The decentralised enforcement of the EU rules.* National courts and competition authorities can and must apply EU competition law, including Article 101(3), and must cooperate in doing so.
● *Enhancement of powers of investigation.* The Commission has greater powers of evidence gathering, including the power of the Commission to visit homes.

These changes gave rise to an increased need for firms to consider strategic issues. For example, telecommunications companies wishing to complain about an anti-competitive practice now need to consider which of the various authorities is best placed/most likely to take action. This will often involve an analysis of whether the Commission, the National Competition Authority (NCA)/National Regulatory Authority (NRA) should be approached or whether direct action through the courts should be taken. Certainly, some national authorities have made more use of their authority to decide infringement cases in the telecommunications sector than others. A review of the 'notice on cooperation'[25] indicates that the authority receiving a complaint will generally continue with the investigation but other factors will be considered. For example, in relation to *TeleKomunikacja Polska*, while the complaint was initially submitted to the Polish authority, the authority believed that the Commission was better able to investigate, and gather information from, the incumbent firm, and, therefore, transferred the complaint to the Commission. Therefore, relevant factors include a determination as to which authority can best gather evidence and impose/enforce any remedies required. The interventionist

---

22   In relation to the application of Article 102, the main 'guidelines' are in the Commission's 'Guidance on the Commission's enforcement priorities and applying Article 102' [2009] OJ C45/2.
23   Council Regulation No 1/2003 on the implementation of the rules on competition laid down in Articles 81 and 82 of the Treaty [2003] OJ L01/2.
24   The guidelines were designed to provide details on how the Commission envisioned the new enforcement rules working in practice. The guidelines remain in place (with some having been updated or replaced) and cover both substantive issues, such as guidance on self-assessment, and procedural issues, such as the handling of complaints.
25   Commission Notice on cooperation within the Network of Competition Authorities [2004] OJ C101/43.

nature of the particular authority as well as other factors (including costs) must also be considered.

2.13   While Regulation 1/2003 provides for the consistent and uniform application of competition law, there have been tensions and inconsistencies particularly as various authorities develop the law on certain issues. As a result, notwithstanding that the ECJ process is lengthy, there have been a number of appeals and references from the national court to the ECJ to determine key issues (such as 'margin squeeze'). Harmonising the approach, and ensuring consistency throughout the EU, is a key task for the Commission. That said, given that national authorities apply Articles 101 and 102, the body of competition law decisions in the telecommunications sector has increased, thus creating a larger pool of 'precedent' decisions from which to draw conclusions.

APPLICATION OF ARTICLE 101 IN THE TELECOMMUNICATIONS SECTOR

2.14   Despite numerous cases on the general application of Article 101, there have been relatively few Commission decisions under Article 101 with respect to the telecommunications.

Of such decisions, a number have related to strategic alliances falling outside the EU Merger Regulation where the Commission granted negative clearance and/or individual exemption.[26] Examples include: *BT/MCI,*[27] *Atlas,*[28] *Iridium,*[29] *Phoenix/ GlobalOne,*[30] *Uniworld,*[31] *Unisource,*[32] *and Cégétel and Télécom Developpement.*[33] The Commission also approved the *GSM MoU Standard International Roaming Agreement,*[34] which enabled GSM mobile telephone users in one country to use networks in another country. In *T-Mobile Deutschland/O2 Germany*, the Commission authorised an agreement that enabled the parties to roam on one another's 3G networks.[35]

2.15   The Commission's assessment of 3G network infrastructure-sharing agreements in relation to the UK and Germany is a useful case study for the sector on the application of Article 101.[36] In 2003, the Commission concluded that the UK arrangements between O2 and T-Mobile fell outside the scope of Article 101(1) of

---

26   See fourth edition of this book, pp 46–49.

27   Case COMP/34.857 [1994] OJ L223/36.

28   Case COMP/35.337 [1996] OJ L239/23.

29   Case COMP/35.518 [1997] OJ L16/87.

30   Case COMP/36.617 [1996] OJ L239/57.

31   Case COMP/35.738 [1997] OJ L318/24.

32   Case COMP/35.830 [1997] OJ L318/1, this decision was subsequently repealed due to changes in the market: IP/01/1, 3 January 2001.

33   Case COMP/36.581 *Télécom Developpement* [1999] OJ L218/24 (IP/99/558, 23 July 1999).

34   See Commission's XXVIIth *Annual Report on Competition Policy* (1997), point 75 and pp 139–140.

35   [2004] OJ L75/32. On appeal, the General Court was critical of the Commission's reasoning and partially annulled the decision: *O2 (Germany) GmbH v Commission* (T-328/03) [2006] ECR II-1231.

36   O2 and T-Mobile entered agreements to share 3G site infrastructure and to roam on their networks in the UK and Germany.

the TFEU in part and otherwise benefited from Article 101(3) of the TFEU.[37] Similar findings were reached for Germany.[38] Despite this 'clearance' of sorts, O2 appealed the Commission's decision. The appeal was successful on the basis that the Commission had not adequately analysed the a priori issue of whether there was an appreciable restriction of competition within the meaning of Article 101(1) of the TFEU.[39]

2.16   In particular, the Commission, in its investigation into the UK agreement (which had two main parts), found that the agreement on site sharing did not restrict competition because the coverage of the agreement was restricted to sharing basic network infrastructure such as masts, power supply, racking, and cooling. The Commission was aware of the history of the agreement, noting that infrastructure sharing was widely promoted at both the national and EU levels for environmental and health reasons. The Commission also noted that network sharing involved varying degrees of cooperation, depending upon the amount of infrastructure shared:

- First level – the shared use of sites, ranging from individual mast sites to sharing of the grid.
- Second level – radio access network sharing, ie the sharing of initial transmission equipment.
- Third level – sharing the core network, including mobile switching centres and various databases, also referred to as the 'intelligent part' of the network.
- Fourth level – the sharing of radio frequencies.

In the Commission's view, the deeper the level of network sharing, the more significant the concern. In assessing the UK agreement, the Commission took the view that while site sharing can raise issues (in particular by reducing network competition), denying competitors access to necessary sites and site infrastructure and, in some cases, facilitating collusive behaviour, access to sites in this case was unlikely to be an issue. There were a number of reasons for this including the regulatory remedy available under Article 12 of the Framework Directive.[40] The Commission also took account of the fact that the parties were sharing a limited number of passive components of the access network. They retained independent control of their networks and the ability to differentiate services downstream. Further, the level of common costs[41] brought about by the site sharing was not significant. As a result, Article 101(1) did not apply.

2.17   The Commission's analysis was different for the roaming arrangements. In the Commission's view, roaming arrangements were considered to restrict competition as they limited network-based competition with respect to coverage, retail prices, quality, and transmission speeds. Nevertheless, the Commission found that the conditions of Article 101(3) were satisfied as the Commission reasoned that the agreement enabled the parties to have a greater density of coverage and a more extended footprint than they would have had individually, and that, given that the parties compete with three other operators, as well as MVNOs at the retail level, the

---

37   Case COMP/38.370 *O2 UK Limited/T-Mobile UK Limited* [2003] OJ L200/59 (IP/03/589, 30 April 2003).

38   Case COMP/38.369 *T-Mobile Deutschland/O2 Germany* [2004] OJ L75/32 (IP/03/1026, 16 July 2003).

39   See *O2 (Germany) v Commission* (T-328/03), judgment of the General Court, 2 May 2006.

40   This allows Member States to impose the sharing of facilities as a remedy even if there is no dominance/SMP. For a more complete discussion, see Chapter 1.89.

41   This is often a factor in assessing the likelihood of coordination.

agreement would lead to better and quicker 3G service coverage, with coverage accelerated in rural areas. National roaming in rural areas was therefore exempted until the end of 2008. The Commission also recognised the benefits of roaming in urban areas so long as it was limited to a short start-up period and would help expedite the availability of new and innovative services to customers. Therefore reciprocal roaming in urban areas was exempted until the end of 2007.

2.18   While the Commission decision is useful in terms of how the Commission considers Article 101(3) of the TFEU if Article 101(1) of the TFEU applies, the judgment of the General Court[42] is highly relevant to the telecommunications sector as it emphasises the importance of the a priori issue of whether there is a violation of Article 101(1) of the TFEU even if two telecommunications sector undertakings enter into an agreement. The General Court emphasised that in order to assess whether an agreement has as its effect (rather than object) a restriction of competition, the state of competition in the absence of the agreement must be examined. The Court emphasised that this is particularly necessary with respect to markets undergoing liberalisation and emerging markets, as in the case of the 3G mobile market, where effective competition may be problematic owing, for example, to the presence of a dormant operator, the concentrated nature of the market, or the existence of significant barriers to entry.

2.19   There have also been some important decisions on the issue of what constitutes a 'by object' restriction. For example, in *T-Mobile Netherlands*,[43] the ECJ affirmed that a one-time meeting between mobile operators in the Netherlands, which evolved into an information exchange on levels of payable commissions, was 'capable' of, and had the potential to, restrict competition. The ECJ concluded, therefore, that the meeting was a 'by object' restriction of competition. No adverse effects needed to be shown to establish the breach, and the limited scope of the discussion did not negate the conclusion.

2.20   It is also important to consider how national courts apply Article 101(3) of the TFEU. As noted above, the Commission has, on many occasions, notwithstanding having engaged in detailed discussions with the parties, decided to close the case subject to significant amendments, or granted an exemption subject to conditions or for a limited period of time. A court, on the other hand, is not able to enter such discussions, being required to assess the arrangement as presented. As such, an agreement which may have been valid in a slightly modified form if discussed with the Commission in advance, may possibly violate Article 101 TFEU. In practice, however, a court faced with the issue (taking account that most such cases would likely settle) will be less interventionist, seeking to preserve commercial arrangements in their entirety if possible.

APPLICATION OF ARTICLE 102 IN THE TELECOMMUNICATIONS SECTOR

2.21   Paragraph 1.73 sets out the method for assessing a dominant position/SMP. The Commission's 'Guidelines on SMP' provide a detailed guide to market definition and assessment of single and collective dominance.

---

42   See *02 (Germany) v Commission* (T-328/03) [2006] ECR II-1231, judgment of the General Court, 2 May 2006, in particular paras 66–69, 71–72 and 116.

43   *T-Mobile Netherlands* (C-8/08) [2009] ECR II I-4529.

2.22   There has been a significant escalation of Commission enforcement policy decisions under Article 102 of the TFEU in the telecommunications sector, commencing with *Wanadoo*[44] and *Deutsche Telekom*,[45] where the Commission issued infringement decisions in 2003, the first in the telecommunications sector for over 20 years. The previous case was in 1982 against BT[46] when it was still a State monopoly. In that case, the Commission held that BT breached Article 102 of the TFEU with respect to the restrictions it imposed on message-forwarding agencies in the UK.[47] The Commission found that BT's practices prejudiced customers located in other Member States, placed message-forwarding agencies in the UK at a competitive disadvantage vis-à-vis their counterparts in other Member States, limited the development of new markets and new technology, and restricted trade between Member States. No fine was imposed due to the circumstances of the case, including the pressure exerted upon BT by other national telecommunication authorities. The appeal of this decision in *Italy v Commission*[48] arguably acted as the catalyst for the subsequent liberalisation of the sector by the Commission. As noted above, there have been a number of decisions subsequently.

2.23   One of the driving forces behind the Commission's increased activity is its desire to foster a competitive broadband Internet market. The Commission is also concerned about the failure of 'local loop' unbundling. More generally, the Commission's decisions can be seen as a 'push', alongside the new regulatory framework, to ensure that the sector is fully liberalised and that competition law is, in practice, acting as a 'punishment' for infringements. The Commission has, therefore, focused heavily on pricing abuses. The decisions in *Wanadoo*, *Deutsche Telekom*, and *Téléfonica* illustrate the determination of the Commission to address pricing issues even in a sector subject to ex ante regulation, and where the Member States play an important role in setting prices. The Commission followed the decisions in *Deutsche Telekom* and *Wanadoo* with further broadband-related cases in *Téléfonica* and *TeleKomunikacja Polska*. Such cases are particularly significant because the communications infrastructure is often owned and controlled by the former State monopolist that is also active in the relevant downstream (often retail) market. There is, therefore, significant scope for pricing abuse by way of predation or margin squeeze. All of these decisions were appealed, with the Commission prevailing in the appeals.

2.24   In *Deutsche Telekom*, the Commission found that Deutsche Telecom ('DT') was engaging in a margin squeeze by charging new entrants higher fees for

---

44   COMP/38.233 *Wanadoo Interactive* (IP/03/1025, 16 July 2003). On appeal, *France Télécom SA v Commission* (T-340/03) [2007] ECR II-117.

45   Case COMP/37.451 *Deutsche Telekom AG* [2003] OJ L263/9. Upheld on appeal, *Deutsche Telekom AG v Commission* (T-271/03) [2008] ECR II 0477 and on appeal to the ECJ Case C-202/07, judgment of 14 October 2010.

46   Case COMP/29.877 *British Telecommunications* [1982] OJ L360/36.

47   The case concerned BT's attempts to comply with the regulations of the International Telecommunication Union (ITU), which culminated in 1978. With reference to recommendations issued by the International Telegraph and Telephone Consultative Committee, one of the permanent organs of the ITU. BT further developed its 'Scheme' restricting the ability of message-forwarding agencies to offer their services as an intermediary where a message was originating outside of the UK and being sent on to a non-UK destination. This Scheme was supported by a written request from BT to the message-forwarding agencies requiring that they provide a written assurance that they would refrain from offering such services.

48   *Italian Republic v Commission* (41/83) [1985] ECR 873, see in particular paras 20 and 22. The fact that BT was a statutory monopoly did not prevent the application of the competition rules.

wholesale access to the local loop than it charged subscribers for retail lines. This discouraged new entry and reduced the choice of suppliers of services as well as price competition. The Commission found an abusive margin squeeze because the difference in DT's retail and wholesale prices was either negative or slightly positive, but in any case insufficient to cover DT's costs of providing its own retail services. The Commission's review[49] revealed that from 1998 to 2000, DT charged competitors more for unbundled access at the wholesale level than it charged its own subscribers for access at the retail level. The Commission rejected DT's argument it was not responsible given that the prices were set by the German regulator. The Commission determined that DT had sufficient freedom of choice in setting its prices to avoid the margin squeeze.

2.25   Notably, the Commission examined the issue of abuse on the basis of total costs, not merely incremental costs, without needing further evidence of adverse impact on the market/anti-competitive intent. In predatory pricing cases, the Commission has looked at variable costs/incremental costs as well as total costs in order to establish abuse. It is only if pricing is below average variable cost that an abuse is clearly established; if above variable but below total costs, evidence of anti-competitive intent is needed (the '*AKZO*' test).[50] In *Deutsche Telekom*, the Commission stated that if there is pricing below total cost, this is sufficient to establish a material adverse effect on competition, and, therefore, an abuse.[51]

2.26   In *Wanadoo*, the Commission fined *Wanadoo* €10.35 million for predatory pricing. The decision, and subsequent appeal, are of importance in that they clarify how the *AKZO* test for predatory pricing is to be applied in emerging market cases. The Commission decision states that the *AKZO* test applies in full, subject to the acquisition costs and revenue for new customers being spread over the lifetime of the subscriber acquired. The General Court did not disagree with this approach and the ECJ rejected the subsequent appeal on the basis that France Telecom/Wanadoo had not raised any point of law (only economics). Highly significant for incumbents considering pricing strategies in emerging markets is the fact that the Commission gave critiqued certain economic methodologies for the assessment of pricing abuses. In particular, it recognised the limitations of 'discounted cash-flow' models as they can conceal periods of predatory pricing. The Commission also rejected various justifications advanced for Wanadoo's pricing below cost, such as a desire to grow the market, 'learning by doing', and economies of scale.[52] Certain national authorities, however, have been more willing to accept such justifications.

2.27   The relationship among the various types of possible price abuse (cross-subsidy, margin squeeze, discrimination, predation, and excessive pricing), and the precise nature of the legal tests have been the subject of much debate. The area has,

---

49   The Commission compared the tariffs for wholesale access to the local loop with those of a number of different retail offers (analogue, ISDN and ADSL) by using a weighted approach, taking into account the number of customers.

50   See *Akzo Chemie BV v Commission* (C-62/86) [1991] ECR I-3359.

51   While some considered this an unmeritorious per se application of the competition rules that ignores economic effects, the Commission's approach appears justifiable. A margin squeeze can be profitable for the vertically integrated firm indefinitely but yet produce anti-competitive effects in the longer term. As such, it seems legitimate in vertical margin squeeze cases to put the burden on the dominant firm to show that there is an objective justification for its pricing. If not, it could set the price at a level that raises no immediate issues for it but which, over time, will distort and hinder competition.

52   A similar case is also before the UK national authorities (*Wanadoo UK plc v The Office of Communications*).

however, been clarified by the Court. In short, a cross-subsidy is at most only an abuse in very limited circumstances,[53] namely, where there has been an acquisition where the funds used were derived from excessive or discriminatory prices or from other unfair practices in a reserved market by the undertaking holding the monopoly. In terms of the relationship between margin squeeze and predation, they are separate abuses. DT had argued that a margin squeeze is a particular form of predation (or excessive pricing) that can be exercised by a vertically integrated dominant[54] firm and that there was no separate abuse. The ECJ rejected this in *Deutsche Telekom* and repeated its view in *Konkurrensverket v Telia Sonera Sverige AB*.[55] In reaching this view, the Court noted the exclusionary effect which margin squeeze may create for competitors and hence considered that it was itself capable of constituting an abuse.[56]

2.28 The question of whose costs to examine when considering pricing abuses has also been settled. As indicated above, one can argue that, for vertically integrated dominant firms, pricing below total costs is presumed to be abusive,[57] given that a margin squeeze can be a long-term, profitable strategy to drive out competitors. Some argued that the test for margin squeeze should be based on the costs of the reasonably efficient competitor, while others argued that this was impractical and one must look at the dominant firm's own costs. Some even argued that both the costs of the dominant firm and the reasonably efficient operator must be considered. The Court in *Deutsche Telekom* held that, as a matter of procedural fairness, the costs of the dominant firm are the ones that must be examined as the court would otherwise not be in a position to assess compliance.

2.29 DT settled a subsequent Commission investigation into an alleged abuse of dominance by way of margin squeeze by making commitments with respect to its future behaviour.[58] The investigation had been triggered by a complaint from a German provider, QSC. QSC complained that DT was imposing a margin squeeze between its retail tariffs for Asymmetric Digital Subscriber Line ('ADSL') broadband Internet connections and the corresponding wholesale tariffs for line sharing, allowing DT to become a quasi-monopolist for ADSL services in Germany. The Commission accepted DT's commitment to significantly reduce line-sharing fees and closed the investigation. Nonetheless, DT is currently being investigated along with its subsidiary Slovak Telekom for abusive margin squeezing in Slovakia. If an infringement is found in this case, the basis for investing DT may have a material impact on how corporate groups comply with competition law and manage competition law risk.

2.30 The Commission has also taken enforcement action against Telia Sonera (Sweden) for having abused a dominant position in the provision of high-speed Internet access.[59] This relates to infrastructure competition rather than retail competition. The matter concerned a contract for the construction and operation of a fibre-optic broadband network on behalf of a regional housing association. The Commission took the view that Telia Sonera's bid for the contract was intentionally

---

53   *UPS Europe v Commission* (T-175/99) [2002] ECR II-1915, paras 61 to 64. cf Whish, *Competition Law*, 4th Ed, p 710.
54   See para 183.
55   Case C-52/09 [2011] ECR I-527.
56   Here the ECJ rejected the argument that it had to also amount to an abusive refusal to supply.
57   *Deutsche Telekom*, para 179.
58   IP/04/281, 1 March 2004.
59   Case COMP/37.663 *B2/Telia* (IP/03/1797, 19 December 2003).

set below cost and did not allow the operator to recover the investments and expenses claimed for the provision of infrastructures and services contained in the contract. In so doing, Telia Sonera prevented the development of alternative infrastructure and the entry of competing service providers, thereby strengthening its dominant position in the markets for the provision of local broadband infrastructure and the provision of high-speed Internet access. To date, the Commission has not reached a decision. Nevertheless, the case illustrates the importance of broadband to the Commission on a policy level; it is taking action in seemingly local cases to pursue its wider objective of promoting competitive broadband provision.

2.31   In terms of non-pricing abuses, the *Microsoft* case[60] is likely to be influential with respect to the analysis of tying. The Commission found that Microsoft had tied its Windows Media Player to the Windows operating system. By offering the two as a package, there was no incentive for competitors to develop alternative media players. Capturing this market also enabled Microsoft to control related markets in the digital media sector. As a result, Microsoft was required to offer manufacturers a version of the Windows PC operating system without the Windows Media Player attached.[61] Notably, the General Court referred to the fact that the IT and communications industry was in constant and rapid evolution, so that what appeared to be separate products at one point in time may subsequently be regarded as forming a single product. The basis for deciding the issue is primarily based on consumer demand.

2.32   Delaying tactics is also a common feature of negotiations when dealing with a dominant incumbent. In *TeleKomunikacja Polska,* the Commission found an abuse for consistent refusals to deal, or making the position more difficult, with respect to access to its network and wholesale broadband services. Polish Telecom ('TP') was (and is) the owner of the only nationwide telecommunications access network and the only supplier of Local Loop Unbundling ('LLU') and bitstream access ('BSA') in Poland. As a dominant company, TP was required to allow remunerated access to its network and broadband services to allow effective competition in downstream markets. The Commission found that the abusive pattern of TP's behaviour included the following elements:

* proposing unreasonable conditions governing access to wholesale broadband products (ie exclusion or modification of contractual clauses and extension of deadlines to the detriment of alternative operators);
* delaying the negotiation process (for example, in 70 per cent of the cases, Telekomunikacja Polska did not meet a 90-day regulatory deadline for concluding negotiations);
* limiting access to its network by, among other things, rejecting alternative operators' orders on unreasonable grounds;
* limiting access to subscriber lines by, among other things, rejecting alternative operators' orders to activate subscriber lines on unreasonable grounds; and
* refusing to provide reliable and complete 'General Information' on TP's network (information which was indispensable to allow alternative operators to make business decisions).

---

60   Case COMP/37.792 *Microsoft/ W2000* (IP/04/382, 24 March 2004).
61   The General Court rejected Microsoft's application for suspension of the remedies imposed by the Commission on 22 December 2004, MEMO/04/305. The Commission's decision was upheld on appeal: see *Microsoft Corpn v Commission* (T-201/04) [2007] ECR II-3601.

As indicated above, since May 2004, NCAs have been required to apply Article 102 of the TFEU whenever they apply national competition law to any abuse prohibited by Article 102 (the position is similar under Article 101 of the TFEU). While some NCAs have begun to utilise these powers, others have been somewhat limited. Decisions of the NCAs need to be monitored, particularly given the network of cooperation among authorities.

SECTORAL INQUIRIES

2.33 Under Article 17 of Regulation 1/2003, the Commission has the power to launch sectoral investigations. These entail general reviews of a market/markets the Commission believes to be problematic with respect to how the market is working rather than an investigation into a specific possible competition law breach (although the evidence uncovered may lead to such an investigation). The Commission has utilised similar powers in the telecommunications sector under the previous legislation.[62] In 1999, it launched an inquiry into three issues: leased lines, mobile roaming services, and unbundling of the local loop. This was only the third occasion on which the Commission had initiated an investigation under the provision.[63] The leased line investigation ended in 2002 as a result of substantial price decreases.[64]

The Commission is using this power more regularly across all sectors (with pharmaceuticals having been the focus). The Commission has recognised that there are certain aspects of markets that may not work effectively. In the telecommunications sector, given the regulatory framework, it is likely that the Commission will look to these market reviews to identify, consider, and address issues, such as international roaming, through regulation such as with international roaming.

RELATIONSHIP OF COMPETITION LAW WITH THE NEW REGULATORY FRAMEWORK

2.34 The relationship between competition law and the new regulatory framework is significant as there is clear scope for overlap and many points of interaction. Indeed, some authorities with dual powers may consider that they are making a decision under the regulatory regime but reach a decision under the competition rules. A number of factors to consider with respect to this relationship are discussed below.

2.35 The closeness of the competition law and the new regulatory framework is illustrated by the fact that there have been some competition law cases that could be dealt with by the regulatory framework, or resolved by way of a regulatory remedy. For example, the cost of call termination on mobile networks was addressed in

---

62 Article 12 of Regulation 17/62.
63 See the Commission's XXIXth Report on Competition Policy (1999), points 74–76; see further the XXXth Report (2000), points 157–160 and XXXIst Report (2001), points 125–131; speech by Sauter 'The Sector Inquiries into Leased Lines and Mobile Roaming: Findings and follow-up of the competition law investigations' 17 September 2001, available at http://ec.europa.eu/competition/speeches/text/sp2001_016_en.pdf
64 See IP/02/1852, 11 December 2002; details of the leased line inquiries can be found at: http://ec.europa.eu/competition/sectors/telecommunications/archive/inquiries/leased_lines/index.html

some instances via competition law. The Commission issued a statement of objections against KPN in March 2002,[65] alleging that KPN abused its dominant position regarding the termination of telephone calls on the KPN mobile network through discriminatory or otherwise unfair behaviour. More generally, however, studies showed that fixed-to-mobile termination rates in Europe could be ten times higher than the average charge for fixed to fixed interconnection. The Commission considered that this resulted in undue barriers for newcomers to the mobile market and high prices for consumers. The Commission, therefore, decided to take action under the regulatory framework which identifies call termination as a recommended market and provides for imposition of material regulatory remedies for anti-competitive conduct.[66]

2.36   The Commission also initially used competition law to challenge international roaming rates. In July 2004, the Commission announced that it had sent two statements of objections to the UK mobile network operators O2 and Vodafone under Article 102. The objections related to the rates that both O2 and Vodafone charged other Mobile Network Operators (MNOs) for international roaming services at the wholesale level. Other MNOs needed to roam on O2's and Vodafone's UK networks in order to enable their own subscribers to use their mobile phones in the UK. The Commission's investigation revealed that Vodafone, since 1997 through to at least the end of September 2003, exploited its dominant position in the UK market for the provision of international roaming services at the wholesale level on its own network. The abuse consisted of charging unfair and excessive prices (otherwise known as 'Inter-operator tariffs') to European MNOs.[67] In September 2007, the first 'Roaming Regulation'[68] was adopted (replaced in 2012), which has addressed the issue.

Impact of the Regulatory Framework on Conditions of Competition

2.37   The regulatory framework affects the assessment of the conditions of competition. The 3G network sharing cases discussed above demonstrate that the regulatory framework, including the availability of remedies thereunder, needs to be taken into account in assessing whether any competition issues arise.

Relationship of Underlying Objectives

2.38   A clear understanding of the different aims of the regulatory framework and competition law is vital given the similar concepts used. Article 8 of the Framework

---

65   The *Wanadoo* abuse of dominance case arose out of the inquiry into the unbundling of the local loop.

66   Case COMP/37.704 *MCI/Mobile Termination Rates* (IP/02/483, 27 March 2002).

67   The Commission is often willing to take a pragmatic view. No action was taken in the German call termination market, for example, due to a 50% reduction in rates by the German operators. In Sweden, where there was also a complaint, the national authority was dealing with the case. In contrast, the UK dealt with similar issues under the licensing provisions by way of an inquiry by the Competition Commission. This resulted in a price cap but no fine. See also Commission Press Release IP/99/298, 4 May 1999.

68   The Commission concluded that each individual network constituted a separate market. The level of IOTs was high particularly compared to the prices charged for similar calls made on their networks by UK subscribers of Independent Service Providers to whom both O2 and Vodafone had supplied wholesale airtime access. See IP/04/994, 26 July 2004.

Directive sets out the policy objectives and regulatory principles of which the NRAs must 'take utmost account' in carrying out their tasks.[69] Article 8(2) states that NRAs 'shall promote competition' by, among other things:

(a) ensuring that users derive maximum benefit in terms of choice, price and quality;

(b) ensuring that there is no distortion or restriction of competition;

(c) encouraging efficient investment in infrastructure and promoting innovation; and

(d) encouraging efficient use and ensuring the effective management of radio frequencies and numbering resources.

While 'competition' is the central theme, the key difference is that NRAs under the regulatory framework have wide latitude to promote competition using a multiplicity of tools. This is, in effect, a continuation of the underlying policy of telecommunications liberalisation, namely a desire to tip the market in favour of new entrants/other operators as opposed to the incumbents, but is much more explicit.

Consistency of concepts

2.39 Given the general alignment of concepts, a mechanism to ensure consistency is necessary.[70] When considering introducing the 2002 regulatory framework, the Commission foresaw the regulatory framework would roll back *ex ante* regulation as competition becomes effective. In doing so, it recognised that there was (and is) a need for consistency of interpretation in both areas. Competition law concepts, therefore, were incorporated into the regulatory framework, in particular, the concept that an operator will, in general, be subject to relevant regulatory obligations only if it is designated as having SMP.[71] An operator is only deemed to have SMP if it is in a dominant position.[72] Further, it was reorganised that whether operators are faced with ex ante regulation or find themselves involved in ex post antitrust proceedings they should have the legal certainty that issues such as 'relevant market' and 'market power' will have the same meaning regardless of whether the proceedings in question are initiated by national regulators or competition authorities. Such consistency is provided for in Article 15 of the Framework Directive.[73]

---

69 Regulation (EC) No 717/2007 of the European Parliament and of the Council of 27 June 2007 on roaming on public mobile telephone networks within the Community and amending Directive 2002/21/EC. Replaced by Regulation (EU) No 531/2012 of the European Parliament and of the Council of 13 June 2012 on roaming on public mobile communications networks within the Union [2012] OJ L172/10.

70 Article 7(1). For a more in depth discussion of the Framework Directive see paras 1.32–1.89 above.

71 The goal was to take the best of both competition law and sector specific legislation, with national regulators applying the resulting principles in a coherent manner aimed at stimulating growth and development in a wide variety of electronic communications services. The Commission envisioned, through the Article 7 mechanism, that DG Competition and DG Information Society would jointly enjoy and exercise review power with respect to the regulatory powers given to the Commission. IP/03/1012, 14 July 2003.

72 Certain other obligations will of course apply to any undertaking, regardless of whether it has SMP. For a more detailed consideration of the concept of SMP in the regulatory framework see paras 1.62–1.78 above.

73 Article 14(2) of the Framework Directive.

Tensions

2.40   Notwithstanding the consistency of concepts, a number of tensions exist, including with respect to the 'recommended markets' that have been identified in the EU regulatory framework.[74] Under competition law and the new regulatory framework, the definition of the relevant market rests on the same economic principles. However, by setting out a list of 'recommended markets,'[75] there is a danger that these have become the 'default' market definitions notwithstanding that they may not align with the true economic markets (although this would breach the Directive). Indeed, the Commission has been very reluctant to allow 'departures' from the recommendation. It is possible, therefore, that this has given rise either to false positives (ie a finding of SMP and, therefore, a remedy where there is in fact no dominance) or to false negatives (ie too wide a market definition, and therefore, no finding of SMP even though it actually exists).

'Precedent value' of market reviews?

2.41   The definition(s) adopted in the market reviews under the regulatory framework are, in practice, the starting point for any subsequent competition investigations, notwithstanding comments where the Commission in its guidance clarified that the market definition may differ on an ex ante and ex post basis. While competition authorities are legally required to examine the issue of market definition in every case,[76] a conclusion reached in the market reviews under the new regulatory framework heavily influences the definition used in subsequent competition cases.

APPLICATION OF THE EU MERGER REGULATION IN THE TELECOMMUNICATIONS SECTOR

A brief outline of the EU Merger Regulation

2.42   There are a vast number (approximately 200) EU merger control decisions related to the telecommunications sector. Telecommunications companies contemplating an acquisition, merger, or joint venture should understand the basic framework and policy.[77]

Jurisdiction

2.43   If a particular transaction constitutes a 'Concentration' [78] with a 'Community dimension' it falls within the scope of the EU Merger Regulation. Under the EU Merger Regulation, notification is mandatory and the transaction cannot, in

---

74   Many NRAs may need some time to adapt to this way of thinking.
75   For a fuller explanation of 'recommended markets' under the Framework Directive see para 1.73 above.
76   Annex 1 to the Framework Directive.
77   *The Coca-Cola Company and Coca-Cola Enterprises Inc v Commission* (T-125/97 and T-127/97) [2000] ECR II-1733, para 82.
78   Council Regulation No 139/2004 on the control of concentrations between undertakings [2004] OJ L24/2.

general, be completed before a decision is reached.[79] The concept of a 'Community dimension' is founded upon turnover thresholds.[80] Some cases that would be best dealt with at Commission level may not have a 'Community dimension' as defined; similarly, some transactions which meet the relevant thresholds would be best examined at the national level.

The current EU Merger Regulation, therefore, has a number of mechanisms to increase flexibility, to address the concern that certain mergers and joint ventures were not being dealt with at the appropriate level.[81] Such mechanisms include, for example, both the use of pre-notification referrals and flexibility on post-notification referrals.[82] The position is that merging parties, prior to notification, can provide a 'reasoned submission', requesting the Commission to take jurisdiction over a case where the turnover thresholds are not satisfied but which could otherwise be notified in three or more Member States.[83] Such an application will not necessarily succeed as some national authorities may be reluctant to lose jurisdiction in a particular case and can easily veto an application. The parties may also request that the Commission refer a case that satisfies the turnover thresholds to one or more Member States on the basis of national or local impact.[84]

Substantive test

2.44   The substantive test under the EU Merger Regulation is whether the concentration 'would significantly impede effective competition, in the common market or a substantial part of it, in particular as a result of the creation or strengthening of a dominant position'. This is a change from the previous substantive test of whether the concentration created or strengthened a dominant position.

---

79   Covering mergers, some joint ventures (if 'full function') and even some other contracts.
80   Articles 4 and 7 of the EUMR.
81   Article 1 of the EUMR.
82   This is a further watering down of the notion of 'one stop shop'. The concept originally meant that if the Commission had jurisdiction, it would examine the merger in the vast majority of cases. This was once fundamental but has been gradually watered down over time as the notion of subsidiarity has become more prominent (or at least that the Commission trusted the Member States more). The recent changes can be seen as an example of this and have lead to some issues in practice
83   See Arts 4, 9 and 22 of the EUMR. Merging parties can notify where they can demonstrate a 'good faith intention to conclude an agreement'. A signed letter of intent or a memorandum of understanding between the parties will suffice. All deadlines are expressed to be in working days rather than months and weeks (but continue to exclude Commission holidays). Phase I investigations last 25 working days, or 35 working days if the merging parties offer commitments or a national authority has requested the referral of a case. The additional four-month in-depth investigation period (Phase II) remains, expressed as 90 working days. This deadline may be extended by a further 20 working days. If the parties offer commitments 55 working days or more after the start of Phase II proceedings, there is an automatic extension of 15 working days. The Commission's powers of investigation are largely consistent with Regulation 1/2003. The powers include the ability to inspect and seal business premises and the ability to conduct interviews (with the consent of the interviewee). Fines are up to 1 per cent of aggregate annual turnover in the preceding financial year for supplying incorrect, misleading, or incomplete information to the Commission or failing to submit to an inspection. Daily penalty payments are up to 5 per cent of daily aggregate turnover for any failure to comply with certain Commission decisions or actions as set out in Article 15.
84   The Commission will refuse to examine a case if any of the Member States that would otherwise have jurisdiction object within 15 working days of receiving a copy of the reasoned submission. Silence, however, will be construed as agreement with the Commission's proposal to take over a case.

Although the 'dominance' test worked well, it was thought to generate a degree of uncertainty as to whether it dealt with non-collusive oligopoly situations where there is a risk that, below a dominance threshold, the merging firms may be able to successfully raise prices to the detriment of consumers, without having to rely on the coordinated response of other members of the oligopoly.

Officially, the revised wording did not signal any shift in the level of the Commission's intervention in merger investigations, and the dominance test was thought to be likely to continue to apply in most scenarios. However, the change has been significant in the telecommunications sector. For example, in the UK, the merger of two of the main mobile telephony operators, T-Mobile and Orange, resulted in the main players being reduced from five to four. While neither single firm nor collective dominance would likely have been created or strengthened as a result of the merger, it was thought to significantly impede effective competition. The parties offered a number of remedies to address the concerns in order to obtain clearance in Phase 1.[85]

2.45 The EU Merger Regulation is accompanied by a number of guidelines. In considering substantive issues, the most significant are the guidelines that describe the approach the Commission takes when assessing horizontal mergers (the Horizontal Merger Guidelines).[86] Although the Commission will look at market shares and market concentration levels, the focus is on competitive harm, including:

- *non-coordinated* (*or unilateral*) *effects* (where a merger leads to or enhances single firm dominance or to a reduction of competitive pressure from non-merging firms even in the absence of coordination); and
- *coordinated effects* (resulting from collective dominance being created and strengthened, ie where the market conditions are such that competitors are able to coordinate their behaviour and raise prices even without entering into an agreement to do so.

Other factors may counterbalance any potential anti-competitive effects. These include countervailing buyer power, ease of market entry, the failing firm defence,[87] and efficiencies. Efficiency claims will only be accepted when they are sufficiently substantiated so as to convince the Commission that the efficiencies will benefit consumers, are merger-specific, and are verifiable. To date, such arguments have had little to no success.

EU Merger Regulation Decisions in the Telecommunications Sector

2.46 For any particular merger, the proposed transaction will need to be assessed in the light of its likely impact on conditions of competition in the relevant market to determine whether the transaction is likely to raise substantive issues. Relevant factors include, among other things, market shares, barriers to entry, and countervailing bargaining power. A study of previous cases can be beneficial. Liberalisation led to many joint ventures designed to exploit the resulting opportunities, and some undertakings, such as BT, Vodafone, and France Telecom have been particularly

---

85   The Commission must issue a decision on such a referral request within 25 days from receipt of the Commission's receipt of the reasoned submission.

86   Case M.5650 *T-Mobile/Orange*.

87   Guidelines on the assessment of horizontal mergers under the Council Regulation on the control of concentrations between undertakings [2004] OJ C31/05.

active. Of particular interest is the *Telia/Telenor* case.[88] In that case, the Commission granted conditional clearance following a Phase II investigation to a proposed concentration between the incumbents of Sweden and Norway. However, by merging to become a single operator in the Nordic region, the parties could gain complete control over the local access network in the home markets (ie the parties would have been in a position to prevent competition by denying access to the 'local loop'). Prior to the merger, neither party had been well equipped to prevent entry into their respective 'captive home markets'. This was because they both needed access to each other's market to provide a number of services to their own countries, and, therefore had an incentive to allow each other entry on mutually beneficial terms. The merger, subsequently abandoned for commercial reasons, was allowed only after the parties committed to giving access to competitors on reasonable terms.

2.47   The Commission granted conditional clearance in the *Telia/Sonera* case,[89] involving the merger of the incumbent operators of Sweden and Finland. This merger was consummated in December 2002. The decision in *Telia/Sonera* indicated that an international calling network may establish a vertical link between networks in different countries. The Commission analysed this point when considering the acquisition of Orange's Danish mobile operations by TeliaSonera.[90] However, it found that TeliaSonera's position in Sweden and Finland did not mean that any such vertical effects would be created in the Danish market as a result of the acquisition.

2.49   There have been a number of merger clearance decisions without remedies or conditions. The Commission cleared Slovak Telecom's acquisition of sole control over EuroTel's mobile phone business from its joint venture partner American West.[91] The Commission found that the change in control would not result in an increase in EuroTel's market share. The fact that Slovak Telecom was already EuroTel's majority shareholder, and, as such, was capable of determining its competitive behaviour, meant that the transaction raised no new competition concerns. The Commission also cleared BT's acquisition of Infonet. The Commission investigated the competitive effects of the proposed transaction on the possible markets for global telecommunications services ('GTS') that are provided to multinational corporations. The Commission found that the transaction would not change significantly the market conditions either on a global or on a European scale as Infonet would bring only a minimal incremental market share to BT, that the combined BT/Infonet would continue to face a number of competitors that are present in these markets, and that customers would still have the possibility to switch to alternative GTS suppliers.

2.50   The Commission has reviewed a number of merger proposals in the mobile sector. In the *T-Mobile/Orange* case, the Commission cleared the proposed merger, conditioned on the divestment of spectrum and the amendment of a network sharing arrangement with a competitor, Hutchison 3G. The Commission also

---

88   The failing firm defence applies where, despite the fact that the proposed transaction is prima facie anti-competitive, the parties are able to show that, absent the deal, the target would exit the market due to its financial difficulties, there is no less anti-competitive alternative than the notified merger and, absent the deal, all the assets of the target would exit the market.

89   Case COMP/M.1439 [2001] OJ L40/1.

90   Case COMP/M.2803 [2002] OJ C201/19.

91   Case COMP/M.3530 *TeliaSonera AB/ Orange AS* [2004] OJ C263/7.

considered T-Mobile's acquisition of Orange in the Netherlands.[92] In the *T-Mobile/tele.ring* case, the Commission required remedies to approve a merger that it considered would give rise to a non-collusive oligopoly in the Austrian mobile sector.[93] A further merger in the mobile sector in Austria between Hutchison 3G and Orange was considered by the Commission, with a conditional clearance decision being issued in December 2012 following an in-depth investigation.[94] To facilitate the entry of new players into the Austrian mobile telecommunications market, Hutchison committed to divesting part of its spectrum to a new entrant as well as entering a Mobile virtual network operator (MVNO) agreement with Liberty global's UPC. The Hong-Kong based company also committed to offer wholesale access to its network to up to 16 MVNO players in the next ten years. This followed another in-depth assessment in 2012, namely that of a joint venture in the UK mobile commerce sector. The Commission's preliminary investigation indicated potential competition concerns in the nascent markets of mobile payment applications supply (so-called 'mobile wallets'), mobile advertising, and related data analytics services, where the joint venture may have very high market shares.[95] Nevertheless, the transaction was cleared unconditionally. The Commission's in-depth investigation revealed that a number of alternatives already exist and much more are very likely to emerge in the near future to ensure adequate competitive pressure on the joint venture's mobile wallet platform. Some of these alternatives may rely on a secure access to the SIM card of the mobile handsets in order to store sensitive data like bank account numbers, etc. This access will be controlled by the mobile network operators, including in particular the three parents of the joint venture. However, other alternatives exist which do not store sensitive data on SIM-cards and it is unlikely that the creation of the joint venture will allow the parent mobile network operators to block these alternative routes to market using technical or commercial means. As regards the joint venture's advertising and data analytics activities, the market investigation revealed that there will be various other players who have access to a comparable set of data and who will offer services in competition with the joint venture.[96]

2.51   The Internet has given rise to a number of issues in the merger context. For example, the Commission prohibited the proposed concentration in the *MCI WorldCom/Sprint* case,[97] which, in the Commission's view, would either have created a dominant position for the merged entity or would have reinforced the dominant position of MCI WorldCom in the provision of 'top-level' or universal interconnectivity on the Internet. This decision was subsequently annulled by the General Court on a technicality.[98]

---

92   Case COMP/M.3561 *DT/ EuroTel*, cleared on 15 December 2004 (IP/04/1492).
93   Case COMP/M.4748 *T-Mobile/Orange*.
94   Case COMP/M.3916 *T.Mobile/tele.ring*.
95   Case COMP/M.6497 *Hutchison 3G Austria / Orange Austria*. See IP/12/1361.
96   See Commission Press Release IP/12/367.
97   P/12/938.
98   Case COMP/M.1741 [2003] OJ L 300/01 – annulled by the General Court on appeal, *WorldCom v Commission* (T-310/00) [2004] ECR II-3253. The General Court considered that the Commission should have found itself without the power to adopt a decision when the parties withdrew their notification. The General Court added that the parties were entitled to expect their letter to the Commission withdrawing notification of the merger to close the file. The Commission granted conditional clearance, following a Phase II investigation, in Case COMP/M.1069 *Worldcom/MCI* [1999] OJ L116/1 in 2000.

2.52 In the *Vivendi/Canal + Seagram* case,[99] Vivendi's acquisition of Seagram, and, through Seagram, Universal, threatened to create a dominant position in the market for Internet portals for Vivendi's subsidiary Vizzavi, if the latter were allowed exclusive access to Universal's music libraries. Universal offered not to discriminate in favour of Vizzavi in the supply of music for downloading or streaming on the Internet to its subscribers in the EU for a period of two years. This commitment, however, was found to be inadequate as it was a behavioural rather than a structural remedy and, further, the duration was too short. Consequently, Vivendi committed to provide access to Universal's music content on a non-discriminatory basis with respect to pricing and terms and conditions. It also committed to provide an arbitration procedure in case of any dispute concerning the access conditions. The commitment was for five years, with the possibility of revision after three years. This revised commitment was accepted by the Commission.

CONCLUSION

2.53 An understanding of competition law is fundamental for any telecommunications undertaking considering its legal position and obligations. Arguments based on competition law are relevant to market reviews and possible obligations that arise thereunder. They also determine many of the obligations of operators in any particular market and impact on any joint venture, strategic alliance, or other arrangement an operator is contemplating, including distribution arrangements. Given the Commission's enthusiasm for bringing competition cases against telecommunications operators, these operators need to be aware of the possible 'punishment' for perceived anti-competitive activity as well as the opportunities that exist in using competition law as a means of attacking the anti-competitive practices of incumbents or competitors.

---

99 The Commission should have found itself without the power to adopt a decision when the parties withdrew their notification) The General Court found that the parties were entitled to expect their letter to the Commission withdrawing the notification of the merger to close the file.

Data Protection and Privacy[1]

Holger Lutz and Caroline Heinickel
Baker & McKenzie, Frankfurt

INTRODUCTION – HISTORY AND PURPOSE

3.1 It is now 17 years since the Directive on the protection of individuals with regard to the processing of personal data (the 'Data Protection Directive')[2] came into force. This Directive sets out the basic provisions for protecting the fundamental rights of individuals with respect to processing of their personal data in Europe.[3] A further Directive dealt with the particular issues which were raised by new advanced technologies being introduced into public telecommunications networks: the Directive on the processing of personal data and the protection of privacy in the telecommunications sector (the 'Telecommunications Privacy Directive').[4] The Telecommunications Privacy Directive complemented the Data Protection Directive. Its ambit was, however, wider. Notably, it also provided protection for subscribers who were legal persons, as opposed to only individuals.

3.2 In 2002, as part of the 2002 EU Regulatory Package, the European Parliament and the Council adopted a further Directive on privacy and electronic communications (the 'E-Privacy Directive').[5] The E-Privacy Directive replaced the Telecommunications Privacy Directive. The Commission's aim was to ensure that people could be confident that their privacy would be respected when they used electronic communications networks and services of all kinds, and that network and service providers have a clear framework in which to operate. As with the Telecommunications Privacy Directive, its provisions complement those of the Data Protection Directive. It carries over much of the previous regime, but there are some

---

1 Editing of this chapter closed on 6 December 2012.
2 Directive 95/46/EC of the European Parliament and of the Council of 24 October 1995 on the protection of individuals with regard to the processing of personal data and on the free movement of such data [1995] OJ L281/31.
3 The rights in this Directive gave substance to the rights contained in the Council of Europe Convention of 28 January 1981 for the Protection of Individuals with regard to the Automatic Processing of Personal Data.
4 Directive 97/66/EC of the European Parliament of 15 December 1997 concerning the processing of personal data and the protection of privacy in the telecommunications sector [1998] OJ L24/1.
5 Directive 2002/58/EC of the European Parliament and of the Council of 12 July 2002 concerning the processing of personal data and the protection of privacy in the electronic communications sector [2002] OJ L201/37.

important changes including clarifying the applicability of the rules on sending unsolicited communications by e-mail and some grey areas.

In 2006, the E-Privacy Directive was supplemented and amended by a further Directive addressing the retention of data generated or processed in connection with the provision of publicly available electronic communications services or of public communications networks (the 'Data Retention Directive').[6] The Data Retention Directive aims to harmonise Member States' provisions concerning the obligations of providers of publicly available electronic communications services and of public communications networks with respect to the retention of certain data (in particular traffic and location data) in order to ensure that the data is available for the purpose of the investigation, detection and prosecution of serious crimes.[7] In 2011, the Commission commenced reviewing the Data Retention Directive.[8]

In 2009, the E-Privacy Directive was further amended by another Directive concerning the processing of personal data and the protection of privacy in the electronic communications sector (the 'Citizens' Rights Directive),[9] which is part of the 2009 EU Regulatory Package.[10] The Citizens' Rights Directive implements changes and amends the E-Privacy Directive, in particular with respect to location data, personal data breaches, and rules on cookies and similar technologies used to store data on or read data from end-user devices (eg web beacons and tracking pixels).

Member States were required to implement the Data Retention Directive by 15 September 2007 and the Citizens' Rights Directive by 25 May 2011.

SCOPE OF APPLICATION

3.3   The E-Privacy Directive is intended to be technology neutral.[11] The Commission wanted to provide an equal level of protection and privacy for users of publicly available electronic communications services regardless of the technologies used.

The E-Privacy Directive covers the processing of personal data in connection with the provision of publicly available electronic communication networks and services in the EU. It therefore addresses public networks and services only. It does not apply to closed or private networks. (However, any personal data processing on closed or private networks would be subject to the general Data Protection Directive. In addition, national implementing regulations may be applicable to private networks).

---

6   Directive 2006/24/EC of the European Parliament and of the Council of 15 March 2006 on the retention of data generated or processed in connection with the provision of publicly available electronic communications services or of public communications networks and amending Directive 2002/58/EC [2006] OJ L105/54.

7   Cf para 3.37 below.

8   Cf para 3.39 below.

9   Directive 2009/136/EC of the European Parliament and of the Council of 25 November 2009 amending Directive 2002/22/EC on universal service and users' rights relating to electronic communications networks and services, Directive 2002/58/EC concerning the processing of personal data and the protection of privacy in the electronic communications sector and Regulation (EC) No 2006/2004 on cooperation between national authorities responsible for the enforcement of consumer protection laws [2009] OJ L337/11.

10   Cf para 1.6 above.

11   Cf para 1.32 above.

3.4   The E-Privacy Directive is primarily concerned with the regulation of the transmission of communications and not the content of those communications. The definition of an electronic communications service clearly excludes the provision of content. It provides that an electronic communications service is:

> 'a service normally provided for remuneration which consists wholly or mainly in the conveyance of signals on electronic communications networks … but excludes services providing, or exercising editorial control over, content transmitted using electronic communications networks and services'.[12]

This definition is based on the concept of the conveyance of signals on electronic communications networks.[13] This means that providers who, for example, provide content to a website would not be covered by the E-Privacy Directive (although they will still be covered by the Data Protection Directive to the extent they collect, process and/or use personal data).

3.5   The Data Protection Directive addresses the rights and freedoms of natural persons. The E-Privacy Directive has a wider scope and, for example, requires Member States to take measures to protect not only natural persons but also corporate subscribers. In this context, the E-Privacy Directive also distinguishes between subscribers and users. Subscribers are defined as:

> 'any natural person or legal entity who or which is a party to a contract with the provider of publicly available electronic communications services for the supply of such services'.[14]

This makes clear that a subscriber can be a natural or a legal person. It is also clear from the E-Privacy Directive that the contractual relationship between the subscriber and the service provider may entail a periodic or one-off payment and that prepaid cards are also considered to be a contract.

The E-Privacy Directive defines a user as:

> 'any natural person using a publicly available electronic communications service, for private or business purposes, without necessarily having subscribed to this service'.[15]

3.6   The intention is clearly to distinguish between those individuals who have a contract for the provision of relevant services and those individuals who have access to the services, notwithstanding the absence of a contract with a service provider, but who, nevertheless, may have rights which require protection, for example members of the same family or household. The rights and protections given to users and subscribers are not always identical.

CONFIDENTIALITY OF COMMUNICATIONS

3.7   The principle of confidentiality of communications is included in the Charter of Fundamental Rights of the European Union.[16]

---

12   Art 2(c) of the Framework Directive; see para 1.34 above.
13   Cf para 1.34 above.
14   Art 2(k) of the Framework Directive.
15   Art 2(a) of the E-Privacy Directive.
16   Art 7 of the Charter of Fundamental Rights of the European Union.

3.8 As set out above, the E-Privacy Directive aims to guarantee the confidentiality of communications and related traffic data[17] by means of public communications networks and publicly available electronic communications services.[18] Member States must prohibit in particular the listening, tapping, storing or surveillance of communications (and the related traffic data) by persons other than users, unless the user has given consent.

3.9 There are a number of exceptions, including for reasons of national and public safety, defence, and the prevention, detection, and prosecution of criminal offences.[19] There is also an exception which permits the recording of communications (and related traffic data) which is carried out in the course of lawful business practice for the purpose of providing evidence of a commercial transaction or any other business communication,[20] provided that confidentiality is ensured. This particular exception is subject to the following conditions:

• the parties to the communications should be informed prior to the recording about the recording, its purpose, and the duration of its storage; and
• the recording must be erased as soon as possible and, at the latest, by the end of the period during which the transaction can be lawfully challenged.[21]

3.10 The E-Privacy Directive places special emphasis on the protection of information stored on a subscriber's or user's terminal equipment. The E-Privacy Directive seeks to control the use of software programs which monitor users' Internet usage where the information collected can then be used for marketing or other purposes. The E-Privacy Directive specifically refers to 'spyware', 'web bugs', and 'cookies'.[22]

Spyware is a type of malicious software installed on the terminal of a user that collects information about the user without the knowledge of the user. Typically, spyware hides its presence from the user.

Web bugs are objects that are embedded in web pages or e-mails and are usually invisible to the user. However, web bugs typically allow checking as to whether a user has viewed a particular page or e-mail.

Cookies are small pieces of information sent to, and stored in, the terminal of a user by a service provider, often without the knowledge of the user. The device then acts as a marker or identifier that can be automatically recognised by the service provider. Cookies are used for a wide range of purposes and can provide benefits to the user, for example by facilitating Internet shopping by remembering a user's preferences and saving the user time when he or she returns to a website. Nevertheless, cookies can contain very sensitive information and often users are completely unaware of them. Other technologies, such as spyware,[23] can be even more invasive.

3.11 Prior to its amendment in 2009, the E-Privacy Directive permitted the use of cookies if the relevant user was sufficiently informed about the use and purpose of

---

17 Art 2(b) of the E-Privacy Directive: see para 3.17.
18 Art 5(1) of the E-Privacy Directive.
19 For details on obligations to retain data see para 3.38 et seq below.
20 Art 5(2) of the E-Privacy Directive.
21 Recital 23 of the E-Privacy Directive.
22 Recitals 24 and 25 of the E-Privacy Directive.
23 Spyware programs can capture data on which websites the user visits or even what a user types, potentially enabling the spyware to record user names and passwords for certain websites.

cookies and was given a right to object.[24] The Citizens' Rights Directive tightened the rules for the application of cookies and similar technologies used to store data on or read data from end user devices (eg web beacons and tracking pixels). Currently, the use of cookies and similar technologies is only permissible if the subscriber or user has given his or her express and informed consent.[25]

Member States were required to transpose the Citizens' Rights Directive into national laws. Article 4(1) of the Citizens' Rights Directive required them to adopt and publish the laws, regulations, and administrative provisions necessary to comply with the Citizens' Rights Directive. The implementation deadline was 25 May 2011. In some Member States, however, the implementation process is still ongoing.

3.12   In order to provide guidance on the permissible use of Cookies, on 22 June 2010, the 'Article 29 Data Protection Working Party'[26] published a Working Paper addressing online behavioural advertising.[27] Although not legally binding, guidance by the Article 29 Data Protection Working Party is usually followed closely by the Member States.

Most notably, the Working Paper contains the statements that:

- the responsibility to comply with the various requirements of the Citizens' Rights Directive (information, consent, etc) ultimately lies with the entity that sends and reads a cookie, understanding joint controllership is possible;
- the consent requirement for online behavioural advertising cookies is only satisfied by opt-in consent;
- browser settings can only deliver consent in very limited circumstances;
- the user's acceptance of a single cookie may also entail acceptance for subsequent readings of the cookie;
- consent regarding the use of cookies should be limited in time;
- users must be enabled to revoke the consent easily;
- 'visible tools' must be prepared and displayed where the monitoring takes place; and
- information on the monitoring must be provided 'periodically'.

The above is not intended to prevent any technical storage or access for the sole purpose of carrying out the transmission of a communication over an electronic communications network, or as strictly necessary for the provider of an information society service[28] explicitly requested by the subscriber or user to provide the service.

Access to specific website content can still be made conditional on the acceptance of cookies or similar technologies if they are used for a legitimate purpose, eg to verify the identity of users engaged in online transactions.[29]

3.13   Network and service providers are required to work together, if necessary, to safeguard the security of the network. The providers of publicly available electronic

---

24   Former Art 5(3) of the E-Privacy Directive.
25   Art 5(3) of the E-Privacy Directive as amended by the Citizens' Rights Directive.
26   The Data Protection Working Party was set up under Art 29 of Directive 95/46/EC. It is an independent European advisory body on data protection and privacy.
27   Article 29 Data Protection Working Party, Opinion 2/2010 on online behavioural advertising adopted on 22 June 2010.
28   The term 'information society' service is defined in the E-Commerce Directive 98/48/EC. It covers any service normally provided for remuneration, at a distance, by electronic means and at the individual request of a recipient of services.
29   Recital 25 of the E-Privacy Directive.

communications services are required to take appropriate technical and organisational measures to safeguard the security of their services.[30] Such measures must at least:

- ensure that personal data can be accessed only by authorised personnel for legally authorised purposes;
- protect personal data stored or transmitted against accidental or unlawful destruction, accidental loss or alteration, and unauthorised or unlawful storage, processing, access or disclosure; and,
- ensure the implementation of a security policy with respect to the processing of personal data.[31]

If there are particular risks of a breach of the security of the network, the service provider must fully inform subscribers and users about such risks, any possible remedies and the likely costs involved.[32] The service provider must fulfil its information obligation even if the existing security risk is outside the scope of remedies that can be implemented by the service provider. Service providers who offer services over the Internet (such as e-mail services) should therefore inform subscribers and users about measures they themselves can take to protect the security of their communications, for example by using encryption technologies.[33]

PERSONAL DATA BREACHES

3.14 Specific notification obligations apply in the case of a 'personal data breach', ie:

> 'a breach of security leading to the accidental or unlawful destruction, loss, alteration, unauthorised disclosure of, or access to, personal data transmitted, stored or otherwise processed in connection with the provision of a publicly available electronic communications service in the Community'.

For example, if a telecommunications network is 'hacked' in a way that unauthorised third parties have access to the data transmitted over such network this is considered a 'personal data breach'.[34]

3.15 If a personal data breach occurs, the service provider must, without undue delay, notify the personal data breach to the competent national authority. The notification to the competent authority must at a minimum describe the nature of the personal data breach and the contact points where more information can be obtained, recommend measures to mitigate the possible adverse effects of the personal data breach, and describe the consequences of, and the measures proposed or taken by the provider to address the breach.[35]

3.16 If the personal data breach is likely to have a negative impact on the personal data or privacy of a subscriber or user (for example, if the personal data breach resulted in unauthorised third parties becoming aware of credit card details or other bank account information of the users of the publicly available electronic communications service), the provider must, in addition to informing the competent

---

30   Art 4(1) of the E-Privacy Directive.
31   Art. 4(1a) of the E-Privacy Directive.
32   Art 4(2) of the E-Privacy Directive.
33   Recital 20 of the E-Privacy Directive.
34   Art 2(i) of the E-Privacy Directive.
35   Art 4(3) sub-paras 1 and 4 of the E-Privacy Directive.

authorities, also notify the subscriber or user of the breach without undue delay. Such notification is not required if the provider has sufficiently demonstrated to the competent authority that it has implemented appropriate technological measures (ie measures that render the data unintelligible to any person who is not authorised to access it) to protect the subscribers' or users' data, and that such measures were applied to the data concerned by the personal data breach.

The notification to the subscriber or user must, at a minimum, describe the nature of the personal data breach and the contact points where more information can be obtained, and must recommend measures to mitigate the possible adverse effects of the personal data breach.[36]

TRAFFIC DATA

3.17 The E-Privacy Directive regulates the use and retention of traffic data, ie 'data processed for the purpose of the conveyance of a communication on an electronic communications network or for the billing thereof'.[37]

This definition replaces the term 'traffic and billing data' in the Telecommunications Privacy Directive.[38] It is much broader than the previous definition, which only encompassed data relating to subscribers and users that was processed to 'establish calls' and stored by the provider. Under the current definition, traffic data includes data with respect to all electronic communications[39] and not only with respect to telephone calls. Traffic data includes data referring to routing, duration, volume, or time of a call. It also includes the format in which the communication is conveyed by the network. It may include 'location data',[40] such as data on the location of the terminal equipment of the sender and the recipient, and it may also include navigation data such as URLs.[41] The definitions of traffic data and location data are, therefore, not mutually exclusive and it is possible for certain data to fall within both definitions.

3.18 The basic rule for the processing of traffic data is that traffic data must be erased or modified so that it is no longer personal data when such data is no longer required for transmission purposes.[42]

The exact moment of the completion of the transmission of a communication will depend on the type of electronic communications service and may vary from case to case. For example, the transmission of a voice telephony call will be completed as soon as either the caller or the called party terminates the connection. For e-mail, the transmission is completed as soon as the addressee collects the message, typically from the server of its service provider.[43]

The service provider may want to keep and use the related traffic information for a longer period, eg for statistical purposes such as monitoring call duration. According to article 6 para 1 of the E-Privacy Directive, this is permissible if such data is first anonymised.

---

36 Art 4(3) sub-paras 2–4 of the E-Privacy Directive.
37 Art 2(b) of the E-Privacy Directive.
38 Cf Art 6 of the Telecommunications Privacy Directive.
39 Art 2(d) of the E-Privacy Directive.
40 Art 2(c) of the E-Privacy Directive: see para 3.20 et seq.
41 The 'Uniform Resource Locator' is the global address of documents and other resources on the World Wide Web.
42 Art 6(1) of the E-Privacy Directive.
43 Recital 27 of the E-Privacy Directive.

3.19   The basic rule for the processing of traffic data is subject to four important exceptions:

(i)   **For billing purposes:** If traffic data is necessary for the purposes of subscriber billing and interconnection payments it may be processed as long as the bill may lawfully be challenged or payment pursued.[44] The service provider must inform the subscriber or user of the types of traffic data which are processed and of the duration of such processing.[45] In addition, only traffic data that is adequate, relevant, and non-excessive for billing and interconnection purposes may be processed. Other traffic data must be deleted.

The Article 29 Data Protection Working Party has been concerned that divergences exist in practice between the electronic communications companies in the Member States with regard to storage periods of traffic data. The working party, therefore, has recommended that there be a routine storage period for billing of a maximum of three to six months, with the exception of particular cases of dispute where data may be processed for a longer period.[46]

(ii)   **For marketing purposes:** Service providers may process traffic data for the purpose of marketing electronic communications services to the extent and for the duration necessary for such marketing, and only after obtaining prior consent from the subscriber or user.[47] This means that the subscriber or user must freely give a specific and informed indication of his or her wishes[48] before the processing takes place. Prior to obtaining this consent, the service provider must inform the subscriber or user of the types of traffic data which are to be processed and of the duration of such processing.[49] Subscribers/users must also be able to withdraw their consent at any time.[50]

The service provider is permitted to market not only its own electronic communications services but also those of third parties.

(iii)   **For the provision of value-added services:** Traffic data may be processed for the provision of value-added services, such as advice on least expensive tariff packages, route guidance, traffic information, weather forecasts, and tourist information. The use of the data requires the prior consent of the subscriber or user.[51] The term 'value-added services' is defined as 'any service which requires the processing of traffic data or location data beyond what is necessary for the transmission of a communication or billing thereof'.[52]

In each of these three exceptions, the processing of traffic data is restricted to persons acting under the authority of providers of the networks and services handling billing or traffic management, customer enquiries, fraud detection, marketing electronic communications services, or providing a value-added service.[53] Where the provider of a service subcontracts the processing of personal data to another entity, the requirements set out in the Data

---

44   Art 6(2) of the E-Privacy Directive.
45   Art 6(4) of the E-Privacy Directive.
46   Article 29 Data Protection Working Party Opinion 1/2003 on the storage of traffic data for billing purposes, adopted 29 January 2003.
47   Art 6(3) of the E-Privacy Directive.
48   Recital 17 of the E-Privacy Directive in conjunction with Art 2(h) of the Data Protection Directive.
49   Art 6(4) of the E-Privacy Directive.
50   Art 6(3) of the E-Privacy Directive.
51   Art 6(3) of the E-Privacy Directive.
52   Art 2(g) of the E-Privacy Directive.
53   Art 6(5) of the E-Privacy Directive.

Protection Directive apply. In this case the subscriber or user should be informed of this forwarding before giving their consent for the processing of the data.

(iv)   **For law enforcement purposes.**[54]

LOCATION DATA

3.20   Additional provisions allow service providers to offer value-added services based on location data. The term 'location data' is defined as:

> 'any data processed in an electronic communications network or by an electronic communications service, indicating the geographic position of the terminal equipment of a user of a publicly available electronic communications service'.[55]

This includes data which refers to the latitude, longitude and altitude of the location of the user's terminal equipment. Such data may also refer to the direction of travel, the level of accuracy of the location information, the identification of the network cell in which the terminal equipment is located at a certain point in time, and to the time the location information was recorded.[56] As mentioned above, some location data may also qualify as traffic data. Where data falls within both definitions, the traffic data provisions apply as Article 9 of the E-Privacy Directive applies only to 'location data other than traffic data'.[57]

The definition of location data has been amended by the Citizens' Rights Directive to also include data processed 'by an electronic communications service'. This extension of the definition is intended to also include 'traffic data collected from devices for data collection and identification that are connected to publicly available electronic communications networks or make use of electronic communications services as a basic infrastructure'.[58]

3.21   As an example of location data, the Citizens' Rights Directive mentions Radio Frequency Identification Devices (RFIDs) that use radio frequencies to capture data from uniquely identified tags which can then be transferred over existing communications networks, and does not exclude other mobile devices such as smart phones. A further example of location data is the data processed by digital mobile networks, which contain more precise information than is necessary for the transmission of communications. This information is potentially useful for providers of value-added services, such as services providing individualised traffic information.

3.22   To the extent that data contains information which is not necessary for the mere transmission of communications (such as information on the time period the mobile device is at a certain position), the specific provisions on location data apply and service providers must comply with the following conditions:

---

54   See para 3.37 below.
55   Art 2(c) of the E-Privacy Directive.
56   Recital 14 of the E-Privacy Directive.
57   Art 9(1) of the E-Privacy Directive.
58   Recital 56 of the Citizens' Rights Directive.

- Location data may only be processed when made anonymous or with the subscriber's or user's consent, and only to the extent and for the duration necessary for the provision of a value-added service.[59]
- The service provider must inform subscribers or users, prior to obtaining their consent, of the type of location data which will be processed, of the purposes and duration of the processing, and whether the data will be transmitted to a third party for the purpose of providing the value-added service.[60]
- Subscribers or users must be able to withdraw their consent at any time.[61] In addition, subscribers or users must have the possibility to temporarily refuse the processing of such data for each connection to the network or for each transmission of a communication by using simple means and free of charge (eg by pressing a button on the user's mobile device).[62]
- In all cases, processing of location data must be restricted to persons acting under the authority of the service provider or the third party providing the value-added service.[63] Consequently, location data may not be provided to unrelated third parties.

3.23 Only in exceptional cases may a service provider override a subscriber's or user's choice regarding the processing of location data. One exception aims to ensure that emergency services can carry out their tasks as effectively as possible. Member States may allow a service provider to override the temporary denial or absence of consent of a subscriber or user for the processing of location data on a per-line basis for organisations dealing with emergency calls, including law enforcement agencies, ambulance services, and fire brigades, for the purpose of responding to such calls.[64] Transparent procedures governing the way such overriding is exercised must be in place. There are other exceptions with regard to national security.[65]

UNSOLICITED COMMUNICATIONS

3.24 The E-Privacy Directive harmonises the conditions under which electronic communications may be used for direct marketing purposes and seeks to prevent 'spamming'. Spamming is the practice of sending unsolicited e-mails, usually of a commercial nature, in large numbers and repeatedly to individuals with whom the sender has had no previous contact.[66] The problems associated with spamming from the individual's point of view include the collection of e-mail addresses without consent, the receipt of unwanted advertising, and the cost of connection time.

3.25 Traditionally, legislators have attempted to deal with the problem of unsolicited communications by setting up systems under which recipients can either 'opt in' to or 'opt out' of receiving such communications. The term 'opt in' means individuals must take some action, such as signing up for the promotional material

---

59   Art 9(1) of the E-Privacy Directive.
60   Art 9(1) of the E-Privacy Directive.
61   Art 9(1) of the E-Privacy Directive.
62   Art 9(2) of the E-Privacy Directive.
63   Art 9(3) of the E-Privacy Directive.
64   Art 10(b) of the E-Privacy Directive.
65   See para 3.37 et seq below.
66   See Communication from the Commission on unsolicited commercial communications or 'spam', Brussels, 22 January 2004 COM(2004) 28 Final, and the CNIL report on Electronic Mailing and Data Protection, October 1999.

in question. Typically, customers are invited to sign up to receive promotional information about one or more categories of products or services. Those who sign up have 'opted in'. An 'opt out' assumes a general permission to send marketing messages to everyone who has not explicitly stated that they do not want to receive such information.

3.26   There is no definition of direct marketing in either the E-Privacy Directive or the Data Protection Directive. The Data Protection Directive, however, refers to direct marketing and provides that:

> 'Member States may similarly specify the conditions under which personal data may be disclosed to a third party for the purposes of marketing whether carried out commercially or by a charitable organisation or by any other association or foundation, of a political nature'.[67]

The Article 29 Data Protection Working Party has expressed the view that the term 'direct marketing' in the E-Privacy Directive covers any form of sales promotion, including direct marketing or fundraising by charities and political organisations.[68]

3.27   The E-Privacy Directive provides that unsolicited communications in the form of electronic mail, facsimile messages, and automated calling systems are only to be permitted with the prior consent of subscribers or users.[69]

3.28   Facsimile machines and automated calling systems were covered in the predecessor to the E-Privacy Directive. Automated calling systems are systems which automatically deliver a recorded message. They operate without human intervention. While it is not entirely clear, it seems that this would not cover power diallers which can dial hundreds of numbers but are designed to establish contact with a human operator rather than a pre-recorded message.[70] In the E-Privacy Directive, electronic mail is defined as:

> 'Any text, voice, sound or image message sent over a public communications network which can be stored in the network or in the recipient's terminal equipment until it is collected by the recipient'.[71]

This broad definition covers any message by electronic communications where the simultaneous participation of the sender and the recipient is not required. This includes basic e-mail, messages left on answering machines, Short Message Services, and Multimedia Messaging Services.

3.29   The requirements for prior consent are the same as under the Data Protection Directive, and therefore any consent will only be valid if it is a specific and informed indication of the subscriber's wishes.[72]

The actual method which must be used to obtain that consent has not been set by the E-Privacy Directive. However, the Directive provides some guidance by stating that consent can be given by any 'appropriate method enabling a freely given specific and informed indication of the user's wishes, including by ticking a box

---

67   Recital 30 of the Data Protection Directive.
68   Article 29 Data Protection Working Party, Opinion 5/2004 on unsolicited communications for marketing purposes under Art 13 of Directive 2002/58/EC, adopted on 27 February 2004.
69   Art 13(1) of the E-Privacy Directive.
70   The Guide to the Privacy and Electronic Communications – Information Commissioner, available at www.ico.gov.uk
71   Art 2(h) of the E-Privacy Directive.
72   Recital 17 and Art 2(f) of the E-Privacy Directive.

when visiting an Internet website'.[73] The Article 29 Data Protection Working Party has stated that it would not be compatible with the E-Privacy Directive to simply send a general e-mail to recipients asking for their consent to receive marketing e-mails, as this would not satisfy the requirement that the purpose be legitimate, explicit and specific. Neither does it consider that pre-ticked boxes on a website would be sufficient.[74]

The marketing communication must include the identity of the sender on whose behalf the communication was sent and an address to which the recipient may send a request that such communication cease.[75] In addition, the communication must comply with the following requirements:

- the communication must be clearly identifiable as such;
- the natural or legal person on whose behalf the communication is made must be clearly identifiable;
- promotional offers, such as discounts, premiums and gifts, where permitted in the Member State where the service provider is established, must be clearly identifiable as such, and the conditions which are to be met to qualify must be easily accessible and be presented clearly and unambiguously;
- promotional competitions or games, where permitted in the Member State where the service provider is established, must be clearly identifiable as such, and the conditions for participation must be easily accessible and be presented clearly and unambiguously.

Furthermore, the communication may not encourage recipients to visit websites that contravene the requirements set out above.[76]

The prior consent requirement for unsolicited direct marketing via automated calling systems, facsimiles, and electronic mail only applies to subscribers who are natural persons. Member States may extend the prior consent requirement to subscribers who are legal persons.[77]

3.30   There is an exception from the requirement for prior consent.[78] This is referred to as 'soft opt-in'. It provides that where there is an existing customer relationship, direct marketing is permitted, provided certain conditions are met. This exception leaves some room for interpretation and some of the key terms, for example 'existing customer relationship', are not defined. The Article 29 Data Protection Working Party has stated that the soft opt-in-exception must be narrowly construed.[79]

The soft opt-in-exception only applies if the following conditions are met:

- Electronic mail may only be sent to customers from whom the electronic contact details for electronic mail have been obtained in the context of the sale of a product or a service.

---

73   Recital 17 of the E-Privacy Directive.
74   Article 29 Data Protection Working Party, Opinion 5/2004 on unsolicited communications for marketing purposes under Article 13 of Directive 2002/58/EC, adopted on 27 February 2004.
75   Art 13(4) of the E-Privacy Directive.
76   Art 13(4) of the E-Privacy Directive in conjunction with Art 6 of Directive 2000/31/EC of the European Parliament and of the Council of 8 June 2000 on certain legal aspects of information society services, in particular electronic commerce, in the Internal Market (Directive on electronic commerce).
77   Art 13(5) of the E-Privacy Directive.
78   Art 13(2) of the E-Privacy Directive.
79   Article 29 Data Protection Working Party, Opinion 5/2004 on unsolicited communications for marketing purposes under Article 13 of Directive 2002/58/EC, adopted on 27 February 2004.

- It must be the same natural or legal entity which collected the data that uses the customer's electronic contact details for direct marketing. Subsidiaries or other companies in the same group of companies do not meet this requirement.
- The direct marketing must be for that specific entity's own similar products or services. This requirement is not further specified. The Article 29 Data Protection Working Party noted that this concept is not an easy one to apply in practice and requires further attention. They felt that similarity of products or services should be judged from the objective perspective (reasonable expectations) of the recipient, rather than the perspective of the sender.
- Customers must be given a clear opportunity to object to the direct marketing, both initially and on each occasion of direct marketing (ie an ongoing 'opt out').
- The initial collection of data must be in accordance with the Data Protection Directive.

3.31   For other forms of unsolicited communications for purposes of direct marketing, for example by telephone, Member States must take appropriate measures to ensure that such unsolicited communications are not allowed, either without the consent of the subscribers or users concerned or in respect of subscribers or users who do not wish to receive such communications. Member States are, therefore, free to choose between an 'opt in' or an 'opt out' protection. The reason for the less stringent provisions with respect to these other forms of communication is that they are more costly for the sender and impose no financial costs on subscribers and users.[80]

As highlighted above, Member States are required to ensure the legitimate interests of subscribers other than natural persons (eg corporate subscribers) are adequately protected.[81] The E-Privacy Directive has, however, left it to the Member States to determine the level of protection to be provided.

ADDITIONAL SERVICES

3.32   The E-Privacy Directive also covers a number of additional services, such as directories and automatic call forwarding. In this context, it includes the following rights for subscribers:

- the right to receive bills that are not itemised;[82]
- the right to prevent calling line identification on outgoing or incoming calls (except in the case of emergency calls, or where necessary to trace malicious or nuisance calls);[83]
- the right to prevent automatic forwarding of calls;[84] and
- the right not to appear in public directories (free of charge) and to determine what if any data can be included in such directories. Subscribers also must be informed in advance as to the purposes of the directory.[85]

---

80   Recital 42 of the E-Privacy Directive.
81   Art 13(5) of the E-Privacy Directive
82   Art 7 of the E-Privacy Directive.
83   Art 8 of the E-Privacy Directive in conjunction with Art 10 of the E-Privacy Directive.
84   Art 11 of the E-Privacy Directive.
85   Art 12 of the E-Privacy Directive.

Itemised Billing

3.33   Subscribers have the right to receive non-itemised bills. This right recognises that, notwithstanding that itemised bills can be useful because they enable subscribers to verify charges, such bills may jeopardise the right to privacy of users, for example where different users share the same telephone. The E-Privacy Directive provides that Member States should ensure that implementing national legislation allows for sufficient methods that do allow subscribers to verify their bills, eg alternative payment facilities or service options. The Directive also refers to the possibility of providing a different type of bill where a certain number of digits of the called number are altered.[86]

Calling and Connected Line Identification

3.34   Calling and connected line identification can be valuable services for users, and the widespread introduction of digital switching technology means that such customer information is widely available. These services do, however, raise serious privacy issues and require data protection safeguards. The E-Privacy Directive carries over from the Telecommunications Privacy Directive a basic set of privacy rights for users making and receiving calls.

The calling user has the right to:

- have a simple means (which must be free of charge) to prevent presentation of its number on the connected line. This option may be exercised on a per-call basis or on a more permanent basis by preventing the display on all calls made from a particular line.[87]

The called subscriber has the right to have:

- a simple means (which must be free of charge for reasonable use) to prevent the display of calling line identification information for incoming calls.[88] This means that certain services, such as help lines, can offer anonymity to callers;
- a simple means of rejecting incoming calls where the display of calling line identification information has been withheld by the caller.[89]

Where connected line identification is offered, the called subscriber must be able, using a simple means and free of charge, to prevent the display to the caller of the actual number to which an incoming call has been connected.[90]

The E-Privacy Directive provides that Member States can override the caller's general right to prevent the display of their calling line identification information to facilitate emergency calls or where authorities are investigating malicious or nuisance calls.[91]

---

86   Recital 33 and art 7(2) of the E-Privacy Directive.
87   Art 8(1) of the E-Privacy Directive.
88   Art 8(2) of the E-Privacy Directive.
89   Art 8(3) of the E-Privacy Directive.
90   Art 8(4) of the E-Privacy Directive.
91   Art (10) of the E-Privacy Directive.

Automatic Call Forwarding

3.35   The provisions on automatic call forwarding have been carried over from the Telecommunications Privacy Directive.[92] Subscribers must have the right to stop, using a simple means and free of charge, any automatic call forwarding by a third party to its terminal equipment.[93]

Directories of Subscribers

3.36   The E-Privacy Directive contains a number of rules on subscriber directories and addresses the issue of reverse or multi-criteria searching services, which raise particular privacy issues.

The provision of directory information is recognised by the Commission as an essential access tool for publicly available telephone services, and, as such, part of universal service obligations which seek to ensure that all end users have access to a defined minimum set of services at an affordable price.[94] However, the concept of a directory has changed over the past few years. Directories are now frequently presented in electronic format and contain the names, addresses and telephone numbers of millions of citizens of different Member States. One of the main innovations with electronic directories is the possibility of providing extended capabilities for the processing of the information contained in these directories. These multi-criteria search facilities go way beyond traditional search facilities and can provide, for example, the names and telephone numbers of all the persons in a particular street. In particular there have been concerns about the potential for individuals to inadvertently disclose their name and address when they hand out their telephone number.

In order to provide an adequate level of data protection with respect to directories, the E-Privacy Directive provides that:

- individuals must be informed, before they are included in the directory, of the purpose of a directory and how it might be used, including any further usage possibilities based on search facilities embedded in electronic versions of the directory;[95]
- individuals can no longer be charged a fee by operators to be excluded from a directory, to specify which of their data is to be included, or to verify, correct or withdraw such data;[96] and
- Member States may impose separate consent requirements for inclusion in any directory including reverse search functions.[97]

These rights apply to subscribers who are natural persons but may be extended to legal persons at the discretion of the Member States.[98]

---

92   Art 10 of the Telecommunications Privacy Directive.
93   Art 11 of the E-Privacy Directive.
94   Recital 4 of the Universal Services Directive. Cf para 1.173 et seq above.
95   Art 12(1) of the E-Privacy Directive.
96   Art 12(2) of the E-Privacy Directive.
97   Art 12(3) of the E-Privacy Directive.
98   Art 12(4) of the E-Privacy Directive.

LEGITIMATE RESTRICTIONS BY VIRTUE OF NATIONAL SECURITY

3.37 The E-Privacy Directive explicitly provides that Member States may deviate from the provisions on confidentiality, traffic, and location data and calling line identification,[99] if necessary, appropriate and proportionate for reasons of national security, defence, public security, the prevention, investigation, detection, and prosecution of criminal offences or of unauthorised use of the electronic communication system. The Directive specifically provides that, to this end, Member States may adopt legislative measures providing for the retention of data for a limited period.[100]

3.38 Based on a legislative proposal submitted by France, Ireland, Sweden, and Great Britain,[101] the Data Retention Directive was issued on 15 March 2006.[102] The Data Retention Directive seeks to harmonise the obligations of providers of publicly available telecommunications services and networks with respect to the retention of specified data for the purpose of 'investigation, detection and prosecution of serious crime, as defined by each Member State in its national law'.[103] Information on the content of communications, including information obtained using an electronic communications network, is outside the scope of the Data Retention Directive.[104]

Furthermore, the Data Retention Directive sets out minimum security requirements for the data to be retained.

3.39 In the context of the Data Retention Directive, data to be retained includes 'traffic data and location data and the related data necessary to identify the subscriber or user'[105] which includes data not only on natural persons but also on legal entities.[106] The categories of data to be retained are further specified in Art of the 5 Data Retention Directive and include the data necessary:

- to trace and identify the source of a communication;
- to identify the destination of a communication;
- to identify the date, time and duration of a communication;
- to identify the type of communication;
- to identify users' communication equipment or 'what purports to be their equipment'; and
- to identify the location of mobile communication equipment.

Following the EU Regulatory Framework's broad approach to defining the scope of electronic communications,[107] the Data Retention Directive defines 'communication' to include fixed and mobile telephony, Internet access, Internet e-mail, and Internet telephony (ie Voice over IP, or 'VoIP').

---

99   Arts 5, 6, 8 and 9 of the E-Privacy Directive.
100 Art 15(1) of the E-Privacy Directive.
101 Document of the Council 8958/04 of 28 April 2004.
102 The ECJ has confirmed that the Data Retention Directive could be issued on the basis of Art 114 TFEU (ex Art 95 ECT); see ECJ judgment of 10 February 2009, *Ireland v European Parliament and Council of the European Union* (C-301/06) [2009] ECR I-00593.
103 Art 1(1) of the Data Retention Directive.
104 Arts 1(1) and 5(2) of the Data Retention Directive.
105 Art 2(a) of the Data Retention Directive.
106 Art 1(2) of the Data Retention Directive.
107 Cf para 1.34 above.

3.40   Member States must ensure that this data is retained for a period of no less than six months and no more than two years.[108] It must be stored in a way so that it can, without undue delay, be transmitted to the competent authority upon request.[109]

3.41   In 2009, the Commission commenced its evaluation of the Data Retention Directive as foreseen in Art 14 of the Data Retention Directive. The evaluation concluded that:

- the Data Retention Directive had not been transposed in all Member States as of 2011[110] (with the lack of full transposition continuing to be an issue in the end of 2012);[111]
- where the Data Retention Directive has been transposed, transposition has been 'uneven' with respect to, among other things, the types of data to be retained, retention periods, requirements for access to data, and data protection standards;[112]
- the Data Retention Directive has, therefore, not fulfilled its purpose of harmonising Member States' approach to data retention and creating a 'level playing field' for operators throughout the EU;[113]
- reimbursement of operators for compliance with their obligations to retain data was lacking and inconsistent between the Member States;[114] and
- the conditions of access to retained data and the retention periods where not limited to the extent necessary for attaining the Directive's objective of combating serious crime and terrorism.[115]

In light of these findings, the Commission decided to review the Data Retention Directive setting out the following three main objectives to be satisfied by the future data retention framework:

(i)   to ensure swift access of the relevant authorities to communications data stored, such data being 'strictly necessary' for combating crime;

(ii)   to implement appropriate limitations on data retention, safeguard against unnecessary infringements of privacy and to ensure protection of personal data retained; and

(iii)   to remove any obstacles to the functioning of the internal market and to ensure consistent reimbursement of providers subject to retention obligations.[116]

To date, the Commission has not yet announced how the future data retention framework will be implemented.[117]

---

108   Art 6 of the Data Retention Directive.
109   Art 8 of the Data Retention Directive.
110   See Report from the Commission to the Council and the European Parliament, Evaluation Report on the Data Retention Directive (Directive 2006/24/EC), 18 April 2011, COM(2011) 225 final ('Data Retention Report'), pp 6 et seq, p 31. See also CEP, Centrum für Europäische Politik, EU Report Data Retention, 14 June 2011.
111   See, e g the infringement proceeding against Germany, Case C-329/12, [2012] OJ C287/23.
112   Data Retention Report, p 31, at 8.2.
113   Data Retention Report, p 31, at 8.3.
114   Data Retention Report, p 31, at 8.4.
115   Data Retention Report, p 32, at 8.5.
116   Roadmap for a Proposal for a review of the Directive 2006/24/EC (Data Retention).
117   Roadmap for a Proposal for a review of the Directive 2006/24/EC (Data Retention).

ENFORCEMENT

3.42 The provisions of the Data Protection Directive on judicial remedies, liability, and sanctions are applicable to the provisions of the E-Privacy Directive.[118] Member States must ensure that penalties and remedies are in place for infringements.[119] Remedies include, among other things, providing compensation for an individual who has suffered damage as a result of any unlawful act.[120]

---

118 Art 15(2) of the E-Privacy Directive.
119 Art 15(2) of the E-Privacy Directive in conjunction with Art 22 of the Data Protection Directive.
120 Art 15(2) of the E-Privacy Directive in conjunction with Art 23 of the Data Protection Directive.

Part 2
International Regulatory Framework

The Law of the International Telecommunication Union and the World Trade Organisation[1]

Joachim Scherer and Serge Pannatier
Baker & McKenzie, Frankfurt/Geneva

THE ITU

History

4.1 The International Telecommunication Union (ITU) was established on 9 December 1932. On 1 January 1949, it became the specialised UN agency for telecommunications by an agreement with the United Nations of 4 September/15 November 1947.[2]

The ITU dates back to the International Telegraph Union, which was founded by 19 European states in 1865.[3]

Following the patenting of the telephone in 1876 and the subsequent growth of the telephony market, the International Telegraph Union began, in 1885, to draw up the first provisions governing the international telephone service. With the invention in 1896 of wireless telegraphy and the growing utilisation of this new radio communication technology, it was decided to convene a preliminary radio conference in 1903 to study the question of international regulations for radio telegraph communications. The first International Radio Telegraph Conference was held in 1906 in Berlin and led to the first International Telegraph Convention (revised London 1912, Washington DC 1927). In 1924, the International Telephone Consultative Committee (CCIF) was set up; the International Telegraph Consultative Committee (CCIT) was established in 1925 and the International Radio Consultative Committee (CCIR) in 1927. These bodies were responsible for coordinating the technical studies, tests and measurements in the various fields of telecommunications and for drawing up international standards.

4.2 At the 1932 Madrid conference, the Union decided to combine the International Telegraph Convention of 1865 and the International Radio Telegraph Convention of 1906 to form the International Telecommunication Convention. It was also decided to change the name of the Union to International Telecommunication Union.

---

1   Editing of this chapter closed on 1 January 2013. Joachim Scherer is the author of the ITU subchapter; Serge Pannatier is the author of the WTO subchapter.
2   UNTS, Vol 30 no 175.
3   For a history of the ITU see Tegge, *Die Internationale Telekommunikations-Union* (Baden-Baden, 1994), pp 28 et seq.

After World War II the ITU became a UN specialised agency, as mentioned above, and the headquarters of the organisation were transferred in 1948 from Bern to Geneva. At the same time, the International Frequency Registration Board (IFRB) was established to coordinate the increasingly complex task of managing the radio frequency spectrum. The Table of Frequency Allocations, which had first been introduced in 1912, was declared mandatory.

In 1956, the two International Consultative Committees, CCIT and the CCIF, were merged to form the International Telegraph and Telephone Consultative Committee, with a view to responding more effectively to the requirements generated by the development of these two types of communication.

4.3 In 1989, the Plenipotentiary Conference held in Nice[4] established the Telecommunications Development Bureau (BDT) in order to promote the development of telecommunication technologies and infrastructures in the developing countries of the world. At the same time, the Nice Plenipotentiary Conference launched an in-depth review of the structure and functioning of the Union with a view to achieving greater cost effectiveness within and between the ITU organs and activities and to improve the Union's structure, organisation, finance, staff, procedure and coordination to ensure that the Union would respond more effectively to the needs of its members. In 1992, an additional Plenipotentiary Conference held in Geneva decided on a number of far-reaching organisational reform measures, including the establishment of three Sectors, corresponding to the ITU's three main areas of activity: the Telecommunication Standardization Sector (ITU-T), the Radio communication Sector (ITU-R), and the Telecommunication Development Sector (ITU-D). For each sector, an advisory group was established, including representatives of Member States and representatives of industry, to review the priorities, programmes, operations and strategies of the sectors and provide guidance for their operation.[5]

Legal Framework

4.4 The legal framework of the ITU comprises three legal instruments, which have international treaty status. They are:

- the Constitution of the International Telecommunication Union ('CS'), which is the 'basic instrument' of the Union;[6]
- the Convention of the International Telecommunication Union ('CV'); and
- the Administrative Regulations, which complement the Constitution and Convention.

4.5 The Constitution contains the basic provisions regarding the purposes of the Union, its composition, the rights and obligations of its members, its legal

---

4   For a brief summary of the reform process initiated at the Nice Plenipotentiary Conference, see Noll, 'The International Telecommunication Union', in MMR 8/1999, pp 465 et seq.

5   See paras 4.35, 4.44 and 4.51 below.

6   Art 4 no 29 CS; in the following, references to the Constitution (CS) and the Convention (CV) are to the versions as amended by the Plenipotentiary Conference Kiyoto, 1994, the Plenipotentiary Conference Minneapolis, 1998, the Plenipotentiary Conference Marrakesh, 2002, the Plenipotentiary Conference 2006, Antalya, and the Plenipotentiary Conference 2010, Guadalajara. References are to the articles and margin numbers of the Constitution. A consolidated version can be found in International Telecommunication Union, Collection of the basic texts of the International Telecommunication Union adopted by the Plenipotentiary Conference, 2011 Edition.

instruments and sets out the organisational structure of the Union, including its three Sectors, their working methods and overall provisions on the functioning of the Union. The Constitution also contains a number of general provisions relating to telecommunications, such as the right of the public to use the international telecommunications service (Art 33 CS), the principle of secrecy of telecommunications (Article 37 CS) and the principle of priority of telecommunications concerning safety of life (Article 40 CS). Furthermore, the CS contains basic substantive provisions regarding radio communications, such as the principles of effective use of the radio frequency spectrum and of the geostationary satellite and other satellite orbits (Article 44 CS), the obligation to avoid harmful interference (Article 45 CS), and the principle of priority for distress calls and messages (Article 46 CS).

4.6   The Convention establishes detailed rules on the functioning of the Union and its organs, contains specific provisions regarding conferences and assemblies, and sets out the details of a voluntary arbitration procedure which may be initiated by Member States to settle their disputes on questions relating to the interpretation or application of the Constitution, the Convention or of the Administrative Regulations.

4.7   The two basic legal instruments of the Union, the Constitution and Convention, are complemented by the Administrative Regulations, which regulate the use of telecommunications and which are binding on all Member States. These Administrative Regulations are:

- the International Telecommunication Regulations; and
- the Radio Regulations.[7]

The standards (Recommendations) which are adopted by ITU-R and ITU-T are not legally binding, unless they are specifically incorporated in the Regulations.[8]

The Radio Regulations

4.8   The Radio Regulations are an international treaty governing the use of the radio frequency spectrum and the geostationary satellite and non-geostationary orbits. The provisions of the radio regulations are legally binding. Under the Radio Regulations, the radio frequency spectrum is divided into frequency bands which are allocated to some 40 radio services for radio communication on an exclusive or shared basis. The list of services and frequency bands allocated in different regions constitute the Table of Frequency Allocations, which is part of the Radio Regulations. The Radio Regulations are regularly amended by the World Radiocommunication Conference.[9]

---

7   The Radio Regulations were signed on 17 February 2012 with a majority of their provisions having entered into force on 1 January 2013.

8   There was consensus that ITU Recommendations should remain legally non-binding at the World Conference on International Telecommunications 2012 in Dubai; see WCIT Highlights, Issue No. 2 (http://www.itu.int/osg/wcit-12/highlights/dec04.html, last visited 28 December 2012).

9   See para 4.28 below.

International Telecommunication Regulations

4.9   The International Telecommunication Regulations ('ITR')[10] were adopted at the World Administrative Telegraph and Telephone Conference in Melbourne (1988) and have been subject to ongoing discussions at least since the Plenipotentiary Conference of Minncapolis 1998. The ITR are binding international instruments[11] subject to revision by the World Conference on International Telecommunications.[12]

4.10   The purpose of the ITR is to establish general principles relating to the provision and operation of international telecommunications services offered to the public as well as to the underlying international telecommunication transport means used to provide such services.[13] The ITR contains statements of principle and specific provisions regarding the routing of international traffic, as well as charging and accounting principles. The ITR obliges Member States to ensure that their telecommunications 'administrations' or recognised private operating agencies cooperate in the establishment, operation and maintenance of the international network to provide a satisfactory quality of service,[14] to promote the implementation of international telecommunication services and to endeavour to make such services generally available to the public international networks.[15] The ITR recognises the right of Member States to allow their administrations and telecommunications organisations to enter into special mutual arrangements provided that no technical harm is caused to the operation of the telecommunication facilities of third countries.[16]

4.11   The ITR establishes the principle that for each applicable telecommunication service, the telecommunications operators concerned shall 'by mutual agreement' establish and revise the accounting rates to be applied between them, ie the mutual compensation for receiving and terminating calls.[17] In 1997, the Federal Communications Commission of the United States ('FCC') issued a 'Benchmark Order' which took effect on 1 January 1998.[18] It obliged US carriers to negotiate cost-based accounting and settlement rates with corresponding foreign carriers according to a time table established by the FCC. Where carriers were unable to do so, the FCC specified what rates American carriers may pay. Both this unilateral challenge to the ITU's accounting rate regime and the methodology applied by the FCC led to considerable controversy.[19] The unilateral enforcement of the FCC's Benchmark Order forced the telecommunications operators in other ITU Member States to

---

10   International Telecommunication Union, Final Acts of the World's Administrative Telegraph and Telephone Conference Melbourne, 1988, International Telecommunication Regulations, Geneva, 1989.

11   Art 54 no 215 CS.

12   Art 25 no 146 CS.

13   Art 1.1 ITR.

14   Art 3.1 ITR.

15   Art 4.1 ITR.

16   Art 9.1 ITR.

17   Art 6.2.1; see also ITU Recommendation D.140 Accounting Principles for International Telephone Services, which established key principles for accounting rates, such as the principle of cost orientation and non-discrimination.

18   Federal Communications Commission, In the matter of International Settlement Rates – Report and Order, FCC 97/280, Docket, no 96–261, adopted 7 August 1997.

19   See William J Drake, 'Towards Sustainable Competition in Global Telecommunications: From Principle to Practice – Summary Report of the Third Aspen Institute Roundtable on International Telecommunications' (Washington, 1999); see also William J Drake, 'The Rise

reduce the rates at which US carriers compensate them for terminating traffic and thus rendered the relevant provision of the ITR de facto irrelevant.[20]

4.12   Given that the ITR had not been changed for a decade, despite the dramatic changes in technology and market structure, the Plenipotentiary Conference (Minneapolis 1998) instructed the Secretary General to review to what extent the needs of Member States were still satisfied by the ITU instruments, especially the ITR.[21] However, neither an expert group nor a Council working group, which was open to all Member States, were able to achieve consensus on how to proceed until 2006. Three approaches had been suggested by Member States, namely: (1) to leave the ITR unchanged, (2) to amend the ITR, including adding new provisions especially regarding the Internet, or (3) to terminate the ITR and transfer certain provisions to the Constitution, Convention and ITU-T Recommendations.[22]

4.13   Whilst the Plenipotentiary Conference Antalya 2006 had agreed to organise a World Conference on International Telecommunications ('WCIT') to review the ITRs in 2012,[23] the major issue amongst Member States remained controversial: there has been no answer to the question whether and to what extent the ITU should gain responsibilities in matters of the Internet with respect to both standardisation and regulation. At present, assignment of IP-addresses is handled by the Internet Corporation for Assigned Names and Numbers (ICANN), a non-governmental organisation tasked with Internet governance. Some countries, in particular Russia, China, Iran, Saudi Arabia and some African States, intend for the ITU to take over this task. Other countries take a very critical stance towards such a shift of competences. They want to maintain the multi-stakeholder Internet governance model and fear that governmental supervision and regimentation can lead to dangers for freedom in cyberspace. As a result of the disagreement on matters of Internet governance the new ITRs, which have been adopted by WCIT-12,[24] merely contain some provisions referring to unsolicited electronic communications ('spam') and cyber-security. However, to some Member States those passages, too, seem to be too extensive. Those states, amongst them the United States, Japan, Australia and many EU Member States, announced that they would not or at least not without further national consultation ratify the new ITRs. Another issue with the new ITRs arises with respect to network neutrality, ie the neutrality of treatment of data in respect of transfer rates and transmission fees. Even after 15 years of debate, the process of ITR reform still has not come to a conclusion.

---

and Decline of the International Telecommunications Regime', in Christopher T Marsden (ed), *Regulating the Global Information Society* (London 2000), pp 124, 170 et seq.

20   See also William J Drake, in Christopher T Marsden (ed), *Regulating the Global Information Society* (London 2000), p 172.

21   Resolution 79.

22   Cf Expert Group on the International Telecommunication Regulations, Executive Summary of the Findings of the Group of Experts on Reform of the International Telecommunication Regulations, May 2000; Working Group on the International Telecommunication Regulations, Report 3 rev 1, 11–13 May 2005.

23   Resolution 146 (Antalya, 2006).

24   See International Telecommunication Union, Draft of the future ITRs; http://www.itu.int/en/wcit-12/Documents/draft-future-itrs-public.pdf (last visited 28 December 2012).

Membership

4.14   Membership of the ITU is open to governments as well as to private organisations (the 'Sector Members').[25] The ITU currently (January 2013) has 193 Member States and over 700 Sector Members. The membership of states is based on the principle of universality: any state which is a Member State of the United Nations or any other state with the approval of two-thirds of the Member States of the Union[26] may accede to the Union. Withdrawal is possible at any time with a one-year denunciation period.[27] Each Member State has one vote at all Plenipotentiary Conferences, all World Conferences and all Sector Assemblies and Study Group Meetings and, if it is a Member State of the Council, all sessions of the Council ('one country, one vote').[28]

4.15   The Sector Members are recognised operating agencies (including carriers, telecommunication service providers, equipment manufacturers), scientific or industrial organisations and financial or development institutions which are approved by the Member States concerned, other entities dealing with telecommunication matters which are approved by the Member State concerned, regional and other international telecommunication, standardisation, financial or development organisations.[29] Sector Members may elect to join one or more of the ITU's three Sectors, depending on their particular interests. They are entitled to participate fully in the activities of the Sector of which they are members and, in particular, may provide chairmen and vice chairmen of Sector Assemblies and meetings as well as World Telecommunication Development Conferences; they are entitled to take part in the adoption of questions and recommendations and in decisions relating to the working methods and procedures of the sector concerned. They do not participate, however, in the Plenipotentiary Conference nor in the Council. They are not entitled to vote on amendments of the Constitution or of the Convention which are the prerogative of the Plenipotentiary Conference[30] nor on the adoption or amendment of administrative regulations, which are the prerogative of the World Conference on International Telecommunications[31] and of the World Radiocommunications Conferences.[32] In an attempt to broaden the participation of industry in the Union's proceedings, the assemblies and conferences of the individual Sectors[33] have been granted the right to admit entities or organisations to participate as 'associates' in the work of a given Study Group or subgroup.[34]

Purposes and Principles of the ITU

4.16   The ITU is an intergovernmental organisation which is based, according to the preamble of the Constitution, on the recognition of 'the sovereign right of each state to regulate its telecommunication'. The Union has been established 'with the object of facilitating peaceful relations, international cooperation among peoples

---

25   Art 2 no 20 CS.
26   Art 2 no 23 CV.
27   Art 57 CV.
28   Art 3 no 27 CV.
29   Annex no 1001 b CS, art 19 no 228–231 CV.
30   Art 8 no 57 CS.
31   Art 25 no 146 CS.
32   Art 13 no 89 CS, art 7 no 114 CV.
33   See below, paras 4.28, 4.30, 4.40, 4.48.
34   Art 20 no 241 A – 241 E CV.

and economic and social development by means of efficient telecommunications services'.[35] To this end, the purposes of the Union are, inter alia:

- to maintain and extend international cooperation among all its Member States for the improvement and rational use of telecommunications of all kinds;
- to promote and enhance participation of entities and organisations in the activities of the Union and foster fruitful cooperation and partnership between them and Member States for the fulfilment of the overall objectives as embodied in the purposes of the Union;
- to promote and to offer technical assistance to developing countries in the field of telecommunications;
- to promote the development of technical facilities and their most efficient operation with a view to improving the efficiency of telecommunication services;
- to promote the extension of the benefits of the new telecommunication technologies to all the world's inhabitants;
- to promote the use of telecommunications services with the objective of facilitating peaceful relations;
- to harmonise the actions of Member States and promote fruitful and constructive cooperation and partnership between Member States and Sector Members in the attainment of those ends; and
- to promote, at the international level, the adoption of a broader approach to the issues of telecommunications in the global information economy and society, by cooperating with other world and regional intergovernmental organisations and those intergovernmental organisations concerned with telecommunications.[36]

4.17   Among the particular purposes of the Union are:

- to allocate bands of the radio-frequency spectrum, allot radio frequencies and register radio-frequency assignments and, for space services, any associated orbital position in the geostationary-satellite orbit or any associated characteristics of satellites in other orbits, in order to avoid harmful interference between radio stations of different countries;
- to coordinate efforts to eliminate harmful interference between the radio stations of different countries and to improve the use made of the radio-frequency spectrum for radio communication services and of the geostationary-satellite and other satellite orbits;
- to facilitate the worldwide standardisation of telecommunications, with the satisfactory quality of service;
- to foster international cooperation and solidarity in the delivery of technically assistance to the developing countries;
- to coordinate efforts to harmonise the development of telecommunication facilities, notably those using space techniques;
- to foster collaboration among Member States and Sector Members with a view to establishing the lowest possible rates; and
- to undertake studies, make regulations, adopt resolutions, formulate recommendations and opinions, and collect and publish information concerning telecommunication matters.[37]

---

35   Preamble CS.
36   Art 1 no 2–9 CS.
37   Art 1 no 10–16, 18 CS.

4.18   Member States have reserved the right to convene regional conferences, to make regional arrangements and to form regional organisations for settling telecommunications questions which are susceptible of being treated on a regional basis, as long as such arrangements are not in conflict with either the Constitution or the Convention.[38] Such arrangements include, for example, the Inter-American Radio Agreement (Washington 1949); the Regional Agreement for the European Broadcasting Area (Stockholm 1961), and the Regional Agreement for the African Broadcasting Area (Geneva 1963).

Organisational Structure of the Union

Overview

4.19   The ITU has three organs which convene periodically and five permanent organs.[39] The supreme organ of the Union is the Plenipotentiary Conference, which is composed of delegations representing the Member States and is normally convened every four years.[40] The Council, which is composed of Members States elected by the Plenipotentiary Conference, acts in the interval between Plenipotentiary Conferences as the governing body of the Union within the limits of the powers delegated to it by the Plenipotentiary Conference.[41]

The World Conference on International Telecommunications may partially or, in exceptional cases, completely revise the International Telecommunication Regulations[42] and may deal with any question of a worldwide character within its competences and related to its agenda; its decisions must in all circumstances be in conformity with the Constitution and Convention of the Union.[43]

The permanent organs of the Union are the General Secretariat, which is directed by the Secretary General,[44] and the three Sectors of the Union, ITU-R, ITU-T and ITU-D.[45]

Plenipotentiary Conference

4.20   The Plenipotentiary Conference determines the general policies of the Union, establishes its strategic plan[46] and the basis for the Union's budget, provides general directives dealing with the staffing of the Union, and examines its account and approves it, if appropriate.[47] The Plenipotentiary is also empowered to elect the Member States which are to serve on the Council, the Secretary General, the Deputy Secretary General and the Directors of the Bureaus, as well as the members of the Radio Regulations Board.[48] At any of these elections, the Plenipotentiary Conference has to give due consideration to an equitable geographical distribution

---

38   Art 43 CS.
39   Art 7 CS.
40   Art 8 no 47 CS.
41   Art 20 no 65, 68 CS.
42   See paras 4.9–4.13 above.
43   Art 25 no 146–147 CS.
44   Art 11 CS.
45   See para 4.26 et seq below.
46   Cf Strategic plan for the Union for 2012–2015, Resolution 71 (Rev Guadalajara 2010), Annex.
47   Art 8 no 49, 51, 52, 53 CS.
48   Art 8 no 54, 55, 56 CS.

amongst the regions of the world. As the Union's supreme organ, the Plenipotentiary is generally empowered to 'deal with such other telecommunication questions as may be necessary'.[49]

The Council

4.21 The Council comprises a maximum of 25 per cent of the total number of Member States, which are elected by the Plenipotentiary Conference with due regard to the need for equitable distribution of the Council seats among the five world regions (Americas, Western Europe, Eastern Europe, Africa, Asia and Australasia). Currently, the Council is comprised of 48 Members.

4.22 In addition to its task to consider, in the interval between Plenipotentiary Conferences, broad telecommunication policy issues and its duty to prepare a report, for consideration by the Plenipotentiary, on the policy and strategic planning of the Union, the Council is also responsible for ensuring the day-to-day functioning of the Union and to exercise effective financial control over the General Secretariat and the three Sectors. Furthermore, the Council has to take all steps to facilitate the implementation by the Member States of the provisions of the ITU's Constitution, the Convention, the administrative regulations, the decisions of the Plenipotentiary Conference and, where appropriate, of the decisions of other conferences and meetings of the Union.[50]

The General Secretariat

4.23 The General Secretariat, which is headed by the Secretary General, is responsible for the overall management of the Union's resources, the coordination of the activities of the General Secretariat and the Sectors of the Union, the coordination of the implementation of the Union's Strategic Plan and for the annual preparation of a four-year rolling operational plan of activities to be undertaken by the staff of the General Secretariat consistent with the strategic plan.[51] Other tasks of the General Secretariat include the management of the administrative and financial aspects of the Union's activities, including the provision of conference services, information services, and corporate functions, eg legal advice, finance, personnel, communications and common services.[52]

4.24 In order to ensure proper coordination among the three Sectors of the Union, a Coordination Committee has been established consisting of the Secretary General, the Deputy Secretary General and the Directors of the three Sector Bureaus.[53] The Coordination Committee is presided over by the Secretary General and acts as:

> '[an] internal management team, which advises and gives the Secretary General practical assistance on all administrative, financial, information system and technical cooperation matters which do not fall under the

---

49   Art 8 no 59 CS.
50   Art 10 no 69–71 CS, see also art 4 CV.
51   Art 5, 84, 85, 86 A, 87 A.
52   Cf art 5 CV.
53   Art 26 no 148 CS.

exclusive competence of a particular sector or of the General Secretariat and on external relations and public information'.[54]

World Conference on International Telecommunications

4.25 World Conferences on International Telecommunications are held at the request at the Plenipotentiary Conference and have treaty-making powers: they can revise the International Telecommunication Regulations[55] and may deal with 'any question of a worldwide character within its competence and related to its agenda'.[56]

Tasks, Structure and Functioning of the Radiocommunications Sector

4.26 The tasks of the ITU's Radiocommunications Sector (ITU-R) are:

- to determine the technical characteristics and the operational procedures for a broad range of wireless communications services;
- to manage, at global level, the frequency spectrum by allocating bands of the radio frequency spectrum, allotting radio frequencies and registering radio frequency assignments and any associated orbital position in the geostationary satellite orbit in order to avoid harmful interference between radio stations of different countries; and
- to coordinate efforts to eliminate harmful interference between radio stations of different countries and to improve the use made of radio frequencies and of the geostationary satellite orbit for radiocommunication services.[57]

Structure

4.27 The Radiocommunication Sector works through:

- World and Regional Radiocommunication Conferences,
- Radiocommunication Assemblies,
- the Radiocommunication Bureau, which is headed by the elected Director,
- Radiocommunication Study Groups,
- the Radiocommunication Advisory Group, and
- the Radio Regulations Board.[58]

World Radiocommunication Conferences

4.28 World Radiocommunication Conferences ('WRC') are normally convened every two to three years. The conferences are composed of delegations of the administrations of Member States. The task of the WRC is to review and to revise, in part or in full, the Radio Regulations. In addition, the WRC may consider any radio communication matter of a worldwide character, and it may instruct the

---

54   Art 26 no 149 CS; see also art 6 CV.
55   See paras 4.9–4.13 above.
56   Art 25 no 146 CS.
57   See also the mission statement in Resolution 71, Annex, Part II, 4.1.
58   Art 12 no 80–85 CS.

Radio Regulation Board and the Radiocommunication Bureau and reviews their activities. Furthermore, the WRC identifies topics to be studied by the Radio-communication Assembly and the Radiocommunication Study Group in prepar-ation for future Radiocommunication Conferences. The general scope of the WRC's agenda is established four to six years in advance with the final agenda being established by the Council, two years before the conference, with the concurrence of a majority of the Member States.[59]

Regional Radiocommunication Conferences

4.29   Regional Radiocommunication Conferences (RRCs) are conferences of either one of the ITU regions or of a group of countries with a mandate to develop an agreement concerning a radio communication service or a frequency band of a regional nature.[60] A regional conference cannot modify the Radio Regulations, unless the proposed modifications are approved by a WRC[61] and the 'Final Acts' of the regional conferences are binding only on those countries that are party to the agreement.[62]

Radiocommunication Assembly

4.30   Radiocommunication Assemblies (RAs) are normally convened every two or three years and may be associated in time and place with Radiocommunication Conferences.[63] Their task is to approve the program of Radiocommunication Study Groups, to establish or dissolve Study Groups according to need, to consider Study Group reports and to approve, modify or reject the draft ITU-R recommendations contained in those reports. The Assembly assigns conference preparatory work and other questions to the Study Groups, responds to requests from ITU conferences, and suggests suitable topics for the agenda of future WRCs.

The Radiocommunication Bureau

4.31   The Radiocommunication Bureau ('BR'), which is headed by a Director elected by the Plenipotentiary Conference, organises and coordinates the work of the Radiocommunications Sector.[64] As the executive arm of the Radiocommunica-tion sector, the Radiocommunication Bureau:

- provides administrative and technical support to Radiocommunication Con-ferences, Assemblies and Study Groups;
- applies the provisions of the Radio Regulations and of the various regional agreements;
- records and registers frequency assignments and orbital characteristics of space services, and maintains the 'Master International Frequency Register';
- provides advice to Member States on the equitable, effective and economical use of the radio frequency spectrum and satellite orbits and investigates and assists in resolving cases of harmful interference;

---

59   Section 8 no 118 CV.
60   Art 9 no 138 CV.
61   Art 13 no 92 CS.
62   Art 9 no 138 CV.
63   Art 13 no 91 CS.
64   Art 16 CS, art 12 no 161 CV.

- coordinates the preparation, editing and dispatch of circulars, documents, and publications developed within the sector; and
- provides technical information and seminars on national frequency management and radio communications.

4.32   The Bureau fulfils its role as global spectrum coordinator through its Space Services Department ('SSD') and its Terrestrial Services Department ('TSD'). The SSD handles the procedures involved in the coordination and registration of satellite systems and earth stations, including the capture, processing and publication of the relevant data and the review of the frequency assignment notices submitted by national administrations with a view either to their inclusion in the official coordination procedure or to their recording in the Master International Frequency Register.

The TSD fulfils technical and regulatory functions in relation to terrestrial radio communication services, including the processing of frequency assignment notices and the maintenance of the Master International Frequency Register, which is regularly updated in accordance with the requirements of the Radio Regulations and of the relevant regional agreements. This Register currently includes over 1.2 million terrestrial frequency assignments and more than 325,000 assignments servicing some 1,500 satellite networks.

Radiocommunication Study Groups

4.33   Radiocommunication Study Groups are expert groups set up by a Radio communications Assembly.[65] Currently, more than 1,500 specialists from telecommunication organisations and administrations throughout the world participate in the work of the Study Groups which encompasses the drafting of the technical bases for Radiocommunication Conferences, the preparation of draft recommendations and the compilation of handbooks on frequency management and use.

4.34   At present, ITU-R has established six Study Groups specialising in spectrum management (Study Group 1), radiowave propagation (Study Group 3), satellite services (Study Group 4), terrestrial services (Study Group 5), broadcasting service (Study Group 6), and science services (Study Group 7).[66] As with other ITU Recommendations, compliance with the ITU-R Recommendations is not mandatory. However, having been developed by recognised radio communication experts, they enjoy a high reputation and are implemented on a worldwide basis.

Radiocommunication Advisory Group

4.35   The Radiocommunication Advisory Group ('RAG') consists of representatives of administrations of Member States, representatives of Sector Members and the Chairman of the Study Groups and other groups. The RAG's tasks are

- to review the priorities and strategies adopted in the ITU-R sector, to monitor the progress of and to provide guidance for the work of the Study Groups; and

---

65 Art 11 no 148 CV.
66 For a detailed description of the work programme of these Study Groups see International Telecommunication Union, Radiocommunication Bureau, ITU-R Study Groups, Geneva 2012.

• to recommend measures for fostering cooperation and coordination with other organisations and with other ITU Sectors.

The RAG acts as an advisory body to the Director of the Radiocommunication Bureau and may receive specific mandates from the Radiocommunication Assemblies.[67]

The Radio Regulations Board

4.36 The Radio Regulations Board ('RRB') consists of 12 elected members who are qualified in the field of Radiocommunications and have practical experience in the assignment and utilisation of frequencies.[68]

The Board Members do not act as representatives of their respective Member States or regions, but as 'custodians of an international public trust'.[69] They perform their duties independently and on a part-time basis.

4.37 The RRB approves the 'Rules of Procedure', which are used by the Radiocommunication Bureau in applying the provisions of the Radio Regulations and registering frequency assignments made by the Member States. These 'Rules of Procedure' clarify and interpret the provisions of the Radio Regulations, regional agreements and resolutions and recommendations of World and Regional Radio communication Conferences. The RRB also addresses matters referred to it by the Bureau which cannot be resolved through application of the Radio Regulations and the Rules of Procedures and considers appeals against decisions made by the Radiocommunication Bureau regarding frequency assignments. Furthermore, the RRB considers reports of unresolved interference investigations which have been carried out by the Bureau at the request of one or more administrations and adopts recommendations. Decisions of the RRB may be brought before the World Radiocommunication Conference.[70]

Tasks, Structure and Functioning of the Standardisation Sector

4.38 The task of the Telecommunication Standardisation Sector (ITU-T) is to study technical, operating and tariff questions and to ensure the production of recommendations with a view to standardising telecommunications on a worldwide basis.[71]

As of December 2012, ITU-T has 280 Sector Members and 146 associates. Well over 3,000 recommendations (standards) are in force; while ITU-T recommendations are legally non-binding, they are generally complied with by manufacturers, network operators and service providers alike.

4.39 The Telecommunication Standardisation Sector operates through:

• World Telecommunication Standardisation Assemblies;
• Telecommunications Standardisation Study Groups;

---

67 For specific matters assigned to the RAG see Resolution ITU-R 52.
68 Art 14 no 93, 93 A CS, see also art 10 CV.
69 Art 14 no 98 CS.
70 Art 7 no 116 CV.
71 Art 17 no 104 CS; for the mission statement of ITU-T see Resolution 71, Annex, Part II, 5.1.

- Telecommunications Standardisation Bureau; and
- Telecommunications Standardisation Advisory Group.

World Telecommunication Standardisation Assembly

4.40   The World Telecommunication Standardisation Assembly ('WTSA') takes place every four years. It brings together delegations of the Member States, representatives of Sector Members and observers of regional telecommunication organisations, other regional organisations or international organisations dealing with matters of interest to the Assembly, and specialised agencies of the United Nations.[72] The WTSA defines the general policy of the Sector and adopts its working methods and procedures.[73] It considers the reports of Study Groups and approves, modifies or rejects draft recommendations. It also approves the work programme and the organisation of the work of ITU-T for each four-year study period, establishes the Study Groups and appoints the Study Group Chairman and Vice Chairman.[74]

Telecommunication Standardisation Study Groups

4.41   The Telecommunication Standardisation Study Groups and their Working Parties conduct the actual standardisation work. They study the questions set forth in the work programme established by the WTSA and elaborate the Recommendations.

For the study period 2013–2016, ITU-T has established 10 Study Groups which cover a broad range of topics, such as economic and policy issues (Study Group 3), environment and climate change (Study Group 5), broadband cable and TV (Study Group 9), protocols and test specifications with a focus on machine-to-machine service layer (Study Group 11), future networks (Study Group 13), transport and access (Study Group 15), multimedia (Study Group 16) and security (Study Group 17).

Telecommunication Standardisation Bureau

4.42   The Telecommunication Standardisation Bureau ('TSB'), which is led by the elected director, organises and coordinates the work of the Telecommunication Standardisation Sector.[75] It provides secretarial support for the work of the ITU sector and services for the participants in ITU-T work, including the coordination of the approval process for recommendations and ensuring the publication of the ITU-T recommendations, handbooks and guides.

4.43   The TSB also coordinates international numbering: Based on an ITU-T recommendation establishing the country codes, which are the basis for the structuring of the international numbering space,[76] TSB provides country code number assignments for telephone, data and other services. It also acts as registrar for Universal International Free Phone Numbers, which enable an international free

---

72   Art 25 no 295–298 f CV.
73   Art 13 no 184 a CV.
74   Art 13 no 188, 191 a, 181 b CV.
75   Art 15 no 198 CV.
76   ITU-T Recommendation E.164.

phone service customer to be allocated a unique Free Phone Number that is the same throughout the world.[77] The TSB also provides administrative support for the regulation of alternative calling procedures (call-back); under a resolution adopted by the World Telecommunication Standardisation Assembly 2004[78] on alternative calling procedures on international telecommunication networks, each country has the right to authorise, prohibit or regulate call-back practices. National regulatory measures regarding call-back must be respected by other countries within the limits of their own legislation. To facilitate the required collaboration between the National Regulatory Authorities in the ITU Member States, a draft guideline has been prepared under which ITU is to collect information once a year on the positions adopted by each country regarding call-back practices and to disseminate the findings among administrations to enable them to take the necessary steps to prevent call-back practices from being supplied to countries which prohibit them.[79]

Telecommunication Standardisation Advisory Group

4.44   The Telecommunication Standardisation Advisory Group ('TSAG') consists of representatives of the administrations of Member States, representatives of Sector Members and the Chairmen of the ITU-T Study Groups and other Groups.[80] Its main task is to review the priorities, programmes, operations, financial matters and strategies for the ITU-T sector, to restructure and establish ITU Study Groups and to provide guidelines for their operation. The TSAG also elaborates recommendations on the work methods and procedures of the ITU-T Study Groups.[81]

Alternative Approval Process (AAP)

4.45   In response to long-standing criticism of ITU-T's slow and cumbersome standardisation procedures, WTSA 2000 adopted a fast-track approval process for technical standards, the 'Alternative Approval Process' ('AAP').

Whereas the Traditional Approval Process ('TAP'), which is still used for recommendations that are considered to have regulatory or policy implications, requires an approval of proposed standards at a Study Group meeting, with prior determination at a previous Study Group or working party meeting, and an announcement by circular before the approval meeting, which adds up to an approval time of six to nine months, the Alternative Approval Process allows for approval of a recommendation within six weeks. Under the AAP, once the text of a draft AAP recommendation is mature, it is submitted for consent at a Study Group or working party meeting. The consent given by the Study Group signals the start of the Approval Process which requires that the mature text is posted on the ITU-T website and an announcement is made that the AAP is in progress. Comments can then be made

---

77   This function is based on ITU-T Recommendation E.169 and Recommendation E.152.
78   Resolution 29 WTSA – 04.
79   See, in this context, International Telecommunication Union, Telecommunication Standardisation Bureau, TSB Circular 30 CUM 3/ST of 2 May 2005: Replies to the questionnaire on conditions for provision of 'call-back'.
80   Art 14 a no 197 a CV.
81   Art 14 a no 197 b – 197 i CV.

during a four-week period. If no comments are received, the recommendation is considered approved by the Study Group Chairman in consultation with TSP.[82]

Tasks, Structure and Functioning of the Telecommunication Development Sector

4.46   The Telecommunication Development Sector ('ITU-D'), which was established in 1989, is the youngest Sector of the Union.

4.47   Its objective is to discharge:

'the Union's dual responsibility as a United Nations specialised agency and executing agency for implementing projects under the United Nations development system or other funding arrangements so it has to facilitate and enhance telecommunications development by offering, organising and coordinating technical cooperation and assistance activities'.[83]

ITU-D is structured similarly to the two other Sectors. It comprises:

* World and Regional Telecommunication Development Conferences;
* Telecommunication Development Study Groups;
* the Telecommunication Development Bureau; and
* the Telecommunication Development Advisory Group.

As of December 2012, ITU-D has approximately 340 Sector Members.

World and Regional Telecommunication Development Conferences

4.48   Telecommunication Development Conferences are held for the discussion and consideration of topics, projects and programmes relevant to telecommunication development and for the provision of direction and guidance to the Telecommunication Development Bureau.[84] The Telecommunication Development Conferences do not produce Final Acts, rather, their conclusions take the form of resolutions, decisions, recommendations or reports.[85] At the Fifth World Telecommunication Development Conference ('WTDC-10') in Hyderabad 2010, an Action Plan was adopted that aims at fostering the global development of information and communication networks and services.[86]

It includes the development of information and communication infrastructure and technology, cyber-security, capacity building, digital inclusion and the building of a global Information Society, environmental issues with a focus on adaption to climate change and special actions for developing and least developed countries.

---

82   For a detailed description see Recommendation H 8.
83   Art 21 no 118 CS.
84   Art 22 no 137 CS.
85   Art 22 no 142 CS.
86   Hyderabad Action Plan, in Final Report, World Telecommunication Development Conference, Hyderabad 2010, ITU 2010, Annex C.

Study Groups

4.49 The current ITU-D Study Groups' mandates are: enabling environment; cyber-security; information and communication technology applications; Internet-related issues; communication infrastructure and technology development; emergency telecommunications and climate-change adaptation.[87] The Study Groups produce recommendations, guidelines, handbooks, manuals and reports.

The Telecommunication Development Bureau

4.50 The Telecommunication Development Bureau ('BDT') is the executive arm of the Telecommunication Development Sector. It is headed by an elected Director. Its tasks include fostering telecommunication development in developing countries through policy advice, the provision of technical assistance, the mobilisation of resources and initiatives with a view to bridge the 'digital divide'. BDT also supervises regional and global projects launch by ITU-D to assist developing countries in modernising their telecommunications systems and regulatory frameworks.

Telecommunication Development Advisory Group

4.51 The Telecommunication Development Advisory Group is open to representatives of Member States, Sector Members and to Chairmen and Vice Chairmen of Study Groups; it meets once a year. Its mandate is to review priorities, programmes, operations, financial measures and strategies for the activities in the ITU-D sector and to advise the Director of ITU-D accordingly.

ITU Reform

4.52 For the last four decades, the ITU has been engaged in a lengthy process of mainly incremental reforms of its structure, its procedures and its management.[88] Many of the reforms were brought about by the transformation of the telecommunications sector which, in turn, has been a consequence of market liberalisation, the convergence of the telecommunications sector with the computing and broadcasting sectors, and the development of the Internet which is transforming the industry.

4.53 Following a debate of the need to adapt the Union's organisational structure to its changing environment, the 1989 Nice Plenipotentiary Conference established the High Level Committee ('HLC') with a mandate to carry out an in-depth review of the ITU's structure and functioning. Based on the HLC's report,[89] a special Plenipotentiary Conference in 1992 overhauled the structure of the Union by creating the ITU-T, ITU-R and ITU-D Sectors. Initiated by the Kiyoto Plenipotentiary Conference of 1994,[90] a task force known as ITU-2000 conducted another

87 Cf http://www.itu.int/net3/ITU-D/stg/index.aspx (last visited 14 December 2012).
88 Cf at last Strategic plan for the Union for 2008–2011, Resolution 71 (Rev Antalya, 2006), Annex 1, Part I, 3.2, Goal 5.
89 Report of the High Level Committee to review the structure and functioning of the International Telecommunication Union, Tomorrow's ITU: The Challenges of Change, Geneva 1991.
90 See Resolution 15, Resolution 39.

in-depth review of the Union's structure and submitted a series of recommenda-tions,[91] including recommendations on enhanced cooperation with the private sector through Sector Members and the membership status termed 'associate',[92] the acceleration of the ITU's standardisation process, and recommendations to improve the ITU's financial situation.

4.54   The Plenipotentiary Conference Minneapolis 1998 approved the streamlined standardisation process[93] and broadened the private sector's rights in the standard-isation process. The Plenipotentiary renewed its commitment to organisational reform by establishing a new 'Working Group for Reform' ('WGR') with the mandate to review the management, functioning and structure of the Union as well as the rights and obligations of Member States and Sector Members. The WGR's final report[94] contained 40 recommendations for the improvement of the Union's budgetary system, the effectiveness of its overall management and of the effectiveness of several of its organs, including the Plenipotentiary Conference, the General Secretariat, the Council and the World Radiocommunications and Development Conferences.

4.55   At the Plenipotentiary Conference in Marrakesh in 2002, only modest steps were made towards increased rights for industry in the standardisation process; the Plenipotentiary instructed the Council to establish a 'Group of Specialists' ('GoS'), composed of five individuals, one from each administrative region, with a mandate to review the management of the Union.[95] In its report, which was submitted in May 2003, the GoS submitted 21 'near-term', 'mid-term' and 'long-term' recom-mendations, including recommendations on the Council's oversight role, the Union's system of budgets, financial management control mechanisms and cost accounting, the need for decentralisation of authority and for comprehensive review of ITU's plans and budgets.[96]

4.56   The Plenipotentiary Conference Antalya 2006 adopted a strategic plan with special regard to bridging the 'digital divide' and improving the ability of develop-ing countries to fully participate in Internet-related technical and policy processes ('broadband inclusion for all').[97] The Plenipotentiary developed strategies in order to implement the outcomes of the World Summit on the Information Society (WSIS) which had been organised by ITU and which was held in Geneva and Tunis in 2003 and 2005.[98] Debates also focused on expanding the ITU's mandate beyond its traditional technological responsibilities; there were proposals for the Union to assume a stronger role when it comes to Internet-related issues, namely cyber-security, network stability, countering spam and managing of critical Internet

---

91   ITU-2000 Recommendations, RAG 98–1/6-E.
92   See para 4.15 above.
93   See para 4.45 above.
94   Document C 2001/25–1 of 1 May 2001.
95   Decision 7 (Marrakesh 2002).
96   See Review of the management of the Union, Report of Group of Specialists (GoS) to review the management of the Union to the ITU Council, C 03/32 (Rev 1)-E; for the implementation of the GoS Recommendations, see Council Resolution 1216 of 16 June 2004.
97   See Strategic plan for the Union for 2008–2011, Resolution 71 (Rev Antalya, 2006), Annex 1, Part I, 3.2, Goals 2 and 6; Resolutions 30 and 123 (Rev Antalya, 2006).
98   See Strategic plan for the Union for 2008–2011, Resolution 71 (Rev Antalya, 2006), Annex 1, Part I, 3.1, 3.2, Goals 1 and 2 and passim and in particular Resolution 140 (Rev Antalya, 2006).

resources including Internet Domain Names and addresses.[99] Neither these proposals nor the proposals to reduce the number of elective ITU posts from five to two (by graduating the posts of directors of ITU-R, ITU-T and ITU-D) have been implemented to date.[100]

Consensus was achieved on the need to organise a World Conference on International Telecommunications (WCIT) to review ITR in 2012.[101]

4.57 Bridging the 'standardisation gap' between developed and developing countries,[102] defining the ITU's role in handling the Internet,[103] reviewing ITR[104] and implementing the outcomes of the WSIS[105] were again key issues to the Plenipotentiary Conference 2010 in Guadalajara, Mexico.[106] Delegates also agreed to improve accessibility of information and communication technology for persons with disabilities,[107] to strive for a better use of information and telecommunication technologies to manage climate change[108] and to open sector membership to academic and research institutions.[109]

4.58 As the debate on ITU reform has focused more and more on narrow and detailed issues of the ITU's management, more basic, structural issues seem to have disappeared from the reform agenda.[110] They include:

- the allocation of functions between the ITU Sectors, in particular ITU-R and ITU-T; and
- an adaptation of the Sectors' organisational structures and their procedural rules to their respective functions.

4.59 The development of telecommunications technology, the privatisation of state-owned communications entities and the liberalisation of telecommunications markets has led, in many Member States of the Union, to a separation of regulatory and operational functions.[111] As part of this functional separation, the preparation and adoption of technical standards, including standards in the telecommunications field, has largely been entrusted to private standardisation bodies.[112]

4.60 Regulatory functions include:

- regulation of market entry and/or supervision of market behaviour;
- regulation of enterprises with significant market power;

---

99 Cf ITU, Final Press Report of the 17th ITU Plenipotentiary Conference held in Antalya, Turkey, 6–24 November 2006.

100 Cf Resolutions 101 and 102 (Rev Antalya, 2006), see para 4.12 ff above.

101 Resolution 146 (Antalya, 2006).

102 Cf Resolutions 30, 123 and 139 (Rev Guadalajara, 2010).

103 Resolution 178 (Guadalajara, 2010).

104 Resolution 171 (Guadalajara, 2010).

105 Cf Resolution 140 (Rev Guadalajara, 2010) and Resolution 172 (Guadalajara, 2010).

106 Cf ITU, Press Release from 22 October 2012.

107 Resolution 175 (Guadalajara, 2010).

108 Resolution 182 (Guadalajara, 2010).

109 Resolution 169 (Guadalajara, 2010).

110 See Note by the Secretary General, Report by the Chairman of the Working Group on Structure – Review of the ITU Structure, Document C 05/34-E, 14 April 2005.

111 For Europe see Art 3 para 2 of the Framework Directive; see para 1.53 above.

112 For an analysis of telecommunication standardisation in Europe as a system of 'regulated self-regulation', see Kerstin Schultheiss, *Europäische Telekommunikationsstandardisierung* (Münster, 2004), p 245 et seq.

- regulation of access and interconnection;
- frequency planning and management including the allocation of frequency bands to specific radio services;
- management of the numbering space, including the allocation of country codes;
- regulation of universal service provision;
- consumer protection; and
- protection of telecommunications secrecy and data protection.

4.61 Despite decades of debate, the ITU has not adapted its organisational structure and its allocation of functions among ITU-R and ITU-T to this universally accepted structural separation: while ITU-R currently discharges mainly regulatory functions with respect to spectrum allocation and frequency management, it also engages in standardisation activity in the radio communications field. On the other hand, ITU-T, while predominantly entrusted with standardisation in the Telecommunications Sector, has traditionally also been engaged in certain regulatory functions, such as, in particular, the administration of the international numbering space.

4.62 Separating regulatory from standardisation functions and allocating them to ITU-R and ITU-T respectively, could have benefits for all stakeholders concerned: The standardisation process could be further streamlined and the role of Sector Members with respect to the adoption of standards could be strengthened. To the extent that technical standards have regulatory implications, ITU-R could be empowered to validate the relevant standards and/or to 'mandate' ITU-T to elaborate certain standards with regulatory implications.

On the other hand, ITU-R, as a 'regulatory' sector could streamline its organisational structure and its procedures and include the national regulatory authorities in its decision-making structure.[113]

4.63 On the basis of a clear allocation of regulatory and non-regulatory (standardisation) functions, the Union would be well positioned to overcome what appears to be one of the major obstacles to its organisational efficiency, namely the Union's 'one size fits all' approach in organising its three Sectors. It has been noted[114] that for historical and political reasons, the three Sectors of the Union have been structured in a broadly identical fashion, despite their completely diverging purposes and objectives; this has led to radical reform proposals to re-organise ITU by establishing three differently structured organisational entities (a regulatory body, a standardisation body and a development agency) under its roof.

4.64 A less radical restructuring of the ITUs' sectors along the lines of regulatory and operational (standardisation) functions would pave the way for a rational discussion of new, additional 'regulatory' tasks to be discharged by ITU-R at international level: they could include, for example, international cooperation to combat spam and the misuse of numbering, the coordination of measures to enhance information security and data protection and contributions to Internet

---

113 To date, the NRAs participate in ITU activities mainly through conferences and regulator.
114 Don McLean, 'Sovereign Right and the Dynamics of Power in the ITU: Lessons in the Quest for Inclusive Global Governance', Manuscript, 2003.

governance, which is currently high on the agenda of communications policy makers in preparation of the 'World Summit on the Information Society in Tunis 2005'.[115]

THE WTO

The WTO in a Nutshell

4.65 The World Trade Organisation ('WTO') is an international, inter-governmental organisation. There are currently 157 Members,[116] including all major trading nations. Key exceptions include Kazakhstan, Algeria, Lebanon and Iran, most of which are currently negotiating their accession to the organisation. The WTO thus enjoys near-global coverage.

4.66 The WTO came into being on 1 December 1995 as result of the 'Uruguay Round' of multilateral trade negotiations launched in 1986 by Contracting Parties to the General Agreement on Tariffs and Trade ('GATT') of 1947. For the first time in the history of successive trade rounds, the agenda covered not only trade in goods but also, inter alia, trade in services and the protection of trade-related intellectual property rights. The round resulted in the Agreement establishing the World Trade Organisation ('WTO Agreement'), concluded in 1994 in Marrakesh, which contained under its umbrella not only the revised GATT with multiple sub-agreements but also, among other things, a new General Agreement on Trade in Services ('GATS') as well as the Agreement on Trade-Related Intellectual Property Rights ('TRIPS') – the three 'pillars' of the WTO system.

4.67 There are numerous other so-called WTO Covered Agreements that, depending upon the subject matter, may or may not be relevant to telecommunications services and products. Other Covered Agreements include:

- Agreement on Technical Barriers to Trade;
- Agreement on Trade-Related Investment Measures;
- Anti-Dumping Agreement;
- Agreement on Customs Valuation;
- Agreement on Pre-shipment Inspection;
- Agreement on Rules of Origin;
- Agreement on Import Licensing;
- Agreement on Subsidies and Countervailing Measures;
- Safeguards Agreement; and
- Government Procurement Agreement.

4.68 While the GATS is the most important of the Covered Agreements for telecommunications, GATT and TRIPS are also of significance to the sector. The GATS provides a framework of rules for the international trade in telecommunications services of all kinds within which firms and individuals can operate. Specific market access commitments undertaken by WTO Members under the GATS include specific access rights for telecommunication services and service providers in a number of so-called 'modes of supply' (see below). In addition, in the landmark

---

115 For a summary of ITU's activities to date see ITU, 'ITU and its Activities Related to Internet Protocol (IP) Networks' (April 2004); see also Working Group on Internet Governance, Report of the Working Group on Internet Governance, June 2005.
116 Status in May 2012.

1997 'Fourth Protocol to the GATS'[117] countries undertook a set of commitments on regulatory disciplines in the basic telecommunications sector by subscribing to the so-called 'Reference Paper'.[118] The GATT, in turn, governs the regulation of international trade in telecommunications-related goods, as well as trade in goods sold via telecommunication means, including the 'physical side' of virtually all forms of e-commerce. The TRIPS establishes a high level of protection of trade-related intellectual property rights ('IPRs'). These include IPRs specifically relevant to telecommunications operators such as patents, trademarks, copyrights, integrated circuits, and business secrets.

4.69   Apart from the substantive rules set out in the Covered Agreements, there is also the Dispute Settlement Understanding ('DSU'), establishing a very effective dispute settlement system, as well as a Trade Policy Review Mechanism ('TPRM') which provides for a regular comprehensive review of every Member's policies relating to the WTO agreements.[119]

The Relevance of WTO Rules to Private Companies

4.70   As the WTO is an intergovernmental organisation, it may be asked why WTO law may be of relevance to private persons. As the WTO system has only been in existence for less than 20 years, businesses have yet to realise the full potential of how the WTO forum and its rules can be of assistance. In developing commercial strategy, a company must take on board important questions of market access, preferential tariffs, licensing requirements, entry tests and recognition of standards. A company can waste significant amounts of time and effort if it has not adequately considered the basic trade and investment framework of a target market. However, where a company keeps abreast of WTO rules and is attuned to their local implementation, it can reduce both trade and investment risks. There are at least three areas where companies will interface with the WTO, namely:

● domestic litigation;
● international dispute settlement; and
● domestic and international rule-making processes.

4.71   In certain jurisdictions, private persons can rely directly on the WTO obligations of their country in private actions before national courts. However, most systems (including the EU, the United States and Japan) generally refuse to recognise the direct effect of WTO obligations within their domestic systems. Notwithstanding this, many courts adhere to a doctrine of consistent interpretation, whereby courts interpret domestic law to be consistent with the relevant country's obligations pursuant to public international law, which will include WTO law. WTO law can, therefore, be a useful mechanism to assist a private person to influence a national court to adopt a certain interpretation of domestic law.

---

117 Fourth Protocol to the General Agreement on Trade in Services, S/L/20, adopted 30 April 1996, entered into force on 5 February 1998.
118 See para 4.113 et seq below.
119 A useful text providing an overview of WTO law is Matsushita, Schoenbaum and Mavroidis, *The World Trade Organization, Law, Practice, and Policy* (The Oxford International Law Library). A number of articles have also been written addressing the impact of the WTO system on the telecommunications industry. See, for example, Luff, 'Telecommunications and Audio-visual Services: Considerations for a Convergence Policy at the World Trade Organization', (2004) 38(6) Journal of World Trade 1059–1086 and also Zhao, *Further Liberalization of Telecommunications Services in the Framework of the WTO in the 21st Century*, International Journal of Communications Law and Policy, Issue 8, Winter 2003/4.

4.72   Even though the WTO Dispute Settlement Mechanism is purely inter-governmental (with no rights for private persons to commence actions),[120] private persons can play a key role in initiating a dispute. It is often private companies that bring to the attention of their government the fact that they are having difficulty penetrating an overseas market and that accordingly an overseas country may be violating its WTO obligations. The company can assist its government to investigate a possible violation by another country by providing trade data and other relevant commercial information. Companies could also be the driving force behind the dispute by funding the legal costs associated with WTO dispute proceedings. A private person can also play a crucial role in monitoring compliance with dispute settlement rulings that are eventually handed down.

4.73   Finally, and perhaps most importantly, companies can also use WTO rules as part of policy advocacy or lobbying initiatives before both national and international fora. At the national level, this may involve, for example, private companies arguing that, in order to ensure compliance with WTO obligations, a national telecommunications regulator must take certain action against dominant telecommunications undertakings to prevent anti-competitive behaviour. At the international level, this could entail companies lobbying their national delegation to the ITU, for example, to argue against relevant ITU policy initiatives in case they could result in a conflict between the ITU and WTO regimes. Therefore, WTO rules can assist companies to play a pivotal role in influencing the rule-making process at both the domestic and international level.

Telecommunications at the WTO – A Brief Historical Overview

4.74   According to the WTO Secretariat, telecommunications services are a global market worth over $1.5 trillion in revenue. Mobile Services account for roughly 40 per cent of this, while mobile subscribers worldwide currently outnumber the use of fixed telephone lines by more than two to one. In the past two decades, the market has witnessed far-reaching changes, with the introduction of competition into a sector that was once principally a monopoly.

At the start of the Uruguay Round in 1986, telecommunications services around the globe were still largely in the hands of state-owned national monopolies. At the time, the United States had just experienced the break-up of AT&T. A year later, in 1987, the European Commission made its first proposals for a partial liberalisation of telecommunications services in the European Community.[121]

4.75   Sectoral talks on telecommunications services began in 1989. The negotiations, however, encountered several specific difficulties. The GATT Contracting Parties agreed to extend sectoral negotiations on basic telecommunications until 1996.[122] These continued negotiations first resulted in a breakdown in 1996 when the United States pulled out, claiming a lack of a critical mass of commitments from other Members. The negotiations ultimately resulted in a significant package of specific commitments in basic telecommunications services undertaken by 69

---

120   There is the possibility for private persons to submit amicus curiae briefs (or so-called friend of the court letter) to WTO panels or the Appellate Body. However, past practice indicates that there is a reluctance to take on board the views of private companies in dispute settlement cases unless the brief is formally adopted by one of the governmental parties to the dispute.

121   See European Commission, Green Paper on the Development of the Common Market for Telecommunications Services and Equipment, COM (87) 290 Final (Brussels, 30 June 1987).

122   Decision on Negotiations on Basic Telecommunications, attached to the WTO Agreement.

countries. In addition to specific market access commitments, all but two of these countries undertook to adhere to a 'Reference Paper' that includes regulatory disciplines.

4.76   In the landmark dispute settlement case of *Mexico – Measures Affecting Telecommunication Services* (*'Telmex'*), the WTO dispute settlement panel found Mexico to be in violation of, inter alia, obligations relating to interconnection and to the prevention of anti-competitive practices, both sets of obligations emanating from the 'Reference Paper'.[123]

'Rule of Law': Dispute Settlement at the WTO

4.77   In contrast to the former GATT system, the WTO emerged as a strictly rules-based system. While a dispute settlement system had in fact gradually evolved under the GATT over the 47 years of its operation, it remained largely a forum for diplomatic, rather than law-based, solutions. Under the previous GATT system, the final adoption of panel verdicts, or 'reports', required the consensus of GATT contracting parties. The reports could, therefore, be – and commonly were – blocked by the losing party. GATT obligations were, therefore, seen as something less than hard law due to the ability to block reports.

4.78   The WTO, in marked contrast, benefits from a two-instance, compulsory and rather expedient dispute settlement procedure under the Dispute Settlement Understanding (DSU), another multilateral agreement that forms part of the 'single undertaking' of all WTO Members. Disputes between WTO Members over alleged violations of the WTO Covered Agreements (eg the GATT, the GATS and the TRIPS) can be brought before a dispute settlement panel. The panel's verdict is issued in the form of a 'report'.[124] The parties to a dispute may then appeal a panel report, in which case the WTO Appellate Body will review the decision. The appeals review process is limited to issues of law.

4.79   The procedure is governed by detailed rules and a fixed timetable. The DSU provides that the time from the request for the establishment of a panel until the adoption of its report should be no longer than nine months and, in the case of an appeal, no longer than 12 months. While these deadlines are sometimes missed, WTO dispute settlement proceedings are still, nonetheless, faster than many domestic judicial proceedings.

4.80   Most importantly, the DSU no longer allows the losing party to block the adoption of the ruling of the panel. Instead of the 'positive consensus' required under the old GATT 1947, which gave each country a veto, the DSU provides for a 'negative consensus' rule, under which a consensus will be required amongst Members to block a panel report.

4.81   The outcome, 'the report', is a legally binding decision, which obliges the state to comply with it. In the vast majority of cases, WTO Members comply with panel or Appellate Body rulings without further enforcement. However, the DSU permits two sanctions if the rulings of the panel or the Appellate Body are not implemented within a reasonable period. The first is compensation payable by the losing party, which may typically consist of additional trade concessions, usually in

---

123   The relevant findings of the Panel are discussed below in the context of the respective rules and commitments.
124   A semantic concession to GATT history. WTO panel or Appellate Body reports are de facto binding judgments.

related economic areas to the dispute, that are acceptable to the winning party as a substitute for maintaining the trade barriers in dispute. Compensation is a voluntary remedy in that it requires the agreement of both parties to the dispute. The second sanction is retaliation (suspension of concessions) against the losing party. Retaliation must be authorised by the Dispute Settlement Body and it must match the level of the impairment suffered by the winning party.

4.82   In the 18 years since its inception, the WTO dispute settlement system has handled nearly 400 cases, more than its predecessor GATT in 47 years. In the landmark *Telmex* case – the first WTO dispute to be resolved solely under the GATS – the United States successfully challenged certain regulations of Mexico's telecommunications law. The United States had, in particular, complained that Mexico failed to ensure that its dominant provider 'Telmex' provided interconnection to US telecom suppliers on reasonable terms and that Mexico failed to prevent Telmex's anti-competitive practices.[125]

THE GATS

Structure

4.83   The GATS aims to cover, in principle, all international trade in services between WTO Members. Broadly modelled on the GATT, the GATS is built on the principles of market access, non-discrimination, transparency, the rule of law, and, more generally, predictability and reliability in relation to national regulations affecting trade in services.

4.84   Unlike the GATT, however, the GATS itself does not provide for absolute market access rights. Such rights are exclusively contained in the specific national commitments embodied in the so-called schedules.

Principles

Four modes of supply

4.85   Article I (2) of the GATS defines four 'modes of supply' of services in international trade, namely:

(a)   services supplied from the territory of one Member into the territory of another Member (cross-border supply, also called 'mode 1');

(b)   services supplied in the territory of one Member to the service consumer of another Member (consumption abroad, also called 'mode 2');

(c)   services supplied by a service supplier of one Member through commercial presence in the territory of another Member (commercial presence, also called 'mode 3'); and

(d)   services supplied by a service supplier of one Member through the presence of natural persons of a Member in the territory of another Member (presence of natural persons, also called 'mode 4').

4.86   These four modes aim to cover any situation where a service is traded internationally. The most important, both generally and for telecommunications

---

125 We discuss the details of the case below in the respective context of the relevant legal provisions.

services, are modes 1 and 3. Under mode 1, the service itself, but not the service provider, crosses national borders. It, therefore, resembles to some extent trade in goods. Under mode 3, service suppliers establish themselves in the territory of another Member. This includes the establishment of a subsidiary or branch as well as the investment in existing service suppliers of that Member. Mode 3, in other words, covers investment in services sectors.

The modes of supply are of crucial relevance for the scheduling of specific market access commitments.[126]

4.87   The classification of a specific provision of a service into the system of the four modes of supply can be difficult. While, for example, mode 1 clearly applies if a lawyer provides legal advice via telephone to a client in another country, the panel in the *Telmex* case had to deal with an argument put forward by Mexico that the cross-border supply of voice telephony pre-supposed that the service provider was using its own lines on both sides of the border. The panel rejected that interpretation and held that a call from the United States into Mexico constituted the cross-border supply of voice telephony services, irrespective of whether the call was carried through on owned or leased network capacity.[127]

Most-Favoured Nation

4.88   Article II GATS provides in para 1:

'With respect to any measure covered by this Agreement, each Member shall accord immediately and unconditionally to services and service suppliers of any other Member treatment no less favourable than that it accords to like services and service suppliers of any other country.'

It should be noted that the Most-Favoured Nation Principle applies independently of whether the respective Member has made specific market access commitments in the respective sector. To the extent that it allows a service provider from any country (not only another WTO Member) to provide a service under any of the four modes of supply, it must grant the same access to services and service suppliers of other WTO Members. It should further be noted that, as under Article I GATT, the Most-Favoured Nation Principle applies unconditionally, ie it is not subject to reciprocity.

4.89   Members of the WTO had the one-time chance to schedule, ie reserve, exceptions to this Most-Favoured Nation Principle at the time when they scheduled their specific market access commitments. For the original Members of the WTO, this was at the time of the conclusion of the Uruguay Round. For Members who have acceded to the WTO after that date, their 'Article II Exemptions' had to be scheduled at the time of accession.

Market access and national treatment

4.90   Article XVI GATS is the provision that links the so-called 'Schedules' of specific commitments relating to market access to the GATS itself. Article XVI incorporates the individual schedules of WTO Members as integral parts into the

---

126 See para 4.97 below.
127 *Mexico – Measures Affecting Telecommunication Services*, Report of the Panel, WT/DS 204/R, para 7.45 (2 April 2004).

GATS. The specific commitments included in a Member's schedule thereby become enforceable WTO law vis-à-vis any other Member.

4.91 Article XVII GATS provides that within scheduled/committed services sectors and modes of supply, a Member has to grant national treatment to services and service suppliers from other WTO Members. This means that they enjoy treatment no less favourable than corresponding national services or service suppliers of that Member.

4.92 The restriction of national treatment to scheduled services is a marked departure from the GATT model. Whereas under Article III GATT, goods generally enjoy national treatment (once they have cleared the border), national treatment under the GATS is firmly restricted to scheduled sectors and modes of supply. This means that outside of such scheduled coverage, service suppliers can only demand Most-Favoured Nation treatment, ie equal treatment with other third country suppliers. They have no right to national treatment unless the services are scheduled. The nature and structure of schedules is further discussed below.

Transparency and domestic regulation

4.93 Article III (1) GATS provides that a Member must publish 'all relevant measures of general application which pertain to or affect the operation of this Agreement' promptly, which means at the latest by the time of their entry into force, except in emergency situations. Further, a Member must notify such measures to the WTO[128] (para 3). Most importantly, a Member is obliged to maintain so-called 'anchor points' where other Members can obtain relevant information.

Domestic regulation

4.94 While the preamble of the GATS explicitly recognises the right of WTO Members to regulate services, Article VI of the Agreement provides for certain disciplines on such domestic regulation. In sectors where a Member has undertaken specific commitments, it is bound to 'ensure that all measures of general application affecting trade and services are administered in a reasonable, objective and impartial manner'.[129] In addition, Members have to provide for an objective and impartial review of administrative decisions relating to trade and services through judicial, arbitral or administrative tribunals or procedures.[130] A Member is further bound to provide for speedy and transparent authorisation procedures.[131] Qualification requirements and procedures, technical standards and licensing requirements should not constitute unnecessary barriers to trade in services. The requirements applied should be based on objective and transparent criteria, should not be more burdensome than necessary to ensure quality and, in the case of licensing procedures, should not in themselves constitute restrictions on the supply of the service.[132]

---

128 Council for Trade and Services.
129 Art VI (1) GATS.
130 Art VI (2) (a) GATS.
131 Art VI (3) GATS.
132 These criteria apply directly in sectors where a Member has made specific commitments, see Art VI (5) GATS. In other sectors, guidelines are provided for further disciplines to be developed under the auspices of the Council for Trade and Services ((Art VI) (4) GATS).

Exceptions

4.95 A number of exceptions apply to the coverage of general GATS rules. The Most-Favoured Nation and National Treatment Principles, as well as specific scheduled commitments, do not apply to government procurement. WTO Members thereby remain free to discriminate against, and not procure from, foreign service suppliers.[133]

4.96 Similar to Article XX GATT, Article XIV contains 'general exceptions' for measures necessary for the advancement of non-trade-related policy goals such as the protection of public morals, the maintenance of public order or the protection of human, animal or plant life or health. Such measures are consistent with the GATS if they 'are not applied in a manner which could constitute a means of arbitrary or unjustifiable discrimination between countries where like conditions prevail, or a disguised restriction on trade and services'. Article XIV b is further more provides for security exceptions.

Schedules of Specific Commitments

4.97 Commitments regarding telecommunications services were first made during the Uruguay Round (1986–1994), mostly in value-added services. After the creation of the WTO, WTO members negotiated on basic telecommunications services. Since 1997, commitments have been made by acceding members upon accession to the WTO or unilaterally at any time.

GATS schedules are relatively complex documents.[134] They usually contain two major sections on horizontal commitments (applying to all scheduled services sectors) and vertical, or sector-specific, commitments (applying specifically to a listed services sector or sub-sector). Both are contained in tables consisting of four columns.

As of today, a total of 108 WTO members have made specific commitments to facilitate trade in telecommunications services. This includes the establishment of new telecommunications companies, foreign direct investment in existing companies and cross-border transmission of telecommunications services. Out of this total, 99 WTO members have committed to extend competition in basic telecommunications. In addition, 82 WTO members have committed to the regulatory principles spelled out in the 'Reference Paper', a blue print for sector reform that largely reflects best practice in telecommunications regulation.

4.98 The first column names and, where necessary, further describes those service sectors or sub-sectors for which commitments are undertaken.[135] Listing sectors or sub-sectors in the first column opens up these sectors for services and service suppliers from other WTO Members under any of the four modes of supply, unless the second column specifies restrictions. The second column, therefore, usually contains a number of specific limitations, specified with respect to each mode of supply with respect to each scheduled sector. Typical market access limitations

---

133 Art XIII (1) GATS. Paragraph 2 of the provision provides for negotiations on disciplines on such government procurement. However, no results have been achieved until now.

134 For background information on schedules and scheduling see Guidelines for the Scheduling of Specific Commitments under the General Agreement on Trade in Services (GATS), S/L/92, 28 March 2001.

135 In the horizontal commitments section this entry usually reads 'All sectors included in this schedule', referring to the specific sectors listed further below in the schedule.

include, for example, maximum percentages of foreign shareholdings in national service supply companies (commercial presence, mode of supply 3).

4.99 Because Article XVII GATS provides in principle for the extension of national treatment to all scheduled services, the third column must contain all limitations on national treatment that the respective WTO Member wants to maintain in these sectors. Any limitation on national treatment not listed in this column would be contrary to WTO law. The fourth column finally contains any additional commitments WTO Members may want to schedule. By way of example, the parties to the Fourth Protocol to the GATS of 1997 included their commitment to the 'Reference Paper' in this column.

4.100 By way of example, the section of the United States' schedule covering basic telecommunications[136] – a relatively simple schedule – looks as follows:

Modes of supply: 1) Cross-border supply 2) Consumption abroad 3) Commercial presence 4) Presence of natural persons

UNITED STATES – SCHEDULE OF SPECIFIC COMMITMENTS
(Excerpt)

Modes of supply: 1) Cross-border supply 2) Consumption abroad 3) Commercial presence 4) Presence of natural persons

Sector or Sub-sector	Limitations on Market Access	Limitations on National Treatment	Additional Commitments
2.C. TELECOM-MUNICATIONS SERVICES:*			
2.C.a. Voice services 2.C.b. Packet-switched data transmission services 2.C.c. Circuit-switched data transmission services 2.C.d. Telex services 2.C.e. Telegraph services 2.C.f. Facsimile services 2.C.g. Private leased circuit services	(1) None (2) None (3) None, other than – Comsat has exclusive rights to links with Intelsat and Inmarsat. – Ownership of a common carrier radio license:	(1) None (2) None (3) None (4) Unbound except as indicated by horizontal commitments.	The United States undertakes the obligations contained in the Reference Paper attached hereto.

---

136 GATS/SC/90/Suppl. 2, as agreed under the Fourth Protocol to the GATS of 11 April 1997.

Sector or Sub-sector	Limitations on Market Access	Limitations on National Treatment	Additional Commitments
2.C.o. Other Mobile Services Analogue/Digital cellular services PCS (Personal Communications services) Paging services Mobile data services * Excluding one-way satellite transmissions of DTH and DBS television services and of digital audio services	Indirect: None Direct: May not be granted to or held by (a) foreign government or the representative thereof (b) non-US citizen or the representative of any non-US citizen (c) any corporation not organized under the laws of the United States or (d) US corporation of which more than 20 per cent of the capital stock is owned or voted by a foreign government or its representative, non-US citizens or their representatives or a corporation not organized under the laws of the United States. (4) Unbound except as indicated by horizontal commitments		

4.101 It should be noted that in the language of GATS scheduling, 'none' indicates 'no limitations', ie full commitments, whereas 'unbound' indicates the opposite, namely 'no commitments'.

Specific Commitments and Rules Relating to Telecommunications under the GATS

Categories of telecommunications services and the distinction between basic and value-added relecommunications

4.102   The GATS Services Sectoral Classification List[137] used by most Members in the Uruguay Round negotiations breaks down telecommunications into 14 sub-sectors (a.– n.) and one 'other' (o.) category. The list did not differentiate between basic and value added telecommunications services. That distinction was introduced into the GATS framework by the United States, reflecting US regulatory categories used to delineate the powers of the FCC.[138] The exact delineation between the two categories is a matter of varying interpretations by Members.[139] US law defines basic services as 'the offering of transmission capacity for the movement of information' while value-added, or enhanced, services are defined as 'any offering over the telecommunications network that is more than a basic transmission service'.[140]

4.103   The distinction played a role not so much in designing schedules, where Members make use of the said 15 categories, but in the negotiations and in particular in the decision to split negotiations in two when it became clear that Members were too far away from an agreement on commitments on basic telecom-munications at the end of the Uruguay Round. While Members did make commit-ments in value-added services at that time, they decided to leave basic telecommunications on the table. The Decision on Negotiations on Basic Telecom-munications annexed to the WTO Agreement required further negotiations that eventually resulted in the Fourth Protocol to the GATS of 1997.[141] The Decision defines basic telecommunications simply as 'trade in telecommunications transport networks and services'.[142] The categories used in the negotiations leading to the 'Fourth Protocol' included a. voice telephone, b. packet-switched data transmission, c. circuit-switched data transmission, d. telex, e. telegraph, f. telefax, g. private-leased circuit and o. 'other' services, including, inter alia, mobile phone, paging and teleconferencing services.[143]

4.104   The distinction between basic and value-added services, however, does play an important role with respect to the 'Reference Paper', which defines its scope as being solely related to 'principles and definitions on the regulatory framework for the basic telecommunications services'.[144]

---

137   MTN.GNS/W/120. Use of the list was not obligatory. Members were free to use other categorisations if they saw fit. However, most Members' schedules make extensive use of the list.

138   See Marco Bronckers & Pierre Larouche, *Telecommunications Services* (2005), p 996.

139   See Telecommunications Services, Background Note by the WTO Secretariat, S/C/W/74, 8 December 1998, para 7.

140   The definitions stem from the FCC's 'Computer Inquiries', see Marco Bronckers & Pierre Larouche, *Telecommunications Services*, p 996 (2005).

141   See para 4.110 below.

142   Decision on Negotiations on Basic Telecommunications, para 1.

143   Use of the 'other' category in relation to the distinction is not uniform.

144   Reference Paper, annexed to the Fourth Protocol to the GATS, see para 4.113 below.

The Annex on Telecommunications

4.105   The Annex on Telecommunications[145] (the 'Annex') provides for additional, specific disciplines beyond the GATS on 'measures of a Member that affect access to and use of public telecommunications transport networks and services'.[146] The preamble to the Annex emphasises 'the dual role [of telecommunications] as a distinct sector of economic activity and as the underlying transport means for other economic activities'. The Annex, consequently, contains disciplines to ensure that other sectors do not suffer indirectly from insufficient commitments in telecommunications.[147] The Annex thereby comes as a 'bonus'[148] to service suppliers that benefit from scheduled commitments.

ACCESS TO AND USE OF NETWORKS

4.106   Paragraph 5 (a) of the Annex states that:

'[e]ach Member shall ensure that any service supplier of any other Member is accorded access to and use of public telecommunications transport networks and services on reasonable and non-discriminatory terms and conditions, for the supply of a service included in its Schedule.'[149]

4.107   These access rights are further specified in some detail.[150] The panel in *Telmex* interpreted 'reasonable terms' to include requirements akin to, even if not as far-reaching as, 'cost-orientation' as required by Section 2.1 (b) Reference Paper.[151] It, therefore, found Mexico's termination rates for incoming international calls in violation of the above provision (in addition to a violation of the Reference Paper) because they were significantly above costs.

RESERVED RIGHTS OF MEMBERS

4.108   Members retain the right to take measures necessary to ensure the security and confidentiality of messages as long as these measures are not discriminating.[152] They also retain the right to impose conditions necessary to safeguard suppliers'

---

145   'Integral part' of the GATS, see Art XXIX GATS.
146   See para 1 of the Annex.
147   Bronckers and Larouche, para 4.102, fn 124 above, p 998, call it 'an insurance policy for suppliers of other services.'
148   Bronckers and Larouche, para 4.102, fn 124 above, at p 999.
149   Section 5(a) of the Annex.
150   Subparagraph (b) specifies that such service suppliers should be allowed to:
   ● purchase or lease and attach terminal or other equipment which interface with the network and which is necessary to supply a supplier's services;
   ● interconnect private leased or owned circuits with public telecommunications transport networks and services; or with other privately owned or leased circuits; and
   ● use operating protocols of the service supplier's choice in the supply of any service, other than as necessary to ensure the availability of telecommunications transport networks and services to the public generally.
   Subparagraph (c) spells out the right of foreign service suppliers to use public telecommunications transport networks for the movement of information within and across borders, including for intra-corporate communications.
151   *Telmex,* Panel Report, para 4.87 above, at paras 7.310–7.344; see, in particular, para 7.344.
152   Section 5 (d) of the Annex

public services responsibilities, to protect the technical integrity of public networks and services or to enforce the limitations of services commitments made.[153]

TRANSPARENCY

4.109   Extending the transparency obligations of Article III of the GATS, the Annex requires Members to ensure that:

'relevant information on conditions affecting access to and use of public telecommunications transport networks and services is publicly available, including: tariffs and other terms and conditions of service; specifications of technical interfaces with such networks and services; information on bodies responsible for the preparation and adoption of standards affecting such access and use; conditions applying to attachment of terminal or other equipment; and notifications, registration or licensing requirements, if any.'[154]

The Fourth Protocol to the GATS

4.110   The Fourth Protocol,[155] at the time of its conclusion in 1997 also referred to as the 'Agreement on Basic Telecommunications', brought two major developments.

4.111   First, it contained as annexes supplements to 55 GATS schedules covering 69 states[156] containing in large part significant market access commitments in basic telecommunications services, including commitments relating to commercial presence – ie total or partial equity investment in local telecoms operators – from 56 countries covering roughly 97 per cent of total revenue from basic telecoms worldwide.[157]

4.112   Secondly, remarkably all but two[158] signatories to the Fourth Protocol agreed to undertake significant additional commitments on regulatory principles in the area of basic telecommunications contained in the so-called Reference Paper.[159]

---

153   Section 5 (e) of the Annex. Section 5 (f) contains examples of such conditions, such as restrictions on resale or shared use of services or technical requirements. An additional exception applies to developing countries. Section 5 (g) entitles them to 'place reasonable conditions on access to and use of public… networks and services necessary to strengthen [their] domestic telecommunications infrastructure and service capacity and to increase [their] participation in international trade telecommunications services. However, this only applies if the conditions are contained in the Members schedule – which was not the case for Mexico in *Telmex*. See Panel Report, para 4.87 above, at paras 7.386–7.389.

154   Section 4 of the Annex.

155   See para 4.68 above

156   The European Communities submitted a single schedule for their (then) 15 Member States.

157   See the very useful unofficial compilation of commitments under the Protocol prepared by the WTO Secretariat, available at www.wto.org/english/tratop_e/serv_e/telecom_e/telecom_commit_exempt_list_e.htm (last visited 31 January 2013) the compilation also contains Members recently acceded to the WTO and other Members not signatories to the Protocol who undertook similar commitments. See also Bronckers and Larouche, para 4.102, fn 124 above, at p 1000 for summaries.

158   Ecuador and Tunisia.

159   While most participants adopted the Reference Paper unmodified, some Members (Bolivia,

The 'Reference Paper'

4.113   The Reference Paper contains a set of rules, or principles, to be applied in the national regulation of telecommunications services by WTO Members in relation to foreign services and service providers. The document has two primary purposes. The first is to provide an effective framework of domestic competitive safeguards for foreign telecommunications service providers, in most cases faced with an entrenched national industry, often dominated by the incumbent former monopolist. The second key purpose is to make such disciplines legally enforceable before the WTO Dispute Settlement Body.

4.114   Both purposes appear to have been put to effect in the recent *Telmex* case. The panel, largely following the complaints brought forward by the United States, found the Mexican law and practice relating to incoming calls – which the panel identified as price cartels and market sharing – to constitute anti-competitive practices in violation of Mexico's commitments, inter alia, under the Reference Paper.

THE NATURE OF THE REFERENCE PAPER: A SET OF ADDITIONAL COMMITMENTS

4.115   The Reference Paper is a very brief (2 $\frac{1}{2}$ page) minimum standard set of pro-competitive regulatory principles for the regulation of basic telecommunications. As the name indicates, it became applicable to those Members who agreed to it by being incorporated by reference in, and annexed to, their respective schedules of specific GATS commitments. The Reference Paper can, in effect, be called a piece of industry-specific competition legislation.

SPECIFIC DISCIPLINES RELATING TO 'MAJOR SUPPLIERS'

4.116   Given the industry's history of monopoly structures it is not surprising that the Reference Paper takes as its point of reference the concept of the 'major supplier', which the Reference Paper, evidently basing itself on established competition law concepts of market dominance, defines as:

> 'a supplier which has the ability to materially affect the terms of participation (having regard to price and supply) in the relevant market for basic telecommunications services as a result of (a) control over essential facilities;[160] or (b) use of its position in the market'.

The panel in *Telmex* had little difficulty in finding that Telmex was such a 'major supplier'.[161]

India, Malaysia, Morocco, Pakistan, the Philippines, Turkey and Venezuela) deleted individual commitments. Others (Bangladesh, Brazil, Mauritius and Thailand) committed to introducing the Reference Paper at a later point in time.

160   The Reference Paper defines 'essential facilities' as 'facilities of a public telecommunications transport network or service that (a) are exclusively or predominantly provided by a single or limited number of suppliers; and (b) cannot feasibly be economically or technically substituted in order to provide a service. For a discussion the 'essential facilities' concept and its counterpart in competition law see Marco Bronckers, 'The WTO Reference Paper on Telecommunications: A Model for WTO Competition Law?', in Bronckers and Quick (eds) *New Directions in International Economic Law* (2000) pp 371, 385–386.

161   *Telmex,* Panel Report, para 4.87 above, at paras 7.146–7.159. In the course of doing so, the panel made an interesting finding on the 'relevant market' in the case. While Mexico had argued that the relevant market would have to include incoming *and* outgoing international

The 'major supplier' is the specific addressee for two sets of disciplines, to be enforced by the WTO Member concerned, namely competitive safeguards and interconnection obligations.

COMPETITIVE SAFEGUARDS

4.117   Section 1.1 of the Reference Paper provides that '[a]ppropriate measures shall be maintained [to prevent] suppliers who, alone or together, are a major supplier from engaging in or continuing anti-competitive practices'. The onus is thus on the Member to ensure, by whatever appropriate means, adequate behaviour by 'major suppliers' within its jurisdiction.

4.118   The question of what is included in the notion of anti-competitive practices is a matter of fierce debate. Section 1.2 Reference Paper notes that it shall 'include in particular' anti-competitive cross-subsidisation, using information obtained from competitors with anti-competitive results and the refusal to provide information about essential facilities and commercially relevant information to other service suppliers. While the examples and the starting point ('major supplier') may suggest that the relevant behaviour must be related to an abuse of dominance, the Panel in *Telmex* applied a more expansive interpretation of the concept to include price-fixing cartels and market-sharing arrangements. This has been heavily criticised by some[162] and defended by others.[163]

4.119   In the case at hand, the Mexican international long distance rules provided that uniform rates for the termination of international calls into Mexico were to be negotiated by the supplier who had the biggest market share of *outgoing* traffic from Mexico in the preceding six months (which was invariably Telmex). The rules further provided that incoming calls were to be distributed among Mexican international gateway providers in proportion to their respective share of outgoing calls in the preceding month. The Panel found that these practices amounted to price-fixing and market-sharing arrangements, which the Panel found to be 'anti-competitive practices' in the sense of Section 1.1 of the Reference Paper.[164]The fact that Mexican law in fact mandated the actions did not change the finding, as the Reference Paper obligation incumbent on Mexico to prevent such behaviour remained unaffected.[165]

4.120   With only one dispute ruled on to date, the jurisprudence is as yet novel and will clearly evolve as more disputes are brought before the Dispute Settlement Body. It is possible that future panels might not apply concepts and case references from national competition laws as freely as this one did. However, generally speaking, regulators and dominant operators should expect to be judged against high standards.

---

calls, as Mexico was not providing termination services but was completing international calls on a shared revenue basis (accounting rates), the United States had argued that a 'demand substitution' analysis suggested the opposite. The Panel followed this latter approach.

162   Marsden, 'WTO Decides Its First Competition – With Disappointing Results', (2004) 16(3) Competition Law Insight 8. See also George, 'WTO panel condemns anti-competitive behaviour in international telecoms case' (2004) 10(5) International Trade Law and Regulation 106.

163   Bronckers and Larouche, para 4.102, fn 124 above.

164   *Telmex,* Panel Report, para 4.87 above, at para 7.238.

165   *Telmex,* Panel Report, para 4.87 above, at paras 7.239–7.245.

INTERCONNECTION

4.121   Section 2 of the Reference Paper imposes obligations on 'major suppliers' relating to interconnection with foreign service providers who enjoy market access under specific scheduled commitments. Section 2.2[166] requires that interconnection be ensured at any technically feasible point in the following manner:

- under non-discriminatory terms ...;
- in a timely fashion, on terms, conditions ... and cost-oriented rates that are transparent, reasonable, having regard to economic feasibility, and sufficiently unbundled ...; and
- upon request at additional termination points, subject to charges.

4.122   The provision contains a number of terms, like 'cost-oriented', 'sufficiently unbundled', 'reasonable', that are rather broad and for which clear definitions are yet to be developed.[167] It will be the task of the Dispute Settlement Mechanism to bring some clarification of the used terms and, thus, strengthen the impact of this provision.

4.123   The Panel in *Telmex* did some first steps in this regard. It found that the interconnection rates offered to US operators under the Mexican ILD rules were significantly above costs,[168] elaborating on the interpretation of 'cost-oriented rates'.[169] The Panel also clarified that relevant costs in the context of international interconnection under the Reference Paper must be those that relate to the actual, attributable cost of providing the service (in this case termination),[170] but may be calculated on the basis of incremental cost methodologies.[171]

---

166 The full text of section 2.2 reads:
   '**2.2   Interconnection to be ensured**
   Interconnection with a major supplier will be ensured at any technically feasible point in the network. Such interconnection is provided:
   (a)   under non-discriminatory terms, conditions (including technical standards and specifications) and rates and of a quality no less favourable than that provided for its own like services or for like services of non-affiliated service suppliers or for its subsidiaries or other affiliates;
   (b)   in a timely fashion, on terms, conditions (including technical standards and specifications) and cost-oriented rates that are transparent, reasonable, having regard to economic feasibility, and sufficiently unbundled so that the supplier need not pay for network components or facilities that it does not require for the service to be provided; and
   (c)   upon request, at points in addition to the network termination points offered to the majority of users, subject to charges that reflect the cost of construction of necessary additional facilities.'
167 Some terms, however, have their origin in US or EU law, so that recourse to EU/US interpretation is possible, e g 'transparency and cost-orientation', 'sufficiently unbundled' in Art 7 of the former EC Interconnection Directive 97/33; 'technical feasible points' in s 251(c)(2)(B) of the US Telecommunications Act.
168 The Panel followed the United States' analysis. The United States had provided four comparisons by proxy, including comparisons with national termination rates that were supposed by law to cover costs. In all four comparisons, the international termination rates were significantly higher. See *Telmex*, Panel Report, 7.186–7.216.
169 See *Telmex*, Panel Report, 7.166–7.185.
170 See *Telmex*, Panel Report, 7.171. The Panel sought and found guidance, inter alia, in ITU-T-series Recommendation 1.40 and 1.50.
171 See *Telmex*, Panel Report, 7.177.

4.124   It further clarified that guidance for the qualifying phrase 'having regard to economic feasibility' could be drawn from the EC Interconnection Directive, in the context of which, the phrase is understood to mean that operators must be allowed a reasonable rate of return on investment.[172]

4.125   Sections 2.3 and 2.4 of the Reference Paper oblige the major supplier to make publicly available its procedures for interconnection negotiations and either its interconnection agreements or a reference interconnection offer. Section 2.5 finally requires that a fast-track independent review procedure is available to suppliers requesting interconnection with a 'major supplier'.

4.126   Based on the *Telmex* experience, it can be said that the interconnection obligations under the Reference Paper are significant. To aggrieved providers, they offer good chances to gain access or reduce disproportionate costs.

UNIVERSAL SERVICE

4.127   An important exemption applies to the benefit of universal service provision. Section 3 of the Reference Paper allows for the implementation of a universal service obligation. These obligations 'will not be regarded as anti-competitive per se, provided they are administered in a transparent, non-discriminatory and competitively neutral manner and are not more burdensome than necessary for the kind of universal service defined by the Member'.

4.128   In the negotiations leading to the Reference Paper the issue of universal service obligations was subject to much debate. While it is generally accepted that the provision of universal service needs some kind of regulatory protection, it was disputed how far-reaching this protection should be. It was argued that universal service exemptions significantly impede market access and are rather used to protect domestic service providers than to enable the provision of universal service.[173] Section 3 Reference Paper, however, makes it clear that every Member retains the right to define the kind of universal service obligation it wishes to maintain, ie which services are to be offered universally and what conditions shall apply.

4.129   Measures under this provision must not be 'more burdensome than necessary'.[174] It remains to be seen whether a reasonably strict necessity test, such as the one applied to measures under the 'general exceptions' provisions of Article XX GATT, will take hold in the interpretation of this exemption.

LICENSING DISCIPLINES

4.130   Where licensing applies, all criteria and time periods normally required as well as terms and conditions of individual licences must be made public. Reasons must be given in case of denial of a licence.[175]

---

172 See *Telmex*, Panel Report, 7.185.
173 See Markus Fredebeul-Klein and Andreas Freytag, 'Telecommunications and WTO discipline', [1997] Telecommunications Policy 477, 482.
174 India, for example, has taken an even broader exception from the provision on anti-competitive practices by stating that universal service obligations are not regarded as anti-competitive per se, *since they would be administered in a transparent and non-discriminatory manner* (GATS/SC/ 42/Suppl.3, 11 April 1997).
175 Section 4 Reference Paper.

Critics have voiced dissatisfaction with the limited scope of this provision, as important issues regarding licensing remain unaddressed.[176]

INDEPENDENT REGULATORS

4.131   Section 5 of the Reference Paper demands an impartial regulatory body that is 'separate from, and not accountable to, any supplier of basic telecommunications services'. While this straightforward rule of the separation of operator and regulator is laudable, issues remain. Unlike in EC Law[177] there is no provision for the structural separation of regulator and (state) owner when a telecoms operator is state-owned or state-controlled,[178] so that conflicts of interests and undue pressures may not be fully excluded.

ALLOCATION OF RESOURCES

4.132   Section 6 of the Reference Paper provides for the objective, timely and non-discriminatory allocation of scarce resources, such as frequencies.

THE GATT

4.133   Whilst the focus of this section has been on the GATS, it is, nonetheless, worth referring to the key obligations of the General Agreement on Tariffs and Trade ('GATT'). The GATT governs the international trade between WTO Members of goods, including telecommunications-related equipment. The three key sets of obligations that apply to the international trade in goods are briefly addressed here.

4.134   Article I GATT guarantees Most-Favoured Nation treatment for the goods of the WTO Members. Under the terms of Article I, any advantage, favour, privilege or immunity granted by any WTO Member to any product originating in or destined for any other country shall be accorded immediately and unconditionally to the 'like product' originating in or destined for the territories of other WTO Members. There is a significant amount of jurisprudence from both the GATT and WTO systems on what constitutes a 'like product'. As the Most-Favoured Nation treatment is only accorded to 'products', whether products are in fact 'like' is always a keenly disputed issue before the panels and the Appellate Body.

4.135   Article III GATT ensures that goods imported from other WTO Members receive national treatment in respect of taxation and other regulations. More specifically, Article III:2 GATT prohibits WTO Members from applying, directly or indirectly, internal taxes or charges of any kind in excess of those applied to like domestic products. Article III:4 requires WTO Members to accord treatment no less favourable to products imported from the territories of other WTO Members than that accorded to like products of national origin 'in respect of all laws, regulations and requirements affecting their internal sale, offering for sale, purchase, transportation, distribution or use'. Once again, any disputes raising issues under Article III will inevitably result in arguments as to whether the relevant products are

---

176   Bronckers and Larouche, para 4.103, fn 124 above, pp 1011–12.

177   Art 3(2) Directive 2002/21 [2002] OJ L108/33.

178   Section 5 does not require that the regulatory body has to be structurally separate from the ministry even in the case of still state owned telecommunications companies. Cf. Fredebeul-Klein and Freytag [1999] Telecommunications Policy 625, 632.

'like'. The national treatment principle embodied within the GATT has played a significant role to bring down trade barriers. Unlike the GATS system, national treatment under the GATT applies unconditionally and does not depend upon WTO Members adhering to or specifying additional commitments.

4.136 Finally, Article XI:1 GATT provides for the general elimination and prohibition of quantitative restrictions relating to both imports and exports. This provision requires WTO Members to remove any and all prohibitions and restrictions, whether made effective through quotas, import or export licences or other measures, in relation to imports from, or exports to, the territory of another WTO Member.

4.137 As with the GATS, the GATT has an exceptions clause that provides a derogation from compliance with the substantive obligations referred to above. Under Article XX GATT, nothing in the GATT prevents the adoption or enforcement of measures that are, inter alia, necessary to protect public morals, necessary to protect human, animal or plant life or health or relating to the conservation of exhaustible natural resources. Article XX GATT is a commonly litigated provision. Any dispute in which a complainant Member establishes a prima facie violation of the GATT under Articles I, III or XI will typically then move to the defendant Member seeking to justify its conduct under Article XX.

4.138 There appear to be no cases under the WTO Dispute Settlement Mechanism involving breaches of the GATT in relation to the international trade in telecommunications equipment. Requests for formal consultations were made in *Japan – Measures Affecting the Purchase of Telecommunications Equipment*[179] and *Korea – Laws, Regulations and Practices in the Telecommunications Procurement Sector.*[180] Both disputes, however, appear to have been resolved bilaterally before any panel decision was handed down.

THE TRIPS

4.139 The Agreement on Trade-Related Intellectual Property Rights ('TRIPS') is another key Covered Agreement that is likely to be of relevance to operators within the telecommunications sector. It is intended to provide minimum guarantees of protection for those who hold intellectual property rights.

4.140 As with the GATS and the GATT, TRIPS provides for the following basic rights:

● under Article 3 of the TRIPS, each WTO Member must accord to the nationals of other Members treatment no less favourable than that it accords to its own nationals with regard to the 'protection' of intellectual property rights (so-called national treatment); and

● under Article 4 of the TRIPS, with regard to the 'protection' of intellectual property rights, any advantage, favour, privilege or immunity granted by a Member to the nationals of any other country shall be accorded immediately

---

179 This involved a claim by the EC against Japan that a US-Japan agreement relating to telecommunications equipment was inconsistent with, inter alia, Articles I and III of the GATT.

180 This case related to a claim by the EC against Korea alleging that the latter's procurement practices in relation to the telecommunications sector discriminated against foreign suppliers contrary to, inter alia, Articles I and III of the GATT.

and unconditionally to the nationals of all other Members (so-called Most Favoured Nation treatment).

For the purposes of both Articles 3 and 4 of the TRIPS, the term 'protection' is defined as including 'matters affecting the availability, acquisition, scope, maintenance and enforcement of intellectual property rights as well as those matters affecting the use of intellectual property rights specifically addressed in this Agreement'.

4.141   The TRIPS governs a broad array of intellectual property rights including the following:

- copyright and related rights;
- trademarks;
- geographical indications;
- industrial designs;
- patents;
- layout designs (topographies) of integrated circuits; and
- protection of undisclosed information.

4.142   Perhaps most importantly, the TRIPS provides for minimum enforcement procedures so as to permit effective action against any act of infringement of intellectual property rights covered by the agreement. Enforcement procedures are required to be fair and equitable and not unnecessarily complicated or costly (Article 41(2) TRIPS). Further, pursuant to Article 41(4), parties to proceedings should be afforded the opportunity to have administrative decisions judicially reviewed. TRIPS also requires WTO Members to ensure that the following remedies are made available in relation to intellectual property infringement proceedings: injunctions (Article 44 TRIPS), damages (Article 45 TRIPS), indemnification (Article 48 TRIPS) and provisional measures (Article 50 TRIPS). In addition, Article 61 TRIPS obliges Members to provide for criminal prosecutions, at least in relation to wilful trademark counterfeiting or copyright piracy on a commercial scale.

THE WTO AND THE ITU

4.143   As the WTO begins to venture into developing rules for subject matters traditionally falling under the auspices of other international and multilateral organisations, the risk of conflict between different international regimes increases. This risk has been most acute in relation to the overlap between the international trading regime, as set out under the WTO Covered Agreements, and multilateral environmental or health agreements. However, the possibility of conflict also exists as between the rules developed by the WTO and the ITU.

4.144   One problem area relates to the size of, and differences in, international settlement rates. The price of each international connection has conventionally been negotiated under the ITU by single operators in the country of origin and destination of the call. Prices could vary significantly and inevitably exceeded costs in developing countries. A so-called peace clause was developed, under which WTO Members accepted, by way of informal gentleman's agreement, that they would not challenge the application of settlement rates, as developed under the ITU regime, before the WTO's Dispute Settlement Mechanism.[181] However, the *Telmex* case challenges this understanding by confirming that, in so far as a WTO Member is bound by the requirements of the Reference Paper, then switched international services will be governed by the rules of the Reference Paper in relation to interconnection. This would suggest that there should be an alignment as between settlement rates and the costs of interconnection. However, this could raise political issues for developing countries, in particular, since they may depend on higher settlement rates in order to help build a more effective domestic telecommunications system. As one commentator notes, '[t]his ruling obviously interferes with ITU rates and poses the politically difficult question of whether the WTO or the ITU has the ultimate economic governance of international telecommunications'.[182]

4.145 Another issue is the extent to which the WTO's trading rules would allow Members to take into account non-trade objectives including, for example, universal and public service or ensuring the safety and development of networks. Whilst this issue was addressed to some extent in the *Telmex* case, further clarity will be required from future WTO case law.[183]

OUTLOOK: RECENT, CURRENT AND FUTURE NEGOTIATIONS

4.146 Like other parts of WTO law, GATS law is in a state of current development through accession and multilateral negotiations. New specific commitments are scheduled by acceding countries at the time of their accession. Recent accessions have, as a rule, included a number of commitments in telecommunications services. Major trading nations now routinely request from accession candidates commitments in key service areas, including financial services and telecommunications services.

4.147 The so-called 'GATS 2000' negotiations mandated by Article XIX(1) GATS were phased into the new comprehensive 'Doha Development Agenda' negotiations launched in November 2001 in the Qatari capital Doha. The negotiations, however, have run into intermittent deadlocks. While initial requests and some offers have been exchanged between WTO Members, it is too early to say whether, and to what extent, significant commitments in telecommunications services can be expected. Given the rapid development of the industry, however, there is an evident need for progressive development. As of July 2008, 39 governments had made offers to improve their existing commitments or to commit for the first time in the telecommunications sector. It is hoped that WTO members will respond to this need by advancing and successfully concluding the negotiations. However, given the current political focus of WTO Members on other more sensitive aspects of WTO negotiations (in particular, agriculture), it is far from clear that the needs of the telecommunications industry will be met in the near-, or even mid-term, future.

---

181 See WTO Report of the Group on Basic Telecommunications to the Council for Trade in Services, S/GBT/4, 15 February, para 5.
182 Luff, 'Telecommunications and Audio-visual Services: Considerations for a Convergence Policy at the World Trade Organization' (2004) 38(6) Journal of World Trade 1059–1086, at 1063.
183 Luff, at p 1064.

Compliance and Risk Management

Sunny Mann, Laura Philippou and Mayuko Roald
Baker & McKenzie LLP, London

INTRODUCTION

5.1   A review of the legal environment applicable to the telecommunications sector would be incomplete without a discussion of the broader risk management and compliance issues that the sector can face. Clearly, risk management can mean different things to different companies, depending on, among other things, the company's precise activities, the countries in which it does business, and the types of third parties with which it interacts. However, in this chapter, we address two particular risk areas that quite commonly affect the telecommunications sector: compliance with anti-bribery and corruption rules, and compliance with export controls and trade sanctions. We note that two other key compliance risk areas include competition law and data protection and privacy law. However, these topics are covered separately in other chapters.

Compliance and risk management issues are among the most troublesome for general counsels and legal teams. Corporate misconduct can result in, among other things, heavy criminal or civil fines, exclusion from public procurement tenders, jail time for individuals, extradition, director disqualifications, and revocation or denial of government authorisations (such as export licences). These are not theoretical penalties as they have been deployed as a result of enforcement actions. In recent years, we have seen a global bribery settlement for one company reaching $1.6 billion (which included settlements in both the United States and Germany), a competition fine by the EU Commission of up to nearly €900 million, and a settlement of a violation of US trade controls for $619 million. Significant penalties have also been imposed on telecommunications companies, including a settlement for violations of US anti-bribery laws for $137 million and an EU Commission fine of €152 million for breaching competition rules prohibiting abuse of dominance. While these penalties alone are enough of a reason for firms to take corporate compliance seriously, corporate misconduct can also irreparably harm corporate reputation (arguably a company's key asset) in the eyes of the company's stakeholders and, ultimately, lead to the demise of an entire corporation.

With respect to export controls and trade sanctions, we focus on the EU regime. However, given that licensing and enforcement related to these rules are both carried out at a national level by national Member State authorities, we provide some national law context as well. With respect to anti-bribery and corruption compliance, there is no pan-EU anti-bribery law as such and, accordingly, we focus on one of the more rigorous anti-bribery laws in Europe, specifically, the recently enacted UK Bribery Act 2010. The UK Act has been one of the most revolutionary and widely discussed compliance developments of recent times due to the breadth of the obligations and the territorial scope of the legislation. We also briefly describe the key tenets of the primary anti-bribery treaties developed under the auspices of the Organisation for Economic Co-operation and Development ('OECD') and the Council of Europe, as many European countries have adopted national legislation intended to comply with them.

European compliance laws are not only relevant to those entities incorporated within European jurisdictions, but can also apply to:

- conduct by non-EU entities outside the EU if, for example, the conduct has an impact within the EU (such as anti-competitive conduct outside the EU, but with an effect in the EU);
- EU nationals outside the EU (for example, under EU trade sanctions laws); or
- non-UK companies that conduct a part of their business in the UK (for example, under the UK Bribery Act).

In light of the fact that the United States has also introduced strongly extra-territorial laws that impose obligations on European companies, it is important to be mindful of US compliance laws as well.

In addition to understanding the legal obligations with which compliance is mandated, it is critical for companies, including telecommunications companies, to understand how to devise, roll out and implement a robust compliance programme. Having a strong compliance programme helps on a number of fronts by:

- reducing the risk of a violation occurring in the first instance;
- in rare circumstances, acting as a complete legal defence to the commission of an offence (for example, under the UK Bribery Act); or
- acting as mitigation in case an offence has been committed such that enforcement authorities may be less likely to bring action.

Accordingly, we also describe what a robust compliance programme entails. Interestingly, the expectations of regulators in terms of what is a good compliance programme are converging, both across different jurisdictions and across different subject matter areas. In this chapter, we also consider the key elements of a good compliance programme.

EU EXPORT CONTROLS

Introduction

5.2   EU Regulation 428/2009[1] ('Dual-Use Regulation') which replaced the former EU Regulation 1334/2000,[2] sets up an EU wide regime for the control of exports of dual-use items and technology. The purpose of the Dual-Use Regulation is to control the export and movement of items that, in themselves are sensitive items or

---

1   Council Regulation (EC) No 428/2009 of 5 May 2009 setting up a Community regime for the control of exports, transfer, brokering and transit of dual-use items (as amended) [2009] OJ L134/1.
2   The EU Council Regulation No 1334/2000 of 22 June 2000 setting up a Community regime for the control of exports of dual-use items and technology [2000] OJ L159/1.

could be put to a sensitive use (for example, civilian use items that can be easily adapted for a more nefarious use, such as in a military or terrorist context).

The Dual-Use Regulation defines a common list of dual-use items which are controlled for certain activities, including transfer, export, brokering, and transit to exports outside of the EU. It is directly applicable, and intended to achieve a uniform and consistent application of controls, throughout the EU. However, enforcement and licensing are left to the 27 national Member State export control authorities. This means that one can find variations of approach among different Member State authorities in terms of how they apply the controls. This inevitably complicates the compliance efforts of companies and makes it critical that they understand how the controls are implemented on the ground in each country. While understanding the Dual-Use Regulation is a necessary step within the compliance process, it is not enough without an understanding of the national component. To provide some context of the national law element, we refer to a number of examples from UK controls that supplement the Dual-Use Regulation. The UK controls are amongst the most rigorous and strictly enforced within the EU. Other EU Member States (in particular, Germany, France and the Netherlands) are also active in terms of licensing and enforcement under the Dual-Use Regulation.

Product Controls

5.3   The EU dual-use control list is based on control lists adopted by the following international export control regimes: the Australia Group ('AG'), the Nuclear Suppliers Group ('NSG'), and the Wassenaar Arrangement and the Missile Technology Control Regime ('MTCR'). The key control list for the telecommunications sector derives from the Wassenaar Arrangement. The list is contained in Annex I to the Dual-Use Regulation. The general rule is that all goods listed in the annex require authorisation for export to countries outside the EU.

The list is divided into the following 10 categories:

Category 0   Nuclear materials, facilities and equipment
Category 1   Materials, chemicals, micro-organisms and toxins
Category 2   Materials processing
Category 3   Electronics
Category 4   Computers
Category 5   Telecommunications and information security
Category 6   Sensors and lasers
Category 7   Navigation and avionics
Category 8   Marine
Category 9   Propulsion systems, space vehicles and related equipment

Within each of the above categories, the list is further subdivided into the following:

- A (systems, equipment and components)
- B (test, inspection and production)
- C (materials)

- D (software)[3]
- E (technology)[4]

The EU dual-use list is a long list that includes complex details of technical specifications of controlled goods, software, and technology. Accordingly, the full list is not reproduced in this chapter. However, set out below are key examples within the categories that the telecommunications sector most commonly encounters. We do not include all relevant specifications within the list below. By way of example, the reference below to 'certain radio equipment' means that only that radio equipment meeting precise specifications (as set out in the dual-use list, but not reproduced in full below) is controlled.

Category 5 Part 1 (telecommunications)

- certain radio equipment;
- certain optical fibre communication cables, optical fibres and accessories;
- certain telemetry and telecontrol equipment, designed or modified for missiles;
- certain telecommunication test, inspection and production equipment including software;
- certain software specially designed or modified for the 'development'[5], 'production'[6] or 'use'[7] of the above listed items; and
- certain technology for the above listed items.

Category 5 Part 2 (information security[8])

Systems equipment and components and related software and technology:

- designed or modified to use cryptography[9] employing a symmetric algorithm with key length in excess of 56 bits;
- designed or modified to use cryptography employing an asymmetric algorithm where the security of the algorithm is based on either factorisation of integers in excess of 512 bits (eg RSA), computation of discrete logarithms in

---

3   'Software' means a collection of one or more 'programmes' or 'microprogrammes' fixed in any tangible medium of expression.

4   'Technology' means specific information necessary for the 'development', 'production' or 'use' of goods. This information takes the form of 'technical data' or 'technical assistance'.

5   'Development' is related to all phases prior to serial production, such as: design, design research, design analyses, design concepts, assembly and testing of prototypes, pilot production schemes, design data, process of transforming design data into a product, configuration design, integration design, layouts.

6   'Production' means all production phases, such as: construction, production engineering, manufacture, integration, assembly (mounting), inspection, testing, quality assurance.

7   'Use' means operation, installation (including on-site installation), maintenance (checking), repair, overhaul and refurbishing.

8   'Information security' is all the means and functions ensuring the accessibility, confidentiality or integrity of information or communications, excluding the means and functions intended to safeguard against malfunctions. This includes 'cryptography', 'cryptanalysis', protection against compromising emanations and computer security.

9   'Cryptography' means the discipline which embodies principles, means and methods for the transformation of data in order to hide its information content, prevent its undetected modification or prevent its unauthorized use. 'Cryptography' is limited to the transformation of information using one or more 'secret parameters' (eg crypto variables) or associated key management.

a multiplicative group of a finite field of size greater than 512 bits (eg Diffie-Hellman over Z/pZ), or discrete logarithms in a group other than the immediately above, in excess of 112 bits (eg Diffie-Hellman over an elliptic curve); or
- designed or modified to perform cryptanalytic functions.

Certain items and technology are exempt from these encryption controls under a number of exceptions set out within the controls. We focus in on two of the exceptions set out under Notes 3 and 4 of Category 5 Part 2. Broadly speaking, Note 3 excludes certain mass-market equipment and software that meet the following four conditions on a cumulative basis:

- generally available to the public;
- having cryptographic functionality that cannot easily be changed by the user;
- designed for installation by the user without further substantial support by the supplier; and
- when necessary, details of the goods are accessible to the competent authorities of the relevant Member State in order to confirm compliance with the requirements of Note 3.

Note 3 is commonly used to decontrol widely available commercial software and goods that have encryption capabilities.

Further, Note 4 excludes items incorporating or using cryptography, which meet the following cumulative requirements:

- the primary function or set of functions is not:
  - 'information security';
  - a computer, including operating systems, parts and components;
  - sending, receiving or storing information (except in support of entertainment, mass commercial broadcasts, digital rights management or medical records management); or
  - networking (includes operation, administration, management and provisioning);
- the cryptographic functionality is limited to supporting their primary function or set of functions; and
- when necessary, details of the goods are accessible to the competent authorities of the relevant Member State in order to confirm compliance with the requirements of Note 4.

Note 4 is commonly used to decontrol certain items where the encryption capability is ancillary to another primary function.

LICENSING REQUIREMENTS

5.4   A licence is required for listed products to be exported to destinations outside of the EU.[10] 'Exports' include both physical/tangible shipment of goods, software and technology, and intangible transfers of software and technology. Intangible transfers include those by e-mail, fax, information networks, and telephone/videoconference. Therefore, by way of example, an employee uploading controlled

---

10   Art 3(1) of the Dual-Use Regulation. It is worth noting (in particular, for telecommunications companies that may be providing support to oil and gas companies offshore) that a transfer to the continental shelf of one of the EU Member States is deemed to be an export to outside of the EU.

technology (for example, design blueprints of controlled telecommunications equipment) to a corporate group intranet site such that it is then accessible to a fellow employee in the United States or elsewhere outside the EU would constitute an 'export'. Transmission may also be by oral means, but only where the technology is contained in a document or the relevant part of that document is either dictated over the telephone or described over the telephone in such a way as to achieve substantially the same result as if it had been dictated. The obligation to obtain a licence lies with the 'exporter'. The 'exporter' is the natural or legal person (or partnership) on whose behalf an export declaration is made, ie the person who, at the time the declaration is accepted, holds the contract with the consignee in the third country and has the power to determine the sending of the item out of the EU. Authorisations must be sought in the Member State where the exporter is established, as opposed to from the Member State from where the controlled item is being dispatched. By way of example, if the exporter is an Irish entity but the controlled good is being dispatched from Germany, the licence should, in principle, be applied for by the Irish entity from the Irish authority.

Under EU controls, there are no restrictions on 're-exports' once the controlled item has left the EU under licence. Thus, no further EU licence is required to re-export the item from one third country to another third country, contrary to the position under US export controls. Further, the EU controls do not go so far as the 'deemed export' controls. By way of example, no licence is required under the Dual-Use Regulation to share or reveal controlled items with a foreign (non-EU) national located within the EU. However, certain EU Member States may choose to adopt a stricter position under national controls.

In general, transfers of controlled items within the EU do not require a prior licence, subject to some key exceptions. First, intra-EU transfers will require a licence if the item is listed under Annex IV of the Dual-Use Regulation. Annex IV is a narrow subset of Annex I, comprising the most sensitive items, such as certain explosives, switching devices, pressure sensors and, perhaps of more relevance to telecommunications companies, cryptanalytic software.

EU Member States are also authorised, in limited circumstances, to impose licensing requirements on other intra-EU movements of controlled items. For example, they can impose a licensing requirement for a transfer to another EU Member State if it is known that the final destination is outside the EU and no processing or work is to be performed to the item or technology within the EU. By way of example, the UK has chosen to exert this competence.[11]

Furthermore, the Dual-Use Regulation provides for restrictions on brokering services out of the EU. Brokering is defined as:

> 'the negotiation or arrangement of transactions for the purchase, sale or supply of dual-use items from a third country to any other third country, or the selling or buying of dual-use items that are located in third countries for their transfer to another third country.'[12]

The brokering controls apply where the broker is aware, or informed by the competent authority, that the relevant items are intended for an end-use related to weapons of mass destruction ('WMD'), broadly speaking, an end-use related to nuclear, chemical or biological weapons, or related missile delivery systems. In such cases, an authorisation from the relevant competent authority (in the country in

---

11   Art 5(1) of the UK Export Control Order 2008.
12   Art 2(5) of the Dual-Use Regulation.

which the broker is resident or established) will be required. The Dual-Use Regulation also gives the EU Member States power to extend these brokering controls so that they can also apply, by way of example, where the items being moved are intended for a military end-use.

End-Use Controls

5.5   Even if the relevant item being exported is not on a control list, it can still be subjected to a licensing requirement if it is being put to a sensitive end-use. It is important to reiterate that the end-use controls apply to non-listed items, as the export of listed items would require a licence in any case.

WMD end-use

5.6   The WMD end-use controls are intended to prevent exports, supplies and technical assistance in furtherance of WMD projects outside the EU. As already noted, broadly speaking, the WMD end-use controls capture an end-use related to nuclear, chemical or biological weapons, or related missile delivery systems. Compliance with the end-use controls is extremely important, in particular in terms of trading with Iran, as the UK (and other Member State) authorities are scrutinising exports to Iran much more closely to ensure that they do not run foul of the end-use controls.

Under the Dual-Use Regulation, an exporter is required to seek a licence to export items outside the EU if the exporter has been informed by the competent authorities of the Member State in which it is established that the items in question are, or may be intended, in their entirety or in part, for use in connection with a WMD end-use.[13] Further, if an exporter is aware that such items which it proposes to export are intended, in their entirety or in part, for any WMD end use, it must notify the relevant authority, which will decide whether to make the export concerned subject to authorisation.

In addition, in the UK, the Export Control Organisation ('ECO') prohibits an export where a person has grounds for suspecting that items are, or may be intended, in their entirety or in part, for any WMD end-use, unless that person has made all reasonable enquiries as to their proposed use and is satisfied that they will not be so used. A significant number (but not all) of the other EU Member States also impose this additional WMD end-use control where the exporter merely has grounds for suspicion.

Military end-use

5.7   The Dual-Use Regulation also applies to military end-use controls that prohibit the supply, without a licence, of any items (regardless of whether they are on the EU dual-use control list) that are, or may be intended for, a military end-use in certain countries subject to military embargoes imposed by the UN, the EU or the Organisation for Security and Cooperation in Europe.[14] The relevant countries subject to an arms embargo are: Armenia, Azerbaijan, Belarus, Burma (Myanmar),

---

13   Art 4(1) of the Dual-Use Regulation.
14   Art 4(2) of the Dual-Use Regulation.

Democratic Republic of Congo, Eritrea, Republic of Guinea, Iran, Iraq, Ivory Coast, Lebanon, Liberia, Libya, North Korea, Somalia, Sudan, Syria, and Zimbabwe.

UNILATERAL DUAL-USE CONTROLS (ADDITIONAL UK CONTROLS ON DUAL-USE ITEMS)

5.8 It is possible for EU Member States to supplement the EU dual-use list and controls. For example, for exports outside of the UK, there is a supplemental UK dual-use list under Schedule 3 of the UK Export Control Order 2008. With respect to telecommunications related-exports, the UK supplemental list includes, by way of example, tropospheric scatter communication equipment using analogue or digital modulation techniques and specially designed components, and technology for the 'development', 'production', or 'use' of such goods.

DOCUMENTARY AND RECORD-KEEPING REQUIREMENTS

5.9 Exporters must keep detailed records of relevant exports for a period of at least three years from the end of the calendar year in which the exports took place. Exporters must be able to produce such records to the relevant competent authorities on request. It is particularly important that exporters comply with such record-keeping requirements as it is one of the first areas that an export control authority will audit during a compliance visit.

Member States are entitled to impose additional record-keeping requirements for encryption items. For example, in the UK, controlled cryptographic items are subject to additional record-keeping requirements with respect to the following information:[15]

- a general description of the goods, software or technology, such as might be contained in a product brochure;
- descriptions of all relevant encryption algorithms and key management schemes, and descriptions of how they are used by the goods, software or technology (eg which algorithm is used for authentication, which for confidentiality and which for key exchange), and details (eg source code) of how they are implemented (eg how keys are generated and distributed, how key length is governed and how the algorithm and keys are called by the software);
- details of any measures taken to preclude user modification of the encryption algorithm, key management scheme or key length;
- details of pre- or post-processing of data, such as compression of plain text or packetisation of encrypted data;
- details of programming interfaces that can be used to gain access to the cryptographic functionality of the goods, software or technology; and
- a list of any protocols to which the goods, software or technology adhere.

For intra-EU movements of controlled items, there is also a requirement to include notices in commercial documents (such as invoices, contracts, and dispatch notes) clearly stating that the items are subject to controls if exported outside of the EU. This is intended to put the recipient of the controlled item on notice that a licence is required to export the item out of the EU.

---

15   Schedule 5 to the Export Control Order 2008 (SI 2008/3231).

Licences

5.10   Except for the EU General Export Authorisation, licences are administered and granted at the Member State level. For example, in the UK, licences are granted by the ECO. The key types of export licences available (in the UK) are as follows (although, broadly similar types of licences are made available by other EU Member State authorities):

- *EU General Export Authorisation ('EU GEA')*
  The EU GEAs are administered at the EU level and are available to all exporters across the EU. The original EU GEA covers all items listed in Annex I to the Dual-Use Regulation (with certain exceptions) and is valid throughout the EU. The EU GEA covers exports to destinations in Australia, Canada, Japan, New Zealand, Norway, Switzerland, the United States and Liechtenstein (the eight 'friendly countries').
  In addition, five new pan-EU GEAs came into force as of January 2012. For telecommunication items, there is an EU GEA that covers specific items including certain radio equipment operating in the 1.5 MHz to 87.5 MHz band and optical fibres of more than 500 m in length, for exports to Argentina, China (including Hong Kong and Macao), Croatia, India, Russia, South Africa, South Korea, Turkey, and Ukraine.
- *Open General Export Licence ('OGEL')*
  OGELs allow the export of specific controlled items by any exporter, removing the need to apply for an individual licence, provided the shipment and destinations are eligible and the conditions of the pre-existing licence are met. Most OGELs require the exporter to register with the ECO their intention to use the OGEL and to reference the relevant OGEL on commercial invoices and shipping documentation accompanying the items being exported.
- *Open Individual Export Licence ('OIEL')*
  An OIEL essentially allows multiple shipments of a range of listed goods to specified destinations and/or consignees. An OIEL is issued to a single exporter, who must submit a licence application. To monitor compliance with many OIELs issued each year, the ECO conducts compliance audits of licence holders on a regular basis.
- *Standard Individual Export Licence ('SIEL')*
  The SIEL covers the export of a specified quantity of goods to a single end-user and is the most widely used licence for goods not benefiting from either the EU GEA, an OGEL or OIEL. Again, an exporter must submit a licence application for a SIEL.

Enforcement

5.11   Breach of export controls can result in criminal sanctions as well as civil penalties. As with licensing, enforcement is undertaken at the national level. In the UK, consequences of export control violations include imprisonment (up to 10 years for the most serious offence) and unlimited fines. Where a corporate offence is committed with the consent, connivance, or negligence of a director (including manager, secretary, officer, or other similar role), the individual may also be found guilty (leading to a maximum imprisonment of 10 years). In the UK, there have been cases in the past where companies have received administrative penalties in lieu of prosecution. Such a penalty may, however, be preferable for companies as the details of the violation will not be revealed, thus enabling the company to protect itself from reputational damage. Other risks associated with violating export controls include extradition, disqualification of directors, confiscation orders resulting in seizure of goods, warning letters (for minor infringements), revocation of licences, and refusal of future licences. Needless to say, such consequences can have a significant impact on the operations of the company.

Where a company finds itself to be in breach of export controls, to mitigate the risk of the above penalties, it is advisable to consider making a voluntary disclosure of the breach to the authorities as it could potentially reduce or eliminate the penalty that would have otherwise arisen.

Compliance

5.12   There is a strong expectation from national export control authorities that companies devise and roll out robust compliance programmes and controls to ensure compliance with export controls. The benefit of a good compliance programme is that it can assist exporters to avoid committing violations. The existence of a compliance programme is also taken into account by export control authorities in considering whether to issue generous and broad export licences. Finally, the existence of a strong compliance programme can constitute good mitigation during enforcement action by the authorities.

Little has been published by authorities as to what constitutes a robust programme, other than by the UK authority, whose Export Control Compliance Code of Practice is increasingly seen by EU companies as a good basis to develop a compliance programme. The Code of Practice is not legally binding, but is intended to set a standard for internal compliance procedures and includes examples of best practice.

The Code sets out the following eight areas of compliance focus:

- *Commitment to compliance* Each company should make a firm commitment to comply with export controls. A corporate statement carrying the authority of a senior officer is considered clear indication of the commitment to compliance. This should be drawn to the attention of all employees and a copy made available to the ECO.
- *Identifying responsible personnel* Each company should nominate the company officer responsible for export control issues and notify the ECO accordingly.
- *Information and training* Each company should establish clear procedures for acquiring, keeping and disseminating information on export controls. Training of staff at all levels should be assessed and satisfied.
- *Company compliance procedure* Exporting companies should draw up and operate export control compliance procedures.
- *Awareness of suspicious enquiries or orders* Companies should develop awareness among their employees to help in identifying suspicious orders. Where suspicion arises, companies should consult with the ECO.
- *Record keeping* Companies exporting controlled goods should, as required by export licences, maintain records of all controlled exports for a minimum of three years.
- *Internal audits* Companies should establish a programme of regular internal audit of the system for export control compliance.
- *Integration with quality management practice* Exporting companies should ensure that procedures and practices for dealing with export control regulations are fully integrated with any quality management systems that may apply to them.

Military controls

5.13 Controls on the export of military items are left to each Member State under national law. However, there is a degree of increasing harmonisation at the EU level. For example, there is a non-binding EU Common Military List to which individual Member States increasingly are adhering. A military item is, broadly speaking, any good software or technology that has been specially designed or modified for military use. This is relevant to telecommunications businesses that supply ministries of defence or defence companies.

While EU Member States typically impose a licensing requirement for the export of a military item out of their country (including to other EU countries), the EU has liberalised to a small extent the movement of military items within the EU. Further, certain countries (such as the UK) also impose a licensing requirement on trafficking and brokering of military items between two third countries (for example, certain types of involvement in the movement of the item from India to Brazil).

SANCTIONS

5.14 Sanctions are increasingly used to apply political and diplomatic pressure on countries and regimes. Unlike the United States, which has comprehensive embargos against a number of countries resulting effectively in a blanket ban on doing business in or with those countries (such as Cuba, Iran, Sudan and Syria), the EU does not impose comprehensive embargos (the recent exception was Iraq, but this was in implementation of UN Security Council resolutions). Instead, the EU operates 'smart' sanctions that target those individuals and groups in relation to which there are concerns (rather than targeting the entire country and population), such as those responsible for nuclear proliferation within Iran, or human rights violations in Syria, Sudan, Zimbabwe, and (until recently) Burma/Myanmar.

There is a common sanctions regime that applies directly across all 27 EU Member States. However, the administration of the EU sanctions measures (including, for example, licensing and enforcement) is left to the individual Member States under national legislation. The EU sanctions regime is, broadly speaking, multilateral in that it is based on UN Security Council resolutions imposing sanctions. However, the EU has also adopted unilateral measures beyond the UN regimes, including, for example, against Syria, Zimbabwe and Burma/Myanmar (none of which are currently subject to UN sanctions), and Iran (which, under EU rules, is subject to stricter trading restrictions than is the case under relevant UN Security Council resolutions). It is worth noting that the EU sanctions may be supplemented by national rules. By way of example, in the UK, there are additional restricted/ designated parties (beyond the list of EU designated persons) and the UK also imposes additional banking restrictions with respect to Iran. However, such additional national measures are generally the exception.

Jurisdiction

5.15 As a starting point, it is important to understand who, from a jurisdictional perspective, must comply with EU sanctions. The EU measures have extraterritorial effect and apply to:

- any person who is a national of an EU Member State, even if based outside the EU;
- any legal person, entity or body incorporated or constituted under the law of a Member State (including their non-EU branches);
- any legal person, entity or body wherever incorporated/constituted, with respect to any business done in whole or in part within the EU;
- any person within the EU, irrespective of their nationality; and
- any acts done within the territory of the EU, including its airspace, or on board any aircraft or vessel under the jurisdiction of an EU Member State.

Types of Controls

5.16   Below are some examples of key sanctions controls that are typically included within sanctions measures, including some specific to the telecommunications sector.

Designated person controls

5.17   A key pillar of the EU sanctions regime is a freeze on the 'funds'[16] and 'economic resources'[17] belonging to designated persons within or associated with targeted countries and groups. The EU measures provide for the following:

- a freeze on all funds and economic resources belonging to, owned, held, or controlled by persons, entities and bodies designated by the relevant sanctions programme;
- a ban on making funds or economic resources available, directly or indirectly, to or for the benefit of designated persons; and
- a prohibition on participating, knowingly and intentionally, in activities the object or effect of which is, directly or indirectly, to circumvent the measures above.

The EU list of designated persons comprises lists compiled by the UN sanctions committees and additional lists compiled by the EU for certain regimes. Currently, there is a freeze on funds and economic resources belonging to designated persons that are within, or associated with, the following countries or groups:

---

16   The term 'funds' is very broadly defined to mean 'financial assets and benefits of every kind.' (see, for example, Art 1(l) of Council Regulation (EU) No 267/2012 of 23 March 2012 concerning restrictive measures against Iran and repealing Regulation (EU) No 961/2010 ('Iran Regulation') [2012] OJ L88/1).

17   The term 'economic resources' is broadly defined as 'assets of every kind, whether tangible or intangible, movable or immovable, which are not funds but which may be used to obtain funds, goods or services.' (see, for example, Art 1(h) Iran Regulation).

Afghanistan	Lebanon[18]
Belarus	Liberia
Burma/Myanmar[19]	Libya
Democratic Republic of Congo	North Korea
Egypt	Somalia
Eritrea	Sudan
Republic of Guinea	Syria
Republic of Guinea-Bissau	Tunisia
Former Republic of Yugoslavia/Serbia	Zimbabwe
Iran	Al Qaida
Iraq	Global terrorist groups
Ivory Coast	

Funds transfers

5.18   With respect to Iran, subject to limited exceptions, all transfer of funds to and from an Iranian person that involve an EU financial or credit institution must be authorised in advance by the competent authority (if over €10,000).[20] In the UK, for example, notifications and applications for authorisation must be sent to HM Treasury.

Foreign transfers of funds (ie transfers of funds taking place outside of the EU) can still be caught by the funds transfer controls (although the precise financial thresholds vary). In addition, transfers of funds taking place outside Iran can be caught as the controls apply to transfers to and from 'Iranian persons', a term which is broadly defined to include not only Iranian residents and entities, but also non-Iranian entities owned or controlled by them. The definition of a 'transfer of funds' is very broad, including transfers by both electronic and non-electronic means (eg Banker's Automated Clearing Services ('BACS') payments, payments in cash, cheques, and accountancy orders, and the mere set-off of funds or provision of credit).[21]

Product controls

5.19   Many sanctions regimes also control the supply of certain equipment, technology and software, together with related services, including in the telecommunications and information security sectors. The EU also imposes arms embargos against a number of countries restricting the supply of military items.

In this section, we focus specifically on sanctions against two countries as these also impose product controls relevant to the telecommunications sector.

---

18   Persons have yet to be designated under the Lebanon regime.
19   The Burma/Myanmar designated person regime has currently been suspended (subject to review).
20   Art 30 of the Iran Regulation.
21   Art 1(t) of the Iran Regulation.

- **Iran**

  It is prohibited to sell, supply, transfer or export, directly or indirectly, certain listed items to Iranian persons or for use in Iran, including controlled dual-use telecommunications/information security items.[22] It is also prohibited to export equipment for monitoring Internet and telephone communications. This restriction is motivated by a desire to prevent the Iranian Government from obtaining equipment used to oppress political opponents.

- **Syria**

  Under the Syria sanctions, there are restrictions on selling, supplying, transferring, or exporting, directly or indirectly, certain listed items, including certain telecommunications/information security items to any person, entity or body in Syria or for use in Syria.[23] These include technology and software which may be used for monitoring or interception of Internet or telephone communications, such as items for speaker recognition, radio frequency monitoring, network interception, remote infection and various other telephonic and IT surveillance and monitoring equipment together with related software and technology.

  In addition, subject to the possibility of obtaining a licence, it is prohibited to supply any kind (listed or non-listed) of telecommunications or Internet monitoring or interception services to Syrian public authorities or persons acting on their behalf (in or outside of Syria). This is intended to cover services used to access incoming and outgoing telecommunications and associated data for the purpose of extraction, recording, decoding or other analytical processes.

Enforcement

5.20 As with violations of export controls, enforcement (including applicable penalties) is left to each of the individual EU Member States. Most Member States have criminal sanctions in place for breaches. By way of example, in the UK, a breach of the funds and economic resources freeze can expose those in violation to up to either seven years' imprisonment or an unlimited fine, or both. A breach of relevant trade-related restrictions related to Iran could result in up to either ten years' imprisonment or an unlimited fine, or both.

Bribery compliance

5.21 Another significant corporate compliance risk for telecommunications companies is bribery and corruption. There is currently no general pan-EU anti-bribery legislation. Anti-bribery laws are instead primarily adopted at the national level. In this chapter, we focus, in particular, on the UK Bribery Act 2010, arguably the

---

22 Other restricted items (less relevant to the telecommunications sector) include: goods and technology related to nuclear proliferation, internal repression items and key oil and gas and petrochemicals equipment and technology. It is also prohibited to sell, supply, transfer or export gold, diamonds and precious metals to the Government of Iran and related parties, and banknotes or minted coinage to or for the benefit of the Central Bank of Iran.

23 Other items (less relevant to the telecommunications sector) include: internal repression items, key oil and gas equipment and technology, luxury goods, and equipment and technology for use in electricity infrastructure projects. It is also prohibited to sell, supply, transfer or export gold, diamonds and precious metals to the Government of Syria and related parties, and banknotes or coinage to the Central Bank of Syria.

strictest and most expansive anti-bribery law anywhere in the world. Given the broad jurisdictional scope of the UK law, it is even of relevance to telecommunications companies outside of the UK. We also set out certain OECD anti-bribery initiatives, which many European countries adhere to.

UK BRIBERY ACT

Historical Context and Overview

5.22   On 1 July 2011, the UK's long-anticipated Bribery Act 2010 (the 'Act') entered into force. [24] The Act replaced the UK's existing legislative[25] and common law framework with an integrated and comprehensive regime designed to quell concerns of the OECD[26] and re-brand the UK as a world leader in the fight against bribery and corruption.[27] It is important that all companies, including telecommunications companies, are familiar with the applicable anti-bribery legislative framework.

The Act exceeds the scope of the United States' Foreign Corrupt Practices Act ('FCPA') in that it applies to behaviour in both the public and private/commercial spheres[28] and provides no exemption for 'facilitation payments'.[29] Further, the Act introduces a strict liability[30] offence for commercial organisations that fail to prevent bribery,[31] shifting the onus onto companies to prove they have put in place 'adequate procedures'[32] to prevent their employees, agents, or subsidiaries from engaging in bribery.

Although the introduction of the Act coincided with a general increase in enforcement activity in the UK (under the old regime), to date only one prosecution has taken place under the Act.

Key Features of the Act

General offences

5.23   The Act creates two general bribery offences. The first, under section 1, catches the offering, promising or giving of a financial or other advantage, either

---

24   Full version of the text available at http://www.legislation.gov.uk/ukpga/2010/23/introduction, last accessed on 17 January 2013.

25   The Public Bodies Corrupt Practices Act 1889, the Prevention of Corruption Act 1906 and the Prevention of Corruption Act 1916.

26   See for instance reports of OECD Working Group demanding that the UK rapidly enact 'adequate anti-bribery laws' in October 2008, available at: http://www.oecd.org/daf/ briberyininternationalbusiness/oecdgroupdemandsrapidukactiontoenactadequateanti- briberylaws.htm, last accessed on 17 January 2013.

27   The old legislation and common law continues to apply to offences committed wholly or partly before the Act's entry into force – s 19(5).

28   The FCPA, on the other hand, applies only to the bribery of foreign public officials.

29   Facilitation payments are small payments to public officials in order to ensure that they perform their routine non-discretionary duties either in a timely manner or at all.

30   The FCPA requires either actual knowledge or substantial certainty on the part of a principal that a payment will be made.

31   S 7.

32   Defence in s 7(2) of the Act.

with the intent that such advantage induces a person (not necessarily the recipient) to perform improperly a relevant function or activity or to reward a person for such improper performance,[33] or in the knowledge that acceptance of the advantage would itself constitute improper performance of the relevant function or activity.[34]

The second general offence, under section 2, covers the requesting, agreement to receive, or acceptance of a financial or other advantage, with the intent that a relevant function or activity will be performed improperly as a result (again, not necessarily by the recipient),[35] where such request, agreement to receive or accept-ance in itself constitutes improper performance,[36] where the advantage is requested, agreed to be received or accepted as a reward for improper performance,[37] or where a relevant activity or function is performed improperly in anticipation or as a result of a person requesting or agreeing to receive such an advantage.[38]

The focus of these general offences is on the intent to induce 'improper' conduct,[39] abandoning the old regime requirement that the conduct be 'corrupt'.[40] Under the Act, a relevant function or activity may be deemed to have been performed 'improperly' if it is performed in breach of a relevant expectation or there is an outright failure to perform the function and this failure in itself breaches a relevant expectation.[41]

Relevant expectations are variously defined as an expectation that the function be performed in good faith, that the function be performed impartially, or that a person in a position of trust by virtue of performing the function performs it in accordance with 'any expectation as to the manner in which, or the reasons for which, the function or activity will be performed that arises from the position of trust' (a somewhat circular definition that could be summarised as a person in a position of trust breaching that trust).[42]

The test for assessing whether such expectations have been met is what 'a reasonable person in the United Kingdom would expect' and no concessions are made to local custom or practice unless such custom or practice is 'permitted or required by the written law' of that country. No concession is made to business norms where these are not officially documented or judicially recognised.[43] In essence, the intent is to avoid defendants arguing that the payment of a bribe is a totally acceptable way of doing business under local cultural norms in an emerging country.

Functions or activities caught by the Act include any function of a public nature, any activity connected with a business, any activity performed in the course of a person's employment, and any activity performed by or on behalf of a body of persons (whether corporate or unincorporated).[44]

---

33   S 1(2).
34   S 1(3).
35   S 2(2).
36   S 2(3).
37   S 2(3).
38   S 2(5).
39   Explanatory Notes to the Act, Summary, available at http://www.legislation.gov.uk/ukpga/ 2010/23/notes/division/2, last accessed on 17 January 2013.
40   The term 'corrupt' had no statutory definition and so parties were obliged to rely on inconsistent and unclear case law.
41   S 4(1).
42   S 4(2) in combination with s 3(3)–(5).
43   S 5(2).
44   S 3(2).

The territorial scope of the Act is extensive, applying to conduct both in and outside the UK. In the case of conduct outside the UK, all that is needed for the Act to apply is that the conduct, be it an act or omission, would have been an offence had it taken place in the UK and that the person involved has a 'close connection'[45] with the UK.[46]

Defences available under the Act are limited. A person otherwise guilty of an offence under the Act must prove that his or her conduct was necessary for the proper exercise of a function of the intelligence service or for the proper exercise of a function of the armed forces 'when engaged on active service'. There is no 'carte blanche'; the relevant heads of service will need to have ensured that arrangements are in place to regulate the conduct and the Secretary of State will need to have signed off on these arrangements.

Bribery of a foreign public official

5.24   The Act creates a separate offence, under section 6, to cover bribery of foreign public officials, designed to 'closely [follow] the requirements of the [OECD] Convention on Combating Bribery of Foreign Public Officials in International Business Transactions'.[47]

The offence will catch the offer, promise or giving of a financial or other advantage to a foreign public official ('FPO'),[48] directly or through a third party, with the intent to influence the FPO 'in his capacity as' an FPO and where the offeror intends also to obtain or retain business or an advantage in the conduct of business. Such intent to influence extends also to any omission by the FPO to perform his functions and to any taking advantage of his position as an FPO, even where such use of his position is outside his authority.[49] It is easier to run foul of the FPO offence than the general offences described above in that there is no need to demonstrate improper performance of a relevant function under the FPO offence, merely an intent to influence the FPO.

Again, no offence is committed where the official is either permitted or required by the written law applicable to him or her 'to be influenced' in such a manner – although this is only likely to apply in very limited circumstances.[50]

Liability of officers of the company

5.25   Where it is shown that one of the offences under sections 1, 2 or 6 of the Act is committed by a company (ie payment of a bribe, receipt of a bribe, or bribing an FPO – but not failure by a commercial organisation to prevent bribery), senior

---

45   This is designed to catch British citizens and variants thereon, UK ordinary residents, bodies incorporated under the law of any part of the UK and Scottish partnerships – s 13.

46   S 12(4).

47   Explanatory Notes to the Act, Section 6, cited above at fn 39.

48   Broadly defined in s 6(5) to include any individual holding a legislative, administrative or judicial position of any kind, whether appointed or elected, of a country outside the UK (or any subdivision of such a country or territory); any individual exercising a public function for or on behalf of a country or territory outside the UK (or any subdivision of such a country or territory), or for any public agency or public enterprise of that country or territory (or subdivision); or any individual who is an agent of a public international organisation.

49   S 6(1)–(4).

50   S 6(3) and (7).

officers of the company or persons 'purporting to act in such a capacity' with whose 'consent or connivance' the offence has been committed will also be deemed guilty of the offence, provided that they have a 'close connection' with the UK.[51]

Penalties under the general and FPO offences

5.26 An individual found guilty of the general or FPO offences could be subject either to up to 10 years' imprisonment or an unlimited fine, or both. A company, meanwhile, will be subject to an unlimited fine.[52]

In addition, the Serious Fraud Office ('SFO'), the key UK enforcement authority in this area, can use its powers under the Proceeds of Crime Act 2002 to recover unlawfully obtained property, even without a prosecution.[53]

Further, a commercial organisation found liable for either the section 1 or 6 offences (ie. payment of a bribe or bribing FPOs but not receiving a bribe) will be automatically debarred from competing for public contracts under regulation 23 of the Public Contracts Regulations 2006.[54] The risk of such debarment is therefore of particular relevance to telecommunications companies that are, or are looking to become involved in, public sector contracting. Since entry into force of the Act, the Regulations have been updated so as to specifically refer to these sections of the Act.

Failure by a commercial organisation to prevent bribery

5.27 The cornerstone of the UK's new Act is the section 7 strict liability offence of failure by a commercial organisation to prevent bribery. This offence has caught the attention of the global business community as it can also apply to entities outside the UK, but having some business activities in the UK. It is therefore of relevance not just to domestic (ie UK) telecommunications companies, but also to overseas (non-UK) telecommunications companies that carry on business in the UK.

Under the UK's previous regime, a company could only be convicted for bribery-related offences where a senior officer deemed to be its 'controlling mind' was responsible for key elements of the offence. Under the new Act, commercial organisations are caught where an 'associated person' (broadly an employee, agent or subsidiary performing services on behalf of the commercial organisation[55]) bribes another person with the intent to obtain or retain business for the commercial organisation or to 'obtain or retain an advantage in the conduct of business'.

---

51 S 14.

52 S 11.

53 Full text available at http://www.legislation.gov.uk/ukpga/2002/29/contents, last accessed on 17 January 2013.

54 A company will equally be debarred if a director or any other person who has powers of representation, decision or control over it has been convicted of such an offence. Full text available at http://www.legislation.gov.uk/uksi/2006/5/contents/made, last accessed on 17 January 2013.

55 Contractors, suppliers, Joint Venture entities and Joint Venture partners may also be caught. Per Ministry of Justice Guidance (discussed below), contractually formed Joint Ventures will more likely be deemed 'associated' with the parent than Joint Ventures that are formed as separate entities. Note that there will be a rebuttable presumption that employees perform services on behalf of the commercial organisation – s 8(5).

There is no need for the associated person to have been individually prosecuted. It is sufficient for the prosecution to show that the person 'would be guilty of the offence were that person prosecuted under [the] Act'. Finally, there is no need for the associated person to have any close connection to the UK.[56] For example, if a telecommunications company in the UK has a subsidiary in China, the UK parent company could be liable for any acts of bribery committed by its Chinese subsidiary if the bribe is intended to result in business or a business advantage for the UK parent.

The territorial scope of this offence is extensive, the definition of 'commercial organisation' encompassing bodies and partnerships not only incorporated or formed under the law of any part of the UK but equally 'any other body corporate (wherever incorporated) which carries on a business, or part of a business, in any part of the [UK]' and 'any other partnership (wherever formed) which carries on a business, or part of a business, in any part of the [UK]'.[57] This would encompass, for example, a US-incorporated telecommunications company providing telecommunications services in the UK.

There is a real risk that non-UK companies will be caught as soon as they have any kind of presence (not necessarily physical) in the UK. (Former) Director of the SFO, Richard Alderman, has counselled against taking an excessively 'technical approach' to interpreting the Act and warns that companies with UK subsidiaries should assume that they are caught: '[t]he safe assumption if there are business activities here is that the group will be covered.'[58] Mr Alderman reassures, however, that:

> 'A mere listing [on a UK Stock Exchange] taken by itself with nothing else is unlikely to involve anything in the UK and certainly no economic engagement with the economy of the UK or a demonstrable business presence in the UK'.

Ultimately, it will be for the courts to decide the precise meaning of 'carrying on business in the UK' and, hence, how widely the UK Act applies.

This is consistent with the position in the UK Ministry of Justice Guidance about procedures which relevant commercial organisations can put into place to prevent persons associated with them from bribing ('Ministry of Justice Guidance'), released prior to the Act's entry into force.[59] The Ministry of Justice Guidance explains that the question as to whether a party can be regarded as carrying on a business or part of a business in any part of the UK will be resolved 'by applying a common sense approach' and that the Government anticipates this meaning that 'organisations that do not have a demonstrable business presence in the United Kingdom would not be caught'. A UK listing alone will be unlikely to suffice. Nor will the mere fact that a company has a subsidiary in the UK, given that a subsidiary 'may act independently of its parent or other group companies'.

---

56   S 7(1)–(3); s 8 for meaning of 'associated person'; and Explanatory Notes to the Act, Section 7, cited above at fn 39 on sufficiency that the associated person 'would be guilty' were they prosecuted.

57   S 7 (5).

58   Speech given on 7 April 2011, 'Managing corruption risk in the real world', available at http://www.sfo.gov.uk/about-us/our-views/director's-speeches/speeches-2011/salans—bribery-act-2010.aspx, last accessed on 17 January 2013.

59   Final guidance released on 30 May 2011. Available at http://www.justice.gov.uk/downloads/legislation/bribery-act-2010-guidance.pdf, last accessed on 17 January 2013.

Once jurisdiction is established and a violation by an associated person observed, the commercial organisation's only real option is to invoke the section 7 'adequate procedures' defence. To escape liability, the commercial organisation must prove that it had in place 'adequate procedures designed to prevent persons associated with [it] from undertaking such conduct'.[60] An indication as to what such procedures might consist of is provided in the Ministry of Justice Guidance,[61] discussed in more detail below.

The consequences for businesses found liable under this provision may be severe. For commercial organisations found guilty on indictment, the fine is unlimited,[62] and, as in the case of offences under sections 1, 2 and 6, the SFO can use its powers under the Proceeds of Crime Act 2002 to recover unlawfully obtained property.[63] Discretionary debarment from procurement is also possible, and this risk should be of particular concern to telecommunications companies involved in public sector contracting (although the Government has declined to extend mandatory debarment under the Public Contracts Regulations 2006 to companies convicted of the corporate offence under section 7 of the Act). Kenneth Clarke QC MP, then Minister of State for Justice, said in a written ministerial statement that:

> 'the Government have also decided that a conviction of a commercial organisation under section 7 of the Act in respect of a failure to prevent bribery will attract discretionary rather than mandatory exclusion from public procurement under the UK's implementation of the EU Procurement Directive'.[64]

UK BRIBERY ACT – COMPLIANCE BEST PRACTICE

Overview

5.28   On 30 March 2011, the Ministry of Justice published its final guidance[65] on procedures commercial organisations can put in place so as to minimise the risk of their associated persons implicating them in bribery (the Ministry of Justice Guidance[66] referenced above).

Rather than adopting too prescriptive an approach, or dictating specific policies commercial organisations should adopt, the Ministry of Justice Guidance sets out key outcome-focussed principles. The guidance is followed by an Appendix of case studies intended to apply the principles to hypothetical scenarios (note that the case studies do not form part of the guidance).

---

60   S 7(2).

61   Cited above at fn 59.

62   S 11(3).

63   Full text available at http://www.legislation.gov.uk/ukpga/2002/29/contents, last accessed on 17 January 2013.

64   Ministerial statement available in Hansard at http://www.publications.parliament.uk/pa/cm201011/cmhansrd/cm110330/wmstext/110330m0001.htm, last accessed on 17 January 2013.

65   The Ministry of Justice had initially published draft guidance as early as October 2010, the consultation on which closed in November 2010. The Ministry of Justice ought then to have published its final Guidance in January 2011 but missed this deadline as a result of industry concerns surrounding its drafting. As a result of the delay in publication, entry into force of the Act itself was pushed back, so as to allow companies a three-month implementation window.

66   Cited above at fn 59.

Meanwhile, the Joint Prosecution Guidance, also published on 30 March 2011 by the Director of Public Prosecutions and the Director of the SFO,[67] explains the approach that these two prosecutorial bodies will adopt when deciding whether to prosecute offences under the Act.

The Ministry of Justice Guidance and Joint Prosecution Guidance are therefore of relevance to all companies, including telecommunications companies, wanting to reduce their exposure to bribery risks.

Adequate Procedures

Ministry of Justice Six Principles

5.29   The Ministry of Justice Guidance is centred around six key principles, namely:

- *Proportionate procedures* A commercial organisation's procedures to prevent bribery by persons associated with it are proportionate to the bribery risks it faces and to the nature, scale and complexity of the commercial organisation's activities, and these procedures are clear, practical, accessible, effectively implemented and enforced.
- *Top-level commitment* The commercial organisation's top-level management are committed to preventing bribery by persons associated with it and foster a culture within the organisation in which bribery is never acceptable.
- *Risk assessment* The commercial organisation assesses the nature and extent of its exposure to potential external and internal risks of bribery on its behalf by persons associated with it and this assessment is periodic, informed and documented.
- *Due diligence* The commercial organisation applies due diligence procedures, taking a proportionate and risk based approach, with respect to persons who perform or will perform services for or on behalf of the organisation, in order to mitigate identified bribery risks.
- *Communication (including training)* The commercial organisation seeks to ensure that its bribery prevention policies and procedures are embedded and understood throughout the organisation through internal and external communication, including training, that is proportionate to the risks it faces.
- *Monitoring and review* The commercial organisation monitors and reviews procedures designed to prevent bribery by persons associated with it and makes improvements where necessary.

Adequate procedures – practical examples

In practical terms, adequate procedures might include:

---

67   'Bribery Act 2010: Joint Prosecution Guidance of the Director of the Serious Fraud Office and the Director of Public Prosecutions', available at http://sfo.gov.uk/media/167348/ bribery_act_2010_joint_prosecution_guidance_of_the_director_of_the_serious_fraud_office_ and_the_director_of_public_prosecutions.pdf, last accessed on 17 January 2013.

- a dedicated compliance function in large organisations;
- codes of conduct or ethics;
- specific policies for gifts and hospitality, due diligence of third parties, political contributions and lobbying;
- tailored corruption risk management procedures for higher risk jurisdictions and transactions;
- escalation procedures for high risk business approval and reporting breaches
- employment procedures (eg vetting of new staff);
- training for all relevant staff;
- whistleblowing hotline to report breaches; and
- application of policies and procedures to subsidiaries, joint ventures, agents and business partners as necessary.

Industry concerns – facilitation payments

5.30   As discussed above, one key difference between the UK and US regimes is that, unlike the US FCPA, the UK Bribery Act 2010 makes no exception for 'facilitation payments' (small payments made to a public official in exchange for the performance of a routine non-discretionary duty either more promptly or at all). Such payments were illegal in the UK before entry into force of the Act (although not necessarily prosecuted) and remain illegal under the new regime.

A case study in the Appendix to the Ministry of Justice Guidance suggests a number of practical steps that companies may take when at risk of being asked for such payments. These steps range from the pragmatic (eg building in longer timescales for clearing customs) to the diplomatic (eg 'Use of any UK diplomatic channels or participation in locally active non-governmental organisations, so as to apply pressure on the authorities' of the host country[68]).

Further practical suggestions include contractually requiring any agent company or its staff to, among other things:

- question legitimacy of demands;
- request receipts and identification details of the official making the demand;
- request consultations with superior officials; and
- try to avoid paying 'inspection fees' if not properly due in cash and directly to an official.

Reassuringly, the Ministry of Justice Guidance makes clear that 'the Government does [...] recognise the problems that commercial organisations face in some parts of the world and in certain sectors'. The eradication of facilitation payments is described as:

> '[a] long term objective that will require economic and social progress and sustained commitment to the rule of law in those parts of the world where the problem is most prevalent'.

Although businesses 'have a role to play' in this evolution, the Government appears at pains to suggest that the onus of reforming corrupt business cultures will not be placed on businesses alone.[69]

The SFO, meanwhile, makes explicit that '[t]here is no exemption in respect of facilitation payments.' Interestingly, however, listed among the SFO's '[f]actors

---

68   Case Study 1, Appendix A of the Ministry of Justice Guidance (cited above at fn 59).
69   Paragraph 46 of the Ministry of Justice Guidance (cited above at fn 59).

tending against prosecution' is that the payment is single and small and would be 'likely to result in only a nominal penalty' and/or that '[t]he payer was in a vulnerable position arising from the circumstances in which the payment was demanded.'[70] However, where the authorities decline to prosecute, such payments may still be problematic from the perspective of the money laundering rules.

Industry concerns – corporate hospitality

5.31   Corporate hospitality and promotional expenditure are a commercial reality that few firms, including telecommunications firms, were ready to relinquish on entry into force of the new Act. Concerns were raised over the potential criminalisation of this important relationship tool.

The Ministry of Justice Guidance (together with statements such as that of Kenneth Clarke QC MP in the Foreword of the guidance that 'no one wants to stop firms getting to know their clients by taking them to events like Wimbledon or the Grand Prix') has gone a long way towards reassuring businesses that bona fide hospitality will not be caught by the Act so long as there is no improper conduct on the part of either the host or recipient and the hospitality is not excessive.

Particular care must be taken when entertaining FPOs. Businesses cannot provide financial or other advantages with the intent that the official be influenced in his official role and business or a business advantage be secured thereby. In testing the existence of a connection between the advantage and intent to influence, 'the totality' of (circumstantial) evidence may be taken into account, including potentially 'matters such as the type and level of advantage offered, the manner and form in which the advantage is provided, and the level of influence the particular public official has over awarding the business'. In other words, from lavish hospitality may be inferred an intent to influence. By contrast, the 'incidental provision of a routine business courtesy' (such as provision of airport transfer services, dinner or event tickets) will be unlikely to raise such an inference.

In terms of what firms may legitimately seek to achieve with the use of hospitality and promotional expenditure, a case study in the Appendix to the Ministry of Justice Guidance recommends the following:

> 'that any hospitality should reflect a desire to cement good relations and show appreciation, and that promotional expenditure should seek to improve the image of [the firm] as a commercial organisation, to better present its products or services, or establish cordial relations'.

The Joint Prosecution Guidance confirms that '[h]ospitality or promotional expenditure which is reasonable, proportionate and made in good faith is an established and important part of doing business' and states explicitly that '[t]he Act does not seek to penalise such activity'. Again, lavishness is suggested as a factor that may support an inference of intent to induce or reward improper performance, and other such factors include that 'the hospitality or expenditure was not clearly connected with legitimate business activity or was concealed'.

---

70   Section 6 of the Joint Prosecution Guidance (cited above at fn 67).

ORGANISATION FOR ECONOMIC COOPERATION AND DEVELOPMENT CONVENTION ON COMBATING BRIBERY OF FOREIGN PUBLIC OFFICIALS IN INTERNATIONAL BUSINESS TRANSACTIONS

5.32   The OECD Convention on Combating Bribery of Foreign Public Officials in International Business Transactions ('OECD Convention')[71] has been adopted by all 34 OECD member countries[72] in addition to five non-member countries – Argentina, Brazil, Bulgaria, Russia, and South Africa. Accordingly, the OECD Convention has widespread application across Europe.

The OECD Convention was signed on 17 December 1997 and entered into force on 15 February 1999. Implementation and enforcement are monitored by the OECD Working Group on Bribery in International Business Transactions, through a process of peer review.

The OECD Convention obliges its members to introduce national legislation making it a criminal offence to bribe foreign public officials in international business transactions. It does this by imposing certain standards to be met, rather than dictating precise wording of any provisions.

Signatory nations are required to adopt:

'such measures as may be necessary to establish that it is a criminal offence under its law for any person intentionally to offer, promise or give any undue pecuniary or other advantage [...] to a foreign public official'.

Any complicity in or authorisation of such conduct should similarly be criminalised.[73] Nations are required to ensure, inter alia, that bribery is 'punishable by effective, proportionate and dissuasive criminal penalties', to 'prohibit the establishment of off-the-books accounts' and similar behaviours and to 'provide prompt and effective legal assistance to another [signatory nation] for the purpose of criminal investigations and proceedings' with respect to offences within the scope of the OECD Convention.

The focus is on transnational, active bribery, and the measures adopted will therefore be of particular relevance to multinational telecommunications companies. The soliciting of bribes is not covered, nor are purely domestic/national instances of bribery. Small facilitation payments are not covered – the definition of bribery covers only advantages given 'in order to obtain or retain business or other improper advantage in the conduct of international business', where improper advantage can be taken to mean 'something to which the company concerned was not clearly entitled'.[74]

The definition of foreign public official is broad, covering 'any person holding a legislative, administrative or judicial office of a foreign country, whether appointed

---

71   Full text available at http://www.oecd.org/daf/briberyininternationalbusiness/anti-bribery convention/38028044.pdf, last accessed on 17 January 2013.

72   Australia, Austria, Belgium, Canada, Chile, Czech Republic, Denmark, Estonia, Finland, France, Germany, Greece, Hungary, Iceland, Ireland, Israel, Italy, Japan, Korea, Luxembourg, Mexico, Netherlands, New Zealand, Norway, Poland, Portugal, Slovak Republic, Slovenia, Spain, Sweden, Switzerland, Turkey, UK, United States.

73   Art 1.

74   Commentaries on the Convention on Combating Bribery of Foreign Public Officials in International Business Transactions, Adopted by the Negotiating Conference on 21 November 1997, available at http://www.oecd.org/daf/briberyininternationalbusiness/anti-bribery convention/38028044.pdf, from p 14 onwards, last accessed on 17 January 2013.

or elected; any person exercising a public function or involved in a public agency or public enterprise; and any official or agent of a public international organisation',[75] but private sector corruption is not caught.

The OECD Convention is complemented by a number of ancillary texts:

- Recommendation of the Council for Further Combating Bribery of Foreign Public Officials in International Business Transactions
- Recommendation of the Council on Tax Measures for Further Combating Bribery of Foreign Public Officials in International Business Transactions
- Recommendation of the Council On Bribery and Officially Supported Export Credits
- Recommendation of the Development Assistance Committee on Anti-Corruption Proposals for Bilateral Aid Procurement
- OECD Guidelines for Multinational Enterprises

OTHER KEY BRIBERY CONVENTIONS

Council of Europe Criminal Law Convention on Corruption

5.33   Adopted in November 1998, the Council of Europe Criminal Law Convention on Corruption[76] aims to develop 'common standards' among the Council's 47 member countries and to ensure criminalisation of both active and passive, national and transnational, public sector and private sector bribery and corruption. Accounting offences are covered, corporate liability is encouraged (although this may be civil rather than criminal), and a number of procedural requirements are adopted (for example, among other things, authorities must work together and witnesses must be protected).

An Additional Protocol was signed in May 2003[77] to address bribery involving arbitrators and jurors.

United Nations Convention Against Corruption

5.34   The United Nations Convention Against Corruption ('UNCAC'),[78] adopted on 31 October 2003 and entered into force on 14 December 2005, boasts 140 signatories.

UNCAC is broad in scope. Private sector bribery is caught together with the bribery of public officials, while international assistance, cooperation and information exchange are encouraged including to facilitate the recovery of assets. There is also a focus on prevention, with a requirement that member countries, among other things, develop 'anti-corruption policies that promote the participation of society and reflect the principles of the rule of law, proper management of public affairs

---

75   Art 1(4)(a).
76   Full text available at http://conventions.coe.int/Treaty/en/Reports/Html/173.htm, last accessed on 17 January 2013.
77   Full text available at http://conventions.coe.int/Treaty/en/Treaties/Html/191.htm, last accessed on 17 January 2013.
78   Full text available at http://www.unodc.org/documents/treaties/UNCAC/Publications/Convention/08–50026_E.pdf, last accessed on 17 January 2013.

and public property, integrity, transparency and accountability'[79] and even put in place 'specific training programmes for [...] personnel responsible for preventing and combating corruption'.[80]

European Union Initiatives

5.35   A number of anti-bribery initiatives have also been adopted at the EU level, including, among others:

- First Protocol of the 1995 Convention on the protection of the European Communities' financial interests;[81]
- Second Protocol of the 1995 Convention;[82]
- Convention of 1997 on the fight against corruption involving officials of the European Communities or officials of member states of the European Union;[83]
- Council Framework Decision 2003/568/JHA of 2003 on combating corruption in the private sector;[84]
- Council Decision 2008/852/JHA of 24 October 2008 on a contact-point network against corruption;[85] and
- Proposal for a Directive on the protection of the financial interests of the EU by criminal law, adopted by the Commission on 11 July 2012, with the aim of reinforcing criminal law by establishing minimum sanctions and common definitions in the Member States for crimes against the EU budget.[86]

Finally, as part of the fight against corruption, consideration is currently being given by the EU to introduce pan-EU legislation that would require companies active in certain sectors (including, telecommunications) to fully disclose all payments to national governments, on a country-by-country and project-by-project basis.

---

79   Ch II, art 5.
80   Ch VI, art 60.
81   Full text and details on related documents available at http://europa.eu/legislation_summaries/ fight_against_fraud/protecting_european_communitys_financial_interests/l33019_en.htm, last accessed on 17 January 2013.
82   Ibid.
83   Full text available at http://eur-lex.europa.eu/Result.do?aaaa=1997&mm=&jj=&type= c&nnn=195&pppp=&RechType=RECH_reference_pub&Submit=Search, details on related documents available at http://europa.eu/legislation_summaries/fight_against_fraud/fight_ against_corruption/l33027_en.htm, last accessed on 17 January 2013.
84   Text and details on related documents available at http://europa.eu/legislation_summaries/ fight_against_fraud/fight_against_corruption/l33308_en.htm, last accessed on 17 January 2013.
85   Full text available at http://europa.eu/legislation_summaries/fight_against_fraud/fight_ against_corruption/lf0002_en.htm, last accessed on 17 January 2013.
86   Full text available at http://ec.europa.eu/anti_fraud/policy/preventing-fraud/index_en.htm, last accessed on 17 January 2013.

Part 3
Telecommunication Laws in EU Member States

The Austrian Market for Electronic Communications[1]

Christoph Kerres & Peter Schludermann; updated by Franz-Josef Arztmann and Gregor Klammer
Baker & McKenzie – Diwok Hermann Petsche Rechtsanwälte GmbH, Vienna

LEGAL STRUCTURE

Basic Policy

6.1 The Austrian approach aims to implement the EU Directives into national law, taking into consideration the state, and unique experience, of the Austrian telecommunications sector. Where the EU Directives provide sufficient flexibility to Member States, the Austrian legislation seeks to strengthen the national telecommunications market, in particular with respect to:

- improving the effectiveness of the NRA's decisions;
- creating a modern electronic infrastructure; and
- establishing effective competition with equal opportunities for all national operators.

6.2 While the national market for fixed telephone connections is still heavily influenced by the former monopoly service provider, Telekom Austria AG, competition in the mobile communications sector exists among various national players wielding considerable influence.

Implementation of EU Directives

6.3 A November 2011 amendment[2] to the *Telekommunikationsgesetz* 2003[3] ('TKG 2003' or 'Telecommunications Act 2003') transposed the 2009 Regulatory Package. Under this amendment, the regulator is tasked with implementing new Regulatory requirements into the existing legislative acts and maintaining the set structure.

---

1 Editing of this chapter closed 15 May 2012. The authors gratefully acknowledge the assistance of Mary B Murrow in the preparation of this chapter.
2 BGBl I 2011/102; said legislation amended other laws as well.
3 BGBl I No 70/2003.

Legislation

6.4   The key piece of legislation implementing the EU Directives is the Telecommunications Act 2003 (as amended). The *Bundesgesetz über Funkanlagen und Telekommunikationsendeinrichtungen*[4] also contains various rules on radio equipment and telecommunications terminal equipment. Although they pre-date the EU Directives, these rules are still in force. The Telecommunications Act 2003 grants various national authorities the power to pass regulations regarding the integrity of networks, the interoperability and quality of services, number portability, the provision of value-added services, the quality of the universal service, interconnection, the management of frequencies, numbers and payments for numbers, telecommunications terminal equipment, the surveillance of communication, itemised billing, and the calculation of fees. These regulations provide additional and more detailed rules on the aforementioned topics.

In general, the legislation and transposition of the EU legislation has considerably achieved the goal of enhancing competition in the Austrian telecommunication markets. In particular, competition in the mobile communications market is one of the strongest within the EU. However, in comparison to other Member States, there is a high barrier of entry into the Austrian electronic communication markets, and the basic principle of technology neutrality is not being observed sufficiently.

REGULATORY PRINCIPLES: IMPLEMENTATION OF THE FRAMEWORK DIRECTIVE

Scope of Regulation

6.5   The definitions of 'electronic communication networks' and 'associated facilities' in s 3 of the TKG 2003 are essentially the same as those in the Framework Directive. The Austrian TKG 2003 defines 'electronic communication services' as a 'commercial'[5] service rather than simply referring to remuneration. Due to the technology-neutral approach, various services previously outside the scope of the telecommunications legislation, such as VoIP, that provide access to or from public switched telephone networks and Conditional Access Systems, are now governed by the new regulatory regime.

'Internet Freedom'

6.6   If a website infringes criminal or copyright laws, it may be shut down to end such perpetration. There are, however, no provisions regarding restrictions of Internet access of an end user; implementation of such a provision was not necessary, given that the European Union did not include similar provisions in any directive.

National Regulatory Authorities: Organisation, Regulatory Objectives, Competencies

6.7   There are numerous authorities in Austria vested with powers with respect to the telecommunication sector. These are divided into two branches: communication

---

4   Bundesgesetz über Funkanlagen und Telekommunikationsendeinrichtungen (FTEG), BGBl I Nr 134/2001; amended by BGBl I Nr 25/2002 and BGBl I Nr 133/2005.

5   S 1 (2) Gewerbeordnung 1994 states that a commercial service needs to be recurrent and must be provided independently. Furthermore, it must be intended to make profits.

authorities, and regulatory authorities. The communication authorities include: the Minister[6] of Transport, Innovation, and Technology ('BMVIT'); the Communications Bureaux; and the Bureau of Radio Communications and Telecommunications Terminal Equipment. The regulatory authorities include: the Rundfunk und Telekom Regulierungs-GmbH ('RTR-GmbH'); Telekom-Control-Kommission ('TKK'); and KommAustria.

6.8 The BMVIT (or 'Minister') is the highest-ranking telecommunications authority. The Minister's sphere of influence includes the whole Federal territory. He manages the frequency spectrum allotted to Austria as well as related international contracts.[7] In addition, he may promulgate regulations regarding number portability, universal service provision, fees for the use of communication parameters, terminal equipment, technical equipment for the surveillance of transmissions, quality of service, integrity of networks, reimbursement of costs incurred to comply with data storage requirements, interoperability of services and interconnection.

6.9 Furthermore, the BMVIT hears appeals from decisions of the Communications Bureaux and the Bureau of Radio Communications and Telecommunications Terminal Equipment.[8]

6.10 The Communications Bureaux are set up in the cities of Graz,[9] Innsbruck,[10] Linz[11] and Vienna.[12] They are given 'subsidiary competence', meaning that they have jurisdiction to handle all matters relating to the TKG 2003 that are not explicitly assigned to another authority.[13]

6.11 The Bureau of Radio Communications and Telecommunications Terminal Equipment deals with the approval of radio equipment and telecommunications terminal equipment where this power is not explicitly given to KommAustria.

6.12 The RTR-GmbH has two major duties. First, it acts as an administrative bureau for the Telekom-Control-Kommission ('TKK') and KommAustria. In these matters, the RTR-GmbH is not independent and must follow instructions by the TKK or KommAustria. Secondly, the RTR-GmbH is given authority in all matters that are assigned to the regulatory authorities but are not explicitly[14] assigned to either the TKK or KommAustria.[15] This includes, in particular, the management of numbers, dispute resolution, and the definition of relevant markets. The RTR-GmbH is responsible for the management of numbers. It develops a plan containing further specifications on the various types of numbers[16] and the prerequisites for an assignment. A special procedure for 'vanity numbers' does not exist.

---

6   In Austria, administrative powers are vested in the Minister. The Ministry merely supports the Minister when exercising these powers. Therefore, Austrian laws always refer to the Minister himself and not to the Ministry.

7   S 51 TKG 2003.

8   S 112 TKG 2003.

9   For the provinces of Styria and Carinthia.

10   For the provinces of Tyrol and Vorarlberg.

11   For the provinces of Upper Austria and Salzburg.

12   For the provinces of Lower Austria, Burgenland and Vienna.

13   S 113 (3) TKG 2003.

14   S 117 and S 120 TKG 2003.

15   S 115 TKG 2003.

16   Various types of service may only be used in specific ranges of numbers, e g enquiry services or erotic services.

6.13   The TKK is an independent authority and consists of a council of three members, with one substitute for each member. One member must be a judge, one must possess relevant technical knowledge, and one must possess relevant economic knowledge.[17] The substitute members must have the same qualifications as the primary members.

6.14   The duties[18] of the TKK consist of:

- decisions regarding the provision of data for enquiry services or directories;
- the objection to and approval of general terms and conditions;
- determination of the markets, which operator possesses SMP and which remedies to impose;
- the allocation of frequencies with a limited number of rights to be granted and changes regarding the allocation;
- decisions regarding spectrum trading;
- exercising enforcement powers as named in s 91(3) and s 91(4) TKG 2003; and
- various other duties.[19]

6.15   The TKK is subject to the general rules of procedure in administrative matters[20] with two exceptions:

(i)   after closing an administrative investigation, the parties involved must not produce any new evidence; and

(ii)   dispute resolution procedures are compulsory in various matters,[21] including site-sharing, interconnection, and the making available of data for directory enquiry services and directories.

6.16   KommAustria is a subsidiary[22] of the Federal Chancellery and thus not independent. It deals with all regulatory matters that concern radio and television broadcasting.[23]

6.17   Generally, the exchange of information between authorities is governed by Article 22 of the Austrian Constitution. Concerning the telecommunications sector, S 126 TKG 2003 provides further specifications. The regulatory authorities are entitled to give to the national competition authorities, and to regulatory authorities of other Member States, any information those authorities need to fulfil their duties in matters of mutual interest. If the European Commission demands information via a written and well-founded request, the regulatory authorities must provide such information.[24] Regulatory authorities must treat confidentially any information they receive if the sending authority has designated the information as confidential. S 128 (1) TKG 2003 is similar to Article 6 of the Framework Directive.

---

17   S 118 (1) TKG 2003.

18   S 117 TKG 2003.

19   Applications to the restrictive practices court, decisions with regards to number portability, non-discrimination, access, leased lines, carrier (pre-)selection, and interconnection, calculation of the amount that operators must pay to the Universal Service Fund, and calculation of the financial compensation payable by the Universal Service Fund, decisions regarding security audits, decisions regarding inoperability, decisions regarding the abuse of a value-added service and ban of such.

20   Allgemeines Verwaltungsverfahrensgesetz 1991.

21   S 121 (2) TKG 2003.

22   S 3 (3) KommAustria-Gesetz.

23   S 120 TKG 2003.

24   S 124 TKG 2003.

The BMVIT and the regulatory authorities must give interested parties the opportunity to comment on draft measures within a reasonable period of time. Consultation procedures and their results (excluding confidential information) must be published. Any procedural time limits are inhibited for the period in which comments are permitted.[25] Regarding individual measures, during the time in which comments are permitted, only the cancellation of the application is admissible.[26]

6.18 If the national regulatory authority suspects that a violation of antitrust law may have occurred, it may (after further investigation) bring the matter to the attention of the Restrictive Practices Court.[27] In some cases, it even has the duty to do so.[28]

Right of Appeal against NRA's Decisions

6.19 There are numerous authorities in Austria which may hear appeals. The BMVIT hears appeals against decisions of the Communications Bureaux and the Bureau of Radio Communications and Telecommunications Terminal Equipment. Appeals against decisions of the TKK and the RTR-GmbH[29] may be brought before the Constitutional Court and the Administrative Court.[30] Appeals against KommAustria's decisions are heard by the Federal Communications Senate (or the Independent Administration Senate when concerning 'administrative penal ties').

The NRA's Obligations to Co-operate with the Commission

6.20 In implementing the consolidation procedure, the TKG 2003 keeps close to the wording of Article 7 of the Framework Directive.[31] However, carrier selection, carrier pre-selection, leased lines, and end-user tariffs are not among the topics listed that require the national regulatory authority to cooperate with the European Commission.

'Significant Market Power' as a Fundamental Prerequisite of Regulation

Definition of SMP

6.21 The basic definition of 'significant market power' in S 35 (1) TKG 2003 is essentially the same as in Article 14(2) of the Framework Directive. The Commission Guidelines on market analysis, which further specify the definition of SMP,[32] have been transposed by the TKG 2003, although not with the same wording.

6.22 The Framework Directive's definition of SMP on closely related markets has been transposed to Austrian law in S 35 (5) TKG 2003. By adding 'horizontally, vertically or geographically' it further specifies and clarifies the term 'closely related markets'.

---

25   S 128 (2) TKG 2003.
26   S 128 (3) TKG 2003.
27   S 127 TKG 2003.
28   S 127 (2) TKG 2003.
29   VfGH 28 November 2001, B 2271/00.
30   S 121 (5) TKG 2003.
31   S 129 TKG 2003.
32   See para 1.63 above.

Definition of relevant markets and SMP designation

6.23   The relevant markets are to be defined by the TKK.[33] Since the TKK has not yet defined the relevant markets, the TKMV 2008 regulation issued by the RTR-GmbH is still applicable.[34] These markets are: access services for residential customers to the public telephone network at fixed locations (retail market); access services for non-residential customers to the public telephone network at fixed locations (retail market); physical network infrastructure access (wholesale market); call connection on the public telephone network at fixed locations (wholesale market); call termination on individual public telephone networks at fixed locations (wholesale market); retail leased lines up to 2.048 Mbit/s (retail market); terminating segments of leased lines for low-broadband up to 2.048 Mbit/s (wholesale market); terminating segments of leased lines with broadband greater than 2.048 Mbit/s up to 155.52 Mbit/s (wholesale market); termination on individual public mobile telephone networks (wholesale market); calls for non-residential customers via the public telephone network at fixed locations (retail market); and wholesale broadband market for the provision of connections to non-residential customers.

6.24   If the Regulatory Authorities identify an undertaking as having significant market power, at least one remedy must be imposed on it. The TKK or KommAustria may impose remedies of non-discrimination, transparency, accounting separation, providing access, price control and cost accounting on non-SMP operators to a certain extent.[35] As neither the TKK nor KommAustria is bound by further conditions, they have discretion to impose those obligations on non-SMP operators.

6.25   Following the definition of the relevant markets by the RTR-GmbH, on 20 October 2003, the TKK initiated 61 proceedings[36] to further investigate the markets (with the exception of the national market for international roaming on public mobile networks) as defined by the RTR-GmbH.[37] On 2 May 2005 the RTR-GmbH defined the market of wholesale broadband access to be a relevant market regarding significant market power and initialised the analysis of said market.

6.26   The TKK concluded that Telekom Austria AG has significant market power in several markets. Regarding the relatively strong influence of the former monopolist in these markets, the remedies of allowing carrier selection and carrier pre-selection, the obligation to provide various standard offers, non-discrimination, the approval of prices and price control, service descriptions and terms of business, accounting separation, obligations of access and interconnection, use of the 'Forward Looking Long Run Average Incremental Costs' Method ('FL-LRAIC'),[38] providing a minimum set of leased lines, as well as transparency, were imposed on Telekom Austria AG.

---

33   S 36, 37 TKG 2003.

34   BGBl II 2008/505, last amended BGBl II Nr 468/2009.

35   The NRA may impose remedies to which an operator agreed when it was assigned frequencies during the procedure in s 55 of the TKG 2003, technical conditions that are necessary for the network to remain operational, and remedies that are needed to fulfill international obligations.

36   See http://www.rtr.at/de/tk/EntscheidungenGesamt (accessed 11 December 2012) for the relevant cases.

37   S 117 (6) TKG 2003.

38   The FL-LRAIC Method simulates a competitive market by using either a bottom-up model or a top-down model and calculates the prices on it.

6.27   In general, the TKK effectively supervises the electronic communication market, which is evidenced by the fact that it instigated various procedures to curb misuse of existing significant market power.

NRA's Regulatory Duties concerning Rights of Way, Co-location and Facility Sharing

Rights of way

6.28   The right of way is defined in S 5 (1) TKG 2003 and may include the following privileges, subject to the decision of the RTR-GmbH or an agreement between the parties involved:

- the construction and maintenance of communication lines, as well as ancillary equipment, with the exception of antenna masts;[39]
- setting up cable lines in buildings and other structures;
- the right to operate, renew or extend the use all of the above mentioned; and
- the right to lop single or multiple[40] trees.

The entering of buildings is, with the exception of emergencies, only permitted during daytime and following prior notification.

Importantly, since implementation of the 2009 Regulatory Package, S 3 TKG 2003, addressing communication lines, includes not only firm transmission paths, but also any existing form, above or below the earth. It is not required that the ancillary equipment constitutes a communication line at the time of the construction, but it must be used as such within considerable time.

6.29   Operators of electronic communication networks, whether public or private, are entitled to rights of way concerning public property, including streets, paths, public plazas and the airspace above. Public waters, however, are not included.

6.30   Operators of public electronic communication networks are entitled to rights of way concerning private property on the following conditions:[41]

- the right of way does not oppose public interests;
- the utilisation of the real estate is not (or, at most, only slightly) restricted; and
- no communication line or facility yet exists on the real estate or an already existing facility is to be expanded; or
- a communication line or facility owned by a third party already exists on the real estate but sharing this line or facility is not possible technically or economically, or the owner of the line or facility is not obliged to share his line or facility.

Undertakings to obtain rights of way regarding private property must include negotiations with the owner of the real estate. If the negotiations remain fruitless for four weeks, either party may call upon the RTR-GmbH to resolve the dispute.

---

39   The construction of antenna masts is usually negotiated on a private basis.
40   Cutting clearings into woods is prohibited, unless it is the only possible way to construct a specific communication line and there is no danger to the preservation of the wood.
41   S 5 (4) TKG 2003.

Co-location and facility sharing

6.31   Co-location and facility sharing are governed by S 7 and 8 TKG 2003. This allows public operators to make use of other lines and facilities (eg electric power lines) when setting up communication lines,[42] if by doing so no further restrictions are imposed on the real estate. S 8 TKG 2003 requires operators to share existing communication lines and facilities. It also obliges owners of cable chutes, pipes and buildings to allow the usage of these. These rights may only be exercised if it is technically possible and economically reasonable and the use of public property is impossible or unreasonable. Antennae or power line poles must be shared with providers of publicly available communication networks, fire departments, ambulance and police, if it is technically possible.

6.32   When asked to do so, public operators who possess any rights under S 8 (1) TKG 2003 must make an offer for the sharing of lines and facilities including aerial masts. If the parties cannot agree within four weeks, the RTR-GmbH can be called upon to decide the matter.[43] In cases of facility sharing under S 7 TKG 2003, the RTR-GmbH and KommAustria have issued regulations regarding compensation of the proprietor of the facility.[44]

REGULATION OF MARKET ENTRY: IMPLEMENTATION OF THE AUTHORISATION DIRECTIVE

The General Authorisation of Electronic Communications

6.33   The TKG 2003 allows any person or entity to provide electronic communication networks or services[45] subject only to prior notification.[46] Notification in written form is required in advance and must contain the name of the operator, the legal form of the undertaking, a short description of the network or the service, and the anticipated date of beginning. Failure to do so is punishable by a fine of up to €58,000.

6.34   Within one week after receipt of the notification, the RTR-GmbH must confirm receipt. If it has reason to suspect that no electronic communication network or service is being operated, the RTR-GmbH must engage in further investigations within one week. If it comes to the conclusion that the designated operator does not actually operate an electronic communication network or service, the RTR-GmbH must communicate these findings in an official notification within four weeks, if the operator demands such notification. All notifications or confirmations of the RTR-GmbH must be made available to the public.[47]

---

42   S 7 TKG 2003.
43   S 9 TKG 2003.
44   Telekom-Richtsatzverordnung 2009; Rundfunkrichtsatzverordnung 2009.
45   S 14 TKG 2003.
46   S 15 TKG 2003.
47   S 15 (5) TKG 2003.

Rights of Use for Radio Frequencies

General authorisations and granting of individual rights

6.35 The BMVIT is responsible for the 'overall management' of frequencies in Austria.[48] However, various authorities may assign frequencies, depending on the type of the frequency concerned. These may be assigned for a limited time[49] only. Operators may lose their rights of use granted to them if they do not use the frequency in accordance with the assignment for a period of six months.[50] If a certain frequency is to be used only in connection with radio communications equipment that falls under the general licence[51] of the BMVIT, then no further assignment is needed.

6.36 If an undertaking decides to apply for a specific frequency, it must submit an application to the appropriate authority, ie the TKK, the Communications Bureau or KommAustria. Rights of use for radio frequencies that are destined to be used for radio or television broadcasting are granted by KommAustria. This is usually done in the form of a 'beauty contest'.[52] If KommAustria wishes to assign any frequency that is not intended to be used for radio and television broadcasting, the approval of the BMVIT is needed. KommAustria must decide on the allocation within six weeks after receipt of the application. This period may be extended by eight months if KommAustria is applying a selection procedure.[53]

Admissible conditions

6.37 To fulfil the objectives of the TKG 2003 and the European Directives, the granting of rights to use frequencies may contain various conditions:[54]

- the declaration of the intended use of the frequency, the type of network and technology used, including exclusive uses of frequencies;
- conditions that are necessary to ensure the effective and efficient use of frequencies, including coverage and start of operation, or such that must be imposed due to other technical reasons or international agreements;
- temporal limitations; and
- conditions regarding spectrum trading.

Limitation of number of rights of use to be granted

6.38 The BMVIT may decide,[55] for certain frequencies, to limit the number of rights of use to be granted[56] and has done so on various occasions. Those

---

48   See para 6.7 above.
49   The period of time must be reasonable, see S 54 (11) TKG 2003.
50   S 54 (12) TKG 2003.
51   Verordnung des Bundesministers für Verkehr, Innovation und Technologie, mit der generelle Bewilligungen erteilt werden (BGBl II No 542/2003; last amendment BGBl II Nr 436/2010).
52   S 10 ff Private Radio Act and s 12 ff Private Television Act.
53   S 54 (5) TKG 2003.
54   S 55 (10) TKG 2003.
55   It lies in the discretion of the BMVIT to decide which frequencies should be affected by the limitation and whether or not they are to be handed down to the TKK for assignment.
56   S 52 (3) TKG 2003 and s 4a Frequenznutzungsverordnung, BGBl II Nr 307/2005 amended last in BGBl II Nr 436/2010.

frequencies are named in the Frequency Usage Ordinance (*Frequenznutzungsverordnung 2005*).[57] Rights to these may be granted by the TKK.[58]

6.39   After public notification by the TKK regarding the availability of a frequency band, the rights to it are then awarded via auction. The TKK will exclude from the auction all undertakings whose applications are incomplete or differing from the conditions set out by the TKK. The TKK then assigns the frequencies in question to the operator who is able to comply with the general prerequisites[59] set out by the TKK and who is best able to make efficient use of the particular frequency. The most efficient use of the frequency concerned is decided on the basis of the operators' bids. The auction must be fair, non-discriminatory and economic.

6.40   Rights to frequencies that have not been named in the Frequency Usage Ordinance, and that are not radio frequencies, are granted by the Communications Bureaux. Whoever first applies for a frequency is awarded the right to use it.[60]

Spectrum trading

6.41   Spectrum trading regarding frequencies assigned by the TKK or Komm-Austria[61] is possible in Austria but, to do so, the prior approval of the RTR-GmbH is required.[62] Both the technical impact as well as the effect on competition must be considered by the RTR-GmbH. The request of the operator and the decision of the RTR-GMBH must be made available to the public. If the frequency is assigned by the TKK, a mere notification is required.[63]

6.42   Furthermore, the TKK must approve any substantial restructuring regarding the ownership of undertakings that were given rights to frequencies according to S 55 of the TKG 2003.

Rights of Use for Numbers

General authorisations and granting of individual rights

6.43   Numbers may be assigned to operators, in blocks of several thousand units, or to users by the RTR-GmbH after formal application.[64] The RTR-GmbH must decide on the application within three weeks after its receipt. Further administration of these blocks is at the discretion of the operator. However, assignees must comply with any conditions[65] imposed on them by the RTR-GmbH and by the TKG 2003. Failing to do so may result in the loss of the right of use.

---

57   BGBl II Nr 307/2005 amended last in BGBl II Nr 436/2010.
58   All previous and future auctions can be found on the website of the RTR-GmbH, www.rtr.at (last accessed 10 December 2012) .
59   S 55 (2) and (10) TKG 2003.
60   S 74 and s 81 TKG 2003.
61   Depending on the type of frequency, either the TKK or the KommAustria would be competent.
62   S 56 TKG 2003.
63   S 56 (4) TKG 2003.
64   The exact procedure is set out in a special regulation of the BMVIT: Kommunikationsparameter-, Entgelt- und Mehrwertdiensteverordnung 2009, BGBl II Nr 212/2009, latest amendment: BGBl II Nr 333/2010.
65   This mainly includes conditions to guarantee the effective and efficient use and conditions that are needed to comply with international agreements.

6.44   The RTR-GmbH's assignment of numbers to operators and users includes the right to use these numbers. They do not, however, gain any property rights from such assignment.[66]

Admissible conditions

6.45   When assigning numbers, the RTR-GmbH may impose the following conditions:[67]

- naming of the type of service for which the assigned numbers may be used;
- time limits;
- conditions that are necessary to maintain the effective and efficient use of numbers; and
- conditions that are necessary to comply with international obligations.

6.46   Undertakings with significant market power must provide the possibility of carrier selection and carrier pre-selection for their subscribers. Remuneration for these services must be cost-oriented. Obligations to provide carrier selection and carrier pre-selection with regard to networks other than public communications networks at fixed locations may be imposed on the same conditions as granting access and interconnection.[68]

Limitation of numbers of rights of use to be granted

6.47   The number of rights of use for numbers and other communication parameters are not limited unlike the number of rights of use for frequencies.

The NRA's Enforcement Powers

6.48   S 90 TKG 2003 grants the RTR-GmbH, the TKK, KommAustria and the BMVIT the power to demand information from operators of communication networks or services. They are permitted to gather information that is needed to monitor compliance with the TKG 2003 and they may obtain information for statistical purposes. In addition, operators of electronic communication services are further obliged to provide administrative authorities with specific information[69] on their subscribers if those subscribers are under suspicion of having committed any administrative crimes by means of a public telecommunications network.

6.49   If the TKK or KommAustria finds an undertaking to violate the TKG 2003, or legal notices and regulations based thereon, the relevant authority notifies the undertaking and gives it an opportunity to remedy the shortcomings or provide a reply within a certain period of time.[70] If the undertaking fails to comply, the RTR-GmbH orders it to do so via official notice. If the undertaking does not comply with the notice either, the RTR-GmbH may suspend the right to provide

---

66   S 66 TKG 2003.
67   S 65 (4) TKG 2003.
68   S 46 (3) and s 41 TKG 2003.
69   This information is limited to name, surname, academic title, address, subscriber number and other contact information, information on the contract with the subscriber and his financial soundness.
70   S 91 TKG 2003.

communication networks or services or revoke any rights of use for frequencies or numbers. If the undertaking's failure to comply poses a serious threat to public safety, security, or health, or causes serious economic or operational problems for other operators or users of communication networks or services, the TKK or KommAustria may issue an injunction.[71]

6.50 The Communications Bureaux monitor the infrastructure[72] used by operators. To do so, they may enter buildings and conduct searches. Furthermore, the Communications Bureaux may execute any measures necessary to protect any telecommunications equipment from interference caused by other telecommunication equipment. These measures must avoid unnecessary costs and need to be appropriate with respect to the circumstances concerned.[73] Any telecommunications equipment that is being operated without authorisation may be put out of operation by the Communications Bureaux without prior warning. Telecommunications equipment that violates the TKG 2003 in any other way may only be put out of operation if this is necessary to maintain or restore the unhindered traffic of communications.

Administrative Charges and Fees for Rights of Use

6.51 Undertakings that are granted rights of use for radio frequencies must pay a monthly fee ('*Frequenznutzungsgebühr*') for this permit.[74] Furthermore, the undertaking usually must pay a remuneration ('*Frequenznutzungsentgelt*') as proposed in its application for the frequency. If rights of use for frequencies are allocated without any remuneration the undertaking must pay a non-recurring fee ('*Zuteilungsgebühr*').

6.52 The BMVIT sets fees for the allocation of numbers.[75]

REGULATION OF NETWORK ACCESS AND INTERCONNECTION: IMPLEMENTATION OF THE ACCESS DIRECTIVE

Objectives and Scope of Access Regulation

6.53 Access and interconnection are seen by the Austrian legislator as a way to stimulate competition and help the smooth the functioning of the Austrian telecommunications markets. The legislator also takes technical standards and the interests of users into consideration.

6.54 While various obligations concerning the access to electronic communication networks may only be imposed on operators with significant market power, all operators of public communication networks are obliged to engage in negotiations concerning interconnection.[76]

---

71 S 91 (4) TKG 2003.
72 This includes, but is not limited to, networks, radio equipment, and telecommunications terminal equipment. See s 86 et seq TKG 2003.
73 S 88 (1) TKG 2003.
74 S 82 TKG 2003.
75 Kommunikationsparameter-, Entgelt- und Mehrwertdiensteverordnung 2009, BGBl II Nr 212/2009, latest amendment: BGBl II Nr 333/2010.
76 S 48 TKG 2003.

Basic Regulatory Concepts

6.55   The definitions of 'access' and 'interconnection' are essentially the same as in Article 2 of the Access Directive. For the definition of interconnection, the term 'operators' has been used instead of 'parties'.

6.56   If two or more operators of publicly available communication networks desire interconnection between their networks, they must first negotiate.[77] If negotiations between operators remain fruitless for six weeks, each operator may turn to the TKK or KommAustria for a decision. In deserving situations, the TKK or KommAustria may initiate proceedings without request from the operators.[78] This gives the competent authority some discretion regarding the imposition of remedies.

Access and Interconnection-related Obligations with Respect to SMP Undertakings

6.57   After one or more undertakings have been identified as having significant market power, the TKK or KommAustria may impose on them the obligations defined in articles 9 to 13 of the Access Directive at its own discretion.[79] These are obligations concerning:

- transparency;
- non-discrimination;
- accounting separation;
- access to and use of specific network facilities; and
- price control and cost accounting.

6.58   To maintain transparency, an undertaking with significant market power may be ordered to provide information on its accounting, technical specifications, characteristics of its network, conditions of use, and tariffs.[80]

6.59   Non-discrimination may be achieved by ordering the undertaking to provide its services under the same conditions to other undertakings that provide similar services.[81] Furthermore, an undertaking with significant market power may be ordered to issue a standard offer regarding its services.

6.60   Regarding access to networks and their facilities, the regulatory authority may order the undertaking to provide access to its network and permission to use its facilities for other undertakings.[82] This also includes the interconnection of networks and network facilities.

6.61   When imposing price control obligations, the regulatory authority may order the undertaking to charge cost-oriented prices, taking into account an adequate rate of return.[83] In addition, the regulatory authority may issue conditions regarding the method of cost accounting.

---

77   S 48 TKG 2003.
78   S 50 (2) TKG 2003.
79   See para 6.22 above.
80   S 39 TKG 2003.
81   S 38 TKG 2003.
82   S 41 TKG 2003.
83   S 42 TKG 2003.

6.62   In order to achieve accounting separation, the regulatory authority may determine the accounting method and its format used by an undertaking with significant market power.[84]

6.63   The TKK has imposed a number of these obligations on undertakings with significant market power.[85] For various markets,[86] the TKK ordered Telekom Austria AG to offer services to joint undertakings and to all undertakings that provide similar services on the same market under the same conditions, and with the same quality the company provided to itself. This also included the provision of various standard offers with specific minimum content. To prevent unauthorised cross-subsidisation, the TKK required Telekom Austria AG to keep records of the costs and profits for each market separately from its other products. Notably, since none of the mobile operators until now have succeeded in gaining significant market power, there are only very few decisions addressed to mobile operators. These few decisions concern the area of pricing of telephone calls between different providers.[87]

Related Regulatory Powers with Respect to SMP Undertakings

6.64   Undertakings with significant market power must provide the possibility of carrier selection and carrier pre-selection for their subscribers. Remuneration for these services must be cost-oriented. The RTR-GmbH may impose the obligation to provide carrier selection and carrier pre-selection with regard to networks other than public communications networks at fixed locations on the same conditions as granting access and interconnection.[88]

6.65   To comply with Annex VII of the Universal Service Directive, S 44 (1) TKG 2003 prescribes the general principles of non-discrimination, cost- orientation, and transparency[89] for the provision of leased lines by an undertaking with significant market power. Tariffs and general terms and conditions of such undertakings regarding leased lines must be approved by the TKK.

6.66   The TKK and KommAustria may impose on an operator with significant market power remedies regarding access in addition to those named in the TKG 2003.[90] Before doing so, however, the TKK, must request the Commission's permission.

Regulatory Powers Applicable to All Market Participants

6.67   To a limited extent, the TKK and KommAustria may impose on non-SMP operators the remedies of non-discrimination, transparency, accounting separation, provision of access, price control, and cost accounting. The RTR-GmbH may impose remedies already announced in the course of the frequency award procedure according to S 55 TKG 2003; technical conditions that are necessary for the

---

84   S 40 TKG 2003.
85   See decisions of the TKK: M1/03, M2/03, M3/03, M6/03, M7/03, M8a/03, M8b-k/03, M10/03, M12/03, M13/03 and M15a-e/03.
86   See decisions of the TKK: M1/03, M2/03, M7/03, M8a/03, M10/03, M12/03 and M13/03.
87   See decisions of the TKK: M13a/06 – M13f/06.
88   S 46 (3) and s 41 TKG 2003.
89   These terms must be interpreted with the help of Annex VII Universal Service Directive.
90   S 47 (1) TKG 2003.

network to remain operational and remedies that are needed to fulfil international obligations may also be imposed. As S 47 (2) TKG 2003 does not name any further prerequisites, the decision whether to impose obligations on non-SMP operators, is in the discretion of the regulator. The regulator, however, still must conduct the consolidation procedure, where applicable.

REGULATION OF UNIVERSAL SERVICES AND USERS' RIGHTS: THE UNIVERSAL SERVICE DIRECTIVE

Regulation of Universal Service Obligations

Scope of universal service obligations

6.68 S 26 TKG 2003 defines the scope of obligations that are imposed on universal service providers.[91] They are essentially the same as the ones named in the Universal Service Directive[92] with minor differences: access to emergency numbers for end users is not mentioned among the provisions. As every end-user must have access to emergency numbers, the Austrian legislator did not mention this provision in S 26 TKG 2003 but made it an obligation for all operators.[93] Special services for disabled users as stated in Article 7 of the Universal Service Directive are not mentioned in the TKG 2003 either. However, the Universal Service Ordinance (*Universaldienst-Verordnung* (UVD)) provides further specifications concerning the obligations of universal service providers.[94]

6.69 The regulatory authorities have no discretion regarding the imposition of these obligations on universal service providers. Universal service providers are required by law to abide by them.

Designation of undertakings obliged to provide universal services

6.70 At least every five years, the BMVIT with the assistance of the RTR-GmbH, must invite operators to tender offers to become universal service providers. The BMVIT then must choose the operator that needs the smallest contribution to provide universal services.[95] If only one operator fulfils the operational conditions required to become a universal service provider, and most likely is able to provide universal services, the BMVIT chooses that operator without prior invitation to tender offers. If no operator makes an offer for providing the universal services, the BMVIT may choose the operator most suited for the task.

6.71 To date, the former monopolist Telekom Austria AG remains the universal service provider. The BMVIT is obliged to review at least every five years whether or not the prerequisites for an invitation to tender are met.[96]

---

91   See para 6.73 below.
92   See para 1.174 above.
93   S 20 TKG 2003.
94   The UVD requires universal service providers to comply with Austrian Standards Institute standards 1600 and 1601 when setting up publicly available telephone equipment. These standards contain conditions with respect to accessibility for disabled persons for the building of structures.
95   S 30 (1) TKG 2003.
96   S 133 (9) TKG 2003.

Regulation of retail tariffs, users' expenditures and quality of services

6.72   The obligations for universal service providers in Annex I Part A Universal Service Directive have been transposed into Austrian law with some differences. The free selective barring for outgoing calls[97] and the obligation to provide itemised billing are not limited to universal service providers alone; they are imposed on all operators of telecommunication services.[98] In addition, all bills must contain information on the possibility of reviewing the bill and on how to contact the operator. At the request of the subscriber, itemised billing must be provided in writing free of charge. Therefore, it is seen as sufficient to provide itemised billing by electronic means, ie the Internet, unless the subscriber wishes otherwise. The RTR-GmbH has the authority to provide further details on which information is required on bills.

6.73   Furthermore, the TKK must approve all prices and general terms and conditions of universal service providers for universal services.[99]

6.74   If a subscriber fails to pay a bill by the due date, the telecommunication services operator may not interrupt the service[100] unless the operator has sent a reminder informing the subscriber about the possible penalties[101] for his or her non-payment and giving him or her at least two weeks to comply. Universal service providers must follow even stricter rules. In addition, they may not interrupt the universal service because of a delay in payment in respect of other contractual relationships with the same subscriber.

6.75   The quality of the universal services is specified in S 27 TKG 2003. The BMVIT has authority to further specify the details mentioned there. The BMVIT may even suspend the obligation to provide publicly available telecommunication devices.[102]

6.76   Universal service providers are required to publish information on their performance regarding the provision of universal service once a year. The RTR-GmbH is permitted to review the performance of the universal service providers and compare it to the information provided.

6.77   If a universal service provider 'severely' fails to comply with the provisions concerning quality of service,[103] the TKK must notify the BMVIT. The BMVIT may then initiate a tendering procedure under S 30 TKG. However, the TKG 2003 does not define 'severe' in this context.

Cost calculation and financing of universal services

6.78   Effective costs relating to universal services may be refunded upon request if they could not have been avoided and are considered an undue burden.[104] If the universal service provider's market share of the relevant market exceeds 80 per cent, the request for a refund is not permissible.

---

97   S 29 (2) TKG 2003.
98   S 100 TKG 2003.
99   S 26 (3) TKG 2003.
100   S 70 TKG 2003.
101   Eg the interruption of the service.
102   S 27 (2) TKG 2003.
103   S 27 (3) TKG 2003.
104   S 31 TKG 2003.

6.79   If deemed necessary,[105] the RTR-GmbH may establish a Universal Services Fund[106] to compensate universal service providers. All operators of telecommunication services whose annual turnover exceeds €5 million must pay a certain amount to the Universal Services Fund depending on their market share. To date, no Universal Service Fund has been established.

Regulation of Retail Markets

Prerequisites for the regulation of retail markets

6.80   S 43 TKG 2003 implements the principle that regulation of retail services is permissible only if regulation at wholesale level does not achieve the regulatory objectives. Except for the market of international telephone services provided at a fixed location for residential customers, the former monopolist Telekom Austria AG has significant market power in all retail markets. Therefore, various remedies have been imposed on Telekom Austria AG.

6.81   Obligations that may be imposed on undertakings with significant market power include the prohibition to demand excessive prices, to hinder the entry of new competitors in the market, to engage in predatory pricing, to unduly favour groups of end-users, and to bundle services without justification. Furthermore, the regulatory authority may impose appropriate measures to maintain upper limits for end-user prices or to control certain tariffs. Format and type of the cost accounting system of the undertaking may be determined and inspected by the regulatory authority. The TKK has imposed such obligations on various occasions.[107] As an undertaking with significant market power, Telekom Austria AG is obliged to submit its general terms and conditions to the TKK for prior approval. Furthermore, Telekom Austria AG's subscriber tariffs must be cost oriented.

End User Rights

Contracts

6.82   Operators of telecommunication networks or services are obliged to use general terms and conditions which provide specific information on the operator, its services, the duration of the contract, the means of dispute resolution, rules regarding compensation, the intervals of billing, the European emergency number, and details on the prices.[108] Additionally, operators must provide an interactive cost control tool.[109] Operators of television or radio networks, and operators that are transmitting radio or television signals, are only required to provide limited information in their general terms and conditions.[110] Universal service providers, however, must provide additional details.[111] The general terms and conditions, as well as any changes to such terms and conditions, must be brought to subscribers' and the TKK's attention. Within eight weeks of the announcement of the general

---

105   Ie if one or more universal service providers apply for refunds.
106   'Universaldienstfonds'.
107   See decisions of the TKK: M1/03, M2/03, M3/03 and M6/03.
108   S 25, 25b TKG 2003.
109   S 25a TGK 2003.
110   S 25 (8) TKG 2003.
111   S 26 (4) TKG 2003.

terms, the TKK may object to the general terms and conditions that do not comply with any provision of the TKG 2003, S 6 and 9 of the Consumer Protection Act, or S 864a and 879 (3) of the Civil Code. Universal service providers must obtain the TKK's approval to use new general terms and conditions.[112] The same obligation may be imposed on operators with significant market power. For other operators, the TKK only has the right of objection (mentioned above) to the general terms and conditions.

6.83   If the changes made to the general terms and conditions do not solely benefit the subscriber, he or she must be notified at least one month in advance before the changes may take effect. During this time, the subscriber has the right to terminate the contract free of charge.[113]

6.84   Operators of public telecommunication services are obliged to conclude contracts with subscribers concerning their services. However, they only need to do so under their own general terms and conditions.[114] That way, operators may still exclude individuals from telecommunication services by means of implementing a check of creditworthiness in their general terms and conditions.

6.85   Besides filing a complaint at court, users, operators, and entities that represent their interests, may take disputes to the relevant regulatory authority. These disputes might in particular cover quality of service, payment, or alleged violations of the TKG 2003. For matters concerning radio and television broadcasting, the relevant regulatory authority is KommAustria; in other matters, the relevant regulatory authority is RTR-GmbH.[115] Operators must co-operate in the process of dispute resolution and provide the regulatory authority with all information and documents it requires to assess the dispute and provide a solution.

6.86   The regulatory authority will try to work out a solution that upon which both parties agree. If the parties are not able to agree to an amicable solution, the regulatory authority will offer a recommendation on how to solve the dispute. This recommendation, however, is not binding on the parties, and the parties may file a complaint after, or even during, the dispute resolution procedure.

6.87   The dispute resolution mechanism regarding the correction of bills (except with respect to radio and television broadcasting) consists of two steps:[116]

(i)   if a subscriber doubts the correctness of a bill, he or she may request the operator to re-inspect it; and

(ii)   the operator then must issue a written confirmation or change the incorrect bill accordingly.

6.88   If the operator and the subscriber are not able to come to an agreement, either party may involve the RTR-GmbH. The disputed amount will not be due until the dispute resolution procedure is finished. The parties are not bound by the RTR-GmbH's decision, as either one can appeal to the court within a certain time period. If the RTR-GmbH decides that the disputed bill was correct from the beginning, then the operator may demand the subscriber to pay interest for the period of time the due date was postponed.

---

112   S 26 (3) TKG 2003.
113   S 25 (3) TKG 2003.
114   S 69 (1) TKG 2003.
115   S 122 TKG 2003.
116   S 71 TKG 2003.

Transparency obligations

6.89   Beside the obligation to use general terms and conditions with the contents mentioned above, other rules in the TKG 2003 aim to accomplish transparency. S 17 (1) TKG 2003 compels operators of public telecommunication services (except with respect to the transmission of radio signals) to provide comparable, adequate, and current information regarding the quality of their services. The BMVIT may provide more detailed rules on the exact type of information and the means of its publication.[117] The RTR-GmbH may inspect the information.

6.90   S 24 TKG 2003 grants the RTR-GmbH authority concerning the transparency of tariffs. The RTR-GmbH has the discretion to publish rules on the numbers usable for value-added services, their prices, the method of calculation and the means of informing the subscribers of the tariffs.[118] The RTR-GmbH must provide rules that allow the adequate protection of users and the transparent provision of value-added services. S 24 (2) TKG 2003 states the control of access regarding specific groups of users, the provision of time limits, rules on dialler programmes, and rules on advertisement as examples of measures the RTR-GmbH may take. Furthermore, the RTR-GmbH must keep names and addresses of operators of value-added services in a public register.

Quality of Service: securing 'Net Neutrality'

6.91   S 17 (3) TKG 2003 authorises the RTR-GmbH to issue regulations to assure a certain standard of quality of services of public communication networks. The Commission of the EU must be notified and may amend the regulation prior to its issuance. Until now, the RTR-GmbH has not issued such a regulation.

Obligations facilitating change of provider

6.92   S 23 TKG 2003 stipulates that operators of fixed and mobile networks are obliged to provide number portability to their subscribers. The NRA issued a regulation regarding number portability, to ensure portability even within one day.[119] The specific type of use of the number may not be altered, however. Location portability of geographical numbers is possible only within the area for which the number was first assigned. Operators are prohibited from charging 'deterrent fees' when providing number portability.

DATA PROTECTION: IMPLEMENTATION OF THE E-PRIVACY DIRECTIVE

Confidentiality of Communications

6.93   Under S 95 (1) TKG 2003, providers of publicly available electronic communication services are obliged to take measures as described in S 14 of the Data Protection Act ('DSG') to ensure the safety of personal data. These measures must

---

117   Such a regulation was only released concerning the universal provider: Universaldienstverordnung, BGBl 1999/192, last amendment BGBl 2006/400.
118   S 24 (1) TKG 2003.
119   Nummernübertragungsverordnung – NÜV, BGBl II 2012/48.

prevent the processed data from being destroyed illegally or accidentally, and ensure that processed data is safe from accidental loss as well as unauthorised access.

6.94   Whenever there is a particular risk of a breach of confidentiality,[120] the provider of publicly available electronic communication services must inform the subscriber; where the risk lies outside the scope of the measures to be taken by the provider, it must inform the subscriber of possible remedies and related costs.

6.95   Providers, and all individuals that assist in the providers' operations, must keep confidential traffic data, location data, and content data (including such data regarding unsuccessful connections).[121] Interception, recording, and any other surveillance of communication; and the traffic, or location data connected to it, are generally prohibited, unless the TKG 2003 explicitly grants the right to process specific kinds of data.[122]

6.96   S 93 (3) TKG 2003 grants exceptions concerning the storage and tracing of emergency calls, investigations concerning harassing calls,[123] the technical storage necessary to transmit communication and the consent of all users involved. In addition, providers of publicly available communication services must provide[124] the technical means to permit the surveillance of telecommunications[125] under the Rules on Criminal Procedure ('StPO').

6.97   Communications that have been intercepted unintentionally must be deleted or destroyed by other means;[126] any other use is prohibited.

Data Retention

6.98   The Data Retention Directive was transposed by amending the TKG 2003,[127] the StPO and the SPG (Security Police Act), after considerable political struggle. These amendments have been in force since 1 April 2012 and are currently being challenged by the province of Carinthia due to alleged breaches of constitutional rights.

Traffic Data and Location Data

6.99   The definitions of the terms 'traffic data' and 'location data'[128] are the same as in the E-Privacy Directive.[129]

---

120   The TKG 2003 chooses not to use the term 'breach of security of the network', but uses 'breach of confidentiality' instead.
121   S 93 TKG 2003.
122   This mainly applies to operators who need to process various types of data regarding their subscribers to provide their services.
123   S 106 TKG 2003.
124   S 94 TKG 2003.
125   Under the StPO, the surveillance of telecommunications requires an order from a criminal court.
126   S 93 (4) TKG 2003.
127   BGBl I 27/2011, for a comprehensive presentation of the amendment see: Tschohl, *Datensicherheit bei der Umsetzung der Vorratsdatenspeicherung in Österreich* (Vienna, 2011).
128   S 92 (3)(4) and 92 (3)(6) TKG 2003.
129   See Art 2(b) and (c) E-Privacy Directive.

6.100   Generally, the storage of traffic data is prohibited unless stated otherwise.[130] Any traffic data must be deleted or anonymised by the provider immediately after the termination of the connection.

6.101   Traffic data that serves the purpose of subscriber billing and the payment of interconnection fees, however, must be stored by the provider and deleted three months after payment. If the bill is challenged, payment not made, or the bill disputed, the traffic data must be stored for the entire period of such proceedings. In this case, operators must provide the decision-making entity with all the necessary traffic data.

6.102   When transposing Article 6(5) of the E-Privacy Directive, the TKG 2003 adds the 'removal of interference' to the list of activities that may be pursued when processing traffic data.[131] This was deemed necessary to provide a secure service and allow the operator to fulfil its contractual obligations. The Austrian legislator, in particular, took into consideration the log files of Internet access providers, as specific information relating to connection is often required to resolve connectivity problems.

6.103   Generally, location data other than traffic data may not be processed unless it is anonymised or the user or subscriber has given consent[132] to the processing. The user or subscriber may withdraw consent at any time. In addition, providers of emergency call services may process and demand location data from providers in case of emergency.[133] The BMVIT is entitled to issue a regulation regarding further details.[134]

6.104   The TKG 2003 does not mention the specific obligations of operators to inform users and subscribers on the processing of location data as provided for in Article 9(1) of the E-Privacy Directive. However, all providers of publicly available communication services, and jointly its operators, are obliged to inform their users and subscribers of the personal data they process, the reason and means of the processing, and how long the personal data will be stored.[135] Additionally, the users have certain rights under the Data Protection Act 2000 (DSG 2000).

Itemised Billing

6.105   Operators must provide itemised billing as long as the subscriber does not object.[136] When concluding the contract, the subscriber must have the right to choose whether itemised billing will be supplied in writing or electronically. Called party numbers are to be anonymised except where the complete number is needed to determine the tariff or the subscriber agrees in writing to inform all present and future users thereof. The RTR-GmbH may issue regulations on the exact form and detail of the bill. The RTR-GmbH has issued a regulation on the exact form and details of itemised billing.[137]

130   S 99 (1) TKG 2003.
131   S 99 (3) TKG 2003.
132   S 102 (1) TKG 2003.
133   S 98 TKG 2003.
134   S 98 (5) TKG 2003; none issued yet.
135   S 96 (3) TKG 2003.
136   S 100 TKG 2003.
137   Einzelentgeltnachweisverordnung 2011 – EEN-V 2011: BGBl. II Nr. 414/2011.

Calling and Connected Line Identification

6.106   Users of publicly available communication services are granted the same rights[138] regarding the presentation and restriction of calling and connected line identification as provided in Article 8(1)–(4) of the E-Privacy Directive. The restriction of the identification of the calling party must be possible generally, or for each call individually, free of charge. However, emergency calls must be identifiable at all times.

Automatic Call Forwarding

6.107   Subscribers must be given the opportunity to suppress automatic call forwarding from third parties to their terminal free of charge.[139]

Directories of Subscribers

6.108   Subscribers must be given the opportunity to decide whether their personal data will be included in a publicly available directory.[140] Furthermore, they must be permitted to verify, correct, or delete their entry. The option of not entering a subscriber's personal data, as well as entering in a directory a subscriber's name, academic title, address, number, and profession, must remain free of charge. Other information may be entered, if the subscriber wishes to do so, albeit not free of charge. Moreover, subscribers may opt out of being entered into electronic directories that permit a more detailed search than just by name. The subscriber must be informed of his rights in an appropriate manner.

6.109   Providers may use the information on subscribers provided in this way solely for the use of publicly available telephone services.[141] In particular, the creation of electronic profiles, or the sorting of subscribers into categories by the provider, unless categories are necessary for the publication of the directory, are prohibited. In addition, all providers are obliged to take measures designed to prevent the duplication of their electronic directories.

---

138   S 104 TKG 2003.
139   S 105 TKG 2003.
140   S 69 TKG 2003.
141   S 103 (1) TKG 2003.

The Belgian Market for Electronic Communications[1]

Updated by Daniel Fesler and Elisabeth Dehareng on the basis of a text originally authored by Arne Gutermann
Baker & McKenzie, Brussels

LEGAL STRUCTURE

7.1 Belgium is a federal state divided into three economic areas and three cultural areas. The economic areas (the 'regions') are the Flemish, Walloon and Brussels-Capital Regions. The three cultural areas (the 'communities') are the Flemish, French, and German-language Communities. At the federal, regional and community level, there are legislative authorities. A description of the Belgian telecommunication regulatory regime is complex because some aspects of telecommunications law in Belgium are organised at the federal and others at the community level.

Basic Policy

Regulatory approach and market conditions

7.2 Prior to 1998, the Belgian telecommunications market was almost entirely controlled by Belgacom, the former incumbent. On 1 January 1998, the Belgian telecommunications market was liberalised consistent with European legislation.[2] Despite this liberalisation, Belgacom continues to control the majority of the market, but pressure on its dominant position is increasing now that saturation of the market has almost been reached.

7.3 *Fixed telephony*: While the markets for business and long-distance calls[3] have become highly competitive, Belgacom remains the principal provider of fixed

---

1   Editing of this chapter closed on 15 December 2012.
2   The Act of 19 December 1997 modifying the Act of 21 March 1991 on the Reform of Certain Public Enterprises in order to make the Regulatory Framework compliant with the Obligations of Free Competition and Harmonization of the Telecommunications Market as laid down in Decisions of the European Union, that entered into force on the 1st of January 1998.
3   As opposed to the market for residential and local calls.

telephony. Alternative operators, however, raised their market share to 31 per cent in 2011.[4]

7.4   *Mobile telephony*: Mobile penetration has significantly increased in recent years. Currently, the penetration rate is estimated at 114 per cent. The market share of the leading cell phone operator, Belgacom's subsidiary Proximus[5], decreased to 40.6 per cent in 2011. Its competitors are Mobistar (30.6 per cent), KPN Group, Belgium-Base (26.8 per cent) and Telenet (2 per cent)[6].

7.5   *Broadband and internet*: The penetration rate for the Belgian broadband market was approximately 32.4 per cent at the end of 2011. In the fixed broadband market, the historical operator, Belgacom, is competing with cable operators, as well as with alternative operators offering broadband based on FWA (Fixed Wireless Access) or on the basis of Belgacom's wholesale DSL products. At the end of 2011, Belgacom's market share was 41.6 per cent, while cable operators owned 47.1 per cent of the market share, and alternative operators owned 11.3 per cent.[7]

At the end of 2011, at least 30 per cent of the fixed broadband subscribers benefited from a download speed of 30 Mbps or more.

7.6   *3G coverage:* At the end of 2011, three operators have 3G networks in Belgium, whose coverage is above 85 per cent of the population, in accordance with applicable requirements. 3G penetration in Belgium stood at 19 per cent of the population at the end of 2011[8].

Implementation of the Revised EU Telecom Package of 2009

7.7   Belgium is one of the countries that did not meet the 25 May 2011 deadline for implementation of the 2009 EU Regulatory Package, ie the Better Regulation Directive, the Citizen's Rights Directive and the BEREC Regulation.

7.8   To date, the process for implementing the 2009 EU Regulatory Package in Belgium has made very good progress. The Act of 13 June 2005 on Electronic Communications was recently amended by the Act of 10 July 2012 containing Various Provisions in the Field of Electronic Communications, implementing Directives 2009/140/EC and 2009/136/EC[9].

Legislation

7.9   With respect to telecommunications, the Electronic Communications Act, as amended (notably by the Act of 10 July 2012), implements the bulk of the 2009 EU

---

4   The source of this market information is: BIPT, 'Situation du secteur des communications électroniques 2011', available at http://www.ibpt.be/FR/189/ShowDoc/3788/Rapports_annuels/Situation_économique_du_secteur_des_télécommunicat.aspx last consulted on 15 December 2012.

5   Belgacom's subsidiary is incorporated under the name Belgacom Mobile SA, but delivers its services under the trade name Proximus.

6   BIPT, 'Situation du secteur des communications électroniques 2011', above, p 14.

7   BIPT, above, p 17.

8   BIPT, above, p 23.

9   This Act amends four existing acts, specifically, the Act of 17 January 2003 on the Status of the Regulator for the Belgian Post and Telecommunications Sectors (the 'BIPT Act'), the Act of 11 March 2003 on Certain Legal Aspects of Information Society Services, the Act of 13 June 2005 on Electronic Communications, and the Act of 6 April 2010 on Market Practices and Consumer Protection.

Regulatory Package. It is supplemented by royal and ministerial implementation decrees, and will be further supplemented with additional ones.

7.10   There are two additional legislative acts related to telecommunications, the most important of which is the Act of 17 January 2003 on the Status of the Regulator of the Belgian Post and Telecommunications Sector (the 'BIPT Act'), which was also amended (again notably by the Act of 10 July 2012). The BIPT Act establishes and governs the organisation, competences and procedural rules of the Belgian Institute for Post and Telecommunications ('BIPT') and sets out its regulatory objectives. In addition, the Act of 17 January 2003 on Remedies and Dispute Settlement governs remedies against BIPT decisions and the settlement of certain disputes between operators.

7.11   The sector is also regulated by decisions, resolutions and recommendations of BIPT (with respect to telecommunications) and by recommendations, decisions and rules of the broadcasting authorities (with respect to radio and television broadcasting).

7.12   A Code for Telecommunication Ethics was adopted by Royal Decree of 9 February 2011, and mainly addresses services payable through telecommunications. A Commission for Telecommunication Ethics is responsible for monitoring compliance with the Code and imposing fines and other sanctions in case of violations.

REGULATORY PRINCIPLES

Scope of Regulation

7.13   The scope of the Electronic Communications Act, which is a federal act, is limited to telecommunications, while broadcasting aspects are dealt with by the Broadcasting Decrees of the various communities.[10]

7.14   The division of competences between the federal level and the communities are also reflected in the wording of the definitions of 'electronic communications network' and 'electronic communications service' in the Electronic Communications Act, which are substantially similar[11] to the definitions in the Framework Directive 2002/21/CE, but explicitly exclude any use of such networks or services for the transmission of broadcasting signals.

---

10   See the coordinated Decree of the French Community of 26 March 2009 on Audiovisual Media Services, as notably amended by the Decree of 1 February 2012 adapting the Decree of 26 March 2009 and implementing into Belgian law Directive 2009/140/EC and Directive 2010/13/EU (the 'French Broadcasting Decree'); and the Decree of the Flemish Community of 27 March 2009 relating to Radio Broadcasting and Television, as recently amended by the Decree of 13 July 2012 modifying the 2009 Decree and implementing into Belgian law the Directives 2009/139/EC and 2009/140/EC and 2010/13/EU (the 'Flemish Broadcasting Decree'), as well as the Decree of the German-language Community of 27 June 2005 on Audiovisual Media Services and Cinematographic Representations, as amended in 2009 and 2012.

11   Notwithstanding some minor differences in the wording, the definitions have the same meaning as the definitions in the Framework Directive.

'Internet Freedom'

7.15   Belgium has not enacted any specific regulation on internet freedom or net neutrality[12] save to state, under article 3 of the Electronic Communications Act, that the provision of electronic communication networks or services is free, except as provided by the law. There is no legal requirement in terms of net neutrality and a draft bill to enact that principle has not made any progress in the Parliament so far.

7.16   On the user's side, there is no specific regulation dealing with restrictions to internet access in case of, e g copyright violations. A draft bill had been filed before the Parliament in early 2010 that would have created a system similar to the one enacted in France under the so-called HADOPI Act and would have foreseen graduated sanctions up to time-limited access barring. In 2011, a second draft bill of the same kind was filed with the new Parliament in parallel with a draft bill that would create a global licence. Both are being examined by the Senate but there is no indication yet as to which of them could be enacted, if any. As the governmental agreement of the current coalition does not give any hint as to the approach the federal executive branch would support, it is doubtful that either solution will be adopted during the current legislature (ending in June 2014).

Regulatory Authorities: Organisation, Regulatory Objectives, Competencies

Telecommunications

Regulatory body and independence

7.17   As noted above, the regulatory authority in Belgium for telecommunications is the Belgian Institute for Post and Telecommunications, or 'BIPT'.

Tasks and competencies

7.18   Under the BIPT Act and the Electronic Communications Act, as amended, the BIPT's tasks include, among other things:[13]

- to ensure that all legislation and regulations regarding electronic communications and telecommunications are observed;
- to advise the Minister regarding the policy the federal government wishes to pursue in telecommunications;
- to assist the Minister in the preparation of legislation regarding telecommunications;
- to manage the national numbering space and radio frequency spectrum; and
- to resolve conflicts between providers of networks, services, and equipment, specifically with respect to interconnection, special access, and shared use.

7.19   To this end, BIPT has been entrusted with powers to impose sanctions upon offenders and to take administrative actions (such as the approval of interconnection tariffs). The BIPT has some discretion in the exercise of these powers.

---

12   See also para 7.127 below.
13   Article 14 § 1 BIPT Act.

7.20   As with other Belgian administrative bodies, the BIPT is subject to rules with respect to the formal motivation (ie justification) of administrative acts,[14] the public nature of administration,[15] and confidentiality.[16] In addition, article 19 BIPT Act offers every person directly and personally involved in a decision of the BIPT the possibility of being heard in advance of such decision. The BIPT is required to send a draft of a decision to interested parties, with an invitation to communicate any comments by a specified date. Interested parties may also be invited to formulate comments during a meeting. Decisions of the BIPT must be published on its website.

Consultation procedures

7.21   To assist in carrying out its functions, the BIPT is entitled to request from any interested party any useful information and may organise an inquiry or public consultation. This right is codified in the BIPT Act[17] as well as in the Electronic Communications Act.[18]

7.22   With respect to individual inquiries, the Electronic Communications Act further specifies that the BIPT's requests for information should be justified and proportionate to the performance of its tasks. The requests should also mention the timeframe for the submission of the requested information.

7.23   If the BIPT intends to adopt a decision that may have a significant impact on a particular market, it must organise a prior public consultation.[19] The consultation procedure must take place within a maximum time frame of two months, and the results must be made available to the public without prejudice to the confidential nature of certain business information. The BIPT has conducted consultations on several topics over the past years.

Relationship with national competition authority

7.24   Article 14 § 2.3, BIPT Act requires the BIPT to cooperate, notably, with the EU Commission, ENISA, the Office and BEREC, as well as other national regulatory bodies, including the Belgian competition authorities. Apparently, the cooperation between the BIPT and the Belgian Competition Council[20] was reported as not going very smoothly in the past, with the main reason being a lack of specific rules and procedures for cooperation.

7.25   The general obligation to work closely with national regulatory authorities as well as the EU Commission and BEREC has been recaptured in article 7 Electronic Communications Act. A concrete example of cooperation can be found in Article 138 Electronic Communications Act, which requires the BIPT to respond positively to any justified request for information of the EU Commission or of any other national regulatory authority, provided it is necessary and proportionate to the accomplishment of their missions.

---

14   Act of 29 July 1991 on the Formal Motivation of Administrative Acts.
15   Act of 11 April 1994 on the Public Nature of the Administration.
16   Article 23 § 3 BIPT Act in conjunction with Article 6 §1, 7° of the Act of 11 April 1994 on the Public Nature of the Administration.
17   Article 14 § 2, 2° BIPT Act.
18   Articles 137 and 139 Electronic Communications Act.
19   Article 140 Electronic Communications Act.
20   'De Raad voor Mededinging'/'Le Conseil de la Concurrence'.

The Electronic Communications Act[21] also provides that, for a series of decisions the BIPT contemplates adopting, a prior consultation procedure with the Belgian Competition Council must take place. This procedure will apply when the BIPT wishes to impose, maintain, or modify certain obligations on SMP undertakings, such as obligations of non-discrimination, and transparency, among others. The Belgian Competition Council's opinion will no longer be required if it fails to deliver an opinion within 30 days following the sending by BIPT of its draft decision.

DISPUTE RESOLUTION POWERS

7.26   In the event of a dispute between operators of electronic communications networks, services, or equipment, the disputing parties may request that the BIPT provide the operators with proposals to resolve the dispute. The BIPT must provide the operators with such proposals within one month from receipt of all required documents by the BIPT.

7.27   Furthermore, the Belgian Competition Council is responsible for the settlement of disputes between operators in relation to interconnection, leased lines, special access, full unbundling, and shared access.[22] The BIPT is also involved in this procedure to the extent that it must assist the Competition Council in the investigation of the dispute. The BIPT is equally responsible for enforcing the decisions of the Competition Council for this type of dispute. The Competition Council must render its decision within a period of four months, it being understood that, where the parties are involved in a reconciliation procedure under the direction of BIPT, the procedure before the Competition Council is suspended.

Broadcasting

7.28   The regulators of the communities are responsible for supervising the market of broadcasting services.

7.29   The Flemish Regulator for Media (Vlaams Regulator voor de Media ('VCM')) oversees the Flemish broadcasting market. This body is the official Flemish regulatory authority (for broadcasting only) pursuant to the Flemish Broadcasting Decree. Its main tasks are to issue licences for broadcasting and to ensure observance of the regulatory framework. To this end, it has powers to impose fines or other sanctions. The VCM is also responsible for conducting market analyses of the broadcasting market. The advisory competence, however, is mainly assigned to the Flemish Council for Culture, Youth, Sport and Media (Raad voor Cultuur, Jeugd, Sport en Media).

7.30   The High Council for the Audiovisual Sector of the French Community (Conseil Supérieur de l'Audiovisuel de la Communauté Française ('CSA')) is the broadcasting regulator of the French Community. The CSA is composed of two colleges – the Advisory College, and the Licence and Supervision College ('LSC'). While the Advisory College is responsible for advising authorities of the French Community, the LSC has substantially the same role as VCM in Flanders.

---

21   Article 55 §§ 4 and 4/1 Electronic Communications Act.
22   Article 4 of the Act of 17 January 2003 on Legal Remedies and Disputes Settlement.

7.31 Pursuant to the German Broadcasting Decree, the Media Council ('Medienrat') is the broadcasting regulator of the German-language Community. It has the same overall powers and tasks as its fellow regulators of the other communities.

7.32 The federal state structure requires that a separate broadcasting regulator be appointed for the 19 municipalities of the Brussels-capital district. The federal legislator has entrusted the BIPT with the supervision of the Brussels broadcasting market, with the French speaking and Dutch speaking broadcasters being monitored by the CSA respectively the VCM.

Convergence

7.33 The Belgian Constitutional Court[23] resolved that any mixed infrastructure, ie networks which can be used for both telecommunication and broadcasting services, requires cooperation between the federal state and the communities. Therefore, on 17 November 2006, the federal state and the communities adopted a cooperation agreement relating to mutual consultation in the elaboration of a legislation on electronic communications networks, for exchange of information and for the exercise of competences with respect to electronic communications networks by regulatory authorities in charge of telecommunications and radio and television broadcasting.

Right of Appeal against NRA's Decisions

7.34 The Act of 17 January 2003 on Legal Remedies and Dispute Settlement introduced a right of appeal against the BIPT's decisions before the Court of Appeal in Brussels. Any person affected by a decision of the BIPT (including the Minister of electronic communications) may submit an appeal. Such an appeal does not suspend the BIPT's decision. The procedure takes the form of summary proceedings but, unlike in short proceedings where only temporary measures are followed, the Court of Appeal rules on the merits of the case. The competence of the Court of Appeal in Brussels for this type of dispute is exclusive. Therefore, an appeal against BIPT decisions cannot be brought to the highest administrative tribunal, the State Council ('Raad van State'/ Conseil d'Etat') in parallel with, or after, an appeal to the Brussels Court of Appeal.

7.35 To date, no special appeal procedures have been introduced at the community level. As with any administrative decision for which no special appeal procedure exists, the decisions of Community regulators can be challenged before the State Council by any person directly and personally affected by such a decision. The State Council may annul such a decision. In addition, any legal action related to acts of the BIPT which do not qualify as a decision (such as, among other things, advices) can be brought before the State Council.

The NRA's Obligations to Cooperate with the Commission

Consolidation procedure

7.36 The general principles of the consolidation procedure (as set forth under Article 7 of the Framework Directive 2002/20/EC) for telecommunications have been implemented by articles 141–143 Electronic Communications Act.

---

23   Decision of the Constitutional Court of 14 July 2004.

7.37 If the BIPT intends to take measures regarding market definitions and analysis, access and interconnection, obligations for SMP operators (or exceptionally non-SMP operators),[24] which may affect trade between or among Member States, it will consult with the European Commission, BEREC, and the other NRAs by submitting a draft decision to them. The BIPT must take into account the comments of these bodies within the month of such notification. The BIPT must communicate final decisions to the European Commission and BEREC.

7.38 If the European Commission so requests within the initial one-month period, the BIPT must wait an additional two months before adopting its decision where the draft measure:

- may affect trade between or among Member States and tends to identify a relevant market other than those already identified by the European Commission, or tends to designate an operator as having (or not having), either individually (or jointly with others) SMP; and
- may, from the perspective of the European Commission, create a barrier to the single market or be contrary to Community law.

If the European Commission requests the withdrawal of the amendment of the draft measure the BIPT must comply with such request within six months.

7.39 If, within the initial one-month period, the European Commission notifies the BIPT that its draft measure tending to impose, modify or withdraw obligations on an SMP operator would create a barrier to the single market or is likely to be contrary to Community law, the BIPT must wait an additional three months before adopting its decision. During those three months, BIPT, the European Commission, and BEREC collaborate to identify the most efficient and appropriate measure with respect to articles 5–8 Electronic Communications Act, taking utmost account of economic stakeholders' opinion and of the necessity to create coherent regulatory measures.

If, within the first six weeks of the three-month period, BEREC delivers an opinion on the Commission's notification indicating that it shares the same doubts with respect to the compatibility of the draft measure with single market or Community law, the BIPT may, before the three-month period expires:

- amend or withdraw its draft measure taking utmost account of the Commission's notification together with BEREC's opinion and advice; or
- maintain its draft measure.

If BEREC does not deliver an opinion or does not share the Commission's doubts as to the draft measure's compatibility with the single market or Community law, or if the BIPT decides to amend or maintain its draft measure, the European Commission may, within one month following the three-month period:

- issue a recommendation requiring the BIPT to amend or withdraw the draft measure ; or
- decide to lift its reservations to the draft measure.
- Within one month following the Commission's decision (or more if the BIPT wishes to organise a public consultation on the draft measure), the BIPT must communicate its final decision to the European Commission and BEREC.

---

24 Obligations can only be imposed on non-SMP market players in order to comply with international obligations and to ensure end-to-end connections.

If the BIPT decides not to amend or withdraw the draft measure notwithstanding the Commission's recommendation, it must provide a reasoned justification. The BIPT may, at any stage of the procedure, withdraw its draft measure.

7.40   Temporary measures within the meaning of article 20 BIPT Act are exempted from the consolidation procedure. This provision considers temporary[25] any measures taken by the BIPT in cases of violation of articles 9, 11, 18, 51, 55, 56 or 64 Electronic Communications Act (or their implementation measures) that create an immediate and serious threat to public safety, public security, or public health, or create serious economic or operational problems for other providers or users of electronic communications networks or services, or other users of the radio spectrum.

7.41   The general principle of the consolidation procedure has also been set out in the Broadcasting Decrees, but only in connection with decisions regarding market definition and analysis as well as obligations for SMP operators.

'Significant Market Power' as a Fundamental Prerequisite of Regulation

Definition of SMP

7.42   Under the Electronic Communications Act, an operator is considered as having a 'Significant Market Power' where;

> 'individually or jointly with others, he is in a position equivalent to dominance, ie he is able to behave, to an appreciable extent, independently of his competitors, his customers, or consumers'.

Undertakings with SMP on one market may also be deemed to have SMP on closely related markets where links between the two markets allow leveraging of market power.[26]

7.43   The Broadcasting Decree's definition of SMP is similar to that in the Electronic Communications Act.

Definition of relevant markets and market analysis

7.44   Pursuant to articles 54 to 56 Electronic Communications Act, the BIPT must define and analyse the relevant markets, taking into account the Commission's guidelines on market analysis, its recommendation on relevant markets, and principles of competition. The public consultation and consolidation procedures[27] are applicable to market analyses.

7.45   If, on the basis of the market analysis, it appears that a market is not effectively competitive, the BIPT must identify the SMP undertakings in that market and impose on them appropriate regulatory obligations, maintain or modify existing obligations. Exceptionally, BIPT may also impose obligations on undertakings which do not have a significant market position within the meaning of the Electronic Communications Act (article 56 § 1).

---

25   The decisions must not be effective beyond a period of three months. This period, however, may be extended by three months, in circumstances where enforcement procedures have not been completed.

26   Article 55 § 3 Electronic Communications Act.

27   See paras 7.21–23 and 7.36–7.41 above, respectively.

NRA's Regulatory Duties concerning Rights of Way, Co-location and Facility Sharing

Rights of way

7.46   In Belgium, the granting of rights of way to network providers has been subject of extensive constitutional debate as to the respective and diverging competences of the Belgian federal government (telecommunications) and the communities (broadcasting) on the one hand, and the regions (public domain) on the other hand. This is due to the fact that rights of way relate to the use of public land on which the networks are installed and such land is within the exclusive competence of the regions. Therefore, the federal government, the communities and the regions all claim (partial) competence for granting rights of way.

7.47   As a result of this debate, installation of telecommunications networks (including rights of way) were left out of the Electronic Communications Act to leave room for further negotiations among the federal government, the communities, and the regions. To date, a cooperation agreement has not been reached. Until such agreement is reached, the old regime of the Act of 1 March 1991 on the Reform of Certain Public Enterprises continues to apply.

7.48   Rights of way have also been regulated in the Flemish[28] and French[29] Broadcasting Decrees. On the basis of these decrees, providers of cable networks have the right to install cables and relevant equipment on public land if they comply with the laws and decrees regarding the public domain, and respect its purpose. Prior to exercising such right, a cable company must submit to the authority responsible for the particular public land information with respect to the location and the cable planning. In general this will be a municipality. In Flanders this authority must decide within two months of the request whether it will authorise the contemplated work. Municipalities in the French Community have three months to reach a decision.

Under both regimes, the relevant authority may also propose amendments to the planning. In addition, providers of cable networks have the right to affix cramps and braces on façades and to install cables over open land or without fixings on private property. In such an event, the work cannot be started until the owners of the property and the tenants are notified. The cable company is responsible for ensuring the competent installation and maintenance of its network. Any damage caused by the installation and exploitation of the cable networks must be compensated by the provider.

Co-location and facility sharing

7.49   Article 25 Electronic Communications Act provides that, in order to protect the environment, public health and public security, or for reasons of town and country planning, and to the extent possible, operators must install antennae on existing sites. Operators who own an antennae site must allow the use of such site by other operators in a reasonable and non-discriminating manner, for which they are entitled to receive compensation to be approved by the BIPT. A database of

---

28   Article 200 of the Flemish Decree.
29   Article 98 French Broadcasting Decree.

antennae sites is managed by the BIPT, with all relevant information to facilitate the evaluation of antennae sites for the purpose of maximal shared use.[30]

7.50   The Flemish Broadcasting Decree also addresses the issue of co-location and facility sharing in a way similar to the Electronic Communications Act.[31]

REGULATION OF MARKET ENTRY: IMPLEMENTATION OF THE AUTHORISATION DIRECTIVE

The General Authorisation of Electronic Communications

7.51   Under the Electronic Communications Act, conditions for undertakings to enter the telecommunications[32] market are significantly simplified. Where, before 2005, a licence was necessary to provide telecommunication networks or telecommunication services, since 2005 an undertaking need only notify the BIPT. Notification must be in the form of a registered letter mentioning the full details of the applicant, its contact person, a succinct description of the networks or services intended to be offered, and the intended commencement date of the activities. A notification form is available on the BIPT website. The BIPT subsequently confirms the notification and enters the notifying party in a public register. The BIPT also informs the operator that it has the right to make an application for the installation of facilities and to negotiate and receive access.

Notifying the BIPT is not required where the provision of telecommunications networks or services:

- does not cross the public domain;
- is exclusively intended for a legal entity in which the provider has a majority holding; or
- is indented for a natural person or a legal entity, provided that the contract simply covers telecommunications networks or services provided on an accessory basis and for support purposes.[33]

7.52   Only in exceptional circumstances (for example, public security, public health, public order, or state defence, among others) may a Royal Decree restrict or even prohibit for a certain period of time the right[34] to provide telecommunications networks and services.[35]

7.53   However, the fact that the provision of networks and services is in principle free does not mean that market entry is not subject to conditions.[36] The Belgian legislator has, in this respect, opted to follow the same approach as the Authorisation Directive, and adopted conditions along the lines of that Directive.

7.54   The community broadcasting decrees mainly focus on the free provision of cable networks subject to the conditions set out in them. Prior notification is

---

30   Article 27 Electronic Communications Act.
31   Article 200 § 1/1, Flemish Broadcasting Decree.
32   The Electronic Communications Act mentions 'electronic' networks and services but, due to the exclusive competence of the communities for broadcasting, 'electronic' must be read as 'telecommunication'.
33   Article 9 §§ 5 and 6 Electronic Communications Act.
34   Article 3 Electronic Communications Act.
35   Article 4 Electronic Communications Act.
36   Article 3 Electronic Communications Act.

required under both the Flemish Broadcasting Decree and the French Broadcasting Decree.[37] In Flanders, a cable company is required only to notify the VCM. A cable network provider in the French Community must notify LSC.

Rights of Use for Radio Frequencies

Granting of individual rights

7.55   The BIPT is responsible for the management of radio spectrum in Belgium. This task covers both the daily management of frequency allocations and the coordination and long-term policy on frequency and readjustment plans. While the BIPT is not responsible for planning broadcasting frequencies, its frequency department does handle day-to-day coordination requests and the application of international agreements that distribute frequencies at international level.[38] This task is particularly important and complicated considering Belgium's small size and the associated issues of overlapping frequencies with neighbouring countries.[39]

To optimise the use of the spectrum and to avoid harmful interference, the BIPT collaborates with the communities, the other NRAs, and the European Commission for the planning, coordination and harmonisation of the use of radio spectrum in the European Community. To this end, the BIPT must take into account, among other things, freedom of expression and economic, security, sanitary and public interest matters.

Principles of frequency allocation, procedural rules

7.56   Because spectrum is considered a scarce resource, the use of radio frequencies in Belgium continues to be subject to the grant of individual user rights rather than being governed by a system of general authorisations. For the purpose of allocating radio frequencies, the BIPT establishes a national frequency plan. Within this national frequency plan, a block of radio frequencies is reserved for broadcasting. The further planning of these broadcasting frequencies is entrusted to the respective communities, which establish their own frequency plans. Therefore, applications for the use of radio frequencies for broadcasting must be addressed to the regulators of the communities. In the Flemish Community, the government grants a right to use a radio frequency as part of the decision to grant a licence for broadcasting. The government makes such a decision after consultation with the VCM. In the French Community, radio frequencies are allocated by the LSC.

7.57   Applications to use radio frequencies for purposes other than the transmission of broadcasting signals[40] are handled by BIPT.

7.58   The Electronic Communications Act establishes two main principles that must be followed in the radio frequency allocation process:

---

37   Article 97 French Broadcasting Decree and Article 161 Flemish Broadcasting Decree.
38   See BIPT Annual Report of 2003, p 23.
39   In Belgium, no single point is more than 60 km away from the border with a neighbouring country.
40   Such uses may include, among other things, those for taxis and other transport companies, security services, and intervention teams.

- the principle of technology neutrality; and
- the principle of service neutrality.[41]

The principle of technology neutrality requires that all types of technologies used for electronic communication services may be used in the radio frequencies that are used entirely or partially for public electronic communication services. This principle can be subject to proportionate and non-discriminatory restrictions by a Royal Decree, but only to the extent necessary to avoid harmful interferences, to ensure the technical quality of the service, to optimise the sharing of radio frequencies, to preserve the efficiency of the spectrum use, and/or to implement a general interest objective. The principle of service neutrality requires that all types of electronic communication services be provided in the frequencies that are used entirely or partially for public electronic communication services. Likewise, this principle may be subject to proportionate and non-discriminatory restrictions by a Royal Decree, but only for the implementation of a general interest objective.

Except in justified cases, the BIPT is prohibited from restraining and withdrawing radio frequencies rights of use before expiry of the grant (article 24/1 Electronic Communications Act).

7.59   In accordance with EU legislation, the communities in Belgium have put in place transparent and non-discriminatory procedures for granting of individual rights for the use of radio frequencies, including public tenders. Such procedures do not, however, apply to the respective incumbents (such as VRT and RTBF), to which a special regime applies.

Transferability and time limitations

7.60   Frequency trading is permitted in Belgium if radio frequencies are entirely or partially used for public telecommunication services. Any operator in Belgium who wishes to transfer or lease user rights for frequencies must notify the BIPT, which will authorise the frequency transfer or lease if it is not likely to distort competition and if it is in accordance with the requirements of effective and efficient management of the spectrum. The BIPT may refuse the transfer or lease if the operator initially obtained the user right for free.

Article 18 § 2 Electronic Communications Act provides that when the BIPT decides to grant rights of radiofrequency use with a time limitation, it must take into account the necessity of an appropriate period of time for investment amortisation when defining the period of time for which the right is to be granted.

7.61   In Flanders, the transfer of rights to use frequencies for broadcasting services requires the authorisation of the VCM. This agency approves the transfer only under very exceptional circumstances on a case-by-case basis. The transfer of frequency rights will be part of the transfer of the broadcasting permit, which also includes compliance with technical conditions for equipment, etc. The French Broadcasting Decree merely prohibits the transfer of the rights of use of radio frequencies.

Admissible conditions

7.62   The conditions for obtaining and exercising individual user rights are set by a Royal Decree of 18 December 2009 after completion of a consultation procedure, which requires the involvement of the BIPT. These conditions relate to:

---

41   Article 18 §§ 1/1 and 1/2 Electronic Communications Act.

- the service, or technology for which user rights are granted;
- the effective and efficient use of radio frequencies;
- the technical and operational conditions to prevent interference with other networks and exposure to electromagnetic fields;
- the maximum duration, subject to modifications of the national frequency plan;
- the transfer of rights at the holder's initiative;
- user fees;
- commitments made by the holder of user rights during the selection procedure;
- obligations ensuing from international agreements regarding the use of radio frequencies; and
- specific obligations concerning the experimental use of radio frequency.

7.63   The communities set the technical and other conditions for the use of radio frequencies for broadcasting purposes independently from the BIPT. The French Community, for example, has imposed the payment of an annual fee for the use of a radio frequency.[42]

Limitation of number of rights of use to be granted

7.64   Article 20 Electronic Communications Act prohibits the BIPT from limiting the number of rights of use that can be granted unless such limitation is necessary to prevent harmful interference caused by insufficient availability of the spectrum or to guarantee efficient and rational use of the radio frequencies. Any limitation to prevent interference must also be proportionate. To date, the procedure the BIPT must follow in the case of limiting the number of user rights has not been determined. The general principles, however, are set out in the Electronic Communications Act and reflect the guarantees required under the Authorisation Directive.

7.65   The respective communities are responsible for limiting the number of user rights within the block of frequencies that is reserved for broadcasting purposes. This competence is not explicitly stated in the Broadcasting Decrees but is considered to be part of the communities' legal mission to establish a frequency plan for broadcasting.

Rights of Use for Numbers

General authorisations and granting of individual rights

7.66   Telephone numbering, like radio frequencies, is considered a scarce resource. Therefore, the allocation of numbers must be fair not only in terms of quantity (there must be enough numbers available to develop a clientele) but also in terms of quality (a number cannot contain too many digits). The BIPT has, therefore, been charged with the general management of the national numbering plan.

7.67   The BIPT assigns the right to use numbers on an individual basis, upon request through an application. The BIPT must publish on its website model forms

---

42   Article 100 French Broadcasting Decree.

for applications. It must assign a right to use numbers within three weeks from receipt of the complete application,[43]

Admissible conditions

7.68   The conditions for obtaining and exercising the rights to use numbers are set by a Royal Decree of 27 April 2007 relating to the management of the national numbering plan. In accordance with Article 11 § 3 Electronic Communications Act, these conditions relate to:

- the indication of the service for which the number shall be used, together with the requirements connected to that service;
- the effective and efficient use of the numbers granted; and
- obligations ensuing from international agreements regarding the use of numbers.

7.69   The BIPT may subject the granting and the exercise of rights of use to a maximum duration, which must be tailored to the service in question.

In addition, Article 11 § 7 Electronic Communications Act requires operators who were granted phone numbers from the national numbering plan to offer number portability to their subscribers. Specific rules regarding number portability, the methodology for calculation of the costs of this facility, and the sharing of the costs between the parties involved, the obligation to provide information concerning the number portability to final users, and the compensation to be paid to subscribers in cases of a later execution of the transfer are set in a Royal Decree of 16 March 2000.

The activation of customers' numbers with their new provider must be performed within one working day. Moreover, the methodology for calculation of the cost and the sharing of the costs cannot result in tariff conditions that would deter subscribers from changing their providers.

Limitation of number of rights of use to be granted

7.70   Article 11 § 5 Electronic Communications Act provides that BIPT, after having carried out a public consultation, may decide to assign numbers with an exceptional economic value through a comparative or competition-based selection procedure.

Such procedure is divided into two phases. The first phase concerns the offer and starts with the publication of specifications on the BIPT's website. The specification sets the minimum conditions for the allocation and the exercise of the rights of use of numbers. It also sets the end-date for the first phase. The second phase concerns the attribution and may exceed three weeks after the end of the first phase. The BIPT may, however, extend the time limit for an additional three weeks. The operator that obtains the right of use is bound by the minimum conditions set in the specification and must abide by the commitments made during the selection procedure.

The NRA's Enforcement Powers

7.71   The BIPT Act contains the majority of the BIPT's enforcement powers.

---

43   Article 11 § 4 Electronic Communications Act.

7.72   As mentioned above, the BIPT is entitled to request information from any person at any time to the extent that this is reasonably necessary for the fulfilment of its tasks.[44] Moreover, in the case of violation of Articles 9, 11, 18, 51, 55, 56 or 64 Electronic Communications Act (or their implementation measures) that create an immediate and serious threat to public safety, public security or public health, or create serious economic or operational problems for other providers or users of electronic communications networks or services or for other users of the radio spectrum, the BIPT may take any interim measures it deems appropriate. However, such measures must remain temporary and not exceed a period of three months, which may be extended by three months in circumstances where enforcement procedures have not been completed.[45]

7.73   Where the BIPT finds evidence that there may have been a breach of the law or of its decisions, it will notify the potential offenders and inform them of the measures contemplated in case the breach is confirmed. The BIPT sets the timeframe (a minimum of 10 days) within which the potential offenders may access the file and submit their written observations. Potential offenders are then invited to appear before the BIPT. If a conclusion is reached that there is indeed an infringement, the BIPT asks the offenders to cease the infringing activity either immediately or within a reasonable period stipulated. The BIPT's decision may include one or several of the following measures:

- imposition of requirements relating to the way of correcting the infringement;
- an administrative fine up to 5 per cent of the last annual turnover in the relevant market or up to €5,000 in case the offender has no activity creating a turnover; and
- order to cease or suspend the provision of services that are likely to distort significantly competition as long as the access obligations imposed as result of a market analysis (carried out in accordance with the Electronic Communications Act) are not being complied with.

If the infringement nonetheless continues, and after following the same procedure, the BIPT can impose an administrative fine of up to twice the percentage or amount mentioned above. In cases of serious and repeated infringements, the BIPT may suspend or withdraw the rights of use for which the conditions have not been respected, or order the partial or entire suspension of the exploitation of the network or service as well as the marketing or use of the product or service concerned.

7.74   Certain special enforcement powers of the BIPT are set out in the Electronic Communications Act. An example is Article 18 § 3, stating that the BIPT may cancel a frequency usage right if not brought into service within a reasonable period.

7.75   The broadcasting regulators in the various communities have similar powers to the BIPT to ensure compliance with the broadcasting regulations. The VCM and the LSC may, among other things, send warnings, impose administrative fines, or suspend licences. In Flanders, administrative fines range between €1,250 and €125,000. The French Community has set the minimum fine at €250, up to a maximum of 3 per cent of annual turnover, or even 5 per cent in the case of repeated offence.

---

44   See paragraphs 7.21 and 7.22 above.
45   Article 20 BIPT Act.

Administrative Charges and Fees for Rights of Use

7.76   The Electronic Communications Act only sets out the general framework regarding administrative charges and fees for rights of use, leaving the further regulation of amounts and specific conditions to the federal government. The general principles of the Electronic Communications Act mirror those of Articles 12 and 13 of the Authorisation Directive. Consequently, administrative charges are allowed only to the extent that they cover the costs incurred by the BIPT in carrying out its tasks, and fees for rights of use can be levied to ensure optimal use of frequencies and numbers. The BIPT is responsible for the collection of all fees and charges. The federal legislator did not (and could not) use the possibility offered by Article 13 of the Authorisation Directive to levy fees for the rights to install facilities (including rights of way), because the regions are competent for this matter. Therefore, fees for rights to install facilities could be addressed separately in a cooperation agreement among the federal government, the communities and the regions.[46]

7.77   The BIPT levies fees for the use of numbers, the communication of access codes, and general information on international and national signalling point codes. Fees include a one-time handling charge and an annual fee, and are accessible on the BIPT website.

Article 30 Electronic Communications Act created a one-time handling charge for operators granted a right of use of radio frequencies. The amount of the charge varies depending on the frequency band[47] and is determined during the process in which frequencies are allocated. Operators have the choice between two modes of payment. They can either pay within 15 days after the commencement of the validity period for the right of use, or by annual instalment. The same procedure applies to operators seeking a renewal of their right of use. Operators who do not pay the charge lose their right of use.

7.78   In addition, the Flemish Broadcasting Decree provides for an annual fee for the use of radio frequencies,[48] the amount of which depends on the broadcasting scale and the market share of the radio broadcasting company.

7.79   Article 100 § 2 French Broadcasting Decree equally provides for the principle of an annual fee for the use of broadcasting frequencies. The amount is to be determined by the government; however, this decree fixes certain fees.[49] For example, a radio station which covers the whole of the French Community and the Brussels area must pay a fee of €50,000 (subject to indexation) per year. Other radio networks and independent radio stations pay either €1,250 or €600 (subject to indexation) per frequency, depending on their advertising revenues.

---

46   See paras 7.51–7.54 above.
47   Article 30 determines the price for frequency bands 880–915 MHz, 925–960 MHz, 1710–1785 MHz, 1805–1880 MHz, 1920–1980 MHz, 2110–2170 MHz and 2500–2690 MHz.
48   Article 202 of the Flemish Broadcasting Decree.
49   Article 109 French Broadcasting Decree.

REGULATION OF NETWORK ACCESS AND INTERCONNECTION: IMPLEMENTATION OF THE ACCESS DIRECTIVE

Objectives and Scope of Access Regulation

7.80   The BIPT's mission with respect to access and interconnection is to ensure access, interconnection, and interoperability of services in such a way as to promote sustainable competition and innovation. The ultimate goal of this policy is to obtain maximum benefit for end users.[50]

7.81   The rules of the Access Directive are transposed into Belgian law through Title III Electronic Communications Act. Title III is subdivided in four chapters:

- Chapter 1 applies to all operators regardless of their market position; it espouses the principle of freedom of access and provides a general framework for the commercial negotiations between operators regarding access and interconnection.
- Chapter 2 contains the provisions with respect to the market analyses to be conducted by BIPT.
- Chapter 3 sets out the special obligations that exist for SMP operators with respect to access and interconnection.
- Chapter 4 sets out obligations that apply to operators that are granted exclusive or special rights in sectors other than electronic communications.

7.82   Some of the provisions of the Access Directive are also relevant for the transmission of broadcasting signals and are thus implemented in the communities' Broadcasting Decrees. They seek to ensure interoperability of services[51] and provide the possibility for the regulator to impose special obligations on SMP undertakings.[52] In a country that is very densely cabled, this is a crucial factor for competition.

Basic Regulatory Concepts

7.83   The Electronic Communications Act[53] defines 'access' as:

> 'the making available of facilities and/or services to an operator, under defined conditions, on either an exclusive or non exclusive basis, for the purpose of providing electronic communications services, including when they serve for the provision of information society service'.

Notably, it covers access to network elements and associated facilities, which may involve the connection of equipment, by fixed or non-fixed means (including, in particular, access to the local loop and to facilities and services necessary to provide services over the local loop); access to physical facilities including buildings, ducts and masts; access to relevant software systems including operational support systems; access to information systems or databases for the preparation of orders, supply, orders, requests for maintenance and repair, and billing; access to number translation or systems offering equivalent functionality; access to fixed and mobile networks, including for roaming; and access to virtual network services.

---

50   See BIPT, Annual Report of 2004, p 23, and Articles 5 to 8 Electronic Communications Act.
51   Article 191 Flemish Broadcasting Decree and Article 95quater French Broadcasting Decree.
52   Article 192 Flemish Broadcasting Decree and Article 96 French Broadcasting Decree.
53   Article 1.18° Electronic Communications Act.

7.84   While the definition of 'access' in the Electronic Communications Act refers to 'operator',[54] the Access Directive mentions 'undertaking'. This difference is meaningless, however, as an 'operator' under the Electronic Communications Act[55] is defined as 'a person who has notified the BIPT in accordance with Article 9', which is a prerequisite to start providing electronic communication networks and services.

7.85   The Electronic Communications Act[56] defines 'interconnection' as:

'a specific type of access consisting of the physical or logical linking of public communication networks used by the same or a different operator in order to allow users to communicate with each other, or to have access to services provided by another operator'.

This definition is substantially the same as that in the Access Directive.

7.86   The French Broadcasting Decree contains definitions of 'access' and 'inter connection'. The Flemish Broadcasting Decree, however, does not define these terms.

Access- and Interconnection-related Obligations with Respect to SMP Undertakings

Telecom

OVERVIEW

7.87   Articles 58 to 65/2 Electronic Communications Act list the access and interconnection-related obligations that the BIPT may impose on telecommunications operators designated as having SMP. In summary they are:

- transparency (Article 59);
- non-discrimination (Article 58);
- access to and use of specific network facilities (Article 61);
- price control and cost accounting obligations (Article 62); and
- accounting separation (Article 60).

7.88   The BIPT is entitled to impose, maintain or modify these obligations as it considers appropriate.[57] The powers of the BIPT, however, are not unconditional. Obligations imposed by the BIPT must be objective, transparent, proportionate, non-discriminatory, and tailored to the specific situation, taking into account the nature of the problem identified.[58] Notwithstanding such limitations, the BIPT still enjoys a considerable level of discretion with respect to the choice of obligations it imposes on SMP operators.

TRANSPARENCY OBLIGATIONS

7.89   The BIPT may require SMP operators to disclose certain access-related information, such as accounting information, technical specifications, network

---

54   See paragraph 7.83
55   Article 1.11° Electronic Communications Act
56   Article 1.19° Electronic Communications Act
57   Article 55 § 3 Electronic Communications Act.
58   Article 5 Electronic Communications Act.

characteristics, modalities and conditions of supply and use, and prices. If the BIPT decides to require SMP operators to disclose such information, it must specify the precise information to be made public, as well as the level of detail required and the manner in which the information should be made available.

7.90   The BIPT may also require the publication of a reference offer for interconnection, unbundled access to the local loop, bitstream access, or any other type of access which the SMP operator involved must allow. Such reference offer must specify, for each type of access, the terms and conditions to gain access, including applicable tariffs. Before being published, the offer must be approved by the BIPT. An operator wishing to modify a reference offer must notify the BIPT, which, in turn, will accept or refuse such modification and may impose adaptations deemed necessary.

NON-DISCRIMINATION OBLIGATIONS

7.91   Article 58 Electronic Communications Act mirrors Article 10 of the Access Directive regarding the definition of 'obligations of non-discrimination'. They are defined as:

> 'obligations ensuring, in particular, that operators apply equivalent conditions in equivalent circumstances to other undertakings providing equivalent services, and provide services and information to others under the same conditions and of the same quality as for their own services, or those of their subsidiaries or partners'.

SPECIFIC ACCESS OBLIGATIONS

7.92   The BIPT is authorised to require SMP operators to grant reasonable requests for access to and use of specific network elements and associated facilities, to be designated by BIPT. Article 61 Electronic Communications Act mirrors the provisions of Article 12 Access Directive.

PRICE CONTROL AND COST ACCOUNTING OBLIGATIONS

7.93   The BIPT may also impose certain obligations relating to cost accounting and price control. In accordance with Article 13 of the Access Directive, the BIPT can only impose such measures if the market analysis indicates that the operator concerned might sustain prices at an excessively high level, or apply a price squeeze to the detriment of end users.

7.94   Even before the entry into force of the Electronic Communications Act, the BIPT had identified three SMP operators in the mobile telephony market (Proximus, Mobistar, and KPN Group Belgium-Base) and imposed on them the obligation to apply cost-oriented prices with respect to charges for 'call termination'. To permit full and fair competition, it is of utmost importance that SMP mobile operators offer this termination service to other operators under transparent, non-discriminatory and cost-oriented conditions. The BIPT has established schedules for the gradual lowering of tariffs of these operators. These schedules are regularly revised to take into account any new trends.

ACCOUNTING SEPARATION OBLIGATIONS

7.95   On the basis of Article 60 Electronic Communications Act, the BIPT may require that separate books be kept with respect to all access-related activities for which an operator has a significant market position. The BIPT specifies the accounting methodology and the format to be used.

7.96   When it deems it necessary, the BIPT may also request submission of accounting records, including data on revenues received from third parties. Such a request must be substantiated.

Broadcasting

7.97   Both the VCM and the CSA are authorised, in the Flemish and French communities respectively, to impose on SMP operators the same types of obliga-tions the BIPT imposes.[59] The French Broadcasting Decree has surprisingly not included specific access obligations, accounting separation, cost accounting, and price control in the list of obligations that may be imposed on broadcasting operators in the French Community.

Regulatory Powers Applicable to All Market Participants

Obligations to ensure end-to-end connectivity

7.98   To the extent necessary to ensure end-to-end connectivity and interoperabil-ity of services, the BIPT may impose obligations (including national roaming) on operators who, with or without SMP, control access to end users[60] ('last mile'). The BIPT may, therefore, determine the conditions for access, as it deems appropriate. Ensuring end-to-end connectivity may also imply an obligation for operators to establish interconnection of their networks if they have not already done so.

Regulation of roaming services

7.99   The BIPT may impose an obligation of national roaming if operators fail to reach an agreement through trade negotiations within a reasonable period. The details of such measure are to be determined by a Royal Decree, including concerning:

- the time span the BIPT is given to impose such measure;
- the operators that are subject to the obligation to offer national roaming and those that are granted the right to receive it;
- the minimal network roll out by an operator that is granted a right to national roaming;
- the services covered by the national roaming contract;
- the geographical scope of the national roaming contract;
- the duration of the national roaming contract; and
- the circumstances which may partially or entirely end the national roaming contract.

---

59   See para 7.88 above.
60   Article 51 § 2 Electronic Communications Act.

Access to digital radio and television broadcasting services

7.100   The communities are exclusively competent to implement the provisions of the Framework and Access Directives in relation to digital radio and television broadcasting services and networks.

7.101   Article 214 Flemish Broadcasting Decree authorises the Flemish Government to impose obligations on providers of Electronic Programme Guides ('EPG'), and suppliers of advanced digital terminals regardless of their market position, with respect to the use of open Interfaces ('APIs') and minimum norms and specifications. These obligations may relate to the use of an open API in accordance with minimum requirements of the relevant standards and specifications, and to the installation, access, and presentation of the EPG. In addition, the Flemish government may require owners of APIs to supply all information necessary to allow other providers of digital interactive television to offer their services using the same interface.

7.102   Articles 210 to 213 Flemish Broadcasting Decree include rules for conditional access systems[61] (e g pay television). The text, for the most part, mirrors the provisions of Article 6(1), and Annex I of Part I to the Access Directive. However, some minor differences include:

- the scope of the rules with respect to conditional access systems are somewhat broader in the Flemish Broadcasting Decree than in the Access Directive (the former imposes obligations on all providers of conditional access systems without any further specification, while the latter adds 'which provide services for access to digital television and radio services', limiting the number of providers to which the obligations apply);
- while the Access Directive refers to 'cost effective' transcontrol, the Flemish Broadcasting Decree refers to 'cheap' transcontrol; and
- the Flemish Broadcasting Decree, contrary to the Access Directive, does not specify that offers for conditional access systems must be compatible with European competition rules. However, in practice this does not mean that such offers should not comply with both the European and Belgian competition rules.

7.103   The French Community has equally adopted the necessary rules to transpose Articles 5(1) and 6(1) of the Access Directive into its legislation. The relevant provisions are in articles 130–131 French Broadcasting Decree (for EPGs) and articles 126–129 French Broadcasting Decree (for conditional access). The text of the French Broadcasting Decree, for the most part, is consistent with that of the Access Directive. However, there are some differences. For example, like the Flemish Broadcasting Decree, the French Broadcasting Decree refers to 'cheap' transcontrol instead of 'cost effective' transcontrol, and the French Broadcasting Decree requires separate accounting 'for the provision of services of conditional access' instead of 'for the activities as provider of conditional access systems', as provided in the Access Directive.

---

61   Article 2, 42° Flemish Broadcasting Decree defines 'conditional access systems' as 'any technical measure or rule whereby access to a protected radio or television program in an understandable form conditional upon subscription or any other form of prior individual authorisation'.

7.104   Furthermore, the French Broadcasting Decree offers additional detail with respect to conditions which may be imposed on providers of EPG (with or without SMP). These conditions could include requirements related to:

- installation of an EPG, which has the technical capability to search a service amongst other services without discrimination;
- maintenance of a sufficient degree of competition in connection with access to EPG for broadcasters; and
- the respect of the principles of pluralism and non-discrimination in relation to the presentation of available services through EPG.

REGULATION OF UNIVERSAL SERVICES AND USERS' RIGHTS: THE UNIVERSAL SERVICE DIRECTIVE

Regulation of Universal Service Obligations

Scope of universal service obligations

7.105   Article 68 Electronic Communications Act lists the services that are considered part of the universal service. The list corresponds to the catalogue contained in the Universal Service Directive and comprises several parts, namely:

- the fixed geographic element of the universal service (including access to the network and the basic telephone voice service, the free routing of emergency calls and the provision of a helpdesk);
- the application of social tariffs, and special measures in the case of non-payment of phone bills;
- the provision of public telephone booths across the country;
- the provision of a directory inquiries service for subscribers; and
- the annual publication of an universal directory.

7.106   These services must be available to all end users, independent of geographic location, at an affordable price and of a specified quality.

7.107   An important feature of the Electronic Communications Act relates to social tariffs. In the past, these tariffs were only applied by Belgacom, in its capacity as provider of the universal service. Currently, an individual who is entitled to such tariffs may go to any operator listed in paragraphs 2 and 3 of Article 74. As further explained below, a separate fund for social tariffs will be created to compensate providers who serve a considerable number of customers who are entitled to social tariffs.

Designation of undertakings obliged to provide universal services

7.108   The Belgian legislator has taken the approach of splitting the universal service into different components (as listed above), allowing it to adopt separate rules in terms of appointment and compensation of providers for each of the components.

7.109   Except for social tariffs, the various components of the universal service will each be entrusted to one (or possibly more) providers. These providers will be appointed through a designation procedure, the rules of which are yet to be adopted by Royal Decree on the basis of proposals from the BIPT. Notwithstanding the possibility of appointing a different provider for each of the components of the universal service, Belgacom likely will continue to be designated as the undertaking that is required to provide all elements of the minimum set of services of the universal service, possibly given the ease of having one operator meeting the national coverage requirement.

Two types of operators are subject to the obligation to apply social tariffs:

  (i) any operator offering a public electronic communications service to con-
       sumers, provided that its turnover for such services exceeds €50,000,000; and
 (ii) any operator offering a public electronic communications service to con-
       sumers, provided that its turnover for such services is less than or equal to
       €50,000,000 and that it declared to the BIPT its intention to provide special
       tariffs on fixed and/or mobile terrestrial networks.

Regulation of retail tariffs, users' expenditures and quality of service

7.110   Rules with respect to permissible end user tariffs[62] for the services which form part of the universal service, as well as requirements regarding the quality of such universal service, are set out in an annex to the Electronic Communications Act (the 'Annex'). By virtue of article 34 of the Annex, end users must have access to publicly available telephone services at a fixed location at prices which are 'affordable'. To ensure that prices are affordable, the Belgian legislator introduced a mathematical formula for the calculation of retail tariffs.[63]

7.111   Article 38 of the Annex sets out the minimum discounts which must be granted to the beneficiaries of social tariffs for telephone and Internet services. To be eligible, customers must fulfil certain conditions with respect to age, disability, or income.[64] More specifically, requests for social tariffs for telephone and Internet services will only be granted if submitted by persons who:

●   are at least 65 years of age;
●   are at least 66 per cent disabled and at least 18 years of age;
●   are entitled to government support with regard to minimum subsistence;
●   have impaired hearing;
●   have had a laryngectomy; or
●   became blind while on active service in wartime.

7.112   To allow customers to control expenditure, articles 117–120 Electronic Communications Act adopt a series of payment facilities (including call barring, pre-payment, phased payment, and selective call barring for outgoing calls). These provisions, however, are merely a confirmation of the general principles, and more detailed rules are yet to be adopted by the Minister of electronic communications.

7.113   The BIPT is responsible for monitoring universal service obligations, including control on tariffs and quality levels.[65] To this end, the BIPT performs field checks and submits each year a report to the minister of electronic communications. Where the BIPT has identified a failure to comply, the minister of electronic communications may impose an administrative fine on the provider involved, which must not exceed an amount equal to 1 per cent of the turnover of the universal

---

62   Articles 34 to 39 of the Annex.
63   Article 35 of the Annex.
64   Article 22 of the Annex.
65   Article 103 Electronic Communications Act.

service provider in the relevant year.[66] The BIPT must notify the European Commission, without delay, of the universal service obligations imposed on providers as well as the amendments brought thereto.

Cost calculation and financing of universal services

7.114   A 'Universal Service Fund' is established for the compensation of undertakings that have been designated to provide universal services.[67] All established providers must contribute to the fund in proportion to their turnover. The Electronic Communications Act is silent with respect to the right to exempt undertakings whose national turnover is less than a set limit. The BIPT, however, has not indicated that undertakings with a national turnover of less than €12,395,000 might not still be exempted.

7.115   For each component of the universal service, the designated provider is entitled to compensation. The amount of the compensation depends on the way the provider was designated. If designation occurred through an open selection procedure, the amount will be equal to the sum determined at the end of the procedure. If, however, the provider was appointed ex-officio, compensation will be calculated on the basis of the net costs of providing the universal service and in accordance with the calculation rules set out in the Annex.[68] The Electronic Communications Act includes the concept of an unfair burden as a condition to compensation.

7.116   A separate fund was created for social tariffs. Any operator applying social tariffs must contribute to the financing of the fund in proportion to its turnover related to public electronic communications services. The fund compensates operators applying social tariffs for which social tariffs create an unjustified burden if they file an application for compensation with the BIPT.

Regulation of Retail Markets

Prerequisites for the regulation of retail markets

7.117   Article 64 Electronic Communications Act sets out the obligations that the BIPT may impose on undertakings with SMP in retail markets. However, regulation of retail services on the basis of article 64 is permissible only if regulation at the wholesale level does not achieve the regulatory objectives established by the federal legislator.

7.118   Currently, no operator is identified as having SMP in the retail market. It cannot be ruled out, however, that, upon completion of the market analysis, the BIPT will identify Belgacom as an operator with SMP in the retail market.

Regulatory powers

7.119   Obligations which the BIPT may impose on SMP undertakings in the retail market seek to prohibit any:

---

66   Article 104 Electronic Communications Act.
67   Article 92 Electronic Communications Act.
68   Articles 40 to 44 of the Annex.

- charging of excessively high prices;
- inhibiting of market entry;
- setting of predatory prices which restrict competition;
- showing of undue preference to specific end users; or
- unreasonable bundling of services.

7.120   Article 64 Electronic Communications Act further provides that the BIPT, if it wishes to control end user tariffs, may determine the necessary and appropriate cost-accounting systems that the targeted undertaking must apply.

End User Rights

Contracts

7.121   Any contract between a subscriber and a telecommunications operator for the provision of a connection to the public electronic communications network or the provision of public electronic communications services must contain, in a clear, detailed, and easily accessible form, at least the following minimum information:[69]

- the identity and address of the operator;
- the services provided (Article 108, § 1, b) Electronic Communications Act);
- where an obligation exists under Article 133 Electronic Communications Act, the subscriber's options as to whether to include his or her personal data in a directory or a telephone directory inquiry service, and the data concerned;
- details on tariffs, the means by which up-to-date information on all applicable tariffs and maintenance charges may be obtained, payment methods offered, and any difference in costs due to payment methods;
- conditions for renewal and termination of the services and the contract ;
- any compensation and the refund arrangements that apply if the elements mentioned in Article 108, § 1, b) Electronic Communications Act are violated;
- dispute mechanisms, including the possibility of appeal and complaint to the mediation service for telecommunications;
- the types of measures that the undertaking might take in reaction to security or integrity incidents, or in reaction to threats or vulnerability; and
- the global price for an offer of several electronic communications services.

7.122   The operator must provide the subscriber with such information at the latest when entering into the contract. The information may be set out in the operator's general terms and conditions. The operator must provide the contract to the subscriber in writing.

7.123   If an operator wishes to change the contractual conditions that govern its relationship with a subscriber, the operator must give the subscriber at least one month's notice of any such proposed modifications and inform the subscriber of his or her right to terminate the contract without penalty until the last day of the month following the effective date of the modifications.[70] Where the proposed modifications relate to a tariff increase, such right of withdrawal continues to exist until the last day of the month following the receipt of the first invoice after the tariff increase has become effective.

---

69   Article 108 Electronic Communications Act.
70   Article 108 § 2 Electronic Communications Act.

Definite terms for a consumer contract cannot exceed an initial period of 24 months[71] and conversion of definite term contracts into indefinite term contracts or vice versa is subject to the subscriber's consent and information duties.[72]

7.124   By using the term 'subscriber', Belgium has taken the opportunity offered in Article 20 of the Universal Directive to extend the above minimum information requirements to all end-users, ie beyond 'consumers' as referred to in the Directive.

Transparency obligations

7.125   Operators must make available to consumers and end users comparative, adequate, and current information regarding access to and use of their networks and services, prices and tariffs, as well as the charges that might be due at the moment of termination of the contract. Such information must be published in a clear, detailed, and easily accessible manner. The BIPT sets out the guidelines with respect to the details of information to be provided and the requirements for publication.[73] The information must be communicated to the BIPT at least 15 days prior to publication.

7.126   To allow end users to benefit from the best price offer tailored to their needs, operators must inform their subscribers at least once a year of the most advantageous tariff plan, taking into account the subscriber's past usage.[74] In the same vein, operators must include on the first page of each bill a note referring to a government website which helps subscribers to find the most advantageous tariff plan.

Quality of services: securing 'net neutrality'

7.127   Article 113 Electronic Communications Act addresses the quality of public electronic communications networks and services. Undertakings providing such networks or services must publish on their website comparative, adequate, and current information concerning the quality of their network and services for end users, and the measures taken to secure an equivalent access for disabled end users. Such information must also be communicated to the BIPT prior to its publication.

The BIPT may set the parameters related to the quality of networks and services with which operators must comply. Furthermore, the BIPT may impose minimum quality of service requirements to prevent the degradation of services and the hindering or slowing down of traffic over networks. The BIPT communicates to the European Commission and to BEREC a summary of the motives on which it bases an intervention and the requirements and the approach that it contemplates.

Article 113/1 Electronic Communications Act gives the BIPT the power to coordinate initiatives related to the safety of public electronic communications networks and services and to provide users with safety-related information. A Royal Decree may set the conditions and modalities of compensation of the subscribers by operators in case of service interruption.

---

71   Article 108 § 3 Electronic Communications Act.
72   Article 108 § 1/1 Electronic Communications Act.
73   Article 111 Electronic Communications Act.
74   Article 110 § 4 Electronic Communications Act.

European emergency call number

7.128   Pursuant to article 108 Electronic Communications Act, any contract between a subscriber and a telecommunications operator for the provision of a connection to the public electronic communications network or the provision of public electronic communications services must contain, in a clear, detailed, and easily accessible form, among others an indication whether access to emergency services and to caller location information is available and whether there are limitations on the availability of the single European emergency call number.

Other obligations

7.129   *Network integrity*:[75] providers of publicly electronic communications networks and services must (taking into account the state of technology and realization costs) take all reasonable technical and organisational steps to ensure the safety of their services. To guarantee uninterrupted access of emergency services, operators must, in the case of defect, give priority to emergency services, hospitals, and physicians, among others, for the repair of such defect, including a back-up service.

7.130   *Helpdesk*: Article 116 Electronic Communications Act provides that operators offering end users a helpdesk must ensure that the communication price per minute does not exceed that of a geographical number.

7.131   *Provision of additional facilities*: Article 121 Electronic Communications Act provides the possibility for the BIPT to require that operators of public electronic communications networks and services offer the additional facilities of calling-line identification and tone dialling. However, these obligations may be waived for all or part of the territory if the federal government, following consultation with the advisory committee for telecommunications and the BIPT, considers that there is already sufficient access to these facilities. Article 121/1 creates an obligation for providers of Internet access services to adopt a code of conduct ensuring minimum requirements regarding, among others:

- access by end users to their electronic addresses based on a trade name and/or brand name if they terminate their contract; and
- access to web space made available to users when they terminate their contract.

7.132   *Telephone directory*: subject to applicable data protection provisions, subscribers to publicly available telephone services have the right to be listed in a telephone directory or registered with a directory inquiry service. A standard entry must be free of charge. To include a subscriber in a telephone directory or in a directory inquiry service, the subscriber's permission is required.

Obligations facilitating change of provider

7.133   A Royal Decree sets the technical methods, the time-limit for execution, and the obligations of information that must be respected by operators when an end-user chooses to change operator. These rules concern the distribution of tasks

---

75   Articles 114 and 115 Electronic Communications Act.

between the parties, the compensation of the subscribers in case of delayed transfer, and the information that operators must provide end users.[76]

Subscribers may terminate their contract in any written manner and without giving any reason. The contract expires at the time set by the subscriber. Terms and conditions making it impossible to change providers or use number portability (or discouraging the same) are void.

For a discussion of number portability, see paragraph 7.69.

DATA PROTECTION: IMPLEMENTATION OF THE DIRECTIVE ON PRIVACY AND ELECTRONIC COMMUNICATIONS

Overview

7.134   The E-Privacy Directive was implemented into Belgian law by the Electronic Communications Act. The relevant provisions complement the existing framework under the Act of 11 March 2003 relating to certain legal aspects of Electronic Services ('Electronic Services Act') and the Data Protection Act of 8 December 1992 ('Data Protection Act').

Confidentiality of Communications

7.135   Except with the authorisation of all persons directly or indirectly concerned, it is illegal for any individual or entity to:[77]

- intentionally acquire knowledge of the existence of information of any kind transmitted by means of electronic communication which is not personally directed to him or her;
- intentionally identify the persons concerned with the transmission of the information and its content;
- intentionally acquire knowledge of electronic communications data relating to another person; or
- modify, delete, disclose, store or make any use of the information, its identification or the data itself, whether or not intentionally obtained.

7.136   Exceptions, however, apply:

- where the law allows or requires the aforementioned acts;
- where those acts are carried out for the exclusive purpose of verifying the good working of the network and to ensure the good working of the electronic communications service;
- where those acts are carried out in order to allow the intervention of the emergency services, in response to requests for assistance;
- where those acts are carried out by the BIPT within the scope of its legal duty of control;
- where those acts are carried out for the sole purpose of providing services to the end user which consist of preventing receipt of undesirable electronic communications, provided the end user has given its consent;
- where those acts are carried out by agents authorised by the Minister in

---

76   Articles 111/2 and 111/3 Electronic Communications Act.
77   Article 124 Electronic Communications Act.

charge of economy within the framework of their regulatory research mission, but only to the extent that such acts do not concern the listening of communications; or

- where those acts are carried out by the Commission for Telecommunication Ethics, its secretariat or as per their request within the framework of their regulatory research mission, but only to the extent that such acts do not concern the listening of communications.

7.137 Without prejudice to the Data Protection Act, the recording of electronic communications and the related traffic data, carried out in the course of lawful business practice or other professional communication, is authorised provided that all parties to that communication are informed beforehand of the recording, the precise purposes thereof, and the period of time for which the recording will be stored.

Traffic Data and Location Data

7.138 The definitions of 'traffic data' and 'location data' are identical to those in the E-Privacy Directive. The main principle[78] is that traffic data relating to subscribers and users, processed and stored by the providers of a public communications network or publicly available electronic communications service, must be erased or made anonymous when it is no longer needed for the purpose of the transmission of a communication. The following exceptions, however, apply:

- providers may store and process traffic data necessary for the purposes of subscriber billing and interconnection payment. Such processing is permissible only up to the end of the period during which the bill can lawfully be challenged or payment pursued;
- providers may process traffic data for the purpose of marketing electronic communications services or services with traffic or location data, to the extent and for the duration necessary for such services or marketing, if the subscriber or user to whom the data relates has given his/her consent. Users or subscribers must be given the possibility to withdraw their consent for the processing of traffic data at any time; and
- traffic data may be processed to detect fraud, and must be transferred to the competent authorities in case of crime or offence.

7.139 A service provider must inform its subscriber or user of the types of traffic data which are processed and of the duration of such processing for the purposes mentioned under the first item above, and, prior to obtaining consent, for the purposes mentioned under the second item above.

7.140 Location data other than traffic data relating to users or subscribers may only be processed if it has been anonymised or if the processing is part of a service concerning traffic or location data, provided the user's consent has been obtained. The consent is only valid if the provider has informed the user or subscriber of the types of location data processed, the purposes and duration of the processing, and third parties to whom the data may be disclosed. This consent may be withdrawn at any time.[79]

78   Article 122 Electronic Communications Act.
79   Article 123 Electronic Communications Act.

Cookies

7.141   The cookie consent requirement set forth in Directive 2009/136/EC was implemented into Belgian law by Article 129 Electronic Communications Act, which provides that:

- the user must be informed about the placing of cookies[80] on his or her system in a clear and detailed manner, and in accordance with the Data Protection Act of 1992 as far as the objectives of the underlying processing and/or his or her rights pursuant to the said Act are concerned;
- cookies may not be placed before the user has provided consent after having received the above information; and
- the data controller must give users the possibility to withdraw their consent freely and in an easy manner.

The prohibition on the placing of cookies without the end users' or subscribers' consent, however, does not apply to the technical recording of information or access to information stored in a subscriber's or end user's terminal (equipment serving the exclusive purpose of sending an electronic communication via an electronic communication network or of providing a service expressly requested by the subscriber or end user where strictly necessary for either of those purposes.

In March 2012, the Belgian Privacy Commission, commenting on the draft bill, complained that the new law would not be clear enough as to the characteristics of the consent to be given by the end user and would not dissipate the uncertainly with respect to the possibility of relying on implicit consent.

However, to rely merely on the browser settings would not be valid under article 129 as the consent must be given after the end user has been informed of the objectives of the processing and of his or her rights.

In practice, it is arguable that websites placing cookies should include a pre-eminent warning mentioning the purposes of such cookies and the end user's rights, and either some implicit consent language with a 'I refuse' button, or explicit 'I accept'/'I refuse' buttons (in which latter case, cookies may only placed after the end user has clicked on the 'I accept' button).

Such websites should also include an easy and free mechanism to withdraw the said consent.

Data Retention

7.142   Article 126 Electronic Communications Act provides that the King (read the Federal Government) may impose on operators the obligation to retain traffic and identification data. For public telephony services, such retention duty must be at least 12 months and cannot exceed 18 months. In the prolonged absence of any implementing decree, such retention duties are however not in force and one may doubt the government's resolution to enforce them. On 27 September 2012, the EU Commission decided to issue a notice of default to Belgium for non-transposition of Directive 2006/24/EC on Retention of Electronic Communications Data (Decision 2012/2152).

---

80   For the purposes of this section, we generally refer to the placing of cookies rather than to the storage of information, which is the correct legal terminology.

Itemised Billing[81]

7.143 Providers must send subscribers who have a maximum of five numbers, a basic itemised invoice at least every three months and free of charge. The level of detail of such invoice is determined by the minister of electronic communications, after consultation with the BIPT. Subscribers may obtain, free of charge and on request, an itemised bill.

7.144 Free calls, calls to emergency numbers, and calls to certain numbers to be determined by the King (ie the federal government) after consultation with the BIPT, are not included in such an invoice.

7.145 At least once per year, a provider must indicate on the invoice for its subscribers the most advantageous tariff plan for the subscriber on the basis of its usage profile.[82]

Calling and Connected Line Identification[83]

7.146 Where calling line identification is offered as a service, the service provider of the calling user must offer the calling user, free of charge and on request, the possibility of preventing the calling line identification on a per-call basis. In addition, the service provider of the called subscriber must offer the called subscriber the possibility, free of charge and on request, to prevent the calling line identification of incoming calls. However, the obligation to provide this service free of charge does not apply when used in an unreasonable way by the subscriber.

7.147 If the calling line identification is displayed prior to the call being established, the service provider of the called subscriber must offer the called subscriber the possibility of rejecting the incoming call on request, where the calling line identification has been prevented on request by the end user or calling subscriber.

7.148 Providers of publicly available electronic communications services must inform the public if calling and/or connected line identification is offered, and of the possibilities relating thereto as described above.

7.149 More detailed rules will be set by Royal Decree, after consultation with the Privacy Commission and the BIPT.

Automatic Call Forwarding[84]

7.150 Providers of public electronic communications services must offer the possibility to their users and subscribers, free of charge and on request, of stopping automatic call forwarding by a third party to the subscriber's terminal.

Directories of Subscribers[85]

7.151 Providers of a telephone service accessible to the public must inform their subscribers, free of charge and before they are included in a directory or in a

---

81 Article 110 Electronic Communications Act.
82 See paragraph 7.126 above.
83 Article 130 Electronic Communications Act.
84 Article 131 Electronic Communications Act.
85 Article 133 Electronic Communications Act.

directory inquiry service, about the purposes of such directory or inquiry service, free inclusion in the directory, and any further usage other than the search of personal data based on the name or residence of the subscriber.[86]

7.152   Providers must ask subscribers whether they wish their personal data to be included in a public directory and, if so, in which directory. Subscribers have the right to verify, correct, or withdraw such data from the directory, free of charge.

7.153   Separate and specific consent from the subscribers is required for any purpose of a public directory other than the search of personal data of persons on the basis of their name and, as the case may arise, residence.

Unsolicited Communications

7.154   Under Belgian law, the sending of unsolicited e-mails ('spam') is subject to the Electronic Services Act and the Royal Decree of 4 April 2003 with respect to advertising by electronic mail. These legislative acts establish an 'opt-in' system whereby the prior consent of the recipients is required to proceed with the sending of unsolicited e-mails.

7.155   There are, however, a number of exceptions to this general 'opt-in' rule. As a matter of law, the sending of unsolicited e-mail is permitted:

- to the sender's own clients if the following conditions are cumulatively met:
  - the contact details were collected directly from the recipient upon the selling of goods or services and the collection is done in accordance with Belgian privacy regulations; and
  - the contact details are used for the exclusive purpose of promoting goods or services similar to those initially sold to the recipient, and the goods or services are offered by the entity which collected the data; and
  - upon collection of a recipient's data, the recipient can, easily and free of charge, object to the processing of his or her data for this purpose; or
- to public or private corporations provided that the following conditions are cumulatively met:
  - the recipient's e-mail address is impersonal (eg 'info@corp.com' or 'reception@justice.gov'); and
  - the promoted services or goods are intended for the recipients' activities.

7.156   The sending of unsolicited e-mails that does not comply with these rules is a criminal offence.

---

86   See paragraph 7.132 above.

The Bulgarian Market for Electronic Communications

Violetta Kunze and Lilia Kisseva
Djingov, Gouginski, Kyutchukov & Velichkov, Sofia

LEGAL STRUCTURE

Basic Policy

8.1   Bulgaria became a full member of the European Union (EU) on 1 January 2007, and the Bulgarian electronic communications market has been fully liberalised since 1 January 2003. The Bulgarian Telecommunications Company ('BTC'), the incumbent operator[1], was successfully privatised in 2004 and, as of 2011, the total number of undertakings that have notified the national regulatory authority of their intention to provide public electronic communications services is 1,264.

In 2011, voice telephony services (fixed, mobile and other voice telephony services) had the highest share (70.03 per cent) of the total volume of the Bulgarian market for public electronic communications services. Data transmission and Internet access services, and radio and TV programme transmission and distribution services are second and third, respectively, with relative market share of 10.73 per cent and 8.28 per cent, respectively. Bundled services are in fourth place; these services are developing rapidly and have 8.10 per cent market share. The total volume of the Bulgarian market for electronic communications services in 2011 represents 3.9 per cent from the total volume of the gross domestic product of Bulgaria[2].

According to the 2011 annual report of the national regulatory authority, the electronic communications sector in Bulgaria is expected to develop in the following aspects: increased competition among operators; development of broadband Internet access (mobile and fixed) services; increased supply of, and demand for, bundled and converged services; and construction of third and fourth generation networks. In addition, the transition from analogue to digital TV is expected to be finalised in 2013. The law envisages, however, that terrestrial analogue television radio broadcasting in the territory of Bulgaria will cease as of 1 September 2013.

---

1   Currently BTC provides a large range of electronic communication services, including mobile services.
2   2011 Annual Report of the Bulgarian Communications Regulatory Commission.

In line with Article 8 of the Framework Directive, the Bulgarian regulatory policy goals include promotion of competition, support of the development of the internal market of electronic communications and protection of the interests of citizens.

Implementation of EU Directives

8.2 Generally, the country is following the principles set forth in the EU Regulatory Package. With the recent amendments to the Law on Electronic Communications effective as of 29 December 2011, Bulgaria has transposed the 2009 Regulatory Package. Implementation of the EU Regulatory Framework is brought by way of amendment of the relevant national laws to implement EU Directives, as well as by adoption by the respective competent executive body or regulatory authority, of secondary legislation, decisions in conformity with the EU Regulations, and decisions and 'soft law' regulatory tools, such as guidelines, recommendations and working papers.

Legislation

8.3 The principal sources of Bulgarian electronic communication legislation comprise the laws passed by the Parliament, supported by secondary legislation. In particular, the Bulgarian electronic communications framework includes:

- the Constitution of the Republic of Bulgaria[3] (the 'Constitution');
- the Law on Electronic Communications[4] ('LEC');
- the Law on Radio and Television[5] ('LRT');
- the Law on Electronic Document and Digital Signature[6] ('LEDDS');
- the Law on Personal Data Protection[7] ('LPDP');
- the Law on Protection of Competition[8] ('LPC'); and
- a number of secondary legislative acts adopted by the competent executive body or regulatory authority.

The laws passed by the Bulgarian Parliament enjoy superiority over any secondary legislation or decisions of the national regulatory authority the Communications Regulatory Commission ('CRC'). The latter acts are designed to provide further clarity on the statutory provisions and to ensure the uniform implementation of law. Generally, national legislation has enhanced competition in the telecommunications markets and provided for technology neutral regulations.

---

3   Promulgated in State Gazette Issue No 56 of 13 July 1991, as subsequently amended and supplemented.
4   Promulgated in State Gazette Issue No 41 of 22 May 2007, as subsequently amended and supplemented.
5   Promulgated in State Gazette Issue No 138 of 24 November 1998, as subsequently amended and supplemented.
6   Promulgated in State Gazette Issue No 34 of 6 April 2001, as subsequently amended and supplemented.
7   Promulgated in State Gazette Issue No 1 of 4 January 2002, as subsequently amended and supplemented.
8   Promulgated in State Gazette Issue No 102 of 28 November 2008, as subsequently amended and supplemented.

REGULATORY PRINCIPLES: THE FRAMEWORK DIRECTIVE

Scope of regulation

8.4   Regulation of transmission is separate from that of content, and therefore broadcasting is regulated by a separate piece of legislation, the LRT.

Pursuant to the LEC, electronic communications are carried out by conveyance, emission, broadcasting, and transmission or reception of signs, signals, written text, images, sound or communications of any kind through wire, radio waves, optical or another electromagnetic media.[9]

The definition of 'electronic communications networks' set out in the LEC corresponds to the one provided for in Article 2(a) of the Framework Directive, ie a system of transmission facilities and, where applicable, switching or routing equipment and other resources, including non-active network elements, which permit the conveyance of signals by wire, by radio, by optical or by other electromagnetic means, including satellite networks, fixed (circuit- and packet-switched, including Internet) and mobile terrestrial networks, electricity cable systems, to the extent that they are used for the purpose of transmitting signals, networks used for radio and television broadcasting, and cable television networks, irrespective of the type of information conveyed ('ECNs').[10]

Furthermore the LEC defines electronic communication service ('ECS') as:

'a service, usually provided for remuneration, which consists wholly or mainly in conveyance of signals over ECNs, including transmission services, provided through broadcasting networks, excluding services, related to content or the control over it. The scope of the electronic communication services does not include information society services, which do not consist wholly or mainly in the conveyance of signals over ECNs'.[11]

Public electronic communications services have been defined as 'electronic communications services available to the public'.[12]

The scope of the pertinent legislation and the regulatory powers are also extended to the 'associated facilities' which, in turn, are described as:

'a system of all or some of the following elements: electronic communications means, including lines, cable systems, poles, towers, ducts, shafts, pipes, masts, cables, wires and facilities, which are used to implement electronic communications, with the exception of electronic communications terminal equipment'.[13]

Depending on the technology employed, VoIP services are either not regulated (such as in 'Skype' type of services) or considered to be data transmission services. In the latter case they are subject to simple notification to the CRC. With respect to allocation of numbers, see 8.37 – 8.40 below.

'Internet Freedom'

8.5   Bulgarian legislation does not provide for the imposition of measures that restrict the end user's access to the Internet. To this end, the introduction of such

---

9   Art 1 (2) LEC.
10   Para 15 of the Additional Provisions of LEC.
11   Para 17 of the Additional Provisions of LEC.
12   Para 40 of the Additional Provisions of LEC.
13   Para 13 of the Additional Provisions of LEC.

measures is not on the legislative agenda of the Bulgarian Parliament, and based on the publicly available information, to date, there have not been any discussions (or planned discussions) on the introduction of such measures.

National Regulatory Authorities: Organisation, Regulatory Objectives, Competencies

8.6 The Bulgarian national regulatory authority is the CRC, an independent authority, vested with the specific powers to regulate and control the compliance of provision of electronic communications with applicable law. The CRC is vested with the powers, amongst others, to:

- determine the relevant markets of ECNs or services subject to regulation under the LEC;
- investigate, analyse and evaluate the level of competition in the relevant markets; and
- determine the SMP undertakings and impose, amend or revoke specific obligations on those undertakings.

The CRC is the authority competent to issue, amend, supplement, transfer, suspend, terminate or revoke permits for use of individually allocated scarce resources.

8.7 There are two independent regulators which exercise their respective competencies over the broadcasting sector: the CRC, overseeing the transmission and the technical issues, and the Council for Electronic Media ('CEM'), regulating the content of the broadcast programmes.

The primary responsibility for enforcement of the competition rules in Bulgaria falls within the competence of the Bulgarian Commission on Protection of Competition ('CPC'). The CRC and the CPC must act in coordination and cooperation.

The Bulgarian Data Protection Commission is an independent authority which protects individuals in the course of processing their personal data and upon access to their personal data, as well as exercising control over the implementation of the LPDP.

8.8 The CRC must exercise the powers and carry out its functions and tasks with the purposes of accomplishing the objectives and principles set forth in LEC. In line with Article 8 of the Framework Directive, those statutory objectives include promotion of competition, support of the development of the internal market of electronic communications and protection of the interests of citizens. The regulatory principles, in turn, consist of compliance with law, predictability, transparency, consultation, publicity, non-discrimination, proportionality, technological neutrality, and minimum regulatory intervention.[14]

The CRC is an independent state body with legal personality. The functional and structural separation of the NRA is ensured by the LEC. The NRA has a separate annual budget and the right to make, once a year, a proposal to the council of ministers for amendments regarding administrative charges. However, there is no

---

14 Art 5 LEC.

explicit provision in Bulgarian legislation prohibiting the CRC from seeking, and taking, instructions from any other body as provided for in the revised Framework Directive.[15]

8.9   For the purposes of fulfilling the CRC's regulatory functions, and in accordance with Article 5 of the Framework Directive, the LEC vests the NRA with the power to request, from the undertakings providing ECNs, all necessary information, including financial information. Such requests must comply with the principle of proportionality and must be based on the objectives set forth in LAC.[16] The information request must not be made prior to or as a condition for a market entry. The CRC must also provide the Commission and any other national regulatory authority of a Member State, after a reasoned request, with the information necessary for carrying out their respective functions.[17] The rules regarding notification of the undertakings concerned and the confidentiality of the information provided are in compliance with Article 5 of the Framework Directive.[18]

Among other powers, the CRC has the power to conduct public hearings and consultations, and request the opinion of the undertakings under the procedures provided for in the LEC.[19] Article 37 LEC implements Article 6 of the Framework Directive and describes the requirements for conducting a consultation procedure. In 2011, the NRA introduced an electronic information system which is expected to facilitate the access of citizens and undertakings to the administrative services of the authority.

8.10   The CRC is also vested with the power to resolve disputes between undertakings providing ECNs or services, as well as between the latter undertakings and entities on which access or interconnection obligations are imposed. The procedures and specific actions that the NRA may undertake are set forth in articles 54–62 LEC inclusive and in general implement the requirements of Articles 20 and 21 of the Framework Directive. Any decision of the CRC, however, may be challenged before the Supreme Administrative Court.

Right of Appeal against NRA's Decisions

8.11   NRA's decisions qualify as individual or general administrative acts and, as such, are subject to appeal under the general proceedings rules of the Bulgarian Administrative Procedure Code ('APC')[20] before the Supreme Administrative Court acting in a chamber of three judges. The latter decision is subject to a final review by the Supreme Administrative Court acting in a chamber of five judges.

The CRC may impose preliminary enforcement should the requirements of Bulgarian general administrative procedure law be in place,[21] and upon issuance of the following groups of decisions:

---

15   Bulgaria 2011 Telecommunication Market and Regulatory Developments, European Commission, Information Society and Media Directorate General, 18 June 2012.
16   Art 40(1) LEC.
17   Art 40(6) LEC.
18   Art 40(7), (8), (9) LEC.
19   Art 30, pt 24 LEC.
20   Promulgated in the State Gazette Issue No 30 of 11 April 2006, as subsequently amended and supplemented.
21   Art 60 APC.

- any decisions whereby information needed for analysis of the relevant markets is requested from the undertakings;
- any decisions on definition and analysis of relevant markets, on designation of undertakings with significant market power in a relevant market, on imposition of specific obligations on undertakings with significant market power on a relevant market and on imposition of provisional obligations;
- any decisions concerning the fulfilment of specific obligations imposed on undertakings with significant market power in a relevant market;
- any decisions on disputes between undertakings; and
- any decisions whereby the Commission grants an authorisation to the candidate, which has won the contest for use of an individually assigned scarce resource – radio spectrum, for implementation of electronic communications over ECNs for digital terrestrial broadcasting.[22]

Every person who has a legitimate interest may appeal a decision of the CRC. The average duration of a court procedure is between one and one and a half years.

The NRA's Obligations to Cooperate with the Commission

Implementation of the consolidation procedure

8.12 The LEC obliges the CRC to cooperate with the Commission, BEREC and the national regulators in other Member States in a transparent manner for the purposes of development of the EU single market and selection of the regulatory remedies and obligations most appropriate for each particular case.[23] The two-tiered consolidation procedure provided in Article 7(3)–(5) of the Framework Directive is implemented into national law. The CRC's practice relating to the consolidation procedure generally meets the requirements set out by the Framework Directive.

The CRC must notify the Commission, BEREC and the national regulators in other Member States, and conduct a consultation procedure before taking a measure which:

- falls within the scope of the powers of the CRC related to determination, analysis and evaluation of the relevant markets, designation of undertaking(s) as having significant market power, and imposing, amending or withdrawing specific obligations on such undertakings, or within the scope of powers related to imposing obligations for access or interconnection; and
- would affect trade between Member States.[24]

8.13 The CRC must make the draft measure available to the Commission, BEREC and the national regulatory authorities in other Member States together with the reasons on which the measure is based. The Commission, BEREC and the national regulators in other Member States then have one month to comment on the draft measure. After the comment period has ended, the CRC may adopt the draft measure, provided that it is not subject to the veto-procedure, taking utmost

---

22   Art 35(6) LEC.
23   Art 41 LEC.
24   Art 42(1) LEC.

account of comments made by the Commission, BEREC and the national regulators in other Member States.[25] The CRC must send the final measure for reference
to the Commission and BEREC.

When the draft measure of the CRC aims to:

- define a relevant market which differs from those defined in the Commission's
  Recommendation on relevant product and service markets; or
- designate an undertaking as having, either individually or jointly with others,
  significant market power, and the Commission has indicated to the CRC that
  it considers that the draft measure would affect trade between Member States
  and create a barrier to the single market, or it has serious doubts as to the
  compatibility of the draft measure with Community law,

the CRC is prevented from adopting the measure for a further two months.[26]

8.14   If, during this two-month period, the Commission adopts a resolution
requiring the CRC to withdraw the draft measure, the CRC must amend or
withdraw the measure within a period of six months following the Commission's
decision.[27] If the CRC amends the measure, the amended measure is subject to
public consultation and re-notification. If during the two-month period, the
Commission takes back its reservations concerning the draft measure, the CRC
must adopt the measure and send its final decision for reference to the Commission
and BEREC.[28]

The CRC may only in exceptional circumstances adopt provisional measures by
way of derogation from the consultation and veto procedures where it considers
that there is an urgent need to act in order to safeguard competition and protect the
interests of users.[29] In such case, the CRC must promptly communicate the adopted
provisional measures, with full reasons, to the Commission, BEREC and the other
national regulators. The CRC may extend the term of such provisional measures or
make them permanent only after following the consultation and veto procedures.[30]

Implementation of the co-regulation procedure

8.15   The co-regulation procedure is also implemented into national law. If, within
a period of one month as of the CRC's notification to the Commission of a draft
measure aiming at imposing, amending or withdrawing a remedy imposed on an
SMP undertaking or an undertaking controlling access to end users, the Commission expresses an opinion that the notified draft measure would affect trade between
Member States and create a barrier to the single market, or that the Commission
has serious doubts as to the compatibility of the draft measure with Community
law, the CRC is prevented from adopting the measure for a further three months.[31]
In the event that no such notification is given by the Commission, the CRC may

---

25   Art 42(2) and (3) LEC.
26   Art 42a(1) and (2) LEC.
27   Art 42a(4) LEC.
28   Art 42a(3) LEC.
29   Art 42B(1) LEC.
30   Art 42B(2) and (4) LEC.
31   Art 426(1) and (4) LEC.

adopt the draft measure, taking utmost account of any comments made by the Commission, BEREC and any other national regulator.[32]

During the three-month period following a notification by the Commission of its opinion that the notified draft measure would affect trade between Member States and create a barrier to the single market, or that the Commission has serious doubts as to the compatibility of the draft measure with Community law, the CRC must cooperate with the Commission and BEREC for the purposes of identifying the most appropriate and effective measure in the light of the objectives laid down in Article 8 of the Framework Directive (and the national provisions implementing it) and taking into account the views of the interested persons and the need to ensure the development of consistent regulatory practice.[33]

8.16   If within six weeks from the beginning of the three-month period, BEREC delivers a reasoned opinion in which it agrees with the doubts of the Commission, the CRC may either amend or withdraw its draft measure, or maintain its draft measure.[34] If the CRC amends or maintains its draft measure, or if BEREC does not share the doubts of the Commission, the Commission may, within one month following the end of the three-month period following its notification of serious doubts, either issue a recommendation requiring the CRC to amend or withdraw the draft measure, or make a decision to withdraw its reservations to the draft measure.[35] The CRC may either follow the recommendation of the Commission or adopt the measure despite the recommendation of the Commission to amend or withdraw the measure; however, it must inform the Commission and BEREC of its final decision and provide a reasoned justification in case it does not follow the Commission's recommendation.[36] The CRC may withdraw its draft measure at any stage of the procedure.[37]

The Commission's power to stipulate standards and specifications

8.17   The LEC reflects the Commission's power set out in the Framework Directive to stipulate standards and specifications and to issue specifications. Pursuant to the LEC, in order to ensure interoperability of electronic communications services and to enhance the freedom of choice of end users, undertakings providing ECNs or services may apply the standards or standardisation documents recommended by the Commission and included in a list published in the Official Journal of the EU.[38] Undertakings providing ECNs or services are obliged to apply the standards or standardisation documents defined as compulsory and published in the Official Journal of the EU.[39] Further, the European and international standards must be introduced as national and be applied pursuant to the provisions of the Bulgarian Law on National Standardisation.[40]

---

32   Art 426(2) and (3) LEC.
33   Art 426(5) LEC.
34   Art 426(6) LEC.
35   Art 426(7) LEC.
36   Art 426(8) and (9) LEC.
37   Art 426(10) LEC.
38   Art 280(1)(2) LEC.
39   Art 280(1)(5) LEC.
40   Art 280(1)(4) LEC.

The Commission's power to issue recommendations

8.18   The LEC obliges the CRC to take utmost account of the recommendations of the Commission where it is established that the national regulators differ in performing their regulatory functions, and such differences may create barriers to the single market of the EU, except for cases related to the management of radio frequency spectrum.[41] Where the CRC chooses not to follow the Commission's recommendation, it must inform the Commission, giving the reasons for its position.[42]

'SIGNIFICANT MARKET POWER' AS A FUNDAMENTAL PREREQUISITE OF REGULATION

Definition of SMP

8.19   One of the many tasks of the CRC is to define and periodically analyse the relevant markets for ECNs or services in order to determine whether effective competition exists.[43] The CRC conducts the analysis in accordance with the methods and principles of competition law, ie effective competition is deemed absent if one or more undertakings have significant market power in a relevant market.[44] In line with article 16(4) of the Framework Directive, the LEC defines SMP as a position equivalent to dominance, ie a position of economic strength vesting in a single undertaking (or a group of undertakings[45]) the power to behave to an appreciable extent independently of competitors, users and end users.[46]

Definition of relevant markets and SMP designation

8.20   The LEC follows the regulatory approach established by the Framework Directive and its Articles 15 and 16. The CRC defines the relevant markets in accordance with the requirements of EU law, taking into account the national specifics. The product and geographical scope of the relevant markets are determined in accordance with a methodology jointly adopted by the CRC and the CPC.[47] On the basis of the market definition and subsequent market analysis, the CRC determines which markets are not effectively competitive and must be subject to regulation. Conversely, markets where effective competition exists may not be subject to sector-specific regulation.[48] In defining those markets, the CRC has administrative discretion which is subject to limited judicial review.

---

41   Art 43a(1) LEC.;'
42   Art 43a(2) LEC.
43   Art 151(1) LEC.
44   Art 154(2) LEC.
45   CRC may determine that two or more undertakings jointly have SMP if, even in the absence of structural or other links between them, they operate in a market which is characterised by a lack of effective competition and in which no single undertaking has significant market power (Art 156(5) LEC).
46   Para 51, Supplementary Provision, LEC.
47   Art 150(3) LEC and Methodology for the terms and procedure of relevant markets definition, analysis and assessment, and criteria for designating undertakings with significant market power, promulgated in State Gazette Issue No 27 of 11 March 2008 (hereinafter the 'Market Methodology').
48   Art 155 LEC.

The CRC must analyse periodically, on a two-year basis, relevant markets for public ECNs or services subject to ex ante regulation.[49] In so doing, the CRC, in principle, follows the Market Recommendation of the Commission; due to national circumstances, however, the CRC may also define relevant markets other than those specified by the Commission.[50] A market would be subject to regulation where:

- there are high and non-transitory barriers to entry, which may be of structural, legal or regulatory nature; and
- development of effective competition is not conceivable within a short time horizon of up to two years; and
- competition law alone is insufficient to adequately address the market failures.

In case an undertaking has SMP in a specific market, it may also be designated as an undertaking having SMP in a closely related market where, on the basis of the analysis, it is ascertained that the links between the two markets allow the market power held by the undertaking in the first market to be leveraged into the second market, thereby strengthening the market power of the undertaking.[51]

Imposition of remedies

8.21   Once the CRC has established the existence of market faults, it must impose specific obligations on SMP undertakings with respect to the relevant market aiming to provide efficient access or interconnection and interoperability of services to the benefit of end users and to encourage effective competition.[52] In selecting the appropriate remedies, the CRC has administrative discretion. If requested, a network operator must negotiate interconnection of its network with those of other public network operators.[53] Exceptionally, the CRC may impose obligations on non-SMP network operators controlling access to end users, as far as may be necessary to secure 'end-to-end connectivity' and interoperability. In implementing its supervisory functions, the CRC must respect the principles of objectivity, transparency, proportionality, and non-discrimination.

The CRC has completed its market analysis of all markets identified in the Market Recommendation and has imposed preliminary measures or remedies with respect to most of these markets. To date, effective specific measures have been imposed with respect to the retail market,[54] where BTC has been identified as a SMP operator, and with respect to wholesale call origination on a public telephone network at a fixed location,[55] where each of the operators is deemed to hold SMP within its own network. These measures include continued obligations on BTC and the other operators to allow carrier selection and wholesale line rental, and additional obligations for non-discrimination, transparency, and cost-oriented pricing.

8.22   While the market analysis process with respect to the entire wholesale level is complete, as most of the relevant decisions were completed at the beginning of

---

49   Art 2 Market Methodology.
50   Arts 4 and 5 Market Methodology.
51   Art 156(6) LEC.
52   Art 166 LEC.
53   See para 8.49 – 8.56 below for more information.
54   See CRC decision No 650 of 25 June 2009, which refers to the six retail markets as per the old Market Recommendation of 2003.
55   See CRC decision No 1361 of 31 May 2012.

2012, they are mostly not yet in force as they are awaiting comments from the Commission. This includes markets 2 (wholesale call origination on the public telephone network at a fixed location), 3 (wholesale call termination on individual public telephone networks provided at a fixed location), 4 (wholesale physical network infrastructure access), 5 (wholesale broadband access) and 7 (voice call termination on individual mobile networks).[56] The analysis of market 6 (wholesale terminating segments of leased lines, wholesale trunk segments of leased lines) was also completed in September 2012.[57] Of these only the analysis for market 2 has been officially adopted and is now in force.[58]

With respect to market 7, the CRC held that each of the three mobile network operators (Mobiltel, Cosmo Bulgaria Mobile and BTC) has SMP in their respective networks and decided to impose obligations for access and interconnection, transparency, non-discrimination, separate accounting, and cost-oriented pricing. In the market for wholesale terminating segments of leased lines (up to 8Mbit/s), BTC has been designated as SMP operator and obliged to provide access to and use of the respective facilities as well as additional pricing restrictions. BTC was also designated as SMP operator with respect to markets 4 and 5, where additional access and transparency obligations were imposed, as well as pricing limitations.

8.23   In general, the CRC must repeat the market analysis within three years from determining specific obligations for the SMP undertaking or undertakings. However this period may be extended for up to three additional years (ie a total of six years), after the CRC has approached the Commission with a reasoned proposal for extension, and the Commission has not objected. Furthermore, the CRC must conduct market analysis within two years after amendment of the relevant act of the Commission defining relevant markets which have not been previously identified as susceptible to ex ante regulation.

NRA's Regulatory Duties concerning Rights of Way, Co-location and Facility Sharing

Rights of way

8.24   Construction of ECNs, facilities and related infrastructure is carried out under the LEC and the Law on Spatial Planning[59] ('LSP'). Such construction must be carried out in compliance with the specific rules governing the construction works. The construction process in Bulgaria goes through several stages, the most important of which are:

- approval of investment designs;
- issuance of a construction permit; and
- issuance of an operational permit or certificate of operation.

Construction or installations developed without the relevant construction papers are considered 'illegal constructions' and are subject to removal. The control over

---

56   See Decision No 884 of 12 April 2012 regarding wholesale markets 2 and 3; Decision No 1683 of 21 December 2011 regarding wholesale market 4; Decision No 1683 of 21 December 2011 regarding wholesale market 5; Decision No 226 of 19 January 2012 regarding wholesale market 7. National proceedings with respect to wholesale market 6 are also near completion.

57   See CRC decision No 1954 of 27 September 2012.

58   See CRC decision No 1362 of 31 May 2012.

59   Promulgated in State Gazette Issue No 1 of 2 January 2001, as subsequently amended and supplemented.

designing, construction, and operation of ECNs, facilities, and related infrastructure must be exercised under the terms and procedures of the LSP.

Undertakings, providing ECNs or services, may install such networks, facilities, and related infrastructure upon entering into a written contract with the owner of a real estate asset owned by the State, a municipality, private individuals, or legal entities.

8.25 In compliance with Article 11 of the Framework Directive, the LEC further provides that, upon installation of new, or extension of existing, overhead and underground ECNs and facilities, for the purposes of achieving the regulatory objectives of the LEC and in pursuance of the public interest, easement rights must arise in favour of the undertakings providing public ECNs or services.[60] The easement rights arising under the LEC must be entered into the Cadastre under the terms and the procedure set forth by the Law on the Cadastre and the Real Estate Register.[61] The easement rights are applicable to all public and privately owned real estate (except where a right of use over public infrastructure might be in place, such as roads, electricity, gas and water and the drainage systems), where there is a detailed zoning plan in force and, in the case of private property, a one-time compensation has been paid to the owner. Easement rights must comprise of:

- rights of way and a right to install networks by the undertakings providing public ECNs or services, including branches from such networks to buildings and other plots; and
- restriction over the use of the real estate where right of way or right of installation has been exercised.[62]

8.26 Upon exercising the easement rights, the undertaking providing public ECNs or services must acquire a right for representatives of the said undertaking to enter and pass through the servicing real estate and to perform their activities related to the installation, development, maintenance and operation of the ECNs, facilities and the related infrastructure, including a right of way for the equipment through the servicing plots in connection with the installation and maintenance of the networks.[63] The undertaking must notify the owners or users of the servicing estate at least seven days prior to the commencement of the above described activities. In case of interruption of the operation of the ECNs or of the facilities to the said networks, caused by unforeseeable or insurmountable event, where urgent action is needed and the seven-day period cannot be observed, the notification must be given within the shortest possible period of time before or immediately after remedying the breakdown or the interruption. The easement right holder must ensure a joint use of the easement strip upon a reasoned request by another undertaking providing public communications networks or services, where this is technically and physically feasible and against payment of a consideration. In fact, the scope, location and specific rules for exercising the easement rights vary depending on the type of the respective ECNs and facilities. Therefore in addition to the general rules of the LEC implementing Articles 11 and 12 of the Framework Directive, secondary legislation (an ordinance) of the Minister of Regional Development and Public Works, the Minister of Agriculture and Food and the Minister

---

60   Art 287 LEC.
61   Promulgated in State Gazette Issue No 34 of 25 April 2000, as subsequently amended and supplemented.
62   Art 288 LEC.
63   Art 290 LEC.

of Transport, Information Technology and Communications address the procedure for exercising of those rights.[64]

The Commission considers the complex procedures for issuing of construction permits and the fragmented national legal framework dealing with the easement rights as a serious obstacle for broadband deployment.[65] Indeed, alternative operators have complained about the significant delays in the administrative procedures. Although, in the course of the transposition of the revised EU regulatory framework, the competent authority must reach a decision within six months, the future implementation of the above described provisions is uncertain.

Co-location and facility sharing

8.27   The CRC may impose on the undertakings providing public ECNs or services co-location or shared use of electronic communications infrastructure facilities, including in buildings, common premises in buildings, building access points, electricity distribution networks, on, over or under real estate owned by the State, a municipality, private individuals, or legal entities. Such obligations may be imposed to protect the environment, public health and security, or to meet town and country planning objectives. Prior to adopting a decision on imposition of an obligation for co-location or shared use of electronic communications network facilities, the CRC must notify interested parties, allowing them an appropriate period of time (which may not be longer than one month) to express their views. When imposing such obligations, the CRC must observe the principles of objectivity, proportionality, non-discrimination, and transparency, and may issue instructions on apportioning the costs of sharing.[66]

REGULATION OF MARKET ENTRY: THE AUTHORISATION DIRECTIVE

The General Authorisation of Electronic Communications

8.28   The LEC implements the principles of the Authorisation Directive and requires that electronic communications be provided freely, upon submission of a notification to the CRC, or upon receipt of a permit from the CRC for use of individually allocated scarce resources (eg radio frequencies, positions of the geostationary orbit, or numbers from the National Numbering Plan).[67] Electronic communications for a company's own needs are provided freely, provided that these are provided through ECNs without use of scarce resources, or radio devices using radio frequency spectrum which does not need to be individually allocated.[68] Public electronic communications must be provided upon submission of a notification to the CRC, provided that no individually allocated scarce resources are needed. In case individually allocated scarce resources are needed, public electronic communications must be provided upon obtaining a permit by the CRC for use of such

---

64   Ordinance No 5 on the Procedure and Manner of the Scope, Location and the specific Rules for Exercising Easement Rights relate to the Electronic Communication Networks, Facilities and the related Infrastructure; Promulgated in State Gazette Issue No 63 of 7 August 2009.

65   Bulgaria 2011 Telecommunication Market and Regulatory Developments, European Commission, Information Society and Media Directorate General, 18 June 2012.

66   Art 281b and Art 281d LEC.

67   Art 64 LEC.

68   Art 65 LEC.

individually allocated scarce resources.[69] Public electronic communications services in the territory of Bulgaria may be provided by sole traders or legal entities, whereas there are no restrictions as to the country of incorporation of the sole trader or legal entity, respectively.[70]

Procedural rules

8.29   The notification procedure is simple and free of charge. Within 14 days of submission of the notification, or of provision of any missing information and correction of any irregularities in the notification, and provided that the verification made by the CRC confirms that no allocation of scarce resources is necessary, the CRC must register the undertaking with the Registry of Undertakings that have Notified the CRC about their Intention to Provide Public Electronic Communications (the 'Registry').[71] Once recorded in the Registry, the operator must inform the CRC about any change in the data provided in the notification within 14 days as of occurrence of the change. The operator may terminate the provision of the notified public electronic communications services at any time, whereas it must notify the CRC in writing of such termination of services.[72]

Content of general authorisations

8.30   The rights and obligations of the undertaking providing public electronic communications arise as of the date of submission of a duly completed notification (assuming no individually allocated scarce resource is needed).[73] An undertaking that has notified the CRC for provision of public electronic communications services has, at a minimum, the following rights:

- to provide ECNs or services as of the date of submission of a duly completed notification (assuming no individually allocated scarce resource is needed);
- to construct, use and dispose of ECNs and devices;
- to receive approval of investment projects and permits for construction of public ECNs, devices and related infrastructure;
- to negotiate and receive assess to and interconnection with networks of other telecoms operators; and
- to provide some or all of the services included in the scope of the universal service when the provision of some or all such services is assigned to it.[74]

An undertaking that has filed with the CRC a notification for providing public electronic communications must comply with certain general requirements adopted by the CRC, depending on the type of the electronic communications network or service, such as, among other things, data and privacy protection obligations, consumer protection obligations, and reporting obligations.[75] The specific obligations which may be imposed on undertakings designated as having SMP are legally separate from the rights and obligations under the general authorisation.

---

69   Arts 66 and 67 LEC.
70   Art 69 LEC.
71   Art 75 LEC.
72   Art 76 LEC.
73   Art 75 LEC.
74   Art 74 LEC.
75   Art 73 LEC and General Requirements to the Providing of Public Electronic Communications (issued by the Chairman of the CRC, promulgated in State Gazette Issue No 24 of 4 March 2008, as subsequently amended and supplemented).

Rights of Use for Radio Frequencies

Strategic planning and co-ordination of spectrum policy

8.31   The use of radio frequency spectrum is regulated by the Council of Ministers (ie the Government), the National Radio Frequency Council and the CRC. The Council of Ministers adopts: (i) state policy on planning and allocation of the radio frequency spectrum upon proposal of the Radio Frequency Council and following a public consultation procedure; and (ii) a national plan on allocation of the radio frequency spectrum, upon proposal of the said Council and following a public consultation procedure.[76] The CRC grants for use the radio frequencies for civil needs and has powers relating to management of the radio frequency spectrum.[77]

The country's spectrum policy is generally consistent with the EU's approach to key issues such as, for example, harmonised and efficient use of the spectrum, the use of the 'digital dividend' spectrum, the flexibility of the GSM band, and application of the principles of 'technological neutrality' and 'service neutrality'. The Radio Frequency Council periodically updates the national plan on allocation of radio frequency spectrum, with the goal of implementing relevant decisions of the EU, CEPT, and the ITU World Radiocommunication Conferences. Bulgaria cooperates with other Member States and the Commission as foreseen by Article 8a of the Framework Directive.

Principles of frequency allocation, procedural rules

8.32   Frequency allocation is based on the principles of technology neutrality, service neutrality and spectrum tradability. Exceptions from the principles of technology neutrality and service neutrality are permissible only in limited cases set forth by the law. The CRC must re-evaluate the need of already introduced exceptions at least once in every two years.[78]

Individual rights of use for radio frequencies are granted by a permit issued by the CRC.[79] The granting of individual rights of use is allowed only in a limited number of cases, namely in order to avoid harmful interference, to ensure technical quality of service, safeguard efficient use of spectrum or fulfil other objectives of general interest as defined in conformity with Community law.[80] The provision of electronic communications through radio devices using radio frequency spectrum which does not need to be individually allocated is governed by rules to be adopted by the CRC.[81] As the relevant legal provision has only been in force since 29 December 2011, the CRC has, to date, not adopted such rules.

Where it is necessary to grant individual rights of use for radio frequencies, the CRC must grant such rights upon request, to any undertaking providing networks or services. The procedure for granting frequency usage rights must be objective, transparent, proportionate and non-discriminatory.[82]

8.33   A permit for use of individually allocated radio frequency spectrum is awarded on a competitive basis (after holding an auction or tender), where the

---

76   Art 8 LEC.
77   Art 30 LEC.
78   Art 130 LEC.
79   Art 79 LEC.
80   Art 67 LEC.
81   Art 65a LEC.
82   Art 80 LEC.

number of applicants exceeds the number of persons that may be granted a permit for the available radio frequencies. A permit is awarded without a competitive procedure in a number of cases explicitly specified by law, including among others:

- where the number of applicants is lower or equal to the number of persons that may be granted a permit for the available radio frequency spectrum;
- for carrying out electronic communications through use of analogue ECNs for terrestrial analogue radio broadcasting; and
- for carrying out electronic communications for own needs.[83]

The CRC must reach a decision on an application for a permit within six weeks after receipt of the complete application, provided that international coordination of the radio frequencies or the technical characteristics of the radio devices is not needed. Should such coordination be needed, the procedure for issuance of a permit may take up to eight months or longer.[84]

Transferability and time limitations

8.34 A permit for use of individually allocated scarce resources is granted for an initial period of up to 20 years, with a possibility for extension upon request of the permit holder.[85]

An undertaking that has obtained a permit for use of individually allocated scarce resources may transfer such permit or part of the rights and the obligations pertaining to the permit, or it may lease the individually allocated radio frequencies after the prior approval of the CRC. The CRC must issue such an approval if the contemplated transfer or lease does not negatively affect the competition or lead to changes in the conditions for use of the scarce resource; if the permit has been granted following an auction or tender procedure, an approval from the CRC may be issued only after expiry of two years from the date the permit was granted.[86]

Admissible conditions

8.35 The granting of frequency usage rights by general authorisation and by individual right of use may be subject to conditions of the type set forth by the law, such as:

- obligations regarding geographical coverage and quality of service;
- conditions for ensuring efficient use of the frequencies;
- the obligation to pay fees for the right of use of the radio frequencies;
- any commitments which the undertaking obtaining the usage right has made in the course of a competitive selection procedure, etc.[87]

Limitations of number of rights of use to be granted

8.36 The CRC may limit the number of rights of use for radio frequencies where it is necessary to ensure the efficient use of radio frequencies, to increase the benefit

---

83   Art 81 LEC.
84   Art 86 LEC.
85   Art 71 LEC.
86   Art 121 LEC.
87   Art 106 LEC.

for consumers or to encourage the competition. The decision to limit the number of rights of use to be granted for radio frequencies must be made after a public consultation procedure. The results from the public consultation and the decision of the CRC must be published on the latter's website. The decision must be reviewed at reasonable intervals or at the request of affected undertakings.[88] Where the granting of rights of use for radio frequencies has been limited, the CRC may grant such rights after holding of an auction or tender procedure.[89] An auction procedure is held in the case when a complex evaluation needs to be made for the granting of rights of use for radio frequencies. A tender procedure is held when the amount of the offered bid price is of utmost importance.[90]

Rights of Use for Numbers

General authorisations and granting of individual rights

8.37   Modeling the regulatory policy on the use of numbers falls within the competence of the CRC. The CRC develops a regulatory policy for use of numbers, addresses and names for carrying out electronic communications. Further, the CRC prepares and adopts the National Numbering Plan, which sets out the allocation of numbers used in the ECNs for identification, routing and charging.[91]

The provisions in the LEC in relation to rights of use for numbers follow broadly those regarding rights of use for radio frequencies. Rights of use for numbers are granted on an individual basis. Rights of use for individually allocated numbers may be granted only to enterprises that carry out electronic communications through:

- ECNs for providing publicly available telephone services ('PATS'); or
- ECNs for providing public electronic communications services, which are accessed through numbers from the National Numbering Plan.[92]

As numbers are considered to be scarce resources, rights of use for numbers are granted by a permit issued by the CRC. A permit for use of numbers is awarded without an auction or tender, for an initial term of up to 20 years, with a possibility for extension.[93] Decisions of the CRC for granting of rights of use for numbers must be made within three weeks as of the receipt of a complete application by the undertaking.[94] The LEC does not envisage a possibility for the CRC to limit the number of rights of use for numbers to be granted or a possibility for numbers of exceptional economic value to be assigned based on competitive or comparative selection procedures.

---

88   Art 90 LEC.
89   Art 89 LEC.
90   Art 94 LEC.
91   Art 30 LEC.
92   Art 3 Ordinance No 1 of 22 July 2010 on the procedures for allocation and sub-allocation, reservation and withdrawal of numbers, addresses and names (adopted by the Chairman of the CRC, promulgated State Gazette Issue No 64 of 17 August 2010, as subsequently amended and supplemented) ('Numbering Ordinance').
93   Art 81(4) LEC.
94   Art 88 LEC.

Admissible conditions

8.38 The granting of number usage rights may be subject to conditions of the type set forth by law, including, but not limited to:

- conditions for the effective and efficient use of numbers;
- conditions regarding the provided service, including conditions regarding transparency of tariff principles and the highest prices which may be applied in a specific number range with a view of protection of consumer rights;
- the obligation to provide public directories subscriber information for the purposes of the universal service;
- the obligation to pay fees for the right of use of the numbers; and
- conditions regarding number portability.[95]

Sub-allocation of numbers

8.39 Operators that have been allocated numbers for providing services through fixed, mobile terrestrial (global system for mobile communications – 'GSM', universal mobile telecommunications system – 'UMTS', or other), mobile virtual network operator ('MVNO'), broadband wireless access ('BWA'), or fixed wireless access ('FWA') networks, as well as operators that have been allocated numbers from the '700' and '800' ranges for non-geographical services, may sub-allocate these numbers for use by end users. Said type of operators may further sub-allocate groups of numbers to another undertaking that does not hold a permit for use of individually allocated scarce resource numbers, and has notified the CRC of its intention to carry out re-sale of the services provided through the respective numbers. In the latter case, the undertaking may use the sub-allocated numbers only for the purposes of re-sale, on its behalf and for its account, of the services provided through these numbers. Except for the described case, sub-allocation of numbers to other undertakings is prohibited. Operators that have been allocated numbers from the '90' range for value-added services, or numbers from the '118' range for directory services, may sub-allocate these numbers to legal entities and sole proprietors for provision by the latter entities of services through numbers from these ranges.[96]

Number portability

8.40 Subscribers of PATS are entitled to retain their numbers independently of the undertaking providing the service, as follows:

- in case of fixed numbers, the numbers may be retained independently of the change of the provider of the fixed telephone service or the address within one and the same geographic national destination code;
- in case of mobile numbers, they can be retained irrespective of the change of the provider of the mobile telephone service; and
- in case of non-geographic numbers, they may be retained irrespective of the change of the provider of the respective service.[97]

Portability took effect for mobile numbers at the beginning of 2008, for fixed in the middle of 2009, and for non-geographical numbers in the middle of 2010.

---

95   Art 107 LEC.
96   Art 43a and 43b Numbering Ordinance.
97   Art 134 LEC.

The NRA's Enforcement Powers

8.41   The CRC has far-reaching powers to exercise control over market players' telecommunications activities. The LEC establishes both procedural and substantive rules to ensure compliance with the conditions of the general authorisations or rights of use, as well as with specific obligations which have been imposed on SMP operators.

The CRC may request from any undertaking performing electronic communications activities information to carry out its regulatory functions. The information which the CRC may request must be proportionate and objectively justified to achieve specific objectives set forth by the law, including, among other things:

- systematic or case-by-case verification of compliance with imposed obligations;
- comparative overviews of quality and price of services; and
- market analysis.[98]

CRC officials are entitled to, among other things, have free access to premises where communications equipment is located, check commercial and accounting documents of undertakings related to the performed electronic communications activity, and require information from third parties for counter-checks.[99]

8.42   The LEC has generally transposed the provisions of Article 10 of the Authorisation Directive regarding the tiered procedure for the enforcement of the conditions of general authorisations or rights of use and the 'specific obligations' of SMP undertakings. Where the CRC finds that an undertaking is not complying with one or more of the conditions of the general authorisation, of rights of use or with the 'specific obligations' imposed on SMP undertakings, it must notify the undertaking of those findings and give the undertaking a period of not less than one month to state its view and remedy the non-performance. If the undertaking does not remedy the non-performance with the specified period of time, the CRC is authorised to impose a financial penalty.[100] In certain cases, specified by the law, such as serious or repeated breaches of relevant conditions or 'specific obligations' the CRC may prevent an undertaking from continuing to provide ECNs or services or suspend or withdraw rights of use.[101]

The CRC may impose urgent interim measures in case of a breach of the conditions of the general authorisation, rights of use or specific obligations of the SMP undertaking, which represents (i) an immediate and serious threat to public safety, public security or public health, or (ii) serious economic or operational problems for other providers or users of ECNs or services or other uses of the frequency spectrum. The CRC must give the undertaking an opportunity to state its view and to suggest measures for remedying the non-performance. The CRC may impose interim measures for a maximum of three months and may be extended by a further three months if the non-performance has not been remedied.[102]

---

98   Art 40 LEC.
99   Art 313 LEC.
100   Art 78 LEC.
101   Arts 118 and 120 LEC.
102   Art 78a LEC.

Administrative Charges and Fees for Rights of Use

Administrative charges

8.43   The CRC imposes on all undertakings providing public electronic communi-cations activities an annual administrative fee for the CRC's control activities. The fee is in the amount of up to 1.2 per cent (for undertakings having annual gross income over BGN 100,000) or 0 per cent (for undertakings having annual gross income below BGN 100,000) over the annual gross income from provision of ECNs or services, VAT not included and following deductions of transfer payments to other operators for interconnection, access, transit, roaming, value added services and expenses for settlement of copyright and related rights for radio and television programmes (if relevant).[103] The annual administrative fee for control activities must be paid in quarterly instalments, with the instalment for the last quarter being a balancing instalment.

The LEC also has three other types of administrative charges:

- a one-time fee for issuance of a permit for use of individually allocated scarce resource;
- a one-time fee for amendment and supplement of a permit, and
- a one-time fee for administrative services by the CRC.[104]

Fees for rights of use

8.44   In addition to administrative charges, the following fees for the rights of use of individually allocated scarce resources are applied:

- an annual fee for use of individually allocated scarce resource-radio frequen-cies or numbers or positions of geostationary orbit; and
- a fee for temporary use of individually allocated scarce resource.[105]

The amount of the annual fee for use of individually allocated scarce resources must be determined on the basis of criteria set forth by the law, such as territorial coverage of the permit, term of spectrum use (in respect of radio frequencies), availability and economic value of numbers from particular number rages (in respect of numbers), etc.[106]

Generally, the amount and terms of payment of administrative charges and fees for rights of use must be determined by a tariff on the charges and fees collected by the CRC. The tariff is adopted by the Council of Ministers upon proposal by the CRC.[107] The administrative charges and fees for rights of use are determined in compliance with the principles of proportionality, non-discrimination, encouraging of the com-petition and provision of new services, ensuring efficient use of the scarce resources and satisfying the needs of end users from quality ECNs and services.[108]

---

103 Art 141 LEC.
104 Art 139 LEC.
105 Art 140 LEC.
106 Art 143 LEC.
107 Tariff on the Fees Charged by the CRC for 2012 under the Law on Electronic Communica-tions (adopted by the Council of Ministers with Order No 374 of 29 December 2011, promulgated in State Gazette Issue No 107 of 31 December 2011).
108 Art 147 LEC.

REGULATION OF NETWORK ACCESS AND INTERCONNECTION: THE ACCESS DIRECTIVE

Objectives and Scope of Access Regulation

8.45   In regulating access and interconnection, the NRA's objectives are efficiency, sustainable competition, efficient investments and innovations, and maximum consumer benefits. The access and interconnection related provisions of the national electronic communications law apply to operators of public communications networks and to undertakings seeking interconnection or access to their networks and associated facilities.

Basic Regulatory Concepts

8.46   With respect to the powers of the CRC in relation to access and interconnection, the LEC distinguishes between general regulatory powers and regulatory powers with respect to SMP undertakings.[109]

The LEC adopts the Access Directive's definition of 'access'. Specifically, the LEC defines access as:

> 'the making available of facilities or services, to another undertaking, on either an exclusive or non-exclusive basis, for the purpose of providing electronic communications services, including when they are used for the provision of information society services or broadcast content'.[110]

The definition is further illustrated by a non-inclusive list of examples, which corresponds to the list of examples provided in the Assess Directive.

Interconnection is defined also in line with the Assess Directive as 'a specific type of access implemented between public network operators'. It is further described as:

> 'the physical and logical linking of public communications networks used by the same or different undertakings in order to allow the users of an undertaking to communication with users of the same or another undertaking, or to access services provided by another undertaking'.

Services of the (interconnected) public communications networks may be provided by the parties involved in the interconnection or by other parties who have access to the network.[111]

8.47   The principle of 'freedom of access' has been implemented into national law and it is upheld in regulatory practice. Pursuant to the LEC undertakings providing public communications networks or services at the territory of another Member State, may request access or interconnection, without a prior notification to the CRC, notwithstanding that they do not provide services and do not have networks at the territory of Bulgaria.[112]

The principle that commercial negotiation takes priority over regulatory intervention is also implemented into national law and upheld in regulatory practice.

---

109   Art 160(1) LEC.
110   Para 1(8) Additional Provisions LEC.
111   Para 1(4) Additional Provisions LEC.
112   Art 165 LEC.

Pursuant to the LEC, undertakings providing public communications network must freely negotiate access and interconnection and execute a contract in writing. For reference purposes, undertakings must provide to the CRC a copy of the signed contract or any amendments thereto.[113] The CRC is empowered to intervene at its own initiative and when this is justified, with respect to access or interconnection matters.[114]

8.48   The LEC further establishes a right of operations of public communications networks to negotiate interconnection with each other. At the request of another authorised undertaking, operators of public communications networks that have been granted a right for use of numbers from the National Numbering Plan are obliged to negotiate interconnection.[115] The purpose of the right and obligation to negotiate interconnection is to ensure provision and interoperability of services.

In line with the Community's policy decision to introduce widescreen television services, pursuant to the LEC, public ECNs established for the distribution of digital television services must be capable of distributing widescreen television services and programmes. Network operators that receive and re-distribute widescreen television services or programmes must maintain the widescreen format.[116]

Undertakings which acquire information from another undertaking during, or in connection with, the process of negotiating access or interconnection arrangements must keep such information confidential and use it solely for the purpose for which it was supplied. Such information may not be provided to entities which may obtain competitive advantages from its use.[117]

Access- and Interconnection-related Obligations with Respect to SMP Undertakings

Overview

8.49   The CRC may impose, maintain, amend or withdraw various access- and interconnection-related obligations on SMP operators where, following its analysis, the CRC finds a lack of effective competition in the relevant market.[118] Furthermore, the authority may intervene on matters of access or interconnection on its own initiative and, where justified, issue individual orders with specific obligations (eg where an operator refuses to conclude an access agreement).[119]

Specific access obligations

8.50   Upon request, or on its own initiative, the CRC may decide to impose on an undertaking with SMP obligations to provide access to and use of network elements or facilities, among other things, in situations where denial of access (or

---

113 Art 159 LEC.
114 Art 163 LEC.
115 Art 158 LEC and Art 3 and 4 Ordinance No 1 of 19 December 2008 on the Terms and Conditions for Access and/or Interconnection (adopted by the CRC with Decision No 2425 dated 19 December 2008, promulgated in State Gazette Issue No 5 of 20 January 2009).
116 Art 161 LEC.
117 Art 162 LEC.
118 Art 166 LEC.
119 Art 163 LEC.

setting prohibitive conditions with similar effect), would hinder competition in the market or otherwise adversely affect end users.[120] In exercising its discretion, the authority must take into account, in particular, the following factors:

- the technological and economic viability of using or installing facilities by competing operators, having regard to the pace of market development and the nature and type of interconnection and access involved;
- the feasibility of providing access in relation to the available capacity;
- the initial investment made by the facility owner, taking into account associated public investment and the risks involved in making the investment;
- the need to safeguard competition, and more specifically economically efficient infrastructure-based competition, in the long-run;
- the relevant intellectual property rights;
- the provision of pan-European services; and
- specific obligations imposed on the same undertaking on neighbouring related markets.[121]

8.51   While the CRC has relative discretion in choosing the appropriate measure, it must ensure that effective competition in the relevant market is restored, and its refusal to act is subject to judicial review. Among the access obligations which CRC may impose are the following:

- to grant access, or not to withdraw access already granted, to specific network elements or facilities, including access to network elements which are not active, for the purpose of, among other things, ensuring unbundled access to the local loop, ensuring access for the purpose of provision of carrier selection services for each call or on subscriber basis, and ensuring access for provision of the wholesale subscriber line rental service;
- to negotiate in good faith with undertakings requesting access;
- to provide specified services on a wholesale basis for resale by third parties;
- to grant open access to technical interfaces, protocols or other key technologies that are indispensable for the interoperability of services or for provision of virtual network services;
- to provide co-location or other forms of sharing of associated facilities;
- to provide specified services needed to ensure interoperability of end-to-end services to users, including means for intelligent network services or roaming on mobile networks;
- to provide access to operational support systems or similar software systems necessary to ensure effective competition in the provision of services;
- to allow interconnection of networks or network facilities; and
- to provide access to associated services.

Transparency obligations

8.52   To ensure transparency of access conditions, the CRC may impose on an SMP operator the obligation to publish, for the benefit of undertakings entitled to access, all such information as is required for use of the relevant access services or facilities, including, in particular: financial statements, technical specifications, network characteristics, terms and procedures for provision of access or interconnection, terms of use, prices, conditions limiting access to or use of services and

---

120   Art 173 LEC.
121   Art 175 LEC.

applications.[122] The CRC, as required by law, specifies the content of the information which must be published, the level of detail required, and the manner of publication, taking into consideration the need to safeguard business secrets. Most transparency obligations imposed in practice relate to publication on company websites of network technical specifications (and network elements), as well as general conditions and detailed information on services offered, including current prices.

If an obligation of non-discrimination has also been imposed, the CRC may require that the operator publish a reference offer.[123] The individual agreements concluded between the undertakings may not conflict with the reference offer.

Non-discrimination obligations

8.53 The CRC may oblige SMP operators to offer access in compliance with objective criteria, on equal terms and quality, and in general to conclude access and interconnection agreements meeting the requirements of fairness and reasonableness.[124] The aim of these obligations is to ensure that the operator applies equivalent conditions to undertakings in similar circumstances, and that it provides services and information under the same conditions and of the same quality to all its commercial partners. In practice such obligations are imposed both with respect to access, and with respect to the prices at which interconnection is achieved.

Accounting separation obligations

8.54 To ensure transparency of pricing, the CRC may require an SMP operator to keep separate accounts for certain activities related to access services or interconnection. In particular, the authority may oblige a vertically integrated undertaking to ensure transparency of its wholesale and internal transfer prices in order to prevent a breach of the prohibition on discrimination and unlawful cross-subsidisation.[125] After consultations with the undertaking concerned, the CRC usually specifies the format and the accounting methodology to be used in setting the prices.[126]

Price control obligations

8.55 Where the CRC issues an order for compulsory access or interconnection, it also retains control over the prices on which the respective services are provided.[127] When setting or approving prices, the CRC must take into consideration the investments made by the SMP operator (including with respect to next generation networks), allowing a reasonable rate of return on capital, as well as any risks specific to a particular new investment network project. The price control may include a price cap, pricing on the basis of a comparative analysis between the

---

122 Art 167(1) LEC.
123 Art 167(3) LEC.
124 Art 168 LEC.
125 Art 169 LEC.
126 See, eg CRC decision No 1049 of 15 April 204, amended by CRC decision No 158 of 28 February 2008.
127 Art 170(1) LEC.

prices set by the undertaking and the prices for the same services in comparable competitive markets of other Member States, or determining a plan for gradual reduction of the prices for a specified period of time after which the level of prices must reach a pre-set level.

The CRC usually restricts the right of SMP undertakings to offer retail price packages (service tie-in) unless the individual services are offered separately. The authority also regulates retail prices of electronic communications services offered by SMP operators by imposing price thresholds, obligations for cost oriented prices, reference pricing etc.[128] For this purpose the authority may require the SMP operator to elaborate and apply a cost accounting system. In the latter case the operator must make a description of the system publicly available, showing at least the main categories under which costs are grouped and the rules used for the allocation of costs.[129] Furthermore, the operator is obliged submit to the CRC detailed information on the costs of the relevant services annually, within four months after closing of the financial year.[130]

Functional separation

8.56   If the CRC determines that effective competition in a relevant market is deterred by a vertically integrated undertaking with SMP, it may order functional separation placing the activities related to wholesale provision of access services in an independently operating undertaking.[131] The separated undertaking must supply wholesale access services to all operators, including to related parties, on the same terms and conditions, including prices and timescales.

Functional separation is an extraordinary measure which has not been used to date, and the law prescribes that it must be applied only where all other measures have failed and there are important and persisting competition problems or distortion in relevant markets for wholesale access.[132] The CRC may impose this obligation after completing public consultations and subject to an authorisation by the Commission.

Regulatory Powers with Respect to SMP-undertakings

8.57   The CRC has imposed specific obligations on all operators providing connection to and use of a public telephone network at fixed locations (wholesale market 2) to offer access and interconnection, not to discriminate and to apply cost-oriented pricing. BTC, the largest (and former monopoly) operator, is also obliged to allow carrier selection on a call-by-call basis, as well as carrier pre-selection.[133]

With respect to wholesale provision of leased lines, the CRC requires BTC to offer to all interested parties wholesale services at non-price conditions and terms

---

128   Art 221 LEC.
129   Art 172(1) LEC.
130   Art 218 LEC.
131   Art 172a(1) LEC.
132   Art 172a(3) LEC.
133   CRC decision No 650 of 25 June 2009. In principle, the CRC may impose obligations to provide call-by-call carrier selection and pre-selection on SMP undertakings on other markets, but the ex ante analysis so far has not indicated a need for such measures.

corresponding to the retail terms offered. However, access deadlines are set significantly shorter than with respect to retail clients.[134] Furthermore, BTC must determine its prices in compliance with the 'retail-minus' approach, where access prices are explicitly set on the basis of the end user or retail prices of the corresponding final services.[135] There is also a general obligation to notify all price changes at least one month before their effective date, providing documents evidencing the pricing methodology.

Regulatory Powers Applicable to All Market Participants

Obligations to ensure end-to-end connectivity

8.58   The CRC is empowered, to the extent that it is necessary to ensure end-to-end connectivity, to impose obligations on undertakings that control access to end users, regardless of their market position, including in justified cases, obligations for interconnection of their networks, if such interconnection has not been made to date. The CRC may also, in justified cases and to the extent necessary, impose interoperability obligations on undertakings controlling access to end users, regardless of their market position.[136]

Regulation of roaming services

8.59   As Bulgaria is a member of the EU, the Roaming Regulation applies directly in Bulgaria. The LEC includes a number of significant monetary sanctions for failure of an undertaking providing roaming services through public electronic networks to comply with the requirements of the Roaming Regulation.[137]

Access to digital and television broadcasting services

8.60   To the extent necessary to ensure access of end users to digital radio and television broadcasting services, the CRC may impose, regardless of an undertaking's market position, fair, reasonable, and non-discriminatory obligations for ensuring access to Application Programming Interfaces (API) and Electronic Programme Guides (EPG).[138] Conditional access systems must have the necessary technical capability for cost-effective control by network operators of the services using such conditional access systems. Operators of conditional access services providing access services to digital television and radio services and upon whose access services broadcasters depend to reach any group of potential viewers or listeners, must offer their services on fair, reasonable, and non-discriminatory terms.[139] The owners of industrial property rights to conditional access products and systems must grant licences for manufacturing of such products and systems under fair, reasonable, and non-discriminatory terms. Such owners must not subject the granting of licences to conditions prohibiting, restricting, or deterring the inclusion in the same product of:

---

134   CRC decision No 226 of 16 February 2012.
135   CRC decision No 650 of 25 June 2009.
136   Art 160(2) LEC.
137   Art 334b LEC.
138   Art 160(2) LEC.
139   Art 179 LEC.

- a common interface allowing connection with one or several other access systems; or
- devices which are specific for another access system, provided that reasonable terms ensuring the security of information exchange with operators of conditional access systems are complied with.[140]

If specific obligations have been imposed on undertakings providing conditional access to digital radio and television programmes, the CRC may amend or withdraw such conditions where, as a result of a market analysis, the CRC concluded that the market is effectively competitive, only to the extent: (i) the access for end users to radio and television broadcasts and broadcasting channels and services specified in the 'must carry' provision, and (ii) the prospects for effective competition in the markets for detail digital television and radio broadcasting services and for conditional access systems and other associated programme or technical devices, must not be adversely affected.[141]

REGULATION OF THE UNIVERSAL SERVICE AND USERS' RIGHTS: THE UNIVERSAL SERVICE DIRECTIVE

Regulation of Universal Service Obligations

Scope of universal service obligations

8.61   In compliance with the Universal Service Directive, the LEC contains provisions regarding the scope, designation of provision and financing of universal service obligations. Universal service ('US') is defined as a set of services with a pre-determined quality that must be offered to all end users at an accessible price, irrespective of their location in Bulgaria.[142] The scope of the universal service obligation (USO) includes:

- connection at a fixed location to a public electronic communications network regardless of the technology used;
- provision of public telephone services that allows for receiving and originating national and international calls;
- securing public pay phones or other public voice telephony access points with pre-determined quality which ensures the possibility to make emergency calls, free of charge, to national numbers and to the single European emergency call number '112';
- provision of directory services;
- provision of directory enquiry services accessible to all end users, including users of public pay telephones or other public voice telephony access points; and
- access to public telephone services by disabled persons.

The scope of US does not include broadband Internet access and such amendment to the scope of US is currently not subject to a wide public discussion.

---

140 Art 180 LEC.
141 Art 155 LEC.
142 Art 182 LEC.

Designation of undertakings obliged to provide universal services

8.62   The CRC must assign (including through a competitive process) to one or more undertakings providing public ECNs or electronic communications services the provision of all or part of the services pertaining to the USO in all or in part of the national territory for the purpose of ensuring US coverage over the whole country.[143] The CRC must notify the Commission on the undertaking(s) designated with the performance of the USO and on the specific obligations imposed as well as on any subsequent changes to such obligations.

Pursuant to Ordinance No 6 on the Requirements and Criteria for the Quality of the US, the specific Measures for the disabled people and the Procedure for Designation of US Provider[144] ('Ordinance No 6') the CRC must conduct a competitive process for designating a US provider within one month after adoption of the analyses of the retail telephony markets. The amendments to the LEC of December 2011 (which also harmonised Bulgarian legislation with the amended Universal Service Directive) and the subsequent secondary legislation regarding US slowed down the process of launching the designation procedure. Currently the incumbent BTC is still imposed with the obligation to provide US.

Regulation of retail tariffs, users' expenditures and quality of service

8.63   The prices and price packages of the USO must be determined in compliance with a Methodology[145] drafted by the CRC and subject to public consultation.[146] The US Provider must submit the prices and price packages together with the underlying documents supporting the calculations for approval by the CRC at least 60 days prior to the entry into effect of the said prices. The CRC must consider the prices and price packages within 30 days after the submission and may demand modifications. The US provider must publish the US prices and price packages as approved by the CRC at least 14 days prior to their effective date by posting the relevant information on the Internet site of the provider, at the latter's commercial premises or in any other appropriate manner.[147] The CRC may oblige the US provider to offer end users and in particular persons with disabilities, with special social needs or with a low income, price packages which depart from those offered under the usual commercial terms.

The US provider must ensure that the end users are able, on their own, to monitor and control their expenditures and to avoid unwarranted disconnection of service by means of:

- free-of-charge itemised bills;
- free-of-charge selective barring for outgoing calls, Short Message Service and Multimedia Messaging Service messages and premium messages and, where technically feasible, of other similar applications;
- payment for access to public communications networks and use of public telephone services on pre-paid terms;
- allowing consumers to pay the fees for connection to public communications networks on the basis of payments phased over time;

---

143   Arts 190 and 191 LEC.
144   Promulgated State Gazette Issue No 32 of 25 March 2008 as subsequently amended and supplemented.
145   Promulgated State Gazette Issue No 94 of 31 October 2008.
146   Art 194a LEC.
147   Art 196 LEC.

- warning beforehand of a possible consequent service interruption or disconnection upon non-payment of bills – any interruption must be confined to the service concerned, as far as this is technically feasible, except in cases of fraud, persistent late payment or non-payment of bills. Within one month prior to disconnection, only calls that do not incur a charge to the subscriber must be permitted;
- provision of information regarding alternative lower-cost tariffs, if available; and
- free-of-charge alerts in case of abnormal or excessive consumer patterns.[148]

The criteria for quality of the US are set out in Ordinance No 6. The latter requires that the quality of the US must be a combination of the criteria for the technical quality of the service[149] and those for quality of provision of the service.[150]

Cost calculation and financing of universal services

8.64   The US provider must be compensated for its net costs where the provision of service represents an unfair burden for the undertaking. The existence of an unfair burden must be determined on the basis of the net costs and taking into consideration the intangible advantages for the US provider associated with the provision of US, provided that the US is provided at a loss or at prices below the reasonable margin of profit.[151] The rules for calculating the net costs are drafted by the CRC.[152]

The means for compensation of the net costs associated with the provision of the US must be raised in a Universal Service Recovery Fund (the 'Fund') and must be contributed by the undertakings providing public telephone services and from other sources. Only undertakings providing public telephone services having a gross annual income above BGN 100,000 are required to make contributions to the Fund. The annual contribution of those undertakings must not exceed 0.8 per cent of the gross revenues from the provision of a public telephone service, exclusive of value added tax, after deduction of the transfer payments to other undertakings for network interconnection and for access, transit, roaming, value added services.[153]

In June 2011, the BTC requested compensation for the net costs of providing universal service in 2010. In October 2011, the CRC opened a tender procedure for the selection of one undertaking which will carry out an examination of the incumbent's system for determination of the net costs and assessment of the net costs for 2009 and 2010. Due to the amendments to the LEC in December 2011, the procedure was cancelled and a new procedure for independent audit of the incumbent's system (in line with the amended legal provisions) has been issued by the CRC. This led to a further delay in the compensation procedure.[154]

---

148   Art 198(1) LEC.
149   Art 11 Ordinance No 6.
150   Art 12 Ordinance No 6 and Decision No 345 of 31 March 2011 of the CRC on the Criteria for the Quality of Provision of the US.
151   Art 200 LEC.
152   Rules on the calculation of the Net Costs for the Provision of the Universal Service, promulgated in State Gazette Issue No 10 of 21 November 2008.
153   Art 206 LEC.
154   Also commented in Bulgaria 2011 Telecommunication Market and Regulatory Developments, European Commission, Information Society and Media Directorate General, 18 June 2012.

Regulation of Retail Markets

Prerequisites for the regulation of retail markets

8.65   In line with Article 17 of the Universal Service Directive, the LEC requires the CRC to safeguard competition to the benefit of consumers and promote, where appropriate, infrastructure-based competition.[155] In principle, the authority may regulate retail prices of SMP operators where imposition of specific obligations is deemed insufficient.[156] Although it is not expressly stipulated in the LEC, therefore, regulation of retail services should be regarded as ancillary and used only where regulation at wholesale level does not achieve the regulatory objectives.[157]

Regulatory powers

8.66   First, the CRC monitors the evolution and level of retail prices and price packages of universal services in relation to national consumer prices and income and prescribes a specific methodology for price formation:[158] see para 8.63 above.

Secondly, where the CRC has established that an undertaking has SMP in a relevant retail market, it may, for the purpose of protecting end users and promoting effective competition, impose ex ante one or several of the following limitations:

- obligation for cost oriented retail prices;
- price ceiling – limiting the growth of retail prices to a predetermined maximum;
- price benchmarking – obligation to align prices with those for same or similar services in comparable relevant markets of (an)other EU Member State(s); or
- control of individual tariffs – direct micromanagement of tariff elements.

The measures must be proportionate, justified, and based on the nature of the identified competition problem.

8.67   Furthermore, the CRC may require SMP undertakings to elaborate and apply a cost accounting system.[159] Costs are derived from the long-run incremental costs of providing the service and an appropriate mark-up for volume-neutral common costs, including a reasonable return on capital employed.[160] In such case the undertakings must submit to the CRC a draft of a cost accounting system which may be modified at its request. The relevant information regarding the principles and main categories under which costs are grouped, as well as the basic rules used for the allocation of costs, must be accessible to the general public, and the undertakings must provide information free of charge upon request. They also must publish annual reports containing analysis of compliance with the cost orientation obligations.

All SMP operators must notify the prices of regulated services to the CRC one month prior to entry into force, and prices of temporary promotional packages

---

155   Art 31, para 4 LEC.
156   Art 221(1) LEC.
157   Art 17(1)(b) Universal Service Directive.
158   Art 194a LEC.
159   Art 222(1) LEC.
160   Art 170(3) LEC.

must be notified at least two weeks prior to implementation.[161] Twice per year, the CRC may require SMP undertakings to prove the cost orientation of prices, allowing them one month to comply. In case they fail to adjust the prices or, respectively, to prove the cost orientation, the authority may impose one or more of the price control mechanisms for a period not exceeding six months.

8.68   Rates for retail services supplied by an SMP operator which are not subject to prior approval may be subject to ex post regulation. The CRC must open an investigation of rates if it becomes aware of facts warranting the assumption that they may be abusive.[162] Abuse is constituted, in particular, by the undertaking levying rates which:

- contain pricing elements based solely on the significant market power of the undertaking on the relevant market;
- contain discounts which impede competition by other undertakings;
- discriminate between users of the same or similar services;
- are below costs levels; and
- are applied for the purpose of a price squeeze.

If the SMP operator fails to demonstrate that its conduct is objectively justified, the CRC will demand modification of prices and may impose further obligations and penalties.

8.69   Retail rates for the provision of leased lines are subject to the same rate regulation provisions as other retail services. To ensure a level playing field for competitors, the CRC has required BTC to offer to all interested parties wholesale leased line and physical network infrastructure access at terms corresponding to the retail terms offered.[163] The purpose of this obligation is to ensure that the SMP operator's competitors are able to provide competing service offerings, based on wholesale products to be provided by the SMP operator, at the same time as the SMP operator provides its retail services.

End User Rights

Contracts

8.70   Pursuant to the LEC, undertakings providing electronic communications services must offer those services to end users in compliance with the principles of transparency and equal treatment with respect to the type of technology used, the categories of subscribers, the amount of traffic, and the means of payment, and must not offer advantages to individual end users or groups of end users for the same services.[164] Only when the execution of individual contracts is not feasible in practice, may undertakings providing connection to public ECNs or public electronic communications services use general terms and conditions ('GTCs') in contracts with end users. Such GTCs must constitute an inseparable part of the individual contracts.

---

161   Art 219(1) and (2) LEC.
162   Art 219(6) LEC.
163   CRC decision No 226 of 16 February 2012.
164   Art 225 LEC.

The LEC establishes minimum content requirements for GTCs,[165] as well as for individual contracts with end users,[166] including those to which GTCs apply. GTCs prepared by operators providing US are subject to approval by the CRC, while operators providing public telephone services must submit the GTCs to the CRC for reference only. In addition, operators providing public electronic communications services must ensure free access of consumers at least to:

- GTCs (if any) applicable to the end user contract;
- up-to-date information about prices and price packages; and
- up-to-date information about the quality of the services offered.

Implementing Article 30(5) and (6) of the Universal Service Directive, the LEC requires that the initial term of contracts between the end users and providers of electronic communications services does not exceed two years and that the undertakings offer to end users the option to enter into a contract with a maximum duration of up to one year. The conditions and procedures for contract termination must not hinder the ability of an end user to change service providers.[167]

Transparency obligations

8.71   Undertakings must publish GTCs, or any amendments to them, at least 30 days prior to their effective date by posting the relevant information on the provider's website, at the provider's commercial premises, or in any other appropriate manner. Providers of public electronic communications networks or services must (through the same means) make available transparent, comparable, adequate, and up-to-date information on, at a minimum:

- the GTCs of the contracts with end users, where applicable;
- name, address, contact number of the undertaking;
- services offered, including (i) type of services offered, (ii) standard tariffs, including the services provided and the content of each tariff element, such as charges for access, usage charges, maintenance charges, standard discounts applied, special and targeted tariff schemes, additional charges and costs with respect to terminal electronic communications equipment, (iii) compensation and refund policies, including a detailed description of any compensation and refund schemes offered, (iv) types of maintenance service offered and (v) standard contract conditions, including any minimum contractual period, termination of the contract and procedures and charges related to the portability of numbers and other identifiers, if relevant,
- dispute settlement procedures, including those developed by the undertakings; and
- information about rights of the end users regarding US.[168]

Such information must be published in a clear and understandable, language and in easily accessible format.

Quality of service: securing 'net neutrality'

8.72   The regulatory framework currently in effect provides for requirements for transparency, non-discrimination, information, and quality of service, to preserve

165   Art 227 LEC.
166   Art 228 LEC.
167   Art 226(4), (5) and (6) LEC.
168   Art 231a LEC.

the openness and neutrality of the Internet. In its 2011 country report, the Commission confirms that net neutrality was not reported to be an issue in 2011.[169] According to the December 2011 amendments to the LEC, the CRC may define and impose on telecommunication providers minimum conditions for quality of service.

European emergency call number

8.73   All emergency services calls in Bulgaria go through the European emergency call number '112'. The 112 call number may be dialed from fixed phones, public pay phones, and mobile phones. National and international roaming is also supported for calls to the 112 emergency call number. There are, however, to date, no special means enabling disabled persons to call the 112 emergency number.

Obligations facilitating change of provider

8.74   Pursuant to the LEC, the porting of numbers must be carried out within the shortest possible time and the interruption of services must not exceed eight hours.[170] The maximum time for porting fixed and mobile numbers is seven working days.[171]

DATA PROTECTION: IMPLEMENTATION OF THE E-PRIVACY DIRECTIVE

Confidentiality of Communications

8.75   The applicable legislation currently in effect requires that undertakings providing public ECNs or services take appropriate technical and organisational measures to manage the risk posed to the security of networks and services. The measures must ensure a level of security appropriate to the risk presented, taking into account the nature of the problems and the costs of implementing the measures, and must aim at preventing and minimising the impact of security incidents on users and interconnected networks.[172]

The LEC imposes on undertakings providing public ECNs or services an obligation not to disclose and disseminate the communications and the related traffic data, location data, and data necessary to identify the user, to which they have gained access in the course of providing ECNs or services. This obligation applies also to the employees of such undertakings.[173]

8.76   There is a prohibition for the recording, interception, surveillance and storing of communications, except in the following cases:

- when the explicit consent of the sender and recipient of communication is obtained;

---

169   Bulgaria 2011 Telecommunication Market and Regulatory Developments, European Commission, Information Society and Media Directorate General, 18 June 2012.
170   Art 134(6) LEC.
171   Bulgaria 2011 Telecommunication Market and Regulatory Developments, European Commission, Information Society and Media Directorate General, 18 June 2012.
172   Art 243 LEC.
173   Art 245 LEC.

- such acts are allowed by a statutory act;
- the storing of data is necessary from technical point of view and is an essential part of the provision of the services; or
- the respective act is part of a technical check of the service, where the latter is performed by authorised persons.[174]

The restrictions do not apply to storage of communications and related traffic data under the following conditions:

- the recording is necessary and is required by a statute for the purpose of providing evidence for the conclusion of commercial transactions; and
- the sender and recipient of the communications have been informed prior to the recording about it, the purposes thereof and the duration of the storage, as well as of their right to object to such recording.[175]

Bulgarian legislation provides for an opt-out mechanism regarding the storing of information or gaining of access to information stored in the terminal equipment of a subscriber or user. The subscriber/user must be provided with clear and comprehensive information on the purposes of storing/access and the purposes of processing of such information, taking into account also the requirements of the data privacy legislation. These requirements do not apply when the storing/access is necessary for the transmission of communication over an ECN or for the provision of information society service, explicitly required by the recipient of services.[176]

8.77   In case of a breach of data secrecy, the service provider, within three days of ascertaining the breach, must notify the Bulgarian Commission on Personal Data Protection and the subscriber or third person(s), provided the breach may negatively impact the privacy of such person(s). Notification of possibly affected subscribers/third persons is not necessary, if the services provider has taken appropriate technical measures for the security of the relevant data.[177]

Violations of the rules on data secrecy and personal data protection are sanctioned with monetary fines. Additionally, Bulgarian legislation has criminalised certain acts leading to disclosure of personal data (eg dissemination of passwords or access codes that enable the disclosure of personal data).[178] The illegal obtaining or disclosure of traffic data is also penalised with criminal sanctions.[179]

Data retention

8.78   The Data Retention Directive has been implemented in the Bulgarian legislation by the inclusion of relevant provisions on data that may be stored and the applicable terms thereof.[180] The categories of data as per the Directive must be retained for a period of 12 months and may be used for the purpose of investigation of serious crimes and of computer crimes and for finding of missing persons. Requests for access to such data may be made by certain categories of officials working at the police authorities, prosecution authorities, national security authorities and military officials. Authorisation for access is issued by the chairpersons of the regional courts.

---

174 Art 246 LEC.
175 Art 247 LEC.
176 Art 4a of the Law on Electronic Commerce.
177 Art 261c LEC.
178 Art 319e Criminal Code.
179 Art 171a Criminal Code.
180 Art 250a LEC et seq.

A public debate preceded adoption of the rules on data retention and access to retained data. The debate mainly concerned the procedure for granting access, and the bodies that might have access to such data. After initial adoption of the rules, they were slightly amended; the main purpose of the amendments was to reach greater clarity and precision.

Traffic Data and Location Data

8.79 The LEC defines 'traffic data' as data processed for the purpose of the conveyance of a communication on an ECN or needed for the billing of the said communication.[181] Stored traffic data may be used after termination of a connection only where required to set up a further connection and for billing purposes. Otherwise, traffic data must be erased by the service provider or must be anonymised.

Additionally, traffic data may be stored and processed also for detecting, locating and eliminating defects and software errors in the ECNs, for detection and cessation of unauthorised use of ECNs and facilities, and for detecting and tracing problematic calls, upon a request by the affected subscriber.

A service provider, to use traffic data for market research purposes or to provide added value services, must obtain the prior explicit consent of the users. An opt-out mechanism must be available to users at any time.

Location data is defined by the law as any data processed in an electronic communications network or by an electronic communications service, indicating the geographic position of the electronic communications terminal equipment of a user of a public electronic communications service.[182] Location data may be processed by services provider after obtaining the prior consent of the subscribers, provided the data is anonymised or the data is necessary for the purposes and duration of provision of value added services requiring further processing of traffic data or location data other than the traffic data necessary for conveyance of the communication or for billing of the communication. An opt-out mechanism must be available at any time to the users.

The services providers must process and provide, for their own account, location data on users in case of emergency calls, even where no prior consent to the processing of such data has been obtained or where such processing has been refused. The data must be provided only to the relevant centres for reception of calls to the single European emergency call number '112' as soon as the call reaches the said centres.

Itemised Billing

8.80 It is the right of subscribers not to receive itemised bills after an express request. Service providers must provide subscribers, free of charge, with an itemised bill for the services used together with a tax invoice, and must provide, free of charge, access to information in an electronic form, regarding the monthly bills for

---

181 Para 1, item 71 LEC.
182 Para 1, item 7 LEC.

the services used. Additionally, service providers must provide, upon request, an itemised bill for the telephone services used by a subscriber.[183]

The LEC requires that the services providers ensure to subscribers the possibility to receive bills on a paper or in digital form.

Presentation and Restriction of Calling and Connected Line Identification

8.81   Service providers are obligated, to the extent technically feasible, to ensure the 'tone dialing', 'calling line identification' and 'connected line identification' functions of the electronic communications network.

Service providers that support the 'calling line identification' function of the electronic communications network, must offer, free of charge, the service 'presentation of calling line identification', giving the users the possibility, free of charge, of activating or deactivating the service 'elimination of calling line identification' via a simple means for each particular call or permanently for their respective line. Such service providers must also offer the called user the possibility, free of charge, via a simple means, to reject incoming calls where the service 'elimination of calling line identification' has been activated on the part of the calling end user.

Service providers that support the 'connected line identification' function of the electronic communications network, must offer, free of charge, the service of 'presentation of connected line identification', giving users the possibility, free of charge, of activating or deactivating the service of 'elimination of connected line identification' via a simple means for each particular call or permanently for their respective line.[184]

Where providing emergency call services, as well as in cases of calls to the services responsible for security, defence and internal order, the service providers must guarantee that the service 'elimination of calling line identification' function may not be activated.

Automatic Call Forwarding

8.82   Service providers that support the 'calling line identification' function of the electronic communications network, must offer the users, free of charge, the service 'stopping automatic call forwarding to the terminal equipment' of the said end users.[185]

Directories of Subscribers

8.83   Undertakings providing public electronic communications services, which prepare and publish telephone directories in a paper or electronic form, must list the name or business name, address and telephone number of the subscribers that have

---

183   Art 260 LEC.
184   Art 257 LEC.
185   Art 257(6) LEC.

explicitly consented to be listed in the telephone directories, free of charge. The telephone directory may also include additional data requested by the subscriber.[186]

Undertakings providing electronic communications services, which assign telephone numbers to subscribers, are obligated to inform their subscribers, in advance and free of charge, of the purposes of the telephone directory in which their data will be listed, as well as of any further possibility to use said data via search functions, in the case of electronic telephone directories, enabling users to find a name or business name and an address of the subscribers only on the basis of a telephone number.

A subscriber has, free of charge, the right to:

• apply for the listing of all or part of his data in a telephone directory; and
• request verification, correction or deletion of all or part of his data from a telephone directory – the data must be deleted or modified upon publication of a new telephone directory or upon updating of an existing telephone directory.

---

186 Art 258(1) LEC. Detailed rules on the publishing of telephone directories are set forth by the Regulation No 5 of 13 December 2007 on the Conditions and Procedure for Publication of Telephone Directories, including Work with Databases, their Transfer and Use, as well as for the Provision of Telephone Directory Services, promulgated in State Gazette Issue No 1 of 4 January 2008, as subsequently amended and supplemented.

The Cyprus Market for Electronic Communications[1]

A K Adamides

Scordis, Papapetrou & Co LLC (incorporating by way of merger Adamos K Adamides & Co), Advocates & Legal Consultants, Limassol

LEGAL STRUCTURE

Basic Policy

9.1 The core regulatory objective of Cyprus is the promotion of consumers' interests through prices, availability of choice, innovation, and economic development through efficient competition, the qualitative control of services, and the guarantee of a minimum bundle of universal services in the market of electronic communications.

The overall objectives of the legislation are, among other things, to create a transparent regulatory and procedural framework which promotes innovative technologies and facilitates the transition to full competition, to promote effective competition, discourage abusive practices, and adopt rules with respect to data protection, consumer protection, and users' rights.

Since the implementation of the 2002 Regulatory package, liberalisation of the Cyprus market for electronic communications has been achieved and new market players, other than the Cyprus Telecommunications Authority (CYTA), a state-owned public utility dominating across the whole spectrum of electronic communications, provide xDSL, cable services and 3.5G services and deploy Backbone fibre networks and pilot fibre access networks. The digital switchover in the broadband sector has been concluded and an alternative undersea fibre network is now available.

Problems regarding rights of way and licensing through public authorities have been resolved through specific secondary legislation. Secondary legislation for customer protection and disable users has been also applied to address consumer needs.

1   Editing of this chapter closed on 31 December 2012 The author is grateful to the Office of the Commissioner of Electronic Communications and Postal Regulation and the Department of Electronic Communications of the Ministry of Communications and Works for their valuable assistance.

Although new players have entered the market since liberalisation of the market in 2003–2004, their accumulated market penetration is still low.[2]

Implementation of EU Directives, Legislation

9.2   Cyprus proceeded with the transposition and implementation of the 2009–2011 European communications-related legislation in 2012. Full transposition of the 2009 EU Regulatory Package has been achieved through enactment of primary and secondary legislation and notification to the EU of all harmonised measures.

There is an holistic approach towards the implementation of the EU Regulatory Framework in Cyprus. Such approach entails that through market analysis the correct regulatory measures are applied to the Cyprus market, thus enabling the development of networks and services, promoting regulatory certainty as incentive for investment and enhancing the security of infrastructures and information.

The two main legislative acts are the Electronic Communications and Postal Regulation Law (L112(I)/2004) ('2004 Electronic Communications Law'), which imposes the legal framework for the regulation of networks and services in the electronic communications and postal services sectors, and the Radiocommunications Law (L146(I)/2002) ('2002 Radiocommunications Law'), which empowers the Director of the Department of Electronic Communications (DEC)[3] to implement and oversee the management and regulation of radiofrequencies, including satellite communications. The two laws were recently amended to transpose the latest 2009 EU Regulatory Package. There are a number of secondary regulations implementing these two laws, some of which took effect prior to the 2004 Electronic Communications Law, providing detailed regulation of specific components of the main legislation such as, inter alia, terminal equipment, collection of information and imposition of administrative fees, quality of services, consumer protection, market definition and designation of operator with significant market power, co-location and facility sharing, cost-calculation methodology, storage and processing of traffic data.

The Cyprus legislation on electronic communications has achieved the best possible result in enhancing competition in the market. The regulatory framework and the measures applied are assessed by the EU on a yearly basis as well as by external auditors. Minor adjustments are being continuously applied to enhance competition and protect consumer interests.

Cyprus is progressing to technology neutral regulation through the amendment of the current mobile authorisations (900MHz and 1800MHz bands) to allow the deployment of other technologies in addition to GSM, through applications for technology neutral licences of wireless access systems in the 3.4–3.8 GHz band, and through the authorisation of the use of the 800MHz and 2500MHz bands.

---

2   The main stakeholders in the market of electronic communications (besides CYTA) are MTN, Primetel, and Cablenet. Their penetration is approximately 11.50 per cent in fixed and 25.50 per cent in mobile telephony and 28 per cent in broadband.

3   The DEC is a department of the Ministry of Communications and Works.

REGULATORY PRINCIPLES: IMPLEMENTATION OF THE FRAMEWORK DIRECTIVE

Scope of Regulation

9.3 The 2004 Electronic Communications Law applies to the regulation of electronic communications networks and services and related facilities required for the implementation of a harmonised regulatory framework within the common market with a view to facilitating convergence of the telecommunications, information technology, and electronic media sectors.[4] This legislation fully conveys the provisions of the Framework Directive on security and integrity of network services, and confers to the Commissioner of Electronic Communications and Postal Regulation (ComECPR) the powers to implement and enforce these provisions pursuant to the relevant provisions of the Framework Directive.[5]

The definitions of 'electronic communications network', 'electronic communications service, and 'associated facilities' in the 2004 Electronic Communications Law as amended[6] are identical to those in Article 2 of the Framework Directive.

Content services are the competency of public authorities other that ComECPR, such as the Ministry of Trade and Industry, Cyprus Broadcasting Authority, Cyprus Police (for criminal issues), etc. The ComECPR may enforce terms and conditions to the electronic communications providers in case of complex services which are set by the relevant competent authorities.

In general terms there is no distinction between PSTN and VoIP telephony. However, special terms and conditions apply in respect to the access to emergency services, customer information and quality of services.

'Internet freedom'

9.4 In order to allow optimal speeds and content there are not restrictions as to access in the internet; however, ComECPR strikes the balance through quality controls and information of the users in relation to the services provided to them, thus, at the same time achieving safety and quality for the users.

National Regulatory Authorities: Organisation, Regulatory Objectives, Competencies

9.5 The ComECPR regulates electronic communications network and services, and the DEC regulates spectrum management.[7]

The ComECPR, in regulating electronic communications network and services, must promote the provision of electronic communications services for the public as a whole, the interest of consumers (with particular reference to the price and quality of services), the introduction of effective competition, and the capability to provide a wide range of electronic communications equipment and services.[8]

---

4   S 2(1) L112(I)/2004 as amended.
5   S 98 L112(I)/2004 as amended.
6   S 4 L112(I)/2004 as amended.
7   See paras 9.12–9.17.
8   S 18 L112(I)/2004 as amended.

Furthermore, the ComECPR must promote, among other things, the interests of the citizens of Cyprus and the EU through access to universal service, an inexpensive dispute resolution system for resolution of matters between consumers and providers, a high level of protection of personal data and privacy, the needs of specific social groups (particularly disabled users, elderly users, and users with special social needs), and greater regulatory coordination pursuant to the requirements of the BEREC.

The 2004 Electronic Communications Law as amended sets a framework for the ComECPR to promote these regulatory principles with objectivity, transparency, proportionality, and non-discrimination.

The ComECPR acts by imposing ex ante regulation in the field of electronic communications, whereas the Commission for the Protection of Competition (CompA) acts by imposing ex post regulation. The ComECPR must consult with the CompA when conducting market analysis;[9] on examination by the CompA of anti-competitive behaviour, the ComECPR may provide relevant information and technical support.

The ComECPR is an independent regulatory authority;[10] it has its own budget, approved by the Council of Ministers and the House of Representatives,[11] and it carries out its own recruitment procedures. The ComECPR and the Deputy Commissioner are appointed by the Council of Ministers, after consultation with the Committee of European Affairs of the House of Representatives, for a term of six years. Notwithstanding that they implement government policies, the ComECPR and the CompA have wide discretion as neither is subject to government oversight or approval.

The CompA's members are appointed for a five-year term.

The powers and duties of both authorities are consistent with the Directives of the 2002 EU Regulatory Package as amended by the 2009 EU Regulatory Package and include the power to demand information.[12]

The ComECPR must obtain information, consult with interested parties,[13] and conduct public hearings.[14] Consultations may refer to measures to be taken and may contain a description of the issues and specific questions. The ComECPR must publish draft measures both on its website and in daily newspapers in printed form and must specify the period for submitting responses, ie 28 days. The ComECPR also, except in confidential matters, must make publicly available the results of consultations and the positions taken by the participants.[15]

All relevant information on rights, conditions, procedures, charges, fees and decisions concerning general authorisations and rights of use must be published on the the ComECPR' s website, subject to the protection of confidentiality of any information which the ComECPR considers confidential.[16]

---

9   See para 9.9 below.
10   S 10(2) L112(I)/2004.
11   S 153(2) L112(I)/2004.
12   Ss 25, 30, 43(1) and 46(6) L112(I)/2004 as amended.
13   S 26 L112(I)/2004 as amended.
14   S 24 L112(I)/2004; PI143/2005.
15   PI144/2005.
16   S 44(1) L112(I)/2004.

The ComECPR has specific resolution powers under which it may summarily deal with a dispute.[17] It may, inter alia:

- undertake to conduct investigations and to resolve disputes either after a complaint or ex officio;[18]
- issue interim orders in cases of urgency in order to safeguard competition and protect the users' interests;[19]
- impose administrative fines to anyone who does not comply with legislation orders or decisions;[20] and
- once notified of a dispute, intervene and resolve the dispute with a binding order within four months of such notification.[21]

In case of a cross-border dispute, the ComECPR, before initiating any procedure, must inform the NRAs of the Member States of the persons involved in the dispute and cooperate with them in order to resolute the dispute. The ComECPR may consult with BEREC and request its opinion as to the necessary action to be taken.[22] Measures adopted by the ComECPR or other NRAs must correspond, to the greatest degree possible, with cooperation agreements between NRAs, taking particular account of the opinion of BEREC.[23]

Without prejudice to the right of consumers to initiate an action in the courts, the ComECPR may conduct a hearing after receiving a complaint from a consumer.[24]

Right of Appeal against NRA's Decisions

9.6   Any act or decision of ComECPR is subject to judicial review by the Supreme Court pursuant to article 146 of the Constitution.[25] The Supreme Court, notwithstanding that its jurisdiction is limited to either annulling or confirming a particular act or decision, widely exercises its jurisdiction.

The NRA's Obligations to Cooperate with the Commission

9.7   The 2004 Electronic Communications Law as amended fully incorporates the consolidation and co-regulation procedure of Articles 7 and 7a of the Framework Directive, as amended.[26]

To ensure that the European Commission has sufficient information to effectively perform its supervisory role over Community law, the ComECPR must, in performing its obligations, cooperate and consult with the European Commission.[27]

The Commission's powers of standardisation and harmonisation detailed in Articles 17 and 19 of the Framework Directive are reflected in ss 39, 50 and 53 of the Electronic Communications Law as amended.

---

17   See Part 7 L112(I)/2004 as amended.
18   Ss 30(1) and 31(1) L112(I)/2004. See para 7.73 below.
19   S 33(2) L112(I)/2004.
20   Ss 33(3) and 20(t) as amended L112(I)/2004.
21   S 33(4) L112(I)/2004. Similarly, in disputes between organisations, ComECPR must decide within four months once notified of the dispute (s 34(2) L112(I)/2004 as amended).
22   S 35(4) L112(I)/2004 as amended.
23   S 35(5) L112(I)/2004 as amended.
24   S 36 L112(I)/2004 as amended.
25   S 158 L112(I)/2004 as amended.
26   Ss 20(z), 47 as amended, 49 as amended, 50 as amended and 50A as amended, L112(I)/2004.
27   S 50(3) L112(I)/2004.

'SIGNIFICANT MARKET POWER' AS A FUNDAMENTAL PREREQUISITE OF REGULATION

Definition of SMP

9.8   An undertaking is deemed to have SMP if, either individually or jointly with others, it enjoys a position equivalent to dominance under Community law. Dominance is defined as a position of economic strength affording an undertaking or undertakings the power to behave, to an appreciable extent, independently of competitors, customers and ultimately, consumers.[28]

'Joint dominant position' refers to cases in which two or more providers function in a market, the structure of which is considered to be conducive to coordinated effects, (ie it encourages parallel or aligned anti-competitive behaviour). The ComECPR must seek the correct interpretation of the term by reference to the Court of Justice of the European Communities (ECJ) case law and the practice of the Commission.[29] Criteria to be used by the ComECPR in making an assessment of joint dominance of two or more undertakings are set out in secondary legislation.[30]

Where an undertaking has SMP in a specific market (the first market), it may also be deemed to have SMP on a closely related market (the second market), where the links between the two markets in question are such as to allow the market power held in the first market to be leveraged into the second market, thereby strengthening the market power of the undertaking in question. Consequently, remedies aimed at preventing such leverage may be applied in the second market pursuant to ss 56 as amended, 57 as amended, 58, and 60 as amended[31] of the 2004 Electronic Communications Law. Where such remedies prove to be insufficient, remedies pursuant to s 65[32] of the 2004 Electronic Communications Law, as amended, may be imposed.[33]

Definition of Relevant Market and SMP Designation

9.9   Under the 2004 Electronic Communications Law as amended, and the relevant orders issued thereunder,[34] the ComECPR, in engaging in market definition and market analysis, taking the utmost account of Community law, defines by order, relevant markets[35] as well as the procedure for defining further relevant markets in line with the competition law principles, taking also into account the prevailing circumstances in Cyprus. If the ComECPR intends to define markets that differ from those listed in the Commission's Market Recommendation and Guidelines it must adhere to the procedures set out in s 46 of the 2004 Electronic Communications Law as amended, as further defined in a relevant order of the ComECPR.

---

28   S 48(3) L112(I)/2004 as amended, see also PI148/2005 as amended.
29   Reg 2 PI148/2005 as amended.
30   PI147/2005 as amended.
31   Imposition of obligations of transparency, impartiality, separate accounts and assessment of price and cost. S 48(4) L112(I)/2004 as amended.
32   Regulatory controls on retail prices.
33   S 48(4) L112(I)/2004 as amended.
34   Ss 47 and 48 L112(I)/2004 as amended; PIs 147/2005 and 148/2005 as amended.
35   S 4 L112(I)/2004 as amended.

Markets defined for the purposes of imposing regulatory obligations under the Law must be without prejudice to markets defined in specific cases under competition law.[36]

After completion of the definition of relevant markets, the ComECPR must conduct an analysis of the effectiveness of competition in such markets, in accordance with Community law and where, as a result of the analysis of competition in a specific market, the market is found not to be effectively competitive, it designates an undertaking or undertakings as possessing SMP in that market and imposes on it or them a minimum proportionate regulatory obligation.[37]

Where, as a result of the analysis on the level of competition in a specific relevant market, the ComECPR concludes that the market is effectively competitive, no remedial measures are imposed and, following a reasonable notice to the affected parties, existing regulatory measures are withdrawn.

After the examination of a relevant market, the ComECPR consults with the interested parties and the CompA on the preliminary draft of the written communication, for the whole of the procedure to be followed.[38] The consultation procedure provides all parties the opportunity to comment on the preliminary draft of the communication and the decision, within a specified time limit, which may not be less than 15 days. The ComECPR must ensure that a centralised information point exists through which all consultations can be accessed, and that the results of the procedure will be published on the ComECPR's website, subject to the right of interested parties to have their confidential information protected.[39]

NRA's Regulatory Duties concerning Rights of Way, Co-location and Facility Sharing

Rights of way

9.10 The consideration by a competent authority to grant rights of way through public or private property, under Article 11 of the Framework Directive, as amended, is fully transposed into Cyprus law.

Specifically, the ComECPR must ensure that a competent authority acts on the basis of simple, efficient, transparent, and publicly available procedures, applied without discrimination and without delay, when it considers:

(a)   an application for the granting of rights to install facilities on, over or under public or private property to an undertaking authorised to provide public communications networks; or

(b)   an application for the granting of rights to install facilities on, over or under public property to an undertaking authorised to provide electronic communications networks other than to the public.

The ComECPR must also ensure that the competent authority makes its decision within six months of the application (except in cases of compulsory acquisition),

---

36   S 47(3) L112(I)/2004 as amended.
37   S 46(3) L112(I)/2004 as amended; see paras 7.27–7.29 above.
38   S 46(4) L112(I)/2004 as amended. Such consultation must take place before the consultation with the Commission, the BEREC and the NRAs of the other Member States as set out in s 50 L112(I)/2004 as amended, as well as before the publishing of the relevant Decision.
39   S 46(5) L112(I)/2004 as amended.

following the principles of transparency and non-discrimination in attaching conditions to any such rights. These procedures may differ depending on whether the applicant is providing public communications networks.[40]

Regarding the installation of facilities and the granting of rights of way, the ComECPR may amend the terms and the procedures only in objectively justified cases and in a proportionate manner. Except where the proposed amendments are of minor importance and agreed with the holder of the rights or the general authorisation, the ComECPR must communicate its intention to amend to interested parties (including users and consumers), giving a reasonable time of at least four4 weeks, for such parties to submit their views on the proposed amendments.[41]

Public communication network providers may acquire immovable property for the purposes of their activities. Property which cannot be acquired by agreement may be acquired under the provisions of the law for compulsory acquisition.[42] Rights of way are regulated through the application of PI10/2012,[43] which has replaced PI322/2008 and harmonises Cyprus legislation with the provisions of the NGA Recommendation of the Commission.

Duly authorised electronic communications network providers may, for the purpose of survey, examination, or investigation, preliminary or incidental to the exercise of any of the functions of a licensed network provider, at all reasonable times, enter upon any land (whether privately or publicly owned) and subject to providing 24 hours' prior notice in writing to its occupier, upon any premises.[44]

For the purpose of carrying out work in connection with any electronic communication network, with the consent of the occupier of immovable property, or by agreement and the payment of an agreed sum of money, after giving 24 hours' prior notice to the occupier of the immovable property, the network provider may enter the property and carry out all necessary work and installations. In the course of such work and installation, the network provider, as may be necessary, may cut or lop trees, remove vegetation, hedges, drywalls or other items.

In the event that no consent is granted or no agreement is concluded between the network provider and the occupier concerning entry or the amount to be paid, the provider may apply to the court which, after considering and weighing the prejudice versus the benefit accruing to the parties involved, will decide whether to permit entry and the amount of compensation to be paid.

An electronic communication network provider may, subject to reasonable notice, execute work upon any street, and, at all reasonable times, enter upon any land, houses or buildings in which installations or machinery have been, are, or will be installed.[45] Prior to executing any work, providers must ensure that it has obtained all necessary rights and permissions.[46] Streets damaged or opened must be reinstated to their previous condition as expeditiously as possible according to the

---

40   S 96B(1) L112(I)/2004 as amended. See also PI10/2012 for procedures and time frames.
41   S 96A(1) L112(I)/2004 as amended.
42   S 89(1) L112(I)/2004.
43   S 89(2) L112(I)/2004.
44   S 89(2) L112(I)/2004.
45   S 90 L112(I)/2004.
46   S 96 L112(I)/2004 as amended.

terms and conditions set by the competent authority.[47] An electronic communication network installation must not interrupt, obstruct, or interfere with passage along the street.[48]

The procedures for obtaining permits from local authorities are fully harmonised.[49]

Co-location and facility sharing

9.11 Article 12 of the Framework Directive has been fully incorporated into Cyprus law via s 62 of the 2004 Electronic Communications Law as amended. The ComECPR, in accordance with the principles of objectivity, transparency, proportionality and impartiality, has the power to impose the sharing of infrastructure or property, including, inter alia, buildings or entries to buildings, building wiring, masts, antennae, towers and other supporting constructions, ducts, conduits, manholes and cabinets, to any person providing electronic communications networks and has the right under national legislation to install infrastructure facilities on, over or under public or private property, or may take advantage of the procedure for the compulsory acquisition or use of property.[50]

The ComECPR may, after public consultations, impose terms and conditions for the sharing of infrastructure or property, including physical co-location, or for taking measures to facilitate public works, or for the sharing of the in-building wiring, or up to the first concentration or distribution point, where such wiring is offsite or for the apportionment of the costs of facility sharing. The ComECPR may, following a referral from any party to a dispute in relation to such an agreement, take measures to resolve the dispute. The aforesaid agreement shall be deemed to be an interconnection agreement for this purpose.[51]

REGULATION OF MARKET ENTRY: IMPLEMENTATION OF THE AUTHORISATION DIRECTIVE

The General Authorisation of Electronic Communications

9.12 Under the latest legislative amendments of 2012[52] the procedures to grant the use of radio frequencies and to grant the use of networks and services are handled by different public bodies. The ComECPR provides general authorisation while the DEC is responsible for the granting of use of radio frequencies.[53] However, in the course of the procedure to grant the use of radio frequencies, the DEC must take into account the opinion of the ComECPR in matters of competition and quality of service.

---

47   S 89(9) L112(I)/2004 as amended.
48   S 89(10)L112(I)/2004.
49   PI10/2012
50   S 62 L112(I)/2004 as amended.
51   Ibid. See also PI338/2006 as amended.
52   L50(I)/2012 amending 2002 Radiocommunications Law and L51(I)/2012 amending 2004 Electronic Communications Law.
53   See para 9.13 below.

Any undertaking may provide electronic communication networks or services in Cyprus subject to a general authorisation or, in exceptional circumstances, to an individual right of use relating to the use of radio frequencies or numbers.[54]

An undertaking seeking to provide electronic communication networks or services pursuant to a general authorisation may commence activities immediately after filing formal notification with ComECPR.[55] Permits from competent authorities are necessary for carrying out construction works.

Undertakings providing cross-border electronic communication services to businesses established in other Member States are not required to file more than one notification for the authorisation of their activity in respect of each Member State involved.[56]

The ComECPR may prohibit or limit the ability of a specific undertaking to provide electronic communication networks or services to protect public order, safety, or health.

Any person who intends to provide an electronic communication network or an electronic communications service must notify the ComECPR in advance, and any changes to the information must be notified within 30 days therefrom.[57]

An undertaking operating pursuant to a general authorisation may provide electronic communication networks or services, as described in its notification, and apply for the necessary rights to install facilities on, over, or under public or private property for the purposes of providing communications networks. Where an authorised undertaking is providing an electronic communication network or service to the public, the general authorisation also gives it the right to negotiate interconnection and obtain access to or interconnection from another undertaking authorised in Cyprus or in another Member State.[58]

The ComECPR, within one week of receiving a request from an authorised undertaking, issues a standardised declaration confirming, where applicable, that the undertaking has submitted a notification and detailing the terms and prerequisites applicable to the exercise of rights by the undertaking. The same declaration may be issued in response to the notification.[59]

The ComECPR must specify in the declaration the obligations of a provider operating pursuant to a general authorisation, and may further specify that certain conditions will not apply to undertakings of a class or type.[60] The conditions set out in Part A of the Annex to the Authorisation Directive have been adopted. General authorisations may set out criteria and procedures for the imposition of specific obligations with respect to interconnection, end users' rights, and universal service, where applicable.

Within its powers, the ComECPR has published a Frequencies Management Plan as to the access to the CYTA's network infrastructure.[61]

---

54   Ss 37(1) and 38 L112(I)/2004 as amended. The authorisation regime is described in detail in PI851/2004, as amended.
55   Ss 37(3) and 38 L112(I)/2004 as amended.
56   S 37(7) L112(I)/2004 as amended.
57   S 38 L112(I)/2004 as amended.
58   S 40 L112(I)/2004.
59   *Ibid.*
60   S 39 L112(I)/2004 as amended.
61   PI450/2008 as amended.

Rights of Use for Radio Frequencies

Principles of frequency allocation, procedural rules

9.13   Radio Frequency regulation is governed by the 2002 Radiocommunications Law[62] as amended. The Minister of Communication and Works ('the Minister') is responsible for the overall policy on all radio matters and the DEC is responsible for the implementation of the said policy, management of the radio spectrum and advises the Minister on radio spectrum policy issues. The DEC develops and maintains the National Radio frequency Plan, authorises use of the radio spectrum (including the assignment of frequencies to broadcasting stations), and monitors spectrum usage.

The legal framework fully adopts the relevant EU legislation: rights of use for frequencies[63] are either granted by way of general authorisations or individual rights of use.[64] The DEC may prescribe categories of radio frequencies and frequency bands that are exempted from the obligation to obtain an authorisation.[65] Such categories include all frequency bands for which CEPT/ECC Decisions[66] provide for exception from individual licensing.

Applications are required for individual rights of use, and registration is required for general authorisations. Generally, authorisations (individual rights of use) that are granted on a 'first come first serve' basis are subject to availability of frequencies and the compliance with the technical requirements of the specified authorisation.

Specifically, authorisations (individual right of use) for fixed links, PMR/PAMR, and satellite uplinks, among others, are granted according to the Authorisations Regulations[67] on a first come first serve basis (an application is submitted and evaluated before the authorisation is granted). Authorisations (individual right of use) for networks such as DTTv, mobile networks, broadband wireless access, (i.e. in case where there is spectrum scarcity and the total market demand cannot be satisfied), are granted through competition procedures (open tender or auction).[68] In some cases authorisations are granted through negotiation procedures.[69] For services such as WiFi/RLAN, MCV, MCA, among others, a general authorisation is granted according to PI376/2012 as amended. Specific devices such as SRDs, RFID devices, among others, are exempted from the obligation to obtain an authorisation based on PI115/2012.

---

62   2002 Radiocommunications Law was enacted to harmonise national law with Directives 87/372/EEC, 90/544/EEC, 91/287/EEC, 710/97/EC, 97/13/EC, 99/128/EC and 1999/5/EC as amended.

63   S 16 L146(I)/2002 as amended.

64   Individual rights of use are granted to avoid harmful interference, ensure technical quality of service, safeguard efficient use of spectrum, and fulfill objectives of general interest (S 18 of the 146(I)/2002 as amended).

65   PI115/2012.

66   ECC/DEC/(03)04, ECC/DEC/(02)08, ECC/DEC/(02)11, ERC/DEC/(01)01 to ERC/DEC/ (01)06, ERC/DEC/(01)08 to ERC/DEC/(01)18, ERC/DEC/(00)03 to ERC/DEC/(00)05, ERC/ DEC/(99)02, ERC/DEC/(99)03, ERC/DEC/(98)22, ERC/DEC/(98)23, ERC/DEC/(98)26, ERC/DEC/(98)27, ERC/DEC/(95)09.

67   PI463/2004 as amended.

68   Ss 23, 24 L146(I)/2002 as amended and PI382/2002 as amended. See para. 7.65 below.

69   S 7(2) of PI382/2002 as amended.

Regulations with respect to frequency allocation fully adopt the EU harmonisation Decisions and follows recommendations of the International Telecommunication Union.[70]

Strategic planning and co-ordination of spectrum policy

9.14   The DEC is charged with efficient and effective spectrum management. The Minister and the DEC must exercise their competences and powers to promote the use of Radiocommunications in Cyprus for the benefit of the public and the availability of spectrum to a wide range of organisations and users and to promote competition in the provision of electronic communication networks.[71] The DEC introduces new technologies and makes radio spectrum available for electronic communication networks in the framework defined by relevant EU legal instruments. It facilitates investment, supports entrepreneurial initiatives, and encourages innovation, aiming at ensuring that all citizens have choices and access to high quality services.

In special cases, defined by the 2002 Radiocommunications Law, authorisations for public radio and television broadcasting services are granted through negotiation procedures and no fees are required.[72]

Cyprus' spectrum policy is fully liberalised and fully consistent with the regulatory framework of the EU. Regarding key issues such as digital dividend, the 800MHz band has been available in Cyprus since July 2011 when Cyprus switched to digital terrestrial television, and the DEC currently is examining the next steps in order to authorise such spectrum. Furthermore, the DEC initiated a procedure to amend the current mobile authorisations (900MHz and 1800MHz band) to allow deployment of other technologies in addition to GSM.

Cyprus cooperates closely with other Member States and the Commission and actively participates in the relevant Commission Committees and Working Groups (eg CoCom, RSC, TCAM, RSPG). Cyprus engages in discussions with other Member States regarding exchange of common practices and information (typically through the exchange of questionnaires).

Transferability and time limitations

9.15   Transfer or lease of frequencies is permitted in specific circumstances.[73] Time limitations to rights to frequency use are set on a case by case basis and are included as terms of the authorisations granted.

Admissible conditions

9.16   A right of use may be issued under such terms, conditions and limitations as the DEC may deem fit, with respect to the 2002 Radiofrequency Law[74] adopting Part B of the Annex to the Authorisation Directive.

---

70   S 5 L146(I)/2002 as amended, National Radiofrequency Plan (available in English at the DEC's website, www.mcw.gov.cy/dec).

71   S 3 L146(I)/2002 as amended.

72   Ss 18(2), 18(4) L146(I)/2002 as amended and s 7(2)(f) of PI382/2002 as amended.

73   S 16A L146(I)/2002 as amended.

74   S 28 L146(I)/2002 as amended.

For the GSM-900 MHz, GSM-1800 MHz and the 3G bands there are only geographical roll-out obligations. The Radio LAN bands (2.4 GHz and 5 GHz) are subject to a general authorisation[75] with the technical requirements[76] prescribed in the relevant EU and CEPT/ECC Decisions.

Special conditions exist for important spectrum bands. Specifically:

- For Wireless Access Systems (WAS) and Radio LAN (RLAN) which are subject to general authorisation, there are power limitations and limitations related to the antenna used with these systems (the terms and conditions are being described in the General Authorisation for the Use of Radiofrequencies by Radio Local Area Networks and by Wireless Access Systems).
- For GSM authorisations (900MHz and 1800MHz), geographical coverage obligations apply. Specifically, CYTA (as the incumbent) must cover geographically 90 per cent of Cyprus, whereas in 2003 MTN (as a newcomer) was required, within two years, to cover 50 per cent of Cyprus, and within 4 years, 75 per cent of Cyprus. For 3G authorisations (2100MHz) both entities (CYTA and MTN) were required (in 2003) to cover geographically 60 per cent of Cyprus within 10 years.
- Cyprus Broadcasting Corporation ('CyBC'), which was granted a digital terrestrial TV (DTTv) network authorisation, must cover the whole of the island whereas Velister (the holder of the commercial DTTv authorisation) must cover geographically 75 per cent of Cyprus. Velister must also use all the frequencies granted to it within three years (in the absence of which, the DEC may take back the frequencies).

Coverage obligations do not include the part of Cyprus occupied by the Turkish army since 1974.

Limitation of number of rights of use to be granted

9.17   There is no limit on the number of authorisations, except to the extent required to ensure the efficient use of radio frequencies.[77]

To optimise the use of frequency spectrum, the DEC may decide whether auctions or invitations for submission of tenders are to be declared, where the total demand is not satisfied or it is anticipated that, in the near future, such a demand will not be satisfied.[78] Spectrum auctions are common in Cyprus. They are conducted by the DEC according to the 2002 Radiocommunications Law and to the Competition and Negotiation Regulations.

Regulations are issued following a procedure safeguarding transparency and giving interested parties the opportunity to express views.[79]

Charges are levied[80] in relation to an individual right of use, for submitting the application, the operation, renewal and amendment and in relation to a general authorisation for the registration, operation, renewal and amendment.

---

75   PIs 376/2010 and 91/2012 respectively.
76   Technical conditions are described in the General Authorisation for the Use of Radiofrequencies by Radio Local Area Networks and by Wireless Access Systems, including the Radio Local Area Networks (WAS/RLAN), PI100/2010.
77   S 19 L146(I)/2002 as amended.
78   Ss 23 (tenders/open contents) and 24 (auctions/closed contents) L146(I)/2002 as amended.
79   S 14 L146(I)/2002 as amended.
80   S 20 L146(I)/2002 as amended and PI464/2004 as amended.

Rights of Use for Numbers

General authorisations and granting of individual rights

9.18   The ComECPR issues decisions granting individual rights to use numbers from the Numbering Plan according to prescribed open, transparent, and non-discriminatory procedures.[81] Rights of use for numbers, or a series of numbers, are issued to providers for their own use and for further allocation to their subscribers.[82]

The ComECPR may impose fees for the right to use numbers.

Admissible conditions

9.19   The ComECPR may impose one or more of the obligations set out in the 2004 Electronic Communications Law which has adopted Part A and Part C of the Annex to the Authorisation Directive.[83]

The ComECPR ensures that all subscribers with numbers from the Numbering Plan of the Republic of Cyprus may, if they so wish, retain their number(s), irrespective of the undertaking providing the service in the case of geographic numbers at a specific location, and, in the case of non geographic numbers, at any location.[84]

Limitation of number of rights of use to be granted

9.20   At reasonable intervals, or at the reasonable request of affected undertakings, the ComECPR may review the limitation on the number of rights of use by withdrawing any limitation or increasing or decreasing the relevant number. If the ComECPR finds that it is possible to expand the scope of the relevant rights of use to include additional numbers, it must amend its decision and determine the type of procedure to be followed for such amendment.[85]

The 2004 Electronic Communications Law as amended provides competitive and comparative selection procedures for rights of use of numbers.[86]

The NRA's Enforcement Powers

9.21   ComECPR is empowered, inter alia to:

- demand and receive information (including information on future network or service developments);[87]

---

81   PI850/2004 as amended.
82   S 41 L112(I)/2004 as amended.
83   S 41(3) L112(I)/2004 as amended.
84   S 75(1) L112(I)/2004 as amended.
85   S 41(9) L112(I)/2004.
86   S 41 L112(I)/2004 as amended.
87   S 25 L112(I)/2004 as amended.

- conduct consultations with commercial and consumer organisations and with representatives of the government;[88]
- supervise compliance with the terms and conditions set out in authorisations;
- impose penalties in the form of administrative fines on any public or non-public provider;
- summon and enforce the attendance of witnesses at inquiries;
- issue decisions necessary to secure compliance with the Law and Orders; and
- upon its own motion or following a complaint, hold an enquiry and summon and compel attendance of witnesses and parties and to examine them personally or through lawyers.[89] Failure to comply, without reasonable cause, with an order or decision constitutes a criminal offence.[90]

ComECPR is also empowered to issue interim decisions and/or orders,[91] upon evidence of a breach of the conditions of a general authorisation or right of use that represents an immediate and serious threat to public safety, public security or public health, or that will create serious economic or operational problems for other providers or users of electronic communication networks or services,[92] and that requires urgent action in order to safeguard competition and protect the interests of users.[93]

Administrative Charges and Fees for Rights of Use

9.22   All authorised organisations must pay appropriate charges and fees.[94]

The ComECPR prescribes and regulates the structure of charges, which may include minimum or maximum price levels required to ensure legitimate and healthy competition, and the principles of transparency and cost orientation of any provider designated as universal service provider or who has been determined as holding a position of SMP in a relevant market.[95]

Application fees for the granting of individual rights of use depend on the activity which is applied for.

REGULATION OF NETWORK ACCESS AND INTERCONNECTION: IMPLEMENTATION OF THE ACCESS DIRECTIVE

Objectives and Scope of Access Regulation

9.23   The ComECPR may confer rights and impose obligations on undertakings in relation to access to, or interconnection of, electronic communication networks

---

88   S 26 L112(I)/2004 as amended.
89   Ss 27, 28 and 30 L112(I)/2004 as amended.
90   S 29 L112(I)/2004 as amended.
91   S 20 (o) L112(I)/2004.
92   S 42(6) L112(I)/2004 as amended.
93   Ss 33(2)(a) and 50(4) L112(I)/2004.
94   Cf for spectrum and for numbers PI464/2004 as amended and for rights of way para 9.10 et seq above.
95   S 20(q) L112(I)/2004.

and services and associated facilities in order to achieve interoperability of electronic communications services and produce sustainable competition between undertakings.[96]

Basic Regulatory Concepts

9.24   The ComECPR, pursuant to the objectives of s 18 of the 2004 Electronic Communications Law as amended, encourages, and where appropriate ensures, adequate access and interconnection, and the interoperability of services,[97] exercising its responsibility in a way that promotes efficiency, sustainable competition, efficient investment and innovation, and gives maximum benefit to end users.

Obligations and conditions imposed must be based on objective, transparent, proportionate and non-discriminatory criteria.[98]

'Access' and 'interconnection' are defined in the 2004 Electronic Communications Law in identical terms to the Access Directive.[99]

The general authorisation also gives an undertaking the right to negotiate interconnection and obtain access to, or interconnection from, another undertaking. An undertaking requesting access or interconnection within Cyprus does not require prior authorisation to operate in Cyprus.[100]

The ComECPR will intervene where appropriate agreement cannot be reached between the undertakings.[101]

Access and Interconnection-related Obligations with Respect to SMP Undertakings

Overview

9.25   The ComECPR may impose on operators designated as having SMP in a relevant market[102] obligations with respect to, inter alia, transparency, non-discrimination, accounting separation, access to and use of specific network facilities, price control, and cost accounting in order to ensure adequate access, interconnection, and interoperability of services for the interests of end users.[103]

In exceptional circumstances, further obligations may be imposed, provided that they are submitted to the European Commission for prior approval.[104] Obligations imposed on operators designated as having SMP in a relevant market must be based on the nature of the problem identified, proportionate and justified in the light of the objectives set out in s 49 of the 2004 Electronic Communications Law as amended (ie promotion of competition in the provision of electronic communication networks and services and contribution to the development of the national

---

96   S 51 L112(I)/2004 as amended.
97   See para 9.5 above.
98   S 53(4) L112(I)/2004 as amended.
99   S 4 L112(I)/2004 as amended.
100   S 52(1) L112(I)/2004 as amended.
101   Ss 53(5) and 51(3) L112(I)/2004 as amended.
102   S 55(1) L112(I)/2004 as amended.
103   Ss 51(2) and 56–65 L112(I)/2004 as amended.
104   Ss 55(3) L112(I)/2004 as amended.

market) and may only be imposed following consultations with interested parties in accordance with the relevant Order[105] and s 50 of the 2004 Electronic Communications Law as amended.[106]

Transparency obligations

9.26 Transparency obligations may require operators to make public or available to the ComECPR specified information such as accounting information, technical specifications, network characteristics, terms and conditions for supply and use, including any conditions limiting access to or use of services and applications (provided such conditions are permitted by the national or EU legislation), and prices. The obligation may involve reference interconnection offers, and the ComECPR may, inter alia, impose amendments to the reference offers submitted by the operators.[107]

Where an operator is required to provide wholesale network infrastructure access and the relevant facilities, the ComECPR ensures the publication of a reference offer containing at least the elements set out in the respective Decision on the relevant market definition, the market analysis and the imposition of regulatory obligations on an undertaking designated as having SMP in the relevant wholesale broadband access market.[108]

Non-discrimination obligations

9.27 Non-discrimination obligations must ensure, in particular, that the undertaking subject to the obligation applies equivalent conditions in equivalent circumstances, and provides services and information to others under the same conditions and of the same quality as for its own services, or those of its subsidiaries or partners.[109]

Specific access obligations

9.28 The ComECPR may impose obligations on operators to meet reasonable requests for access to, and use of, specific network elements and associated facilities, inter alia, where development of a sustainable competitive market may be hindered at the retail level or end users' interests are not served. Such obligations may, inter alia, require that operators provide or do not withdraw access to specified network elements or facilities, to, inter alia, allow carrier selection, pre selection, or subscriber line resale offer, negotiate in good faith, provide specified services on a wholesale basis for resale, grant open access to technical interfaces, and provide co-location or other forms of facility sharing. In assessing the imposition of obligations, the ComECPR will take into account viability in the light of market development, feasibility of providing the access proposed in relation to the capacity available, the initial investment by the facility owner, the need to safeguard

---

105 PI144/2005. See para 9.5 above.
106 S 55(4) L112(I)/2004. See also paras 7.27–7.28 and 7.33 above.
107 S 56 L112(I)/2004 as amended and PI112/2007.
108 S 56(3) L112(I)/2004 as amended. Related are PI112/2007 as amended and Individual Administrative Decisions (IADs) 736 and 737 of 16/11/2012.
109 S 57 L112(I)/2004 as amended.

competition in the long term, any intellectual property rights, and the provision of pan-European services.[110]

9.29   In the mobile telephony market, the incumbent must offer interconnection, including carrier selection (cost-oriented pricing as derived from the incumbent's long-run incremental cost system audit), and national roaming.

Price control obligations

9.30   The pricing system of the incumbent is reviewed on an annual basis by external auditors to evaluate the input data, the allocation factors used, and the results generated. The system includes operating costs and cost of capital.

Data entered the system is financial data from the general ledger and the fixed asset register, and actual data relating to the number of customers, traffic volume (minutes), number of customer applications, and allocation bases. The ComECPR carried out an audit, the results of which confirmed that the incumbent's pricing system is reliable.

The ComECPR has adopted reference interconnection offers and reference unbundling offers. Modifications include immediate access for local loop unbundling to all network nodes of the incumbent, and full and shared access pricing.

Functional separation

9.31   Where the ComECPR concludes that effective competition does not exist, it may, subject to the provisions of s 55(3) of 2004 Electronic Communications Law as amended,[111] impose an obligation on vertically integrated undertakings to place activities related to the wholesale provision of relevant access products in an independently operating business entity.[112]

Undertakings with SMP in one or several relevant markets may voluntarily transfer their local access network assets, or a substantial part thereof, to a separate legal entity under different ownership, or establish a separate business entity in order to provide to all retail providers, including its own retail divisions, fully equivalent access products. To that end, they must inform the ComECPR in advance, and in a timely manner, in order to allow it to assess the effect of the intended transaction.[113]

Accounting separation obligations

9.32   The ComECPR may impose obligations for accounting separation and, in particular, may require a vertically integrated company to make transparent its wholesale prices and its internal transfer prices, inter alia, to ensure compliance where there is a requirement for non-discrimination and to prevent unfair cross-subsidies. It may also require the submission of accounting records, including data on revenues received from third parties.[114]

---

110   S 59 L112(I)/2004 as amended.
111   See para 9.26 above.
112   S 60A L112(I)/2004 as amended.
113   S 60B L112(I)/2004 as amended.
114   S 58 L112(I)/2004.

Regulatory Powers with Respect to SMP Undertakings

9.33 The ComECPR may impose appropriate regulatory obligations on undertakings with SMP in a particular retail market when that market is not effectively competitive and the obligations imposed under Part 10[115] of the 2004 Electronic Communications Law as amended, would not result, according to the ComECPR's assessment, in achievement of the objectives of that law.[116]

Regulatory Powers Applicable to All Market Participants

9.34 Regardless of any measures taken with respect to undertakings found to hold SMP, ComECPR may impose:[117]

(a)   obligations on undertakings that control access to end users, including, in justified cases, the obligation to interconnect networks which are not already interconnected;

(b)   to the extent that it is necessary to ensure accessibility for end users to digital radio and television broadcasting services in Cyprus, obligations on operators to provide access on fair, reasonable and non-discriminatory terms, to the following facilities:

(i) Application Programme Interfaces (APIs); and

(ii) Electronic Programme Guides (EPGs).

Regardless of the transmission mode used, an open API must be used for digital interactive television services which are being transmitted by digital interactive television platforms and distributed within the EU.[118]

The ComECPR ensures that the conditions set out by order apply with respect to conditional access to digital television and radio services broadcast to viewers and listeners in Cyprus, regardless of the means of transmission.[119]

REGULATION OF UNIVERSAL SERVICES AND USERS' RIGHTS: THE UNIVERSAL SERVICE DIRECTIVE

Regulation of Universal Service Obligations

Scope of universal service obligations

9.35 The ComECPR ensures that a minimum set of services is made available at the level of quality specified to all end users, independent of their geographic location and, in light of specific national conditions, at an affordable price.[120]

Universal service is defined as including connection on a permanent basis to the public telephone network and access to the relevant telephone services, information service by way of telephone directory and provision of the subscriber list in printed and electronic formats, provision of public telephones, services or facilities for

---

115   See paras 9.26–9.32.
116   S 65(1) L112(I)/2004 as amended.
117   S 53(2) L112(I)/2004 as amended.
118   S 63 L112(I)/2004 as amended.
119   S 64 L112(I)/2004 as amended.
120   S 108(1) L112(I)/2004 as amended.

individuals with special needs, low income or with special social needs, and free access to emergency services by making use of the European emergency call number '112' or of other emergency numbers.[121]

The ComECPR may specify requirements applicable to undertakings providing publicly available electronic communication services to ensure that disabled end users have access to electronic communications services equivalent to that enjoyed by the majority of end users, and benefit from the choice of undertakings and services available to the majority of end users.

Designation of undertakings obliged to provide universal services

9.36   The ComECPR designates the undertakings to provide universal service for a specified period, so that such universal service may be available across the whole of the geographic territory of the Republic of Cyprus.[122]

The ComECPR issued a decision designating CYTA as a universal service provider for three years.[123] The decision includes, inter alia, the criteria procedures used to designate universal service providers.

These criteria include the prerequisite of prior authorisation of the candidate for fixed network and fixed telephony, the percentage of coverage of the territory and the population by the candidate's network, the quality of the service as specified from time to time by relevant orders, and the financial and operational viability of the candidate.

A universal service provider must provide, inter alia, access to the public fixed network upon reasonable request by any person, at affordable prices, and according to transparent and non-discriminatory procedures.

Regulation of retail tariffs, users' expenditures and quality of service

9.37   Specific facilities including price control provisions and specific services (eg itemised billing and call barring) that a universal service operator must provide are set out in ss 108–113 of the 2004 Electronic Communications Law as amended, implementing the provisions of the Universal Service Directive; details are covered by a relevant order.[124] The ComECPR monitors billing on retail level by the universal service operator, especially in relation to national consumer prices and the average income.[125]

Under s 70 of the 2004 Electronic Communications Law as amended, the Com-ECPR may require operators to publish to end users and consumers transparent, comparable, adequate, and up-to-date information,[126] on applicable prices and tariffs, so that end users and consumers have comparable information to enable them to independently evaluate the cost of alternative usage patterns.

---

121   S 108(2) and ss 110–113 L112(I)/2004 as amended, for an analysis of the specific services.
122   S 109 L112(I)/2004 as amended and PI137/2005 as amended, which also provides, inter alia, for the criteria and procedure for designation.
123   IAD 170/2019.
124   PI142/2005.
125   S 114 L112(I)/2004 as amended.
126   Indicative information includes, for example, the name and address of the provider, the description of the offered service, and a dispute resolution mechanism.

The ComECPR may also require operators to regularly inform disabled subscribers of details of products and services designed for them.[127]

Operators must collect, maintain, and deliver to the ComECPR comparable, adequate and up-to-date information for end users on the quality of their services and on measures taken to ensure equivalence in access for disabled end users.

The ComECPR may impose on operators minimum quality of service requirements in order to prevent the degradation of service and the hindering or slowing down of traffic over networks.[128] The ComECPR may impose administrative sanctions in case of breach of such obligations.[129]

Cost calculation and financing of universal services

9.38   Universal services are financed through the universal service fund according to specified procedures.[130] Any undertaking providing services or electronic communications within the Republic of Cyprus must contribute to the fund, with the exception of any categories of authorised persons that the ComECPR has exempted through a duly reasoned decision. Exemptions may be granted for beneficiaries of the fund but not to legal entities connected to them, not under the obligation to provide universal services,[131] or providers of services or electronic communication networks within the Republic of Cyprus whose annual gross income does not exceed €427,150.[132]

The ComECPR calculates the costs of the universal services according to specified methodology and procedure.[133] For this purpose, the ComECPR has developed a long-run average incremental costing model.

Regulation of Retail Markets

Prerequisites for the regulation of retail markets

9.39   The ComECPR may impose appropriate regulatory obligations on undertakings identified as having SMP in a given retail market if, as a result of a market analysis, it concludes that the market is not effectively competitive, and that obligations imposed on the wholesale markets would not achieve the objectives set out in the 2004 Electronic Communications Law as amended.[134]

Regulatory powers

9.40   Retail price regulation is limited to the market of public telephone network at a fixed location comprising PSTN and ISDN connection[135] and to the market of

---

127   S 70 L112(I)/2004 as amended.
128   S 70A(3) L112(I)/2004 as amended.
129   PI74/2005 as amended.
130   PI141/2005.
131   PI74/2005 as amended.
132   Reg 7 PI141/2005.
133   PI140/2005.
134   S 65(1) L112(I)/2004 as amended.
135   PI800/2009.

publicly available local and/or national telephone services provided at a fixed location.[136] The minimum retail prices are set from costing controls and budgeted data of the incumbent following public hearings.[137]

End User Rights

Contracts

9.41   The ComECPR ensures that consumers and other end users, wishing to subscribe to the public telephone network, have the right to a contract with the provider of such services;[138] such contracts will provide minimum obligations in accordance with Article 20 of the Universal Service Directive as amended.

Transparency obligations

9.42   The ComECPR ensures that transparent and current information on applicable prices and tariffs, and on standard terms and conditions, is made available to end users and consumers with respect to access to and the use of publicly available telephone services.[139]

Operators must, inter alia, supply the end users and consumers with competition comparatives, information on invoicing, details on discount offers and premium rates and annual reports. To this end, they must make available specified procedures securing correct information to end users and consumers, in particular, so that subscribers are informed of price increases prior to their implementation, printed invoices and operators' websites are duly updated, and personnel in charge, their resellers and their associates are effectively trained to supply correct and comprehensible information to end users with respect to the provision of electronic services.[140]

Quality of service: securing 'net neutrality'

9.43   Quality of service is promoted and net neutrality is secured through ss 70A and 56 of the 2004 Electronic Communications Law as amended. Under this section, the ComECPR may require operators to publish comparable, adequate, and up-to-date information on the quality of their services, based on quality factors established by the ComECPR.[141]

Obligations facilitating change of provider

9.44   ComECPR ensures that all subscribers may retain their number(s), independently of the undertaking providing the service in the case of geographic numbers at a specific location, and, in the case of non-geographic numbers, at any

---

136   PI801/2009.
137   PI800/2009 and PI801/2009, in the Preamble.
138   S 69(1) L112(I)2004 as amended.
139   S 70 L112(I)/2004 as amended and PI139/2005 as amended.
140   Reg 14 PI139/2005 as amended and PI259/2006.
141   PI74/2005 as amended. Also, see para 9.26 above.

location.[142] The ComECPR also ensures that the price for number portability reflects the cost and does not work as a disincentive to changing service providers.[143] The ComECPR does not impose retail tariffs for porting numbers in a manner that would distort competition.[144] The ComECPR ensures that number portability is carried out within the shortest possible time.

A subscriber who has entered a contract with the operator must have its number activated within one working day.[145]

Contracts between consumers and undertakings must not exceed 24 months, and providers must offer the possibility to subscribe to a contract with a maximum duration of 12 months.[146] Without prejudice to any minimum contractual period, The ComECPR ensures that conditions and procedures for contract termination do not act as a disincentive to changing a service provider.[147]

Number Portability is regulated by PI565/2003 as amended by PI206/2004.

DATA PROTECTION: IMPLEMENTATION OF THE E-PRIVACY DIRECTIVE

Confidentiality of Communications

9.45 Undertakings providing public networks and/or electronic communication services to the public must take all necessary technical and organisational measures for the appropriate risk management in order to safeguard the security of their networks and services.[148]

No person, other than a user communicating with another user, may listen to, tap, store, intercept, or undertake any other form of surveillance of communications without the consent of the users concerned,[149] except interceptions of communications in circumstances provided for by law and with the authorisation of a court.[150] Legally authorised recording of electronic communications in the course of lawful business practice, for the purpose of providing evidence of a commercial transaction and/or of any other business communication, is permitted.[151]

Under the latest (sixth) amendment of the Cyprus Constitution, a person's right to the respect and safeguarding of the confidentiality of his or her communication can

---

142 S 75(1) L112(I)/2004 as amended; Also, see para 7.70 above.
143 S 75(2) L112(I)/2004 as amended.
144 S 75(3) L112(I)/2004 as amended.
145 S 75(4)(a) L112(I)/2004 as amended.
146 S 75(5) L112(I)/2004 as amended.
147 S 75(6) L112(I)/2004 as amended.
148 S 98(1) L112(I)/2004 as amended.
149 S 99(2) L112(I)/2004.
150 S 8 L92(I)/96. The application to the court must be in writing, made by or on behalf of the Attorney General of the Republic, and supported by affidavit sworn by an appropriate person. The court may allow interception if it is satisfied, inter alia, that there is reasonable suspicion that a person is committing, has committed, or is about to commit an offence, that the private communication is connected with the offence, that usual investigation methods have been adopted without success, that there is reasonable suspicion that the apparatus which is to be intercepted is being, will be, or has been, used with respect of such an offence, and that it is in the interest of justice for the order applied for to be issued.
151 S 99(4) L112(I)/2004 as amended.

be expropriated in the interest of national security or the deterrence, investigation, or prosecution of serious criminal offences such as manslaughter, trafficking, and offences related to child pornography and narcotics.[152]

The storing of information, or the gaining of access to information stored, in the terminal equipment of a subscriber or user is permitted only if the subscriber or user concerned has consented (having been provided with clear and comprehensive information about, inter alia, the purposes of the processing), in accordance with the provisions of the Processing of Personal Data (Protection of Individuals) Law of 2001 as amended.[153]

Public provider must take appropriate technical and organisational measures with respect to network security.[154] In the case of risk of a breach of network security, public providers must notify their subscribers of the risk.[155] In the case of an actual breach, providers must notify the ComECPR and affected subscribers.

The 2004 Electronic Communications Law as amended provides detailed require-ments with respect to the content of such notifications.[156] 2004 Electronic Commu-nications Law also provides for the ComECPR's duty[157] to issue instructions concerning the circumstances in which providers are required to notify personal data violations, and the implementation of appropriate technological protection measures in cases of personal data violation.[158]

Pursuant to the provisions of the 2004 Electronic Communications Law as amended, the ComECPR established a Computer Security Incident Response Team ('CSIRT') and Computer Emergency Response Team ('CERT'), which are respon-sible for incidents related to security of information and networks. These teams are comprised of specialists on information security matters whose duty is to respond to the 'clients/users'[159] in matters of security of information. The ComECPR supervises the activities of these bodies.[160]

Under PI253/2011, the ComECPR defines the providers' minimum obligations regarding the security of information and networks. The goal of these regulatory obligations is to ensure the integrity and the business continuity of the networks and the services provided to end users/consumers in cases of destructive damage or force majeure.

The ComECPR intends to enact and implement further measures to ensure security of information and networks.

Data Retention

9.46   Directive 2006/24/EC has been fully implemented in Cyprus through the enactment of the Retention of Telecommunications Data for the Investigation of Serious Criminal Offences Law (Law 183(I)/2007) as amended. The provisions of

---

152   Art 17 of the Constitution of the Republic of Cyprus as amended.
153   S 99(5) L112(I)/2004 as amended.
154   S 98A(1) L112(I)/2004 as amended.
155   S 98A(3) L112(I)/2004 as amended.
156   S 98(4) L112(I)/2004 as amended.
157   Duty carried out together with the Commissioner for the Protection of Personal Data.
158   S 98A(4)–(6) L112(I)/2004 as amended.
159   Sic.
160   PI358/2010.

this legislation related to the access to the data by the police have been challenged in the Supreme Court of Cyprus[161] where the Court ruled that those provisions went beyond the 2006 Directive. The judgement of the Supreme Court, however, was given in the light of article 17 of the Constitution before the 2010 amendment.[162]

Traffic Data and Location Data

9.47   'Traffic data' are defined as 'any data processed for the purpose of the conveyance of a communication on an electronic communication network or for the billing thereof', and 'location data' as 'any data processed in an electronic communication network, indicating the geographic position of the terminal equipment of a user of a publicly available electronic communications service'.[163]

Traffic data concerning subscribers and users submitted to processing so as to establish communications, and which are stored by organisations, must be erased or made anonymous at the end of a call, except for the purpose of subscriber billing and interconnection payments processing, and only up to the end of the period in which a bill may be lawfully challenged or the payment pursued, and provided that the subscriber or user consents that such data may be processed for the purpose of commercial promotion of the services of electronic communications or for the provision of added value services. The consent may be withdrawn at any time.[164]

Location data may only be processed when made anonymous, or with the consent of the user or subscriber, to the extent, and for the duration, necessary for the provision of a value-added service. The consent may be withdrawn at any time.[165]

Itemised Billing

9.48   Subscribers must have the right to receive non-itemised bills. The Com-ECPR, after consultation with the Commissioner for the Protection of Personal Data, must, by order, prescribe alternative methods of communication among associated users and called subscribers, in order to reconcile their respective rights to privacy.[166]

Calling and Connected Line Identification

9.49   Where the presentation of calling-line identification is offered, the calling user must be able, easily and free of charge, to eliminate this function on a per-call basis and, likewise, the called subscriber, for the reasonable use of this function, must be able, easily and free of charge, to prevent the presentation of the calling line identification of incoming calls. Where the calling-line identification is presented prior to the call being established, the called subscriber must be able, using simple means, to reject incoming calls where the presentation of the calling line identification has been eliminated by the calling user or subscriber. The called subscriber

---

161   Joint Civil Applications Nos 65/2009, 78/2009, 82/2009 and 15/2010–22/2010.
162   See para 9.45 above.
163   S 4 L112(I)/2004 as amended.
164   S 100 L112(I)/2004 as amended.
165   S 101 L112(I)/2004 as amended.
166   S 100(3) L112(I)/2004.

must be able, easily and free of charge, to eliminate the presentation of the connected line identification to the calling user.[167]

A provider of a fixed or mobile network or electronic communication services may, through transparent procedures, terminate the possibility of:

- the non-presentation of calling line identification on a temporary basis, upon subscriber request seeking the tracing of malicious or nuisance calls; or
- the deletion of the calling line's identity presentation and of the temporary denial or lack of consent of a subscriber or user for the processing of location data for specifically defined organisations dealing with emergency calls including police authorities, first aid services and fire brigades in order to ensure that calls to the emergency services are duly answered and handled.[168]

Automatic Call Forwarding

9.50   Subscribers must be provided with the possibility to, easily and free of charge, stop automatic call forwarding by a third party to the subscriber's terminal equipment.[169]

Directories of Subscribers

9.51   Personal data contained in printed or electronic directories of subscribers, available to the public, or obtainable through directory enquiry services, must be limited to that which is necessary to identify a particular subscriber, unless the subscriber has given his unambiguous consent. The providers of directory inquiry services must provide their subscribers with the possibility of an entry free of charge, and the choice as to which aspects of their personal data will be included in publicly available directories. Subscribers may request and obtain, free of charge, the verification, correction or withdrawal of their personal data from directories.[170]

The providers of directory inquiry services must obtain additional consent by the subscriber prior to the addition of his or her name in the directories, and prior to the disposal or use of the directories for services of reverse, or on the basis of multiple, search criteria.[171]

Unsolicited Communications

9.52   The use of automated calling systems without human intervention is permitted only with respect to subscribers who have given their prior consent. Unsolicited communications for the purposes of direct marketing, by means other those mentioned, are not permissible without the consent of the subscribers concerned. Rights conferred apply to subscribers who are natural persons.[172]

---

167 S 102 L112(I)/2004.
168 S 103 L112(I)/2004 as amended.
169 S 104 L112(I)/2004.
170 S 105 L112(I)/2004 as amended.
171 S 105(3) L112(I)/2004
172 S 106 L112(I)/2004 as amended.

The practice of sending electronic mail for the purposes of direct marketing promotion, which disguise or conceal the identity of the sender or of the person by which, or for whose benefit, the message is sent, is prohibited.[173]

The ComECPR ensures, within the framework of EU Law and the national legislation in force, that the legitimate interests of subscribers other than natural persons, with respect to unsolicited communications, are sufficiently protected.

Any natural or legal person adversely affected by infringements of the provisions regarding unsolicited communications, including an electronic communications service provider protecting its legitimate business interests, may commence legal proceedings with respect to such infringements.[174]

---

173   S 106(4) L112(I)/2004 as amended.
174   S 106(6) L112(I)/2004 as amended.

The Czech Market for Electronic Communications[1]

Tomas Skoumal, Petra Ledvinkova & Patrik Kastner
Baker & McKenzie, v.o.s., Prague

LEGAL STRUCTURE

Basic Policy

10.1   The Czech voice telephony market was first opened to competition in 2001. Liberalisation continued with the introduction of:

- carrier selection, carrier pre- selection services and fixed number portability in 2002;
- local loop unbundling in 2003; and
- mobile number portability in 2006.

10.2   Liberalisation of the telecommunications market has led to greater competition in both fixed line and mobile services. Telefonica O2 Czech Republic, a.s. ('Telefonica'), the incumbent operator with more than 7 million lines, keeps its leading position in both the fixed and mobile market. Other significant operators in the fixed market are GTS Novera, a.s., Radiokomunikace, a.s., Tiscali Telekomunikace ČR, a.s and T-Systems Pragonet, a.s. Mobile penetration has exceeded 100 per cent and is close to saturation. There are three nationwide mobile operators: Telefonica O2, a.s., T-Mobile Czech Republic, a.s., and Vodafone Czech Republic, a.s.

10.3   The overall policy objectives of the Czech Telecommunications Office ('CTO') and the Ministry of Trade and Commerce ('Ministry') are to:

(i)   compensate for a lack of competition to date;
(ii)   create conditions to foster competition going forward; and
(iii)   protect customers and other market participants.

Implementation of EU Directives

10.4   The Czech Republic was one of the last Member States to transpose the 2002 EU Regulatory Package. This transposition was carried out by the adoption of one single act: Act No 127/2005 Coll, on Electronic Communications ('Act on

---

1   Editing of this chapter closed on 23 January 2013.

EC'),[2] which became effective as of 1 May 2005. The Act on EC provides a legal basis for the electronic communications regime and sets out a framework in which the CTO regulates the market.

Two regulations of note implementing the Act on EC include the Data Retention Directive 2006/24/ES (previous relevant provisions regarding data retention were cancelled by the Constitutional Court of Czech Republic in 2011), and Regulation (EU) No 531/2012 of the European Parliament and of the Council of 13 June 2012 on roaming on public mobile communications networks within the Union.

10.5   The Act on EC provides a legal basis for the electronic communications regime and sets out a framework in which the CTO regulates the market.

Legislation

10.6   The Act on EC replaced the previous Act on Telecommunications, No 151/2000 Coll ('Telecom Act'). Besides the Act on EC, electronic communications are also regulated by:

- nine Ministerial Decrees regarding, for example billing, security and network integrity, universal service, rules of assessment of market power of ECS providers and ESN operators, among others;
- a governmental decree regarding administrative fees charged for use of frequencies; and
- numerous CTO Provisions and Decisions regarding, for example, price regulation, use of frequencies, quality of services of electronic communications, among others.

10.7   The regulator is entitled to issue general provisions regarding various issues specified in the Act on EC.

10.8   Generally, the CTO's decisions have had a significant influence on the telecommunications market. The CTO has so far held a relatively strong, impartial, and independent position in regulation, and has shown an apparent effort to support competition in telecommunications for the benefit of end-users.

REGULATORY PRINCIPLES: IMPLEMENTATION OF THE FRAMEWORK DIRECTIVE

Scope of Regulation

10.9   The Act on EC fully implements the Framework Directive and constitutes an overall legal regulation of electronic communications services, including state administration.

The Act on EC's definitions of 'electronic communications network', 'electronic communications service', and 'associated facilities' are identical to those in the Framework Directive.[3] Voice over IP ('VoIP') services are covered by the definition of electronic communications services. The provisions of the Act on EC do not apply to content transmitted through electronic communications networks.

---

2   Published in the Collection of Laws on 31 March 2005.
3   S 2 Act on EC.

'Internet Freedom'

10.10   The Czech Republic has not passed any regulation regarding 'Internet Freedom'.

National Regulatory Authorities: Organisation, Regulatory Objectives, Competencies

10.11   The Act on EC defines the powers of the two principal regulators: the CTO and the Ministry of Trade and Commerce ('Ministry'). Their regulatory objectives are:

- to promote competition in the communications market;
- to contribute to the development of the EU internal market; and
- to promote the interests of end-users.[4]

10.12   The Ministry is primarily responsible for the overall telecommunications policy of the Czech Republic, international cooperation, and the fulfilment of international obligations by the Czech Republic in the telecommunications sector.[5]

10.13   The CTO is the principal regulator of telecommunications activities in the Czech Republic. It is an independent body, headed by the Chairman of a Council. Members of the Council are appointed by the government.[6] The CTO is not directly subordinate to the Ministry. Rather it is responsible for ensuring compliance with obligations regarding the provision of, and access to, electronic communications services and networks. The CTO issues general authorisations, administers frequency spectrum and numbers, engages in market analysis, imposes obligations on service providers with significant market power and other operators, issues price decisions, resolves disputes between operators, and brings prosecutions. It is also entitled to request information in order to monitor compliance with the Act on EC.[7]

10.14   The CTO is obliged to cooperate closely with the Office for Protection of Competition ('OPC')[8] and the Council for Radio and Television Broadcasting ('CRTB'), by exchanging information and engaging in other forms of collaboration.[9] The CTO must undertake a public consultation process if it intends to issue a general provision, or a price decision or other decision which could have a significant impact on the electronic communications market.[10]

10.15   The CTO Chairman resolves disputes between electronic communications service providers.[11] Any party may initiate proceedings; the CTO is obliged to issue a decision within four months. Only in exceptional circumstances may the deadline for issuance of a decision be prolonged. The CTO's decisions must be reasoned and published. The CTO may also decide not to initiate proceedings if, in its view, there are other more effective means of resolution available to address the dispute.[12] The Act on EC also stipulates a procedure to deal with customer complaints against

---

4   S 4 Act on EC.
5   S 105 Act on EC.
6   S 107 Act on EC.
7   S 108 Act on EC.
8   S 111 Act on EC.
9   S 112 Act on EC.
10   S 130 Act on EC.
11   S 127 Act on EC.
12   S 128 Act on EC.

providers of public communications services.[13] If a dispute also falls within the jurisdiction of a regulator from another state, the CTO cooperates with the involved regulator.

Right of Appeal against NRA's Decisions

10.16   Any party to proceedings may lodge an appeal against a decision of the Chairman of the CTO or the CTO itself.[14] Appeals must be submitted within 15 days from delivery of the contested decision, in writing, to the CTO.

10.17   Appeals against the Chairman's decisions are heard by a five-person permanent Council of the CTO.[15] The Council may examine witnesses, enforce their attendance and compel the production of documents.[16]

10.18   The decision of the Council is final and conclusive and cannot be further appealed.[17] The decision must contain reasoning, be delivered to the parties and published. The parties have the right to file a court action against the Council's decision.

The NRA's Obligations to Cooperate with the Commission

10.19   The Consultation Procedure has been implemented fully in accordance with the Article 6 of the Framework Directive.[18] The Act on EC also fully implements the 'consolidation procedure' (including the 'veto procedure') as defined in Article 7 of the Framework Directive.

10.20   An undertaking that provides electronic communications networks or services must use standards and specifications for the provision of its services, determination of technical interfaces and network functions, which list is published by the *Official Journal* of the European Union.[19] The CTO drafts and publishes network plans based on the standards and specifications issued by the Commission, which are binding for all operators and electronic service providers.

'Significant Market Power' as a Fundamental Prerequisite of Regulation

Definition of SMP

10.21   The definition of an SMP undertaking contained in section 53 Act on EC does not deviate from the 'SMP undertaking' definition in Article 14 of the Framework Directive.

Definition of relevant markets and SMP designation

10.22   The CTO determines the relevant markets in electronic communications in a general provision on the basis of the Commission's decisions, recommendations

---

13   S 129 Act on EC.
14   S 123 Act on EC.
15   S 107 Act on EC.
16   The rules of the proceedings are stipulated in S 122 Act on EC and in the Act No 500/2004 Coll, on Administrative Proceedings.
17   S 123 Act on EC.
18   S 131 Act on EC.
19   S 62 Act on EC.

and instructions, taking into account public consultations and consolidation procedures. CTO also takes into consideration the opinion of the OPC.[20]

The CTO has determined the following SMP undertakings:

(1)   Telefonica O2 Czech Republic, a.s. on the market of :
    (i) access to public telephony network in fixed places;
    (ii) publicly accessible national and international telephony services provided in fixed places;
    (iii) minimum set of leased circuits;
    (iv) origination of calls in public telephony network in fixed places;
    (v) termination of calls in each of the public telephony networks provided in fixed places;
    (vi) wholesale full (or shared) access to end-users' metal lines;
    (vii) wholesale broadband access to EC networks;
    (viii) wholesale provision of end parts of leased lines in EC networks; and
    (ix) termination of calls in each public mobile telephony network;
(2)   T-Mobile Czech Republic, a.s. on the market of termination of calls in each public mobile telephony networks;
(3)   Vodafone Czech Republic, a.s. on the market of termination of calls in each public mobile telephony networks;
(4)   RADIOKOMUNIKACE, a.s. on the market of services of broadcasting of radio and television signal in EC networks to end-users;
(5)   T-Systems PragoNet, a.s. on the market of termination of calls in each of the public telephony networks provided at a fixed location;
(6)   TISCALI Telekomunikace Česká republika s.r.o. on the market of termination of calls in each of the public telephony networks provided in fixed places;
(7)   RADIOKOMUNIKACE a.s. on the market of termination of calls in each of the public telephony networks provided in fixed places;
(8)   GTS Novera Next, s.r.o on the market of termination of calls in each of the public telephony networks provided in fixed places;
(9)   GTS Novera Contact, s.r.o. on the market of termination of calls in each of the public telephony networks provided in fixed places;
(10)   GTS NOVERA a.s. on the market of termination of calls in each of the public telephony networks provided in fixed places;
(11)   ČEZnet, a.s. on the market of termination of calls in each of the public telephony networks provided in fixed places;
(12)   ČD-Telematika a.s. on the market of termination of calls in each of the public telephony networks provided in fixed places;
(13)   Czech On Line, a.s. on the market of termination of calls in each of the public telephony networks provided in fixed places;
(14)   BT Limited, organizační složka on the market of termination of calls in each of the public telephony networks provided in fixed places; and
(15)   ETEL, s.r.o. on the market of termination of calls in each of the public telephony networks provided in fixed places.

10.23   The CTO determines the SMP operators based on the outcomes of market analyses. To date the CTO has published 18 market analyses. In its decision, the CTO imposed on the above SMP operators one or more access-related obligations.[21] With the consent of the Commission, the CTO is also entitled to impose on

---

20   S 52 Act on EC.
21   S 51 Act on EC; see para 10.56 et seq below.

an SMP operator access-related obligations other than those specified in the Act on EC. The CTO can also under certain conditions[22] impose access[23] or co-location[24] obligations on non-SMP operators or electronic communications service providers.

The NRA's Regulatory Duties concerning Rights of Way, Co-location and Facility Sharing

Rights of way

10.24 Any provider of a public electronic communications network is in the public interest and, in accordance with a permit granted by the building authority, entitled to establish and operate its network on or in another owner's land, based on a written agreement on right of way with the land owner.[25] The right of way is established for a lump sum compensation based on a written agreement with the landowner. If no agreement is reached, or if the landowner is unknown or inactive or inaccessible, the building authority may establish a right of way by its decision. Such right of way may be granted under conditions stipulated in Act No 183/2006 Coll, Building Act.[26] Such a decision can be appealed to the building authority at the district level. An administrative decision on the appeal is subject to judicial review. Czech law does not distinguish between rights of way over public and private property.

10.25 The communications line of a public communications network may cross various types of lines, areas or zones.[27]

10.26 The provider of a public communications network is, after prior notification to the owner of the property, entitled to enter the owner's property to the extent necessary to maintain, build, or repair the network or electronic communications equipment or to cut or lop trees.[28]

Co-location and facility sharing

10.27 The CTO is entitled to impose on SMP operators an obligation to meet the reasonable requirements of another undertaking in terms of use of and access to its

---

22 The access obligation may be imposed on an operator, who controls access to end-users or who controls access to certain interfaces. The co-location obligation might be imposed on a provider of public electronic communications network, who uses imovable property of third parties and it is not possible to build a separate device due to environmental protection, public health or security protection or other public interests..

23 S 79 Act on EC.

24 S 84 Act on EC; see para 10.27 below.

25 S 104 Act on EC.

26 The conditions are the following: the establishment of the right of way is in the public interest; the aim of the establishment of the right of way cannot be reached otherwise; the establishment of the right of way is not in contradiction to the aims of the decision about the area management; and the rights of the landowner are injured only to the minimum necessary extent, and compensation is paid to the landowner.

27 Electricity, water, sewage and other lines, natural water reservoirs, territories protected under special legal regulations, railway tracks, public roads, water management structures or any other such schemes, including their protective zones.

28 S 104 Act on EC.

specific network elements and associated facilities.[29] These obligations include provision of co-location or any other form of equipment sharing in compliance with Article 12 of the Framework Directive.

REGULATION OF MARKET ENTRY: IMPLEMENTATION OF THE AUTHORISATION DIRECTIVE

The General Authorisation of Electronic Communications

10.28   The general authorisation regime has replaced the licensing system that was previously in use. The Act on EC provides that the CTO issues general authorisations as a general provision, in which it sets out conditions applicable to all or some electronic communications services and networks and the operation of equipment.[30] The provisions of Czech law regarding general authorisations are in compliance with the provisions of the Authorisation Directive. Operators are obliged to notify the CTO in advance of their intention to provide a network or service.[31] A foreign entity must notify the CTO of its intention to provide electronic communications services in the territory of the Czech Republic only if it has established its branch or subsidiary in such territory and such branch or subsidiary is registered with the Czech Commercial Registry.

10.29   If no electronic communications services are provided in the territory of the Czech Republic, no notification is required by undertakings applying for access to, or interconnection of, networks

10.30   If an operator meets all legal requirements, the CTO is obliged to issue a confirmation of the notification within one week from delivery of the notification form and the related documentation.[32] Providers may allowed to start service once they have fulfilled their notification obligation.

10.31   Authorised operators have a wide range of rights, the most important being:

- the right to provide electronic communications services or networks;
- the right to apply for assignment of frequencies[33] and number allocation;[34]
- the right to negotiate and request interconnection with public electronic communications networks of other operators;[35] and
- the right to build communications lines in accordance with a permit issued by the building authority.

10.32   In compliance with the Authorisation Directive, the CTO is entitled to issue a general authorisation and therein specify conditions for the provision of electronic communications services or operation of communications networks. Such general authorisations have been issued by the CTO and they contain conditions relating to issues specified in the Act on EC.[36] The list of such conditions is in conformity with Part A of the Annex to the Authorisation Directive.

---

29   S 84 Act on EC.
30   S 9 Act on EC.
31   S 13 Act on EC.
32   S 14 Act on EC.
33   S 17 Act on EC.
34   S 30 Act on EC.
35   S 79 Act on EC.
36   S 10 Act on EC.

Rights of Use of Radio Frequencies

General authorisations and the granting of individual rights

10.33   The CTO manages the radio frequency spectrum.[37] In this role, the CTO, among other things, drafts a plan of frequency band allocation, grants individual authorisations for use of radio frequencies, assigns radio frequencies and provides consent to the transfer of radio frequencies. Recently, the CTO announced its intention to carry out an auction of the following frequencies: 800 MHz, 1800 MHz and 2600 MHz, which will be used for 4G EC services.

10.34   Radio frequencies may be used based on individual authorisations for the use of radio frequencies or based on general authorisations if the issuance of an individual authorisation is not necessary. The CTO has discretion to decide when the issue of an individual authorisation is not necessary, but it has not made such a decision to date. Any authorised operator, user of an electronic communications network, or any other person, may acquire an individual authorisation for the use of radio frequency, based on a written application. The CTO is obliged to reach a decision on an application as soon as possible. If there are more applicants requesting permission for use of the same frequencies, the CTO will issue its decisions based on the sequence of applications.[38] If frequencies for broadcasting radio or television signals are requested, the CTO may issue such individual authorisations only to holders of licences issued by the CRTB or with the prior consent of the CRTB.

10.35   The CTO may refuse to grant an individual authorisation for use of radio frequencies, based on the reasons specified in the Act on EC.[39]

Admissible Conditions

10.36   In the individual authorisation, the CTO may impose additional conditions regarding protection from harmful interference and radiation, or regarding obligations arising from international treaties which are binding on the Czech Republic.[40] The list of additional conditions conforms with the conditions contained in Annex B to the Authorisation Directive. Special conditions may be imposed in the permit for use of radio frequencies, if these frequencies were allocated to an operator based on a public tender.[41]

Limitation of number of rights of use to be granted

10.37   The CTO may limit the number of rights for use of radio frequencies, compared to the scheduled number, in order to ensure that the radio frequencies are used effectively.[42] The intention of the CTO to limit the number of rights to use radio frequencies is subject to the requirement for prior public consultations. In

---

37   S 15 Act on EC.
38   S 17 Act on EC.
39   S 17 Act on EC
40   S 18 Act on EC.
41   S 22 Act on EC.
42   S 20 Act on EC.

compliance with Article 7 of the Authorisation Directive, the CTO has to carry out a tender for granting frequencies, where the number is limited.[43]

10.38   The Act on EC specifies annual fees for use of radio frequencies. The individual fees depend on the service provided and the frequency assigned.[44]

Frequency Trading

10.39   Frequency trading is allowed only with the prior consent of the CTO.[45] The CTO is authorised to issue a general provision, in which it will lay down the generally applicable conditions and procedures for transfer of the frequencies. Such provision has been issued by the CTO on 30 June 2005.

Rights of Use for Numbers

General authorisation and granting of individual rights

10.40   To ensure that numbers, number series and codes, addresses and names (except internet addresses), are effectively managed and reasonably utilised, the CTO is responsible for the administration of numbers in compliance with the Community's harmonisation objectives.[46] The CTO arranges the numbering plans, promulgates rules for creating addresses and names, and grants, amends or withdraws authorisations to utilise numbers.

10.41   Numbers in the numbering plan may only be used based on an individual authorisation.[47] Provisions of Czech law regarding the use of numbers do not deviate from those contained in Article 7 of the Authorisation Directive. The transfer of allocated numbers to another undertaking is admissible only with the prior consent of the CTO.

10.42   The CTO may, after a public consultation process, decide to announce a tender for the issue of authorisations to utilise numbers with special economic value ('golden numbers'). The criteria for evaluation of bids are set by the CTO.

10.43   Numbers are not subject to ownership rights; they constitute nonproprietary data and no person may claim ownership of the assigned numbers.

10.44   The CTO may, in the authorisation to use numbers, impose conditions. The list of such conditions is similar to the conditions contained in Part C of the Annex to the Authorisation Directive.[48]

10.45   Any provider of a public telephony service must ensure full number portability both in fixed and mobile networks.[49] In the case of geographical numbers, number portability is offered only in a given location. The obligation of number portability does not apply to telephone number portability between public fixed and public mobile telephony networks.

---

43   S 22 Act on EC.
44   S 24 Act on EC.
45   S 23 Act on EC.
46   S 28 Act on EC.
47   S 30 Act on EC.
48   The conditions regarding number portability requirements and the provision of public directory subscriber information are excluded.
49   S 34 Act on EC.

10.46 In its Decision dated 26 April 2006, the CTO imposed carrier selection and carrier pre-selection obligations on Telefonica O2 Czech Republic, a.s., as the SMP operator in the market of connection of end-users to a public telephony network.[50]

The NRA's Enforcement Powers

10.47 The CTO may request information from electronic communications network operators or service providers, including information which is considered to be a business secret, in order to verify compliance with the obligations set out by the Act on EC, the CTO's decisions, general authorisations, or individual authorisations for frequency and number use.[51]

10.48 If the CTO learns that a liable person or entity has failed to comply with conditions or obligations specified in the general authorisation, authorisation to use radio frequencies, or authorisation to use numbers, or other obligations set out in the Act on EC or in a CTO decision, the CTO may request an operator to correct the identified irregularities within one month. The CTO is entitled to issue a decision on preliminary injunction to remedy the situation, if there is an imminent danger threatening public interest or third persons.[52]

10.49 The CTO may also impose sanctions for breaches of obligations specified in the Act.[53] The maximum penalty which can be imposed is up to CZK 20,000,000 (€800,000). In determining the amount of the penalty to be imposed, the CTO must consider the relevance of the offence, including but not limited to, the manner in which the breach was committed, its consequences, duration, and the circumstances under which it was committed. The CTO may exercise simultaneously or separately its power to request that irregularities be corrected and its power to impose sanctions.

Administrative Charges and Fees for Rights of Use

10.50 The Act on Administrative Charges[54] contains provisions regarding the following fees:

- fees for the issue of a confirmation of the notification under general authorisation of CZK 1,000 (€40);
- fees for the issue of an authorisation to use numbers of CZK 5,000 (€200) per authorisation; and
- fees for the issue of an authorisation to use frequencies from CZK 3,000 (€120) up to CZK 7,000 (€280) per authorisation.

10.51 In addition, the Act on EC provides that the holder of an individual authorisation for use of frequencies (or numbers) must pay an annual fee for the allocated frequencies (or numbers).[55]

---

50 S 70 Act on EC.
51 S 115 Act on EC.
52 S 114 Act on EC.
53 S 118 Act on EC.
54 No 634/2004 Coll.
55 S 24 Act on EC.

REGULATION OF NETWORK ACCESS AND INTERCONNECTION: IMPLEMENTATION OF THE ACCESS DIRECTIVE

Objectives and Scope of Access Regulation

10.52   Effective competition is among the principal objectives of the current regulatory regime.[56] The CTO, therefore, through its regulatory powers, must ensure that access to networks and interconnection effectively enables the entry of competitors to the market for the benefit of end-users.

10.53   Provisions regarding access to networks and interconnection apply to operators designated to have SMP, to other public communications network operators, and to authorised undertakings seeking interconnection or access to these networks.

Basic Regulatory Concepts

10.54   Although wordings of the definitions of 'access' and 'interconnection'[57] are slightly different from the ones in the Access Directive, they have the same meaning as those in the Directive.

10.55   Any authorised operator is entitled to negotiate mutual access to or interconnection with networks of an undertaking providing a public communications network in order to facilitate publicly accessible services of electronic communications on the whole territory of the Czech Republic.[58] If no agreement is reached within two months from commencement of the negotiations, any of the involved parties may request the CTO to issue a decision substituting conclusion of an access or interconnection agreement.

Access- and Interconnection-related Obligations with Respect to SMP Undertakings

Overview

10.56   Based on the outcomes of market analyses in which the CTO engages every one to three years, the CTO may impose on an SMP undertaking access-related and interconnection-related obligations specified in the Act on EC.[59] Such obligations may be imposed only in the event that the relevant markets are not effectively competitive. Access-related and interconnection-related obligations which are not listed in the Act on EC may be imposed only with the previous consent of the Commission.

10.57   The CTO has carried out analyses of 18 markets and has imposed certain access related obligations on the SMP operators.

As regards the incumbent operator, Telefonica O2 Czech Republic, a.s., the CTO imposed a number of obligations including, but not limited to:

- an obligation to enable access to specific network components and use of facilities in the public fixed telephony network;

---

56   S 4 Act on EC.
57   S 78 Act on EC.
58   S 79 Act on EC.
59   S 51 Act on EC.

- an obligation to enable carrier selection and pre-selection;
- accounting separation obligations;
- price regulation;
- an obligation to provide a minimum set of leased circuits in the whole territory of the Czech Republic;
- an obligation of non-discrimination;
- transparency obligations; and
- an obligation of non-discrimination as regards access to the network and interconnection.

CT imposed on other SMP operators in the market of mobile telephony networks such as Vodafone Czech Republic, a.s., and T-Mobile Czech Republic, a.s, the following obligations:

- an obligation to enable access to specific network components and use of facilities in the public mobile telephony network;
- transparency obligations;
- non-discrimination obligations with respect to network and interconnection;
- accounting separation obligations; and
- price regulation obligations.

CTO imposed on RADIOKOMUMIKACE, a.s., the SMP operator in the market of broadcasting of radio and television signals, certain obligations, including:

- an obligation to enable access to use of facilities and capacity sharing;
- transparency obligations;
- non-discrimination obligations; and
- accounting separation obligations.

Transparency obligations

10.58   The transparency obligation under the Act on EC encompasses, in accordance with the Access Directive, the obligation to publish specified accounting information, technical specifications, network characteristics, contractual conditions and pricing conditions. The CTO may also require the SMP operator to publish its reference offer regarding access and interconnection and is also entitled to implement changes to it.[60] The CTO has already exercised such right, and changed the reference offer of Telefonica O2 Czech Republic.

Non-discrimination obligations

10.59   Provisions of the Act on EC regarding non-discrimination obligations do not deviate from the respective provisions of the Access Directive.

Specific access obligations

10.60   A Telecom Act amendment introduced local loop unbundling into Czech law during the second half of 2003. Currently, Telefonica O2 Czech Republic must enable access to its local loop by other operators. The Act on EC provides that the

---

60   S 82 Act on EC.

CTO may impose the obligation of local loop unbundling on an SMP operator.[61] In addition, the CTO may impose the obligations of access to, or use of, facilities on an SMP operator. The CTO has imposed such obligations on the SMP operators mentioned above at para 10.57. Czech legal provisions regarding access obligations do not deviate from similar provisions in the Access Directive.

Price control obligations

10.61   The CTO has issued numerous price decisions setting out the maximum prices or method of price calculation for specified electronic communications services. The CTO issues such a decision in the event that, according to the outcome of its market analyses, the CTO determines that the relevant market is not effectively competitive and other CTO measures have not remedied the situation.[62] The CTO can define a price based on prices in comparable markets.[63]

Accounting separation obligations

10.62   The CTO may also impose accounting separation obligations[64] – and has done so repeatedly – on SMP operators in the relevant markets: for details see para 10.57 above. These do not deviate from the accounting separation obligations contained in the Access Directive.

Related Regulatory Powers with Respect to SMP Undertakings

10.63   Based on the outcome of its market analyses, the CTO may impose carrier selection, and carrier pre-selection, obligations on an operator with SMP, for the provision of connection to and use of the public telephone network and use at a fixed location.[65]

10.64   The CTO may also impose on an SMP operator the obligation to provide the lease of telecommunications lines service (lease of capacity between end points of electronic communications networks) in the relevant market. Such operator must provide a minimum set of leased lines on a non-discriminatory basis, and must publish the general terms and conditions applicable to provision of these services.[66] The CTO may, in justified cases, change the general terms and conditions of an SMP operator regarding supply of leased line services.

10.65   Prices for leased line services must be independent of the mode of use of the leased lines. Prices for the installation and lease of circuits must be set separately. The wholesale prices for leased line services must be cost oriented.

---

61   S 85 Act on EC.
62   S 57 Act on EC.
63   Based on the CTO's price decision issued under the old regime, the following telecommunications prices for wholesale services are regulated: interconnection charges for both mobile and fixed termination; carrier selection and pre-selection services; local loop unbundling; interconnection charges for the use of virtual mobile operators services; interconnection charges for ADSL wholesale services; and interconnection charges for dial-up internet services.
64   S 86 Act on EC.
65   S 70 Act on EC.
66   S 76 Act on EC

Regulatory Powers Applicable to All Market Participants

Obligations to ensure end-to-end connectivity

10.66   The CTO may, upon consultation, issue a decision to impose obligations enabling connection of an end point with another end point, including, in justified cases, interconnection of networks on an undertaking which controls access to end-users.[67]

10.67   The CTO may, upon its own initiative or on the initiative of any of the interested parties, enter into the negotiations between undertakings about interconnection or access agreements. The CTO may also issue its opinion about the disputed part of the draft agreement. If no agreement is reached within two months of the beginning of negotiations, the CTO may issue its decision completing the interconnection or access agreement.

Access to digital and television broadcasting services

10.68   The CTO is also entitled to impose on an operator an obligation to provide access to Application Programming Interfaces (APIs) or Electronic Programme Guides (EPGs) under equitable, fair, reasonable, and non-discriminatory conditions.[68]

REGULATION OF UNIVERSAL SERVICES AND USERS' RIGHTS: THE UNIVERSAL SERVICE DIRECTIVE

Regulation of Universal Service Obligations

Scope of universal service obligations

10.69   The scope of the universal service obligation under Czech law is similar to the one contained in the Universal Service Directive.[69]

10.70   The Czech universal service definition additionally covers supplemental services such as phased payment of the price for connection to the public telephone network for consumers, selective barring of outgoing calls, and itemised billing.

10.71   The CTO has imposed a universal service obligation on the incumbent operator in fixed lines networks, Telefonica O2 Czech Republic, a.s. The scope of the imposed universal service obligation is limited to the following obligations:

- operation of public telephony booths;
- provision of access for disabled persons to fixed public telephony networks comparable to such access for other end-users; and
- provision of special tariffs to persons with special social needs.

Designation of undertakings obliged to provide universal service

10.72   The CTO must carry out a consultation process before imposing a universal service obligation on any operator. Such obligation, or some of the comprised

---

67   S 79 Act on EC.
68   S 79 Act on EC.
69   S 38 Act on EC.

obligations, can be imposed on an undertaking based on a public tender carried out by the CTO or by the CTO's decision on an operator designated as having SMP on the relevant market. If there is no undertaking with SMP on the relevant market, the universal service obligation may be imposed on an undertaking best meeting the selection criteria.[70]

10.73 Currently, Telefonica O2 Czech Republic, a.s,. is the only operator designated under the old regime as having an obligation to provide universal service.

Regulation of retail tariffs, users' expenditures and quality of service

10.74 In its numerous price decisions, the CTO has set out maximum retail prices for specified services provided by Telefonica O2 Czech Republic, a.s.[71]

10.75 Users may control their expenditure through using the following additional free of charge services: selective call barring service, itemised billing service, and the service of phased payment of the price for connection to the public telephone network.

10.76 The Act on EC obliges the universal service provider to provide special (lower) tariffs to persons with special social needs, or the disabled.[72]

10.77 A universal service provider must comply with the quality parameter levels and mandatory performance targets of the individual universal services set out by a general provision issued by the CTO.[73]

Cost calculation and financing of universal services

10.78 The CTO calculates the net costs of provision of the universal service obligation based on information supplied by the provider of the universal service. A universal service provider is entitled to compensation for the costs incurred in connection with fulfilling the universal service obligation, if the amount of these costs represents an unfair burden to the operator. Compensation is paid from the universal service fund, to which other authorised providers of public electronic communications services contribute. If an obligation to provide supplemental services (phased payment of price for connection to the public telephone network for consumers, selective barring of outgoing calls and itemised billing) is imposed within the universal service obligation on an operator, costs for these services would also be compensated from the universal service fund. This contradicts the Universal Service Directive.[74]

---

70 S 39 Act on EC.
71 Price caps are set for the establishment or transfer of end-users' telephony station, tariffs for telephone calls originating in fixed networks, and monthly line rental.
72 S 38 Act on EC.
73 S 47 Act on EC.
74 S 49 Act on EC.

Regulation of Retail Markets

Prerequisites for the regulation of retail markets

10.79   Regulation of retail services is permissible only if regulation at a wholesale level does not achieve the regulatory objectives.[75] Such regulation may be implemented if a given retail market is not effectively competitive.

Regulatory powers

10.80   Based on the outcomes of its market analyses, the CTO may impose carrier selection, or pre-selection, obligations or a leased line obligation on an SMP operator.[76] Such obligations have already been imposed on the incumbent operator, Telefonica O2 Czech Republic.

The CTO may, by its decision, also change the general terms and conditions of a public electronic communications service, if these are in contradiction to the law or secondary legislation.[77] In addition, the CTO may oblige an undertaking providing a public electronic communications service to publish an overview of its current prices, quality and conditions of services provided, in a form which enables the end-users to compare the data with information provided by other electronic communications service providers.[78]

10.81   The CTO may also apply price regulation to services provided by an SMP undertaking in the relevant market.[79] The CTO may issue a price decision if competition in the relevant market is limited, because the negotiated prices are unreasonably high or unreasonably low to the detriment of end-users,[80] or if the charges for carrier selection or pre-selection services or number portability services discourage subscribers from using such services.

End-user Rights

Contracts

10.82   The scope of the minimum terms of a contract on provision of publicly accessible services of electronic communications contained in the Act on EC[81] is in conformity with the list of these terms set out in Article 20(2) of the Universal Service Directive. Some minimum terms are in addition to those in the Universal Service Directive.[82] The CTO is entitled to change the general terms and conditions of an operator if these are in contradiction to the law or secondary legislation.

---

75   S 57 Act on EC.
76   See paras 10.65–10.67 above.
77   S 63 Act on EC.
78   S 71 Act on EC.
79   S 56 Act on EC.
80   S 57 Act on EC.
81   S 63 Act on EC.
82   The following terms are added: information about the dates and methods of billing and payment, conventional fines for failure to fulfil contractual obligations, and information about how the customer will be informed of any change to contractual conditions.

Transparency obligations

10.83   Any provider of public electronic communications services is obliged to prepare a draft contract regarding provision of the offered services, which must also contain obligations specified in the Act on EC. The draft contract, together with general terms and conditions of the services provided, must be published in the premises of the operator and on its websites.

Quality of service: securing 'net neutrality'

10.84   Net neutrality is secured in the Act on EC as one of the key principles.

Dispute resolution

10.85   The Act on EC provides that a customer may file a complaint regarding charges for communications services provided by an operator within two months of receipt of a statement of account. The operator is obliged to handle the complaint within one month after its delivery. If the customer does not agree with the result of the complaint procedure, he or she may apply to the CTO to resolve the dispute.[83]

Other obligations

10.86   Providers of public electronic communications services must provide their services uninterrupted each day of the year to a quality specified in the Act on EC. They also must maintain an updated database of their customers and must provide uninterrupted access to emergency numbers.[84]

10.87   End-users have a right to have their number or address information excluded from telephone directories and a right to request identification of the telephone number from which malicious or annoying calls originated.

10.88   Providers of public electronic communications services must ensure that it is possible to carry out all international calls to the European Telephone Numbering Area.

DATA PROTECTION: IMPLEMENTATION OF THE E-PRIVACY DIRECTIVE

Confidentiality of Communications

10.89   The operators of public communications networks and providers of publicly available electronic communications services are obliged to take appropriate technical and organisational measures in order to safeguard the security of their services, especially in relation to personal data protection of natural persons (users), protection of traffic data and location data, and privacy of communication of natural persons and legal entities.

---

83   S 64 Act on EC.
84   S 61 Act on EC.

10.90 The rights and obligations relating to the protection of personal data, which are not specifically regulated in the Act on EC, are governed by Act No 101/2000 Coll,[85] which implemented the provisions of Directive 95/46/EC.[86]

10.91 In particular, operators and service providers must prevent listening, tapping, storage, or other kinds of interception or surveillance of communications and related traffic data by persons other than the users, without the consent of the users concerned.

10.92 This, however, must not prevent technical storage, which is necessary for the conveyance of a communication without prejudice to the principle of confidentiality. Moreover, Act No 141/1961 Coll defines exceptions to the general confidentiality rule in the case of criminal proceedings concerning a serious criminal offence or other malicious criminal offences which must be prosecuted according to a promulgated international agreement.[87]

10.93 The measures adopted by service providers, in order to ensure security protection, must include adoption of an internal technical and organisational statute, which may be reviewed, upon request, by the CTO.

10.94 The measures to be taken in the case of a particular risk of a breach of network security are identical to those stipulated in the E-Privacy Directive. The provider of a publicly available electronic communications service must inform subscribers of such risk and, where a risk exceeds the scope of measures taken by the service provider, of any possible remedies, including an indication of the likely costs involved.

Traffic Data and Location Data

10.95 The wording of the definitions concerning traffic data and location data set out in sections 90 and 91 Act on EC is consistent with the E-Privacy Directive. Traffic data is defined as 'any data processed for the purpose of transmission of a message via the electronic communications network or for the billing thereof'; and location data is defined as:

> 'any data processed within the electronic communications network which defines the geographical location of terminal equipment of a user of a publicly available electronic communications service'.

10.96 If the operator of a public communications network or the provider of a publicly available electronic communications service performs processing of traffic data, including the relevant location data related to subscribers and users, such data must be deleted or made anonymous when it is no longer needed for the purpose of transmission of a communication, unless it is necessary for the purposes of subscriber billing, interconnection payments, marketing of electronic communications services, or the provision of value added services.

10.97 Traffic data necessary for the purposes of subscriber billing and interconnection payments may be processed only until the end of the period during which

---

85 Act No 101/2000 Coll on Protection of Personal Data and Amendments to Certain Other Laws.
86 Directive 95/46/EC of the European Parliament and of the Council of 24 October 1995 on the protection of individuals with regard to the processing of personal data and on the free movement of such data [1995] OJ L281/31.
87 S 88 Act No 141/1961 Coll. on Criminal Court Procedure.

the bill may be lawfully challenged or payment pursued. For the purposes of marketing of electronic communications services or for the provision of value added services, data may be processed to the extent and for the duration necessary for such services or marketing if the subscriber or user to whom the data relates has given his or her consent. The consent for processing of the traffic data may be withdrawn at any time.[88]

10.98   Location data other than traffic data, relating to users or subscribers of public communications networks or publicly available electronic communications services, may only be processed when it is made anonymous, or with the consent of users or subscribers to the extent and for the duration necessary for provision of a value added service.[89] Users or subscribers must be permitted (using simple means, at any time, and free of charge) to withdraw their consent to, or temporarily refuse, the processing of location data other than traffic data.[90]

10.99   Processing of location data other than traffic data by an operator of a communications network, a provider of a publicly available communications service and a provider of a value added service must only be conducted by persons empowered and authorised for processing by the relevant state authorities, and the processing must be restricted to the extent necessary for the purpose of providing the respective services.[91]

Data Retention

10.100   Directive 2006/24/EC ('Directive') was implemented into Czech law by Act No 247/2008 Coll amending the Act on EC. The relevant provision of the Act on EC is Section § 97(3).The respective provision of the Act on EC was challenged and subsequently cancelled by the Czech Constitutional Court in its decision No 94/2011. In addition to the respective provision of the Act on EC, the Constitution Court cancelled also the implementing Regulation No 485/2005 Coll on the scope of operational and localisation data, duration of its storage and manner of its transfer to competent authorities. Following the decision of the Constitutional Court, the relevant regulation in the Directive was implemented in the Act on EC by an amendment No 273/2012 Coll effective as of 1 October 2012. In connection with the above legislative changes, the Czech Criminal Procedural Code was also amended. The original Section 88a of the Code cancelled by the Constitutional Court has been replaced with a new Section 88a by act No 273/2012 Coll.

Itemised Billing

10.101   The provider of a publicly available electronic communications service, provided via a public telephone network, must provide free of charge, either electronically or in printed form, as the subscriber or user may choose, either:

- a bill itemised by the type of service provided; or
- a summary bill, indicating one total item.[92]

---

88   S 90 Act on EC.
89   S 91 Act on EC.
90   S 91 Act on EC.
91   S 91 Act on EC.
92   S 64 Act on EC.

Bills must not contain items regarding calls for which the subscriber is not supposed to pay, including calls to numbers identified as free call numbers.[93]

10.102   A provider that submits a bill containing an itemised list of individual calls must also offer, for consideration, a suitable alternative to the bill, if so requested by the subscriber, in order to provide increased protection of the subscriber's privacy. Such an alternative may consist, inter alia, in non-indication of a certain part (ie digits) of the dialled numbers in the bill.[94]

Calling and Connected Line Identification

10.103   The provider of a publicly available telephone service must, where presentation is offered of the calling line identification, offer:

- the calling user the possibility (using a simple means and free of charge) of preventing the presentation of the calling line identification on a per-call basis (the calling subscriber must have this possibility on a per-line basis); and
- the called subscriber the possibility (using a simple means and free of charge), for the reasonable use of this function (eg in crisis centres, hotlines), of preventing presentation of the calling line identification of incoming calls;
- the calling line identification and where the calling line identification is presented prior to the call being established, to offer the called subscriber the possibility, using a simple means, of rejecting incoming calls where presentation of the calling line identification has been prevented by the calling user or subscriber; and
- the called subscriber identification, to offer the called subscriber the possibility, using a simple means and free of charge, of preventing the presentation of the called line identification.[95]

10.104   The provisions stipulated in the first bullet point in para 10.103 above also apply to calls to third countries originating in the Community, and the provisions in the second and third bullet points also apply to incoming calls originating in third countries.

10.105   The operator of a public communications network or provider of a publicly available electronic communications service is entitled to cancel the prevention of presentation of the calling line identification under the terms and for the period stipulated in Act on EC.[96] The information must be communicated to the public, by means allowing for remote access, about the procedures regarding these measures.

Automatic Call Forwarding

10.106   The operator of a public communications network or provider of a publicly available electronic communications service must ensure that every subscriber has the possibility (using simple means and free of charge), to stop automatic call forwarding by a third party to the subscriber's terminal.[97]

---

93   S 64 Act on EC.
94   S 64 Act on EC.
95   S 92 Act on EC.
96   S 92 Act on EC.
97   S 94 Act on EC.

10.107   In the event that, during provision of a publicly available electronic communications service, calls are automatically or disguisedly forwarded to another service or to a service provided by another operator, or a new connection is realised and, thus, raises the price to be charged, an operator must notify the user (free of charge) about this fact and allow him or her to stop the call before it is forwarded or a new connection is established.[98]

Directories of Subscribers

10.108   Anyone gathering a subscriber's personal data in order to issue a directory of subscribers must inform the subscriber about, and obtain prior consent of the subscriber to, the inclusion of his or her data in the directory and its publication according to the terms stipulated in the Act on EC.[99]

10.109   Non-inclusion in a public directory of subscribers, verifications, corrections and removals of information from the directory and information about a subscriber's preference not to be contacted for marketing purposes must be free of charge.

10.110   No person or entity may offer, via a public communications network or a publicly available electronic communications service, any marketing, advertising or other method of offering goods or services to subscribers who have stated in a public directory that they do not wish to be contacted for such purposes. The provider of an information service, regarding subscribers' numbers or other information, may not provide information about subscribers that is not included in a public directory. The provisions in this paragraph apply, mutatis mutandis, to information about subscribers who are legal persons.

Unsolicited Communications

10.111   The promotion and advertising of products and services is regulated primarily in Act No 40/1995 Coll.[100] According to this Act, the dissemination of unsolicited advertising that causes expense on the part of the addressee, or is viewed by the addressee as annoying, is prohibited. The Act further stipulates that advertising is considered annoying where it is addressed to a particular addressee who has previously expressed that he or she does not wish to receive such advertising.

10.112   In addition to the general restrictions set out in Act No 40/1995 Coll, Act No 480/2004 Coll[101] on Certain Services of Information Society (so called 'anti-spam law') regulates the dissemination of advertising in electronic form. This anti-spam law implements the provisions of the Directive on electronic commerce and the E-Privacy Directive, and restricts the sending of electronic commercial messages without the prior consent of the addressee (ie it applies the opt-in principle).

---

98   S 94 Act on EC.
99   S 95 Act on EC.
100 Act No 40/1995 Coll. on Regulation of Advertising and on Amendment to Act No 468/1991 Coll. on Radio and Television Broadcasting.
101 Act No 480/2004 Coll. on Certain Services of Information Society.

The Danish Market for Electronic Communications[1]

Henning Hansen and Niels M Andersen
Bech-Bruun law firm, Copenhagen

LEGAL STRUCTURE

Basic Policy

11.1   The Danish electronic communications market underwent complete liberalisation during the 1990s following almost a century of virtual state monopoly. All relevant European directives pre-dating 1999 were implemented as part of the liberalisation process.

11.2   Planning and regulation of the telecommunications sector during the decade 2000–2010 is outlined in a second political framework agreement dating from 1999 (the '1999 Agreement').[2] The regulatory emphasis has changed from sector regulation to competition-based regulation with a gradual phasing-out of parts of the regulatory framework that have become redundant due to increasing competition. The number of applicable acts has been reduced considerably, as has the number of contradictory provisions, while regulatory flexibility has increased.

11.3   The 2009 EU Regulatory Package revised the 2002 EU Regulatory Package. The Act on Electronic Communications Networks and Services (the 'Tele Act' or 'L169'),[3] and its implementing regulations, implemented the 2009 EU Regulatory Package (which replaced the 2002 EU Regulatory Package) into Danish law.[4] The Tele Act delegates extensive power to the Minister/Ministry for Business and Growth ('the Minister' or the 'Ministry'), and, in some cases, directly to the Danish Business Authority ('DBA'), 'Erhvervsstyrelsen', which is a part of the Ministry, to issue detailed regulations to implement the Tele Act".[5] Applying this authority, the Minister and the DBA have issued a number of detailed Ministerial Orders ('bekendtgørelser').

11.4   Overall market conditions in Denmark are such that the former telecommunications monopoly, TDC A/S (formerly Tele Danmark) ('TDC'), continues to hold a strong position, particularly in infrastructure ownership and access to end users in

---

1   Editing of this chapter closed on 29 June 2012.
2   Dated 8 September 1999.
3   Consolidated Act no 169 of 3 March 2011.
4   Directive 2009/136/EC and Directive 2009/140/EC.
5   These activities were previously handled by the Danish National IT and Telecom Agency.

fixed network markets, whereas the mobile communication sector is characterised by stronger competition.

Implementation of EU Directives

11.5   The 2009 EU Regulatory Package was implemented into Danish law in May 2011.

Legislation

11.6   The key parts of the legislative framework in relation to the 2009 EU Regulatory Package are:

- **Acts**
  - Consolidated Act No 169 of 3 March 2011 (Tele Act)[6]
- **Ministerial orders issued pursuant to the Tele Act**
  - Ministerial Order No 382 of 21 April 2011 ('MO382')[7]
  - Ministerial Order No 385 of 27 April 2011 ('MO385')[8]
  - Ministerial Order No 398 of 2 May 2011 ('MO398')[9]
  - Ministerial Order No 390 of 21 April 2011 ('MO390')[10]
  - Ministerial Order No 374 of 27 April 2011 ('MO374')[11]
  - Ministerial Order No 399 of 2 May 2011 ('MO399')[12]
  - Ministerial Order No 715 of 23 June 2011 ('MO715')[13]
  - Ministerial Order No 435 of 9 May 2011 ('MO435')[14]
  - Ministerial Order No 991 of 6 November 2011 ('MO991')[15]
  - Ministerial Order No 701 of 26 June 2011 ('MO701')[16]
  - Ministerial Order No 710 of 25 July 2011 ('MO710')[17]

---

6   Concerning Electronic Communications Networks and Services (Lov om elektroniske kommunikationsnet og –tjenester).

7   Concerning Delegation of the Minister for Science, Technology and Innovation's Authorities Pursuant to the Act Concerning Electronic Communications Networks and Services (Bekendtgørelse om delegation af ministeren for videnskab, teknologi og udviklings beføjelser i lov om elektroniske kommunikationsnet og – tjenester).

8   Concerning Price Control (Bekendtgørelse om priskontrol).

9   Concerning Alternative Disputes Settlement between Suppliers of Public Electronic Communications Networks and Services (Bekendtgørelse om alternativ tvistbilæggelse mellem udbydere af offentlige elektroniske kommunikationsnet og -tjenester).

10   Concerning International Roaming (Bekendtgørelse om roaming).

11   Concerning Audit Rules for Certain Suppliers of Public Electronic Communications Networks and Services (Bekendtgørelse om regnskabsregler for visse udbydere af offentlige elektroniske kommunikationsnet og -tjenester).

12   Concerning Consulting Procedures in Connection with Market Analyses of the Market for Electronic Communications Networks and Services (Bekendtgørelse om høringsprocedurer i forbindelse med markedsundersøgelser på markedet for elektroniske kommunikationsnet og -tjenester).

13   Concerning Provision of Electronic Communications Networks and Services (Bekendtgørelse om udbud af elektroniske kommunikationsnet og -tjenester).

14   Concerning Number Information Databases (Bekendtgørelse om nummeroplysningsdatabaser).

15   Concerning Service 900 Services (Bekendtgørelse om service 900-tjenester).

16   Concerning Universal Service Obligations (Bekendtgørelse om forsyningspligtydelser).

17   Concerning Payphones (Bekendtgørelse om betalingstelefoner).

- Ministerial Order No 425 of 14 April 2011 ('MO425')[18]
- Ministerial Order No 384 of 21 April 2011 ('MO384')[19]
- Ministerial Order No 393 of 2 may 2011 ('MO393')[20]
- Ministerial Order No 396 of 21 April 2011 ('MO396')[21]
- Ministerial Order No 445 of 11 May 2011 ('MO445')[22]
- Ministerial Order No 383 of 21 April 2011 ('MO383')[23]

11.7   The regulation of the telecommunications market has always been very dynamic; however, since the implementation of the 2009 EU Regulatory Package, the regulation of the telecommunications market has been steady.

REGULATORY PRINCIPLES: THE FRAMEWORK DIRECTIVE

Scope of Regulation

11.8   The Tele Act defines the two key terms 'electronic communications network' and 'electronic communications service'. It defines 'electronic communications networks' as 'any form of radio frequency or cable-based telecommunications infrastructure used for handling electronic communications services';[24] and 'electronic communications services' as 'services consisting wholly or mainly in electronic conveyance of communications in the form of sound, images, text or combinations thereof, by means of radio or telecommunications techniques, between network termination points, including two-way and one-way communications'.[25]

11.9   Article 2(e) of the Framework Directive defines 'associated facilities' as:

'those associated services, physical infrastructures and other facilities or elements associated with an electronic communications network and/or an electronic communications service which enable and/or support the provision of services via that network and/or service or have the potential to do so, and include, inter alia, buildings or entries to buildings, building wiring, antennae, towers and other supporting constructions, ducts, conduits, masts, manholes, and cabinets'.

11.10   While the Tele Act does not separately define 'associated facilities', it does, in the opening paragraph, refer to Article 2(e) of the Framework Directive. One could infer from this reference that, in practice, the term is likely to be interpreted consistent with that article. Note, however, that to date, the DBA has not interpreted this term in practice.

---

18   Concerning the Overall Danish Number Plan (Bekendtgørelse om den samlede danske nummerplan).
19   Concerning Coordinated Use of Network Elements in Electronic Communications Networks, etc (Bekendtgørelse om koordineret anvendelse af netelementer i elektroniske kommunikationsnet mv).
20   Concerning Digital Radio and TV Services (Bekendtgørelse om digitale radio- og tv-tjenester).
21   Concerning the Scope of the Information Security and Preparedness (Bekendtgørelse om rammerne for informationssikkerhed og beredskab).
22   Concerning Information Security and Preparedness for Electronic Communications Networks and Services (Bekendtgørelse om informationssikkerhed og beredskab for elektroniske kommunikationsnet og -tjenester).
23   Concerning the Telecommunications Complaints Board (Bekendtgørelse om Teleklagenævnets virksomhed).
24   S 2(1)(4) L169.
25   S 2(1)(7) L169.

11.11   Voice over Internet Protocol ('VoIP') services are covered by the same regulatory framework as other electronic communications services.

'Internet Freedom'

11.12   On 20 July 2012, the Danish Minister of Culture announced a series of initiatives aimed at making it easier to use creative content online legally while contributing to the ongoing efforts to limit the illicit piracy of copyright protected materials. In a press release accompanying the announcement, the Minister of Culture officially abandoned the previous contemplations of enacting the so-called 'letter model' according to which Internet providers were to automatically issue warning letters to Internet subscribers whose connections had been used for illegal file sharing. Rather the Minister of Culture emphasises the existing remedies, including that a copyright owner may take legal actions against an Internet provider in order to force such Internet provider to block the access to a web page containing illegal and infringing material. Such judgment will only be binding on the Internet provider in question, but Danish Internet providers and copyright owners are in the process of preparing a code of conduct which will imply that all other Internet providers must also comply with such judgment and thus block the access. Further, Internet providers are entitled to – but not obliged to – block an end user's Internet access due to that end user having infringed any copyrights and failed to observe the Internet provider's guidelines.

National Regulatory Authorities: Organisation, Regulatory Objectives, Competencies

11.13   The DBA is responsible for administration of the telecommunication laws in Denmark. The DBA's tasks include supervision, ensuring compliance with legislation, decision-making, conciliation, promotion of competition, and consumer protection. As noted above, the DBA is part of the Ministry of Business and Growth in Denmark. All telecommunications-related issues fall within the jurisdiction of the Ministry.

11.14   The Minister is authorised to define by regulation what decisions by the DBA may be subject to extended consultation procedures and how such procedures will be conducted.[26] The DBA is required to apply the procedures outlined in Articles 6 and 7 of the Framework Directive as part of the extended consultation procedure, including application of the Commission Guidelines.

11.15   The DBA consults and coordinates with the Danish competition authorities (the Danish Competition and Consumer Authority ('DCCA')[27] and the Danish Competition Council ('DCC'))[28] in matters involving competition issues. The DBA must consult with the DCCA on issues involving the Competition Act.[29] The DBA and the DCCA and DCC are independent of one another, the DCC being responsible for overall administration of the Competition Act, and the DCCA being the secretariat of the DCC. The DCCA and DCC are, like the DBA, part of the Danish Ministry of Business and Growth.

---

26   S 57 L169.
27   'Konkurrence- og Forbrugerstyrelsen'.
28   'Konkurrencerådet'.
29   Eg s 39 L169 and guidelines prepared by the DBA.

11.16   The powers and duties of the DBA and the DCCA are consistent with the requirements of the 2009 EU Regulatory Package and EU competition regulation. Both are vested with powers to demand information from undertakings in certain defined circumstances. The DBA may impose fines for failure to comply with statutory requirements for provision of information.[30]

11.17   The DBA has a duty to publish information concerning telecommunication sector issues, e g comparisons of prices charged by service providers. Such comparative studies are published regularly and are available on the DBA website.

11.18   The DBA has sweeping powers to conduct market analyses and consultations that must be conducted in co-operation with the DCCA where appropriate and expedient.

11.19   The DBA supervises compliance with the majority of the provisions in the Tele Act.

Right of Appeal against NRA's Decisions

11.20   Decisions by the DBA are subject to administrative review by the Telecommunications Complaints Board ('TCB').[31] The decisions of the TCB may not be brought before other administrative authorities. The decisions of the TCB may be brought before the courts no later than eight weeks after the date on which the decision was communicated to the party concerned. The TCB has extensive powers to demand information deemed necessary to discharge its duties and to facilitate its handling of specific complaints. The TCB seeks to make decisions regarding appeals against the DBA's decisions no later than three months after the date on which the appeal was submitted to the TCB.

The NRA's Obligation to Cooperate with the Commission

11.21   The consolidation procedure provided for by Article 7 Framework Directive has not been directly restated in the Tele Act. However, it follows from DBA Guidelines and the Ministerial Order concerning Consulting Procedures, that the procedure in Article 7 will be employed. Furthermore, the Tele Act provides for a consultation procedure in matters involving the imposition of certain obligations on SMP undertakings for which the consent of the EU Commission is required.[32] The DBA, in assessing questions of dominance when conducting market analyses, must consider both Commission Recommendations in relevant markets and Commission Guidelines.[33]

---

30   S 79 L169.
31   'Teleklagenævnet'.
32   S 41 L169.
33   S 37 and S 38 L169.

'Significant Market Power' as a Fundamental Prerequisite to Regulation

Definition of SMP

11.22   The Tele Act adopts the Framework Directive's definition of significant market power, or SMP.[34]

11.23   Determination of whether an undertaking has SMP status requires a market analysis by the DBA leading to the identification of relevant markets appropriate to Danish circumstances. The Tele Act contains detailed provisions governing these procedures, including section 37(4) stipulating that the DBA may request assistance from the Body of European Regulators for Electronic Communications ('BEREC') in the event that the DBA is not able to carry out a market analysis within the timescale set by current EU regulation.

Definition of relevant markets

11.24   The DBA, at regular intervals, must conduct market analyses to facilitate decisions involving the regulation of SMP undertakings.[35]

11.25   In determining relevant markets, the DBA may consult with the NRAs of other Member States where the Commission has identified a transnational market.[36]

11.26   The delineation of relevant markets should follow the Commission Recommendation on relevant markets and include criteria outlined in the Commission Guidelines on market analysis.

11.27   The DBA has conducted thorough investigations on competition in the Danish telecommunications market. These investigations have resulted in identification of eight separate markets which the DBA is currently studying.

11.28   The former monopoly provider, TDC, is currently deemed to have SMP status in six of the markets[37], and seven other telecommunications companies are deemed to have SMP status each in one of the markets.

Imposition of remedies

11.29   The DBA, if it deems necessary, may impose on SMP undertakings specific remedies such as with respect to network access, non-discrimination, transparency, and price control.[38]

---

34   Art 14(2) of the Framework Directive and s 40(2) L169.
35   S 37(1) L169.
36   S 37(5) L169.
37   Retail market for fixed network subscriptions to private and business customers (market 1), wholesale market for fixed network origination (2), wholesale market for physical network infrastructure access (4), wholesale market for broadband connection (5), wholesale market for terminating segments of fixed networks (6) and wholesale market for termination of SMS.
38   S 41 L169.

NRA's Regulatory Duties concerning Rights of Way, Co-location and Facility Sharing

Rights of way

11.30   Anyone providing or operating public electronic communications networks is entitled to:

- open or use public roads to establish infrastructure: the relevant road authority must be notified four weeks in advance of commencing such work, regardless of whether it is an overground or underground structure, construction or maintenance of infrastructure under or along public roads or railway sites.[39] Consent of the relevant road authority is required.[40] Cables or other infrastructure facilities installed must be registered with the Land Register.[41] The operator must pay compensation to the landowner concerned and cover the cost of repairs or reinstatement of the road concerned.[42]
- relocation of infrastructure: anyone undertaking work to carry out construction or digging work that may disturb or damage underground cables must notify the cable owners no later than eight days before commencing works that may affect the cable.[43] Costs associated with relocation of infrastructure are generally payable by the infrastructure owner.[44]

Co-location and facility sharing

11.31   The Danish Act concerning the Establishment and Joint Utilisation of Masts for Radio Communication Purposes, etc ('L681') provides for a particular form of right of way involving joint utilisation of masts erected for radio (including mobile) communications purposes and the mounting of antenna systems on masts, buildings and other high structures. Owners have a statutory duty to accommodate requests for joint utilisation. This includes joint use of associated buildings, but only to the extent that joint utilisation is possible and there are no technical obstacles achieving it. The rules apply if the property is not already being fully utilised. Authority to impose obligations on owners, leaseholders, or those who hold rights of use rest with the local municipal authorities who may issue an order for access to joint utilisation. Initial installation of antenna systems, among other things, requires permission from the local municipal council.

REGULATION OF MARKET ENTRY: THE AUTHORISATION DIRECTIVE

The General Authorisation of Electronic Communications

11.32   No individual licence or authorisation is required to provide telecommunication networks or services or to establish and operate fixed or mobile networks.

---

39   L662 of 10 July 2003 ('L662') Concerning Cable Laying Access and Expropriation, etc for Telecommunications Purposes, s 1(7).
40   L1048 of 3 November 2011 ('L1048') Concerning Public Roads, s 101.
41   S 6 L662.
42   S 7 L662.
43   S 5 L662.
44   S 106 L1048.

Networks or services may be provided on the terms set out in MO715.[45] A service provider does not need a licence to provide or establish services or infrastructure covered by MO715. Service providers must, however, register their undertaking with the Telecommunications Centre of the Danish National Police. Furthermore, operators of mobile communications services must obtain authorisation to use the (radio) frequencies concerned prior to commencing operations.

Rights of Use for Radio Frequencies

Strategic planning and co-ordination of spectrum policy

11.33 The authorisation regime applicable to the use of radio frequencies is governed by the Danish Act Concerning Radio Frequencies ('L475'),[46] which, among other things, requires the Minister to issue an annual spectrum policy framework mandate containing guidelines for the general prioritisation of frequencies in Denmark. The Minister issued the most recent framework in 2012.[47] The DBA prepares a nationwide frequency plan based on the mandate and international and EU frequency co-operation.

Principles of frequency allocation, procedural rules

11.34 The use of radio frequencies requires a licence issued by the DBA, except in cases in which express exemption is available (eg for the police under certain circumstances and matters comprised by MO459 concerning the Use of Radio Frequencies Without Licence). Acquiring the right to use a particular radio frequency requires an application to be filed with the DBA. The DBA will generally issue licences on a 'first come first serve' basis. However, if more than one application is received on the same day for the same frequency, the DBA will investigate if there are other frequencies which are just as suitable as the requested frequency in which case licenses will be issued based on the drawing of lots. The winner will be issued the requested frequency and the other applicants will be issued the other suitable frequencies. If there is a scarcity of frequency licenses will usually be issued based on an auction.

Transferability and time limitations

11.35 While transfer of licences to others is generally permitted without prior DBA approval, notification to the DBA is required. The Minister may issue rules stating that transfer of licences issued on the basis of public tenders or auctions may only take place subject to prior approval of the DBA.

11.36 Licences for the use of radio frequencies will generally be limited in time.[48] Licences become effective on the day they are issued. Upon expiry of a licence, the licensee must apply for a new licence. The licensee must pay an annual fee (calculated on an individual basis for each type of licence) for the use radio of frequencies.

---

45   General obligations include access to: the national emergency number; service providers' text phone service and related emergency numbers; at least one national call based directory enquiry service and a call based charge information facility.

46   Consolidated Act no 475 of 12 June 2009 (Lov om radiofrekvenser).

47   MO no 402 of 3 May 2012.

48   S 18 L475.

Admissible conditions

11.37   When issuing a licence, the DBA prepares terms for the use of such licences. Such terms may include limits with respect to use of a certain technology if the DBA assess that such limits are necessary in order to:[49]

- avoid unacceptable disturbances;
- protect public health against electromagnetic fields; or
- observe a restriction of the supply of services.

Such terms may include requirements:

- relating to radio engineering;
- aimed at avoiding interference;
- aimed at realising international and EU frequency co-operation;
- restricting the geographical extension of the application area of the licence; and
- aimed at meeting broader societal needs.

Limitation of number of rights of use to be granted

11.38   The DBA may limit the number of rights of use to be granted in the case of an existing or imminent frequency scarcity.

The DBA has issued a number of licences which have been granted on the basis of public tenders and auctions.

L475 authorises the Minister to determine whether to initiate public tenders or auctions as the basis for issuing licences where a shortage is deemed to prevail. Auctions and tenders are conducted by the DBA.[50] Following a decision to initiate an auction or public tender, the Minister must issue detailed rules for the particular auction or tender.

Rights of Use for Numbers

General authorisation and granting of individual rights

11.39   The administration and allocation of Danish numbering resources is managed by the DBA and governed by the Tele Act and secondary legislation. Rights of use for numbers are granted by the DBA in accordance with Part 3 of Ministerial Order No 425 concerning the Overall Danish Numbering Plan. Numbers may only be used in accordance with the National Numbering Plan.

Admissible conditions

11.40   The DBA grants numbers and number series through an application process. It will not automatically grant authorisations based on applications for specific numbers or number series, but rather will set out specific terms for the allocation of such numbers or number series, for example:

---

49   S 14 L475.
50   S 9 L475.

- specify what services the numbers may be used for and requirements associated with such services;
- require that actual, effective and efficient use must be made of the numbers concerned;
- set a deadline for commencing use of numbers; and
- specify the maximum time validity of the numbers allocated.[51]

11.41   Providers of electronic communications networks or services must ensure that end users are able to retain their subscription numbers when changing providers within fixed networks and mobile networks respectively (number portability).[52]

Providers of electronic communications networks or services must meet all requests from other providers of electronic communications networks or services for establishing agreements to transfer subscription numbers for the purpose of enabling number portability as requested by an end user.

Generally, it must be possible for end users to have subscription numbers ported no later than by the end of the next working day following receipt of the request by the transferring provider. However, porting of subscription numbers must not be made earlier than the date on which the end user's subscription under the provider intended to receive the subscription numbers has entered into force.

Limitation of number of rights of use to be granted

11.42   Numbers and number series may not be assigned or transferred to other providers without prior approval by the DBA. The DBA may withdraw or replace numbers or number series in certain circumstances.

The NRA's Enforcement Powers

11.43   The DBA has extensive powers to demand, from all undertakings whose activities are governed (in full or in part) by the Tele Act, such information as the DBA deems relevant to enable it to discharge its duties as NRA.

11.44   The DBA may, in certain circumstances, impose fines for violation of particular provisions of the Tele Act.

11.45   Decisions made by the DBA may be brought before the TCB. Complaints regarding decisions made by DBA must be submitted to the TCB within four weeks. The TCB seeks to render a decision no later than three months after the date of submission of a complaint. The decisions of the TCB may not be brought before other administrative authorities, but may be brought to court within eight weeks of receipt of the TCB's decision. The TCB collects a fee of DKK 4,000 (approx €530) for handling complaints. The fee is refunded if the complainant wins the case in full or in part.

---

51   S 7 MO425.
52   Part 7 L169.

Administrative Charges and Fees for Rights of Use

11.46   Revenues collected from licences for use of radio frequencies and allocated numbers contribute towards the costs of operating the DBA. All applicable fees are set annually as part of the Finance and Appropriation Act[53] and published by way of Ministerial Order, ensuring a transparent fee structure. The charges are collected by the DBA and are generally payable at the beginning of each year.

REGULATION OF NETWORK ACCESS AND INTERCONNECTION: THE ACCESS DIRECTIVE

Objectives and Scope of Access Regulation

11.47   Providers of public electronic communications networks or services must negotiate agreements with one another on interconnection, for the purpose of providing publicly available electronic communications services, in order to ensure provision and interoperability of such services throughout the EU and EEA.[54] Interconnection agreements must be concluded on commercial terms.[55]

11.48   Access and interconnection related provisions of the Tele Act apply to operators of public communications networks and services and to undertakings seeking interconnection and/or access to their networks or associated facilities. Danish regulation of SMP undertakings applies equally to operators in the fixed and mobile markets.

Basic Regulatory Concepts

11.49   The DBA's regulatory powers in matters involving access and interconnection are primarily set forth in the Tele Act. If agreements on commercial terms cannot be reached, the DBA may impose obligations to the extent necessary to ensure connection between end users in individual networks or to create interoperability in relation to providers of electronic communications networks or services who control access to one or more end users, including the obligation to interconnect their networks.[56]

11.50   The Tele Act defines 'interconnection' as 'a form of network access established between providers of electronic communications networks or services, consisting of physical and logical linking of electronic communications networks, used by the same or a different undertaking to allow communication or to get access to electronic communications services.'[57]

11.51   The Tele Act defines 'network access' as 'access to a provider's electronic communications networks or services and associated facilities for another provider for the purpose of providing electronic communications networks or services.'[58]

---

53   The Finance and Appropriation Act is a bill which the Constitution requires Parliament to pass annually approving the State budget.
54   S 33 L169.
55   S 34 L169.
56   S 33 L169.
57   S 2(1)(12) L169.
58   S 2(1)(12) L169.

Access- and Interconnection-related Obligations with Respect to SMP Undertakings

Overview

11.52   Upon identification of an undertaking as having SMP, the DBA must impose certain obligations on the undertaking.[59] Determination of precisely what obligation(s) to impose is left to the discretion of the DBA. Once imposed, obligations remain in force until such time as the DBA withdraws them, ie upon determination that the undertaking no longer has SMP.

11.53   The DBA operates on terms which are virtually identical to those described in Articles 9–13 of the Access Directive.

11.54   The DBA may impose on SMP undertakings one or more of the obligations described in the paragraphs below.[60]

11.55   In addition to the obligations specifically described below, the DBA may impose other obligations on SMP undertakings in exceptional circumstances but only following consultations with, and approval from, the European Commission.[61]

11.56   The emphasis of the regulatory scheme is on individual decisions based on findings resulting from market analyses. Based hereupon the DBA has imposed obligations on the identified SMP undertakings in Denmark.

11.57   Where an obligation to accommodate reasonable requests for access to interconnection has been imposed, requests may be refused by the DBA to safeguard competition in the long term and the provision of pan-European services.

Transparency obligations and accounting separation obligations

11.58   The transparency and accounting separation obligations are identical to those contained in Articles 9 and 11(1) of the Access Directive. They include a duty to publish pertinent information and prepare separate accounts for each specific activity that forms part of interconnection.

Non-discrimination obligations and reference offers

11.59   The Tele Act, in adopting non-discrimination obligations, implements Article 10 of the Access Directive. This includes, for example, a duty to grant competitors the same terms as those applied to its own undertakings or to those of its subsidiaries. The DBA may also impose an obligation to publish reference offers to ensure that other providers of public electronic communications networks or services are not required to pay for facilities which are not necessary for the network access requested, giving a description of the relevant offerings broken down into components and the associated terms and conditions, including prices.

---

59   S 41 L169.
60   S 41(1) L169.
61   S 41(3) L169.

Specific access obligations

11.60 Specific access obligations include a requirement that the SMP accommodate reasonable requests for access to interconnection, including access to interconnection product(s), to negotiate agreements in good faith, and to maintain access to the facilities concerned.

Price control obligations and accounting obligations

11.61 These obligations include requirements that the SMP use cost based pricing[62] and specific cost accounting systems to support price controls. These price control and cost accounting obligations implement Article 13 of the Access Directive.

Related Regulatory Powers with Respect to SMP Undertakings

11.62 As a consequence of the deletion of Articles 18 and 19 of the Universal Service Directive, the equivalent rules in Danish law have been deleted. Consequently, Danish law does not provide for obligations related to provision of leased lines/carrier (pre-) selection which previously could be imposed separate from access obligations.

Regulatory Powers Applicable to All Market Participants

Obligations to ensure end-to-end connectivity

11.63 To ensure end-to-end connectivity, the DBA may impose obligations on providers or operators who control access to end users similar to those that may be imposed on SMP undertakings in relation to interconnection agreements, including in exceptional circumstances, an obligation to connect their networks.[63]

Access to digital radio and television broadcasting services

11.64 Part 15 of the Tele Act implements Access Directive requirements[64] concerning digital radio and television services. The obligations that may be imposed on multiplex operators, regardless of their market power, are regulated by Ministerial Order concerning Digital Radio and TV Services[65] and Part 15 of the Tele Act. Additional regulation is contained in the Act concerning Standards for Broadcasting of Television Signals, etc.[66]

11.65 The DBA has discretionary powers to initiate market analyses in the broadcasting and conditional access sectors. Previously imposed obligations may only be amended or withdrawn where this will not adversely affect competition in the relevant market or accessibility for end users.

---

62   S 46 L169.
63   S 33 L169.
64   Arts 5 and 6 of the Access Directive.
65   MO no 393 of 2 May 2011.
66   Act no 664 of 10 July 2003.

REGULATION OF UNIVERSAL SERVICES AND USERS' RIGHTS: THE UNIVERSAL SERVICE DIRECTIVE

Regulation of Universal Service Obligations

Scope of universal service obligations

11.66   The purpose of appointing universal service providers is designated as '... ensuring end users' access to basic electronic communications services on reasonable terms and at reasonable prices'.[67] Universal service obligations include the provision of:

- access to a public electronic communications network at a fixed location;
- access to a publicly available voice telephony service via the electronic communications network referred to above;
- special universal services for certain defined groups of persons with disabilities; and
- an exhaustive directory containing all numbers in the overall Danish numbering plan assigned to end users. [68]

11.67   Appointed universal service providers have a duty to supply or offer all of the above services to anyone applying for them. The DBA may determine maximum prices and other terms for the relevant universal services.

Designation of undertakings obliged to provide universal services

11.68   The designation procedures authorise the DBA to determine whether providers must be appointed as universal service providers, and if so, what obligations must be imposed. It is within the discretion of the DBA to set the terms on which the appointed universal service providers must implement their obligations.[69]

11.69   The Minister may issue detailed regulations governing the DBA's handling of the appointment and applicable terms (eg by public tender). These include the terms of an appointment; the basis on which the DBA may fix such terms; and content requirements for the terms designated.[70] MO701 concerning Universal Service Obligations provides the framework for the appointment of universal service providers.

11.70   TDC is the only undertaking appointed as a universal service provider.

Regulation of retail tariffs, users' expenditures and quality of service

11.71   The Minister may adopt specific rules with respect to requirements for, and calculation of, maximum prices for universal services, including the framework for the DBA's determination of such prices, and for the price proposals to be prepared by universal service providers. In setting the maximum prices, the DBA may not impose obligations that do not permit overall coverage of the costs incurred in supplying the services.

---

67   S 14 L169.
68   S 14(2) L169.
69   S 15(2) and (3) L169.
70   Eg quality requirements, assessment procedures and publication of their findings.

11.72   Since 2003, the regulation of prices for universal services is being phased out. At this point, universal service providers' prices charged to end users are no longer regulated except for few exceptions, including, but not limited to the situation in which a universal service provider must charge the same price for installation and transfer, regardless of the geographical location of the end user.

Cost calculation and financing of universal services

11.73   Designated universal service providers are entitled to be compensated for any documented net costs incurred in providing universal services if the DBA considers that the provision of universal service represents an unfair burden on the universal service provider.[71] Net costs are calculated as the universal service provider's overall loss in providing and delivering all the universal services that the individual universal service provider is obliged to provide by virtue of its designation as a universal service provider, deducting the value of any intangible benefits derived by the universal service provider from handling the universal service obligation. Rules governing calculation of contributions towards losses are adopted as part of the Finance and Appropriation Act and published by the DBA.

Regulation of Retail Markets

Prerequisites for the regulation of retail markets

11.74   The DBA may impose further obligations on a provider with significant market power at the retail level if the DBA considers that the ordinary obligations mentioned above are not suitable to solving a competitive problem identified under a market analysis.[72]

Regulatory powers

11.75   The Tele Act stipulates the supervisory duties of the DBA.[73]

11.76   The DBA may engage in supervisory activities either on its own initiative or following a complaint. The DBA may impose fines, the levels of which may vary according to the nature of the infringement.[74]

End User Rights

Contracts

11.77   Section 4 of Tele Act and MO715 implement Article 20 of the Universal Services Directive. Service providers must enter into end-user contracts,[75] To ensure consumer protection, minimum requirements for services provided by electronic

---

71   S 18 L169.
72   S 41(4) L169.
73   S 20, s 32 and s 52 L169.
74   S 81 L169.
75   S 4(2) L169 and s 9 MO715.

communications networks and service providers include a basic requirement entitling end users to a contract that meets specific minimum requirements.[76] MO715 sets out statutory rights ensuring that a contract includes the minimum information outlined in Article 20(2) of the Universal Services Directive.

Transparency obligations

11.78   Undertakings have a statutory duty to provide information to end users on tariffs and terms and quality of services specified in Article 21 and Annex 2 of the Universal Service Directive.[77] The DBA may require providers of electronic communications networks or services and others to provide information that the DBA deems relevant to discharge its supervisory duties under the Tele Act. The DBA must prepare and publish, at regular intervals, statistics and documentation concerning issues that the DBA deems relevant.[78]

Quality of service: securing 'net neutrality'

11.79   Section 4(7) of the Tele Act implements Article 8(4)(g) of the Framework Directive regarding net neutrality. Pursuant to section 4(7) of the Tele Act, the DBA may lay down rules for the purpose of requiring providers of electronic communications networks or services to ensure end users the ability to access and distribute information and to run applications and services of their choice. The DBA has not laid down such rules and it will only do so if deemed necessary.

Other obligations

11.80   Danish law, primarily the Tele Act, implements the additional obligations described in the Universal Service Directive, in particular the obligation relating to the change of providers.[79]

DATA PROTECTION: THE DIRECTIVE ON PRIVACY AND ELECTRONIC COMMUNICATIONS

Confidentiality of Communications

11.81   Service and network providers, and their employees and former employees, may not, without authorisation, disclose or utilise information about other persons' use of the network or the service or the content thereof which they learn in connection with the provision of electronic communications networks or services. Providers must take measures necessary to ensure that information about other persons' use of the network or service or the content thereof will not be available to unauthorised persons.[80]

11.82   Service and network providers must ensure the confidentiality of communications by taking appropriate technical and organisational precautions to safeguard the security of their services. If necessary, they must do so in conjunction with the relevant network operators.

---

76   MO715 appendix 1, cf s 9.
77   MO715, cf L169 s 4.
78   S 75 L169.
79   See at 9.40.
80   S 7(1) L169.

11.83   Section 10 of the Tele Act includes exceptions to the generally applicable principle of prohibition on interception or surveillance of communications For example, one exception provides that the police must be permitted access to interception and surveillance of communications for investigatory purposes, provided compliance with the requirements of the Danish Administration of Justice Act.[81] Another exception provides that carrying out interception and immediate transmission of telecommunications to another Member State under Articles 18(5)(a), cf (2)(a) and (c) of the Convention of 29 May 2000 on Mutual Assistance in Criminal Matters between the Member States of the European Union is permitted following a request by the police.

11.84   Access to, or storage of, information on a subscriber's or user's terminal equipment and the processing of such information generally requires express consent.[82] The information to be provided based on which the consent is to be given must be clear and comprehensive. It is an offence to use an electronic communications network to store, or gain access to, information included on a user's terminal equipment (eg by means of 'cookies') without first providing clear and comprehensive information regarding the intent, scope, and purpose of processing. An exception to this prohibition is for technical storage or access for the sole purpose of transmitting a communication or providing services expressly requested by the subscriber or user.

Data Retention

11.85   Ministerial Order No 988 of 28 September 2006[83] implements Directive 2006/24/EC (Data Retention Directive). According to MO988, providers of electronic communications networks and services to end users must register and retain data concerning telecommunications traffic which is generated or processed in the provider's network, in order for such data to be used in connection with investigations and criminal prosecutions. MO988 lists different categories of data which providers must register and retain for a period of one year.

Traffic Data and Location Data

11.86   'Traffic data' is defined as 'data processed for the purpose of the conveyance of a communication on an electronic communications network or for the billing thereof'. 'Location data' is defined as 'data processed in an electronic communications network, indicating the geographic position of the terminal equipment of a user of a publicly available electronic communications service'.[84]

11.87   Subscribers must always be advised of the types of data processed and the duration of such processing.

---

81   Act No 1063 of 17 November 2011 ('Retsplejeloven').

82   Ministerial Order No 1148 of 9 December 2011 on Information and Consent Requiring in Case of Storing or Accessing Information in End User Terminal Equipment (Cookies)

83   Ministerial Order No 988 of 28 September 2006 concerning Providers of Electronic Communications Networks and Services' Registration and Retention of Data regarding Telecommunications Traffic (Logging) ('MO988'). MO988 is issued pursuant to s 786 of the Danish Administration of Justice Act.

84   S 2(2) and 2(3) MO715.

11.88   Service providers are permitted to store and process traffic data for the purpose of billing subscribers and invoicing for interconnection.[85] Such data may only be retained for the period of time during which the bill may be lawfully challenged and payment pursued (or the completion of any legal proceedings initiated during that time).

11.89   Traffic data must be erased or anonymised when it is no longer required for the purpose of transmitting communications. Subject to obtaining consent, operators may process data for the purpose of marketing electronic communications services or providing value-added services. Consent may be withdrawn at any time.

11.90   A service provider may process location data only upon obtaining the subscriber's or user's consent, or upon anonymising the data[86] and only to the extent, and for the period, required to deliver a value- added service. Consent may be withdrawn at any time.

11.91   Service providers must offer the provision of either itemised bills or tariff specific invoices.[87] Specified bills prepared in connection with complaints must always be offered free of charge.

Presentation and Restriction of Calling and Connected Line Identification

11.92   Service providers offering calling line identification services must permit users to withhold their numbers on a per-call and per-line basis, free of charge. The same applies to facilitating the blocking of numbers of incoming calls and rejecting incoming calls automatically where the caller has withheld identification.[88] The service may be suspended temporarily during a police investigation of suspected malicious or nuisance calls or calls to emergency services.[89]

Automatic Call Forwarding

11.93   Service providers must offer their customers, free of charge, the right to request that automatically forwarded calls resulting from third party actions be discontinued.[90]

Directories of Subscribers

11.94   Anyone has the right to request not to be included in the telephone directory. Inclusion in the directory requires express consent from the individual concerned in relation not only to inclusion but also to the nature of the personal data.

---

85   S 23(2) MO715.
86   S 24(1) MO715.
87   S 19 MO715.
88   S 20 and s 21 MO715.
89   S 22 MO715.
90   S 16 MO715.

The Estonian Market for Electronic Communications[1]

Pirkko-Liis Harkmaa, Katri Paas-Mohando, Martin-Kaspar Sild
LAWIN Attorneys at Law, Tallinn

LEGAL STRUCTURE

Basic Policy

12.1   Estonia has a stable and well-developed electronic communications sector. Since regaining independence in the early 1990s, electronic communications have played a central role in the country's economic development. The lack of an entrenched, inflexible legal system, which typically stifles innovation, has contributed to the rapid spread of electronic and mobile communications throughout the country and across sectors.

12.2   The telecommunications market has been open to competition since 2001, when the exclusive rights of the incumbent national operator, Estonian Telecom (Eesti Telekom), expired. Unbundling is fully implemented and pro-competitive requirements of access to telecommunications networks is in place. Conditions have been created for the successful roll-out of 3G services and licences have been issued to three national mobile operators.

12.3   The latest policy documents are 'The Information Society Development Plan until 2013', approved by the Government in November 2006, and 'Implementation Plan for 2010–2011 of the Information Society Development Plan until 2013' ('Development Plan'), approved by the Government in February 2010. The government adopted the Development Plan, taking into account the 'EU Policy Framework for the Information Society and Media 2005–2009' ('EU Policy Framework i2010'). The overall goal of the Development Plan is to develop the information society to include participation of all citizens, thereby improving quality of life and strengthening the economy.

Implementation of EU Directives

12.4   By 1 May 2004 Estonia had transposed the main elements of the 1998 EU Regulatory Package into the Estonian Telecommunications Act that entered into force in March 2000. Since 1 January 2005, the telecommunications market has

---

1   Editing of this chapter closed on 15 May 2012.

been regulated by the Electronic Communications Act ('ECA'),[2] which replaced the Telecommunications Act and served to transpose the 2002 EU Regulatory Package, and, as of 2011, the 2009 EU Regulatory Package.

Legislation

12.5   The ECA is the principal legislation governing the telecommunications.[3] A number of secondary acts referenced in the ECA describe in more detail certain requirements and procedures set out in the ECA.

12.6   The national regulatory agencies, the Estonian Technical Surveillance Authority ('ETSA') and the Estonian Competition Authority ('CA'), have the right to issue individual administrative acts setting out obligations for performance of the duties provided under the ECA.[4] These acts could take the form of either administrative precepts or decisions or misdemeanour sanctions. ETSA and CA (collectively referred to as 'ENRAs', or, individually, as 'ENRA') share authority in the electronic communications sector.

REGULATORY PRINCIPLES: IMPLEMENTATION OF THE FRAMEWORK DIRECTIVE

Scope of Regulation

12.7   Since enactment of the ECA, communications regulation in Estonia does not focus solely on 'telecommunications networks and services', but rather on 'electronic communications networks and services'. With respect to infrastructure and networks, and the technicalities of provision of respective services, telecommunications, IT and broadcasting all fall under the scope of the general regulatory framework set out in the ECA. While the ECA's general regulatory framework also covers VoIP, it does not specifically address such services.

12.8   The definition of the term 'electronic communications networks'[5] is identical to the definition in the 2002 Framework Directive. The definition of 'electronic communications service'[6] is, however, slightly different, but the overall meaning remains the same as in the Framework Directive. 'Associated facilities' are not separately defined, but are described in the context of provision of access as facilities and services necessary to provide services over the local loop.

12.9   Content is regulated separately under the Media Services Act[7] (which also regulates broadcasting licensing), as well as under the Information Society Services Act[8] and the Product Conformity Act.[9]

---

2   Riigi Teataja I ('RTI') 2004, 87, 593 (as amended periodically).
3   Eg Estonian Number Plan Riigi Teataja ('RTL' or 'RT') 2007, 49, 891, Estonian Frequency Plan RT I, 31.03.2011, 3, Requirements of Number Portability upon Changing the Provider of Communications Services RT I, 16.06.2011, 15, Terms and Conditions for Booking Numbers RTL 2005, 30, 420, and others.
4   Art 145 ECA.
5   Art 2(8) ECA.
6   Art 2(6) ECA.
7   RT I, 06.01.2011, 1.
8   RTI 2004, 29, 191 (as amended from time to time).
9   RT I 2010, 31, 157.

'Internet Freedom'

12.10   End users' access to the Internet is not restricted and current information society policies outline goals to further enhance the overall accessibility of the Internet.

National Regulatory Authorities: Organisation, Regulatory Objectives, Competencies

12.11   Consistent with the Framework Directive, the ENRAs are the independent regulators. The Data Protection Inspectorate and Consumer Protection Board also have certain supervisory functions with respect to the electronic communications sector. The Ministry of Economic Affairs and Communications also has certain functions in the electronic communications sector, but these relate mostly to strategic planning and policy making.

12.12   The ENRAs are both governmental agencies under the Ministry of Economic Affairs and Communications. Both ENRAs have their own statutes and their own budget that are financed from the State budget. The Minister of Economic Affairs and Communications (upon proposal by the Chancellor of the Minister) appoints a Director General to both ENRAs.

12.13   Although the Ministry of Economic Affairs and Communications exercises a certain amount of supervisory control over the ENRAs, they are structured in a manner to make independent decisions and take independent actions.

12.14   Article 134 ECA sets out the ENRAs' national regulatory objectives, which mirror the objectives in Article 8 of the Framework Directive. The ENRAs may request from undertakings providing electronic communications and networks and other persons information to enable the ENRAs to perform the duties dictated to them by the ECA[10] The ENRAs publish on their respective websites information related to their regulatory activities, including the specific tasks assigned to them.[11] They hold public consultations prior to performing an act, assigning an obligation or application of a measure, or adopting legislation which may significantly affect the relevant electronic communications market or the rights of end users and consumers. For these purposes, the relevant ENRA will publish an according notice on its website.[12]

12.15   The CA, in addition to serving as the national competition authority, also serves as a sector regulator governing market specific issues such as access and interconnection, SMPs and universal services. ETSA oversees technical issues such as safety, data retention, frequency allocation, and number usage. Although authority in electronic communication matters is shared between these two authorities, their fields of supervision do not overlap.

12.16   The ENRAs settle disputes in circumstances outlined in the ECA: the CA settles disputes related to access or interconnection;[13] and the ETSA settles disputes

---

10   Art 148 ECA.
11   Art 151 ECA (ie decisions on declaring undertakings as undertakings with SMP, concerning assignment of obligations to undertakings or defining of electronic communications markets, decisions made in disputes between undertakings, etc).
12   Art 152 ECA.
13   Art 68 ECA.

related to line facilities.[14] In order to initiate dispute resolution procedures, a party to the dispute must submit a written petition. The relevant ENRA must resolve the dispute without undue delay, but in any case within no more than four months after receipt of a petition. However, if the dispute is particularly complicated, the ENRA may take longer to resolve the dispute, but must explain why the dispute is considered to be particularly complicated and communicate the term for settlement. The ENRA settles a dispute by passing a resolution granting or denying the petition, and depending on the circumstances, such resolution is prepared in the form of either a decision or an administrative precept. If the petitioner so desires, the ENRA may participate in the dispute as the conciliator but in such case, the ENRA may not make a binding resolution. The ENRA does not settle private law disputes between end users and undertakings, or consumers' complaints against undertakings providing electronic communications networks or services. Should a specific dispute also fall within the competence of a supervisory authority from another EU Member State, the ENRA must cooperate with such supervisory authority in settling the dispute, and, if necessary, also consult with the Body of European Regulators for Electronic Communications (BEREC).[15]

Right of Appeal against NRA's Decisions

12.17   Administrative precepts and decisions of the ENRAs as administrative acts can be challenged pursuant to the procedures set out in the Administrative Procedures Act.[16] An individual who believes that his or her rights have been violated, or freedoms restricted, by an administrative act or in the course of administrative proceedings, may file a challenge with the relevant ENRA within 30 days of the date the person became, or should have become, aware of the challenged administrative act or measure. An individual whose challenge is dismissed or whose rights are violated in the course of the proceedings may, within 30 days, file an action with an administrative court under conditions and pursuant to procedures provided by the Code of Administrative Court Procedure.[17]

The NRA's Obligations to Cooperate with the Commission

12.18   The consolidation procedure and co-regulation procedure have been implemented into articles 48 and 48.1 ECA in full consistency with the relevant provisions of article 7 and 7a of Framework Directive.

12.19   While the ECA does not explicitly refer to Article 19 of the Framework Directive and the obligation of the ENRA to take utmost account of the Commission's recommendations, article 133(3) ECA stipulates that, upon performing duties and carrying out the supervision proceeding delineated in the ECA, the ENRA should refer to EU laws, including regulations, directives, decisions and recommendations.

12.20   The Commission's power to stipulate standards and specifications[18] is reflected in article 124 ECA, whereby, to the extent that a piece of equipment is manufactured in conformity with EU standards and specifications, it is presumed that the equipment is also in conformity with the requirements of ECA.

---

14   Art 120 ECA.
15   Art 149 ECA.
16   RTI 2001, 58, 354 (as amended from time to time).
17   RT I, 23.02.2011, 3.
18   Art 17 of the Framework Directive, Art 24 ECA.

'Significant Market Power' as a fundamental prerequisite of regulation

Definition of SMP

12.21 The definition of significant market power in the ECA is similar to the definition set out in Article 14 of the Framework Directive, ie the CA designates an undertaking as having SMP in a specific electronic communications service market and in the region where the services are provided if, individually or together with other undertakings, the undertaking has significant market power which enables the undertaking to operate, to an appreciable extent, independently of competitors, parties, and end users.[19]

12.22 The CA may designate one or several SMP undertakings provided that it has established that competition is not present in the respective electronic communications service market and the undertaking(s) meet(s) the SMP criteria. The CA may also find that several undertakings have a collective dominant position in a specific communications service market and may designate an undertaking having SMP in one electronic communications service market as also having SMP in a closely related market.[20]

12.23 In practice, the CA has designated only one undertaking as having SMP in most relevant markets, but in some markets it has also designated several undertakings as having SMP (eg it has designated ten such undertakings in the market of termination of calls in a fixed telephone network and three such undertakings in the termination of calls in a mobile telephone network).

Definition of relevant markets

12.24 The CA must define the relevant markets and their geographical area in accordance with the principles of EU competition law and on the basis of the European Commission recommendations and guidelines concerning the list of markets, the decisions of the European Commission, and the rulings of the European Court of Justice (ECJ). If justified by the national competitive situation, the CA may deviate from the recommendations of the European Commission, but only after notifying the European Commission. [21] In practice, the CA has occasionally slightly deviated from the European Commission recommendations when defining relevant markets.

Imposition of remedies

12.25 While the ECA does not clearly indicate whether the CA must impose remedies on undertakings identified as having SMP, in practice the CA typically imposes such remedies. The CA may impose one, or several, relevant obligations on an undertaking with SMP. Upon selecting the obligations, the CA must follow the requirements detailed in the ECA and must also consider recommendations and opinions of the European Commission concerning the electronic communications

---

19   Art 45 (2) ECA.
20   Art 45 (4), (5) ECA.
21   Art 43 (1), (1.1) ECA.

market as well as the corresponding practices developed in co-operation with the EU communications market regulators.[22]

NRA's Regulatory Duties concerning Rights of Way, Co-location and Facility Sharing

Rights of way

12.26 With respect to the regulation of rights of way, the ECA contains provisions only concerning line facilities[23] and the restrictions applied to activities carried out in the exclusivity zones thereof.[24] Other aspects of rights of way are regulated by the Law of Property Act,[25] the Act on Implementation of the Law of Property Act,[26] and the Building Act.[27]

12.27 The owner of immovable property, regardless of whether it is in the private or public domain, must permit line facilities to be built on the property if the building of such line facilities:

- is necessary for the intended use or management of other immovable property;
- is not possible without using the property; or
- would be excessively expensive at an alternate location.

The owner of the immovable property on which the line facilities are built may demand that the other immovable would be encumbered with a private easement, in which case a fee payable to the owner of the immovable on which the line facilities are built by the owner of the other immovable will be determined upon agreement. If the building or maintenance of the line facility damages the immovable property, the owner of the line facility must eliminate the consequences of the damage or compensate for the damage caused to the owner of the immovable property. The owner of the immovable property, may demand that the owner of the line facility relocate the line facility on the immovable property, if technically feasible, and if the owner of the immovable property compensates the owner of the line facility for the costs related to relocation.[28]

12.28 The owner of immovable property must permit line facilities to be built on his or her immovable property if universal services are provided through the line facilities by a universal service provider and there is no other technically and

---

22 Art 46(2) ECA.
23 Art 2(24) ECA defines 'line' as a set of technical facilities which connects the termination point with the connection point of terminal equipment. Art 2(25) ECA defines 'line facility' as a part of an electronic communications network permanently attached to subsoil, which includes an underground cable, cable in the bottom of a body of water, cable conduit or duct, a set of cables or wires installed on buildings and poles together with switching devices, distribution equipment and cable termination equipment, regenerator, equipment container and a radio mast, as well as utility networks and constructions within the meaning of the Building Act and the Law of Property Act Implementation Act.
24 Art 117 ECA defines the protective zone of a line facility as an area where any activity likely to damage or harm the line facility is permitted only with the permission of the owner of the line facility.
25 RTI 1999, 44, 509 (consolidated text, as amended from time to time).
26 RTI 1993, 72/73, 1021 (as amended from time to time).
27 RTI 2002, 47, 297 (as amended from time to time).
28 Art 158 Law of Property Act.

economically more expedient possibility to connect to line facilities the consumption site of a person who wishes to connect to the line facilities or to develop the line facilities. Upon termination of the contract for the provision of universal services, the obligation to tolerate does not cease if the provision of services offered to all persons through the line facilities is continued pursuant to the general procedure. The owner is not subject to such an obligation if the restriction arising from the line facilities to the owner is significantly greater than the public interest in the line facilities, or the interest of the person who wishes to connect to the line facilities, and there is a possibility of building the line facilities so that the owner of another immovable property is not placed in an equivalent or worse situation.[29] The owner of the immovable property may demand payment for tolerating a line facility erected on its immovable property.[30]

12.29   The ECA delegates to the ETSA the power to resolve disputes concerning line facilities.[31]

Co-location and facility sharing

12.30   The CA may impose on an undertaking operating an electronic communications network an obligation to share or co-locate network equipment or other property used for the provision of electronic communications services, including line facilities and cabling inside or outside of buildings, up to the intermediate distribution point. The CA may impose the facility sharing or co-location obligations particularly if other providers of electronic communications services or networks do not have alternative possibilities for access due to environmental, health protection, building and planning requirements or public security. [32] The facility sharing or co-location obligation may result in the respective undertaking incurring a proportional share of the costs relating to facility sharing or co-location or tolerating line facilities, equipment, or other property being used by another undertaking.[33]

REGULATION OF MARKET ENTRY: IMPLEMENTATION OF THE AUTHORISATION DIRECTIVE

The General Authorisation of Electronic Communications

12.31   The ECA sets the legal framework for provision of all public electronic communication services, including fixed, mobile, and satellite services.[34] An operator, in order to provide electronic communications services, must have an undertaking or a branch office registered in the Estonian Commercial Register or the register of non-profit associations and foundations.[35] This is also consistent with the Commercial Code,[36] which stipulates that, if a foreign undertaking wishes to permanently offer its products and services in Estonia under its own name, such

---

29   Art 158.1 Law of Property Act.
30   Art 158.2 (1) Law of Property Act.
31   Art 120 ECA.
32   Art 63(3) ECA.
33   Art 63(4) ECA.
34   Art 3(1) ECA.
35   Art 3(2) ECA.
36   RTI 1998, 91/93, 1500 (consolidated text as amended).

foreign undertaking should establish a branch office in Estonia and register it in the Commercial Register. The undertaking or the branch office wishing to provide electronic communications services must submit a written notice to the ETSA prior to commencing activities.[37]

12.32   Upon written request from the service provider, the ETSA must issue, within seven days of receiving the request, a written confirmation of receipt of the request, and, if the service provider so requests, an overview of the respective rights and obligations of the service provider arising from the ECA.[38]

12.33   The ECA, and respective government regulations, set out the conditions for provision of public electronic communications services. In general, service providers must guarantee the security, integrity, and interoperability of networks, secure the protection of transmitted or saved information, observe health-related and environmental requirements, guarantee the quality of services, avoid harmful interferences, secure public order and national security, and avoid activities hindering free competition.

Rights of Use for Radio Frequencies

Strategic planning and co-ordination of spectrum policy

12.34   To date, Estonia has not adopted policies specific to radio spectrum. In adopting the general manners, purposes and regime for the use of the radio frequency bands, the Estonian Frequency Plan draws upon the radio regulations arising from the Constitution and Convention of the International Telecommunications Union.[39]

12.35   The Ministry of Economics and Communication has adopted a plan for the use of digital dividend spectrum. This plan determines the various possibilities of usage of the digital dividend as a limited technical resource in Estonia as well as to map further courses of action.

Principles of frequency allocation, procedural rules

12.36   The use of radio frequencies requires a frequency permit issued by an ETSA decision on the basis of an application submitted by the electronic communication service provider. The ETSA must issue such a permit within six weeks of receiving the application, provided that the use of the respective frequency does not require international coordination, and within eight months where use of the respective frequency requires international coordination.[40] On written request from the holder of the frequency permit, the ETSA must submit to the applicant a written confirmation of the rights and obligations under the frequency permit within three working days of receipt of the application.

---

37   Art 4(1) ECA.
38   Art 4(4) ECA.
39   Art 1(1) Estonian Frequency Plan
40   Art 13(1) ECA.

12.37   Generally, before the grant of a frequency permit or amendment of its conditions, the ETSA will submit the conditions of the frequency permit for approval to the Health Board. [41]

12.38   The Minister of Economic Affairs and Communications may also determine that certain frequencies may be used without a frequency permit, provided that the respective requirements established for the use of such frequencies are observed.[42]

Transferability and time limitations

12.39   In principle, article 17 ECA permits trading of the spectrum licences, provided that the right to trade the respective frequencies has been addressed in the Estonian Frequency Plan and that the transfer of frequencies would not result in distortion of competition. In order to trade the radio frequencies, the prospective transferor and transferee must submit an application to the ETSA. The procedure for the transfer of the right to radio frequencies is detailed in a regulation of the Minister of Economic Affairs and Communications.[43]

12.40   The period of validity of a frequency permit is generally one year,[44] unless the applicant requests a shorter period of validity. The frequency permit is extendable on the basis of an according application submitted by the electronic communication service provider.

Admissible Conditions

12.41   The ECA sets out explicit terms and conditions to be included in a frequency permit. The ECA adopts most of the terms and conditions set out in Part B of the Annex to the Authorisation Directive. Those terms and conditions in items 1, 6, 7 and 9 of Part B of the Annex, however, are not included in the ECA.

12.42   The ECA does not contain any specific provisions related to 3G services, the initial roll-out of which started on the basis of the previous Telecommunications Act, which also set out specific UMTS licence conditions (including coverage requirements, data transfer rates, and license validity period).

Limitation of number of rights of use to be granted

12.43   Upon receipt of several, simultaneously submitted, applications for the use of the same radio frequency, the Estonia National Communications Board ('ENCB') will organise an auction to issue a permit for such frequency.[45] In addition, certain frequencies set out in the frequency plan must be allocated through public tender.

---

41   Art 13(3.1) ECA.
42   Art 20 ECA.
43   Procedure for transfer of the right to use radio frequencies and for granting the right to use radio frequencies on the basis of use agreement (RT I, 06.07.2011, 5).
44   Art 11(3) ECA.
45   Art 19 ECA.

Rights of Use for Numbers

General authorisations and granting of individual rights

12.44   The ETSA issues permits for the use of numbers. Such permits are issued within 10 business days of receiving an application, provided that the applicant has paid the relevant State duties applicable to the issuance of number permits.[46] Number permits may not be transferred or traded. The number permit is valid for one year and is extendable on the basis of application.[47]

12.45   A number use permit does not confer property rights in the number. Intellectual property issues may, however, arise in connection with certain short numbers. For example, short numbers '1188' and '1184' are parts of trademarks registered by providers of directory and general information services.

Admissible conditions

12.46   A number permit grants the holder of the permit the right to reserve numbers, as a result of which a right to use a particular number is granted. Such reservation is not limited in time and the reservation for a particular portable number is transferred to another operator if the customer decides to change the service provider.

12.47   The holder of the number permit may use geographical and non-geographical numbers (telephone numbers) or mobile telephone numbers and grant these to their subscribers or clients for their own use or for use as service numbers for the provision of other services rendered by means of an electronic communications service.

12.48   In addition to the conditions for the use of numbering contained in the ECA, the Minister of Economic Affairs and Communications may establish certain other conditions. These conditions, however, differ somewhat from those set out in Part C of the Annex to the Authorisation Directive. For example, the Minister may establish conditions for reserving numbers, as well as conditions for using numbers in order to ensure public order and national security.[48] The admissible conditions under the ECA also do not contain conditions referred to under items 2, 3, 7, 8 as well as partly (with regard to tariff principles and maximum prices) item 1 of Part C of the Annex.

12.49   Undertakings designated as having SMP in the market of access to the public telephone network at a fixed location for residential customers may be subject to the obligation to enable its end users to access the services of any interconnected provider of publicly available telephone services by dialling a carrier selection code and by means of pre-selection, with a facility to override any pre-selected choice on a call-by-call basis by dialling a carrier selection code.[49]

Limitation of number of rights of use to be granted

12.50   Upon receipt of several applications for permits to use the same short number or identification code, and it is not possible to grant joint use of the short

---

46   Art 34 ECA.
47   Art 33(4) and 35(2) ECA.
48   Art 29(2) ECA.
49   Art 51(1) clause [10] ECA.

number or identification code, the ETSA will organise an auction for issuance of a number permit. The Minister of Economic Affairs and Communications may establish specific procedural rules for organising the auction.[50]

The NRA's Enforcement Powers

12.51   The ENRAs supervise the fulfilment of the requirements set out in the ECA. If violations are detected, the respective ENRA with authority over the specific matter, depending on the circumstances, may:

- issue an administrative precept requiring the elimination of a violation or the performance of certain acts together with the right to use a coercive measure, in the form of a penalty payment of up to €9,600 if the precept of the authority is not voluntarily complied with by the deadline given;[51]
- suspend a frequency permit if the ETSA has notified the holder of the permit of a detected violation and the holder of the permit has failed to eliminate the violation within one month after receipt of the ETSA's respective notice;[52]
- revoke a frequency permit, for example where use of the rights granted by the frequency permit has not commenced within six months after the grant of the frequency permit, the holder of the frequency permit has materially or repeatedly violated the conditions of the frequency permit, use of the radio frequencies is suspended and the user of the radio frequencies has not eliminated the circumstances on which the suspension is based within one month of the date on which the decision on suspension is made;[53]
- restrict the rights of the holder of the number permit if the holder of the number permit has violated the established requirements and has failed to eliminate the violation within the prescribed term;[54] or
- carry out extra-judicial proceedings of handling misdemeanours and impose sanctions in the form of fines according to the procedures set out in the General Part of the Penal Code[55] and the Code of Misdemeanour Procedure,[56] which in the case of natural persons can be 3 to 300 penalty units, where one penalty unit is €4, and in the case of legal persons up to €3,200.[57]

Administrative Charges and Fees for Rights of Use

12.52   There is no fee required for submission of a notice of commencement of the provision of electronic communications services. There is, likewise, no general charge or fee for undertakings benefiting from general authorisations without having obtained rights of use for frequencies or numbers, except the universal service fee.[58]

12.53   The granting, amendment and extension of frequency permits and number permits is subject to the payment of State duties by the applicant. The amount of

---

50   Art 39 ECA.
51   Art 146(1) ECA.
52   Art 18(1) ECA.
53   Art 18(3) ECA.
54   Art 37 ECA.
55   RTI 2002, 86, 504 (consolidated text as amended from time to time).
56   RTI 2002, 50, 313 (as amended from time to time).
57   Art 188(3)–(3.1) ECA.
58   See para 12.76 below.

the particular State duty varies: in the case of frequency permits, the exact amount depends on the type of frequencies used and the nature and purpose of such use, and in the case of number permits on the type of numbers used. The Act on State Duties lists detailed rates of State duties.[59]

REGULATION OF NETWORK ACCESS AND INTERCONNECTION: THE ACCESS DIRECTIVE

Objectives and Scope of Access Regulation

12.54   The basic principles of access and interconnection as embodied in the ECA are derived from the Access Directive. The purpose of regulating access and interconnection is to ensure competition, efficient investment and innovation, the interoperability of communications services and protection of the interests of end users.[60] General access- and interconnection-related provisions of the ECA, eg the obligation to enter into interconnection negotiations and to disclose information necessary for interconnection, apply to all electronic communications service providers. The CA may impose additional, more specific obligations on such SMP undertakings.

Basic Regulatory Concepts

12.55   'Access' is defined as the making available of networks, line facilities and network facilities or services provided by one communications undertaking to another undertaking for the purpose of providing communications services.[61] 'Interconnection' is defined as a special type of access which means the technical and logical linking of two or more communications networks in a manner which enables provision of communications services to the subscribers of the connected communications networks.[62] The ECA expressly stipulates the principle of the 'freedom of access' as set out in Article 3(1) of the Access Directive, entitling communications undertakings to agree freely on the technical and commercial conditions for access and interconnection, taking into account certain obligations in connection with access and interconnection and the possible SMP obligations imposed on communications undertakings.[63]

12.56   An undertaking providing electronic communications network services is required, at the request of another communications undertaking, to negotiate interconnection in good faith if necessary for the provision of electronic communications services. An undertaking may terminate pre-contractual negotiations and refuse to enter into an access or interconnection agreement if the creation of technical conditions for interconnection or access is unreasonably burdensome or the interconnection or access would damage the integrity of its network. [64] The

---

59   RT I 2010, 21, 107 (as amended from time to time).
60   Art 59 ECA.
61   Art 60(1) ECA.
62   Art 61(1) ECA.
63   Art 62 ECA.
64   Art 65(1) ECA.

ETSA becomes involved if it receives a complaint with regard to access or interconnection. [65]

Access- and Interconnection-Related Obligations with Respect to SMP Undertakings

12.57 The obligations that may be imposed on SMP undertakings are identical to those listed in Articles 9–13b of the Access Directive.

Transparency obligations

12.58 The ENCB may impose on SMP undertakings an obligation to publish information in relation to access and interconnection, relating to accounting information, technical specifications, network characteristics, terms and conditions for provision of services, including any conditions restricting access to services and their application and use, and prices, as well as obligations to publish a reference offer regarding a specific access or interconnection service which should contain the conditions for provision of the corresponding service.[66] The ECA also sets out a detailed list of conditions that must be contained in a reference offer.[67]

Non-discrimination obligations

12.59 The CA may impose on SMP undertakings an obligation of non-discrimination which should ensure that SMP undertakings, and, in particular, vertically integrated SMP undertakings, which provide services to undertakings with which they compete at the retail level, apply equivalent conditions in equivalent circumstances to other undertakings providing equivalent services, and provide services and information to others under the same conditions and of the same quality as they provide for their own services, or those of their subsidiaries or partners.[68]

Specific access obligations

12.60 The ENCB may impose on SMP undertakings an obligation to meet reasonable requests of other providers of electronic communications services or networks for access to, and use of, specific network elements and associated facilities, if denial of access or unreasonable terms and conditions having a similar effect would hinder the emergence of a sustainable competitive market at the retail level, or would not be in the end users' interests.[69]

---

65   Art 68 ECA.
66   Art 50 (1) clauses [1], [2] ECA.
67   Art 53 ECA.
68   Art 50 (1) clause [3] ECA.
69   Art 50(1) clause [5] ECA.

Price controls

12.61   The CA may impose on SMP undertakings an obligation relating to the recovery of costs for access or interconnection and price controls and obligations for cost orientation of prices and obligations concerning cost-accounting systems.[70]

Accounting separation

12.62   The CA may impose on SMP undertakings an obligation to maintain separate records of activities related to interconnection or access in connection with which the CA may require a vertically integrated undertaking to make transparent its wholesale prices and its internal transfer prices.[71]

Regulatory Powers with Respect to SMP Undertakings

12.63   If the CA concludes, as a result of market analysis, that the appropriate obligations imposed have failed to achieve effective competition and that there are important and persisting competition problems or market failures identified in relation to the market of wholesale provision of certain access products, it may, as an exceptional measure, impose an obligation on vertically integrated undertakings to place activities related to the wholesale provision of relevant access products in an independently operating business entity.[72]

Regulatory Powers Applicable to All Market Participants

Obligations to ensure end-to-end connectivity

12.64   The CA may impose on an undertaking providing electronic communications networks, and controlling access to end users, any obligations necessary to ensure end-to-end connectivity, including obligations for the interconnection of networks.[73]

Access to digital radio and television broadcasting services

12.65   The CA may impose on an undertaking providing electronic communications networks, obligations to ensure access to application program interfaces (APIs) and electronic programme guides (EPGs) on fair, reasonable, and non-discriminatory terms, if necessary to ensure accessibility for end users to specified digital radio and television broadcasting programmes, as well as facility sharing or co-location obligations.[74]

---

70 Art 50(1) clause [7] ECA.
71   Art 50(1) clause [4] ECA.
72   Art 55 ECA.
73   Art 63(1) ECA.
74   Art 63(2) ECA.

12.66   An undertaking providing conditional access systems must ensure that such systems permit the technical conduct of cost-oriented cross-checks of services provided by other communications undertakings providing conditional access systems.[75]

12.67   If the access of a provider of television or radio services to the potential viewers and listeners depends on conditional access services, the communications undertaking providing the conditional access to the provider of television and radio services must provide to the provider of television or radio services on fair, reasonable, and non-discriminatory terms and conditions, technical services which allow the viewers or listeners equipped with decoding devices to receive the digitally transmitted services of the provider of television or radio services and to keep separate accounts of its activities as a provider of conditional access services.[76]

REGULATION OF UNIVERSAL SERVICE AND USERS' RIGHTS: THE UNIVERSAL SERVICE DIRECTIVE

Regulation of Universal Service Obligations

Scope of universal service obligations

12.68   A universal service is a set of services which conforms with the technical and quality requirements established by EU law, which is of specified quality and available to all end users requesting it, independently of their geographical location, uniformly and at an affordable price.[77] Article 69 ECA defines the scope of universal services to include the connection to a communications network in a fixed location enabling telephone services, public pay phone service, or other publicly accessible communications service enabling calls and the accessibility of an electronic Public Number Directory and directory enquiry services.

Designation of undertakings obliged to provide universal services

12.69   A public procurement (tender process) or public competition serves to designate providers of universal services If these processes fail to designate a universal services provider, the CA designates as an interim provider of universal services the undertaking who, at the time of the public competition or public tender, held the position of designated universal services provider. The interim provider is subject same conditions effective at the time the public procurement or public competition commenced, and such designation lasts until a service provider is chosen under the public consultation or public procurement.[78] A service contract between the State and the relevant designated undertaking sets out the details of the provision of universal service.

12.70   As of 31 December 2010, Elisa was the only undertaking in Estonia required to provide the universal service, with 11 end users. The universal service must enable originating and receiving national and international calls, sending and receipt of faxes and a data communication service with a download speed of up to

75   Art 67(1) ECA.
76   Art 67(2) ECA.
77   Art 69 ECA.
78   Art 73(2) ECA.

556kbit/s. As 31 December 2010, public pay phone service and universal electronic Public Number Directory and directory enquiry services are not considered universal services.[79]

Regulation of retail tariffs, user expenditures and quality of service

12.71   The affordable price charged for the universal service to end users by the provider of universal service is included in the conditions of the public tender or the tender documents relating to the public procurement and will be also fixed in the universal service contract. The CA recommends to the Minister of Economic Affairs and Communications the rate it deems affordable, and the Minister establishes the rate.[80]

12.72   A universal service provider, upon commencement of service, must provide the end users with several possibilities to control expenditures relating to the service (eg itemised bills, call barring, access on pre-paid terms, deferred payment of connection charges).[81]

12.73   Pursuant to concepts and methods of measurement provided in Estonian standard EVS 874:2003, a universal service provider, to enable monitoring of its service quality, must make available to the public, and submit to the CA, at a minimum, the information listed in Annex III Universal Service Directive (as listed prior to amendments to Annex III) related to the provision of universal services.[82]

Cost calculation and financing of universal services

12.74   Upon determining the additional costs and revenue involved in the provision of the universal service, a universal service provider must take into account only the costs necessary for performance of universal service obligation; the costs which a universal service provider would incur regardless of the universal service obligation (such as ordinary business expenses), and costs which have been incurred before the beginning of the calendar year of submission of the tender, must not be taken into account.[83]

12.75   A universal service provider may submit an application to the CA for compensation of unfairly burdensome costs relating to the performance of the universal service obligation. The CA may decide to compensate the universal service provider for costs related to the universal service obligation to the extent to which the charges paid by end users do not cover the costs related to performance of the universal service obligation or do not ensure a reasonable profit.[84]

12.76   Universal service is financed by means of a separate universal service fee, which will, commencing in 2017, be payable to the State budget by all electronic communication service providers whose annual turnover from the provision of electronic communication services exceeds €383,500. The rate of the fee is 0.01–1% will be calculated on the basis of the turnover of the previous financial year. The

---

79   Annual Report for year 2010 of the Estonian Competition Authority, p 61
80   Art 74(2) ECA.
81   Art 79 ECA.
82   Art 78 ECA.
83   Art 76(2) ECA.
84   Art 75(4) ECA.

exact rate of the fee is established by the Government on the proposal by the Minister of Economic Affairs and Communications for each calendar year.[85]

Regulation of Retail Markets

Prerequisites for the regulation of retail markets

12.77   The CA only regulates a retail market if, in the course of market analysis, the CA determines that competition in the particular relevant retail market is ineffective, and that wholesale remedies will not ensure effective competition. In such a case the CA will designate an SMP undertaking in the retail market and impose relevant obligations on the SMP undertaking.[86] To date, the CA has not designated an undertaking as having SMP in a retail market.

Regulatory powers

12.78   The CA may, among other things, prohibit an SMP undertaking from:

- sustaining prices at an excessively high level;
- preventing competitors from entering a market or limiting competition by applying excessively low prices;
- showing undue preference to certain end users; and
- unduly bundling services.[87]

The CA may impose other obligations on an SMP undertaking upon receiving appropriate permission from the European Commission,[88] although no such permission requirement is set out in the Universal Service Directive.

12.79   An SMP undertaking with such obligations must use necessary and appropriate methodology of cost accounting, and the SMP undertaking with universal service obligations must use the cost accounting methodology determined by the CA.[89]

End User Rights

Contracts

12.80   Electronic communications services are provided to end users on the basis of electronic communications service contracts. As a general rule, undertakings providing electronic communications services and end users are free to agree on the conditions of an electronic communications service contract. However, any condition of an electronic communications service contract which restricts the rights of the end user, as compared to the rights provided by the ECA, is null and void.[90]

---

85   Art 84 ECA; Art 83.1 ECA (provision will enter into force as from the year 2016).
86   Art 54(1) ECA.
87   Art 54(2) ECA.
88   Art 54(3) ECA.
89   Art 54(4) ECA.
90   Art 92(2) ECA.

12.81   The ECA sets out an exhaustive list of grounds under which an electronic communications service provider may refuse to enter into a subscription contract.[91] If no such ground exists, the service provider must enter into the contract.

12.82   The ECA also lists the mandatory terms and conditions of an electronic communications service contract.[92] These terms and conditions are consistent with Article 20(1) of the Universal Service Directive.

12.83   A consumer has the right to cancel an electronic communications service contract at any time without prior notice by notifying the undertaking providing the electronic communication services.[93]

Transparency obligations

12.84   An electronic communications service provider must publish the mandatory terms and conditions of its end user contracts, as well as any other general conditions applied to such contracts, on its website.[94]

Quality of Service: securing 'Network Neutrality'

12.85   The ECA contains a several general references requiring that the principle of neutrality be observed in sector-specific regulation of markets,[95] in preparing frequency allocation plans,[96] and in implementation of the ECA.[97] Certain obligations relating to the quality of compulsory technical standards, which are related to securing the security of communications networks and data, minimising the possible adverse effects related to service interruptions and performing maintenance works are set out in a regulation of the Government of the Republic.[98] The ECA also requires that a communications undertaking make information on the quality of the communications services publicly accessible to end users on its webpage. If the undertaking does not have a website, it must make the information available in another reasonable manner.[99]

European emergency call number

12.86   Communications undertakings providing telephone or mobile services must guarantee the establishment of connection to the national emergency numbers and the single European emergency number '112' free of charge over each communications network and also make available the telephone number of the caller and information on the location of the caller to the national emergency service, the alarm centre, and the security authority. Upon providing mobile telephone services,

---

91   Art 93(2) ECA.
92   Art 96(1), (2) ECA.
93   Art 100(1) ECA.
94   Art 96(3) ECA.
95   Art 40(3) ECA.
96   Art 9(1.1) ECA.
97   Art 134(5) ECA.
98   Regulation of the Government No 140 of 22 June 2006 'Requirements for Provisions of Communications Services and Technical Requirements for Communications Networks' (RT I 2006, 31, 237).
99   Art 87(3) ECA.

a communications undertaking is required to ensure access to the single European emergency call number '112' by SMS for notification of emergencies over its communications network.[100]

Obligations facilitating change of provider

12.87   A subscriber has the right to keep a number (which belongs to the Estonian numbering plan) the use of which has been granted to the subscriber by the service provider when changing the service provider or the geographical location of the subscriber's access point. A service provider must provide the subscriber with information, free of charge, concerning number portability through telephone enquiries and on its website. The charge for number portability must be cost-oriented. The charge is paid by the service provider with whom the subscriber has entered into a new subscription contract providing, as a condition, that the subscriber may keep the current telephone number.[101]

A regulation of the Minister of Economic Affairs and Communications sets out the procedures and specific requirements for number portability. While the regulation stipulates the procedure for the collaboration of the service providers (the recipient operator and the donor operator), it does not require that number portability takes effect within one working day.[102]

DATA PROTECTION: IMPLEMENTATION OF THE DIRECTIVE ON PRIVACY AND ELECTRONIC COMMUNICATIONS

Confidentiality of Communications

12.88   An undertaking providing electronic communications services must maintain the confidentiality of all information which becomes known to it in the process of providing electronic communications services and which concerns subscribers and other persons using electronic communications services with the consent of the subscriber. Such information may be disclosed only to the relevant subscriber and, with the consent of the subscriber, to third persons. A subscriber has the right to withdraw his or her consent at any time. An electronic communications service provider must guarantee the security of the communications network and prevent third persons from accessing such information without legal grounds.[103]

12.89   The ECA requires electronic communication service providers to release certain information to respective governmental surveillance agencies or enable these agencies access to their networks.[104]

12.90   An undertaking providing electronic communications services may process subscriber information if the undertaking notifies the subscriber, in a clear and unambiguous manner, of the purposes of processing the information, and gives the subscriber an opportunity to refuse the processing. Such an obligation does not,

---

100   Art 89 ECA.
101   Art 89 ECA.
102   Regulation No 44 of the Minister of Economic Affairs and Communications of 14 June 2011 'Requirements of Number Portability upon Changing the Provider of Communications Services' (RT I, 16.06.2011, 15)
103   Arts 101, 102 ECA.
104   See also paras 12.92–12.94 (Data retention).

however, restrict the right of the undertaking to collect and process, without the consent of a subscriber, information which must be processed for the purposes of recording the transactions carried out in the conduct of business activities and for other business-related exchange of information, as well as the right to store or process data without the consent of a subscriber if the sole purpose of such activity is the provision of services through the communications network, or if such activity is necessary for the provision of information society services which are directly requested by the subscriber.[105]

12.91   If an electronic communications service provider wishes to process a subscriber's information for marketing purposes, the service provider must inform the subscriber, prior to obtaining consent, of the type of information needed for such purposes and the duration of the intended use of such information.

Data Retention

12.92   The ECA, in adding specific provisions on data retention, transposes Directive 2006/24/EC (the Data Retention Directive) into Estonian law.[106] These provisions incorporate the most important aspects of the Directive (eg provisions relating to the obligation to retain data, types of data to be retained, data protection, and safety, among other things.). Some more technical matters are regulated by the Minister.[107]

12.93   In general, the data retention obligations set out in the ECA follow the obligations set out in Article 5 of the Data Retention Directive, although with some difference regarding the arrangement of the list of obligations and use of some terms. However, the ECA, unlike the Data Retention Directive, sets out general retention obligations. Under the ECA, communications undertakings must retain data necessary for the performance of the following acts:

- tracing and identification of the source of a communication;
- identification of the destination of a communication;
- identification of the date, time and duration of a communication;
- identification of the type of communications service;
- identification of users' terminal equipment or what purports to be their terminal equipment; and
- identification of the location of terminal equipment.[108]

This obligation is of general nature only and is not referenced in other provisions of the ECA regulating among other things, the quality, maintenance, and use of the data to be retained.

12.94   There has not been much public debate on the regulation of data retention, and as far as we are aware, to date, legislation relating to data retention has not been challenged.

---

105   Art 102(4) ECA.
106   Art 111.1 ECA
107   Regulation No 56 of the Minister of Economic Affairs and Communication of 25 June 2008 'The procedure for retention, passing over to Technical Surveillance Board, deleting and destroying data, inquiries, log files and applications' (RTL 2008, 56, 774).
108   Art 111. (1) ECA.

Traffic Data and Location Data

12.95   The ECA does not contain definitions for 'traffic data' or 'location data'. Electronic communications service providers have the right to process subscribers' location data only if such data is rendered anonymous prior to processing.[109] In order to provide other services in the process of using the electronic communications services, service providers also have the right to process, with the consent of subscribers, location data to an extent, and during the term, necessary for processing and without rendering the data anonymous. A subscriber has the right to withdraw his or her consent at any time. A subscriber who has granted consent for the processing of location data must be able easily, and free of charge, to temporarily prohibit processing the data regarding the establishment of connection or transmission of information specifically indicated by the subscriber.[110]

Itemised Billing

12.96   A subscriber has the right to request that a bill presented to it omit the details of provision of the service.

Presentation and restriction of Calling and Connected Line Identification

12.97   If offering calling-line identification, a service provider must provide users with a possibility via a simple means, and free of charge, to eliminate the presentation of the calling-line identification and, where technically possible, provide such opportunity with respect to each separate call and number. A service provider must guarantee that the identity and telephone number of the caller is not disclosed to the person receiving the call even after the call is terminated.[111]

Automatic Call Forwarding

12.98   An undertaking providing electronic communications services is required to provide the end user, where technical capability for such a function exists, with the possibility via a simple means, free of charge, to eliminate automatic routing of calls by third persons to its terminal equipment.[112]

Directories of Subscribers

12.99   Undertakings wishing to publish data on subscribers in telephone directories, or through telephone enquiries, must, prior to publication of such data, provide subscribers with free information concerning the purposes of the databases of the telephone directories or telephone enquiries.[113] Undertakings must provide subscribers with an opportunity to decide whether, and to what extent, they wish

---

109   Art 105(1) ECA.
110   Art 105(2), (3), (4) ECA.
111   Art 108 ECA.
112   Art 109 ECA.
113   Art 107(1) ECA.

such data to be made public. Subscribers must also have the opportunity to verify and amend their data, and to terminate the publication of such data.[114]

---

114 Art 107(2) ECA.

The Finnish Market for Electronic Communications[1]

Henriikka Piekkala and Markus von Schrowe
Attorneys at Law Borenius, Helsinki

LEGAL STRUCTURE

Basic Policy

13.1   The Communications Market Act[2] ('CMA') seeks to promote the provision and use of services within communications networks and to ensure availability of the networks and services under reasonable conditions to all telecommunications operators and users throughout the country. The CMA also seeks to ensure services that are competitive, technologically advanced, of high quality, reliable, safe, and inexpensive.[3]

The regulatory policy seeks to ensure technology neutrality and to optimise the quality, price and availability of services. Despite limited frequencies, a sparse population, and a small communications market, Finland offers communications services that are inexpensive and represent high standards compared to other countries. The regulatory policy also emphasises a citizen's right to participate in the information society and the digital world freely, regardless of wealth, state of health, economic status, or place of residence.[4]

The national broadband agenda seeks to secure national broadband coverage by 2015. The specific goal is that, by the end of 2015 over 99 per cent of the population, including permanent residences, business offices and permanent offices of public-sector organisations, will be located within 2 kilometres of an optic fibre network or a cable network that enables data connections with a transfer speed of 100 Mb/s. Operators are expected to build fast data connections on market terms, reaching population coverage of approximately 95 per cent. Public funding is available to support the rollout of fibre networks to the last 5 per cent of the market.[5]

Mobile services play an important role in Finnish telecommunications markets both in speech and data services. The number of mobile subscriptions totals approximately 8.8 million (160 per cent of the population) while fixed subscriptions

---

1   Editing of this chapter closed on 29 January 2013.
2   Viestintämarkkinalaki 23.5.2003/393.
3   Art 1 CMA.
4   Ministry of Transport and Communications, Communications policy 2011–2015.
5   Ministry of Transport and Communications, Broadband for all 2015.

continue to decline, totalling approximately 1.1 million (20 per cent of the population) in 2011.[6] Finland is EU's leader in mobile broadband implementation. There currently are four licensed national mobile network operators, three of which offer full nationwide services.

A special characteristic of the Finnish telecommunications market is the large number of small local fixed network incumbents. There are currently 42 local network operators, some of which are very small, having significant market power in their respective local operating areas.

The digital switchover of terrestrial television was completed in August 2007. The Government seeks to create competition in the digital terrestrial television ('DTT') market, and has granted network licences to three operators. Currently there are two DTT networks:

- incumbent operator Digita operates a network using high mast infrastructure; and
- DNA Oy has built a network based on telecommunication mast infrastructure.

The third network licensee, Anvia Oy, operates within Digita's network. Currently, the incumbent DTT network operator, Digita, offers only standard definition broadcast while the two other operators may also send high definition broadcasts. Some changes to the licensing policy and licence terms are foreseen to take place after 2016 when most of the DTT network and broadcasting licences expire. There are several local cable TV networks, operated mostly by the local fixed network incumbents. The cable TV operator is competing with the local telecommunications incumbent only in the Helsinki region. Cable networks cover 47 per cent of the population. Satellite television penetration is 4 per cent. IPTV market share has been growing but is still only 2 per cent.[7]

Implementation of EU Directives

13.2   Finland has transposed the 2009 Regulatory Package into national legislation by an amendment to the CMA and other relevant legislation. The amendment came into force on 25 May 2011.[8]

Legislation

13.3   The CMA is the main legislative act governing the electronic communications market, and it has been revised a number of times since its adoption in 2003. Provisions relevant to the communications market can also be found in the Act on Television and Radio Operations[9], the Act on Radio Frequencies and Telecommunications Equipment,[10] the Act on Auctioning Certain Radio Frequencies[11] and the Act on the Protection of Privacy in Electronic Communications.[12]

---

6   FICORA market review 3/2011.
7   FICORA market review 1/2011.
8   Laki viestintämarkkinalain muuttamisesta 8.4.2011/363.
9   Laki televisio- ja radiotoiminnasta 9.10.1998/744.
10   Laki radiotaajuuksista ja telelaitteista 16.11.2001/1015.
11   Laki eräiden radiotaajuuksien huutokaupoista 26.6.2009/462.
12   Sähköisen viestinnän tietosuojalaki 16.6.2004/516.

The legislative acts are complemented by decrees issued by the Government and the Ministry. The national regulatory authority has competence to give technical regulations. This authority has also issued a number of non-binding technical recommendations and regulatory guidelines regarding. eg regulatory pricing and non-discrimination.

The Ministry of Transport and Communications ('Ministry') currently is conducting a legal reform, whereby the legislation concerning electronic communications currently scattered among more than 10 acts will be compiled into a single Code for Information Society and Communications Services. The reform seeks to remove overlapping legislation and reduce regulation. The licensing regime will be renewed and regulations concerning, among other things, SMP obligations, consumer protection, and privacy will be revised. The Ministry plans to adopt the first phase of the reform in 2012–2013.

REGULATORY PRINCIPLES: THE FRAMEWORK DIRECTIVE

Scope of Regulation

13.4 The CMA applies to communications markets, meaning markets of network services, communications services, and related services. Other relevant acts and regulations cover spectrum issues and security of communications. The regulations do not apply to the content of messages transmitted in a communications network. The communications services are interpreted widely to cover, among other things, IP telephony services.

A 'communications network' is defined as a system comprising cables and equipment joined to each other for the purpose of transmitting or distributing messages by wire, radio waves, optically or by other electromagnetic means.[13]

A 'communications service' is defined as a service provided by a service operator. A service operator, in turn, is defined as an operator that transmits messages over a communications network in its possession or obtained for use from a network operator or distributes or provides messages in a mass communications network.[14]

The term 'associated facilities' is not defined in national legislation but is intended to be in line with the EU Directives.[15]

'Internet Freedom'

13.5 The Act on Measures Preventing the Distribution of Child Pornography[16] permits telecommunications operators to voluntarily restrict access to Internet services providing child pornography. In addition, restriction measures may be imposed under the national Copyright Act.[17] The District Court of Helsinki has ordered telecommunications operator Elisa, under the penalty of a fine, to cease making copyright-infringing material publicly available through Pirate Bay.[18]

---

13   Art 2(1.1) CMA.
14   Art 2(1.19) and 2(1.20) CMA.
15   Art 36a CMA.
16   Laki lapsipornografian levittämisen estotoimista 1.12.2006/1068.
17   Tekijänoikeuslaki 8.7.1961/404.
18   District Court of Helsinki, decision 11/41552, 26 October 2011. The case is under appeal.

National Regulatory Authorities: Organisation, Regulatory Objectives, Competencies

13.6   General telecommunications guidance and development are the responsibility of the Ministry of Transport and Communications. The Ministry of Transport and Communications is assisted by the Communications Administration Advisory Board. The Advisory Board monitors the activities of communications administration, prepares initiatives for developing communications administration, and issues opinions. The Communications Administration Advisory Board has a chairperson, deputy chairperson and no more than 16 members, who are appointed by the Ministry of Transport and Communications for three years at a time. Each member is also appointed a personal deputy. The Advisory Board includes representatives of the Ministry of Transport and Communications, operators in the sector, and the main user groups. The Advisory Board convenes at the invitation of the chairperson or deputy chairperson.[19]

The Finnish Communications Regulatory Authority ('FICORA') is the national regulatory authority for communications markets in Finland. FICORA has far-reaching responsibilities within the communications markets, including supervision of communications networks and services, planning and administering the use of radio frequencies, information security, consumer affairs, supervision of media regulations, and granting Internet domain names for the .fi root. FICORA's objective is to make the provision of communications services more versatile, improve the availability of basic communications services, and develop the functionality and security of communications networks and services.[20]

The government acts as a licencing authority for mobile network licences, digital terrestrial television network licences, and broadcasting licences .

Both FICORA and the Consumer Ombudsman have competence over issues regarding consumer contracts. FICORA monitors general contract terms, and the Consumer Authority deals with individual consumer complaints.[21] The Consumer Ombudsman also has competence in certain cases to close a number or a service that is used to for unlawful financial benefit.[22]

Both the Ministry and FICORA must work in cooperation with the competition authorities and the consumer authorities whenever necessary.[23] To avoid overlapping investigations, FICORA and the Finnish Competition Authority ('FCA'), on 14 March 2003, signed a co-operation memorandum in which they clarify the division of tasks in cases where both authorities have competence. Pursuant to this memorandum, FICORA will mainly deal with cases concerning the level of regulated prices, and the FCA will concentrate on discriminatory practices, such as engaging in price squeezing. The memorandum, however, does not legally limit the competences of either authority and does not prevent both authorities to investigate the same case.

According to Article 119(3) CMA, the Government must ensure that activities relating to the regulation of telecommunications operators and to Government ownership or decision-making power are separated from each other in a structurally

---

19   Art 119(1) and 119(4) CMA.
20   FICORA's Strategy 2020.
21   Art 83(2) CMA.
22   Art 121b CMA.
23   Art 120 CMA

efficient manner. Currently, the State does not have majority ownership in any telecommunications operator; it does, however, have minority ownership in Elisa Oyj (10 per cent) and TeliaSonera AB (13 per cent).

The Ministry and FICORA have the right to collect information from telecommunications operators and from any other company in possession of information that is essential and significant for the supervision and regulation purposes. The information, including even business and professional secrets, must be supplied without delay, in the form requested by the public authority and without charge.[24]

FICORA has the right to perform technical inspections of telecommunications operators in order to supervise compliance with the obligations imposed in this Act and in provisions issued under it. FICORA may perform an economic inspection only if an operator has not provided the requested information or if the information is incomplete and there are special reasons to suspect that the operator is in breach of its obligations. The inspections are not permitted to cover private homes.[25]

National consultation procedures and public hearings are covered by general administrative law that requires all public authorities to conduct their duties in accordance with the principles of good administration.[26] The publication of documents and decisions is regulated by the Act on the Openness of Government Activities. According to the Act, all official documents are public, unless specifically otherwise provided by law.[27]

The international consultation procedures regarding market definitions and SMP decisions comply with the relevant EU directives.[28]

Right of Appeal against NRA's Decisions

13.7   Any Government or FICORA decision may be appealed. The Government's decisions are appealed directly to the Supreme Administrative Court.[29] FICORA's decisions are appealed either to the local administrative court or directly to the Supreme Administrative Court, depending on the subject matter of the decision. Decisions relating to market analyses and SMP obligations, designation of the universal service operator, and resolution of disputes under article 126 CMA are appealed directly to the Supreme Administrative Court.[30] Decisions whereby FICORA prohibits an operator from applying unfair contract terms or whereby the Consumer Ombudsman orders an operator to close a number or bar the use of a service are referred to the Market Court.[31] All other matters, including matters falling within the Act on Radio Frequencies and Telecommunications Equipment, the Act on Television and Radio Operations, and the Act on the Protection of Privacy in Electronic Communications are appealed to the local Administrative Court, serving as a first appeal instance. The Administrative Court's ruling may be further appealed to the Supreme Administrative Court.

---

24   Art 112(1) and 112(2) CMA.
25   Art 124 CMA.
26   Hallintolaki 6.6.2003/434.
27   Laki viranomaisten toiminnan julkisuudesta 21.5.1999/621.
28   Arts 21, 21a and 22 CMA.
29   Art 127(3) CMA.
30   Art 127(3) CMA.
31   Art 121a(4), Art 121b(4) and Art 127(4) CMA.

The right to appeal is governed by general administrative law. According to the Administrative Judicial Procedure Act,[32] any person to whom a decision is addressed or whose right, obligation or interest is directly affected by a decision may appeal the decision. In addition, an authority may appeal a decision pursuant to an express provision in an Act, or if it is essential to exercise the right of appeal to protect a public interest supervised by the authority. FICORA has an explicit right to appeal an Administrative Court decision in which the Administrative Court has repealed or amended a decision of the Ministry or FICORA's.[33]

The decisions of the Ministry and FICORA are directly enforceable and must be complied with despite any appeal unless the appellate authority orders otherwise.[34] The Supreme Administrative Court has ruled that the suspension of FICORA's decision may be granted only if there are strong arguments in favour of the suspension.[35]

According to article 127(5) CMA, appeals must be dealt with urgently. However, in practice, an average appeal process takes several years.

The NRA's Obligations to Cooperate with the Commission

13.8   The consolidation procedure (Article 7 of the Framework Directive) and the co-regulation procedure (Article 7a of the Framework Directive) have been fully implemented in national legislation, with the relevant procedural provisions in articles 21 and 21a CMA. FICORA has, to date, fully complied with these provisions.

There are no specific provisions in the national legislation regarding the Commission's power to stipulate standards and specifications (Article 17 of the Framework Directive) or to issue specifications (Article 19 of the Framework Directive).

'SIGNIFICANT MARKET POWER' AS A FUNDAMENTAL PREREQUISITE OF REGULATION

Definition of SMP

13.9   The national definition of SMP is in line with the EU rules. FICORA has not defined SMP operators based on collective dominance or dominance in closely related markets.

Definition of relevant markets

13.10   FICORA issues decisions at regular intervals defining the relevant communications markets. In doing so, FICORA must consider the European Commission recommendation on relevant markets and BEREC opinions on the matter.[36] FICORA has not deviated from the recommendations on relevant markets and has not defined any markets outside the recommendation.

---

32   Hallintolainkäyttölaki 26.7.1996/586.
33   Art 127(2) CMA.
34   Art 127(1) and 127(3) CMA.
35   Supreme Administrative Court ruling KHO 01.08.2005/1904.
36   Art 16 CMA.

In Finland, most markets are geographically segmented. There are currently 42 local SMP operators in the fixed network operating in their respective geographical operating areas, some of which are very small and cover only couple of thousands subscribers.

Imposition of remedies

13.11   When FICORA has identified a SMP operator, it must impose at least one obligation on that operator. FICORA must impose obligations if they are needed to eliminate barriers to competition or to promote competition. When imposing obligations, FICORA must work in appropriate cooperation with the Commission and BEREC. The obligations must be in correct proportion to the aim being addressed, and in imposing them, the FICORA must consider the following:[37]

- the appropriateness of access rights in technical and economic terms, taking into account the degree of development of the markets and the type of access rights;
- the feasibility of access rights, taking into account the capacity available;
- requirements concerning protection of privacy and information security;
- the investment made and risks taken by the operator with significant market power;
- the need to safeguard competition in the long term;
- relevant industrial property rights and copyrights; and
- the provision of services at the European level.

The available regulatory measures are listed in article 18 CMA. The list is exhaustive and FICORA does not have authority to impose obligations on an SMP beyond those listed: access to network elements and associated facilities, interconnection, roaming, pre-selection, pricing and non-discrimination, transparency of fees and terms, cost accounting, accounting separation, and structural separation.

FICORA may impose certain obligations on operators that do not have significant market power. For example, it may impose on a non-SMP a requirement to give access to local loop and equipment facilities, antenna sites and cable ducts, electronic programme guides ('EPG') or programming interface for television or radio systems. It may also require a non-SMP operator to interconnect its networks, publish delivery terms and tariff information, use non-discriminatory terms and prices, and apply cost-oriented pricing.[38]

To date, FICORA has not imposed obligations on non-SMP operators.

NRA'S REGULATORY DUTIES CONCERNING RIGHTS OF WAY, CO-LOCATION AND FACILITY SHARING

Rights of way

13.12   The CMA and the Land Use Building Act[39] govern the right to install a telecommunications cable and related minor equipment in an area owned or controlled by a third party. Wherever possible, a telecommunications cable must be

---

37   Art 18(1) CMA.
38   Art 19 CMA
39   Maankäyttö- ja rakennuslaki 5.2.1999/132.

installed in a highway area or other public area.[40] A telecommunications cable and related equipment, minor structures, and poles may be installed in an area owned or controlled by another if the parties reach agreement on the installation.[41] According to the Building Act, the owner or the holder of the property must allow the location of cables and related minor equipment on its property if the location of such equipment benefits a community or a real estate. The right of way applies only if the location cannot be organised satisfactorily and at reasonable cost by using some other means.[42]

Pursuant to the Expropriation Act[43], an owner or holder of a property is entitled to be paid compensation for harm and damage caused by the location of cables or other equipment. If the parties cannot reach an agreement on compensation, the matter is resolved pursuant to requirements set forth in the Expropriation Act.[44] The property owner is entitled full compensation based on fair market values.[45]

13.13   If the parties do not reach an agreement on the installation, the telecommunications operator must create a 'cable route plan' for installing the telecommunications cable for which it must obtain an opinion from the municipal authorities and the competent Centre for Economic Development, Transport and the Environment and, where necessary, from other competent authorities.[46] Prior to obtaining an opinion from such authorities, it must place the cable route plan on public view through a public notice in order to communicate the plan to all interested parties.[47] A property owner or other party whose benefit or right is affected by the cable route plan has the right to file an objection with the telecommunications operator within 30 days of the publication of the cable route plan.[48]

In case no agreement on the installation is reached, the municipal building supervision authority may grant the right to install the cable by validating the cable route plan. A decision regarding rights of way must be made within six months of the application.[49] The municipal building supervision authority may order the decision to be directly enforceable. The decision can be appealed to the Administrative Court.[50]

In addition, if more extensive rights to others' assets are needed in installing and maintaining telecommunications cables and related infrastructure, the telecommunications operator may have the right to redeem property and specific rights in accordance with the Expropriation Act.[51]

The installation and maintenance of a telecommunications cable must not cause hindrance or damage that could be avoided at reasonable expense. Existing zoning and other land-use planning and landscape and environmental aspects must be considered when installing a cable.[52]

---

40   Art 101(1) CMA.
41   Art 106(1) CMA.
42   Art 161(1) Building Act.
43   Laki kiinteän omaisuuden ja erityisten oikeuksien lunastuksesta 29.7.1977/603.
44   Art 161(3) Building Act.
45   Art 29(1) Expropriation Act.
46   Arts 103 and 104 CMA.
47   Art 103 CMA.
48   Art 105 CMA.
49   Art 106(1) CMA.
50   Art 106(3) and (4) CMA.
51   Art 109 CMA.
52   Art 101(2) and (3) CMA.

However, if it is necessary for the implementation of a cable route plan, a telecommunications operator may, without the permission of the owner or holder, fell trees and remove other plants from the cable route plan area, affix necessary equipment to buildings and structures, and undertake other construction work in the area. Nevertheless, the operator has a specific obligation to restore the condition of the area after the work is completed and to compensate for any hindrance and damage caused by these measures.[53]

Co-location and facility sharing

13.14   If a network operator has installed a telecommunications cable, related equipment, minor structures, or poles based on a confirmed cable route plan in an area owned or controlled by another, or has affixed necessary equipment to buildings and structures, FICORA may require the network operator to allow sharing and co-location of such property for other telecommunications operators. An obligation of co-location and facility sharing may be issued if the construction and location cannot otherwise be organised satisfactorily and at a reasonable cost. A further requirement for imposing the obligation is that it shall not prevent or unreasonably restrict the network operator's own use. In the event that the parties concerned do not agree on costs related to sharing or colocation, FICORA may issue orders on apportioning the costs.[54]

A wider obligation to allow co-location and facility sharing regarding radio mast antenna sites and cable ducts may be imposed on SMP operators. The obligation may be imposed also on non-SMP operators, if the construction of a parallel cable duct or radio mast is not appropriate for reasons of environmental protection, nature conservation, land use planning, or other comparable reason. On the same grounds, if an entity leases out an antenna site to a telecommunications operator, notwithstanding that the antenna site owner is not itself a telecommunications operator, it may be subject to facility sharing obligations.[55]

FICORA has issued co-location and facility sharing obligations in the SMP decision regarding market 18 (terrestrial television and radio networks).[56] To date, it has not imposed obligations on non-SMP operators or companies that are not telecommunications operators.

REGULATION OF MARKET ENTRY: THE AUTHORISATION DIRECTIVE

The General Authorisation of Electronic Communications

13.15   Entry to the Finnish telecommunications market has been liberalised and does not, for the most part, require any authorisation. Before beginning operations, a service provider must submit to FICORA a written notification of the intention to operate public telecommunications.[57] The notification is for information purposes only, and does not impose any rights or obligations on the operator. However,

---

53   Art 107 CMA.
54   Art 107a CMA.
55   Art 26 CMA.
56   FICORA's decision on 10 November 2008 (1668/934/2008)Päätös huomattavasta markkin-avoimasta TV- ja radiolähetyspalvelujen tukkumarkkinalla.
57   Art 13(1) CMA.

the operator may request that FICORA provide a confirmation notice, confirming receipt of its telecommunications notification (which FICORA must provide within a week), and this notice indicates the rights and obligations of telecommunications operators in Finland under the CMA.

The requirement to submit a notification does not apply to public telecommunications services that are temporary in nature, aimed at a small audience, or otherwise of minor significance.[58] A telecommunications service is considered of minor importance, and therefore excluded from the notification duty, if the annual turnover of the operator is less than €300,000.[59]

The notification must contain all information necessary for the purposes of supervision, including contact information of the operator, description of the group of companies to which the operator belongs, description of the services, the geographical operating area, and estimation of the starting date of operations.[60] The operator must notify FICORA of any change in the information entered in a telecommunications notification. If the operator discontinues operations, it must notify FICORA no later than one week before the discontinuation of operations. If the operator is a service operator, the network operator whose communications network the service operator uses must also notify FICORA. FICORA, upon receipt of reliable evidence of terminated operations, may state on its own initiative that the operations of a telecommunications operator have ceased.

13.16   A licence is required to provide a network service that uses radio frequencies in a digital terrestrial mass communications network or in a public mobile network.[61] A broadcasting licence is required for operations of television and radio services. The main licensing authority is the Government.

The Ministry may grant licences for wireless broadband services in the special case where the operator has previously been granted a radio licence to the frequency in question and the operator wishes to convert the fixed radio service into mobile service.[62]

FICORA grants short-term licences for digital terrestrial television networks as well as licences for short-term broadcasting and mobile broadcasting.

Most licences are granted by a comparative selection process ('beauty contest'). If a licence cannot be granted to all applicants due to the scarcity of radio frequencies, it must be granted to applicants whose operation best promotes the objectives of the CMA,[63] which are referenced in para 13.1 above.

Provisions regarding issuance of licences through auction processes, and modification and transfer of such licences, are set out in the Act on Auctioning Certain Radio Frequencies. Frequency auctions are discussed in more detail in para 13.26 below.

13.17   A licensing procedure commences when frequencies that are technically appropriate, and appropriate for efficient frequency use, become available for digital

---

58   Art 13 CMA.
59   Valtioneuvoston asetus merkitykseltään vähäisestä teletoiminnasta 3.7.2003/675.
60   Liikenne- ja viestintäministeriön asetus toimilupahakemusten ja teletoimintailmoitusten sisällöstä 3.7.2003/695.
61   Art 4(1) CMA.
62   Art 8(3) CMA. The procedure is intended for transition from fixed to mobile Wimax technology.
63   Art 9(3) CMA.

terrestrial television or public mobile networks. The Government will make a public announcement when a licence is available for application.[64] An application fee of €1,000 is charged for all applicants, except for a licence application concerning a public authority network.[65]

The government grants licences for a fixed period of up to 20 years. The government must decide whether to grant an application for a licence within six weeks of the close of the application period. In special cases, the government may extend the six-week deadline by eight months at most if necessary to ensure that the application procedure is fair, reasonable, clear, and transparent; to supplement the information in the applications, or for other special reasons. It must announce publically any extension to the deadline.[66]

The government must grant a licence if it finds the applicant to have sufficient economic resources to meet the network operator obligations and has no justifiable reason to suspect that the applicant will violate the provisions of the CMA, the Radio Act, the Act on the Protection of Privacy in Electronic Communications,[67] or any other legislation governing telecommunications. The government may grant a licence for providing network service in a public authority network only if the applicant, in addition to fulfilling all other licensing requirements, demonstrates that it has the ability and professional skills related to the special nature of the operation.

13.18   The geographical operating area of the licensed operator is included in the licence. Other licence terms may be defined by the licensing authority. Such terms may relate to the technical characteristics of communications networks or the efficient use of frequencies. Such terms must be consistent with the objectives of the CMA.[68]

In addition, a licence for digital terrestrial television network may contain terms relating to the particular broadcasting technology. A television network licence may also contain terms stating that the broadcasters must have access to transmission capacity and terms noting the particular capacity reserved for a programming licensee or requiring cooperation between programming licensees in matters relating to capacity distribution or electronic programme guides.[69]

Upon application by the licensee, the terms of an operating licence may be amended on the licensee's application. Before issuing a decision on such an application, the government must inform the licensee of how the re-examination would influence the operating license, and allow the licensee a reasonable time limit to withdraw the application.[70]

The licensing authority can, on its own initiative, alter the licence terms during the license's validity period with the consent of the licensee. The terms of a licence may be changed without a licensee's consent if the government deems such change necessary for technical development or an essential change in the operating conditions of the licensed activity.[71]

---

64   Art 5 CMA.
65   Art 7 CMA.
66   Art 8 CMA.
67   sähköisen viestinnän tietosuojalaki 16.6.2004/516.
68   Art 10(1) and 10(2) CMA.
69   Art 10(3) and (4) CMA.
70   Art 11(2) CMA.
71   Art 11(1) CMA.

13.19   The Government may cancel a telecommunications operator's licence, in part or in full, if the operator has repeatedly and seriously violated the provisions of the CMA, other relevant communications legislation, or the terms of the licence, or no longer has sufficient economic resources to meet its obligations in view of the nature and extent of the operation. The licence may also be cancelled if the operator fails to start the licensed operations within a reasonable time, unless the Government, following the licence holder's application, orders otherwise due to technological development or other conditions for the operations.[72]

Before cancelling a licence, the operator must be given a possibility, within a reasonable period of at least one month, to rectify its conduct, replenish its economic resources to a sufficient level, or prove it has started operations.[73]

A licence granted by beauty contest is non-transferable. The Government may cancel a licence if the effective control of the licensee changes. Any such change must be notified immediately to the licensing authority. The Government must decide on whether to cancel the licence within two months of the notification.[74]

A licensee may apply for a pre-ruling concerning the acceptability of a change of control. The licensing authority must issue a decision within two months of receipt of the application. If a change in the effective control concerns a company acquisition that must be reported to the Finnish Competition Authority or to the Commission as a merger notification, the licensing authority must issue a decision no later than two months after the definitive decision concerning the company acquisition was made.[75]

The internal transfer of a licence within a group between a parent company and a wholly owned subsidiary is not considered to be a licence transfer that would require cancellation. However, such a transfer must be notified immediately to the licensing authority.[76]

The transfer of an auctioned licence is addressed in para 13.26 below.

Rights of Use for Radio Frequencies

Strategic planning and co-ordination of spectrum policy

13.20   The Act on Radio Frequencies and Telecommunications Equipment ('Radio Frequency Act') states the goal of the national spectrum policy to promote efficient, appropriate, and sufficiently interference-free use of radio frequencies, to safeguard the fair availability of radio frequencies, and to promote the efficiency of the communications market and the provision of network and communications services in a technology and service neutral manner.[77]

FICORA oversees the use of radio frequencies in Finland and, in so doing, seeks to offer to all users radio frequencies that are as free from interference as possible. Radio spectrum management is intended to ensure that technically and economically feasible radio frequencies may be assigned to both present and future radio systems.

---

72   Art 12(1) CMA.
73   Art 12(2) CMA.
74   Art 12(3) CMA.
75   Art 12(4) CMA.
76   Art 12(5) CMA.
77   Art 1 Radio Frequency Act.

The Government sets general guidelines for frequency usage as well as the frequency allocation plan for the most important frequencies. It also allocates frequencies for mobile telecommunications networks, for television and radio broadcasting, for development, testing and educational purposes, and for any other use that has a significant impact on the general development of the communications market. The radio frequency utilisation plan, which includes detailed provisions on the use of these frequency bands, is confirmed by a decree of the Ministry.

13.21   FICORA, in the Radio Frequency Regulation,[78] sets the overall frequency allocation. In national frequency planning, FICORA considers international regulations and recommendations on radio frequency usage. The Radio Frequency Regulation contains information on the intended use of frequency bands and on the most important radio technical characteristics required of radio equipment using the frequency bands.

The Finnish national spectrum policy is consistent with the EU spectrum policy. Finland was among the first countries to permit flexible use of the GSM band to other mobile techniques and it has committed to assign digital dividend spectrum to mobile broadband.

In all spectrum matters, Finland must consider its international commitments with non-EU countries. These international commitments may sometimes delay or hinder Finland from implementing EU spectrum decisions. Coordination and negotiations with the neighbouring country Russia, with whom Finland shares a 1340 kilometre-long border, plays an important role in Finnish spectrum policy.

Principles of frequency allocation, procedural rules

13.22   The possession and use of a radio transmitter requires a technical radio licence from FICORA.[79]

No licence is required for the possession and use of radio receivers or transmitters permanently rendered technically inoperable.[80] No licence is required if the radio transmitter functions only on the collective frequencies designated for it by FICORA.[81] FICORA's Regulation on Collective Frequencies for Licence-exempt Radio Transmitters and on Their Use[82] lists specific radio transmitters that have been exempted from licensing.

Radio licences are granted on a first-come first-serve basis. In the case of competing licence applications, licences are granted using a comparative selection process ('beauty contest'). According to the Radio Frequency Act, if a licence cannot be granted to all applicants due to the insufficiency of radio frequencies, a licence must be granted to those applicants whose operations best promote the following goals:

- efficient, appropriate and sufficiently interference-free use of radio frequencies;
- safeguarding the fair availability of radio frequencies;
- maximising the unrestricted mobility of telecommunications equipment; and

---

78   Radiotaajuusmääräys 4 N/2011 M.
79   Art 7(1) Radio Frequency Act.
80   Art 7(3) Radio Frequency Act.
81   Art 7(2) Radio Frequency Act.
82   Määräys luvasta vapaiden radiolähettimien yhteistaajuuksista ja käytöstä 15AC/2011 R.

- promotion of the efficiency of the communications market within public telecommunications.[83]

The terms of a radio licence may be amended on the licensee's application. FICORA must, before issuing a decision, inform the licensee of how the re-examination would influence the license, and allow the licensee a reasonable time limit to withdraw the application.[84]

13.23   The licensing authority may amend the licence conditions on its own initiative during the validity period of the radio license. The licence conditions may be amended without the consent of the licence holder if it is necessary due to changes in the confirmed utilisation plan or other regulations or international treaty obligations. The licence conditions may also be amended if justified for the prevention or removal of interference in radio communications or on the basis of the radio frequency band's primary purpose of use. Licence conditions may be amended for reasons relating to competitive conditions of the market, eg if the amendment is necessary due to a change in the economic or technical operating prerequisites of a telecommunications operator, the arrival of a new operator, or the need to reorganise radio frequency usage arising from a change in market circumstances.[85]

Transferability and time limitations

13.24   Radio licences may be transferred within a group of companies. Transfer to a third party is permitted only if the licence conditions so specify. FICORA must be notified of the transfer without delay.[86]

If the licence holder merges with another limited liability company, the radio licence will be transferred to the receiving company. If the business activity performed by the licence holder, and to which the radio licence pertains, is given up completely, the radio licence will be transferred to the receiving legal person or natural person. If the holder of the radio licence is declared bankrupt, and the administration of the bankrupt licence holder's estate notifies FICORA without delay that the estate is to continue the business activity of the licence holder, the radio licence will be transferred to the bankrupt licence holder's estate.[87]

Radio licences are granted for up to maximum of 10 years at a time. In case of a transmitter to be used in licensed mobile networks or terrestrial mass communications networks, the licence may be granted for up to maximum of 20 years.[88]

Admissible conditions

13.25   Conditions may be attached to a radio licence if they are necessary to ensure the efficient and appropriate use of frequencies, ensure efficiency in the communications market, or ensure prevention or removal of interference in radio

---

83   Art 10(8) Radio Frequency Act.
84   Art 8(4) Radio Frequency Act.
85   Art 8(3) Radio Frequency Act.
86   Art 11(1) Radio Frequency Act.
87   Art 11(3) Radio Frequency Act.
88   Art 10(2) Radio Frequency Act.

communications. FICORA may order that the radio licence be kept in the immediate vicinity of the radio transmitter.[89] Licence conditions for radio transmitters presenting a considerable risk of interference may include a requirement that such transmitters may only be put into circulation upon FICORA's approval on the basis of an inspection.[90]

Radio licences commonly include terms relating to the radio technology in use, location of transmitters, transmitter power and other similar technical characteristics. There are no roll-out or coverage obligations for radio licences.

Limitation of number of rights of use to be granted

13.26 FICORA may limit the number of radio licences only if licences cannot be granted to all applicants due to the insufficiency of radio frequencies (see para 13.22 above).

An annual frequency fee is collected from radio licensees. The frequency fee is defined according to the usability of the frequencies in the radio license. To date, the level of such fees has been moderate.

The Act on Auctioning of Certain Radio Frequencies[91] sets the legal framework for spectrum auctions. The law is under reform due to the upcoming auction of the 800 MHz band in 2013.

In its current form, the Auction Act applies only to the 2.6 GHz band which was auctioned in 2009 (the first spectrum auction in Finland). The auctioned licences are valid for 20 years. Licences may be transferred or leased to third parties under certain conditions and only after Government consent. At the request of a licence holder, the Government may transfer the license, provided that it has no significant reasons to suspect that the transfer might prevent competition, endanger interference-free radio communications, or pose a risk to national security.[92] Upon a licence holder's application, the Government may approve the lease of the right to frequencies, provided that it has no significant reasons to suspect that the lease would pose a risk to national security.[93]

Rights of Use for Numbers

General authorisations and granting of individual rights

13.27 FICORA decides which numbers and identifiers are to be issued for the use of telecommunications operators and other persons.[94] A decision with respect to the assignment of numbers or identifiers must be made within three weeks of receipt of an application. However, if a number or identifier is of exceptional economic value, the numbering decision may be made within six weeks of receipt of the application.[95]

---

89   Art 8(1) Radio Frequency Act.
90   Art 8(2) Radio Frequency Act.
91   Laki eräiden radiotaajuuksien huutokaupoista 26.6.2009/462.
92   Art 16 Auction Act.
93   Art 18(2) Auction Act.
94   Art 48(1) CMA.
95   Art 48(3) CMA.

Admissible conditions

13.28   FICORA may order that the holder of a number or identifier must start using the number or identifier within a reasonable time,[96] or that the number or identifier be used to offer a specified service. FICORA may impose other conditions.[97]

Number portability is mandatory both for fixed and mobile numbers. Fixed numbers may be ported within the same numbering area.[98] Portability is not mandated between fixed and mobile numbers.[99]

No portability fees may be charged from the end customer. Operators may charge each other a one-off payment equivalent to the cost of transferring the telephone number if the technical process of transferring the number generates one-off costs. The one-off payment may not, however, be so high as to deter the use of the service. In individual cases, FICORA may decide on a maximum amount of the one-off payment .[100] The assigning and receiving operator are each responsible for meeting half of any per-call costs incurred from transfer of the number.[101]

Telecommunications operators are jointly responsible for maintaining a public, comprehensive, and free-of-charge service providing information on transferred telephone numbers.[102]

Among other SMP obligations, FICORA may impose carrier pre-selection requirements.[103] To date, however, FICORA has not imposed such obligations on any operator.

Limitation of number of rights of use to be granted

13.29   FICORA must distribute numbers and identifiers in a manner that treats telecommunications operators and other persons as fairly as possible, taking into account the nature and extent of operations.[104] In case of competing applications, and if the case cannot be solved by negotiations, FICORA may divide the numbers by lot.

The NRA's Enforcement Powers

13.30   FICORA promotes cooperation among telecommunications operators and seeks to resolve disputes between telecommunications operators primarily through mediation.[105] FICORA may order a telecommunications operator to correct its actions. For example, FICORA may impose a conditional fine or a temporary order on a company or an individual, if the company or individual fails to rectify the

---

96   Art 48(4) CMA.
97   Art 48(5) CMA.
98   Art 51(1) CMA.
99   Art 51(3) CMA.
100 Art 51(2) CMA.
101 Art 51(4) CMA
102 Art 51(5) CMA.
103 Art 24a CMA.
104 Art 48(2) CMA.
105 Art 126(3) CMA.

relevant actions within a reasonable period of at least one month.[106] Conditional fines are issued only in rare cases.

FICORA may also prohibit the use of unfair contract terms.[107] This relates mainly to consumer contracts.

In case of violation of SMP obligations, a telecommunications operator who fails to rectify its actions within a reasonable period of at least three months may be ordered to pay a penalty. The penalty may not be ordered if the action has no significant effect on the market, or if the ordering of the penalty is otherwise manifestly unjustified with regard to the safeguarding of competition.[108] The minimum amount of the penalty is €1,000 and the maximum is €1 million.[109] The penalty is determined by the Market Court on the proposal of FICORA.[110] To date, FICORA has not made any proposals regarding penalty payments.

Ultimately, if all other enforcement means fail and an operator seriously and significantly breaches or fails to comply with its obligations, FICORA may prohibit the operator from providing telecommunications services, in full or in part. FICORA must provide the operator a reasonable period of at least one month to rectify its actions before issuing the prohibition.[111]

Administrative Charges and Fees for Rights of Use

13.31 FICORA collects fees from telecommunications operators to cover the costs it incurs in regulating telecommunications markets. The fee is determined on the basis of the operator's annual total turnover from telecommunications activities in Finland, excluding turnover from television and radio broadcasting activities. Operators are assigned to payment categories in order to take into account the average costs incurred to FICORA for carrying out the duties related to operators in the respective category. There are 22 payment categories ranging from two payment units for operators with a turnover of less than €1 million up to 4007 units for an operator with a turnover of €1,843 million or more. One payment unit equals €350. The fee is not refundable even if the operator were to discontinue its operations.[112]

Annual spectrum fees are collected from radio licensees.[113] The licence fees for the auctioned licences are paid annually in equal installments during the licence period.[114]

Annual numbering fees are collected from holders of numbers and identifiers.[115]

Transitional Regulations for Existing Authorisations

13.32 There are no transitional regulations in place.

---

106 Art 121(1) CMA.
107 Art 1221a CMA.
108 Art 122(1) CMA.
109 Art 122(4) CMA.
110 Art 122(5) CMA.
111 Art 123 CMA.
112 Arts 15a, 15b, 15c and 15d CMA.
113 Liikenne- ja viestintäministeriön asetus taajuusmaksuista ja Viestintäviraston radiohallin- nollisista suoritteista perittävistä muista maksuista 21.12.2010/1222.
114 Art 14(2) Auction Act.
115 Art 49 CMA.

REGULATION OF NETWORK ACCESS AND INTERCONNECTION: THE ACCESS DIRECTIVE

Objectives and Scope of Access Regulation

13.33 The goal of access and interconnection regulation is to ensure interoperability of networks and services and competitive telecommunications markets.

Access and interconnection related provisions apply mainly to SMP operators. FICORA may issue certain access and interconnection obligations on non-SMP operators, but, to date, it has not imposed any such obligations.

All network operators must negotiate interconnection in good faith.[116] All network operators and service providers are subject to obligations regarding the interconnection charge structure.[117]

Basic Regulatory Concepts

13.34 'Access' is not a legal term of art in Finnish legislation. Rather, the CMA includes a comprehensive list of the various access obligations available to FICORA (see para 13.35).

Interconnection is defined as the physical and functional connecting of different communications networks and communications services to ensure that users can access communications networks and communications services of other telecommunications operators.[118]

Access- and Interconnection-related Obligations with Respect to SMP Undertakings

13.35 FICORA may impose specific access obligations to SMP operators. The available obligations are listed in Article 18(2) CMA. The list is comprehensive and the NRA may not impose any other access obligations.

The available access obligations include access to mobile networks, local loop and associated facilities, leased lines, antenna sites and cable ducts, cable television network capacity, terrestrial mass communications network, smart cards (eg mobile SIM cards), EPGs and application programming interfaces ('APIs'). Article 36a CMA gives the NRA power to impose also other reasonable access rights.

The access obligations do not apply if the object of the access rights is used by the operator itself or if it is necessary for the reasonable future needs of the obliged operator.[119]

To date, FICORA has imposed access obligations with respect to local loops and associated facilities (in markets 4 and 5), terminating segments of the leased lines (market 6) and terrestrial radio and television networks (market 18 of the old recommendation).

---

116   Art 39(1) CMA.
117   Arts 43 and 44 CMA.
118   Art 2(1.13) CMA.
119   Art 38 CMA.

FICORA may impose interconnection obligations on a SMP operator, meaning an obligation to connect a communications network or communications service to the communications network or communications service of another telecommunications operator. The SMP operator must thereafter negotiate on interconnection with the other telecommunications operator under terms and conditions consistent with interconnection obligations.[120]

To date, interconnection obligations have been issued on over 30 fixed network SMP operators, both on call origination and termination, and on five mobile network operators in the market of mobile call termination.

13.36 Both access and interconnection obligations may be accompanied by further obligations regarding transparency, non-discrimination, accounting separation, price controls and cost accounting.

Transparency obligations include an obligation to publish important information regarding leasing obligations, access rights or interconnection, such as information on service delivery terms, tariff information and agreements made, to the extent they do not include business secrets or confidential information. Transparency obligations may be imposed even without access or interconnection obligations.[121] In practice, transparency obligations have not been issued independent of other obligations.

To date, transparency obligations have been issued in relation to all SMP markets and operators.

Non-discriminations obligation may be imposed on pricing, on other terms, or on both.[122] Non-discrimination means a requirement that telecommunications operators in similar situations be treated equally. If a telecommunications operator uses a certain service itself or provides it to a subsidiary or other similar party, it must also offer an equivalent service on equivalent terms to any competing telecommunications operators.[123] FICORA has published guidelines regarding the assessment of the non-discrimination obligation.[124]

To date, non-discrimination obligations have been issued in relation to all SMP markets and operators.

13.37 FICORA may impose obligations to apply cost oriented pricing. FICORA may also set the maximum price for local loop unbundling and leased lines and for a maximum period of three years at a time. In addition, the maximum price may be set in exceptional cases only, if the price charged for the access rights clearly exceeds the general price level or is otherwise necessary in order to meet the purpose of access rights.[125] In 2012, FICORA, for the first time, proposed to set a maximum price on copper loops.

The cost orientation obligation means a price that is reasonable, taking into account the costs incurred and the efficiency of the operation. In assessing reasonableness, a reasonable return on capital must also be considered, which is affected by the

---

120 Art 39(2) CMA.
121 Art 33 CMA.
122 Art 37(1) CMA.
123 Art 84(2) CMA.
124 Viestintäviraston arviointiperiaatteet säänneltyjen tukkutuotteiden hinnoittelun ja ehtojen syrjimättömyydestä 14.12.2011, Dnro 712/9319/2011.
125 Art 37 CMA.

investment of the telecommunications operator and related risks.[126] FICORA assesses the cost orientation using an approach based on fully allocated current costs. FICORA announced that it will start using an approach based on fully allocated historical costs for certain regulated products, namely for copper loops and digital terrestrial television services, from 1 January 2013.[127]

To date, cost accounting obligations have been imposed on all SMP operators in market 4 regarding copper loops, on all SMP operators regarding call origination in the fixed network, on 33 incumbent operators in fixed network termination market, on the three major network operators in mobile termination market, and on sole SMP operator in the digital terrestrial television network market.

13.38   Accounting separation may be imposed if it is necessary in order to monitor pricing in regard to leasing out of access rights and interconnection. Accounting separation consists of an obligation to separate in the accounts the functions with respect to access rights and interconnection from other service provision activities of the operator.[128] The Supreme Administrative Court has ruled that the accounting separation calculations are business secrets and FICORA may not require operators to publish the accounts of such calculations.

Carrier pre-selection obligations apply only to the services provided in the fixed network and include both a selection code per call and pre-selection that, if necessary, may be overridden with a selection code.[129] To date, no carrier pre-selection obligations have been issued.

An obligation regarding functional separation[130] has been available since 2011 but it has not been used to date.

Regulatory Powers with Respect to SMP-undertakings

13.39   There are no further regulatory powers provided for in the national legislation with respect to SMP undertakings on wholesale or retail markets.

Regulatory Powers Applicable to All Market Participants

Obligations to ensure end-to-end connectivity

13.40   FICORA may impose interconnection obligations on a non-SMP operator, if the operator controls user connections to the communications network and if the imposition of the obligation is necessary to ensure that communications networks can interconnect.[131] To date, FICORA has not imposed such obligations.

Regulation of roaming services

13.41   EU roaming regulations are directly applicable in Finland.

---

126   Art 84(1) CMA.
127   Viestintäviraston arviointiperiaatteet käyttöoikeuden luovuttamisen hinnoittelusta 14.12.2011, Dnro 712/9319/2011.
128   Art 89 CMA.
129   Art 24a CMA.
130   Art 89a CMA.
131   Art 39(3) CMA.

Access to digital radio and television broadcasting services

13.42   FICORA may impose an obligation on SMP operators to grant access to an electronic programme guide to digital television or radio. It may also impose this obligation on a non-SMP operator, if it is necessary to ensure that information on digital television and radio broadcasts covered by the must carry obligation are made available to the public in an electronic programme guide.[132]

FICORA may impose an obligation on SMP operators to grant access to Aplication Programming Interface to digital television or radio. The obligation may be imposed also on a non-SMP operator, if it is necessary to ensure that information on digital television and radio broadcasts covered by the must carry obligation may be connected to the programming interface used.[133]

To date, no obligations regarding EPGs of APIs have been issued.

REGULATION OF THE UNIVERSAL SERVICE AND USERS' RIGHTS: THE UNIVERSAL SERVICE DIRECTIVE

Regulation of Universal Service Obligations

Scope of universal service obligations

13.43   Universal service includes a subscriber connection to the public communications network at the user's permanent place of residence or location at a reasonable price. The connection must allow all users, including those with disabilities, to use emergency services, make and receive national and international calls, and use other ordinary telephone services. The subscriber connection must also allow an appropriate Internet connection for all users, taking into account prevailing rates available to the majority of subscribers, technological feasibility and costs.[134]

According to a ministerial decree,[135] the minimum rate of downstream traffic of universal service Internet access is 1 Mbit/s. It is sufficient that the average minimum rate of downstream traffic of an Internet access is 750 Kbit/s in a measuring period of 24 hours and 500 Kbit/s in any 4-hour measuring period.

Designation of undertakings obliged to provide universal services

13.44   FICORA designates as universal service operators one or more telecommunications operators, operators providing a directory inquiry service, or operators providing a telephone directory service, if necessary to ensure universal service provision in a certain geographic area. The designation procedure must be efficient,

---

132   Art 31 CMA.
133   Art 32 CMA.
134   Art 60c CMA.
135   Liikenne- ja viestintäministeriön asetus tarkoituksenmukaisen internet-yhteyden vähimmäisnopeudesta yleispalvelussa 7.10.2009/732.

unbiased, open, and non-discriminatory. An operator with the best possible prerequisites to provide universal service will be designated as the universal service
operator.[136]

In practice, FICORA issues universal service obligations only in geographical areas
where there are fewer than three competing service providers. Mobile telephone
services are regarded as substitutes to fixed telephone services in regard to universal
service. To date, FICORA has designated four operators to provide universal
telephone services and 27 operators to provide Internet services in specific geographical areas.

Regulation of retail tariffs, users' expenditures and quality of service

13.45   Pricing of the universal service must be reasonable.[137] FICORA monitors
the pricing of universal service, compares it to the general price level of communications services and assesses the pricing of universal service in relation to the
general consumer price level and income level of the population.[138] When assessing
the reasonableness of the price, FICORA takes into account also the costs of the
service provision. The price can vary according to local circumstances and costs.

Telecommunications legislation does not provide for special price controls or other
arrangements for those with low incomes or special needs as these are covered by
the social security scheme.

The CMA provides for measures to control expenditure, including itemised billing
and call barring. These cover all consumer subscriptions, including but not limited
to universal service.

Cost calculation and financing of universal services

13.46   Universal service operators have a legal right to compensation for the net
cost of the relevant universal service. The part of the net costs constituting an
unreasonable financial encumbrance with regard to the size of the operator, type of
business activities, turnover of the operator's telecommunications, directory inquiry
service and telephone directory service, or other similar elements must be paid to
the universal service operator from State funds, if the operator so requests.[139]

In practice, to date, no operator has asked for, or received, any compensation for net
costs.

Regulation of Retail Markets

Prerequisites for the regulation of retail markets

13.47   Under Article 20 CMA, FICORA may impose SMP obligations in retail
markets only if it conducts a market analysis and finds that no competition exists
and that the obligations imposed on a SMP operator in the wholesale market do

136   Art 59 CMA.
137   Art 60c(1) CMA.
138   Art 60 CMA.
139   Art 60b(1) CMA.

not sufficiently promote competition in the retail market, and that the imposition of additional obligations is necessary to secure efficient competition.

Regulatory powers

13.48   FICORA may order that a SMP operator in retail markets may not charge unreasonable prices, prevent access to the market or restrict competition by unjustifiably low pricing, favour certain service recipients in an unwarranted manner, or tie a specific product or service to other products or services.[140]

Any obligation imposed in the retail market must be in correct proportion to the aim being addressed.[141] If there are significant changes in the competitive situation, the SMP decision and obligations must be amended accordingly.[142]

To date, all retail markets are regarded competitive and therefore no SMP obligations have been issued.

End User Rights

Contracts

13.49   A telecommunications operator has an obligation to adopt standard agreement terms for consumer agreements on telephone network subscriber connections and to use them when entering agreements with consumers. Such agreements must not include any terms or limitations unfair to the consumer.[143]

Agreements on any communications services must be made in writing. They may also be made electronically, provided that the content of the electronic agreement may not be amended without the consent of the other party and that the agreement remains available to both parties.[144]

13.50   Minimum contract terms are regulated in Article 67 CMA. The agreement must specify:

* the name and contact information of the telecommunications operator;
* the validity of the agreement and a possible renewal procedure;
* the nature and features of the services and the types of maintenance service provided;
* the data transfer rate variation for broadband services;
* the delivery time of a communications service;
* the procedure for giving notice to terminate the agreement and the reasons for termination;
* the sanctions for any error or delay;
* the means the user is to be informed of amendments to the agreement terms;
* the user's rights if the agreement terms are amended;
* the pricing basis or applied tariffs;
* the user's right to obtain information on the calculation of his or her bill;
* the user's right to complain about a telecommunications bill;

---

140   Art 20(2) CMA.
141   Art 20(3) CMA.
142   Art 20(4) CMA.
143   Art 66(1) CMA.
144   Art 67(1) CMA.

- the sanctions for neglect of payment;
- the right of the telecommunications operator to terminate the provision of a service or to restrict the use of a service;
- the spending limit and consumer instructions on how to monitor the amount due on the bill;
- whether the subscriber connection allows access to emergency services and whether caller location information is provided in an emergency situation;
- information on any procedures put in place by the telecommunications operator to measure and shape telecommunications traffic so as to avoid overfilling a network link and information on how these procedures could impact service quality;
- types of customer services provided;
- any restrictions imposed on the use of the terminal equipment supplied;
- the user's options to choose whether or not to include his or her contact information in a telephone directory and the data he or she wishes to include;
- payment methods offered and any differences in price due to payment method; and
- the type of action that might be taken by the telecommunications operator in reaction to security threats.

In addition, the agreement must state the right of the consumer to refer a dispute on the agreement for the decision of the Consumer Complaint Board.

Transparency obligations

13.51   A telecommunications operator must publish standard agreement terms and tariff information on communications services and ensure that they are easily available to users without charge.[145] The transparency requirement applies to both consumer and business agreements.

Quality of service: securing 'net neutrality'

13.52   There are no specific regulations regarding net neutrality. Instead, net neutrality is preserved through end user rights and quality of service.

According to Article 67 CMA, an operator may not restrict a user's right to choose a service provider.

FICORA may impose an obligation on any telecommunications operator to publish comparable and up-to-date data on the quality of the services it offers.[146] To date, FICORA has imposed an obligation on 39 service providers to publish data on the response times of customer services. The information must be published in the operator's Internet site.

---

145   Art 66(2) CMA.
146   Art 82 CMA.

European emergency call number

13.53 A telecommunications operator must, ensure that users are able to access the universal emergency call number 112 by phone and SMS message free of charge.[147]

Other obligations

13.54 End users are entitled to a standard compensation in case of a delay or defect in the delivery of the communications service. The minimum amount of the compensation is €20 for each full or part week of delay but not more than €160.[148] End users are also entitled to damages exceeding the standard compensation.[149]

The tie-in sales of terminal equipment and mobile subscriptions are regulated by Article 70 CMA. Tie-in sales are not permitted in agreements concerning GSM subscriptions but are permitted for other mobile and fixed subscriptions. The service must always be available also without the tie-in. One of the objectives of the regulation is encourage the sale of 3G subscriptions and terminals.

The duration of consumer agreements are regulated by Article 70a CMA. Time-limited contracts with consumers may not exceed two years. A 12-month agreement must be available for the consumer if the operator offers agreements exceeding 12 months. An automatic chaining of time-limited consumer contracts is forbidden. The time-limited agreement cannot be extended by another time-limited agreement without concluding a new agreement in writing with the consumer.

Mobile subscriptions may not be marketed to consumers by phone. The restriction is temporary and valid until May 2015.[150]

Obligations facilitating change of provider

13.55 An end user has the right to select a content service provider. The terms of an agreement on a telephone network subscriber connection, and any other agreement on receiving a communications service, may not restrict such right.[151]

In order to ensure users' freedom of choice, FICORA may impose an obligation on a housing company, a real estate company, or a similar entity that owns or manages a fixed communications network connected to a public communications network on the property, that entity must relinquish (on non-discriminatory terms), to a telecommunications operator chosen by a user, access rights to the available capacity on the communications network to transmit communications services to the user's terminal equipment on the property.[152]

Number portability is mandated in Article 51 CMA. Numbers may be ported within fixed or mobile networks but not between the two. Number portability must be offered free of charge to the end user. The operator can collect a one-off payment equivalent to the costs of transferring the telephone number from the

---

147 Art 55(1) CMA.
148 Art 67b and 67f CMA.
149 Art 67c and 67g CMA.
150 Art 65a CMA.
151 Art 68 CMA.
152 Art 69a(1) CMA.

other operator involved, if the technical process of transferring the number generates one-off costs. The one-off payment cannot, however, be so high as to deter the use of the service. In individual cases FICORA may decide on a maximum amount of the one-off payment.

According to FICORA's regulation on number portability,[153] the porting time, in addition to the standard delivery time of a communications service, must not exceed five working days, unless the subscriber has agreed on a later delivery time with the recipient operator. The loss of service between the technical closure of the old service and the technical opening of the new service must not exceed 10 minutes for a mobile network, and 60 minutes for a fixed telephone network.

DATA PROTECTION: THE DIRECTIVE ON PRIVACY AND ELECTRONIC COMMUNICATIONS

Confidentiality of Communications

13.56   The right to confidential communications is based on the Constitution of Finland. The Act on the Protection of Privacy in Electronic Communications ('PPEC')[154] contains a general provision on confidentiality of messages, identification data and location data.[155]

Service providers and network providers are defined in the PPEC as 'telecommunications operators'. Pursuant to the PPEC, current and former employees of telecommunications operators must not disclose knowledge obtained through their employment about messages, identification data, or location data without the consent of a party to the communication or the party to whom the location data applies, unless otherwise provided by law. This obligation of secrecy also covers all persons who are, or have been, acting on behalf of a telecommunications operator.[156]

Furthermore, telecommunications operators must maintain the information security of their services. Maintaining such information security means taking measures to ensure operating security, communications security, hardware and software security, and data security. These measures must be commensurate with the seriousness of threats, level of technical development, and costs.[157]

13.57   The PPEC contains a provision on the guidance and supervision authorities' right of access to information[158] as well as a provision on disclosing information to emergency services authorities.[159] Pursuant to these provisions, a telecommunications operator must disclose certain information to FICORA, the Data Protection Ombudsman, an Emergency Response Centre, a Marine Rescue Coordination Centre, a Marine Rescue Sub-Centre, or the Police.

The right of authorities to receive identification data for the purposes of preventing, uncovering or investigating crimes is laid down in the Police Act (578/2005), the

---

153   Viestintäviraston määräys puhelinnumeron siirrettävyydestä 46 H/2011 M.
154   Laki sähköisen viestinnän tietosuojasta (516/2004).
155   Art 4 PPEC.
156   Art 5 (3–4) PPEC.
157   Art 19 (1) PPEC.
158   Art 33 PPEC.
159   Art 35 (1) PPEC.

Act on the Processing of Personal Data by the Border Guard (579/2005), the Customs Act (1466/1994), and the Coercive Measures Act (450/1987).[160]

Provisions on telecommunications interception for the purpose of investigating an offence are laid down in the Coercive Measures Act. Provisions on telecommunications interception for the purpose of preventing or detecting an offence are laid down in the Police Act.

A service provider may save cookies or other data concerning the use of the service in the user's terminal device, and use such data, if the user has given his or her consent thereto and the service provider gives the user comprehensible and complete information on the purposes of saving or using such data. The saving and use of data is permitted only to the extent required for the service, and it may not limit the protection or privacy any more than is necessary.[161]

13.58   A telecommunications operator must, without undue delay, notify FICORA of significant violations of information security in network services and communications services and of any information security threats to such services that come to the attention of the telecommunications operator. The operator must also notify FICORA of any consequences of information security violations and of measures undertaken to prevent the reoccurrence of such violations and threats of such violations. If, according to FICORA, the notification of information security violations referred to above is in the public interest, it may order the telecommunications operator to provide information regarding the matter.[162]

If a specific violation or threat is posed to the information security of a service, the telecommunications operator must immediately notify the subscriber and the user and inform them of the measures available to them for combating the threat, of the probable costs of such measures, and inform the sources of further information available to them.[163]

If anyone violates the PPEC or provisions issued under it, and, despite being requested to do so, fails to rectify his or her actions within a specified reasonable period, FICORA, or the Data Protection Ombudsman, may order him or her to rectify his or her error or neglect. FICORA, or the Data Protection Ombudsman, may impose a conditional fine or a threat of having the act done at the defaulter's expense. If the violation is severe, the threat may also involve terminating the violator's business in part or in full. FICORA and the Data Protection Ombudsman may also submit any matter processed by them to pre-trial investigation.[164]

13.59   The penalties for communications secrecy violation and aggravated communications secrecy violation are provided in Chapter 38(3 and 4) of the Penal Code, and the penalty for unauthorised access to data in Chapter 38(8) of the Penal Code. The penalty for a breach of the obligation of secrecy is subject to Chapter 38(1 or 2) of the Penal Code, unless the offence is punishable under Chapter 40(5) of the Penal Code or unless a more severe penalty is provided elsewhere. A breach of the confidentiality requirements is punished pursuant to Chapter 38(2)(2)

---

160   Art 36 (1–2) PPEC
161   Art 7 PPEC.
162   Art 21 PPEC, also Art 128a CMA.
163   Art 21a PPEC.
164   Art 41 PPEC.

of the Penal Code unless a more severe penalty than in s 38(1) of the Penal Code is laid down elsewhere in law.[165]

Furthermore, pursuant to the PPEC, anyone who deliberately violates certain prohibitions or neglects certain duties provided in the PPEC, must be fined for a violation of protection of privacy in electronic communications as set out in more detail in the PPEC, unless a more severe penalty is provided elsewhere.[166]

Data Retention

13.60   The Data Retention Directive was implemented into Finnish legislation through amendments to PPEC. The amendments took effect on 1 June 2008. The retention obligation is specified in the Regulation on the Obligation to Retain Identification Data.[167]

Traffic Data and Location Data

13.61   The concept of 'traffic data' in the Data Retention Directive does not as such appear in Finnish law. Under Finnish law, 'identification data' is defined as data which may be associated with a subscriber or user and which is processed in communications networks for the purposes of transmitting, distributing or providing messages. 'Location data' means data which shows the geographic location of a subscriber connection or terminal device and which is used for a purpose other than the provision of a network service or communications service.[168]

Identification data (as defined above) may be processed with the consent of the sender or intended recipient of such a message or if so provided by law.

Pursuant to the PPEC,[169] and subject to the limitations set out therein, telecommunications operators may process identification data as described below.

- Identification data may be processed for providing and using a network service, communications service or value added service and for the purpose of ensuring information security.
- Telecommunications operators and value added service providers may process identification data necessary for defining fees between themselves and for billing purposes. Telecommunications operators must inform subscribers or users about what identification data is being processed and how long the processing will last.
- Identification data may be processed for the purpose of marketing communications services or value added services, to such an extent and for such a period of time as the marketing requires if the subscriber or user to whom the data applies has given his or her consent thereto. Telecommunications operators must, prior to obtaining consent, inform subscribers or users about what identification data is to be processed and how long the processing would last. The party giving such consent must have the opportunity to cancel his or her consent regarding the processing of identification data.

---

165   Art 42 (1) PPEC.
166   Art 42 (2–3) PPEC.
167   FICORA 53/2008 M.
168   Art 2 (8–9) PPEC.
169   Chapter 3 PPEC.

- Identification data may be processed for the purpose of technical development. Subscribers or users shall be informed of what identification data is to
be processed and how long the processing will last.
- Identification data may be processed for the purposes of statistical analysis.
- Identification data may be processed for detecting, preventing or investigating
any nonpaying use of fee-based network services, communications services or
value added services, or any similar cases of misuse.

13.62   Processing of identification data is only permitted to the extent necessary
for the purpose of such processing, and it may not limit the confidentiality of
messages or the protection of privacy any more than is necessary. Identification
data may only be disclosed to those parties entitled to process it in the given
situation. After processing, identification data must be destroyed or rendered such
that they cannot be associated with the subscriber or user involved, unless otherwise
provided by law.[170]

Telecommunications operators may process location data (as defined above) subject
to the provisions of Chapter 5 of the PPEC for the purpose of providing and using
value added services if the subscriber has not forbidden it. The telecommunications
operator shall ensure that the subscriber can easily and at no separate charge
prohibit processing of location data.

Processing of location data is permitted only to the extent required for the purpose
of the processing, and it shall not limit the protection of privacy any more than is
necessary. After processing, the location data must, unless otherwise provided by
law, be destroyed or rendered such that it cannot be associated with a specific
subscriber or user.

The telecommunications operator must ensure that the subscriber has easy and
continuous access to information on the precision of the location data processed,
the purpose of the processing and whether location data may be disclosed to a third
party for the purpose of providing value added services.

Itemised Billing

13.63   A telecommunications operator must, without charge, provide itemised
bills on the use of the telephone network subscriber connection and, provided that
the bill is more than €50, without being separately requested to do so. Calls to
Freephone numbers must not be indicated in an itemised bill.[171]

Regardless of the amount of the bill, a telecommunications operator must itemise
the fees for services other than communications services without being requested to
do so and without charge. The user has the right to obtain a non-itemised bill on
request.[172]

---

170   Art 8 PPEC.
171   Art 80(1) and (3) CMA.
172   Art 80(2) and (4) CMA.

Presentation and Restriction of Calling and Connected Line Identification

13.64   A telecommunications operator must provide a service enabling a call recipient to see the calling number before answering a call.[173]

Automatic Call Forwarding

13.65   Automatic call forwarding is not regulated.

Directories of Subscribers

13.66   A telecommunications operator must ensure that users have access to a generally available, comprehensive, and reasonably priced directory inquiry service.[174] End users with fixed or mobile subscriptions have the right to have their name, address and telephone number published in a generally available, comprehensive, and reasonably priced telephone directory that is updated at least once per year. The telephone directory may be in printed or electronic form.[175] All directory information must be handled in a non-discriminatory manner by the operator providing the directory service.[176]

According to Article 25(4) of the PPEC, an end user has the right to to prohibit, at no charge, the inclusion of any part or all of his or her contact information in a telephone directory, other subscriber directory or directory inquiry service.

A telecommunications operator, and any company with which it has an agreement on maintaining the contact information, must release, on request, the directory contact information in a useable form to another company for the purposes of preparing a telephone directory or providing a directory inquiry service. The contact information must be released at a cost-oriented price and on non-discriminatory terms.[177] According to FICORA's ruling,[178] an operator must release all the information the user has given to the operator to be published in a directory on a price that covers the cost of handing over the information to a third party.

---

173   Art 64 CMA.
174   Art 56(1) CMA.
175   Art 57(1) CMA.
176   Art 56(2) and 57(2) CMA.
177   Art 58 CMA.
178   FICORA's decision on 22 June 2011, Dnro 248/539/00.

The French Market for Electronic Communications[1]

Christian Blomet & Magalie Dansac
Baker & McKenzie SCP, Paris

LEGAL STRUCTURE

Basic Policy

14.1 The French telecommunications sector has experienced important changes since 1 January 1998, when telecommunications services were opened to competition. The implementation of the 2002 EU Regulatory Package and the taking into account of the purposes and procedures defined at Community level led to a revision due to changes in the markets' needs and obligations, and the desire to relax certain rules in the interests of promoting effective competition. The main purposes of the French legislator were as follows:

- to promote effective and fair competition for the benefit of users – competition is not the only purpose, it should provide consumers with a better quality service, at better prices and with many service offerings meeting their requirements and needs;
- to control the supply and financing of all components of the public telecommunications service;
- to control the development of employment, innovation and competitiveness in the electronic communications sector – competition is useful only if it is a factor in the development of the market and the economy; and
- to take into account the interest of territories and users concerning access to services and equipment – city planning remains a central concern.

The legislative reform that occurred in France in Summer 2004 to implement part of the provisions of the 2002 EU Regulatory Framework was marked by four major considerations:

- freedom to exercise electronic communication activities and reinforcement of competitiveness in a simplified regulatory context;
- reinforcement of the role of the legislator;
- city planning and the widening of powers of local authorities; and
- modernisation and simplification of the rules governing the freedom of communication.

---

1 Editing of this chapter closed 21 December 2012.

While France Telecom, the incumbent operator, is still very powerful on most markets, competition is gradually making its way into the sector.

14.2   The rules which govern the electronic communications sector in the EU were revised in November 2009 by two amending Directives:[2] Directive 2009/140/EC (Framework, Authorization and Access directives) and Directive 2009/136/EC (Universal Services and E-privacy directives). The 2009 EU Regulatory Package aimed at liberalising the European market by harmonising the EU Member States' legislations. It covers all forms of fixed and wireless telecoms, data transmission and broadcasting services. The regulation of the content carried by such services is, however, dealt with under separate rules.

Beyond these purposes, the implementation of the provisions of the 2009 EU Regulatory Package was also governed by the several challenges which arose in France after the legislation reform of 2004:

- strengthening consumer rights;
- giving consumers more choice by reinforcing competition between telecoms operators;
- promoting investment into new communication infrastructures, in particular by freeing radio spectrum for wireless broadband services;
- making communication networks more reliable and more secure, especially in case of viruses and other cyber-attacks.

Implementation of EU Directives, Legislation

Implementation of the 2002 EU Regulatory Package

14.3   The Directives of the 2002 EU Regulatory Package were properly implemented by the French legislator even if not fully on time with the expected schedule. Three acts were adopted by the French Parliament to implement the 2002 EU Regulatory Package and reform the entire electronic communications sector and complete the existing Act No 96–659. All these texts have been codified in the Code for Post and Electronic Communications ('CPCE'):

- Act No 2003–1365[3] relating to the obligations of telecommunications public service and France Telecom. It includes the regulatory modifications resulting from the implementation of the Universal Service Directive,
- Act No 2004–575[4] on confidence in the digital economy, specifying the terms and conditions to exercise specific telecommunications activities such as satellite services; and
- Act No 2004–669[5] relating to electronic communications and audiovisual communications services. This act, implementing the most important part of the EU Directives, was passed according to an emergency procedure in order to avoid the parliamentary discussions slowing down the process.

These acts have been complemented by many decrees, notably:

---

2   For further details see fifth edition of this book, para 1.6.
3   Act No 2003–1365, dated 31 December 2003.
4   Act No 2004–575, dated 21 June 2004.
5   Act No 2004–669, dated 9 July 2004.

- Decree No 2004–1222[6] regarding Public Service obligations and electronic communications universal service financing;
- Decree No 2004–1301[7] regarding the regulation of operators having significant market power on the electronic communications market;
- Decree No 2005–75[8] regarding universal service price monitoring in the sector of electronic communications;
- Decree No 2005–400[9] specifying:
  - the deadlines (i) to grant authorisations to use frequencies, and (ii) to notify their renewal conditions; and
  - the obligations incumbent to authorisation holders to enable the monitoring of their conditions of use.
- Decree No 2005–399[10] amending the third part of the CPCE. It specifies notably the conditions of the communication of information between the French Regulatory Authority, the other National Regulatory Authorities and the European Commission;
- Decree No 2005–605[11] amending the second part of the CPCE. It notably inserts provisions regarding numbering resources. In a Decision dated 25 April 2007,[12] the French Administrative Supreme Court (Conseil d'Etat) voided some of its dispositions;
- Decree No 2005–862[13] regarding the conditions of networks implementation and operation and the provision of electronic communication services. It specifies operators obligations regarding services quality and public security;
- Decree No 2007–1532[14] regarding fees for the right of use of radio frequencies; and
- Decree No 2011–219[15] dated 25 February 2011, regarding the storage and the communication of the personal data identifying individuals contributing to an online content creation.

Implementation of the 2009 EU Regulatory Package

14.4   France has partially implemented the two Directives of the 2009 EU Regulatory Package. The European Regulation No 1211/2009 dated 25 November 2009 which is part of the 2009 EU Regulatory Package and which established the Body of European Regulators for Electronic Communications ('BEREC') and the Office, is directly applicable and enforceable in France. It entered into force as of 7 January 2010 and no implementation measures were necessary. Concerning the Better Regulation Directive and the Citizen's Rights Directive, the French Parliament adopted on 22 March 2011, Act No 2011–302[16] enabling the Government to implement the 2009 EU Regulatory Package by Governmental Orders. By enacting this Act, the goal of the French Parliament was to transpose the Directives as soon as possible, to avoid France being sanctioned by the European Commission for not

---

6   Decree No 2004–1222 dated 17 November 2004.
7   Decree No 2004–1301 dated 26 November 2004.
8   Decree No 2005–75 dated 31 January 2005.
9   Decree No 2005–400 dated 25 April 2005.
10   Decree No 2005–399 dated 27 April 2005.
11   Decree No 2005–605 dated 27 May 2005.
12   Administrative Supreme Court, Decision No 287486 dated 25 April 2007.
13   Decree No 2005–862 dated 26 July 2005.
14   Decree No 2007–1532 dated 27 October 2007.
15   Decree No 2011–219 dated 25 February 2011.
16   Act No 2011–302 dated 22 March 2011.

complying with the implementation deadline (25 May 2011).[17] Pursuant to the Act No 2011–302, the transposition ordinance may contain:

- the necessary legislative provisions to implement Directive 2009/140/EC 'Better Regulation' and the Directive 2009/136/EC;
- legislative provisions aiming to improve efficiency in the management of radio electric frequencies, (in particular by encouraging the development of a secondary market for frequencies and by strengthening control systems for preventing interference);
- legislative provisions to:
  - enhance the protection of privacy and electronic communication confidentiality by amending the offences regulated by article 226–3 of the French Criminal Code;
  - prevent and remedy infringements and serious threats to the security of communication systems;
- any other provisions required to amend errors and clarify provisions of the CPCE.

On 24 August 2011, the French Government adopted Governmental Order No 2011–1012[18] on the ground of Act No 2011–302. The Order is divided into the four domains described by Act No 2011–302. The French Government adopted three decrees implementing the Governmental Order No 2011–1012:

- Decree No 2012–436[19] regarding notably operator's obligations, personal data protection and the security of interception means;
- Decree No 2012–488[20] amending operator's obligations; and
- Decree No 2012–513[21] regarding the communication to the State and local authorities of information regarding infrastructures and networks established on their territory.

Implementing decrees are to be adopted in order to complete the legislative texts. While the acts and decrees establish the new framework and are binding upon the French Regulatory Authority (*Autorité de Régulation des Communications Electroniques et des Postes* ('ARCEP')), the latter's decisions also play a significant role in shaping the telecommunications policy of the country. As a matter of fact, ARCEP's role is to apply the dispositions of the legislative texts.

REGULATORY PRINCIPLES: IMPLEMENTATION OF THE FRAMEWORK DIRECTIVE

Scope of Regulation

14.5   The implementation of the 2002 and 2009 EU Regulatory Package resulted in a revision of the CPCE and other legal instruments.

---

17   France has already been sanctioned in the past because of a late transposition. European procedure for imposing penalties begins automatically immediately after the relevant deadline has passed. France was ordered in 2008 to pay a €10 million fine for its delay in implementing Directive 2001/18/EC regarding the release into the environment of genetically modified organisms. The fact that France had implemented the Directive by the time the ruling was made did not prevent France from being sanctioned.
18   Governmental Order No 2011–1012 dated 24 August 2011.
19   Decree No 2012–436 dated 31 March 2012.
20   Decree No 2012–488 dated 13 April 2012.
21   Decree No 2012–513 dated 18 April 2012.

The 2009 EU Regulatory Package aimed at raising standards of competition and defining the role and powers of the national regulatory authorities (the 'NRAs'). It has set out a number of principles and objectives for NRAs to follow for the regulation of the market. It did not, however, address issues of content delivered through electronic communications networks using electronic communications services, such as broadcasting content (including television and radio programmes, which are specifically regulated by the Audiovisual Media Services Directive of 10 March 2012), financial services and certain services specific to the information society which are subject to other regulations.[22]

14.6   In 2004, the French legislator did not strictly implement the definitions contained in the Directives but it kept their spirit.

Thus, 'electronic communications network' is defined as 'any installation or group of installations of transport or broadcasting as well as, if necessary, the other means ensuring the routing of electronic communications, in particular switching and routing means'.[23] The following networks are considered as electronic communications networks: satellite networks, mobile and terrestrial networks, systems using the electric network if they are used to route electronic communications, and networks ensuring the broadcasting or used for the distribution of audiovisual communication services. There is no reference to the difference between fixed networks and mobile networks since both networks are subject to the same development and operating conditions, subject to the frequency granting conditions. The legislator also deleted the reference to cable networks whose system is now in line with the system of the other electronic communications networks.

'Electronic communications services' are defined by the CPCE as:

> 'services consisting, totally or mainly, in the provision of electronic communications. The services aiming at editing or distributing communications services to the public electronically are excluded'.[24]

Contrary to the definition in Article 2(c) of the Framework Directive, there is no reference to the fact that a fee will be charged for the service.

French law defines the 'electronic communications' provided as part of the Electronic communications services as 'emission, transmission or reception of signs, signals, writings, images or sounds electronically'.

In addition to these elements, the criteria set up by the French Regulatory Authority (ARCEP) suggested in a survey report of June 2011, using a two stage qualification test, must be taken into account to help identifying an electronic communications service for regulatory purposes: the first stage consists of the identification of an electronic communication service; the second one consists in the qualification of the entity which provides the service mentioned (an operator or electronic communication service provider).

According to the above-mentioned test, there is an electronic communication service if the four following conditions are met:

- the service includes, entirely or mainly, the transmission or routing of signals;
- the service provider is responsible for such transmission;

---

22   For further details see fifth edition of this book, para 1.7.
23   Art L32(2) CPCE.
24   Art L32(6).

- the service is provided 'to the public'; and
- the service is provided in return for some kind of payment.

14.7   The qualification of operator will in turn depend on the following:

- if the entity provides an electronic communication service to the public;
- if the entity provides transmission or routing facilities; and
- if the facilities are mainly used for the provision of these communications and are located in France.

Conversely, an electronic communications service provider is the person/entity whose main activity is to provide electronic communications, but who does not establish or operate an electronic communication network. The regulatory regime applicable to these entities will depend on the qualification applicable to them with respect to their participation in the provision of the electronic communication services.

Numerous definitions contained in the Framework Directive have not been included under French law: notions of associated facilities, conditional access systems or application programme interfaces are not defined under French law.

However, the 2009 Regulatory Package brought changes to the national legal framework governing electronic communications by emphasising certain concepts and objectives such as net neutrality and internet freedom.

'Internet Freedom'

14.8   The 2009 Regulatory Framework introduced, in Article 1(3a) of the Framework Directive, a provision which provides for limitations to 'measures taken by Member States regarding end users' access to, or use of, services and applications through electronic communications networks' (the 'Internet Freedom' provision). In 2009, the French government initiated a national legislative initiative to combat online infringements of copyright, allowing the French administration, inter alia, to restrict accused French citizens from accessing the internet.

The HADOPI law, enacted in May 2009, allows users that have been caught illegally downloading copyrighted content, or who have failed to secure their system again such illegal downloads to be disconnected from the Internet; in August 2009, this law was supplemented by the HADOPI 2 law to improve the rights of defendants as corresponding provisions of the HADOPI 1 law were cancelled by the *Conseil d'Etat*, the French administrative supreme court.

The LOPPSI 2 law, adopted on 14 March 2011, allows for the blocking of Internet access to a site deemed as having 'obvious' child pornographic content, without a court order. This law adds to a growing number of security measures adopted in France since the terrorist attacks of September 2001 that have continually extended the powers of police forces, the amount of surveillance and the strengthening of criminal sanctions.

Net neutrality

14.9   Net neutrality emerged progressively during the 1990s following convergence and digitalisation, requesting a new regulatory approach. The French regulator espoused this concept extensively, considering that introducing net neutrality into electronic communication regulation could help laws to be forward-looking. The desirability of technology neutral legislation has become generally accepted. The implementation of the concept, however, is complex.

In France, Article 18 of Act No 2011–302[25] – enabling the Government to implement the 2009 EU Regulatory Package by Governmental Orders – completed the list of principles governing regulation of the electronic communications sector, by adding to the objectives already listed in CPCE Article L.32–1:

> 'That no discrimination exists, under analogous circumstances, in the relationship between the operators and providers of public online electronic communication services in traffic routing and access to these services'.

ARCEP is thereby mandated to ensure that the principle of neutrality is respected.[26]

National Regulatory Authorities: Organisation, Regulatory Objectives, Competencies

Overview

14.10   Regulation of the electronic communications sector is undertaken by the Minister for Electronic Communications and ARCEP under their respective attributions[27] with one exception: the Prime Minister manages and grants frequencies to ARCEP and the Superior Audiovisual Board ('CSA'), which are in charge of frequency management.[28]

The Competition Council is also an important authority for the telecommunications sector.

The Minister for Electronic Communications

14.11   The Minister for Electronic Communications holds numerous exclusive subject-matter competencies. The main ones concern:

- the appointment of operators in charge of providing components of the universal service;[29] and
- the departure from the obligation on ARCEP to cooperate with the European Commission.

The Telecommunications Regulation Authority

STATUS AND COMPOSITION

14.12   ARCEP (formerly 'ART') is an independent administrative authority in charge of preparing and assisting the opening to competition of these sectors and ensuring the provision and financing of universal telecommunications services

---

25   Act No 2011–302 dated 22 March 2011
26   For further developments on the net neutrality concept, please refer to the sections below relating to the Universal Directive.
27   Art L32(1) CPCE.
28   Art L41 CPCE.
29   Art L35(2) CPCE.

created under the Act dated 26 July 1996,[30] and implemented as from 1 January 1997. Originally, ARCEP had a sectoral regulation role whereby it resolved interconnection disputes and regulated tariffs. Its powers have been increased through the implementation of the 2002 and 2009 EU Regulatory Package. Its seven members[31] hold an irrevocable and non-renewable term of office of six years.

To ensure the independence of ARCEP as provided for in Article 3(3) of the Framework Directive, article L.13–1 CPCE provides that the function of membership of ARCEP is not compatible with any other professional activity, national electoral office, public employment or the holding of interests in the electronic communications, postal, IT, audiovisual sectors, and members shall not communicate their opinion publicly concerning any subject matter of a decision of ARCEP.

REGULATORY POWERS OF ARCEP

14.13   ARCEP's main missions are the following:

* to define the conditions for the deployment of optical fibre over the entire territory and prepare the allocation of frequencies;
* to regulate through prior notification requirements covering the contemplated activities for each operator purporting to exploit an electronic communication network or service—ARCEP will then deliver a receipt enabling them to exercise their rights (such as interconnection rights) and listing their obligations (financial obligations, mainly payment of an annual administrative tax and contribution to the universal service funding and technical, commercial and more general obligations);
* to impose on SMP operators specific obligations (as set out below) to guarantee fair competition in the electronic communications sector; and
* to ensure that end users (both individuals and legal entities) have access to quality electronic communications that are transparent in terms of both content provided and rates charged.

14.14   In addition, pursuant to Governmental Order no 2011–1012 of 24 August 2011, ARCEP's powers were broadened to include the settlement of disputes relating to the reciprocal technical and pricing terms governing traffic routing between an operator and an undertaking providing public online electronic communication services in application of Article 36–8, II of the French Postal and Electronic Communications Code.

ARCEP holds the power to settle disputes[32] between operators in the following fields:

* refusal of interconnection, failure of commercial negotiations or disagreement on conclusion and execution of agreements of interconnection or conditions of access to a telecommunications network;
* technical and financial terms of communication of subscriber lists (subscriber or user to whom one or several numbers were affected);
* performance of operator's obligations provided by the French Code of telecommunication (Code des Postes et des Télécommunications);

---

30   Act No 96–659, dated 26 July 1996 for the regulation of telecommunications.
31   Five members are appointed by the Government and the others are appointed by the Presidents of the parliamentary chambers.
32   Art L36(8) CPCE.

- technical and financial terms of shared use of public infrastructure of civil engineering;
- technical and financial conditions of performance of:
  - operator activities by local government as provided by article L.1425–1 of the French Code of local government (Code des collectivités territoriales); or
  - the establishment, provision, or sharing of electronic communications infrastructure and networks by local government as provided by article L. 1425–1 of the French Code of local government (Code des collectivités territoriales);
- mutual technical and pricing terms of carrying Internet traffic between an operator and a company providing online communication services to the public;
- adjustment of agreements including clauses excluding or limiting, from a legal or technical viewpoint, the provision of telecommunications services over cabled networks; and
- possibilities and conditions for shared use of the existing installations located on the public domain or on private property.

14.15   ARCEP shall also ensure the settlement of cross-border disputes: when the case is also brought before the Regulatory Authority of another Member State, the Authorities shall coordinate their actions.

ARCEP shall take a decision within four months. Under exceptional circumstances, this period may be increased to six months. Common law courts settle consumer/ provider disputes.[33]

ARCEP also defines the rules concerning:

- rights and obligations relating to the operation of the various categories of networks and services;
- requirements applicable to the technical and financial conditions of interconnection and access, and the technical and financial conditions of local roaming; and
- conditions of use of frequencies and frequency bands.

Contrary to Article 3 of the Framework Directive, the CPCE does not contain any reference to the promotion of cultural diversity and media, or disputes between providers and consumers.

STRENGTHENED REGULATORY POWERS

14.16   Several provisions of the 2009 EU Regulatory Package have come to reinforce the Authority's regulatory powers. The regulator's overall independence has been increased. New provisions stipulate that ARCEP members and representatives will perform their duties with no instruction from the Government, nor any other institution. Like other independent regulatory authorities, ARCEP provides its expertise as an administrative body fully integrated into the governmental organisation system, but fulfils its regulatory duties in a completely independent manner– as required by European law and jurisprudence.

ARCEP has been given the power to impose functional separation on a vertically integrated operator with significant market power (SMP), in accordance with the

---

33   Art R11–1 CPCE.

new CPCE Article L.38–2. This regulatory instrument is viewed as an exceptional, last recourse measure, when all other means of regulation have failed to create a free and fair competition environment in the marketplace.

Symmetrical regulation, imposed by the legal provisions that apply to all operators, has been strengthened with the addition of a new Article L.34-8-4 to the French Postal and Electronic Communications Code (CPCE), on pooling land resources. This article applies to all operators who enjoy significant market power in a portion of the country, regardless of their status of SMP or alternative operator on the national scale.

Imposition of penalties may be swift, now that – in accordance with the EU 2009 Regulatory Framework – the minimum period of one month allowed by the Director General to any operator suspected of failing to comply with its obligations has been removed from Article L.36–11.

ARCEP's POWER TO DEMAND INFORMATION

14.17   Pursuant to Article 5 of the Framework Directive, ARCEP has a right to information and powers of investigation, jointly exercised with the Minister for Electronic Communications.[34] Transparency is guaranteed, subject to compliance with business confidentiality.

The obligation to provide information, incumbent on operators, set out in Article 5(1) of the Framework Directive, is included in the various articles relating to the services for which such information is necessary to enable ARCEP to carry out its functions.[35]

ARCEP is also entitled to request the communication of interconnection and access agreements concluded between operators.[36] Agreements concerning local roaming shall be communicated to ARCEP.[37]

Pursuant to article L.32(4) CPCE, ARCEP has investigation powers which permit its agents to enter premises, and to demand and copy documents relevant to the investigation.

ARCEP, during the preparation of its annual report, may prepare expert reports, studies, collect data, and carry out any action required to obtain information regarding the electronic communications sector. In this context, operators have to provide ARCEP with statistics about the use, area of coverage, and conditions of access to their service.

In other respects, under its contentious powers, ARCEP performs 'investigations and expertises'.[38]

---

34   Art L32(4) CPCE.
35   Arts L32(4), L36(13), L38, L39(4) CPCE.
36   Art L34(8) CPCE.
37   Art L34(8)(1) CPCE.
38   Art L36(11)(2) CPCE.

COOPERATION WITH THE OTHER AUTHORITIES

14.18   The President of ARCEP may refer to the Competition Council any anti-competitive practices implemented in the electronic communications sector.[39] The Competition Council can be consulted on any matter falling within its jurisdiction and, typically, in the context of the analysis of relevant markets.

ARCEP shall consult the CSA (Superior Audiovisual Board) before taking any decision that may have an impact on radio and television broadcasting, whether it is concerning interconnection and access,[40] dispute settlement[41] or relevant market analysis.[42]

In the event of cross-border disputes,[43] French law provides that ARCEP shall coordinate its action with the authorities which the case is referred to.[44] The procedure rules applicable to national disputes are applicable, except those relating to time limits.

To allow a comparison between the regulatory measures taken by other NRAs, article L.36(14) CPCE requires ARCEP to analyse, in its annual report, the main decisions made by the electronic communications regulation authorities of the Member States of the European Union during the past year. When a dispute is also referred to an NRA of another Member State, ARCEP shall coordinate the NRA of such state.[45] Finally, markets analysis must be notified to other Member States' NRAs.

ESTABLISHMENT OF BEREC AND ORECE

14.19   ARCEP participates in the work of BEREC, created by the 2009 EU Regulatory Package and composed of the national regulatory authorities of EU Member States to advise European institutions on the establishment and implementation of regulation in the sector.

Consumer protection is one of the key new objectives of the European regulation and ARCEP's missions in this field have been reasserted. In a market as complex as electronic communications, it is vital that consumers be fully aware of the terms and conditions available to them so that they can then make informed choices. Proper consumer information is guaranteed, in particular by CPCE Article L.33–1 and by several legal provisions contained in the Consumer Code.

In accordance with CPCE article L.33–1, disabled users have the right to have access to electronic communications and emergency services that are equivalent to those available to other users.

A decree dated 30 March 2012, which serves to complete the CPCE, details the measures the operators must introduce to the benefit of disabled users so that they might get all of the components of the universal service:

- access to pricing information, contractual and billing documents through a means adapted to their disability;

---

39   Art L36(10) CPCE.
40   Art L36(6) CPCE.
41   Art L36(8) CPCE.
42   Art L37(1) CPCE.
43   Art 21 Framework Directive.
44   Art L36(8)(V) CPCE.
45   Art L36(8)(V) CPCE.

- free access to the universal directory for the visually impaired; and
- installation of public payphones that are accessible to those with motor disabilities, the blind and visually impaired in sufficient numbers to serve the population concerned.

ARCEP also works to ensure that a balanced relationship between vendors and consumers is maintained. To this end, it has taken steps to implement a procedure for enabling price comparisons for retail market mobile services, in application of Article 21 of the Universal Service directive, and more generally the principles contained in the laws on electronic communications, notably the obligation of transparency with respect to services.

TRANSPARENCY AND CONSULTATIONS

14.20   Pursuant to Article 6 of the Framework Directive, article L.32–1 III CPCE imposes on ARCEP an obligation to make public its consultations. The ARCEP publishes all such information on its website.[46]

Article L.36(14) CPCE imposes on ARCEP the obligation to prepare, every year, a public report concerning its activity and the enforcement of the legal and regulatory provisions relating to electronic communications. It includes in the report an analysis of the main decisions reached by its European counterparts in order to make a comparison between the different types of control performed and their consequences on the markets. This report is sent to the Government and the Parliament as well as to the Superior Commission of the Public Service of Post and Electronic Communications. ARCEP may suggest, in the report, any legal or regulatory modification deemed relevant to take into account changes in the electronic communications sector and the development of competition. ARCEP shall also report its activities to the parliamentary standing committees for the telecommunications sector.

Right of Appeal against NRA's Decisions

14.21   The decisions of ARCEP[47] may be cancelled or modified on appeal to the Court of Appeal in Paris within one month from their notification to the parties. Only the parties to the dispute may institute an appeal against ARCEP's decisions. The remedy does not suspend the decision.[48] The suspension of the decision may be ordered if it is likely to result in excessive consequences or if new, extremely serious events occurred after its notification. Interim measures granted by ARCEP may be the subject of a remedy before the same court within 10 days from their notification. In such a case, the Court shall examine the remedy within one month. Finally, the decision of the Court of Appeal in Paris may be referred to the French Supreme Court of Appeal (Cour de Cassation) within one month from the notification of the appeal decision. The sanctions taken pursuant to article L.36(11) CPCE may be the subject of a remedy before the French Administrative Supreme Court (Conseil d'Etat).

---

46   www.arcep.fr
47   Art L36(8) CPCE.
48   Art L36(8) CPCE.

The NRA's Obligations to Cooperate with the Commission

14.22 Cooperation with the Commission occurs mainly in relation to definition of the relevant markets and proposals for remedies.

The CPCE requires ARCEP to cooperate with the European Commission in two respects:

- ARCEP shall notify any measure relating to conditions of access and interconnection;[49] and
- it shall notify draft decisions relating to analysis of the relevant markets.[50]

The draft decisions on analysis of the markets are notified to the European Commission, which holds a 'right of veto' concerning the definition of relevant markets and the designation of the main operators.[51] Other Member States' NRAs are also notified of the decision as part of an information and coordination process. Article L.37(3) CPCE provides that, under exceptional circumstances, it is possible to depart from the notification 'for a limited term'. The conditions of application of this article will be specified in a decree which has not yet been published.

Concerning the measures adopted in the interconnection sector, ARCEP shall have a public consultation and notify the measures to the relevant authorities of the Member States concerned and the European Commission.[52]

ARCEP promotes respect for standards set by European and international authorities. The CPCE[53] describes the procedure for evaluating conformity in France. During dispute resolutions, ARCEP may issue recommendations on conformity. Although there is no formal provision that ARCEP may cooperate with the Commission on conformity matters, the latter's advice could be sought.

ANFR

14.23 The CPCE gives the National Frequency Agency, ANFR (Agence nationale des fréquences) – which is a public State body– a central role in managing radio frequencies, and the licensed operators authorised to use them. As a result, ARCEP works closely with ANFR. An ARCEP representative is a member of the ANFR Board of Directors, and therefore takes part in its operation.

ANFR is responsible for managing national spectrum assignment records. As the authority responsible for allocating spectrum, ARCEP informs the National Frequency Agency of the frequency assignments it has authorised, and submits the Agency with any plans to create or alter radio stations operating in the frequency bands for which ARCEP is responsible. In some instances, and particularly networks open to the public, ARCEP delegates this obligation to declare any changes to the spectrum licence-holders themselves. ANFR supervises the use of spectrum, and is therefore required to verify that undertakings licensed to use frequencies comply with the technical terms set by ARCEP. The Agency also investigates interference complaints.

Furthermore, working together with licence-holders, ANFR performs a periodical examination of their use of their spectrum, and recommends any necessary

---

49   Art L34(8) CPCE.
50   Art L37(3)(2) CPCE.
51   Art L37(3)(1) CPCE.
52   Art L34(8)(I) CPCE.
53   Art L34(9) CPCE.

adjustments. It regularly issues the national frequency allocation table, which is ratified by the Prime Minister.

ANFR is responsible for preparing France's position and for coordinating its representation at international radio spectrum negotiations. It does the preparatory work for the ITU radiocommunication conferences (WCR/RRC) and for the European Conference of Postal and Telecommunications Administrations (CEPT), as well as European Union conferences devoted to these issues that fall under its purview.

ARCEP assists ANFR in international negotiations on the use of radio spectrum for electronic communications. The Authority is thus a member of the French delegation led by ANFR for the various CEPT working groups on frequencies. At the national level, ARCEP implements the agreements that ANFR has negotiated on the terms of use for radio spectrum in the frequency bands it is responsible for.

Finally, ARCEP subcontracts technical advisory work to ANFR in connection with the issuance of spectrum licences in two specific fields:

- professional mobile radiocommunications; and
- temporary networks, notably for special events broadcasting.

Here, ARCEP and ANFR are bound by an agreement that has been renewed every year since 1997.

'Significant Market Power' as a Fundamental Prerequisite of Regulation

Definition of SMP

14.24   Article L.37(1) CPCE sets out a definition that is nearly identical to the Framework Directive's definition, even though the French legislator preferred the words 'significant influence' to 'significant power'. French law, while mentioning[54] that an operator exercising a significant influence may also be deemed as exercising such an influence on an associated market, does not define the notion of associated market. The same provision also stresses that significant influence may be exercised jointly.[55] ARCEP imposes obligations on operators exercising significant influence.[56] For ARCEP, an operator has significant market power (SMP) if, individually or jointly with others, it commands a position equivalent to a dominant position, ie it has considerable ability to behave without regard to its competitors, its customers and ultimately, consumers.[57] These obligations are described in the CPCE.[58]

The European Commission's Recommendation 2005/698/EC of 19 September 2005 imposes on operators that have significant market power ('SMP operators') in relevant markets a duty to implement accounting separation and cost accounting systems which allows NRAs to verify that:

---

54   Art L37(1) CPCE.
55   Art L37(1) CPCE.
56   Art L37(2)(2) CPCE.
57   ARCEP Annual Report, 2011, glossary.
58   Art L38 CPCE.

- their financial information reflects as closely as possible the performance of parts of the relevant SMP operator's business as if they had operated as separate businesses; and
- they comply with fair, objective and transparent criteria in allocating their costs to services (in situations where they are subject to obligations for price controls or cost-oriented prices).

The 2009 EU Regulatory Package increased NRAs' independence and regulatory powers. For example, the NRAs have gained the power to:

- set minimum quality levels for network transmission services;
- mandate access to ducts even on operators without SMP; and
- impose on SMP operators, as a last resort remedy, the duty to separate communication networks from their service branches (functional separation).

Definition of relevant markets and SMP designation

14.25   The Framework Directive sets out specific rules for the designation of SMP operators and establishes criteria and procedures to ensuring a coherent assessment of the SMP operators throughout the European Union.[59] The analysis of markets is the basis for adapting regulations specifically to suit the level of restriction on competition, if any, observed in each individual market. Its main objective is to limit ex ante regulation to markets where the level of competition is low (which is currently the case in the majority of the wholesale markets), and to apply ex post regulation to markets where the level of competition is high (currently the case in most retail markets).

The Framework Directive provides that Member States must impose obligations on SMP operators proportional to the distortion of competition in the market in question. In order to define the relevant markets, NRAs have to follow:

- European Commission guidelines 2002/C165/03 of 11 July 2001 (on market analysis and the assessment of SMP under the Community regulatory framework for electronic communications networks and services); and
- the Commission Recommendations (on relevant product and service markets within the electronic communications sector susceptible to ex ante regulation).

To this end, the initial Recommendation 2003/311/EC of 11 February 2003 identified 18 relevant markets. Adapting its recommendations to the evolution of the telecommunication market (and in accordance with the objective of diminishing the ex ante regulation), the last Commission's Recommendation 2007/879/EC of 17 December 2007, reduced the number of relevant markets from 18 to seven (and excluded old market no 18).

14.26   In France, the conditions of enforcement of article L.37(1) CPCE concerning the definition of SMP in France are set out in sections D.301 et seq of the CPCE, inter alia, the conditions of renewal and the minimum frequency of the market analysis.

ARCEP is granted the following missions and powers with respect to market analysis as set forth in further detail in the CPCE:

- to identify operators with SMP (ie the SMP operators) in relevant markets within the electronic communications sector (article L.37–1 CPCE);

---

59   For further details see fifth edition of this work, para 1.63 et seq.

- to monitor SMP operators' activities by determining a set of mandatory disclosure requirements and obligations that they shall comply with (article L.38 CPCE), such as, notably, to provide interconnection services or access in accordance with non-discriminatory terms and conditions, to facilitate access to their networks and facilities, and to refrain from applying predatory or excessive prices and tariff rates;
- more particularly, to fix a common set of accounting rules to be applied by SMP operators for monitoring purposes (eg to separate accounts by activity involved); and
- where appropriate, in exceptional circumstances, to have SMP operators meet all other requirements set by ARCEP, after prior agreement of the European Commission, to remove or lower barriers to the development of effective competition identified during the analysis of the market (article L.38 CPCE).

In addition, further to the implementation of the 2009 EU Regulatory Package, the following additional powers were granted to ARCEP:

- to enable extension of the remedies imposed on an SMP operator in a market to a related market that might be affected by the position of the operator in the first market (article L.37–2 3° CPCE pursuant to the French transposition ordinance); and
- the ability to impose, as a last resort remedy, SMP operators to separate their networks from their service branches—known as 'functional separation'.

The different steps of the market analysis process followed by ARCEP are compliant with the procedure described in Article 16 of the Framework Directive.

14.27   In order to collect the information it considers as 'necessary to assess the power of operators on any market',[60] ARCEP published in July 2003 quality and quantity questionnaires to which the parties concerned were invited to reply before 30 September 2003.

Since then the ARCEP regularly conducts public consultations and subsequent market analysis near the end of the three-year regulation cycle applicable to each relevant market so as to identify and propose, based on the results of its new analysis of the market, the regulatory measures and remedy which it deemed necessary to compensate the lack of or restriction on competition it may have identified during its analysis.

After this internal process, pursuant to Article 7 of the Framework Directive, ARCEP submits the corresponding draft decisions to the Commission and the NRAs of the other Member States. ARCEP shall take into account the comments made by the Commission and other NRAs in the draft decision that it will eventually adopt. The decision can, however, be dropped if the Commission vetoes it. Article L.37(3) CPCE provides that, in exceptional circumstances, if the electronic communications minister or ARCEP considers that it is urgent to act in order to preserve competition and protect the interests of users, appropriate measures, applicable for a limited term, may be adopted without consulting the Commission and the other NRAs.

14.28   In practice, ARCEP has regularly completed its cycle analysis for markets 1 to 7. The work performed enabled ARCEP to fine tune the decisions taken during the first cycles and take into account the comments received from the industry through the public consultation process and the remarks received from the Competition Authority and the European Commission. In certain decisions ARCEP has

---

60   Commission Guidelines on the definition of the relevant markets, point 121.

provided 'rendez-vous' clauses midway through the three-year cycle to review its analysis if the situation of the market makes it necessary.

In addition to that, one market has been the object of several specific developments: former market no 18 (or the 'Market 18'). Although Recommendation 2007/879/EC of 17 December 2007, reduced the number of relevant markets from 18 to 7, thereby excluding from the scope of ex ante market analysis and regulation, the terrestrial broadcasting market entitled 'Broadcasting transmission services, to deliver broadcast content to end users' (the Market 18), it is still subject to ex ante regulation in France. Indeed, on the basis of the three criteria set forth by the EU Commission in Recommendation 2007/879/EC ((1) the presence of high and non-transitory barriers to entry, whether of a structural, legal or regulatory nature; (2) a market structure which does not and will not tend towards effective competition within the relevant time horizon; and (3) the application of competition law alone would not adequately address the market failure(s) concerned), ARCEP considered that there entry barriers on the broadcasting transmission services market in France remained which justified an ex ante regulation.

ARCEP has submitted Market 18 to public consultation pursuant to subsequent analysis cycles since 2006 (first cycle: 2006–2009, second cycle: 2009–2011, and more recently the third cycle: 2012–2015), leading to formal advice issued by the French Competition Authority (the 'FCA') and the CSA respectively, and most recently:

• Advice n°09-A-09 of the FCA; and
• Advice dated 7 April 2009 of the CSA.

Based on the foregoing methodology, ARCEP concluded in its Decision n°2009–0484 dated 1 June 2009 that there is a sound rationale for maintaining ex ante regulation in Market 18. ARCEP further specified in same Decision:

• the scope of Market 18 through the study of the degree of substitutability among coexisting offers therein;
• the current competition level and how it may evolve within such Market 18 and its impact on the SMP operator status; and
• the list of obligations that the SMP operator must comply with in such Market 18. This Decision applied until 9 July 2012.

14.29 In a new Decision n°2012–1137 dated 11 September 2012 (and enforceable as from 17 September 2012 for a three-year period) ARCEP has set forth the rules and recommendations applicable to the third regulatory cycle (2012–2015). ARCEP confirmed there is a sound rationale for maintaining ex ante regulation in Market 18 on a geographical scope including both the French territory and all overseas French departments/regions and communities ('Overseas Territories'). The ARCEP maintained its position in considering that TDF remains an SMP operator for the following reasons:

(1)   Entry barriers remain high for alternative operators due to the historical situation of broadcasting infrastructure, notably in the principal network on which TDF owns the main sites (eg the Eiffel Tower), thereby resulting in the non-replicability of a significant number of sites in the principal network. Other barriers prevent alternative operators from further investing in the secondary network due to significant construction costs, cumbersome administrative procedures and other constraints to building alternative sites in the vicinity of historical sites (most of which TDF owns).

(2)   The structure of Market 18 does not allow for effective competition to take place – to date, competition has risen but remains fragile despite the ex ante

regulation – which is to say that in the absence of regulation, the competition level would be further weakened..

(3) The application of competition law would certainly have an adverse effect on competition (as stated in point 2). Conversely, the implementation of a specific regulation appears necessary, such as the obligation to orientate tariffs imposed on the SMP operator (TDF) due to the large number of non-replicable sites and to limit SMP operator's monopoly and its associated effects on Market 18.

NRA's Regulatory Duties Concerning Rights of Way, Co-location and Facility Sharing

Rights of way

RIGHTS OF WAY ON THE PUBLIC DOMAIN

14.30 The CPCE distinguishes between rights of way on the public domain and easements on private properties. Article L.45(1) CPCE distinguishes between the rights of way of 'operators of public networks open to the public' and those of 'operators of electronic communications networks': only 'operators of networks open to the public' benefit from a right of way on the public road domain whereas the possibilities to access the public domain with the exception of carriageways are extended to all 'operators of electronic communications networks'.

For the public road domain, public networks operators benefit from a right of way, pursuant to articles L.45(1) and L.46 CPCE. Such occupancy is subject to an authorisation issued by the relevant authorities, according to the nature of the road, under the conditions defined by the Road System Code (*Code de la voirie routière*).[61] The authorities delivering the authorisation shall make a decision within two months following the application for authorisation.

Rights of way may only be impeded in order to ensure compliance with the essential requirements of conformity with standards,[62] environmental protection and compliance with the rules of city planning.

Following authorisation, fees must be paid to the public authorities according to the principle of equality between all operators. Thus, to avoid any discrimination, the maximum annual amount of these fees is set by decree. In the case of dispute concerning the fees for public domain occupancy, the administrative courts have jurisdiction.

The works necessary for the installation and maintenance of networks are carried out pursuant to the road regulations.

Concerning the public road domain, with the exception of carriageways, no right of access has been granted to telecommunications operators by the legislator; the managing authorities having a discretionary power to allow access to this domain.

When the authorities authorise this access, they shall do it under an occupancy agreement, subject to open and non-discriminatory conditions. The occupancy shall be compatible with the allocation of the public domain or with the available capacities of the managing or concessionary authorities of the public domain.

---

61   Art L113(3) *Code de la Voirie Routière*; arts L46, L47 CPCE.
62   Art L32(12) CPCE.

Article L.45(1) CPCE provides that the fees payable by operators of networks for the occupancy of non-road public domain shall be reasonable and in proportion to the effective use of the domain and in compliance with the principle of equality between all operators.

EASEMENTS ON PRIVATE PROPERTY

14.31   Operators authorised to establish public networks benefit from easements on private property in order to allow the installation and operation of network equipment:

- in parts of collective buildings and allotments allocated to a common use;
- on soil and subsoil of open property; and
- above private property insofar as the operator only uses the installation of a third party benefiting from easements without hindering, if applicable, the function of public service assigned to this third party.[63]

The implementation of easements is subject to an authorisation issued in the name of the state by the mayor. Prior to the authorisation, concerned parties – landlords or, in the case of co-ownership, the managing agent of its union – are given justifications and explanations on the easement, on which they can comment within three months. The works may not start before the expiry of such time period. In case of dispute, the chief judge of the district court determines the terms of implementation of the easement.

Co-location and facility sharing

PUBLIC DOMAIN

14.32   In order to rationalise occupancy of the public domain and to limit civil engineering works, the relevant authorities may encourage an operator or impose on an SMP operator obligations to share existing infrastructures or use co-location.[64] Specific provisions must be included in the established infrastructure sharing agreements.[65] ARCEP is entitled to request from operators the communication of the infrastructure sharing and collocation agreements in particular the agreements relating to the sharing of infrastructure for the installation of ultra-fast broadband networks.[66] ARCEP is also competent for the settlement of disputes between operators related to the sharing of infrastructures.[67]

The operator has a right of way under the same conditions as an authorised occupant, through use of existing facilities, if such use does not compromise the public service function of such occupant. In order to ensure such right, the relevant authorities may invite the concerned parties to meet in order to determine the technical and financial conditions of shared use of the facilities in question.

---

63   Art L48 CPCE.
64   Arts L47 and D310(6) CPCE.
65   Art D99(9) CPCE.
66   Art D98(11)(2)(a) CPCE.
67   Art L36(8)(II) CPCE.

PRIVATE PROPERTY

14.33   Article L.48 CPCE provides that, if infrastructure sharing does not impede the exercise of the public service functioning of the beneficiary of the easement, the mayor acting in the name of the state may invite both parties to meet in order to define the technical and financial conditions of the shared use of the concerned facilities. In this case, except as otherwise agreed, the facilities' landlord receiving the authorised operator shall be liable, within the limits of the agreement concluded between the parties, for the maintenance of the infrastructure and equipment located in its facilities and placed under its liability, against the payment of compensation negotiated with the operator.

The same rule has been extended to ultra-fast broadband networks, and more specifically FTTH (Fibre To The Home) networks, as specified in the first paragraph of article L48 CPCE.

ARCEP may settle disputes arising between operators relating to the possibilities and conditions of the shared use of existing infrastructures located on the public domain or on private property. ARCEP shall carry out a public consultation of all the parties concerned prior to any decision requiring the shared use of existing facilities.

14.34   The principle of Network Sharing has been introduced by the Law on modernising the economy ('LME') of 4 August 2008 to guarantee competition in the supply of ultra-fast broadband without increasing the number of undertakings required to do work on private property.

The law states that an operator who installs fibres in a building must respond favourably to all reasonable requests made by other operators to access the last metres of the network (mainly the indoor cabling) beyond the point of demarcation of the indoor network and the public networks named 'point of mutualisation'.[68] The operators must publish a technical and pricing offer for access to the indoor network infrastructure.[69] The access is provided under transparent and non-discriminatory conditions. Any refusal must be justified.[70] The Competition Authority has officially warned France Telecom not to keep its own infrastructure for itself and also reminded ARCEP that the deployment of ultra-fast fibre networks was an issue of regulation.[71] The agreement entered into between an operator and the owner of a building for the installation of a fibre network must include the authorisation that any other operator can use the same infrastructure, considering the capacity and that the first operator's service is not impaired.[72]

The use of the infrastructure for the installation of fibre shall not be subject to any financial consideration and cannot be subject to the provision of services other than audiovisual or electronic communications.[73] The work needed for the fibre installation has to be done in six months from the signature of the agreement. The operator is liable for all damages caused by this work[74]

The tenant asking for fibre must notify the owner beforehand. If the owner wants to refuse the fibre installation and if he/she does not intend to install it in another

---

68   Art L34(8)(3) CPCE.
69   Art D308 CPCE.
70   Art L34(8)(3) CPCE.
71   Decision No 08-D-02 from the Competition Authority dated 12 February 2008 and Decision No 2010–1312 from ARCEP dated 14 December 2010.
72   Art L33(6) CPCE.
73   Art R9(2) CPCE.
74   Art R9(4) CPCE.

way, he/she must file a claim at the Tribunal d'Instance within six months after the notification.[75]

REGULATION OF MARKET ENTRY: IMPLEMENTATION OF THE AUTHORISATION DIRECTIVE

The General Authorisation of Electronic Communications

14.35   According to article L.33(1) CPCE, there are no limitations on the development and operation of public networks and the provision to the public of electronic communications services, subject to prior notification to ARCEP.

However, the notification is not required for the establishment and operation of internal networks open to the public and for the provision to the public of electronic communication services on those networks.

Nevertheless, under certain circumstances the new framework maintains the granting of individual authorisations for the allocation of scarce resources (eg frequencies or numbers).

Due to the implementation of a general authorisation system, ARCEP no longer reviews applications for individual authorisation and the electronic communications minister does not grant licences. However, operators must provide ARCEP with a notification[76] and ARCEP must issue a receipt allowing them to enforce their rights (interconnection, rights of way, etc) and to be aware of their obligations (taxes, participation in the financing of the universal service, etc).

Concerning the content of the applicant's file and the forms required for the declarations, the law refers to a decree published on 26 July 2005, the provisions of which are codified in articles D.98(1) to D.99(3) CPCE. An individual or entity, whose right to develop and operate a network open to the public or to provide the public with an electronic communications service has been withdrawn or suspended, or who has been the subject of a sanction as provided for in article L.39 of the CPCE in case of breach or violation of its obligations, may not make a new notification.[77]

Article L.33(1) CPCE lists the conditions which are imposed on public network operators and service providers providing electronic communications services to the public. These conditions are detailed in articles D.98(3) to D.98(12) CPCE.

Operators obligations concern mainly:

- continuity, quality, availability, security and integrity of the network and of the service;
- notification of the transfer of an operator's facilities;
- communications confidentiality;
- communications security;
- net neutrality;
- universal services;
- interconnection and access;
- network and service standards and specifications;

---

75   Decree No 2009–53 dated 15 January 2009.
76   Art L33(1) CPCE.
77   Art L33(1) CPCE.

- tax payment;
- intellectual property protection – access blocking;
- personal data protection;
- public order, national defence and public security requirements;
- free transportation and localisation of emergency calls;
- services interoperability;
- users protection and information; and
- disabled users protection.

Telephone service operators are subject to additional specific obligations, such as, for example, the obligation to allow their customers, freely and easily, to oppose the identification of the customers' number, the obligation to inform their customers when they offer an identification service, or the obligation to answer interconnection demands by allowed operators from countries ensuring the equivalence of treatments.[78]

Rights of Use for Radio Frequencies

Strategic planning and co-ordination of spectrum policy

14.36   French Act no 2007–309 dated 5 March 2007 stated that the frequencies freed by the end of analogical television (other than the frequencies necessary for the deployment of the digital terrestrial television services already authorised) will be re-affected by the Prime Minister in a national re-affectation plan. In this plan, the frequency band called '800 MHz' was re-affected to the 4 G mobile services from 1 December 2011. The rights to use the band '800 MHz' were granted on 22 December 2011 to three telecommunication operators: Orange, SFR and Bouygues Telecom.

14.37   The remaining band, between 470 MHz to 790 MHz, is used for broadcasting digital terrestrial television. However, the allocation of this band to the television services may be again partially challenged concerning the highest part of the band before 2020 according to the steps provided by the world conference on radiocommunication dated January 2012.

14.38   Under French law, frequencies assignment is subject to significantly different regulatory regimes depending of the nature of the frequencies and their use. For example, frequencies are assigned for free to televisions channels in consideration of some obligations, notably regarding the financing of creation. The telecommunication sector does not benefit from such exemption.

The national frequency allocation table

14.39   Frequency bands are allocated by the International Telecommunication Union (ITU) Radio Regulations RR), to one or several radiocommunication services: this international treaty governs the use that signatory countries make of radio frequency spectrum.

In Europe, the European Conference of Postal and Telecommunications Administrations, CEPT, keeps a European table of frequency applications and allocations – the aim being to harmonise spectrum use across the 48 Member States. In addition,

---

78   Art D98(1) CPCE referring to art D98(5)(II)(3),(4) and (5) and art D98(9) CPCE.

some frequency bands are covered by harmonisation decisions from the European Commission, which therefore apply to all EU Member States.

These provisions are listed in the national frequency allocation table ratified by the Prime Minister, and which specifies the rights of each undertaking to whom spectrum has been allocated spectrum, and the methods for their coordination.

In France, because of the possibilities offered by the RR and the international treaties that France has signed, it is the Prime Minister who ratifies the allocation of spectrum between services and licence-holders, in accordance with Article 41 CPCE:

> 'after having received the opinion of the Broadcasting Authority, CSA, and the ARCEP, the Prime Minister will define the radio frequencies or frequency bands that are assigned to State administrations, and those to be assigned by CSA or ARCEP'.

The administrations concerned, as well as ARCEP and CSA are referred to as 'spectrum assignees'. ANFR amends the table on a regular basis to take account of changing spectrum requirements. These changes are then brought into force by the Prime Minister, after having consulted with CSA and ARCEP.

General authorisations and granting of individual rights

14.40   The Prime Minister defines, after consultation with the CSA (Superior Audiovisual Board) and ARCEP, the frequencies or radio-electric frequency bands granted to administrations of the state and those which may be assigned by NRAs, namely CSA and ARCEP.[79]

Subject to the exceptions set out in article L.33(3) CPCE,[80] the use of frequencies to ensure the transmission or both the transmission and reception of electronic signals is subject to an individual administrative authorisation when it is necessary to avoid interference, to ensure services' technical quality, to maintain the efficiency of radio frequency use, or to realize one of the general interest purposes mentioned in article L.32(1) and L.42 CPCE . The use of radio-electric frequencies is considered, under French law, as a private use of the public domain of the state.

ARCEP determines, for each frequency or frequency band which it is empowered to assign:

- the technical conditions for use of the frequency or of the frequency band; and
- the cases in which the use of the frequency is subject to a administrative authorisation,
- the cases in which the use of the frequency is subject to the notification under article L.33(1) CPCE.

ARCEP can limit the type of equipment, network, technologies used or services for which the use of the frequency is reserved when necessary to comply with the principles and purposes under article L.42 CPCE.

ARCEP grants authorisations to use frequencies under objective, transparent and non-discriminatory conditions, taking into account city planning requirements. Frequency assignments may be refused only in the following cases:

---

79   Art L41 CPCE.
80   Facilities that do not use frequencies specially assigned or radio-electric facilities making the sending or arrival of mobile communications inoperative in theatres and prisons.

- maintaining public order, or requirements of national defence or public security;
- improper use of frequencies;
- technical or financial incapacity of the applicant to continuously meet the obligations resulting from the conditions of exercise of its activity; and
- the applicant was sanctioned under articles L.36(11), L.39, L.39(1) and L.39(4).

Admissible conditions

14.41   The authorisation specifies the conditions of use of the frequency. Article L.42(1)(II) CPCE repeats the content of Part B of the Annex to the Authorisation Directive. The maximum term of authorisation is 20 years. The authorisation must also mention the minimum time period during which the conditions of renewal and the grounds of a refusal to renew apply; this time must be in proportion to the term of the authorisation and must take into account the level of investment undertaken by the holder.

The time limits within which the authorisations are granted and the conditions of their renewal, and the obligations imposed on holders of the authorisation in order to allow control of the conditions of use of frequencies by ARCEP, are set out in a decree.

Limitation of number of rights of use to be granted

14.42   If necessary for the proper use of the frequencies, ARCEP may, after a public consultation, propose to limit the number of authorisations in a way ensuring effective competition conditions.[81]

The electronic communications minister, upon a proposal of ARCEP, determines the conditions of allocation and modification of the authorisations of use corresponding to these frequencies. With respect to the frequencies allocated to electronic communications in the context of the national re-allocation scheme of the freed frequencies following the shutting down of analogical broadcasting transmissions, the opinion of the Committee of digital dividend was also considered by the electronic communications minister.

The choice of the holders of these authorisations is made via:

- an invitation to tender under objective, transparent and non-discriminatory conditions; or
- an auction sale.

ARCEP controls the selection procedure and allocates the corresponding frequencies. Article L.42(1) of the CPCE lists conditions which successful candidates must fulfil, such as the technical and financial capability to comply with its obligations and a clear criminal record. The candidate must not be a threat to public order and must be able to meet requirements of any international agreements concerning frequencies, etc.

---

81   Art L42(2)) CPCE.

When operators obtain an authorisation, they are liable for 'all fixing up costs necessary for the provision of frequencies granted to them'.[82] An advanced payment of part of those costs can be made by the spectrum redevelopment fund managed by the National Frequencies Agency. The amount and conditions of such contribution will be fixed by the National Frequencies Agency under the conditions defined by a decree.

Frequency trading

14.43   The 'trading' of frequencies has been introduced under French law by Act No 2004–669. The frequencies or frequency bands that may be 'transferred' are determined by the Minister.[83]

Any project of frequency transfer shall be notified to ARCEP. ARCEP 's consent is necessary when the project concerns a frequency granted pursuant to article L.42(2) CPCE or is used to perform a public service mission. A decree determines:

● procedures of notification and approval;
● conditions under which ARCEP may refuse the assignment contemplated or provide for conditions aimed at ensuring compliance with the purposes mentioned in the CPCE or continuity of the public service; and
● cases in which the assignment must be accompanied by the issue of a new authorisation to use and the withdrawal or modification of rights and obligations transferred to the transferee as well as those which may remain incumbent upon the transferor.

Low power systems

14.44   Frequencies used in connection with low power systems are not subject to an authorisation regime, the corresponding frequencies are not individually assigned and users can use them freely (for instance the Wi-Fi frequencies) but they do not benefit from any warranty against potential interferences.

Rights of Use for Numbers

General authorisations and granting of individual rights

14.45   The national numbering plan is prepared by ARCEP and managed under its control.

ARCEP identifies the numbers or blocs of numbers that can be priced with a premium and can set the pricing principles and the maximum prices applicable to such numbers.

ARCEP also grants, under objective, transparent and non-discriminatory conditions, prefixes and numbers or blocks of numbers, the codes used for the transportation of electronic communications which are not part of the domain name system against the payment of an annual fee (including the year of the granting). The method used to determine the licence fee is described in article L.44 CPCE.

---

82   Art L41(2) CPCE.
83   Art L42(3) CPCE.

However, the allocation of the following resources is not subject to the payment of any tax:

- granting of codes used for the transmission of electronic communication that are not part of the domain name system;
- when not made to the benefit of a specific operator, the granting of resources of two or three numbers beginning by the number 1 or the resources affected by ARCEP to the provision of services regarding an access offer to an electronic communications network; and
- in the context of a restructuration of the numbering national plan, the granting by ARCEP of new resources replacing the prior resources granted to an operator until the term of the replacement of the old resources by the new ones.

ARCEP ensures the efficient use and management of number resources. The operators have the obligation of regularly reporting to ARCEP about how the numbers are being used, or if they are being used at all. If they are not being used, ARCEP can retrieve the numbers, so as not to waste any resources. This obligation is provided for in the individual authorisations granted to the operators.

14.46   Article L.44 CPCE states that the national numbering plan 'guarantees equal and simple access by users to all networks and electronic communications services and equivalent numbering formats'.

The same article further provides that, subject to technical and economic feasibility, users located in other Member States of the European Community may access non-geographic numbers accessible on the whole national territory.

Article L.44(5) CPCE excludes any industrial or intellectual property rights on prefixes, numbers, blocks of numbers and codes allocated. It sets out that they may be transferred with the prior consent of ARCEP.

Blocks of numbers are generally allocated to operators who request them under the conditions specified by ARCEP and according to the category of number in question (geographic, non-geographic, etc). The operator in turn allocates numbers to its subscribers. These numbers will be returned to ARCEP if, for example, changes to the national numbering plan are made.

ARCEP applies specific fees for certain numbers, which are more attractive either because they are short numbers or attention grabbing. In France, specific numbers may be allocated through a draw since auctions are excluded as a selection procedure. As an example, enquiry services numbers were allocated by this method.

Admissible conditions

14.47   ARCEP's decision on allocation specifies the conditions of use of these prefixes, numbers or blocks of numbers concerning:

- the type of service for which the use of the resources granted is reserved;
- the requirements necessary to ensure the correct use of the resources allocated;
- the requirements, if any, relating to number portability; and
- the term of the allocation, which shall not exceed 20 years. The term shall be adjusted to the services concerned and take into account the length needed to pay off the investments.

Operators must give their subscribers, at a reasonable price, the option to keep their geographic number when they change their operator without changing their geographic location, and to keep their fixed or mobile non-geographic number when they change their operator while remaining in the metropolitan territory, in the DOM, at Mayotte or at Saint-Pierre-et-Miquelon. Fixed-to-mobile and mobile-to-fixed portability is currently not possible. To implement number portability, operators have to include the necessary provisions in the access and interconnection agreements, at prices reflecting the corresponding costs.[84]

Limitation of number of rights of use to be granted

14.48   French law excludes the allocation of number resources by comparative or competitive procedures. Operators are free to choose the available prefixes, numbers or blocks of numbers from the national numbering plan. The numbers are allocated subject to availability on a 'first come first served' basis unless a draw is organised for the allocation. To this end, ARCEP publishes on its website the list of number resources available. The numbers are allocated through a transparent and non-discriminatory process and a fee is required from the operator for the resource.[85]

The NRA's Enforcement Powers

14.49   ARCEP can impose sanctions on operators or service providers that do not meet their obligations. It exercises this power ex officio or upon the request of the Minister for Electronic Communications, of a professional entity, an authorised users' association or any concerned individual or legal entity.

Pursuant to article L.36(11) CPCE, ARCEP may formally request compliance, within a time limit, with its regulatory decisions or CPCE provisions in case of breach by a network operator or service provider. ARCEP may impose interim obligations within the delay. This mechanism also applies to violations of:

- European Regulation No 717/2007; and
- of decisions granting or assigning frequencies pursuant to article 26 of Act No 86–1067 dated 30 September 1986.

In case of serious and immediate breach of such regulations, ARCEP may take protective orders for at maximum three months, renewable once.

When a service provider or an operator does not comply with a compliance request (as described below) or to a decision taken pursuant to article L.36(8) CPCE, ARCEP may take financial sanctions and finally suspend or withdraw partially or totally the frequency or numbers.[86] If a breach is likely to cause serious damage to an operator or the entire market, the President of ARCEP may request the President of the litigation section of the French Administrative Supreme Court (*Conseil d'Etat*) for a ruling under summary proceedings to require the liable person to comply with the applicable rules and decisions and to remedy the consequences of the breach. Facts dating back more than three years may not be referred to ARCEP except if some investigation, reporting or sanction actions have been taken. Decisions relating to sanctions must be justified, and they may be the subject of remedy before the French Administrative Supreme Court.

14.50   ARCEP's power to impose sanctions may be exercised regardless of the fact that the operator is subject to a general authorisation or an individual authorisation.

---

84   Art L44 CPCE.
85   Art L44 CPCE.
86   Art L36(11) CPCE.

Article L.36(11) CPCE lists the sanctions that ARCEP may order in the case of a breach of its regulatory obligations by an operator or an electronic communications service provider. ARCEP can notably decide:

- depending on the seriousness of the breach, total or partial suspension of the right to develop an electronic communications network/provide an electronic communications service for up to one month is possible. The right may be removed for up to three years;
- depending on the seriousness of the breach, total or partial suspension up to one month, term reduction up to one year or the withdrawal of the granting or assigning decision issued pursuant to article L. 42(1) or L. 44 CPCE. The authority may notably withdraw the rights of use in certain geographical zones included in the decision, on all or part of the frequencies, prefixes, numbers, or blocks of numbers or for all or a part of the remaining term of the authorisation as stated in the decision.
- a financial sanction proportionate to the breach is imposed for non-criminal offences. It cannot exceed 3 per cent of the previous year's turnover. When there is a repeated offence, a 5 per cent sanction can be imposed.
- Pursuant to article L.44(3) CPCE, ARCEP is involved in the battle against fraudulent or abusive services and the use of numbers that enable such fraud or abuse. In this context, the President of ARCEP may request the President of the Paris First Instance Court, to issue an order under summary proceedings to demand operators to block the access to the numbers and the fraudulent or abusive services and the retention of the benefits coming from the connexion or other services.

Administrative Charges and Fees for Rights of Use

14.51   The general authorisation system excludes the payment of a fee upon the submission of the request for authorisation: instead, operators shall pay an annual administrative tax. The amount of such tax is defined in the finance law.[87] All operators who provide an electronic service to the public or operate a network which is open to the public pay these charges.

However, there are two limitations:

- exoneration of operators whose turnover related to electronic communications activities mentioned at article L.33(1) CPCE is inferior to €1 million; and
- limitation for operators whose turnover is between €1 million and €2 million.

In addition, the allocation of frequency and number resources is subject to the payment of fees. These fees are also determined in the finance law.[88]

Transitional regulations for existing authorisations

14.52   Individual authorisations to use frequencies which were still in existence on 19 December 2011 will be brought in line with the new provisions of the CPCE (articles L.42(1) and L.42) by 19 December 2011 at the latest.

Where the application of this rule results in a reduction of the rights or in the extension of the obligations under an authorisation already in force, ARCEP can

---

87   Act No 2003–1312 dated 31 December 2003.
88   Act No 2003–1312 dated 31 December 2003.

extend the validity of those authorisations until 30 September 2012, provided that the rights of other undertakings are not affected thereby. ARCEP will notify to the European Commission such extension mentioning its justification.

The beneficiary of an authorisation to use radio frequencies which remains valid for a period of at least five years from 25 May 2011 may request ARCEP before 24 May 2016 to reconsider the restrictions on spectrum use provided by the authorisation in regards to the provisions of article L.42 II and III CPCE. The Authority shall review it in order to retain only the necessary restrictions under these provisions. A decree taken by the Conseil d'Etat determines the terms of this review.

As of 25 May 2016, ARCEP will take the necessary measures to maintain, in the authorisations to use frequencies which are still in existence on 24 May 2016, only frequencies using restrictions that are required under II and III of article L.42 CPCE.

In the context of such authorisations reviews, ARCEP shall take appropriate measures in order to respect the principle of equality between operators and the conditions of effective competition.

REGULATION OF NETWORK ACCESS AND INTERCONNECTION: IMPLEMENTATION OF THE ACCESS DIRECTIVE

Objectives and Scope of Access Regulation

14.53   ARCEP is empowered to regulate interconnection and access. It ensures that the pricing and operational conditions of interconnection and access favour the development of fair and lasting competition and provide the possibility, for all users, to communicate freely.

In its reply to the public call for comments launched by the Government prior to the preparation of the electronic communications act, ARCEP submitted that the powers it held under the 1996 law were limited. Thus, ARCEP wished to have widened and appropriate powers in order to comply fully with its functions of control and surveillance.

The implementation of the Access Directive increased the powers of ARCEP. It defines the scope of its intervention by determining, among other things, the obligations that ARCEP could impose on operators exercising a significant influence on a relevant market concerning their offers of interconnection and access.

All provisions relating to access and interconnection provided for in article L.34(8) CPCE are applicable to operators of public networks, including public service providers.

Basic Regulatory Concepts

14.54   Pursuant to article L.32(1)(II) CPCE, ARCEP defines the public network access and interconnection conditions which guarantee equal market conditions and the possibility of unrestricted communication between users. Furthermore,

ARCEP can impose access and interconnection conditions if needed.[89] It can also settle disputes concerning refusal to grant access or interconnection.[90]

As per article L.32(8) CPCE, 'access' shall mean 'any provision of means, hardware or software, or services, in order to allow the beneficiary to provide electronic communications services'. However, and contrary to the Access Directive which applies, in particular, to conditional access systems for digital TV, article L.32(8) CPCE excludes audiovisual communications services which are governed by specific regulations.[91] This exclusion is a consequence of the fact that the CPCE does not govern audiovisual communications: all provisions relating to audiovisual communications are included in Act No 86–1067 relating to the freedom of communication, reformed upon the implementation of the 2002 EU Regulatory Package.

Regarding the exclusion of audiovisual communications services, the French definition of access is quite similar to the European Community one. However, the French legislator decided not to include information aiming at illustrating the definition. For the words 'resources and/or services', French law preferred 'means, hardware or software, or services', ie a wider notion and consequently likely to apply regardless of the future technologic innovations the sector will experience.

Article L.32(9) CPCE defines interconnection and repeats more or less the definition from the Access Directive: to the word '*undertaking*' the legislator preferred the word '*operator*'. In other respects, the French text refers to '*the parties authorised to access the network*' whereas the Access Directive mentions the '*parties having access to the network*'. Nevertheless, the word '*authorised*' shall not be construed as a regulatory authorisation but as an operator fulfilling the conditions necessary to benefit from access.

French law provides that interconnection or access is freely negotiated between the parties and is subject to private law agreements.[92] The non-discriminatory conditions the operators have to comply with are not specific to the electronic communications sector: article L.442(6) of the French Commercial Code prohibits discriminatory practices between professionals when they are not justified by any compensation and create an advantage or disadvantage in terms of competition.

Access- and Interconnection-related Obligations with Respect to SMP Undertakings

Overview of the NRA's regulatory powers

14.55   In compliance with the provisions of the Framework Directive which provides that Member States must impose obligations on SMP operators proportional to the distortion of competition in ta relevant market, ARCEP must follow European Commission guidelines on market analysis and the assessment of SMP, and Commission Recommendation 2007/879/EC of 17 December 2007 on relevant product and service markets within the electronic communications sector susceptible to ex ante regulation, and identify operators deemed to have a significant influence on the market of electronic communications.

---

89   Art L34(8) CPCE.
90   Art L36(8) CPCE.
91   Act No 86–1067 dated 30 September 1986.
92   Art L34(8)(I) CPCE.

ARCEP has the power to impose obligations on undertakings held to have SMP, on the matters of interconnection and access. Article L.38 CPCE thus requires SMP operators to publish information concerning interconnection or access. It also requires that interconnection and access be provided under transparent and non-discriminatory conditions, and that tariffs charged reflect the corresponding costs. Account separation is also required. A decree specifies the application of this article.[93]

Transparency obligations

14.56   An operator who has SMP can be required by ARCEP to publish a detailed technical and price offer of interconnection or access.[94] ARCEP can review at anytime this offer so that it complies with the CPCE.

Non-discrimination obligations

14.57   An operator who has SMP can be required by ARCEP to also provide interconnection or access services under non-discriminatory conditions.[95] It must offer equivalent conditions to its subsidiaries and other operators, in the same circumstances[96] and accept reasonable requests for access to elements of the network or means associated therewith.

Price-control obligations

14.58   SMP operators can also be required by ARCEP to use interconnection tariffs which reflect costs and to prove this.[97] ARCEP can require them to justify their tariffs or modify them if need be.

Accounting separation obligations

14.59   SMP operators can be required by ARCEP to furthermore distinguish, in their accounting system, interconnection or access activities, or hold an accounting system allowing the control of compliance with SMP cost orientation obligations.[98] Compliance with the cost accounting system is verified, at the operator's expense, by an independent entity appointed by ARCEP. The operators can also be required by ARCEP to render their accounting methods public. ARCEP specifies the formats of the documents needed and the mechanism used for accounting systems.[99]

These measures are not applicable on emergent markets, in particular those created by technological innovation, unless the purposes of article L.32(II) CPCE are not achieved. In this case, ARCEP may impose the obligations described above only via

---

93   Decree No 2004–1301 dated 26 November 2004.
94   Art L38(I)(1) CPCE.
95   Art L38(I)(2) CPCE.
96   Art D309 CPCE.
97   Art D311(I) CPCE.
98   Art L38(I)(5) CPCE.
99   Art D312 CPCE.

a decision justified by specifying, on a case-by-case basis, which purposes are not achieved and by justifying the adequacy of the obligations provided for.[100]

The CPCE, unlike the Access Directive, makes a very subtle distinction at article L.38. Indeed, the CPCE first elaborates the obligations to be imposed on SMP undertakings on any electronic communications market[101] and then enumerates the obligations for SMP undertakings on the retail market.[102] Article L.38(1) is to be applied if Article L.38(I) does not achieve its objectives. Concerning the obligations to be imposed on SMP undertakings, French law has very closely transposed the obligations detailed in the Access Directive.

Related Regulatory Powers with Respect to SMP Undertakings

14.60   Pursuant to Article L.38(II) CPCE as modified by the Governmental Order No 2011–1012 of 24 August 2011 implementing the provisions of the Access Directive, ARCEP can impose obligations on operators exercising a significant influence on the market of connection to fixed public telephone networks. The types of obligations that ARCEP may impose are defined in Articles L.38(I) and L.38(1) CPCE. Such obligations notably relate to the provision to any operators with the necessary interconnection and access services, or to the minimum provision of leased lines on the wholesale market. In practice, these obligations will be imposed only in the absence of effective and sustainable competition, identified as a result of the market analysis performed under Article L.37(1) CPCE. ARCEP withdraws them once such a competition exists.[103]

Since 2011, the European Commission or BEREC can prevent ARCEP from taking certain measures if those are an obstacle to the Single Market or incompatible with EU law.[104]

Regulatory Powers Applicable to All Market Participants

Obligations to ensure end-to-end connectivity

14.61   As per Article 4 of the Access Directive, operators of public networks, regardless of their influence on the market, are obliged to negotiate interconnection with other operators of public networks, including those located in another Member State of the Community or party to the EEA agreement.[105] However, it is specified in the CPCE that the application for interconnection may not be refused if it is justified considering the needs of the applicant and if the operator has the capacity to meet such an application.[106] Any interconnection refusal shall be justified and may be the subject of a remedy before ARCEP under the procedure of dispute settlement. ARCEP can force operators who have control on access to end

---

100   Art L38(1)(II) CPCE.
101   Art L38(I) CPCE.
102   Art L38(1) CPCE.
103   Art L37(2) CPCE.
104   Art L37(3) CPCE.
105   Art L34(8)(II) CPCE.
106   Art L34(8)(II) CPCE.

user obligations to interconnect their networks and to establish interoperability of services provided over those networks or other networks.[107]

In addition, pursuant to Governmental Order No 2011–1012 of 24 August 2011, ARCEP's powers were broadened to include settlement of disputes relating to the reciprocal technical and pricing terms governing traffic routing between an operator and an undertaking providing public online electronic communication services in application of Article 36–8, II of the French Postal and Electronic Communications Code.

Regulation of roaming services

14.62   The Regulation on roaming on public mobile communications networks within the EU aims at ensuring that users of public mobile communications networks do not pay excessive prices for regulated roaming calls, as well as regulated roaming SMS messages when travelling in the EU.[108] The CPCE imposes objective, transparent and non-discriminatory conditions to operate roaming. ARCEP can review the agreement signed between operators.[109] SMP operators have an obligation to provide special services so that interoperability and roaming are guaranteed for users.[110]

A French law extended the EU roaming regulation for overseas.[111]

Access to digital radio and television broadcasting services

14.63   Article 95 of the Act relating to communication freedom repeats the requirements of Article 6 of and Annex I to the Access Directive.[112] The 1986 Act makes an additional specification by providing that access to any group of terminals of reception of TV or sound broadcasting services provided to the public via digital signals shall also be offered under 'equitable, reasonable and non-discriminatory conditions to any distributor or editor of TV or sound broadcasting services wishing to use it to provide the authorised public with its offer'.

Conditional access system operators are required to allow the distributors of bundled service offers to use conditional systems of their choice, at reasonable prices.[113]

Finally, article 95 of the 1986 Act requires that:

'the operators or providers of public conditional access digital TV or sound broadcasting shall hold a separate financial accounting showing their entire activity of operating or provision of these systems'.

---

107   Art D99(11) CPCE.
108   Regulation (EU) No 531/2012 dated 13 June 2012.
109   Art L34(8)(1) CPCE.
110   Art D310(7) CPCE.
111   Act No 2012–1270 dated 20 November 2012.
112   Act No 86–1067 dated 30 September 1986.
113   Art 95 Act No 86–1067 dated 30 September 1986.

REGULATION OF UNIVERSAL SERVICES AND USERS' RIGHTS: THE UNIVERSAL SERVICE DIRECTIVE

Regulation of Universal Service Obligations

Overview

14.64　Pursuant to article L.35(3) CPCE, ARCEP shall:

- determine principles and methods of the universal service;
- determine the amounts of participation in the financing of the obligations of the universal service, based on turnover made through these services (except interconnection);
- ensure the control of financing systems; and
- impose sanctions on any operator who fails to pay.

Scope of universal service obligations

14.65　The components of the French universal service obligations set out in article L.35(1) CPCE are identical to those provided for in the Universal Service Directive:

- a quality telephone service at a reasonable price meeting the conditions set in Article 4(2) of the Universal Service Directive – concerning Internet access, the French authorities have held this to be the equivalent of a dial-up connection via the telephone line;
- an inquiry service and directory of subscribers, in printed and electronic format;
- access to public telephone booths installed in the public domain or other points of access to public telephone service; and
- special measures in favour of disabled individuals to ensure access to the universal service which is equivalent to that available to other end users and the affordability of these services.

Article R20(30) CPCE[114] specifies the conditions attached to the provision of the universal service: the universal service is also to be provided to the French overseas territories. Article L.35(2) further mentions that the provider of the universal service must ensure that calls can be made to and received from the overseas territories and other foreign countries. In addition, operators selected to provide the obligations of article L.35(1) must offer preferential tariffs for connections to the French overseas territories at non-peak hours.

Designation of undertakings obliged to provide universal services

14.66　Any operator may be given the responsibility of providing the universal service as long as it accepts providing it nationwide.

However, one or more operators may be designated to provide either one component, more than one or some elements of the components of the universal

---

114　Decree No 2004–1222 dated 17 November 2004.

service.[115] Complementary obligations are imposed to operators in order to permanently ensure the availability of the service to all users within the geographical area for which they have been appointed by Decree No 2012–436 dated 30 March 2012.

The operator(s) appointed to provide either one component, more than one or some elements of the components of the universal service are subject to the provisions of the CPCE and must comply with a statement of works ('*Cahier des charges*') in which their obligations under their function of universal service are listed.

14.67   When an appointed operator intends to transfer a substantial part or all of its local access network assets to a separate legal entity, it shall inform in advance the electronic communications Minister and ARCEP who may adapt its obligations, provide a new statement of works and if necessary, launch a new invitation to tender.

After an invitation to tender concerning technical and price conditions and the net cost to provide these services, the electronic communications Minister appoints operators to provide the different components of the universal service. If an invitation to tender proves to be unsuccessful the Minister appoints one or more operators who can ensure the service in question throughout the whole French territory. Obviously the criteria for this decision are the financial and technical capacity of the selected operator to provide the service

On the last call for tenders of 14 December 2009, France Telecom was designated by the Minister to be responsible for public telephones booths and telephone service respectively until 2011 and 2012. The Yellow Pages operator was designated to be responsible for printed universal directory and universal information service respectively until November 2011 and December 2011.

Regulation of retail tariffs, users' expenditures and quality of service

PRICE CONTROL PROVISIONS

14.68   The prices of offers for the provision of components of the universal service are defined by the operator so as to comply with the principles of transparency, non-discrimination and cost orientation, and do not depend on the nature and use of the service by users.[116] The prices of the universal service are established to avoid any discrimination based on geographic location. The legislator maintained the principle of price standardisation, subject to exceptional circumstances under which the operator may apply different prices which shall be published.[117]

Article L.35(2) CPCE provides for a decree, adopted in January 2005,[118] determining the conditions under which the universal service prices are controlled and specifying, inter alia, the cases in which these prices may be subject to a long-term control measure or a refusal or a prior consent of ARCEP. This decree, codified at article R.20(30)(11) CPCE, provides that tariffs can be controlled by ARCEP over a number of years. Where this type of control is not carried out, the decree states that

---

115 Art L35(2) CPCE.
116 Art L35(3) CPCE.
117 Art L35(1) CPCE.
118 Decree No 2005–75.

the tariffs are transmitted to the ARCEP together with elements allowing their appraisal, and ARCEP gives its opinion within three weeks.

The new legal system of price control applicable to the universal service waives the ex-ante price approval system under which the minister approved, after receiving notice from ARCEP, the prices of the universal service before their application.

USERS' EXPENDITURES

14.69   The operator providing the universal service component defined at article L.35(1)(1) CPCE is under an obligation to maintain a limited telephone service for one year to users who have not paid their bills or who are in debt with the operator. The operator must also provide itemised billing to its customers.

The operator providing the universal service offers barring for the following outgoing calls: international, national, national calls made to mobiles and calls to numbers of the national numbering plan which enable call reverse mechanisms so that it is the final recipient who pays for the communication.[119] Itemised billing is also provided.[120]

QUALITY OF SERVICE

14.70   The service quality obligations to be complied with by universal service operators are detailed in their respective statements of works. Operators publish the values resulting from the application of the quality indicators: these indicators include those mentioned in Annex III to the Universal Service Directive as well as the rights of users on networks and electronic communications services as listed in the Universal Service Directive.[121]

14.71   The conditions under which universal service quality is controlled are set out in Decree No 2004–1222.[122] ARCEP has jurisdiction, pursuant to article L.36(11) CPCE, to impose sanctions on operators that do not comply with their obligations. Operators also have the obligation of informing their customers of the universal service offer, its tariffs and any potential modifications. A time limit of six months is set for any modification or termination the operator might bring about. ARCEP must be informed of any technical or tariff-related alterations.

Cost calculation and financing of universal services

14.72   Article L.35(3) CPCE provides that the net costs resulting from the universal service obligations are assessed on the basis of the accounts held by the operators designated to ensure these obligations and audited, at their own expense, by an independent entity appointed by ARCEP. As per Article 12(1)(a) of the Universal Service Directive, the assessment of these net costs shall take into account the advantage obtained on the market by operators subject to universal service obligations, if any. The net costs likely to be offset under the universal service

---

119   Art R 20–30(1) Decree No 2004–1222 on the obligations of public service and the funding of Universal Service.
120   Art R 20–30(1) Decree No 2004–1222 on the obligations of public service and the funding of Universal Service.
121   Art 22 of the Universal Service Directive.
122   Art R20–30 (7) CPCE.

financing cannot exceed the commitments made by the operator under the invitations to tender in which it participated.

Contrary to Article 13 of the Universal Service Directive, French law did not introduce a mechanism of participation in the financing of the universal service upon request from a designated undertaking, but set the rules relating to the participation of each operator in the financing of universal service obligations.

Thus, each operator shall participate in the financing of the universal services on a pro-rated basis considering its turnover, excluding turnover from interconnection and access services and other services provided or billed on behalf of third operators.

However, pursuant to article L.35(3) CPCE, operators whose turnover is below an amount determined in Decree No 2004–1222 of 17 November 2004 do not participate in the financing of the universal service.

When an operator agrees to provide universal services under the price and technical conditions suitable to some categories of users, the net cost resulting from this service is deducted from its contribution to the universal service fund.

An electronic communication universal service fund ensures the financing of the net costs of the universal service obligations.

A setting-off mechanism is in place, where the operator providing a universal service sets off the costs incurred in its activities, except where these costs are not excessive for the operator.[123]

France has chosen a setting-off system with exceptions, and not the Community system which requires the company to prove it incurred an unjustified charge.

The amount of the net participations that the operators shall pay to the fund and the amounts due by the fund to the operators are determined by ARCEP[124] according to their turnover.

The accounting and financial management of the fund is ensured by the French Deposit and Consignment Office (*Caisse des Dépôts et Consignations*) on a specific account. The management costs incurred by the Office are charged to the fund.

14.73   In the case of non-payment by any operator of its contribution, ARCEP orders one of the sanctions provided for in article L.36(11) CPCE. In the case of repeated failure, it may impose on the operator a prohibition from operating a public network or providing a publicly available electronic communications service. If the amounts due are not paid within one year, they are charged to the fund during the next fiscal year.

Decree No 2004–1222 defines the enforcement conditions of article L.35(3) CPCE and specifies the allocation conditions, the assessment methods if the requirements of transparency and publicity are met, setting off and sharing of the net costs of the universal service, and the management methods of the electronic communications universal service fund. This decree determines the categories of activity for which, due to their nature, operators do not participate in the financing of the costs resulting from the universal service obligations. Hence, the turnover from interconnection and access agreements negotiated under article L.34(8), and from the routing and broadcasting of television and radio services and the operation of

---

123   Art L35(3)(III) CPCE.
124   Art L35(3)(III) CPCE.

collective antennas, are not taken into account when calculating the prorated contributions. Moreover, the methods of evaluation of the net costs of universal service obligations have also evolved with the new legal framework. ARCEP who carries out this evaluation takes into consideration the capital used for these obligations and looks at certain elements which will determine the compensation of the operator for the provision of the universal service – social tariffs, universal directory, public payphones and geographic adjustment.

Regulation of Retail Markets

Prerequisites for the regulation of retail markets

14.74   The general rule is that retail markets are not regulated, since both ARCEP and the Competition Authority agree that regulation should only intervene on wholesale markets. The only retail market regulated in France is the one for the universal service, where prices are controlled by the authorities. It could happen eventually that ARCEP and the Competition Authority might decide to regulate a retail market if competition was seriously impeded.

Regulatory powers

14.75   According to article L.38(1)(I) CPCE, the following obligations may be 'imposed' on providers with SMP on a retail market:

- supply of retail services under non-discriminatory conditions and without abusively tying services;
- not to apply excessive or predatory prices on the markets concerned;
- to apply prices reflecting the corresponding costs;
- to comply with long-term control of prices as defined by ARCEP;
- to communicate the prices to ARCEP prior to their implementation, insofar as these prices are not controlled under the universal service. ARCEP may refuse the implementation of a price communicated to it by a founded decision setting out the (economic) analysis explaining its refusal; and
- to hold an accounting system allowing the control of compliance with the cost orientation obligations. Compliance with the cost accounting system is verified, at the operator's expense, by an independent entity appointed by ARCEP.

These different obligations are established, maintained or withdrawn according to market analysis. These obligations are not applicable on emerging markets, in particular those created by means of technologic innovation, unless the purposes of the CPCE are breached. In such a case, ARCEP may impose the obligations described above only through a founded decision, specifying, on a case-by-case basis, the purposes breached and justifying the adequacy of the obligations required.[125]

The offer of leased lines on both retail and wholesale markets falls within the scope of complementary services included in the French public service, pursuant to article L.35-5 of the CPCE. The French public service consists of the universal service,

125   Art L38(1) CPCE.

complementary services to the universal service and general interest missions.[126] Leased lines, although not part of the universal service, are provided under the complementary services.[127]

When any operator is considered as exercising a significant influence on all or part of the market of the supply of the minimum set of leased lines mentioned in Article 18 of the Universal Service Directive, it shall provide these lines under technical and price conditions defined in Article D369 to D377 CPCE).[128]

End User Rights

Contracts

14.76   Provisions concerning agreements relating to electronic communications services concluded with consumers are mainly included in the French Consumer Code and not in the CPCE. Articles L.121–83 and L. 21-83-1 of the Consumer Code list electronic communication service providers' obligations with respect to the information that must be made available to consumers, and the information that must appear in their service contracts with users. However, if article L.121(83) of the Code provides that any agreement concluded by a consumer with an electronic communications service provider shall include all information mentioned in Article 20(1) of the revised Universal Service Directive, point (1)(b)(5°) relating to the types of maintenance service offered are not mentioned under French law.

For the modification of contractual conditions, article L.121(84) of the French Consumer Code implements Article 20(2) of the revised Universal Service Directive by providing that the client may terminate the agreement without penalty within four months after the new conditions have come into force, unless he expressly accepted the new conditions notified.

Transparency obligations

14.77   Contractual information obligations increased transparency towards end users. Article L33(1)(n) CPCE refers to articles L.121(83) and L.121(83)(1) of the Consumer Code. Article L.121(83) imposes, in particular, on a provider of an electronic communications service a duty to specify in a clear, detailed and easily accessible form the information mentioned in Article 20(1) of the revised Universal Service Directive.

Operators must appoint a mediator to settle conflicts with their customers (article L.121-84-9 of the Consumer Code).

Better serving consumer interests

14.78   In a market as complex as electronic communications, it is vital that consumers be fully aware of the terms and conditions available to them so that they can then make informed choices. Proper consumer information is guaranteed, in particular by Article L.33–1 CPCE and by several legal provisions contained in the

---

126 Art L35 CPCE.
127 Decree No 2004–1301 dated 26 November 2004.
128 Decree No 2004–1301 dated 26 November 2004.

Consumer Code. In accordance with Article L.33–1 CPCE, disabled users have the right to have access to electronic communications and emergency services that are equivalent to those available to other users.

A decree dated 13 April 2012, which has completed the CPCE, details the measures the operators must introduce on behalf of disabled users so that they might benefit from all of the components of the universal service:

- access to pricing information, contractual and billing documents through a means adapted to their disability;
- free access to the universal directory for the visually impaired; and
- installation of public payphones that are accessible to those with motor disabilities, the blind and visually impaired in sufficient numbers to serve the population concerned.

For a market to operate properly, a balanced relationship between vendors and consumers is key. ARCEP works to ensure this balance is maintained. It is to this end that it will implement a procedure for enabling price comparisons for retail market mobile services, in accordance with Article 21 of the Universal Service Directive, and the principles contained in the laws that govern electronic communications, notably the obligation of transparency with respect to services.

Quality of service: securing 'net neutrality':

14.79   According to ARCEP the principle of network and nternet neutrality assumes that every user must have access, via the Internet and, more generally, electronic communications networks (regardless of distribution platform) to all of the content, services and applications carried over these networks, regardless of who is supplying or using them, and in a transparent and non-discriminatory manner.

If French law does not currently refer expressly to internet and network neutrality, article L.32–1 CPCE states that the electronic communications Minister and ARCEP must take measures whilst ensuring technological and service neutrality.

However, ARCEP's prerogatives have been expanded and intend to enforce this principle. For instance, ARCEP is entitled to settle disputes arising between operators and internet service providers according to there financial and technical reciprocal traffic exchange and routing agreements (article L.36–8 II 5° CPCE). It also has the possibility of setting minimum quality of service requirements (article L.36–6 CPCE).

In September 2012, ARCEP issued a report to Parliament and the Government on net neutrality. This report follows a report dated 2010 containing 10 proposals and recommendations with regard to internet and network neutrality which marked at the time the start of a cycle of work and monitoring of internet players' practices to be performed in an open and collaborative way involving all of the stakeholders.

The 2012 report includes, inter alia, the work in progress in relation to transparency, quality of service, interconnection and traffic management.

14.80   First, new measures provided by the French Consumer Code contribute to ensure the enforcement of the principle of neutrality through more transparency such as information on any procedures put in place by the undertaking to measure and shape traffic so as to avoid filling or overfilling a network link, and information on how those procedures could impact on service quality as well as information on any restrictions imposed by the provider on the use of terminal equipment supplied.

Secondly, an ARCEP decision to track the quality of internet access services is about to be adopted. It will specify the quality of service indicators for fixed networks, which will be measured and made public, in addition to those already measured for mobile networks. This investigation will make it possible to compare network performance, to strengthen competition between operators and, taking a preventive approach, to ensure that quality of service does not decline.

It is to be noted that operators with more than 100,000 subscribers are obliged to make available to the public each quarter on their website, the results of measuring the quality of their service by type of fixed telephone service (switched telephone network , ADSL, cable, etc).

Thirdly, ARCEP has undertaken an inventory of traffic management practices implemented by operators, eg throttling, blocking or priority queues – if the market fails to make sufficient progress on its own, the current legislation gives the ARCEP the powers needed to intervene.

Lastly, the regular collection of information on technical and pricing terms governing interconnection and routing introduced by the NRA's decision n°2012– 0366 dated 29 March 2012 allows the Authority to keep track of these trends, to analyse them and take action accordingly.

Meanwhile, the Competition Authority has addressed for the first time the issue on neutrality in a decision dated 19 September 2012 relating to practices concerning reciprocal interconnection services in the area of internet connectivity. It considered that a network operator is entitled to charge a content provider for opening additional capacity subject to compliance with contractual conditions of trans-parency in order to detect potential margin squeeze practices or unfair discrimin-ation.

Other obligations

14.81   The transmission of emergency calls is free and all operators of public telephony must provide it.[129] Access to the European emergency number '112' must also be provided and operators need to take necessary measures for its availability.

The number portability legal system results from articles L.44, D.406–18 and D.406–19 CPCE. Article L.44 imposes on operators a duty to include in their interconnection agreements measures taken to implement number portability.

Art. L44 CPCE states that operators are required to offer to their subscribers at a reasonable price to retain their geographical number when changing operator without changing geographical location and retain their non-geographic numbers, either fixed or mobile, when they change operator. In either case, the waiting period for actually porting a number, is one business day, subject to access availability unless expressly requested by the subscriber.

Effective number porting causes concomitant termination of the contract between the former operator and the subscriber.

Fixed number portability is, since its inception, based on the principle of one-step process. The user goes directly to the new operator when subscribing to his new contract. However, the fixed number portability does not apply to changes of geographical location.

---

129   Art L33(1)(f) CPCE.

14.82   Mobile number portability follows a one-step process discharged by operators with the unit in charge of mobile number retention at GIE EGP (*Groupement d'intérêt économique – Entité de gestion de la portabilité*), a special entity formed among mobile operators who operates a central IT system connected to operators' information systems. GIE EGP has been working under the aegis of ARCEP to reduce the time to portability, to simplify the customer process and increase the information available to subscribers.

ARCEP has clarified the conditions for the implementation of the obligation of number portability for fixed and mobile call (ARCEP, Decree No 2006–0381, 30 March 2006), even if a bill has been unpaid. It considers also that termination of a contract for legal reasons is consistent with the conservation of number. Hence ARCEP reminded operators that they must ensure that subscribers who terminate their contract through portability while they have a right to termination for not accepting new financial conditions are not subject to termination fees.

DATA PROTECTION: IMPLEMENTATION OF THE E-PRIVACY DIRECTIVE

Confidentiality of Communications

14.83   When service and network providers notify their activity to ARCEP, their project is approved if they comply with certain rules as listed by the CPCE, one being the rules on confidentiality and neutrality of all communications.[130] Confidentiality is guaranteed by French law, but certain exceptions are provided for, in particular for billing purposes and public order reasons.[131] To comply with the law, operators must take the necessary measures to ensure confidentiality of content transmitted on their networks. Operators must not discriminate between messages transmitted, that is between voice or data, and they must ensure their integrity whatever their nature.[132]

Art 241(1) of the Code for national security[133] states that the secrecy of messages is guaranteed, except the state can intervene if the public interest is at stake. Indeed, messages can be intercepted if they concern information relevant to national security, the safeguard of elements essential to the scientific and economical potential of France, or the prevention of terrorism, criminality, organised delinquency and the reconstruction or maintenance of groups dissolved.[134]

Such interception must, however, be carried out within very strict conditions.[135] The National Commission for the Control of Interceptions oversees the operation so that the law on the subject is respected. Authorisation to intercept is given in writing by the Prime Minister and needs to be thoroughly justified, at the request of the Minister for Defence, the Home Minister and the Customs Minister. Such an authorisation cannot exceed four months, is renewable, and the records of the interception have to be destroyed within 10 days. The information gathered cannot be used for any other purpose that the one described in the authorisation.

---

130 Art L33(1)(I)(b) CPCE.
131 Art L241(1) *Code de la Sécurité Intérieure* (CSI).
132 Art D98(5) CPCE.
133 Art L241(1) CSI.
134 Art 241(2) CSI.
135 Art 243(1) CSI.

Transcriptions can be operated under strict conditions.[136] Revealing the existence of an interception or refusing to execute an order of interception may be subject to criminal sanctions[137]

14.84 Under the provisions of the CPCE,[138] data allowing the localisation of the user's terminal equipment cannot be used during the communication for any other purpose than the transmission of the message. This information can, however, be used if it is required in judicial investigations and if the user is properly informed of how the data will be used, for how long and provided he or she can withdraw their consent at any time, free of charge.

The storage of or access to information on the terminal equipment of the subscriber or user is permitted under certain conditions. The subscriber or user used to only have an opposition right. Since the transposition of the e-privacy directive and its modification from 2009[139], the information of the filing of a cookie is prior to the filing itself. The consent of the subscriber or user has to be obtained beforehand and specifically[140]. There are two exceptions : when the cookie exclusively aims to allow or facilitate telecommunications and when it is strictly necessary to provide an online telecommunications service expressly asked by the user.

Breaches of the secrecy of communications are offences.[141]

Data Retention

14.85 Directive 2006/24/EC has been transposed by a decree in 2006.[142] Art 34(1) CPCE allow data retention in three cases :

- for the purposes of research, recognition and prosecution of criminal offences;
- for the purposes of billing and payment services of telecommunications;
- to commercialise the own telecommunications services of operators or provide value-added services and ensure safety of operators' networks.

A list of data that can be kept is fixed. There are no details on proportionality, transparency, data security or a claim. It only refers to Act No 78–17.[143]

The legislation has not yet been challenged.

Traffic Data and Location Data

14.86 The CPCE defines traffic data as all the data which is processed so as to transmit a communication through a communication network or to charge for this communication.[144] It is however questionable whether this definition is consistent with the 2009 EU Regulatory Framework. Traffic data is rendered anonymous by

---

136 Art 242(5) and (7) CSI.
137 Art 245(1) to (3) CSI.
138 Art L34(1) CPCE.
139 Ordonnance No 2011–1012 dated 24 August 2011.
140 Art 32(II) Act No 78–17 dated 6 January 1978.
141 Art 226(13), 226(15) and 432(9) *Code Pénal*.
142 Decree No 2006–358 dated 24 March 2006.
143 Act No 78–17 dated 6 January 1978.
144 Art L32(18) and R10(12) CPCE.

providers of electronic communications. There are some provisions for exceptions to this requirement.

Traffic data can be processed under two exceptions:[145]

- If needed in criminal prosecutions by the judicial authorities, it can be stored for up to one year before being rendered anonymous. The National Commission for Information Technology and Liberties ('CNIL') oversees this operation and specifies which data can be stored and for how long.
- For billing purposes, operators can store and use traffic data over the period where the bill can be legally challenged, that is one year. They can transmit this data to concerned third parties. This is all supervised by the CNIL. The operators can further process traffic data so as to market their own electronic communications services or to provide value added services if subscribers expressly give their consent.

Location data allows the localisation of the user's terminal equipment.[146]

Location data cannot be used during communication for any purpose other than the transmission of the communication. It can be stored and processed after the transmission only if the subscriber gives his consent after being properly informed about which data will be processed, for how long and that the data will not be transferred to third parties.[147] The subscriber must be able to withdraw his consent at any time, free of charge.

Traffic and location data that are stored and processed can only relate to the identification of users, the technical characteristics of the services provided by the operators and the localisation of terminal equipment. They cannot relate to the content of the information, irrespective of its form, consulted during those communications.

The conservation and processing of these data has to respect the provisions of Act No 78–17[148] 'relating to information technology, files and liberties'.

Itemised Billing

14.87   The CPCE provides that subscribers are entitled to receive itemised bills free of charge if they request it.[149] When such a request is made, the bills must contain sufficient details which permit the verification of the sums billed. It should not mention the calls that are free of charge for the user and it should not display the last four digits of dialled numbers unless the customer asked for it.[150]

The customer has a choice in the way in which dialled numbers are displayed on his bills: either the last four digits of the numbers are displayed, or they are hidden. The operator must be able to provide both.[151]

---

145   Arts L34(1)(II), (III), and R10(14) CPCE.
146   Art L34(1)(IV) CPCE.
147   Art L34(1)(IV) CPCE.
148   Act No 78–17 dated 6 January 1978.
149   Arts D98 (5)(II)(1) CPCE and R20(30)(1)(III) CPCE for the universal service.
150   Art D98(5)(II)(2) CPCE.
151   Art D98(5)(II)(2) CPCE.

Calling and Connected Line Identification

14.88 CPCE asserts that the operator must inform subscribers that it offers calling and connected line identification.[152] When calling line identification is offered, the operator must enable the subscriber to choose whether he wants the service or not through a simple, free of charge method. When connected line identification is offered, the operator must permit the user to prevent the identification of his line, either on a permanent or call-by-call basis. Furthermore, when calling line identification is offered and is indicated before the call is made, the user must be able to block access to non-identified incoming calls.

Automatic Call Forwarding

14.89 The operator must enable the user to whom calls are transferred to interrupt or have interrupted this service by a simple, free of charge method.[153]

Directories of Subscribers

14.90 The publication of subscriber lists is free but is subject to the protection of individual rights.[154] Every user can choose whether or not he appears in the directory. Users can also prevent certain personal data from being displayed in the directory.[155] Users can prohibit the use of their personal data in marketing operations and must be able to alter, update, withdraw or clarify their personal data, as provided for by Act No 78–17.[156] Pre-paid subscribers who do not have any contractual relationship with their operator can still be included in the directory upon request to the operator. Mobile subscribers need to give their consent in order to be included in any directory being compiled by the operator or information service.[157] The lists obtained for the compilation of a directory cannot be used for any other purpose, nor can they be sold.[158]

Unsolicited Communications

14.91 Act No 2004–575[159] has implemented new provisions concerning unsolicited communications into the CPCE. Under the new regime, unsolicited communications to a natural person, irrespective of their nature, are prohibited unless the addressee has given their prior and express consent. However, when it comes to unsolicited messages for legal entities, prior consent is not needed if the message is sent to a professional address. But if a professional's email address can allow their identification, then their prior consent must be sought.

French law also specifies that messages can be sent to a professional without their prior consent if the message is directly linked to their professional activity.

---

152 Art D98(5)(II)(4) CPCE.
153 Art D98(5)(II)(5) CPCE.
154 Art L34 CPCE.
155 Art R10 CPCE.
156 Act No 78–17 dated 6 January 1978.
157 Art L34 CPCE.
158 Art R10(4) CPCE.
159 Art 22 Act No 2004–575 dated 21 June 2004.

There exists one exception to the general prohibition: if a person has previously entered into a contract with an entity for similar products and services, the latter may contact them again for marketing purposes. Of course, the person must be given the possibility to prevent this eventuality at the time of the said transaction.[160]

---

160 Art 22(II) Act No 2004–575 dated 21 June 2004.

The German Market for Electronic Communications[1]

Joachim Scherer and Caroline Heinickel
Baker & McKenzie, Frankfurt

LEGAL STRUCTURE

Basic Policy

15.1 The German market for electronic communication services is characterised by lively competition both between mobile and fixed network operators and among operators within the mobile and fixed telecommunications markets.[2]

In the market for fixed telephony, the former incumbent operator Telekom Deutschland GmbH (formerly Deutsche Telekom AG ('Telekom')) is faced with strong competition. The classic PSTN connections are being slowly replaced by Voice over IP ('VoIP') telephony via (unbundled) DSL and TV cable. In 2011, the market share in the fixed telephony market held by Telekom's competitors (more than 150 alternative network operators and several cable operators) increased to 37.9 per cent (from 20 per cent in 2004). At the end of 2011, Telecom's competitors had a market share of 55 per cent with respect to broadband connections. Fixed broadband penetration in Germany reached 32.7 per cent in the first half of 2011 (as compared to 27.2 per cent as an EU average). At the end of 2011, 99 per cent of German households had access to broadband connections with a minimum bandwidth of 1 Mbit/s.

In 2011, the four mobile communications operators in Germany achieved 140 per cent market penetration, increasing the number of users to approximately 114 million. In the third quarter of 2012, the market shares based on subscribers were approximately as follows – Telefónica Germany GmbH & Co OHG (formerly O2 Germany): 16.7 per cent, E-Plus Mobilfunk GmbH & Co KG: 21 per cent, Vodafone D2 GmbH: 30.7 per cent and Telekom (formerly T-Mobile GmbH): 31.5 per cent.

All four mobile operators offer services that allow their users to be called under a fixed-network telephone number. At the end of 2011, about 6.5 million mobile users used a fixed-network number via their mobile plans. In 2011, the amount of mobile minutes reached 107 billion, which represents a growth of about 5 per cent from

---

1   Editing of this chapter closed on 30 January 2013.
2   The following is based on the Federal Network Agency's Annual Report 2011 and the current market data published on the Federal Network Agency's homepage.

2010. This shows that fixed-to-mobile substitution is a growing concern for fixed network operators.

The percentage of mobile customers which regularly use UMTS-services has increased to 28.6 per cent in 2011. Currently, all four mobile operators heavily invest in mobile broadband infrastructure. At the end of 2011, about 3000 mobile base stations were equipped to be operated under the LTE-standard.

15.2 The German NRA was formerly known as the Regulatory Authority for Telecommunications and Post (*Regulierungsbehörde für Telekommunikation und Post* ('RegTP'), and was renamed, in July 2005, the Federal Network Agency for Electricity, Gas, Telecommunications, Post and Railways – Federal Network Agency (*Bundesnetzagentur für Elektrizität, Gas, Telekommunikation, Post und Eisenbahnen* ('BNetzA')).

The BNetzA defines its regulatory objectives with respect to the telecommunications sector annually in its Strategic Plan which is published, after public consultation, as part of the BNetzA's Annual Report.[3]

The BNetzA's current strategic objectives include, among other things, the promotion of broadband infrastructure roll-out, the regulation of mobile and fixed termination fees in accordance with the Commission's Termination Recommendation,[4] the prosecution of abuses of numbering resources[5] and unsolicited communications[6], frequency management and flexibilisation,[7] and actively participating in the work of BEREC.

In regulating the German electronic communications markets, the BNetzA, in accordance with the EU regulatory framework, follows the principle of proportionality and prioritises the regulation of wholesale markets before any regulation of retail markets.

15.3 One of the major upcoming challenges for the BNetzA is the (re-)assignment of the former GSM frequencies in the 900 MHz and 1800 MHz bands whose current assignment to the four German mobile network operators terminates on 31 December 2016.

After public consultation in May 2012, the BNetzA has published four possible scenarios for the assignment of the former GSM spectrum and other spectrum bands, including the 700 MHz band.[8]

In its consultation paper, the BNetzA has developed four scenarios:[9]

---

3   Available in German at: http://www.bundesnetzagentur.de/SharedDocs/Downloads/DE/
     BNetzA/Presse/Berichte/2012/Jahresbericht2011pdf.pdf?__blob=publicationFile
4   Commission Recommendation of 7 May 2009 on the Regulatory Treatment of Fixed and
     Mobile Termination Rates in the EU, OJ L 124/67, 20.5.2009 ('Termination Recommendation'); see at para 15.78 below.
5   See para 15.62 below.
6   See para 15.117 below.
7   See para 15.55 et seq below.
8   http://www.bundesnetzagentur.de/SharedDocs/Downloads/DE/BNetzA/Sachgebiete/Telekom
     munikation/Regulierung/Frequenzordnung/OeffentlicherMobilfunk/DrahtloserNetzzugang/
     Projekt2016/SzenarienpapierProjekt2016_pdf.pdf?__blob=publicationFile (German).
9   Further information is available at http://www.bundesnetzagentur.de/cln_1911/EN/Areas/
     Telecommunications/TelecomsRegulation/FrequencyManagement/ElectronicCommunication
     sServices/DemandIdentificationProceedings_Basepage.html;jsessionid=2E65ECDEE17D405
     8FC9B620741273779 (English).

- extension of the existing frequency assignments for 900/1800 MHz frequencies until 2020/2025;
- frequency assignments with respect to the 900/1800 MHz frequencies three years prior to the termination of the current assignments;
- frequency assignments with respect to the 900/1800 MHz frequencies together with other available frequencies, which may include spectrum at 700 MHz, 1452–1492 MHz, 2 GHz (available in 2017) and 3.5 GHz (available in 2022); and
- joint assignment (possibly in 2023) of the entire wireless access frequency spectrum (400 MHz – 4 GHz) after 31 December 2025. This scenario would require that all existing frequency assignments ('frequency licenses') for the mobile wireless spectrum terminate by the end of 2025.

Implementation of EU Directives

15.4   The EU Regulatory Framework as amended by the 2009 Regulatory Package[10] has been transposed into German law with the Telecommunications Act of 22 June 2004 (*Telekommunikationsgesetz* ('TKG')) as last amended by the Act for the Amendment of the Telecommunications Law Provisions,[11] which entered into force in May 2012, almost one year after the transposition deadline as mandated by EU law.[12]

The TKG follows the regulatory approach of the EU Regulatory Package by granting broad decision-making powers as well as broad discretion to the BNetzA.

Legislation

15.5   The TKG is the main legislative act governing electronic communications in Germany. It is complemented by a number of ordinances (*Rechtsverordnungen*)[13], which have been adopted by the executive branch of government on the basis of the TKG and have the force of law. Furthermore, the BNetzA is entitled to pass orders in certain areas, eg in the context of numbering regulation[14] and frequency management,[15] which have a binding effect.

---

10   The 2009 Regulatory Package comprises two directives, the 'Better Regulation Directive' 2009/140/EC amending the Framework Directive, the Access Directive and the Authorisation Directive as well as the 'Citizens' Rights Directive' 2009/136/EC amending in particular the Universal Services Directive and the e-Privacy Directive; for further details see at 1.6 above.
11   Federal Gazette (*Bundesgesetzblatt* ('BGBl')) I 2004, 1190, last amended BGBl I 2012, 958. For a summary of the 2012 amendments to the TKG, cf Scherer/Heinickel, Die TKG Novelle 2012, NVwZ 2012, 585.
12   The 2009 EU Regulatory Package was due for transposition into national law by 25 May 2011.
13   These include: the Frequency Fee Ordinance· BGBl I 2000, 1704, last amended by BGBl I 2005, 1970; the Ordinance on Charges to Secure Interference-free Use of Frequencies, BGBl I 2004, 958, last amended by BGBl I 2012, 1815; the Telecommunications Numbering Ordinance, BGBl I 2008, 141; the Telecommunications Numbering Fee Ordinance, BGBl I 1999, 1887 last amended by BGBl I2010, 582; and the Ordinance on Emergency Connections, BGBl. I 2009, 481, last amended by BGBl. I 2012, 2347.
14   See paras 15.57 et seq below.
15   See paras 15.40 et seq below.

REGULATORY PRINCIPLES: IMPLEMENTATION OF THE FRAMEWORK DIRECTIVE

Scope of Regulation

15.6   The TKG governs 'telecommunications' (the German equivalent of 'electronic communications'), which is defined as the technical process of sending, transmitting and receiving signals by means of telecommunications systems.[16] Telecommunications systems are technical facilities or equipment capable of sending, transmitting, switching, receiving, steering or controlling electromagnetic or optical signals identifiable as messages.[17] Whereas the Federal Government is competent for the regulation of 'telecommunications', most content-related regulation, particularly in the area of radio and television broadcasting, is governed by legislation of the Federal States (State Broadcasting Treaty – *Rundfunkstaatsvertrag*). Telemedia (eg online shops) are subject to the Telemedia Act (*Telemediengesetz*) for which the legislative power lies with the Federal Government. Telemedia with journalistic and editorial content (eg Internet newspapers) are, in addition to that, subject to provisions of the State Broadcasting Treaty for which the legislative power lies with the Federal States.[18]

The definitions of the terms 'telecommunications services', 'telecommunications network' and 'public telecommunications network' broadly correspond with the definitions set out in Article 2(a), (c) and (d) of the Framework Directive.[19]

15.7   Where complex, convergent services[20] are concerned, it may be difficult to clearly qualify the service as either telecommunications service or content service. In the BNetzA's practice, where a service has elements of both telecommunications and content/ media services, telecommunication and media law apply to each of the respective service element(s).

15.8   The BNetzA has found that VoIP services that are not entirely confined to the IP networks they are provided over but allow for a breakout to the public telephony network ('PSTN-breakout') and thereby enable any-to-any-connections into national/international fixed networks are substitutes for traditional PSTN calls.[21] The German regulatory practice considers VoIP Services that are (partial) substitutes for PSTN Services as publicly available telephony services ('PATS').

---

16   S 3 no 22 TKG.
17   S 3 no 23 TKG.
18   BGBl. I 2007, 179.
19   S 3 no 24 TKG defines telecommunications services as 'services normally provided for remuneration consisting in, or having as their principle feature, the conveyance of signals by means of telecommunications networks and includes transmission services in networks used for broadcasting'. The term 'telecommunications network' is defined as 'transmission systems and, where applicable, switching or routing equipment and other resources, including non-active network elements, which permit the conveyance of signals by wire, by radio, by optical or by other electromagnetic means, including satellite networks, fixed circuit and packet switched networks including the internet, and mobile terrestrial networks, electricity cable systems, to the extent that they are used for the purpose of transmitting signals, networks used for radio and television broadcasting, and cable television networks, irrespective of the type of information conveyed' (S 3 no 27 TKG). S 3 no 16a TKG defines the term 'public telecommunications network' as 'a telecommunications network used wholly or mainly for the provision of electronic communications services available to the public which supports the transfer of information between network termination points'.
20   See at 1.7 above.
21   See BNetzA, Market definition and analysis regarding the markets for access to the public

'Internet Freedom'

15.9 At present, there are no specific provisions in Germany that allow the imposition of measures restricting end user's access to the Internet and no such measures are planned.[22]

National Regulatory Authority: Organisation, Regulatory Objectives, Competencies

Overview

15.10 The BNetzA is a higher Federal Authority responsible to the Federal Ministry of Economics and Technology ('BMWi'). It is the German regulatory body for the telecommunications and postal sectors and – as from 13 July 2005 – also for electricity and gas and railways.

With respect to European and international telecommunications policy, in particular as regards the participation in European and international institutions and organisations,[23] the BNetzA acts on behalf of the BMWi which remains the governmental body representing the Federal Government in European and international organisations.[24]

15.11 Although the BNetzA is part of the Federal Government and operates under the supervision of the BMWi, the TKG aims at ensuring a certain degree of independence of the BNetzA from political influences. In particular, the Ministry is obliged to publish all directives which it issues in relation to the BNetzA's regulatory tasks in the Federal Gazette.[25]

15.12 The BNetzA is run by a president who represents the BNetzA in and out of court, and lays down the administration and order of business by rules of procedure which require confirmation by the BMWi. The president and the two vice-presidents are nominated by the Federal Government upon the proposal of BNetzA's advisory council which, in turn, consists of 16 members of the German Bundestag and 16 representatives of the German Bundesrat.[26]

Regulatory objectives of BNetzA

15.13 BNetzA discharges the functions and exercises the powers that are assigned to it under the TKG. The aims of regulation, as stated in section 2 para 2 TKG, transpose Article 8 paras 2 to 4 of the Framework Directive. They are:

---

telephone network at a fixed location, public national calls at a fixed location and public international calls at a fixed location (ex markets 1–6), pp 8–11 and pp 60–70, Official Gazette 4/2010.

22 In January 2012 the BMWi published a study of possible measures to counter copyright infringements, accessible at: http://bmwi.de/BMWi/Redaktion/PDF/Publikationen/Tech nologie-und-Innovation/warnhinweise-lang,property=pdf,bereich=bmwi,sprache=de,rwb= true.pdf (German) which does not promote restrictions to Internet access as sanction as foreseen, e g under French law, see para 14.8 above.

23 Including the International Telecommunications Union ('ITU').

24 S 140 TKG; see also Act on the Federal Network Agency for Electricity, Gas, Telecommunications, Post and Railways, BGBl I 2005, 2009 as last amended by Art 2 of the law of 26.7.2011 BGBl I 2011, 1554 (the 'BNetzA Act').

25 S 117 TKG.

26 Ss 3, 5 BNetzA Act.

- to safeguard user, most notably consumer, interests in telecommunications and to safeguard telecommunications secrecy, this goal was extended to include an obligation of the BNetzA 'to promote the ability of the end customer to access and process information, or to use services and applications of their choice';[27]
- to secure fair competition and to promote telecommunications markets with sustainable competition in services and networks and in associated facilities and services, in rural areas as well;
- to promote development of the internal market of the European Union;
- to ensure provision throughout the Federal Republic of Germany of equivalent basic telecommunications services (universal services) at affordable prices;
- to speed-up the roll-out of high-speed next generation telecommunications networks;
- to promote telecommunications services in public institutions;
- to secure efficient and interference-free use of frequencies, account also being taken of broadcasting interests;
- to secure efficient use of numbering resources; and
- to protect public safety interests.

These regulatory aims are complemented by 'regulatory principles' which the BNetzA has to apply in the course of pursuing the regulatory aims. Section 2 para 3 TKG sets out a non-exhaustive list of these principles which closely follow Article 8 para 5 of the Framework Directive including:

- promoting regulatory predictability by applying consistent regulatory concepts over appropriate review periods;
- ensuring, that, in similar circumstances, that operators of telecommunications networks and providers of telecommunications services are not discriminated;
- safeguarding competition to the benefit of consumers and promoting, where appropriate, infrastructure-based competition;
- promoting efficient investment and innovation in new and enhanced infrastructures, inter alia by ensuring that any access obligation takes appropriate account of the risk incurred by the investing undertakings and by permitting various cooperative arrangements between investors and parties seeking access to diversify the risk of investment, whilst ensuring that competition in the market and the principle of non-discrimination are preserved;
- taking due account of the variety of conditions relating to competition and consumers that exist in the various geographic areas within Germany;
- imposing ex-ante regulatory obligations only where there is no effective and sustainable competition and relaxing or lifting such obligations as soon as that condition is fulfilled.

The latter regulatory principle confirming the subsidiarity of ex-ante regulation will, in practice, only have a clarifying function should the BNetzA continue to revoke remedies[28] if they find during their review of an existing market definition

---

27   As a consequence of this extension, 'net neutrality' is now codified as a Regulatory Aim in German telecommunications law, albeit in a rather generic way. Due to the reference to 'end customers', this objective is not limited to consumer services but also relevant for providers of services to business customers. For further details on securing 'net neutrality', see para 15.103 below.

28   S 13(1) TKG.

and analysis that a market should not be subject to further regulation. [29] This principle could, however, become of relevance should the BNetzA deem it necessary to extensively 'loosen' regulatory measures as soon as the BNetzA recognizes that competitive developments on a given market can be observed.

Tasks and competences of the BNetzA

15.14 The tasks and competences of the BNetzA are defined in the TKG. Its main tasks include the definition of relevant telecommunications markets warranting ex ante regulation, conducting market analyses with a view to determine whether there is effective competition in the relevant market,[30] the adoption of 'regulatory orders' (*Regulierungsverfügungen*) imposing remedies on operators with significant market power, [31] and the management of numbering[32] and frequency [33] resources.

15.15 Other tasks include consumer protection in the telecommunications sector,[34] the granting of rights of way for telecommunications lines and mandating shared use of infrastructure where applicable,[35] ensuring the provision of universal services,[36] dispute resolution,[37] safeguarding telecommunications secrecy and data protection and ensuring safety of telecommunications.[38]

Powers of the BNetzA

15.16 The BNetzA has broad powers to ensure compliance with the provisions of the TKG by taking remedial action. In the case of serious or repeated breaches of obligations by an undertaking or failure to comply with measures for remedial action ordered by the BNetzA, the undertaking may be prohibited from operating its telecommunications network or providing telecommunications services.[39] Furthermore, the BNetzA is empowered to impose fines for violations of specific provisions of the TKG[40] as well as to impose measures to secure compliance with numbering-related rules.[41]

In addition, BNetzA may request, from network operators and service providers, the provision of any information that is required for the execution of the TKG. This includes information for the systematic or case-by-case verification of compliance with obligations ensuing from or by virtue of the TKG. The BNetzA may also request information for the purposes of case-by-case verification of compliance with obligations when the BNetzA has received a complaint or has other reasons to assume non-compliance with obligations or when it has opened investigations on its

---

29 See para 15.30 below.
30 See para 15.29 et seq below.
31 See para 15.32 below.
32 See para 15.40 et seq below.
33 See para 15.57 et seq below.
34 See para 15.96 et seq below.
35 See para 15.33 et seq below.
36 See para 15.85 et seq below.
37 See para 15.22 below.
38 See para 15.106 et seq below.
39 S 126(3) TKG; cf para 15.18 below.
40 S 115(2) TKG.
41 S 67 (1) TKG.

own initiative. Furthermore, the BNetzA is entitled to request information for the publication of comparative overviews, and information on quality and price of service for the benefit of end users, statistical purposes, market definition or market analysis procedures.[42] The BNetzA is also entitled to request, from operators of telecommunications networks and from undertakings and legal entitics under public law which have facilities suitable for the use for telecommunications purposes, information which is necessary to compile a public register on these facilities.[43]

Representatives of the BNetzA are entitled to have access to the offices and business premises of undertakings and associations of undertakings during normal business or working hours; searches, however, may be carried out solely by order of the local court.[44]

The BNetzA may conduct formal investigations and take evidence, including testimonies and expert opinions,[45] and it may seize objects which may be important as evidence in its investigations.[46]

15.17   The BNetzA's decisions relating to market regulation and its decisions mandating the shared use of infrastructure, decisions regarding the assignment of frequencies in situations of frequency scarcity, decisions in frequency award proceedings, on spectrum trading, and on the imposition of universal service obligations are issued by the BNetzA's Ruling Chambers.

The Ruling Chambers are decision-making bodies which consist of a chairman and two assessors. The chairman and the assessors shall be qualified to hold office in the senior administrative grade of the civil service and at least one member of the Ruling Chamber shall be qualified to exercise the functions of a judge.[47] The Ruling Chambers institute proceedings on their own initiative or upon a motion. Participants in the proceedings are the person presenting the motion, the network operators and service providers against whom the proceedings are directed and persons and associations of persons whose interests are likely to be affected by the decision and to whom BNetzA has sent a summons to attend proceedings in response to their request.[48] The Ruling Chamber takes its decisions on the basis of public oral proceedings; subject to the consent of the parties concerned, it can take its decisions without oral proceedings.[49] The parties concerned have a right to be heard and, where appropriate, the Ruling Chamber may give persons representing 'business circles affected by the proceedings', such as industry associations, the opportunity to state their views.[50]

The BNetzA's enforcement powers

15.18   BNetzA has general powers to enforce the obligations of network operators and service providers set out in the TKG which apply in such cases where the TKG

---

42   S 127(1) TKG.
43   S 77a(3) TKG.
44   S 127(6) TKG.
45   S 128 TKG.
46   S 129 TKG.
47   S 132 TKG.
48   S 134 TKG.
49   S 135(3) TKG.
50   S 135(1), (2) TKG.

does not grant the BNetzA more specific enforcement powers (eg to revoke frequency or numbering assignments[51]).

Under the TKG's general enforcement provision, where the BNetzA finds that an undertaking is failing to meet its obligations by or under the TKG, it shall require the undertaking to state its views and to take remedial action within a given time limit.[52] If the undertaking fails to meet its obligations within the time limit set, the BNetzA may order such measures as are necessary to secure compliance with the obligations concerned. Again, the BNetzA has to set a reasonable time limit to allow the undertaking to comply with the measures. In case of serious or repeated breaches of obligations by the undertaking or failure to comply with an order for remedial action, the BNetzA may prohibit the undertaking from acting as a network operator or service provider;[53] for reasons of proportionality such prohibition can only be issued as a 'last resort' measure. The BNetzA may take provisional measures where a breach of obligations constitutes a direct and serious threat to public safety and order, or where a violation of duties creates serious economic and operational problems for other providers or users of telecommunications networks or services. If provisional measures have been taken, the BNetzA has to give the undertaking concerned the opportunity to state its views within a reasonable period and to decide whether the provisional measures shall be confirmed, withdrawn or modified.[54]

To enforce its orders against non-compliant undertakings, the BNetzA may impose an administrative enforcement fine of up to €500,000.

Regulatory concepts

15.19 Section 15a TKG enables the BNetzA to pass so called 'regulatory concepts' in the form of administrative rules (*Verwaltungsvorschriften*) with an aim to further the predictability of regulation. This provision has been introduced particularly with a view to supporting investment in next generation network infrastructure.[55] Whether or not such regulatory concepts will be suitable to create or increase planning certainty for investors will largely depend on the BNetzA's practice since administrative rules are not legally binding and only result in a 'certain self-commitment of the BNetzA with regard to its regulatory practice'.[56]

The BNetzA's cooperation duties on the national level

15.20 In specified cases, the BNetzA must cooperate with the Federal Cartel Office (*Bundeskartellamt* ('BKartA')) which is competent for the regulation of all markets that are not subject to ex ante regulation but to ex post control under general competition law, and with the State Media Authorities, ie the authorities, at State level, which are in charge of the regulation of radio and television broadcasting and media services.[57]

---

51   See paras 15.49 and 15.62 below.
52   S 126(1) TKG.
53   S 126(3) TKG.
54   S 126(5) TKG.
55   See para 1.37 above.
56   BT-Drs. 17/5707, p 56.
57   S 123 TKG.

In relation to the definition of telecommunications markets, the market analysis,[58] decisions relating to functional separation, decisions regarding the exclusion of an applicant from participation in frequency award proceedings and establishing the terms and conditions for frequency trading, BNetzA is required to take its decisions 'in agreement' with the BKartA. Where the BNetzA takes decisions on specific remedies, on anti competitive practices or on mandated infrastructure-sharing, it is obliged to give the BKartA the opportunity to state its views 'in good time before closure of the case'.[59]

The national consultation procedure

15.21   The BNetzA is in charge of conducting the national consultation and consolidation procedures[60] in conjunction with the market definition, market analysis and the imposition of remedies. In accordance with Article 6 of the Framework Directive, the TKG provides that a public consultation procedure shall also be conducted in the case of all measures 'having a 'significant impact' on the relevant market'.[61]

Dispute resolution

15.22   In addition to its regulatory tasks, the BNetzA also acts as a dispute resolution body. In the event of a dispute arising in connection with obligations under the TKG between undertakings operating public telecommunications networks or offering publicly available telecommunications services or between such undertakings and other undertakings which benefit from access or interconnection obligations under the TKG, the BNetzA – acting through its Ruling Chambers[62] – is empowered to issue a binding decision to resolve the dispute at the request of either party and after consultation with the parties concerned. In the case of such a dispute, the Ruling Chamber is obliged to adopt its decision within a period not exceeding four months, from the date of the request from one of the parties concerned.[63] In the event of a dispute arising between undertakings in different Member States where such dispute falls within the competence of the NRAs of more than one Member State, any of the parties may refer the dispute to the NRA concerned. In this case, the Ruling Chamber is obliged to take its decision in consultation with the NRA concerned as well as to coordinate its measures with the other competent NRAs.[64] The BNetzA may also consult the Body of European Regulators for Electronic Communications ('BEREC') in such cases.[65]

Right of Appeal against NRA's Decisions

15.23   In accordance with the general rules of German constitutional and administrative law and procedure, not only the decisions of BNetzA's Ruling Chambers,

58   See para 15.28 et seq below.
59   S 123(1) sentence 1 TKG.
60   Ss 12 et seq TKG.
61   S 15 TKG.
62   See para 15.17 above.
63   S 133(1) TKG.
64   S 133(2) TKG.
65   BEREC was established by Regulation (EC) No 1211/2009 of and of the Council of 25 November 2009 establishing the Body of European Regulators for Electronic Communications (BEREC) and the Office [2009] OJ L337/1..

but any administrative act issued by the BNetzA and any other BNetzA action which adversely affects an individual's or a company's right, are subject to court review.[66]

15.24   Decisions of the BNetzA are subject to judicial review by the administrative courts. In an attempt to accelerate the judicial review procedure, section 137 TKG provides that decisions of the administrative court of first instance which relate to decisions by the BNetzA's Ruling Chambers[67] are not, as are most decisions of the administrative courts, subject to appeal on issues of fact and law before the Superior Administrative Court, but merely subject to appeals on procedural issues before the Federal Administrative Court. Furthermore, decisions of the BNetzA's Ruling Chambers are not subject to the administrative appeal procedure.

15.25   Administrative appeals and court actions against decisions of the BNetzA do not have suspensive effect. In accordance with the general rules of the Code of Administrative Court Procedure, however, a suspension of the BNetzA's decisions can be brought about by the BNetzA or, upon application, by the administrative court.

The NRA's Obligations to Co-operate with the Commission

15.26   The consolidation procedure set out in Article 7 of the Framework Directive has been transposed into German law, which requires that this procedure shall take place prior to the BNetzA's final decision on:

- the definition of a telecommunications market warranting regulation;
- the determination whether there is effective competition in the market being analysed and which undertaking is deemed to have significant market power;
- the imposition of remedies as a result of the market analysis; and
- the imposition of remedies in the case of trans-national markets.[68]

The consolidation procedure is initiated by the BNetzA making available its proposals to the Commission and to the NRAs of the other Member States. The BNetzA is obliged not to give effect to its proposals prior to the expiry of the deadlines set out in Article 7 para 3, 7a of the Framework Directive.[69]

In taking its final decision, the BNetzA is obliged to take the utmost account of the comments of the Commission and of the NRAs and to communicate the resulting draft to the Commission.

15.27   With respect to regulatory decisions which are subject to the Commission's veto powers,[70] detailed procedural rules apply, which reflect the provisions of Article 7 para 4 of the Framework Directive. Where the Commission takes a decision requiring the BNetzA to withdraw its draft, the BNetzA is bound by such decision. It may again consult the parties concerned on the Commission's decision. Where the BNetzA wishes to accept the amendments proposed by the Commission, it shall amend the draft in accordance with the Commission's decision and submit the amended draft to the Commission. Otherwise, it shall inform the BMWi of the

---

66   This follows from article 19 para 3 of the German Constitution.
67   See para 15.16 above.
68   S 12(2), (3), 13 (1) TKG.
69   See paras 1.55 et seq above.
70   See paras 1.55 et seq above.

Commission's decision.[71] It is then up to the BMWi to decide whether or not to bring an action against the Commission's decision before the European Court of Justice.

With regard to the imposition of remedies Sec. 13 (4) TKG transposes the procedure for the consistent application of remedies set out in Article 7a of the Framework Directive.[72]

'Significant Market Power' as a Fundamental Prerequisite of Regulation

Definition of significant market power

15.28 The TKG defines, in line with Article 16 para 2, 4 of the Framework Directive, the existence of effective competition in terms of the market power of the undertakings that are active in the relevant market. Effective competition is deemed absent if one or more undertakings have significant market power ('SMP') in a relevant market.[73] The definition of SMP is almost identical to the terminology of Article 16 para 4 of the Framework Directive. An undertaking is deemed to have significant market power if, either individually or jointly with others, it enjoys a position equivalent to dominance, ie a position of economic strength affording it the power to behave to an appreciable extent independently of competitors and end users.[74]

Definition of relevant markets and designation of SMP

15.29 The TKG's regulatory approach follows the concept of Articles 15 and 16 of the Framework Directive. On the basis of a market definition and a subsequent market analysis, the BNetzA defines those markets that are not effectively competitive and which are therefore subject to regulation. Those markets where effective competition exists are not subject to sector-specific regulation but rather to general competition law.[75]

15.30 The BNetzA is obliged to identify the relevant product and geographic telecommunications markets warranting regulation under the TKG. This market definition must be reviewed at three-year intervals unless the BNetzA decides to exceptionally extend the review period to up to six years[76] or becomes aware that the current market definition is no longer in accordance with the realities of the respective market in which case the BNetzA reassesses the relevant market in question.[77] The TKG establishes three cumulative criteria for relevant markets that are subject to regulation. Potentially subject to regulation are markets:

* with high, non-transitory entry barriers of a structural or legal nature;
* which do not tend towards effective competition within the relevant time horizon; and

---

71   S 12(2)(3) TKG.
72   See para 1.58 above.
73   S 11(1) sentence 2 TKG.
74   S 11(1) sentence 3 TKG.
75   S 2(4) TKG.
76   S 14(2) TKG.
77   S 14(1) TKG.

- in respect of which the application of competition law alone would not adequately address the market failure concerned. [78]

In defining those markets, the BNetzA has discretion which is subject to limited court review only.[79] In identifying the markets that are subject to regulation, the BNetzA is obliged to 'take the utmost account' of the Market Recommendation.[80]

15.31 To date, BNetzA has concluded its market analysis of all markets identified in the 2007 Market Recommendation[81] and has imposed remedies on SMP undertakings in these markets. In all fixed line wholesale markets (markets 2 to 6), the BNetzA has found the former incumbent Deutsche Telekom AG (now Telekom Deutschland GmbH) to have SMP. Additionally, on markets 2 and 3, all alternative access network operators have been designated as SMP providers. In regulating markets 2 and 3, the BNetzA has applied the 'one network, one market' approach and concluded that each network operator has 100 per cent market share for call termination in their network.

On the only regulated wholesale mobile market, market 7, the BNetzA has found the four German mobile network operators, Telekom Deutschland GmbH, Telefónica Germany GmbH & Co OHG, E-Plus Mobilfunk GmbH and Vodafone D2 GmbH to have SMP. Again, this finding is based on the 'one network, one market' approach. Additionally, the BNetzA has designated Lycamobile GmbH, a 'full' Mobile Virtual Network Operator ('MVNO'), ie an MVNO which enters into its own interconnection agreements and provides 'virtual' mobile call termination on this basis, to have SMP.

On the retail market 1 Deutsche Telekom AG has been designated with SMP.

On market 18 of the 2003 Commission Recommendation on relevant markets[82] the BNetzA has found four cable network operators to have SMP.

In German regulatory practice, the designation of SMP is not limited to the regulated undertaking as such but also to all undertakings of the SMP provider's company group which are active on the relevant markets.

All regulatory orders of the BNetzA (together with the underlying market definition and analysis) are available on the BNetzA's homepage in German language. [83]

15.32 The TKG provides that the BNetzA is obliged to impose one or more suitable remedies on undertakings which are designated to have SMP on a relevant market. In selecting the appropriate remedies, the BNetzA has broad administrative discretion, the scope of which is defined in the TKG's provisions on access regulation and on rate regulation.[84]

Exceptionally, BNetzA may, in justified cases, impose obligations on network operators which do not have significant market power, provided that such network operators control access to end users. Upon request, the network operator can be obliged to interconnect its network with those of other public network operators, as

---

78 S 10(2) TKG.
79 S 10(2) sentence 2 TKG ; see eg Federal Administrative Court, Decisions BVerwG, 6 C 14.07 to 17.07 of 2 April 2008 and BVerwG, 6 C 39.07 of 28 January 2009.
80 S 10(2) sentence 3 TKG, see also para 1.74 above.
81 See para 1.73 above.
82 See para 1.73 above.
83 http://www.bundesnetzagentur.de/cln_1931/DE/EinheitlicheInformationsstelle/ Einheitliche_Informationsstelle_node.html
84 See paras 15.70 et seq and 15.77 et seq below.

far as may be necessary to secure user communication, the provision of services and service interoperability.[85] In addition, the BNetzA may impose further access obligations on network operators controlling access to end users, as far as may be necessary to secure 'end-to-end connectivity'. The BNetzA has, so far, not imposed such obligations.

NRA's Regulatory Duties Concerning Rights of Way, Facility Sharing and Shared Use of Infrastructures

Rights of way

15.33   The right to use transport routes, including public ways, squares, bridges, and public waters, for telecommunications lines serving public purposes free of charge ('right of way'), lies with the German Federation.[86] The German Federation, acting through the BNetzA, transfers its rights of way to operators or owners of public telecommunications networks upon written application.[87] The right of use has to be granted if the applicant has the specialist knowledge, reliability and efficiency necessary to install telecommunications lines and if the transfer is in accordance with the regulatory aims. The right of use will be granted for the duration of the public activity; the BNetzA has to render its decision on complete applications within a period of six weeks.

15.34   The installation of new, and the modification of existing telecommunications lines requires the written consent of the authorities responsible for the construction and maintenance of public ways. The TKG does not favour the installation of overhead lines and requires that, in this case, the interests of the authorities responsible for public ways, of the network operators and the requirements of town planning shall be weighed. Where the installation can be coordinated under a comprehensive building project to be carried out close in time to the application for consent, lines shall typically be installed underground. The authorities in charge of public ways may grant their consent subject to non-discriminatory conditions which may, however, make stipulations solely on the way in which a telecommunications line is to be installed, the rules of engineering to be observed in doing so, the safety and ease of traffic, local documentation requirements, and traffic safety obligations.[88]

In using traffic ways for the installation of telecommunication lines, any hindrance to their maintenance and any temporary restriction of their use is to be avoided as far as possible; where maintenance is hindered, the party enjoying the right of use is obliged to reimburse the party liable for maintenance for costs arising from the hindrance. After completion of work on the telecommunication lines, the transport route has to be restored without undue delay at the expense of the party enjoying the right of use unless the party liable for the maintenance has declared its willingness to undertake restoration itself. Any expenses incurred in the course of the restoration must be reimbursed by the party enjoying the right of use.[89] Trees planted on and around traffic ways are to be protected as far as possible and the

---

85   See para 15.82 below.
86   S 68(1) TKG.
87   S 69(1) TKG.
88   S 68(3) TKG.
89   S 71 TKG.

cutting-down of such trees may be required only to the extent necessary to install the telecommunications line or to prevent interruption of service.[90]

15.35   The use of private property is subject to negotiation and private agreement, under Civil Law, between the network operator and the private landowner unless the private property is subject to mandated infrastructure sharing.[91] A private landowner cannot prohibit the installation, operation or renewal of telecommunications lines on his property in so far as:

- an existing line or installation (eg an electricity line) that is secured by a right (either a contractual right or an easement) is used also for the installation, operation or renewal of a telecommunications line and the usability of the property is not thereby additionally restricted on a lasting basis; or
- the property is not, or is not significantly, affected by such use.[92]

Facility sharing and shared use of infrastructure

15.36   Section 70 TKG provides for a right of network operators to the 'shared use' of installations intended for the accommodation of telecommunications cables. Where it is not possible, or is possible only at disproportionately high expense, to establish new telecommunication lines, other operators are obliged to acquiesce in the shared use of existing installations, provided that the shared use is economically reasonable and no major additional construction work is needed. In this case, the party enjoying the right of shared use is obliged to pay adequate compensation to the party obliged to grant shared use.

Section 77a TKG which transposes Article 12 of the Framework Directive entitles the BNetzA to mandate the shared use of cables and cable ducts in buildings or outside buildings up to the first distribution or concentration point where a duplication of the infrastructure would be economically unfeasible or practically impossible. The obligation to allow for the shared use of such infrastructure may be imposed on the owners of cables or cable ducts, on operators of telecommunications networks who have been granted rights of way or a similar usage right or who are entitled to benefit from proceedings aimed at the expropriation or usage of immovable property. When mandating the shared use of cables or cable ducts the BNetzA has to set an appropriate usage fee which may be appropriately adjusted for risks.

According to Section 77b TKG, undertakings and legal entities under public law which have facilities suitable for the installation and extension of next generation networks are obliged to provide operators of public telecommunications networks with an offer for the shared use of such facilities against appropriate remuneration upon written request. In case that the parties do not agree on the conditions for the shared usage of such facilities they may approach the BNetzA for dispute settlement; however, the parties are not obliged to accept the BNetzA's settlement decision.

Furthermore, operators of public telecommunications networks are entitled to request the shared use of Federal highways, public railways and Federal waterways (Sections 77c-77e TKG).

---

90   S 73 TKG.
91   See para 15.36.
92   S 76(1) TKG.

15.37   Section 77a para 3 TKG imposes an information obligation on telecommunications operators as well as on undertakings or legal entities under public law which are in possession of facilities which can be used for telecommunications purposes. These information obligations are intended to strengthen the role of the so-called 'infrastructure atlas' which is maintained by the BNetzA in order to gather information on the existing infrastructure in Germany which can be used for the roll-out of next generation access networks (NGA) and which was previously based on voluntary contributions.

REGULATION OF MARKET ENTRY: IMPLEMENTATION OF THE AUTHORISATION DIRECTIVE

The General Authorisation of Electronic Communications

15.38   In accordance with the provisions of the Authorisation Directive, the TKG does not provide for a prior approval for the operation of telecommunications networks or the provision of telecommunications services.[93] Network operators and service providers are merely obliged to notify the BNetzA without undue delay of beginning to provide services, of changing the service provision or ceasing to provide services as well as of any changes in their undertaking.[94] Upon request, the BNetzA confirms within a period of one week that the notification is complete and certifies that the undertaking has the rights granted by or under the TKG.[95] At regular intervals, the BNetzA publishes a list of notified undertakings. A failure to file a notification or the filing of a false, incomplete or otherwise wrongful notification, as well as the delayed filing of a notification, are administrative offences subject to a fine.

15.39   The TKG establishes a number of obligations which apply, by operation of law, to specific categories of operators: for example, all public telecommunications network operators and providers of publicly available telecommunications services are obliged to provide the BNetzA, upon request, with all information that it requires to fulfil its reporting requirements in relation to the Commission and other international bodies.[96] All providers of publicly available telephone services are obliged to provide all users with access to emergency services by using, free of charge, the single European emergency call number '112' and additional national emergency call numbers set out in an ordinance.

Rights of Use for Radio Frequencies

Overview

15.40   Frequency management in Germany is based on the Frequency Ordinance ('*Frequenzverordnung*')[97] and on the Frequency Plan (*Frequenzplan*).[98] The Frequency Ordinance which requires the approval of the German Bundesrat sets out

---

93   For the prior approval ('assignment') requirement with respect to frequencies, see paras 15.41 et seq below.
94   S 6(1) TKG.
95   S 6(3) TKG.
96   S 4 TKG, S 108(1), sentence 2 TKG.
97   Replacing the National Table of Frequency Allocations.
98   Replacing the Frequency Usage Plan.

the frequency allocations for Germany and may include further specifications, taking into account applicable international agreements including the ITU's Radio Regulations, harmonisation at the EU level, and technical development.[99] In the Frequency Plan the BNetzA allocates, to the various frequency ranges, frequency usages and corresponding usage conditions, based on the provisions of the Frequency Ordinance.[100] The BNetzA publishes the Frequency Plan in its Official Gazette. With respect to mobile access spectrum, the TKG expressly provides for technology and service neutrality in setting out frequency usage and usage conditions.[101]

General authorisation and granting of individual rights

15.41   Each frequency usage requires a prior frequency assignment, unless otherwise provided in the TKG.[102] The frequency assignment is the authorisation given by the BNetzA or by operation of law to use particular frequencies under specified conditions in accordance with the Frequency Plan. A frequency assignment is not required where usage rights can be exercised by virtue of another statutory regulation.

15.42   Frequencies are assigned by administrative act, either ex-officio or upon application. Ex-officio assignments are 'general assignments' which allow for the use of particular frequencies by the general public or by a group of persons defined or capable of being defined by general characteristics (e g all operators of a specific type of radio installation). Such 'general assignments' are published in BNetzA's Official Gazette.[103] Where a general assignment is not possible, frequencies for particular usages are assigned by BNetzA to natural persons, legal entities and associations of persons upon application ('individual assignments'). This applies in particular in cases where the risk of harmful interference cannot otherwise be ruled out or if an individual assignment is necessary in order to secure efficient frequency use.

15.43   Applications for individual assignments which have to be made in text form[104] have to specify the area in which the frequencies are to be used. Furthermore, the applicant has to show that the subjective requirements for frequency assignment with regard to the efficient and interference-free use of frequencies and other conditions[105] are satisfied. The BNetzA is obliged to take a decision on a complete application for an individual assignment within a period of six weeks[106] and has to publish its decision.[107]

Frequencies are generally assigned subject to:

- their designation for the planned usage in the Frequency Usage Plan;
- their availability;

---

99   S 53(2) TKG.
100   S 54 TKG.
101   S 54(2) TKG.
102   S 55 TKG.
103   For a list of general assignments in force see http://www.bundesnetzagentur.de/cln_1912/DE/
Sachgebiete/Telekommunikation/RegulierungTelekommunikation/Frequenzordnung/Allge
meinzuteilungen/AllgemeinzuteilungenBasepage.html (German).
104   S 126b German Civil Act ('Bürgerliches Gesetzbuch' ('BGB')).
105   As specified in Part B of the Annex to the Authorisation Directive, cf para 1.112 above.
106   S 55(4) TKG.
107   S 55(3) TKG.

- their compatibility with other frequency usages; and
- their efficient and interference-free use by the applicant being secured.[108]

15.44   Applicants are not entitled to any particular frequency[109] and are obliged to notify BNetzA without undue delay of the beginning and the cessation of frequency usage.[110] They must also notify BNetzA of any change of name, change of address, change in ownership structure and any identity-preserving transformations.[111]

15.45   Changes in the frequency assignment are subject to BNetzA's prior approval; BNetzA has to approve of such change where the change does not lead to any distortions to competition of the relevant market and where an efficient and interference-free use of the respective frequencies is ensured.[112] Frequencies are typically assigned for a limited period and the time limit for the frequency usage must be appropriate to the service concerned and allow for an appropriate amortisation of investments. The BNetzA must extend the time limitation to the assignment upon request where the requirements for an individual assignment[113] continue to be fulfilled.[114]

15.46   A frequency assignment may be denied in full or in part where the use intended by the applicant is incompatible with the TKG's regulatory objectives.[115] Where the interests of the Federal States relating to broadcasting within their jurisdiction are concerned, BNetzA is obliged to consult with the competent state authority.[116]

Admissible conditions

15.47   Frequency assignments generally specify, in particular, the type and extent of the frequency usage as far as necessary to secure efficient and interference-free use of frequencies.

In order to secure the efficient and interference-free use of frequencies and to ensure that the regulatory objectives are fulfilled, frequency assignments may be made subject to specific conditions. Where, after assignment, it is established that usage is being significantly restricted on account of increased use of the radio spectrum or that considerable efficiency gains are possible on account of technological progress, the type and extent of the frequency usage may subsequently be modified.[117] The frequency assignment may contain references to the parameters for the receiving equipment on which BNetzA has based its specifications on the type and extent of the frequency usage.[118]

15.48   The TKG sets out special preconditions for the assignment of frequencies for broadcasting within the jurisdiction of the Federal States. In particular, BNetzA

---

108   S 55(5) TKG:
109   S 55(6) TKG.
110   S 55(8) TKG.
111   S 55(7) TKG.
112   Cf s 55(8) TKG.
113   Cf para 15.42 above.
114   Cf s 55(9) TKG.
115   Cf para 15.13 above.
116   S 55(5) TKG.
117   S 60(2) TKG.
118   S 60(3) sentence 1 TKG.

is obliged to consult with the relevant state authorities with respect to their coverage requirements and before using frequencies allocated to the broadcasting service for purposes other than broadcasting. Frequency usages of the Federal Ministry of Defence in the bands designated in the Frequency Usage Plan exclusively for military purposes do not require an assignment. Special conditions apply with regard to frequencies designated in the Frequency Usage Plan for public safety or radio communications.[119] The TKG allows for the assignment of frequencies to more than one party for shared use if frequency usage by one party alone is not expected to be efficient.[120]

15.49   Frequency assignments may be revoked where use of the assigned frequency for the intended purpose has not commenced within one year of the assignment or where the frequency has not been used for the intended purpose for more than one year.[121] Furthermore, frequency assignments may be revoked, among other things, if an obligation arising from the assignment is repeatedly violated, has not been fulfilled despite repeated requests for fulfilment, if competition or the introduction of new spectrum-efficient technologies is prevented or unreasonably hindered as a result of a scarcity of frequencies arising after the assignment, or if a distortion of competition in the relevant market is to be expected as a result of a change in ownership structure in the person of the assignee.[122] Furthermore, revocations are permissible in accordance with the general rules of the Administrative Procedure Act.[123]

Limitation of number of rights of use to be granted

15.50   In situations of frequency scarcity, ie where frequencies are not available for assignment in sufficient numbers or where more than one application has been made for particular frequencies, BNetzA may order, following a public hearing, that the frequency assignment be preceded by award proceedings.[124] Where such an order has been issued, BNetzA may, after hearing the parties concerned, either conduct an auction or invite tenders for the relevant frequencies. Decisions on the choice of proceedings, and the determinations and rules for the conduct of the proceedings, are to be published by BNetzA. The TKG provides that, as a general rule, award proceedings shall be conducted in the form of an auction, except where such proceedings are not likely to secure the regulatory objectives set out in the TKG.[125] This may be the case, in particular, when frequencies have already been assigned, without a prior auction or where an applicant can claim a legal right to preference for the frequencies to be assigned.

In practice, frequencies for the provision of mobile communications services are predominantly assigned by way of an auction. The most prominent recent example for this is the auction of the 'digital dividend' spectrum and further spectrum for wireless mobile access services which took place in April/May 2010.[126]

---

119 S 57(1) TKG.
120 S 58(1) TKG.
121 S 63(1) TKG.
122 S 63(2) TKG.
123 Cf Quaas, in Ruster (ed) *Business Transactions in Germany*, § 7.03 [2].
124 S 55(9) TKG.
125 See para 15.13 above.
126 Information on the auction rules and its outcome are available at http://www.bundesnetz

15.51   The objective of award proceedings (both auctions and tender proceedings) is to determine which of the applicants is or are best placed to make efficient use of the frequencies to be assigned. Prior to carrying out award proceedings, BNetzA is obliged to determine:

- the minimum specialist and other requirements to be met by applicants in order to qualify for the award proceedings;
- the relevant product and geographic market for which the frequencies to be assigned may be used in accordance with the Frequency Usage Plan;
- the basic spectrum package required for commencement of the telecommunications service, where necessary; and
- the frequency usage conditions, including the degree of coverage with the frequency usage and the time required to achieve such degree of coverage.[127]

15.52   If BNetzA decides to conduct an auction, it shall, prior to the award proceedings, detail the rules for conducting the auction; such rules must be objective, transparent and non-discriminatory and have regard to the interest of small and medium-sized enterprises. BNetzA is entitled to stipulate a minimum bid for participation in the auction.[128]

15.53   In the case of tender proceedings, BNetzA shall, prior to the award proceedings, determine the criteria against which tenderers' eligibility will be assessed. Such criteria include the tenderers' specialist knowledge and efficiency, the suitability of their plans for providing the telecommunications service for which the tender has been invited, and the promotion of sustainable competition in the market. Preference is to be given in the selection procedure to tenderers' ensuring a higher degree of coverage with the particular telecommunications service. Where the outcome of tendering shows several tenders to be equally well placed, the decision shall be made by drawing lots.[129]

Any commitment entered into by bidders in the course of an auction or by tenderers in the course of a tendering procedure becomes a constituent part of the frequency assignment.

15.54   BNetzA is empowered to charge fees and contributions for frequency assignments and usage. The exact charges are set out in the Frequency Fee Ordinance[130] and in the Ordinance on Charges to Secure Interference-free Use of Frequencies.[131]

Flexibilisation

15.55   BNetzA may, after a public hearing, release specific frequency bands for trading, lease or cooperative shared usage[132] based on pre-set conditions to enable a flexible use of frequencies.[133] The conditions of and the procedure for trading shall

---

agentur.de/cln_1912/EN/Areas/Telecommunications/TelecomsRegulation/FrequencyManage ment/ElectronicCommunicationsServices/FrequencyAward2010_Basepage.html (English).

127   S 61(3) TKG.
128   S 61(4) TKG.
129   S 61(5) TKG.
130   BGBl I 2000, 1704, last amended by BGBl I 2005, 1970.
131   BGBl I 2004, 958, last amended by BGBl I 2012, 1815.
132   See BNetzA, Notice 458/2010, Official Gazette 15/2010, pp 2730; BNetzA Notice 152/2005, Official Gazette 12/2005, pp 1021.
133   S 62(1) TKG.

ensure in particular that spectrum efficiency is increased or maintained, that the original award proceedings do not preclude frequency assignment, that no distortion of competition in the relevant markets is to be feared, that other legal conditions, in particular the conditions of use and international agreements on spectrum use, are complied with and, generally, that the regulatory objectives of the TKG are secured.[134] Decisions on the conditions of and the procedure for spectrum trading are to be published. The proceeds from spectrum trading, less the administrative costs incurred, are due to the party selling, leasing or allowing for the shared use of the frequency usage rights.[135]

15.56 To transpose the amended GSM-Directive,[136] the BNetzA President's Chamber has provided for the flexibilisation of frequency usage rights for wireless access for the provision of telecommunications services in the bands 450 MHz, 900 MHz, 1800 MHz, 2 GHz and 3.5.[137]

Rights of Use for Numbers

Overview

15.57 The BNetzA has the sole competence for structuring and configuring the numbering space and for the allocation of numbers to telecommunications network operators, service providers and end users. To implement international obligations and recommendations and to ensure sufficient availability of numbers, The BNetzA may modify the structure and configuration of the numbering space and the national numbering plan. Proposed modifications need to be made known in good time prior to becoming effective.

15.58 The criteria and guidelines for the structuring, configuration and administration of the numbering plans, for the acquisition, the extent and the loss of rights to use numbers including the requirements for telecommunications-based services, and to transpose international recommendations and obligations into national legislation, are set out in the Telecommunications Numbering Ordinance.[138]

---

134 S 62(2) TKG.
135 S 62(3) TKG.
136 Directive 2009/114/EC of the European Parliament and of the Council amending Council Directive 87/372/EEC on the frequency bands to be reserved for the coordinated introduction of public pan-European cellular digital land-based mobile communications in the Community [2009] OJ L274/25.
137 Decision BK 1a-09/001; a non-official English translation of the decision is available at http://www.bundesnetzagentur.de/SharedDocs/Downloads/EN/BNetzA/Areas/ Telecommunications/TelecomRegulation/FrequencyManagement/FlexibilisationFrequency/ DecisionPresidentChamberFlexibilisation101022pdf.pdf?__blob=publicationFile; documents on the public consultation with respect to the flexibilisation of the GSM spectrum can be accessed at http://www.bundesnetzagentur.de/cln_1912/EN/Areas/Telecommunications/Tele comsRegulation/FrequencyManagement/FlexibilisationFrequencyUsageRights/Consultation FlexibleGSM_Basepage.html
138 BGBl I 2008, 141.

General authorisations and granting of individual rights

15.59   The BNetzA issues numbering plans detailing in particular the numbering structure, conditions of use and assignment and further usage conditions for the individual numbering ranges.[139]

Furthermore, the BNetzA issues an annual numbering concept which describes the current developments with respect to telecommunications services and assesses the impact of these developments on the management of numbering resources.[140]

15.60   The right to use numbers is subject to prior assignment. The assignment is either:

- a 'direct assignment' by BNetzA of numbers for the assignee's own use; or
- an 'original assignment' by BNetzA to an operator of a telecommunications network or a provider of telecommunication services for use of the numbers by the assignee for the purposes of a 'derived assignment'; or
- by way of a 'derived assignment', whereby an operator of a telecommunications network or a provider of telecommunications services assigns a number for the assignee's own use; or
- exceptionally, by way of a 'general assignment' issued by BNetzA.[141]

15.61   Both direct and original assignments are based on administrative acts issued by BNetzA upon request.

Only 'derived assignments' can be transferred on the basis of contractual arrangements; otherwise, the 'sale' of numbers is not permissible.[142]

Transferral of 'direct assignments' and 'original assignments' by way of succession requires the BNetzA's written confirmation and change of the assignment which is granted upon prior application; such application has to be submitted without undue delay.[143]

Admissible conditions

15.62   The assignment of numbers may be limited in time and may be subject to conditions, including a deadline by which an assigned number needs to be used, as well as conditions for the procedure to assign numbers to end customers ('derived assignment'); such conditions are detailed in the BNetzA's numbering plans. A number assignment may be refused, at BNetzA's discretion, if BNetzA has reason to believe that an applicant will not be reachable in Germany, and that it will not be able to ensure the proper usage of the assigned numbers from a technical and organisational viewpoint. Number assignments can be revoked, inter alia, in cases of unlawful numbering usage, where numbers are not used continuously or where

---

139 Information on the German numbering plans is available at http://www.bundesnetzagentur.de/ cln_1912/EN/Areas/Telecommunications/TelecomsRegulation/NumberManagement/number management_node.html (English)

140 The 2011 numbering concept is available at http://www.bundesnetzagentur.de/SharedDocs/ Downloads/DE/BNetzA/Sachgebiete/Telekommunikation/Regulierung/Nummernverwaltung/ Nummerierungskonzept/Nummerierungskonzept2011pdf.pdf?__blob=publicationFile (German).

141 See S 4(2) Telecommunications Numbering Ordinance.

142 S 4(3) Telecommunications Numbering Ordinance.

143 S. 4(6) Telecommunications Numbering Ordinance.

numbering plans are amended to implement international obligations, to secure the availability of numbering resources or to fulfil the TKG's regulatory objectives.[144]

15.63 In order to ensure number portability, BNetzA may require the providers of public telecommunications services to participate in automated data exchange procedures to ensure the portability of numbers.

Limitation of number of rights of use to be granted

15.64 German law does not provide for the granting of rights of use for numbers through 'competitive' or comparative selection procedures. The assignment of numbers is subject to procedural rules to be determined by BNetzA in accordance with the Telecommunications Numbering Ordinance.[145] Decisions on assignments of numbers shall be taken on a 'first come, first served' basis, and, in the case of simultaneous receipt of several applications, by lot.[146] BNetzA is obliged to take its decision on the allocation of numbers as fast as possible and within three weeks at the latest.

Administrative Charges and Fees for Rights of Use

15.65 BNetzA charges fees and expenses for a number of its regulatory measures, including:

- decisions on the grant of rights of use for frequencies;
- decisions on the grant of rights of use for telephone numbers;
- the processing of publications for the registration of diallers using premium rate numbers;
- the case-by-case coordination, advance publication, assignment and notification of satellite systems;
- measures to counteract violations of the TKG or of ordinances issued by virtue of the TKG;
- decisions on the transfer of rights of way;
- decisions in conjunction with access or rate regulation; and
- decisions in abuse proceedings.[147]

The chargeable acts and the level of fees are set out in specific ordinances.[148]

15.66 In addition to the fees and expenses for the granting of the right to use frequencies, the BNetzA levies annual contribution charges to recover costs it incurs for the management, control and enforcement of general assignments and rights of use for spectrum and orbit usage.[149] This 'frequency usage contribution charge' is to be paid by all those who have been assigned frequencies.

---

144 S 9(2) Telecommunications Numbering Ordinance; see also S 67(1) TKG.
145 See para 15.58 above.
146 S 5 Telecommunications Numbering Ordinance.
147 S 142(1) TKG
148 S 142 TKG; see e g Frequency Fee Ordinance, BGBl I 1997, 1226, last amended by BGBl I 2012, 130; Telecommunications Numbering Fee Ordinance, BGBl I 1999, 1887, last amended by BGBl I 2010, 582.
149 S 143 TKG; Ordinance on Contribution Charges for the Protection of Frequencies, BGBl I 2004, 958, last amended by BGBl I 2012, 1815.

REGULATION OF NETWORK ACCESS AND INTERCONNECTION: IMPLEMENTATION OF THE ACCESS DIRECTIVE

Objectives and Scope of Access Regulation

15.67   The Access Directive has been transposed by sections 16–26 TKG. The provisions distinguish between interconnection[150] and access,[151] and empower BNetzA to impose access obligations on both network operators with and without SMP.

Basic Regulatory Concepts

15.68   The Act defines 'access' as 'the provision of services and/or the making available of facilities to another undertaking, under defined conditions, for the purpose of providing telecommunications services, including their use for the provision of information society and broadcasting services'.[152] The definition further includes the non-exhaustive list of different types of access set out in Article 2(a) of the Access Directive.[153] The definition of the term 'interconnection' is almost identical to the definition set out in Article 2(b) of the Access Directive.[154]

15.69   All operators of public telecommunications networks must make an interconnection offer to other public telecommunications network operators upon their request in order to secure user communication, the provision of telecommunications services and service interoperability throughout the European Community.[155] In addition to this general obligation which applies to all operators of public telecommunication networks regardless of their market position, the TKG allows for the imposition of access- and interconnection-related obligations to SMP undertakings[156] and network operators controlling access to end users.[157] The access provisions of the TKG are predicated on the principle that commercial negotiations shall have priority over access orders (possibly subject to non-discrimination obligations[158]).

Access- and Interconnection-related Obligations with Respect to SMP Undertakings

Overview

15.70   The BNetzA is empowered to impose access- and interconnection-related obligations on SMP operators ('remedies') on the basis of regulatory orders following a market analysis,[159] and by way of individual access orders as and when

---

150   S 16 TKG.
151   S 18–22 TKG.
152   S 3 no 32 TKG.
153   S 3 no 32 lit a) to h).
154   Cf s 3 no 34 TKG.
155   S 16 TKG.
156   See para 15.70 et seq below.
157   See para 15.81 below.
158   See para 15.72 below.
159   S 13 TKG, cf para 15.28 et seq above.

a regulated operator and another operator fail to conclude an access agreement.[160] Where SMP has been found on a relevant market, the BNetzA must impose at least one remedy[161] but has broad regulatory discretion, subject to only limited court review, regarding the choice of remedies. [162]

Transparency obligation

15.71 In order to ensure transparency of access conditions, the BNetzA may impose on an SMP operator the obligation to publish, for the benefit of undertakings entitled to access, all such information as is required for use of the relevant access services and/or facilities, in particular accounting information, information on technical specifications, network characteristics, terms and conditions of supply and use (including information on all conditions that limit access to and use of services and applications), and the charges payable.[163] In particular, the BNetzA may require the SMP operators to provide the BNetzA with copies of their access agreements in a public and a non-public version. The BNetzA then publishes information on where the public versions of the agreements may be accessed by undertakings requesting access. The BNetzA regularly imposes transparency obligations on SMP undertakings.

Non-discrimination obligations

15.72 The BNetzA regularly imposes obligations on an SMP operator requiring access agreements to be based on objective criteria, to be transparent, to grant equally good access and to meet the requirements of fairness and reasonableness.[164] These obligations of non-discrimination aim at ensuring, in particular, that the operator applies equivalent conditions in the same circumstances to other undertakings providing like services, and provides services and information to others under the same conditions and of the same quality as it provides for its own services or those of its subsidiaries or partners.

Specific access obligations

15.73 The BNetzA may also, upon request or on its own initiative, impose specific access obligations on network operators with SMP, including the obligation to provide unbundled access and technical facilities enabling carrier (pre-)selection.[165]

In exercising its discretion, BNetzA has to take into account, in particular, the following factors:

- the technical and economic viability, having regard to the pace of market development, of using or installing alternative facilities, bearing in mind the nature and type of interconnection access proposed and taking into account the feasibility of upstream access products such as ducts;

---

160 S 25 TKG.
161 S 9(2) TKG
162 See e g Federal Administrative Court, Decision BVerwG, 6 C 42.06 of 28 November 2008.
163 S 20(1) TKG.
164 S 19(1) TKG.
165 S 21 TKG.

- the feasibility of providing the access proposed, in relation to the capacity available;
- the initial investment by the facility owner, bearing in mind any investments already made and the risks involved in making the investment;
- the need to secure competition in the long term, taking into account in particular an economically efficient competition, by providing incentives for efficient investment into infrastructures, among other things;
- industrial and intellectual property rights;
- the provision of services that are available throughout Europe; and
- the already imposed obligations or non-mandated services available in and taken up by a large part of the market as sufficient to ensure the regulatory objectives.[166]

15.74   The TKG distinguishes between two types of access obligations: those that BNetzA may, at its regulatory discretion, impose on SMP operators; and those that it 'should' impose. The latter are obligations which shall be imposed unless BNetzA has overriding reasons not do so.

Among the access obligations which BNetzA may impose, at its discretion, are the following:

- to grant access to specified network elements and/or facilities, including unbundled broadband access, and not to refuse access already granted;
- to grant access on a wholesale basis to particular services offered by the operator as offered to end users, for the purpose of resale by third parties in their own name and for their own account;
- to create the necessary prerequisites for the interoperability of end-to-end communication, including the provision of facilities for intelligent network services and roaming;
- to grant access to operational support systems or similar software systems required to secure fair competition in the provision of services, while ensuring the efficient use of existing facilities; and
- to grant access to connected services such as an identity-, location- or presence service.[167]

These specific access obligations also include very detailed access provisions in relation to billing and collection services.

15.75   Whereas this list of specific access obligations which BNetzA 'may' impose is non-exhaustive, the TKG provides for six specific obligations which BNetzA 'should' impose on SMP operators, namely:

- the granting of access to passive infrastructure components;
- the granting of fully unbundled access to the local loop and shared access to the local loop;
- the interconnection of telecommunications networks;
- the granting of open access to technical interfaces, protocols and other key technologies essential for service interoperability and virtual network services;
- the provision of co-location and other forms of facility sharing, including building, duct and mast sharing, and the grant, to users or their agents, of access to these facilities at any time;

---

166   S 21(1) TKG.
167   S 21(2) TKG.

- the granting of access to specific network components, facilities and services to enable carrier selection and carrier pre-selection.[168]

In practice, the BNetzA applies the factors set out at para 15.73 above also in cases of the above access obligations.

15.76   Limitations on the imposition of access obligations exist where an operator shows that use of the facility would endanger the maintenance of network integrity or the safety of network operations. The maintenance of network integrity and the safety of network operations are to be judged on the basis of objective standards, and the burden of proof lies with the SMP operator.[169]

Where the BNetzA has imposed an access obligation, the BNetzA may require the regulated operator or the users of the access to fulfil certain technical conditions required to secure normal functioning of the network.[170]

Obligation to publish a reference offer

15.77   The BNetzA may impose, on SMP operators, an obligation to publish a reference offer for access services for which there is a general demand. The BNetzA assesses whether the submitted draft reference offer is in accordance with the principles of promoting equal opportunities, reasonableness and timeliness and may require the regulated operators to change their reference offer to make it conform to these principles. The BNetzA approves the reference offer and sets a minimum term. The regulated operator must include the approved reference offer in its terms and conditions. [171]

Price control obligations

15.78   The rates charged by an SMP public telecommunications network operator for access services and/or facilities mandated by way of an access order are subject to prior approval by the BNetzA. In derogation from this principle, the BNetzA may subject such rates to mere ex-post regulation where an ex post control is sufficient to ensure that the TKG's regulatory objectives are met. [172]

15.79   When approving rates in the ex-ante procedure, such rates may not exceed the 'cost of efficient service provision'[173] unless the BNetzA exceptionally applies a different cost standard.[174] While the TKG also foresees the possibility of a price cap regulation, this option is of no relevance in regulatory practice.[175]

The cost of efficient service provision 'are derived from the long run incremental costs of providing the service and an appropriate mark-up for volume-neutral common costs, inclusive of a reasonable return on capital employed, as far as these costs are required to provide the service'.[176]

---

168 S 21(3) TKG.
169 S 21(4) TKG.
170 S 21(5) TKG.
171 S 23 TKG.
172 S 30(1) TKG.
173 S 31(1) no 1 TKG.
174 S 31(2) TKG.
175 S 31(1) no 2 TKG.
176 S 32(1) TKG.

This cost standard differs from the Pure-Long Run Incremental Cost (Pure-LRIC) cost standard set out in Commission Recommendation of 7 May 2009 on the Regulatory Treatment of Fixed and Mobile Termination Rates in the EU[177] as the cost of efficient service provision include volume-neutral common costs. In its recent preliminary decisions on the approval of fixed and mobile termination rates, the BNctzA, nevertheless, refuses to give up ex-ante controls according to the cost of efficient service provision standard.[178] At the time of writing, consultation of the BNetzA's draft decisions with the Commission had not yet been concluded.

Accounting separation obligations

15.80   In order to ensure transparency of pricing, BNetzA may require an SMP operator to keep separate accounts for certain activities related to access services and facilities. In particular, BNetzA shall require, as a rule, a vertically integrated undertaking to make its wholesale prices and its internal transfer prices transparent in order to prevent a breach of the prohibition on discrimination and unlawful cross-subsidisation.[179] The BNetzA has, so far, not applied this obligation where an SMP undertaking was subject to cost control obligations as, in the BNetzA's view, such obligation provided sufficient transparency and control.

Functional separation

15.81   As a last resort measure, the BNetzA may impose functional separation[180] on an SMP undertaking.[181] The TKG transposes the requirements of Article 13a of the Access Directive[182] almost verbatim.

Regulatory Powers Applicable to All Market Participants

Obligations to ensure end-to-end connectivity

15.82   In order to ensure end-to-end connectivity, BNetzA may oblige both SMP operators[183] and non-SMP operators controlling access to end users[184] to interconnect their networks with those of other telecommunications network operators.

Access to digital radio and television broadcasting services

15.83   Rights holders of application programming interfaces are obliged to provide on fair, reasonable and non-discriminatory terms and against appropriate

---

177   [2009] OJ L124/67.
178   See BK 3-12-089 (fixed termination rates) and BK 3-12-084 to -087 (mobile termination rates).
179   S 24(1) TKG.
180   Functional separation describes 'an obligation on vertically integrated undertakings to place activities related to the wholesale provision of relevant access products in an independently operating business entity'.
181   See para 15.28.
182   See above at para 1.164.
183   See para 15.28 et seq above.
184   See para 15.32 above.

remuneration, manufacturers of digital television receivers and third parties claiming legitimate interest with all such information as is necessary to provide all services supported by the application programming interface in fully functional form.[185]

15.84   Providers of conditional access systems are obliged to ensure that these have the necessary technical capability for the cost-effective transfer of control functions, allowing the possibility for full control by public telecommunications network operators at local or regional level of the services using such conditional access systems.[186]

Holders of industrial property rights to conditional access systems are obliged to grant licences to manufacturers of digital television receivers or to third parties demonstrating a legitimate interest on fair, reasonable and non-discriminatory terms, if and when they decide to grant such licences. The licences may not be made subject to conditions hindering the installation of a common interface allowing connection with other conditional access systems or components specific to another conditional access system, for reasons of transaction security with regard to the content to be protected.[187]

REGULATION OF UNIVERSAL SERVICES AND USERS' RIGHTS: THE UNIVERSAL SERVICE DIRECTIVE

Regulation of Universal Service Obligations

Scope of universal service obligations

15.85   The TKG defines universal services in almost identical terms to Article 2(j) of the Framework Directive.[188]

The list of services that have been determined as universal services under German law is identical with the list set out in Articles 4 to 6 of the Universal Service Directive.[189] In the course of transposing the 2009 EU Regulatory Package, there has been a heated political debate in Germany on whether to include access to the Internet at broadband speed in the scope of the universal service. Ultimately, such access has not been made part of the universal service.[190]

The BNetzA may, after consulting the undertaking with universal service obligations (the 'designated universal service provider'), identify general demand for the universal services in terms of the needs of end users with regard to, in particular, geographical coverage, number of telephones, accessibility and quality of service. The BNetzA also has the power to impose obligations on undertakings in order to secure provision of the service and of service features. It may choose not to impose

---

185   S 49(2) TKG.
186   S 50(1) TKG.
187   S 50(2) TKG.
188   Cf s 78(1) TKG.
189   See at para 1.174 et seq above.
190   Cf BT-Drucksache 17/6912 (request from the Group of the Left); BT-Drucksache 17/7527 (request from the Group of the Social-Democratic Party of Germany); BT-Drucksache 17/7528 (request from the Group of Alliance 90/Green Party); BT-Drucksache 17/7521 (resolution recommendation and report of the Committee on Economics and Technology); Plenary Protocol of German Bundestag no 17/136 p 16099 A, B, D.

such obligations for all or part of its territory if it is satisfied, after consulting the interested parties, that these service features or comparable services are deemed widely available.[191]

Designation of undertakings obliged to provide universal services

15.86   If a universal service is not being adequately or appropriately provided by the market or where there is reason to fear that such provision will not be secured, each provider operating in the relevant product market and achieving, within the area of application of the TKG, at least 4 per cent of total sales in this market or having significant market power in the relevant geographic market is obliged to contribute to making possible the provision of the universal service.[192] This statutory obligation can result either in an obligation to provide the universal services as such or to contribute to the funding of universal service provision.

15.87   If the BNetzA finds that a universal service is not being adequately or appropriately provided, it announces its intention to impose universal service obligations, unless an undertaking declares itself willing, within a period of one month of the publication of notice, to provide such universal service without compensation.[193]

After consulting the undertakings likely to be concerned, BNetzA shall decide whether and to what extent to oblige one or more of these undertakings to provide the universal service.

Where an undertaking that is to be obliged to provide a universal service can demonstrate by prima facie evidence that, in the case of such obligation, financial compensation will be necessary, BNetzA is obliged to invite tenders for the provision of the universal service and award it to a qualified applicant requiring the least financial compensation for providing the universal service in compliance with the requirements of the Act.[194]

At present, universal services are provided by Deutsche Telekom AG. If Deutsche Telekom AG intends to stop providing universal services or to offer them under less favourable conditions, it is obliged to notify BNetzA of its intentions one year prior to their taking effect, to allow the regulator time to take the necessary measures under the Act.[195]

Regulation of retail tariffs, users' expenditures and quality of service

15.88   The TKG requires, in accordance with the Universal Service Directive,[196] that universal services shall be provided at affordable prices. The price for providing a connection at a fixed location to a public telecommunications network and access to publicly available telephone services via this connection[197] is deemed affordable if it does not exceed the real price of the telephone services required on average by a household situated outside a town or city with a population of more than 100,000

---

191   S 78(4) TKG.
192   S 80 sentence 1 TKG.
193   S 81(1) TKG.
194   S 81(3) TKG.
195   S 150 para 9 TKG.
196   See para 1.162 above.
197   S 78(2) no 1, 2 TKG.

on 1 January 1998. In its assessment of affordability, the BNetzA shall take into account the quality of service levels, including supply times at that time and the rate of growth in productivity up to 31 December of the year prior to the previous one.[198]

All other universal services are deemed affordable if the rates charged by the universal service provider are not abusive.[199]

15.89   The BNetzA is empowered to monitor the provision of universal services, including their quality, and applies the parameters, definitions and measuring methods established by EU law.[200]

Cost calculation and financing of universal services

15.90   If the BNetzA grants compensation for the provision of a universal service, each undertaking operating in the relevant product market and achieving, within the area of application of the TKG, at least 4 per cent of total sales in this market or having SMP[201] shall share, by means of a universal service contribution, in funding the compensation. The sharing mechanism is assessed on the basis of the proportion of the sales of the particular undertaking to the total sales of all those that are obliged to contribute to the funding.[202]

15.91   The compensation payable for the provision of a universal service is determined by calculating the difference between the cost for a designated undertaking of operating without the universal service obligation and the cost of operating in observance of the obligation. Benefits and proceeds accruing to the universal service provider, including intangible benefits, are to be taken into account.[203] To calculate the amount of compensation, BNetzA may ask the designated universal service provider for the necessary documentation. The results of the cost calculation and of the examination are to be published.

Regulation of Retail Markets

Prerequisites for the regulation of retail markets

15.92   Where the BNetzA is of the view that access measures are insufficient to fulfil the TKG's regulatory objectives, the BNetzA may subject end user tariffs of an undertaking having SMP on a retail market to a prior rate approval requirement.[204]

Regulatory powers

15.93   The regulation of end user tariffs may be subject to ex-ante approval or to ex-post regulation by BNetzA.

---

198   S 79(1) TKG.
199   S 79(2) TKG in conjunction with S 28 TKG.
200   S 84 (3) TKG.
201   See para 15.28 et seq above.
202   S 83(1) TKG.
203   S 82(2) TKG.
204   S 39(1) TKG.

The BNetzA 'should' limit imposing prior rate approval requirements to those markets in which the sustainable competition is not expected to develop in the foreseeable future, unless exceptional circumstances prevail.[205] Rates which require prior approval are eligible for approval if they do not exceed the costs of efficient service provision[206] unless the BNetzA has decided to apply a different cost standard. [207]

15.94   Rates for retail services supplied by an SMP operator which the BNetzA has not subjected to prior approval are subject to ex-post regulation. Under the rules for ex-post regulation, the BNetzA is obliged to open an investigation of rates if it becomes aware of facts warranting the assumption that the rates may be abusive.[208] Abuse is constituted, in particular, by the undertaking levying rates which:

- prevail solely as a result of it having significant market power in the particular telecommunications markets;
- considerably prejudice the competitive opportunities of other undertakings in a telecommunications market; or
- create advantages for particular users in relation to other users of the same or similar telecommunications services.[209]

In the two latter instances, the SMP operator is allowed to show that its conduct is objectively justified.

Abusive pricing is presumed where:

- the price for the service in question does not cover its long-run incremental costs, including a reasonable return on capital employed;
- the margin between the price that the SMP public telecommunications operator charges competitors for an access service of facility and the corresponding retail price is not enough to enable an efficient undertaking to achieve a reasonable return on capital employed in the retail markets (margin squeeze); or
- an undertaking bundles its products in an objectively unreasonable manner.[210]

15.95   The BNetzA may further oblige an SMP undertaking to inform it of proposed end user rates two months prior to their planned effective date. If the BNetzA finds that the proposed rates could be abusive, it shall, within two weeks of receiving notice of the measure, prohibit the introduction of the proposed rates until it has completed its examination.[211]

In order to ensure a level playing field for competitors, the TKG provides that an undertaking with SMP in a retail market and obliged to grant access to a service and/or a facility which includes components that are likewise essential to a service offer in the retail market, is obliged to submit at the same time as its planned rates measure for the retail service an offer for the wholesale product which meets, in particular, the requirements of fair pricing. The purpose of this provision is to ensure that the SMP operator's competitors are able to provide competing service

---

205   S 39(1) TKG.
206   S 39 para 1, 31 para 1 TKG, see para 15.78 above.
207   S 39 para 1, 31 para 2 no. 2 TKG, see para 15.78 above.
208   S 38(2) TKG.
209   S 28(1) TKG.
210   S 28(2) TKG.
211   S 38(1) sentences 1 and 2.

offerings, based on wholesale products to be provided by the SMP operator, at the same time as the SMP operator provides its retail services.[212]

End User Rights

Contracts

15.96   Providers of public telecommunications services have to provide, in contracts with end users, information on:

- the provider's name, address, legal form, seat of business and court of registry;
- the kind of services provided and the services' key technical features – this has to include information on the availability of emergency services, on any restrictions to the availability of access to services, information on minimum quality of service, information on any traffic management measures foreseen by the provider, and any restrictions to the use of terminal equipment, subject to further specification by the BNetzA;
- the time necessary for the making available of the connection;
- the maintenance and customers services offered including the possibilities to contact such services;
- details on prices;
- where the providers pricing lists can be accessed;
- the term of contract;
- the conditions for extension and termination of supply of individual services and the contract as a whole including the conditions for a change of provider;[213]
- details on compensation and refunds for cases where the provider did not offer the key technical requirements of the services;
- extrajudicial settlement of disputes;
- the entitlement of the subscriber to have their data listed in a public directory;
- measures foreseen by the provider to counter breaches of security or integrity;
- the entitlement of subscribers to have certain numbering ranges blocked; and
- the blocking and billing of value added services provided over mobile connections.[214]

With regard to end users who are not consumers these information requirements apply only upon request.

15.97   The maximum contract term of a contract between a consumer and a provider of public telecommunications services may not exceed 24 months. Providers of public telecommunications services must enable subscribers to sign contracts with a maximum period of 12 months.[215]

---

212   S 39(4) TKG.
213   See para 15.104 et seq below.
214   S 43a(1), (2) TKG.
215   S 43bTKG.

Transparency obligations

15.98   Before the recent amendment of the TKG, the law contained transparency and publication obligations directly applicable to all providers of public telecommunication services. These direct obligations were replaced by an entitlement of the BNetzA[216] to issue an ordinance including detailed transparency obligations, including: [217]

- the provider's name, address, legal form, seat of business and court of registry;
- the kind of services provided and the services' key technical features as well as maintenance services including information on whether the services provided are billed separately or in connection with other services;
- details on the prices of the services provided and on contract termination costs;
- details on compensation and refunds;
- the provider's Terms and Conditions as well as information on the minimum contract terms offered;
- general and provider-specific information on extrajudicial settlement of disputes;
- information about the basic rights of end users of telecommunications services especially with regard to itemised billing, call barring, prepaid services, the possibility to pay the cost of setting up a connection in instalments, the consequences of delays in payment and certain service features such as calling-line identification and tone dialling;
- information with regard to technical features of their services including details on quality of service;
- information on the implementation of emergency call functionalities and any changes thereto;
- information on the rights of subscribers in conjunction with directory services; and
- information on any traffic management measures and on the possible impact of such measures on service quality.

The ordinance may also determine whether and to what degree the transparency obligations will apply to telecommunications providers offering their services to business customers only.

Other obligations

15.99   Providers of public telecommunications services have the following obligations towards (i) subscribers and (ii) resellers of voice services on behalf of their subscribers: [218]

- Subscribers may request that their data is included, free of charge, in a publicly accessible directory with the following information: number, surname and first name, address. The provider does not necessarily have to provide the directory themself. The actual form of the directory entry may be determined

---

216   S 1 Ordinance on the Transferal of Competencies to issue Ordinances under the German Telekommunications Act and the Act on the Electromagnetic Compatibility of Electrical Equipment ('TKEMÜbertrV'), BGBI I 2013, 79.
217   S 45nTKG.
218   S 45m TKG.

by the provider. The subscriber is free to determine which data is included in the directory.[219]

- Subscribers are entitled to demand from their provider that existing directory entries are deleted.
- Subscribers also have a right to request correction of incorrect directory entries.
- Subscribers may demand that co-users of their connection are included in the directory with their name and surname, provided that this is not in violation of data protection rules.[220] The provider may demand remuneration for such directory entry.

15.100   The provision of the possibility to make emergency calls from all public pay telephones free of charge, simply by the use of the number '112' and the national emergency call numbers determined in an ordinance, is part of the universal service obligations under the TKG.[221] In addition, any person offering public telecommunications services enabling the caller to place outgoing national calls to a number/numbers from the national numbering plan must provide all users with access to emergency services by using, free of charge, the single European emergency call number '112' and the additional national emergency call number 110.[222] Details on the obligation are set-out in the Ordinance on Emergency Connections.[223]

15.101   Providers of public telecommunications services enabling the caller to place outgoing national calls to a number/numbers from the national numbering plan, providers of access to such services and operators of telecommunications networks used for the provision of such services including the transit of calls must ensure, or assist to the extent necessary, that emergency calls are immediately transferred to the competent emergency centre and that the following information is transmitted to the competent emergency centre together with the emergency call:

- the number of the connection from which the emergency call connection originates; and
- the data which are necessary to determine the location from which the emergency call connection originates

The transmission of emergency calls must be prioritised.

Details on the technical implementation of this obligation are set-out in a Technical Directive issued by BNetzA. [224]

15.102   To ensure Community-wide electronic communications, public telephone network operators are obliged to make provision in their networks for handling all calls to the European telephone numbering space.[225]

---

219   S 104 (2)TKG, see also para 15.116 below.
220   S 104 (3)TKG, see also para 15.116 below.
221   S 78(2) no 6 TKG.
222   S 108(1) TKG.
223   BGBl. I 2009, 481, last amended by BGBl. I 2012, 2347.
224   Available in German at http://www.bundesnetzagentur.de/SharedDocs/Downloads/DE/ BNetzA/Sachgebiete/Telekommunikation/TechnischeRegulierung/Notruf/ TechRichtlinieTRNotruf1.pdf?__blob=publicationFile
225   S 46(6) TKG.

Quality of service: securing 'net neutrality'

15.103 There is no direct obligation with regard to net neutrality under the TKG.[226] The BNetzA is, however, empowered to pass an ordinance imposing on providers of telecommunications networks general requirements to ensure non-discriminatory data transmission and non-discriminatory access to content and services in order to prevent an arbitrary deterioration of services and an unjustified disruption or slowing-down of data traffic in the network.[227] The BNetzA may also issue a technical directive setting out minimum quality of service requirements after consulting the Commission and BEREC.[228] At the time of editing, the BNetzA has not issued such ordinance or technical directive.

Obligations facilitating change of provider

15.104 Providers of public telecommunications services and operators of public telecommunications networks must ensure that service provision to a subscriber changing provider is not discontinued before the contractual and technical precon-ditions for the change of provider are met unless requested otherwise by the subscriber. Service provision must not be discontinued for longer than one working day. If the change of provider cannot be implemented on time, the releasing provider has to continue providing telecommunication services to the subscriber but generally at reduced tariffs.[229]

In order to ensure such change of provider, operators of public telecommunications networks have to ensure, in particular that subscribers may keep their numbers independently of the undertaking providing their telecommunications services as follows:

●   in the case of geographic numbers, at a specific location; and
●   in the case of non-geographic numbers, at any location.

This obligation to ensure number portability applies only within the numbering ranges and sub-ranges designated for a telephone service. The transfer of telephone numbers for telephone services provided at a fixed location to those not provided at a fixed location and vice versa is not permitted.[230] Subscribers may be charged only at cost-based rates for the porting of numbers allocated to them.

15.105 When changing their residence, consumers have a right to retain their telecommunications services if these services are also offered at their new resi-dence.[231]

---

226 Several political groups, among others, had demanded that net neutrality be expressly and directly included in the TKG (see e g BT-Drs. 17/3688; BT-Drs. 17/4843; BT-Drs. 17/5367). This demand was refused by the legislator, see Plenary Protokol of the German Bundestag no 17/136 p 16099, B to D.
227 S 41a(1) TKG.
228 S 41a(2) TKG.
229 S 46(1), (2) TKG.
230 S 46(1) TKG.
231 S 88(2) TKG.

DATA PROTECTION: IMPLEMENTATION OF THE E-PRIVACY-DIRECTIVE

Confidentiality of Communications

15.106   The principle of telecommunications secrecy is enshrined in article 10 of the German Federal Constitution. On this basis, the TKG provides that the content and detailed circumstances of telecommunications, in particular the fact of whether or not a person is or was engaged in a telecommunications activity, is subject to telecommunications secrecy which also covers the detailed circumstances surrounding unsuccessful call attempts. Every service provider is obliged to maintain telecommunications secrecy; this obligation also applies after the end of the activity through which such commitment arose.[232]

15.107   The interception or surveillance of communications is permissible only on the basis of specific legislative permissions and, in principle, subject to a court order. The operators of telecommunications systems by means of which publicly available telecommunications services are provided are obliged to provide, at their own expense, the technical facilities which allow for the implementation of telecommunications interception measures provided for by law and to make organisational arrangements for the implementation of such measures.[233]

Traffic Data and Location Data

15.108   Traffic data, ie data collected, processed or used in the provision of a telecommunications service,[234] may only be collected to the extent required for purposes specifically set out in the TKG. This applies, in particular, to:

- the number or other identification of the lines in question or of the terminal, personal authorisation codes, the card number (when customer cards are used), and the location data when mobile handsets are used;
- the beginning and end of the connection, indicated by date and time and, where relevant to the charges, the volume of data transmitted;
- the telecommunications service used by the user;
- the termination points of fixed connections, the beginning and end of their use, indicated by date and time and, where relevant to the charges, the volume of data transmitted; and
- any other traffic data required for set up and maintenance of the telecommunications connection and for billing purposes.[235]

15.109   Collected traffic data may only be processed or used to the extent required for the purposes set out above or in other applicable statutory provisions or to set up further connections. Otherwise, traffic data is to be erased by the service provider without undue delay following termination of the connection.[236]

15.110   Location data, ie data collected or used in a telecommunications network or by a telecommunications service indicating the geographic position of the terminal equipment of an end user of a publicly available telecommunications

---

232   S 110(1) TKG.
233   S 3 No 30 TKG.
234   S 96(1) sentence 1 TKG.
235   S 96(1) sentence 2 TKG.
236   S 3 No 19 TKG.

service,[237] may be processed to the extent and for the duration necessary for the provision of value added services only when they have been made anonymous or with the consent of the subscriber. In these cases, the provider of the value added service shall inform the user in case of each identification of the location of the mobile terminal by means of sending a text message to the terminal whose location data was identified (an exception applies if the location is only displayed on the terminal whose location data was identified). If the location data are processed for a value added service whose purpose is the transmission of location data of a mobile terminal to another subscriber or to a third party that is not the added value service provider, the subscriber's consent must be collected explicitly, separately and in writing. The subscriber shall inform his co-users of all such consent given and the consent may be withdrawn at any time.[238] In respect of calls to the emergency call numbers '112' and '110' and to the telephone numbers '124 124' and '116 117', the service provider shall ensure that the transmission of location data is not ruled out on a per-call or a per-line basis.[239]

Data Retention

15.111   At present, there exists no obligation to retain communications data under the TKG as mandated in the Data Retention Directive.[240] After a ruling of the German Constitutional Court of 2 March 2010 which invalidated the provisions of the TKG regarding telecommunications data retention[241] there is currently no data retention legislation in force in Germany. Germany is subject to infringement proceedings following its non-transposition of the EU Data Retention Directive.[242]

Itemised Billing

15.112   If a subscriber has requested, in textual form, an itemised bill, he or she shall be informed of certain traffic data in relation to calls for which he or she is liable to pay.[243] In respect of residential lines, the disclosure of such information is permitted only if the subscriber has declared, in textual form, that he or she has informed all co-users of the line, and will inform future co-users without undue delay, of the disclosure to him or her of the traffic data underpinning the bill. In respect of lines in businesses and public authorities, the disclosure of such information is permitted only if the subscriber has declared, in textual form, that the employees have been informed, new employees will be informed without undue delay and the works council or the staff representation has been involved in accordance with the statutory requirements, or that such involvement is not necessary.[244]

15.113   The itemised bill may not allow calls to persons, public authorities or organisations in the social or the church domain who or which offer anonymous counselling wholly or predominantly by telephone to callers in emotional or social

---

237   S 98(1) TKG.
238   S 98(3) TKG.
239   See para 3.38 et seq above,
240   BVerfGE 125, 260 et seq.
241   Case C-329/12, OJ C 287/23, 22.09.2012.
242   S 99(1) sentence 1 TKG.
243   S 99(1) sentences 2 and 3 TKG.
244   S 99(2) TKG.

distress and who or which themselves or whose employees therefore have a special duty not to disclose confidential information, to be identified. To this end, BNetzA keeps a register where such called lines are listed.[245]

Calling and Connected Line Identification

15.114 Service providers offering calling line identification shall ensure that the calling and the called parties have the possibility, using a simple means and free of charge, to prevent presentation of the telephone number on a per-line or a per-call basis. Called parties shall be given the possibility, using a simple means and free of charge, of rejecting incoming calls from a calling party that has prevented presentation of its telephone number. On application by the subscriber, service providers are obliged to provide lines on which presentation on the connected line of the telephone number of the calling line is ruled out, free of charge. With regard to calls to the emergency call numbers '112' and '110' and to the telephone numbers '124 124' and '116 117' the service provider is obliged to ensure that calling line identification presentation is not ruled out on a per-call or on a per-line basis.[246]

Automatic Call Forwarding

15.115 Service providers are obliged to give their subscribers the possibility, using a simple means and free of charge, of stopping calls being automatically forwarded to their terminal as a result of action taken by a third party, to the extent that this is technically feasible.[247]

Directories of Subscribers

15.116 Upon request, subscribers may have their name and address, and additional information such as occupation, branch and type of line, entered in public printed or electronic directories. They may specify what information is to be published in the directories. At the subscribers' request, co-users may also be entered, provided they agree.[248] Information on telephone numbers included in the directories may be provided if the subscriber has been suitably informed that he may object to his telephone number being passed on and has not exercised his right to object; information on data published in subscriber directories other than telephone numbers may be provided only if the subscriber has given its consent to such additional data being passed on.[249]

Unsolicited Communications

15.117 The recipients of unsolicited electronic communications ('spam') can avail themselves of legal remedies under the Unfair Competition Act and the German Civil Code. In addition, BNetzA is empowered to take regulatory action against

---

245 S 102 TKG.
246 S 103 TKG.
247 S 104 TKG.
248 S 105(2) TKG.
249 Ping calls are calls which consist in the mere transmission of a single signal or with a view to soliciting a return call.

providers that use their telecommunications numbers for spamming via email, unsolicited telefax or SMS or so called 'ping' calls.[250] The regulatory measures taken by BNetzA in these cases include the blockage of the relevant numbers or administrative cease and desist orders.

---

250   S 67 TKG.

The Greek Market for Electronic Communications

Alkistis Christofilou, Paris Passias and Christos Papadochatzakis
I K Rokas & Partners, Athens

LEGAL STRUCTURE

Basic Policy

16.1   Unlike mobile telephony, where competition has been active since 1993, Greece started free competition in the fixed voice telephony market in 2002. The following decade, however, has been characterised by intense competition in voice telephony and broadband services, and a continuous decrease in the market share of the incumbent, Greek Telecommunications Organisation ('OTE'). The policy of the national Regulator, the National Telecommunications and Post Commission ('EETT'), to strictly supervise the OTE's retail pricing policy and wholesale activities, although highly criticised by the incumbent, has proven to be substantially effective. In terms of outgoing traffic, the OTE has seen its market share decrease to 60,6 per cent in 2011, in favour of the three largest operators that survived the turbulence of the first years of the market liberalisation, which now hold a market share of 27.2 per cent.[1] OTE's management, currently controlled by Deutsche Telekom AG,[2] has initiated a major restructuring focusing on the decrease of personnel and operational costs, while the company is in the process of fully integrating the very successful mobile telephony activities of its subsidiary COSMOTE.[3]

Broadband access has experienced a boost in recent years, showing in 2011 a penetration of 21.8 per cent. The growth of the broadband penetration rate in Greece during 2010 (2.9 per cent) was the highest in the EU and substantially higher than the European average (1.7 per cent), and amongst the highest of EU Member States for the first half of 2011, with 0.9 lines per 100 inhabitants compared to the 0.6 respective European average figure. The growth rate has

---

1   Figures based on the Telecommunications and Post Commission Annual Report for 2010.
2   Deutsche Telekom today holds 40 per cent of OTE's share capital, and holds the management following a Shareholders Agreement with the Greek State, which now holds 10 per cent. The remaining share capital is free floated. OTE is listed on the Athens Stock Exchange. In 2010 OTE applied for a delisting from the New York Stock Exchange.
3   COSMOTE is the market leader with a market share of approximately 40 per cent.

recently started to decline, making the convergence with the rest of Europe (average penetration rate 25 per cent) seem a far target.[4]

The recent economic crisis of the country has had a serious impact on the overall financial performance of the operators as well as the overall market performance.

Following the implementation of the 2002 Regulatory package in 2006, EETT has set as a goal the creation of a fully liberalised and competitive market, aiming primarily to attract investments in broadband network infrastructures.[5]

The unbundling of the local loop has caused alternative operators to invest in new, independent infrastructure, enabling them to detach from the existing OTE infrastructure and offer consumers new competitive products. In the years following 2004, OTE has shown remarkable flexibility, adapting its strategy to the new environment, and setting aside a major part of the legacy deriving from its former state monopoly position. Its solid financial position has enabled its management to invest in state of the art broadband technologies throughout its operations, offering to its own customers, as well as to customers of alternative operators, access to new services, and contributing to the substantial increase of broadband penetration.

Implementation of EU Directives

16.2   Greece has implemented the 2009 EU Regulatory Package with Law 4070/2012,[6] which was published in the Government Gazette on 10 April 2012 and became effective on the same date. According to its initiators, the law not only intends to harmonise local legislation on electronic communications to the new European law, but also to adjust some of the rules contained in the existing legal framework to the new needs and environment.

The main objectives of the new Law are to:

● liberate access to networks and services of electronic communications;
● liberate the right of all enterprises to offer electronic communication services as well as install, expand, operate, control and dispose electronic communication networks;
● protect competition and, to the extent possible, technology neutral regulation;
● promote competition in the provision of networks and electronic communication and similar services;
● protect the public interest;
● contribute to the development of a single European market; and
● protect user interests.

Greece implemented the 2002 EU Regulatory Package by enacting Law 3431/2006; it has also implemented the previously applicable legal regimes in the past. As a general rule, the Greek legislator, when harmonising EU directives, abides by their provisions, on several occasions almost literally. In supplementing the legislative framework, EETT has adopted a proactive attitude in issuing regulations, decisions and rulings incorporating the gradually evolving EU regulation.

Beyond harmonising the latest telecoms package, the new law intends to facilitate investment in the electronic communications sector by cutting through bureaucratic

4   BEREC Annual Report 2011, p 9 and EETT Annual Report 2011, p 49.
5   EETT Strategy for Regulation of Electronic Communications (2008–2011).
6   'Law 4070/2012 on Regulation of Electronic Communications, Transportations, Public Works and Miscellaneous Provisions' hereinafter referred to as 'Law 4070/2012', 'L4070/2012', or 'the new Law', interchangeably.

complications which create heavy friction and are significantly time-consuming. Pursuant to the new law, the telecoms NRA is responsible for the issuance of all relevant licences required for the completion of the licensed activity.

Legislation

16.3 The sources of law in the Hellenic Republic are laws ('L'), presidential decrees ('PD'), ministerial decisions ('MD'),which with regard to the matters in hand are issued by the Minister of Infrastructure, Transport and Networks (Ypourgos Ypodomon, Metaforon kai Diktion – 'MITN'), and Joint Ministerial Decisions ('JMD'). These are supplemented by decisions of the NRA, 'EETT'.

Law 4070/2012 is the principal legislation in the field of electronic communications, and includes the harmonised text for Directives 2002/19/EC, 2002/20/EC, 2002/21/EC, 2002/22/EC and 2002/77/EC as amended by Directives 2009/136/EC and 2009/140/EC of European Parliament and Council.

EETT has issued numerous decisions which constitute secondary law and regulate more specific matters and procedures, including the numbering plan, licensing regulations, pricing principles, SMP, radio frequency fees, universal service, etc. EETT, within its proactive regulatory approach, has been issuing decisions and rulings which incorporate the evolving EU regulation prior to new regulatory packages becoming wholly adopted by law.

The legal framework is supplemented by MDs issued by Ministers with peripheral competences, such as for example the city planning and environmental permissions for antenna installations.

The new legislative framework aims at further enhancing the liberalisation of the Greek market in line with the European status quo. However the extent to which this task will be achieved depends not only on the regulatory framework, but primarily on the financial viability of the operators in the current financial situation. The investments shortcut, the recession and the consolidation of operators in order to optimise their financials, may lead to considerable restrictions of the competition and revival of old market structures, dominated by one or two operators.

REGULATORY PRINCIPLES: THE FRAMEWORK DIRECTIVE

Scope of Regulation

16.4 Law 4070/2012 provides the legal framework for electronic communications networks and services, associated facilities and related services. Excluded from its ambit are the state's electronic communications, the networks and individual radio stations of the radio amateur service, the radio amateur service via satellite, those used solely for experimental or research and demonstration purposes, and the citizen band service (CB). Content and the relevant audiovisual policy, analogue TV and free streaming radio are also excluded, except for the provisions on surveillance and control of radio spectrum use and enforcement of relevant sanctions and/or penalties. This exception does not include the electronic communications infrastructure used to transport radio and TV signals to the transmission point, and the obligations of undertakings for signal transmission and additional facilities provision.

Law 4070/2012 defines 'electronic communications networks' as the:

'transmission systems and, where applicable, switching or routing equipment and other resources, including not active network elements, which permit the conveyance of signals by wire, by radio, by optical or by other electromagnetic means, including satellite networks, fixed (circuit- and packet-switched, including Internet) and mobile terrestrial networks, electricity cable systems, to the extent that they are used for the purpose of transmitting signals, networks used for radio and television broadcasting, and cable television networks, irrespective of the type of information conveyed'.

'Electronic communications service' is defined as:

'a service normally provided for payment which consists wholly or mainly in the conveyance of signals on electronic communications networks, including telecommunications services and transmission services in networks used for broadcasting, but exclude services providing, or exercising editorial control over, content transmitted using electronic communications networks and services; it does not include information society services, as defined in Article 2 of PD 39/2001, as applicable, which do not consist wholly or mainly in the conveyance of signals on electronic communications networks'.

'Associated facilities' are defined as:

'the material infrastructure and related services and other facilities or elements associated with an electronic communications network and/or an electronic communications service which enable and/or support the provision of services via that network and/or service or have that possibility. They include, among others, buildings or entrances of buildings, building wirings, masts, towers, and other supporting structures, ducts, pipes, poles, manholes, and cabinets'.

In terms of complex services, Art 13 of the new Law specifically regulates the terrestrial television and radio services. The provision of such services through frequencies allocated for television and radio broadcasting is defined as provision of electronic communication services, and requires both a network provider as well as a content provider. With the exception of the state owned radio and television company ERT, the law requires that the two providers are two different legal entities.

VoIP services are not specifically regulated in Greece; they fall under the communication services.

'Internet Freedom'

16.5   Law 4070/2012, in article 3(2) has endorsed the principles set out in Article 3a of the Framework directive by providing that the regulatory principles of objectivity, transparency, impartiality and proportionality are applicable in order to attain the regulatory goals specifically defined in Article 3(1). Via article 3(2) subsections ζ, ζα and ζβ, the new Law goes on to endorse almost verbatim the wording of Article 3a of the Framework Directive, as an application of the above basic principles.

As a matter of legal evolution and the law's adaptation to social advancement, the necessity to monitor internet end-usage and to restrict or punish illicit online behaviour in terms of violations falling within criminal, civil, competition or intellectual property law, during recent years has been driving Greek legislation to evolve and address the core issues of defining the role of internet service providers (ISP's) and identifying infringing users.

With regard to the role of ISPs, article 11 of PD 131/2003[7] introduces the exclusion of ISPs' liability arising from data they transmit, but on the condition that they solely forward signals within e-communication networks, without being the source of the information disseminated or choosing the recipient of the information, nor selecting or modifying the transmitted information. Article 14 of the afore-mentioned PD clarifies that there is no generalised obligation for the ISPs to monitor the access provided regarding the information transmitted or stored, or regarding indications of illegal use or behaviour. Nonetheless, this virtual 'immunity' enjoyed by the ISPs is not absolute, since upon the authority of a judicial or administrative decision issued to that end, measures can be imposed for the cessation or prevention of any infringement regarding information disseminated via the internet. Such measures primarily aim at removing any infringing material, or at blocking access to such material, or filtering the transmitted data for infringements of intellectual property rights. Moreover, when hosting, the ISPs must notify the competent authorities on any indications of illegal data or illegal activities they identify, and provide to the authorities any information and help required for the identification of parties receiving such services with whom they are contracted in storage agreements, subject to the provisions of the law of privacy and personal data. When in breach of such obligations, an ISP may be held liable in criminal or tort law.

The above, in conjunction with the provisions of copyright law[8], may give rise to applications seeking the imposition of interim measures upon ISPs mainly regarding the following:

- seizure/confiscation of any technical equipment (incl. servers) which may contain proof of the infringement;
- disclosure of the contents of the servers;
- providing information regarding the identification of the counterparty to the services agreement;
- temporary removal of the content in question from the servers;
- temporary cessation of user access to the data in question;
- cessation of the user's connection;
- listing of end users to blacklists barring access to the internet; and
- temporary installation of filters to block the accessibility to the content or service in question.[9]

According to recent case law coming out of the Athens Single Member Court of First Instance,[10] a generalised barring or exclusion of end user accessibility to resources of the Internet or parts thereof, is to be considered, as a matter of principle, as violating fundamental law provisions; specifically regarding article 51 para 2 of the Hellenic Constitution which provides for the right to participate in the information society, as applied in conjunction with articles 5 para 1, 5a para 1, 14

---

7   PD131/2003 on the 'Liability of Intermediaries in Service Provision', incorporating Directive 2000/31/EC.
8   Copyright Law 2121/1993.
9   Bagena, E, 'Problems and Solutions regarding the implementation of copyright in the Internet', article published in the booklet *Safe Internet Navigation Affects All of Us, 1st Safe Internet Navigation Conference 2012*, (Livanis Publications, Athens, 2012), p 149.
10   Athens Single Member Court of First Instance Decision No 4658/2012, Interim Measures.

para 1 and 16 para 1 of the Constitution, providing respectively for the right to freely develop one's personality and to participate to the economic, political and social life of Greece, the right to information, the right to expression and the freedom of science, research and the arts, interpreted by reference to article 10 of the European Human Rights Convention, article 19 para 2 of the International Covenant on Civil and Political Rights and articles 11 and 36 of the Charter of Fundamental Rights of the European Union (subject to the limitations of article 52(3)). The abovementioned constitutional rights include the right to access the technical infrastructure of the information society, and, with reference to the relation between users and providers, such rights may be claimed directly by the users, without requiring any further legal specialisation. Based upon the above, the court went further and defined agreement terms and conditions enabling providers to block or restrict access to the Internet as void and ineffective.

Such technical measures restricting access conform with the law only when imposed by the enforcement authority of a court order and when they restrict user access to specific Internet content of a website where the infringement takes place. This ruling agrees with judgments in other EU Member States where applications for interim measures have recently been accepted by national courts implementing Directives 2001/29 and 2004/48, such as the Appellate Court of Belgium in the case of *VZW BAF v NV Telnet and NV Publiek Recht Belgacom* (339/2011) or the British High Court in *Twentieth Century Fox Film Corp & Ors v British Telecommunications Plc* [2011]. At this point it should be noted that the Court of Justice of the European Union (ECJ) in November 2011 ruled in Scarlet Extended SA v Société belge des auteurs, compositeurs et éditeurs SCRL (SABAM) (C-70/10) that the Directives are contrary to the installation of filters because among a number of other reasons:

> '[such a] filtering system is to be regarded as not respecting the requirement that a fair balance be struck between, on the one hand, the protection of the intellectual property right enjoyed by copyright holders, and, on the other hand, that of the freedom to conduct business enjoyed by operators such as ISPs'.[11]

National Regulatory Authorities: Organisation, Regulatory Objectives, Competencies

16.6   The MITN takes policy decisions for the electronic communications sector and introduces legislation. It regulates satellite and geostationary satellite orbits. It determines, following the recommendation of EETT, the content of the Universal Service and the conditions and procedure establishing the criteria for the selection of its providers. It harmonises the use of radio frequencies with other EU Member States. It issues the National Regulation for the Allocation of Frequency Bands jointly with the Minister of National Defence, and the National Numbering Plan following a recommendation by EETT. It determines technical requirements for networks jointly with the Minister of Environment, Energy and Climate Change, and Frequencies Maps jointly with the competent Ministers.

Radio and television broadcasting is governed principally by Law 2328/95 as amended. The licensing authority is the National Council for Radio and Television

---

11   Judgement of the Court of Justice of the European Union (Third Chamber) of 24 November 2011 *Scarlet Extended SA v Société belge des auteurs, compositeurs et éditeurs SCRL (SABAM)* (C-70/10), available at http://eur-lex.europa.eu/LexUriServ/LexUriServ.do?uri=CELEX:62010CJ0070:EN:HTML, accessed 22 October 2012.

(*Ethniko Symvoulio Radiotileorasis* ('NCRTV')), which is also responsible for content supervision.

Greece's independent telecommunications monitoring body, the EETT was introduced pursuant to the provisions of Law 2075/1992, and is now regulated by Law 4070/2012. The EETT's funding is achieved by the licence levies on telecommunications companies, both public and private, and by fines imposed on such companies by itself or the courts.

The EETT is an independent authority, enjoys administrative and economic independence and does not request or receive instructions from any ministry or other supervisory body in relation to the tasks assigned by the relevant law, so fulfilling the requirements set out in articles 3(2), 3(3) and 3(3a) of the Framework Directive. It is governed by the plenary, which is composed of nine members, including a President and two Vice Presidents. The President, Vice Presidents and the members of EETT are selected by the Conference of Chairs of the Greek Parliament, following a recommendation by the Committee on Institutions and Transparency in accordance with the Regulation of the Parliament. The other members are appointed by the MITN and must be higher government officials. They also must fulfil criteria such as scientific competence, social recognition and professional esteem in the technical, economic or legal area. EETT members enjoy personal and functional independence in the exercise of their duties. Their term of service is four years and they can be appointed for only two terms.

Article 12 of Law 4070/2012 sets out EETT's powers and duties, which are consistent with the EU Regulatory Framework and cover the ambit of the e-communications regulation within the Hellenic territory to the extent it does not fall within MITN's competence. Amongst its duties are:

- the definition of the relevant markets;
- licensing and the supervision and control of network and service providers;
- the imposition of sanctions;
- the issue of Ethics Codes for the electronic communications market; keeping record of all information necessary for the overview of the electronic communications market in Greece;
- the provision of an extra-judicial disputes settlement facility;
- the compliance with electronic communications and postal services legislation and the application of the provisions of Law 3959/2011 on the protection of competition and Articles 101 and 102 of the TFEU and Regulation 1/2003/EC;
- the cooperation and exchange of information on issues of public interest with any public authority, particularly with the MITN, the Competition Commission, the NCRTV, the Hellenic Data Protection Authority, the Hellenic Authority for Communication Security and Privacy, the General Secretariat of Consumer Protection, the Consumer Ombudsman and the Financial Intelligence Unit;
- ensuring the same level of confidentiality as the Authorities mentioned above;
- the conduct of hearings to determine violations of Law 4070/2012;
- the issuance of the Hearings Regulation;
- notification to the European Commission, to NRAs of other Member States and to BEREC of its Draft Measures;
- ex officio or upon MITN's request to conduct public consultations on the matters of its competence;
- licensing;
- keeping and managing the National Register of Radio Frequencies and the Register of Networks and Electronic Communications Providers;

- monitoring the undertakings operating in the electronic communications market and physical or legal entities operating in the radio and telecommunications terminal equipment field;
- determining the frequencies or frequency bands for which rights of use are required, and granting, revoking or restricting frequency rights of use by the issue of relevant Regulations;
- managing the use of radio frequencies or radio frequency spectrum bands which fall within its competence;
- supervising and controlling the use of radio spectrum applying the relevant sanctions;
- managing the National Numbering Plan and allocating numbers;
- monitoring number portability;
- conducting the tenders for frequencies and/or numbers rights of use;
- regulating the issues of domain names ending in '.gr';
- regulating the issues of electronic signatures and supervising the relevant authorities;
- exercising its responsibilities for the provision of universal service and submitting recommendations to MITN;
- regulating consumer protection issues in electronic communications;
- granting construction licences for antenna stations on land, including broadcasting antennas;
- dealing with issues relating to conditions of use and marketing of terminal and radio equipment;
- issuing decisions in order to regulate internet issues;
- regulating issues related to network technology neutrality;
- controlling and supervising the implementation of wholesale access provisions and associated facilities, price control and cost accounting, disclosure and non-discriminatory treatment; and
- issuing guidelines and recommendations, imposing fines and other administrative sanctions on undertakings involved in electronic communications pursuant to applicable law, including penalties and sanctions provided by Law 3959/2011 referring offenders to the competent judicial authorities.

The EETT provides a dispute resolution facility (mediation and arbitration) for conflicts between market participants or between undertakings, which have their establishment in Greece or in another EU Member State and their users, or with the state. The designated procedure for the dispute resolution function of the EETT is provided in articles 34–36 of Law 4070/2012. The EETT is entitled to adjudicate on matters arising in relation to, inter alia, network installation, installation and operation of mobile telephone antennas and terminal equipment access, interconnection, universal service obligation, competition and consumer protection.

Pursuant to article 36 of Law 4070/2012, a roster of arbitrators is drawn up annually, principally from members of the Athens Bar and the Chamber of Engineers with experience in telecommunications and/or competition. Decisions must be rendered within three months from the final hearing. Arbitrators' fees and costs are proportionate to the value of the dispute. In practice, much of the dispute resolution function of the EETT is managed without recourse to arbitration procedures, following the notification of problems to the regulator.

In terms of facilitating the market opening and integration, the EETT has proved to be an efficient regulator. Although in the past there were queries to be cleared as to drawing the line between its competences and those of the MITN on one hand, and the Competition Commission on the other, competences are now rather delineated which causes less friction in the market. The recently allocated 'one-stop-shop' identity to the EETT is expected to further contribute to this goal.

Right of appeal against NRA's decisions

16.7   The EETT's regulatory decisions are subject to appeal (*aitisi akirosis*) before the Supreme Administrative Court (Symvoulion tis Epikrateias), within 60 days from the day the person became aware of the decision. The EETT's decisions imposing sanctions can be challenged (prosfigi) before the Athens Administrative Court of Appeal within 30 days of their date of publication. Other individual administrative decisions of EETT can be subjected to an appeal (aitisi akyrosis) before the Athens Administrative Court of Appeal within 60 days from the day the person became aware of the decision. Moreover, the decisions of the Athens Administrative Court of Appeal are subject to appeal before the Supreme Administrative Court.

The relevant limitation period allowed for filing an appeal or challenge accordingly, and the respective filing itself does not suspend the implementation of the contested decision of EETT except in case the court, upon a request by the applicant or the challenger and with a justified and reasoned decision, suspends wholly or partially the decision on the grounds of the applicable provisions.

The admissibility of challenges before the Athens Administrative Court of Appeal against the EETT's decisions imposing fines is subject to the advance payment of 30 per cent of the fine, which may not exceed the amount of €500,000.

The procedures before the courts are long. The average time for a trial to conclude may exceed three years. It is for this reason that judicial protection is not considered adequate. Provisional measures are available, within a reasonably efficient time frame.

The NRA's Obligations to Cooperate with the Commission

16.8   The EETT informs the European Commission and the General Secretariat for Telecommunications and Post of the MITN of undertakings with significant market power and the obligations imposed on them, the identification of the specific products and services and geographic markets, the rights of users to a Universal Service and information on competition and a detailed description of market structure, access and interconnection, provision of infrastructure and subscriber line services. Changes affecting the obligations imposed on undertakings are notified to the Commission.

Article 40 of Law 4070/2012 introduces, for the provision of services, technical interfaces and/or network functions, the implementation of mandatory standards or requirements adopted at Community level and published respectively in a list of standards and/or specifications in the Official Journal of European Communities. However, when it is absolutely necessary to ensure interoperability of services and improve users' options, non-binding standards or requirements adopted at Community level and published in a list of standards and/or specifications in the Official Journal of European Communities are applicable.

If the standards and/or specifications do not exist, the existing relevant national ones are implemented and a decision of the MITN must be issued to this end. In the absence of all of the above, the standards and/or specifications adopted by the

European Standardisation Bodies (ETSI, CENELEC, CEN, CEPT) or international standards or recommendations adopted by the ITU) ISO or the IEC are applicable.

'Significant Market Power' as a Fundamental Prerequisite of Regulation

Definition of SMP

16.9 In line with the definitions of the Framework Directive, the new Law on Electronic Communications has abolished the 25 per cent test. Article 41 determines, using the same language as Article 14(2) of the Framework Directive, that an undertaking is considered to have significant market power, if either individually or jointly with others, it enjoys a position equivalent to dominance. In order to comply with this test, the undertaking shall be in a position of economic strength affording it the power to behave to a relative extent independently of competitors, customers and ultimately consumers.

Article 41 of the new Law effectively repeats the provisions of Article 14(3) of the Framework Directive. Should an undertaking have SMP in one market (the primary market), then it may be declared as having a SMP in another market as well (secondary market), if the two markets are linked in such a way that the SMP in the primary market can be used in favour of the second one.

Definition of relevant markets

16.10 The whole territory of Greece has been defined as the relevant geographic market in leased lines[12] and in mobile telephony for both network and services.[13]

The new Law has granted the Regulator power to perform market analysis, including the definition of the relevant markets, as well as an analysis on the efficiency of competition. The EETT is further entrusted with the power to determine the providers with SMP and to impose regulatory restrictions in connection with a relevant market. In order to fulfil this task, the EETT shall perform public consultations, and have access to all data deemed necessary in order to impose ex ante regulations, and monitor the performance of the providers.

In the process of defining the relevant markets, the EETT is required by law to take into consideration the Recommendations and Guidelines of the European Commission. In the definition of the markets subject to ex ante regulation, the EETT is following the Recommendations of the European Commission, dated 17 December 2007. After the finalisation of the market definition procedure, the EETT is required to submit to the European Commission, BEREC and the European Regulators the draft measures paper, and to consider their suggestions.

EETT has so far performed three rounds of Analysis on markets 1–7 as defined in the EC Market Recommendation 5406/2007 and 3, 5, 7, 10, 14 and 15 of the EC Market Recommendation 497/2003. While the outcome of certain analysis segments is still pending, OTE has been defined to have exclusive SMP in all analysed markets of the 2007 Recommendation and all analysed markets of the 2003

---

12   EETT Decision 251/77/2002.
13   EETT Decision 248/68/2002 as supplemented by Decision 278/65/20.3.2003.

Recommendation, with the exception of Market 15, where no provider with SMP has been identified. In Market 3 and 7 of the 2007 recommendation, more providers have been identified as having SMP.

In May 2012, the EETT submitted to BEREC the Draft Plan relating to the second round analysis and proposed ex ante regulatory measures for markets 7 and 14 of the 2003 Recommendations, and Market 6 of the 2007 Recommendation.[14] So far, the EETT has not defined sub-national markets.

The performed market analysis should give sufficient evidence to the Regulator, to determine whether a relevant market is competitive enough or not. If a relevant market is found to be competitive, the EETT is required to waive all obligations imposed on providers with SMP.

Should competition be distorted in the relevant market, the EETT may trigger the procedures regarding remedial measures. Communication with BEREC and the regulatory authorities of the other Member States is required if there is a spillover of the effects.[15]

NRA's Regulatory Duties Concerning Rights of Way, Co-location and Facility Sharing

16.11   The previous law on granting rights of way proved inefficient due to complicated secondary legislation governing the various public entities involved and a certain level of legal ambiguity. The new Law attempts to introduce adjustments, aiming at facilitating new investment in infrastructure. It has adopted the distinction made by the Framework Directive (Art 11(1)) between undertakings authorised to provide public e-communications networks and undertakings authorised to provide e-communications networks other than to the public (art 28). While undertakings belonging to the first category are entitled to be granted with rights of way on or under private and public land, undertakings of the second category have the same rights only in relation to public land and land of common use.

The rights of way over private property can be granted through the procedure stipulated in Art 1188 of the Greek Civil Code, as a personal easement, and shall be accompanied by reasonable compensation to the owner of the private property in question; it is the latter who grants such rights. The lack of a complete and centrally monitored land registry (cadastre) in order to identify owners of private property and the requirement for all joint owners of a property to consent (all the owners of flats in an apartment block, for example) frequently impede the use of private property, including roofs and open spaces.

The procedure for obtaining rights of way over public property is outlined in the law. The procedure by which they acquire such rights is by submitting an application to the relevant governmental body, which should grant the rights of way within a certain timeframe, provided that the applicant has submitted all necessary documents. An additional authorisation is required in special cases (archaeological sites, protected areas and areas dedicated to national defence). Should the authorities not respond, the application is considered as having been approved. Under the old law however, appeals against decisions of local authorities refusing access or applying inappropriate criteria cause significant delays.

---

14   The paper distinguishes between leased lines with a capacity of up to 2Mbps and higher than 2 Mbps.

15   Article 45 of Law 4072/2012.

The competent authority has to grant the rights of way or otherwise give a justified reply on a fully documented application within 30 days of the receipt of the application, which is extended if the applicant is the provider of a non-public network. If the deadline expires, the permission for access is presumed to be granted automatically, which deviates from the general administrative law practice applicable in Greece. Police authorities keep record of the relevant documentation. Decisions denying the grant of rights of way must be specifically justified on the ground of environmental protection, public health, defence and the protection of archeological areas. The Administrative Court of Appeal has jurisdiction over relevant complaints.

The law provides for secondary legislation to be issued on the recommendation of the EETT following a public consultation, determining among others the exact procedure, the fees and the entities entitled to receive the fees for granting rights of way.

Article 29 of Law 4070/2012 provides for the power of the EETT to enforce the co-location or the co-use of a facility or a building assigned to an undertaking with other providers. The EETT shall issue a regulation determining the terms and conditions for the assignment of such obligations, based on transparency, neutrality and proportionality.

The law governing the installation and operation of antennas and its implementation in practice proved to be one the most important aspects of the development of public communication. Sector specific responsible public authorities used to authorise rights of way in their area of authority. For instance the Ministry of Environment authorised rights of way to protected areas or traditional villages, the Hellenic National Defence General Staff for areas of the Ministry of Defence and the Armed Forces, and the local Archeological Service for areas near monuments, archeological sites and historic landmarks. The new Law tries to address this issue by introducing more flexible and anti-bureaucratic procedures by nominating a single web based point of entrance for the applications concerning the constructions of antennas. The new Law appoints the EETT as the entity responsible for granting the licence to construct and operate antennas and sets four months as the ultimate deadline to respond, however it has to clear the interaction with the respective competent authorities.

Since the new Law provides for a significant amount of secondary legislation, it cannot currently be assessed to what extent the new system will provide a substantial improvement of the procedures. Until the issuance of such regulations, JMD 725/23 issued on 05 January 2012 by the Ministers for Internal Affairs, Finance, Defence, Development, Environment, Infrastructure, Transport and Networks, Citizen Protection, Tourism and Culture is still applicable.

Co-location agreements between undertakings are subject to review by the EETT for compliance with the law. If no agreement on co-location and common use of facilities is achieved within 45 days of the beginning of the negotiations, the interested party may request the intervention of the EETT. In resolving the dispute the EETT will take into consideration the following:

- the cost and the possible difficulties for independent installation and operation of the relevant equipment or systems;
- the implications for competition on the level of the services provided by the parties taking into account geographical coverage, the pricing and the quality of the services;
- the benefit to consumers taking into account the price of the services, the

extent of coverage, the development and quality of the network and the protection of the environment and the public safety;
- the possible existence of alternative competitive facilities, and their technical and economic viability, taking into account the peculiarities of the domestic market and any environmental restrictions, public health and safety and city planning objectives.

REGULATION OF MARKET ENTRY: THE AUTHORISATION DIRECTIVE

The General Authorisation of Electronic Communications

16.12   The provision of electronic communication networks and/or services is regulated under a General Authorisation regime. General Authorisations are issued in accordance with article 18 of Law 4070/2012 and the Regulation on General Authorisations of the EETT (Government Gazette B 748/21.06.2006). The EETT has held a public consultation which was open between 18 October 2012 and 19 November 2012, on the amendment of the Regulation on General Authorisations, in order to bring the Regulation into line with the new Law.

Under Law 4070/2012 the EETT may require the submission of a Registration Declaration by interested providers of electronic communications, including cross-border e-communication service providers, in order for them to be subjected to the General Authorisation regime. Nevertheless, the issuance of an individual administrative act is not required in terms of exercising the rights that arise from the General Authorisation. Upon submitting the Registration Declaration, the undertaking may commence its operations, subject to the legal reservations on rights of use. Undertakings which provide cross-border e-communication services to undertakings based in other Member States are not obliged to submit a Registration Declaration, as long as they have already submitted a notification in another member state.

The Regulation on General Authorisations defines as a mandatory field the submission of the Registration Declaration, under article 4, only for entities that provide public networks of communication or offer electronic communication services to the public, as well as for entities that operate specific radio networks, as defined in Annex A of the Regulation. Via the Registration Declaration, the interested party declares the intention to start one or more electronic communication activities, which are then described and registered in the Registry of Electronic Communication Network and Service Providers, kept by the EETT.

Within one week of filing the application, the EETT issues a certificate on the submission of the Registration Declaration. The certification disambiguates the conditions subject to which the provider becomes entitled to apply for authorisation to install facilities, negotiate access and/or gain access or interconnection in order to be facilitated in exercising the respective rights.

All entities operating under the General Authorisations regime must pay administrative fees[16] which represent costs for management, control and enforcement of the General Authorisations, fees for the grant of rights of use of radio frequencies and/or numbers and also special fees, provided for in Law 4070/2012. These administrative fees do not include number and frequency allocation fees, which according to the applicable EETT Regulations are payable upon the submission of

---

16   Art 74 of Law 4070/12 et seq.

the application for number and/or frequency allocation. The administrative fees are paid only by undertakings which provide public electronic networks or electronic communication services to the public, whether for profit or not. All entities operating under the General Authorisations regime, who provide public electronic network or electronic communication services to the public, must pay the annual administrative fee, calculated as a percentage of the total gross income from the provision of public electronic communication networks or electronic communication services to the public. Apart from the abovementioned fees, when applying for a Registration Declaration, an administrative fee of €300 applies; for any addition or amendment to the original Registration Declaration a fee of €100 is due.

Any entity providing network and/or electronic communication services shall comply with the regulations of the National Numbering Plan,[17] the Regulation on Management and Allocation of Numbering Resources of the National Numbering Plan,[18] the Regulation of Use and Grant of Rights of Radio Frequencies[19] under a General Authorisation, and to any amendment, addition or replacement thereof, as well as with any terms which the MITN or the EETT may impose on specific lines of numbers or radiofrequencies, according to the provisions of Law 4070/2012.

Any entities providing public networks and/or e-communication services to the public, undertakes all the Universal Service Obligations,[20] which can be imposed on it, under the current legislation and is obliged, if necessary, to participate in the sharing of the Universal Service net costs, according to the current regulations, which is charged on the persons who are obliged to provide Universal Service.

Simple resale of electronic communication services to end-users, and own use of terminal radio equipment based upon a non-exclusive use of special radio frequencies (e.g. CB use) are exempt from the provisions of articles 18–27 on the General Authorisation regime.

Rights of Use for Radio Frequencies

Strategic planning and co-ordination of spectrum policy

16.13   The MITN, and occasionally the EETT cooperate with the competent authorities of other EU Member States and with the European Commission, under article 20(3) of Law 4070/2012, regarding the strategic planning, co-ordination and harmonization of spectrum use in the European Union. The MITN and the EETT further consider matters of economy, safety, general interest, freedom of expression and cultural, scientific, social and technical aspects of the EU policies and along with the interests of groups of radio spectrum users, in order to optimise the use of spectrum and avoid harmful interference.

Spectrum frequency management and radio transmission supervision are performed by the authorised bodies, in accordance with national requirements, international agreements and the provisions of the Charter, the Convention and Radiocommunications Regulations of the International Telecommunications Union, and taking into account the decisions of the competent bodies of the CEPT and the EU Directives, as applicable following their ratification, under the article 28

---

17   See 'Rights of use for numbers' below
18   See 'Rights of use for numbers' below
19   See 'Rights of use for radio frequencies' below
20   See 'Regulation of the Universal Service And Users' Rights' below

para 1 of the Constitution; laws adopting international conventions prevail over other national laws regarding the subject matter.

Under the Regulation for Use-Granting of Rights to Use Radio Frequencies, in order to provide electronic communications networks or services, the public networks of electronic communications, the networks and individual stations for radio communications of the radio amateur service, the radio amateur satellite service and anything used exclusively for experimental or research purposes and for demonstration, as well as analogue TV, free radio and satellite digital broadcasting are outside its scope.

The MITN Minister and the Minister assigned with the General Secretariats of Information and Communication and of Media, after consulting with the EETT, cede a part of the digital terrestrial broadcasting spectrum for the Greek region to the Hellenic Radiotelevision Company ERT SA, being a network provider serving public interest purposes.

Greece has implemented the transition from analogue to digital television in the largest part of its territory, with Article 14 of Law 3592/2007 providing for the fundamentals for the transition.

Auctions have been held in relation to mobile telephony bandwidths. A successful tender procedure was completed in autumn 2011 for the granting of rights of use in the 900 MHz and 1800 MHz frequency bands, raising a total amount of €380.5 million. Although not all 2G licences expire in September 2012, all 14 lots of 2×2.5 MHz available in the 900 MHz band (including spectrum previously allocated to the use of the Army Forces) were auctioned as well as four lots of 2×5 MHz in the 1800 MHz band, so that all rights of use expire in 2026. The procedure chosen was a multi-round tender procedure, open also to new entrants.

EETT cooperates with other Member States' NRAs order to share know-how and experience gained from the organisation and outcome of tendering procedures.

Transferability and time limitations

16.14 A transfer, lease, change of beneficiary, or change of the beneficiary's control of a right to use a radio frequency, wholly or in part, is subject to the approval of the EETT, upon the joint application filed by the company granted with the right of use of the radio frequencies and the future beneficiary. For a transfer to be completed the following conditions must be cumulatively satisfied:

- the use of radio frequencies has to remain unchanged, when such use has been harmonised via the implementation of Decision 676/2002/EU or other Community measures;
- the radio frequency's terms of use, which had been imposed upon the previous beneficiary, have to be respected by the new beneficiary; and
- in the case of radio frequencies which are subject to international coordination procedures, the new beneficiary must continue providing support to the YYMD for the completion of such procedures.

On approving the transfer, the EETT must ensure that competition law is not violated, and that the new beneficiary fulfills any conditions deemed necessary out of those under which the above-mentioned rights were granted, indicatively taking into consideration the technological changes, the time at which the rights were granted, the development of networks and the level of competition.

The above-mentioned approval is notified in writing to the undertakings in question and is published on the EETT website.

Antenna systems which are used in conjunction with the transferred radio frequencies, may also be transferred, in accordance with the laws in force and provided that the owner of the property where the antenna systems are installed consents to such transfer. In the cases of antenna systems' transfer or lease, providers are obliged to notify the EETT.

Upon the EETT's recommendations, an MD issued by the MITN Minister defines the terms, conditions, criteria and the procedure for the partial transfer or lease of a right of use of radio frequencies. Such decision shall take into consideration the implementation measures adopted by the European Commission for the determination of the frequency zones where such transfer or lease among undertakings is allowed.

Terms connected to the individual rights of use remain in effect after the transfer or lease, unless the EETT specifies otherwise.

If the grant is for a term of ten years or more, which cannot be transferred or leased among undertakings under the abovementioned procedure, the EETT ensures that the granting criteria continue to be valid throughout the entire duration of the right, especially if the right holder submits a justified application to the EETT. If the criteria are no longer valid, the specific right is converted into a general permit for the use of radio frequencies, always subject to a prior notice and after a reasonable period of time either becomes freely transferable or can be leased between undertakings, under the above-mentioned procedure.

Under Law 4070/2012, a right of use of a radio frequency may be granted either on a temporary basis, which cannot exceed a term of two months and may be renewed once for a maximum of two additional months, or on a permanent basis without a defined time limit.

Admissible conditions

16.15   The National Regulation on Frequency Band Allocation[21] provides for the allocation of frequency bands of the spectrum from 9 KHz to 1000 GHz in one or more radio communication services. The Regulation on the Terms of Use of Individual Radio Frequencies or Frequency Bands[22] specifies the category in which every use of individual radio frequency or frequency band for the provision of networks and/or electronic communication services is included. It also defines the technical terms of use of individual radio frequencies or frequency bands for applications or radio communication services. The technical terms concern the permissible uses, the technical features of the equipment and the current plans of channel spacing.

When the Regulation of Terms of Use does not provide for the use of a specific radio frequency or frequency band, the National Regulation on Frequency Band Allocation is applicable.

Bands 880–915 MHz, 1710–1785 MHz and 1805–1880 MHz are used in accordance with the provisions of Decision 2009/766/EU of the European Commission, as

---

21   JMD 20490/525, Government Gazette Issue B' 1444/02.05.2012.
22   MD 624/216/2011, GG Issue B' 2512/07.11.2011.

amended by the Implementing Decision 2011/251/EU of the Commission 'on the amendment of the Decision 2009/766/EU on the harmonisation of frequency bands of 900 MHz and 1800 MHz for terrestrial systems capable of providing electronic communication services in the Community' and the JMD 58626/2224/Φ1/2010,[23] GG B' 918/2010 'on the frequency bands to be reserved for the coordinated introduction of pan-European cellular digital public land-based mobile communications in the Community'.

According to the above-mentioned JMD, the frequency bands of 880–915 MHz and 925–960 MHz (900 MHz band), are applicable for GSM and UMTS systems, as well as for other land-based systems capable of providing electronic communication services, which may co-exist with GSM systems, according to the technical measures adopted by the implementation of 676/2002/EU Decision of the European Parliament and the Council on the regulatory framework for the radio spectrum policy in the European Community (Radio Spectrum Decision, EE L 108, 24 April 2002).

The EETT submits a report to the MITN suggesting whether the current allocation of the 900 MHz band to competitive mobile telephony undertakings may distort competition.

The use of frequency bands falls under the General Authorisation regime, concerning frequency bands of non-exclusive use where the operating devices are not protected from interferences (ie WiFi@, 2.4 GHz, 5GHz), and therefore no personal right of use is needed.

On December 2012, the EETT published the results of a public consultation held on the amendment of the Regulation for Use – Granting of Rights to Use Radio Frequencies, where three providers/operators participated. The EETT partially held one of the three proposed amendments. This concerned the implementation of objective criteria when looking into the actual use of spectrum, in order to avoid the phenomenon of users stockpiling spectrum, and in case such a phenomenon occurs, to impose such penalties as provided in article 77 of Law 4070 upon the responsible juristic person. In general, amendments which shall be adopted in the near future primarily aim at the harmonisation of the regulation in question with Law 4070/2012 and consequently the Framework Directive.

Limitation of number of rights of use to be granted

16.16   The number of rights of use of radio frequencies to be granted is unlimited, unless such limitation is deemed necessary to ensure the effective use of the radio frequencies. If limiting is considered, maximising the benefit for the users and facilitating competition shall be taken into account.

The EETT may proceed with a public consultation to examine whether it is essential to limit the number of rights of use of radio frequencies, the granting procedure thereof, the need to extend the duration of the currently existing rights in some way other than as described in these rights.

When the public consultation is over, the MITN Minister, on the recommendation of the EETT, may limit the number of rights of use of radio frequencies to be

---

23   On the compliance to the provisions of Directive 2009/114/EU of the European Parliament and the Council of September 16, 2009 on the amendment of Directive 87/372/EU of the Council.

granted or extend the duration of the currently existing rights in a way different than the one described in these rights. This decision provides for the type of tender procedure for these rights to be granted.

The EETT is responsible for the publication of the invitation to tender for rights of use and the procedure, as defined in the MITN Decision.

The MITN Minister is entitled, either ex officio or upon request, to review the limitation on the number of rights of use of radio frequencies and raise or reduce that number and/or the extent of the duration of the currently existing rights, provided that there has been an EETT recommendation to that effect and a relative public consultation.

The parties to whom the rights will be granted are selected on the basis of objective, transparent, non-discriminatory and proportionate criteria.

Rights of use for numbers

General authorisations and granting of individual rights

16.17 Law 4070/2012, the National Numbering Plan and the Regulation on Management and Allocation of Numbering Resources of the National Numbering Plan[24] regulate number allocation in the Greek region.

Granting rights of use of the numbering resources of the National Numbering Plan is distinguished by primary and secondary allocation. Tertiary allocation of numbering resources is prohibited. Primary allocation is defined as the EETT's granting the right(s) of use of specific numbering resources, after thoroughly examining the application of the electronic communications network and service provider, for the applicant's own use or for such numbering resources to be secondarily provided to other users by the applicant, under the terms, conditions and limitations defined by the law. Secondary allocation is defined as the granting of rights of use of numbering resources by the provider of electronic communication networks and services, granted primarily to the provider by the EETT under the terms, conditions and limitations set by the law.

The providers of electronic communication networks and services have the right to apply for a primary allocation of numbering resources, if the network or the provided service justifies the use of the requested numbering resources. The application for primary allocation shall be specific and definite and must include specific numbering resources.

Applications for the allocation of numbering resources are reviewed by the EETT on the basis of a time-priority principle, as determined by the protocol number attributed to each application. If it is required to complete the application with additional information, the submission date is the date that the complete application is submitted.

Primary allocation of numbering resources is for an indefinite term. If the General Authorisation is recalled or the operations or activity of providing electronic communication network or services under a General Authorisation are terminated, the decision granting the numbering resources is repealed by the EETT. It is forbidden to reserve numbering resources of the National Numbering Plan.

---

24   See below

The EETT grants the rights of use of numbers under the National Numbering Plan within three weeks of the submission of the complete application.

As regards 'golden' or 'silver' numbers, ie numbers which have been characterised by an EETT decision as of exceptional economic value, the EETT decides after a consultation that such numbers shall be granted via a tender process, and rights of use of such numbers shall be granted within six weeks of the beginning of the process.

Primary and secondary allocations only provide rights of use over the numbers and do not bring about the acquisition of any property rights on these numbers by the assignee. Therefore no natural or legal person may raise proprietorship claims on the numbers.[25]

Only a provider who has been primarily allocated the numbers may allocate numbers secondarily. Providers are not allowed to use internal network numbers, which contradict the National Numbering Plan.

Admissible conditions

16.18   The allocated numbers shall be used in accordance with the conditions and provisions of the National Numbering Plan, the Regulation on Management and Allocation of Numbering Resources of the National Numbering Plan and the Decisions of the European Commission on harmonised use of numbering resources throughout Europe, as well as with any additional terms defined by the EETT in Annex VII, Part C' of Law 4070/2012.

The evaluation of applications for primary allocation of numbering resources by the EETT is performed while considering the following:

- the provision of an e-communications network or e-communication services under a General Authorisation offered by the competent authority and subject to the conditions set thereof;
- the necessity of efficient usage of the National Numbering Plan resources and especially their scarcity;
- the resources applied for and their use in accordance with the law, public order and the principles of morality;
- observance of principles of equal treatment of interested users and the transparency in secondary allocation procedures;
- the need to ensure effective competition and equal treatment of interested parties;
- public interest requirements in the social, economic and/or other sectors;
- compliance with international rules and conventions and with EU legislation;
- the possibility of alternative numbering solutions; and
- availability in terms of time of the service for which the application is submitted.

The entity that primarily allocates the numbers is obliged to provide the EETT with any information on the current situation of the numbering resources which have been allocated or used (ie in use, out of use, portability to some other network) under Law 4070/2012.

In respect of number portability, the provider is obliged to ensure the portability of geographical numbers, so that subscribers may be able to preserve the geographical

---

25   Art 10, S A, Ss 3 ΚΔΕΑΠΕΣΑ (441/121/21-06-2007).

number(s) within the same geographical region, even if they change network/ services provider.[26]

Fixed network providers and/or electronic communication service providers shall perform the procedures regarding geographic number introduction and termination to/from their networks regarding the availability of geographical number portability in accordance with the Regulation on Number Portability in the Greek Market.[27]

New market entrants shall provide number portability in the region within one month of commencing operations.[28]

Mobile telephony network and/or service providers must also ensure the portability of mobile numbers, so that subscribers may retain their numbers upon changing network or/and service provider.

The provider initiating a call is responsible for routing it to the receiver's network, regardless of the network to which the respective number group has been primarily allocated by the EETT.

In particular the obligation to properly route calls initiated within the Greek territory to the recipient's network is set upon the provider where a call is initiated; on the other hand, the obligation to properly route incoming calls from areas outside Greece towards the recipient's network, is imposed upon the provider whose network first receives the call within Greek territory.

The provider may either properly route the calls to the recipient's network or route the call to another provider, on the basis of a relevant agreement, and make use of the routing services of this provider.

According to Regulation 366/48/2006 on the Introduction of Provider Pre-selection to the Greek Market, fixed public telephony SMPs must provide their subscribers, including those using ISDN, with the pre-selection facility.[29]

This facility consists of providing access to switched telecommunication services of any interconnected organisation providing public telecommunication services or any virtual telecommunication provider. This option must be accompanied by the concurrent ability of cancelling the pre-selection by dialing a per call short call pre-fix (provider selection code) of some other telecommunication provider while making the particular call.

Limitation of number of rights of use to be granted

16.19   Decisions issued by the EETT define the procedures, conditions and any relevant details regarding the granting of rights of use for numbers, but Law 4070/2012 does not provide for a specific framework on such procedures, apart from requiring for them to be transparent, objective, unbiased and open.

The NRA's Enforcement Powers

16.20   In exercising its supervisory authority and monitoring the proper functioning of the market, the EETT has the full investigative powers provided by Law

---

26   Art 68 Law 4070/2012.
27   Art 3, S 2 Regulation on Number Portability (EETT 566/016/2010).
28   Art 3, S 3 Regulation on Number Portability (EETT 566/016/2010).
29   Art 3, para 1 366/48/2006 Regulation on the Introduction of Provider Pre-selection to the Greek Market.

3959/2011 on Competition Protection, in order to establish whether the law is violated, such as the powers afforded to tax auditors. The EETT has no power to seize or take away the tax books and elements of subjects of its investigations. EETT officers may take sworn or unsworn depositions of individuals involved. Articles 38 and 39 of Law 3959/2011 specify such powers in detail, to include the power to request a party to provide information upon a deadline, to obtain permission to search the domiciles of company executives when there are indications that company books and information are purposely withheld there, to impose penalties when parties do not comply with its requests, to demand the assistance of any public authority, etc. In exercising these powers, the EETT personnel are subject to a confidentiality obligation.[30]

Sanctions

16.21   The breach of regulations that concern the rights of use of radio frequencies and numbers, or their unauthorised use, illegal trade or use of terminal equipment and radio equipment, is punishable by at least six months of imprisonment and a monetary penalty ranging from €3,000 to €1,500,000. Any related technical equipment is seized and may be confiscated, subject to an irrevocable criminal sentence.

Apart from the administrative penalties provided for in Article 16 of PD 44/2002 which range from €3,000 to €60,000 and are imposed upon breaches of the legislation on radio equipment and telecommunications terminal equipment and the mutual recognition of their conformity, the EETT, upon taking notice that an e-communication provider is breaching any of the terms of the General Authorisation, the rights of use of radio frequencies and/or numbers, the special obligations imposed[31] or the obligations of designated undertakings, the e-communication legislation, or the Regulation of the European Commission on International Roaming, or does not provide the information requested as defined in Article 38 of Law 4070/2012, notifies the breaching provider of it becoming aware of the breach, providing the breaching party with a chance to be heard or remedy any breaches within a reasonable term of time.

Upon issuing a justified decision and after having heard the parties in question, the EETT may demand the cessation of such breach as described in the paragraph above, either henceforth or within a reasonable deadline, take appropriate and proportionate measures in order to ensure compliance, and may impose one (or more) of the following penalties:

- a formal recommendation/warning;
- a fine of up to €3,000,000, payable in accordance with the Code of Public Revenue Collection, which may include retroactive periodic penalties. The EETT can provide for its payment in installments;
- order for the suspension or revocation of the right to provide networks or/and e-communication services under a General Authorisation, as well as of the rights of use and/or special obligations when grave and repeated breaches are recorded. In such cases, the EETT may impose effective, proportionate and deterrent penalties that will cover the whole term of the breach, even if the breach has ceased to exist.

---

30   Such powers further delegated to the EETT by Art 14 of Law 4070/2012.
31   Arts 44, 47 Ss1, 2,4,5, and 49 of Law 4070/2012.

- An order to stop or delay the provision of a service or a group of services which upon its continuation would produce a gravely distorted effect on competition, while compliance is pending in respect of access obligations imposed after a market analysis.

The decision of the EETT is notified to the undertaking concerned within 10 working days. Prior to this notification, the EETT does not inform of the decision or of any part of it to any third party.

If a penalised entity pays an administrative fine within 30 days of it being notified of the EETT's decision, the fine is reduced to two thirds of the initial fine imposed. This provision also applies to penalties imposed by the EETT under PD 44/2002.

In exceptional circumstances where EETT has sufficient indications that a breach of legal provisions on e-communications poses a direct, serious and imminent threat to public safety, public order or public health, or may cause serious economic or operational problems to other undertakings or e-communication network users or other users of radio spectra, may take exceptional temporary measures in order to address the situation, prior to reaching a final decision, which is taken after a hearing of the undertaking concerned. The decision of the EETT on the temporary measures is implemented immediately and it may impose an administrative fine of up to €150,000 per day of non-compliance. The procedure of adopting temporary measures is defined by the Regulation on Hearings of the EETT, which is published in the Government Gazette. The concerned undertaking may present its views and propose rectification measures. If these measures are considered sufficient, or via a final decision by the EETT, the temporary measures are revoked and the proposed measures are validated by the EETT. The temporary measures of the EETT present a maximum effectual term of three months, which may be extended for another three months in cases of incomplete compliance.

Furthermore, undertakings operating under a General Authorisation are obliged to provide any and all information to the authorities upon the EETT's request, including all financial information required to ensure compliance with the laws on e-communications and specifically with regard to the General Authorisation's terms, terms of rights of use of radio frequencies or numbers and rights to install facilities or special requirements set by Law 4070/2012.

If there is no deadline, information shall be provided to the EETT within 20 working days of the submission of the application. In any case, the time defined may not be less than five working days.

All information relevant to rights, terms, procedures, charges, fees and decisions on General Authorisations and rights of use of radio frequencies and numbers, rights, rights to install facilities, definition of special markets for products or services and geographical markets, as well as any other information that contributes to an open and competitive market, are published on the website of the EETT in a manner that it is accessible to all interested parties, subject to business confidentiality.[32]

Administrative Charges and Fees for Rights of Use[33]

16.22 Where applicable, decisions issued by the EETT per case impose on providers of electronic communications the following fees:

---

32   Art 39 Law 4070/2012.
33   Arts 74 and 75 Law 4070/2012.

- fees for General Authorisations and especially for General Authorisations management and control;
- fees for the granting rights of use, especially for the management and review of the providers' applications;
- fees for the special obligations imposed on undertakings;
- fees for domain name assignment; and
- fees for spectrum control and supervision.

Beyond the above-mentioned administrative fees, the EETT imposes fees on e-communication providers for the right of use of radio frequencies and numbers, which reflect the need to ensure the best possible use for these resources. Furthermore, the EETT imposes fees for the rights of use of domain names, in order to ensure efficient use of resources. The EETT imposes the fees mentioned above in a way which is objective, transparent, non-discriminatory and proportionate to the objectives of L4070/2012.

The Regulation on Fees of Spectrum Use and on Fees of Radio Frequencies' Allocation[34], as well as the Regulation on Management and Allocation of Numbering Resources of the National Plan of Numbering[35] govern the matter of the fees of use.

Transitional Regulations for Existing Authorisations

16.22 Except for the provisions on the adaptation of already existing rights of use of radiofrequencies,[36] the EETT must adapt the general authorisations and individual rights of use that already existed as of 31 December 2009 to accord with the provisions of Law 4070/2012 within six months of its entry into force. With regard to the exception mentioned above for radiofrequencies, the new Law defines that for a term of five years, beginning from 25 May, 2011, holders of rights of use of radiofrequencies, where such rights had been granted prior to that date and which are still valid five years after that date, may apply to the EETT for a reevaluation of the restriction of their rights in accordance to the principles and provisions of Law 4070/2012.

As of the entry into force of Law 4070/2012, tender procedures carried out by the EETT or the MITN which are currently in progress are to be completed in accordance with the relevant proclamation.

Pending Applications submitted to EETT before the entry into force of Law 4070/2012 shall be examined under Law 4070/2012.

REGULATION OF NETWORK ACCESS AND INTERCONNECTION: THE ACCESS DIRECTIVE

Objectives and Scope of Access Regulation

16.23 The EETT is assigned with the task of ensuring the availability of both network access and interconnection of all telecommunication undertakings.[37] In this role, the EETT's objectives are expressly stated as guaranteeing the access,

---

34 EETT Decision 276/49/14-2-2003.
35 EETT Decision 441/121/21-06-2007.
36 Arts 24 and 20 of Law 4070/2012.
37 Art 1 A of Law 4070/2012.

interconnection and interoperability of the services. To that end, the EETT is required to take measures aiming to achieve maximum economic outcome, sustainable competition, return on investment and innovation, while ensuring the maximum possible benefit to end users.

A key element of the new provisions (Articles 46 to 54) is the ability of network and service providers to enter into access and interconnection agreements without any restrictions. Non-resident EU operators do not need to have general authorisation in order to enter into such an agreement, unless they operate in Greece.

The principle of the priority of commercial negotiations[38] has been expressly provided for in Article 46(3) of the new Law. Providers of public communication networks are required to enter into negotiations with holders of a General Authorisation, while the terms and the conditions for the provisions of these services are subject to the supervision of the EETT.

Basic Regulatory Concepts

16.24   The powers and obligations of the EETT in regulating access and interconnection are set out in Articles 46 to 53 of the new Law. Network providers are required to enter into interconnection agreements with holders of an authorisation, under terms and conditions that are to be defined by an EETT Regulation.

The terms 'access' and 'interconnection' are defined in Law 4070/2012 in the same terms as in the Access Directive.

In order to ensure the access, interconnection and interoperability of the services, EETT can impose on all undertakings the following remedies, based on objective, transparent and proportional criteria:

● to providers having control over the access to end users specific obligations, including the obligation to provide interconnection and services subject to interoperability. [39]
● to providers the obligation to provide access to API and EPG under non discriminatory, equal and fair terms, in order to ensure that end users have access to certain digital radio and television broadcasting services[40].

The new Law deviates from the obligation approach of the Access Directive, relying upon the discretion of the EETT, whether it is necessary or not to impose remedies on an undertaking.

The EETT is also entitled to initiate investigations in order to ensure that the market remains competitive. Should the EETT, after conducting a market analysis, come to the conclusion that a provider has an SMP, then it can impose additional transparency, non-discrimination and accounting separation obligations.[41] The new Law has adopted the additional safeguards stipulated by the Access Directive, and requires the EETT to first submit a request to the European Commission, which makes a decision following consultation with BEREC.[42]

---

38   Art 3(1) of the Access Directive.
39   Art 47(1)(a) Law 4070/2012.
40   Art 47(1)(b) Law 4070/2012.
41   Art 50(1) Law 4070/2012.
42   Art 47(4),(45) Law 4070/2012.

Access- and Interconnection-related Obligations with Respect to SMP-undertakings

Specific access obligations

16.25   Article 51 of the new Law aims to implement the scope of Article 12 of the Access Directive, adopting effectively the same language.

The new Law restricts the circle of providers subject to the EETT's powers to impose special access obligations to SMP undertakings.[43] Should the NRA come to the conclusion that restricted access or access on onerous terms may have a negative impact on the end users or on the competition, then it may impose additional obligations regarding access and use of the network or value added services.

The EETT is empowered to impose obligations on SMP undertakings to meet reasonable requests for access to and use of specific network elements and associated facilities. The EETT should impose the obligations in particular in situations where the NRA considers the denial of access or unreasonable terms and conditions having a similar effect would hinder a sustainable competitive market at retail level or would not be to the end users' interests.[44] In line with the provisions of the Directive, Law 4070/2012 provides the EETT with the authority to impose on operators the same requirements as those provided for by Article 12 of the Access Directive.[45]

Price control and cost accounting

16.26   Should, following a market analysis, the EETT come to the conclusion that that the operator concerned might sustain prices at an excessively high level, or apply a price squeeze, to the detriment of end users, then it can include obligations relating to cost recovery and price controls, including obligations for cost orientation of prices in relation to the provision of specific types of interconnection and/or access. In order to encourage further infrastructure investments in next generation access networks, Article 51 para 1 provides, in line with Article 13(1) sentence 3 of the Access Directive, for a duty of the EETT to be to 'take into account the investment made by the operator and allow it a reasonable rate of return on adequate capital employed, taking into account any risks specific to a particular new investment network project'.

Regarding pricing of services that involve interoperability and operators' interconnection, according to an EETT Press elease dated 21 December 2012, starting 1 January 2013, the termination fees in the wholesale market for mobile networks will be reduced to 1.269 cents per minute from 4.95 cents per minute since 31 July 2012, before the gradual drop in charges was applied. Retail call prices from fixed phones to mobile phones are also expected to be reduced, generating significant economic benefits for the end consumer. Overall, it is estimated that the billing accounts of consumers in the Greek market will drop by about €47 million euros within 2013. Termination fee charges for calls to mobile networks will be further applied in 2014 (1.168 cents per minute) and in 2015 (1.099 cents per minute) plus

---

43   Art 51(1) Law 4070/2012.
44   Art 51(1) Law 4070/2012.
45   Directive 2002/19/EC of the EU Parliament and of the Council.

inflation rate, thus implementing the EETT's policy for a stable and regulated market to the benefit of consumers.[46]

Functional separation

16.27   Under the new Law, the Regulator is entitled to impose functional separation. If the appropriate obligations imposed under Articles 50, 51 and 52 of Law 4070/2012 have failed to achieve effective competition and there are important and persisting competition problems and/or market failures identified in relation to the wholesale provision of certain access product markets', the EETT may impose 'an obligation on vertically integrated undertakings to place activities related to the wholesale provision of relevant access products in an independently operating business entity' as an exceptional measure. The EETT's decision is subject to approval by the European Commission.

Regulatory Powers Applicable to All Market Participants

Obligation to ensure end-to-end connectivity, roaming services and access to digital radio and television broadcasting services.

16.28   Subject to the conditions of fairness, reasonableness and timeliness, the EETT has the authority to oblige operators to provide specified services needed to ensure interoperability of end-to-end services to users, including facilities for intelligent network services or roaming on mobile networks.[47]

Apart from the measures enforced especially on SMPs, the EETT may impose upon companies controlling end-user access any appropriate requirements, even the requirement to interconnect or render their services interoperable.[48] Moreover, undertakings must install all required equipment to ensure that they can carry telephone calls to the emergency number '112' even through national roaming, or even without having identified the caller's SIM card.

Regulation of roaming services

16.29   With regard to tariffs, Greek law is in conformity with the EU guidelines and regulations on pricing.

Access to digital radio and television broadcasting services

16.30   Operators offering services of Digital Interactive Television which are transmitted in whatever manner within other Member States must use the open API and be in accordance with European standards.[49] Law 3592/2007, as amended, harmonised Directives 2002/19/EC, 2002/20/EC, 2002/21/EC,2002/22/EC and 2002/77/EC and concerns the acquisition of control on electronic mass media.

---

46   Press release of 21 December 2012 from the official website of the EETT, http://www.eett.gr/opencms/opencms/admin_EN/News/news_0159.html, (accessed 18 January 2013
47   Art 51(1ζ) of Law 4070/2012.
48   Art 47(1) of Law 4070/2012.
49   Art 48 of Law 4070/2012, Law 3592/2007 as amended.

REGULATION OF THE UNIVERSAL SERVICE AND USERS' RIGHTS: THE UNIVERSAL SERVICE DIRECTIVE

Scope of Universal Service Obligations

16.31   The provision of Universal Service, according to Article 55 of Law 4070/2012 and the MD 440/2007 on the Context of the Universal Service, includes at least the following services:

- access to fixed positions and telephone services;
- directories and directory information service;
- public telephones and other access points for the public telephony service; and
- special arrangements for end users with disability or special social needs, such as the elderly, or patients suffering from heart, kidney, transplant conditions, etc.

The MITN, upon the EETT's recommendation, may specify the context of the Universal Service and define any additional services. If deemed necessary and in the same way, it may define the technology of the Universal Service in a way that minimises market distortions, especially regarding the provision of services at a price or under terms and conditions that deviate from ordinary commercial conditions.

The provided connection in a fixed position to the public fixed network has to enable end users to make calls (local, national or international) and use fax and data services. Data services and capacity/speed should allow for operational access to the Internet, provided this is technologically possible on the basis of the prevailing technology used by the majority of subscribers. This obligation of the Universal Service provider concerns the user's connection to a public fixed telephone network with a single narrowband connection, but does not extend to Integrated Services of Digital Networks (ISDN).[50]

Under Article 60 of Law 4070/2012, Ministerial Decision 440/2007 and Ministerial Decision 44867/1637 on Measures for Disabled End-users, the EETT supervises the Universal Service providers regarding the following:

- the imposition of terms and conditions which financially burden the subscribers for facilities or services which are not included within the provisions regarding the Universal Service, and are neither essential nor mandatory for the requested service; and
- the provision of special facilities and services as described in Annex I of Ministerial Decision 440/2007, to enable subscribers to monitor and control their expenses and avoid unjustified service disconnections.

The above are effective when the Universal Service provider provides facilities and services beyond those due according to the provisions of the general legal framework, beyond the special measures regarding disabled end users and beyond the provisions on ensuring affordable tariffs, under the Universal Service.

The MITN may take special measures to provide disabled end users with the right to choose between undertakings and providers available to the majority of end users, regardless of whether they also provide Universal Service.

---

50   Art 4 of MD 440/2007 on Defining the Contents of the Universal Service.

Designation of Undertakings Obliged to Provide Universal Services

16.32   Article 56 of Law 4070/2012 and the MD 281/2002 determine the conditions, choice criteria and selection process for providers designated to provide universal services.

Each public network and/or electronic communication provider to the public, operating under the General Authorisation regime, is entitled to be a Universal Service candidate provider for the whole or part of the service.

The EETT may designate different undertakings or groups of undertakings for the provision of various Universal Service services or the coverage of different areas of the Greek territory, provided that they meet the relevant eligibility criteria, in order to ensure the provision of the Universal Service.

An undertaking may assume the obligation to provide a part or elements of the Universal Service, if the following criteria are satisfied:

- the undertaking is a provider of public networks and/or electronic communication services, under a General Authorisation;
- the undertaking is a reliable provider, regarding the capability of fulfilling the Universal Service obligations that may be assigned to it. Reliability criteria are examined, depending on the group of the Universal Service services that the undertaking wishes to provide:
   (i) the public telephony network operation which can cover the whole geographical region where this specific undertaking has to provide the access to fixed positions;]
   (ii) the geographical coverage, the extent and density of the public telephone network of the undertaking, and the capability of the above-mentioned network to react to unexpected situations based on clearly defined provider's projects of action;
   (iii) the number of years of total business activity and the candidate's published financial data of the last three financial years;
   (iv) the existence of a specific development plan for the public telephone network;
   (v) the ability to provide Universal Service services at least of a defined minimum quality to the whole Greek region or in a specific territory; and
   (vi) especially for the edition of a Telephony Directory in electronic or written format and the provision of information services of a unified telephone directory, the reliability criteria (i), (ii) and (iv) are not mandatory.

The selection of a Universal Service provider follows the principles of technological neutrality, objectivity, transparency and impartiality.

If no undertaking is interested in providing the Universal Service wholly or partly, or none meets the above-mentioned criteria, the selection of the provider is performed as follows:

- The EETT designates an undertaking with significant power in the market of public telephony network for domestic users and this will be the one to become the provider. If the EETT had designated more than one undertaking, then the provider with the largest share in the market will be selected.
- If the EETT has come to the conclusion that no undertaking has significant power in the said market, then the undertaking with the largest share in the specific market will be selected.

When several undertakings meet the criteria to becoming a provider of Universal Services, the EETT will choose the provider(s) via a tender competition. The terms of this competition are defined by the EETT in an objective, clear, non-discriminatory way and the candidates are informed prior to the beginning of the procedure.

The designated undertaking's compensation and the Universal Services' funding are defined in the Decisions of the Finance and the MITN Ministers and the EETT. The aggregate compensation amount for the provision of Universal Services can by no means exceed the net cost.[51]

The minimum term of time set for a designated undertaking to provide Universal Service services is three years. After the expiration of the specified term, the procedure of designating a Universal Service provider is repeated when the designated undertaking wishes to discontinue providing the service, or when another undertaking that meets the criteria applies for the service.

The minimum appropriate geographical area for the designation of the obligation to provide the Universal Service is a 'Region' as defined by Greek legislation. The EETT has the power to otherwise divide the Greek territory into separate areas in order to designate the appropriate undertaking per region.

Regulation of Retail Tariffs, Users' Expenditures and Quality of Service

16.33   The EETT, in its duty to ensure affordable pricing for the services rendered within the Greek market, monitors the evolution and levels of retail pricelists regarding services falling within the Universal Service and which are either provided by designated undertakings or are offered within the market with no specific undertakings having been designated for the provision of such services; the EETT performs this monitoring process especially with reference to the consumer price index and by taking into account the purchasing power of consumers.[52] In pursuit of the above, and further in order to ensure that consumers of low income and special social needs are not excluded from access to networks, the EETT is given the authority to impose on designated providers the obligation to offer consumers with pricing options or packages that differ from those offered under regular commercial terms. Additional supportive measures may be enforced by competent governmental authorities and EETT.

The Universal Service provider implements geographically adapted pricelists for the whole of the geographical area falling within its responsibilities.

The Universal Service provider must apply tariffs for the provision of Universal Services equal to or less than the maximum cap price set by the EETT to the SMP undertaking in the market in question.

In the case of subscribers' debts towards the Universal Service provider, the following are applicable:

- People with disabilities and people with special social needs, such as the elderly, people suffering from heart diseases or kidney problems, who have for

---

51   Art 64 Law 4070/2012.
52   Art 61(1) of Law 4070/2012.

any reason lost their telephone connection, enjoy priority in terms of connection or repair. They can receive calls and reach emergency services without any restriction.

- In case of a dispute over excessive billing for premium rate services, subscribers maintain their access to all basic telephone services, until the dispute is resolved.

The Universal Service provider ensures the provision of a minimum level of analytical billing, which must be offered free of charge, as defined in the MITN's decision on the definition of the content of the Universal Service.[53] There must be a standard form of analytical billing to enable customers to verify and control the billing for the use of the public telephone landline networks at fixed locations and/or relevant available telephone services, as well as for the appropriate monitoring of use and expenses, with which users are charged, controlling in that way their bills.

If necessary, subscribers can be offered a detailed analysis of the bill subject to a minimum or no charge. When the subscribers make calls which are free of charge (ie emergency calls) they are not to appear on billing analysis.

In a two-month period, the Universal Service provider sends an intermediate bill to the subscriber if this is technically possible and justifiable by the traffic volume. At the subscriber's request, and if it is technically possible, the Universal Service provider informs the subscriber on the value of his or her telephone billing per month.

The EETT supervises the designated undertakings:

- to not impose terms and conditions which financially burden the subscribers regarding the provision of facilities and services beyond those constituting the USO; and
- to provide certain facilities and services,[54] to enable the consumers to monitor or control their expenses and to avoid disconnecting the service to their detriment.[55]

When such facilities are regarded as widely available, the EETT may not impose the above requirements on the Greek region as a whole or on any part thereof.

The designated undertakings shall publish on both their website and at least in one wide-circulation newspaper adequate and updated information on their performance regarding the Universal Service provision, based on the parameters, definitions and methods of measuring the quality of the service found in Annex V of Law 4070/2012. The published information is notified to the EETT within seven working days of its publication.

The EETT may define the content, format, as well as the means of publication, so that the end users and consumers have access to complete, comparable and useful information.

If necessary, the EETT may:

- define additional quality standards of service, when the relevant parameters have been set, for the evaluation of the undertakings' performance regarding the provision of services to end users and consumers with disabilities;

---

53   Appendix I of MD 440/2007.
54   See Annex III, Part A of Law 4070/2012.
55   Art 62 of Law 4070/2012.

- set performance objectives for the undertakings with Universal Service obligations, after a consultation; and
- take appropriate measures in order to meet the aforementioned objectives. More specifically the EETT can order for independent controls or examinations of performance records, whose cost is covered by the concerned undertakings, in order to ensure the accuracy and comparability of data held by undertakings with Universal Service obligations.[56]

Persistent failure of an undertaking to meet the performance objectives may cause the imposition of the penalties provided for in Article 77 of Law 4070/2012, including administrative penalties and fines.

Cost calculation and financing of universal services

16.34   The compensation mechanism regarding the net cost for the provision of Universal Services is made upon the submission of a net cost research on the provision of the undertaking's Universal Service and control of this research by the EETT or an independent appointed auditor. The imposed research should include the calculation of possible intangible benefits, which the EETT takes into account. The submission of the research accompanies the request for compensation.

The EETT estimates the net cost of the Universal Service, either taking into account the market profit that a designated undertaking receives under Annex VI, Part A of Law 4070/2012, or uses the net cost of the Universal Service, which is calculated under Article 56 of the Law.

The sharing mechanism abides by the principles of transparency, minimum market distortion, non-discrimination and proportionality, according to the principles of Annex VI, Part B' of Law 4070/2012.

The EETT decides on the charge to be imposed on each undertaking individually regarding the sharing of the Universal Services obligation cost.

The EETT, subject to business confidentiality obligation, publishes on its official webpage an annual report, which states the estimated cost of the Universal Service obligation and defines the stakeholders' contributions and possible market benefits that the designated undertakings may receive for the provision of the Universal Service.[57]

The bills and other information, upon which the calculation of the cost is based, are audited by the EETT or an independent body defined by the EETT. The cost calculation and review results are published in a daily newspaper and on the Internet. There is a Compensation Mechanism designated to apportion the financing of the net cost of the Universal Service if a designated undertaking is overcharged.

For the EETT to calculate the net cost of the Universal Service of the provider, the technical economical model may be used, with an average long-term incremental cost.

Regulation of Retail Markets – Prerequisites for the Regulation of Retail Markets

16.35   The EETT imposes appropriate obligations upon SMP undertakings specifically within the retail market of electronic communication services under

---

56   Art 63 of Law 4070/2012.
57   Art 64(5) of Law 4070/2012.

Article 41 of Law 4070/2012 if this market is not sufficiently competitive and the imposed obligations are not sufficient for the objectives of the law to be fulfilled.

The imposed obligations must be justified by, and proportionate to, the objective pursued. The imposed obligations may address SMP undertakings to prevent them from overcharging, impeding new entries in the market, restricting competition by undercutting prices to attract customers, providing benefits to specific end users or bundling services without a justified cause.

Regulatory Powers

16.36   The EETT may impose on undertakings appropriate measures to reduce retail prices, measures to control individual price-lists or measures to orient price-lists towards the cost or prices existing in comparable markets so that the interests of end users and, simultaneously, effective competition between undertakings are promoted.

The EETT ensures the implementation of all necessary and appropriate cost accounting systems when an undertaking is subjected to pricelist regulation or other relevant retail controls. The EETT may specify the format and accounting methodology that is to be used. The compliance of an appropriate accounting system for the registration of the cost is controlled by another qualified body, private or public, independent from the EETT and the principal operator, as defined by the EETT, which ensures the annual publication of the declaration of compliance.

The EETT does not impose retail service control mechanisms on individual markets, where effective competition is considered to exist.

End User Rights

Contracts[58]

16.37   Consumers and end users who are subscribers of services connecting to a public communication network and/or electronic communication services available to the public, if required, have the right to contract such undertaking(s). The contract must at least include the following, in a clear, comprehensive and easily accessible format:

- the name and address of the company;
- the services provided, including particularly:
  - access to emergency services, caller location/identification and any restrictions regarding the provision on emergency services of Law 4070/2012;[59].
  - information on additional terms that restrict access to services and applications and/or their use, when such terms are permitted under national and EU law;
  - information regarding methods used by the undertaking to monitor and reduce traffic at any connection point, and also information regarding how such methods affect the quality of the service;

---

58   Art 65 of Law 4070/2012.
59   Art 70 of Law 4070/2012.

- minimum service quality standards, especially during the initial connection and, where appropriate, other aspects of quality of service, as defined by the EETT;
- the types of maintenance offered and customer support, as well as available ways of getting in contact with them;
- restrictions imposed by the provider concerning the use of the terminal equipment;

- options available to the subscribers regarding whether their personal data are included in the subscriber's directory and also regarding the nature of such data;
- details on prices and pricelists, the way to obtain updated information on pricelists and maintenance fees, available payment methods and cost differences attributed to payment methods;
- the effective duration/term of the contract and the terms for renewal and termination of the provision of services and the contract, including the following:
  - minimum limit of use or duration needed in order to benefit the subscriber;
  - any charge for the portability of the number;
  - any charge on the termination of the contract, including the recovering of the terminal's equipment cost;
- any regulation on compensation and reimbursement in case of breach of contract related to the quality level of the service;
- the mechanism to initiate extra-judicial dispute resolution;
- the measures by which the undertaking will confront incidents concerning security, integrity, threats and other vulnerabilities of the system; and
- the use of the Greek language for any provided service.[60]

The subscribers have the right to terminate their contracts without any penalty, upon being notified of amendments of contractual terms that are proposed by the provider. Providers must inform their subscribers through their bill about the modifications and their right to terminate the contract, at least one month prior to their entry into force, subject to cases of pricelist reductions.

The Consumers' Ombudsman, collaborating with the EETT when deemed necessary, has the competency to address unresolved disputes between network and/or electronic communications service providers on one hand and small and medium enterprises' consumers and other end users on the other, regarding the contractual terms and/or performance of the contracts. Pending is the issuance of a Ministerial decision which will determine a specific dispute resolution procedure; in the meantime disputes are handled by the Consumers' Ombudsman. Consumers and end users retain their rights to any other available legal protection offered by the law.[61] The law does not differentiate between consumers and small and medium enterprises. In this respect the law extends the notion of consumer in comparison to the general consumer protection law, which may raise interpretation matters.

Transparency Obligation

16.38   The EETT, following a public consultation, will demand that public network and/or electronic communication service providers publish transparent,

---

60   Art 65 of Law 4070/2012.
61   Art 65(4) of Law 4070/2012.

comparable, appropriate and updated information on applicable prices and pricelists, contract termination charges, information on the standard terms and conditions concerning access to services provided to end users and consumers, and the use of such services, under Annex IV of Law 4070/2012. Such information must be published in a clear, understandable and easily accessible format. By virtue of its decision, the EETT may specify additional requirements with respect to the publication format of the said information.

The EETT, by adopting the appropriate measures, shall ensure the provision of facilities which will assist end users and consumers in performing an independent evaluation of the cost of alternative service packages through interactive applications or similar techniques. Should the EETT notice that such facilities are not available to the public free of charge or at a reasonable pricing, it shall ensure that either the EETT or via a third party/accredited body, will offer them to the public. The EETT may, upon request grant a compliance certificate to natural or legal entities. Upon issuing a decision the EETT will regulate any matter, including any incurring fees and especially the procedure for the submission of the application, along with the criteria for granting the above-mentioned certificate of compliance.

Third parties have the right to use the published information free of charge, in order to offer at a fee or provide the above-mentioned interactive applications or other relevant techniques.

Following a public consultation, the EETT can demand that providers of public electronic communication networks and/or publicly available electronic communication services:

- provide information to the subscribers on the applicable pricelists or any other service specially priced;
- inform subscribers of the changes in terms of access to emergency services or of location data regarding the caller subscribed in a given service;
- inform the subscribers of any changes in the terms that limit access to services and applications and/or the use thereof, when such terms are allowed under national and EU legislation;
- provide information regarding the methods applied by the provider for traffic measurement and formulation, which aims to prevent overloading the connection by reaching its maximum capacity or to prevent it from becoming overloaded and also provide information on how these methods may affect the quality of the service;
- inform the subscribers of their right to decide whether they wish to be included in a public directory and on the format of this list, under the legislation on personal data protection; and
- regularly inform disabled subscribers regarding the details of available products designed especially for them.

Prior to the imposition of any obligation, the EETT may promote measures of self-regulation or co-regulation, as it will deem necessary.

The EETT, may decide to require from electronic communication public network and/or services providers to give information of public interest to current and new subscribers, where necessary, using means commonly used by undertakings for their communication with their subscribers. In this case, all information provided by the competent public authorities concerns the following matters:

- the most common uses of electronic communication services for participation to illegal activities or distribution of material with harmful content, especially in sectors that could endanger the principles of respect of rights and freedoms, including infringements of intellectual property rights and other related rights and their legal implications; and

- the means of subscriber protection against risks of personal safety, privacy and personal data, when using electronic communication services.[62]

The EETT recently took firm action against violations of the law which resulted from practices injuring consumers interests. In particular, after carrying out a thorough investigation on allegations of arbitrary and exorbitant charges to subscribers mainly concerning Internet access via mobile devices, the EETT Plenary unanimously decided to impose fines totalling €6.65 million on three mobile operators. The EETT specifically found that the service of data transfer was activated in violation of the law, without prior notice to subscribers, resulting in high charges. These charges concerned mainly users of smartphones, due to automatic updates of their devices involving transfers of large amounts of data. The fines were defined for each company based on the extent of the infringement, the total number of affected subscribers, the economic harm caused to consumers, the increased company revenue emerging from the infringements and the need to discourage such malpractice in the future.[63]

Quality of service: securing 'net neutrality'

16.39 Law 4070/2012 introduces the promotion and establishment of net neutrality by a combination of cross-referred provisions commencing from Article 12, which outlines the powers of the EETT. In particular, the EETT regulates issues concerning the technological neutrality of networks according to the principles set out in Article 3, and Article 3 in turn mandates the NRA to impose objective, transparent, unbiased and analogous regulation principles, especially respecting the fundamental human rights and basic freedoms as established by the European Convention for the Protection of Human Rights and Fundamental Freedoms.[64]

European emergency call number[65]

16.40 Emergency calls making use of the common European emergency number '112', as with national emergency numbers such as the ones set in the National Numbering Plan, are enabled for outgoing national calls through any electronic communication provider, including all public telephones, free of any charge.

The competent body for the organisation and operation of the Common European Emergency Number Service is the General Secretariat for Civil Protection of the Ministry of Citizens Protection.

The emergency call shall be enabled by linking any person calling number 112 with the appropriate and local competent bodies of emergency services (Hellenic Police Force, Fire Brigade, Port Authority) depending on the type of incident reported by the caller, as well as the Children SOS National Telephone Line '1056' and the Open European Telephone Line for Missing Children '1160000'.

---

62 Art 66 of Law 4070/2012.
63 Press release dated 26.11.2012 from EETT's official website [http://www.eett.gr/opencms/opencms/admin_EN/News/news_0153.html], accessed 18.01.2013
64 Arts 12(μβ) + 3(2)(ζ+ζα) of Law 4070/12.
65 Art 70 of Law 4070/2012.

Obligations Facilitating Change of Provider[66]

16.41   All subscribers with numbers registered in the National Numbering Plan have the right, upon request, to retain their number(s) regardless of the service provider (number portability) in a specific place as for geographical numbers and anywhere regarding non-geographical numbers. The transfer must be realised within one working day.

The pricing between operators and service providers, as far as the portability provision is concerned, is cost-oriented and any charge should not be a disincentive for a change of service provider.

The EETT does not define retail pricelists for number transfers, in a manner that would distort competition, such as by introducing special or common retail pricelists.

The EETT takes measures, if needed, in order to ensure the subscribers' protection during the process of changing a service provider. The EETT may impose penalties on service providers, including the obligation to compensate subscribers in cases of delayed or abusive transfer, carried out either by them or on their behalf.

Providers may request that any outstanding charges including gifts and subsidies are paid up prior to the transfer.

The EETT monitors whether contractual terms and termination processes may deter subscribers from changing their service providers.

DATA PROTECTION: THE DIRECTIVE ON PRIVACY AND ELECTRONIC COMMUNICATIONS

Confidentiality of Communications

16.42   Electronic communications by means of public communication network and the related traffic and location data are protected by the confidentiality of communications. Law 3471/2006 on the protection of personal data and of privacy in the electronic communications sector (the E-privacy law) prohibits listening, tapping, storage and any kind of interception of communications and the related traffic and location data, unless legally authorised. The provisions of Law 2472/1997 on the protection of individuals with regard to the processing of personal data ('Data Protection Law') also apply.

The processing of personal data, including traffic and location data, must be restricted to the extent necessary for the purposes it occurs. The provider of a publicly available electronic communications service must use anonymous or pseudonymous data where possible. Processing of personal data is permitted under the following conditions:

- the subscriber or user has given his/her consent after having been informed about the sort of data, the purpose and the extent of the processing, the recipient or the categories of recipients (Article 5 (2)(a)); and
- the processing is necessary for the performance of the contract, to which the subscriber or user is party, or the implementation of a pre-contractual stage, upon the subscriber's request (Article 5 (2)(b)).

---

66   Art 68 of Law 4070/2012; see 'Rights of use for numbers; Admissible Conditions' above.

The subscriber's or user's consent must be given in writing or by electronic means. In this latter case, the data controller shall ensure that the subscriber or the user is fully aware of the consequences of his statement. The statement is recorded in a secured way; it is accessible to the user or subscriber and can be recalled anytime.

The provider of a publicly available electronic communications service must take appropriate technical and organisational measures to safeguard security of its services and of the public communications network. These measures shall be taken if necessary in conjunction with the provider of the public communications network and shall ensure a level of security appropriate to the risk presented, having regard to the state of the art and the cost of implementation.

In case of a particular risk for breach of the network security, the provider of a publicly available electronic communications service must inform the subscribers concerning such risk. Where the risk lies outside the scope of the measures to be taken by the service provider, the provider must also inform the subscribers of any possible remedies, including an indication of the likely costs involved.

Without prejudice to Article 10 of the Data Protection Law that provides for the confidentiality and the security of processing, the respective measures shall at least:

- ensure that personal data can be accessed only by authorised personnel for legally authorised purposes;
- protect personal data stored or transmitted against accidental or unlawful destruction, accidental loss or alteration, and unauthorised or unlawful storage, including processing, access or disclosure; and
- ensure the implementation of a security policy with respect to the processing of personal data. Relevant special provisions and regulations of independent authority continue to apply.

The competent authorities are authorised to issue recommendations about best practices concerning the level of security which those measures should achieve.

Recording of communications and the related traffic data is considered as legally authorised interception when carried out in the course of lawful business practice for the purpose of providing evidence of a commercial transaction or any other business communication with a prior consent of the parties involved.

Further, exceptions to the prohibition on interception or surveillance of communications are permitted only under the conditions provided in Article 19 of the Greek Constitution. Legislative Decree 47/2005 and Law 2225/1994 regulate the grounds, procedures and technical and organisational guarantees for the withdrawal of communications' confidentiality. National security, the investigation, detection and prosecution of certain criminal offences and the protection of human rights and freedoms are legal grounds for the competent authorities to service a warrant authorising the withdrawal of confidentiality.

Storing information or gaining access to information already stored in the terminal equipment of a subscriber or user is only allowed on the condition that the subscriber or user concerned has given his or her informed consent, ie having been provided with clear and comprehensive information, in accordance with the Data Protection Law, about the purposes of the processing. The exception is when the sole purpose of the technical storage or access is to carry out the transmission of a communication over an electronic communications network. In addition, the same applies when the technical storage or access is considered strictly necessary for the provider of an information society service to provide a service explicitly requested by the subscriber or user (Article 4(5) of Law 3471/2006).

In the event of a personal data breach, the provider of publicly available electronic communications services shall, without undue delay, notify the personal data breach to the Hellenic Data Protection Authority ('HDPA'), responsible for the application of the Data Protection Law and the Hellenic Authority for Communication Security and Privacy ('ADAE') which is responsible for the application of the E-Privacy Law. When the personal data breach is likely to adversely affect the personal data or privacy of a subscriber or individual, the provider shall also notify the subscriber or individual of the breach without undue delay.

Greek law provides for administrative remedies, civil penalties and criminal sanctions applicable to infringements of the privacy and of the data protection rules in the electronic communication sector. The HDPA and ADAE are the authorities that can impose administrative penalties to infringing providers regarding the data protection rules and the communications security and privacy accordingly. Full compensation is imposed in the event of financial losses and indemnity of a minimum of €10,000 for moral damage. The criminal sanctions escalate depending on the kind of breach, on the provider's extent of non-compliance or not with the administrative penalties, and the size of the illegal profits, from 1 to 10 years and €10,000 to €350,000.

An example of recent case law concerned the following infringement of the privacy and data protection laws. A mobile network operator contacted an individual, ie the claimant in the respective litigation, advertising its mobile services. The claimant has given some of his personal data, including his name, his tax registration number and his address for the operator to provide him with an offer for a mobile programme. Eventually, no contract was concluded. However the provider had stored and processed his personal data without the claimant's prior consent and sent the claimant bills for three mobile contracts! For the above breach, the civil law court convicted the provider, requiring them to indemnify the claimant for moral damage and to destroy the stored personal data of the claimant.

Data Retention

16.43   Law 3917/2011 has transposed Directive 2006/24/EC on the retention of data generated or processed in connection with the provision of publicly available electronic communications services or of public communications networks into the Greek legislation.

This legislation has not yet been challenged in the national or European courts. However, there is a number of issues have arisen regarding employment law and the permissibility of video surveillance in the workplace.

Traffic Data and Location Data

16.44   Article 2 of the E-Privacy Law provides the definition for 'traffic data' as the data processed for the purpose of the conveyance of a communication on an electronic communication network or for the billing thereof. Traffic data may, inter alia, consist of data referring to the routing, duration, time or volume of a communication, to the protocol used, to the location of the terminal equipment of the sender or recipient, to the network on which the communication originates or terminates, to the beginning, end or duration of a connection. They may also consist of the format in which the communication is conveyed by the network. In the same article 'location data' is defined as the data processed in an electronic communications network, indicating the geographic position of the terminal equipment of a user of a publicly available electronic communications service.

Traffic data relating to subscribers and users processed and stored by the provider of a public communications network or a publicly available electronic communications service must be erased or made anonymous, without prejudice to Law 3917/2011 on the retention of data. Traffic data necessary for the purposes of subscriber billing and interconnection payments may be processed. The electronic communication service provider shall inform the subscriber as to the type of data to be processed and the duration of processing. Such processing is permissible only up to 12 months from the communication date, unless the billing was challenged or not settled. In this case the data may be processed until the final resolution of the dispute.

The transmission of traffic data and personal data relating to the contract to another provider is permitted for the billing and payment of the services, provided that the subscriber or user is informed in a clear and appropriate manner, in writing or by electronic means, at the conclusion of the contract or prior to the transmission.

For the purpose of marketing electronic communications services or for the provision of value added services, the provider of a publicly available electronic communications service may process the traffic data to the extent and for the duration necessary for such services or marketing, if the subscriber or user to whom the data relates has given his or her prior consent after being properly informed. Users or subscribers can withdraw their consent for the processing of traffic data at any time.

Exceptionally, location data processing is permitted, without the user's or subscriber's prior consent, by the providers of a public communications network or publicly available e-communications service, in order to assist organisations dealing with emergency calls, including law enforcement agencies, ambulance services and the fire brigade, for the sole purpose of locating the caller and responding to such calls.

Another exception applies when the EETT is informed by the interested parties on traffic data, with the aim of resolving disputes relating mainly to interconnection or payments.

Itemised Billing

16.45   Subscribers shall have the right to receive non-itemised bills (Article 7 of Law 3471/2006). When a connection is used by numerous users, or when the subscriber is liable for the payment of a connection used by multiple users, the subscriber must provide a statement that the users have been informed or shall be informed, in the most appropriate manner in each case, as to the itemised billing of the subscriber. In the case of toll-free communication, the connection called shall not be included in the itemised billing. If so requested by the subscriber, the provider of a public communications network or publicly available electronic communications service must erase the three last digits of the called connections-numbers from the itemised bill.

Pursuant to Decision 588//2010 of the EETT, operators have been asked to make available two types of detailed bills: the minimum level of itemised billing ('MLIB') and the enriched MLIB. MLIB contains information about the past debt balance, the fixed charge, cumulative information on prepaid service and extra cost service, and information about other discounts and tolls (e g end connection or disconnection toll, outgoing call barring service, etc – Article 3 of the EETT Decision). The enriched MLIB is sent only upon the subscriber's request and contains all the abovementioned data plus certain more detailed data regarding the above categories of information (Article 4 of the EETT Decision).

Providers of public telephone communications service may offer their subscribers information beyond MLIB or enriched MLIB in the form of greater analysis of each service and/or other information at a reasonable price or free of charge.

Presentation and Restriction of Calling and Connected Line Identification

16.46   Where presentation of calling line identification is offered, the service provider must offer the calling user the possibility, using a simple means and free of charge, of preventing the presentation of the calling line identification on a per-call basis, which applies with regard to calls to third countries outside the European Union as well. The calling subscriber must have this possibility on a per-line basis. Moreover, the service provider must offer the called subscriber the possibility, using a simple means and free of charge, of preventing the presentation of the calling line identification of incoming calls. Where the calling line identification is presented prior to the call being established, the service provider must offer the called subscriber the possibility, using a simple means, of rejecting incoming calls where the presentation of calling line identification has been prevented by the calling user or subscriber. Where presentation of connected line identification is offered, the service provider must offer the called subscriber the possibility, using a simple means and free of charge, of preventing the presentation of connected line identification to the calling user.

Where presentation of calling or connected line identification is offered, publicly available electronic communications service providers must inform the public and their subscribers, using all appropriate means and methods, regarding the existence of calling or connected line identification services, based on the identification of the calling or connected line and the possibilities described above.

The provider of a public communications network or publicly available electronic communications service may override the calling line non-identification option under the following conditions:

- On a temporary basis, upon application of a subscriber requesting the tracing of malicious or nuisance calls. In this case, the data containing the identification of the calling subscriber or user will be stored and be made available by the provider of a public communications network and/or publicly available electronic communications service only to the subscriber or user who has requested the identification and are subsequently erased, unless otherwise determined by Law 3471/2006, as amended.
- For emergency calls to the competent public organisations dealing with such calls or to private emergency assistance organisations, recognised by the State, for the purpose of responding to such calls, irrespective of the existence of the subscriber or user's temporary consent. In this case, the data containing the identification of the calling subscriber will be stored and be made available by the public organisation or private emergency assistance organisation for the sole purpose of immediately replying and dealing with the emergency and only for the period required to complete this purpose, and are subsequently

erased. In both cases, the specific procedures, manner, duration of the option's cancellation and all other necessary details to secure the procedure's transparency are defined by a decision of the ADAE.

- For calls subject to withdrawal of caller identification restriction, according to the effective legislation.

Automatic call forwarding

16.47   Subscribers have the right to stop call forwarding by third parties to their terminal pursuant to Article 9 of Law 3471/2006. The provider of a public communications network or publicly available electronic communications service must offer this technical option free of charge.

Directories of Subscribers

16.48   Article 10 of the E-Privacy Law regulates the inclusion of subscribers' personal data in directories. Under this article subscribers shall be informed, free of charge, in an appropriate and comprehensive manner, about the purpose of a printed or electronic directory of subscribers available to the public or obtainable through directory enquiry services, in which their personal data can be included. Subscribers shall also be informed of any further usage possibilities based on search functions embedded in electronic versions of the directory. Subscribers are included in the directory, if they have not expressed their refusal and shall be given the option not to be included in a printed or electronic directory. The non-registration, verification, correction or withdrawal of personal data from the public subscribers' directory is free of charge.

Personal data contained in the printed or electronic directory of subscribers available to the public or obtainable through directory enquiry services must be limited to those that are necessary for the identification of a specific subscriber (name, surname, father's name, address), unless the subscriber has provided written consent for the publication of additional personal data.

If a third party collects the data from the subscriber or any third party to whom the data have been transmitted wishing to use the data for an additional purpose, the renewed consent of the subscriber must be obtained. The provider of the public subscriber directory may not depend on the provision of the public subscriber directory services to the subscriber on their consent to the processing of such data for purposes other than those for which they have been collected.

These rights apply to individual subscribers. Where the subscriber is a legal entity, the data published in the public subscriber directory are limited to those necessary to ascertain the identity of the legal entity (title or trading name, seat, legal form, address), unless the legal representative of the legal entity has provided written consent on the publication of additional data.

The Hungarian Market for Electronic Communications[1]

Tamás Kaibinger, Emese Szitási, and Péter Vörös, with Ines Radmilovic
Baker & McKenzie, Budapest

LEGAL STRUCTURE

Basic Policy

17.1 Hungary opened up its telecommunications market at the end of 2001. With its accession to the EU on 1 May 2004, it ensured compliance with the rules of the 2002 EU Regulatory Package. This led to the adoption of a new electronic communications act, which harmonises Hungarian rules with those of the EU. The electronic communications market is constantly changing and continuously developing since the implementation of the 2009 Regulatory Package.

17.2 Since 2010, Hungary has had a powerful independent national regulatory authority, the National Communication and Media Authority ('NRA'), which emerged from the merger of the National Communications Authority and the National Radio and Television Board. The NRA is responsible for the supervision of the electronic communication market and the media market.

Implementation of EU Directives

17.3 Hungary undertook to fully harmonise its laws with the applicable EU legislation. The electronic communications rules are set out in Act 100 of 2003 on electronic communications ('elektronikus hírközlésröl szóló törvény' ('EHT')), the basic structure of which was elaborated when the 2002 EU Regulatory Package was implemented. The implementation of the 2009 Regulatory Package required only amendment of the EHT and the related legislation.

Legislation

17.4 The basic rules on electronic communications are set out in the EHT, which provides an overall framework for market players. According to the Hungarian Constitution, the EHT is a basic Hungarian act, the amendment of which requires a two-thirds majority of the Members of the Parliament who are present. In

---

1   Editing of this chapter closed on 20 December 2012.

addition to the EHT, there were several decrees adopted by the Government and the relevant Minister, and recently also by the President of the NRA. The decrees of the NRA partly replace (renew) the previous Government Decrees and are partly new. This new legal source provides the opportunity to take a flexible approach and to react quickly to market changes. The decrees contain special rules, eg on data protection, number portability, etc. In addition, the NRA is empowered to carry out regulatory as well as supervisory tasks, including but not limited to the designation of SMP undertakings, imposing remedies, etc.

17.5   In general, the implementation of the 2009 EU Regulatory Package has been successful, as a result of which Hungary has a technology neutral legislation. New market players entered the relevant markets, including the mobile telephony segment, and new services were introduced. However, because of the economic downturn, the consumer segment has been decreasing; the business sector experienced slight growth. The Government's tax policy also has a major effect on the markets.

REGULATORY PRINCIPLES: THE FRAMEWORK DIRECTIVE

Scope of Regulation

17.6   The EHT defines its scope similar to the relevant directives: it applies to electronic communication activities and to all other activities where radio-frequency signals are generated. The term 'electronic communication activity' covers activities related to electronic communication networks and electronic communication services. These terms are similarly defined as in the Framework Directive. The territorial scope of the EHT covers all electronic communication activities performed in, or directed to, the territory of Hungary. The EHT applies to service providers and customers as well. It contains no restrictions regarding the nationality of service providers. The EHT does not apply to information society services. Among others, separate legislation[2] regulates radio and television activities, including the digital switch-over.

17.7   The EHT defines electronic communications activity as:

'an activity in the course of which signals, signs, texts, images, voice or messages of any other nature and generated in any form that can be interpreted, are transmitted via electronic communications networks to one or more users, including, in particular, electronic communications services, the operation of electronic communications networks and equipment, distribution of terminal equipment and related services'.[3]

Electronic communication service and electronic communication network are defined similarly as in the Framework Directive.

17.8   Hungarian laws contain no specific guidance on the provision of complex services.

17.9   There are no VoIP specific laws in Hungary. Basically, VoIP services have to be assessed under the general electronic communications regime which seems to apply to VoIP in limited cases only. If the given service qualifies as an electronic

2   Act CLXXXV of 2010 on media services and mass communication ('Media Act').
3   S 188 EHT.

communication service, the EHT applies and the service provider must comply with the above legislation. This is likely to be the case if the service complies with the ITU-T and ETSI telephony recommendations.

'Internet Freedom'

17.10   The electronic communication laws do not contain any rules relating to measures that restrict the end user's access right to the internet, eg for copyright violation. We are not aware of any legislative plans regarding the adoption of measures based upon which Internet access may be restricted.

National Regulatory Authorities: Organisation, Regulatory Objectives, Competencies

17.11   In the electronic communications sector, the NRA is the most important regulator. As described below, it has strong rights and basic influence on the electronic communications market.

17.12   The Hungarian Government has high level general rights, such as the elaboration of the national electronic communications policy, which defines the basic principles and conditions of the operation of the market. It is also responsible for the elaboration and adoption of legislation that contributes to the implementation of the national electronic communications policy. As a result of recent changes in connection with the implementation of the 2009 Regulatory Package, the Electronic Communications Minister's responsibilities were extended. The responsibilities of the Minister, cover, among others, the obligation to ensure that subscribers receive appropriate information, the right to adopt decrees on the principles of the market definition, market analysis and the obligations which may be imposed on SMPs and obligations regarding the providers of universal services, among others, tender proceedings in connection with the selection of the above.

17.13   There is also a special consultative entity, the National Communication and IT Council, which has several consultative tasks in respect of the Government in IT and communication cases.[4]

17.14   The following regulatory authorities are entitled to enforce certain provision of the EHT, or their activities otherwise affect the electronic communications market: the Office of Economic Competition ('Competition Office'), the National Consumer Protection Agency and the National Data Protection and Freedom of Information Office. These regulators are explicitly mentioned in the EHT.

17.15   The regulatory objectives of the NRA are defined in the EHT as in the Framework Directive.

17.16   The NRA is the regulator responsible for the supervision of the electronic communications market. Other authorities, mentioned above, have responsibilities that relate to their specific task. For example, the National Consumer Protection Agency is responsible for the enforcement of certain consumer protection rules of the EHT. The EHT requires the NRA to cooperate with the above-mentioned regulatory bodies and contains some basic cooperation-related provisions as well.

---

4   The Media Act contains detailed rules regarding this organ. In this regard, we note that the EHT contains only some basic rules regarding the NRA, because the organizational and other rules are incorporated in the Media Act.

17.17   In general, the Competition Office, as an independent national regulator, has similar responsibilities to the competition agencies of other Member States. In respect of electronic communication, among others, when defining the relevant markets, assessing the competition and identifying SMPs, the NRA is required to consider the opinion of the Competition Office. If it deviates from the professional opinion of the Competition Office, it must provide its reasons for the deviation.

17.18   The NRA is a fully independent, state administrative entity conducting its own financial management, covering the expenditures incurred in the course of performing its duties from its own revenues. As mentioned above, the amendment of the EHT requires a qualified majority which ensures that the responsibilities of the NRA always serve as guidance for its activities. Further, the Head of the NRA is elected for nine years, which ensures independence and continuity. The Head of the NRA has significant rights under the EHT. The EHT is in line with the requirements of the Framework Directive regarding the independence and powers of the NRAs.

17.19   As an independent regulator, the NRA is only required to provide an annual report to the Parliament. The NRA takes part in the enforcement of the Government's policy regarding frequency management and electronic communication, as defined by law. Only acts of Parliament or such legislative means may create additional responsibilities for the NRA, which are issued based on the authorisation granted in an act.

17.20   The powers and obligations of the NRA related to the electronic communication industry are consistent with the Framework Directive. As the NRA emerged from the merger of the National Communications Authority and the National Radio and Television Board, it also has several responsibilities relating to the media market. The NRA is a powerful national regulator able to achieve the aims of the EHT.

17.21   The NRA has significant powers to demand information. It is entrusted with a wide array of options mainly relating to evidence gathering, inspections and information requests. If information is required from any third party to clarify a particular issue, the relevant person or organisation is obliged to supply the necessary information and make available the documents associated with the matter.[5] Such request for information may be challenged before the Metropolitan Court. A person's failure to cooperate could result in a procedural fine.

17.22   The EHT regulates the cooperation obligation of the NRA with other regulators. It is worth mentioning that even before the implementation of the cooperation obligation, the NRA considered cooperation as an important task, and, therefore, signed a cooperation agreement, among others, with the Competition Office.

17.23   The NRA takes its responsibility regarding publishing information very seriously. The effective decisions of the NRA and the courts are available on the website of the NRA. Further, it has also published important market information, statistical data, research results, studies, etc.

17.24   The EHT implemented the requirements related to consultation obligation as follows:

'The NRA, prior to:

---

5   S 35 EHT.

(a) adopting a decision concerning entities identified as having significant market power and on the obligations imposed under this Act upon service providers with significant market power in the course of the identification procedure,

(b) rendering – by means of a resolution – obligations upon service providers that do not have significant market power,

(c) adopting a decision relating to reference offers,

(d) adopting a decision relating to frequency management,

and where it is deemed necessary by the NRA, shall open a dialogue with the parties concerned in cases falling within its jurisdiction. To this end, the NRA shall publish the draft of its decision at least thirty days in advance, as well as the preparatory documents necessary for the consultations relating to the decision on hand.'[6]

17.25   Under the EHT, the NRA has specific dispute resolution power. Any service provider or other business entity whose right or lawful interest related to electronic communications as regulated in any electronic communications regulations or under contract governed by such regulations, or under a network contract specified in the EHT, is violated by another service provider, may seek remedy before the NRA.[7] The applicant has to submit a detailed request to the NRA which establishes a chamber in order to decide the dispute. At the request of any party, the NRA holds a hearing.

17.26   The provisions of the EHT on the Permanent Arbitration Court for Communications Cases were deleted as of 1 January 2012, as a result of which the EHT does not envisage any role for the arbitration court in case of legal disputes. It is not clear whether the arbitration court still operates or ceased to exist.

Right of Appeal against NRA's Decisions

17.27   The right of appeal follows the division of tasks between the President of the NRA and the NRA itself. Any decision delivered by the NRA, as a first instance regulatory authority, may be appealed to the President of the NRA,[8] except for procedural orders and certain other orders specified in the act. The judicial review of the President's decision, adopted either as a first instance authority or as an appellate body, may be requested from the Metropolitan Court,[9] but such an action does not automatically suspend the President's decision; the suspension of the decision may be requested from the civil court.[10]

17.28   Only the parties participating in the first instance procedure have a right to appeal or request the full judicial review of the decision. All other participants in the procedure (such as witnesses, experts, etc) may appeal only those parts of the decision which relate to them.[11]

17.29   In general, the Metropolitan Court has jurisdiction to review the President's decision. The Metropolitan Court's ruling on the President's decision adopted as a first instance authority may be appealed to the Metropolitan Court of

---

6   S 40 EHT.
7   S 57 EHT.
8   S 44 EHT.
9   Ss 44 (3) and 45 EHT.
10   Ss 37 and 46–48 EHT.
11   Ss 44(3)and 46–48 EHT.

Appeal (there is no appeal against the Metropolitan Court's decision reviewing the President's decisions adopted as an appellate authority). As an ultimate remedy, the extraordinary review of final and binding court decisions can be requested from the Kúria (the supreme court of Hungary). Courts only review issues of the breach of law and may not and do not review any decisions adopted within the President's or the NRA's discretionary powers on the merits.

17.30   The President of the NRA must decide on an appeal in 45 days.[12] Courts must review the decisions in an expedited procedure,[13] and – if suspension is requested – must decide on the suspension of the decision within eight days. In fact, this deadline is often exceeded, and expedited procedure can last a relatively long time. Administrative decisions are only rarely suspended.

The NRA's Obligations to Cooperate with the Commission

17.31   The EHT does not deviate in any material respect from the Framework Directive.[14] The NRA must take into consideration – within the framework of the applicable laws – the Commission recommendations and must take into consideration, to the extent possible, the applicable specifications. If the NRA does not follow the recommendations, it informs the Commission thereof.[15]

17.32   When defining relevant markets or identifying SMP undertakings, the Commission's and BEREC's involvement must be ensured. The procedural rules of the consolidation procedure[16] are mirrored in the applicable laws,[17] with the technical exception that, instead of the two- and three-month deadlines, 60- and 90-day deadlines are set out, respectively. Legislation also provides for the President's right to adopt provisional measures in exceptional circumstances, and obliges the President of the NRA to decide on the maintenance of the provisional measure within 15 days from the receipt of comments or objections. As a derogation from the general rule, there is no specific remedy available against the President's decision ordering provisional measures, it may be challenged only in remedies available against the decision maintaining the provisional measure.

17.33   Co-regulation procedure is also implemented into Hungarian law.[18]

'Significant Market Power' as a Fundamental Prerequisite of Regulation

Definition of SMP

17.34   The definition of significant market power ('SMP') follows the definition and the logic of that in the Framework Directive, namely it is based on the dominance test.[19] Furthermore, similar to EU legislation, SMP may relate to individual or collective dominance. Collective dominance may arise particularly if

---

12   S 31 (1) EHT.
13   S 46 (1) EHT.
14   Ss 63–66, 71 EHT.
15   S 24 (2) EHT.
16   Article 7 of the Framework Directive.
17   S 71 EHT.
18   Ss 64 EHT and 71 (5) EHT.
19   S 62 (3) EHT.

there is no effective competition between two or more undertakings in the relevant market, or the same two or more undertakings are jointly in a dominant position against the other providers in the relevant market. Collective dominance may also exist without any structural or other relationship between the service providers if the relevant service providers operate in a market the structure of which facilitates the coordination of actions. Furthermore, an SMP undertaking on one market may be designated as an SMP undertaking on a closely related market if, as a result of the connection between the relevant market and the closely related market, the market power of the undertaking held in one market may be leveraged in the other market, thereby strengthening its market power.

17.35   The President of the NRA has identified only one SMP undertaking on each relevant market and has not established collective dominance to date. The President's approach has been relatively simple: it has defined the owner of the (dominant) network as the SMP undertaking. The most important recent development in this regard is that the President of the NRA has introduced technology neutrality, because it has defined as SMP undertakings, in addition to the incumbents, the operators of CATV networks and ISPs having physical infrastructure on the fixed location call termination markets (market No. 3/2007) and imposed remedies on them.

Definition of relevant markets

17.36   The President of the NRA defines relevant markets following a thorough investigation and data collection process on the basis of the guidelines issued by the Communications Minister, the European Commission's decisions and recommendations, on the basis of the applicable competition law rules, by taking into consideration the differences between competition conditions and consumer characteristics within the geographic market.[20] The rules on market definition are set out in a Communications Minister Decree and the so-called 'Methodology' issued by the NRA.[21] These documents, which describe the criteria for designating SMP undertakings, the way market definition should be handled and the procedure for designating SMP undertakings, are in line with the Commission Guidelines on market analysis and EU case law. The procedure is also in line with Articles 7 and 7a of the Framework Directive, since the procedural rules implemented the consolidation and the co-regulation rules of the Directive. Further, in the procedure leading to the identification of SMP undertakings and the imposition of remedies and obligations on SMP undertakings the President of the NRA must launch public consultation by publishing its draft decision and the supporting documents at least 30 days prior to the decision's adoption. Any person or entity can comment on the draft decision within 20 days from the draft's publication, although the NRA does not have to take such comments into consideration.[22] Markets must be reviewed every three years or even more frequently if it is required or requested due to changes on the market.

17.37   The President's predecessor, the Council of the National Communication Authority, has followed the Commission Recommendation and guidelines and has defined 18 relevant markets, The Council and its successor, the President of the NRA started new procedures (also in light of EU developments) and re-assessed

---

20   S 62 (2) EHT.

21   Decree No 16/2004 of the Communications Minister and the NRA's Methodology, 30 June 2004.

22   S 40 EHT

markets on the basis of the Commission's guidelines and recommendation. As of June 2012, the President has adopted new decisions[23] defining relevant markets 2–7 (2007), and the decision of the Council on market 1[24] is still in force. Further, the President of the NRA adopted a new decision[25] on market 7 (2003) and established that it can not be considered as a relevant market any more.

17.38   The President of the NRA has defined sub-national markets with regard to all fixed-line services. This has traditionally been the regulator's practice, because prior to liberalisation, different incumbents had owned the PSTN network and had operated the fixed line services in the various geographic regions (numbering zones) in Hungary. After liberalisation, these incumbents remained the owners of the infrastructure (although other operators also built some limited infrastructure, predominantly for providing broadband services) and maintained their leading market position in most of the retail markets. Since some of these incumbents merged, as of June 2012, three incumbents are designated as SMP undertakings, each in their respective geographic region/numbering zones. Further, with regard to call termination, every service provider which provides voice services to its own customers on its own network (3 incumbents + 28 other operators) has been designated as an SMP undertaking in the separate relevant market defined by its own network. The mobile market is national because each provider's network covers the entire country's territory.

Imposition of remedies

17.39   The President of the NRA is obliged to impose at least one remedy on SMP undertakings which mirrors the provisions of the Access and Universal Services Directives.[26] The President of the NRA [27] may impose individual remedies,[28] details of which are subject to deliberation or mandatory/determined remedies detailed by law.[29] Remedies must be proportionate and justified in light of the restrictions of competition revealed by the market analysis, keeping in mind the European Commission's harmonised decisions and recommendation, the principles established by the Minister's decree and competition law rules.

17.40   In addition to the remedies imposed on SMP operators, the President of the NRA is also entitled to impose remedies on undertakings not designated as SMP undertakings. To achieve connection between subscriber access points, the subscriber access service provider can be required to interconnect its network with

---

23   HF/1944–18/2011, HF/1948–28/2011, HF/44–10/2011, HF/56–12/2011, HF/1930–15/2011, HF/1595–34/2011.
24   DH-8664–17/2010.
25   HF/1586–12/2011.
26   S 62 (1) b) and Chapter XII EHT.
27   The EHT's wording is inconsistent on whether the President or the NRA may impose the remedies, but in practice the President has adopted the decisions defining markets, identifying SMPs and imposing remedies.
28   Individual remedies can be: transparency, accounting or functional separation, facility sharing and co-location, cost-based prices and controllability of prices, non-discrimination, obligations related to access and interconnection or to subscriber services fees (in case of an SMP undertaking in a given retail market), including the prohibition on applying unjustified abusive pricing policies or the obligation to provide a minimum set of leased line services in respect of an SMP undertaking in the leased line market.
29   Mandatory remedies are carrier selection and internet access offer.

the network of another service provider and to ensure the cooperation of services.[30] Furthermore, to the extent that is necessary to ensure accessibility for end users to digital radio and television broadcasting services, the obligation to provide access to other service providers to the other facilities under fair, reasonable and non-discriminatory terms can also be imposed on these undertakings and, if duplicating the infrastructure would be economically ineffective or physically impractical.[31]

NRA's Regulatory Duties concerning Rights of Way, Co-location and Facility Sharing

Rights of way

17.41   All service providers, both public and non-public, have to use existing electronic communications structures, or must place their own structure(s) on public property, or use the facilities of a public utility service provider. If the placement of a public service provider's electronic communications structure is not possible by using existing structures or on public property and provided that no agreement has been reached between the public utility service provider or the owner of the private property and the public service provider, the structure in question may be installed by using the facilities of the public utility service provider as the first choice, or using private property as the second choice.[32] The developer of a structure is also entitled to use waterways, canals, natural lakes and the beds and channels thereof together with the airspace above the country for electronic communications purposes.[33]

17.42   The NRA/local government, upon request, grants rights of way to the service provider.[34] If private property is to be used, the NRA may restrict, upon request of the service provider, the use of the property by its owner in the interest of the public. The NRA may, by granting rights of way, among others permit the authorised representative of the service provider to enter the affected property for checking the electronic communications structures and for maintenance and (emergency) repair purposes.[35] The owner of the private property is entitled to indemnification and may exercise his rights in accordance with the provisions of the Civil Code.

17.43   Upon completion of the construction work, the service provider installing an electronic communications structure is obliged to restore the environment to its original condition; however, the parties can agree to restore it to a better condition.[36]

Co-location and facility sharing

17.44   The regulations concerning co-location and facility sharing fully implement Article 12 of the Framework Directive with respect to compulsory facility sharing

---

30   See paras 17.84–17.85 below.
31   Communications Minister Decree No 11/2004, S 100 (3),101 EHT.
32   Ss 94–95 EHT.
33   S 98 EHT.
34   Ss 94–96 EHT.
35   S 95(2) EHT.
36   S 96 EHT.

in the case of lack of access to viable alternatives, as well as to the encouragement of voluntary agreements about (possible) shared facilities.[37]

REGULATION OF MARKET ENTRY: THE AUTHORISATION DIRECTIVE

The General Authorisation of Electronic Communications

17.45   Hungarian legislation applies a general authorisation regime. Under the general authorisation regime, the rights and obligations derive from an act of law and are not subject to any approval from the NRA.[38] Individual licences are only required for using certain radio frequencies, using numbers, and acquiring authorisation for the building of electronic communications structures.[39]

17.46   Any natural and legal person or organisation without legal personality intending to provide electronic communications services or wanting to operate an electronic communication structure shall notify the NRA of its intention to commence the provision of such service, as well as the planned date of commencement, together with some basic information, amongst others, on the person wanting to offer the services and a short description of the services to be offered.[40] The NRA registers the notifying entity, based on the data disclosed and confirms the fact of registration within eight days from the date of notification.[41] The NRA may refuse the registration only if the NRA cannot identify, from the submitted data, either the service provider or the activities to be offered. In the latter case, simultaneously with the refusal, the NRA obliges the service provider to re-submit the notification within eight days.[42] In addition to being responsible for the notification process, the NRA is also in charge of issuing an authorisation for the installation, occupancy, continuation, removal and dismantling of electronic communications structures. Authorisation, however, is not required for construction works for non-public service providers.[43]

---

37   S 90 EHT.
38   Ss 74 and 76 EHT; see para 17.28 below.
39   S 74(2) EHT.
40   S 76(2) EHT.
41   S 76(3) EHT.
42   S 76(5) EHT.
43   S 83 (2) EHT.

Rights of Use for Radio Frequencies

Strategic planning and co-ordination of spectrum policy

17.47   Hungary's radio spectrum strategy for 2012–2015 has been published in December 2012, and is consistent with the EU's radio spectrum policy programmes.

Principles of frequency allocation, procedural rules

17.48   The rules for using radio frequencies are generally laid down in the EHT[44] but detailed in various decrees.[45] The frequencies that may be used are set out in the national table of frequency allocation. Any natural or legal person or other organisation having no legal personality can request the use of the civilian-purpose frequency bands set out in the table. The operation of radio equipment for radio applications with a harmonised frequency or frequency band is not subject to an individual licence and their distribution does not have to be notified either. On the other hand, to operate radio equipment, radio stations and radio electronic communications networks, an individual radio licence is required and the installation of these is also subject to a frequency assignment in certain cases listed set out in the applicable regulation.

17.49   The NRA, which deals with frequencies allocated for civilian purposes, grants the civilian-purpose frequency assignments and radio licences in cases defined by the law by an authorisation to use frequencies through the general administrative procedure or, in case of frequency assignments, through auctions or tenders. These frequencies are allocated on a 'first come, first served' basis through individual licensing; however, certain frequencies set out in the law are distributed through tenders or auctions. In other cases set out by the legislation, frequencies may be used under general authorisation. Licensing and allocation are made on the basis of open, objective, transparent and non-discriminatory procedures.[46]

Transferability and time limitations

17.50   Frequency assignment, frequency reservations and radio licences are generally not transferable, except in respect of those frequencies specifically indicated in a decree issued by the NRA' President which are transferable upon the approval of the NRA.[47]

17.51   Frequency assignments are limited in time. The time limit[48] is either the validity period set out in the tender specification of the auctions/tenders for the relevant frequency or 1 year, which may be extended by another year upon request[49].

Admissible conditions

17.52   The frequency use has to be in compliance with legislation concerning the national allocation of frequency bands and the rules for the utilisation of frequency

---

44   Ss 55 and 84 EHT.
45   NMHH Decrees No. 7/2012 and 4/2011 of the NRA's President.
46   S 55 EHT.
47   NMHH Decree No 7/2011 of the NRA's President.
48   NMHH Decree No 7/2012 of the NRA's President.
49   This 1-year period can be extended to 7 years in case investments are to realised under a procurement procedure

bands, as well as regulations concerning public health and the emission of and protection against interference.

17.53 If frequencies are granted through auctions or tenders, the NRA may prescribe certain additional conditions in the tender specifications in connection with e.g. the provision of services and the applicable technologies relating to the frequency use, the transferability and the validity period of the right.[50]

17.54 GSM, UMTS 900 MHz, DCS 1800 MHz, WiFi and 2.5 GHz and 3G are already in use in Hungary. As the majority of the frequencies were assigned under the old telecommunications regime, the operators only have to comply with obligations such as equal treatment and account separation.[51]

17.55 For broadcasting services, special provisions are set forth in Act 74 of 2007 on the rules of broadcasting and digital switchover ('Digital Broadcasting Act') regarding the frequency assignment, radio licence and the frequency usage fee.

Limitation of number of rights of use to be granted

17.56 The conditions and the number of rights of use to be granted depends on the legislation concerning the national allocation of frequency bands, the utilisation of frequency bands and the general provisions of Hungarian administrative procedure rules. Frequency auctions and tenders are prepared and organised by the NRA[52] and should be conducted according to Hungarian administrative procedure rules. Auctions and tenders are generally open to the public and there are no limitations on the number of applicants. After the proceedings, the NRA determines the winner(s) of the auction/tender and declares the auction/tender as valid and successful. The NRA, in its decision, either determines the deadline for the submission of the application for the frequency assignment by the winner(s) or concludes an administrative contract with the winner(s) if it is allowed according to the tender specification. The auction for the E-GSM band in the 900 MHz frequencies was conducted in 2012; however, as the decision was challenged by some of the tenderers, the decision on these frequencies is only likely to be final in 2013.

17.57 Operators are obliged to pay a one-time frequency reservation fee, but they are also subject to a regular frequency usage fee.[53] The frequency usage fee must be established reflecting the need to ensure the optimal use of resources. The fees have to be objective, transparent, non-discriminatory and proportionate with respect to the goal to be achieved, and they should also serve the goals of frequency management.[54]

---

50   S 55 EHT.
51   Part III of Act 40 of 2001.
52   NMHH Decree No 4/2011 of the NRA's President.
53   NMHH Decree No 1/2011 of the NRA's President.
54   S 84(7) EHT.

Rights of Use for Numbers

General authorisations and granting of individual rights

17.58   Identifiers, save for IP addresses, e-mail addresses and domain names, may be used only based on assignment licences subject to prior reservation.[55] Certain numbers (eg area codes, special numbers and prefixes for carrier selections) are, however, not subject to the individual licensing regime, as these numbers are generally allocated by law for the various tasks.[56] The NRA, at the service provider's request, issues the number reservation and/or the assignment licences. The assignment of numbers is carried out on a 'first come, first served' basis and, once assigned, the numbers cannot be assigned to other service operators except in case of succession.[57] For the usage and reservation of numbers, a number reservation and usage fee is payable. A number's allocation can be revoked if the assigned number cannot be used for the assigned purpose in the future, eg due to obligations arising from international agreements, or the service provider does not start the actual use of the number within 90 days from the date when the assignment licence has become final.[58]

Admissible conditions

17.59   Conditions relating to the use of numbers include, amongst others, number portability and carrier pre-selection.[59] Other conditions such as the transfer of allocated numbers, the duration of the reservation and use of the number, or the obligation to provide public directory subscribers' information are set out in the EHT and in the various implementing regulations.[60]

17.60   Number portability is already available for both mobile and fixed line services. The service provider is obliged to enable the subscriber to retain his subscriber number for fixed line or mobile telephone services when the subscriber changes the service provider providing subscriber access. Furthermore, the service provider providing subscriber access and the recipient provider have to agree on number portability if an offer of interconnection is received from the recipient service provider.[61]

17.61   Conditions relating to carrier pre-selection may be imposed upon the SMP service provider by the NRA. The obliged service provider must enable their subscribers' carrier selection regarding all publicly available fixed telephone calls. The subscriber contracts of service providers required to provide carrier selection may not contain any clause restricting or limiting carrier selection.[62]

The NRA's Enforcement Powers

17.62   The NRA, under its general tasks as a market supervisory authority, must also ensure compliance with the applicable rules in respect of the use of numbers

---

55   NMHH Decree No 2/2011 of the NRA's President.
56   NMHH Decree No 3/2011 of the NRA's President.
57   NMHH Decree No 2/2011 of the NRA's President.
58   NMHH Decree No 2/2011 of the NRA's President.
59   Government Decree No 73/2004.
60   Ss 146–150 EHT; NMHH Decree No. 2/2011 of the NRA's President.
61   S 150 EHT.
62   S 111 EHT.

and frequencies, eg it has the right to revoke the various licences or impose sanctions on service providers for non-compliance, etc. For further information on the NRA's enforcement rights, see para 17.11 et seq above.

Administrative Charges and Fees for Rights of Use

17.63 The NRA's activities are subject to administrative charges payable for granting rights of way, individual licences for numbers and in other cases when a procedure is initiated upon request. The administrative charge has to be paid in advance by the party initiating the procedure, as detailed in the legislation relating to the various procedures.[63] In addition to the administrative charges, service providers are obliged to pay an annual supervisory fee based on their turnover from the year preceding the year in question, together with an annual fee for the use of frequencies and numbers.[64]

REGULATION OF NETWORK ACCESS AND INTERCONNECTION: THE ACCESS DIRECTIVE

Objectives and Scope of Access Regulation

17.64 The EHT's definitions of access and interconnection are in line with EU law, as the EHT[65] mirrors the definitions in the Access Directive. However, the EHT is rather silent about any obligations or guidance on what principles and objectives the President/NRA should follow when identifying undertakings having SMP and/or when imposing remedies and obligations on them. In general, the EHT prescribes that remedies must be justified by and proportionate to any barriers to competition, must expressly refer to the European Commission's decisions and recommendations on the harmonised application of laws, and must contain further principles among the specific rules relating to the various remedies, but the President has wide discretion in applying remedies. In practice, the regulation of access and interconnection are based on the principles set out in the Access Directive.[66]

Basic Regulatory Concepts

17.65 The NRA has all the powers the Community legislation prescribes: it may collect information from market participants in individual procedures and in sector inquiries; it has the power to review the market; it is empowered to conduct market analysis, to identify undertakings having SMP and to impose obligations or remedies on them; to review, modify or terminate the designation and the remedies if they are not justified or proportionate any more; and to monitor compliance with the laws and obligations. There are very limited restrictions on the use of these powers. The restrictions also come from Community legislation (eg the obligation to impose remedies only if and to the extent they are justified and proportionate; the obligation to require functional separation only if other, less restrictive remedies

---

63   NMHH Decree No 5/2011 of the NRA's President.
64   NMHH Decrees No 9/2012, 5/2012 and 1/2011 of the NRA's President.
65   S 188 EHT.
66   See para 1.130 et seq above.

are insufficient). However, other principles are not expressly implemented, eg the priority of commercial negotiations over regulation is not expressly mentioned in the EHT.

Access- and Interconnection-related Obligations with Respect to SMP Undertakings

Overview

17.66   The access- and interconnection-related obligations which may be imposed on SMP undertakings correspond to those set out in the Access Directive:

- transparency, including the obligation to provide a reference offer;
- non-discrimination;
- accounting separation;
- obligations related to access and interconnection;
- functional separation;
- joint use of facilities and co-location; and
- price control and cost-accounting obligations.

The various obligations are applicable both to mobile and fixed line service providers; the EHT does not make any distinction between the different types of operators.

17.67   The President imposes remedies/obligations in administrative decisions. These are individual administrative actions binding upon the addressees of the decision who are parties to the procedure leading to the adoption of the decision, and who, therefore, have a right to request the judicial review of the decision.

17.68   If the President identifies an SMP undertaking, it must impose at least one remedy on it, but it may choose the most appropriate remedy/remedies in order to create or maintain competition. When deciding on the applicable obligations, the NRA has to take into account relevant factors described in detail in the laws in general or with regard to the specific remedies, such as proportionality, the creation or maintenance of competition, investments made by efficient service providers, the related risks and fair return on capital invested, and the prices available on comparative competitive markets. The NRA also may consider criteria such as the prices applied by service providers who are in a situation similar to that of the SMP undertaking.[67]

Transparency obligations

17.69   The NRA may impose transparency obligations on SMP undertakings in wholesale markets in connection with access and interconnection, and may oblige SMP undertakings to disclose certain information in a comparable, accurate and timely format. Such information includes:

- accounting and technical information;
- the conditions of the provision or purchase of the service;

- prices; and
- access for disabled people.[68]

17.70   As a transparency remedy, the NRA may oblige SMP undertakings to submit their contracts to the NRA. Lastly, the NRA may oblige SMP undertakings to prepare reference offers. SMP undertakings must prepare reference offers if they are subject to an access obligation to physical infrastructure.[69]

17.71   In practice, the President has obliged the incumbent SMP operators to prepare and publish reference offers. The decision usually provides guidance and conditions regarding the content of the reference offers on the basis of the EHT.[70] In addition, the President has imposed other types of transparency obligations on non-incumbent SMP undertakings and on mobile operators, eg to publish their termination rates and certain technical and business information, including planned changes, relating to access and interconnection on their websites. The President usually prescribes that such information should be accessible by a maximum of two clicks from the opening page of the given operator. In addition to this, in relation to the non-discrimination principle, it has obliged the incumbents on the wholesale broadband access market (market 5/2007) to publish those conditions of the wholesale services under which it provides such services to its affiliates.

Non-discrimination obligations

17.72   Non-discrimination obligations must primarily aim to ensure that SMP undertakings:

- apply substantially the same conditions towards other providers providing substantially the same services under substantially the same circumstances; and
- provide services and information of at least the same quality and under at least the same conditions to independent operators which it applies to its own services or to the services provided by its subsidiaries.[71]

The EHT provides a non-exhaustive list of discriminative behaviour, which includes, inter alia:

- setting such unjustified technical conditions to the provision of a service which can only be fulfilled by one or a few providers;
- applying such a condition in its subscriber contract which excludes the purchase of other provider's service;
- to apply such pricing conditions (eg volume discount) under which the best prices can only be met by purchasing only one or only a few providers' services.

Further, in practice the President of the NRA also prescribes that as part of the non-discrimination remedy, SMP undertakings must provide to all service providers the more preferential conditions they are applying towards other service providers.

---

68   S 102 EHT.
69   Ss 102 (1) and 103 EHT; see also Article 9 (4) of the Access Directive.
70   See also Government Decree 277/2003 (XII.24.) on reference offers.
71   S 104 EHT.

Specific access obligations

17.73   Section 106 EHT implements the non-exhaustive list of Article 12(1) of the Access Directive relating to the various obligations that the NRA may impose on an SMP undertaking. It directly obliges SMP undertakings to ensure access to physical infrastructure or services in accordance with the NRA's decision on the basis of a justified request. The EHT contains a non-exhaustive list of the types of obligations, which are practically identical to Article 12(1) of the Access Directive. In addition to this, the EHT also names as a possible obligation that SMP undertakings may be obliged to comply with specific technical or operational conditions if it is necessary for the proper functioning of the network (which is practically the implementation of Article 12(3) of the Access Directive).

17.74   The EHT, in line with Article 12(2) of the Access Directive and Article 8(5) of the Framework Directive, lists the conditions which the NRA must take into consideration when choosing among the various obligations. The EHT contain special rules on co-location and facility sharing.[72] It prescribes that co-location must be implemented by the lowest possible cost. Further, it lists some issues which must be regulated in the decision imposing obligations or in the reference offer (if the SMP undertaking is obliged to issue a reference offer). These include:

- location of relevant network places;
- co-location possibilities;
- entry into the relevant buildings and facilities;
- security standards;
- the conditions of the review of refused co-location requests and the rules of appeal; and
- access to IT systems; etc.

17.75   The SMP undertaking must ensure power supply and the possibility of connecting to the SMP undertaking's network. The SMP undertaking may set conditions relating to the other service provider's equipment only in certain limited cases, eg in order to protect human life and health, to avoid electromagnetic interference, to ensure compliance with interface or cable network standards, size of the space provided and fire protection.

17.76   In practice, the NRA has imposed several access-related obligations, each specific to the SMP undertaking and the service concerned. These related to the preparation of a reference offer, to technical and practical issues, and to the publication of certain information, etc. In a recent development, the President of the NRA has obliged incumbent SMP undertakings to grant access to the subscriber parts of NGNs in market 4 in order to provide voice or broadband services, with the exception of CATV networks ending in coaxial networks.

Cost-based prices and the controllability of prices

17.77   Section 108 EHT, reflecting the wording of Article 13 of the Access Directive,[73] states that a market analysis indicates that the absence of efficient competition could result in the application of unjustifiably high fees or price squeeze, the NRA can impose various price-related obligations on SMP undertakings on wholesale markets relating to certain access or interconnection services in

---

72   S 107 EHT
73   See paras 1.157–1.161 above.

order to promote efficiency and sustainable competition and to enforce consumer advantages. These price-related obligations include:

- the obligation to apply cost-based fees;
- the obligation to apply certain cost calculation or price setting mechanisms;
- the obligations ensuring the controllability of prices; or
- the NRA's right to apply a cost calculating method which is different from the one applied by the SMP undertaking in order to control costs.

In applying these powers, the NRA may oblige SMP undertakings to modify prices, and may establish the ratio of wholesale and retail services or the fee applicable to network services.[74]

17.78 As with the general principles, the factors to be taken into account by NRAs when applying this obligation listed in Article 13(1) and (2) of the Access Directive are implemented (the need to promote investments, particularly into NGNs; reasonable return on investments; risks assumed). However, the EHT's relevant section does not include the first sentence of Article 13(2) of the Access Directive which, as a general rule, obliges the NRAs to ensure that the cost recovery mechanisms must promote efficiency, sustainable competition and must maximise consumer benefits.

17.79 In practice, the NRA imposed the various types of price and cost control mechanisms listed below:

- SMP undertakings were obliged to apply cost-based prices;
- the applicable cost calculation method (LRIC –long-run incremental cost[75] or FDC – fully distributed costs[76]) was set;
- the maximum prices calculated on the basis of the cost calculation method were set;[77]
- a benchmark and a price formula were applied which are based upon the incumbent's prices;[78] and
- retail minus method was applied.[79]

Functional separation

17.80 Several provisions of the EHT relate to functional separation: different rules implemented the procedural rules, particularly on the involvement of the European Commission and BEREC in the adoption of the decision[80] and the substantive rules of Article 13a of the Access Directive.[81] These practically mirror the directives' provisions. The NRA has not imposed functional separation obligation on any SMP undertaking yet.

---

74   S 108 (5) EHT.
75   Eg markets 4, 7 and 5 (local and regional bitstream service) 2007.
76   Market 18 2003.
77   Market 7 2007.
78   Market 3 2007.
79   Market 5 2007, access to national bitstream service.
80   Ss 66 and 71 EHT.
81   S 108/A EHT.

Accounting separation obligations

17.81   The EHT,[82] mirroring the wording of the Access Directive,[83] empowers the NRA to prescribe, among other things, that an SMP undertaking should make its wholesale and transfer prices transparent. It can require the SMP undertaking to assume additional obligations either related to transparent operation and equal treatment or related to providing data required for checking the prohibition on unjustified pricing methods. An independent auditor must review the accounting separation records annually at the cost of the SMP undertaking. After the review the auditor issues a certificate, which must be published, about the compliance with the obligations.

Related Regulatory Powers with Respect to SMP Undertakings

17.82   The EHT, in addition to the obligations set out above, can still impose obligations relating to the spread of Internet usage on a service provider having SMP, but the detailed rules were entirely changed.[84] According to these rules, undertakings having SMP on a wholesale market must notify their intention to transfer all or a significant part of their local access network equipment to another independent entity which is controlled by third parties, or to establish an independent business unit to provide totally equivalent access services to all retail service providers, including to their own retail business units, to the NRA at least 90 days in advance. They must also notify the NRA if such transaction is not completed and of the results of the separation.

17.83   The EHT still authorises the NRA to impose obligations relating to carrier pre-selection on service providers having SMP on the market of subscriber access to public electronic communication networks. If such obligations are imposed, the service provider must ensure carrier (pre-)selection as it is described in its subscriber contract, must not prohibit use of carrier (pre-)selection in its subscriber contract, and must comply with the specific rules contained in separate legislation. The EHT obliges the SMP undertaking to bear the costs of making its network capable of carrier (pre-)selection.

Regulatory Powers Applicable to All Market Participants

Obligations to ensure end-to-end connectivity

17.84   The NRA can oblige the service provider controlling access to end users to provide access to or interconnect with its network out of consideration of efficiency and sustainable competition, in order to encourage and promote investment and to enforce consumer rights. In particular, the service provider can be obliged to interconnect its network with the networks of other service providers, to ensure interconnection between subscriber access points. The NRA may also request, when appropriate, that service providers ensure that 'services cooperate' when and to the extent necessary for interoperability. To achieve this, obligations may be imposed on equal treatment, access, interconnection, co-location and facility sharing.

---

82   S 105 EHT.
83   See paras 1.162–1.163 above.
84   S 112 EHT

17.85   When duplication of infrastructure is economically inefficient or physically impracticable, the NRA can impose on service providers the obligation to share facilities with any other service provider who requests it.[85]

Regulation of roaming services

17.86   The Regulation on roaming on public mobile communications networks within the EU[86] (the 'Roaming Regulation') also applies to Hungary. The Roaming Regulation sets out the ceilings on retail and wholesale prices of roaming calls, SMS messages and data roaming services and regulates the transparency of these prices. The price limits, in the Hungarian currency (Forint), are determined by the average of the reference exchange rates published in the Official Journal of the European Union.[87]

Access to digital radio and television broadcasting services

17.87   The rules on digital television are regulated by the Digital Broadcasting Act. Broadcasters and content providers operating a digital transmission network suitable for providing digital interactive television services shall make their best effort, regardless of transmission method, to apply an open Application Programming Interface.[88] To the extent required for the displaying and establishing of user interfaces, the supplier of the Electronic Programme Guide shall grant access to the Electronic Programme Guide service to all content providers and supplementary content providers under fair and reasonable conditions and in compliance with the principle of equal treatment.[89]

17.88   Obligations relating to Conditional Access Systems are set out in the Digital Broadcasting Act. The rules are in line with those regulated in the Annex to Part I of the Access Directive. According to the Framework Directive, if the NRA, as a result of the revision of the obligations relating to Electronic Programme Guides and Conditional Access Systems, consider that one or more conditional access operators have no significant market power in a particular market, the NRA may exempt these conditional access operators from such obligations, or may, in certain cases, impose new obligations in line with the Access Directive.

17.89   In order to enable end users to access digital radio and television broadcasts, service providers shall grant other service providers access to the relevant facilities under conditions fulfilling the requirements of fair, reasonable and equal treatment.[90]

---

85   S 100 EHT.
86   Regulation (EU) 531/2012 of the European Parliament and of the Council of 13 June 2012 on roaming on public mobile communications networks within the Union [2012] OJ L172/10.
87   Art 1(7) of the Roaming Regulation.
88   S 31 Digital Broadcasting Act.
89   S 33 Digital Broadcasting Act.
90   S 100(4) EHT.

REGULATION OF UNIVERSAL SERVICES AND USERS' RIGHTS: THE UNIVERSAL SERVICE DIRECTIVE

Regulation of Universal Service Obligations

Scope of universal service obligations

17.90   The definition of universal service[91] and the scope of the universal service obligations under the EHT[92] are in line with Articles 3 to 7 Universal Service Directive. As universal service obligations, the service provider has to provide, at an affordable price, connection at a fixed subscriber access point which permits the originating and receiving of national and international phone calls, facsimile and data transmission, accessing emergency services, as well as Internet connection at data rates that are sufficient to permit functional internet access. Functional Internet access means such a service which allows Internet connection of at least 9600 bit/s data rates.[93] In addition, the service provider must also provide, at an affordable price, national directory services, access to directory subscriber information, itemised bills, calling line identification and selective call barring. Furthermore, it must operate at least one public telephone site per 2,500 inhabitants or in each settlement with a population of less than 2,500.[94]

17.91   At least 3 per cent of the universal service provider's compulsory public telephone facilities must accommodate hearing-impaired and disabled persons, and the universal service provider also has to provide special packages and to subsidise low-income or disabled subscribers.[95]

Designation of undertakings obliged to provide universal services

17.92   If one of the universal services is not available throughout the entire country, the President of the NRA must designate the universal service provider ensuring the coverage of the entire country with universal services, and the least distortion to competition in the market.

17.93   The rules of EHT on designation procedure are in line with the provisions of the Universal Service Directive: universal services are to be provided by a service provider which is able to offer such services most efficiently and the designation procedure should be based on transparent and objective criteria and should be non-discriminative. [96] The detailed rules and conditions of the designation procedure are to be regulated in a decree to be issued by the NRA's President, however these details are not yet known to the market participants.

17.94   There is no designated universal service provider at this moment; designation is in progress, but it is expected to be carried out in 2013. Currently, universal services are now provided by the market and not under a designation.

---

91   S 188(11) EHT.
92   S 117 EHT.
93   Government Decree No 97/2010.
94   Ss 117 and 148 EHT.
95   S 117 EHT, Government Decree No 97/2010.
96   S 119 EHT.

Regulation of retail tariffs, users' expenditures and quality of service

17.95 The provisions allowing the subscribers to control their expenditures are in compliance with the Universal Service Directive. Service providers must, for example, provide their subscribers with itemised bills and cost control facilities, such as free-of-charge alerts in case of perception of abnormal or excessive consumption habits.[97]

17.96 The NRA supervises the universal service provider with regard to the execution of its activities on an ongoing basis. The President of the NRA is entitled to monitor the affordability of the universal services. The universal service provider is obliged to submit the data required for controlling compliance with its obligations to the NRA on an ongoing basis. The data providing evaluation on compliance with the obligations should be publicly available. The detailed rules of the universal service providers' supervision will be regulated in a Decree of the President of the NRA which has not yet entered into force. The NRA, of course, can also use its enforcement measures in case of non-compliance.[98]

Cost calculation and financing of universal services

17.97 The financing system of the universal service provider is in line with the Universal Service Directive. The principles for calculating the net avoidable costs, the detailed rules of compensation will be set out in a Decree of President of the NRA.[99]

17.98 The universal service provider is entitled to compensation on the basis of calculation of the net avoidable costs and the unfair burden related to providing universal services. The subsidy may only cover those net avoidable costs which exceed the 1 per cent of the service provider's net revenue arising from the provision of electronic communication services in the relevant year and which are therefore considered an unfair burden to the universal service provider. The compensation is provided by the NRA upon the request of the universal service provider.[100]

Regulation of Retail Markets

17.99 The EHT fully implements the principles and regulatory rules relating to the retail market under the applicable Directives.[101] Namely, it practically translates Article 17(1)(b) of the Universal Service Directive by stating that remedies on undertakings having an SMP status on the retail service market may be imposed only in order to protect the users' or subscribers' interests and to facilitate effective competition if it can be established on the basis of market analysis that competition is not sufficiently effective on a retail service market, and the objectives of the act could not be achieved by imposing wholesale remedies.

17.100 Undertakings having SMP on a retail market are identified in accordance with the general rules of competition law. In practice, national and regional fixed line incumbents are identified as SMP undertakings on the retail market.

---

97   S 119 EHT.
98   See paras 1.179–1.182 above.
99   S 121 EHT.
100 S 121 EHT.
101 S 109 EHT.

17.101   One notable difference from the Directives is that the EHT only lists the following obligations. The NRA may prohibit that SMP undertakings from:

- charging excessive or predatory prices;
- applying unjustified discrimination; and
- unreasonably bundling services.

Further, the NRA may oblige the service provider having SMP in a retail market to keep a cost calculation record, and may set the applicable principles, format and method, and the content of the records.

17.102   In practice, the NRA has prohibited excessive prices by setting a cap. The increase of prices in excess of the published inflation rate of the National Statistical Office is considered as excessive, and therefore is prohibited.[102] In other words, SMP undertakings cannot increase their fixed line prices by more than the inflation rate. Further, as a specific type of discrimination, the NRA prohibited SMP undertakings from applying such conditions as terminating the fixed term subscriber contract or the early exit from a tariff which is unjustified by and disproportionate to the costs of the performance of the contract or the discounts provided to the user.[103]

End User Rights

Contracts

17.103   The subscriber contract consists of the general terms and conditions (eg detailing the terms of the services, the procedural rules for concluding the agreement, data necessary for providing the services, suspension of the services, customer services, etc) and the individual subscriber contract. The individual subscriber contract sets out the specifics of the services and the service provider, eg details of the parties, duration, fees, termination, etc.[104] Only the universal service provider is obliged to conclude a subscriber contract.

17.104   Pursuant to the individual subscriber contract, the subscriber will be entitled to connect electronic communications terminal equipment that complies with the essential requirements of the subscriber interface provided in the network and to make use of the given service at any time during the term of the contract. The service provider cannot unjustifiably tie their services to other services.[105]

17.105   The individual subscriber contract must include, in addition to the provisions set out in Article 20(2) of the Universal Service Directive, further information, including:

- details of the subscriber;
- the consent of the subscriber to handle his or her data;
- the place of installation of the subscriber terminal equipment and the calling number of the subscriber;
- statements and data concerning the carrier service provider selected by pre-selection;
- a statement requesting an itemised bill; and

---

102   DH-8664–17/2010.
103   DH-8664–17/2010.
104   Ss 127–130 EHT.
105   S 128 EHT.

- accessibility to the general terms and conditions and the statement of the subscriber under which he or she accepts the provisions of the individual subscription contract.[106]

Transparency obligations

17.106   The service provider is obliged to inform its users about the content of the written general terms and conditions, and it also has to make them available to the customers at the service provider's customer service centre and on its website, free of charge. The general terms and conditions must be published and must also be sent to the NRA. The NRA regularly reviews and ensures compliance by the general terms and conditions with the applicable rules.

17.107   The general terms and conditions must contain at least the provisions set out in Annex II of the Universal Services Directive and the following issues:

- the period agreed for the installation of the subscriber access point and the commencement of its operation;
- terms of connection of the subscriber's terminal equipment;
- data protection;
- number portability rules, if applicable;
- rules of carrier selection;
- details of the supervisory authority; and
- accessibility of the general terms and conditions.[107]

17.108   When legislation requires that a subscriber is notified of an event, the service provider can inform its subscriber by mail, by email or any other form of electronic communications or through public announcement. In order that consumers have adequate information on the quality of services, prices and fees and can compare individual services and make rational decisions, the NRA can require communications service providers to provide data on the quality, accessibility and price of the services provided by them to the NRA or to disclose such data. The NRA publishes comparative data on the basis of information submitted by service providers.

Quality of Service: securing 'Net Neutrality'

17.109   Similarly to article 8(4)(g) of the Framework Directive, the EHT regulates the concept of the 'net neutrality' as a fundamental principal in respect of consumers.[108] In addition, to ensure 'net neutrality', Hungary[109] has implemented the provisions of the Universal Service Directive regarding the rules of transparency and the power of the NRA to impose minimum quality of service obligations. According to these rules, the service providers are obliged, among others, to indicate the content, quality and the security of the subscriber service in their general terms of contract.[110] Moreover, the NRA may require that the service providers provide them with comparable information regarding the quality, the

---

106   S 129 EHT.
107   S 131 EHT.
108   S 2 ba), bc), bf) EHT.
109   NMHH Decree No 6/2011 of the NRA's President, NMHH Decree No 13/2011 of the NRA's President.
110   S 131 EHT.

availability and the price of their services.[111] The 'quality of service parameters' are defined by the Decree of the NRA's President.[112]

Other obligations

17.110   Other obligations on the universal service provider, including obligations to provide access to emergency call numbers, and directory enquiry services, are also incorporated into the EHT on the basis of the Universal Service Directive.[113]

17.111   Under the applicable rules, end users can decide whether they wish to select their carrier through call-by-call prefix selection or by using pre-selection for all types of calls including VoIP calls. SMP undertakings have to ensure carrier selection; they cannot, therefore, exclude or restrict carrier selection in their respective subscriber contracts. Service providers providing subscriber access and the recipient provider also have to agree on number portability if an offer on interconnection is received from the recipient service provider.[114]

DATA PROTECTION: THE DIRECTIVE ON PRIVACY AND ELECTRONIC COMMUNICATIONS

Confidentiality of Communications

17.112   The EHT contains a chapter on the confidentiality of communications, which contains several security and security risk management related requirements.

17.113   Service providers must take appropriate technical and organisational measures – jointly with other service providers if necessary – to safeguard the security of their services in order to block any unauthorised attempt to intercept, store or monitor communications transmitted and any related traffic data and to prevent any unauthorised or accidental access to communications transmitted and any related traffic data. According to the EHT, the technical and organisational measures must also be sufficient – with regard to best practices and the costs of the proposed measures – to afford a level of security appropriate to the risk presented in connection with the services. The President of the NRA issued Decree 4/2012[115] ('Data Protection Decree') which contains more detailed security requirements and which contains data protection rules as well. Government Decree 226/2003 on the same subject matter is also effective.

17.114   The EHT provides only a limited statutory authorisation to process personal data. Service providers may process end users' and subscribers' personal data only to the extent required and necessary for their identification for the purpose of concluding the relevant contracts, to define and amend the contents of

111   S 144 (10) EHT.
112   NMHH Decree No 13/2011 of the NRA's President.
113   For further details see paras 1.172 et seq above.
114   S 111 EHT.
115   Decree No 4/2012. (I.24.) NMHH of the National Media and Communication Authority's Head on public electronic communication services related data protection and confidentiality obligation, special conditions on data processing and security, network security and integrity, processing of traffic and invoicing data, and on the rules applicable to ID display and redirection of calls. Government Decree No 226/2003, which contains similar requirements on the same subject matter, is still valid.

these contracts, to monitor contractual performance, charges and fees as contracted and for enforcing any related claims together with personal data which is technically essential for providing the services. Furthermore, personal data can be processed in connection with charges for the services only for calculating and billing charges (in particular the data relating to the date, duration and place of service to which it pertains). The service provider is also authorised to process personal data that is necessary from a technical point of view to provide the services. The Data Protection Decree contains additional special data processing rules and requirements.

17.115   In the absence of statutory authorisation to process personal data, with a few exemptions, the service provider must acquire the informed voluntary consent of the user to the data processing. Exact details of personal data processing and related rules must be set out in the service providers' data protection policy, which must be made available to the public at their customer services centre and on the Internet.

17.116   There are a few exceptions to the prohibition on interception or surveillance of communications. The investigating authorities and national security agencies may monitor, intercept and store communications by virtue of another act, and the frequency management authorities when exercising their powers conferred in the EHT or may otherwise intrude communication for surveillance purposes. There is also another limited exemption, when the investigating authority is entitled to tap into the telephone conversations, electronic communications and e-mail messages: in case of any alleged threat of murder or physical violence or blackmail, the user or subscriber threatened may authorise in writing the investigating authority to do so.

17.117   According to the EHT:

> 'Storing of information and or the gaining of access to information already stored in the terminal equipment of a subscriber or user is allowed only on the condition that the subscriber or user provides consent, having been provided clear and comprehensive information, inter alia, about the purposes of the processing.'

Since the EHT only refers to some information which has to be provided to subscribers, the general rules of Act CXII of 2011 on Information Rights and the Freedom of Information (the 'DPA') have to be applied, according to which subscribers must be informed about the person of the data controller, purpose and duration of the processing, whether data processors are applied and the rights of the subscribers. It is worth mentioning that since the EHT applies to electronic communication activities, but not to information society services, the EHT does not affect the cookie policy of the information society service providers.

17.118   As a result of the recent amendment of the EHT, the EHT contains the same requirements in respect of personal data breaches as the E-Privacy Directive. The Data Protection Decree has introduced special requirements affecting the performance of the personal data breach related obligations of the service providers. Among others, besides the general requirement to report data security breaches as soon as possible, the Data Protection Decree contains a 48-hour deadline. It contains the same deadline for informing the subscribers. It also contains requirements regarding the content of the report and notification.

17.119   Hungarian legislation contains effective mechanisms to sanction privacy and data protection breaches. In this regard, the NRA and the National Authority for Data Protection and Freedom of Information must cooperate. The authorities have to conclude a cooperation agreement. Both the EHT and the DPA contain adequate sanctions. Based on the legislation, it is not entirely clear how the above authorities proceed if the EHT and the DPA were infringed.

Data Retention

17.120   The EHT transposed the Data Retention Directive. The retention period is the following:

- in the case of unsuccessful calls, the relevant data has to be retained for six months;
- in any other cases, the relevant data has to be retained for one year.

According to our information, these rules of the EHT were not challenged, although the former Data Protection Commissioner expressed his concerns about the retention obligation.

Traffic Data and Location Data

17.121   The EHT defines location data as any data processed in an electronic communications network, indicating the geographic position of the terminal equipment of a user of an electronic communications service. Traffic data is not defined as such; however, the EHT uses this expression in line with the E-Privacy Directive.

17.122   The EHT contains a few new provisions regarding the processing of traffic and location data. According to these rules, where the provision of a value added service requires that processing of traffic or location data, the service provider must inform the subscribers or users concerning the type of data required, the purpose and duration of data processing, and as to whether or not the data needs to be disclosed to third persons. Pursuant to the strict rules of the EHT, providers of electronic communications services are authorised to process traffic or location data – excluding the data processing related to the data retention obligation – only upon the prior consent of the subscribers or users to whom the data is related, and only to the extent and for the duration as it is necessary for the provision of value added services. Users and subscribers are entitled to the right to withdraw their consent at any time. The consent has to be voluntary and informed as required by the DPA.

17.123   In case of emergency calls, even in the absence of consent, or the withdrawal of the above, the service provider must provide the operator of the emergency service with location and user identification data.

Itemised Billing

17.124   Service providers have to provide an itemised billing statement, free of charge. In connection with such billing, service providers are entitled to process various data including personal data. Operators are required to make available different types of detailed bills.

Presentation and Restriction of Calling and Connection Line Identification

17.125   Service providers, upon the written request of the subscriber but without charge, must allow users to withhold their number on a per-call or per-line basis.

Users must also be provided with the possibility of blocking the numbers of incoming calls or to reject those incoming calls where the caller has withheld the caller identification. Withholding the caller identity can, however, be limited in case of emergency calls or in those institutions which are considered to be vital for the operation of the state.[116]

Automatic Call Forwarding

17.126   Users are entitled to request the service provider to forward calls from their phone number to another phone number free of charge, and to ensure that the caller receives no information about the phone number or the subscriber, to whose phone number the call is forwarded. Users have the right to request, without charge, the cancellation of automatic call forwarding, if another user has ordered call forwarding to their phone number.

Directories of Subscribers

17.127   Service providers have to prepare directories of subscribers of fixed network telephony services each year in printed format or in electronic format, listing all subscribers of the service provider. Address registers may be created as well.

17.128   Subscriber directories and address registers may contain only as much data of a subscriber as is essential for the identification of the subscriber unless the subscriber concerned clearly approves, on a voluntary basis, to the publication of more personal data.

17.129   Subscribers are entitled to require that the service provider, free of charge, leaves them out of the printed or electronic directory; indicates in the telephone books that the subscriber's personal data may not be used for the purposes of direct marketing, information, public-opinion polling and market research; or indicates personal address in the telephone books in part only.

---

116 Decree No 4/2012. (I.24.) NMHH and Government Decree No 226/2003.

The Irish Market for Electronic Communications[1]

Claire Waterson
William Fry, Dublin

John Handoll
Amarchand Mangaldas, New Delhi

BASIC POLICY

18.1 The Irish telecommunications market is characterised by diverse market segments, such as large corporate customers with integrated data/voice requirements, a large number of small and medium enterprises ('SMEs') increasingly demanding data products, and domestic customers seeking inexpensive voice and broadband services. With the recent economic difficulties, the stated overall policy objectives of the Department of Communications, Energy and Natural Resources include developing Ireland as a 'digital Island' in order to promote economic recovery and employment. To this end, it has set out details of required policy intervention across a range of areas, including facilitating the roll out of high-speed broadband services, developing online trading platforms and developing a digitally enabled workforce.[2]

Policy is implemented on a day-to-day basis by the national communications regulator, the Commission for Communications Regulation ('ComReg'). ComReg has noted a fall in the revenues of the electronic communications sector as consumers and business seek to cut costs to deal with the recession. Nonetheless, revenues in the communications sector have grown as a proportion of GDP, indicating that overall the sector has remained relatively healthy. ComReg has noted its responsibility to deliver a transparent, predictable, and stable regulatory environment and to foster a competitive market offering quality and choice for consumers, as well as stimulating the next wave of investment and innovation. [3]

Implementation of EU Directives

18.2 The 2009 EU Regulatory Package was transposed on 1 July 2011.

Transposition into Irish law has been by Regulations[4] made under the European Communities Acts 1972–2009. The Regulations were adopted by the Minister for

---

1   Editing of this chapter closed on 1 July 2012.
2   Department of Communications, Energy and Natural Resources Statement of Strategy 2011–2014.
3   Strategy Statement 2010–2012: ComReg document 10/47.
4   In the form of Statutory Instruments, a form of delegated or secondary legislation.

Communications, Energy and Natural Resources (the 'Minister') after a period of public consultation. They are:

- SI 333 of 2011, the European Communities (Electronic Communications Networks and Services)(Framework) Regulations 2011 (the 'Framework Regulations');
- SI 335 of 2011, the European Communities (Electronic Communications Networks and Services)(Authorisation) Regulations 2011 (the 'Authorisation Regulations');
- SI 337 of 2011, the European Communities (Electronic Communications Networks and Services)(Universal Service and Users' Rights) Regulations 2011 (the 'Universal Service Regulations');
- SI 334 of 2011, the European Communities (Electronic Communications Networks and Services)(Access) Regulations 2011 (the 'Access Regulations'); and
- SI 336 of 2011, the European Communities (Electronic Communications Networks and Services)(Privacy and Electronic Communications) Regulations 2011 (the 'E-Privacy Regulations').

The Regulations provide the legal basis for the regulatory regime and set out the framework in which ComReg regulates the market on an ongoing basis.[5]

Legislation

18.3   As well as the Regulations implementing the new regime, there are a number of legislative acts relating to electronic communications. The principal act is the Communications Regulation Act 2002 (the '2002 Act') which establishes and governs the operation of the regulator, together with some transferred functions contained in the Telecommunications (Miscellaneous Provisions) Act 1996. Com-Reg was granted competition law powers in relation to electronic communications and services by the Communications Regulation (Amendment) Act 2007 (the '2007 Act'). Responsibility for the regulation of premium rate services was transferred to ComReg in 2010 pursuant to the Communications Regulation (Premium Rate Services and Electronic Communications Infrastructure) Act 2010 (the '2010 Act'). The Postal and Telecommunications Services Act 1983 (as amended) contains a number of provisions relating to interception. The regulation of spectrum and licensing of wireless telegraphy apparatus are governed by the Wireless Telegraphy Acts 1926–2009 and a number of statutory instruments.

REGULATORY PRINCIPLES: THE FRAMEWORK DIRECTIVE

Scope of Regulation

18.4   Irish legislation has adopted the technology-neutral approach of the EU Directives. The definitions of 'electronic communications network' and 'electronic communications service' are identical to those in the Framework Directive.[6] The

---

5   The 2011 Regulations, in each case, replace Regulations adopted in 2003 under the previous regime.

6   References to the Framework Directive relate to the Directive as amended by the Better Regulation Directive.

definitions of 'associated facilities' and 'associated services', although slightly different in wording, have the same meaning as in the Framework Directive.[7]

The need to adapt the regulatory system to complex services (ie non-traditional services, including services which may include the provision of content as well as features of electronic communications services) has been recognised.[8] A framework to facilitate the introduction of Voice over Internet Protocol ('VoIP') services in Ireland was put in place in 2004, when a range of numbers was opened specifically for IP-based services. Requirements relating to number portability, directory services, calling line identification, access to directories of subscribers, quality of service and network integrity and the treatment of consumers have since been established.[9] Separately, the regulation of premium rate services has been brought onto a statutory footing.[10]

'Internet freedom'

18.5   There are no specific provisions under Irish law concerning the imposition of measures to restrict end user access to the Internet. The European Union (Copyright and Related Rights) Regulations 2012 enable copyright holders to seek an injunction against an intermediary which provides facilities that may be used by third parties to infringe copyright.[11] Separately, the operator eircom has reached agreement with an association representing Irish music companies to implement a system known as 'graduated response' aimed at preventing infringement of copyright by end users by, ultimately, terminating Internet services to infringing users.[12]

National Regulatory Authorities: Organisation, Regulatory Objectives, Competencies

ComReg

18.6   ComReg is an independent commission, consisting of one to three members, established under the 2002 Act. Members of ComReg are appointed by the Minister following a competition. ComReg's objectives are established in s 12 of the 2002 Act (as amended) and include:

- 'in relation to the provision of electronic communications networks, electronic communications services and associated facilities —
    - to promote competition;
    - to contribute to the development of the internal market; and
    - to promote the interests of users within the Community;
- to ensure the efficient management and use of the radio frequency spectrum

---

7   Definitions are contained in Reg 2 Framework Regulations.
8   ComReg document 10/47.
9   ComReg documents 04/103, 05/50, 06/45 and 07/99.
10   See the 2010 Act.
11   These Regulations (SI 59 of 2012) were enacted after a High Court finding (in *EMI Records (Ireland) Ltd & Ors v UPC Communications Ireland Ltd* ([2010] IEHC 377)) that this remedy was not clearly available in Irish law due to a failure to transpose fully certain relevant EU Directives, including the E-Commerce Directive (2000/31/EC).
12   A 2011 declaration by the Data Protection Commissioner that this agreement was unlawful has been overturned in the High Court: *EMI Records (Ireland) Limited and others v Data Protection Commissioner*, 27 June 2012. This decision is under appeal.

and numbers from the national numbering scheme in the State in accordance with [a Ministerial direction]'.

ComReg is responsible for ensuring compliance with obligations regarding the supply of, and access to, electronic communications networks and services. While it manages spectrum and the national numbering resource and regulates the placing on the market of radio and communications equipment,[13] content is regulated separately under the Broadcasting Act 2009. ComReg is also responsible for regulating the provision of premium rate services.[14] Its functions are consistent with the NRA tasks identified in the Framework Directive.

ComReg is independent in the exercise of its functions, in accordance with the requirements of the Framework Directive,[15] and is required to apply objective, transparent, non-discriminatory and proportionate regulatory principles in pursuit of its objectives.[16] In exercising its duties, ComReg must follow policy directions given by the Minister.[17] The Minister may not give policy directions in respect of individual operators or the performance of ComReg's functions in relation to individuals.

ComReg has significant investigation powers (including powers to require the provision of information)[18] and may bring both civil and criminal actions for breaches of the relevant legislation.[19] Subject to certain specified exceptions, the Freedom of Information Acts 1997 and 2003 provide a right of public access to records held by ComReg.

Co-operation with other regulators – national level

18.7 A number of other regulatory authorities have a role to play in the electronic communications sector, in particular:

- the Office of the Data Protection Commissioner ('ODPC') (responsible for enforcing the Data Protection Acts 1988 and 2003 and certain provisions of the E-Privacy Regulations);
- the National Consumer Agency (responsible for enforcing specific regulations regarding the interoperability of consumer television equipment under the Universal Service Regulations);
- the Broadcasting Authority of Ireland ('BAI') (responsible for the regulation of broadcasting content); and
- the Competition Authority.

ComReg liaises and co-operates with these bodies as appropriate. It has also established a joint working group with the communications regulator for Northern Ireland (Ofcom) on cross-border issues.

Under the 2007 Act, ComReg and the Competition Authority have concurrent competition powers in the field of electronic communications. Consultation and co-operation between the regulators is facilitated by two complementary

---

13 Section 10 of the 2002 Act as amended.
14 Under the 2010 Act.
15 Section 11 of the 2002 Act.
16 Regulation 16(2) Framework Regulations.
17 Section 13 of the 2002 Act as amended.
18 See, for example, Section 13D and Part 3 of the 2002 Act (as amended).
19 Regulation 10 Framework Regulations.

co-operation agreements.[20] The first agreement sets out general procedures for the exchange of information and consultation, and for identifying situations in which one party may agree to forbear to perform any of its functions. The second agreement governs the concurrent exercise of competition functions. ComReg liaises with the Competition Authority with regard to market analysis and definition for the purposes of designating operators with significant market power ('SMP').

Co-operation at EU level

18.8   ComReg's obligations to publish information, to conduct public hearings or consultations and to co-operate with other NRAs and BEREC are contained in Regulations 12 and 13 of the Framework Regulations.

ComReg must actively support BEREC's goal of promoting greater regulatory co-ordination and coherence and must take the utmost account of opinions and common positions adopted by BEREC when adopting decisions for the Irish market.[21] ComReg is required to provide the European Commission with the information it reasonably requests in order to carry out its tasks under the EU Treaties.[22]

Where ComReg intends to take a measure which has a significant impact on a market for electronic communications networks or services, it must undertake a public consultation process, procedures for which are set out in Regulation 12 of the Framework Regulations.

Dispute resolution

18.9   The Framework Regulations confer specific powers and duties on ComReg with regard to dispute resolution. The exercise of these functions must comply with Article 8 of the Framework Directive and Section 12(2)(c)(ii) of the 2002 Act (containing an obligation to ensure the availability of simple and inexpensive dispute resolution procedures). Operators are required to establish procedures for the resolution of disputes with end users, and ComReg has a role in resolving unresolved disputes.[23]

Dispute resolution between operators is governed by Regulation 31 of the Framework Regulations and ComReg's published procedures.[24] Any party may initiate an investigation and ComReg is normally obliged to make a determination within four months. Decisions must be reasoned and published. ComReg's approach to dispute resolution is flexible: it may decide not to initiate an investigation where it is satisfied that other means of resolution (such as through informal contacts or negotiation) are available.

---

20   Agreements dated 16 December 2002 and 23 June 2008.
21   Regulation 16(3) Framework Regulations.
22   Regulation 10(7) Framework Regulations.
23   Regulation 27 Universal Service Regulations.
24   ComReg document 10/18R.

Right of Appeal against NRA's Decisions

18.10 Appeals may be taken against decisions made by ComReg under the Framework, Authorisation, Access, Universal Service or E-Privacy Regulations,[25] with some exceptions concerning notifications and opinions of non-compliance. Any user or operator affected by a decision of ComReg may appeal to the High Court within 28 days of notification of the decision.[26] ComReg is required to provide to the Court all documents that were before it in connection with the proceedings to which the appeal relates.[27]

An appeal does not of itself affect the operation of the decision or prevent action being taken to implement the decision. However, the High Court may make an order affecting the operation or implementation of ComReg's decision if it is appropriate for the purpose of securing the effectiveness of the hearing and determination of the appeal.[28] After hearing the appeal, the Court may affirm or set aside (in whole or in part) the contested decision, or remit the case to ComReg for reconsideration in accordance with directions of the Court.

The NRA's Obligations to Co-operate with the Commission

18.11 Regulation 13 of the Framework Regulations implements the consolidation procedure (Article 7 of the Framework Directive). ComReg has a duty to cooperate with NRAs of other EU Member States, the European Commission and BEREC, and to work with the Commission and BEREC to agree on the most appropriate types of instruments and remedies to address particular types of situations in the marketplace. The co-regulation procedure (Article 7a of the Framework Directive) has been implemented by Regulation 14 of the Framework Regulations. Both procedures have been respected in practice by ComReg.

The Commission's power to draw up and publish standards and specifications is recognised in Regulation 28 of the Framework Regulations. ComReg must encourage the use of standards and specifications published by the Commission for the provision of services, technical interfaces or network functions, to ensure interoperability of services and to improve users' freedom of choice. Regulation 30 establishes similar conditions in relation to harmonisation.

'Significant Market Power' as a Fundamental Prerequisite of Regulation

Definition of SMP

18.12 An operator shall be designated as having SMP[29] where ComReg is satisfied that, in relation to any relevant market, the operator (whether individually or jointly with others) enjoys a position which is equivalent to dominance of that market, that is to say a position of economic strength affording it the power to

---

25 Regulation 3 Framework Regulations.
26 Regulations 4 and 5 Framework Regulations. The appeal must be served on ComReg.
27 Regulation 8 Framework Regulations.
28 Regulation 7 Framework Regulations.
29 Regulation 25(1) Framework Regulations.

behave to an appreciable extent, independently of competitors, customers and, ultimately, consumers.[30]

When assessing whether one or more operators has SMP in a relevant market, ComReg must act in accordance with EU law and take the utmost account of European Commission guidelines on market analysis pursuant to Article 15(2) of the Framework Directive. In addition, in the case of an assessment of joint dominance, it must take account of the criteria set out in the Schedule to the Framework Regulations (which mirror those set out in Annex II of the Framework Directive).[31]

An operator with SMP in one market may also be designated as having SMP in a closely related market where links between the markets are such as to allow the market power held in the first market to be leveraged into the second market, thereby strengthening the market power of the operator.[32]

Definition of relevant markets

18.13   ComReg must, taking utmost account of the Commission Market Recommendation and the Commission Guidelines for market analysis, define markets appropriate to national circumstances, in particular the relevant geographic markets within the State, in accordance with the principles of competition law.[33] Before defining markets that differ to those identified in the Recommendation, ComReg must follow the consultation and transparency procedure and the consolidation procedure.[34]

In practice, ComReg has followed the Market Recommendation and Guidelines, although it has occasionally departed from these where this was necessitated by the market structure and conditions of competition in Ireland. ComReg has identified national markets (and not sub-national markets) as the relevant geographic market in each of its current SMP decisions. Further details of the markets that have been defined by ComReg are set out below.[35]

Imposition of remedies

18.14   Where ComReg determines that a relevant market is not effectively competitive, it must designate operators which individually or jointly have SMP on that market and impose on such operators (following the appropriate procedure) such specific regulatory obligations as ComReg considers appropriate. Subject to obligations as to appropriateness and proportionality, the selection of the specific obligations to be imposed is at ComReg's discretion. The obligations which may be imposed by ComReg are set out in Regulations 9 to 14 of the Access Regulations and (in relation to retail markets) Regulation 13 of the Universal Service Regulations.

---

30   The question of collective dominance was considered in relation to the market for wholesale mobile access and call origination on public mobile telephony networks (ComReg document 05/14). However, that decision was annulled on appeal.
31   Regulation 25(2) Framework Regulations.
32   Regulation 25(3)(a) Framework Regulations.
33   Regulation 26(1) Framework Regulations.
34   Regulations 12 and 13 Framework Regulations.
35   See para 18.18 below.

ComReg may impose certain obligations on operators which have not been designated as having SMP. Regulation 6 of the Access Regulations enables ComReg to impose obligations in relation to end-to-end connectivity, interoperability and (after consultation with the BAI) the provision of access to application programme interfaces and electronic programme guides.

NRA's Regulatory Duties Concerning Rights of Way, Co-location and Facility Sharing

Rights of way

18.15 Persons providing or operating an electronic communications network, whether public or private, are entitled to the following rights:

- *Opening of public road to establish underground infrastructure*:[36] consent of the relevant road authority is required and exempts the operator from the requirement to hold a licence under s 254 of the Planning and Development Act 2000. Charges may be imposed to cover administrative costs and costs incurred in repairing or reinstating a road following work by an operator.

- *Use of public road to establish overground infrastructure*:[37] the erection, construction or maintenance of overground infrastructure and associated physical infrastructure on, under or along a public road requires a licence from the local authority.[38] An operator will be responsible for all costs incurred in the reinstatement of a road to a satisfactory standard where it has opened a road to establish, maintain or repair overground infrastructure.

- *Lopping of trees*:[39] operators may lop or cut trees, shrubs or hedges which interfere with physical infrastructure (but not trees interfering with radio signals) on giving 28 days' notice to the landowner and may enter land at any reasonable time to do so.

- *Relocation of infrastructure due to road improvements*:[40] road authorities undertaking work to improve a road shall pay all reasonable costs incurred by an operator in relocating its infrastructure (with specified exceptions).

Co-location and facility sharing

18.16 Section 57 of the 2002 Act entitles network operators to negotiate infrastructure sharing agreements with other providers. Operators may serve notice on ComReg of such negotiations. If requested, or on its own initiative, ComReg will specify a timeframe within which negotiations shall be completed. If an agreement is not reached, ComReg will take steps necessary to resolve the dispute and may impose conditions for physical infrastructure sharing. Conditions imposed by ComReg may be enforced by way of application to the High Court.[41]

ComReg may require the holders of rights to install facilities on, over or under public or private property to enter into negotiations with other physical infrastructure providers for the sharing of physical infrastructure where ComReg considers

---

36   Section 53 of the 2002 Act as substituted by s 21(2) of the 2010 Act.
37   Section 54 of the 2002 Act.
38   Section 254 of the Planning and Development Act 2000.
39   Section 58 of the 2002 Act.
40   Section 55 of the 2002 Act as substituted by s 21(3) of the 2010 Act.
41   Section 57A of the 2002 Act as inserted by the 2007 Act.

that this is necessary in order to protect the environment, public health or public security, or to meet planning objectives.[42] Furthermore, where ComReg considers it justifiable on the grounds that duplication of infrastructure would be economically inefficient or physically impracticable, it may require the holder of such rights to enter into negotiations with other physical infrastructure providers in relation to the sharing of wiring inside buildings or up to the first connection or distribution point where this is located outside the building. Where agreement cannot be reached on the sharing of the infrastructure within a time period set by ComReg, ComReg may make decisions in accordance with s 57 of the 2002 Act.

REGULATION OF MARKET ENTRY: THE AUTHORISATION DIRECTIVE

The General Authorisation of Electronic Communications

Authorisation process

18.17   There is no requirement to apply for a licence to provide an electronic communications network or service. Any person may do so provided they comply with the conditions set out in a General Authorisation. Operators must notify ComReg in advance of their intention to provide a network or service. Failure to notify is an offence.[43] Where the proposed network and services are designed wholly for own use by an operator, including use by connected entities,[44] the operator is exempt from the requirement to make a prior notification and is deemed to be authorised, but must comply with the conditions of the General Authorisation. Separate conditions apply to the use of spectrum.

Notification is made by submitting a completed notification form to ComReg. Where networks or services are provided by different group companies, a separate notification form should be completed by each legal entity. A register of authorised operators is maintained on ComReg's website.[45]

Rights and obligations of operators

18.18   Authorised operators may apply for consent to carry out road works and for a licence to establish overground infrastructure. In addition, operators providing services or networks to the public have the right to negotiate interconnection with and, where applicable, obtain access to or interconnection from, another authorised operator and to be given an opportunity to be designated under the Universal Service Regulations.[46]

---

42   Regulation 21 Framework Regulations.
43   See Regulation 4(6) (offence) and Regulation 25 (penalties) Authorisation Regulations.
44   'Connected entities' are entities directly or indirectly owned by a common entity, and wholly owned subsidiaries: ComReg document 03/90. The legal basis for the exemption is Regulation 4(7) Authorisation Regulations.
45   www.comreg.ie Parties authorised in accordance with the 2003 regime are deemed to be authorised under the Authorisation Regulations by virtue of Regulation 27(9) Authorisation Regulations.
46   Regulation 7 Authorisation Regulations.

The conditions for authorisation (which are binding) have been specified by ComReg,[47] which is charged with monitoring compliance with the conditions. The general conditions for authorisation are:

- provision of information to ComReg;
- compliance with decisions on emergency services during disasters;
- compliance with radiation emission standards;
- ensuring no harmful interference with other networks;
- compliance with decisions on maintenance of the integrity of public electronic communications networks;
- use of apparatus for wireless telegraphy in accordance with applicable conditions; and
- having regard to issued notices or guidelines on the use of standards or specifications.

Operators providing a network or service that is not wholly for their own use are also subject to conditions regarding;

- universal service funding;
- administrative charges;
- interconnection;
- compliance with the National Numbering Conventions;
- co-location and facility sharing;
- misuse of data;
- consumer protection rules; and
- security of public networks.

Rights of Use for Radio Frequencies

Strategic planning and co-ordination of spectrum policy

18.19   ComReg is responsible for the effective management of radio frequencies for electronic communications services[48] in accordance with Government policy and EU requirements. It issues a Strategy Statement for the managing of the radio spectrum in Ireland every three years.[49] Current policy reflects the essential role of radio spectrum for the continuing provision of mobile communications and in the wireless reception of broadcast services, as well as the role of spectrum in the day-to-day operation of the defence forces, emergency services and air and maritime transport, and is consistent with the EU's approach to key issues, including the digital dividend.

Principles of frequency allocation, procedural rules

18.20   Authorisations to use spectrum are granted in accordance with the Wireless Telegraphy Acts 1926–2009 and the Authorisation Regulations. ComReg is required to establish open, objective, transparent, non-discriminatory, and proportionate

---

47   ComReg document 03/81R3 (conditions specified in accordance with Regulation 8 of the Authorisation Regulations).
48   Regulation 17 Framework Regulations.
49   At the time of writing, the current Strategy Statement covers the period 2011–2013: ComReg document 11/89.

procedures for the granting of rights of use for radio frequencies.[50] The principles of technology and service neutrality have also been reflected in the national legislation.[51]

Rights to use radio frequencies for the provision of electronic communications networks or services must normally be granted under a general authorisation. Any general authorisation for the granting of rights of use for radio frequencies must be facilitated by way of an Order made by ComReg under s 3(6) of the Wireless Telegraphy Act 1926 (the '1926 Act').

Section 5 of the 1926 Act applies to licences granting individual rights of use, conferring the right to keep and have possession of wireless telegraphy apparatus. The conditions that can be attached to licences granting individual rights of use must be in accordance with Regulation 10 of the Authorisation Regulations. ComReg may grant individual rights by way of a licence where it considers that it is necessary, applying one or more of the following criteria:

- to avoid harmful interference;
- to ensure technical quality of service;
- to safeguard the efficient use of spectrum; or
- to fulfil other objectives of general interest.

ComReg must make any decision on the grant of rights of use for radio frequencies as soon as possible after receipt of the complete application, and in the case of frequencies allocated for use by electronic communications services within the national frequency plan, within six weeks of receipt.

Transferability and time limitations

18.21   When granting rights of use for radio frequencies, ComReg must specify whether such rights may be transferred by the holder of the rights and under what conditions such a transfer may take place. The time limitations to rights for frequency use established in Article 5(2) of the Authorisation Directive have been transposed.[52]

Admissible conditions

18.22   The Schedule to the Authorisation Regulations (Part B) lists the conditions which may be attached to rights of use for radio frequencies, repeating the conditions set out in the Authorisation Directive. In certain cases, specific obligations are imposed (for example in the case of the 900MHz, 1800 MHz and 800 MHz bands, conditions relating to minimum coverage, minimum quality of service conditions and compliance with international obligations).

Limitation of number of rights of use to be granted

18.23   ComReg may limit the number of rights of use to be granted for radio frequencies where necessary to ensure their efficient use, giving due weight to the

---

50   See, generally, Regulation 9 Authorisation Regulations.
51   Regulations 17(2) and (4) Framework Regulations.
52   References to the Authorisation Directive relate to the Directive as amended by the Better Regulation Directive.

need to maximise benefits for users and to facilitate the development of competition. When limiting the number of rights of use, ComReg must grant rights on the basis of objective, transparent, non-discriminatory and proportionate selection criteria.[53] Spectrum auctions have been used as an award mechanism for bands where the number of licences to be awarded was limited and demand was likely to exceed supply (eg advanced high speed fourth generation mobile services).

ComReg may impose fees for rights of use for radio frequencies which reflect the need to ensure the optimal use of the radio frequency spectrum.[54] Fees must be objectively justified, transparent, non-discriminatory and proportionate in relation to their intended purpose and must be consistent with ComReg's statutory objectives.[55]

Rights of use for numbers

General authorisations and granting of individual rights

18.24   ComReg is responsible for the administration of the national telecommunications numbering resource.[56] It establishes National Numbering Conventions (the 'Conventions')[57] setting out eligibility criteria, application procedures, and conditions for allocation and use of numbers. It is a condition of the General Authorisation that operators comply with the Conventions. Numbers constitute non-proprietary data of which no particular organisation, institution, or individual may claim ownership.[58]

Primary allocation of numbers is made to operators following application to ComReg, which should be done not more than six months before the planned activation date. In the case of numbers for which designations exist, ComReg will normally notify the applicant of its decision within three weeks of application. Refusal to make an allocation, or the attachment of conditions, may be appealed in accordance with the normal appeals procedure.[59] Operators then make a secondary allocation of the numbers to end users. A refusal to make an allocation, or the attachment of conditions to an allocation, may be appealed to ComReg.

ComReg may, after carrying out a public consultation, decide that rights of use of numbers with exceptional economic value will be granted through a competitive or comparative selection procedure (although this has not been done in practice).[60]

Operators have a right to use the numbers allocated to them in accordance with the Conventions. ComReg may decide that certain conditions may not apply to persons of such class or type as it objectively determines to be appropriate. The conditions of allocation can only be amended by ComReg in objectively justified cases and in a proportionate manner.[61]

End users have a right to use numbers allocated to them subject to directions set by the operator and/or ComReg. Their rights of use include the allocation of telephone numbers that are not subject to frequent misdialling, a change of telephone

---

53   Regulations 9(10) and 11 Authorisation Regulations.
54   In accordance with ss 13 and 37 of the 2002 Act.
55   Regulation 19 Authorisation Regulations.
56   Section 12 of the 2002 Act; Regulation 20 Framework Regulations.
57   ComReg document 11/17.
58   Section 8 of the Conventions.
59   See further para 18.10 above.
60   Regulation 13 Authorisation Regulations.
61   Section 8.1 of the Conventions.

number if an existing number is subject to unacceptable levels of nuisance or malicious calls, and having numbers or address information excluded from telephone directories.[62]

Admissible conditions

18.25   The Schedule to the Authorisation Regulations lists the conditions which may be attached to rights of use of numbers, repeating the conditions set out in the Authorisation Directive. General conditions of use and conditions for specific number types are set out in the Conventions.

All fixed and mobile network operators are obliged to offer full number portability to their customers. In the case of geographic numbers, an operator may also offer location portability, but only within the area for which the number was originally allocated.[63] As SMP operator in the retail narrowband access markets, eircom is subject to obligations in relation to carrier pre-selection/indirect access.

The NRA's enforcement powers

18.26   ComReg's enforcement powers are set out in Regulations 16 to 26 of the Authorisation Regulations. These powers echo the powers of the NRA set out in the Authorisation Directive and apply to conditions for authorisation, licences for spectrum, rights to use of numbers, regulatory controls on retail markets, universal service, access and interconnection obligations, and SMP obligations.

ComReg may require the provision of information in order to verify compliance with the conditions for authorisation or with any direction issued to an operator.[64] It also has general powers to require the provision of information in order to carry out its functions and to conduct investigations (including entry onto operators' premises).[65]

Where it identifies a failure to comply, ComReg will notify the operator concerned and give it an opportunity to state its views. If ComReg believes the operator has not complied with the condition or direction, it may apply to the High Court for an order compelling compliance, and for the imposition of a financial penalty in respect of the failure to comply.[66]

ComReg may direct immediate compliance in the case of a breach representing an immediate and serious threat to public safety, security or health, or a breach which could in ComReg's opinion create serious economic or operational problems for operators or for end users.[67] Authorisations and rights of use for radio frequencies or numbers may also be suspended or withdrawn in the case of serious or repeated breaches of the relevant conditions.[68]

---

62   Section 8.2 of the Conventions.
63   Section 10.5 of the Conventions.
64   Regulation 21 Authorisation Regulations.
65   Section 13D and s 39 of the 2002 Act (as amended).
66   Any financial penalty shall be paid to and retained by ComReg as income: Regulation 16(10)(c).
67   Regulation 16(12) Authorisation Regulations.
68   Regulation 17 Authorisation Regulations.

Certain breaches may be prosecuted criminally as well as on a civil basis, although civil and criminal proceedings may not be taken in respect of the same breach.[69] Offences under the Authorisation Regulations are punishable on summary conviction by a fine of up to €5,000. Certain offences, such as failure to comply with conditions for authorisation or for the use of numbers, may, on conviction on indictment, attract fines of up to €50,000 (in the case of a natural person) or €500,000 (in the case of a body corporate). Complicit officers are also liable to prosecution.[70]

Administrative Charges and Fees for Rights of Use

18.27   There is no fee for notification in accordance with the General Authorisation. However, authorised operators providing a public network or service with an annual turnover of €500,000 or more are subject to an annual levy of 0.2 per cent of their turnover to meet ComReg's expenses in the discharge of its functions.[71] ComReg may impose fees for rights of use for radio frequencies or numbers which reflect the need to ensure the optimal use of the radio frequency spectrum and the national numbering scheme. Fees vary in accordance with the rights granted.[72]

REGULATION OF NETWORK ACCESS AND INTERCONNECTION: THE ACCESS DIRECTIVE

Objectives and Scope of Access Regulation

18.28   ComReg is mandated to encourage and, where appropriate, ensure adequate access, interconnection, and interoperability of services in such a way as to promote efficiency, sustainable competition, efficient investment, and innovation, and to give maximum benefit to end users.[73]

The Irish provisions on interconnection and access apply to operators of publicly available communications networks and to authorised operators seeking interconnection or access to these networks or associated facilities.

Basic Regulatory Concepts

18.29   The Irish definitions of 'access' and 'interconnection' mirror those in the Access Directive.[74] ComReg may, without prejudice to any measures that may be taken in respect of operators with SMP:

- to the extent that is necessary to ensure end-to-end connectivity, impose obligations on operators that control access to end users including, in justified cases, the obligation to interconnect their networks where this is not already the case;

---

69   Regulation 23 Authorisation Regulations.
70   Regulation 24 Authorisation Regulations.
71   SI 346 of 2003, Communications Regulation Act (Section 30) Levy Order 2003. A number of operators are exempt from this obligation, ie providers of satellite, radio and television terrestrial transmission networks.
72   Regulation 19 Authorisation Regulations.
73   Regulation 6 Access Regulations.
74   References to the Access Directive relate to the Directive as amended by the Better Regulation Directive.

- in justified cases and to the extent that is necessary, impose obligations on operators that control access to end users to make their services interoperable; and
- impose obligations in relation to conditional access systems and other facilities.[75]

Obligations must be objective, transparent, proportionate, and non-discriminatory and must be applied in accordance with Regulations 12 (consultation and transparency obligations), 13 (provisions in respect of consolidating the internal market) and 14 (procedure for the consistent application of remedies) of the Framework Regulations.[76] The imposition, amendment or revocation of obligations under the Access Regulations must be published.[77]

ComReg may apply to the High Court for an order to secure compliance with an obligation, requirement, condition or direction imposed under the Access Regulations.[78]

ComReg is precluded from maintaining or imposing administrative measures which oblige operators, when granting access or interconnection, to offer different terms and conditions to different operators for equivalent services or to impose obligations that are not related to the actual access and interconnection services provided.[79]

Operators, whether established in Ireland or in another Member State, are entitled to negotiate with any other operator an agreement on technical and commercial arrangements for access or interconnection in the State in accordance with EU law for the purpose of the provision of electronic communications services. An operator requesting access or interconnection in Ireland does not need to be authorised if it is not providing services and does not operate a network in Ireland.[80]

In accordance with the principle of the priority of commercial negotiations, ComReg may exercise its powers on its own initiative where justified.[81] In practice, this will only occur where ComReg considers that negotiation or other means of resolution cannot be or have not been effective.

Access- and Interconnection-related Obligations with Respect to SMP-undertakings

18.30   Where an operator is designated as having SMP, ComReg may impose such of the following obligations as it considers appropriate on the relevant operator:[82]

- transparency;
- non-discrimination;
- accounting separation;
- access to and use of specific network facilities; and
- price control and cost accounting obligations.

---

75   Regulation 6(2) Access Regulations.
76   See para 18.14 above.
77   Regulation 16 Access Regulations.
78   Regulation 19(4) Access Regulations.
79   Regulation 4(3) Access Regulations.
80   Regulation 4 Access Regulations.
81   Regulation 6(4) Access Regulations.
82   Regulations 9 to 13 Access Regulations.

Obligations imposed must be based on the nature of the problem identified, must be proportionate and justified, and may only be imposed following the appropriate consultation and consolidation procedure. Any proposal to impose obligations other than those listed above must be approved by the European Commission.[83]

eircom has been designated as having SMP in the markets for higher- and lower-level retail narrowband access from a fixed location;[84] the markets for wholesale call origination and for wholesale national call transit services (both on the public telephone network at a fixed location);[85] the market for wholesale (physical) network infrastructure access;[86] the market for wholesale broadband access;[87] and the market for wholesale terminating segments of leased lines.[88] Obligations of access, transparency, accounting separation, non-discrimination and price control/cost accounting have been imposed in all markets.

A number of operators, including eircom, have been designated as having SMP in the market for wholesale call termination on individual (fixed) networks.[89] All designated operators are subject to obligations of transparency, non-discrimination and price control; eircom is subject to additional obligations of access, accounting separation and cost accounting.[90]

In the mobile sector, individual operators have been designated as having SMP in the market for wholesale call termination on individual mobile networks,[91] with obligations of access, non-discrimination, transparency, price control, cost accounting and accounting separation.[92]

Further market reviews are underway, and the scope of a number of specific obligations is under consideration, including price control for fixed and mobile termination rates,[93] proposed remedies in next generation access markets,[94] and eircom's obligation not to unreasonably bundle retail fixed narrowband access with other retail services.[95]

ComReg is entitled to impose, as an exceptional measure, the remedy of functional separation,[96] where it concludes that the normal SMP obligations previously imposed have failed to achieve effective competition and that there are important and persisting competition problems or market failures identified in relation to the

---

83 Regulation 8 Access Regulations.
84 ComReg document 07/61.
85 ComReg document 07/80.
86 ComReg document 10/39.
87 ComReg document 11/49.
88 ComReg document 08/103.
89 ComReg document 07/109.
90 ComReg documents 07/109, 10/67 and 11/67.
91 O2, Vodafone, Meteor and Hutchison 3G Ireland ('H3GI') were designated under the previous regime (ComReg document 04/82). The original designation was overturned on appeal by H3GI, leading to a separate re-designation (ComReg document 08/92). At the time of writing, ComReg was considering proposals to re-designate these operators and in addition to designate Lycamobile and Tesco Mobile as having SMP in the relevant markets (ComReg document 12/46).
92 The obligations of cost accounting and accounting separation apply only to Vodafone and O2, but have not been further detailed. It is proposed to remove the obligation of accounting separation and, possibly, the cost accounting obligation (ComReg document 12/46).
93 ComReg document 12/67.
94 ComReg document 12/27.
95 ComReg document 10/01.
96 Regulation 14 Access Regulations (in accordance with Article 13a of the Access Directive).

wholesale provision of certain access product markets. ComReg must submit a request to the European Commission before imposing functional separation.

Regulatory Powers with Respect to SMP-undertakings

18.31   The obligations which may be imposed on SMP operators are identified above. Obligations related to the provision of leased lines and carrier selection and pre-selection, formerly contained in Articles 18 and 19 of the Universal Service Directive, have been removed from the new Universal Service Regulations and may only be imposed under the Access Regulations.

Regulatory Powers Applicable to All Market Participants

Obligations to ensure end-to-end connectivity

18.32   Without prejudice to any measures that may be taken in respect of operators with SMP, ComReg may, to the extent that is necessary to ensure end-to-end connectivity, impose obligations on operators that control access to end users including, in justified cases, the obligation to interconnect their networks where this is not already the case.[97]

Regulation of roaming services

18.33   All mobile operators are subject to the Roaming Regulation. ComReg may also require an SMP operator to provide specified services needed to ensure interoperability of end-to-end services to users, including facilities for intelligent network services or roaming on mobile networks.[98]

Access to digital radio and television broadcasting services

18.34   ComReg is required to encourage providers of digital interactive television services for distribution to the public in the EU on digital interactive television platforms, regardless of the transmission mode, to use an open application pro-gramme interface. It is also required to encourage providers of all enhanced digital television equipment deployed for the reception of digital interactive television services on interactive digital television platforms to comply with an open appli-cation programme interface in accordance with the minimum requirements of the relevant standards or specifications. Finally, it must encourage providers of digital television services and equipment to co-operate in the provision of interoperable television services for disabled end users.[99]

To the extent that it is necessary to ensure accessibility for end users to digital radio and television broadcasting services specified by the BAI (and after consultation with the BAI), ComReg may impose obligations on operators to provide access to

---

97   Regulation 6(2) Access Regulations.
98   Regulation 12(2)(g) Access Regulations.
99   Regulation 29(1) Framework Regulations.

application programme interfaces ('APIs') and electronic programme guides ('EPGs') on fair, reasonable and non-discriminatory terms.[100]

The conditions for conditional access systems as laid down in Annex I, Part I of the Access Directive have been transposed in accordance with Article 6(1) of the Access Directive.[101]

REGULATION OF THE UNIVERSAL SERVICE AND USERS' RIGHTS: THE UNIVERSAL SERVICE DIRECTIVE

Regulation of Universal Service Obligations

Scope of universal service obligations

18.35   A number of universal service obligations may be imposed on designated operators, namely provision of access at a fixed location and provision of telephone services, directory enquiry services and directories, public pay telephones and other public voice telephony access points, the implementation of measures for disabled users, and the affordability of retail tariffs.[102]

Broadband Internet access is not currently included within the scope of universal service obligations. A review of the position is planned for 2014, and ComReg has committed to monitoring the position in the interim to establish whether there is a demonstrable case for including it.[103]

ComReg must specify obligations applicable to designated operators for the purpose of ensuring that disabled users can enjoy access to, and afford, publicly available telephone services equivalent to that enjoyed by other users, as well as access to directory enquiry services and directories.[104] A number of obligations have been imposed on the universal service provider, including a Code of Practice on the provision of services to disabled users and specified measures in respect of hearing, speech, mobility and sight impaired users.[105]

Designation of undertakings obliged to provide universal services

18.36   ComReg may designate one or more operators to provide universal services. In the latter case, it can designate different operators or sets of operators to comply with one or more of the obligations or to cover different parts of the State. The designation procedure must be efficient, objective, transparent and non-discriminatory and must ensure that the obligations imposed are provided in a cost-effective manner.[106] Following a public consultation, eircom has been

---

100   Regulation 6(2)(c) Access Regulations.
101   Regulation 7 Access Regulations.
102   Regulations 3 to 9 Universal Service Regulations.
103   Section 5.1 ComReg document 12/71.
104   Regulation 6 Universal Service Regulations.
105   ComReg document 12/71. A separate consultation is planned on measures to do with accessibility of telecommunications services in accordance with Regulation 17 Universal Service Regulations.
106   Regulation 7 Universal Service Regulations.

re-designated as the universal service provider throughout the State for a period of two years from 1 July 2012.[107]

Regulation on tariffs, users' expenditures and quality of service

18.37   eircom is required to apply geographically averaged prices throughout the State in respect of its universal service obligations. Affordability is also maintained through a number of different mechanisms, including:

- a minimum level of itemised billing (free of charge);
- offering call barring facilities; and
- a scheme for the phased payment of connection fees.[108]

eircom must publish information on its universal service performance based on the service parameters and measurement methods set out in Annex III to the Universal Service Directive.[109] Performance targets have been developed for connections, fault rate occurrence and fault repair times.[110]

If ComReg finds that the universal service provider has not complied with an obligation, it may apply to the High Court to enforce compliance, including the imposition of a financial penalty.[111]

Cost calculation and financing of universal services

18.38   The onus is on the universal service operator to claim that the universal service obligation is an undue burden, in which case ComReg will determine how to share the costs among operators.[112] The net cost of the universal service obligation is calculated by means of the Historic Cost Accounting methodology (adjusted for efficiencies and taking account of costs that could have been avoided by the universal service provider without having the universal service obligation).[113]

Regulation of Retail Markets

Prerequisites for the regulation of retail markets

18.39   eircom has been designated as having SMP in the retail narrowband access markets, specifically a national market for lower level retail narrowband access (including access via analogue exchange lines and integrated services digital network basic rate access carried over copper, cable or fixed wireless access) and a national market for higher level retail narrowband access, including access via integrated services digital network fractional rate access and integrated services digital network primary rate access.[114]

---

107   ComReg document 12/71.
108   ComReg document 12/71.
109   References to the Universal Service Directive relate to the Directive as amended by the Citizens' Rights Directive.
110   ComReg document 08/37.
111   Regulation 31 Universal Service Regulations.
112   Regulations 11 and 12 Universal Service Regulations.
113   ComReg document 11/42.
114   ComReg document 07/61.

In accordance with Article 17(1)(b) of the Universal Service Directive, regulation of retail services is permissible only if ComReg finds that regulation at wholesale level would not achieve the relevant regulatory objectives.[115] This principle has been applied in practice, for example in relation to the analysis leading up to the imposition of obligations on the retail narrowband access markets.[116]

Regulatory powers

18.40   In retail markets, obligations may be imposed to ensure that the operator concerned does not:

- charge excessive prices;
- inhibit market entry or restrict competition by setting predatory prices;
- show undue preference to specific end users; or
- unreasonably bundle services.

Measures to control individual tariffs, retail price cap measures or measures to orient tariffs towards costs or prices on comparable markets may also be imposed.[117]

Obligations of access, transparency, non-discrimination, accounting separation, price control, and cost accounting have been imposed on eircom in the retail narrowband access markets.[118] The access obligations imposed include that eircom enable its subscribers to access the services of any interconnected providers of publicly available telephone services: on a call-by-call basis, by dialling a carrier selection code; by means of pre-selection with a facility to over-ride any pre-selected choice; and by carrier access. The price-control obligations require eircom to ensure that its pricing for such access and interconnection is cost-oriented.

eircom is subject to an access obligation in respect of wholesale access products, services, features or associated facilities which enable operators to provide equivalent retail products to those offered by eircom in the retail narrowband access markets, including various obligations in respect of single billing wholesale line rental.[119] eircom is also obliged not unreasonably to bundle fixed narrowband access. A net revenue and margin squeeze test is currently applied in this regard.[120]

End User Rights

Contracts

18.41   Operators providing connection to a public communications network or publicly available electronic communications services to consumers, and other end users so requesting, must do so in accordance with a contract containing a specified

---

115   Regulation 13(1)(b) Universal Service Regulations.
116   ComReg document 07/26.
117   Regulation 13 Universal Service Regulations.
118   ComReg document 07/61.
119   ComReg document 08/19.
120   At the time of writing, ComReg was considering whether the net revenue test should be revised: ComReg documents 11/72 and 12/63.

minimum level of information including the requirements established in Article 20 of the Universal Service Directive.[121]

ComReg has issued Guidelines setting out the level of detail to be included in contracts with end users.[122] These do not distinguish between consumers and business users. Separate guidelines have been issued for VoIP service providers on the treatment of consumers.[123]

In order for terms and conditions to be valid they must be brought to the attention of the end user before any agreement is concluded. This may be done by providing a written contract or by indicating where written terms and conditions can be found. Standard terms and conditions should be published in a transparent and accessible manner and a paper copy should be provided if requested.

Operators must establish a Code of Practice for handling customer complaints, including procedures, time frames and appropriate cases where reimbursement/payments in settlement of losses will be made.[124] The Code of Practice must be clearly referred to in the customer contract, and must explain ComReg's role in the resolution of disputes.

Transparency obligations

18.42   Operators may be required to publish transparent, comparable and up-to-date information on tariffs and prices.[125] Details of prices and tariffs must be included in the customer contract, including the types of charges, connection costs, rebates, peak and off-peak calling times, billing frequency and billing and payment mechanisms.[126] A direct link must be provided from the homepage of an operator's website to the tariff information section.[127] ComReg has published a detailed Code of Practice for the presentation of tariff information[128] and has developed an interactive online tariff guide for consumers to facilitate comparison of operators' rates.[129]

Quality of service: securing 'net neutrality'

18.43   In accordance with Article 8(4)(g) of the Framework Directive, one of ComReg's objectives is to promote the ability of end users to access and distribute information or to use applications and services of their choice.[130] There are a number of specific national provisions that enable ComReg to secure net neutrality,[131] including the setting of minimum quality of service requirements on operators providing public communications networks in order to prevent the degradation of service and the hindering or slowing of traffic over networks. ComReg may also

---

121   Regulation 14 Universal Service Regulations.
122   ComReg document 03/129.
123   ComReg document 05/50.
124   Regulation 27 Universal Service Regulations.
125   Regulation 15 Universal Service Regulations.
126   ComReg document 03/129.
127   ComReg document 03/86.
128   ComReg document 04/86.
129   www.callcosts.ie
130   Regulation 16(d)(ii) Framework Regulations.
131   Regulation 15 Universal Service Regulations.

require the provision of a wide variety of information to subscribers, including information on any procedures in place to measure and shape traffic and how those procedures could impact on service quality.

European emergency call number

18.44   Operators providing end users with an electronic communications service for originating national calls to a number or numbers in the national numbering scheme (including from public pay telephones) must ensure that such end users are able to call the emergency services free of charge by using the single European emergency call number '112' or the national emergency call number '999'.[132]

Other obligations

18.45   ComReg is required to ensure that the '00' code is the standard international access code.[133] Operators are also required to facilitate the making of calls to Northern Ireland by means of a national access code ('048') in addition to the international UK country code '00 44'.[134]

Obligations Facilitating Change of Provider

18.46   Operators are required to ensure that a subscriber with a number from the national numbering scheme can retain his or her number independently of the operator providing the service in the case of geographic numbers, at a specific location; and in the case of non-geographic numbers, at any location.[135] Portability between fixed and mobile networks is excluded.

ComReg has established global processes for portability, taking into account contract provisions, technical feasibility, the need to maintain continuity of service and subscriber protection issues. The obligations referred to in the Universal Service Regulations apply to all operators with a role in facilitating change of provider, including the old operator, the new operator, and any wholesale operator involved in the process.

Prices related to number portability must be cost oriented and direct charges to subscribers, if any, must not act as a disincentive to switching. The porting of numbers must be carried out within the shortest possible time, and the number must be activated within one working day. Loss of service during the porting process must not exceed one working day. Subscribers must be compensated in case of delay in porting or abuse of porting (in accordance with requirements specified by ComReg).

An operator providing electronic communications services must not conclude contracts with consumers which mandate an initial commitment period that exceeds 24 months and shall offer users the possibility to subscribe to a contract with a maximum duration of 12 months. Conditions and procedures for contract termination must not act as a disincentive to switching.

---

132   Regulation 20 Universal Service Regulations; Conventions, section 3.2.1.
133   Regulation 21 Universal Service Regulations.
134   Conventions, section 12.
135   See generally Regulation 25 Universal Service Regulations.

DATA PROTECTION: THE DIRECTIVE ON PRIVACY AND ELECTRONIC COMMUNICATIONS

Confidentiality of Communications

18.47   Subject to limited exceptions (generally relating to legally authorised data interception or retention), the listening to, tapping, storage or other kinds of interception or surveillance of communications and the related traffic data by persons other than users, without the consent of the users concerned, is prohibited.[136]

Operators providing publicly available electronic communications networks or services are obliged to take appropriate technical and organisational measures to safeguard the security of their services (if necessary in conjunction with the relevant network operators).[137] The minimum security measures required reflect the requirements of the E-Privacy Directive.[138]

Exceptions to the prohibition on interception or surveillance are contained in s 98 of the Postal and Telecommunications Services Act 1983 and in s 2 of the Interception of Postal Packets and Telecommunications Messages (Regulation) Act 1993. This legislation permits interception to take place in certain circumstances (in particular, for the purpose of supporting criminal investigations or to protect the interests/security of the State). Interception may be authorised on foot of an application to the Minister for Justice by the Irish police or Irish defence forces, or where it is carried out by a person acting 'under other lawful authority'.

The use of electronic communications networks to store information or to gain access to information already stored in the terminal equipment of a subscriber is prohibited, unless the subscriber has given consent to that use, after having received clear and comprehensive information in accordance with the Data Protection Acts 1988 and 2003.[139] This information must be prominently displayed and easily accessible, and must include the purposes of the processing of the information. The technical storage of, or access to, information for the sole purpose of carrying out the transmission of a communication over an electronic communications network or which is strictly necessary in order to provide information society services explicitly requested by the subscriber, is permitted.

Where there is a risk of security breach, subscribers must be informed without delay of the risk and possible remedies (as well as cost implications). When a personal data breach has already occurred, the operator must notify the ODPC and, if such a breach could affect the personal data or privacy of a subscriber, the subscriber. Operators must maintain an inventory of personal data breaches comprising the facts of the breach, its effects and any remedy taken.[140]

The ODPC may, following a complaint or on its own initiative, investigate, or cause to be investigated, breaches of the E-Privacy Regulations. If the ODPC believes a breach has occurred, it may serve on the concerned person an enforcement notice

---

136   See, generally, Regulation 5 E-Privacy Regulations.
137   Regulation 4 E-Privacy Regulations.
138   References to the E-Privacy Directive relate to the Directive as amended by the Citizens' Rights Directive.
139   Regulation 5(3) E-Privacy Regulations.
140   Regulation 4 E-Privacy Regulations.

requiring the person to take specified steps. Failure to comply with a requirement specified in an enforcement notice is an offence.[141]

Data Retention

18.48 The Data Retention Directive has been transposed into Irish law by the Communications (Retention of Data) Act 2011 (the 'Data Retention Act 2011'). The Data Retention Act 2011 governs the retention of Internet and telephone traffic and location data by 'service providers', defined as a person engaged in the provision of a publicly available electronic communications service or a public communications network by means of fixed line or mobile telephones or the Internet. Internet data must be retained for one year, while telephone data must be retained for two years.[142] The duty to retain data arises automatically (and is not dependent on the receipt of a request from any authority). The retention obligation does not apply to the content of communications.[143] Requests for disclosure of retained data may be made by certain senior members of the Garda Siochána, the Permanent Defence Force or the Revenue Commissioners where the data is required for specified purposes (generally relating to the investigation of offences or state security).[144] The retained data may also be accessed in accordance with the consent of the person to whom the data relates, a court order, or as may be authorised by the ODPC.

In 2010, a non-governmental non-profit organisation concerned with the promotion and protection of civil and human rights in the context of telecommunications technologies brought a High Court action against the Minister and other parties, challenging data retention measures on various grounds. The High Court has made a reference to the European Court of Justice to determine whether the Data Retention Directive is fully compatible with the EU Treaties and the Charter of Fundamental Rights.[145]

Traffic Data and Location Data

18.49 The definitions of 'traffic data' and 'location data' mirror those in the E-Privacy Directive.[146] Service providers must inform subscribers of the types of data processed and the duration of such processing. Traffic data processed for the purpose of transmitting communications must be erased or anonymised when it is no longer needed for that purpose. Operators may process data for the purposes of marketing electronic communications services and pursuing payment (or the determination of proceedings if taken during that time). Location data may only be processed if it has been anonymised and the user's consent has been obtained to the extent and for the duration necessary for the provision of a value added service. This consent may be withdrawn at any time.[147]

---

141 See, generally, Regulation 17 E-Privacy Regulations. Prosecutions may be taken by the ODPC.

142 Section 3 of the Data Retention Act 2011.

143 Section 2 of the Data Retention Act 2011.

144 Section 6 of the Data Retention Act 2011.

145 *Digital Rights Ireland Limited v The Minister for Communication, Marine and Natural Resources, The Minister for Justice, Equality and Law Reform, The Commissioner of an Garda Siochána, Ireland and the Attorney General* [2010] IEHC 221. The reference is Case C-293/12.

146 Regulation 2(2) E-Privacy Regulations.

147 Regulations 6 and 9 E-Privacy Regulations.

In an exception to the above rule, the Data Retention Act 2011 provides for the retention of traffic and location data for specified periods.

Itemised Billing

18.50   Users have the right to request service providers *not* to provide itemised bills. As universal service provider, eircom has been directed to make a minimum level of itemised billing available to customers free of charge.

Presentation and Restriction of Calling and Connected Line Identification

18.51   Service providers offering calling line identification services must allow users to withhold their number on a per-call and per-line basis, using simple means and free of charge. Users must also have the facility to block the numbers of incoming calls and to reject incoming calls automatically in cases where the caller has withheld the caller identification.[148] This service may be eliminated temporarily during a police investigation into suspected malicious or nuisance calls. An exception also lies in respect of calls to emergency services and law enforcement agencies.[149]

Automatic Call Forwarding

18.52   Users to whom calls have been automatically forwarded as a result of third party actions have the right, without charge, to request that these be ceased as soon as practicable after receipt of the request.[150]

Directories of Subscribers

18.53   The universal service operator and any other person making subscribers' data available for inclusion in a directory must inform all subscribers in advance of the purposes of the directory and any further usage possibilities based on search functions embedded in electronic versions of the directory. Subscribers must have the opportunity, without charge, to determine whether and to what extent their personal data is included in the directory and be given the opportunity to verify, correct or withdraw the data. [151]

---

148   Regulation 8 E-Privacy Regulations.
149   Regulation 10 E-Privacy Regulations.
150   Regulation 11 E-Privacy Regulations.
151   Regulation 12 E-Privacy Regulations.

The Italian Market for Electronic Telecommunications[1]

Raffaele Giarda and Andrea Mezzetti
Baker & McKenzie, Rome

LEGAL STRUCTURE

Basic Policy

19.1   As one of the founding Member States of the European Community, Italy has followed the EC's regulatory approach in the telecommunications sector, thus liberalising the national telecommunications market[2] and adopting the Harmonisation Directives.[3]

19.2   In addition, and differently from other EU Member States, throughout the years, Italy has privatised to a large extent the former Public Telecommunications Operator so that the Italian Treasury has now fully divested its participation in the corporate capital of the former incumbent, Telecom Italia. On the other hand, national and local utilities (directly or indirectly owned by the State) continue to hold interests in a number of players.

19.3   Telecom Italia still holds a significant market share in the fixed telephony and leased line markets. At the same time, other competitors (both national and local) have increasing access to such markets, mostly in larger cities. The mobile, data services/Internet and broadband markets are more competitive with numerous alternative providers, while the cable services market is still very small compared to the satellite and direct to home ('DTH') services markets.

19.4   The main regulatory principles followed by the Italian policy-makers are the freedom to use electronic communications and the right of economic initiative in a competitive environment. The provision of communications networks and services is the primary regulatory objective: in addition to the regulatory objectives set out in the 2002 and the 2009 Regulatory Packages,[4] under Italian law, the regulator must guarantee the right of information pursuant to Article 19 of the UN Universal Declaration of Human Rights.[5]

---

1   Editing of this chapter closed on 10 November 2012.
2   See para 1.8 et seq above.
3   See para 1.20 et seq above.
4   Art 8 of the Framework Directive. For an analysis, see para 1.32 et seq above.
5   Adopted by UN General Assembly Resolution 217 A (III) of 10 December 1948.

19.5   Since the implementation of the 2002 Regulatory Package, the Italian market has faced new challenges, mainly related to the evolution of the electronic communications market. In particular, the significant expansion of smartphones in Italy is triggering a growing demand for mobile broadband which must be faster and more efficient, and, in turn, triggers the need for additional allocation of frequencies. Moreover, recent years have seen the rise of new players which provide their services through electronic communication networks but which are not telecommunications providers, the so called 'Over-the-Top' players. In this respect, Italian policy-makers must find a delicate balance between the interest of network providers (to protect their investments in the infrastructures) and the interests of Over-the-Top players (which invoke the net neutrality principle to utilise the network so as to provide their services without surcharges).

19.6   In this rapidly evolving scenario, the main regulatory objectives focus on broadband, both fixed and mobile. With respect to fixed broadband, network providers are currently looking at the shift to 'next generation' networks, which should align Italy with other EU countries and promote better connectivity. On the mobile side, in 2011 the Ministry of Economic Development ('Ministry') awarded, through public tender, certain frequencies to be used for the provision of LTE mobile services.

Implementation of EU Directives

19.7   With the enactment of Legislative Decrees Nos 69 and 70 of 28 May 2012, which entered into force on 1 June 2012, Italy has finally implemented the 2009 Regulatory Package. In particular, Legislative Decree No 69/2012 essentially contains a set of amendments to the Code of Personal Data Protection ('Privacy Act'),[6] while Legislative Decree No 70/2012 amended the Code of Electronic Communications ('CEC').[7]

19.8   The amendments to the CEC and to the Privacy Act implemented the 2009 Regulatory Package following the same structure and approach. The main aspects of the new regulation are examined in the following paragraphs.

Legislation

19.9   The CEC is the main piece of legislation on the regulation of electronic communications in Italy, which abrogated or amended most parts of the former regulatory regime.[8] Accordingly, the entry into force of the CEC has simplified and consolidated the Italian sector-specific regulation, reducing significantly the number of legislative measures governing the electronic communications sector. At the same time, the CEC has maintained, or only partially amended, parts of the previous legislative measures, thus giving rise to interpretation and harmonisation issues.

19.10   In addition to the CEC, the main legislative measures in the sector are the laws enacted before the adoption of the CEC and not abrogated by the latter,

---

6   Legislative Decree No 196 of 20 June 2003, which entered into force on 1 January 2004.
7   Legislative Decree No 259 of 1 August 2003, published in the Official Gazette No 214 of 15 September 2003.
8   Among others, the main legislative acts of the former regulatory regime which have not been abrogated, but only supplemented by the CEC, are the laws and decrees setting out the legal status, powers, and duties of the Ministry and AGCOM.

including legislative decrees and law decrees. The latter are statutes in the Italian legal system. In addition, other regulatory provisions are contained in ministerial decrees and regulations which, under Italian law, are secondary legislative measures to be adopted in compliance with the (higher-ranking) laws. Finally, the sector is also regulated through decisions, resolutions and recommendations of the Ministry, the Italian Communications Regulatory Authority (*Autorità per le Garanzie nelle Comunicazioni* – 'AGCOM'); and the Italian Data Protection Authority (*Garante per la Protezione dei Dati Personali* – 'IDPA'), which are administrative provisions under Italian law.

19.11   Over the years, Italian legislation has enhanced competition, particularly in the mobile sector, which has become even more competitive after AGCOM opened the market to virtual operators (mobile virtual network operators, enhanced service providers, and air time resellers) through Resolution No 46/06/CONS.[9] The fixed communications arena also includes a number of players, but the incumbent, Telecom Italia, operating a significant portion of Italian network, still plays one of the most important roles in the market. However, the number of competitors and the forthcoming deployment of next generation networks will provide additional competitive pressure.

REGULATORY PRINCIPLES: THE FRAMEWORK DIRECTIVE

Scope of Regulation

19.12   The following sectors and activities fall within the scope of the CEC:

- public electronic communications networks and services, including networks used for audio or video broadcasting and cable television networks;
- electronic communications activities for private use;
- protection of submarine electronic communications apparatus; and
- radio electrical services.

19.13   The CEC definitions of 'electronic communications networks', 'electronic communications services', and 'associated facilities' are identical to those in the Framework Directive, as amended by the 2009 Regulatory Package.[10]

19.14   The CEC does not regulate the following:

- services which provide content transmitted through electronic communications networks and services, and services which provide editorial control over content;
- radio equipment and telecommunications terminal equipment, except for the apparatus utilised by digital TV users; and
- electronic commerce and information society services which do not consist wholly or mainly in the conveyance of signals on electronic communications networks.

19.15   The CEC does not expressly address VoIP services, which are regulated by AGCOM Resolution No 11/06/CONS.[11] Depending on their technical features, these services could qualify as nomadic voice communication services (if they allow users to originate and receive domestic and international voice communications

---

9   Published in the Official Gazette No 46 of 24 February 2006.
10   For the relevant definitions, see paras 1.33, 1.34 and 1.35 above.
11   Published in the Official Gazette No 87 of 13 April 2006 – Ordinary Annex No 95.

from any network termination point) or as publicly available telephone services (if a limited nomadic use of the service is permitted only within the relevant area code district in Italy).

'Internet Freedom'

19.16   Italian law does not provide for the imposition of measures to restrict end users' access to the Internet per se, except for certain provisions which sanction crimes committed via the web (eg unlawful access to an internet system).[12]

19.17   On 8 July 2011, AGCOM launched a public consultation concerning the regulation of copyright protection on electronic communication networks which contained a number of rules that, if passed, could restrict end users' access to the Internet.[13] However, after such public consultation, considering the public opinion criticising the proposed rules, AGCOM decided not to issue the regulation. While, currently, the topic seems to no longer be at the top of AGCOM's agenda, this does not exclude the possibility that the AGCOM may decide to adopt measures in this regard.

National Regulatory Authorities: Organisation, Regulatory Objectives, Competencies

19.18   In Italy, regulatory powers and competences are divided between the Ministry and AGCOM.[14] Such powers are consistent with the provisions set out in the EU regulatory framework. Specifically, the Ministry:

- issues general authorisations and manages, controls and applies the general authorisation regime for electronic communications services and the rights for use of radio frequencies and numbers;
- monitors compliance with universal service obligations in the electronic communications sector;
- controls the allocation of national numbering resources and the management of the national numbering plan; and
- monitors radio frequencies so as to ensure compatibility with human health.

19.19   AGCOM is an independent body, whose members are appointed by the Parliament, responsible for implementing the legal framework for telecommunications, as well as with respect to press and audio-visual matters. More specifically, AGCOM:

- develops and issues the national numbering plan and procedures for the assignment of numbering resources;
- develops the frequency allocation plan;
- maintains the public register of communications operators (*Registro degli Operatori di Comunicazione*);
- issues regulations regarding the general quality of service levels and oversees the application of quality service standards by communications operators;

---

12   Art 615*ter* Criminal Code.

13   AGCOM Resolution No 398 /11/CONS.

14   The Ministry has the regulatory powers set out by Legislative Decree No 300 of 30 July 1999, as amended. AGCOM has the regulatory powers set out under Laws No 481 of 14 November 1995 and No 249 of 31 July 1997, as amended.

- provides the European Commission with the list of operators with significant market power (SMP) and their obligations; and
- has dispute resolution powers in cases of disputes between providers as well as between providers and users.

19.20   The Ministry and AGCOM are legally and functionally independent from all telecommunications operators. AGCOM, in performing its tasks, makes its own decisions, independent of the Government.

19.21   The functions of the Ministry and AGCOM are complementary. Coordination issues may arise, particularly in areas where the Ministry and AGCOM have complementary powers.

Pursuant to article 8 CEC, the Ministry, AGCOM, and the Italian Competition Authority (*Autorità Garante della Concorrenza e del Mercato* – 'ICA') must exchange information necessary for application of the EU regulatory framework and must adopt, through specific agreements, procedures for reciprocal consultation and cooperation in areas of common interest.[15] In carrying out their regulatory activities, the Ministry and AGCOM must promote technological neutrality[16] where possible, and with certain exceptions in case of frequency allocation. [17]

19.22   The Ministry, AGCOM and the ICA each have the power to request information from operators and undertakings. In particular, the CEC provides that the Ministry and AGCOM may do so in order to ensure that the operators comply with the provisions of the CEC or with decisions adopted pursuant to the CEC. The Ministry and AGCOM must publish the relevant information to the extent it contributes to creating a free and competitive market, in compliance with European and national legislation on confidentiality.

19.23   When the Ministry and AGCOM intend to adopt a decision that may have a significant impact on the relevant market, they must allow interested parties to submit their observations on the proposed decision within at least 30 days following the date of notification of the proposed decision.[18] In addition, the Ministry and AGCOM must publish information about the relevant consultation procedure on their websites and in their Official Bulletins.[19] In the case of confidential information, the right of access is granted to the extent necessary to guarantee the right of defence.

The Ministry and AGCOM must promptly publish on their websites all disclosable information regarding a decision to open a consultation procedure, the results of such consultation, and the proposed final decision.[20]

19.24   AGCOM must cooperate with other EU Member States' NRAs, with the European Commission, and with BEREC in order to ensure that the provisions set out in the 2002 and 2009 Regulatory Packages are fully implemented in all Member States. To this end, AGCOM must undertake activities in order to reach agreements

---

15   To this end, on 28 January 2004, AGCOM and the ICA entered into a collaboration agreement which covers market analysis procedures, the transfer of rights of use of radio frequencies, and access to documents and confidential information.

16   Art 13(2) CEC.

17   See para 19.59 et seq below.

18   Art 11 CEC.

19   To this end, AGCOM, by Resolution No 453/03/CONS, published in the Italian Official Gazette on 28 January 2004, adopted a specific regulation on the consultation procedure.

20   See para 19.35 below.

with other Member States' NRAs, with the European Commission, and with BEREC on the most appropriate means and solutions.[21]

19.25　AGCOM has the power to resolve disputes between providers of electronic communications networks or services. AGCOM must adopt a binding decision within four months from submission of a claim. If the parties agreed to derogate from the competence of the AGCOM by choosing to use an alternative dispute resolution method and the parties did not settle within four months from the beginning of the alternative proceedings, AGCOM must adopt a binding decision on the dispute within the four months. AGCOM must publish its decision on the AGCOM website and in the Official Bulletin.[22]

19.26　AGCOM must administer transparent, simple, and inexpensive procedures to resolve disputes between operators and users, in order to ensure fair and prompt resolution of such disputes by providing, when justified, a reimbursement and indemnification system.[23]

19.27　AGCOM also has dispute resolution powers in cases of transnational disputes where one of the parties is established in another EU Member State. In this case, AGCOM must coordinate with the NRA of the other EU Member State in order to resolve the dispute, also consulting BEREC. Again, if the parties agreed to derogate from the competence of NRAs by choosing to use an alternative dispute resolution method, and the parties did not settle within four months from the beginning of the proceedings, AGCOM and the other EU Member State's NRA must adopt a binding decision on the dispute.[24] All such AGCOM decisions may be challenged as outlined in the following paragraph.

Right of Appeal against NRA's Decisions

19.28　All decisions and resolutions adopted by AGCOM and the Ministry pursuant to the CEC may be challenged before the administrative court (*Tribunale Amministrativo Regionale* ('TAR') of Lazio), based in Rome.[25]

The TAR may grant temporary restraining orders and may rule on the merits of any such decision or resolution. The decisions of the TAR may be appealed before the Council of State (the highest administrative court). The Council of State may also reverse the decision and grant temporary restraining orders. Except for significant proceedings and highly visible matters, the heavy workload of the TAR and the Council of State at times results in the handling of cases in a manner less efficient than would be required for the rapidly evolving telecommunications market.

The NRA's Obligations to Cooperate with the Commission

19.29　AGCOM must cooperate in a transparent manner with the NRAs of the other Member States in order to ensure full compliance with the EU regulatory

---

21　Art 12 CEC.

22　Art 23 CEC. By Resolution No 352/08/CONS, published in the Italian Official Gazette on 7 August 2008, the NRA passed a regulation for the resolution of disputes among operators.

23　Art 84 CEC. By Resolution No 173/07/CONS, published in the Italian Official Gazette on 25 May 2007, AGCOM adopted a regulation for the resolution of disputes between operators and users.

24　Art 24 CEC.

25　Art 9 CEC.

framework as implemented by the CEC. To this end, AGCOM must seek to reach an agreement with the other NRAs, the European Commission, and BEREC on the most appropriate instruments and solutions to be adopted.[26] Furthermore, and in addition to the consultation procedure,[27] whenever AGCOM intends to take a decision regarding market definitions and analysis, access and interconnection, or obligations for SMP operators, which affects trade between EU Member States, it must make the draft decision available to the Commission, BEREC and the other NRAs. AGCOM must refrain from adopting the draft decision for one month from the date of its communication to the Commission, BEREC, and the other NRAs. If, during the one-month period, the Commission so requests, AGCOM must wait an additional two months before adopting the draft decision and must amend the same, if:

- the draft decision identifies a market different from the markets identified in the relevant Commission recommendations,[28] or
- the draft decision designates SMP operators, affects trade between Member States, and the European Commission believes that it may create a barrier to the EU market or has doubts as to its compatibility with Community law or with the objectives of the EU Regulatory Framework.

19.30   The AGCOM may derogate from the procedure set out above in urgent cases and when needed to protect competition and users' rights. In these cases, AGCOM may adopt appropriate temporary measures with immediate effect and must promptly inform the Commission, BEREC and the other NRAs. Any decision of AGCOM regarding the extension of the term of such temporary measures or their adoption as definitive decisions must follow the procedure set out above.

19.31   The CEC reflects the Commission's power to stipulate standards and issue specifications. Specifically, the CEC requires the Ministry to monitor the use of technical provisions and specifications published in the Official Journal of the European Union for the harmonised provision of services, technical interfaces, and network functions to the extent necessary to guarantee interoperability of services and improve the users' freedom of choice. Until the Commission adopts such technical provisions and specifications, the Ministry must promote the application of technical specifications and provisions adopted by European standardisation organisations.[29]

'Significant Market Power' as a Fundamental Prerequisite of Regulation

Definition of SMP

19.32   The CEC requires AGCOM to determine whether an undertaking has significant market power by conducting a market analysis procedure.[30] AGCOM must conduct the market analysis procedure after consulting with the ICA and taking into account the recommendations and guidelines of the Commission. With

---

26   Art 12 CEC and para 19.24 above.
27   See para 19.23 above for further details.
28   Commission Recommendation 2007/879/EC of 17 December 2007 on relevant product and service markets within the electronic communications sector susceptible to ex ante [2007] OJ L344/65.
29   Art 20 CEC.
30   Art 19 CEC.

respect to the outcome of such market analysis procedure, the CEC reflects exactly the provisions set out in Article 16 of the Framework Directive.[31]

19.33   The CEC defines dominance with respect to closely related markets in exactly the same way as the Framework Directive.[32] When evaluating whether two or more undertakings are in a joint dominant position in a market, the CEC requires the AGCOM to take into account the guidelines of the European Commission.[33]

Definition of relevant markets

19.34   The AGCOM, taking into account the recommendations and guidelines of the European Commission, must define the relevant markets in accordance with the principles of competition law and on the basis of the structure and characteristics of the Italian market for electronic communications.[34] Before defining markets in a manner different from the EU Commission Recommendation on relevant markets no 2007/879/EC dated 17 December 2007 ('Recommendation'), AGCOM must follow the consultation and consolidation procedure outlined above.[35]

19.35   AGCOM has carried out public consultations in relation to market analysis in each market identified in the Recommendation.

Telecom Italia, the former monopolist, is designated as having SMP in the following markets:

- access to the public telephone network at a fixed location for residential and non-residential customers;[36]
- call origination on the public telephone network provided at a fixed location;[37]
- call termination on individual public telephone networks provided at a fixed location, together with a number of other fixed operators each of them having SMP on call termination on its own fixed network;[38]
- wholesale (physical) network infrastructure access (including shared or fully unbundled access) at a fixed location;[39]
- wholesale broadband access;[40]
- wholesale terminating segments of leased lines, irrespective of the technology used to provide leased or dedicated capacity;[41] and
- voice call termination on individual mobile networks, together with the other three mobile network operators, Vodafone Omnitel N.V., WindTelecomunicazioni S.p.A. and H3G S.p.A., each of them having SMP on call termination on its own mobile network.[42]

31   See para 1.72 et seq above.
32   Cf art 17 CEC. For the definition of SMP as set out in the Framework Directive, see para 1.62 above.
33   Commission Guidelines on market analysis [2002] OJ C165/6.
34   Art 18 CEC.
35   See para 19.23 above.
36   AGCOM Resolution No 314/09/CONS.
37   AGCOM Resolution No 179/10/CONS.
38   AGCOM Resolution No 179/10/CONS.
39   AGCOM Resolution No 314/09/CONS.
40   AGCOM Resolution No 314/09/CONS.
41   AGCOM Resolution No 2/10/CONS.
42   AGCOM Resolution No 621/11/CONS.

Consequently, Telecom Italia must comply with non-discrimination, transparency, accounting separation and price control obligations as set forth by AGCOM in the relevant resolutions and in the CEC.

Imposition of remedies

19.36 If, on the basis of the market analysis procedure, AGCOM determines that a market is not effectively competitive, it must identify the SMP undertakings in that market and impose appropriate specific regulatory obligations (remedies) or maintain or amend the existing obligations.

AGCOM may also impose obligations on other undertakings not identified as having SMP, such as:[43]

- for providers controlling access to end users, the obligation to interconnect their networks to the extent necessary to guarantee point-to-point interconnection;[44]
- obligations for enterprises controlling end users' access, so as to make their services interoperable, but only in justified cases and to the extent necessary; and
- the obligation to provide access to Application Programming Interfaces (APIs) and Electronic Program Guides (EPGs) on fair, reasonable and non-discriminatory terms in order to ensure accessibility for end users to digital radio and TV broadcasting services.[45]

AGCOM periodically reviews its market analysis, to assess whether the conditions of the market have changed.

NRA's Regulatory Duties concerning Rights of Way, Co-location and Facility Sharing

Rights of way

19.37 The CEC establishes the principles for the grant of rights of way.[46] Although expressly allowed under the Framework Directive, no distinctions are drawn between rights of way for undertakings authorised to provide public electronic communications networks and undertakings authorised to provide electronic communications networks other than to the public. Similar rules apply to the grant of rights of way in relation to electronic communications infrastructures used for radio-electronic systems and civil infrastructures, digging works, and the occupation of public land. In these cases, local governmental entities ('local entities') or the land owner concerned must grant the rights of way for the installation of the electronic communications infrastructures.

19.38 The CEC also governs the grant of rights of way in relation to electronic communications infrastructures for radio-electronic systems.[47] Such infrastructures include radio base stations for mobile GSM/UMTS communications networks and for point-to-multipoint broadband radio networks using ad hoc frequencies (WLL networks). Both an express and an implicit authorisation regime can apply. More specifically:

---

43   Art 42 CEC.
44   See para 19.113 below.
45   See para 19.115 below.
46   Art 86 CEC.
47   Art 87 CEC.

- Under the express authorisation regime, undertakings must file an application with the relevant local entity, giving evidence that the infrastructure is compatible with the electromagnetic fields exposure limits set out by applicable laws.[48] Once the competent administration bodies have confirmed the infrastructure's compatibility, the local entity may grant the rights of way. The application must be approved within 30 days. However, if there is a disagreement among the administrations involved in the processing, the time period may be extended.

  It is not necessary to file an application when the installation involves systems based on UMTS or other technologies with single antenna power not in excess of 20 Watts. In this case, a notification describing, among others, the infrastructures to be installed is sufficient.

- Under the implicit authorisation regime, the application and the declaration are deemed as approved if the local entities do not reject them within 90 days from receipt of the relevant documents.

- A simplified procedure is set forth in order to promote investments in the mobile broadband. This procedure applies to the installation of systems based on UMTS or its evolution, as well as to other technologies based on infrastructures for existing radio-electric systems or which only modify transmission features. In these cases, a notification describing, among others, the infrastructures to be installed, is sufficient. The notification is considered as rejected if a refusal is served on the applicant by the local authority within 30 days from the notification's filing.[49]

19.39   Operators are solely responsible for the costs related to such works, and for restoring the site within the timeframes set by the local entities.

19.40   Authorisation is required to install civil infrastructures, carry out digging works, or occupy public land. Such authorisation is granted by the local entities through an express or implicit authorisation regime similar to that provided for infrastructures for radio-electronic systems highlighted above.[50] The period for the grant of the implicit authorisation is reduced from 90 days to 30 days for digging works pertaining to crossroads and for any work of less than 200 metres in length.

19.41   The CEC contains a number of provisions aimed at facilitating the installation of electronic communications networks systems. Such provisions include, among other things, the expropriation of real estate, limitations on ownership rights, and limitations on rights of easement.

19.42   A different regulation may apply to public and private networks depending on whether they qualify as 'public utility' infrastructures. In particular, public electronic communications networks automatically qualify as public utility infrastructures, while private electronic communications networks may be so qualified only through a decree of the Ministry.[51]

19.43   Undertakings authorised to install public or private networks qualified as public utility infrastructures are entitled to expropriate the necessary real estate. The expropriation, however, will be allowed only if it was impossible to reach an amicable agreement with the owner of the real estate concerned.

---

48   This matter is governed by Law No 36 of 22 February 2001 and implementing legislation (eg Prime Minister Decree dated 8 July 2003).
49   Art 87*bis* CEC.
50   Art 88 CEC.
51   Art 90 CEC.

19.44 Aerial wires or cables which are part of public or private networks may be placed above public or private properties as well as on those sides of the buildings where there are no windows.[52] Such installation may be effected without the owner's consent. Further, the owner may not object to the installation of antennas, masts or ducts, wires, or any other systems necessary to meet the service needs of other occupants of the same building. The service provider is also entitled to start legal action to restrict any behaviour which prevents or disturbs the installation of such infrastructures. The owner is not entitled to any indemnity.

19.45 The CEC expressly provides for the right to obtain easements for the deployment of wires, cables, and apparatus (of public and private networks) on, over, or below private or public land, without the landowner's consent.[53] If the easements concern public land, they are subject to the conclusion of an ad hoc master agreement with the relevant local entities. The latter are entitled to an indemnity. Special rules apply in relation to easements on highways.[54]

19.46 The CEC provides for a structural separation mechanism equivalent to that set out in the Framework Directive.[55]

Co-location and facility sharing

19.47 The CEC contains rules for co-location and facility sharing which mirror those set out in the Framework Directive.[56] Under the CEC, however, if the installation of infrastructures requires digging works within inhabited areas, the operator must file with the Ministry a notice describing the relevant project. Within 30 days from such filing, operators interested in co-location or facility sharing may agree on a shared co-location or facility plan with the operator that filed the notice.

19.48 Upon public consultation, AGCOM may impose obligations for the sharing of wiring inside buildings (or up to the first concentration or distribution point, if this is located outside the building) within the same limits set forth in the Framework Directive.[57] The Ministry may request enterprises to provide any information necessary to elaborate a detailed inventory of the nature, availability, and location of relevant infrastructures, so as to make it available to interested parties and AGCOM.

REGULATION OF MARKET ENTRY: THE AUTHORISATION DIRECTIVE

The General Authorisation of Electronic Communications

19.49 The provision of electronic communications networks and services is subject only to a general authorisation.[58] This does not prevent the Ministry from supplementing such a 'general' authorisation with regulatory decisions with respect to specific obligations related to network access, interconnection, universal service, and individual rights to use frequencies and/or numbers.

52　Art 91 CEC.
53　Art 92 CEC.
54　Art 94 CEC.
55　Art 86 CEC.
56　Art 89 CEC. Cf para 1.87 et seq above.
57　Art 89(5*bis*). Cf also para 1.88 above.
58　Art 25 CEC.

19.50   To obtain a general authorisation, the interested individual or, in the case of an entity, the authorised representative, must file a declaration with the Ministry, stating the intent to commence the provision of electronic communications networks or services. Such declaration is equivalent to the 'notification' set out in Article 3(3) of the 'Authorisation Directive. The declaration must contain the information necessary to allow the Ministry to keep a current register of electronic communications network and service providers.

19.51   After filing the declaration, the undertaking concerned may begin its activity immediately, subject to the specific provisions on rights to use frequencies or numbers. Within 60 days of the filing, the Ministry must verify the compliance of the declaration with necessary requirements. In the case of non-compliance, the Ministry may order the undertaking concerned to cease its activity.

19.52   The general authorisation may be granted to individuals or entities of the EU and individuals or entities of non-EU countries under condition of reciprocity (but particular limitations deriving from international treaties may apply to the latter).

19.53   The duration of a general authorisation may not exceed 20 years, but it may be renewed by filing a new declaration at least 60 days before its expiration. General authorisations do not entail the issue of any paper permit. However, at the operator's request, and within one week thereafter, the Ministry must issue a statement to confirm that the operator has filed a declaration under the rules,[59] indicating the conditions under which the operator that provides electronic communications networks or services is entitled to install facilities, negotiate interconnection agreements with, or obtain access from, other operators or government entities.

19.54   Authorised undertakings have the right to:[60]

● provide electronic communications networks and services to the public, and
● apply for specific authorisations, or file the necessary declarations, to exercise the rights to install facilities, in compliance with the provisions set out in the CEC.[61]

19.55   If an undertaking intends to provide electronic communications networks or services to the public, the general authorisation allows the undertaking to:

● negotiate interconnection with other authorised providers of publicly available electronic communications networks and services and, where applicable, obtain network access and interconnection anywhere in the EU, subject to the access and interconnection conditions set out in the CEC;[62] and
● be designated as provider, in all or part of the national territory, of one or more services which fall within the obligations of the universal service.

19.56   The 'maximum' number of conditions which may be attached to the general authorisation are those listed in Part A of Annex 1 CEC, which, in essence, mirrors Part A of the Annex to the Authorisation Directive. Among these conditions, the CEC specifies that the general authorisation must always contain the specific obligation to enable legal interception by the relevant judicial authorities.[63]

---

59   See para 19.50 above.
60   Art 26 CEC.
61   Such provisions are arts 86, 87 and 88 CEC. See para 19.33 above.
62   See para 19.95 below.
63   Point 11, Part A, Annex 1 CEC.

However, the general authorisation must not duplicate conditions that are applicable to undertakings by virtue of other national legislation.[64]

19.57   In granting rights to use frequencies and numbers, the Ministry applies only the conditions listed in Parts B and C respectively of Annex 1 CEC, which mirror those listed in Parts B and C of the Annex to the Authorisation Directive.

19.58   The specific obligations which may be imposed on providers of electronic communications networks and services designated as having significant market power, or undertakings designated for the provision of universal service, are separate from the rights and obligations attached to the general authorisation. However, in order to ensure transparency, the general authorisations for such undertakings must specify the additional obligations so imposed.

Rights of Use for Radio Frequencies

Strategic planning and co-ordination of spectrum policy

19.59   New article 14 CEC contains the Italian spectrum policy and strategic planning rules. Considering that frequencies belong to the State and have an important social, cultural, and economic value, the Ministry and AGCOM must ensure that radio frequencies for electronic communications services are managed efficiently. When preparing allocation and assignment plans, the Ministry and AGCOM must use objective, transparent, non-discriminatory, and proportionate criteria. The same criteria must be used when allocating frequencies for electronic communication services and when granting general authorisations or rights of use. In carrying out these activities, the Ministry and AGCOM must comply with applicable international conventions, including the ITU Radio Regulations and CEPT rules, and may take into account specific exigencies of public interest.[65]

19.60   The Ministry must promote harmonisation in the use of radio frequencies within the EU so as to grant an effective and efficient utilisation of the same frequencies, as well as to foster consumers' wellbeing, such as with economies of scale and interoperability of services, in compliance with Commission decision No 676/2002/EC.[66]

19.61   The Ministry and AGCOM must ensure that, consistent with EU rules, all technologies used for electronic communication services may be utilised in the frequency bands available for electronic communication services pursuant to the National Frequencies Allocation Plan ('NAFP').[67] The Ministry and AGCOM may, however, impose proportionate and non-discriminatory restrictions with respect to the type of wireless access or radio network technologies that may be used for electronic communication networks, if necessary for the purposes of:

- avoiding harmful interference;
- protecting public health from electromagnetic fields;
- ensuring technical quality of service;
- ensuring radio frequency sharing at the maximum level;

---

64   Art 28 CEC.
65   Art 14(1) CEC.
66   Art 14(2) CEC.
67   Ministerial Decree dated 13 November 2008, published in the Appendix to the Official Gazette No 273 of 21 November 2008.

- safeguarding the efficient use of spectrum; or
- promoting the general public interest.[68]

19.62   The Ministry and AGCOM must ensure that, consistent with EU rules, all electronic communication services may be provided in the frequency bands available for electronic communication services. The Ministry and AGCOM may, however, impose proportionate and non-discriminatory restrictions to the type of electronic communication services that may be provided.[69]

19.63   Under the CEC, the Ministry may require undertakings to provide any given electronic communication service in a specific band available for electronic communication services if necessary to promote the public interest pursuant to EU rules, such as, for example:

- safeguarding human life;
- promoting social, local or territorial cohesion;
- avoiding an inefficient use of radio frequencies; or
- promoting cultural or linguistic diversity and media pluralism.[70]

The Ministry and AGCOM may prohibit the provision of any given electronic communication service in a specific band only necessary to safeguard human life.[71]

19.64   When addressing strategic planning and harmonisation in the use of spectrum within the EU, the Ministry must cooperate with the relevant authorities of the other Member States and with the Commission. To this end, the Ministry must take into account, among other things, any economic aspects and any issues related to safety, health, public interest, freedom of speech, as well as cultural, scientific, social and technical issues of the EU policies. The Ministry must also consider the various interests of the spectrum users in order to optimise the use of frequencies and avoid harmful interference.[72] The Ministry grants rights of use of frequencies, upon request, to any undertaking providing or using network services under a general authorisation.

19.65   Legislative Decree No 177/2005 includes special provisions on the grant of rights of use of frequencies favouring radio and video broadcasting content providers.[73]

Principles of frequency allocation, procedural rules

19.66   The CEC[74] requires that, except for the specific regulation on the grant of rights to use frequencies to providers of radio and video broadcasting content, such rights of use be granted through public, transparent, and non-discriminatory procedures.

19.67   The Ministry must adopt and publish its decisions on the rights to use frequencies immediately after receipt of the relevant application or, in the case of frequencies that have been allocated for specific purposes under the NAFP, within

---

68   Art 14(3) CEC.
69   Art 14(4) CEC.
70   Art 14(5) CEC.
71   Art 14(6) CEC.
72   Art 13*bis* CEC.
73   Legislative Decree No 177 dated 31 July 2005, published in the Official Gazette on 7 September 2005.
74   Art 27(5) CEC.

six weeks, without prejudice to the international agreements on frequencies coordination and satellite orbits.

19.68   Where the use of radio frequencies has been harmonised, and subject to the other conditions set out in article 30 CEC, the Ministry must grant the right of use for such frequencies in accordance with such conditions, provided that the applicant has complied with all national requirements related to the rights to use frequencies. The Ministry may not impose any further conditions or procedures which would restrict, alter, or delay the correct implementation of the common assignment of such radio frequencies.

19.69   As a general rule, the utilisation of radio frequencies must not be subject to the issuance of individual rights of use. However individual rights of use may be granted when necessary to:

- avoid harmful interference;
- ensure technical quality of services;
- ensure efficient spectrum usage; and
- achieve other purposes of general interest in compliance with EU rules.[75]

Transferability and time limitations

19.70   The Ministry must specify, at the time of the assignment of the right of use of frequencies, whether, and under which conditions, those rights may be transferred at the initiative of the relevant holder.[76] Without prejudice to specific radio and video broadcasting regulations, the rights to use frequencies with limited bandwidth availability which have been granted to a limited number of operators may be transferred against consideration between operators that are authorised to provide electronic networks based on similar technology. Such transfer is allowed only with the express consent of the Ministry. An undertaking must notify the Ministry and AGCOM of its intent to transfer rights of use of radio frequencies. The Ministry must consent or object within 90 days from the operator's notification. Based on the opinion issued by the ICA that competition will not be distorted as a result of the transfer, the Ministry may consent to the transfer subject to specific conditions. Any such transfer must be made public and must not result in a change of use of those radio frequencies whose use has been harmonised through the application of the Radio Spectrum Decision or other Community measures.

19.71   Individual rights of use of radio frequencies are granted for a duration which is adequate in relation to the type of service for which the frequencies are intended, but in no case may exceed the duration of the general authorisation.[77]

Admissible conditions

19.72   The right to use radio frequencies may be granted for a limited period of time, provided that the duration is appropriate for the service concerned. As indicated above, the grant of rights to use frequencies may be subject only to the conditions listed in Part B of Annex 1 CEC.

---

75   Art 27(1) CEC.
76   Art 27(5*bis*) CEC.
77   Art 27(4) CEC.

19.73   Where the number of rights to use frequencies has been limited through competitive bidding procedures, the undertaking must comply with all special commitments made in the course of the relevant competitive bidding procedure.

19.74   There are no special conditions specifically for important spectrum bands. However, in Italy, the rights to use spectrum, concerning, eg GSM, 3G, WLL, WiMAX or 4G, have always been granted through competitive selection procedures.

19.75   Examples of special conditions imposed during competitive selection procedures include the obligations to:

●   start the service within the time indicated by the AGCOM;
●   ensure certain territorial and population coverage;
●   comply with minimum service quality standards;[78] and
●   pay penalties in case of failure to fulfil the targets set out under the licence.

Limitation of the number of rights of use to be granted

19.76   AGCOM is in charge of adopting all decisions on the limitation of the number of rights to use frequencies.

19.77   The relevant procedure as set out in article 29 CEC mirrors that in Article 7 of the Authorisation Directive.[79] The main difference is that the Italian legislature has deemed it appropriate to specify that AGCOM, in considering the possibility of limiting the number of rights to use to be granted, must take into account not only the need to maximise users' benefits and the development of competition, but also the sustainability of investments in relation to market needs, pursuing the efficient and effective use of radio frequencies.

19.78   In the case of competitive selection procedures, the CEC requires the Ministry to administer the procedure and to grant the rights to use pursuant to rules established by AGCOM on the basis of objective, transparent, proportionate, and non-discriminatory selection criteria, aimed at developing competition and pursuing efficient and effective use of radio frequencies. The awards are made within eight months, and usage fees can be levied under auction procedures, provided that such fees are proportionate and reflect the need to ensure optimal use of the radio spectrum. In all other cases, fees for rights to use for radio frequencies or numbers are defined by the Ministry on the basis of the criteria indicated below.[80]

19.79   In the case of competitive selection procedures of particular national importance, AGCOM may propose to the Ministry and the Prime Minister that a Committee of Ministries is established to coordinate the procedure for the grant of individual rights of use.

19.80   The latest significant nationwide public tender for the award of rights of use of frequencies was launched and completed in 2011 for 4G frequencies in the 800, 1800, 2000 and 2600 MHZ bands.[81]

---

78   See para 19.138 below.
79   See para 1.118 above.
80   See paras 19.92–19.93 below.
81   AGCOM Regulation No 282/11/CONS of 18 May 2011.

Rights of Use for Numbers

General authorisations and granting of individual rights

19.81   The Ministry assigns the rights to use numbers on an individual basis upon request by any undertaking which provides or uses networks or services under a general authorisation. The assignment is effected immediately after receipt of the relevant application, or within three weeks in the case of numbers dedicated to specific purposes under the National Numbering Plan issued by AGCOM ('NNP').[82]

19.82   The Ministry is responsible for management of the NNP and is required to ensure that adequate numbering resources be allocated to all public electronic communications services. Further, the Ministry must monitor the numbering resources to ensure that they are used pursuant to the types of services to which such numbers are allocated under the NNP.

19.83   AGCOM defines and publishes the NNP, and all subsequent additions or amendments thereto, as well as the procedures for the assignment of numbering resources. Such assignment must be effected in compliance with the principles of objectivity, transparency, and non-discrimination, in order to ensure that an undertaking that has been assigned a range of numbers does not discriminate against other providers of electronic communications services with respect to the numbering sequences to be used for access to their services. The undertaking that has been assigned the right to use numbers does not obtain property rights in such numbers.

Admissible conditions

19.84   Part C of Annex 1 CEC sets out a comprehensive list of conditions which may be attached to rights of use for numbers. These include the effective and efficient use of numbers, the obligation to pay the relevant fees, and compliance with number portability rules.

19.85   In this regard, AGCOM ensures that all subscribers to public telephony services, including mobile services, may maintain their own number(s), regardless of the undertaking providing the service. There is no number portability between fixed and mobile services. AGCOM must take steps to ensure that interconnection charges related to number portability are cost-oriented and that the possible charges on end users do not result in a decreased demand for number portability. AGCOM may also impose on operators the obligation to grant to third party operators access to certain network elements or resources, including access to non-active network elements or unbundled access to local network, also in order to allow carrier selection or pre-selection.[83]

Limitation of the number of rights of use to be granted

19.86   Whenever, after public consultation, AGCOM determines that rights of use for numbers of exceptional economic value must be granted through competitive selection procedures, the same procedural rules and principles as those described with reference to the limitation of rights to use radio frequencies apply.

---

82   AGCOM Resolution No 26/08/CIR of 14 May 2008, as amended.
83   Art 49(1)(a) CEC.

The NRA's Enforcement Powers

19.87   Undertakings providing electronic communications services or networks under a general authorisation or which have been granted rights to use numbers or frequencies must provide the Ministry with the information necessary to verify compliance with the conditions attached to the general authorisation or the rights of use. In addition, undertakings must provide AGCOM with the information necessary to verify compliance with the 'separate conditions' which are imposed on undertakings designated as having SMP. The Ministry and AGCOM may only request information that is proportionate and objectively justified and must inform the undertakings of the specific purpose for which the information is to be used.[84]

19.88   If an undertaking fails to provide AGCOM with the information within the required timeframe, AGCOM may impose administrative fines ranging from €15,000 to €1,150,000.[85]

19.89   Where the Ministry or AGCOM finds that an undertaking has not complied with one or more conditions of the general authorisation, the rights of use, or the specific obligations imposed on SMP undertakings, it must notify the undertaking of those findings and give the undertaking a reasonable opportunity to state its view and remedy any breaches within one month after notification. If the undertaking does not remedy the breach within the one-month period, the Ministry or AGCOM must take appropriate and proportionate measures aimed at ensuring compliance, and, in so doing, may impose administrative fines ranging from €15,000 to €2,500,000.[86] Should the breaches concern specific obligations imposed on SMP undertakings, AGCOM may impose an administrative fine ranging from 2 per cent to 5 per cent of the turnover generated by the defaulting undertaking in the market concerned[87] in the previous financial-year.

19.90   In cases of serious breaches repeated more than twice in a five-year period, and if the measures aimed at ensuring compliance have failed, the Ministry and/or the AGCOM may prevent an undertaking from continuing to provide electronic communications networks or services or suspend or revoke the relevant rights of use.[88] Should the breaches entail the installation and provision of public electronic communications networks or the offer of public electronic communications services without general authorisation, the Ministry may impose an administrative fine from €15,000 to €2,500,000.[89]

19.91   The Ministry and the AGCOM may take urgent temporary measures whenever they have evidence of a breach of the conditions of the general authorisation, rights of use, or specific obligations of undertakings which would entail an immediate and serious threat to public safety, public security, or public health or are likely to create a barrier to criminal investigations or serious economic or operational problems for other providers or users of electronic communications networks or services.[90]

---

84   Art 33 CEC.
85   Art 98(9) CEC.
86   Art 32 CEC.
87   Art 98(11) CEC.
88   Arts 32(4) and 98(12) CEC.
89   Art 98(2) CEC.
90   Art 32 (5) CEC.

Administrative Charges and Fees for Rights of Use

19.92   Administrative fees ranging from €600 (for each site where a switching apparatus is located) to €111,000, depending on the type of service and its geographical coverage, are imposed on undertakings providing a communication service or network under the general authorisation. These fees must cover only the administrative costs incurred in the management, control, and enforcement of the general authorisation regime, the rights of use and the specific obligations attached (eg to SMP operators or service providers).[91]

19.93   Fees for the rights to use frequencies or numbers are defined by the Ministry on the basis of the criteria set out by AGCOM and are indicated in Annex 10 CEC. In essence, the relevant amounts depend on the frequencies and bandwidth used as well as on the number and type of apparatus utilised.

Transitional Regulations for Existing Authorisations

19.94   Individual licences and general authorisations for public telecommunications networks and services which were already in existence on the date of entry into force of the CEC continue to be valid until their natural expiration, and the provisions set out in the CEC apply.

REGULATION OF NETWORK ACCESS AND INTERCONNECTION: THE ACCESS DIRECTIVE

Objectives and Scope of Access Regulation

19.95   The CEC specifies both the aim and objectives of access and interconnection regulation.[92]

19.96   In particular, the regulation of electronic communications networks and services must guarantee flexible rules on access and interconnection in relation to broadband electronic communications networks, in order to ensure a sustainable degree of competition, innovation, and benefits for consumers.[93]

19.97   Also, the Ministry and AGCOM must contribute to the development of the electronic communications market through the adoption of flexible regulation of access and interconnection.[94]

19.98   Access and interconnection rules apply to all undertakings authorised to provide electronic communications services and networks in Italy as well as to operators similarly authorised in another EU Member State. Such foreign operators do not need a general authorisation under Italian law in order to obtain access or interconnection if they do not manage a network or offer electronic communications services within the Italian territory.

Basic Regulatory Concepts

19.99   AGCOM must encourage and guarantee adequate access, interconnection and interoperability of services. AGCOM must also exercise its responsibilities in

---

91   Arts 34 and 35 CEC.
92   Arts 4 and 13 CEC.
93   Art 4(3) CEC.
94   Art 13 CEC.

order to promote economic efficiency, sustainable competition and provide maximum benefit to end users. [95]

19.100   AGCOM may apply ex ante regulatory obligations on SMP undertakings as well as on other market players regardless of their market power. Unlike under the previous regulatory framework, these obligations include specific conditions on digital television and radio broadcasting services.[96] In the exercise of its regulatory powers, AGCOM must comply with the principles of objectivity, transparency, proportionality, and non-discrimination. All obligations are subject to consultation procedures.[97]

19.101   The CEC contains a definition of 'access' which is almost identical to that contained in the Access Directive.[98]

19.102   'Interconnection' is defined almost in the same terms as in the Access Directive, with a particular difference deriving from the use of the expression 'operator' (contained in the CEC) as opposed to the expression 'undertaking' (contained in the Access Directive).[99] 'Operator' is defined by the CEC as an 'undertaking authorised to provide a public communications network or an associated facility'.[100] Although an almost identical definition of 'operator' is contained in the Access Directive, the latter does not use the term 'operator' in the main section of the definition of interconnection (rather using the term 'undertaking').[101] This difference may entail interpretation issues, because a literal reading of the definition of 'operator' could lead to the conclusion that interconnection regulation under the CEC applies only to undertakings authorised to provide electronic communications networks while omitting undertakings offering only electronic communications services.

19.103   The principle of freedom of access as set out in Article 3(1) of the Access Directive has been reproduced almost verbatim in the CEC.[102]

19.104   The principle that commercial negotiations take priority over regulatory intervention is set out in a number of provisions contained in the CEC,[103] which mirror Articles 3(1) and 5(4) of the Access Directive. The CEC also regulates the confidentiality obligations applicable to access and interconnection agreement negotiations. The relevant provision is identical to that set out in Article 4(3) of the Access Directive.[104]

---

95   Art 42 CEC.
96   See para 19.115 below.
97   Arts 11 and 12 CEC.
98   Art 1(1)(b) CEC.
99   Art 1(1)(m) CEC.
100   Art 1(1)(u) CEC.
101   Art 2 of the Access Directive.
102   Art 40 CEC.
103   Arts 40, 41 and 42(5) CEC.
104   Art 41(3) CEC.

Access- and Interconnection-related Obligations with Respect to SMP Undertakings

Overview

19.105 If an undertaking has been designated as having SMP in a specific market, AGCOM must, at its discretion, impose one of the obligations detailed under the following subheadings. Obligations imposed as indicated under these subheadings shall be based on the nature of the issues investigated, and they must be proportionate and justified in light of the objectives set out in article 13 CEC.[105]

Specific access obligations

19.106 The CEC sets forth specific obligations for SMP operators to accept reasonable requests for access to, and use of, specific network elements and associated facilities.[106] The relevant CEC provision is almost identical to Article 12 of the Access Directive. The Italian text, however, slightly differs from the European rule with respect to some of the specific obligations. In particular, Article 49 CEC refers to obligations to grant 'operators' access to specified network elements and facilities, including local loop unbundling, and to negotiate in good faith with operators requesting access (as opposed to 'third parties' referred to in the corresponding European provision).[107]

Transparency obligations

19.107 Transparency obligations are regulated in the same manner as under Article 9 of the Access Directive.[108]

Non-discrimination obligations

19.108 Non-discrimination obligations correspond to those contained in Article 10 of the Access Directive. The relevant provision of the Access Directive, however, refers to equivalent conditions to be applied to '*other undertakings*' while the corresponding rule of the CEC refers to '*other operators*' (the latter being a more restricted definition than the former).[109]

Accounting separation obligations

19.109 The CEC implements almost verbatim Article 11 of the Access Directive.[110]

---

105 Art 40 CEC.
106 Art 49 CEC.
107 See para 19.102 above for the possible consequences of such discrepancy between the Access Directive and the CEC.
108 Art 46 CEC.
109 Art 47 CEC.
110 Art 48 CEC.

Price control and cost accounting

19.110   The CEC contains certain obligations relating to cost recovery and price controls which correspond exactly to those set out in Article 13 of the Access Directive.[111] In determining cost-oriented prices, AGCOM must take into account the investment made by the operator and allow a reasonable rate of return on the capital invested, considering the risks involved and the investments related to the development of innovative networks and services. This particular element (which is not contained in the corresponding provision of the Access Directive) seems to constitute an additional incentive for operators to invest in advanced infrastructures and technologies, such as broadband.

Carrier (pre-)selection is regulated in the same manner as under Article 12(1)(a) of the Access Directive.[112]

Functional separation

19.111   Functional separation is regulated in the same manner as under Article 13a of the Access Directive.[113]

Regulatory Powers with Respect to SMP-Undertakings

19.112   Article 68 CEC, which originally allowed AGCOM to impose obligations for the provision of part or all of the minimum set of leased lines on undertakings notified as having SMP in the relevant market, has been abrogated as a result of the implementation of the 2009 Regulatory Package.

Article 69 CEC, which originally set out carrier selection and carrier pre-selection obligations corresponding to those already contained in Article 19 of the Universal Service Directive, has been abrogated as a result of the implementation of the 2009 Regulatory Package.

Regulatory Powers Applicable to All Market Participants

Obligations to ensure end-to-end connectivity

19.113   End-to-end connectivity obligations are set out in the CEC. These apply to all market players along the same lines as those contained in Article 5(1) of the Access Directive.[114] The AGCOM may impose such obligations to encourage and, where appropriate, ensure adequate access and interconnection, and interoperability of services in order to promote efficiency and sustainable competition, and give the maximum benefit to end users.

---

111   Art 50 CEC.
112   Art 49(1)(a) CEC. See also para 19.85 above.
113   Art 50*bis* CEC. See also paras 1.164–1.166 above.
114   Art 42 CEC.

Regulation of roaming services

19.114   Under article 1(b) CEC, which reflects Article 2(a) of the Access Directive, roaming is a specific type of access. Roaming services are regulated under the Roaming Regulation.[115] Moreover, AGCOM may impose on operators the obligation to provide, inter alia, specific services to ensure interoperability of end-to-end services for the benefit of users, including roaming on mobile networks.[116]

Access to digital radio and television broadcasting services

19.115   In addition to the 'traditional telecommunications' interconnection services, article 42(2)(b) CEC also regulates access to digital radio and television broadcasting services. These obligations correspond to those set out in Article 5(1)(b) of the Access Directive. Article 42(2)(b) should be read in conjunction with article 43(1) and Annex 2, Part I, to the CEC, on conditional access systems, which reproduces Article 6 of the Access Directive. Unlike the Access Directive, however, the CEC expressly provides for the possibility to modify the list of conditions as set out in Annex 2, Part I, to the CEC.

19.116   Nonetheless, AGCOM must encourage providers of digital interactive television services and providers of enhanced digital television equipment to use and comply with Application Programme Interfaces (APIs).[117]

REGULATION OF UNIVERSAL SERVICES AND USERS' RIGHTS: THE UNIVERSAL SERVICE DIRECTIVE

Regulation of Universal Service Obligations

Scope of universal service obligations

19.117   In line with Article 3(1) of the Universal Service Directive, article 53 CEC requires that those services falling within the definition of universal service[118] be made available to all end users in the Italian territory, at a specified quality, regardless of the end users' geographical location. AGCOM must establish the most effective and appropriate method to guarantee the provision of universal service at an affordable price.[119]

19.118   The catalogue of universal services follows the list set out in the Universal Service Directive with certain exceptions, as outlined below:

• In implementing Article 4 of the Universal Service Directive, article 54 CEC

---

115   See para 1.30 above.
116   Art 49(1)(g) CEC.
117   Art 21 CEC.
118   Mirroring the definition contained in Art 2(j) of the Framework Directive, art 1(ll) CEC defines 'universal service' as a 'minimum set of services, of a specified quality, which is available to all users [not only end-users] regardless of their geographical location and offered, in light of the specific national conditions, at an affordable price'.
119   Art 53 CEC.

replaced the term 'undertaking' with the term 'operator' which, as noted above,[120] has a stricter meaning.

- The provision of at least one comprehensive directory to be provided to any end user is limited to the urban network to which the end user belongs.[121] Each operator must make all its directories (including directories of pre-paid mobile users as these are identified at the time of the first purchase) available to the Ministry of Internal Affairs so that judicial authorities may access the relevant data for investigation purposes. The provision of these services, as well as the provision of directory inquiry services, falls outside the scope of universal service because there are 'various offers in terms of availability, quality and affordable price' in the market. The Ministry may apply universal service obligations to these services if, in the future, it will determine that the market conditions are no longer satisfied.[122]
- The provision of public pay telephones may be excluded by decree of the Ministry in those locations where, after consultation with the interested parties (to be carried out on an annual basis), the Ministry determines that these facilities or comparable services are widely available.[123]

19.119   The list of obligations falling within the universal service is comprehensive. However, under article 65 CEC, the Ministry, after having consulted with AGCOM, must review the scope of universal service every two years. The CEC contains no express reference to the 'twin test' set out in Annex V Universal Service Directive. Nonetheless, this test seems to be a mandatory reference given that the CEC requires the Ministry to review the universal service obligations on the basis, inter alia, of the guidelines of the European Commission.[124]

19.120   In addition, the Ministry, after consultation with the *'Conferenza Unificata'*,[125] may decide to make additional services publicly available on a mandatory basis, but outside the scope of the universal service.[126] This means that the relevant costs may not be subject to sharing or compensation mechanisms such as the universal service fund.[127] Such decision on new mandatory services will likely need to be coordinated through the periodic review process described above.

Designation of undertakings obliged to provide universal services

19.121   AGCOM must establish the procedure for designation of undertakings in charge of the universal service. In so doing, AGCOM must follow principles, among other things, of efficiency, objectivity, transparency, and non-discrimination.[128] The procedure not only must ensure that the universal service is provided in a cost-effective manner but must also be capable of being used as a means to determine the net cost of universal service.

---

120 See para 19.102 above.
121 Art 55(1)(a) CEC.
122 Art 55(3) CEC.
123 Art 56 CEC.
124 Art 65 CEC.
125 This is a public body created by Legislative Decree No 281/97 with the mission to foster the cooperation between the State and local entities in all those matters where they share a common interest.
126 Art 82 CEC.
127 See para 19.129 below.
128 Art 58 CEC, which mirrors almost verbatim Art 8 of the Universal Service Directive.

19.122   Until such designation is made, Telecom Italia continues to be the only universal service provider in the entire Italian territory.

Regulation of retail tariffs, users' expenditures and quality of service

19.123   AGCOM must monitor the evolution and level of retail tariffs for those services which fall within the scope of universal service. The relevant provision of the CEC captures the wording of the entire Article 9 of the Universal Service Directive except for the third paragraph whereby Member States may, in addition to any provision for designated undertakings to provide special tariff options or to comply with price caps, geographical averaging or other similar schemes, ensure that support be provided to consumers with low income or special social needs.[129]

19.124   An additional benefit of the affordability of tariffs is the possibility for subscribers to control their expenditures and avoid unwarranted disconnection of services in the case of non-payment. To this end, Article 10 of the Universal Service Directive has been imported into the CEC,[130] thus requiring designated undertakings to provide:

- itemised billing;
- selective call barring (free of charge for outgoing calls);
- pre-payment systems for the provision of access to the public telephone network and the use of publicly available telephone services;
- phased payment of connection fees;
- specific measures for non-payment of bills, including, for example, warning obligations before the disconnection of the services in the case of non-payment of bills;
- tariff advice; and
- cost control.

19.125   One of the elements that characterises universal service obligations is the 'specified quality'. For this reason, AGCOM must not only obtain and publish information concerning undertakings' performance in the provision of universal service, [131] but also set performance targets to be met by undertakings with universal service obligations. As under the Universal Service Directive, AGCOM may adopt 'specific measures' in the case of persistent failure by such undertakings to meet performance targets. These specific measures may go as far as prohibiting an undertaking from providing all or part of its networks or services.[132]

Cost calculation and financing of universal services

19.126   If AGCOM considers that the provision of universal service may present an 'unfair burden' for the designated undertaking(s), it must calculate the net cost of such provision so that the cost may be shared among operators.[133]

---

129   Art 59 CEC.
130   Art 60 CEC.
131   AGCOM must also specify the content, form, and manner for such publication (see art 61(3) CEC).
132   Art 61(6) CEC.
133   Art 62 CEC.

19.127   The calculation is based on avoidable long-run incremental costs and revenues incurred and generated, respectively, in serving customers/areas (or providing services) that are 'non viable'[134] plus a reasonable return on the incremental capital invested for the provision of the universal service. Additional elements, including, but not limited to, branding recognition, the possibility of applying economies of scale, benefits stemming from the transformation of non-viable customers/areas into viable ones, and the availability of market information, must be taken into account in calculating the net cost. AGCOM must appoint an independent body to verify the calculation, and the independent body's fees are included in the net cost of the universal service.

19.128   The net cost must be shared among undertakings that operate public communications networks, provide publicly available telephone services (in proportion to their usage of public communications networks), and/or provide mobile and personal communications services in the Italian territory. Undertakings that provide private communications networks, telephone services to closed user groups, data transmission, value-added services (such as video conference or telephone banking), and Internet access are not required to share such net cost. Furthermore, each year AGCOM may exempt from the cost sharing all those 'undertakings that do not exceed certain turnover thresholds and those that are new entrants, taking into account their financial situation and the competitive conditions of the market'.[135] While the CEC does not contain a definition of new entrant, since 1999 AGCOM has consistently applied a 1 per cent net revenue threshold (on the total net revenues) to allow undertakings to benefit from the exemption.

19.129   Undertakings designated to provide the universal service may obtain reimbursement of the eligible net cost by drawing from a specific fund administered by the Ministry and funded from the contributions of the above-mentioned operators.

19.130   The amount of the contribution owed by each operator is based on a mathematical formula described in Exhibit 11 to the CEC which, in essence, takes into account the percentage of the costs and revenues of each operator required to contribute over the total costs and revenues of the other operators.

Regulation of Retail Markets

Prerequisites for the regulation of retail markets

19.131   The CEC reproduces Article 17 of the Universal Service Directive on the re-examination of existing obligations related to retail tariffs for access services.[136]

19.132   Accordingly, the regulation of retail services is permissible if regulation at the wholesale level does not achieve the competition and regulatory objectives established by the Italian legislature. Currently, Telecom Italia is the only operator identified as having SMP in retail markets.

---

134 Under art 1 of Exhibit 11 to the CEC, a non-viable customer/area is a customer/area that would not be served if the undertaking was not subject to universal service obligations. Likewise, a non-viable service is a service whose incremental cost of provision is higher than the incremental revenue stemming therefrom.

135 Art 63(3) CEC.

136 Art 67 CEC.

Regulatory powers

19.133   In line with Article 17(2) of the Universal Service Directive, AGCOM has broad discretion in the application of regulatory measures in retail markets.[137] The non-exhaustive list of tariff obligations which may be imposed on SMP undertakings in a given retail market, as set out in article 17(2) Universal Directive, has been adopted almost verbatim in the CEC. Slight differences exist with respect to conditions under which AGCOM may apply such measures. In fact, whereas the EU allows the application of such tariff measures 'in order to protect end users' interests whilst promoting effective competition', article 67(2) CEC expressly states that tariff obligations are permitted if measures related to wholesale carrier selection or pre-selection services are not able to ensure effective competition and the public interest. The list of tariff regulations includes the application of appropriate retail price cap measures which currently apply to the retail voice telephony services offered by Telecom Italia.[138]

19.134   The provisions allowing for end user tariff regulation are complemented by mandatory rules[139] regarding the implementation of cost accounting systems, as required by Article 17(4) of the Universal Service Directive.

End User Rights

Contracts

19.135   The CEC implements the principles set out in Article 20 of the Universal Service Directive, thus requiring that 'consumers[140] and other end users that so request have the right to enter into contracts with one or more undertakings which provide connection services to a public communication network or publicly available electronic communication services'.[141] These contracts must contain the same minimum information and details as those required under Article 20(1) of the Universal Service Directive. The contractual terms and conditions may be changed only according to the same rules as those set out by Article 20(2) of the Universal Service Directive. Under the CEC, if subscribers do not accept such changed contractual terms and conditions, when they withdraw from the contract, the operators are prevented from applying not only 'penalt[ies]' (just as per Article 20(2) of the Universal Service Directive), but also any 'disconnection charges'.[142]

Transparency obligations

19.136   In terms of transparency, publication of information, and quality of service, the CEC affords the same protection as that granted by Articles 21 and 22 of the Universal Service Directive.[143]

---

137   Art 67(2) CEC.
138   AGCOM Resolution No 289/03/CONS of 23 July 2003.
139   Art 67(4) CEC.
140   'Consumer' is defined as the 'individual end user who utilises or who asks to utilise a publicly available electronic communication service for purposes outside his/her business, trade or professional activity' (art 1(j) CEC).
141   Art 70(1) CEC.
142   Art 70(4) CEC.
143   Arts 71 and 72 CEC.

Quality of service: securing 'net neutrality'

19.137   Although the CEC does not expressly contain the term 'net neutrality', it nonetheless provides that 'AGCOM, in order to prevent service deterioration and network traffic limitation or slowdown, may impose obligations in relation to minimum quality of service upon the undertaking or undertakings which provide public communication networks'.[144] To date, AGCOM has not issued specific resolutions to regulate 'net neutrality'. Regardless, the contracts mentioned above must indeed contain, among other things, information on the procedures put in place by the undertaking to measure and shape traffic in a network link, in compliance with end users' right of choice and data protection rules, to avoid network saturation or overfilling, as well as information on how those procedures could affect service quality.[145]

19.138   Quality of service has been specifically regulated by AGCOM Resolution No 179/03/CSP of 24 July 2003 as further supplemented by specific resolutions for specific services.[146] Under articles 10(2) and 3(8) of the Resolution, quality of service indicators and relevant general and specific standards must be reported in the 'charter of services'. This is a 'manifesto' that each operator must publish and the mandatory effect of which has been established by Directive of the Prime Minister of 27 January 1994[147] and then confirmed by, inter alia, Law No 481 of 14 November 1995.[148] The charter of services must be updated annually to ensure continual improvement of effectiveness and efficiency of services. The CEC treats quality of service as a parameter whose publication is designed to help end users exercise their right to choose. On the other hand, when quality of service is addressed in the context of universal service obligations, quality becomes also a technical specification to be specifically met by universal service providers in compliance with those quality levels that have been established by AGCOM resolutions and/or the CEC.[149]

European emergency call number

19.139   The regulatory measures concerning the European emergency call number ('112') are the same as those set out in article 26 of the Universal Service Directive.[150] The Ministry of Internal Affairs, together with the Ministry, is empowered to take all necessary measures for the full implementation of the European emergency call number.[151]

---

144   Art 72(2bis) CEC.

145   Art 70(1)(b)(4) CEC.

146   AGCOM Resolutions No 254/04/CSP, 79/09/CSP on fixed voice telephony, 104/05/CSP and 79/09/CSP on mobile and personal communications, and 131/06/CSP and 244/08/CSP on Internet access from a fixed location.

147   The 1994 Prime Minister Directive established that all public services (such as electronic communications services) must be rendered according to principles of non-discrimination, impartiality, efficiency, effectiveness, continuity, the right to choose and right to participate in the decision-making process.

148   Law No 481/95 seeks to guarantee appropriate quality levels for all public interest services, ensuring their availability and in a homogeneous manner throughout the Italian territory, thus promoting the protection of users' and consumers' interests.

149   Arts 61 and 72 CEC.

150   Art 76 CEC.

151   Art 75bis CEC.

Other obligations

19.140   The regulatory measures concerning the availability of services, equivalence in access and choice for disabled end users, operator assistance and directory inquiry services, the European standard international access code ('00'), harmonised numbers for harmonised services of social value (including missing children hotline numbers), non-geographic numbers, additional facilities (tone dialling or DTMF and calling line identification) ,and number portability are the same as those set out in articles 23–30 Universal Service Directive.[152]

19.141   With particular reference to number portability, article 80(4*bis*) CEC provides that end users that wish to port their numbers to another operator have the right to obtain the activation of the ported number within one working day.

DATA PROTECTION: THE DIRECTIVE ON PRIVACY AND ELECTRONIC COMMUNICATIONS

Confidentiality of Communications

19.142   It is prohibited to use electronic communications networks to obtain access to information stored in users' terminal equipment (eg by way of 'spyware', 'web bug' or 'cookies'), to store information or to monitor users' activities without first:

- providing clear and comprehensive information regarding the purposes of the data processing and storage; and
- collecting the user's express consent.[153]

19.143   The above does not prohibit the possible technical storage or access to already stored information, if this is only to convey a communication on an electronic communication network, or to the extent necessary, to let an information society service provider provide a service expressly requested by a subscriber or user.

19.144   Operators providing publicly available electronic communications services must inform subscribers and, if possible, users of situations which unintentionally may allow third parties to access the content of communications or conversations. Subscribers must inform users when third parties may have access to the content of communications or conversations due to the terminal equipment or transmission links used at subscribers' premises. Users must inform the other users when equipment used during the conversation allows third parties to hear the conversation.[154]

19.145   In the case of a data breach, the publicly available electronic communication service provider must promptly inform the IDPA. If the data breach can damage personal data or the subscriber's or another person's privacy, the provider must promptly also inform such subscriber or other person, unless the provider demonstrates to the IDPA that it has put in place all technological measures to ensure anonymisation of the data involved. The data breach that triggers such notification obligations is defined as any breach of security leading to the accidental or unlawful destruction, loss, alteration, unauthorised disclosure of, or access to, personal data transmitted, stored or otherwise processed in connection with the

---

152   Arts 73–80 CEC.
153   Art 122 Privacy Act.
154   Art 131 Privacy Act.

provision of a publicly available electronic communications service. Furthermore, providers must keep an up-to-date registry listing all data breaches.[155]

19.146   Non-compliance with the above notification obligations with respect to the IDPA triggers an administrative fine ranging from €25,000 to €150,000, while the breach of notification obligations with respect to subscribers or other persons, if due,[156] triggers an administrative fine ranging from €150 to €1,000 per customer involved. Failure to keep the up-to-date registry of data breaches triggers an administrative fine ranging from €20,000 to €120,000.[157]

Traffic Data and Location Data

19.147   The definitions of 'traffic data' and 'location data' are identical to those in the E-Privacy Directive. Service providers must inform subscribers of the types of data processed and the duration of such processing.[158]

19.148   Storage of traffic data for invoicing or interconnection purposes is permitted for a maximum period of six months; however, in the case of litigation, storage is permitted for longer periods.[159] In addition, providers must store voice and Internet traffic data for 24 and 12 months, respectively, for law enforcement purposes. This does not apply to the content of voice or Internet communications which may be intercepted, processed, and stored only upon order of the judicial authority and in compliance therewith.[160]

19.149   Location data may be processed if the data has been made anonymous and the user's consent has been obtained to the extent and for the duration necessary for the provision only of the requested value-added services. The user's consent may be withdrawn at any time. To obtain consent, service providers must inform users and subscribers about the nature of the location data subject to processing, the purposes and duration of such processing, and the possibility that such data may be transferred to third parties for the provision of the value added service requested.[161] Moreover, the data controller must provide advance notification to the IDPA (using an online tool available on IDPA's website) that it intends to process location data.[162]

Itemised Billing

19.150   Users have the right to obtain, free of charge, itemised bills from service providers. When invoicing subscribers, service providers must cancel the last three digits of the called numbers from the bills, unless subscribers request such three digits to appear for claims against specific bills and for limited periods of time.[163]

---

155   Art 32*bis* Privacy Act.
156   See para 19.145 above.
157   Art 162*ter* Privacy Act.
158   Art 123(4) Privacy Act.
159   Art 123(2) Privacy Act.
160   Art 132 Privacy Act.
161   Art 126 Privacy Act.
162   Art 37(1)(a) Privacy Act.
163   Art 124 Privacy Act.

19.151   Service providers must allow users to communicate and request services from any terminal equipment, using payment means alternative to billing, such as credit, debit, or pre-paid cards.[164]

Presentation and Restriction of Calling and Connected Line Identification

19.152   If calling line identification services are available, service providers must allow calling users and subscribers to withhold their numbers on a per-call and (in case of subscribers) per-line basis, through simple means and free of charge. Called subscribers must also have the possibility to block the numbers of incoming calls and to reject incoming calls automatically in cases where the caller has withheld the caller identification.[165]

Automatic Call Forwarding

19.153   Service providers must adopt the necessary measures to allow users, to whom calls have been automatically forwarded as a result of third party actions, to request (using simple means and free of charge) that these be stopped.[166]

Directories of Subscribers

19.154   The Italian Data Protection Authority, in cooperation with AGCOM, sets out the modalities for inclusion and use of subscribers' personal data in paper and electronic directories, also with reference to data already processed prior to the entry into force of the Privacy Act.[167]

19.155   The Data Protection Authority, in cooperation with AGCOM, also sets out the modalities for subscribers' consent to the inclusion of their personal data in such directories, based on criteria of maximum simplification, and subscribers' right to verify, modify and cancel such data free of charge.[168]

---

164   Art 124 Privacy Act.
165   Art 125 Privacy Act.
166   Art 128 Privacy Act.
167   Art 129 Privacy Act.
168   Art 129 Privacy Act.

The Latvian Market for Electronic Telecommunications[1]

Sarmis Spilbergs
LAWIN, Riga

LEGAL STRUCTURE

Basic Policy

20.1 The telecommunications service markets in Latvia have been fully opened to competition since 2003. Over the years the markets have grown rapidly and are expected to continue to do so. Currently there are approximately 400 electronic communications undertakings operating in the market. Most are Internet Service Providers ('ISPs), with providers of voice telephony in second position.

20.2 Latvian policy for the electronic communications sector is determined within the boundaries of common EU policy.[2] The goal of the policy at the national level for the period 2011–2016 is to ensure the availability of high quality electronic communications services throughout the entire territory of Latvia by introduction of an investment-friendly regulatory environment and use of innovative technologies. The policy identifies four areas for action to achieve this goal:

- facilitation of electronic communications services at a defined quality and provision of services corresponding to the needs of end users;
- introduction of preconditions for use of innovative technologies;
- development of state private electronic communications network for continuous and effective state governance; and
- ensuring stable investment environment.

20.3 In order to ensure unified regulation in the field of electronic communications, creating open and transparent relations, the regulatory approach is to achieve mutual cooperation between the Public Utilities Commission ('PUC', the Latvian telecommunications regulatory authority), the Ministry of Transport, the Competition Council, the Consumer Rights Protection Centre, and the Electronic Communications Office.

20.4 The PUC, in its role as telecommunications regulator, is responsible for monitoring the telecommunications sector to ensure that the set objectives are

---

1   Editing of this chapter closed on 11 January 2013.
2   'Basic policy of electronic communications sector in Republic of Latvia for years 2011–2016', adopted by decree of Cabinet of Ministers No 151, 13 April 2011, ('LV', 60 (4458), 15.04.2011.)

reached, the interests of all stakeholders are observed, and that the regulatory regime is current and compliant with the EU Regulatory Package. The EC has initiative a number of infringement procedures (approximately ten since 2004 when Latvia joined the EU) against Latvia for various irregularities and failure to comply with the EU Regulatory Package. Latvia deals with the majority of these cases at the pre-trial stage by taking the necessary practical steps and amending local legislative enactments. The most significant and illustrative challenges have been with respect to the division of regulatory functions apart from functions related to proprietary rights and control over undertakings (ie the PUC has simultaneously performed both functions), with respect to the provision of location data of callers to emergency service providers, and ensuring publicly available directory list of subscribers. The PUC continues to monitor the sector for any issues that call for attention and to follow up on implementation of the determined policy objectives.

Implementation of EU Directives

20.5 Latvia has transposed the 2009 Regulatory Package, passing a total of 16 legislative acts to implement the Better Regulation Directive and the Citizens Rights Directive (in most cases through amendments to existing legislative acts, with a few new laws, instead of introduction of a single new act). The BEREC Regulation did not require transposition at the national level. Furthermore, the PUC continues work on drafting further legislative amendment proposals to ensure compliance with the determined principles, and to make regulation more simple, transparent, and effective consistent with the common EU policy.

Legislation

20.6 The most significant legal acts in the telecommunications sector as adopted by the Parliament of Latvia (Saeima) are:

- the Electronic Communications Law ('2004 Act');[3]
- the Law on Regulators of Public Utilities ('2000 Act');[4] and
- the Electronic Mass Media Law.[5]

Based on these primary acts, there have been numerous Cabinet of Ministers Regulations and PUC regulations and decisions adopted. Although the most material rules arise from the laws and regulations of the Cabinet of Ministers, the role of PUC is still significant as it not only passes further technical regulations, but also adopts individual decisions with interpretation of applicable rules. Nonetheless, the laws and regulations remain the primary regulatory source (with decisions of the PUC consulted as secondary).

Given that the number of undertakings operating in the sector continues to grow, the overall legislative approach has achieved enhanced competition. Most companies that had previously provided one type of service are now entering other markets. For example, traditional voice telephony service providers (both mobile and fixed) and cable TV operators are now also providing Internet access services,

---

3   Electronic Communications Law, adopted on 28 October 2004, (LV 183 (3131), 17 November 2004; Ziņotājs, 23, 09 December 2004.).
4   Law on Regulators of Public Utilities, adopted on 19 October 2000, (LV, 394/395 (2305/2306), 07 November 2000.; Ziņotājs, 22, 23 November 2000.)
5   Electronic Mass Media Law, adopted on 12 July 2010, (LV, 118 (4310), 28 July 2010.)

and voice telephony service providers are also providing cable TV services, competing with the traditional cable TV network operators. Accordingly, despite the difference in underlying technology and infrastructure for each of these services (for example, traditional copper lines, optical fibre lines, wireless 3G or 4G, satellite, among others), undertakings are competing with one another in each of these markets, demonstrating a regulatory landscape that is technology neutral and enhances competition.

REGULATORY PRINCIPLES: IMPLEMENTATION OF THE FRAMEWORK DIRECTIVE

Scope of Regulation

20.7   The 2004 Act, which is the primary regulatory act for the telecommunications market, determines the competence, rights, and obligations of users, electronic communications undertakings, private electronic communications network owners, and state administrative institutions, and governs the provision of electronic communications networks and services, and the use and administration of scarce resources. The 2004 Act also applies to the electronic communications networks that are necessary for the distribution of radio or television programmes; however the Electronic Mass Media Law determines the procedures for the establishment, registration, operation, and supervision of broadcasting organisations. The 2004 Act does not apply to the provision of information society services and the information content thereof, which are transmitted or received in electronic communications networks.

Despite differences in wording, the definitions of 'electronic communications networks', 'electronic communications service', and 'associated facilities' are substantially the same as those in the Framework Directive.

According to PUC published guidelines regarding electronic communications undertakings' notification forms, VoIP in Latvia is considered 'voice telephony service', requiring prior notification registration with the PUC.[6] This qualification, however, is not binding. Therefore, the qualification of VoIP under Latvian laws is subject to debate.

Internet Freedom

20.8   To date Latvia has not introduced a mechanism that would oblige ISPs, or would allow other entities, to monitor Internet traffic and restrict end users' access to the Internet in the case of intellectual property rights violations. While the possibility of the introduction of such mechanism has been debated by stakeholders, ISPs and other interest groups voiced concerns, blocking the adoption of any such mechanism. Accordingly, the only obligations of ISPs in this regard are those arising from the Data Retention Directive, and those with respect to the processing of traffic and location data.

---

6   Art 1, PUC Recommendation for filling out form 'Information on provided electronic communications networks and provided electronic communications services in specific area and the administrative territory codes of Republic of Latvia', available at http://www.sprk.gov.lv/doc_upl/ieteikumi.doc

Temporary measures to restrict a user's access to the Internet are permitted only if a user takes actions that threaten the integrity and safety of the network.[7]Recently, ISPs have been required to cooperate with competent court requests in civil matters to disclose the identity of a user who has committed a tort online (usually defamation). Previously, only criminal investigative authorities were entitled to obtain such information form ISPs, but not private parties. Accordingly, the 2004 Act was amended providing that where a civil matter is before the court, the court is entitled to request that the ISP discloses the identity of the user and also certain traffic data (to the extent necessary and reasonable). However, if the existing infrastructure of the ISP does not generate such data, the ISP is not required to make additional investments in order to be able to comply with such requests.[8]

National Regulatory Authorities: Organisation, Regulatory Objectives, Competences

20.9   The Ministry of Transport ('Ministry') oversees the telecommunications sector, issuing top level policy decisions and legislation in the field of telecommunications. The PUC, however, as the sector regulator, is the most closely involved in supervising market participants. Other institutions have specific functions, such as the Electronic Communications Office (which manages limited resources such as numbering and radiofrequencies and supervises the technical development of infrastructure) and the Data State Inspection ('the Inspection') which safeguards the personal data.

20.10   The PUC has various competences, obligations, and powers vested through articles 8 and 9 2004 Act, pursuant to which the PUC regulates the electronic communications market. In this role, the PUC promotes the development of the electronic communications market, supervises and ensures compliance with legislation, and promotes competition in the sector so that undertakings providing electronic communications networks are treated equally to undertakings offering electronic communications services. The PUC also issues decisions and administrative acts that are binding upon undertakings and consumers of electronic communications. The 2004 Act and the 2000 Act both adopt general regulatory objectives and principles to be observed by the PUC.

20.11   The powers vested in, and duties imposed on, the PUC and the Electronic Communications Office, as well as regulatory objectives and principles, are consistent with the requirements of the Framework Directive. The relevant powers and duties are also generally in compliance with the requirements set out in Article 3 of the Framework Directive, except for the lack of a legal framework for cooperation on matters involving questions of competition.

20.12.   The establishment, operational structure, and independence of the PUC are stipulated in article 7 2000 Act. The PUC is an independent authority that is not accountable to the Ministry or any other institution. Its highest decision making body is the 'Council', which consists of five members elected by parliament. Article 9 2000 Act stipulates the right for the PUC to request information necessary to fulfil its functions.

20.13   The PUC has a duty to secure transparency of its actions by making public its yearly reviews, and compiling and publishing information on the electronic

---

7   Art 9(1)(5), 'Information technology safety law', adopted 28 October 2010, (LV 178 (4370), 10 November 2010.)

8   Art 71.[2] 2004 Act.

communications sector. Such information and reviews are regularly published and are available on the PUC's website. Information on regulation in the electronic communications sector can also be found on the Ministry's website. The cooperation requirement (exchange of information with other domestic and foreign institutions as well as with EU institutions, and following BEREC opinions and goals) is also stated in article 8 2004 Act.

The PUC recently revised Regulations on Consultation Procedure with Participants of the Market,[9] implementing Art 6 of the Framework Directive. Pursuant to these revised regulations, the PUC will draft consultation documents which it will publish in the official magazine *Latvijas Vestnesis* ('LV'), place a copy on the PUC website, and consider proposals submitted by market participants.

20.14   Section VII 2000 Act establishes the power of the PUC to settle disputes in the sector. As a settlement body separate from the court system, the PUC is entitled to review disputes between electronic communications undertakings as well as between undertakings and end users. Nonetheless, the parties are entitled to settle the dispute also without PUC involvement by submitting the relevant claim in courts under civil procedures. Where the party to a dispute is not satisfied with a PUC decision, further recourse to courts is available.

Right of Appeal against NRA's Decisions

20.15   Decisions and actions of the PUC and the Electronic Communications Office are subject to an appeal procedure in the Administrative Court. Pursuant to the Latvian Administrative Procedure Law, an appeal may be filed by persons against whom a decision or action is taken or by third parties whose rights are infringed by the relevant decision or action.[10]

The submission of an appeal against a PUC decision or action does not suspend the effectiveness of the decision or action while the appeal is pending.[11] Where a specific request is made to order suspensive effect, the courts usually are reluctant to grant such suspension

The NRA's Obligations to Cooperate with the Commission

20.16   The general obligation of the PUC to cooperate with the Commission and the BEREC is stipulated in article 8 2004 Act. More specific obligations (depending on the particular situation or decision, as provided in Articles 7 and 7a of the Framework Directive) are included in various other articles of the 2004 Act.

Under point 28 of the General Authorisation Terms,[12] electronic communications undertakings are required to comply with, among other things, the specifications and standards published in the Official Journal of the European Union.

---

9   Art 13, 'Regulations on Consultation Procedure with Participants of the Market', adopted by PUC decision No 1/20, 24 August 2011, (LV 135 (4533), 30 August 2011.).

10   Art 76, 'Administrative Procedure Law', adopted 25 October 2001, (LV, 164 (2551), 14 November 2001; Ziņotājs, 23, 13 December 2001).

11   Art 11(5) 2000 Act.

12   'General authorisation terms', adopted by PUC decision No 1/19, 17 August 2011, (LV, 131 (4529), 23 August 2011).

'Significant Market Power' as a Fundamental Prerequisite of Regulation

Definition of SMP

20.17   Article 29(2) 2004 Act defines Significant Market Power ('SMP') the same way it is defined in Article 14(2) of the Framework Directive and also notes the obligation to take into account the guidelines on market analysis and the assessment of significant market power published by the Commission.[13] Consistent with the obligation to cooperate with Commission, any deviations from the Commission recommended market definitions must be coordinated with the Commission.

Definition of relevant markets

20.18   The PUC determines the specific electronic communications services markets, taking into account the geographic distribution of electronic communications services and other special circumstances, as well as the recommendation of the European Commission. The PUC must consult with electronic communications undertakings and, if necessary, with the Competition Council. The PUC must conduct market analyses consistent with the European Commission market analysis guidelines.[14]

20.19   In practice, the PUC has closely followed the Market Recommendation 2003's definitions of the Commission. In most of the electronic communications markets (markets 1–13) the PUC has designated SIA Lattelecom ('Lattelecom') as the SMP operator. Lattelecom is the historic monopoly company in the fixed landline voice telephony market; therefore it carries the most developed infrastructure. However, with respect to call termination markets (9 and 3 for fixed telephony and 16 and 7 for mobile) each company that has its own network infrastructure is usually regarded as having an SMP in its own network.

Imposition of remedies

20.20   If, as a result of a market analysis, the PUC determines that there is a lack of effective competition in a particular market, the PUC issues a decision regarding the imposition, maintenance, amendment, or withdrawal of adequate and proportional special obligations with respect to particular electronic communications undertakings.[15] If the PUC determines that effective competition exists, on the other hand, it does not apply remedies or revokes the imposed remedies on the undertakings having SMP.[16]

NRA's Regulatory Duties concerning Rights of Way, Co-location and Facility Sharing

20.21   According to article 16 2004 Act, public electronic communications network undertakings which provide or operate electronic communications networks

---

13   Art 29(2) 2004 Act.
14   Art 30 2004 Act.
15   Art 31(2) 2004 Act.
16   Art 31(3) 2004 Act.

may install public electronic communications networks and construct the necessary structures (such as cable ducts, manholes, poles, masts, towers, containers, and payphones, among others) on state, local government, and private property territory, if they coordinate the design in advance with the owners or possessors of the immovable property. Owners of residential and non-residential buildings, risers, horizontal cable channels, facilities for the installation of cable distribution, and electronic communications network facilities in public premises, must make their facilities accessible to undertakings without discrimination, subject to applicable laws on property rights.

Pursuant to article 18 2004 Act, a public electronic communications network operator has the right of use (servitude) to maintain and operate a public electronic communications network. The right of use is exercised by mutual agreement between the operator and the owner of the real estate. If the parties fail to reach agreement, the court will resolve the dispute.

Pursuant to article 44 2004 Act, the PUC may impose specific access obligations on undertakings having SMP in relevant markets. The relevant undertakings are required to draft and publish their basic offers on gaining access to their infrastructure; however, if the basic offerings hinder competition, the PUC is entitled to impose specific obligations as a remedy on such undertakings.

20.22   All undertakings, after installing, exploiting, or developing electronic communications networks, must repair any damages or unwarranted alterations caused to the property.

REGULATION OF MARKET ENTRY: IMPLEMENTATION OF THE AUTHORISATION DIRECTIVE

The General Authorisation of Electronic Communications

20.23   The PUC prepares and publishes a list of electronic communications services which are subject to the requirement of prior registration with the PUC.[17] The PUC publishes a list of the undertakings that have filed their registration notifications and issues a registration certificate to the relevant undertakings.

20.24   General Authorisation Terms are applicable to all undertakings providing electronic communications services that require registration notification to the PUC. If an undertaking repeatedly violates the General Authorisation Terms, it risks being restricted from providing relevant services for up to five years.[18] Certain undertakings may be subject to additional obligations (for example, those having SMP).

20.25   In accordance with Article 34 2004 Act, the provisions of the General Authorisation Terms may cover:

● the financing of investments in the universal service;
● information regarding State fees;
● interoperability of electronic communications services and interconnection of electronic communications networks;
● routing of user calls in conformity with the national, and European, numbering plans, Universal International Freephone Numbers and, if technically possible, numbering plans of other European Union Member States;

17   Art 32 2004 Act.
18   Art 33(3) 2004 Act.

- environmental, city, and rural territorial planning requirements;
- access to privately and publicly owned land;
- shared use of infrastructures (including technical and financial guarantees);
- mandatory transmission of radio or television programmes;
- protection of user data including personal data in the electronic communications sector;
- specific requirements for the protection of consumer rights in the electronic communications sector and availability of electronic communications services for persons with disabilities;
- restriction of the transmission of information with unlawful contents;
- information which must be submitted to the PUC for its supervision of the implementation of the general authorisation regulations;
- provision of electronic communications services between emergency service operators in emergency situations, for the '112' service, for state administrative institutions, and to inform individuals in emergency situations;
- limitation of the impact of electronic communications network electromagnetic radiation;
- access for electronic communications undertakings, as well as special access requirement specification and criteria for electronic communications undertakings with SMP;
- technical regulations related to electronic communications network connection and requirements to prevent electromagnetic interference in electronic communications networks;
- protection of public electronic communications networks against unauthorised access;
- use of common radio frequency spectrum for commercial activities; and
- conformity to the standards or specifications published in the Official Journal of the European Communities.

Rights of Use for Radio Frequencies

General authorisations and granting of individual rights

20.26   An electronic communications undertaking wishing to use radio frequencies for commercial purposes must apply to the PUC for the right of use of radio frequency. The PUC then decides whether to grant such application for right of use. If the requested radio frequency band has been determined by the Cabinet of Ministers as of limited use, the PUC must organise a tender for rights of use of such frequencies.[19] Certain frequency bands have been defined as common use bands and the use such bands in commercial application is permitted without separate assignments or licencing, instead the general authorization terms issued by PUC should be observed.

Admissible conditions

20.27   The PUC may set the following specific terms and conditions for use of the radio frequency spectrum:

- requirements for electronic services, quality, networks or technologies;
- requirements for the efficient use of the radio frequency spectrum and to ensure adequate coverage;

---

19   Art 47 2004 Act.

- technical requirements with respect to assessing potentially harmful radio disturbances;
- the term of validity of the rights of use;
- conditions for the transfer of the right of use of the radio frequency spectrum allocated for commercial activities;
- the fee for the right of use of the spectrum;
- obligations to be met if the rights of use are granted as a result of a tender or auction; and
- requirements resulting from international agreements on use of radio frequency spectrum.[20]

20.28   The right to use radio frequency spectrum is generally transferable, except where the undertaking has not paid for the right of use or where the undertaking has obtained the right of use for a period in excess of ten years before these rights are transformed into common use radiofrequency spectrum permission.[21]

Limitation of number of rights of use to be granted

20.29   Article 47(5) 2004 Act delegates to the Cabinet of Ministers the right to define radio frequency spectrum bands, in which, for the purpose of efficient utilisation, it is necessary to limit granting of the rights to use radio frequency spectrum to businesses in the electronic communications sector.[22] In these bands the PUC will organise a tender or auction proceedings and will grant the rights to use the radio frequency spectrum to the winner of the tender or auction, respectively.

Commercial activities without receipt of the right of use of the radio frequency spectrum allocated by the PUC is permitted if it is performed in radio frequency spectrums or radio frequency channels for which a common radio frequency allocation use permit has been specified.[23]

Rights of Use for Numbers

20.30   The PUC grants, reserves, annuls, and withdraws numbering resources. The Electronic Communications Office, on the other hand, manages the numbering and maintains the database of numbering as allocated to undertakings by the PUC. The procedures under which the PUC and the Electronic Communications Office perform these activities are set out in the Cabinet of Ministers and PUC regulations.[24] The Cabinet of Ministers also approves the national numbering plan.

20.31   The right to use of numbers or number series is granted to an electronic communications undertaking based on an application to the PUC. The PUC may

---

20   Art 47(7) 2004 Act.
21   Art 47(3¹) 2004 Act
22   'Regulations on radio frequency spectrum bands, in which, for the purpose of efficient utilisation, it is necessary to limit granting of the rights to use radio frequency spectrum to businesses in the electronic communications sector', adopted by Cabinet of Ministers Regulation No 143, 16 February 2010, (LV' 29 (4221), 19 February 2010.)
23   Art 47(51) 2004 Act.
24   'Regulations how the Electronic Communications Office manages numbering by setting up and maintaining the numbering database', adopted by Cabinet of Ministers Regulation No 656, 11 August 2008, (LV, 124 (3908), 13 August 2008.) and 'Regulations on the rights to use numbering', adopted by PUC decision No 1/5, 16 June 2011, LV', 97 (4495), 22.06.2011.).

also decide to use a tender for rights to use numbers. Typically, the electronic communications undertaking will acquire the rights in numbering for indefinite period of time; however, in exceptional cases a fixed term can be set. The undertaking that has acquired numbering rights from the PUC may transfer the number to another undertaking as long as the number has not already been issued to end users. An undertaking that has acquired a number from another undertaking is not entitled to transfer the number further.[25]

20.32   Under article 47(8) 2004 Act the PUC may determine specific terms and conditions with respect to the rights of use for numbers, including:

- requirements in relation to electronic communications services, the provision of which the right of use of numbering has been allocated and requirements in relation to the tariff principles and maximum prices applicable in the specific number range for the purposes of ensuring consumer protection;
- requirements with respect to services for the efficient use of numbering resources;
- requirements to ensure availability of a list of subscribers;
- requirements with respect to maximum time periods for the operation of right of use of numbering;
- requirements for procedures for further transfer of the rights of use of numbers;
- requirements with respect to terms in respect for payment for the rights of use of numbers;
- obligations to be met if the rights of use of numbers are granted as a result of tender or auction; and
- requirements resulting from international agreements on the use of numbering resources.

Under article 57 2004 Act, when changing electronic communications service providers, a subscriber must be able to retain the number allocated to him or her by the electronic communications undertaking for use in the geographic numbering territory in the national numbering plan, or in any other location if the end user number is not associated with geographic numbering. The PUC has issued regulations for the number portability service.[26] Pursuant to these regulations, an electronic communications undertaking must enter into an agreement with an end user regarding the transfer of the number. The agreement must include, among other things, provisions with respect to the time period for the transfer of the number and the amount of the compensation for non-observance thereof and other provisions shall be provided. The electronic communications undertaking must activate a number within one working day.

The NRA's Enforcement Powers

20.33   The PUC has the right to request and receive, within a specified timeframe, information from undertakings necessary for performance of its functions (including information that contains commercial secrets), as well as to request written or

---

25   'Regulations on the rights to use numbering', adopted by PUC decision No 1/5, 16 June 2011, ('LV', 97 (4495), 22 June 2011.)

26   'Regulations on ensuring number portability services', adopted by PUC decision No 1/6, 16 June 2011, (LV, 97 (4495), 22 June 2011.)

oral explanations from the respective undertakings.[27] The PUC also has the right, by giving prior notice, to visit the premises and buildings and gain access to the equipment which is used for the supply of electronic communications services or network operation and to request permits, certificates, and other documents.[28] If the PUC discovers violations of the applicable rules, the Chairperson of the PUC, or his or her authorised official, may draft an administrative violation report.[29] When evaluating the report the PUC is entitled to impose administrative penalties. The maximum administrative penalty in Latvia currently is LVL 10,000 (€14,000).[30]

Administrative Charges and Fees for Rights of Use

20.34   All undertakings providing electronic communication services or networks must pay an annual fee to cover regulation of public services.[31] The rates are determined by the Cabinet of Ministers; however they may not exceed 0.2 per cent of the net turnover of the provided regulated services of the undertaking in the previous calendar year.[32] Undertakings, upon commencing activities, must pay the State fee from the planned net turnover of the regulated services.[33]

REGULATION OF NETWORK ACCESS AND INTERCONNECTION: THE ACCESS DIRECTIVE

Objectives and Scope of Access Regulation

20.35   The objectives of access and interconnection regulation are to encourage competition, and reduce the cost of service, in the market for electronic communications with respect to interconnection, joint use of network infrastructure, and unbundled access to the local loop. The PUC encourages cooperation between electronic communications undertakings, oversees the execution of agreements on interconnection of electronic communications networks which govern how these networks will be connected, decides what electronic communications services the undertakings will render to each other and how much will they cost, regulates the joint use of electronic communications network infrastructure, and facilitates the approximation of the rates of these services to the costs thereof.

20.36   The provisions of the 2004 Act regarding access and interconnection are binding on operators of public electronic communications networks and electronic communications undertakings who wish to obtain access or interconnection.[34]

Basic Regulatory Concepts

20.37   'Access' is a service rendered to another electronic communications undertaking on specific conditions with respect to gaining access to services and

---

27   Art 9(1) 2004 Act.
28   Art 9(1) 2004 Act.
29   Art 9(2) 2004 Act.
30   Art 26, 'Code of Administrative Offenses of Latvia', adopted 7 December 1984, (Ziiņotājs, 51, 20 December 1984.)
31   Art 30(1) 2000 Act
32   Art 31(2) 2000 Act.
33   Art 31(2¹) 2000 Act.
34   Art 36–37 2004 Act.

equipment needed to render electronic communications services, including for use for information society services or content distribution services. It includes:

- access to electronic communications network elements and their associated facilities with wire or non-wire connections, in particular access to the subscriber line, as well as equipment and services which are necessary to ensure services in the subscriber line;
- access to physical infrastructure (including buildings, cable lines, cable ducts and antenna masts and towers used to ensure electronic communications networks);
- access to the relevant software systems (including operational support systems);
- access to information systems and databases in order to carry out orders, deliveries, maintenance, damage prevention and preparation of bills;
- access to number translation or systems which offer similar possibilities;
- access to electronic communications networks (in particular for roaming);
- access to conditional access systems for digital television services; and
- access to virtual network services.[35]

20.38 'Interconnection' is defined as physical and logical connections among one and the same or various electronic communications undertakings on public electronic communications networks, which allow the users of one electronic communications undertaking to communicate with the users of the same or another electronic communications undertaking, or to access electronic communications services that are provided by another electronic communications undertaking.[36]

20.39   The PUC is vested with broad regulatory powers with respect to access and interconnection. In this role, the PUC has the right:

- upon their own initiative, or if justifiably requested by one of the parties, to ascertain the conditions to be included in access, interconnection, common use of associated facilities, leased lines, access to data flow or unbundling of the access subscriber lines (local loops) contracts, as well as to impose what needs to be observed by one or several of the contracting parties, in order to amend or delete conditions or to agree regarding contract conditions;[37]
- to request the amendment of agreements that have already been executed, on interconnection, access or joint use of equipment, if necessary to ensure active competition, maximum economic efficiency, or the interoperability of electronic communications networks or electronic communications services;[38]
- upon its own initiative or, if reasonably so requested by any of the parties, to set the date by which negotiations on the execution of access or interconnection agreements must be concluded (the time period specified by the PUC, however, may not be longer than three months from the time the PUC's decision takes effect);[39] and
- to specify the access and interconnection obligations of SMP undertakings.[40]

Pursuant to Article 3(1) of the Access Directive, undertakings may freely enter into mutual commercial negotiations on access and interconnection. Article 37 2004 Act

---

35   Art 1(38) 2004 Act.
36   Art 1(46) 2004 Act.
37   Art 9(1)(3) 2004 Act.
38   Art 9(1)(4) 2004 Act.
39   Art 9(1) 2004 Act.
40   See para 20.40 below.

stipulates that each undertaking has the right to request and, if requested by other undertakings, to reach an agreement on, access or interconnection to public electronic communications network. The PUC will exercise its rights with respect to execution of interconnection agreements in cases where negotiations between the undertakings have reached an impasse and the parties are unable to agree.[41]

Access- and Interconnection-related Obligations with Respect to SMP Undertakings

20.40   With regard to the regulation of access and interconnection with respect to SMP undertakings, according to articles 31[42] and 38(1) 2004 Act, based on the results of a market analysis, the PUC has the right to impose the obligations set out in articles 9–13a of the Access Directive,[43] specifically:

- transparency;
- non-discrimination;
- accounting separation;
- access to and use of specific network facilities;
- price control and cost accounting obligations; and
- obligation relating to functional separation.

20.41   The same regulatory regime applies to operators of fixed and mobile networks. The PUC, in imposing any obligations on operators, must observe the principles of objectivity, transparency, reasonableness, and non-discrimination and must take into account regulatory goals and nature of the issue. Before deciding to imposing obligations on an operator, the PUC must consult with electronic communications market participants.[44]

20.42   The PUC may impose the following additional requirements on SMP undertakings in the market for fixed voice telephony services:

- approximation of rates with costs, based on the methodology of the PUC;
- provision of access to the communication services of other suppliers of public telecommunications services connected to the telecommunications network;
- provision of a universal telecommunications service;
- ensuring special technical conditions for the supply of telecommunications services to disabled persons; and
- ensuring access to the access network and related equipment.

Under article 43(1) 2004 Act, an undertaking with SMP in the market for public fixed voice telephony network supply services must ensure carrier selection or carrier pre-selection services to its subscribers. In other cases and in other networks, carrier selection and pre-selection obligations may be imposed as part of access obligations as provided in article 12 Access Directive, but are not obligatory.[45]

20.43   The PUC may impose the following additional requirements on SMP undertakings in the market for interconnection services:

---

41   Art 9(1)(3) 2004 Act
42   See paras 1.145–1.166 above.
43   Art 38(2) 2004 Act.
44   Art 43(2) 2004 Act.
45   'Regulations on leased-lines minimum service coverage', adopted by PUC Decision No 143, 15 June 2005, (LV, 104 (3262), 06 July 2005.).

- ensuring connection of own public telecommunications network to other public telecommunications networks;
- meeting the demands of suppliers of telecommunication services in respect of special access; and
- submitting information to the PUC on the basic offer of interconnection, the basic offer of commercial calls, and special access agreements.

20.44 The PUC may intervene in accordance with the dispute resolution procedures if other operators have difficulties obtaining access or interconnection from SMP undertakings.

Regulatory Powers with Respect to SMP Undertakings

20.45 The PUC has issued regulations determining the scope of minimum services of leased lines applicable to SMP undertakings in the market of leased line services.[46]

Regulatory Powers Applicable to All Market Participants

20.46 In order to ensure end-to-end connectivity between two public electronic communications networks, the PUC may impose particular obligations on all market participants (regardless of whether they have SMP) with respect to access and interconnection. In order to ensure subscriber access to digital radio and television broadcasting services, the PUC may impose on public electronic communications network operators (regardless of whether they have SMP), obligations for access to application programming interfaces and electronic programme guides. All such obligations, however, must be applied fairly, reasonably, transparently, and without discrimination, (with respect to radio and television broadcasting services). Furthermore, the PUC, before imposing such obligations, must engage in consultations with market participants, other EU Member State regulators, and the Commission. [47]

REGULATION OF UNIVERSAL SERVICES AND USERS' RIGHTS: THE UNIVERSAL SERVICE DIRECTIVE

Regulation of Universal Service Obligations

Scope of universal service obligations

20.47 The PUC has determined that the following services are to be covered under the scope of universal services at fixed locations of public telephone network:[48]

- ensuring access to end users;
- voice telephony services;
- data and electronic message transmission services at public telephone network with a speed of at least 9600 bit/s;

---

46 Art 36 2004 Act.
47 'On Regulations regarding Universal Service in the Electronic Communications Sector', adopted by the PUC decision No 152, 30 May 2007, (LV, 89 (3665), 05 June 2007.).
48 Art 6–7, Ibid fn 47 above.

- payphone services to ensure;
  - — local, national and international voice telephony services;
  - — State fire and rescue services, State police, ambulance and emergency gas services and 112 toll-free calls; and
  - — free of charge call initiation service.

The universal service provider must provide to the end users of such service:

- at least one comprehensive telephone directory inquiry service;
- access to comprehensive list of subscribers;
- payphone service and related services:
  - — opportunity to apply for damages;
  - — access to at least one comprehensive directory service; and
  - — access to comprehensive list of subscribers.

    In order to ensure 'equivalent accesses' to disabled users, the universal service provider must take special measures to ensure that the electronic communications services in general are accessible, but in particular that public payphone services are available, and to ensure discounts to disabled users.[49]

    The PUC may require that a public network operator takes specific measures to ensure that disabled users have access to publicly available electronic communications services, including access to emergency services, comprehensive directory service, and comprehensive subscriber directory. These services must be provided on terms comparable to those provided to other users.[50]

Designation of undertakings obliged to provide universal services

20.48   The PUC specifies one or more undertakings which are required to supply universal services, and determines the scope, territory, users and the term for the supply provisions of the universal service.[51] The PUC has specified Lattelecom as the universal service provider in Latvia, and periodically amends the obligations imposed on it.[52]

Regulation of retail tariffs, users' expenditures and quality of service

20.49   The PUC sets the methodology that electronic communications undertakings required to provide universal services must follow in determining acceptable tariffs for such services.[53] The PUC also determines the minimum quality of services.[54]

20.50   Universal service undertakings must provide at least one optional tariff package under which the subscription price for a telephone subscription line does not exceed an acceptable price.[55] Such undertakings must provide services in the most economically effective manner and may not require subscribers to pay for any services which are not needed to provide universal service the subscriber requests.

49   Art 63 2004 Act.
50   Art 64(3) 2004 Act.
51   'On universal service obligations', adopted by PUC decision No 427, 7 December 2009.
52   'On Methodology regarding calculation and determination of Universal Service Obligation net cost', adopted by PUC decision No 153, 30 May 2007, (LV, 89 (3665), 05 June 2007.)
53   Above, fn 48.
54   Art 8, above, fn 47.
55   Art 64(6) 2004 Act.

20.51 Consistent with article 64(7) 2004 Act, the PUC controls universal service tariff levels, taking into account the retail prices and income of residents in the country. The PUC may impose specific obligations on the supplier of universal services with respect to itemised billing to enable users to verify and expenses.[56]

Cost calculation and financing of universal services

20.52 Pursuant to article 66 2004 Act, a universal service fund or another financing mechanism should be created for the purpose of compensation of undertakings required obliged to provide universal services. The Cabinet of Ministers must, by 1 July 2013, determine the procedures pursuant to which contributions to the fund are made and how the financing is utilised to compensate the universal service provider's losses. Absent such a mechanism, losses are compensated from State budget.[57]

20.53 The costs of universal service obligations are calculated according to the methodology for calculation and determination of universal service obligations developed by the PUC.[58] Net costs are calculated on an annual basis separately for each universal service obligation component imposed. Net costs of the universal service obligation must be calculated as the total of net costs derived from the components of universal service obligations, deducting intangible benefits. Within seven months following each financial year, the universal service provider must submit to the PUC its calculated costs, followed by sworn auditor's confirmation.

Regulation of Retail Markets

20.54 Chapter IX 2004 Act implements the principle that regulation of retail services is permissible only if regulation at wholesale level does not achieve regulatory objectives.

20.55 Articles 38–44 2004 Act regulates permissible remedies in the retail market. The PUC may impose obligations on SMP undertakings with respect to:

- ensuring access to elements and equipment of the electronic communications network; and
- providing specific wholesale services to third parties for the supply of electronic communications retail services.

End User Rights

Contracts

20.56 Operators providing connection or access to the public telephone network must enter into written agreements with subscribers with respect to the electronic communications services it will provide.[59] The term 'subscriber' encompasses both 'consumers' and other end users.

20.57 Such agreements must specify the information as provided in Article 20 of the Universal Service Directive. In addition article 22 2004 Act dictates that the following be included:

56 Transitional provision 14, 2004 Act.
57 Above, fn 52.
58 Art 19(1)(3) 2004 Act.
59 Art 23(3) 2004 Act.

- type of electronic service provided, term, subscriber number or address, access to network and service receipt location (to the extent possible);
- terms of payment and issuing of invoices;
- terms of use of service provided; and
- information on permission to process the consumer's data, in order to publish and use them for commercial purposes,

Agreements with 'consumers' for set duration must:

- not initially exceed 24 months (but the undertaking must offer the option to conclude the contract initially within 12 months);
- include easily accessible information on overall costs (and compare the costs with the costs of open-ended contracts, as well as information on penalties and the value of terminal equipment supplied, or lease payment if provided); and
- include a provision for penalties for premature termination that is proportional to the actual term of use of the services, dividing it in at least three-month periods.

If an end user requires terminal equipment for receipt of the service (ie a decoder) which cannot be used for receipt of analogous service from another service provider, it must be stated in the purchase or lease agreement for such equipment that the equipment cannot be used with other service providers, and the service provider must offer to lease the equipment on objectively justifiable and cost-based fees.

20.58 Subscribers have the right to terminate contracts without penalty if, upon receipt of notice of changes to terms and conditions in the agreement, they do not agree to the notified changes. Subscribers must be informed of changes to the terms and conditions in the agreement not less than one month prior to the actual modification.[60] No contractual penalty may be applied for a subscriber's termination of an agreement, if the basis for such termination is the failure of the service provider to meet the defined quality levels of the service. Prior to termination, upon initiative of the subscriber, the PUC will determine the actual service quality levels.

Quality of service: securing 'net neutrality'

20.59 Operators must ensure that rates, rate plans, and rate discounts of services that are supplied to consumers are made publicly available through publication and other means.[61]

20.60 Subscribers have a right to receive invoices without detailed records of the services that they have used.[62] The PUC sets requirements for a basic level of detail for invoices to enable the end users to examine and control payments and supervise costs, thereby maintaining control over his or her invoices.[63]

20.61 No specific measures concerning 'net neutrality' have been adopted in Latvia; instead the noted aim is pursued through service quality requirements. Article 59 2004 Act delegates to the PUC the respective powers in this regard. The

---

60   Art 60 2004 Act.
61   Art 75 2004 Act.
62   Art 75(2) 2004 Act.
63   'Regulations on quality of electronic communications service levels, quality overview report submission and publication', adopted by PUC Decision No 1/17, (LV, 121 (4519), 04 August 2011).

PUC has laid down the quality requirements of services as well as procedures for submission and publication of quality overviews by service providers.[64] The PUC, on an annual basis, conducts a quality report on services on markets in the previous year. In order to prevent the possibility of degradation of service levels, including slowing down of data flows, the PUC is also entitled to define minimum service quality levels for public network operators. However, before implementing such requirements, BEREC should be consulted.

20.62   Additional obligations as described in articles 23 to 26 of the Universal Service Directive[65] are all incorporated in the 2004 Act.

Obligations facilitating the change of provider

20.63   Pursuant to article 57(2) of 2004 Act, an electronic communications undertaking offering voice telephony services must provide number portability service. The PUC determines the procedures whereby the number portability service is to be provided, and the rights and obligations of the involved parties.[66] A ported number must be activated within one business day.

DATA PROTECTION: IMPLEMENTATION OF THE E-PRIVACY DIRECTIVE

Confidentiality of Communications

20.64   Both service and network providers have an obligation not to disclose data on users or subscribers, as well as information on electronic communications services or value added services received by subscribers, except in cases where such information is necessary for the performance of the functions specified in the regulatory enactments of such institutions as pre-trial investigation institutions, persons performing investigative field work, state security institutions, the public prosecutor's office, and the courts in order to protect state and public security interests or to ensure the investigation of criminal offences, criminal prosecution and criminal court proceedings. Recent amendments allow disclosure of information for the purpose of ensuring the protection of the rights and legal interests of individuals whose rights have been infringed in the electronic environment in civil cases.[67]

20.65   Unless the law provides for such a specific exception, service providers are prohibited, without consent of users or subscribers, to disclose information being transmitted, or which was previously transmitted, in the provision of electronic communications services.

20.66   An electronic communications undertaking may only be granted a connection to the electronic communications network to obtain information about a user or subscriber if such user or subscriber is the subject of operational activities (eg by

---

64   See paras 1.201–1.203 above.
65   Above, fn 26.
66   Art 68 2004 Act.
67   'Procedures whereby electronic communications undertaking installs equipment on electronic communications network which, in cases prescribed by law, ensures gathering of operative information from technical resources and operative listening to conversations', adopted by Cabinet of Ministers Regulation No 591, 9 August 2005, (LV, 126 (3284), 11 August 2005).

the police or the prosecutor's office). A decision to grant such access must be issued by the court. The Cabinet of Ministers has approved regulations which stipulate the procedures by which electronic communications undertakings must ensure that operative institutions can attach phone-tapping equipment to the electronic communications network.[68]

20.67   The Personal Data Protection Law[69] ('Data Protection Act'), and regulations deriving from it (such as the Obligatory Technical and Organisational Requirements for Protection of Personal Data Processing Systems)[70] regulate personal data protection in all sectors, not only the electronic communications sector. These legislative acts are closely based on the EU data protection directives[71] and electronic communications sector undertakings must implement the applicable requirements, including those pertaining to safety and information.

20.68   In addition to the general personal data protection laws and regulations, the 2004 Act contains certain sector specific rules. Specifically Section XVI of the 2004 Act deals exclusively with data protection matters. For example, in addition to general data privacy rules, the electronic communications undertakings shall ensure:

- only authorised personnel get access to personal data and use them only for the previously defined purposes;
- personal data is protected from accidental or unlawful erasure, loss, storage, access or disclosure; and
- pursuant to applicable regulations,[72] internal regulations for investigations and monitoring of personal data protection breaches are documented.

20.69   Since 2011, in case of personal data protection breaches the electronic communications undertakings are required to inform the Data State Inspector immediately (with a basic incident report) and provide a detailed analysis within 30 days.[73]

If a data breach may affect data subjects, end users or subscribers, the electronic communications undertaking must also notify the data subject, end user or subscriber accordingly, except where the undertaking has convinced the Data State Inspector that sufficient technical and organisational measures have been taken to ensure that the information will not be legible (ie has been encrypted) for persons who did not have access to it.[74]

All data protection breaches must be documented, including measures taken and notification filed, and information shall be maintained for at least 18 months.[75]

---

68   'Personal Data Protection law', adopted 23 March 2000, (LV, 123/124 (2034/2035), 06 April 2000; Ziiņotājs, 9, 04 May 2000).
69   'Obligatory technical and organisational requirements for protection of personal data processing systems', adopted by Cabinet of Ministers Regulation No 40, 30 January 2001, (LV, 19 (2406), 02 February 2001)
70   See para 1.4 above.
71   'Obligatory requirements to be observed upon drafting of internal regulations for investigations and monitoring of personal data protection breaches', adopted by Cabinet of Ministers Regulation No 627, 9 August 2011, (LV, 128 (4526), 17 August 2011).
72   Art 68² 2004 Act
73   Art 68³ 2004 Act
74   Art 68⁴ 2004 Act
75   Art 7.¹, 'Information Society Services Law', adopted 4 November 2004, (LV, 183 (3131), 17 November 2004)

20.70   The storing of information or the gaining of access to information already stored in the terminal equipment of a subscriber or user is only permitted if the subscriber or user concerned has given his or her consent (having been provided with clear and comprehensive information, in accordance Data Protection Act, inter alia, about the purposes of the processing). Consent, however, is not necessary for any technical storage or access for the sole purpose of carrying out the transmission of a communication over an electronic communications network, or as strictly necessary in order for the provider of an information society service explicitly requested by the subscriber or user to provide the service.[76]

20.71   Violations with respect to personal data protection rules in activities of electronic communications undertakings are examined by the Data State Inspectorate, rather than the PUC. The Latvian Administrative Violations Code[77] provides that, for violations concerning personal data processing matters, a monetary fine up to LVL 10,000 (approximately €14,000) may be imposed, with or without confiscation of assets used for breaches. The Data Protection Act provides that the Data State Inspectorate, may, among other things, request information, investigate for compliance with applicable rules, and request data blocking or erasure of incorrect or unlawfully obtained data, or impose permanent or temporary prohibitions on data processing.[78]

Data Retention

20.72   Article 71 2004 Act transposed the provisions of the Data Retention Directive. Article 71 stipulates the general obligation to retain data, to whom data should be disclosed, and the obligation to inform the Data State Inspectorate regarding requests for data retained by competent authorities. Annexes 1 and 2 of the 2004 Act stipulate the type of data to be retained depending on the electronic communications service provided.

The data retention legislation has not been challenged in Latvia.

Traffic Data and Location Data

20.73   The definitions of 'traffic data' and 'location data' are provided in article 1 2004 Act:

> 'Location data' ... 'data, which is processed in an electronic communications network or processed using electronic communications services and indicates the location of the terminal equipment of an electronic communications service user. For public mobile electronic communications networks, satellite networks and non-wire networks, which are utilised for the distribution of radio or television signals, it shall be the geographic location (address) of the terminal equipment of an electronic communications service user, but for public fixed networks, cable television and cable radio networks, and electricity cable systems to the extent that they are utilised in order to transmit electronic communications signals – the access point address.'

---

76   'Code of Administrative Offences of Latvia', adopted 7 December 1984, (Ziņotājs, 51, 20 December 1984.)
77   Art 29(4) Data Protection Act
78   Art 70(4) 2004 Act.

'Traffic data' ... 'any information or data, which is processed in order to transmit information by an electronic communications network or to prepare accounts and register payments, except the content of transmitted information.'

20.74   Traffic data processing is permitted for distribution of electronic communications services and provision of value-added services, if the user or subscriber has given consent in accordance with the relevant service agreement. The user or subscriber is entitled, at any time, to withdraw consent to the processing of traffic data.[79] Traffic data are processed for the period of time within which the user or subscriber can dispute the invoice and make payments.[80]

20.75   Location data processing is permitted only in order to ensure the provision of electronic communications services. The processing of the such data for other purposes is permitted upon consent of the user or subscriber (after having informed the user regarding the purposes for which the data will be processed and whether the data will be transferred to third parties), and only within the period of time necessary for provision of value added services. The user or subscriber is entitled at any time to withdraw consent to the processing of location data for other purposes.[81] No consent is needed where location data are provided to emergency service operators for fulfilment of their legal obligations.

Itemised Billing

20.76   Pursuant to article 75 of 2004 Act, subscribers are entitled to receive bills without detailed description of services used. The PUC has set the requirements with respect to the basic level of detail of bills, which the service provider must provide subscribers free of charge.[82] The subscriber is also entitled to request a more detailed bill than the basic level set by PUC, either free of charge or for a cost-based fee.

Calling and Connected Line Identification

20.77   Service providers must inform users and subscribers of the cases in which calling and connected line identification is performed. Calling users are entitled (free of charge) to prohibit calling line identification for each call separately, and called subscribers are entitled (also free of charge) to reject calling line identification for incoming calls. Called subscribers may also request that the operator ensure the refusal of calls for which the user or subscriber has prohibited calling number identification. Called subscribers are entitled (free of charge) to prohibit the connected line identification for the calling user. These rules may be overridden if emergency service operators request such information.[83]

Automatic Call Forwarding

20.78   Under article 73 2004 Act, subscribers are entitled (free of charge) to prohibit the forwarding of calls by third persons to the subscriber.

---

79   Art 70(2) 2004 Act.
80   Art 71 2004 Act.
81   'On Regulations on subscriber bill itemisation base level', adopted by PUC decision No 275, 8 November 2006, (LV, 184 (3552), 16 November 2006).
82   Art 72 2004 Act.
83   Art 74 2004 Act.

Directories of Subscribers

20.79 Personal data of subscribers may be included in a publicly available subscribers' directory only upon consent of the subscribers. Before inclusion of data in such a directory, subscribers must be informed (free of charge) of the name of the publisher of the directory and the purpose of the directory. Subscribers are entitled (free of charge) to state which personal data may be included in the directory, and verify, recall, or amend his or her personal data.

The Lithuanian Market for Electronic Communications[1]

Jaunius Gumbis and Tomas Kamblevicius
LAWIN, Vilnius

LEGAL STRUCTURE

Basic Policy

21.1 The Lithuanian Communications Regulatory Authority ('CRA') is entrusted by law with the basic policy task of developing effective competition in the field of electronic communications, efficient use of electronic communications resources and ensured protection of the rights of consumers of electronic communications services.

21.2 As its current mission, the CRA sets the acceleration of the expansion of the 'information society' by creating greater opportunities for the development of information and communication technology ('ICT') as well as by securing a wide range of technologically advanced, high-quality, safe and affordable ICT services and products to benefit the citizens of Lithuania.[2]

21.3 The basic foundations for continuous and sustainable growth of the Lithuanian electronic communications sector[3] have resulted from the process of Lithuania's accession to the European Union ('EU') and the implementation of its *acquis communautaire*, including the 2002 Regulatory Package, which completely transformed the face of Lithuania's electronic communications markets.

21.4 While Lithuania has made great efforts to implement the 2002 Regulatory Package, it did not avoid formal infringement proceedings on such issues as

---

1   Editing of this chapter closed on 27 December 2012. The authors would like to give credit to Agne Makauskaite and Giedre Valentaite who were co-authors of the previous edition of this chapter.

2   Strategic Activity Plan of 2012–2014, approved by the Order of the Director of the Lithuanian Communications Regulatory Authority ('CRA') of 25 October 2011, No 1V-1020 (as amended).

3   For more information and data on the Lithuanian electronic communications sector, see Annual Report 2010, CRA, 2010.

directory services,[4] number portability,[5] caller location information for 112,[6] and independence of the CRA,[7] all of which have been resolved to the satisfaction of the Commission.

21.5   The short-term regulatory priorities of the CRA include maintenance of competition in the broadband communication services market (by creating favourable conditions for access to the physical network infrastructure) and efficient management of radio frequencies (by creating the conditions for investment into the next generation wireless communication networks).[8]

Implementation of EU Directives

21.6   The 2009 Regulatory Package was fully transposed into Lithuanian law through revision of the Law on Electronic Communications ('LEC').[9] The revised LEC took effect on 1 August 2011. The CRA has been actively engaged in reviewing related secondary legislation to ensure conformity with the revised LEC.

21.7   As with earlier regulatory packages, the 2009 Regulatory Package was transposed into the LEC by meticulously mirroring the provisions of the Better Regulation Directive and the Citizens' Rights Directive. This method of transposition minimised the risk of inconsistencies and thus guaranteed a higher degree of legal certainty and predictability.

21.8   In addition to the transposition of the 2009 Regulatory Package, the revised LEC resolved the long-standing issue of a lack of effective structural separation of regulatory functions, which has been subject to the Commission's reasoned opinion[10] and reference to the European Court of Justice ('ECJ')[11] (the proceedings were suspended on 19 May 2011).

Legislation

21.9   The main legislative act in the area of electronic communications is the LEC. Next in the legislative hierarchy are the resolutions of the Government of the Republic of Lithuania ('Government'), such as resolutions concerning the strategy for assigning radio frequencies to broadcast and transmit radio and television

---

4   EU telecom rules: Commission takes action against 11 Member States to ensure effective implementation (IP/05/875) (7 July 2005).
5   Telecoms: Commission opens new round of infringement proceedings, but also sees positive results of previous ones (IP/05/1585) (14 December 2005).
6   EU telecoms rules: Commission takes steps to ensure that emergency services can locate callers (IP/06/464) (6 June 2006).
7   Commission opens three new cases on independence and effectiveness of telecoms regulators in Latvia, Lithuania and Sweden (IP/08/1343) (18 September 2008).
8   Strategic Activity Plan of 2012–2014, approved by the Order of the Director of the CRA of 25 October 2011, No 1V-1020 (as amended).
9   Law on Electronic Communications of the Republic of Lithuania, approved by the Parliament of the Republic of Lithuania on 15 April 2004, No IX–2135 (as amended) ('LEC').
10   Telecoms: Commission urges Lithuania to separate regulatory and ownership functions in telecoms (IP/09/1040) (25 June 2009).
11   Digital Agenda: Commission acts against Lithuania and Romania to ensure impartial regulation of telecoms (IP/10/1557) (24 November 2010).

programmes[12] and rules and price caps for universal services[13]. Other legal acts, detailing the provisions of the LEC as well as of the resolutions of the Government, are issued by the CRA, such as rules on the provision of electronic communications services,[14] on market analysis,[15] and on dispute resolution between service and network providers,[16] among others.

21.10   Lithuania's accession to the EU and the introduction of the EU regulatory regime for electronic communications resulted in the complete transformation of Lithuania's electronic communications sector, gradually enabling competition in its markets. Further efforts of the CRA in implementing the EU regulatory packages as well as in applying regulatory remedies has contributed significantly towards this goal. The CRA has demonstrated that it is committed to the principles of technological neutrality and functional equivalence.

REGULATORY PRINCIPLES: THE FRAMEWORK DIRECTIVE

Scope of Regulation

21.11   In line with the Framework Directive, the LEC regulates electronic communications services and networks, associated facilities and services, use of electronic communications resources as well as radio equipment, terminal equipment and electromagnetic compatibility.

21.12   The definitions of 'electronic communications network', 'electronic communications service', and 'associated facilities' used in the LEC are identical to those provided in the Framework Directive.

21.13   Electronic communications services, such as Voice over Internet Protocol ('VoIP'), are not specifically covered by the LEC. They are governed, therefore, by the common regulatory framework. Generally, VoIP services of categories 2, 3 and 4, as classified by the ERG,[17] are deemed to be 'electronic communications services' by the CRA.

'Internet Freedom'

21.14   Currently, neither the LEC nor other laws of Lithuania provide for the possibility to impose measures that restrict end users' access to, or use of, services and applications through electronic communications networks. This was explicitly noted in the preparatory documents during the transposition of the 2009 Regulatory Package.

---

12   Strategy for Assigning Radio Frequencies to Broadcast and Transmit Radio and Television Programs, approved by the Resolution of the Government of the Republic of Lithuania of 27 March 2003, No 376 (as amended).

13   Rules on Compensation of Losses Related to Universal Electronic Communications Service and on Price Caps of Electronic Communications Services, approved by the Resolution of the Government of the Republic of Lithuania of 27 October 2011, No 1248.

14   Rules on Provision of Electronic Communications Services, approved by the Order of the Director of the CRA of 23 December 2005, No 1V-1160 (as amended).

15   Rules on Market Analysis, approved by the Order of the Director of the CRA of 17 September 2004, No 1V-297 (as amended).

16   Rules on Resolution of Disputes between Providers of Electronic Communications Networks and/or Services and of Disputes between Providers of Postal Services and/or Courier Services, approved by the Order of the Director of the CRA of 21 October 2011, No 1V-1017.

17   ERG Common Position on VoIP, December 2007, ERG (07) 56rev2.

National Regulatory Authorities: Organisation, Regulatory Objectives, Competencies

21.15 The Government, together with its authorised institutions, is empowered to formulate policies on electronic communications activities in Lithuania.[18] The regulation of electronic communications activities, however, is exclusively reserved for the CRA and other State institutions within the scope of their competence defined by the LEC (for example, the Competition Council of the Republic of Lithuania ('Competition Council'), the State Data Protection Inspectorate, and the State Consumer Rights Protection Authority).[19]

21.16 The CRA is an independent institution of the State. It is headed by a Director and has a Council composed of seven members. The Director and the members of the Council are appointed for five years by the President on proposal from the Prime Minister.[20] The CRA has no direct subordination to the Government; notably, the latter has no power to suspend or overturn orders or decisions of the Council or the Director. The CRA is financed from the national budget and a separate budget of its own comprised of revenues from the charges for the work and services of the CRA.[21]

21.17 The CRA and other state institutions are required to follow the regulatory objectives established by the EU Regulatory Framework, including in particular, the promotion of competition in the markets for the electronic communications networks and services as well as associated facilities and services, the protection of user interests, and the development of the internal market.[22] The secondary objectives listed in Article 8 of the Framework Directive, including those newly introduced by the 2009 Regulatory Package, are transposed into the LEC as additional objectives or functions of the CRA.[23]

21.18 The LEC defines the terms of cooperation between the CRA and other state institutions participating in the regulation of electronic communications activities.[24] However, the division of competences is vague, which resulted in a recent court ruling on the interaction of competences of the CRA and the Competition Council.[25] The LEC, therefore, permits the CRA and other state institutions to enter into inter-institutional agreements and to set the specific terms and conditions of the cooperation, which, in turn, helps to ensure a unified practice and avoids overlaps and inconsistencies.[26]

21.19 As required by the revised Article 5(1) of the Framework Directive, the LEC entitles the CRA (and the State Data Protection Inspectorate, within the scope of its competence) to request all information necessary for the performance of its

---

18 Arts 4, 5 LEC. See also Grant of Authorisations for Implementation of the Law on Electronic Communications of the Republic of Lithuania, approved by the Resolution of the Government of the Republic of Lithuania of 6 December 2004, No 1593 (as amended).
19 Arts 4, 12 LEC.
20 Art 7 LEC.
21 See para 21.54 below.
22 Art 1(5) LEC.
23 See paras 1.40–1.44 above. Arts 8, 9 LEC.
24 Art 12 LEC.
25 10 November 2010 ruling of the Supreme Administrative Court of Lithuania in administrative case No A-858-1309-10. In this ruling the court has reaffirmed that the competences of the CRA and the Competition Council may not overlap and there is a need for the regulatory authorities to cooperate.
26 Art 12(12) LEC.

functions, regardless of whether such information is confidential.[27] The information must be provided within a reasonable period of time and be of the level of detail set by the CRA. The CRA must disclose the purpose for which the information is requested and the request must be proportionate and objectively justified. The CRA also must protect confidential information.

21.20   The powers of the CRA are not limited to the right to request information. Subject to the permission of the court, the officials of the CRA, among other things, are entitled to enter into and inspect premises, territories and vehicles used by an undertaking, review documents, and obtain copies and extracts thereof, and gain access to information stored in computers and magnetic media.[28] In urgent cases, such actions may be taken under the decision of the Director of the CRA; such actions, however, subsequently must be confirmed by the court.

21.21   In line with the Framework Directive,[29] the LEC requires the CRA to publish information, conduct public hearings or consultations, and cooperate with other state institutions. For example, the CRA must publish information contributing to an open and competitive market as well as information related to the implementation of the LEC.[30] The CRA also must adopt an extensive list of instances when public hearings or consultations must be conducted, including the terms and conditions for conducting the hearings.[31] Further, article 12 LEC lists a number of cooperation obligations that apply to the network of state institutions participating in the regulation of electronic communications activities.

21.22   The LEC grants the CRA two non-judicial dispute resolution powers. Specifically, the CRA is authorised to issue binding decisions on any dispute between undertakings providing electronic communications networks or services and on any dispute between end users and electronic communications service providers arising under the LEC.[32] While, in the latter case, end users are free to choose between the court and the dispute resolution procedures of the CRA, providers of electronic communications networks or services must bring their matters to the CRA prior to bringing them to court.

21.23   In the case of a dispute between providers of electronic communications network or services, the CRA must render its decision within four months, unless there are exceptional circumstances requiring a longer period. The CRA's decision may be appealed to the court within 14 days. Once the term for appeal expires, the CRA's decision takes effect and becomes binding. The CRA adopts detailed rules of procedure for such cases.[33] If requested, the CRA may also act as a mediator or conciliator. In such a case, the CRA does not issue a binding decision.[34]

---

27   Art 71 LEC.
28   Art 73 LEC.
29   See paras 1.47–1.48 above.
30   Arts 6(5)–6(6) LEC.
31   Rules of Public Consultations on the Decisions of the CRA, approved by the Order of the Director of the CRA of 16 September 2004, No 1V-295 (as amended).
32   Arts 28, 36 LEC.
33   Rules on Resolution of Disputes between Providers of Electronic Communications Networks and/or Services and Disputes between Providers of Postal Services and/or Courier Services, approved by the Order of the Director of the CRA of 21 October 2011, No 1V-1017.
34   Rules on Mediation and/or Reconciliation of Undertakings Providing Electronic Communications Networks and/or Services in order to Resolve Disputes in an Amicable Manner without Issuing Binding Decision, approved by the Order of the Director of the CRA of 11 April 2005, No 1V-354.

21.24   The CRA also adopts detailed rules of procedure for hearing disputes between end users and electronic communications service providers.[35] Once the CRA renders a decision, the parties have 30 days (from the day of its adoption) to appeal the decision to a court of general jurisdiction; in such case, the procedural status of the parties does not change. As in the case of a dispute between providers, upon expiration of the term for the appeal, the decision takes effect and becomes binding.

Right of Appeal against NRA's Decisions

21.25   Any person who feels that his or her rights or interests are affected by the action or inaction of the CRA may file an appeal in the administrative court.[36] The filling of an appeal does not suspend the legal act, unless the court decides otherwise. However, the suspension of the validity of legal act is rather rare and the practice of suspension often inconsistent.

21.26   Additionally, the LEC provides for the right to appeal to the Director of the CRA against illegal actions of its officials, thus giving an opportunity to resolve a matter without going through the court procedure.[37] An appeal must be filed within 10 days after learning about the actions, and the Director must adopt a decision on the appeal within 10 days of its filing. The matter may be taken to court if no decision is adopted or a person disagrees with it.

The NRA's Obligations to Co-operate with the Commission

21.27   In line with the Framework Directive, article 13 LEC imposes an obligation on the CRA to cooperate with the EU institutions, BEREC, other EU Member States, and their national regulatory authorities as required under the EU legal acts and mutual agreements. Both the consolidation and the co-regulation procedures are reflected in the LEC, as well as the Commission's power to stipulate standards and specifications, and to issue recommendations.

21.28   Article 7(3)–(9) of the Framework Directive was implemented into the LEC by closely mirroring the consultation and veto procedures established therein.[38] A similar approach has been taken in respect to the new Article 7a of the Framework Directive, which was introduced by the 2009 Regulatory Framework and which provides for a co-regulation procedure.[39]

21.29   The LEC also reflects the Commission's power to stipulate standards and specifications. It does not, however, recognise their automatic application (ie without a separate decision of the CRA or other state institution).[40] As required by Article 19 of the Framework Directive, the LEC requires state institutions to

---

35   Rules on Resolution of Disputes between End Users and Providers of Electronic Communications Services and Disputes between Users and Providers of Postal Services and/or Courier Services, approved by the Order of the Director of the CRA of 21 October 2011, No 1V-1015.
36   Art 6 LEC.
37   Art 73 LEC.
38   Arts 16(12)–(13), (17)–(18) LEC.
39   Arts 16(14)–(17) LEC.
40   Art 27 LEC.

consider the Commission's recommendations and, if such recommendations are not followed, to inform, and give reasons to, the Commission.[41]

'Significant Market Power' as Fundamental Prerequisite of Regulation

Definition of SMP

21.30   The LEC's definition of SMP is identical to that in Article 14(2) of the Framework Directive.[42] The LEC also adopts the concept of joint dominance and the concept of a closely related market without deviating from the Framework Directive.[43] Generally, in practice, the CRA has closely followed the Commission's recommendations and guidelines and the practice of the European courts in assessing whether an undertaking has significant market power.[44]

Definition of relevant markets

21.31   Undertakings are designated to have SMP by an individual decision of the CRA, subject to a prior market analysis.[45] The CRA engages in a market analysis in three cases:

  (i)   upon adoption of the recommendation on relevant product and service markets;
  (ii)   upon adoption of the decision on the EU market; or
  (iii) upon revision of these legal acts.[46]

It may also engage in a market analysis at its own initiative, at the request of the interested undertakings, or at the request of the state or municipal institutions. The CRA approves detailed rules and procedures for conducting market analyses.[47]

21.32   The stages of market analysis set by the LEC and the Rules on Market Analysis are in line with those provided by Article 16 of the Framework Directive.[48] Under the LEC, during all stages of the market analysis, the CRA must follow local laws and regulations and the EU law, and strongly consider the Commission's guidelines and recommendations as well as BEREC's opinions and common positions.[49] The CRA also has the right to consult the Competition Council but must always receive the opinion of the Competition Council in cases where its market definition differs from that of the Commission.[50]

---

41   Art 1(4) LEC. See also Art 16(6) LEC.
42   Art 15(1) LEC.
43   Art 15(1), (2) LEC.
44   See paras 1.63–1.71 above.
45   Art 15(3) LEC.
46   Art 16(3)–(4) LEC.
47   Rules on Market Analysis, approved by the Order of the Director of the CRA of 17 September 2004, No 1V-297 (as amended).
48   Art 16(2) LEC; see paras 1.72–1.77 above.
49   Art 16(6) LEC.
50   Art 16(7) LEC.

21.33   In line with the 2009 Regulatory Package, the LEC has introduced mandatory time limits for the CRA's market analysis procedures.[51] In addition, article 16(11) LEC requires that such market analysis procedures be completed within
four months (which does not include time for consultation and veto procedures).[52]
While the CRA has the right to prolong the period, it must attempt to complete the
market analysis within the shortest time possible.

Imposition of remedies

21.34   Once the CRA determines that competition on a relevant market is not
effective, it must identify undertakings with significant market power and impose
appropriate remedies.[53] Since implementation of the 2009 Regulatory Package, the
CRA has no discretion to choose whether to impose such remedies.[54] In exceptional
cases, and only with the approval of the Commission, the CRA may impose access
and interconnection obligations on SMP undertakings beyond those provided by
the LEC.[55]

NRA's Regulatory Duties concerning Rights of Way, Co-location and Facility Sharing

Rights of way

21.35   As a general rule, providers of electronic communications networks may
install electronic communications infrastructure on the land owned by them, for
which servitude has been established, or where the providers have the right to use it
on any other basis without changing the purpose of the land.[56] The CRA adopts
detailed rules regulating installation, protection, sharing, maintenance and use of
electronic communications networks.[57]

21.36   Every natural person or legal entity, upon coordination with the State or
municipal institutions, is entitled to use state and municipal roads, squares, pipe-
lines, waters and their coasts, bridges, viaducts, tunnels and other constructions for
building of public communications networks. While such use is free of charge, upon
completion of the work, the roads and other constructions must be reinstated at the
expense of the public communications networks owner.[58]

21.37   If the provider of public communications networks is not able to build the
network either through joint effort with other persons or through infrastructure
sharing,[59] and the negotiations with the owners of the property fail, the provider of
public communications networks may apply to the court for servitude.[60] The
servitude may be placed on state, municipal or private property, if the court

---

51   Art 16(9) LEC; see para 1.77 above.
52   See paras 21.27–21.29 above.
53   See para 1.62 above.
54   Art 17(1), (7) LEC.
55   Art 17(4) LEC.
56   Art 37(1) LEC.
57   Rules on Installation, Marking, Maintenance and Use of Electronic Communications Net-
     work, approved by the Order of the Director of the CRA of 14 October 2011, No 1V-978.
58   Art 38 LEC.
59   See paras 21.38–21.40 below.
60   Art 40 LEC.

considers that this would not constitute an undue burden for the owner. The court must set a reasonable price for the use of such property.

Co-location and facility sharing

21.38   Persons who build electronic communications networks must make public information about the start of construction works and the possibilities for other persons to jointly build electronic communications networks.[61] The CRA, however, following public consultation with interested parties, may also request the person building electronic communications networks to offer the possibility for other persons to participate in construction sharing.

21.39   Moreover, a person controlling electronic communications infrastructure must permit infrastructure sharing, if:

(i)   a potential user of the electronic communications infrastructure cannot realise the right to install the necessary electronic communications infrastructure or the costs of realisation of such a right are disproportionately high; and

(ii)   such sharing is cost-efficient and does not require significant additional work.[62]

Any refusal to permit infrastructure sharing must be reasoned, and made in writing.

21.40   The procedure and conditions for shared use of electronic communications infrastructure must be established in a contract between the person controlling and the person planning to use the respective infrastructure. Detailed rules address handling requests for infrastructure sharing and concluding contracts.[63] The user of the electronic communications infrastructure must pay a reasonable fee to the person whose infrastructure is being used.

REGULATION OF MARKET ENTRY: THE AUTHORISATION DIRECTIVE

The General Authorisation of Electronic Communications

21.41   In line with the Authorisation Directive, electronic communications activities may be provided without any prior licence or permit in Lithuania ('general authorisation'). Nevertheless, the CRA approves a list of activities requiring prior notification:[64]

●   provision of public fixed telephone networks and/or public fixed telephone services;

---

61   Art 37(3) LEC. Presently, there are no detailed rules established on construction sharing; however, discussions are going on between the CRA and market participants on the subject.

62   Rules on Installation, Marking, Maintenance and Use of Electronic Communications Network, approved by the Order of the Director of the CRA of 14 October 2011, No 1V-978.

63   Rules on Installation, Marking, Maintenance and Use of Electronic Communications Network, approved by the Order of the Director of the CRA of 14 October 2011, No 1V-978. Disputes between the controller and user of electronic communications infrastructure are heard by the CRA: see paras 21.22–21.23 above.

64   Art 29(3) LEC; General Terms and Conditions for Engaging in Electronic Communications Activities, approved by the Order of the Director of the CRA of 8 April 2005, No 1V-340 (as amended).

- provision of public mobile telephone networks and/or public mobile telephone services;
- provision of public communications networks and/or public electronic communications services by using communications systems ensured through power lines;
- provision of public satellite communications networks and/or public satellite communications services;
- provision of call transfer services.[65]

The CRA must confirm receipt of the notification, and inform the provider whether it complies with the set requirements, within seven days of such receipt.[66] Upon request of the provider, the CRA must also issue a standardised declaration, as specified in Article 9 of the Authorisation Directive.[67]

21.42 Rights deriving from, and conditions which are (or may be) attached to, the general authorisation generally correspond to those provided in Article 4 of the Authorisation Directive and in the Annex to the Authorisation Directive.[68] The specific obligations for SMP providers as well as providers of universal services are legally separate from the rights and obligations under the general authorisation.

Rights of Use for Radio Frequencies

Strategic planning and co-ordination of spectrum policy

21.43 The CRA focuses, in particular, on efficient use and management of radio frequencies.[69] In addition, recently, the CRA has focused its efforts on compliance with EU radio spectrum harmonisation measures. For example, the CRA implemented the amended GSM Directive and other harmonisation decisions.[70] In accordance with Article 8a of the Framework Directive, the CRA, in strategic planning, coordination, and harmonisation of radio spectrum use in the EU, is actively cooperating with other Member States, the Commission, and other countries.

Principles of frequency allocation, procedural rules

21.44 The LEC sets a special regime for allocation of radio frequencies. Use of radio frequencies is subject to a general authorisation, unless the law prescribes that specific radio frequencies may be used only with an individual authorization

---

65 Undertakings providing public and commercial telephone services independently of the technology or the networks (including Internet) used for provision of services, in case the services are offered as an alternative to the publicly available telephone services existing on the market, shall be considered as providing public fixed or public mobile telephone services and thus shall be subject to notification requirement.
66 Art 29(5) LEC.
67 Art 29(6) LEC; see para 1.94 above.
68 General Terms and Conditions for Engaging in Electronic Communications Activities, approved by the Order of the Director of the CRA of 8 April 2005, No 1V-340 (as amended).
69 See Annual Report of 2010, CRA, 2010.
70 See paras 1.105 and 1.108 above.

(permit).[71] In the latter case, and subject to the conditions provided by the LEC, the authorisations may be issued:

(i)   directly to a person applying for them;
(ii)   by tender; or
(iii) by auction.[72]

The CRA has adopted detailed rules on the assignment and use of radio frequencies.[73] Radio frequencies must be also assigned in accordance with the National Radio Frequency Allocation Table.[74]

Transferability and time limitations

21.45   Article 57 LEC allows for the transfer and lease of the rights to use radio frequencies, unless such radio frequencies are intended for broadcasting (rebroadcasting) of radio and/or television programmes or for other pre-defined special needs (national defence, national security, and maintenance of public order, among others). The CRA has adopted detailed procedures for transfer or lease of such rights.[75] Provisions regarding time limitations on the use of radio frequencies closely follow those in the Authorisation Directive.[76]

Admissible conditions

21.46   The LEC adopts the same list of conditions as specified in Part B of the Annex to the Authorisation Directive and requires that such conditions be non-discriminatory, proportionate, and transparent.[77] For individual authorisations, the CRA may impose obligations related to network build-out, geographical coverage, and quality, among other things, particularly when such obligations result from a tender or auction.

Limitation of number of rights of use to be granted

21.47   As a general rule, the number of authorisations for use of radio frequencies is unlimited. However, in accordance with the Authorisation Directive, the CRA may limit the number of such authorisations when necessary to ensure the effective use of radio frequencies.[78] In such cases, the CRA must follow substantive and procedural rules that correspond to those provided in Article 7 of the Authorization

---

71   Art 50(2) LEC.
72   Arts 5255 LEC; Rules on Assignment of Electronic Communications Resources by Auction, approved by the Order of the CRA of 28 September 2005, No 1V-824 (as amended); Rules on Assignment of Electronic Communications Resources by Tender, approved by the Order of the CRA of 13 September 2005, No 1V-777 (as amended). See also para 21.47 below.
73   Rules on Assignment and Use of Radio Frequencies (Channels), approved by the Order of the Director of the CRA of 6 October 2005, No 1V-854 (as amended).
74   National Radio Frequency Allocation Table, approved by the Order of the Director of the CRA of 24 December 2008, No 1V-1160 (as amended).
75   Rules on Assignment and Use of Radio Frequencies (Channels), approved by the Order of the Director of the CRA of 6 October 2005, No 1V-854 (as amended).
76   See para 1.111 above.
77   Art 58(1), (2) LEC.
78   Art 51(5) LEC; see para 1.113 above.

Directive, including the obligation to grant the rights of use for radio frequencies on the basis of a tender or auction.[79]

Rights of Use for Numbers

General authorisations and granting of individual rights

21.48 As in the case of radio frequencies, the LEC sets a special regime for allocation of telephone numbers. In practice, however, the use of telephone numbers is subject to an individual authorisation (permit) issued by the CRA, unless the law prescribes that specific telephone numbers (eg specific short numbers) may be used without such an authorisation (ie provides for a general authorisation).[80] Telephone numbers are allocated in accordance with the National Telephone Numbering Plan[81] and in accordance with the CRA's rules on allocation and use of telephone numbers.[82]

21.49 Individual authorisations to use telephone numbers (except service numbers and telephone numbers designated for non-telecommunication service providers and non-telecommunications services) may only be issued to providers having the right to provide a public fixed (or mobile) telephone network or publicly available fixed (or mobile) telephone services. Such authorisations may be issued:

(i) directly to the person applying for them;
(ii) by tender (in case of social service numbers); or
(iii) by auction (in case of more than one application (e.g. numbers of exceptional economic value)).[83]

21.50 A telephone number may be transferred upon application to the CRA, but not earlier than one year from its allocation. This time constraint is not applicable when complying with number portability obligations (in such case there is also no need to apply to the CRA for approval) or when transferring the telephone number to the subscriber (in the case of refusal of publicly available telephone services). Transfer of the telephone number is also exempt from any requirement to make public the application for the transfer.

Admissible conditions

21.51 The list of conditions which may be attached to the authorisation to use telephone numbers closely corresponds to the list provided by Part C of the Annex to the Authorization Directive.[84] The LEC also requires that such conditions be applied in a non-discriminatory, proportionate, and transparent manner.

---

79 Art 51 LEC; see para 1.113 above. See also para 21.44 above.
80 Art 50(2) LEC.
81 National Telephone Numbering Plan, approved by the Order of the Director of the CRA of 13 December 2005, No 1V-1104 (as amended).
82 Rules on Allocation and Use of Telephone Number, approved by the Order of the Director of the CRA of 13 December 2005, No 1V-1104 (as amended).
83 Arts 52–55 LEC; see para 21.44 above.
84 Art 58(3) LEC; see para 1.117 of the EU Law Chapter. For obligations related to number portability and carrier (pre-) selection, see paras 21.67 and 21.88–21.91 below.

Limitation of number of rights of use to be granted

21.52   As in the case of radio frequencies, the number of authorisations for use of telephone numbers is unlimited, except when such numbers have an exclusive economic value or they are scarce.[85] In such cases, procedural rules similar to those applicable to the grant of authorisations for use of radio frequencies apply.[86]

The NRA's Enforcement Powers

21.53   The CRA's enforcement powers, including the power to request information and the power to ensure compliance with the conditions of the authorisations, are generally in line with those provided by the Authorisation Directive.[87] They are equally applied with respect to individual authorisations and general authorisations. Financial penalties may reach 5 per cent of the undertaking's annual gross income from activities associated with electronic communications or, if it is difficult or impossible to calculate the volume of such activity, approximately €145,000. While the CRA actively enforces rules, the number of economic sanctions imposed is generally low.[88]

Administrative Charges and Fees for Rights of Use

21.54   A large part of the CRA's budget is comprised of revenues from one-time or periodic (monthly) charges which are paid by market participants for the services and work the CRA provides.[89] For example, charges are set for the supervision of compliance with the conditions for electronic communications activities and for the supervision of use of radio frequencies and telephone numbers, among others.[90] The CRA sets specific charges, based on amounts, formula, and coefficients.[91]

Transitional Regulations for Existing Authorisations

21.55   Where necessary, laws and regulations provide for transition provisions to comply with Article 17(1) and (2) of the Authorisation Directive.

REGULATION OF NETWORK ACCESS AND INTERCONNECTION: IMPLEMENTATION: THE ACCESS DIRECTIVE

Objectives and Scope of Access Regulation

21.56   Through regulation of access and interconnection, the CRA seeks to promote efficiency, sustainable competition, efficient investment and innovation, all

---

85   Art 51(5) LEC.
86   See paras 21.47 and 21.49 above.
87   Arts 71–76 LEC; see paras 1.1191.125 above.
88   See Annual Report of 2010, CRA, 2010.
89   Art 6(3) LEC.
90   Terms and Conditions for Payment for Services and Works provided by the CRA, approved by the Order of the Director of the CRA of 7 April 2011, No 1V-367 (as amended).
91   Payment Tariffs for Services and Works provided by the CRA, approved by the Order of the Director of the CRA of 7 April 2011, No 1V-367 (as amended).

of which benefit end users.[92] Such regulation applies to undertakings that provide, or are authorised to provide, public communications networks or associated facilities, as well as to undertakings seeking interconnection of, or access to, such networks or associated facilities.[93]

Basic Regulatory Concepts

21.57   In general, all basic regulatory concepts, including the definitions of 'access' and 'interconnection', and the majority of other provisions related to access and interconnection (for example, with regard to regulatory powers of the CRA), were transposed verbatim from the Access Directive to the LEC.[94]

21.58   In line with the Access Directive, the provisions of the LEC do not discriminate between undertakings negotiating for access or interconnection in the same Member State or in different Member States, and establish a rather clear priority for commercial negotiations over regulatory intervention.[95]

Access- and Interconnection-related Obligations with Respect to SMP Undertakings

21.59   As required by Article 8(1) of the Access Directive, with regard to the regulation of access and interconnection for SMP undertakings, the CRA may impose obligations provided in Articles 9 to 13a of the Access Directive.[96] In so doing, the CRA must observe the basic regulatory principles, most of which are set out in the Access Directive.[97]

Obligations of transparency

21.60   In line with Article 9(1) of the Access Directive, to ensure efficient access and interconnection, the CRA may require SMP operators to publish access- and interconnection-related information.[98] The list of examples of such information corresponds to the list provided in the Access Directive.[99] The LEC also grants the CRA other powers established by Article 9 of the Access Directive, and the CRA approves detailed provisions on the implementation of these obligations.[100]

---

92   Art 22(2) LEC.
93   Art 22(1), (6) LEC.
94   Art 22 LEC; see paras 1.133–1.142 above.
95   Art 22(1) LEC. The LEC also sets obligations with regard to wide-screen television services and confidentiality during negotiations; see paras 1.139–1.140 above.
96   Art 17(1) LEC.
97   Art 17 LEC; see para 21.34 above; see also paras 1.146–1.147 above.
98   Art 18 LEC.
99   See paras 1.148–1.151 above.
100 Rules on Provision of Access and Interconnection, approved by the Order of the Director of the CRA of 10 October 2011, No 1V-960.

Obligations of non-discrimination

21.61   The LEC's non-discrimination obligation mirrors the obligation in Article 10 of the Access Directive.[101] Additionally, the LEC requires that the CRA impose obligations of non-discrimination in all cases in which such obligations are necessary to ensure that vertically integrated undertakings controlled by the State or municipalities, providing electronic communications networks established subject to the exclusive or special rights, and which have SMP in the relevant market, do not discriminate against other undertakings resulting in advantages to their own activities.

Specific obligations of access

21.62   The non-exhaustive list of specific obligations of access which the CRA may impose upon SMP undertakings matches the list provided in Article 12(1) of the Access Directive.[102] The LEC also transposes the factors which the NRAs must consider when assessing whether access obligations comply with the principle of proportionality. The CRA has issued detailed rules on access and interconnection, including technical and operational conditions, which the providers or beneficiaries of such access must meet.[103]

Price control and cost accounting obligations

21.63   The LEC's provisions on obligations relating to cost recovery and price controls, including obligations for cost orientation and accounting systems, are consistent with Article 13 of the Access Directive.[104] The CRA ensures cost orientation of prices using the following cost-accounting methods: Fully Distributed Cost (FDC)[105] and Long Run Average Incremental Cost (LRAIC) (using price-caps).[106]

Obligation of accounting separation

21.64   Article 20 LEC sets out the obligation of accounting separation in a general manner, by stating that the CRA may require an operator having SMP in the relevant market to keep separate accounting of the activity or activities related to access. The CRA approves specific rules on accounting separation and related requirements.[107]

---

101 Art 19 LEC.
102 Art 21 LEC. For more information on the obligations related to carrier (pre-) selection, see para 21.67 below.
103 Rules on Provision of Access and Interconnection, approved by the Order of the Director of the CRA of 10 October 2011, No 1V-960.
104 Art 23 LEC; Rules for cost accounting according to the fully distributed costs method, approved by the Order of the Director of the CRA of 28 December 2005, No 1V-1164 (as amended); see also paras 1.157–1.161 above.
105 Rules for cost accounting according to the fully distributed costs method, approved by the Order of the Director of the CRA of 28 December 2005, No 1V-1164 (as amended).
106 For more information on cost accounting, price control and accounting separation by markets, see http://rrt.lt/en/for-business/promotion-of-competition/regulatory-accounting-and-6a63.html (accessed on 13 December 2012).
107 Rules on Accounting Separation and Related Requirements, approved by the Order of the Director of the CRA of 14 June 2006, No 1V-738 (as amended); see paras 1.162–1.163 above.

Obligation to implement functional separation

21.65 Consistent with Articles 13a and 13b of the Access Directive introduced by the 2009 Regulatory Package, the LEC delegates to the CRA authority to impose the obligation on undertakings to implement functional separation, and imposes an obligation on vertically integrated undertakings having SMP to notify the CRA about any voluntary separation.[108] As in the case with most obligations described above, the related rights and obligations of the CRA are identical to those mandated by the Access Directive.

Imposition of obligations in practice

21.66 Access- and interconnection-related obligations have been imposed on a number of SMP undertakings in Lithuania in the markets defined by the Commission in 2003 and 2007.[109] The CRA regularly publishes the complete list of the SMP undertakings, and the respective obligations imposed on them.[110]

Regulatory Powers with Respect to SMP Undertakings

21.67 Since transposition of the 2009 Regulatory Package, in addition to the access and interconnection obligations mentioned above, the CRA may impose on undertakings having SMP for the provision of connection to and use of the public telephone network at a fixed location the obligation to provide access to the services of any interconnected provider of publicly available telephone services.[111] Access prices must be cost-oriented; for this purpose, the CRA may set the price caps.

Regulatory Powers Applicable to All Market Participants

Obligations to ensure end-to-end connectivity

21.68 Consistent with Article 5(1), sub-para 2(a) of the Access Directive, the CRA may impose obligations ensuring end-to-end connectivity on undertakings controlling access to end users (regardless of their market position), including the

---

108 Arts 23–1, 23–2 LEC; see also paras 1.164–1.166 above.

109 Commission Recommendation 2003/311/EC of 11 February 2003 on relevant product and service markets within the electronic communications sector susceptible to ex ante regulation in accordance with Directive 2002/21/EC of the European Parliament and of the Council on a common regulatory framework for electronic communication networks and services [2003] OJ L114/45; Commission Recommendation 2007/879/EC of 17 December 2007 on relevant product and service markets within the electronic communications sector susceptible to ex ante regulation in accordance with Directive 2002/21/EC of the European Parliament and of the Council on a common regulatory framework for electronic communications networks and services [2007] OJ L344/65.

110 List of Markets and Undertakings having SMP, and Obligations Imposed on them, approved by the Order of the Director of the CRA of 9 September 2010, No 1V-897. For the up-to-date list of SMP undertakings, including obligations imposed on them, see http://rrt.lt/en/for-business/promotion-of-competition/undertakings-having-significant-kv81.html (accessed on 13 December 2012).

111 Art 33 LEC; Terms and Conditions for Ensuring Subscriber's Right to Access Services of Any Publicly Available Telephone Service Provider, approved by the Order of the Director of the CRA of 28 November 2005, No 1V-1037 (as amended).

obligation to interconnect networks.[112] Similarly, in accordance with Article 5(1), sub-para 2(ab) of the Access Directive, the CRA may impose interoperability requirements on undertakings controlling access to end users.[113] The CRA may also impose other requirements on undertakings controlling access to end users.

Regulation of Roaming Services

21.69   Under the Roaming Regulation, which does not require any transposition, operators must observe the maximum prices set for the regulated roaming services and must comply with related requirements.[114]

Access to digital radio and television broadcasting services

21.70   To the extent necessary to ensure that end users may access specified digital radio and television broadcasting services, the CRA may also impose obligations on operators (regardless of their market position) to provide access to the Application Programming Interfaces and Electronic Programme Guides on fair, reasonable and non-discriminatory terms.[115]

21.71   Pursuant to article 25 LEC, conditional access systems, operators of conditional access services, and holders of industrial property rights to conditional access products and systems must meet requirements identical to those set out in Part I, Annex I Access Directive. The CRA has reserved the right to establish more detailed rules for the implementation of these requirements.[116]

21.72   Owners of Application Programming Interfaces must disclose, against due remuneration, and on fair, reasonable, and non-discriminatory conditions, any information necessary for digital television service providers to provide, in a fully functional manner, all services supported by such Application Programming Interfaces (including services for disabled end users).[117]

REGULATION OF UNIVERSAL SERVICE AND USERS' RIGHTS: THE UNIVERSAL SERVICE DIRECTIVE

Regulation of Universal Service Obligations

Scope of universal service obligations

21.73   The following minimum set of services of specified quality must be available to all end users requesting them, regardless of their geographical location, and at an affordable price (ie universal services):[118]

---

112   Art 22(2)(1) LEC.
113   Art 22(2)(3) LEC.
114   See para 1.30 above.
115   Art 22(2)(2) LEC.
116   Art 25(3), (5) LEC.
117   Art 27(6) LEC.
118   Art 31(1) LEC. With respect to broadband access, under art 37 LEC, the State may develop a broadband communications infrastructure in areas where there is no such infrastructure or where there is no competition in the provision of broadband communications services.

- connection to the public fixed communications network and provision of publicly available fixed telephone services;
- publicly available telephone services over pay telephones or in other public places;
- information on subscribers of publicly available telephone services;
- universal services for disabled users.

21.74   The CRA approves rules for the provision of universal services regulating their scope, quality, procedures and conditions for provision of such services, the procedures, conditions, and cases for imposition of universal services obligations on providers of electronic communications services, and rules for the provision of information about the quality of the services.[119]

Designation of undertakings obliged to provide universal services

21.75   Public electronic communications service providers designated by the CRA as universal services providers or as having SMP in the market for connection to the public fixed telephone network must provide universal services.[120] Other providers may apply to the CRA (upon their own initiative or in response to an invitation by the CRA) for the provision of universal services without compensation. The CRA may also impose obligations on providers which are not designated as universal services providers, if it is necessary for proper provision of universal services. When designating universal services providers, the CRA must follow the regulatory principles established by the LEC. To date, only the incumbent TEO LT, AB must provide universal services in Lithuania.

Regulation of retail tariffs, users' expenditures and quality of service

21.76   Designated universal services providers, must, among other things, ensure that:

- their prices are not dependent on the geographic location of the user and do not exceed the price caps set for universal services;
- the users of public electronic communications services are given transparent and updated information on the prices, tariffs, and conditions for the use of universal services; and
- the service quality complies with the requirements for the quality of universal services.[121]

Retail tariffs for universal services are also subject to the price control and cost accounting obligations that are applicable to SMP operators.

---

119   Art 31(3) LEC. Rules on Provision of Universal Electronic Communications Services ('Rules on Universal Services'), approved by the Order of the Director of the CRA of 20 September 2011, No 1V-889.
120   Rules on Universal Services, approved by the Order of the Director of the CRA of 20 September 2011, No 1V-889.
121   Rules on Universal Services, approved by the Order of the Director of the CRA of 20 September 2011, No 1V-889. Requirements for quality of universal services are set by the Regulation on Requirements for Quality of Universal Services, approved by the Order of the Director of the CRA of 15 February 2006, No 1V-214 (as amended) and other legal acts. Price caps for universal services are set by the Price Caps of Electronic Communications Services, approved by the Resolution of the Government of Lithuania of 27 October 2011, No 1248.

Cost calculation and financing of universal services

21.77   Providers of universal services may request compensation for loss associ-ated with the provision of universal services, if such services can only be provided at a loss and would constitute an 'unfair burden'.[122] The loss is calculated pursuant to the methodology approved by the CRA,[123] and is financed from the funds of publicly available telephone service providers which meet certain conditions, or from other sources determined by the Government. As an additional measure, the LEC allows for the reconsideration of the set price caps.

Regulation of Retail Markets

Prerequisites for the regulation of retail markets

21.78   In cases where the CRA considers that 'traditional' SMP obligations (on wholesale markets) are insufficient, it must impose additional obligations on SMP undertakings in relevant retail markets.[124] Market analysis is a prerequisite, and regulation of the retail market is permissible only if regulation at the wholesale level does not result in achievement of regulatory objectives. Imposition of these obligations must be reasonable in the light of the particular problem, and propor-tionate and justifiable with respect to the particular objectives.

Regulatory powers

21.79   The LEC includes a list of examples of remedies available to the CRA which corresponds to the list provided in Article 17(2) of the Universal Service Directive.[125] The LEC also grants the right to the CRA to regulate end user tariffs by taking regulatory measures provided in the same article. These regulatory measures are complemented by mandatory rules regarding the implementation of cost accounting systems.[126] To date, retail market obligations are imposed on the incumbent TEO LT, AB and covers markets from 1 to 7 as defined by the Commission in 2003.[127]

---

122   Art 31(2), (5) LEC; Rules on Compensation of Losses Associated with Provision of Universal Electronic Communications Services, approved by the Resolution of the Government of Lithuania of 27 October 2011, No 1248.

123   Art 31(5) LEC; Rules on Calculation of Losses Associated with Provision of Universal Electronic Communications Services, approved by the Order of the Director of the CRA of 28 April 2006, No 1V-574.

124   Art 32(1) LEC.

125   Art 32(1) LEC.

126   Art 32(2) LEC. See para 1.189 above.

127   Commission Recommendation 2003/311/EC [2003] OJ L114/45.

End User Rights

Contracts: obligation to contract and minimum standards

21.80   Pursuant to the LEC, both consumers and end users may enter into a contract for the provision of electronic communications services.[128] While the law differentiates between consumers and end users, in practice this differentiation is far less evident. All end users are treated equally, without differentiating between SMEs and large business customers, mainly because currently there is no social need for such differentiation.

21.81   The CRA establishes minimum requirements for contracts,[129] and, in some cases, these requirements go beyond those contained in Article 20(1) Universal Services Directive, as revised by the 2009 Regulatory Package.[130]

21.82   Generally, subscribers (consumers and end users) have the right to terminate their contracts at any time with a reasonable notice; the consequences of termination, however, differ depending on the type of the contract (indefinite term contract or fixed term contract). As provided by Article 20(4) Universal Service Directive, subscribers may withdraw from their contracts without penalty if the provider modifies the terms and conditions of the contract, including the prices, or materially breaches the contract.

Transparency obligations

21.83   Providers of publicly available electronic communications services must publish transparent, comparable, adequate, and current information on applicable prices and tariffs, any charges due in connection with contract termination, on standard terms and conditions of provision of services, and on quality of services, among other things.[131] The CRA approves the detailed list of information to be published in accordance with this rule.[132] The rule applies equally with respect to services provided to consumers and end users.

Quality of Service: securing 'Net Neutrality'

21.84   The CRA may impose minimum quality of service requirements on public electronic communications network providers;[133] to date, however, it has not imposed any such requirements.[134] Likewise, to date, it has not adopted any other regulatory instruments specifically targeted to secure net neutrality. Due to the increasing amount of data being transmitted over the networks, however, such

---

128   Art 34(1) LEC.
129   Rules on Provision of Public Electronic Communications Services, approved by the Order of the Director of the CRA of 23 December 2005, No 1V-1160 (as amended).
130   See para 1.194 above.
131   Art 34(2) LEC.
132   Rules on Provision of Public Electronic Communications Services, approved by the Order of the Director of the CRA of 23 December 2005, No 1V-1160 (as amended).
133   Art 34(3) LEC.
134   The Rules on Provision of Public Electronic Communications Services, approved by the Order of the Director of the CRA of 23 December 2005, No 1V-1160 (as amended), however, include some quality-related provisions. Quality of service requirements are also set for universal services, see para 21.76 above.

practices as blocking or throttling of traffic are becoming increasingly popular among providers in Lithuania. Therefore, the CRA is likely to focus on this area in the future.

European emergency call number

21.85   Providers of public electronic communications networks or publicly available electronic communications services must ensure that subscribers or users, including public pay phone users and disabled subscribers or end users, are able to use emergency services (by using the number 112 and other national emergency numbers).[135] Use of emergency services must be free of charge (ie not requiring any form of payment) and without the requirement to use personal identification numbers (PIN), codes or cards; they must be available regardless of whether the provision of services has been restricted (in the case of public mobile telephone services, on any public mobile communications network); and they must be available in all cases as long as technically feasible.[136]

21.86   The CRA adopts other terms and conditions for provision of access to emergency services.[137] For example, providers of public electronic communications networks or publicly available electronic communications services must transmit to emergency services the telephone numbers of the subscribers or users making the call and the location data (including traffic data) of the caller's terminal equipment.[138] Moreover, they must establish reserve communications routes of sufficient capacity for direction of calls to other emergency services in the case of breakdowns in the public communications network, and give absolute and immediate priority to communications with emergency services, among other things.

Other obligations

21.87   Providers of electronic communications networks or services must also secure functioning of the public electronic communications networks and services in the case of catastrophic network failure or force majeure, and in other extraordinary circumstances.[139] They must give absolute and immediate priority to communications with emergency services, institutions servicing emergency calls, and with other selected organisations. The CRA adopts the terms and conditions for the implementation of these obligations.[140] In addition, the LEC sets the obligations related to directory enquiry services, additional facilities, among others.

---

135   Art 34(10) LEC.
136   Terms and Conditions for Access to Services Provided by Emergency Service Providers by Subscribers and/or Users, approved by the Order of the Director of the CRA of 7 November 2011, No 1V-1087.
137   Terms and Conditions for Access to Services Provided by Emergency Service Providers by Subscribers and/or Users, approved by the Order of the Director of the CRA of 7 November 2011, No 1V-1087.
138   Lithuania has experienced some difficulties with the provision of caller location information to emergency services, see EU telecoms rules: Commission takes steps to ensure that emergency services can locate callers (IP/06/464) (6 June 2006).
139   Art 78 LEC.
140   Rules on Priorities of Telecommunications, approved by the Order of the Director of the CRA of 13 June 2006, No 1V-736 (as amended); Priorities for Securing the Functioning of Public Communications Networks and Services in cases of Catastrophic Network Failure or

Obligations facilitating change of provider

21.88   Providers of public electronic communications networks or publicly available electronic communications services must ensure that subscribers retain their numbers where there is a change of the service provider, the location of service or the way in which the services are provided.[141] They must do so at their own cost and in accordance with the terms and conditions adopted by the CRA.[142] Related access prices must be cost oriented.

21.89

Providers must ensure number portability in the following cases:

- when changing the provider of public fixed telephone services or public mobile telephone services;
- when changing the place of provision of public fixed telephone services;
- when changing the method of provision of public fixed telephone services (from PSTN to the integrated services digital network ('ISDN') and vice versa);
- when changing the method of payment for public mobile telephone services; or
- when changing the method of provision of public mobile telephone services (from the digital mobile cellular communications system ('GSM/DCS') to the universal mobile telecommunications system ('UMTS') and vice versa).

21.90   Under the terms and conditions set forth by the CRA, a donor network or service provider ('donor') must not refuse number portability, except when:

- the data held by the donor about the subscriber wishing to enforce its right to number portability differs from the data provided by the recipient; or
- the donor does not possess the data about such subscriber (unidentified subscribers), if the donor provides the possibility for the subscribers, at no charge, to identify themselves using the Internet.

21.91   Once a subscriber submits an application for number portability, the recipient of such application is responsible for ensuring that a proper basis for number portability exists. The recipient must instruct the Central Database Administrator (a pre-selected undertaking that administers the central data base for number portability) to start the process of porting. During the process, all parties (the donor, the recipient, and the Central Database Administrator) must closely cooperate and exchange information. As required by the revised Universal Service Directive, the process of porting must be completed within one working day.[143] Upon completion thereof, the recipient must inform the subscriber of such completion.

Force Majeure, as well as in other Extraordinary Circumstances, approved by the Order of the Minister of Communications of 3 April 2006, No 3–125.

141   Art 34(11) LEC.

142   Terms and Conditions for Ensuring Subscriber's Right to Retain Subscriber Number when Changing the Provider of Telephone Services or Place and Method of Provision of Services, approved by the Order of the Director of the CRA of 29 April 2011, No 1V-460 (as amended).

143   See paras 1.208–1.209 above.

DATA PROTECTION: THE DIRECTIVE ON PRIVACY AND ELECTRONIC COMMUNICATIONS

Confidentiality of Communications

21.92   The LEC prohibits listening to, tapping, storage or other kinds of interception or surveillance of communications including the related traffic data by persons other than users, without consent of the users concerned.[144] Exceptions to this prohibition correspond to those provided in the E-Privacy Directive: prevention, investigation, detection and prosecution of criminal offences; technical storage; provision of evidence of a commercial transaction; and unauthorised use of electronic communications systems, among others.

21.93   Providers of public electronic communications networks and publicly available electronic communications services are obliged to take appropriate technical and organisational measures to safeguard confidentiality of communications and the related traffic data.[145] The State Data Protection Inspectorate is responsible for the supervision of the implementation of this obligation in accordance with the Rules on Conduct of Confidentiality Assessments.[146]

21.94   Providers of publicly available electronic communications services must also implement appropriate technical and organisational measures to safeguard security of its services, if necessary in conjunction with network providers with respect to the network security.[147] These measures must ensure a level of security appropriate to the risk presented. In the case of a particular risk of breach of network security, network providers or service providers must inform subscribers or registered users.

21.95   In accordance with the E-Privacy Directive, storage of, or access to, information in the terminal equipment is only permitted if the subscriber or user has given his or her consent ('opt-in' rule).[148] Before such consent, they must be provided information specified in Article 10 of the 1995 Directive on the protection of individuals with regard to the processing of personal data and on the free movement of such data.[149] The State Data Inspectorate has issued recommendations in relation to the implementation of this rule.[150]

21.96   The LEC requires providers of publicly available electronic communications services and providers of electronic communications networks to notify the State Data Protection Inspectorate about personal data breaches.[151] National notification requirements are consistent with those provided for in the E-Privacy

---

144   Art 61 LEC.
145   Art 61(3) LEC.
146   Art 61(3) LEC; Rules on Conduct of Confidentiality Assessments, approved by the Resolution of the Government of 20 July 2005, No 807 (as amended).
147   Art 62 LEC.
148   Art 61(4) LEC. The exceptions to this rule are identical to those provided in Article 5(3) of the E-Privacy Directive.
149   Directive 95/46/EC of the European Parliament and of the Council of 24 October 1995 on the protection of individuals with regard to the processing of personal data and on the free movement of such data [1995] OJ L281/31, as amended by Regulation (EC) No 1882/2003 of the European Parliament and of the Council of 29 September 2003 [2003] OJ L284/1.
150   Recommendations for Use of Cookies and Similar Tools (2011), available in Lithuanian at http://www.ada.lt/images/cms/File/naujienu/slapuk_DV.pdf (accessed on 13 December 2012).
151   Art 62(4)–(7) LEC.

Directive. The State Data Protection Authority has issued instructions detailing the notification obligations.[152]

21.97   In light of Article 15a of the E-Privacy Directive, the laws of Lithuania establish rules on penalties applicable to infringements of the provisions adopted pursuant to the E-Privacy Directive. Such rules provide for administrative and criminal sanctions, including the power to order cessation of the infringements and the power to obtain information.[153] In the wider context of enforcement of data protection rules, however, administrative sanctions have been criticised for being too low to be effective and dissuasive.

Data Retention

21.98   The Data Retention Directive is fully transposed into the LEC.[154] The categories of data to be retained and provided to the competent authorities by the public electronic communications network or publicly available electronic communications services providers correspond to those listed in Article 5 of the Data Retention Directive. The data must be retained for six months from the date of the communication, unless there is a request by the competent authority to retain the data for a longer period, which however must not exceed additional six months. The costs related to the retention of data for the additional six months are paid by state funds in accordance with the procedures established by the Government.

Traffic Data and Location Data

21.99   The LEC adopts the definitions of the E-Privacy Directive for traffic data and location data. As a general rule, public electronic communications network or publicly available electronic communications services providers must generate, store, and process only such personal, traffic, and other related data of the subscriber or user needed for the identification of the subscriber/user, provision of services, billing, and payment.[155]

21.100   As provided in the E-Privacy Directive, processing of traffic data for the purpose of marketing electronic communications services or processing of traffic and location data for the provision of value added services is subject to prior consent of the subscriber or registered user.[156]

21.101   Before collection or processing of traffic data or location data and, where applicable, prior to obtaining consent, public electronic communications networks or publicly available electronic communications services providers must inform the subscribers and registered users of electronic communications services about the data processed, the purpose of processing, and the period of processing.[157]

---

152   Rules on Submission of Notification of Personal Data Breach, approved by the Order of the Director of the State Data Protection Inspectorate of 22 July 2011, No 1T-37(1.12).

153   See, eg Art 214–23 Code of Administrative Violations, approved by the Highest Council of the Republic of Lithuania on 13 December 1984 (as amended); Arts 166, 196–198–2 Criminal Code, approved by the Parliament of the Republic of Lithuania on 26 September 2000, No VIII-1968 (as amended); Arts 71–72 LEC.

154   Arts 65, 66, 77 LEC.

155   Art 65 LEC.

156   Arts 66, 68 LEC.

157   Arts 66(2) LEC.

Itemised Billing

21.102   Itemised bills must be presented only with the consent or at the request, of the subscriber. The State Data Protection Inspectorate establishes basic requirements for itemised bills.[158] The requirements currently do not allow for different types of detailed bills (eg in which a certain number of digits of the called number have been deleted).

Presentation and Restriction of Calling and Connected Line Identification

21.103   The provisions of the LEC on presentation and restriction of calling and connected line identification for the most part repeats the respective provisions of the E-Privacy Directive.[159] Service providers and network providers may not impose elimination of the presentation of calling line identification upon application of a subscriber requesting the tracing of malicious or nuisance calls, and regarding specific lines operated by institutions dealing with emergency calls (eg law enforcement agencies, ambulance services, and fire brigades) for the purpose of responding to such calls by the subscriber or the actual user of electronic communications services.

Automatic Call Forwarding

21.104   Service providers must ensure that any subscriber or registered user has the possibility, free of charge and using a simple means, of stopping automatic call forwarding by a third party to the subscriber's or registered user's terminal equipment.[160]

Directories of Subscribers

21.105   Subscribers must be informed, free of charge and before they are included in a printed or electronic directory of subscribers available to the public or obtainable through directory enquiry services, about the purpose of a subscriber directory in which their data can be included, and of any further usage possibilities based on search functions embedded in electronic versions of the directory.[161]

21.106   Subscribers have the right to decide whether their data will be included in a public directory and which personal data meets the purpose of the directory as declared by the provider. Subscribers may also verify, correct, or withdraw such data or request the provider to do so. The decision as to whether to be included in a public directory, and the verifying, correcting or withdrawing of data must be free of charge.[162]

---

158   Art 67(4)–(5) LEC; Requirements for Itemised Bills, approved by the Order of the Director of the State Data Protection Inspectorate of 5 July 2005, No 1T-95.
159   Art 64 LEC.
160   Art 63 LEC.
161   Art 67(1) LEC.
162   Art 67(2) LEC.

21.107   For any purpose of a public directory, other than the search of contact details of persons on the basis of their name, a subscriber's consent for the inclusion of his or her data in such a directory must be obtained.[163]

---

163   Art 67(3) LEC.

The Luxembourg Market for Electronic Communications

Audrey Rustichelli and Raphaël Collin,
Baker & McKenzie, Luxembourg

LEGAL STRUCTURE

Basic policy

22.1 The implementation in Luxembourg of European regulation relating to telecommunications has been a complex process. Indeed, historically, the provision of telecommunications services was controlled by the state administration of Postal and Telecommunications.[1]

The Luxembourg legislator implemented parts of the ONP Directives with the law of 21 March 1997 on telecommunications[2] ('1997 Law'), which initiated the liberalisation of the telecommunications market. The 1997 Law set a new legislative framework for the provision of telecommunications services and networks and completed the separation of regulatory functions and service provision functions with the creation of an independent regulatory authority in charge of monitoring the telecommunications sector.[3]

In implementing the 2002 EU Regulatory Package, the Luxembourg Government, given the fundamental discrepancies existing between the regulatory framework in place and the new European directives, considered it appropriate to repeal the existing legislation in order to implement a consistent set of rules.[4] During the process of implementation of the 2002 Regulatory Package in Luxembourg, the objectives of the Government were to adopt a regulation in line with the new technological challenges and features and adapted to the opening up of the markets. The 2002 Regulatory Package was implemented in Luxembourg with the adoption of the following four laws of 30 May 2005, in force from 1 July 2005 (the '2005 Laws'):

● the law concerning electronic communications networks and services (the '2005 E-Law')[5], which repeals the 1997 Law;

---

1 The P&T Administration.
2 Memorial A, no 18 of 27 March 1997 p 761.
3 Annual report of the Luxembourg Institute of Telecommunications.
4 Chamber of Deputies, Report of the Commission de la fonction publique, no 5178.
5 Memorial A, no 73 of 7 June 2005 p 1144.

- the law concerning the organisation of the management of radio frequencies (the '2005 RF Law');[6]
- the law concerning the organisation of the *Institut Luxembourgeois de Régulation* (ie the Luxembourg Regulatory Institute ('LRI')) (the '2005 LRI Law');[7] and
- the law concerning specific provisions regarding the protection of privacy in relation to the processing of personal data in the electronic communications sector (the '2005 E-Privacy Law').[8]

Implementation of EU Directives

22.2   The Luxembourg Government has always been eager to further develop the telecommunications sector in line with major industry trends and has been active in negotiating and defending the interests of Luxembourg in the adoption process of the 2009 Regulatory Package. Aware of the fact that further adjustment of the 2005 Laws were necessary, due to the increasing convergence between information technology, media and telecommunications, the legislator enacted in 2010 and 2011 a new set of rules implementing the 2009 Regulatory Package. The Luxembourg Government supports the principle of network neutrality through keeping a free architecture, with open and non-discriminatory access without unjustified conditions on electronic communications networks.

Legislation

22.3   Luxembourg's legal provisions on electronic communications consist of the following:

- the law of 27 February 2011 concerning electronic communications networks and services, which repealed the 2005 E-Law (the '2011 E-Law');[9]
- the law of 27 February 2011 amending the law concerning the organisation of the management of radio frequencies (the '2011 RF-Law', the coordinated law being referred to as the 'RF-Law');[10]
- the law of 28 July 2011 amending the law concerning specific provisions regarding the protection of privacy in relation to the processing of personal data in the electronic communications sector (the '2011 E-Privacy Law', the coordinated law being referred to as the 'E-Privacy Law');[11] and
- the law of 26 July 2010 amending the law concerning the organisation of the *Institut Luxembourgeois de Régulation* (the '2010 LRI Law', the coordinated law being referred to as the 'LRI Law').[12]

In addition to the four laws implementing the 2009 Regulatory Package, the Luxembourg legal framework on telecommunications includes the following laws:

---

6   Memorial A, no 73 of 7 June 2005 p 1159.
7   Memorial A, no 73 of 7 June 2005 p 1162.
8   Memorial A, no 73 of 7 June 2005 p 1168.
9   Memorial A, no 43 of 8 March 2011 p 610.
10   Memorial A, no 43 of 29 July 2010 p 630.
11   Memorial A, no 172 of 10 August 2011 p 2938.
12   Memorial A, no 132 of 12 August 2010 p 2184.

- the law of 27 November 1996 approving the Convention for the establishment of the European Radiocommunications Office ('ERO');[13] and
- the law of 8 April 1999 approving the Convention creating the European Telecommunications Office ('ETO').[14]

The telecommunications sector is broad and diversified, with numerous other laws applying to specific aspects of the sector, including, but not limited to:

- the law of 27 July 1991, as amended, on electronic media;[15]
- the law of 14 August 2000, as amended on electronic commerce;[16] and
- the law of 2 August 2002, as amended, regarding the protection of individuals as to the processing of personal data (the 'Data Protection Law'). [17]

The Luxembourg legal framework is also composed of Grand-Ducal regulations, implementing the provisions of the above-listed laws.

REGULATORY PRINCIPLES: THE FRAMEWORK DIRECTIVE

Scope of Regulation

22.4   The provisions of the 2011 E-Law provide for a technology-neutral approach to regulation. The definitions of 'electronic communications network', 'electronic communications service', and 'associated facilities' as contained in the 2011 E-Law, are identical to those contained in the Framework Directive.

Consistent with the Framework Directive, electronic communications networks and services installed and operated by the State for its own needs are excluded from the scope of the 2011 E-Law.

'Internet Freedom'

22.5   There is no specific provision in Luxembourg providing for the imposition of measures that restrict the end user's access to the Internet. So far, there are no plans to implement such measures.

National Regulatory Authorities: Organisation, Regulatory Objectives, Competencies

22.6   The national regulatory authority for Luxembourg is the Luxembourg Regulatory Institute ('LRI'). Created under the 1997 Law, the LRI regulates electronic communications networks and services, as well as the electrical power supply and distribution, natural gas supply and distribution, the rail transport sector, and the postal services sector.[18]

The Luxembourg legislator has deemed it preferable to define the general framework, ie the status, organisation and operational rules of the LRI, in a separate law,

---

13   Memorial A, no 87 of 12 December 1996 p 2468.
14   Memorial A, no 38 of 16 April 1999 p 993.
15   Memorial A, no 47 of 30 July 1991 p 972.
16   Memorial A, no 96 of 8 September 2000 p 2176.
17   Memorial A, no 91 of 13 August 2002 p 1836.
18   Art 2 LRI Law.

given the fact that this regulatory authority is also competent in sectors other than the electronic communications market. This framework is contained in the LRI Law, whereas the 2011 E-Law, RF Law and e-Privacy Law define the LRI's missions with regard to the electronic communications market.

22.7   In principle, the LRI regulates upstream by preventing any hindrance to competition in regulated sectors and freedom of economic activity while the Luxembourg competition authority (*Conseil de la concurrence*) regulates downstream by sanctioning such anti-competitive hindrances.[19] The LRI operates in close cooperation with the Luxembourg competition authority and, if necessary, with the Ministry of Economy and Foreign Trade in charge of consumer protection. The LRI also takes into account the opinion of BEREC.[20] This cooperation results in the LRI's obligation to obtain prior approval from the Luxembourg competition authority for any planned measure concerning the regulation of electronic communications markets,[21] access and interconnection markets[22] and of the right of ways on the public domain.[23] The Luxembourg competition authority has one month to accept, amend, or oppose (based on competition law), the proposed measure.[24]

Notwithstanding the obligation of professional secrecy binding the LRI, its board of directors may share confidential information and documents with supervisory authorities[25].

The LRI is an independent public authority, being a legal person, placed under the authority of the Minister for Media and Communications and it enjoys financial and administrative autonomy.[26] The LRI Law provides that the LRI executes its assignments independently within the limits of regulations and laws.[27]

22.8   The LRI Law has been amended in order to comply with the new requirements of the Framework Directive as amended by the Better Regulation Directive.[28] Specifically, the Grand Duke of Luxembourg no longer has the power to suspend, revoke, or transfer a member of the LRI's board of directors for fundamental disagreement regarding LRI's policy execution of its assignments. The LRI Law stipulates that, during their term of office, members of the board of directors may not be suspended, revoked or transferred except for infirmity or misconduct. In the latter cases, the mandate of the concerned may only be challenged by the LRI's Council after the conduct of hearings with the defendant, and the Council's decision shall be published at the defendant's request.[29]

The 2011 E-Law has transposed all tasks and duties that must be granted to the LRI under the Framework Directive.

The LRI is entrusted with collecting of notifications sent by undertakings planning to provide electronic communications networks and services ('notified undertakings') and maintains a registry of notified undertakings.

---

19   Q&A, Introductory Booklet of the LRI, 2007.
20   Art 76(1) E-Law.
21   Art 17 et seq E-Law.
22   Art 22 et seq E-Law.
23   Art 37 et seq E-Law.
24   Art 76(2) E-Law.
25   Art 15(2) LRI Law and Art 77(3) LRI Law.
26   Art 1 LRI Law.
27   Art 2 LRI Law.
28   Bill of the 2010 LRI Law.
29   Art 11(2) LRI Law.

When necessary to control an undertaking's compliance with the E-2011 Law, the LRI may request specific information from the undertaking, The LRI may also set the deadlines, and the level of detail required, for the provision of such information.[30]

22.9   In the interest of promoting an open and competitive market, the LRI may publish all information provided by undertakings, taking into consideration requirements of business confidentiality.[31] The LRI must periodically consult with relevant notified undertakings, manufacturers, the consumers' representatives, on matters relevant to the market.[32] Before taking a measure which would have a significant impact on the market, however, the LRI must commence a procedure of consultation with all concerned parties, who may, in turn, submit comments on the measure within one month. The LRI must publish a notice of consultation on its website and in the official gazette ('Mémorial'). The LRI website must also provide information on current consultations and the results of the past consultations, except for confidential information.[33]

The LRI must also consult with the European Commission, BEREC, and the regulatory authorities from the other EU Member States when the planned measure involves access and interconnection, or would significantly affect **trade** between Member States. The adopted measure must be communicated to the European Commission and BEREC.[34]

22.10   At the request of an interested party, the LRI may resolve disputes between notified undertakings on the interpretation of the 2011 E-Law, its associated regulations and decisions, at the request of one of the party. The LRI, after having heard the arguments of parties in an adversarial procedure, must issue a decision within four months from the date of receipt of the request. The decision may be appealed before the administrative court.[35] In the case of a cross-border dispute where the opinion of BEREC has been requested, except in urgent circumstances, the LRI must postpone the commencement of proceedings until BEREC issues its opinion.[36]

Right of Appeal against NRA's Decisions

22.11   Any interested legal or natural person may appeal a regulation or decision of the NRA to the administrative court.

The NRA's Obligations to Cooperate with the Commission

22.12   As noted above in para 22.9, the LRI must cooperate with the European Commission in the framework of the consolidation procedure, when the planned measure to be adopted by the LRI involves access and interconnection or would significantly affect exchanges between Member States.

The co-regulation procedure has been partially transposed considering that, as opposed to the Framework Directive, only the European Commission (and not BEREC) is empowered to limit the LRI.

---

30   Arts 14, 29, 46, 62 and 74 E-Law.
31   Art 77(1) E-Law.
32   Art 80(1) E-Law.
33   Art 78 E-Law.
34   Art 79(1) E-Law.
35   Art 6 E-Law.
36   Art 82 E-Law.

The European Commission is entitled to postpone for two months the adoption of a planned measure to be adopted by the LRI which involves access and interconnection or would significantly affect exchanges between Member States, where the definition of the market is not relevant for the European Commission or where the European Commission considers as questionable the supposed significant impact on market of the relevant notified undertaking's power.

The opposition of the European Commission to a measure is binding on the LRI,[37] and it can notify the LRI to withdraw such adopted measure within six months. The LRI can opt for the amendment of the withdrawn measure; in such case, the LRI must commence a new consultation procedure.[38]

The 2011 E-Law does not reflect the power of the European Commission to stipulate standards and specifications and to issue specifications.

'Significant Market Power' as a Fundamental Prerequisite of Regulation

Definition of SMP

22.13   The definition of an undertaking with significant market power contained in the 2011 E-Law[39] is identical to the definition set out under Article 14(2) and (3) of the Framework Directive. The 2011 E-Law requires the LRI to consider the criteria set out in Annex II to the Framework Directive, which have been reproduced in article 19(2) of the law.

Definition of relevant markets and imposition of remedies

22.14   According to article 19(1) of the 2011 E-Law, if the LRI determines that, based on its analysis of a market in the electronic communications sector, the market is not competitive, it then identifies the undertakings with significant market power in that market. In order to evaluate the significance or power of one or several undertakings jointly in a market, the LRI takes into account the following criteria, among others:

- low flexibility of the demand;
- similar market shares;
- important economic and juridical constraints at the entry;
- vertical integration with collective refusal of supplying;
- lack of buyer's counter-power; and
- lack of potential competition.

The LRI then imposes specific and appropriate obligations on undertakings with significant market power in accordance with the provisions of the 2011 E-Law, or it maintains or modifies these obligations, if they already exist.

The LRI performed a first cycle of market analysis between 2006 and 2008 and started a second cycle in 2010.

Specific obligations may be imposed by the LRI on undertakings with significant market power as detailed under the sections of the 2011 E-Law concerning access and interconnection.

---

37   Art 79(2) E-Law.
38   Art 79(3) E-Law.
39   Art 2(13) E-Law.

NRA's Regulatory Duties Concerning Rights of Way, Co-location and Facility Sharing

Rights of way

22.15   Title V 2011 E-Law provides specific requirements for rights of way. Such requirements apply to any notified entity and grant rights over public property of the State and of local authorities but also private property. There is only one provision applicable to rights on private property. This provision requires that a notified undertaking that intends to establish facilities and associated facilities on private property must enter into a written contract with the owner of the property that is to be used. The contract must regulate the possibility of sharing facilities and associated facilities with another notified undertaking.[40]

In principle, according to the 2011 E-Law, any notified undertaking has a right of way on public property of the State and local authorities. This right permits access to, and installation of, technical infrastructures, facilities, and equipment.[41] The installation of facilities and associated facilities must be carried out under the least detrimental conditions for the public property concerned, having due regard to the environment and aesthetic quality of the locations.[42]

22.16   In compliance with the Framework Directive, for rights of way on public property other than the property of the state road or railway networks, the authorities managing such public property grant access to such property by way of contract. Such contract may not contain provisions relating to the commercial conditions of the activity. The notified undertaking must disclose a copy of the contract to the LRI within one month from the date it takes effect.[43]

The right of way over public property pertaining to roads and railways is subject to an authorisation issued by the competent authority.[44] No tax, fee, toll fee, remuneration, or indemnity of any nature may be imposed for the passage through public property.[45]

The owner of a road or railway must negotiate the terms of a contract with the notified undertakings that will use the right of way with respect to the same property.[46]

Consistent with new Article 11(1)(3) of the Framework Directive, the 2011 E-Law requires that public authorities in charge of the establishment of the written conventions or the authorisations (in the case of roads and railway properties) issue their decision within a period of six months of receiving a request from the undertaking. An authority's failure to act on a request is considered as grant of the request.[47] Additionally, new article 38(5) 2011 E-Law requires that public or local authorities retaining ownership or control of undertakings operating public electronic communications networks or publicly available electronic communications services, must notify the LRI of such activity and install an effective structural separation of the function responsible for granting the rights from the activities

---

40   Art 43 E-Law.
41   Art 37(1) E-Law.
42   Art 37(2) E-Law.
43   Art 38(1) E-Law.
44   Art 38(2) E-Law.
45   Art 38(3) E-Law.
46   Art 39 E-Law.
47   Art 38(4) E-Law.

associated with ownership or control. The LRI must monitor this separation to ensure that it is effective and remains in place, and must publishes the results of such monitoring on the LRI website.

Co-location and facility sharing

22.17 Provisions related to co-location and facility sharing in the 2005 E-Law[48] differed drastically from the provisions of the 2002 Regulatory Package, as the 2005 E-Law did not contain or implement any of the two articles relating to co-location and facility sharing under the Framework Directive. When implementing the provisions of the Better Regulation Directive related to this area, the Luxembourg legislator considerably amended the 2005 E-Law. Indeed, the provisions related to co-location and facility sharing in the 2011 E-Law[49] are identical to the provisions contained in Article 12 of the Framework Directive.

The 2011 E-Law, however, includes an additional provision[50] already contained in the 2005 E-Law that differs from Article 12(2) of the Framework Directive. Specifically, the 2011 E-Law provides that, when a notified company, who has a right of way in accordance with article 37 2011 E-Law, in order to install its equipment, wishes to use a land which is already used by another notified undertaking, the owner of the land requires the two undertakings to negotiate the terms of a sharing agreement for the existing facilities. The agreement must contain provisions regarding the allotment of maintenance costs related to the shared equipment and facilities. Where no agreement is found or in the case of a dispute, each of the parties concerned, including the owner, may request that the competent authority (in its dispute resolution role) make decide the matter,

The LRI is the competent authority for the application of rules regarding co-location and facility sharing.

REGULATION OF MARKET ENTRY: THE AUTHORISATION DIRECTIVE

The General Authorisation of Electronic Communications

22.18 Under article 7 2011 E-Law, the provision of electronic communications services and networks can be freely exercised. Any undertaking, however, wishing to engage in such activities must first notify the LRI. The undertaking must initiate the notification procedure at least 20 days before commencing. The LRI provides a standard notification form to the undertakings. The notification form must fully describe the undertaking and the networks or services to be provided, and must indicate the launch date of its activities.[51] The LRI compiles the information in a public registry[52] and must publish the list of the notified undertakings.[53] Upon receipt of the notification, the LRI issues within one week, at the request of the

---

48   Art 69 to 71 2005 E-Law.
49   Art 43 and Art 44 E-Law.
50   Art 43 E-Law.
51   Art 8(1) LRI Law.
52   Art 8 LRI Law.
53   Art 9 LRI Law.

concerned undertaking, a standardised certificate, proving that the entity has duly filed a notification.[54]

When such activities are offered by public electronic communications network providers such undertakings are entitled to negotiate interconnection with other networks and communication services providers throughout the entire territory of the EU, subject to the compliance to applicable laws.[55] Voice service providers must provide to any end user access to telephone inquiry services and must cooperate with notified undertakings whose activities include the production of telephone directories, the provision of telephone inquiry services, or telephone support service. Such cooperation entails transmitting the relevant data of willing clients.[56]

The notification procedure applies in the same manner, and to the same extent, to specific providers such as SMP providers or universal service providers.

Right of Use for Radio Frequencies

Strategic planning and co-ordination of spectrum policy

22.19   The management and use of radio spectrum is restricted to the State, which is entitled to grant it to third parties, in compliance with international treaties, European and regional agreements and with the RF Law.[57]

Broadcasting services are regulated by the 2011 E-Law and the RF Law, as well as by the two regulations of 17 March 1993 with respect to television broadcasting and attribution of the authorisations for Luxembourg programmes by cable, and by one regulation of 5 April 2001 on applicable rules regarding advertising, sponsorship, telemarketing, and self-promotion in television programmes.

Principles of frequency allocation, procedural rules

22.20   The Minister for Media and Communications grants licences to undertakings for rights to use radio frequency channels.[58] The licence constitutes an administrative authorisation.[59]

The process for granting such licences must be based on objective criteria and be transparent, non-discriminatory, and proportionate.[60] This process is carried out on the basis of an individual authorisation procedure and therefore does not meet the criteria of the general authorisation procedure based on the notification, as required for the provision of electronic communications services and networks.

Undertakings wishing to use frequencies or channels must apply to the LRI, the entity which examines applications on behalf of the Minister.[61] A decision of the Minister will be based on the frequency plan, which sets out the plan of the

---

54   Art 8(3) LRI Law.
55   Art 10 E-Law.
56   Art 12 E-Law.
57   Art 2 RF Law.
58   Art 6(1) RF Law.
59   Art 1(2) RF Law.
60   Art 6(1) RF Law.
61   Art 7a RF Law.

allotment and allocation of radio frequencies[62] and on the public registry of frequencies that registers all the assigned frequencies.[63]

Transferability and time limitations

22.21 The RF Law has been amended to remove the earlier provision stating that such a licence is personal and non-transferable, consistent with the Better Regulation Directive[64] and to empower the Minister to condition the licence grant to on compliance with a transfer procedure (in case the transferability of the licence has been authorised).[65]

Licences to use frequencies or channels are of set duration, with the maximum duration a period which must be appropriate for the service concerned in view of the objective pursued (and taking due account of the need to allow for an appropriate period for investment).[66]

Admissible conditions

22.22 The special conditions attached to spectrum licences are identical to the optional conditions listed under Annex B of Authorisation Directive, except for the sixth condition, as fees for rights of use are mandatory under the RF Law.[67]

Limitation of number of rights of use to be granted

22.23 The RF Law does not provide for a maximum number of rights of use to be granted, except for technical reasons in accordance with the frequency plan.[68]

The fees due for the use of spectrum include the taxes on frequency use as well as the administrative costs of the LRI,[69] which was previously informally, and is since the amendment of the RF Law officially, the main administrative body in charge of all tasks related to spectrum management.[70]

In case several candidates request a licence to use the same frequency or frequencies, the Minister will initiate a procedure of public call for tenders (with either a competitive or comparative selection process) to grant such a licence.[71]

The RF Law has been amended so that if several candidates request a licence to use frequencies to set up a network with the primary purpose of providing electronic communications that are accessible to the public, the licence will be granted according to a public consultation organised by the LRI, not to last more than six months.[72]

---

62   Art 5(1) RF Law.
63   Art 5(2) RF Law.
64   Bill of the 2011 RF Law.
65   Art 7(1)(g) RF Law.
66   Art 7(1)(d) RF Law.
67   Art 8 RF Law.
68   Art 6(1) RF Law.
69   Art 8(2) RF Law.
70   Art 7a RF Law.
71   Art 6(2) RF Law.
72   Art 6(3) RF Law.

Rights of Use for Numbers

General authorisations and granting of individual rights

22.24   Numbers are regulated by a national numbering plan established and controlled by the LRI, taking into account consumers' interests and fair competition between notified undertakings. The national numbering plan is public and therefore published on the website of the LRI. The LRI issues decisions regarding the numbering plan, amendments to the numbering plan, the use and the structure of numbers, the allocation of numbers and series of numbers to each notified undertaking and each electronic communications service, and number portability. Since the amendment of the 2005 E-Law, the LRI also provides decisions concerning services access and the pricing of such access.[73]

The LRI, in granting individual numbers or series of numbers to notified undertakings must be objective, proportional, transparent, and non-discriminatory, and must issued the numbers in a timely manner.[74] There is no provision for 'golden numbers' (ie vanity numbers) in the 2011 E-Law or in the decisions of the LRI. The allocation of numbers is carried out in chronological order of request.[75] If there are several applications for the same individual number on the same date (which might be the case for the allocation 'golden numbers'), the LRI must create a lottery procedure for assignment of the number.[76]

Operators or users have only a right of use of the numbers. The numbers are, under Luxembourg law, considered as public goods and therefore the property of the State. Undertakings holding rights of use of numbers are not entitled to sell such numbers or to transfer their rights to use the numbers to third parties, except for to their customers in the framework of their activities.[77]

Admissible conditions

22.25   The rights of use of numbers are conditioned on the payment of fees to the LRI, which are set by decisions of the LRI.[78]Numbers allocated to notified undertakings must be put into service within six months of the allocation.[79] Notified undertakings that use series of numbers may not discriminate against other undertakings that provide electronic communications services with regard to the sequences of numbers that are used in order to gain access to their services.[80]

The obligation for operators to provide number portability for mobile numbers is absolute,[81] must be achieved by the concerned operator at the request of the user within three working days, and may not result in breach of service during transfer.[82]

---

73   Art 47(1) E-Law.
74   Art 47(2) E-Law.
75   Art 2.2.4. Decision 99/17/ILT of 19 April 1999.
76   Art 2.2.5. Decision 99/17/ILT of 19 April 1999.
77   Art 2.2.1. and 2.4.2. Decision 99/17/ILT of 19 April 1999.
78   Art 2.4.1. Decision 99/17/ILT of 19 April 1999.
79   Art 2.4. Decision 99/17/ILT of 19 April 1999.
80   Art 47(3) E-Law.
81   Art 2 Decision 04/77/LRI of 6 July 2004.
82   Art 6 Decision 04/77/LRI of 6 July 2004.

Limitation of number of rights of use to be granted

22.26   There are no competitive or comparative selection procedures for the allocation of numbers under Luxembourg law.

The NRA's Enforcement Powers

22.27   The LRI is empowered to impose sanctions on notified undertakings not complying with the 2011 E-Law, related regulations, specifications made in their implementation, and the regulatory measures of the LRI.[83]

The 2011 E-Law increases the maximum fine that the LRI may impose on notified undertakings to €1,000,000. The LRI may also impose a daily fine of an amount between €200 and €2,000, fixed according to the economic capacity of the undertaking and the nature of the infringement. Such fine may be doubled for a second offence.[84]

The LRI is further empowered to take complementary or alternative disciplinary sanctions, including, among other things, warnings, prohibitions on carrying out certain operations, or temporary suspension of one or more managers or directors of an undertaking.[85]

The LRI is entitled to suspend temporarily or definitely, without giving rise to any right to compensation, the services provided by a notified undertaking after having notified such undertaking of its infringement of the law.[86]

The amount of the fines imposed by the LRI to infringing undertakings has typically been between €2,500 and €7,500.

Administrative Charges and Fees for Rights of Use

22.28   The 2011 E-Law provides that notification of the LRI to obtain the general authorisation will be understood as acceptance of the conditions of contributing to the costs borne by the LRI for the management of the sector.[87]

In addition to the notification requirement, annual fees are payable to the LRI for its supervision, unless a provider has fewer than 500 end users and a net annual turnover of less than €300,000. The fees are follows:[88]

- a fixed fee of €2,500 (this fee is doubled to EUR 5,000.for each market where the operator is considered by the LRI as having significant market power); and
- a variable fee calculated on the basis of net-turnover generated by the service provider with the regulated activities in Luxembourg. This fee is set out by the LRI each year for the following year in a Grand-Ducal regulation. For 2012 the fee is of 0.9 per cent of net turnover generated by the notified entity in Luxembourg.

---

83   Art 83(1) E-Law.
84   Art 83(1) E-Law.
85   Art 83(1) E-Law.
86   Art 83(3) E-Law.
87   Art 11(1) E-Law.
88   Art 11 E-Law.

The fees for individual rights of use for spectrum and numbers are set by the LRI and published[89].

REGULATION OF NETWORK ACCESS AND INTERCONNECTION: THE ACCESS DIRECTIVE

Objectives and Scope of Access Regulation

22.29   Provisions related to access and interconnection are set out in title IV 2011 E-Law, with the objectives of regulating the access to electronic communications networks in order to ensure sustainable competition, guaranteeing the interoperability of electronic communications services, and providing benefits to consumers.

Provisions on access apply to notified entities seeking access to facilities or services for the purpose of providing electronic communications services, while provisions on interconnection apply to the physical and logical linking of public communications networks used by the same or a different undertaking in order to allow the users of one undertaking to communicate with users of the same or another undertaking, or to access services provided by another undertaking. Interconnection is a specific type of access implemented between public network operators.

Basic Regulatory Concepts

22.30   The definitions of 'access' and 'interconnection' contained in the 2011 E-Law are identical to those set out in the Access Directive.

In line with the principle of freedom of access as set out under Article 3(1) of the Access Directive, according to article 22 2011 E-Law, a notified entity freely negotiates with another notified entity, or with an undertaking authorised in another EU Member State, contracts establishing the technical and commercial aspects of access or interconnection. An undertaking that does not provide electronic communications services and does not operate an electronic communications network in Luxembourg is not required to notify the LRI of its activities to the LRI in order to request access or interconnection.

Upon request by another notified undertaking, operators must negotiate reciprocal interconnection to provide electronic communications services that are accessible to the public in order to guarantee the provision of services and their interoperability in the whole EU. Operators must offer access and interconnection to other undertakings according to terms and conditions that are compatible with the obligations imposed upon them by the LRI in accordance with the provisions of the 2011 E-Law.

22.31   According to article 24 2011 E-Law, the LRI may impose the following obligations in order to ensure, to the extent possible, adequate access and interconnection and interoperability of services:

- on notified undertakings that control access to end users, to the extent necessary in order to ensure end-to-end connectivity – obligations of access and interconnection, including, where it is justified, the obligation to ensure

---

89   Art 9(1) E-Law.

interconnection of their networks where such interconnection has not yet been realised;

- on operators, to the extent necessary in order to ensure access by end users to services of specific digital radio and television broadcasts – obligations of access, under fair, reasonable and non-discriminatory conditions, to application programme interfaces and to electronic programme guides; and
- in justified cases and to the extent necessary, obligations on entities controlling access to end users in order to ensure the interoperability of their services.

The LRI may also:

- set out a mandatory procedure with precise timeframes for the completion of the negotiation of any contract on access to the network(s), including on unbundled access to the local loop or on an interconnection contract;
- set out the terms and conditions of access or interconnection, including the financial terms and conditions, if no contract is entered into within the specified timeframe or in the event of failure of negotiations; and
- impose amendments to an existing contract, including of the relevant financial terms and conditions, in exceptional cases justified by requirements of interoperability of the services or accounting obligations imposed on one of the parties. The LRI may set a deadline for implementation of the amendment. After expiration of the deadline, the LRI may impose terms and conditions of access and interconnection, as set out above in this paragraph.[90]

According to article 78 2011 E-Law, before taking measures that are deemed to have an important impact on a market, the LRI must give the concerned parties a period of one month to provide their observations on the future measure. To that end, the LRI sets up a consultation procedure which is published to the memorial and on its website, unless the information are confidential.

Access- and Interconnection-related Obligations with Respect to SMP-undertakings

22.32   Undertakings that have significant power in the market of access and interconnection must comply with obligations identical to those imposed on other undertakings. However, Title IV 2011 E-Law sets out additional obligations that are specific to SMP undertakings. According to article 28(1) 2011 E-Law, when the LRI, further to a market analysis, designates an undertaking as having significant power in the market of access and interconnection, it may impose the following obligations:

- Obligations of transparency regarding the access and interconnection. .According to this obligation, the undertaking must publish specific information including, but not limited to, accounting information, technical specifications, characteristics of the network, modalities and conditions of the provision, including any condition limiting the access or the use of the services.
  In line with article 9(2) Access Directive, the LRI may require an SMP undertaking to publish a reference offer, which must be sufficiently unbundled to ensure that undertakings are not required to pay for facilities which are not necessary for the service requested, giving a description of the relevant offerings broken down into components according to market needs, and the

---

90   Art 27(1) E-Law.

associated terms and conditions including prices. The LRI details the specific information to be provided, including the level of detail, and may impose modifications to the offer.

- Non-discrimination obligations as set out under article 30 2011 E-Law which is identical to Article 10(2) of the Access Directive.
- Accounting separation requirements as set out under article 31 2011 E-Law which is identical to Article 11(1) of the Access Directive.
- Obligation to satisfy reasonable demands of access to, and use of, specific network facilities (the non-exhaustive list of requirements that may be imposed on operators in this respect and which is contained in Article 12(1) of the Access Directive has been transposed verbatim into article 32 2011 E-Law).
- Obligation of price control and cost accounting in line with Article 13 of the Access Directive.

In exceptional circumstances, should the LRI decide to impose on SMP undertakings measures other than the above listed obligations, it must submit a request to the European Commission who has the final decision as to the application of the requested measure.

Regulatory Powers with Respect to SMP-undertakings

22.33   The 2011 E-Law provides some specific obligations with respect to SMP undertakings in wholesale markets.

Specifically, consistent with new Article 9(4) of the Access Directive, according to article 29(2) E-Law, when an SMP undertaking must comply with the obligations of article 28(1) 2011 E-Law concerning wholesale network infrastructure access, the operator must publish a reference offer contained specific information, as listed in article 29(2) 2011 E-Law. The non-exhaustive list of information that may be imposed on operators and which is contained in Annex II to the Access Directive has been transposed verbatim into article 29(2) 2011 E-Law.

Additionally, consistent with Article 13(a) of the Access Directive, article 34 2011 E-Law requires the LRI, if it wishes (in exceptional circumstances) to impose an obligation on vertically integrated undertakings to place activities related to the wholesale provision of relevant access products in an independently operating business entity, to conclude that appropriate obligations imposed under article 28 2011 E-Law have failed to achieve effective competition and that there are important and persisting competition problems or market failures identified in relation to the wholesale provision of certain access product markets. In such a situation, the LRI must submit a request to the European Commission containing the elements listed in article 34(2) 2011 E-Law and Article 13(a)(2) of the Access Directive.

The only provision remaining in the 2011 E-Law regarding carrier pre-selection is contained in article 32 2011 E-Law under which the LRI may require SMP undertakings to give third parties access to specified network elements or facilities (including access to network elements which are not active), or unbundled access to the local loop to, among other things, allow carrier selection or pre-selection.

There are no provisions regarding leased lines in the 2011 E-Law.

Regulatory Powers Applicable to All Market Participants

Obligations to ensure end-to-end connectivity

22.34 In order to encourage, and, where appropriate, ensure, adequate access and interconnection and interoperability of services, the LRI may impose (to the extent necessary to ensure end-to-end connectivity) obligations on undertakings that control access to end users, including (in justified cases) the obligation to interconnect their networks if they have not already done so.[91]

According to article 32(g) 2011 E-Law the LRI may require SMP undertakings to provide specified services needed to ensure interoperability of end-to-end services to users, including facilities for intelligent network services or roaming on mobile networks.

Regulation of roaming services

22.35 The LRI is charged with monitoring notified entities and making sure that they act in compliance with the European Roaming Regulation.[92]

Access to digital radio and television broadcasting services

22.36 In line with Article 5(1) sentence 2(b) of the Access Directive, under article 24(c) 2011 E-Law the LRI may require operators, after consultation with concerned parties, and to the extent necessary, to provide end users access to specified digital radio and television broadcasting services, Application Programming Interfaces ('API') and Electronic Programme Guides ('EPG').

Obligations contained in Part I Annex I to the Access Directive have been implemented in Luxembourg under articles 25 and 27 2011 E-Law. Such articles are consistent with the Annex.

REGULATION OF THE UNIVERSAL SERVICE AND USER'S RIGHTS: THE UNIVERSAL SERVICE DIRECTIVE

Regulation of Universal Service Obligations

Scope of universal service obligation

22.37 Universal service obligations are contained in Title IX of the 2011 E-Law. In line with the Universal Service Directive, as amended by the Citizen's Rights Directive in 2009, all end users have a right to universal service in electronic communications.

According to article 48 2011 E-Law, universal service in Luxembourg must include the following:

- The provision of access at a fixed location and of telephonic services.

---

91 Art 24(a) E-Law.
92 Cf point 1.30 Electronic Communication Law and Policy of the European Union Chapter.

- The availability of public pay telephones and other public voice telephony access points.
  In accordance with the new Article 6(1) of the Universal Service Directive, the LRI must ensure that public pay telephones or other public voice telephony access points are provided to meet the reasonable needs of end users in terms of the geographical coverage, the number of telephones or other access points and accessibility to disabled end users and the quality of services.[93]
  Public pay telephones must offer the possibility to call, free of charge, the European emergency number 112 and other emergency numbers and must display information to end users regarding, at a minimum, the tariffs of use, the terms and conditions of use, the telephone number for assistance services, emergency services, and inquiry services, and the telephone number of the public pay telephone.[94]
- The availability, free of charge and publication of at least one telephone directory including all subscribers to the publicly available telephone service. Such directory must be issued consistent with the E-Privacy Law obligations and be updated once a year.
- The provision of one telephone directory inquiry service.

In order to comply with Article 7 of the Universal Service Directive with respect to disabled users, the 2011 E-Law requires that public pay telephones be accessible to disabled end users.[95] Article 70(2) was added to the 2011 E-Law providing that the LRI may require notified companies providing universal services to make offers specifically designed for the needs of disabled users in order to guaranty equivalent access.

Designation of undertakings obliged to provide universal services

22.38   The 2011 E-Law provides that universal service may be offered by one, several, or groups of, notified undertakings which provide different parts of the universal service, or which cover different parts of the national territory.[96] The LRI must ensure that the entire national territory is covered.

If the LRI discovers that all or part of the universal service is not covered, or is not sufficiently or adequately covered, the LRI must organise a call for tenders for the provision of the universal service. The LRI will attribute to the notified company having demonstrated the most adequate aptitude to provide such service the provision of all or part of the universal service for all or part of the Luxembourg territory.[97]

If the function of providing the universal service cannot be attributed to a notified undertaking pursuant to the call for tenders, the LRI may impose on any undertaking with significant market power the obligation to contribute to the provision of the public service. Pursuant to article 70(1)[98] 2011 E-Law, a notified undertaking may be required, by decision of the Minister, upon advice of the LRI, to render electronic communications services, other than those regarding universal services obligations, accessible to the public.

---

93   Art 51(1) E-Law.
94   Art 51(2) E-Law.
95   Art 51(1) E-Law.
96   Art 49 E-Law.
97   Art 63 E-Law.
98   Art 64 E-Law.

Universal service has not been implemented in practice in Luxembourg as, to date, no specific undertaking has been designated in to provide such service.

Regulation of retailed tariffs, user's expenditures and quality of service

22.39   The LRI is in charge of monitoring the evolution and level of retail tariffs applicable to the different elements of the universal service, in particular in relation to national consumer prices.

Consistent with new Article 9(2) of the Universal Service Directive, article 58(2) 2011 E-Law requires that notified undertakings provide to consumers tariff options or packages which depart from those provided under normal commercial conditions, in particular to ensure that individuals with low incomes or with special social needs are not prevented from accessing the service. The LRI may also require the notified entity to comply with price caps or geographical averaging.

Article 60 2011 E-Law requires any undertaking providing universal service to comply with the obligations detailed in Part A of Annex 1 to the Universal Service Directive. The entity providing universal service, therefore, must provide subscribers of its services with additional services such as complimentary itemised billing, pre-payment systems, phased payment of connection fees, and alternative tariff offers corresponding to the specific subscriber's situation.

According to article 61 2011 E-Law, the LRI specifies the minimum quality criteria for the services. The entity providing universal service must provide the LRI once a year any data necessary for the LRI to verify compliance with the established quality criteria.

Cost calculation and financing of universal services

22.40   The undertaking with significant market power which has been designated by the LRI to contribute to the provision of universal service pursuant to article 64 2011 E-Law, may receive financial compensation, at its request, when the LRI finds that the obligation to provide such service would represent an unfair burden on the undertaking designated to provide universal service.[99] The LRI must calculate the net costs of its provision as set out under Article 12(1) of the Universal Service Directive.

To the contrary, no compensation will be offered to notified companies that have been appointed after a call for tenders.

Article 68 2011 E-Law provides for the creation of a fund for the maintenance of the universal service managed by the LRI. The financial management of the fund is subject to dual control by an external auditor and by the *Cour des Comptes*.

Any notified entity must, if necessary, contribute to the fund for the maintenance of universal service. The amount of contribution is determined by the LRI according to the proportion between the global sales generated by all the notified companies and the sales of each notified entity. Such contributions are defined separately for each notified entity.

The amount of the contribution for each calendar year is determined, for each notified company, on the basis of sales in the previous year. The LRI publishes an

---

99   Art 66 E-Law.

annual report indicating the cost of the obligations of universal service as calculated, issuing the contributions made by the notified companies, and highlighting
the commercial advantages resulting for each notified company from the provision
of the universal service.[100]

Regulation of Retail Markets

Prerequisites for the regulation of retail markets and regulatory powers

22.41   According to article 21(1) 2011 E-Law, if the LRI discovers that a retail
market is not competitive and concludes that the obligations as set out by the 2011
E-Law with respect to access and interconnection or the numbering rules established under title VIII of the 2011 E-Law are not sufficient to ensure effective
competition in the market, it may impose adequate obligations on entities that have
significant power in such market.

Additionally, article 21(2) 2011 E-Law requires that, an entity subject to obligations
related to retail tariffs or to other controls regarding the retail market must put in
place necessary and appropriate systems for costs accounting. The LRI may specify
the format and methodology for such systems. The conformity of the systems is
monitored by an independent entity which must publish an annual declaration of
conformity.

End User Rights

Contracts

22.42   The Luxembourg legislator favours the application of general consumer
regulation and contract law, with no differentiation among sectors (rather than
sector-specific consumer protection, for instance with respect to the public telephone network)

The provisions of article 20 Universal Service Directive have, nonetheless, all been
implemented by article 73 2011 E-Law.

Transparency obligations

22.43   Consistent with Article 21 of the Universal Service Directive, article 72
2011 E-Law requires that any entity (with no specific differentiation) providing
electronic communications services accessible to the public and public electronic
communications networks publish transparent, adequate, comparative, and current
information on applicable prices and tariffs, costs due at the time of the contract
termination, and standard terms and conditions with respect to access to and use of
the services to end users and consumers.

Such information must be complete, comparable, and easy to read. The information
is disclosed to the LRI before publication, which also determines the content and
the form of the publication as well as the method of publication.[101]

---

100   Art 69(2) E-Law.
101   Art 72(1) E-Law.

The LRI may require providers of electronic communications services accessible to the public and of public electronic communications networks to issue a list of information, as included in Article 21(3) of the Universal Service Directive.

Third parties may use the information issued by entities providing electronic communications services accessible to the public and public electronic communications networks to make an independent evaluation of the cost of alternative usage patterns, by means of, for example, interactive guides.[102]

Quality of service: securing 'net neutrality'

22.44 Consistent with Article 22(2) of the Universal Service Directive, the LRI may specify, among other things, the quality of service parameters to be measured, and the content, form and manner of information to be published, in order to ensure that end users have access to comprehensive, comparable and user-friendly information.

European emergency call number

22.45 Public pay telephones must offer the possibility to call, free of charge, and without the use of any means of payment, the European emergency number 112 and other emergency numbers.[103] The telephones must also display such numbers and indicate that they are free of charge.[104]

Additionally, entities providing electronic communications services accessible to the public and public electronic communications networks must inform their subscribers regarding access to emergency services.

The service provider providing access to the unique European emergency number 112, and to other emergency numbers identified by the LRI, must, for each call directed to such numbers, provide the available data regarding the calling person, including location data.[105]

Obligations Facilitating Change of Provider

22.46 Pursuant to article 9(1)(b) 2011 E-Law, the LRI publishes, on its website, for each notified entity, the procedures and direct costs for the portability of numbers or other identifiers.

In accordance with article 47(1) 2011 E-Law, the LRI determines the rules applicable to the portability of numbers. In parallel, any consumer or end user who subscribes to services providing access to electronic communications services accessible to the public or public electronic communications networks has the right to be receive from the provider of the services a written agreement containing information on any costs related to the portability of numbers and other identifiers.

DATA PROTECTION: THE DIRECTIVE ON PRIVACY AND ELECTRONIC COMMUNICATIONS

22.47 The 2011 E-Privacy Law implements in Luxembourg the amendments to the E-Privacy Directive introduced by the Citizen's Rights Directive.

---

102 Art 72(2) E-Law.
103 Art 51(2) E-Law.
104 Art 52(4) E-Law.
105 Art 5(a) E-Privacy Law.

As did the 2002 E-Privacy Law, the 2011 E-Privacy Law contains one major difference with the E-Privacy Directive with respect to the definitions of 'user' and 'subscriber'.[106] Specifically, contrary to the E-Privacy Directive, legal entities (in addition to natural persons) are included in the scope of these definitions, in addition to natural persons.

The 2011 E-Privacy Law, therefore, remains consistent with the objectives of the Luxembourg legislator to include legal entities (which was already explicitly set out with the Data Protection Law relating to the protection of natural persons or legal entities with regard to the processing of personal data, which implemented Directive 1995/46/EC of the European Parliament and of the Council of 24 October 1995 on the protection of individuals with regard to the processing of personal data and on the free movement of such data, which also applies to the processing of data regarding legal entities).

Confidentiality of Communications

22.48   The obligations imposed on service providers and network providers to ensure the confidentiality of communications in articles 4(1) and 4(2) 2011 E-Privacy Law are identical to those in Article 5(1) of the E-Privacy Directive

In line with the E-Privacy Directive, the E-Privacy Law contains exceptions to provisions 4(1) and 4(2). Namely, article 4(1) and 4(2) do not prevent:

- technical storage required for the conveyance of a communication;[107]
- data processing done in the course of business practice for the purpose of providing evidence of a commercial transaction or any other business communication;[108]
- processing of data, collected by the use of cookies or other similar techniques, with regard to information stored in the terminal equipment of a subscriber, user, or end user;[109] and
- data processing undertaken by the competent authorities with regard to the safeguarding of national security, defence, national safety, and the prevention, investigation, detection and prosecution of criminal offences.[110]

22.49   The 2011 E-Privacy Law, however, goes further than the E-Privacy Directive by including additional exceptions. Specifically, articles 4(1) and (2) E-Privacy Law do not apply to communications made in the context of emergency calls (unique European emergency number 112) and to the related traffic data. The listening, tapping, and storage of such communications must have been made only for the purposes of listening again to certain messages in the case of incomprehension or ambiguity, documenting false alerts, abusive or threatening calls and producing evidence in case of a dispute with respect to events concerning emergency interventions. The related traffic data, including location data, must be erased once help has been provided and the content of communications must be erased within six months.

With respect to interception, article 4(2) 2011 E-Law sets out a specific exception applying to notified companies. Specifically, such entities are required to make

---

106   Art 2(a) and (i) E-Privacy Law.
107   Art 4(3)(a) E-Privacy Law.
108   Art 4(3)(d) E-Privacy Law.
109   Art 4(3)(e) E-Privacy Law.
110   Art 4(3)(b) E-Privacy Law.

available to the requesting competent authority, free of charge, any technical data and equipment that would allow it to perform its legal mission of communications supervision.

Intercepted information must be transported without delay to the requesting government agency or agencies, in accordance with a technical protocol set out in the Regulation on the interception of public electronic communications.[111]

22.50   In order to comply with their intercept obligations, notified entities must:

- observe secrecy with regard to the intercepted data;
- ensure that data requested on the basis of intercept obligations is protected against examination by unauthorised persons;
- ensure that the interception does not modify or delay the provision of services to users, is undetectable to the users, and is of a quality comparable to the original communication; and
- decrypt any encrypted signals (telecommunication signals that are transferred via a switch to another public telecommunications network must also be capable of interception).

Article 4(3)(e) 2011 E-Privacy Law sets out specific requirements with respect to the storage of or access to information on the terminal equipment of a subscriber or user. This article sets out, in line with Article 5(3) of the E-Privacy Directive, that a prior consent must be obtained by the subscriber or user, after being provided with clear and comprehensive information about the purposes of the processing. The 2011 E-Privacy Law, however, goes further, requiring that:

- the methods of providing information and offering the right to refuse should be as user-friendly as possible; and
- where technically possible and effective, the user's consent to processing may be expressed by appropriate browser or other application settings.

Security of Processing

22.51   Article 3(1) 2011 E-Privacy Law is identical to the requirements set out in Article 4(1) and 4(1)(a) of the E-Privacy Directive. The notification required in case of a breach of personal data is also identical to Article 4(3) and (4) of the E-Privacy Directive.

Failure to comply with the above-mentioned provisions of the 2011 E-Privacy Law is subject to a prison sentence of eight days to one year and/or a fine of €251 to €125,000.[112]

The Luxembourg National Commission for the Protection of Personal Data ('CNPD') is the competent authority in Luxembourg to receive notifications, monitor any security measures taken by the providers of publicly available electronic communications services, and issue recommendations related to best practices on the degree of such security of such measures.[113]

The CNPD issues on its website a notification form that providers can complete and send online to the authority. When discovering a first failure by a provider to

---

111   Luxembourg Regulation 08/134/LRI of 1 December 2008 on the technical specifications for the interception of public electronic communications in Luxembourg.
112   Art 3(5) E-Privacy Law.
113   Art 3(1) E-privacy Law.

comply with its notification requirement, the CNPD sends the provider a warning. Repeated failure to comply is subject to a maximum fine of €50,000.[114]

Data Retention

22.52   Directive 2006/24/EC has been implemented by the law dated 24 July 2010 amending articles 5 and 9 2005 E-law, respectively regarding traffic data and location data other than traffic data.[115]

Adoption of the bill of law implementing Directive 2006/24/EC has been extremely long and complex, specifically, with respect to the parliamentary work, due to the fact that the legislator had to reconcile diverging interests of the telecommunications sector and the justice authorities.[116]

Traffic Data and Location Data

22.53   The definition of the terms 'traffic data'[117] and 'location data'[118] in the 2011 E-Privacy Law are identical to those contained in the E-Privacy Directive.

Obligations with respect to traffic data and location data are contained in article 5 and 9 of the 2011 E-Law, which remained unchanged, as amended by the law of 24 July 2010.[119]

Any service provider or operator which processes or generates traffic data in the course of the provision of its services must keep such data for a period of six months for the purposes of investigation, detection and prosecution of criminal offences, and with the sole aim making available (if necessary) information to judicial authorities.[120]

A regulation dated 24 July 2010[121] determines the categories of traffic data which are necessary for the purposes of investigation, detection and prosecution of criminal offences.

Specifically, the following categories of data must be kept for the period of six months:

- data necessary to find and identify the source of a communication with respect to
    (i) fixed and mobile telephony; and
    (ii) access to Internet web mail and telephony over the Internet;
- data necessary to identify the destination of a communication with respect to:
    (i) fixed and mobile telephony; and
    (ii) access to Internet web mail and telephony over the Internet;
- data necessary to determine the date, time and duration of a communication with respect to:

---

114   Art 3(3) E-Privacy Law.
115   Memorial A, no 122 of 29 July 2010 p 2059.
116   Deputy Chambers – Ordinary session 2009–2010.
117   Art 2(e) E-Privacy Law.
118   Art 2(f) E-Privacy Law.
119   Cf point 1.127.
120   Art 5(1)(a) E-Privacy Law.
121   Memorial A, no 122 of 29 July 2010 p 2061.

    (i) fixed and mobile telephony; and
    (ii) access to Internet web mail and telephony over the Internet;
- data necessary to determine the type of communication with respect to:
    (i) fixed and mobile telephony; and
    (ii) access to Internet web mail and telephony over the Internet;
- data necessary to identify the communication material of the users; and
- data necessary to localise mobile communications equipment

22.54   The 2011 E-Privacy Law further provides that traffic data concerning subscribers or users must be erased or rendered anonymous after the expiry of the six-month period.[122]

During the period of retention of the traffic data, any service provider or operator must render access to the data impossible when such data is no longer required for the conveyance of a communication or for billing purposes. Access must, however, still be granted to certain competent official authorities acting in accordance with the provisions of the law, such as criminal prosecution authorities acting in the context of an investigation relating to a criminal offence.[123]

Traffic data that are necessary to establish subscribers' bills or for the purpose of interconnection payments may be processed. Such processing is only lawful up to the date until which the bill may lawfully be contested or until which legal proceedings for the payment of such bill may be brought, but may not exceed a period of six months if the bill has been paid or is not the object of legal action or dispute.[124] Traffic data may also be processed in order to provide value-added services or for the marketing of electronic communications services in accordance with Article 6(3) of the E-Privacy Directive, which has been implemented as such by the 2011 E-Privacy Law.[125] The traffic data must be stored in compliance with the Data Protection Law.

The provisions of the 2011 E-Privacy Law on location data other than traffic data[126] are similar to the provisions on traffic data.

Violation of the provisions on the processing of traffic data or location data contained in the 2011 E-Privacy Law is subject to a prison sentence of eight days to one year and/or a fine of €251 to €125,000.[127]

Itemised Billing

22.55   Under the 2011 E-Privacy Law, every subscriber has the right to receive a non-itemised bill.[128] Itemised bills may not identify any calls that are free of charge (including calls to the emergency services) and may not contain any information which would make it possible to identify the called person.[129]

---

122 Art 5(1)(b) E-Privacy Law.
123 Art 5(2) E-Privacy Law.
124 Art 5(3) E-Privacy Law.
125 Art 5(4) E-Privacy Law.
126 Art 9 E-Privacy Law.
127 Art 5(6) and Art 9(6) E-Privacy Law.
128 Art 6(1) E-Privacy Law.
129 Art 6(2) E-Privacy Law.

Presentation and Restriction of Calling and Connected Line Identification

22.56   The requirements contained in article 7 2011 E-Privacy Law with respect to calling and connected line identification arc identical to the requirements contained in the E-Privacy Directive.

With regard to information provided to a subscriber with respect to rights of presentation and restriction of calling and connected line identification by the service provider, the 2011 E-Privacy Law requires that such information be provided by appropriate means and, at the latest, at the time a contract is entered into.[130]

Article 6 2011 E-Privacy Law however, goes further that the E-Privacy Directive and adds the following requirements:

- The service provider providing an access to the unique European emergency number 112 and to other emergency numbers identified by the LRI must, for each call directed to such numbers, provide the available data regarding the calling person, location data included.[131]
  Available data are defined as data related identification such as, among other things, the phone number, name, address, company name, and place of establishment, of a user or subscriber, as long as this latter is identified or identifiable, the public or private character of the data, together with any data processed within an electronic communications network indicating the geographic position of the terminal equipment of a user of a service of electronic communications available to the public (location data).
  In the case of calls directed to the unique European emergency number 112 and to other emergency numbers identified by the LRI, the identification of the calling line must always be presented, even if the calling person has prevented it.[132]
  Such provisions were not contained in the 2005 E-Privacy Law.
- A called subscriber claiming to be the victim of malicious anonymous calls may, in certain circumstances, ask for the identification of the calling or connected line.[133]

Automatic Call Forwarding

22.57   When the automatic call forwarding (or diversion) is offered as a service, the service provider must offer to any subscriber (free of charge and in an easy manner) the possibility to stop the automatic call forwarding by a third party to the subscriber's terminal, as long as the service provider may identify the origin of the forwarded calls. If applicable, the identification of such origin must be implemented in cooperation with other service providers.[134]

Directories of subscribers

22.58   Subscribers must be informed, free of charge, and before being included in the directory, of the purposes of any printed, or electronic directory of subscriber

---

130   Art 7(7) E-Privacy Law.
131   Art 5(a) E-Privacy Law.
132   Art 7(5) E-Privacy Law.
133   Art 7(8) E-Privacy Law.
134   Art 8 E-Privacy Law.

available to the public or available by consultation through directory inquiry services, in which their personal data can be included and of any further usage possibilities based on search functions embedded in electronic versions of the directory.[135]

Subscribers must have the possibility to clearly indicate (when subscribing or at any time when the directory is updated or new editions are published, ie rendered available) whether their data should appear on a public directory. Subscribers must also have the possibility, free of charge, to verify, withdraw, and correct the data.

A provider failing to comply with these provisions of the 2011 E-Privacy Law is subject to a prison sentence of eight days to one year and/or a fine of €251 to €125,000.[136]

---

135 Art 10(1) E-Privacy Law.
136 Art 10(3) E-Privacy Law.

The Maltese Market for Electronic Communications

Paul Micallef Grimaud[1]
Ganado Advocates, Valletta

LEGAL STRUCTURE

Basic Policy

23.1   In December 1997 the Maltese Government started the process of liberalising the telecommunications sector in Malta. Specifically, it established an independent telecommunications regulator, the Malta Communications Authority ('MCA'), thereby paving the way for the gradual introduction of competition in the various telecommunications markets. In 2000 the Maltese Government approved a National Plan for the Reform of the Telecommunications Sector[2] detailing the process from the position at that time, and culminating in the full liberalisation of the various telecommunications markets in January 2003. Today the Maltese telecommunications sector enjoys a satisfactory level of competition with operators providing triple and quadruple play options to their end users.

23.2   The overall policy objectives as reflected in the mission statement of the MCA, and the objectives as established at law, focus on achieving sustainable competition and enabling customer choice and value for money, while contributing to the development of an environment that is conducive to investment and continued social and economic growth. While striving to achieve these objectives through the implementation of the EU Regulatory Framework, the MCA's overall approach is a 'light touch' approach and attention is paid not to overburden the operators with obligations that are not strictly necessary to attain the stated objectives. This is consistent with its obligation to impose ex-ante regulatory obligations 'only where there is no effective and sustainable competition and to relax and lift such obligations as soon as that condition is fulfilled.'[3]

---

1   Mr Victor Zammit, Dr Paul Edgar Micallef, and Mr Ian Agius assisted the author by providing inputs to various parts of this contribution. All three are officers within the Malta Communications Authority.

2   This Plan was included as an annex to the Act XXVIII of 2000. This Act amended the Telecommunications (Regulation) Act, whilst enacting the Malta Communications Authority Act.

3   Article 4(2)(f) of Electronic Communications (Regulation) Act, Cap 399 ('ECR Act').

Implementation of the EU Directives

23.3   The 2009 EU Regulatory Package was transposed into Maltese law through amendments to the legal framework that had implemented the 2002 EU Regulatory Package, inter alia, the Malta Communications Authority Act, Cap 418 ('MCA Act'), the Electronic Communications (Regulation) Act, Cap 399 ('ECR Act'), the Utilities and Services (Regulation of Certain Works) Act, Cap 81, and the subsidiary legislations under the same Acts, most notably the Electronic Communications Networks and Services (General) Regulations, 2004[4] ('ECNS Regulations'), as well as the publication of regulatory decisions and modifications to previously published decisions implementing measures catered for by the new framework.[5] Moreover, various other pieces of legislation deriving from previous frameworks that are no longer pertinent today were rescinded by Legal Notice 273 of 2011.

Legislation

23.4   The pieces of legislation mentioned above reflect the technology-neutral approach of the EU Directives, both in the terminology used and in the scope being achieved through their implementation. As in the EU Framework, certain provisions, such as those relating to publicly available telephony services ('PATS')) are directed towards a particular market.

REGULATORY PRINCIPLES: THE FRAMEWORK DIRECTIVE

Scope of Regulation

23.5   Maltese legislation has adopted the technology-neutral approach of the Framework Directive, and imposes on the MCA an obligation to take 'the utmost account of the desirability of making regulations technologically neutral, in particular with regards to those designed to ensure effective competition.'[6] Moreover the definitions of 'electronic communications network', 'electronic communications service', and 'associated facilities' in the Framework Directive have been transposed verbatim.[7] In so doing Maltese law does not specify how certain services which include features of both content and transmission services are to be regulated, leaving room for determination of ad hoc issues to the NRAs involved who must first decide whether they have the power to deal with the issue in question depending on the nature of the service. The MCA, as the NRA responsible for the regulation of electronic communications services and networks in Malta, is not given the power to intervene in matters relating to content services. In this vein, VoIP services are not treated as a special ad hoc set of services but each service is analysed so as to determine the nature of the service and whether it constitutes a mere application on an existing Electronic Communications Service, a PATS, or an 'Other Publicly Available Electronic Communications Service', and will be regulated accordingly.

---

4   As per Legal Notice 412 of 2004.
5   These include a decision published by the MCA in May 2010 relating to the new interconnection strategy which derives from the EC Recommendation on Fixed and Mobile Termination Rates (2009/396/EC), and a decision on Functional Internet Access as an obligation forming part of the Fixed Access Universal Service Obligation which was published by the MCA in June 2011.
6   Art 4(2)(g) ECR Act.
7   Art 2 ECR Act.

Internet Freedom

23.6   No specific provision has been introduced in Maltese law pursuant to Article 1(3)(a) of the Framework Directive. The MCA has the power, under the Electronic Commerce (General) Regulations,[8] to utilise its enforcement powers under the MCA Act, as discussed below, to ensure compliance with the Electronic Commerce Act, including the provisions relating to the obligations of intermediary services. Although not required to monitor the information which they transmit or store or to actively seek facts or circumstances indicating illegal activity in connection with their activities of mere conduit, caching or hosting, intermediary service providers must promptly inform the public authorities competent in the matter of any alleged illegal activity undertaken or information provided by recipients of their service and upon request provide the authorities with information enabling the identification of recipients of their service with whom they have storage agreements.[9]

23.7   The Copyright Act, Cap. 415, provides for remedies for breach of copyright. Specifically, the First Hall of the Civil Court may require the breaching party to pay damages to the injured party for a breach of copyright. This court may also issue, upon request, an injunction ordering the perpetrator to suspend the alleged wrongful act until such time as the court rules on the merits of the case.

National Regulatory Authorities: Organisation, Regulatory Objectives, Competencies

23.8   As of 1 January 2001, the MCA is the designated communications regulator for Malta. Its structure, powers and limitations are set out in the MCA Act. The MCA is composed of a board consisting of a Chairman and four to six other members appointed by the Minister responsible for communications. Notwithstanding the fact that these appointments are political, the MCA retains its independence from Government.

23.9   The objectives of the MCA in the exercise of its functions in relation to electronic communications include[10] promoting of competition, contributing to the development of the internal market, promoting the interests of users within the European Communities, and ensuring, to the extent practicable, that electronic communications services in Malta are provided in a manner that satisfies all reasonable demands for such services including emergency services, public call services, and directory information services.

23.10   The MCA is, among other things, responsible for ensuring compliance with obligations regarding the supply of and access to electronic communications networks and services, and for managing the national numbering resources. In accordance with its objectives stated in the MCA Act, and subject to the national radio frequency plan adopted by the Minister responsible for communications, the MCA is by virtue of the ECR Act responsible for the effective management of the radio frequencies assigned to it under this plan.

23.11   The MCA is empowered to require any person to provide it with any information, including financial information, which it considers necessary to ensure compliance with the laws it enforces and with any decisions or directives it may

---

8   Subsidiary Legislation 426.02.
9   Art 22 Electronic Commerce Act, Cap. 426.
10   Art 4 ECR Act.

issue. The obligations on the MCA to publish information, to conduct consultations, and to cooperate with other NRAs are addressed in provisions in various laws, including article 4A of the MCA Act, article 9 ECR Act and regulations 5,7 and 11 ECNS Regulations. In this regard, under article 4A of the MCA Act, if the MCA were to propose to take a measure that has a significant impact on a market for electronic communications networks or services, it must first undertake a public consultation process.

23.12 The Minister responsible for communications may, in relation to matters that he believes affect the public interest, give the MCA directions of a general nature in writing on the policy that the MCA must follow in carrying out its functions under the MCA Act. Such directions, however, must not be inconsistent with the provisions of the said Act.[11] The MCA Act clarifies, however, that this must not diminish the independence of the MCA, which must 'act independently and shall not seek or take instructions from any other body on matters related to ex-ante market regulation and the resolution of disputes between undertakings'.

23.13 The MCA and the Malta Competition and Consumer Affairs Authority ('MCCAA') are required to provide one another with such information as is necessary for the application of the provisions of the MCA Act. The two bodies have a memorandum of understanding in place in relation to the cooperation and coordination of investigations between the two authorities, particularly with respect to competition issues that may involve both authorities.[12] The MCA, the Data Protection Commissioner, and the Malta Security Services are, where appropriate, required to consult and cooperate with one another in enforcing the relevant laws and regulations that require the intervention of any one or more of these bodies.

23.14 Article 43 MCA Act establishes the procedure to be followed in dealing with disputes involving authorised undertakings. In such cases the MCA is required to determine the dispute within four months from the date the dispute was notified to the MCA, unless there are circumstances which the MCA considers to be exceptional or if the MCA decides not to proceed with the investigation because it is satisfied that there are other means of redress available to the parties for resolving the dispute in a timely manner. The MCA may, on its own initiative, investigate any dispute of which it becomes aware. Decisions of the MCA must be published, subject to the requirements of commercial confidentiality, and be consistent with the principles of natural justice. Although such decisions may be appealed,[13] undertakings must comply immediately with the MCA's decisions, unless the appellate forum suspends the appealed decision.

23.15 Disputes between end users and undertakings are regulated by article 44 MCA Act. The end user must prima facie demonstrate that he or she has suffered prejudice as a result of the undertaking's violation of any law, decision, directive, or authorisation condition which the MCA is entitled to enforce. The MCA may also undertake an investigation in relation to a dispute between an end user and an undertaking on its own initiative. The MCA establishes the procedure which must be followed when dealing with such disputes. The MCA must ensure that such a procedure is transparent, simple, inexpensive, and conducive to a prompt and fair settlement. Moreover, the MCA makes publicly available the administrative rules it establishes periodically to deal with such disputes. In resolving disputes the MCA

---

11 Art 6 MCA Act.
12 'Memorandum of Understanding between the Malta Communications Authority and the Consumer and Competition Division', May 2005.
13 See below.

may issue directives to the undertaking concerned, requiring it to comply with any measures the MCA may specify, which may include an order to effect reimbursement or make compensation payments to the affected end user(s), which may include legal costs. The MCA must publish a notice of the decision. It may decide not to investigate a complaint where it is satisfied that there are other means to resolve the dispute in a timely manner or if other proceedings in relation to the same dispute have been initiated by any party to the dispute.

23.16   Article 44A MCA Act establishes the procedure to be used in the event of a dispute between parties in different Member States, where the dispute is within the competence of both the MCA and the NRA of such other State. The MCA, in dealing with such disputes, must coordinate with the other NRAs and consult with BEREC in accordance with the objectives stated in Article 8 of the Framework Directive.

Right of Appeal against NRA's Decisions

23.17   Part VIII MCA Act establishes the right of appeal to contest any decision or directive issued by the MCA. Any person, including an undertaking, aggrieved by a decision or directive of the MCA may, within 20 days from the date on which it was notified of the decision, lodge an appeal before the Administrative Review Tribunal. In so doing, the appellant must explain his or her juridical interest in contesting the decision or directive of the MCA. The MCA has 20 days from the date it received the appeal application to respond to it.

23.18   The Administrative Review Tribunal is independent and impartial in the exercise of its functions. It is set, created under and regulated by the Administrative Justice Act, Cap. 490. Although the Tribunal is competent to review all administrative decisions regardless of the sector involved, there are various compositions (sections) of the same Tribunal depending on the subject matter under review.[14] The Tribunal consists of a Chairperson who must be a person who holds, or has held, the position of a judge or magistrate in Malta. If the Chairperson is a former Judge or former Magistrate, he or she may only serve a four-year term. The Chairperson is appointed by the President of Malta, acting on the advice of the Prime Minister, and may only be removed in the same manner that a judge or magistrate is ordinarily removed, namely by the President after a qualified majority vote (two thirds of the Members) in the House of Representatives is obtained following a request for the removal of the judge or magistrate on grounds of proved misbehaviour or inability to perform his or her functions.

The Tribunal (ie the Chairperson) is assisted by two assistants with whom the Tribunal may consult, and who sit together with the Tribunal during the hearing of the cases. The assistants for a particular case are selected on the basis of their technical competence in the subject matter of the case. The President of Malta, acting on the advice of the Prime Minister, appoints the assistants, or panels of assistants. The term of office of an assistant is four years, although this may be renewed for further terms. An assistant may be removed from office in the same manner as the Chairperson. Assistants must act impartially and independently, and only be subject to the direction or control of the Chairperson. Both the Chairperson and assistants must take an oath of office.

---

14   The designation of categories of cases to the various sections of the Tribunal is regulated by the Administrative Review Tribunal (Establishment of Panels) Regulations, S.L. 490.04.

23.19 The Administrative Review Tribunal, in the exercise of its functions, has the same powers as the First Hall of the Civil Court and may, subject to any regulations that the Minister responsible for justice establishes, regulate its own procedures.

23.20 The Administrative Review Tribunal when determining an appeal, may, in whole or in part, confirm or annul the decision appealed. In so doing the Tribunal must in writing give the reasons for its decision, make the decision public, and communicate it to the parties to the appeal.[15] All parties to the proceedings before the Tribunal may contest the decision of the Tribunal before the Court of Appeal.

23.21 While proceedings are still pending before the Administrative Review Tribunal or the Court of Appeal, the decision of the MCA stands and must be adhered to by all parties involved. Any party to the appeal may, however, apply to the Tribunal or the Court of Appeal to suspend the decision or directive of the MCA that is being contested pending the final outcome of the appeal.[16]

The NRA's Obligations to Cooperate with the Commission

23.22 The consolidation procedure[17] has been implemented into Maltese Law by Regulation 7 ECNS Regulations, while the co-regulation procedure[18] has been transposed into Maltese Law by Regulation 8 ECNS Regulations.

23.23 With respect to the powers of the European Commission to issue standards and specifications, the ECNS Regulations[19] impose on regulated undertakings an obligation to give due regard to any notices or guidelines that the MCA may issue with respect to standards, as well as any relevant voluntary standards and, or specifications published by the European Commission in accordance with Article 17(1) of the Framework Directive, and, or those that may be adopted by the European Standards Organisations or internationally recognised standardisation bodies where no compulsory standards have been issued.

Moreover the Authority must encourage the use of the non-compulsory standards or specifications referred to in Article 17(1) of the Framework Directive, for the provision of services, technical interfaces, or network functions, to the extent strictly necessary to ensure interoperability of services and to improve freedom of choice for users.[20]

'Significant Market Power' as a Fundamental Prerequisite of Regulation

Definition of SMP

23.24 The definition of 'significant market power' under the ECR Act is similar to that in the Framework Directive. SMP is defined as being a position equivalent to dominance, a position of economic strength affording an undertaking the power

---

15   Art 39 MCA Act.
16   Art 42 MCA Act.
17   Art 7 of the Framework Directive.
18   Art 7a of the Framework Directive.
19   See condition 12 of the Ninth Schedule (Section B) ECNS Regulations.
20   Reg 87 ECNS Regulations.

to behave to an appreciable extent independently of competitors, customers and, ultimately, consumers.[21] In October 2004, the MCA published a document entitled 'Market Review Methodology' detailing the manner in which it assesses significant market power.[22]

Definition of relevant markets and SMP designation

23.25   Article 9 ECR Act stipulates that the MCA must define relevant markets in accordance with the principles of competition law, taking the utmost account of any relevant recommendations and guidelines that the European Commission may issue.

23.26   To date, the MCA has followed the Commission's Market Recommendation and Guidelines in market analysis and has not defined sub-national markets. This being said, the MCA has recently proposed to define two additional markets that currently are not included among those recommended by the Commission, namely wholesale trunk segments of leased lines and retail leased lines. The Commission has recently approved this proposal and the final decision relating to the analysis of, and finding of SMP in, these markets has been published in December 2012.

Imposition of remedies

23.27   The MCA must impose ex-ante regulatory obligations 'only where there is no effective and sustainable competition and to relax and lift such obligations as soon as that condition is fulfilled.'[23] In accordance with the EU Regulatory Framework, therefore, where the MCA determines that a relevant market is not effectively competitive and designates undertakings with SMP, it is required to impose on such undertakings appropriate regulatory obligations and controls set out in the law, namely the ECNS Regulations.

NRA's Regulatory Duties Concerning Rights of Way, Co-location and Facility Sharing

Rights of way

23.28   The authority responsible for Transport in Malta (Transport Malta – 'TM') is empowered, under article 4 Utilities and Services (Regulation of Certain Works) Act, Cap. 81, to order that cables and wires be placed or other works be carried out either below, above, or adjacent to any tenement, and that trenches, pits, poles, stays, brackets, and all other accessories essential to the proper working of the electrical power and telecommunication systems be cut, placed, erected in, or affixed to any tenement. Decisions of the TM must be reasoned and are subject to the principles of transparency and non-discrimination, and the levy of fees must be proportionate. Decisions must be notified to the affected party ten days in advance of the carrying out of the ordered works. The order becomes effective ten days from

---

21   Art 2 ECR Act, and see also reg 6 ECNS Regulations.

22   Market Review Guidelines, Malta Communications Authority, 8 October 2004 (Market Review Guidelines 2004).

23   Article 4(2)(f) ECR Act.

notification. A person providing electronic communications networks or services, or associated facilities who is aggrieved by any decision may appeal to the Administrative Review Tribunal under the same principles applying to an appeal from a decision by the MCA. In so doing the appellant must show his or her juridical interest in challenging the contested decision. Moreover, within eight days from the order, the owner of a tenement affected by the order may submit a request to the MCA asking that the route of the cable, or other accessory to be erected or affixed, be deviated. The MCA must honour such request if such deviation does not cause interference or inefficiency with the service to be provided, create further liability or prejudice to other property, or give rise to a greater expense to the MCA. Such a decision may be appealed to the Court of Appeal by any person aggrieved by the decision. Additionally, the owner of a tenement affected by a right of way decision may request the Court of Appeal to order the payment of compensation for damages suffered. The law stipulates certain situations in which inconvenience is deemed not to be caused and compensation not due.[24] Moreover, operators enjoying rights must pay the MCA a fee which is set in accordance with the Right of Way for Utilities and Services (Fees) Regulations.[25]

Co-location and facility sharing

23.29   The TM is also empowered, under article 4(2) Utilities and Services (Regulation of Certain Works) Act, after consultation with the MCA and giving the affected undertaking reasonable time to express its views, to impose collocation or facility sharing obligations on an undertaking. The said undertaking may levy a reasonable fee on the undertaking to whom it must offer collocation or facility sharing. The fee must be cost-oriented and must not include charges for overheads such as marketing, personnel, or maintenance costs, other than those directly incurred on the facilities used.[26] Where the amount of this fee is disputed, the MCA will resolve the dispute and determine the charge to be levied. Where the person requesting collocation or facility sharing is an electronic communications service provider, the ordinary procedures (including those relating to an appeal) relating to dispute resolution will apply.[27]

REGULATION OF MARKET ENTRY: THE AUTHORISATION DIRECTIVE

The General Authorisation of Electronic Communications

23.30   The ECR Act introduces the concept of a general authorisation regime, expressly providing that no exclusive or special rights for the establishment or provision of networks or services will be granted or maintained in force.

23.31   An authorised undertaking is, in accordance with the provisions of the ECR Act and with the procedure under the ECNS Regulations, entitled to provide electronic communications services or to establish, extend, or provide electronic communications networks. In so doing, an undertaking must act in compliance with the applicable general authorisation conditions established under the ECNS Regulations, and, in particular, must first notify the MCA of its intention to provide the service or network.

---

24   Art 5 Utilities and Services (Regulation of Certain Works) Act.
25   S.L. 499.37.
26   Art 4(4) Utilities and Services (Regulation of Certain Works) Act.
27   See above.

23.32   The ECNS Regulations establish different categories of authorisation based on the nature of the service offered, reflecting the various rights and obligations applicable to these services. The categories of general authorisation are:

- public communications networks;
- publicly available telephone services;
- television and radio distribution services;
- other publicly available electronic communications services;
- non-public electronic communications services;
- publicly available telephone directories and directory enquiry services; and
- private electronic communications networks and/or services.[28]

23.33   A notification of a general authorisation is made by completing a notification form provided by the MCA. An undertaking is required to inform the MCA if it ceases to provide the network or service as notified, or if there is any change to the information supplied.[29] The MCA must maintain a register of those authorised undertakings that have notified it of their intention to provide a network or service. The register must include such information as the MCA considers appropriate, and which is not of a confidential nature.[30]

23.34   Undertakings acting under a general authorisation have a right to provide the electronic communications networks or services as described in the notification made to the MCA.[31] In addition, such undertakings are entitled to:

- where applicable, have their applications for rights of use of numbers and radio frequencies considered in according with the ECR Act and ECNS Regulations;[32]
- request the MCA to issue a declaration to facilitate the exercise of rights to install facilities and rights to interconnection;[33] and
- have their applications for rights to install facilities considered in accordance with applicable legislation.[34]

Authorised undertakings providing publicly available electronic communications networks or services enjoy additional rights to negotiate interconnection with and, where applicable, obtain access to or interconnection from another authorised undertaking and to be given an opportunity to be designated to carry out universal service obligations.[35]

23.35   General conditions for authorisation are established in the Ninth Schedule to the ECNS Regulations. The MCA, with the approval of the Minister responsible for communications, may amend the schedule periodically, but, regardless, it may not attach to general authorisations further obligations other than those listed in the Seventh Schedule to the ECNS Regulations. The MCA may also establish that certain conditions do not apply to specific categories of undertakings. As in all its regulatory dealings, the MCA must exercise these powers in accordance with the principles of non-discrimination, proportionality, transparency and objectivity.

---

28   Reg 65 ECNS Regulations.
29   Reg. 66 ECNS Regulations.
30   Reg. 68 ECNS Regulations.
31   Reg 69 ECNS Regulations.
32   Reg 69 ECNS Regulations.
33   Reg 69 ECNS Regulations.
34   Reg 69 ECNS Regulations.
35   Reg 69 ECNS Regulations.

23.36   Consistent with the EU Regulatory Framework, the general authorisation obligations may be supplemented by other specific obligations, including those relating to SMP and universal service operators, use of spectrum and numbering, and the provision of publicly available electronic communications services. This possibility is codified in clause 3, section B of the Ninth Schedule of the ECNS Regulations. This section specifies that all obligations, decisions, and directives adopted by the MCA in accordance with the applicable laws will apply and form an integral part of the general authorisation, making a breach of such obligations a breach of an undertaking's general authorisation.

23.37   A General Authorisation does not in any way exempt an authorised undertaking from its obligation to apply for and obtain other required permits (such as planning permits) that may be ancillary, but equally necessary, to providing the authorised service or network.

Rights of Use for Radio Frequencies

Strategic planning and co-ordination of spectrum policy

23.38   Article 38 ECR Act gives the MCA responsibility for the effective management of radio frequencies assigned to it in the National Frequency Plan. The National Frequency Plan is created and amended by the Minister responsible for communications after consultation, with the MCA.[36]

23.39   Regulation 75 ECNS Regulations transposes into Maltese law Article 8a of the Framework Directive. Under this regulation, the Minister and the MCA must, in their respective functions, cooperate with other Member States and with the European Commission in the strategic planning, coordination, and harmonisation of the use of radio spectrum in the European Union. To this end, they must take into consideration, among other things, the economic, safety, health, public interest, freedom of expression, cultural, scientific, social and technical aspects of EU and national policies as well as the various interests of radio spectrum user communities with the goal of optimising the use of radio spectrum and avoiding harmful interference. Such cooperation must promote the coordination of radio spectrum policy approaches in the European Union and, where appropriate, harmonised conditions with respect to the availability and efficient use of radio spectrum necessary for the establishment and functioning of the internal market in electronic communications.[37]

Principles of frequency allocation, procedural rules

23.40   Authorisations to use radio frequencies, with the exception of authorisations to use radio frequencies for radio or television broadcasting services with a view to pursuing general interest objectives and any other frequencies not assigned to the MCA under the National Frequency Plan, are granted by the MCA under articles 37 and 38 ECR Act. Under these provisions the MCA is prohibited from granting exclusive or special rights of use for the provision of electronic communication services.

23.41   The MCA may limit rights of use only when necessary to ensure the effective use of radio frequencies. When so doing, the MCA must follow the

---

36   Art 39 ECR Act.
37   Reg 75(3) and (4) ECNS Regulations.

procedure set out in regulation 73 the ECNS Regulations. Under this regulation, when the MCA is considering whether to limit the rights of use of spectrum, it must embark on a consultation process and publish its final decision. Following this, the MCA must invite applications, consider applications received, and award the rights of use in a non-discriminatory manner, through a competitive or comparative procedure. The award is considered a decision of the MCA and, therefore, subject to appeal. The MCA, on a number of occasions, has utilised such procedures for the assignment of limited rights of use, with respect to the award of 3G, GSM, DTTV , D-TAB, and BWA radio frequencies. The MCA has used both beauty contests and auction processes, as well as a combination of the two procedures.

23.42   All assignments of radio frequencies must be in accordance with open, objective, transparent, non-discriminatory,and proportionate procedures that are publicly available.[38]Except in instances where rights of use must be limited, and competitive or comparative procedures put in place for the purpose of assigning such frequencies, the MCA must assign radio frequencies within six weeks of receipt of an application.[39]

23.43   Unless otherwise restricted and specified in the Frequency Plan on grounds of efficiency, the need to limit harmful interference or ensure the technical quality of service, all forms of technology may be deployed over those radio frequencies set aside for use for the purpose of electronic communication services in the same Plan.[40]

23.44   Although in principle all types of electronic communications services may be provided in the radio frequency bands declared available for electronic communications services, the Minister, or the MCA with the approval of the Minister, may provide for proportionate and non-discriminatory restrictions to the types of electronic communications services to be provided, including, where necessary, to fulfil a requirement under the ITU Radio Regulations.[41]

23.45   The imposition of an obligation to provide a particular service or to use a particular type of technology for which the rights of use for the frequency is granted is permissible under the Seventh Schedule of the ECNS Regulations. In fact, the MCA has, almost invariably, resorted to this measure.

Transferability and time limitations

23.46   Rights of use of radio frequencies may be transferred or leased only where expressly authorised.[42] Given that the MCA must ensure efficient use of spectrum and avoid spectrum hoarding, individual rights of use typically are issued subject to a spectrum trading limitation. Where not excluded a priori spectrum rights licences generally require the prior approval of the MCA following a detailed process of due diligence of the assignee and the effect of the contemplated transfer on the market.

23.47   Under Reg 76(2), the MCA is required to ensure that when it grants rights of use for a limited period of time, the duration is appropriate for the service concerned taking due account of the need to allow for an appropriate period of investment amortisation. In practice, licences for the use of radio frequencies are

---

38   Reg 72(2) ECNS Regulations.
39   Reg 72(3) ECNS Regulations.
40   Art 40 ECR Act.
41   Art 41 ECR Act.
42   Art 45 ECR Act.

issued for a definite period of time. The period of a licence is generally announced at the call for applications stage and, prior to that, in the consultation seeking comments on the proposed policy and procedure to be utilised by the MCA for the award of the frequencies.

Admissible conditions

23.48   The conditions attached to individual rights of use are established by the MCA and contained in a licence but cannot exceed the maximum conditions set out in the Seventh Schedule to the ECNS Regulations. Roll out and coverage obligations are generally included in the licences issued by the MCA. In practice, the MCA has always published its draft licence together with the Call for Applications. This allows for greater transparency. However, the MCA generally reserves the right to increase or amend the obligations contained in the draft licence, with obligations made by the undertaking in the course of the competitive or comparative selection procedure.

Limitation of numbers of rights of use to be granted

23.49   As mentioned above, the MCA may, and in fact has on a number of occasions limited the number of licences granted with respect to a particular radio frequency. The MCA has utilised beauty contests, auctions, a mix of the two procedures, and negotiation procedures in assigning radio frequencies. The assignment procedure is one of the aspects of the consultation that commences the assignment process in cases where the number of rights of use are to be limited.

23.50   The annual fees to be levied are established by law.[43] In addition to such fees, the award price (where an auction process is employed) is paid upon licence grant.

Rights of Use for Numbers

General authorisations and granting of individual rights

23.51   The MCA is responsible for establishing and managing the national numbering plan for electronic communications services and for controlling the assignment of all national numbering resources.[44] It also has a statutory obligation to put in place procedures to ensure that the allocation of numbers is carried out in an objective, transparent, equitable, non-discriminatory, and timely manner. Any undertaking or person may apply to the MCA to have numbering resources assigned in accordance with regulation 77 ECNS Regulations.

23.52   Where the MCA deems numbers to be of exceptional value, it will issue a public consultation and such numbers will be allocated following a transparent and non-discriminatory comparative or competitive procedure.[45] The MCA is required to allocate a number within three weeks from a receipt of an application, except in cases of numbers of exceptional value, in which case the term may be extended.

---

43   Eighth Schedule to the ECNS Regulations.
44   Art 10 ECR Act.
45   Reg 77 ECNS Regulations.

Admissible conditions

23.53   In accordance with regulation 78 ECNS Regulations, the maximum conditions that may be imposed with respect to rights of use of numbering resources are
those set out in Part C of the Seventh Schedule ECNS Regulations, in line with
Part C of the Annex to the Authorisation Directive. All undertakings providing
publicly available telephone services (including mobile network operators and VoIP
providers) are required to provide full number portability facilities to their subscribers, consistent with regulation 47 ECNS Regulations. The MCA issued a decision[46]
on number portability highlighting the obligations and procedures to be followed. It
also issued a decision relating to the charging mechanism for number portability
that may be applied by operators.[47]

23.54   Under its decision 'Wholesale call origination services provided over fixed
networks', the MCA imposed carrier selection and carrier pre-selection on GO plc
as the undertaking with SMP in this particular wholesale market.[48]

Limitation of number of rights of use to be granted

23.55   As stated above, the MCA may, after public consultation, assign numbering
resources deemed to have an exceptional economic value, by using a comparative or
competitive selection process, therefore limiting the number of rights of use of these
numbers.

The NRA's Enforcement Powers

23.56   The enforcement powers of the MCA are primarily addressed in Part VII
MCA Act. Under Article 29 MCA Act, the MCA may, among other things, enter
premises, inspect books and documentation, and require the production of any
documentation, books, records, or information. Any person who impedes or
obstructs the MCA in carrying out its functions prescribed by law, including failing
to produce information the MCA requests, may lead to the imposition of a fine of
not less than €11,645, to imprisonment for a period not exceeding three months, or
to both.[49]

23.57   In the majority of cases of violation of a law or regulation enforced by the
MCA, or of a decision or directive issued by the MCA, the MCA is empowered to
impose administrative fines on the undertaking or person acting in breach of the
law, regulation, decision, or directive. Unless otherwise stated by law,[50] the MCA
may impose a maximum administrative fine of €349,406 for each infringement or
failure to comply and/or €11,646.86 for each day of infringement or non-
compliance. The amount of the fine imposed must reflect the seriousness and extent
of the infringement, its duration, and its impact on the market and on consumers.[51]
Where the infringement committed by the undertaking has particularly significant
effects on the market to the detriment of other competing undertakings or

---

46   'Introducing Number Portability in Malta', March 2005 (updated March 2010).
47   'Charging for Number Portability', March 2006 (updated January 2012).
48   Published 18 January 2010.
49   Art 29(5) MCA Act.
50   Certain provisions establish the maximum administrative fine that can be imposed.
51   Art 33(2) MCA Act.

consumers, the maximum limit of the administrative fine may be exceeded, provided it does not exceed 5 per cent of the turnover of the undertaking in the calendar year immediately preceding the year when the infringement was committed.[52]

23.58 In addition to imposing fines the MCA may order the cessation of any act or omission which is in breach of a law or regulation, or order the delay of a service or bundle of services which, if continued, may result in significant harm to competition, pending compliance with access obligations imposed following a market analysis.[53]

23.59 In cases of serious and repetitive breaches, the MCA may suspend or withdraw an authorisation to provide electronic communications services or networks.[54]

23.60 In each of the above cases, the MCA must, prior to taking any measures, provide the undertaking or person concerned a written warning of the measure to be taken, the specific reason for the measure, and the time within which the measure will take effect. With respect to timing, the MCA must allow for at least 15 days within which the undertaking or person concerned may make submissions, unless the MCA considers that the continuance of the infringement would hinder the ability of the MCA to carry out its regulatory functions or warrants immediate intervention. Where the measure to be taken is an administrative fine the person concerned must also be informed of the amount of the fine. In issuing the warning, the MCA may impose such conditions as it may consider reasonable in the circumstances.

23.61 If the alleged infringement constitutes an immediate and serious threat to public safety, public security or public health, or creates or may create serious economic or operational problems to other undertakings providing communications services or networks, or for consumers, the MCA may take urgent interim measures to remedy the situation, which may also include the imposition of administrative fines. Even in such instances, the person or undertaking against whom the measures are being contemplated must be afforded a reasonable opportunity to comment and propose alternative remedies.[55]

23.62 Notwithstanding an undertaking or person's right to appeal the MCA's decision to impose a fine or other measure, the fine or measure will be effective immediately upon its imposition. The undertaking or person, however, may request the Tribunal for the Administration of Justice to suspend the fine or measure until the final determination on the merits by the same Tribunal or Court of Appeal (in case the Tribunal's decision is appealed).[56]

23.63 A fine imposed by the MCA is subject to interest at the rate of 8 per cent per year.[57]

Administrative Charges and Fees for Rights of Use

23.64 The general principles relating to administrative charges are established in article 18 ECR Act, which, in substance mirrors the provisions of the Authorisation

---

52 Art 33(1) MCA Act.
53 Art 31(1) MCA Act.
54 Art 31(2) MCA Act.
55 Art 33(5) MCA Act.
56 Art 33(6) MCA Act.

Directive, and requires the levy of such fees as necessary to cover the administrative costs of the MCA. No fee is charged when a person or undertaking notifies the MCA of the intention to provide a network or service. However, authorised undertakings are required to pay an annual set fee depending on the category of network or service provided. Providers of television and radio distribution services must also pay a fee of €0.35 per subscriber, and providers of publicly available telephone services, television and radio distribution services, other publicly available electronic communication services and non-public electronic communications services, must also pay a percentage of their total gross revenues, which will vary depending on the amount, decreasing as the revenue band increases.[58]

23.65   Undertakings are required to pay usage fees for radio frequencies on an annual basis. The fees are listed in Part B of the Eighth Schedule to the ECNS Regulations.

23.66   Undertakings are required to pay usage fees for numbers on an annual basis. For geographic and mobile numbers, these fees are €0.35 for each individual number and €230 for each block of 10,000 numbers. For carrier select or pre-select codes, this fee amounts to €2,325 for each code.[59]

REGULATION OF NETWORK ACCESS AND INTERCONNECTION: THE ACCESS DIRECTIVE

Objectives and Scope of Access Regulation

23.67   Article 13 ECR Act requires the MCA to ensure adequate access, interconnection, and interoperability of services in such a way as to promote efficiency, sustainable competition, efficient investment, and innovation, with a goal of benefitting end users. The MCA may not impose restrictions that prevent undertakings from negotiating between themselves agreements on technical and commercial arrangements for access or interconnection, in accordance with EU law.[60] The manner in which the MCA may regulate access and interconnection in practice is further detailed in the ECNS Regulations.[61]

23.68   The provisions dealing with access and interconnection apply to operators of public communications networks on whom access obligations may be imposed, and to authorised undertakings seeking access. The term 'operator' is defined as 'an undertaking providing or authorised to provide a public communications network or an associated facility'.[62]

Basic Regulatory Concepts

23.69   The powers of the MCA with respect to access and interconnection are clearly delineated by the ECNS Regulations, which reflect the provisions of the Access Directive. The MCA has the power to impose access obligations on undertakings identified as having significant market power following the market

---

58   Eighth Schedule Part A ECNS Regulations.
59   Eighth Schedule Part C ECNS Regulations.
60   Art 14(1) ECR Act.
61   See Part IV of the ECNS Regulations.
62   Art 2 ECR Act.

review process.[63] In addition, the MCA has the power to impose obligations on all undertakings to ensure end-to-end connectivity and accessibility for end users, including those of digital radio and television broadcasting services.[64]

23.70   The definitions of access and interconnection are similar to those in the Access Directive.[65]

23.71   An undertaking requesting access or interconnection in Malta does not require a general authorisation to operate in Malta if it does not provide electronic communications services and/or does not operate a network in Malta. Furthermore, no restrictions may be imposed that prevent undertakings in Malta, or undertakings in Member States, from negotiating between themselves agreements on technical and commercial arrangements for access and/or interconnection, in accordance with EU law.[66]

23.72   The MCA may intervene on own initiative where justified or, in the absence of agreement between undertakings, at the request of either of the parties involved, in order to secure the policy objectives of the ECNS Regulations.[67]Any access and interconnection obligations the MCA imposes must be objective, transparent, proportionate, and non-discriminatory, and implemented following a consultation process.[68]

Access- and Interconnection-related Obligations with Respect to SMP Undertakings

Overview

23.73   The obligations that the MCA may impose following a finding of SMP reflect those in the Access Directive, specifically, transparency, non-discrimination, accounting separation, access to and use of specific network facilities, and price control and cost accounting obligations.[69] Furthermore, if the MCA deems that the obligations imposed have not achieved effective competition and that there are important and persistent competition problems, and/or it identifies market failures in relation to the wholesale provision of certain access product markets, it may, as an exceptional measure, request the European Commission to authorise it to impose an obligation on vertically integrated undertakings to place activities related to the wholesale provision of relevant access products in an independently operating business entity.[70] In all cases, any obligations imposed must be based on the nature of the problem identified, be proportionate and justified in the light of the objectives of ECR Act, and must be imposed following consultation.

Transparency obligations

23.74   The MCA may impose transparency obligations in relation to access, requiring operators to make public specified information, such as accounting

---

63   Reg 15 ECNS Regulations.
64   Reg 9 ECNS Regulations.
65   Art 2 ECR Act.
66   Art 14(1) ECR Act.
67   Reg 9(3) ECNS Regulations.
68   Reg 9(2) ECNS Regulations.
69   See Regs 12 to 16 ECNS Regulations.
70   Reg 17 ECNS Regulations.

information, technical specifications, network characteristics, terms and conditions for supply and use, and prices.[71] Where an operator has an obligation of non-discrimination, the operator may be required to publish a reference offer which must be sufficiently unbundled to ensure that undertakings are not required to pay for facilities which are not necessary for the services requested, giving a description of relevant offerings broken down into components according to market needs, and providing relevant terms and conditions for the provision of those offerings, including prices. The MCA may specify precise information to be made available, the level of detail required and the manner of publication. The obligation to publish a Reference Interconnection Offer has in fact been imposed in relation to various markets,[72] and the MCA has also imposed the obligation to publish a Wholesale Line Rental Offer, a Reference Unbundling Offer and wholesale prices in relation to other markets[73]

Non-discrimination obligations

23.75   With respect to the provision of access or interconnection, the MCA may also impose an obligation of non-discrimination to ensure that an SMP operator applies the same conditions in equivalent circumstances to other undertakings providing equivalent services. Such an obligation also requires that services and information are provided to others under the same conditions and of the same quality as the SMP operator provides for its own services, or for those of its subsidiaries or partners.[74] The MCA has imposed this obligation in all the six markets that it found not to be competitive.

Specific access obligations

23.76   If the MCA considers that denial of access hinders the emergence of a sustainable competitive market at the retail level, or is not in the end users' interest, the MCA may impose an obligation on an SMP operator to meet reasonable requests for access to, and use of, specific network elements and associated facilities. Operators may be required, among other things, to provide third parties with access to specified network elements, to allow carrier selection and/or pre-selection, and to offer subscriber line resale.[75] When considering whether to impose such an obligation, the MCA is required to take into account the technical and economic viability of using or installing competing facilities, available capacity and initial investment, among other factors. The MCA imposed access obligations in all the six markets that it found not to be competitive.

Price control obligations

23.77   Where lack of effective competition means that the operator concerned may sustain prices at an excessively high level, or apply a price squeeze, to the detriment of end users, the MCA may impose price controls in the provision of access, including an obligation that prices are cost-oriented while allowing for a

---

71   Reg 12 ECNS Regulations.
72   Namely, Markets 2, 3 and 7.
73   Namely, Markets 4, 1 and 6 respectively.
74   Reg 13 ECNS Regulations.
75   Reg 15 ECNS Regulations.

reasonable return on capital employed, and cost accounting obligations.[76] The MCA is required to ensure that any cost recovery mechanism or pricing methodology that it mandates serves to promote efficiency and sustainable competition and maximise consumer benefits. The MCA imposed wholesale price control and cost accounting obligations, mainly cost orientation, in all the six markets that it found not to be competitive

Accounting separation obligations

23.78 The MCA may also impose accounting separation obligations for specified activities related to interconnection or access,[77] such as requiring a vertically integrated company to make transparent its wholesale prices and its internal transfer prices. The MCA imposed accounting separation obligations in all the six markets that it found not to be competitive.

Functional separation obligations

23.79 Where the MCA has properly imposed the above access-related obligations, and concludes that they have failed to achieve effective competition and that there are important and persistent competition problems or it has identified market failures in relation to the wholesale provision of certain access product markets, it may, as an exceptional measure, following consultation with the Commission, impose an obligation on vertically integrated undertakings to place activities related to the wholesale provision of relevant access products in an independently operating business entity. Such business entity must supply access products and services to all undertakings, including to other business entities within the parent company, on the same timescales, terms, and conditions, including those relating to price and service levels, and by means of the same systems and processes.[78]

Regulatory Powers Applicable to All Market Participants

Obligations to ensure end-to-end connectivity

23.80 In accordance with the provisions of the Access Directive, without prejudice to any measures that may be taken in relation to SMP operators, the MCA may, to the extent necessary to ensure end-to-end connectivity, impose obligations on undertakings that control access to end users including, in justified cases, the obligation to interconnect their networks (if they have not already done so), and to make their services interoperable.[79]

Regulation of roaming services

23.81 The Roaming on Public Mobile Network Regulations (S.L. 399.29, or Roaming Regulations) were introduced in 2007 and amended in 2010 and 2012 to reflect the EU Roaming Regulation. The MCA is the authority in Malta responsible

---

76 Reg 16 ECNS Regulations.
77 Reg 20 ECNS Regulations.
78 Reg 17 ECNS Regulations.
79 Reg 9 ECNS Regulations.

for ensuring compliance with the Roaming Regulation, and, in so doing is authorised to exercise its powers under the MCA Act. In addition, the MCA is authorised to issue a compliance order requiring a person or undertaking in breach of the Roaming Regulations to cease and desist from its unlawful activity.

Access to digital radio and television broadcasting services

23.82   The MCA may impose access obligations on non-SMP operators to ensure accessibility for end users to specified digital radio and television broadcasting services, subject to the pre-conditions of objectivity, transparency, proportionality, and non-discrimination.[80] Moreover, the MCA may impose those conditions set out in Annex 1, Part 1 of the Access Directive in relation to operators of conditional access services who provide access services to digital television and radio services and holders of industrial property rights to conditional access products and systems.[81]

23.83   To the extent necessary to ensure accessibility for end users to digital radio and television broadcasting services specified by the MCA, the MCA may impose obligations on operators to provide access to the application programme interfaces (APIs) and electronic programme guides (EPGs) on fair, reasonable and non-discriminatory terms.[82]

REGULATION OF UNIVERSAL SERVICES AND USERS' RIGHTS: THE UNIVERSAL SERVICE DIRECTIVE

Regulation of Universal Service Obligations

23.84   The MCA published a decision entitled 'Universal Service Obligations on Electronic Communication Services' in April 2010 which was subsequently amended in September 2011.

23.85   The said Universal Service Decision set out the universal service obligations, and designated GO plc as the operator required to provide universal services, in the absence of expressions of interest by other operators. The defined universal service obligations are:

- the provision of access at a fixed location to the public telephone network and access to publicly available telephone services, whereby it was clarified that any request by any person in Malta for such connection or access is to be considered reasonable and that a connection must be capable of allowing end users to make and receive local and international calls, facsimile communications and data communications at data rates that are sufficient to permit functional internet access;
- the provision of broadband internet at a speed of at least 4Mbps, unless such speed is impossible to achieve due to technical or economical reasons, in which case the speed shall not be less than 2Mbps – 97 per cent of all installed lines must be capable of achieving a speed of 4Mbps;
- the provision of a comprehensive electronic telephone directory free of charge and a printed directory including the numbers of all subscribers of publicly

---

80   Reg 9 ECNS Regulations.
81   Second Schedule, Part A ECNS Regulations.
82   Reg 9 (3) ECNS Regulations.

available telephone services at a fixed location to be distributed to all said subscribers free of charge;

- the provision of a comprehensive telephone directory enquiry service made available to all end users, including users of public payphones at an affordable rate;
- the provision of public payphones;
- the provision of one call free of charge per week to a directory enquiry service number of the designated provider's choice to eligible visually impaired persons which are included in a list specifically provided by the responsible Ministry or Government Department;
- the provision of a 'Telecare' type of service allowing easy access to emergency services;
- the provision of reduced tariff options which would contribute to render the universal service affordable to eligible consumers, particularly vulnerable users on low incomes or with special social needs which are included in a list specifically provided by the responsible Ministry or Government Department;
- a call barring facility free of charge to block mobile calls, international calls, premium rate services and all outgoing calls with the exception of '112' calls; and
- the provision of a prepaid service which allows a subscriber to prepay for fixed lines services rather than pay rent or receive a bill.

23.86   Under the said Universal Service Decision, the designated undertaking may submit to the MCA a request for funding. This request must be submitted in writing to the MCA no later than nine months following the end of the financial year. The relevant period of assessing a request for funding is the most recent completed financial year of the undertaking. The undertaking requesting funding must provide the MCA with sufficient and detailed evidence supporting the claim that it has suffered an unfair burden in the provision of the universal service. This evidence must include a consideration of net costs, taking into account any market benefit accrued to the undertaking as a result of the universal service provided and follow the requirements of the Seventh Schedule to the ECNS Regulations. The undertaking bears the burden of proof for each universal service.

End User Rights

Contracts

23.87   Under Article 22 of the ECR Act, an undertaking providing connection or access to the public telephone network is required to provide the person subscribing to the service with a written contract containing at least the information stipulated under Regulation 35 of the ECNS Regulations. These include the details of the service provider, specific details of the service, prices and tariffs and the duration of the contract. A service provider may opt to enter into written contracts to provide other services to its subscribers, in which case such contracts must include the same detail as those required for contracts for connection or access to the public telephone network.

23.88   Before an undertaking makes modifications to any of the conditions in a contract, it must, at least 30 days before modifications take effect, notify every subscriber to that service of the modifications, informing him or her of the right to withdraw without penalty from the contract if he or she does not accept the modification. Moreover, the undertaking must also inform the MCA of its proposed modifications to the contract.

23.89   In October 2011, the MCA published a decision entitled 'Modifications to the Terms and Conditions of subscriber contracts'. Among other things, this decision clarifies that, in relation to a TV service, a change in channel line-up constitutes a change in the terms and conditions of service, and the service provider, therefore, is subject to the above contract modification requirements.

Quality of service: securing 'net neutrality'

23.90   The MCA has set Quality of Service parameters through a decision entitled 'Measuring Authorised Operator Quality of Service Performance', which was published in June 2005 and updated in March 2012. The decision requires the universal service fixed telephony provider to publish QoS information relating to:

- average time for initial connection;
- fault rate per access line;
- fault repair time;
- response time for operator services;
- response time for directory enquiry services;
- proportion of coin and card operated public pay telephones in working order;
- bill correction complaints.

With respect to mobile services, the publication of QoS performance results is not mandated, but encouraged. The designated operator providing leased lines is required to publish QoS performance results for the delivery period and repair time parameters as reported in the European Commission's Annual Report.

European emergency call number

23.91   An undertaking providing public pay telephones or comparable services must ensure that users of such facilities are able, free of charge and without the need to use coins or cards or any other means of payment, to make emergency calls using the single European emergency call number 112, and any national emergency call number that may be specified by the Authority.[83] Moreover, where a service is suspended, calls to these numbers must still be permitted.[84]

23.92   An undertaking providing end users with an electronic communications service for originating national calls to a number or numbers in a national telephone numbering plan, including public pay telephones, must ensure that, in addition to any other national emergency call number that may be specified by the MCA, all end users are able to call the emergency services free of charge, without the use of any means of payment, by using the single European emergency call number 112.[85]

23.93   In addition to the above, the 'Single European Emergency Call Service ('112' Number) And The European Harmonised Services Of Social Value ('116' Numbering Range) Regulations' (S.L. 399.43) have been promulgated to specifically regulate the handling of calls to the Emergency Numbers'112' and '116'. This subsidiary legislation includes, among other things, measures for the benefit of disabled end users and the provision and dissemination of information relating to these services.

---

83   Reg 25(4) ECNS Regulations.
84   Reg 36(5)(b) ECNS Regulations.
85   Reg 43(1) ECNS Regulations.

Obligations Facilitating Change of Provider

23.94   Number portability was introduced by a decision dated March 2005 (updated in 2010) and accompanying Specifications.[86] The MCA also published a decision on charges related to portability.

23.95   The obligation to allow for number portability extends to both fixed and mobile operators. The decision lists limited grounds for the refusal of porting. Moreover, the decision also prohibits operators from attempting to convince subscribers to remain with them or return to them (known as 'win back' tactics).

23.96   The prohibition of 'win back' tactics during and after the porting process is the subject of another decision published by the MCA in December 2006 (updated in August 2011). A distinction is made between such tactics and exit surveys which are permitted to the extent that they are not aimed at disrupting, and do not constitute a, disruption of, a smooth porting process. Exit surveys must be carried out in writing and no contact may be initiated with the subscriber prior to the passage of two months from effective porting. Moreover, a subscriber may not port his or her number back to the donor operator prior to the passage of two months from effective porting.

DATA PROTECTION: THE DIRECTIVE ON PRIVACY AND ELECTRONIC COMMUNICATIONS

Confidentiality of Communications

23.97   Data protection in electronic communications is regulated by the Processing of Personal Data (Electronic Communications Sector) Regulations (S.L. 440.01), administered by the Data Protection Commissioner. Regulation 4 of these regulations prohibits any form of interception or surveillance of communications without the consent of the user concerned. This prohibition does not extend to the recording of communications as part of lawful business practice or for the purpose of providing evidence of a commercial transaction. This provision in its entirety is excluded from applicability with respect to measures taken in accordance with legislation for the following purposes:[87]

- national and public security and defence;
- the prevention, investigation, detection and prosecution of criminal or administrative offences or of breaches of ethics for regulated professions;
- important economic or financial interests, including monetary, budgetary and taxation matters; and
- the protection of the subscriber or user or of the rights and freedoms of others.

23.98   Persons wishing to use electronic communications system to gain access to information stored in terminal equipment are required to inform the subscriber of the purposes of such processing. The subscriber or user is entitled to object to, or refuse, such processing at any time.[88]

---

86   The specifications related to fixed number portability have recently (July 2012) been amended to include an obligation to complete the process within one day from the conclusion of the contract.

87   Reg 10 Processing of Personal Data (Electronic Communications Sector) Regulations.

88   Reg 5 Processing of Personal Data (Electronic Communications Sector) Regulations.

23.99   The technical storage or access to information stored in terminal equipment for the sole purpose of carrying out or facilitating the transmission of a communication or providing an information society service explicitly requested by the subscriber or user is not subject to these requirements.[89]

Data Retention

23.100   The Data Retention Directive has been transposed into Maltese law in the Processing of Personal Data (Electronic Communications Sector) Regulations. Under these regulations, a provider of publicly available electronic communications services or of a public communications network must retain:

- data they have generated or processed in supplying the service that is necessary to trace and identify the source, destination, date, time and duration, and type of communication;
- data necessary to identify users' communications equipment (or what purports to be their equipment); and
- data necessary to identify the location of mobile communication equipment as specified and defined in these same regulations, to the extent that the said data is generated or processed by the said providers of the service or network in the process of supplying the service.

No data revealing the content of any communication may be retained.[90]

23.101   Unless a conservation order is issued by a Magistrate or a competent Court, or criminal proceedings have been commenced, the periods of retention of this data are as follows:

- communications data relating to Internet access and Internet e-mail – for a period of six months from the date of communication; and
- communications data concerning fixed network telephony, mobile telephony, and Internet telephony – for a period of one year from the date of communication.[91]

23.102   The retained data may only be disclosed to the Police or the Security Services where such data is required for the purpose of the investigation, detection, or prosecution of a serious crime (i.e., a crime punishable by a term of imprisonment of not less than one year).[92]

Traffic Data and Location Data

23.103   The definitions of 'traffic data' and 'location data' are the same as those in the E-Privacy Directive.[93]

23.104   Undertakings are required to erase or render anonymous traffic data processed for the purpose of transmitting communications as soon as the data is no longer needed for that purpose. However, traffic data necessary for billing purposes, including interconnection payments, may be retained for the period during which

---

89   Reg 5(3) Processing of Personal Data (Electronic Communications Sector) Regulations.
90   Reg 18 Processing of Personal Data (Electronic Communications Sector) Regulations.
91   Reg 21 Processing of Personal Data (Electronic Communications Sector) Regulations.
92   Reg 19 Processing of Personal Data (Electronic Communications Sector) Regulations.
93   Reg 3 Processing of Personal Data (Electronic Communications Sector) Regulations.

the bill may legally be challenged. The processing of data for marketing purposes or for the provision of value-added services is subject to the consent of the subscriber.

23.105   Where data processing is permitted, the undertaking concerned is required to inform the subscriber or user of the data being processed and the duration of such processing.

23.106   The rules for location data are the same as those for traffic data. Such data may be processed if it has been rendered anonymous, or to the extent and for the duration necessary for the provision of a value-added service. In the latter instance, such use is subject to the consent of the user. Specific rules dictate the information to be provided to the user prior to obtaining such consent.[94]

Itemised Billing

23.107   The contract between an undertaking and a subscriber, for connection to a public communications network and/or provision of publicly available electronic communications services must specify, among other things, the subscriber's' right to request a basic level of itemised bill, free of charge and through the subscriber's preferred medium.[95]

Presentation and Restriction of Calling and Connected Line Identification

23.108   The presentation and restriction of calling and connected line identification facilities are regulated by the ECNS Regulations. Where calling and connected line identification facilities are offered, the undertaking providing the publicly available electronic communications service must enable the caller or the called subscriber, to easily and free of charge, restrict the presentation of the calling line identification (and where the caller restricts the presentation of identification for the called subscriber to reject the call).[96] Moreover the restriction of these facilities may be overridden by the undertaking providing the public communications network or publicly available electronic communications service if a subscriber has requested in writing the tracing of malicious or nuisance calls and the undertaking is satisfied that such an action is necessary and expedient for the purposes of tracing such calls.

Automatic Call Forwarding

23.109   An undertaking providing a public communications network or publicly available electronic communications services must ensure that any subscriber is able to, easily and free of charge, stop automatic call forwarding by a third party to its terminal without delay.[97]

Directories of Subscribers

23.110   The Processing of Personal Data (Electronic Communications Sector) Regulations require any persons or undertakings producing a directory of subscribers to inform all subscribers in advance of the purposes of the directory and any

94   Reg 7 Processing of Personal Data (Electronic Communications Sector) Regulations.
95   Reg 35(1)(e) ECNS Regulations.
96   Reg 59(1) and (2) ECNS Regulations.
97   Reg 61 ECNS Regulations.

further usage possibilities based on search functions of any electronic versions of the directory. Data may only be included subject to the subscribers' consent. In giving their consent, subscribers may indicate which personal data is to be included in the directory. Subscribers who have given their consent must be given the opportunity to verify, correct, or withdraw the data.[98] The personal data included in directories is required to be limited to the data necessary to identify the subscriber and his or her number. Any additional information is subject to further consent, over and above that obtained for the inclusion of the basic data in the directory.

Unsolicited Communications

23.111   It is illegal to use any publicly available telecommunications service to make unsolicited communications for the purpose of direct marketing by means of an automatic calling machine, by facsimile, or electronic mail to a subscriber, unless the subscriber has given prior explicit consent in writing agreeing to receive such communications.[99]

---

98   Reg 8 Processing of Personal Data (Electronic Communications Sector) Regulations.
99   Reg 9 Processing of Personal Data (Electronic Communications Sector) Regulations.

The Dutch Market for Electronic Communications[1]

Robert Boekhorst, Maarten Goudsmit, and Kevin van 't Klooster
Baker & McKenzie, Amsterdam

LEGAL STRUCTURE

Basic Policy

24.1 The telecommunications market in the Netherlands has undergone some important shifts in the last decade. The original focus was to stimulate competition and disempower the former incumbent, KPN Telecom. This has resulted in robust competition in many markets and the creation of many new fields in which parties can compete on a level playing field.[2] Much still remains to be done in the Netherlands, but there has been a marked shift of focus from ex ante regulation to ex post regulation. Moreover, there has been an increased interest in regulation of telecommunications services provided to end users and the many issues related to privacy, security, and quality of service.

24.2 In the Netherlands, the legislator has not been satisfied to see the European Commission take the lead in strengthening consumer protection. The Dutch NRA has, therefore, become more focused on enforcing consumer rights, imposing fines for spam, regulating roaming tariffs, and emphasising the importance of a new cookie law.[3]

24.3 The NRA's role as a market regulator remains important as the Dutch incumbent KPN continues to have significant market power in many markets.[4] There still remains a challenge to further open these markets. In the next decade, therefore, ex ante regulation likely will remain an important tool for the NRA.

---

1 Editing of this chapter was concluded on 18 September 2012.
2 KPN was not considered to have significant market power in the low quality wholesale broadband access market. *Marktanalyse wholesale breedbandtoegang*, 27 April 2012, OPTA/AM/2012/201220.
3 *OPTA's Focus op 2012: internetveiligheid, ongevraagde telemarketing en de zakelijke telecommarkt*, 19 March 2012, www.opta.nl/nl/actueel/alle-publicaties/publicatie/?id=3566
4 The NRA found that there was a risk that KPN would have significant market power in the retail market for fixed telephony in the absence of regulation, and that KPN had significant market power in the wholesale market for fixed telephony. *Marktanalyse Vaste Telefonie*, 1 May 2012, OPTA/AM/2012/201189.

Implementation of EU Directives

24.4   The framework for Dutch telecommunications law is set out in the Telecom Act of 1998 (*Telecommunicatiewet* (Tw)),[5] which was overhauled as part of the 2002 Regulatory Package. This led to the enactment of an almost completely redrafted version of the Tw in 2004. The Dutch implementation of the 2009 Regulatory Package lagged in Parliament, and the Netherlands (like many Member States) did not meet the 25 May 2011 deadline for implementation. On 5 June 2012, the 2009 Package was finally implemented in Dutch law.[6] The revised legislation also necessitated numerous changes in governmental regulations.[7]

Legislation

24.5   The Tw provides the overarching framework for the regulation of telecommunications in the Netherlands. Many of the specifics of regulation are left to the government, which issues decrees, often corresponding to the fields of telecommunications regulation set out by the European directives, such the Interoperability Decree[8], the Decree on Terminal and Radio Equipment[9], the Decree on End User Rights,[10] and the Conditional Access Decree.[11] Several of these decrees delegate certain rule-making to even lower-level legislation, such as the Regulation on End User Rights.[12]

Regulatory Principles: The Framework Directive

Scope of regulation

24.6   The Tw covers all electronic communications services and networks, including communications services in networks used for broadcasting. In line with Article 2(c) of the Framework Directive, services providing, or exercising editorial control over, content transmitted using electronic communications networks and services, are excluded from the scope of the Tw, if these services do not consist wholly (or mainly) of the conveyance of signals on electronic communications

---

5   *Wet van 19 oktober 1998, houdende regels inzake de telecommunicatie* (*Telecommunicatiewet*). Bulletin of Acts and Decrees 1998, 610.

6   *Wet van 10 mei 2012 tot wijziging van de Telecommunicatiewet ter implementatie van de herziene telecommunicatierichtlijnen*, Bulletin of Acts and Decrees 2012, 235.

7   *Besluit van 30 mei 2012 tot wijziging van het Besluit interoperabiliteit, het Besluit randapparaten en radioapparaten 2007, het Besluit universele dienstverlening en eindgebruikersbelangen, het Besluit vergoedingen Telecommunicatiewet, het Besluit voorwaardelijke toegang en het Frequentiebesluit, ter implementatie van de herziene telecommunicatierichtlijnen* (*Besluit implementatie herziene telecommunicatierichtlijnen*). Bulletin of Acts and Decrees 2012, 236.

8   *Besluit interoperabiliteit*, 7 May 2004, Bulletin of Acts and Decrees 2004, 205, as amended from time to time.

9   *Besluit randapparaten en radioapparaten 2007*, 20 July 2007, Bulletin of Acts and Decrees 207, 20, as amended from time to time.

10   *Besluit universele dienstverlening en eindgebruikersbelangen*, 19 May 2004, Bulletin of Acts and Decrees 2004, 203, as amended from time to time.

11   *Besluit voorwaardelijke toegang*, 19 May 2004, Bulletin of Acts and Decrees 2004, 204, as amended from time to time.

12   *Besluit universele dienstverlening en eindgebruikersbelangen*, 19 May 2004, Bulletin of Acts and Decrees 2004, 203, as amended from time to time.

networks. Such 'content services' are typically governed by, among other things, the Dutch Media Act.[13]

24.7   Dutch telecommunications law only regulates *public* electronic communications networks and services. In general, an offer to provide a network or service that is only available to one group of customers, which is not accessible to the general public, is not considered to be a public network or service and, therefore, is not subject to regulation. The fact that those customers use the network or service to provide a public network or service themselves is irrelevant.[14]

24.8   The provision of Voice over the Internet Protocol ('VoIP') falls within the scope of telecommunications regulation.[15] In many cases, the Dutch telecommunications regulator, the Independent Post and Telecommunications Authority (*Onafhankelijke Post- en Telecommunicatieautoriteit* ('OPTA')) considers VoIP a public telephony service. As such, end user rights[16] apply to those services. VoIP services that do not allow the end user to call to, and be called at, numbers from the numbering plan, are in principle not considered public telephony services.

'Internet Freedom'

24.9   The Dutch Parliament has implemented a net neutrality provision, which prohibits providers of public electronic communication networks and services from restricting or impairing traffic. The Netherlands is the first Member State to implement such a far-reaching net neutrality provision.[17]

24.10   Dutch law currently provides no basis to impose a restriction of end user access to the Internet based on an end user's violation of a third party's intellectual property rights. However, courts can grant orders to Internet service providers to block their end users from accessing certain websites which infringe on the intellectual property of third parties.[18]

National Regulatory Authorities: Organisation, Regulatory Objectives, Competencies

Overview

24.11   While the OPTA derives its authority from the Tw, the agency was created by the OPTA Act of 1997.[19] This Act also establishes the independence of OPTA from undue government influence through various safeguards. Some specific issues under the Tw remain under the authority of the Ministry of Economic Affairs.

---

13   *Wet van 29 december 2008 tot vaststelling van een nieuwe Mediawet*, Bulletin of Acts and Decrees 2008, 583.
14   Lower Court of Rotterdam, 27 March 2009, LJN: BH9324 (affirmed by College van Beroep voor het Bedrijfsleven, 22 June 2012, LJN: BX0230).
15   *Standpunt eindgebruikersverplichtingen Voice over IP diensten.* OPTA/AM/2008/201405, 23 June 2008.
16   These end user rights are set out in the Tw and lower level regulations.
17   See paras 24.134 et seq.
18   For a recent example in the context of the on-going litigation regarding torrent website, see *The Pirate Bay* Lower Court of The Hague, 11 January 2012, LJN: BV0549.
19   Wet Onafhankelijke post- en telecommunicatie autoriteit, 5 July 1997 Bulletin of Acts and Decrees 1997, 320.

24.12   The General Administrative Law Act (*Algemene wet bestuursrecht* ('Awb')) sets out the majority of procedural rules regarding regulation by administrative bodies.[20] The Awb permits regulatory authorities to enter private premises (with the exception of homes) in the exercise of their tasks.[21] Moreover, these authorities are entitled to copies of any relevant papers and documents and may order parties to disclose relevant information.[22] These competencies are not unrestricted, however, as regulators must exercise these measures proportionally.

Tasks and competencies of OPTA

24.13   The OPTA is an independent administrative body (*zelfstandig bestuursorgaan*), a status that enables it to operate independently of the State. This independence was initially intended to prevent favouritism towards the fixed line incumbent operator, KPN. At the time OPTA was established, the Dutch government held a significant portion and a 'golden share' voting power in KPN. In September 2006, the State divested all its shares, however. The Minister of Economic Affairs bears political responsibility for a number of the OPTA's tasks, but has no influence on the decisions made by the OPTA.

24.14   The tasks and competence of the OPTA are defined in the Tw and in the OPTA Act. The Tw, for example, delegates to the OPTA the important task of defining relevant markets, identifying parties with SMP in the markets, and determining the obligations to be imposed on such parties.

24.15   The OPTA is also tasked with settling disputes between providers regarding access to, and interconnection between, networks. The OPTA must, except in rare circumstances, render a decision within 17 weeks after receiving a request for dispute resolution.[23] In urgent matters, the OPTA may render a provisional decision that will bind the disputing parties until a final decision is made.

24.16   The scope of the OPTA's enforcement duties has been expanded to cover certain aspects of privacy regulation. For example, the OPTA actively regulates the use of unsolicited electronic communications ('spam').[24] The implementation of the 2009 Regulatory Package has added the responsibility for OPTA to ensure that data breaches are reported properly and to oversee the use of 'cookies' on the Internet.[25] Many of these responsibilities give OPTA jurisdiction to oversee parties who do not provide telecommunication services or networks.

24.17   Other tasks of OPTA include:

- approving or rejecting interconnection rates and/or end-user tariffs of SMP undertakings;[26]
- issuing telephone numbers;[27]

---

20   *Algemene wet bestuursrecht*, 4 June 1992, Bulletin of Acts and Decrees 1992, 315, as amended from time to time.
21   Art 5:15(1) Awb.
22   Art 5:17(2) Awb.
23   Art 12.5(1) Tw.
24   See paras 24.154 et seq.
25   See paras 24.142 et seq.
26   Art 6a.7 Tw (interconnection rates) and art 6a.13 Tw (end-user tariffs). See paras 24.94 et seq and para 24.126, respectively.
27   Art 4.2 Tw. See para 24.71.

- regulating certification providers for electronic signatures;[28] and
- safeguarding the legal minimum of services to be provided in the area of fixed telephony.[29]

Tasks and competencies of the Minister of Economic Affairs

24.18 One important task under the Tw has not been assigned to OPTA, and remains the responsibility of the Minister of Economic Affairs: the management and allocation of radio spectrum (ie frequency planning, issuing licences for frequency use, and enforcement of frequency use). In practice, this task is carried out by the Telecom Agency (*Agentschap Telecom*), a government agency operating under the responsibility of the Minister of Economic Affairs. The Agency is also tasked with enforcing rules regarding lawful intercept of communications and the retention of traffic data and ensuring that the European emergency number is accessible from all telecommunications services.

24.19 In order to enforce regulations, the Minister of Economic Affairs is authorised, among other things, to collect information from regulated market parties, to levy fines in the event of violations, and to issue threats of fines in order to ensure compliance with legal obligations.

Relationship between OPTA and the Dutch Competition Authority

24.20 The OPTA issues sector-specific ex ante regulatory decisions in order to promote competition in the electronic communications sector. The Dutch Competition Authority (*Nederlandse Mededingingsautoriteit* ('NMa')) enforces the prohibition against cartels or abuse of a position of economic power in all markets, and determines ex post whether a violation to the Competition Act has taken place. The NMa is competent to decide whether companies that submit an application will be permitted to merge. Given that the ex ante regulatory duties of the two agencies coincide, they work closely together in this area. In 1999, the two organisations developed a cooperation protocol,[30] which was revised in June 2004 to reflect the amendments in the new Tw.[31]

24.21 At the time of writing, a proposal to merge OPTA, the NMa, and the Dutch Consumer Authority into one Authority for Consumer and Market Affairs ('ACM') was pending before the Second House of Parliament.[32] The government expects that the legislative act instituting ACM will enter into force by January 2013. A second legislative act is expected to be introduced to streamline the rules and regulations that currently govern the three regulatory authorities. The merger should negate the overlap that currently exists between the regulatory authorities.

Relationship with the Dutch Data Protection Authority

24.22 As explained above, the OPTA has assumed an increasing number of regulatory responsibilities with respect to data protection. This results in regulatory

---

28   Art 15.1(3) and 18.15 Tw.
29   Art 15.1(3) and 9.1 Tw.
30   *Samenwerkingsprotocol OPTA/NMa*, Official Gazette 1999, 2, p 5.
31   *Herzien samenwerkingsprotocol OPTA/NMa over de wijze van samenwerking bij aangelegen heden van wederzijds belang*, Official Gazette 2004, 121, p 34.
32   *Regels omtrent de instelling van de Autoriteit Consument en Markt* (*Instellingswet Autoriteit Consument en Markt*). Second Chamber 2011–2012, 33.186, nr 2.

overlap with the Dutch Data Protection Authority (*Commissie bescherming persoonsgegevens* ('Cbp')), which is charged with the enforcement of the Data Protection Act (*Wet bescherming persoonsgegevens* ('Wbp')). In 2005, the OPTA and the Cbp published a cooperation protocol that sets out the delineation of regulatory activities of each body.[33] In general, the OPTA is responsible for the data protection rules that are set out in the Telecom Act. The Cbp is responsible for the enforcement of the provisions set out in the Wbp. The implementation of the 2009 Regulatory Package introduced a number of additional data protection rules into the Tw, such as the data breach notification duty and specific provisions regarding the use of cookies on the Internet.[34]It is expected that these developments will result in an updated cooperation protocol, though this has not yet been announced.

The national consultation procedure

24.23   Where OPTA intends to take certain measures concerning access and interconnection,[35] the OPTA must follow a national consultation procedure whereby it:[36]

- prepares a draft measure and publishes it in the Dutch Government Gazette (Staatscourant);
- makes all relevant information available for interested parties;
- consults, where appropriate, with the Dutch Competition Authority (NMa);
- provides any interested party the opportunity to comment on the draft measure within one month after its publication; and
- issues the measure, which thereby becomes legally binding (usually on its website).

24.24   Only 'interested parties' (ie those who have a direct interest in the draft measure) are permitted to comment on a draft measure. Such parties have six weeks to submit comments.[37] If the intended measure does not have a 'significant impact on the relevant market', the OPTA may refrain from conducting the national consultation procedure described above. As the Tw does not specify how 'a significant impact on the relevant market' is to be assessed, the OPTA has a certain amount of discretion in deciding whether to utilise the national consultation procedure for a particular intended measure.

Right of Appeal against NRA's Decisions

24.25   Under Dutch law, not all acts by an administrative body are considered 'decisions' which are open to administrative appeal. A 'decision' is any written statement by an administrative body, which entails a change in the legal position of a party under public law. Verbal statements by OPTA officials, therefore, are not

---

33   *Samenwerkingsprotocol CBP-OPTA*. Official Gazette 2005, 133, p. 127.
34   Art 11.7a Tw.
35   The consultation procedure is mandatory when the OPTA makes a decision based on 6.2, 6a.2, 6a.3, 6a.4a, 6b.2(5)(a) Tw.
36   Art 6b.1(1) Tw.
37   Dutch law provides for a shorter term than suggested by the European Commission in paragraph 145 of the 'Commission Guidelines on market analysis and the assessment of significant market power', where it states that 'a period of two months would be reasonable for the public consultation' for decisions related to the existence and designation of undertakings with SMP.

'decisions' subject to appeal. Moreover, a written statement by the OPTA which simply recounts a state of affairs is not a 'decision' as it does not involve a change in the legal position of a party; it is simply a statement of fact. Finally, the change must involve public law, not civil law. If the OPTA signs a contract, it can be sued in civil law court for disputes arising out of that contract, but not an administrative court.

24.26 Any interested party may, in principle, challenge a decision by the OPTA. A party is interested when it has a direct, personal and individual interest in the decision. A direct interest means that the decision must affect the party directly (and not, for example, through a contractual relationship with a party who is affected by the decision). The interest must be personal in the sense that the party's own interests must be at stake, not those of a third party. Finally, the right to appeal exists only if the party's individual interests are affected (ie the individual's interest must be distinguishable from the interests of the general public).

24.27 Interested parties may appeal most OPTA decisions directly in court, without first having to submit an objection to the decision with the OPTA itself. This does not apply to decisions by OPTA to impose fines or to issue a prohibition to provide telecommunications services or networks, an objection to which must be submitted to the OPTA first before appeal becomes available. The Tw also stipulates that most OPTA decisions may be challenged by way of a proceeding at the Appellate Tribunal for Trade and Industry (*College van Beroep voor het Bedrijf-sleven* ('CBb')).[38] In most instances, there is no option to appeal the CBb judgment and the verdict in first instance is, therefore, final. This does not apply to fines and a prohibition to provide telecommunications services or networks, which must be challenged first in the Rotterdam court and then appealed to the CBb.

The NRA's Obligations to Cooperate with the Commission

24.28 The consultation procedure applies in situations in which the OPTA intends to make a decision to identify a relevant market or to identify a party with significant market power and this intended measure would affect trade between Member States. In such case, the OPTA must submit the draft measure (stating the reasons behind the draft measure) to the Commission, BEREC, and the other NRAs. The Commission, BEREC and the other NRAs have one month to comment on the draft measure.

24.29 Once the comment period has ended, the OPTA may adopt the draft measure, taking into account 'as much as possible' the comments of the Commission, BEREC, and the other NRAs.[39] The OPTA, therefore, may adopt the measure despite objections raised by the other bodies.

24.30 If the Commission notifies the OPTA that it believes the draft measure would create a barrier to the single market, or that it has serious doubts as to its compatibility with Community law (and in particular the objectives referred to in Article 8 of the Framework Directive), the OPTA may not adopt the measure for a further two months. During this two-month period, the Commission may decide to

---

38   Art 17.1 Tw.
39   Art 6b.2(3) Tw.

require the OPTA to bring the draft measure in line with Community law, or to withdraw the draft measure.[40]

24.31   The international consultation procedure set out in the Tw complies with the Framework Directive. If the OPTA prepares a measure to impose, extend, revoke, or amend certain obligations on a party which has significant market power, OPTA must also open a European consultation, which includes waiting one month to finalise the measure. The Commission may decide to notify the OPTA that it believes the draft measure would create a barrier to the single market, or that it has serious doubts as to its compatibility with Community law, and in particular the objectives referred to in Article 8 of the Framework Directive. In such a case, the decision to finalise the measure is postponed by four months. During this four-month period, the Commission and BEREC may try to convince the OPTA to withdraw or amend the measure. If the Commission and BEREC have issued their recommendation, or withdrawn their objections before the end of the four months period, the OPTA may choose to follow the recommendation or withdraw its draft measure altogether. If the OPTA decides to do the former, it must restart the national consultation procedure. The OPTA may also decide to ignore the recommendation from the Commission and BEREC but has to explain its reasons for this decision. However, the OPTA decision to ignore the recommendation from the Commission and BEREC applies only to remedy decisions (Article 7b (5)(a) of the Framework Directive). The Commission does have a veto power with regard to decisions related to market definitions and market analysis.

24.32   The Tw does not specify whether the international consultation procedure must be preceded by the national consultation procedure,[41] or whether both procedures can be held at the same time. The OPTA, therefore, is free to decide the order. For market analyses, the OPTA usually finalises the national consultation before submitting the decision for European consultation.

24.33   The 2002 Regulatory Package gave the Commission authority to set non-binding, as well as compulsory, technical standards. The Tw has delegated to lower level government decrees the specific requirements for compliance with compulsory standards. To date, however, the government has not issued any regulations with respect to the implementation of standards requirements.

24.34   Article 19 of the Framework Directive grants the Commission the authority to issue recommendations which are not binding on the OPTA. The Directive states, however, that an NRA must take 'utmost account' of these recommendations in carrying out its tasks.[42] If the OPTA sets aside a recommendation, therefore, it must notify the Commission and the Ministry of Economic Affairs of the reasons for that decision.

24.35   The CBb has ruled that reliance on these non-binding Commission recommendations is not a sufficient defence to a claim that an OPTA measure has violated the Tw.[43] The CBb ruling came in a case where CBb decided that OPTA had violated the Tw notwithstanding that the OPTA set the rates in accordance with the Commission's recommendation on fixed and mobile termination rates. The OPTA was forced to reconsider the measure and establish rates that were inconsistent with those in the Commission recommendation.

---

40   Art 6b.2(5) Tw.
41   See paras 24.23 et seq above.
42   Implemented in art 1.3(2) Tw.
43   CBb, 31 August 2011, LJN: BR6195 (*Providers/OPTA*).

'Significant Market Power' as a Fundamental Prerequisite of Regulation

Definition of SMP

24.36 The definition of SMP in the Tw is identical to that in the Framework Directive. In order to find that an undertaking has SMP, the OPTA must establish that:

'either individually or jointly with others, it enjoys a position equivalent to dominance, that is to say a position of economic strength affording it the power to behave to an appreciable extent independently of competitors, customers and ultimately consumers.'

24.37 The OPTA has struggled with the identification of parties with SMP, and the CBb annulled several OPTA decisions with respect to SMP designations during the first round of market analyses.[44] In the second round of market analyses, OPTA's SMP designations passed scrutiny in all cases under review.[45] Nevertheless, many of the OPTA's market analyses were annulled by the CBb for other reasons, often due to incorrect designations of the relevant market.

Definition of relevant markets

24.38 The OPTA must determine the relevant market in the Dutch telecommunications sector for products or services that the Commission considers eligible for ex ante regulation in its Recommendation on relevant markets.[46] The OPTA has generally adhered to these recommendations from the Commission. In addition to the markets listed by the Commission, the OPTA may, at its discretion, identify other relevant markets.[47]

24.39 The OPTA must investigate these markets to determine:

- whether they are effectively competitive;
- whether they include undertakings with SMP; and
- which obligations are appropriate for these undertakings.

24.40 Whether a market is susceptible to ex ante regulation is established using the three-criteria test, as set out by the Commission in their Recommendation regarding relevant product and service markets:[48]

---

44 P Glazener & Q Kroes, *De rechterlijke toetsing van OPTA's marktanalyses: Materiële aspecten*, Mediaforum 2007, 11/12, p 334.

45 Q Kroes & P Glazener, *De rechterlijke toetsing van OPTA's marktanalyses: de tweede ronde*, Mediaforum 2012, 6, p 193.

46 Commission Recommendation on relevant product and service markets within the electronic communications sector susceptible to ex ante regulation in accordance with Directive 2002/21/EC of the European Parliament and of the Council on a common regulatory framework for electronic communications networks and services, C(2007) 5406 rev 1, recital 5.

47 Art 6a.1(2) Tw.

48 Commission Recommendation on relevant product and service markets within the electronic communications sector susceptible to ex ante regulation in accordance with Directive 2002/21/EC of the European Parliament and of the Council on a common regulatory framework for electronic communications networks and services, C(2007) 5406 rev 1, recital 5.

(1)   there are high and non-transitory barriers to entry in the relevant market;
(2)   there is no tendency towards competition; and
(3)   general competition law itself is insufficient.

24.41   The OPTA investigates whether this is the case in each market analysis. In the most recent round of market analyses, OPTA has found the following relevant markets (and the corresponding market number from the Annex of the Commission Recommendation):

● the retail market for fixed telephony (market 1);
● the wholesale market for fixed telephony (market 2);
● the market for fixed and mobile call termination (markets 3 and 7);
● the market for unbundled access (market 4);
● the market for low quality wholesale broadband access (market 5); and
● the market for high quality wholesale broadband access (market 5 and 6).

24.42   The OPTA also published a market analysis of the television market in 2011, but concluded that the market for television services did not meet the three-criteria test and therefore did not proceed to identify SMP undertakings in that market.[49]

Imposition of remedies

24.43   If the OPTA determines that a market lacks effective competition and a party in that market has significant market power, it must impose 'appropriate' and 'adequate' obligations on such party. An 'adequate' obligation is one that is based on the nature of problem identified in the specific market and is justified and proportional in light of the promotion of competition, the development of the internal market, and promoting end user interests.[50] In addition, the Ministry of Economic Affairs has issued a policy statement that instructs the OPTA to impose the obligations in such a way that minimizes the reduction of the incentive to develop innovative infrastructure.[51]

24.44   Three years after imposing the obligation, OPTA must re-evaluate the decision and potentially revoke the obligation if the market has reached the desired level of competition or the market party has lost its SMP.[52] The OPTA may, however, impose measures for an indefinite period of time.[53]

NRA's Regulatory Duties Concerning Rights of Way, Co-location and Facility Sharing

Rights of way

24.45   Any owner or supervisor of public lands is obliged to tolerate the installation and maintenance, as well as the clearance, of cables for a public electronic

---

49   *Analyse televisie*, 20 December 2011, OPTA/AM/2011/202885.
50   Art 6a.2(3) and 1.3(1) Tw.
51   *Beleidsregels van de Minister van Economische Zaken over door het college uit te oefenen taken in de elektronische communicatiesector*, Official Gazette 2005, nr 109.
52   Art 6a.4 Tw.
53   *Memorie van Toelichting*, Second Chamber 2002/2003, Bullet in of Acts and Decrees 28 851, nr 3, p 6.

communications network in and on that land.[54] In the 1998 Tw, the obligation to allow the installation of cables in public or private land was restricted to cables that were actually being used.[55] In the current Tw, this obligation also covers the installation of unused cables or empty 'ducts' that are to be filled with cables at a later stage.[56] The Tw provides for the right to compensation for landowners who are obliged to tolerate the installation of cables, though these compensation rights are rather restricted.[57]

24.46   Dutch municipalities are responsible for coordinating the work carried out within their territories by providers of public electronic communications networks in connection with the installation and maintenance of cables.[58] A municipality may require separate providers to carry out the installation of cables under public roads at the same time, in order to reduce the inconvenience to users of the public roads. In any event, providers may only begin to perform digging on the municipality's land if they have notified the municipality concerned of their intention to do so, and if they have received permission from the municipal executive with respect to the time, place, and method of carrying out the work.

24.47   If a landowner is under an obligation to tolerate installation, maintenance, or clearance of cables is a private party, the provider must try to reach an agreement with the landowner with respect to the time, place, and method of carrying out the work. If the parties fail to reach an agreement, the landowner or the provider may request the OPTA to decide the matter.[59] The OPTA must issue a decision within eight weeks after receiving a request. In the interim, the provider may not commence the intended work.

24.48   Cables placed underground are considered real property in their own right, separate from the land under which they are placed.[60] Therefore, underground networks must be registered with the land register (*kadaster*), and the transfer of underground networks must be carried out by notarial deed, requiring payment of transfer tax.

Co-location and facility sharing

24.49   Licensees for the use of sets of frequencies intended for the provision of electronic communications networks or services must fulfil reasonable requests to share the use of antenna sites (site sharing).[61] In the event that parties fail to reach an agreement, they may request OPTA to resolve their dispute. In the past, OPTA has also published guidelines on co-location of equipment in connection with access to the local loop.[62]

---

54   Art 5.2(1) Tw.
55   See *Telecommunication Laws in Europe* (4th edn) (1998), paras 12.129–12.131.
56   Art 1.1(z) Tw, art 5.1(1) Tw.
57   Art 5.7 Tw.
58   Art 5.2 Tw.
59   Art 5.3(2) Tw.
60   Art 5:20(2) Dutch Civil Code.
61   Art 3.11 Tw.
62   *Richtsnoeren over collocatie en eenmalige kosten met betrekking tot toegang tot de aansluitlijn*, 20 December 2000, 2000/OPTA/IBT/2000/203357, Official Gazette 21 December 2000, 248.

REGULATION OF MARKET ENTRY: THE AUTHORISATION DIRECTIVE

The General Authorisation of Electronic Communications

24.50   Any person or entity may provide public electronic communications networks, public electronic communications services, or associated facilities, upon notification to the OPTA.[63] Notification is carried out by completing a standard notification form. The OPTA subsequently confirms the notification and enters the notified parties in a public register, which can be accessed through OPTA's website.[64] Parties registered with OPTA are required to contribute to the cost of supervision, in proportion to their telecommunications-related turnover in the Netherlands.

24.51   Although the provision of electronic communications networks and services is, in principle, open to all, persons or entities providing such services must adhere to a number of obligations (described below). The Tw imposes specific obligations on all providers,[65] on universal service providers,[66] on providers who offer services to end users,[67] and persons or entities using telecommunications networks or services reach end users.[68]

24.52   Parties are required to apply for permission only when the utilisation of scarce resources is involved. For example, licences are required for the use of specific frequencies,[69] and numbers must be assigned to a party before they may use a number from a numbering plan.[70]

Rights of Use for Radio Frequencies

Strategic planning and co-ordination of spectrum policy

24.53   In 2005, the Dutch Government published a study on the economic merits of its frequency policy. [71] Based on this review, the Government submitted a proposal to amend the Tw in 2008.[72] The goal of the proposal was to introduce a more flexible approach with respect to frequency allocation. The 2009 Regulatory Package contained many similar changes. Parliament, therefore, decided to incorporate the 2008 proposal as part of the implementation of the 2009 Regulatory Package.

24.54   In May 2012, the Dutch Parliament approved both amendments to the Tw. These amendments entered into force upon publication by the government. The

---

63   Art 2.1(1) Tw.
64   www.opta.nl
65   See e g para 24.124.
66   See para 24.115 et seq and Chapter 9 Tw.
67   See, e g para 24.103 et seq for obligations regarding interconnection which apply to all providers of public electronic communications networks and services controlling access to end users, as set out in Chapter 6 Tw.
68   For example, the Tw contains provisions regarding unsolicited electronic communications ('spam') and the use of cookies, which apply to all persons or entities, and is not limited to those persons or entities offering telecommunications services, see art 11.7 and 11.7a Tw.
69   Art 3.3 Tw, see para 24.58 below.
70   Art 4.2 Tw see para 24.72 below.
71   *Nota Frequentiebeleid 2005*, Parliamentary Records II, 2005–2006, 24 095, nr 188.
72   *Wijziging van de Telecommunicatiewet in verband met de Nota frequentiebeleid 2005*, Parliamentary Records II, 2007–2008, 31 412, nr 2.

bulk of these amendments to the Tw has been published, and, therefore, has entered into force. At the time of writing, the new frequency provisions are awaiting publication. The Government expects to publish the law by 1 January 2013.[73]

24.55   The new 2012 policy emphasises the following objectives:

- the purposes for which frequencies may be used will be expanded;
- joint use is encouraged;
- the number of frequencies which require licences will be reduced;
- the allocation procedure is streamlined; and
- there is more opportunity to trade licences.[74]

24.56   The National Frequency Plan, established periodically by the Minister of Economic Affairs, describes which frequency usages require a licence.[75] The contents of the Frequency Plan are predetermined to a large extent by arrangements made on an international level under the auspices of the International Telecommunications Union (ITU), the European Conference of Postal and Telecommunications Administrations (CEPT), and the EU. The frequency policy as formulated in the National Frequency Plan is described in further detail in the Frequency Table, which indicates which frequencies can be used, whether they are subject to a licence and which method of allocation will be used. The Frequency Plan must be changed using a national consultation procedure. This allows market parties to provide their input on any amendments.

24.57   In 2010, the Minister of Economic Affairs released a 'conceptual note' regarding future policy on mobile development for the period 2011–2017, which includes radio spectrum policy for mobile communications,[76] and incorporates many of the suggestions in the first Radio Spectrum Policy Programme.[77] The Government identified a quickly growing demand for wireless broadband access, which will be satisfied in part using the 'digital dividend' band in the 800 MHz range. The most important objective for the coming years will be to safeguard effective competition. Therefore, the government reserved two 10 MHz bands for newcomers. Moreover, in order to optimise the use of the available radio spectrum, the Government will allow parties to trade and share frequencies for the use of mobile communications.

Principles of frequency allocation, procedural rules

24.58   A limited number of radio frequencies may be used without obtaining an individual licence. These licence-free frequencies are either frequencies that may be used by anyone, together with categories of radio transmission equipment to be designated by ministerial regulation (eg mobile telephones, remote controls) or frequencies used by government bodies such as the armed forces and the police. In certain cases, the government requires the user of a license-free frequency to notify the Telecommunications Agency of their intention to do so. The Minister of

---

73   This chapter discusses the law as enacted in May of 2012, although it has not entered into force at the time of writing.

74   *Wijziging van de Telecommunicatiewet in verband met de Nota frequentiebeleid 2005, Memorie van Toelichting*, Parliamentary Records II, 2007–2008, 31 412, nr 3.

75   The last revision entered into force on 1 January 2012, Official Gazette 2011, 23518.

76   *Strategische Nota Mobiele Communicatie*, Parliamentary Records II, 2010–2011, 24 095, nr 264.

77   Proposal for a decision of the European Parliament and of the Council establishing the first radio spectrum policy programme, COM(2010) 471 final, 20 September 2010.

Economic Affairs may also establish 'passive' frequencies in the National Frequency Plan, which are used for receiving signals only. This option has been introduced mostly for scientific applications, such as radio astronomy.[78]

24.59   The National Frequency Plan also sets aside frequencies for public broadcasting services. The law dictates that the Minister of Economic Affairs must, to the extent that this is technically possible, provide sufficient frequency for three national public television channels and five public radio channels. In addition, the Minister of Economic Affairs must set aside radio frequencies for at least one public station per province and, if it does not interfere with the functional allocation of the spectrum, one station at the local level.

24.60   The use of all other radio frequencies requires a licence. These licences are granted by the Minister of Economic Affairs, rather than the OPTA.[79] The Tw provides for allocation of frequencies for public use in the areas of defence, public safety, law enforcement, science, traffic safety and emergency services, at the request of the responsible governmental departments. These frequencies are then designated as such in the National Frequency Plan. The relevant governmental department must restate the justification for the designation after three years.

24.61   Pursuant to the Tw, the Minister of Economic Affairs may assign the remaining frequency bands in the order of receipt of the applications ('first come, first serve'), by means of a 'beauty contest' which may or may not include a financial bid, or by means of an auction.[80] The Frequency Decree adopted in 1998 however, determines, to a certain extent, which of these allocation methods must be applied utilised for a certain radio frequency.[81] The 'first come, first serve' method is only applied for frequencies that are not scarce (ie where demand does not exceed supply), and for non-commercial frequencies. For the economically most valuable frequencies (such as frequencies for GSM/UMTS and commercial FM radio frequencies), the Minister of Economic Affairs has the choice between a beauty contest (which can include a financial bid) or auction. For example, the Minister of Economic Affairs chose to allocate both the GSM and UMTS frequencies through auction.

24.62   An important new feature of the 2012 legislation is 'allocation upon request': the right of market participants to request that a certain frequency band be allocated, rather than waiting for the Government to open a frequency up for allocation. If the Government receives such a request from a market participant, it publishes the request and gives other market participants the chance to express their interest in the specific frequency. If no other party expresses an interest in the frequency, the Minister of Economic Affairs allocated the frequency without charge. If interested parties outnumber the available licences, an auction is used to determine the licence holders.

24.63   The government has, at the time of publication, not appointed any frequencies suitable for 'allocation upon request'. However, the government has indicated that this method will mostly be used for the allocation of frequencies with 'niche' applications.

---

78   *Wijziging van de Telecommunicatiewet in verband met de Nota frequentiebeleid 2005, Memorie van Toelichting*, Parliamentary Records II 2007–2008, 31 412, nr 3.
79   Art 3.1 Tw.
80   Art 3.3(2), 3.3(4) Tw.
81   *Frequentiebesluit*, Bulletin of Acts and Decrees 1998, 638.

Transferability and time limitations

24.64 A licence is, in principle, transferable to a third party with permission from the Minister of Economic Affairs.[82] The Minister of Economic Affairs bases its decision to permit a frequency licence transfer on the same criteria on which it based the initial decision to grant the license. Additionally, the Minister of Economic Affairs may refuse to permit a licence transfer such refusal is necessary to achieve or maintain effective competition. The Minister of Economic Affairs must involve the OPTA if the transfer could seriously restrict the effective competition. The Minister of Economic Affairs has the opportunity to amend the conditions imposed on the new licence holder. If the licence is only partially transferred, the Minister of Economic Affairs may amend the conditions that apply to the original licence holder and issue a new licence to the new licence holder.

24.65 All licences are limited in time.[83] The duration of a licence is specified for each license. Licences which were granted on a 'first come, first serve' basis are automatically renewed, unless the Minister of Economic Affairs decides to terminate the licence. The Minister of Economic Affairs must give notice of a decision to terminate a licence two years prior to the date that the licence would normally automatically renew. The duration of the licence is often tied to the duration it would reasonably take a market party to obtain a return on the investment in the network infrastructure. In the case of the 2,6 GHz band, for example, this was estimated to take 20 years.

Admissible conditions

24.66 The Minister of Economic Affairs may impose additional restrictions (beyond time limitations) and obligations on the licence holder in the interest of an optimal allocation and effective use of the radio spectrum.[84]

24.67 For example, the Minister of Economic Affairs may require a licence holder to:

- offer certain services using the frequency;
- pay a lump sum (but not a recurring fee, and the fee must be calculated in relation to the economic value of the benefits that would be derived from the use of the frequency during the term of the licence);[85] and
- roll out a network that utilises the frequency in a timely and comprehensive manner.

24.68 The extent of the last obligation will increase over time, so that the licence holder has an opportunity to roll out its network in a phased manner. The Dutch court has ruled that the government may impose an obligation for each licence holder to use its own network. Market parties are, therefore, in principle free to jointly set up network infrastructure, as long as they each use their own frequency on that network.[86]

---

82   Art 3.20 Tw.
83   Art 3.17 Tw.
84   Art 3.14 Tw.
85   Art 3.15 Tw.
86   Lower Court of Rotterdam, 27 May 2010, LJN: BM5977 (*Telfort and Vodafone/State Secretary of Economic Affairs*).

Limitation of number of rights of use to be granted

24.69   As noted above, the Government may identify in the National Frequency Plan certain frequency bands that require a licence. The Tw does not dictate guidelines the government must follow in its determination. However, the prevailing policy is to impose as few limits as possible. Limitations are only necessary where demand exceeds supply. The instrument of 'allocation upon request' has been introduced as a way to allow the market to decide whether scarcity exists.

Rights of Use for Numbers

General authorisations and granting of individual rights

24.70   The Minister of Economic Affairs and the OPTA together institute and maintain numbering plans which set out the purpose for which numbers may be used.[87] A numbering plan may also state that the same number can be allocated to multiple applicants and fix a maximum cost in order to protect the consumer. Amendments to the numbering plans are subject to a national consultation procedure, unless they are the result of a decision of an international governing body (e.g., the European Commission).[88]

24.71   Numbers from one of the number plans are allocated on a 'first come, first serve' basis to providers of electronic communications networks or services and to natural persons or legal entities for use on an electronic communications service. The OPTA allocates these numbers at the request of such parties. If parties request the same number on the same day, OPTA decides by lot.[89] OPTA's decision must be made within three weeks. The procedure is slightly different for numbers with exceptional economic value. These are auctioned off where this has been decreed in the numbering plan.[90]

24.72   Pursuant to Article 4.6 Tw, the holder of a number assignment or reservation may transfer that assignment or reservation to a third party, provided that it obtains prior permission from the OPTA.

Admissible conditions

24.73   The number holder may only use the number for the purpose indicated in the number plan, and may not use a number in the numbering plan for a purpose assigned to another number range.[91]

---

87   *Nummerplan pakket- en circuitgeschakelde datadiensten*, 19 July 1996, Official Gazette 1996, 144; *Nummerplan identiteitsnummers voor internationale mobiliteit* (*IMSI*), 11 January 1999, Official Gazette 1999 15; *Nummerplan internationale signaleringspuntcodes*, 11 July 1997, Official Gazette 1997, 137; *Nummerplan internationale signaleringspuntcodes*, 31 March 1998, Official Gazette 1998, 76; *Nummerplan telefoon- en ISDN-diensten*, 11 January 1999, Official Gazette 1999, 14, each as revised from time to time.

88   Art 4.1 Tw.

89   Art 4.2 Tw.

90   Rules with regards to allocation by lot and auction are set out in the *Besluit alternatieve verdeling nummers*, Bulletin of Acts and Decrees 2004, nr 206 and the *Regeling veilingprocedure en lotingprocedure nummers*, Official Gazette 2006, 96 (WJZ6028957).

91   Art 4.1(4) Tw.

24.74   The Decree on number portability[92] requires providers of publicly available telephone services, including mobile services, to allow their subscribers to retain their numbers when switching to a different provider.[93] These rules for number portability, which lessen the obstacles for switching mobile providers are intended to enhance competition and consumer choice.[94]

The NRA's Enforcement Powers

24.75   OPTA is charged with enforcement of the provisions in the Tw and underlying regulations, except for the rules regarding the management, allocation and protection of radio spectrum, the enforcement of which is the responsibility of the Minister of Economic Affairs.

24.76   For the proper implementation of the provisions of the Tw and underlying regulations, the OPTA and the Minister of Economic Affairs may demand information from anyone at any time insofar as this is reasonably necessary for the fulfilment of their tasks. Both entities may also enter any locations where this is necessary. Any party from whom such information is demanded must provide the information (and all further cooperation that can be reasonably demanded) without delay, and within the time limit stipulated by OPTA or the Minister of Economic Affairs.[95]

24.77   In the event that a provider fails to comply with the obligations set forth in the Tw, OPTA or the Minister of Economic Affairs (if the non-compliance concerns radio spectrum issues) may impose administrative sanctions on that provider. OPTA and the Minister of Economic Affairs may also impose fines of up to €450,000 per infraction.[96] This maximum fine does not apply to providers with SMP. For such providers, OPTA may impose fines of up to 10 per cent of the provider's turnover in the Netherlands. The amount of the fine, however, must be proportional to the gravity and duration of the violation, as well as to the extent to which the offender can be deemed to be at fault. On 7 November 2004, OPTA published guidelines regarding the manner in which it exercises its authority to impose fines.[97] These guidelines provide an insight into the factors that determine the scale of a fine.

24.78   Although certain alternative operators are of the view that OPTA has not always used its enforcement powers under the 1998 Tw adequately, the OPTA has performed various administrative enforcement activities, in which it imposed fines. In 2003, OPTA imposed fines twice on KPN for violating the principle of non-discrimination.[98] In January 2005, OPTA imposed on KPN a penalty of €450,000 (the highest it had imposed at that time) for offering new business

---

92   *Besluit nummerportabiliteit*, Bulletin of Acts and Decrees 1998, 635, as amended from time to time.

93   The Tw does not provide for transferring numbers between fixed and mobile networks.

94   Aanpassing beleidsregels nummerportabiliteit mobiele telefonie, Government Gazette 2003, 50, p 21.

95   Art 18.7 Tw and Art 5:15, 5:16 and 5:17 Awb.

96   Art 15.4 Tw.

97   *Boetebeleidsregels OPTA*, Official Gazette 2010, nr 5163.

98   Decision of 11 March 2003, *KPN Telecom (Informatievoorziening RA ULL)*, OPTA/IBT/2003/201837, Decision of 19 December 2003, *KPN Telecom (ontbundelde toegang)*, OPTA/IBT/2003/204596.

subscribers financial inducements without first obtaining OPTA approval.[99] OPTA again fined KPN €540,000 in 2010 for a similar offence. Fines have increased steadily as OPTA has established its authority in the field. For example, OPTA imposed on Telfort, a subsidiary of KPN, a fine of €5 million in 2009 for not using its UMTS frequency adequately.

24.79   OPTA and the Minister of Economic Affairs may also prohibit a provider from offering its electronic communications networks or services for a certain period, if that provider has repeatedly and substantially failed to comply with applicable regulations, and use of administrative sanctions or financial fines have failed.[100] This measure, however, may be used only in the most extreme cases, and, to date, neither OPTA nor the Minister of Economic Affairs has used it.[101]

Administrative Charges and Fees for Rights of Use

24.80   Regulated market participants cover 90 per cent of OPTA's costs: 10 per cent are covered by the Ministry of Economic Affairs.[102] Parties for whose benefit OPTA has performed work or services under the provisions given by or pursuant to the Tw must reimburse OPTA's costs. Article 16.1 Tw, the Telecommunication Fees Decree,[103] and the Independent Post and Telecommunications Authority Act provide the legal basis for such reimbursement.[104] The fees in any given year are based on the turnover from party's telecommunications activity in the Netherlands two years prior.[105] Depending on the turnover, the party must pay to OPTA either a set amount or a percentage of its turnover.

24.81   The cost-covering tariffs to be charged to the market parties are approved each year by the Minister of Economic Affairs, and are published annually in the Dutch Government Gazette as the 'OPTA fee regulation'.[106] Market participants must pay an annually recurring fee to cover the costs of OPTA's task of supervising the electronic communications sector. The Ministry of Economic Affairs (not the providers) cover the costs of OPTA's tasks with respect to individual objections and appeals.

REGULATION OF NETWORK ACCESS AND INTERCONNECTION: THE ACCESS DIRECTIVE

Objectives and Scope of Access Regulation

24.82   The Access Directive has been implemented mainly in Chapters 6 and 6a Tw, which regulate the relationships between suppliers of networks and services and

---

99   KPN launched a marketing campaign in July 2004 offering to new clients up to €5,000 in exchange for signing up to a fixed-line business subscription. Being an operator with SMP in the market for fixed telephony, KPN is required to seek OPTA's prior permission before introducing such permanent discounts.
100   Art 15.2a(2) Tw.
101   Consideration 27 of the Authorisation Directive.
102   *Jaarverslag OPTA 2011*, April 2012.
103   *Besluit vergoedingen telecommunicatiewet*, 12 March 1999, Bulletin of Acts and Decrees 1999, 130, as amended from time to time.
104   *Wet onafhankelijke Post- en Telecommunicatieautoriteit*, 5 July 1997, Bulletin of Acts and Decrees 1997, 320, as amended from time to time.
105   For example, the fees for 2013 are calculated on the basis of the turnover from 2011.
106   The most recent fee regulation entered into force on 1 January 2012, *Regeling vergoedingen OPTA 2012*, Official Gazette 2011, nr 22274.

are aimed at creating or maintaining sustainable competition, interoperability of electronic communications services, and consumer benefits.

24.83 Chapter 6 contains rules that apply regardless of the market position of undertakings, and is mainly aimed at ensuring interoperability of services. Chapter 6a contains the obligations that exist with respect to SMP undertakings. Specific access obligations with regard to digital television and radio broadcasting services are set out in chapter 8 Tw.

Basic Regulatory Concepts

24.84 'Access' is broadly defined as:

> 'the making available of network elements, associated facilities and/or services, to another undertaking, under express conditions on either an exclusive or non-exclusive basis, for the purpose of providing electronic communications services, offering services of the information society and/or distributing programmes to the public'.[107]

This includes not only access to physical infrastructure or the connection of equipment, but also access to relevant software systems, number translation systems, and virtual network services. This definition is the same as that in the Access Directive.

24.85 'Interconnection' is defined as 'a specific type of access implemented between public network operators, consisting of the physical and logical linking of public communications networks used by the same or a different undertaking in order to allow the users of an undertaking to communicate with users of the same or another undertaking, or to access services provided by another undertaking'.[108]

Access- and interconnection-related obligations with respect to SMP-undertakings

Overview of NRA's regulatory powers

24.86 Chapter 6a Tw lists the access- and interconnection-related obligations that OPTA may impose upon SMP undertakings. OPTA may not impose such obligations until it has completed the market analysis procedure, which entails delineating the relevant markets, determining whether the relevant markets are competitive and, for non-competitive markets, determining which parties have SMP.

24.87 With respect to the regulation of access and interconnection for SMP undertakings, OPTA may impose the following obligations:

- obligations of access to, and use of, specific network facilities (article 6a.6 Tw);
- obligations relating to price control and cost accounting (article 6a.7 Tw);
- obligations of non-discrimination (article 6a.8 Tw);
- obligations of transparency (article 6a.9 Tw);

---

107 Art 1.1(l) Tw.
108 Art 1.1(m) Tw.

- obligations of accounting separation (article 6a.10 Tw); and
- obligations of functional separation (article 6a.4a Tw).[109]

24.88   If an undertaking has been designated as having SMP in a specific market, the OPTA must impose the obligations set out above 'as appropriate'. A remedy is considered appropriate if it is proportional and justified and takes into account 'the nature of the problem identified' and the objectives set out in Article 8 of the Framework Directive.[110] This leaves OPTA a considerable level of discretion with respect to the choice of these access- and interconnection-related obligations.

Specific access obligations

24.89   Under Article 6.a.6 Tw, OPTA may impose obligations on SMP undertakings to meet reasonable requests for access to, and use of, specific network elements and associated facilities, that the OPTA will designate. OPTA may impose such access obligations, among other things, in situations in which OPTA considers that denial of access or unreasonable terms and conditions having a similar effect would hinder the emergence of a sustainable competitive market at the retail level, or would not be in the end user's interest. Article 6a.6(2) Tw sets out a non-exhaustive catalogue of specific access obligations, which are identical to those listed in Article 12(1) of the Access Directive. When imposing such access obligations, OPTA may attach conditions ensuring fairness, reasonableness, and timeliness.

Obligations of transparency

24.90   OPTA may require SMP undertakings to disclose information in relation to access to their public communications networks.[111] Such information may include tariffs and other terms and conditions for supply and use, as well as technical specifications and network characteristics. OPTA may specify the precise information to be made available and the level of detail required.

24.91   OPTA also has the authority to require the publication of reference offers, which include a description of those types of access designated by OPTA. For each type of access, the reference offer must separately mention the applicable tariffs and other terms and conditions. If the reference offer concerns unbundled access to the local loop, the reference offer must contain at least the elements set out in Annex II to the Access Directive.

Obligations of non-discrimination

24.92   OPTA may require SMP undertakings to provide certain types of access (to be designated by OPTA) under equivalent conditions in equivalent circumstances.[112] This means that the SMP undertaking must apply to other undertakings the same conditions as it provides for its own services, subsidiaries, or partners.

Accounting separation obligations

24.93   Article 6a.10 Tw authorises the OPTA to impose on SMP undertakings obligations for accounting separation in relation to specified types of access. OPTA

---

109   These measures correspond the obligations set out arts 12, 13, 10, 9, 11,13a, respectively, of the Access Directive.
110   Art 6.1.2(3) Tw.
111   Art 6a.9 Tw.
112   Art 6a.8 Tw.

may specify the accounting methodology to be used and the format of the accounting records to be provided to it, including data on revenues received from third parties. Separated accounting records give OPTA an insight into the wholesale prices and internal transfer prices of SMP undertakings, allowing OPTA to ensure compliance with non-discrimination obligations and to prevent unfair cross-subsidising practices.

Price control and cost accounting obligations

24.94 OPTA may impose upon SMP undertakings obligations relating to cost accounting and price controls in relation to the provision of specific types of interconnection or access, which OPTA will determine.[113] OPTA may only impose these price control measures if a market analysis has indicated that, due to a lack of effective competition, an operator might maintain prices at an excessively high level, or apply a margin squeeze, to the detriment of end users. Article 6a.7(2) Tw expressly mentions that the price control obligations imposed by OPTA may include the obligation to apply cost-oriented prices, which effectively amounts to the ex ante regulation of prices. In addition, the cost-accounting methods that SMP undertakings use may be made subject to OPTA's prior approval. The burden of proof that prices are cost-oriented lies with the SMP undertaking.

24.95 In 2010, OPTA designated all providers of fixed and mobile telephone call termination services (not just KPN) as SMP undertakings and imposed obligations – including price control – on all these carriers.[114] The termination rates are more closely regulated than the originating tariffs, because no competition is possible for call termination. For determining the level of cost-oriented terminating tariffs, OPTA calculates what the costs would be if the network were operated in a sufficiently efficient manner under pressure from market mechanisms. This is known as the BULRIC[115] model. In this way, needlessly high or inefficient costs may not be charged to competitors. KPN has been designated as SMP undertaking in the wholesale market for call origination on the fixed public telephone network[116] and is required to set cost-oriented tariffs.[117] For calculating cost-oriented originating tariffs, OPTA permits KPN to use its embedded direct cost ('EDC') cost-allocation model. The EDC model uses the figures from KPN's own accounting records to calculate KPN's actual costs.

24.96 Recent case law suggests that the directive in the Tw to impose 'cost-oriented' tariffs on SMP-undertakings limits OPTA's (and the Commission's) ability to tighten tariff controls. The CBb ruled that the pure BULRIC method of calculating termination rates did not take into account all costs, and was, therefore, not cost-oriented in violation of the Tw. The court directed OPTA to re-calculate the costs based on the plus BULRIC method.[118]

Carrier (pre-)selection obligations

24.97 Prior to implementation of the 2009 Regulatory Package, the Tw contained a generic obligation for SMP undertakings to allow their subscribers to make use of

---

113 Art 6a.7 Tw.
114 *Marktanalyse vaste en mobiele gespreksafgifte*, 7 July 2010, OPTA/AM/2010/201951, p 180.
115 Bottom Up Long Run Incremental Costs.
116 *Marktanalyse vaste telefonie*, 1 May 2012, OPTA/AM/2012/201189, p 216.
117 Embedded Direct Costs.
118 CBb, 31 August 2011, LJN: BR6195 (*Providers/OPTA*)

the service of other carriers by using either a selection or by enabling pre-selection. While, with the implementation of the 2009 Regulatory Package, however, this blanket obligation no longer exists, the OPTA may impose on SMP undertakings obligations with respect to carrier selection.

Functional separation

24.98   If OPTA concludes that the foregoing obligations have failed to achieve effective and lasting competition which is based on infrastructure, it can order an SMP undertaking to place any activities that relate to offering specific types of access in an independently operating business unit. This business unit must then offer such activities to all market parties under the same conditions and for the same prices using the same systems and processes.[119]

24.99   When OPTA makes such a decision, it specifies the following elements:

● the exact nature and level of the separation, making note of the legal status of the independently operating business unit;
● the identification of the assets of the independently operating business unit and the products or services that will be provided by the business unit;
● bylaws to ensure the independence of the employees of the business unit;
● the measures to ensure compliance with legislation;
● the measures to ensure transparency of the operational procedures;
● an instrument to measure the extent of compliance with the obligations; and
● publication in the annual financial statement of this measurement.

24.100   OPTA must submit the draft measure to the Commission and must follow the national consultation procedure. The material and procedural requirements of imposing an obligation of functional separation are consistent with the Access Directive.

24.101   OPTA has not, to date, employed functional separation. The Government commissioned a study in 2007 to investigate the possibility of functional separation after it was employed by Ofcom to separate the BT business and network. The Government concluded that, at that time, functional separation of KPN was disproportional.[120]

Regulatory Powers with Respect to SMP-undertakings

24.102   With implementation of the 2009 amendments to the Universal Service Directive, obligations regarding carrier (pre-)selection and leased lines are no longer specifically set out in the Tw. OPTA, however, still has the regulatory power, where it deems appropriate, to impose such obligations on SMP undertakings.[121]

Regulatory Powers Applicable to All Market Participants

Obligations to ensure end to end connectivity

24.103   Any provider of public electronic communications networks or public electronic communications services which controls access to end users (regardless of

---

119   Art 6a.4a Tw.
120   *All-IP: beleidsregels en functionele scheiding*, 2 March 2007, OPTA/TN/2007/200309.
121   *Wijziging van de Telecommunicatiewet ter implementatie van de herziene telecommunicatier-ichtlijnen, Memorie van Toelichting*, Parliamentary Records II 2010–2011, 32 549, nr 3, p 57.

market power) must upon request of another such provider, enter into negotiations with the other provider, to secure an agreement on measures necessary to bring about end-to-end connectivity. Such measures can (and usually do) include interconnection of the respective networks.[122] In that case, establishing such end-to-end connectivity may require further technical or organisational) measures. Therefore, the negotiation obligation is not limited to interconnection agreements.[123]

24.104   The goal of this requirement is for providers to come to an agreement regarding access without the interference of OPTA. The parties must conduct these negotiations in good faith and may only cease negotiations if a request is demonstrably unreasonable. In such a case, the provider must state the reasons for ceasing negotiations. If a provider, requesting access to end users, feels that the other provider is not meeting its obligation to negotiate, it may request OPTA to set the conditions under which the negotiation must take place.[124] While the Tw does not state what these conditions may entail, it does prohibit OPTA from requiring the parties to reach a specific agreement.

24.105   If the negotiations fail entirely, however, OPTA may set the conditions necessary to achieve end-to-end connectivity.[125] OPTA may do this at the request of either party, or of its own accord. If a dispute is brought before OPTA by a party, the scope of the dispute is limited by the request of the party who initiated the proceedings. OPTA must consider whether the request submitted is reasonable. Although OPTA generally has no right to impose cost-oriented tariff obligations on providers without SMP, it may decide to take costs into account when setting conditions for interoperability.

24.106   If OPTA decides to impose obligations regarding end-to-end connectivity on its own accord, the motivation must be the interests of eusers and sustainable competition. A decision to impose obligations must be published, leaving out any sensitive commercial information.

Regulation of roaming services

24.107   The Tw appoints OPTA as NRA for purposes of the Roaming Regulation.[126] OPTA may impose fines where providers impose rates for roaming higher than those permitted under the Roaming Regulation.[127]

Access to digital radio and television broadcasting services

24.108   The Government may impose an obligation on providers of public electronic telecommunications networks, which consist of radio broadcasting equipment capable of distributing radio programming, to carry certain public radio broadcasts.[128] The government may also impose technical standards for television

---

122   Art 6.1(1) Tw.
123   Art 6.1(2) Tw imposes an obligation on providers to use any information obtained as part of these negotiations or obtained in the exercise of the agreement. The information may not be shared within the business of the provider or with third parties.
124   Art 6.1(3) Tw. Such a decision need not follow the national consultation procedure.
125   Art 6.2 Tw.
126   Art 18.2a Tw.
127   See for example Lower Court of Rotterdam, 24 May 2012, LJN: BW6593 (*Tele-2*).
128   Art 8.3 Tw.

broadcasts in a widescreen format, or television broadcasts intended to be transmitted digitally over a public electronic communications network.[129] These technical standards impose requirements on the network, but also on the terminal equipment, such as television sets and decoders. The government may also impose obligations for providers of Application Programming Interfaces (APIs) and Electronic Programme Guides (EPGs), regardless of their market position, to provide access to APIs and EPGs on fair, reasonable, and non-discriminatory terms.[130]

24.109 A government decree on conditional access sets the rules for conditional access systems.[131] This decree implements the obligations set out in Annex I to Part I of the Access Directive. These obligations apply to all providers of conditional access systems providing access to digital television and radio services, regardless of their market position.

24.110 Providers of conditional access systems are required to offer broadcasters of digitally transmitted services those technical services which are necessary to enable the end user to receive the broadcasters' digitally transmitted services. Such technical services must be offered on a fair, reasonable, and non-discriminatory terms consistent with Community competition law. Providers of conditional access systems must also keep separate financial accounts regarding their activity as conditional access providers.[132]

24.111 Furthermore, providers of conditional access systems must ensure that their systems have the necessary technical capability for cost-effective transfer of control. This means that network operators broadcasting services to the public must be enabled to have full control of the services using such conditional access systems.[133]

REGULATION OF THE UNIVERSAL SERVICE AND USERS' RIGHTS: THE UNIVERSAL SERVICE DIRECTIVE

Regulation of universal service obligations

Scope of universal service obligations

24.112 Article 9.1 Tw lists the minimum set of services which constitute 'universal service'. The list is identical to the catalogue provided by the Universal Service Directive. These services must be made available to all end users, independently of geographical location, at an affordable price and at a specified quality.

24.113 Tw implementing regulations require that universal service providers offer data communication speeds which are sufficient for functional Internet access,[134]

---

129 Art 8.4a Tw, see the *Regeling breedbeeldtelevisiediensten en normen digitale consumenten-apparaten*, Official Gazette 2004, nr 92, for a specification regarding widescreen and digital television transmission.
130 Art 8.6 Tw.
131 *Besluit voorwaardelijke toegang*, last revision: 5 June 2012, Bulletin of Acts and Decrees 2012, nr 236.
132 *Besluit voorwaardelijke toegang*, art 2.
133 *Besluit voorwaardelijke toegang*, art 3.
134 Art 2.1 of the *Besluit universele dienstverlening en eindgebruikersbelangen*, 7 May 2004, Bulletin of Acts and Decrees 2004, 203, as amended from time to time.

and indicate that speeds of 56 kb/s are sufficient for such access.[135] The Government, however, has not introduced a specific obligation to provide broadband access.

24.114 The 2009 Regulatory Package introduces the requirement to provide disabled users 'equivalent access' to the public telephone service, directory service and directory inquiry service. The government has concluded that these facilities can best be provided to end users with hearing disabilities through an intermediary service. This intermediary service converts text or sign language into speech. The Government also concluded that visually impaired end users require a special directory service.[136] At the time of writing, the Government had not appointed any party as the universal service provider with regards to equivalent access for disabled end users.

Designation of undertakings obliged to provide universal services

24.115 KPN is designated as the universal service provider for almost the entire catalogue of services set out in Article 9.1 Tw.[137] KPN, however, is not designated as the universal service provider for equivalent access for disabled users. In deviation from the financing mechanism set out in article 9.3 Tw, KPN is not entitled to any remuneration of net costs involved in providing universal service. KPN is authorised, however, unilaterally to terminate universal service wholly or partially, subject to a one-year notice term.[138]

24.116 Should KPN cease the provision of (one or more) universal services, and should this lead to a situation in which the availability, affordability, or quality of one or more elements of the universal service cannot be guaranteed by normal market processes, the Minister of Economic Affairs may designate one or more undertakings to provide different elements of the universal service or to cover different parts of the national territory. If the Government determines that designating an alternative universal service provider in this case will not unfairly burden the provider, the Government makes the designation as follows:

- in the case of the provision of a connection to a public electronic communications network at a fixed location – the provider of the network to which most end users are connected in the relevant service area;
- in the case of the provision of any other service – the provider of that particular service with the most end-users in the relevant service area; or
- in the case of the provision of a facility – the provider of that particular facility with the most end users in the relevant service area.

---

135 *Besluit van 7 mei 2004, houdende regels met betrekking tot universele dienstverlening en eindgebruikersbelangen* (*Besluit universele dienstverlening en eindgebruikersbelangen*), *Nota van Toelichting*, Bulletin of Acts and Decrees 2004, 203, p 18. See also *Besluit van 2 september 2011 tot wijziging universele dienstverlening en eindgebruikersbelangen i.v.m. de levering van de openbare telefoondienst via een mobiel network*, *Nota van Toelichting*, Bulletin of Acts and Decrees 2011, 441, p 5.

136 *Besluit van 17 juli 2012 tot wijziging van het Besluit universele dienstverlening en eindgebruikersbelangen ter implementatie van de herziene universeledienstrichtlijn in verband met diensten voor eindgebruikers met een fysieke beperking, alsmede wijziging van het Besluit randapparaten en radioapparaten 2007 en het Frequentiebesluit*, 17 July 2012, Bulletin of Acts and Decrees 2012, nr 353.

137 Art 20.1(1) Tw.

138 Art 20.1(2) Tw.

24.117   If, on the other hand, the Government finds that the designation of a party as a universal service provider will impose an on unfair burden on that party, the Government must issue a public notice requesting bids for the provision of such services, and must designate the party who makes the lowest offer for the provision of the required services.

Regulation of retail tariffs, users' expenditures and quality of services

24.118   The Decree on Universal Services and End User Interests,[139] and the underlying Regulation on Universal Service and End User Interests,[140] establish rules regarding permissible end user tariffs for, and quality of, universal services. Pursuant to the Decree, consumers must have access to publicly available telephone services at a fixed location, to public pay phones and to the directory and directory enquiry services for tariffs that are 'no higher than reasonable'. An end user tariff is reasonable if the scale of the tariff is in reasonable proportion to the economic value of the service rendered, plus a reasonable return. This is different from the principle of cost orientation.[141]

24.119   In addition, end users who wish to use their fixed telephone connection mainly for the purpose of receiving (rather than making) calls must have access to a specific type of 'low budget' subscription with relatively low monthly fixed charges, and relatively high usage charges. The Regulation on Universal Services and End User Interests sets the maximum scale of these charges.[142]

24.120   Furthermore, undertakings with universal service obligations must apply common tariffs throughout the territory where they provide such services. They may not oblige subscribers to pay for facilities or services which are not necessary or not required for the service requested. A universal service provider is obligated to provide an itemised bill of charged incurred in using the service.[143]

Cost calculation and financing of universal services

24.121   As discussed above, the Government (OPTA) must determine whether designation as a universal service provider imposes an unfair burden. If it is found that such designation would not unfairly burden the provider, the provider may cover its costs through the provision of the service. Otherwise, remuneration for the provision of the universal service is accomplished through a public bid procedure.[144]

24.122   OPTA must publish in the Official Gazette its intention to solicit public bids for the provision of universal service. The publication must notify providers of the services or facilities with the most end users in the relevant service areas. A party interested in being designated as a universal service provider must submit a bid

---

139   *Besluit universele dienstverlening en eindgebruikersbelangen*, 7 May 2004, Bulletin of Acts and Decrees 2004, 203, as amended from time to time.

140   *Regeling universele dienstverlening en eindgebruikersbelangen*, 10 May 2004, Official Gazette 2004, 92, as amended from time to time.

141   OPTA may still impose cost-orientation obligations on providers of public telephone services at a fixed location that have been designated as SMP undertakings, on the basis of arts 6a.2 and 6a.13 Tw.

142   Art 2.1, *Regeling universele dienstverlening en eindgebruikersbelangen*.

143   As set out in accordance with Annex I, Part A of the Universal Service Directive.

144   Art 9.3(5) Tw.

within eight weeks following publication. OPTA must designate the lowest bidder to provide the universal service.[145]

24.123   Compensation for undertakings that have been designated for the provision of universal services is based on a sharing of the net cost of universal service obligations between providers of electronic communications networks and services.[146] Each provider that has realised an annual turnover of more than €2 million[147] must contribute to the compensation of the designated undertaking. The amount of the contribution must be proportional to the relevant turnover.

Regulation of Retail Markets

Prerequisites for the regulation of retail markets

24.124   Articles 6a.12 – 6a.15 Tw set out the obligations that OPTA may impose upon undertakings with SMP in retail markets. OPTA may impose such measures at the retail level only if the relevant retail market is not effectively competitive and access-related obligations would not be sufficient to resolve the problems identified in the relevant retail market.[148]

Regulatory powers

24.125   On the basis of article 6a.12 Tw, OPTA may prohibit SMP undertakings from discriminating between end users (in order to prevent undue preference to specific end users), and from unreasonably bundling end user services. In addition, OPTA may require undertakings to announce specified information to end users, such as pricing information, applicable terms and conditions, information regarding consumers' right to submit a dispute with the SMP undertaking to a dispute resolution committee, or information regarding the quality of the service.[149]

24.126   The most far-reaching authority that OPTA has in relation to end user markets is the power to regulate tariffs.[150] In order to prevent an SMP undertaking from charging excessively high prices, or from setting predatory prices, OPTA may set both a floor and a ceiling for the undertaking's end user tariffs. Where OPTA regulates end user tariffs, it must also require the implementation of cost-accounting systems. OPTA may specify the format and accounting methodology to be used for cost-accounting systems. OPTA must also require SMP undertakings to publish annually a statement concerning compliance with the cost-accounting requirements.

24.127   Once OPTA regulates a particular SMP undertaking's end-user tariffs once, it may also prohibit the undertaking from implementing any new end user tariffs in the future without first obtaining authorisation from OPTA.[151]

---

145   Art 9.4(1) Tw.
146   Art 9.5 Tw.
147   This amount is determined in art 2.6 of the Regulation on Universal Service and End User interests and may be subject to change.
148   Art 6a.2(2)(b).
149   Art 6a.12 Tw.
150   Art 6a.13 Tw.
151   Art 6a.14 Tw.

End User Rights

Contracts

24.128   All providers of public electronic communication services must, when entering into a contract with a consumer (ie any natural person that uses or requests the publicly available electronic communications service for purposes which are outside his or her trade, business or profession), provide, at a minimum, the following information to the consumer:[152]

- name and address of the provider;
- the services to be delivered;
- the tariff structure, the most important charges, the manner in which the consumer may obtain information about the charges and maintenance costs, the methods of payment and any costs connected with these methods of payment;
- the duration of the agreement and terms under which the agreement may be terminated or extended;
- the compensation method or refund rights in case the provider does not meet the quality levels set out in the agreement;
- the manner in which the consumer can submit a dispute with the provider to the dispute resolution committee;
- the choice to incorporate the consumer's personal data in a directory and which data would be incorporated; and
- the measures that the provider may or will take in the case of a security breach.

24.129   The provider must supply the above information to the consumer prior to, or at the moment of, entering into the contract. The information may set out in the provider's general terms and conditions. Upon request, such information must also be provided to others.

24.130   If a provider of public electronic communication services intends to amend the contractual conditions of existing contracts with subscribers (including consumers and end users), the provider must give the subscribers adequate notice of such proposed amendments. The provider must notify their subscribers at least one month prior to any such amendment. Subscribers must also be informed of their right to withdraw from contracts without penalty[153]

24.131   The Tw gives a consumer the right to terminate an agreement for the provision of an electronic communications service for an indefinite term free of charge at any time. An agreement for a fixed term can last no longer than 24 months. Such an agreement may be automatically and tacitly extended, as long as the consumer has the right to terminate the agreement at all times, free of charge.

Transparency obligations

24.132   Providers of public telephony must disclose to their potential end users information regarding standard tariffs, compensation and refund policies, the type

---

152   Art 7.1(1) Tw.
153   Art 7.2 Tw.

of maintenance service offered, standard contract conditions (including any minimum contractual period), and dispute settlement mechanisms.[154] This information must be disclosed 'in a satisfactory manner', ie at a minimum, the provider must make the information available on its website. There is no distinction between consumers and non-consumers when it comes to the provision of information regarding charges.

24.133 Furthermore, providers of public telephone services at fixed locations, providers of public payphones that have been designated as providers of universal services, and any other provider of fixed public telephone services or public payphones that has been active in the Dutch market for more than one year, must publish an annual overview of the quality of their services, in accordance with Annex III of the Universal Service Directive.[155] The published information must include, among other things, the supply time for initial connection, fault rate per access line, fault repair time, unsuccessful call ratio, call set-up time, and other parameters. A new requirement is that the provider must also provide information on any measures taken to make the service more accessible to end-users with a disability.

Quality of service: securing 'net neutrality'

24.134 During the legislative round related to the implementation of the 2009 Regulatory Package, the Dutch Parliament issued amendments to the Tw that introduced 'net neutrality' into the Tw.[156] The Netherlands was the first European nation to implement net neutrality at the time. The rules are intended to prevent providers of telecommunications services which offer access to the Internet from hindering or delaying traffic, except in the following cases:[157]

- to reduce the consequences of network congestion, where equal traffic is treated equally;
- to ensure the integrity and security of the network and the service or the terminal equipment of the end user;
- to block unsolicited commercial, charitable or ideological communications, at the request of the user; or
- to comply with a statutory obligation or a judicial order.

24.135 Service providers are also prohibited from basing the price of the service on what services and applications are offered or used.

European emergency call number

24.136 Providers of electronic communications networks which are used to offer outgoing calls to a number in a national numbering plan, public pay phones, and public telephony services must provide a free and unencumbered connection to emergency numbers to all users of these services.

---

154 Art 7.2 Tw, in conjunction with Art 3.2 of the Decree on Universal Service and End User Interests.
155 Art 7.4 Tw.
156 *Wijziging van de Telecommunicatiewet ter implementatie van de herziene telecommunicatierichtlijnen*, Parliamentary Records 2010–2011, 32 549, nr 10, 17 and 29.
157 Art 7.4a Tw.

Other obligations

24.137   Providers of Internet access service to end users may only terminate or suspend the service in certain circumstances, such as default of payment or in accordance with a statutory obligation or court order.[158]

Obligations Facilitating Change of Provider

24.138   Subscribers are entitled to retain the number they are using with a public communication service when they switch to another provider who offers the same service.[159] The provider who will receive the number may charge a fee to cover the administrative expense involved. This fee is capped in the Decree on Number Portability.[160]

DATA PROTECTION: IMPLEMENTATION OF THE E-PRIVACY DIRECTIVE

Confidentiality of Communications

24.139   Without prejudice to the Wbp,[161] operators providing publicly available electronic communications networks or services must take appropriate technical and organisational measures to safeguard the security of the networks and services they provide.[162] Taking account of the state of technology and the costs, the measures must guarantee a level of security proportionate to the risks involved. Where there is a special risk of security breach on the network or service, subscribers must be informed of these risks. The provider must also supply information about possible safety measures and the cost implications these measures might have.[163]

24.140   In principle, providers of publicly available telecommunications networks or services are not permitted to wiretap, intercept, or otherwise control data that is transmitted over the network or service, except in the following cases:

- the provider has obtained prior consent from the subscriber for interception or wiretapping;
- wiretapping or interception is required to safeguard the integrity and safety of the network and services of the provider;
- interception is necessary in order to transmit information over the network and or the services; or
- the interception is required based on a request from law enforcement or a court order.[164]

24.141   The provider may not receive compensation for the costs of making the telecommunications network or service technically capable of being wiretapped.

---

158   Art 7.6a Tw. This provision will enter into force on 1 January 2013.
159   Art 4.10 Tw.
160   See paragraph 24.74.
161   *Wet bescherming persoonsgegevens*, 6 July 2000, Bulletin of Acts and Decrees 2000, 302.
162   Art 11.3(1) Tw, see also art 13 WBP.
163   Art 11.3(3) Tw.
164   Art 11.2a(2) Tw.

Only the administrative and personnel costs incurred by the provider as a direct result of carrying out an individual wiretapping order may be compensated by the State.[165]

Rules regarding so-called 'cookies'

24.142   The Netherlands has opted for a strict interpretation of the Directive in relation to the storage of or access to information on the terminal equipment of users (ie placement of cookies).[166] Article 11.7a Tw requires any person who wishes to store or access information on the terminal equipment of users to obtain prior consent. Users must, therefore, be provided with clear and complete information regarding the purposes of cookies. The user must also consent (ie opt-in) to the use of cookies, whereas previously only an opt-out right was available to the user. These rules apply to all cookies, with the exception of:

- cookies that are strictly necessary to carry traffic data over an electronic communications network; and
- cookies that that are strictly necessary to fulfil a service on the website requested by the user (such as shopping cart cookies that are placed in order to enable an Internet purchase).[167]

24.143   The foregoing is no different from what has been set out in the European legislation. In addition to this opt-in regime for cookies, however, the Netherlands has also legislated the use of so-called 'tracking cookies'. Those who use cookies to collect, combine or analyse the use by users of different services of the information society are presumed to process personal data.[168] This rule transfers the burden of proof to the party placing the cookie to show that it does not process the user's personal data. This makes it much easier for the Cbp and the data subject to enforce privacy law. In general, the Wbp is applicable to an act of processing taken in the context of activities of an establishment of a controller in the Netherlands.

24.144   OPTA is primarily in charge of the enforcement of the new cookie legislation, and has the ability to impose fines of up to €450,000, apply administrative sanctions, and/or impose an order for periodic penalty payments.[169] In addition, the Cbp may impose monetary penalties of up to €4,500 and other administrative penalties in the event a party fails to notify data processing activities and transfers of data in breach of a Commission decision.[170]

Data breach notification

24.145   The Netherlands has implemented the data notification breach obligations set out in Articles 4(3) and 4(4) of the Directive in article 11.3a of the Tw. The national implementation is identical to the procedure in the Directive. In case of a data security breach with detrimental effects for the protection of personal data, the Tw imposes an obligation on providers of public electronic communication services to notify the OPTA as soon as possible. In addition, the provider must notify the

---

165   See Chapter 13 Tw.
166   Art 11.7a Tw.
167   Art 11.7a(3) Tw.
168   The legal presumption with respect to tracking cookies enters into force on 1 January 2013.
169   OPTA has provided an FAQ on its website to provide guidance on the new cookie legislation.
170   Art 66 WBP.

relevant data subjects if their personal data is at risk. If the provider fails to notify the data subjects, OPTA may order the provider to do so.

24.146   While currently, the notification obligation only applies to providers of public electronic communications services, the Dutch government has announced its intent to introduce legislation to expand this obligation to all processors of personal data.[171] The European Commission has included the same obligation in its proposal for a new Data Protection Regulation.[172]

Data Retention

24.147   Directive 2006/24/EC has been transported into the Telecommunications Data Retention Act (*Wet Bewaarplicht Telecommunicatiegegevens* ('WBT')) which amends Chapter 13 of the Tw.[173] In the Netherlands, providers of public electronic communication networks and services must retain traffic and location data relating to wired and mobile telephony for a maximum and minimum period of twelve months. A shorter data retention period of six months applies to the retention of Internet access, e-mail, Internet telephony traffic, and location data. At the end of the data retention period parties are obliged to destroy the data. In order to adequately process requests from law enforcement, all providers of public electronic communication networks or services that store traffic and location data are requested to sign up to the Central Information point for Investigation Telecommunication (*Centraal Informatiepunt Onderzoek Telecommunicatiegegevens* ('CIOT')). Via the CIOT, law enforcement can request traffic and location data from providers of public electronic communication networks and services. The Dutch Telecom Agency (*Agentschap Telecom-* ('AT')) has been appointed to ensure that providers comply with the data retention obligations.[174] The enforcement capabilities of the AT are similar to those of the OPTA and include imposing fines of up to €450,000, administrative fines, and periodic penalty payments. To date the AT has not imposed sanctions for data retention breaches.

---

171 *Wijziging van de Wet bescherming persoonsgegevens en enige andere wetten in verband met de verruiming van de mogelijkheid van het gebruik van camerabeelden van strafbare feiten ten behoeve van de ondersteuning van de rechtshandhaving en de invoering van een meldplicht bij de doorbreking van maatregelen voor de beveiliging van persoonsgegevens (gebruik camerabeelden en meldplicht datalekken)* (*versie consultatie en advise*), no official publication, available as of 18 September 2012 at http://www.internetconsultatie.nl/camerabeelden

172 Proposal for a Regulation of the European Parliament and of the Council on the protection of individuals with regard to the processing of personal data and on the free movement of such data, 25 January 2012, COM(2012) 11 final.

173 *Wet van 18 juli 2009 tot wijziging van de Telecommunicatiewet en de Wet op de economische delicten in verband met de implementatie van Richtlijn 2006/24/EG van het Europees Parlement en de Raad van de Europese Unie betreffende de bewaring van gegevens die zijn verwerkt in verband met het aanbieden van openbare elektronische communicatiediensten en tot wijziging van Richtlijn 2002/58/EG (Wet bewaarplicht telecommunicatiegegevens)*, 30 July 2009, Bulletin of Acts and Decrees 2009, 333.

174 In 2010, the AT performed a baseline measurement in to assess the extent to which undertakings comply with data retention obligations.

Traffic Data and Location Data

24.148   The definitions of 'traffic data' and 'location data' are identical to those in the E-Privacy Directive.[175] As a general rule, traffic data processed for the purpose of transmitting communications must be erased or anonymised when no longer needed for the purposes for which they were collected. There are two exceptions:

- providers may retain traffic data if necessary for billing purposes, but only for the period during which the bill may be lawfully challenged and payment pursued; and
- providers may process traffic data for the purposes of marketing electronic communications services or the provision of value added services, provided that consent from the user or subscriber has been obtained prior to processing the traffic and location data.[176]

In addition, users or subscribers must be given the opportunity to withdraw their consent at any given time. Moreover, providers must inform subscribers of the types of traffic data that is being processed and the duration of such processing.[177]

24.149   Location data other than traffic data may only be processed if they have been anonymised or the user's prior consent has been obtained to the extent and for the duration necessary for the provision of a value added service. The consent is only valid if the provider has informed the user or subscriber of the types of location data processed, the purposes and duration of the processing, and the third parties to whom the data may be disclosed prior to processing the personal data. This consent may be withdrawn at any time.[178]

Itemised Billing

24.150   At the request of a subscriber, the provider of a public electronic communications service must issue completely or partially non-itemised bills.[179] The Minister of Economic Affairs may issue a ministerial decree with more detailed rules regarding the itemisation of bills for electronic communications services, but, to date, has not done so.

Calling and Connected Line Identification

24.151   Providers offering calling line identification must permit any calling subscriber or user to easily, and free of charge, block the provision of the calling number on a per-call and per-line basis. Users or subscribers must also be able to block the numbers of incoming calls and to reject incoming calls automatically in cases where the caller has withheld the caller identification.[180] The Regulation on Universal Services and End User Interests sets out more detailed rules, including rules regarding international line identification.[181]

---

175   Art 11.1(b), (d) Tw.
176   Art 11.5(3) Tw, was amended on 5 June 2012 in order to implement the updated Directive.
177   Art 11.5 Tw.
178   Art 11.5a Tw.
179   Art 11.4(1) Tw.
180   Art 11.9 Tw.
181   *Regeling universele dienstverlening en eindgebruikersbelangen*, 10 May 2004, Official Gazette 2004, 92, as amended from time to time.

Automatic Call Forwarding

24.152   Providers of public electronic communications services must enable their subscribers to easily, and free of charge, block automatic call forwarding from a third party to their terminal.[182]

Directories of Subscribers

24.153   Universal service operators, and any other operator making subscribers data available for inclusion in a directory, must provide advance notification to subscribers of the purposes of the directory and any further usage possibilities based on search functions embedded in electronic versions of the directory. A subscriber's personal data may only be included in the directory if, and to the extent, the subscriber has given his or her consent. A provider may not charge a fee to a subscriber who chooses not to have his or her information included in a public subscriber directory not to verify, correct or withdraw personal data from the directory.[183]

Prohibition of Unsolicited Communications

24.154   The Tw provides for an opt-in system for unsolicited communications ('spam'). The use of automatic calling systems without human intervention, faxes, or electronic messages (beyond e-mail, and also including, for example, text or video messages on mobile devices) for transmitting unsolicited communications to subscribers for commercial, idealistic or charitable purposes (which is broader than direct marketing) will only be permitted if the sender can demonstrate that the subscriber concerned has given prior permission.[184]

24.155   An exception applies if a sender has obtained electronic contact details for electronic messages in the context of a previous sale of a product or a service from its existing customers. This person or entity may use these electronic contact details for transmitting communications for commercial, idealistic or charitable purposes in connection with its own similar products or services, provided that customers clearly and distinctly are given the opportunity to object, free of charge and in an easy manner, to such use of electronic contact details when they are collected and on the occasion of each message in case the customer has not initially refused such use. This amounts to an opt-out system. The anti-spam protection covers not only individuals but also businesses.

24.156   OPTA has a website[185] specifically for submission of complaints against violators of this spam prohibition. Since 2004 OPTA has imposed a number of fines on distributors of spam through e-mail, mobile text messages, and social media networks. The imposed fines ranged from a few thousand euros to €450.000.[186] OPTA is also involved with NRAs from other EU Member States in

---

182   Art 11.4(1) Tw.
183   Art 11.6 Tw.
184   Art 11.7 Tw.
185   See www.spamklacht.nl (only available in Dutch).
186   OPTA 31 May 2011.

initiatives to combat spam.[187] Moreover, the Dutch Ministry for Economic Affairs has created a Do Not Call Me Register (*'Bel-me-niet-register'*) for consumers and small companies in which they can indicate that they do not want to receive unsolicited telephone calls from undertakings.[188] Undertakings must check the register prior to calling consumers and small companies. If companies breach this obligation, the OPTA may impose fines.

24.157   In addition to the statutory prohibition of spam in the TW, various forms of self-regulation have emerged in the Netherlands. After the implementation of the spam regulation a self-regulatory code on direct marketing was created by direct marketing associations. By adhering to this code participating undertakings have made clear that they will not be involved in the distribution of spam.

---

187 On the initiative of the European Commission, an informal group was created consisting of NRAs involved with the enforcement of Article 13 of the Privacy and Electronic Communi-cation Directive 2002/58/EC called 'the Contact Network of Spam Authorities' (CNSA). In December 2004, the CNSA established a cooperation procedure aimed at facilitating the transmission of complaint information between NRAs.

188 Art 11.7(6) Tw and *Besluit Bel-me-niet-Register*, 26 February 2009, Bulletin of Acts and Decrees 2009, 129.

The Polish Market for Electronic Communications[1]

Justyna Michalak-Królicka, Natalia Marczuk
Baker & McKenzie, Warsaw

LEGAL STRUCTURE

Basic Policy

25.1   At the beginning of the 1990s, the Polish telecommunications market had a monopoly structure with Telekomunikacja Polska SA ('TPSA') being the monopolist. In the mid-1990s, selected sectors of the market were opened up to private investors; however TPSA still had exclusivity in the main telecommunications services (long-distance and international telecommunications services). The liberalisation process progressed through the 1990s and the early 2000s and included the successful two-stage privatisation of the incumbent operator. Full liberalisation of the market was completed by the end of 2003, when the last foreign ownership restrictions were lifted. A new Telecommunications Law was enacted in 2004, the core of which transposes the EU Directives 2002/21/EC, 2002/22/EC and 2002/19/EC.

25.2   The most rapidly developing market in the Republic of Poland ('Republic of Poland' or 'Poland') is the mobile telephony sector, in which four lead operators have their own telecommunications infrastructure covering over 94 per cent of the territory of Poland: Polska Telefonia Cyfrowa Sp z o.o., Polska Telefonia Komórkowa Centertel Sp z o.o., Polkomtel SA and P4 Sp z o.o., all of which are privately owned. Several smaller operators also appeared on the market. All operators provide their services in the GSM standard, including P4, which, as a result of the conclusion of agreements on telecommunications access to the terrestrial network (national roaming), ensures that P4's customers have access to services provided through the GSM networks belonging to Polkomtel. All operators hold licences for the provision of UMTS services and provide such services. The President of the Office of Electronic Communications (President of the UKE) keeps a list of radio licenses for mobile telephony base stations (E-GSM, GSM900, GSM1800, UMTS and LTE) on its website and publishes the area of UMTS coverage. The largest operator in the fixed line telephony market with a market share of over 68.4 per cent is TPSA, which also dominates several other market segments. It is expected that the consolidation processes, which started several years ago, will continue in the coming years. In March 2012, the Management Board of

---

1   Editing of this chapter closed on 15 May 2012.

Telekomunikacja Polska decided to rebrand all fixed line services. While Telekomunikacja Polska and PTK Centertel will not be merged and will remain as separate companies through the end of the second quarter of 2012, Orange (the brand previously used by PTK Centertel) will become the commercial brand of all of Telekomunikacja Polska's products and services.

25.3   With the adoption of the Telecommunications Law of 16 July 2004 ('TL'),[2] the core of which was the transposition of EU Directives 2002/21/EC, 2002/22/EC and 2002/19/EC, Poland was tasked with introducing regulations implementing the law, aligning Polish legislation to changes in Community Telecommunications Law, and abolishing inconsistent regulations.

25.4   The Telecommunications Law of 16 July 2004 ('TL') states the overall policy objectives of the President of the Office of Electronic Communications ('the President of UKE'):

- the support of effective competition and equal rights with regard to the provision of telecommunications services;
- the development and support of a modern telecommunications infrastructure;
- the assurance of proper numbering, frequency and satellite resource management;
- the assurance of maximum benefits in terms of diversity, price and quality of telecommunications services; and
- the assurance of technological neutrality.[3]

Implementation of EU Directives

25.5   The 2002 EU Regulatory Package was transposed into Polish law through the TL in July 2004 (which entered into force on 3 September 2004) with only a three-month delay. In principle, the TL appropriately implements the 2002 Regulatory Package. The TL has been amended more than 20 times since 2004. These amendments were based on comments from the European Commission with respect to alignment of the national telecommunications regulations to the EU Directives. This was, in particular, the nature of the amendment of 24 April 2009 on the amendment of the Telecommunications Law and certain other Acts,[4] referred to as the 'EU Revision', and the amendment currently being prepared, which is at the stage of a government bill. The EU Revision, both in the case of subscribers and users of mobile pre-paid telephones, abolished the one-off fee for transferring an allocated number at the time of changing the operator of public mobile telephone networks. It introduced major changes in the provision of premium rate services, which will be provided on the basis of an agreement on the provision of telecommunications services. The next pro-consumer change specified that, in the case of unilateral termination of the agreement by the subscriber, or by the service provider through the subscriber's fault before the end of the term set in the agreement, the subscriber should refund the equivalent of the allowance granted as at the date of termination of the agreement and not as at the date of its signature, as has been the case to date.

The revision also introduced changes in conducting market analyses. The changes introduced enable the President of the UKE to define the relevant markets in

---

2   Journal of Laws, No 171, item 1800.
3   Art 1.2(1)–(5) TL.
4   Journal of Laws, No 85, item 716.

accordance with the European Commission's recommendation. The President of the UKE will issue decisions, in which, in the first instance, he will specify the relevant market, assess competition problems in the market, specify the undertaking (or undertakings) with significant market power ('SMP'), and impose regulatory obligations on such SMP provider (or providers).

New Article 180a is the first phase of implementation of the EU Directive on Telecommunications Data Retention, (Directive 2006/24/EC) into national legislation. This article specifies that data retention will serve the purpose of investigating crimes against State defence and security, public safety and order, and fiscal offences. Public telecommunications network operators and providers of publicly available telecommunications services will be required to retain and store data for 24 months.

Therefore, EU regulations have only been partly implemented into national legislation. A number of EU regulations are yet to be transposed, which will occur through further amendments to the TL, the most recent of which is currently under consideration, in a pending government bill.

On 12 October 2012, the Sejm of the Republic of Poland adopted an amendment to the Telecommunications Law. The proposed act introduces a range of facilities for Polish citizens and it also implements into the Polish legal system the provisions of the Citizens' Rights Directive (Directive 2009/139/EC) and the Better Regulation Directive (2009/140/EC). The proposed act takes into account the content of the judgment of the European Court of Justice (ECJ) in Case C-522/08 on the ban on tied sales. Currently work is being done in the Senate on this act.

25.6   The main sources of Polish telecommunication legislation are the laws passed by the Parliament, supported by secondary regulations. The Polish telecommunications framework consists of:

- the Constitution of the Republic of Poland of 1997;[5]
- the TL;
- the Broadcasting Act of 29 December 1992;[6]
- the Act on the support of the development of telecommunications services and networks of 7 May 2010 (the so-called Broadband Act);[7] and
- regulations of the minister responsible for communications (which is currently the Minister of Administration and Digitisation) and the Chairperson of the National Broadcasting Council ('NBC').

25.7   The objectives stated in the TL reflect the EU regulatory agenda in the area of telecommunications. The changes in the TL and the proactive nature of the Office of Electronic Communications ('regulator') are resulting in rapid development on the telecommunications market in Poland. Apart from directly supporting consumers, the regulator primarily stimulates the development of effective competition in the market and the support of investment processes. Furthermore, acting in the interests of consumers, the activities of telecommunications operators are supported through the preparation of long-term and transparent regulatory plans for the incumbent operator, as well as support in the use of the existing infrastructure for alternative operators. As a result, operators can expect non-discriminatory treatment when using the incumbent operator's network.

---

5   Constitution of the Republic of Poland of 2 April 1997, Journal of Laws, No 78, item 483 as amended.
6   Journal of Laws, No 253, item 2531 of 2004.
7   Journal of Laws, No 106, item 675.

REGULATORY PRINCIPLES: THE FRAMEWORK DIRECTIVE

Scope of Regulation

25.8 Polish legislation adopts the technology neutral approach of the EU Directives. The definition of a telecommunications network in the TL[8] has the same meaning as the term 'electronic communications network', in Article 2(a) of the Framework Directive. Telecommunications services, on the other hand, are defined as services 'which consist mainly in the conveyance of signals in a telecommunications network; electronic mail is not considered as such a service'[9] and differs from the definition of electronic communications services, as defined in Article 2(c) of the Framework Directive by excluding the reference to remuneration and adding the express exclusion of electronic mail. The exclusion of electronic mail is clearly inconsistent with the Framework Directive. Notwithstanding that this definition does not expressly refer to VoIP services, it may be assumed that such services are treated as telecommunications services. The provision makes it clear, however, that such services exclude services providing or exercising editorial control over transmitted content, similar to the case in the Framework Directive. Regardless, an issue which will also be regulated in the planned amendment of the TL is the relationship between the new definition of 'call' and the definition of 'publicly available telephone service' (Article 2(c) of the Universal Service Directive), which, after the amendments, also included VoIP technology. A practical problem which can arise is the technical ability to implement number portability services in this technology. However, it appears that, based on the current regulations, no major changes will be necessary.

The appropriate solution, which is already functioning, is the power of the President of the UKE to examine whether it is technically possible to implement this service and the competence to issue a decision suspending the ability of subscribers to exercise this right. The definition of telephone call, as before, also applies to teleconferences conducted within the framework of publicly available telecommunications services. The wording of the definition of 'associated facilities'[10] differs slightly from its equivalent in the Framework Directive, but the meaning is the same.

Internet Freedom

25.9 Poland was ready to ratify the international Anti-Counterfeiting Trade Agreement ('ACTA'). However, after waves of protests across Poland, the Prime Minister decided that, until Polish society establishes a meaningful consensus, ACTA would not be sent for ratification. The conflict between Internet freedom and the legal protection of copyrights was the main point of controversy.

In principle, only after such protests did the process of the social discussion on the freedom to use third party intellectual property rights begin. Organisations involved in the protection of copyright supported the work of the Polish government on the adoption of ACTA.

---

8 Art 2.35 TL.
9 Art 2.48 TL.
10 Art 2.44 TL.

National Regulatory Authorities: Organisation, Regulatory Objectives and Competencies

25.10   The Polish regulator of the communications sector is the President of the Office of Electronic Communications (President of the UKE). The President of the UKE is a single-person, independent governmental body with an extensive range of powers, situated at the highest level in the public administrative structure. The President of the UKE is appointed by the Sejm (Lower house of the Polish Parliament), with the Senate's consent, at the request of the Prime Minister, for a period of five years. The Minister responsible for communications (this is currently the Minister of Administration and Digitisation) is also a supervisory body of the President of the UKE.

25.11   The statutory objectives of both communications authorities (the President of the UKE and the Minister responsible for communications)[11] are:

- to encourage competition in the provision of telecommunications networks, associated services or the provision of telecommunications services;
- to support the development of the domestic market;
- to promote the interests of the citizens of the European Union;
- to implement the policy of promoting cultural and language variety, as well as pluralism of the media; and
- to guarantee technological neutrality in the accepted legal standards.

25.12   The powers of the President of the UKE are listed in the TL and include both regulatory and supervisory tasks. The main tasks are:

- intervening in matters regarding the functioning of the telecommunications services market and access to the telecommunications infrastructure;[12]
- settlement of disputes between telecommunications undertakings;[13]
- keeping telecommunications registers;[14]
- coordination of frequency reservation;[15]
- preparation of drafts of secondary regulations;[16] and
- initiation and support of scientific research related to telecommunications.[17]

The implementation of the amended Article 3 of the Framework Directive was included in the government bill on the amendment of the Telecommunications Law.

25.13   At governmental level, the Minister responsible for communications is responsible for the telecommunications sector. He is authorised to issue secondary regulations to the TL. The Minister is not, however, authorised to interfere with the day-to-day administration of the telecommunications sector – this falls within the scope of duties of the President of the UKE. The Minister appoints and recalls the Deputy President of the UKE on the request of the President of the UKE.

25.14   As of 2005, the Chairperson of the National Broadcasting Council ('NBC') has not been awarded rights in the telecommunications sector under the Telecommunications Law. The TL requires cooperation between the President of the UKE and the Chairperson of the Office for Competition and Consumer Protection

---

11   Art 189.1 TL.
12   Art 192.5 TL.
13   Art 192.6 TL.
14   Art 192.10 TL.
15   Art 192.11 TL.
16   Art 192.4 TL.
17   Art 192.12 TL.

('Competition Authority'), and with the Chairperson of the NBC. Such cooperation consists of the exchange of information and consultation between those bodies.[18] The President of the UKE has already liaised with the Competition Authority with regard to market analysis and the definition for the purposes of designating SMP operators.

25.15   When the President of the UKE takes (or repeals) decisions related to market analysis and determination of an SMP operator, imposing, withdrawing, maintaining or amending regulatory obligations with regard to SMP operators, and those relating to telecommunications access, he must permit interested parties to express their positions on the proposed decision (or proposed repeal of a decision) in writing and within a specific deadline.[19]

25.16   The President of the UKE has competences to resolve disputes between consumers and providers of telecommunications services. In particular, the President of the UKE conducts mediation proceedings at the consumer's request, or at his own discretion.[20] Furthermore, the President settles disputes between undertakings if they cannot come to an agreement on access or interconnection.[21]

Right of Appeal against the NRA's Decisions

25.17   Decisions determining whether a given entity has significant market power, and the imposition of regulatory duties and penalties, are subject to appeal before the District Court in Warsaw – the Court of Competition and Consumer Protection. Other decisions cannot be directly appealed against in the first instance but an interested party may request the President of the UKE to re-examine a case. If the party is dissatisfied with a decision issued as a result of the review of the application for the re-examination of the case, it may file a complaint with the administrative court requesting the decision to be overruled. The party must file such complaint within 30 days of the delivery of the adjudication in the case.[22]

The NRA's Obligations to Cooperate with the Commission

25.18   The TL implements the requirements of Article 7 of the Framework Directive regarding cooperation with the Commission. The President of the UKE must cooperate with the NRAs of the EU Member States and with the European Commission. In particular, the President of the UKE must grant the NRAs of other Member States access to information collected from telecommunications undertakings and submit draft decisions together with their justifications to the Commission and the regulatory authorities of other EU Member States in cases where its decisions might influence commercial relations between Member States. The 'veto procedure' has been implemented in accordance with Article 7 of the Framework Directive; when determining significant market power and the extent of the intention to define the relevant market as a market other than the markets specified in the Commission Recommendation on relevant markets, the President of the UKE must take into account the Commission's position. Should the Commission state that the proposed solution may hamper the development of 'the single

---

18   Among others, Art 25c in connection with Art 23c.1 or Art 24
19   Art 15 TL.
20   Art 109 TL.
21   Art 28.1 TL.
22   Art 53 of the Law on Proceedings before Administrative Courts, Journal of Laws of 2002, No 153, item 1270.

European market', or would result in a breach of Community law, the President of the UKE must delay issuance of a decision for a specified period of time and may then be forced to withdraw the draft decision during this period (following a demand from the European Commission) by discontinuing the proceedings in the case. However, Directive 2009/140/EC introduced amendments into Articles 6 and 7 of the Framework Directive and has added Article 7a, which provides for a procedure for the consistent application of remedial measures, which strengthens their re-implementation into national legislation. In addition, in connection with the appointment of the Body of European Regulators for Electronic Communications ('BEREC'), it is required that this institution also be included in the procedure of consolidation proceedings. These amendments have been included in the government bill on the amendment to the Telecommunications Law.

'Significant Market Power' as a Fundamental Prerequisite of Regulation

Definition of SMP

25.19   According to the TL, a telecommunications undertaking has significant market power if it has an economic position that reflects dominance in the relevant market, in accordance with the provisions of EU law.[23] SMP may refer to individual or collective dominance, with the latter being applicable in the event that two or more undertakings hold a dominant economic position in the relevant market in accordance with the provisions of EU law, even if there are no organisational connections or other relations between them.[24] However, the Government bill on the amendment of the TL provides for the implementation of
Article 14(3) of the Framework Directive, according to which, where an undertaking has significant market power on a specific market, it may also be deemed to have SMP in a closely related market, where the links between the two markets are such as to allow the market power held in one market to be leveraged into the other market, thereby strengthening the market power of the undertaking.

25.20   After determination of the relevant markets, the President of the UKE initiates proceedings to establish whether there is effective competition in these markets. Should there be no effective competition, the President of the UKE initiates proceedings to determine which undertaking or undertakings have significant market power in the markets.[25]

Definition of relevant markets

25.21   A 'relevant market' is a market of goods and services considered by their purchasers to be substitutes because of their intended use, price or properties, including quality, and which are offered in an area where there are similar competitive conditions because of the type and properties of the goods and services or because of hindered market access, consumer preferences, significant price differences, and transport costs.[26]

---

23   Art 25a TL.
24   Art 25a.3 TL.
25   Art 22–24 TL.
26   The Telecommunications Law does not contain a legal definition of 'relevant market'. Rather,

25.22   The TL requires the President of the UKE to analyse the markets of telecommunications products and services.[27] The objective of conducting an analysis of the market is to determine whether there is effective competition. After completing the analysis, the President of the UKE conducts proceedings to specify the relevant market and to determine whether there is a telecommunications undertaking with significant market power or a telecommunications undertaking occupying a significant collective position on the market. If the given market is not a competitive market, the President of the UKE makes a decision recognising a telecommunications undertaking as one having significant market power, which, in turn, is related to the imposition of the additional obligations set out in the Act on this undertaking. The market analysis also serves the purpose of maintaining, amending or repealing regulatory obligations with respect to undertaking with significant market power.

25.23   The President of the UKE must conduct the proceedings no less frequently than every two years from the end of the previous proceedings. However, the President of the UKE must conduct proceedings immediately after an EC recommendation is issued or amended.

In addition, current implementing regulations to the TL regarding the specification of the relevant market take into consideration allegations of the EC finding previous regulations addressing the definition of the relevant markets defective (specifically Regulation of the Minister of Infrastructure of 25 October 2004 on the definition of the relevant markets to be analysed by the President of the Office of Telecommunications and Post). The Minister of Infrastructure set out the substantive scope of the specified market in detail in the regulation within the framework of the awarded individual competence. The main allegation regarding the solution adopted applied to the inability to effectively appeal against the settlement regarding the setting and definition of the relevant market. The current solution, including that the President of the UKE must specify the relevant markets, satisfies the requirements of the Framework Directive regarding guaranteeing effective appeal remedies, because it creates the ability for telecommunications undertakings to challenge the decision of the President of the UKE.

Imposition of remedies

25.24   After conducting the proceedings, in the event that it is established that there is a telecommunications undertaking with significant market power in the relevant market, the President of the UKE issues a decision in which the case is settled regarding the significant market power of the undertaking and its regulatory obligations. The decision may not include imposition of obligations not related to services provided in the regulated market. The President of the UKE must specify adequate and proportional measures which the entity subject to regulation must perform. The obligations should be specified in a clear manner and specifically targeted to address the particular problem.

The obligations imposed by the President of the UKE on undertakings with significant market power include, among other things: provision of telecommunications access for other telecommunications operators, including the use of network components and associated facilities; the obligation of equal treatment of telecommunications operators regarding telecommunications access; the obligation to

---

the definition of a relevant market is contained in Art 4.8 of the Act on Competition and Consumer Protection of 15 December 2000, Journal of Laws of 2003, No 86, item 804.

27   Art 21 TL.

announce or make information available on matters related to the assurance of telecommunications access, accounting information, technical specifications of the telecommunications network and equipment, network characteristics, rules and conditions for the provision of services and the use of the network, and the charges for such services; the obligation to keep regulatory accounts in a way which enables the identification of internal flows of transfers related to telecommunications access activities; and the obligation to prepare and submit a draft reference offer on telecommunications access within a specified period, the level of detail of which he will specify in the decision and the lack of setting of over-stated prices of services.[28]

NRA's Regulatory Duties concerning Rights of Way, Co-location and Facility Sharing

Rights of way

25.25   The owners, perpetual usufructuaries, or administrators of real estate or real property (collectively, 'property'), and their administrators, must permit operators and entities such as diplomatic and consular offices, military organisational units, and security units to lay cable lines underneath or over their property to install telecommunications equipment.[29] These duties also apply when the property is the subject of an agreement on use, rental, lease, or permanent management. The property owner, usufructuary, or administrator must fulfil these duties unless doing so would make their reasonable use of the real estate impossible.

25.26   The conditions for an operator's use of such property must be detailed in an agreement between the owner, usufructuary, or administrator and the requesting operator, which must be executed within 30 days from the date of the request for access. Generally, such access and use is subject to a fee.[30] If, however, the property owner, user, or administrator requests that the operator provide telecommunications services, and the telecommunications equipment is to be used for providing these services, the operator must not be charged for such access and use.

The amount of charge is in the parties' discretion. It is a commonpractice of operators to negotiate the access to be granted free of charge. Should the parties not agree on the wording of the respective contract within 30 days, the operator may request the local administrative authority to issue a decision granting those access rights and specifying where the lines or the equipment are to be installed. These procedures are also used by undertakings in the energy and gas sectors. Before access is granted, the requesting operator must attempt to negotiate access rights in good faith with the landowners. Good faith may be demonstrated by presenting documents on the negotiations held in pursuant to the procedures set out in the TL.

Co-location and Facility Sharing

25.27   The operator of a public telecommunications network must provide access for other public operators to telecommunications buildings and infrastructure and, in particular, to install, operate, supervise and maintain telecommunications devices if:

---

28   Arts 34–40, 42, 44, 45, 46, 47, 48 TL.
29   Art 33 of the Broadband Act.
30   Art 33.2 of the Broadband Act

- the fulfilment of these activities without access to the telecommunications buildings and infrastructure is impossible;
- doing so without such access might jeopardise land planning, human health, or the environment; and
- there is no technical or financial justification for duplicating the existing telecommunications infrastructure.

The conditions for providing access must be specified in an agreement between the two operators. If the parties cannot agree on the content of such an agreement, the President of the UKE will set out the conditions in an administrative decision.[31]

REGULATION OF MARKET ENTRY: IMPLEMENTATION OF THE AUTHORISATION DIRECTIVE

The General Authorisation of Electronic Communications

25.28   An operator must obtain a general permit from the national regulatory authority in order to conduct telecommunications activities. This general permit replaced concessions and individual permits, which were required for many years. Under the new regulatory regime, individual authorisations are only required for the use of radio equipment (through a radio permit) and scarce resources (ie frequencies and numbers). If a telecommunications undertaking of another Member State, or of a state which has entered into an agreement with the European Community and its Member States on the freedom to provide services, temporarily wishes to provide services in the Republic of Poland under the terms and conditions specified in the provisions of the Treaty establishing the European Community, the Agreement on the European Economic Area or in the provisions of another agreement regulating the freedom to provide services, as appropriate, will also be subject to entry in the register.

25.29   A party wishing to provide telecommunications services must complete a registration form and submit to the President of the UKE, who then issues the provider with a 'registration certificate', upon receipt of which the provider may commence providing services. If, after 14 days of receipt of a properly completed registration form, the President of the UKE has not issued the provider with a registration certificate, the undertaking may, once it notifies the President of the UKE, commence providing services. The registration procedure is free of charge.

25.30   If an undertaking provides telecommunications services without having going through the registration procedures described above, the undertaking may be fined up to 3 per cent of its annual income from the previous financial year.[32] Regardless of the financial penalty imposed on the undertaking, the President of the UKE may impose a financial penalty on the person in charge of the undertaking (ie the person performing managerial functions, or a member of a management body of the undertaking or of an association of such undertakings) of up to 300 per cent of the person's monthly remuneration, as calculated for the compensation for unused paid holidays. The person may also be subject to arrest, a restriction of freedom or a fine, which can be imposed simultaneously to the penalty mentioned above.

---

31   Art 30–31 of the Broadband Act.
32   Art 209 TL.

Rights of Use of Radio Frequencies

Strategic planning and coordination of the spectrum policy

25.31   An operator intending to use frequencies must apply to the President of the UKE for an individual decision (frequency reservation) and, in the case of digital television, to the President of the UKE in consultation with the National Broadcasting Council. Only a selected range of frequencies (those in the 2.4 GHz band) has been opened up to all interested parties without the need to apply for the reservation. When assigning frequencies, the President of the UKE must observe the National Frequency Designation Plan, as well as specific plans for the use of the relevant frequencies. The National Frequency Designation Plan is a general document with limited information on the designated use of each frequency range. Specific plans are far more detailed and extensive, but these plans only exist for selected frequencies. The lack of a specific plan for a particular range does not hinder the allocation of frequencies. Frequencies are allocated to all interested parties, but, if there are more applicants than the number of available frequencies, the President of the UKE must hold a tender before allocating the frequencies.[33]

25.32   The use of radio equipment requires a radio permit,[34] except for selected radio equipment, as listed in the TL[35] or in the Regulation of the Minister of Infrastructure.[36]

Admissible conditions

25.33   Frequency reservations may regulate the conditions which apply to the use of the frequencies,[37] requirements regarding the prevention of harmful electromagnetic interference, and the obligation to protect against electromagnetic radiation and the arrangements arising from the tender or competitive bidding proceedings.

Limitation of the number of rights of use to be granted

25.34   As noted above, if there are more applicants than the number of available frequencies, the President of the UKE must hold a tender (*przetarg*) before allocating the frequencies.[38] The main difference between competitive bidding and a tender is the selection criteria; while the amount of the declared fee and the maintenance of competitive conditions are the main factors taken into account in the tender process, only the latter criterion (maintaining of competitive conditions) is taken into account in the case of the competitive bidding. Both the tender and competitive bidding proceedings are preceded by consultation proceedings.

---

33   Art 116 TL.
34   Art 143 TL.
35   Art 144 TL, which exempts, for instance, radio equipment used solely for receiving or such radio equipment that is used in amateur radio-communications services.
36   Regulation of the Minister of Infrastructure of 3 July 2007 on radio transmitters and transmitter-receivers which may be used without a permit, Journal of Laws No 138, item 972, which exempts, for instance, radio equipment in the 2.4 GHz band.
37   Art 146.1 TL in connection with Art 115.2, item 1 TL.
38   Art 116 TL.

Frequency trading

25.35   Polish law only allows for limited trading in frequencies. Operators are not entitled to transfer frequencies on their own, but may request that the President of the UKE transfer them. The President of the UKE may only transfer a frequency reservation to another entity at the request of an operator already using these frequencies if the decision on the frequency reservation allows for such a transfer and the new operator satisfies applicable legal requirements.[39] The conditions for the transfer of rights to frequencies are set out in the frequency reservation.[40]

Rights of Use of Numbers

General authorisations and award of individual rights

25.36   The President of the UKE grants individual numbering resources to operators by way of an administrative decision issued on the motion of operators. When granting those rights, the President of the UKE must observe limitations specified in the National Numbering Plan. The allocation of numbers gives the operator the right to use, and allow access to, the particular numbers. VoIP products now also use geographic telephone numbers.

Admissible conditions

25.37   The decision on the allocation of numbers may specify conditions for using the numbers or for provision of access to numbering, in particular, the requirement for non-discriminatory access to telecommunications services using numbers allocated to other undertakings.[41] An entity having received the numbers must provide access to the allocated numbering to entities which interoperate with its telecommunications network and entities providing telecommunications services.[42]

25.38   Operators of public telephone networks (including mobile network operators) must offer number portability to their customers. In the case of geographic numbers, an operator is only obliged to offer portability within the same geographic area.[43]

Limitation of the number of rights of use to be awarded

25.39   In the case of insufficient numbering resources, undertakings to which numbers will be granted are selected by tender, the deciding criterion of which is the declared price.[44]

The NRA's Enforcement Powers

25.40   The President of the UKE is authorised to conduct reviews regarding compliance with laws, decisions, and regulations on telecommunications, frequency

---

39   Art 122 TL.
40   Art 115.1, item 7 TL.
41   Art 126.7 TL.
42   Art 128.1 TL
43   Art 70 TL
44   Art 126.6 TL.

management and satisfying the requirements regarding electromagnetic compatibility of the equipment on the market. UKE employees enjoy extensive supervisory powers.[45] After post-audit recommendations are issued, the President of the UKE may issue a decision ordering elimination of the irregularities found, and may also indicate measures for eliminating those irregularities, set a deadline for adopting such measures, and impose an administrative fine on the audited entity.

25.41   If the irregularities have taken place in the past, are serious, and the inspected entity has not responded to such a prior decision, the President of the UKE may prevent the entity from conducting telecommunications activities, or change or withdraw the reservation to the entity of frequencies, satellite resources or numbering allocations.[46]

Administrative Charges and Fees for Rights of Use

25.42   Under the TL individual authorisations are subject to a one-time fee as well as, in some instances, an annual fee. The annual fee must be paid by any undertaking having generated revenues from telecommunications activities in excess of PLN 4m (approximately €1,000,000) during the financial year falling two years before the year in question. The undertaking must commence payment of the fee after the first two years of conducting telecommunications activities. The amount of this annual charge is specified in the secondary regulation to the TL.[47]

The annual fee may not exceed 0.05 per cent of a telecommunications undertaking's annual revenues from telecommunications activities performed, obtained in the financial year two years before the year for which this fee is due.

One-time fees include:

- one-off fees for a general exclusive frequency licence in an amount declared in this procedure, not lower than 50 per cent of an annual fee for the right to use the frequency specified in accordance with the conditions provided for in the general exclusive frequency licence; and
- one-off fees of the amount declared by an entity applying for a numbering assignment.

25.43   Entities obtaining rights of use for numbers, and those obtaining rights of use for frequencies, must pay an annual fee for such rights. The fees are collected by the UKE and constitute income to the state budget. Interest is charged in arrears.[48]

Transitional Regulations for Existing authorisations

25.44   Undertakings holding a telecommunications permit, or those having submitted a notification of their telecommunications activities under the previous

---

45   Arts 199 and 200 TL.

46   Art 201.4 TL.

47   Regulation of the Minister of Infrastructure on the amount, the mode of establishment and the terms and manner of making payments of the annual telecommunications charge of 27 December 2004, Journal of Laws, of 2004, No 285, item 2857.

48   At the same level as for tax arrears, as defined by the Tax Ordinance of 29 August 1997, Journal of Laws No 137, item 926 as amended.

telecommunications law (the Telecommunications Act of 21 July 2000),[49] are entered ex officio into the register of telecommunications undertakings by the President of the UKE.

25.45 Frequency reservations and number allocations, including those contained in telecommunications permits issued under the previous regulation, automatically became reservations and allocations under the TL.[50]

REGULATION OF NETWORK ACCESS AND INTERCONNECTION: IMPLEMENTATION OF THE ACCESS DIRECTIVE

Objectives and Scope of Access Regulation

25.46 The objective of regulating network access and interconnection (as with other provisions of the TL) is to support effective competition in the provision of telecommunications services on equal terms, as well as to assure maximum benefits to users regarding the diversity, price and quality of telecommunications services.[51]

25.47 The TL's regulations on telecommunications access apply to all telecommunications undertakings, including those which have not been identified as having significant market position.

Basic Regulatory Concepts

25.48 Telecommunications access is defined in the TL as the use of telecommunications facilities, associated facilities or services provided by another telecommunications undertaking, under defined conditions, for the purpose of providing telecommunications services.[52] This includes:

- the connection of telecommunications equipment, in particular access to the local loop and to facilities and services necessary to provide services over the local loop;
- access to buildings and telecommunications infrastructure;
- access to relevant software systems including operational support systems;
- access to number translation or systems offering equivalent functionality;
- access to telecommunications networks, in particular for roaming;
- access to conditional access systems; and
- access to virtual network services.

25.49 Priority is given to commercial negotiations. Each operator of a public telecommunications network is obliged to negotiate a telecommunications access agreement at the request of another telecommunications undertaking for the purpose of providing publicly available telecommunications services and ensuring interoperability of services. Information obtained in connection with the negotiations may be used exclusively in accordance with the purpose for which it is collected and must be kept confidential.[53] Only if the operators cannot agree on the content of the agreement may the President of the UKE intervene.

---

49 Journal of Laws No 73, item 852 as amended.
50 Art 227.1 TL.
51 Art 1.2 TL.
52 Art 2.6 TL.
53 Art 26.1 TL.

25.50 The TL has implemented the freedom of access rule, as specified in Article 3(1) of the Access Directive. Under these provisions, an undertaking requesting access does not need to apply for entry into the register of telecommunications undertakings if it is not providing services in Poland.[54]

Access- and Interconnection-related Obligations with Respect to SMP Undertakings

25.51 The TL provides for a number of remedies that the President of the UKE may impose on an undertaking with significant market power.[55] These include such obligations as the duty to ensure equal treatment of telecommunications undertakings with regard to telecommunications access,[56] the duty to keep specific regulatory accounting,[57] and the duty to pay fees for telecommunications access based on the costs incurred.[58]

25.52 The President of the UKE may require an SMP undertaking to publish or make information available on issues of the provision of telecommunications access, issues related to accounting data, technical specifications of network and telecommunications equipment and network characteristics.[59]

25.53 The President of the UKE may require a SMP undertaking to treat other telecommunications undertakings equally with respect to telecommunications access, in particular, by offering equal conditions in comparable circumstances.[60]

25.54 The President of the UKE may also authorised to impose specific access obligations, such as obligations to ensure the possibility of managing end user services and to specify the details regarding the provision of those services, to grant access to interfaces, protocols and other technologies required for the interoperability of services, and to provide other undertakings with systems supporting operational activities and other software systems, including tariff systems, billing systems, and receivables collection systems.[61]

25.55 The President of the UKE may also require an SMP undertaking to fix fees for telecommunications access on the basis of the costs incurred.[62]

25.56 The purpose of regulatory accounting is to separate and allocate the assets, liabilities, revenues and expenses of the telecommunications undertaking to given operations, as if each type of operation would be performed by an alternative telecommunications operator and the obligation to apply such accounting rules may be imposed on an SMP undertaking.[63] The Minister responsible for communications in, agreement with the Minister responsible for public finance, must issue an

---

54   Art 26.4 TL.
55   Art 36–40 TL.
56   Art 36 TL.
57   Art 39.1.1 TL.
58   Art 39.1.2 TL.
59   Art 37 TL.
60   Art 36 TL.
61   Art 34.2 TL.
62   Art 40.1 TL.
63   Art 49.1 TL.

ordinance specifying the methods of assigning assets and liabilities, revenues and expenses to operations, and methods and procedures for cost calculation.[64]

25.57 The President of the UKE, after having prepared a market analysis, defined the relevant market, and nominated the undertaking with SMP, typically issues a regulatory decision imposing on the SMP undertaking the obligation to provide telecommunications access, the obligation of equal treatment of telecommunications undertakings regarding telecommunications access, the obligation of transparency, the obligation of regulatory accounting, the obligation to set charges for telecommunications access on the basis of the costs incurred, and the obligation to prepare and present a reference offer for telecommunications access.

The President of the UKE may impose on a SMP operator an obligation to make available specific telecommunications network elements, including cables, lines or local loops; the obligation to make local loops available may relate to a loop or a sub-loop, with full or shared access, together with collocation and access to cable lines and relevant information systems, providing telecommunications infrastructure, collocation and other forms of shared use of buildings.[65]

Regulatory Powers with Respect to SMP Undertakings

25.58 A subscriber who is a party to an agreement with a service provider which ensures access to a fixed line public telephone network of an SMP undertaking may choose any provider of publicly available telephone services, the services of which are available in interconnected networks.[66]

25.59 In addition to the obligations listed above which the President of the UKE may impose on an SMP provider, he may also require such an undertaking to offer services on wholesale terms for the purpose of their future sale by another undertaking,[67] as well not to restrict competition by fixing the price for services below the cost of their provision, and not to apply preferential treatment to particular end-users.[68]

The proposed act[69] includes a provision on functional separation in Article 44b which will be transposed into Polish law as an implementation of Article 13a of the Framework Directive. This provision states that where the national regulatory authority concludes that the appropriate obligations imposed have failed to achieve effective competition and that there are important and persisting competition problems or market failures identified in relation to the wholesale provision of certain access product markets, the President of the UKE may, as an exceptional measure, impose an obligation on vertically integrated undertakings to place activities related to the wholesale provision of relevant access products in an independently operating business entity.

---

64   Art 51 TL.
65   Art 34 TL.
66   Art 72.1 TL.
67   Art 34.1(3) TL.
68   Art 46.2 TL.
69   See para 25.5 above.

Regulatory Powers Applicable to All Market Participants

Obligation to ensure end-to-end connectivity

25.60   The President of the UKE may, upon the written request of any of the parties to negotiations regarding the conclusion of a telecommunications access agreement, specify the end date of such negotiations. The end date, however must not fall later than 90 days from the day of submission of the motion for the conclusion of the agreement. Furthermore, in the case of negotiations which have not yet started, the refusal to grant telecommunications access by the obliged entity or the failure to conclude the agreement within the deadline specified above, either party may file a motion with the President of the UKE to issue a decision on any contentious issues or a decision setting out the conditions for cooperation.[70] These rules follow from the obligation to encourage and ensure access and interconnection, as specified in Article 5(1)(a) of the Access Directive.

Regulation of Roaming Services

25.61   Under the TL, roaming services are a form of telecommunications access, which encompasses the use of telecommunications equipment, associated facilities, or services provided by another telecommunications operator, on specified conditions, for the purpose of providing telecommunications services.[71] National roaming refers to an agreement among operators to use each other's networks to provide services in geographic areas where they have no coverage.

An operator using national roaming service is a fully independent mobile network operator ('Mobile Network Operator' or 'MNO') with regard to the services provided, but coverage of their access infrastructure does not, temporarily or permanently, cover the whole of the country, but only certain areas ('insular network access'). In order to provide services on a national scale, therefore, such an operator must sign a national roaming agreement with another MNO with a mobile telecommunications network to use its network to complement its network coverage.

In accordance with the decision of the President of the UKE, if there is no telecommunications undertaking with SMP in the domestic market for the provision of access services and call initiation in public mobile telephone networks, or a telecommunications undertaking holding a significant collective position, there is effective competition on the market.

However, in terms of international roaming (in particular Community roaming), according to the President of the UKE, imposing, through a regulation, the access obligation connected with the obligation of non-discrimination, would be an effective remedy to anti-competitiveness encountered in the wholesale roaming market. Such a solution would force operators who receive requests for access to conclude agreements according to commercial rules (the price will also be of significance) and to hold negotiations in good faith.

---

70   Art 26 TL.
71   Art 34.1–2.

Access to digital radio and television broadcasting services

25.62   The obligation to ensure access to associated API and EPG facilities may be imposed on telecommunications undertakings in order to give an end user access to digital radio and television transmission.[72] Telecommunications undertakings providing conditional access systems must offer technical services to broadcasters on equal and non-discriminatory terms, which enable the receipt of digital radio and television transmissions using decoders installed in the networks or at the subscriber's premises. Telecommunications undertakings providing conditional access systems are obliged to keep separate accounts for this activity.

REGULATION OF UNIVERSAL SERVICES AND USER RIGHTS: THE UNIVERSAL SERVICE DIRECTIVE

Regulation of Universal Service Obligations

Scope of universal service obligations

25.63   Universal services are defined as a set of telecommunications services provided by a designated telecommunications undertaking,[73] which should be available to all end users of fixed-line public telephone networks within the territory of Poland, and which should be of the required quality and offered at an affordable price.

25.64   Universal services include all services as prescribed in the Universal Service Directive. In the case of specifically mentioned entities (schools, public libraries, and universities), the provider of universal services will also be obliged to offer an additional service in the form of broadband access to the Internet.[74] The costs of this service are borne by the state budget.[75] The details regarding accessibility and quality are determined in a separate regulation to be issued by the Minister responsible for communication.[76]

Designation of undertakings obliged to provide universal services

25.65   The TL provides two procedures for the designation of undertakings obliged to provide universal services. Under the first procedure, to be applied initially, the undertaking is selected through competitive bidding organised by the President of the UKE, in which any telecommunications undertaking may submit an offer. The selection is based on two criteria: the lowest cost of public telephony services and the quality of the services provided. In the event that no offer is submitted, in the second procedure, the President of the UKE designates the provider of telecommunications services specified by the authority, which has significant market power on the retail market in the area, to provide universal services. If no provider of publicly available telecommunications services in public fixed line telephone networks has gained significant market power in the relevant market in the area specified by the President of the UKE, the provider of fixed line

---

72   Art 136, item 1 TL.
73   Art 81 TL.
74   Art 81.5 TL.
75   Art 100 TL.
76   Art 81.6 TL.

telecommunications services with the largest number of subscriber lines will be designated as the provider of universal services.[77]

25.66   After holding competitive bidding, in a decision of 5 May 2006, the President of the UKE designated Telekomunikacja Polska S.A. to provide universal services involving:

- the connection of a single network termination at the subscriber's main location, with the exception of an integrated services digital network ('ISDN');
- keeping the subscriber loop with the network termination referred to above ready for the provision of telecommunications services;
- national and international telephone calls, including to mobile networks as well as the provision of fax transmission and data transmission, including Internet connections;
- the provision of a directory enquiry service and the provision of subscriber directories;
- the supply of facilities for the disabled; and
- the provision of telephone services using public payphones throughout the entire country.

To date, Telekomunikacja Polska S.A. has been the only such designated operator.

Regulation of retail tariffs, user expenditures and quality of service

25.67   Service providers must set tariffs on the basis of clear, objective and non-discriminatory criteria. The tariffs must be published and the subscribers must be notified of any increase in advance. A subscriber has the right to terminate the service agreement without any financial consequences in the event that the price increase is not accepted. Providers of public telecommunications services are also obliged to adhere to quality of services standards as set out by the minister responsible for communications in a regulation. Service providers must publish data on the quality of their services. In the event of non-compliance with applicable standards, the provider may be fined up to 3 per cent of its income from the preceding year.

25.68   Other guarantees provided for in the TL include the empowerment of the regulatory authority to review price lists and general terms and conditions of universal services. In addition, a provider of universal services is must provide detailed billing free of charge.

Cost calculation and financing of universal services

25.69   A provider of universal services sets the prices for these services on the basis of reasonable costs, calculated in accordance with the regulation of the minister responsible for communications, taking into consideration the financial standing of the end users, including the disabled.[78] The undertaking designated as the provider of universal services is also entitled to receive special compensation if the provision of such services proves unprofitable.[79]

---

77   Arts 82 and 83 TL.
78   Art 90 TL.
79   Arts 91 and 95 TL.

25.70   The amount of such compensation is set by the President of the UKE who must follow the instructions on the calculation of the respective figure provided in the regulation issued by the Minister responsible for communications. The purpose of such compensation is to reimburse the provider of universal services for losses (costs) incurred in connection with the provision of universal services. The calculation of the costs should include the costs directly incurred in connection with the provision of the universal services, revenues from the provision of such services, as well as other indirect benefits connected with the provision of universal services.[80] The reimbursement will be paid from a special fund administered by the UKE.[81] Contributions to this fund are to be made by telecommunications undertakings with revenues exceeding PLN 4m (approx €1m) in a given year.[82] The maximum contribution must not exceed 1 per cent of the revenue of the contributing entity.[83]

Regulation of Retail Markets

Prerequisites for the regulation of retail markets

25.71   Under the TL a retail market will be regulated if it is determined that:

- there is no effective competition in the market;
- the obligations related to ensuring access to telecommunications on the wholesale market would not lead to the desired results; and
- the obligations related to carrier pre-selection have not led to the desired results in accordance with the provisions of the TL.[84]

Regulatory powers

25.72   The President of the UKE may impose the following obligations on undertakings with significant market power on retail markets:

- not to apply excessive pricing;[85]
- not to hinder market entry for other undertakings;[86]
- not to limit competition by setting prices of services below cost;[87]
- not to apply unjustified preferences for specific end users, except as provided for in the TL;[88] and
- not to unduly bundle services.[89]

25.73   The President of the UKE may require an undertaking with significant market power in in the retail market of the provision of all or some of the minimum set of leased lines to, among others, provide leased lines on transparent and non-discriminatory terms, to maintain regulatory accounts in accordance with the instruction approved by the President of the UKE, to calculate the costs of

---

80   Art 95 TL.
81   Art 99 TL.
82   Art 97 TL.
83   Art 98 TL.
84   Art 46 TL.
85   Art 46.2, item 1 TL.
86   Art 46.2, item 2 TL.
87   Art 46.2, item 3 TL.
88   Art 46.2, item 4 TL.
89   Art 46.2, item 5 TL.

providing all or a part of the minimum set of leased lines in accordance with the description of the cost calculation approved by the President of the UKE, and to set prices on the basis of reasonable costs incurred in connection with the provision of such services.[90]

End User Rights

Contracts

25.74   The designated universal services undertaking may not refuse to enter into an agreement regarding universal services or individual services making up the universal service or, in the case of 'authorised entities', a network connection service for the provision of broadband Internet access when the user satisfies the required conditions set out in the general terms and conditions for providing universal.[91] The agreement on the provision of the universal service must be concluded within 30 days of such a request. The agreement must, in particular,specify the date on which the provision of services will start.

25.75   The TL provides for mandatory elements of an agreement on the provision of telecommunications services.[92] In particular, the agreement must cover such issues as the quality of the service, the scope of the services, prices, the term of the agreement, and complaint procedures.

Transparency obligations

25.76   The TL imposes on providers of telecommunications obligations related to transparency, such as the obligationto make its list of prices for telecommunications services publicly available and to provide the list to subscribers upon request, and free of charge. Any increase in a provider's prices of telecommunications services must announced one billing period in advance. The provider must, at the request of the regulatory authority, submit the price list for review. In addition, the provider must publish information on the quality of services offered. The President of the UKE publishes information on the rights and obligations of end users in the Bulletin of the UKE and on the authority's official website.[93]

Quality of service: securing 'net neutrality'

25.77   The TL currently has no rules on network neutrality. However, they have been included in the government bill on the amendment to the Telecommunications Law. The relevant provisions of the TL are in need of modification to bring the TL in line with Article 20 of the Universal Services Directive. This article awards national regulatory authorities the right to:

- specify, inter alia, the quantifiable indicators of the quality of services and content, the form and the method of providing information intended for publication, on the possible mechanisms on quality certification; and

---

90   Art 47.1, 2 and 3 TL.
91   Art 86 TL.
92   Art 56.3 TL.
93   Art 61 and 62 TL.

- impose minimum requirements on an undertaking or undertakings providing public communications networks regarding quality of services, to prevent a deterioration of the quality of services, blocking access to the network and obstructing or slowing down traffic in networks,

The proposed amendments apply the concept of network neutrality consistent with the definition accepted by BEREC in the Report 'A framework of quality of services in the scope of network neutrality' published on 8 December 2011.

European emergency call number

25.78   Under the TL, a provider of publicly available telecommunications services must provide enable its network end users, including people using public payphones, to call emergency numbers free of charge. A provider of publicly available telecommunications services must ensure the routing of calls to the emergency call centre for the 112 emergency number and the ability to the statutory emergency services which are appropriate for a given area for calls to other emergency numbers.[94]

Other obligations

25.79   Pursuant to the TL, an operator of a public telephone network must provide end users with the possibility of dual-tone multi-frequency signalling (DTMF),[95] a directory enquiries service[96] and telephone directories, and must provide information on the location of a network termination from which a call was made to the 112 emergency number and other emergency numbers, in real time, as far as technically possible, on every request by the services officially appointed to provide assistance, to enable them to take immediate action.[97]

Obligation facilitating a change of provider

25.80   When changing service providers, a subscriber, who is a party to an agreement with an undertaking providing connections to a public telephone network or a pre-paid end user, may request the assigned number to be ported to an existing network of an operator[98] in:

- a geographic area (for geographic numbers); and
- the entire country (for non-geographic numbers).

The undertaking may not charge a fee to the subscriber or pre-paid end user in the public mobile telephone network for porting an assigned number. When requesting an assigned number to be ported, the subscriber referred to above may terminate an agreement with the existing service provider without the observance of terms of notice specified in the terminated agreement. In such a case, the subscriber will be obliged to pay the charge to the existing service provider at an amount which is no more than the subscription fee for the notice period; however, no more than the subscription fee for one billing period plus a claim related to the allowance granted

---

94   Art 77 TL.
95   Art 75 TL.
96   Art 66 TL.
97   Art 78 TL.
98   Art 71 TL.

to the subscriber, calculated in proportion to the time that remains to the end of the agreement.[99]

DATA PROTECTION: IMPLEMENTATION OF THE DIRECTIVE ON PRIVACY AND ELECTRONIC COMMUNICATIONS

Confidentiality of Communications

25.81   The TL defines the scope of confidentiality of communications and imposes several related obligations on providers of publicly available electronic communications. In particular, the TL prohibits access, storage, transmission or any other use of the content or data without the consent of the users concerned,[100] except when legally authorised to do so.[101] Entities involved in telecommunications activities must take all necessary precautions to safeguard the security of their services. In the case of a risk of a security breach, the operator must inform subscribers that the technical measures applied do not guarantee security of communications. The operator must also inform the users about possible remedies that may be applied and their related costs.[102]

25.82   The use of an electronic communications network for the purpose of storing information or gaining access to information in a user's terminal equipment constitutes an offence (subject to a fine) if the user or the subscriber is not provided with easy to understand information regarding the purpose of the processing. The user or the subscriber must also be given the opportunity to refuse processing.[103]

25.83   The amended provisions of the Privacy Directive have not yet been implemented. The implementation has been included in the government bill on the amendment of the Telecommunications Law.

Data Retention

25.84   An operator of a public telecommunications network and the provider of publicly available telecommunications services must, at their expense:

- retain and store the data (referred to in Article 180c TL) which is generated in a telecommunications network or processed by that operator or provider, in the territory of the Republic of Poland, for a period of 24 months from the date of the call or unsuccessful call attempt, and to erase the data as soon as this period expires, excluding data protected under separate provisions of the law;
- make available such data to authorised entities and to the court and public prosecutor on the terms, and pursuant to the procedures specified in separate provisions of the law; and
- protect the data against accidental or unlawful destruction, loss or alteration, unauthorised or unlawful storage, processing, access or disclosure, in accordance with the TL (provisions of Articles 159–175 and Article 180e).

The TL provisions referenced constitute the implementation of the Data Retention Directive.

---

99   Art 71a TL.
100   Art 159.3 TL.
101   Art 159.4 TL.
102   Art 175 TL.
103   Art 173 TL.

An important amendment in the proposed act is the shortening of time of storing (retention) end users' telecommunications data for law enforcement agencies and services from 24 to 12 months. The proposed act foresees the possibility of retention only in the matters of utmost importance, e g fighting terrorism, defensibility, public good.

Traffic Data and Location Data

25.85   Operators of publicly available telecommunications networks and providers of telecommunications services processing traffic data must store such data for a period of 24 months (due to certain obligations regarding state security and national defence). After that period, the traffic data must be erased or made anonymous.[104]

25.86   The processing of traffic data necessary for billing and interconnection payments is permissible, subject to the notification of the subscriber or user. Such processing is only possible up to the end of the period during which the bill may be lawfully challenged or payment claimed.[105] The providers of publicly available telecommunications services must inform the subscriber or user of the traffic data which will be processed for the purpose of marketing or for the purpose of providing value added services. The provider must obtain consent from the user or subscriber for such processing.[106]

25.87   Location data may only be processed when such data is made anonymous, or with the consent of the user or subscriber. In obtaining consent from the user or subscriber, the service provider must informed the user or subscriber of the type of location data which is subject to processing, the purpose and duration of the processing, and whether the data will be transferred to another entity for the purpose of providing value added services.[107]. Users or subscribers may withdraw their consent, at which time, the provider must cease processing the location data

Itemised Billing

25.88   A provider of publicly available telecommunications services must provide the subscriber, free of charge, with a list of all services provided, together with the invoice and information on the calls for which the charge was made, stating the number of billing units representing the value of calls made by the subscriber. At the subscriber's request, the provider must supply a detailed itemisation of the telecommunications services for which a charge may be made, at the rate specified in the price list.[108]

Presentation and Restriction of Calling and Connected Line Identification

25.89   An operator of a publicly available telecommunications network must provide users with the capability of ID presentation of a network termination from

---

104   Art 180a et seq TL.
105   Art 165.2 TL.
106   Art 165 TL.
107   Art 166 TL
108   Art 80 TL.

which the call is originated, before answering the call.[109] At the same time, the service provider must notify subscribers that the network the subscriber uses allows for the presentation of the calling line ID and the called line ID.[110] If the subscriber chooses to cancel or restrict the call identification services, the operator should do so free of charge.[111] The service provider may override the cancellation of the caller identification in cases specified by law.

Automatic Call Forwarding

25.90   The provider of services in publicly available telecommunications networks offering automatic call forwarding must enable the subscriber to easily restrict third party automatic call forwarding to the subscriber's terminal equipment.[112]

Subscriber Directories

25.91   The TL defines the scope of personal data that may be used in the preparation of telephone directories without obtaining the subscriber's consent. Such data includes the subscriber's number or identification mark, his name and surname, the name of the town and street where the termination made available to the subscriber is located (for fixed line public telephone networks) and the permanent registration (for mobile public telephone networks).[113] Before this data may be included in the directory, subscribers must be informed, free of charge, about the purpose of the directory and further possibilities to use the directory.

Unsolicited Communications

25.92   The Law on the Provision of Services Electronically ('EL') regulates the unsolicited commercial information.[114] Pursuant to the EL, it is prohibited to send unsolicited commercial information to a particular recipient through means of electronic communications and by e-mail in particular.[115] Commercial information is considered solicited if the recipient has agreed to receive such information and has disclosed his or her electronic address which identifies the recipient for that purpose.[116] Means of electronic communications are defined as technical solutions, including telecommunications devices and supporting software, which allow communication through the use of data transmission between telecommunication systems, including e-mail in particular.[117]

---

109   Art 171.1 TL.
110   Art 171.5 TL.
111   Art 171.6 TL.
112   Art 171.4 TL.
113   Art 169 TL.
114   The Law on the Provision of Services Electronically of 18 July 2002, Journal of Laws No 173, item 1808, as amended ('EL').
115   Art 10.2 EL.
116   Art 10.2 EL.
117   Art 2.5 EL.

25.93   Non-compliance with these rules is considered an act of unfair competition under The Act on the Combating of Unfair Competition.[118] The unsolicited transmission of commercial information is also considered a misdemeanour and is subject to a fine.[119]

---

118   The Act on the Combating of Unfair Competition of 16 April 1997, Journal of Laws No 47, item 211, as amended.
119   Art 24 EL.

The Portuguese Market for Electronic Communications[1]

António de Mendonça Raimundo and Miriam Brice
Albuquerque & Associados – Law Firm, Lisbon

LEGAL STRUCTURE

Basic Policy

26.1 Following the complete market liberalisation and opening to competition in the early 2000s, and the development of a comprehensive legal framework with the implementation of the 2002 EU Regulatory Package, the Portuguese telecommunications market continues to be developed within the EU framework and standards.

26.2 Portugal has a medium-sized telecommunications market with a technological development pattern consistent with EU standards. The market is characterised by a very strong mobile sector with three major competitive players (TMN, Vodafone, and Optimus) and with the number of mobile phones in operation exceeding the Portuguese population.

26.3 Currently, the telecommunications market is also characterised by a notable growth of next generation networks and optical fibre and, from a commercial point of view, the dissemination of multiple play offers by the two major telecommunications operators, ZON and PT. The universal electronic communications service provider is currently PT, which must guarantee a minimum set of quality services available to all users regardless of their geographical location and, in light of national conditions, at an affordable price. However, the current Portuguese Government plans to renegotiate the concession agreement with PT and launch a new public tender to choose new universal services suppliers.

26.4 From a regulatory standpoint, the major challenge, and first objective, is to consolidate market growth and competitiveness evidenced in the last decade and to continue to promote open and competitive markets, ensuring conditions for innovation, investment, efficiency and fair competition among the different technological platforms. An additional significant goal is the assurance and protection of the rights of users and the general public under the principles of universal access, transparency, and non-discrimination.

26.5 In order to achieve these major objectives, the current governmental telecommunications policy underscores the need for stronger and more efficient

---

1   Editing of this chapter closed on 11 September 2012.

regulation. Improving the telecommunications regulator's efficiency and perform-ance capacity, therefore, is paramount, with respect to market monitoring and supervision, and adoption of measures necessary to rectify irregularities. Promotion of institutional and technical cooperation, and participation in the development of the EU internal market, are also key goals to be pursued by the Portuguese telecommunications regulator.

Implementation of EU Directives

26.6   Law No 5/2004, of 10 February 2004 (the 'Electronic Communications Law, 'Lei das Telecomunicações Electrónicas', or 'REGICOM') implemented the 2002 EU Regulatory Package.

26.7   Directive 2002/58/EC of the European Parliament and of the Council, of 12 July 2002 concerning the processing of personal data and the protection of privacy in the electronic communications ('E-Privacy Directive') was implemented in Portugal by Law No 41/2004, of 18 August 2004 ('E-Privacy Law'). Recently, Law No 46/2012 of 29 August 2012 (which implemented Directive 2009/136/EC of the European Parliament and of the Council, of 25 November 2009 amending the E-Privacy Directive) introduced amendments to the E-Privacy Law.

26.8   Portugal implemented the 'Better Regulation Directive' and the 'Citizens' Rights Directive' through Law No 51/2011, of 13 September 2011, which intro-duced the sixth amendment to REGICOM. In addition, Law No 51/2011, of 13 September 2011 produced the third amendment to Decree No 177/99, of 21 May 1999, which regulates access to and provision of audiotext services and value-added message-based services.

Legislation

26.9   REGICOM establishes the legal regime applicable to electronic communica-tions networks and services and to associated facilities and services, and defines the assignments of the national regulatory authority, Autoridade Nacional de Comuni-cações ('ANACOM').

26.10   The provisions of REGICOM do not affect the application of provisions pursuant to:

- the regime of free circulation, placing on the market and putting into service radio equipment and telecommunications terminal equipment, or the regime of the respective conformity assessment and marking procedures;[2]
- the regime of infrastructure construction suitable for the accommodation of electronic communications networks, the set-up of electronic communications networks and the construction of infrastructure for telecommunications in housing developments, urban settlements and groups of buildings;[3]
- the regime applicable to radio-communications networks and stations;[4] or
- the regime applicable to the use of the Personal Radio Service – Citizen's Band (SRP-CB).

---

2   Decree no 192/2000, of 18 August)
3   Decree no 259/2000 of 25 September, Decree-Law No 123/2009, of 21 May, as amended by Decree No 258/2009, of 25 September.
4   Decree no 151-A/2000 of 20 July 2000, amended by Decree No 167/2006, of 16 August and Decree No 264/2009, of 28 September.

In addition to REGICOM, there are several Laws and Decrees applicable to telecommunication matters. ANACOM is governed by statutes (bylaws) approved by Decree No 309/2001, of 7 December 2000.[5] Decree No 31/2003, of 17 February 2003, provides for the bases of the telecommunications public service concession, which was granted thereby to Portugal Telecom, the concessionaire and former incumbent. However, currently, there are three ongoing tender procedures, limited by prior qualification, and published in the EU Official Journal. These tender procedures seek to replace the current concession with Portugal Telecom in the fields of:

● universal service of connection to public telecommunications network and publicly available telephone services;
● public payphones; and
● complete phonebook and directory services.

The regulatory decisions of the ANACOM and the implementation of its measures are based on REGICOM, specifically on the principles set forth in article 5, establishing the regulatory objectives to be pursued by ANACOM.

REGULATORY PRINCIPLES: THE FRAMEWORK DIRECTIVE

Scope of Regulation

26.11   REGICOM covers electronic communications networks and services and associated facilities and services, and also defines role of ANACOM.

REGICOM does not apply to:

● information society services,[6] which do not consist wholly or mainly in the conveyance of signals on electronic communications networks;
● services which provide or which exercise editorial control over content transmitted over electronic communications networks and services, including television and radio programme services, audiotext, and value-added message-based services;
● private networks of, or under the responsibility of, the Ministry of National Defence or of the security and emergency forces and services; and
● the Portuguese Government computer network managed by the Government Computer Network Management Centre ('*Centro de Gestão da Rede Informática do Governo*' ('CEGER')).

The definitions of 'electronic communications network', 'electronic communications service', and 'associated facilities' are provided in article 3 REGICOM.

26.12   'Electronic communications network' is defined as:

'transmission systems and, where applicable, switching or routing equipment and other resources, including network elements which are not active, which permit the conveyance of signals by wire, radio, optical or other electromagnetic means, including satellite networks, fixed (circuit- and packet-switched, including Internet) and mobile terrestrial networks, electricity cable

---

5   ICP – *Instituto de Comunicações de Portugal* – was established by the Decree-law No 188/81, of 2 July; the name was changed to ICP-ANACOM by Decree-law No 309/2001, of 7 December 2001.
6   As defined in Decree-Law No 58/2000, of 18 April 2000.

systems, to the extent that they are used for the purpose of transmitting signals, networks used for radio and television broadcasting, and cable television networks, irrespective of the type of information conveyed'.[7]

26.13 'Electronic communications service' is defined as 'service usually provided against remuneration which consists wholly or mainly in the conveyance of signals through electronic communications networks, including telecommunications services and transmission services in networks used for broadcasting.'[8]

The definition of electronic communications service differs from the EU definition as the former clearly states that it includes telecommunications services and transmission services in networks used for broadcasting and does not include information society services (defined in Decree No 58/2000, of 18 April 2000)[9] that do not consist wholly or mainly in the conveyance of signals through electronic communications networks.

Moreover, the definition does not include services which provide, or which exercise editorial control over, transmitted content through electronic communication networks and services, including radio and television programme services, audio text services, and value-added services based on the delivery of messages.

26.14 'Associated facilities' are defined as:

'those associated services, physical infrastructures and other facilities or elements associated with an electronic communications network and/or an electronic communication service which enable and/or support the provision of services via that network and/or service or have the potential to do so, and include, inter alia, buildings or entries to buildings, building wiring, antennae, towers and other supporting constructions, ducts, conduits, masts, manholes, and cabinets.'[10]

26.15 The Portuguese approach with respect to regulation of complex services (services which include features of both electronic communications as well as content services such as VoIP or Cloud Computing Services) is generally to consider such services as electronic communication services.

26.16 VoIP services are considered to be within the definition of electronic communications services. In 2005, ANACOM engaged in a public consultation on VoIP, and in May 2006 issued an extensive report describing its understanding with respect to the issues raised during the consultation. As a result, in the interim, ANACOM has issued rules which affect VoIP, notably with respect to numbering.

'Internet Freedom'

26.17 To date, Portugal has not adopted rules restricting end users' access to the Internet, and REGICOM does not establish an autonomous principle of Internet neutrality. The only requirements are with respect to copyright or criminal law, and these requirements do not contravene the European Convention for the Protection

---

7   Article 3(cc) REGICOM.
8   Article 3(cc) REGICOM.
9   This decree implemented the EU Directive 98/48/EC of the European Parliament and of the Council, of July 20, that amended the EU Directive 98/34/EC, of June 22, of the European Parliament and of the Council sets out 'a procedure for the provision of information in the field of technical standards and regulations and of rules on Information Society services'.
10   Art 3(bb) REGICOM.

of Human Rights and Fundamental Freedoms. Moreover, in such cases, the presumption of innocence, the right to privacy, and the right to be heard principles apply.

As a result of the implementation of the EU Directives, no substantive amendments to existing national provisions were inserted in regard to issues of 'Internet Freedom'.

National Regulatory Authorities: Organisation, Regulatory Objectives, Competencies

26.18   The current NRA in Portugal is ANACOM; it succeeded the '*Instituto das Comunicações de Portugal*' ('ICP'). It is a public corporation with administrative and financial independence and its own assets. It regulates and supervises the telecommunications sector and represents Portugal in national and international telecommunications organisations.

Pursuant to REGICOM, ANACOM is an independent organisational and financial body, which:

- is functionally separated from the Government;
- is endowed with financial and human resources necessary for execution of its functions, including active participation in BEREC;
- is functionally separated from undertakings which provide electronic communications networks, services, and equipment, with separate regulatory functions from powers associated with the ownership or control of undertakings of the sector upon which the State retains ownership or control; and
- exercises its powers in a neutral, transparent and timely manner.[11]

As such, Article 3(2), (3) and 3(a) of the Framework Directive, has been duly implemented in Portugal.

26.19   The Government appoints ANACOM's board of directors.[12] ANACOM must send to the Government an annual report of its regulatory activities, which is also submitted to the Parliament. The chairman of the board of directors must appear before Parliament whenever requested, to be heard by the appropriate committee of the Parliament.[13]

26.20   The regulatory objectives and principles to be pursued by ANACOM are established in article 5 REGICOM and are similar to those established in Article 8 of the Framework Directive. These objectives are:

- the promotion of competition in the provision of electronic communications networks, electronic communications services and associated facilities and services;
- the contribution to the development of the internal market of the European Union; and
- the promotion of the interests of citizens.

26.21   In order to promote competition in the provision of electronic communications networks, electronic communications services and associated facilities and services, ANACOM must:

---

11   Art 4 REGICOM.
12   Art 21 ANACOM's Bylaws (approved by Decree-law No 309/2001, of 7 December 2000).
13   Art 51 ANACOM's Bylaws.

- ensure that users, including disabled users, elderly users and users with special social needs, obtain maximum benefit in terms of choice, price, and quality;
- ensure that there is no distortion or restriction of competition in the electronic communications sector, including in the scope of electronic communications networks and services used for the provision of such services; and
- encourage an efficient use and ensure an effective management of radio frequencies and numbering resources.[14]

26.22   In order to contribute to the development of the internal market within the European Union, ANACOM must:

- remove existing obstacles to the provision of electronic communications networks, of associated facilities and services and of electronic communications services at a European level;
- encourage the establishment and development of trans-European networks, the interoperability of pan-European services, and end-to-end connectivity;
- work in a transparent manner with the Commission, BEREC, and other communications regulatory authorities of other Member States of the European Union so as to ensure the development of a regulatory practise and consistent application of a common regulatory framework for electronic communications networks and services.[15]

26.23   In order to promote the interests of citizens, ANACOM must:

- ensure that all citizens have access to the universal service as defined in this law;
- ensure a high level of consumer protection in their relationship with undertakings providing electronic communications networks and services, in particular through the establishment of simple and inexpensive dispute resolution procedures, put in place by a body that is independent of the parties in dispute;
- contribute to guarantee a high level of protection of personal data and privacy;
- promote the provision of clear information, requiring in particular that tariffs and conditions for using publicly available electronic communications services are transparent;
- address the needs of specific social groups, in particular users with disabilities, elderly users and users with special social needs;
- ensure that the integrity and security of public communications networks are maintained; and
- promote the ability of end users to access and distribute information and to run applications and services of their choice.[16]

26.24   In pursuit of such objectives, Article 4(5) REGICOM states that, in all decisions and measures adopted, ANACOM must apply objective, transparent, non-discriminatory and proportionate regulatory principles, being responsible in particular for:

- promoting regulatory predictability by ensuring a consistent regulatory approach over appropriate review periods;

---

14   Art 5(2) REGICOM.
15   Art 5(3) REGICOM.
16   Art 5(4) REGICOM.

- ensuring that, in similar circumstances, there is no discrimination in the treatment of undertakings providing electronic communications networks and services;
- safeguarding competition to the benefit of consumers and promoting, where appropriate, infrastructure-based competition;
- promoting efficient investment and innovation in new and enhanced infrastructures, including by ensuring that any access obligation takes appropriate account of the risk incurred by the investing undertakings and by permits cooperative arrangements between investors and parties seeking access to diversify the risk of investment, while ensuring that competition in the market and the principle of non-discrimination are preserved;
- taking into account the variety of conditions relating to competition and consumers that exist in the various national geographic areas; and
- imposing ex-ante regulatory obligations only where there is no effective and sustainable competition and smoothing or lifting such obligations as soon as that condition is fulfilled.

26.25 ANACOM may request undertakings subject to the obligations provided for in REGICOM all information related to their activities, including financial information and information concerning future network or service developments that could affect the wholesale services that they make available to competitors, so that ANACOM is able to exercise all powers provided for in the law. For such purposes, the undertakings must identify information deemed confidential. The information requests made by ANACOM must be proportionate and objectively justified.[17]

26.26 Article 7 REGICOM establishes a cooperation principle between ANACOM and the Portuguese Consumer General Directorate (*'Direcção Geral do Consumidor'* – 'DGC') and with the Portuguese Competition Authority (*'Autoridade da Concorrência'* – 'ADC') in the area of consumer protection and competition, respectively.

26.27 Pursuant to article 6 REGICOM, ANACOM must contribute to the development of the internal market by working in a transparent manner with other national regulatory authorities, with the Commission, and with BEREC, to ensure consistent application of the regulatory framework for electronic communications. Specifically, ANACOM must:

- support the goals of BEREC of promoting greater regulatory coordination and coherence, giving significant weight to opinions, guidelines, and common positions adopted by that body when adopting its decisions on the definition and assessment of relevant markets; and
- work with the Commission and BEREC to identify the types of regulatory instruments and remedies best suited to address particular types of situations in the marketplace.

26.28 ANACOM must, in the performance of its functions, take into account the recommendations of the European Commission on the harmonised application of the regulatory framework applicable to electronic communications, considering the pursuit of the regulatory objectives of REGICOM. If ANACOM decides not to follow such a recommendation, it must inform the European Commission of this decision, and explain the grounds for such decision.

---

17 Arts 108 and 109 REGICOM.

26.29   REGICOM requires ANACOM to adopt, and publish, a general consultation procedure, to be used whenever ANACOM, in the exercise of its competencies, intends to take measures that have a significant impact on the relevant market. According to this procedure, ANACOM must publish a draft measure to be adopted, and give interested parties the opportunity to comment within a specified period of no less than 20 days.[18]

REGICOM allows for ANACOM to establish provisions for urgent measures in exceptional circumstances, to be applied where ANACOM considers that there is an urgent need to act in order to safeguard competition and protect the interests of users, within the terms of Article 7(6) of the Framework Directive.[19] Articles 10 and 12 REGICOM provide for an administrative dispute resolution procedure whereby, at the request of any of the parties, ANACOM issues binding decisions to resolve disputes in connection with obligations arising under REGICOM between undertakings and subject thereto in the national territory, or between such undertakings and other undertakings benefiting from obligations of access in the national territory, without prejudice to the possibility of judicial review.

26.30   Parties seeking ANACOM dispute resolution, must request that ANACOM intervene no later than one year from the date of the beginning of the dispute. Under this procedure, ANACOM must issue its decision within four months from the date of the request,[20] and must notify the parties involved of its decision, including a complete statement of the grounds on which it based the decision.

26.31   The ANACOM may deny requests for intervention in dispute resolution only in the following cases:

- where the request does not concern compliance with obligations arising from REGICOM, where a period of more than a year has elapsed since the date of the beginning of the dispute; or
- where ANACOM finds that other mechanisms, including mediation, exist and would better contribute to the resolution of the dispute in a timely manner in accordance with ANACOM's regulatory objectives.[21]

26.32   In addition, article 48-B REGICOM includes the option for out-of-court settlement of disputes. In accordance with such provision, without prejudice to the recourse to courts and to bodies responsible for promoting and fostering consumer rights, end users may submit any disputes with electronic communications undertakings to legally established out-of-court dispute settlement mechanisms. ANACOM must encourage the development of mechanisms that are simple, transparent, and economic according to the various types of end users, and non-discriminatory, for the expedient, fair and impartial settlement of disputes, notably those concerning contract conditions or conditions for implementing contracts governing the provision of electronic communications networks and services between electronic communications undertakings and end users. For these purposes, ANACOM may establish cooperation agreements or participate in the establishment of bodies that seek to ensure these mechanisms.

---

18   Art 8 REGICOM.
19   Art 9 REGICOM.
20   Under exceptional circumstances, there may be an extension.
21   Art 12(3) REGICOM.

Right of Appeal against ANACOM's Decisions

26.33   Under article 13 REGICOM, decisions, orders, and other measures adopted by ANACOM in the area of administrative offence proceedings ('*contraordenações*'), resulting from the application of the regulatory framework on electronic communications, may be appealed before the Competition, Regulation and Supervision Court.[22]

Other actions performed by ANACOM may be appealed before the administrative courts pursuant to applicable Portuguese law. In this case ANACOM must maintain current information on such appeals,[23] and shall, upon reasoned request, provide such information to the Commission and to BEREC.

26.34   Appeals against ANACOM decisions, which, with respect to administrative offence proceedings, determine the application of fines or additional sanctions, will have suspensive effects, while appeals against other decisions, orders, and further measures, including decisions to apply penalty payments, adopted within administrative offence proceedings initiated by the ANACOM, will have a mere devolutive (non-suspensive) effect.

26.35   ANACOM is entitled to autonomously appeal against decisions issued within the impugnation proceedings, where appeal is permitted.

26.36   Decisions of the Competition, Regulation and Supervision Court which allow appeal, pursuant to the general regime of administrative offences ('*Regime Geral das Contraordenações*'), may be appealed before the Court of Appeals ('*Tribunal da Relação*') with jurisdiction over the area of the referred Court's location being the last instance court, ie the decision on the appeal is final.

ANACOM's Obligations to Cooperate with the Commission

26.37   ANACOM's obligation to cooperate with the European Commission is set out in articles 6, 57 and 57-A of REGICOM. Article 6 requires that ANACOM, in carrying out its tasks, contribute to the development of the internal market, by working in a transparent manner with other national regulatory authorities, with the Commission, and BEREC to ensure consistent application of the regulatory framework for electronic communications. Specifically, ANACOM must:

- support the goals of BEREC of promoting greater regulatory coordination and coherence, giving significant weight to opinions, guidelines and common positions adopted by that body when adopting its decisions on the definition and assessment of relevant markets; and
- work with the Commission and BEREC to identify the types of regulatory instruments and remedies best suited to address particular types of situations in the marketplace.

26.38   Furthermore, ANACOM must, in the performance of its functions, take into account the recommendations of the European Commission on the harmonised application of the regulatory framework applicable to electronic communications, having regard to the pursuit of the regulatory objectives. In the event that

---

22   Recently created by Law No 46/2011, of 24 June 2011.

23   These include, notably, information on the number of requests for appeal, the subject-matter and duration of the appeal proceedings, and the number of decisions to grant interim measures.

ANACOM decides not to follow such recommendations, it must inform the European Commission of this decision, including the grounds for such decision.[24]

26.39 Moreover, articles 56, 57, and 57-A REGICOM implement Articles 7, 7a, and 7b of the Better Regulation Directive. Specifically, when ANACOM decisions (such as identification of relevant markets, determination of whether a relevant market is effectively competitive, declaration of SMP, and imposing, maintaining, amending, or withdrawing obligations with respect to undertakings regardless of whether they have significant market power, including the imposition of technical and operational conditions on the provider or beneficiaries of access) are likely to affect trade between Member States, REGICOM requires a 'specific consultation procedures' (article 57 REGICOM, 'Specific consultation procedure') and a 'procedure for the consistent application of regulatory obligations' (article 57-A REGI-COM).

26.40 With respect to implementation in Portugal of Article 17 of the Framework Directive, article 29 REGICOM states that, without prejudice to rules defined as mandatory at EU level, ANACOM, to the extent strictly necessary to ensure interoperability of services and to broaden freedom of choice for users, must encourage the use of non-mandatory technical standards and specifications, in order to foster the harmonised provision of electronic communications networks and services and associated facilities and services.

26.41 Such standards and specifications must be based on the list created by the European Commission and published in the Official Journal of the European Communities. ANACOM must post on its website the reference to the publication in the Official Journal of the European Communities of the list of standards and specifications regarding harmonised provision of electronic communications networks and services and associated facilities and services. While such list has not been published, ANACOM must encourage the implementation of standards and specifications adopted by European standards organisations. In the absence of these standards, ANACOM must encourage implementation of international standards or recommendations adopted by the ITU, CEPT, ISO, and IEC. ANACOM, however, also stated that, despite the existence of such standards and specifications, technical specifications may be issued at the national level.

'Significant Market Power' as a Fundamental Prerequisite of Regulation

Definition of SMP

26.42 Article 60 EGICOM provides a definition of 'significant market power' similar to the one used by the Framework Directive (that an undertaking will be deemed to have significant market power if, either individually or jointly with others, it enjoys a position equivalent to dominance, ie a position of economic strength affording it the power to behave to a considerable extent independently of competitors, customers, and consumers). Additionally, REGICOM states that ANACOM, when assessing whether two or more undertakings have a joint dominant position in a market, must, act in accordance with Community law, taking its guidelines into account).

---

24 Art 6(4) REGICOM.

26.43   ANACOM may determine that two or more companies are in a 'joint dominance' situation where they operate in a market with a structure that leads to coordinated effects, even in the absence of structural or other links between them.

26.44   Pursuant to REGICOM, without prejudice to the case law of the Court of Justice of the European Communities on joint dominance, ANACOM must take into account the following factors in its assessment:

● low elasticity of demand;
● similar market shares;
● vertical integration with collective refusal to supply;
● high legal or economic barriers to entry;
● lack of countervailing buyer power; and
● lack of potential competition.

In addition, where an undertaking has SMP in a specific market, it may also be deemed to have significant market power in an adjacent market, where the links between the two markets permit the market power held in the former market to be leveraged into the latter, thereby strengthening the market power of the undertaking.

26.45   In accordance with article 61 REGICOM, ANACOM's draft measures with respect to market analysis and determination of whether an undertaking holds significant market power are subject to the prior opinion of the Portuguese Competition Authority, which must be issued within 30 days upon request.

Definition of relevant markets

26.46   ANACOM must define and analyse the relevant markets, identify undertakings with SMP, and determine suitable measures with respect to undertakings providing electronic communications networks and services.[25]

In the course of market definition, ANACOM, considering national circumstances, must also consider the European Community Recommendation and Guidelines on market analysis and assessment of significant market power.[26] However, ANACOM may define markets that differ from those mentioned in the Recommendation of the European Community, following the 'specific consultation procedure' set forth in article 57 of REGICOM.

To date, ANACOM has identified 19 relevant product markets.

Imposition of remedies

26.47   Where ANACOM determines that a relevant market is not effectively competitive, it identifies undertakings which individually or jointly have significant power in that market, imposing thereon the appropriate specific regulatory obligations, or maintaining or amending such obligations where they already exist.

26.48   REGICOM adopts the following SMP-undertaking related obligations:

---

25   Art 18 REGICOM.
26   Art 58 REGICOM.

- obligation of transparency in relation to the publication of information, including reference offers;[27]
- obligation of non-discrimination, in relation to the provision of access and interconnection and the respective provision of information;[28]
- obligation for accounting separation in respect of specific activities related to access and interconnection;[29]
- obligation to respond to reasonable requests for access;[30]
- obligation of price control and cost accounting;[31] and
- obligation for functional separation.[32]

ANACOM may also impose remedies on undertakings not identified as having SMP. For instance, ANACOM may impose access and interconnection obligations:

- on undertakings that control access to end users, to the extent required to ensure end-to-end connectivity, including in justified cases the obligation to interconnect their networks;
- on undertakings that control access to end-users, in justified cases and to the extent required to ensure the interoperability of their services; and
- to provide access to APIs (application programme interfaces) and EPGs (electronic programme guides), on fair, reasonable and non-discriminatory terms, to the extent required to ensure that digital radio and television programme services as specified by the competent authorities under the law are accessible to end-users.

26.49 REGICOM also establishes that all operators of conditional access services which, irrespective of the means of transmission, provide access services to digital radio and television programme services, whereby television and radio operators depend on such services in order to reach any group of potential viewers or listeners, shall:

- offer technical services to all television and radio operators, on a fair, reasonable and non-discriminatory basis compatible with EU competition law, enabling the digital radio and television programme services to be received by viewers or listeners duly authorised by means of decoders managed by operators of conditional access services, as well as comply with EU competition law (the conditions of distribution, including prices, disclosed by distribution operators shall specify whether or not material related to conditional access is supplied); and
- keep separate financial accounts regarding their activity as conditional access providers.

Such operators shall notify ANACOM of the technical procedures adopted to ensure the interoperability of the different conditional access systems within five days of their implementation and ANACOM shall publish on its website the references to the applicable technical specifications. Operators providing conditional access services shall also adopt systems with suitable technical capability for a cost-effective transfer of control, to be agreed with the support network operators. Such transfer shall allow the full control by network operators, at local or regional level, of services using such conditional access systems. Moreover the

---

27   Art 67–69 REGICOM.
28   Art 70 REGICOM.
29   Art 71 REGICOM.
30   Art 72 REGICOM.
31   Art 74–76 REGICOM.
32   Art 76-A REGICOM.

holders of industrial property rights in respect of conditional access products and systems shall ensure that licences to manufacturers of user equipment are granted on fair, reasonable and non-discriminatory terms. Such granting of licences shall also obey certain principles established by REGICOM. The conditional access obligations described above may be amended or removed by ANACOM, giving the appropriate prior notice to the undertakings affected by such measures. ANACOM shall also decide on the imposition of obligations in respect of the presentation of electronic programme guides and similar listing and navigation facilities.

ANACOM's Regulatory Duties concerning Rights of Way, Co-location and Facility Sharing

Rights of way

26.50   Undertakings providing public communications networks or publicly available electronic communications services must be ensured:

- the right to request, pursuant to general law, the expropriation and the constitution of public easements indispensable for the installation, protection and maintenance of the respective systems, equipment and further resources; and
- the right to use public domain, in conditions of equality, for implanting, crossing or passing over necessary for the installation of systems, equipment and further resources.[33]

Undertakings providing electronic communications networks and services not available to the public are ensured the right to request the use of public domain necessary for the installation of systems, equipment and further resources.

26.51   Pursuant to REGICOM, the granting of rights of way over private property is achieved through an expropriation request (to compulsorily deprive a person of his property by the State). The procedures for granting rights of way must be clear and duly published, applied without discrimination and without delay, and the conditions attached to any such rights must follow the principles of transparency and non-discrimination.[34] All authorities with legal power over public domain[35] must create and publish clear, timely and non-discriminatory procedures on the exercise of the right of use of public domain.

REGICOM requires that the authority responsible for granting or defining the conditions for the exercise of these rights have effective structural separation from activities associated with ownership or control of undertakings operating in the sector over which public authorities, including local authorities, retain ownership or control.

Such rights granted for the use of the public domain may not be extinguished prior to the expiry of the period for which such right was granted, except where justified, and without prejudice to applicable provisions in respect of compensation.

26.52   Undertakings providing public communications networks or publicly available electronic communications services must negotiate and promote the conclusion

---

33   Art 24(1) REGICOM.
34   Art 24(3) and (4) REGICOM.
35   The public domain is managed by the entities to which title is granted, notably Ministries of the Government and Public Institutes, among others.

of agreements towards the sharing of property or facilities, already installed or to be installed. The conclusion of said agreements must be communicated to ANACOM.[36]

If, for reasons of environmental protection, public health, public security, country planning, or to preserve landscapes, there are no viable alternatives in specific situations regarding the installation of new infrastructures, ANACOM may impose obligations relating to the sharing of facilities, even if the owners thereof are undertakings providing electronic communications networks and services, ensuring that the measures put in place are objective, transparent, non-discriminatory, and proportionate. Nevertheless, such determination may include rules for apportioning the costs thereof, and ANACOM may also require adoption of measures limiting the function of the facilities to be installed, notably the reduction in the maximum transmitted power levels.[37]

Co-location and facility sharing

26.53   Undertakings providing public communications networks or publicly available electronic communications services must negotiate and promote the conclusion of agreements towards the sharing of property or facilities, already installed or to be installed. The conclusion of said agreements must be communicated to ANACOM.[38]

As noted above with respect to rights-of-way, if, for reasons of environmental protection, public health, public security, country planning, or to preserve landscapes, there are no viable alternatives in specific situations regarding the installation of new infrastructures, ANACOM may impose obligations relating to the sharing of facilities, even if the owners thereof are undertakings providing electronic communications networks and services, ensuring that the measures put in place are objective, transparent, non-discriminatory and proportionate. Nevertheless, such determination may include rules for apportioning the costs thereof, and ANACOM may also require the adoption of measures limiting the function of the facilities to be installed, notably the reduction in the maximum transmitted power levels.[39]

REGULATION OF MARKET ENTRY: IMPLEMENTATION OF THE AUTHORISATION DIRECTIVE

The General Authorisation of Electronic Communications

26.54   In accordance with article 19(2) and 21 REGICOM, undertakings which intend to provide electronic communications networks and services, regardless of whether they are publicly available, must first submit to ANACOM a short description of the network or service they wish to initiate and give notice of the date upon which they plan to commence the activity (submitting also the elements necessary for their full identification).

The provision of electronic communication services is only subject to the general authorization regime, not being dependent on any prior decision or act of

---

36   Art 25(1) REGICOM.
37   Art 25(2), (3) and (4) REGICOM.
38   Art 25(1) REGICOM.
39   Art 25(2), (3) and (4) REGICOM.

ANACOM. After performing the referred notification, undertakings may immediately commence activity.

26.55 The use of numbers and frequencies is also subject to the general authorisation regime and depends, additionally, on the allocation by ANACOM of rights of use, in all cases for numbers, and exceptionally for frequencies.[40]

ANACOM must approve the procedures pursuant to which interested parties as regards the beginning of the provision of services, as well as the related notification model for general authorization and corresponding form are approved by ANACOM.

ANACOM, within five days of the receipt of said notification, issues a statement confirming its delivery. Such statement shall describe in detail the rights provided for in REGICOM in respect of access and interconnection and of implementation of facilities.

26.56 Among other elements, undertakings must provide the address which is to be used for notifications and other communications to be carried out by ANACOM. Undertakings must notify ANACOM of a change in address within 30 days.

Undertakings that provide publicly available electronic communications networks and services are entitled to the following rights:

- to negotiate interconnection with and obtain access to or interconnection from other providers of publicly available communications networks and services, and
- to be given an opportunity to be designated to provide different elements of a universal service and/or to cover different parts of the national territory in accordance with the provisions of REGICOM.[41]

The amendments to the conditions, rights and procedures concerning the provision of electronic communications networks and services, including the rights of use or rights to install facilities, are subject to a general consultation procedure.[42]

26.57 Undertakings providing electronic communications networks and services, regardless of SMP, may only be subject to the general conditions in article 27 REGICOM:

- interoperability of services and interconnection of networks;
- certain obligations of access;
- transparency obligations on operators of public communications networks providing electronic communications services available to the public to ensure end-to-end connectivity, disclosure regarding any conditions limiting access to or use of services and applications where such conditions are allowed in conformity with the law, and, where necessary and proportionate, access by ANACOM to such information needed to confirm the accuracy of such disclosure;
- maintenance of the integrity of public networks, including conditions to

---

40   The use of frequencies for electronic communications services, regardless of whether they depend on the allocation of rights of use, is subject to the conditions for use of radio spectrum in Decree No 151-A/2000, of 20 July 2000, as amended by Decrees No 167/2006, of 16 August 2006, and 264/2009, of 28 September 2009.

41   Art 22 REGICOM.

42   Except in rare circumstances, the consultation period may be no less than 20 days.

prevent electromagnetic interference between electronic communications networks and/or services;[43]

- terms of use for communications from public authorities to the general public such as warnings of imminent threats and mitigating the consequences of major catastrophes, and during major disasters or national emergencies to ensure communications between emergency services and authorities;

- security of public networks against unauthorised access according to legislation governing personal data and privacy protection in respect of electronic communications;

- environmental and town and country planning requirements, and requirements and conditions linked to granting access to public or private land and conditions linked to co-location and facility sharing, including, where applicable, any financial or technical guarantees necessary to ensure the proper execution of infrastructure works;

- personal data and privacy protection specifically related to electronic communications, in accordance with legislation governing personal data and privacy protection;

- terms of use for frequencies,[44] where that use is not subject to the allocation of rights of use, as specified in the National Frequency Allocation Plan ('NFAP');

- accessibility by end users to numbers of the National Numbering Plan, numbers of the European Telephone Numbering Space, Universal International Freephone Numbers, and, where technically and economically feasible, numbers of numbering plans of other Member States, and respective conditions provided for in REGICOM;

- consumer protection rules specific to the electronic communications sector and conditions on accessibility for users with disabilities;[45]

- measures regarding limitation of exposure of the general public to electromagnetic fields caused by electronic communications networks in accordance with applicable law;

- measures of standardisation;

- installation, at the undertaking's own expense, and provision of systems of legal interception to competent national authorities, and supply of means of decryption or decoding where these facilities are present, in accordance with legislation governing personal data and privacy protection within the scope of electronic communications;

- 'must carry' obligations;[46]

- restrictions on the transmission of illegal content,[47] and the transmission of harmful content;[48]

- financial contributions to the funding of the universal service;[49]

---

43   In accordance with Decree-Law No 325/2007, of 28 September 2007, as amended by Decree-Law No 20/2009, of 19 January 2009.

44   Pursuant to Decree-Law No 151-A/2000 of 20 July 2000, as amended by Decree-Laws No 167/2006, of 16 August 2006, and 264/2009, of 28 September 2009.

45   In accordance with art 91 REGICOM.

46   In accordance with art 43 REGICOM.

47   In accordance with Decree-Law No 7/2004, of 7 January 2004, as amended by Decree-Law No 62/2009, of 10 March 2009.

48   In accordance with Law No 27/2007, of 30 July 2007, as amended by Law No 8/2011, of 11 April 2011.

49   In accordance with arts 95 to 97 REGICOM.

- fees;[50] and
- information to be provided under the procedure of notification set out in article 21 REGICOM.[51]

26.58 ANACOM must specify, among the conditions referred to above, those conditions that are applicable to electronic communications networks and services, and, if it deems convenient, identifying the relevant categories for that purpose. Such categories must be objectively justified with respect to the relevant network or service, particularly considering its availability to the public, and must be non-discriminatory, proportionate and transparent.[52]

According to article 28 REGICOM, ANACOM may, without prejudice to determining conditions, decide the imposition of obligations regarding access and interconnection, control over retail market, and universal service.

Rights of Use for Radio Frequencies

Strategic Planning and co-ordination of spectrum policy

26.59 ANACOM is responsible for spectrum management (ie the set of frequencies associated with radio waves). Portuguese legislation formally recognises that frequencies have an important social, cultural, and economic value.[53] REGICOM requires that ANACOM cooperate with the Commission and with the competent bodies for spectrum management of other Member States in the strategic planning, coordination, and harmonisation of the use of radio spectrum in the European Union, notably under the scope of multi-annual radio spectrum policy programmes approved by the European Parliament and the Council (taking into consideration, among other things, economic, safety, health, public interest, freedom of expression, cultural, scientific, social, and technical aspects of EU policies and interests of radio spectrum users). In addition, REGICOM requires ANACOM to promote harmonisation of the use of radio frequencies across the European Union, consistent with the need to ensure effective and efficient spectrum use, and in pursuit of benefits for the consumer such as economies of scale and interoperability of services, in accordance with the Radio Spectrum Decision.[54]

Principles of frequency allocation, procedural rules

26.60 ANACOM allocates spectrum, develops frequency plans, and assigns frequencies based on objective, transparent, non-discriminatory, and proportionate criteria.[55]ANACOM also develops frequency plans to include management of pursuant to the availability of radio spectrum, guarantee of conditions of effective competition in the relevant markets, effective and efficient use of frequencies, and assessment of interests of radio spectrum users.[56]

ANACOM, in managing spectrum, must follow the principles of technology neutrality (ie all types of technology used for electronic communications services

---

50   In accordance with art 105 REGICOM.
51   For the purposes set forth in art 109 REGICOM.
52   For the purposes set forth in art 109 REGICOM.
53   Art 15(1) REGICOM.
54   Art 15(4) REGICOM.
55   Art 15(5) REGICOM.
56   Art 15(2) REGICOM.

may be used in frequency bands declared to be available for electronic communications services, and published in the NFAP as such) and service neutrality. (ie all types of electronic communications services may be provided in frequency bands declared to be available for electronic communications services, and published in the NFAP as such). ANACOM also must publish annually, and keep current, the National Frequency Allocation Table ('NFAT').[57]

26.61 The use of numbers and frequencies is subject to the general authorisation regime and may only depend on the allocation by ANACOM of rights of use, where provided for in the NFAT.[58]

The use of frequencies for electronic communications services, regardless of whether they depend on the allocation of rights of use, is subject to specific conditions for use of radio spectrum.[59]

ANACOM may grant rights of use for frequencies through an application process, to providers of electronic communication networks or services or to entities that use those networks or services.[60] The ANACOM must reach a decision to grant rights of use, communicated the decision, and make the decision public, within 30 days of receipt of an appropriate request,[61] in the case of frequencies that have been allocated for specific purposes within the NFAT, without prejudice to any applicable international agreements relating to the use of radio frequencies or of orbital positions.

Transferability and time limitations

26.62 Under article 34 REGICOM, undertakings may transfer or lease their rights of use of frequencies to other undertakings in accordance with conditions attached to those rights of use and with procedures established in this article, where the transfer or lease of such rights has not been explicitly prohibited by ANACOM and published in the NFAP.[62]

Holders of rights of use of frequencies must notify ANACOM of their intention to transfer or lease those rights, as well as the conditions to do so, and, in case such rights are transferred or leased, it is ANACOM that must ensure the publicity of

---

57 Art 16 REGICOM. The NFAT must comprise: (i) the frequency allocation table, corresponding to the radio spectrum subdivisions, breaking down radio-communications services for each frequency band, in accordance with allocations in ITU Radio Regulations applying to Portugal; (ii) the frequency bands and radio spectrum allocated to undertakings providing public communications networks or publicly available electronic communications services, including the date on which each allocation is to be reviewed; (iii) the frequency bands which are reserved and which are available, in respect of electronic communications networks and services, whether publicly available or not, specifying, for each frequency band, the cases where rights of use are required and the respective procedure of allocation; and (iv) the rights of use of frequencies that cannot be sold or leased, as well as bands that cannot be sold or leased
58 Art 19(3) and Art 27(2) and (3).
59 See Art 19(4) REGICOM, Decree No 151-A/2000, of 20 July, as amended by Decrees No 167/2006, of 16 August, and No 264/2009, of 28 September.
60 Art 30(2) and (6) REGICOM.
61 Art 35(2) REGICOM.
62 Art 34(3) REGICOM prohibits ANACOM from preventing the transfer or lease of rights of use in the bands for which this is provided in the implementing measures approved for the purpose by the European Commission, in accordance with the Framework Directive.

such transfer or lease, that such transfer does not distort competition, that the frequencies are efficiently and effectively used, that there is compliance with frequency use where it has been harmonised through the Radio Spectrum Decision or other Community measures, and that the restrictions set forth in the law regarding radio and television broadcasting are safeguarded.

26.63   ANACOM, based on duly justified reasons, is entitled to oppose a transfer or lease of rights of use, as well as to impose conditions necessary for compliance with these elements (consulting the Portuguese Competition Authority, if needed).

The transfer or lease of rights of use may not suspend nor interrupt the period for which the respective rights were granted and the original conditions continue to apply after the transfer or lease of those rights, unless otherwise specified by ANACOM.

Where a right of use of frequencies is not transferable, or cannot be leased under the terms of ANACOM's decisions as referred above, ANACOM must ensure that the reasons that required the allocation of the right of use, as well as the impossibility to transfer or lease it, remain for the full duration of the right and where such reasons no longer exist, ANACOM, at a substantiated request from the holder of the right, shall adopt all necessary measures to revoke the right of use (being the use of frequencies subject to the general authorisation regime), or to amend the referred right of use, removing the impossibility to transfer or lease it.

Admissible conditions

26.64   Without prejudice to the conditions attached to the general authorisation, article 32 REGICOM implements the list of conditions that ANACOM may impose as regards rights of use of radio frequencies, per Annex B Authorisation Directive.

ANACOM may provide for proportionate, non-discriminatory, and substantiated restrictions to the technology used for electronic communications services where necessary to avoid harmful interference, protect the population against electro-magnetic fields, ensure technical quality of service, ensure maximisation of radio frequency sharing, ensure efficient use of spectrum, or ensure the fulfilment of a general interest objective.[63] ANACOM may also, consistent with the same principles, impose restrictions on the types of electronic communications services to be provided, including, where necessary, to fulfil a requirement under ITU.[64]

ANACOM may also adopt measures that require an electronic communications service to be provided in a specific band available for electronic communications services, where justified in order to ensure fulfilment of a general interest objective or the provision of a specific electronic communications service in a specific band, while excluding any other service, where justified by the need to protect safety of life services or, exceptionally, to fulfil other general interest objectives.

---

63   'General interest objective' is defined in REGICOM as 'safety of life, the promotion of social, regional or territorial cohesion, the avoidance of inefficient use of radio frequencies, as well as the promotion of cultural and linguistic diversity and media pluralism, for example by the provision of radio and television broadcasting services'.
64   Art 16-A(3) REGICOM.

Limitation of number of rights of use to be granted

26.65 ANACOM may limit the number of rights of use to be granted only when necessary to ensure the efficient use of radio frequencies.[65] When ANACOM is considering whether to limit the number of rights of use to be granted for frequencies, it must, in particular, give significant weight to the need to maximise benefits for users and to facilitate the development of competition.

ANACOM may also, in procedures for the allocation of rights of use for frequencies, limit the amount of spectrum to be allocated to the same holder, and, in a specific case, if competition concerns justify it, order a holder to transfer or lease its rights of use for frequencies.[66]

Rights of Use for Numbers

General authorisations and granting of individual rights

26.66 Article 17 REGICOM provides ANACOM with powers concerning the availability of numbering resources adequate for all publicly available electronics communications services. In this regard, ANACOM must, among other things, define the guidelines for, and manage, the National Numbering Plan, and allocate numbering resources. ANACOM's competencies with respect to numbering resources were recently increased to include requirements to:

- ensure that an undertaking assigned a right to use a range of numbers does not discriminate against other providers of electronic communications services with respect to the number sequences used to give access to its services;
- support harmonisation of specific numbers or numbering ranges within the European Union in order to promote both the functioning of the internal market and the development of pan-European services; and
- where appropriate to ensure full and global interoperability of services, coordinate its position with other competent bodies of the EU with respect to international organisations and forums which make decisions on numbering issues.[67]

The use of numbers may only be subject to the general authorisation regime and additionally depends on allocation by ANACOM of rights of use.[68]

26.67 Article 36 REGICOM provides for the allocation of rights of use of numbers. Rights of use for numbers must be allocated to providers of electronic communications services or networks and to bodies that use such networks or services, under applicable rules, by means of procedures which are open, objective, transparent, non-discriminatory, and proportional.

Without prejudice to previous considerations, ANACOM may decide, after the general consultation procedure, whether rights of use of numbers of exceptional economic value should be granted through competitive or comparative selection procedures (ie either tender or auction).

The decision on the allocation of rights of use for numbers shall be taken, notified and made public within the following maximum periods:

---

65   Art 31 REGICOM.
66   Art 35(2) REGICOM.
67   Art 17(2)(e)(f) REGICOM.
68   Arts 19(3) and 27(2) and (3) REGICOM.

- 15 days, in the case of numbers allocated for specific purposes within the National Numbering Plan; and
- 30 days, where rights of use for numbers are subject to competitive or comparative selection procedures.

Admissible conditions

26.68 Without prejudice to the conditions attached to the general authorisation, article 34 REGICOM implements the list of conditions that ANACOM may attach to the rights of use for radio frequencies pursuant to Annex C of the Authorisation Directive. Rights of use for numbers may only be subject to the following conditions:

- designation of service for which the number will be used and any requirements linked to the provision of that service, including tariff principles and maximum prices that can apply in the specific number range for the purposes of ensuring consumer protection;
- effective and efficient use of numbers;
- number portability requirements;
- obligations related to directory services;
- transfer of rights at the initiative of the right holder and conditions for such transfer;
- fees;
- any commitments which the undertaking obtaining the right of use has made in the course of a competitive or comparative selection procedure; and
- obligations under relevant international agreements relating to the use of numbers.

26.69 Pursuant to REGICOM, all subscribers with numbers in the National Numbering Plan who so request are entitled to retain their number(s), related to the same service, regardless of the providers of the service, in the case of geographic numbers, at a specific location, and in the case of the remaining numbers, throughout national territory.[69]

Moreover, the entity responsible for the portability process must ensure that the transfer of a subscriber from one provider to another, and the portability activation, is carried out within the shortest possible time, respecting the express wishes of the subscriber. The effective porting of the number to the new provider must occur within one working day, and the loss of service must not exceed that period of time.[70]

According to Article 38 REGICOM, the rights of use of numbers may be transferred by their respective holders, under conditions to be implemented by ANACOM, which must provide the instruments intended to safeguard, in particular, the effective and efficient use of numbers and rights of users.

---

69   Arts 39(3)(j) and 54 REGICOM.
70   Arts 39(3)(j) and 54 REGICOM.

Limitation of number of rights of use to be granted

26.70 ANACOM may decide, after the general consultation procedure, if rights of use for numbers of exceptional economic value are to be granted through competitive or comparative selection procedures, specifically, either tender or auction.[71]

ANACOM's Enforcement Powers

26.71 ANACOM must enforce the provisions of REGICOM and respective regulations, through its monitoring agents or representatives duly qualified by the Management Board, without prejudice to powers granted to other entities.[72]

Undertakings subject to obligations[73] must submit to ANACOM all information related to their activities, including financial information and information concerning future network or service developments that could affect the wholesale services that they make available to competitors, to enable ANACOM to exercise its powers provided for in the law. Undertakings must identify information deemed confidential. The information requests made by ANACOM must be proportionate and objectively justified.[74]

26.72 The administrative offences listed in article 113 REGICOM are punishable with a fine of up to €5m. ANACOM conducts proceedings related to such offences. Where an undertaking fails to comply with a legal duty or an order of ANACOM, the application of sanctions, or the compliance therewith, do not exempt the undertaking from, where possible, complying with the duty or order. In such cases, ANACOM may impose, where justified, a compulsory penalty payment[75] consisting of the payment of a pecuniary amount for each day exceeding the time limit set by ANACOM for compliance.

Where the significance of the infringement and the fault of the offender so justify, with respect to certain offences, ANACOM may apply additional sanctions such as the removal by the State of property, equipment and illicit devices, prohibition on engaging in the respective activity for a period of up to two years, or revocation, for a period up to two years, of the right to participate in tenders or auctions promoted within the scope of REGICOM.[76]

Administrative Charges and Fees for Rights of Use

26.73 REGICOM,[77] in implementing the Authorisation Directive's provisions with respect to administrative charges and fees imposed on undertakings to which a right of use has been granted, follows closely the wording of the Authorisation Directive. In accordance with such provision, fees may be imposed on:

- declarations supporting rights issued by the ANACOM pursuant to article 21(5) REGICOM;

---

71 Art 36(4) REGICOM.
72 Art 112 REGICOM.
73 This includes conditions of the general authorisation or of rights of use and specific obligations.
74 Arts 108 and 109 REGICOM.
75 Art 116 REGICOM.
76 Art 114 REGICOM.
77 Art 105 REGICOM.

- the exercise of the activity of electronic communications networks and services provider, on an annual basis;
- the assignment of frequency usage rights;
- the assignment of rights of use for numbers and the reservation thereof;
- the use of numbers; and
- the use of frequencies.

Except for the use of frequencies, the amount of fees is established by administrative rule of the member of the Government responsible for the communications sector, and constitutes revenue for ANACOM. Such fees must be determined keeping in mind the administrative costs incurred in the management, control and enforcement of the general authorisation scheme and of rights of use and of specific obligations as referred to in article 28 REGICOM, which may include costs for international cooperation, harmonisation and standardisation, market analysis, monitoring of compliance and other market control, as well as regulatory work involving the preparation and enforcement of secondary legislation and administrative decisions, such as decisions on access and interconnection. Such fees must be imposed upon undertakings in an objective, transparent and proportionate manner which minimises additional administrative costs and associated charges.

26.74 The fees for the use of numbers and the use of frequencies must reflect the need to ensure optimal use of frequencies and numbers, which must be objectively justified, transparent, non-discriminatory, and proportionate in relation to their intended purpose and must take into account the regulatory objectives set forth in article 5 REGICOM.

Administrative Rule No 1473-B/2008, of 17 December 2008, rectified by Statement No 16-A/2009, of 13 February 2009, and amended by Administrative Rules No 567/2009, of 27 May 2009 and No 1307/2009, of 19 October 2009, approved the amount of fees due to ANACOM. This administrative rule combined in a single legal instrument the fees provided for in REGICOM, making a fundamental change to the spectrum tariff model, as well as other fees scattered in administrative rules and orders that implement the respective establishment instruments, notably fees applicable in the scope of the amateur and amateur-satellite services, the Personal Radio Service – Citizens' Band, the construction of infrastructures for telecommunications in buildings (ITED), audio text services, value-added message-based services, and postal activities.

Transitional Regulations for Existing Authorisations

26.75 REGICOM includes a transitional provision regarding the reassessment of rights of use for frequencies allocated before 25 May 2011 which remain valid until 25 May 2016.[78] The holders of such rights of use have until that date to submit an application to ANACOM for a re-assessment of the technology and service neutrality restrictions on their rights and regularisation of registers and licences issued pursuant to prior law. When examining the applications, ANACOM must take appropriate measures to promote fair competition. ANACOM must notify the rights holder of the result of its reassessment, and must allow the holder a time limit of no less than 10 days to address the issue or to withdraw the application.[79]

---

78 Art 122 REGICOM.
79 Art 121 REGICOM.

REGULATION OF NETWORK ACCESS AND INTERCONNECTION: IMPLEMENTATION OF THE ACCESS DIRECTIVE

Objectives and Scope of Access Regulation

26.76 ANACOM must encourage and, where appropriate, ensure, adequate access and interconnection, as well as interoperability of services, aimed at promoting efficient and sustainable competition, and efficient investment and innovation, and at providing maximum benefit to end users.[80]

According to articles 66 and 77 REGICOM, access and interconnection-related obligations apply to undertakings that provide electronic communications networks and services available to the public. Some obligations are applicable only to SMP undertakings[81] while other obligations are applicable to all undertakings, regardless of whether they have SMP.[82]

Basic Regulatory Concepts

26.77 Article 3(a) REGICOM implements in precise terms the definition of 'access' in Article 2(a) of the Access Directive, duly amended by the Better Regulation Directive. The definition of 'interconnection' in article 3(j) REGICOM is also the same as that in Article 2(b) of the Access Directive.

According to article 62 REGICOM, undertakings providing electronic communications networks and services are entitled to negotiate and enter into technical and commercial agreements between themselves for access and interconnection.

Operators must have the right, and, when requested by other undertakings, the obligation, to negotiate interconnection with each other for the purpose of providing publicly available electronic communications services, in order to ensure provision and interoperability of services.[83]

26.78 ANACOM has the power to impose obligations related to access and interconnection matters on undertakings providing electronic communications networks and services and to intervene on its own initiative where justified or, in the absence of agreement between undertakings, at the request of either of the parties involved, in order to achieve the objectives of REGICOM.[84]

Access- and Interconnection-related Obligations with Respect to SMP Undertakings

26.79 According to article 66 REGICOM, ANACOM is entitled to impose, maintain, amend or withdraw the following obligations applicable to undertakings with significant market power:

- obligations of transparency in relation to the publishing of information, including reference offers;

---

80 Art 63(1) REGICOM.
81 Art 66 REGICOM.
82 Art 77 REGICOM.
83 Art 64(2) REGICOM.
84 Art 63(2) REGICOM.

- obligations of non-discrimination regarding the provision of access and interconnection and of the relevant information;
- obligations as to accounting separation concerning specified activities related to access and interconnection;
- obligations to meet reasonable requests for access;
- obligations of price control and cost accounting; and
- obligations for functional separation under the terms of the recent article 76-A.

The implementation of these obligations by REGICOM follows closely the wording of Articles 9 to 13 of the Access Directive.

26.80   The transparency obligation consists of the requirement to publish specified information in relation to operator access and interconnection, such as accounting information, technical specifications, network characteristics, terms and conditions for supply and use, including prices and any conditions limiting access to or use of services and applications.[85] The obligation of non-discrimination consists, in particular, of the requirement to apply equivalent conditions in equivalent circumstances to undertakings providing equivalent services.[86] The obligation of accounting separation consists, in particular, of the requirement on operators, especially those that are vertically integrated, to make their wholesale prices and internal prices transparent in order to prevent unfair cross-subsidy.[87] The obligations to meet reasonable requests for access consist of the requirement that operators meet reasonable requests for access to, and use of, specific network elements and associated facilities, in particular where the denial of such requests within reasonable conditions would hinder a sustainable market at the retail level or end users' interests.[88] Obligations of price control and cost accounting may be imposed where market analysis indicates a lack of effective competition in which an operator might sustain prices at an excessively high level, or apply a price squeeze, to the detriment of end users.[89]

26.81   The ANACOM must impose appropriate obligations, considering the nature of the issue identified, which must be proportionate and justified consistent with ANACOM's regulatory objectives. In exceptional circumstances, and where appropriate, the ANACOM may impose obligations on operators with SMP other than those specified in articles 9 to 13 of the Access Directive, provided that the ANACOM obtains prior authorisation from the European Commission, pursuant to article 7 Framework Directive.[90]

Other Regulatory Powers with Respect to SMP Undertakings

26.82   The provisions regarding the obligation to provide leased lines and carrier pre-selection, required by the rules implementing the 2002 EU Regulatory Package, were repealed with the implementation of the 2009 EU Regulatory Package in

---

85   Arts 67 to 69 REGICOM.
86   Art 70 REGICOM.
87   Art 71 REGICOM.
88   Art 72 REGICOM.
89   Art 74 REGICOM.
90   Art 66(4) REGICOM.

Portugal.[91] Such requirements were included within the obligations of access to, and usage of, specific network facilities established in article 72 of REGICOM.[92]

Under said article ANACOM may impose obligations on operators to meet reasonable requests for access to and use of specific network components and associated facilities, particularly in situations where the denial of access or the setting of unreasonable conditions would hinder the emergence of a sustainable competitive market at the retail level or harm the interest of end-users. ANACOM may, in particular, impose the following obligations on operators:

- to give third parties access to a specific network elements and/or facilities, including access to network elements which are not active and/or unbundled access to the local loop;
- not to withdraw access to facilities where access has already been granted;
- to interconnect networks or network facilities;
- to provide specific services needed to ensure interoperability of end-to-end services to users, including facilities for intelligent network services or roaming on mobile networks;
- to grant open access to technical interfaces, protocols or other key technologies that are indispensable for the interoperability of services or virtual network services;
- to provide specific services on a wholesale basis for resale by third parties;
- to provide access to operational support systems or similar software systems necessary to ensure fair competition in the provision of services;
- to allow carrier selection and pre-selection and/or subscriber line resale offer; and
- to negotiate in good faith with undertakings requesting access.

Regulatory powers applicable to all market participants

Obligations to ensure end-to-end connectivity

26.83   ANACOM may impose access and interconnection obligations on undertakings that control access to end users:

- to the extent required to ensure end-to-end connectivity, including in justified cases the obligation to interconnect their networks; and
- in justified cases, to the extent required to ensure the interoperability of their services.

Such imposition of obligations must be objective, transparent, proportionate, and non-discriminatory.[93]

Regulation of roaming services

26.84   The amended definition of 'access' in Article 3(a) REGICOM, covers, among other things, access to fixed and mobile networks, in particular to roaming. Therefore, and in accordance with REGICOM provisions, obligations with respect to roaming may be imposed on undertakings providing electronic communications networks and services.

---

91   Former Art. 82 to 84 REGICOM.
92   Cf Para 26.48 above.
93   Art 77(1)(a)(b) REGICOM.

Access to digital and television broadcasting services

26.85   ANACOM may impose access and interconnection obligations on any undertaking, regardless of whether the undertaking has significant market power, to provide access to application programme interfaces ('APIs') and electronic programme guides ('EPG'), on fair, reasonable, and non-discriminatory terms, to the extent required to ensure that digital radio and television programme services as specified by the legally competent authorities are accessible to end users. Such imposition of obligations must be objective, transparent, proportionate and non-discriminatory.[94]

26.86   All operators of conditional access services which, regardless of the means of transmission, provide access services to digital television and radio services, whereby broadcasters depend on such services in order to reach any group of potential viewers or listeners, must:

● keep separate financial accounts regarding their activity as conditional access providers; and
● offer technical services to all broadcasters, on a fair, reasonable and non-discriminatory basis compatible with Community competition law, enabling the digitally-transmitted services of broadcasters to be received by viewers or listeners duly authorised by means of decoders administered by the service operators, and comply with EU competition law.

Such conditions of provision, including prices, disclosed by broadcasters of digital television must specify whether material related to conditional access is supplied.[95]

26.87   Such operators must notify ANACOM of the technical procedures adopted to ensure the interoperability of the different conditional access systems, within five days from the implementation thereof. ANACOM must publish the reference to the applicable technical specifications, through a notice in Series III of the Official Gazette (*'Diário da República'*) and in a digital format on the Internet.[96]

REGULATION OF UNIVERSAL SERVICES AND USERS' RIGHTS: THE UNIVERSAL SERVICE DIRECTIVE

Regulation of Universal Service Obligations

Scope of universal service obligations

26.88   Pursuant to the REGICOM, universal service obligations consist of the provision of a minimum set of services, with specified quality and made available to all end users, regarding their geographical location, and at an affordable price.[97] The scope of the universal service must reflect the progress in technology, market developments and changes in user demand, to be modified where such developments require. Universal services include:

● connection to a public communications network at a fixed location and provision of a publicly available telephone service over that connection;

---

94   Art 77(1)(c) REGICOM.
95   Art 78(1)(2) REGICOM.
96   Art 78(3)(4) REGICOM.
97   Art 86 REGICOM.

- provision of a comprehensive directory and of a comprehensive telephone directory inquiry service; and
- adequate provision of public pay telephones. [98]

26.89   REGICOM requires that the public communications network allow end users to originate and receive calls supporting voice, facsimile, and data communications, at data rates that are sufficient to permit functional Internet access, taking into account prevailing technologies used by the majority of subscribers and technological feasibility.[99] The telephone service must allow subscribers and users to originate and receive national and international calls, and to access, through the national emergency number defined in the National Numbering Plan, the various emergency services.[100]

The directory must be printed or provided in electronic form and must be updated and made available once per year. The inquiry service must be provided through a short number and involves disclosure of data in the directory.

26.90   Universal service providers must make available specific services in order to ensure access for disabled end users, equivalent to those enjoyed by other end users, to publicly available telephone services, including access to emergency services, directory inquiry services, and directories.[101]

Universal service providers must provide, free of charge:

- handset amplifier, to increase the earpiece volume, for hearing impaired people;
- call indicator light, which consists of a device that activates a visual signal when the terminal equipment receives a call;
- simple braille bills;
- a fixed destination line, enabling the customer to make calls automatically to a specific destination he or she has defined; and
- the possibility of making a pre-defined number of free calls to directory inquiry services.

26.91   Additionally, pursuant to REGICOM, ANACOM must, following the general consultation procedure, to assess the need for universal service undertakings to provide specific offers to disabled users, as well as to define the terms and conditions by which such provisions are to be made available. ANACOM also may take specific measures to ensure that end users with disabilities may also benefit from the choice of service providers which is available to the majority of end users.

Designation of undertakings obliged to provide universal services

26.92   Article 99 REGICOM provides for the designation of undertakings required to provide universal services. More than one undertaking may provide the universal service in different geographic areas or with different obligations, without prejudice to the provision of universal services throughout the national territory.

The Government must designate the undertaking(s) responsible for the universal service provision following a public tender, in terms to be approved by members of

---

98   Art 88 REGICOM.
99   Art 88(2) REGICOM.
100   Art 88(3) REGICOM.
101   Art 91 REGICOM.

the Government with competence in the areas of finance and electronic communications. The designation process must be efficient, objective, transparent, and non-discriminatory, ensuring that no undertaking is excluded a priori from being designated.[102]

Regulation of retail tariffs, user's expenditures and quality of service

26.93 REGICOM provides rules to ensure that universal service prices are affordable on the basis of national consumer prices and income.[103] REGICOM also requires undertakings to have a minimum set of facilities and mechanisms to permit the control of expenditure by subscribers, including, free of charge:

- itemised billing;
- selective and barring of outgoing calls of or to defined types of numbers, or of premium SMS or MMS or other services or applications of value-added message-based services;
- pre-payment systems;
- payment by instalments;
- measures applicable to non-payment of telephone bills; and
- tariff advice service and control of charges with telephone services, including warnings free.[104]

With respect to the price regime, ANACOM must monitor the evolution of prices charged and must assess and determine the most suitable means to guarantee affordable prices, whereby it may determine:

- the availability of tariff options or packages different from those provided under common commercial conditions, in particular to ensure that consumers with low income or special social needs are not prevented from accessing an electronic communications network at a fixed location or from using any of the services included in the universal service;
- the imposition of price caps and the application of common tariffs, including geographical averaging of prices, throughout the territory; or
- other similar schemes.[105]

26.94 With respect to the control of expenditure, in accordance with REGICOM, the following minimum level of detail must be ensured, free of charge and without prejudice to legislation applicable in matters of protection of personal data and privacy:

- initial price of the connection to the public communication network at a fixed location and for the provision of the telephone service over that network, where appropriate;
- subscription price, where applicable;
- price of use, identifying the different traffic categories, indicating each call and the respective charge;
- periodical equipment rental prices, where applicable;
- price for the installation of additional material and equipment requested subsequent to the commencement of service provision;
- subscriber's debts; and

---

102 Art 99 REGICOM.
103 Art 93 REGICOM.
104 Art 94 REGICOM.
105 Art 93 REGICOM.

- compensation resulting from reimbursement.

In addition, universal service providers may provide, at the request of the subscriber, itemised bills with higher levels of detail, either free of charge or at reasonable tariffs, and, regardless, must not include in billing details calls that are free of charge to the calling subscriber, such as calls to help-lines.[106]

Article 92 REGICOM on the quality of universal service sets out obligations for the Universal Service Providers, notably to provide information to end users and to the ANACOM on their performance, establishing ANACOM's competencies in this regard, including the ability to monitor compliance through independent audits and similar reviews of performance data.

Cost calculation and financing of universal services

26.95   Where ANACOM considers that the universal service has net costs and finds such costs to be unfair, the Government must, after request of the respective providers, give appropriate compensation by means of one or both of the following mechanisms:

- compensation from public funds; and
- sharing the net cost with other undertakings providing public communications networks and publicly available electronic communications services on national territory.[107]

26.96   On the calculation of the net cost, in accordance with article 96 REGICOM, the following assumptions apply:

- all means to ensure appropriate incentives, so that providers comply with universal service obligations in a cost efficient manner, is to be considered;
- the cost of universal service obligations is to be calculated as the difference between the net cost, for an organisation, of operating with the universal service obligations and of operating without the universal service obligations, whether the network is fully developed or is still undergoing development and expansion (due attention is to be given to correctly assessing the costs that providers would have chosen to avoid had there been no universal service obligation);
- the calculation of net cost should take into account the benefits, including intangible benefits, obtained by the universal service operators;
- the calculation of the net cost of specific aspects of universal service obligations is to be made separately to avoid the duplication of any direct or indirect benefits and costs; and
- the net cost of universal service obligations is to be calculated as the sum of the net costs arising from the specific components of universal service obligations.

The recently adopted Decree No 35/2012, 23 August 2012, establishes a compensation fund for the electronic communications universal service, provided for in the Electronic Communications Law, for the financing of net costs arising from the provision of the universal service.

---

106   Art 94 REGICOM.
107   Art 95 REGICOM.

Regulation of Retail Markets

Prerequisites for the regulation of the retail markets

26.97   ANACOM must impose adequate regulatory obligations on undertakings identified as having SMP in a given retail market, previously defined and analysed pursuant to REGICOM, where cumulatively it concludes that:

- such retail market is not effectively competitive; and
- the imposition of obligations set out in the access and interconnection chapter of the REGICOM would not result in the achievement of the regulatory objectives. [108]

Regulatory powers

26.98   The regulatory obligations imposed must be based on the nature of the problem identified and be proportionate and justified with respect to the objectives of regulation, and may require that the identified undertakings:

- do not charge excessive prices;
- do not inhibit market entry or restrict competition by setting predatory prices;
- do not show undue preference to specific end-users; and
- do not unreasonably bundle services.[109]

In order to protect end user interests and to promote effective competition, ANACOM may apply appropriate price cap measures, measures to control individual tariffs, or measures to orient tariffs towards costs or prices in comparable markets.[110]

26.99   Without prejudice to articles 93 (price regime) and 94 (control of expenditure) REGICOM, ANACOM may not apply retail control mechanisms to geographical or user markets where it is satisfied that there is effective competition.[111]

Undertakings subject to price regulation, or subject to other relevant retail controls, must implement analytical accounting systems which are appropriate for the application of the imposed measures. ANACOM, or an independent body which it has appointed, must conduct an annual audit of the cost accounting system supporting price controls, in order to verify the compliance thereof, and must issue and publish the respective statement.[112]

End User Rights

Contracts

26.100   Under article 48 REGICOM, and without prejudice to rules on consumer protection, the provision of public communications networks or publicly available electronic communications services must be subject to a contract that must specify, in a clear, comprehensive, and easily accessible form, the following elements:

---

108   Art 85(1) REGICOM.
109   Art 85(2) REGICOM.
110   Art 85(3) REGICOM.
111   Art 85(4) REGICOM.
112   Art 85(5)(6) REGICOM.

- the identity and address of the supplier;
- the services provided (including the minimum service quality levels offered, in particular the time for the initial connection, as well as other quality of service parameters, as defined in REGICOM);
- restrictions imposed on the use of terminal equipment supplied, any conditions limiting access to or use of services, and procedures put in place to shape traffic to avoid filling or overfilling the contracted capacity, indicating in this case how those procedures could impact the service quality;
- information as to whether access to emergency services is provided, caller location information, and information of any limitations on the provision of emergency services;
- the types of maintenance service offered and customer support services provided, as well as the means of contacting these services;
- details of prices, the means by which current information on all applicable tariffs and maintenance charges may be obtained, payment methods offered and any charges or penalties due to payment method;
- the duration of the contract and the conditions whereby the contract or services may be renewed, suspended or terminated;
- any compensation and the refund arrangements which apply if contracted levels of service quality are not met;
- the means of initiating procedures for the settlement of disputes in accordance with REGICOM; conditions for the provision of itemised bills;
- explicit indication of the subscriber's willingness in respect of the inclusion or not of their respective personal information in a public directory and on its disclosure through the directory inquiry service, regardless of whether the transfer to third parties is involved, pursuant to legislation on protection of personal data;
- indication of the possibility of entering subscriber's data on the database that enables identification of subscribers who have failed to meet their payment obligations with respect to executed contracts;
- the type of action that might be taken by the provider in reaction to network security or integrity incidents or threats and vulnerabilities; and
- means of subscriber protection against risks to personal security, privacy and personal data.

Additionally, information on the duration of contracts must indicate whether there is any minimum contractual period, notably associated to the provision of promotional terms, any charges with terminal equipment or related to portability of numbers and other identifiers, as well as any charges due on early termination of the contract on the subscriber's initiative, including any cost recovery with respect to terminal equipment.[113]

26.101   Contracts executed between consumers and undertakings providing electronic communications services may not mandate an initial commitment period that exceeds 24 months.[114]Undertakings providing publicly available electronic communications services must offer all users the possibility to subscribe to a contract with a maximum duration of 12 months.[115] ANACOM may determine that undertakings that provide public communications networks, or publicly available electronic communications services, cease or adapt immediately the use of standard contracts

---

113   Art 48(2) REGICOM.
114   Art 48(3) REGICOM.
115   Art 48(4) REGICOM.

where it verifies the failure to comply with legal rules it must enforce or with any determination issued under its competencies.

Transparency obligations

26.102   Undertakings providing publicly available telephone networks and services must make available to the public, transparent, comparable, and current information on standard terms and conditions, with respect to access to, and use of, services provided to end users and consumers, setting out in detail the applicable prices and any other charges, and, where appropriate, those due on termination of a contract.[116] For the purposes of this set of obligations, such undertakings must publish, make available, and notify ANACOM, of the following information:

- identification of the provider, indicating the name, contact details and head office address of the undertaking providing public communications networks or publicly available services;
- information on publicly available electronic communications services being provided, including, the description of the services offered, as well as of the several features and functionalities included, indicating the geographical area where they are provided and the levels of quality of service provided;
- standard tariffs indicating the services provided and the content of each tariff element, specifically including charges for access, usage and maintenance, details of standard discounts applied and special and targeted tariff schemes, any additional charges, as well as costs with respect to terminal equipment and charges due on termination of a contract;
- compensation or refund systems, including specific details on the respective schemes, where offered;
- types of maintenance service offered;
- standard contract conditions, including any minimum contractual period, conditions for termination of the contract and procedures and charges related to the portability of numbers and other identifiers, if relevant, as well as formalities and documents to be submitted with the portability application to terminate the contract; and
- dispute settlement mechanisms, including those developed by the undertaking providing the network or service.[117]

26.103   Without prejudice to information published pursuant to article 47, the recent article 47-A REGICOM establishes that ANACOM may require undertakings providing public electronic communications networks and publicly available electronic communications services to provide subscribers with information on:

- applicable tariffs regarding any number or service subject to particular pricing conditions;
- any change to access to emergency services or caller location information;
- any change to conditions limiting access to or use of services and applications;
- any procedures put in place by the provider to measure and shape traffic so as to avoid filling or overfilling a network link, and on how those procedures could impact the service quality;
- their right to determine whether to include their personal data in directories; and

---

116   Art 47(1) REGICOM.
117   Art 47(2) and (3) REGICOM.

- details of products and services designed for disabled subscribers, where appropriate.

ANACOM must determine the form and frequency of the provision to subscribers of such information, and, in the case of information regarding applicable tariffs for any number or service subject to particular pricing conditions, ANACOM may require such information to be provided immediately prior to connecting the call.[118]

26.104   Additionally, such undertakings must distribute to subscribers, upon request from the competent public authorities, public interest information free of charge, where appropriate, by the same means they ordinarily used in their communications with such subscribers. Such information must be provided by the relevant public authorities in a standardised format and must, among other things, cover the legal consequences of using electronic communications services to engage in unlawful activities or to disseminate harmful content, including infringements of copyright and related rights, as well as information on means of protection against risks to personal security, privacy and personal data when using electronic communications services.[119]

The public authority requesting the disclosure of the information must be exclusively responsible for it, and such information must be limited to the space defined by undertakings subject to the obligation to publish it, without hindering or preventing the clear perception of information on conditions for the provision of electronic communications services.[120]

Quality of service: securing 'net neutrality'

26.105   Under article 40 REGICOM, undertakings that provide public communications networks or publicly available electronic communications services must publish, and provide end users with, comparable, clear, comprehensive and current information on the quality of their services and on measures taken to ensure equivalent access for disabled end-users. ANACOM, following a general consultation procedure, may:

- specify, among other things, the quality of service parameters to be measured and the content, form, and manner of the information to be published, including possible quality certification mechanisms, in order to ensure that end users, including disabled end users, have access to clear, comprehensive, reliable and comparable information;[121] and
- where appropriate, in order to prevent the degradation of services or the hindering or slowing down of traffic over networks, impose minimum quality of service requirements on undertakings providing public communications networks.

26.106   The general consultation procedure must be preceded by a notification to the Commission and to BEREC, with the proposed course of action as well as a summary of the respective grounds. When setting quality of service requirements, ANACOM must take the utmost account of the European Commission's comments

---

118 Art 47-A(2) REGICOM.
119 Art 47-A(3) REGICOM.
120 Art 47-A(5) REGICOM.
121 Art 40(2) REGICOM.

and recommendations, to ensure that the proposed requirements do not adversely affect the functioning of the internal market. [122]

Undertakings must also provide ANACOM with regular and current information on the quality of their services and must provide end users with information on the quality of services. [123]

European emergency call number

26.107   Pursuant to Article 51 REGICOM, end users of electronic communications services capable of originating national calls to numbers included in the National Numbering Plan, including users of public pay-phones, have the right to call the emergency services free of charge by using the single European emergency call number 112 and any national emergency call number specified by ANACOM, duly identified as such in the referred Plan. Such providers must, therefore, ensure the right to such access including for disabled end users, following, to the greatest extent possible, European standards or specifications published, without prejudice to the adoption of additional, and more demanding, requirements in order to ensure access to the referred services. [124]

Other obligations

26.108   Pursuant to REGICOM, end users also have the right to:

- to obtain information on European telephone access codes;
- have access to complaint handling procedures; [125]
- access directory information services;
- obtain, where technically and economically viable, the additional resources of dual-tone multifrequency operation (DTMF) and calling-line identification; and
- utilise out-of-court dispute settlement mechanisms as referred above. [126]

Obligations facilitating change of provider

26.109   It has been considered, bearing in mind the weaker position of the individual consumer, that consumers need additional protection deriving from the law and therefore some additional protective provisions are usually applied to consumers. This is the case in the general contractual clauses regime and also in some field of telecommunication laws in Portugal. For instance, in accordance with article 48(5) REGICOM, the contracts concluded between consumers and undertakings providing electronic communications services shall not mandate an initial commitment period that exceeds 24 months.

Also the above referred transparency obligations under which the provider may be required to provide comparable information are obligations that facilitate the change of provider and the effective competition.

---

122   Art 40(4), (5) and (6) REGICOM.
123   Arts 40(7) and 47-A(5) REGICOM.
124   Art 51 REGICOM.
125   Art 48-A REGICOM regarding end user's complaint handling procedures.
126   Art 39(2)(b) REGICOM.

A special role is attributed to the portability obligation. In accordance with Portuguese law, the provider responsible for the portability process must ensure that the transfer of a subscriber from one provider to another, and the portability activation, is carried out within the shortest possible time, respecting the wishes expressly disclosed by the subscriber. The effective porting of the number to the new provider shall occur within one working day at the most, and the loss of service shall not exceed that period of time.[127]

DATA PROTECTION: IMPLEMENTATION OF THE E-PRIVACY DIRECTIVE

Confidentiality of Communications

26.110   The E-Privacy Directive was implemented in Portugal by the E-Privacy Law. Law No 46/2012 of 29 August 2012 (which implemented Directive 2009/136/EC of the European Parliament and of the Council, of 25 November 2009), introduced amendments to the E-Privacy Law. The E-Privacy Law complements and specifies the rules governing personal data protection matters contained in the Data Protection Act,[128] and governs data processing in the context of networks and publicly available electronic communications.

26.111   Operators providing network and publicly available electronic communications services must ensure the confidentiality and security of communications and related traffic data. Listening, tapping, storage or other kinds of interception or surveillance of communications and the related traffic data by persons other than users is prohibited, without the prior and explicit consent of the users concerned, except for cases provided for in the law. This does not affect any legally authorised recording of communications and the related traffic data, when carried out in the course of lawful business practice for the purpose of providing evidence of a commercial transaction, or of any other communication made in the scope of a business relationship, provided that the data holder has been informed thereof and given his consent thereto. Recordings of communications by and for public services intended to provide for emergency situations of any nature shall be authorised.[129]

26.112   Moreover, under Portuguese legislation, providers of electronic communication services may be required to install, at their own expense, and provide systems of legal interception to competent national authorities, as well as supply means of decryption or decoding where these facilities are present, in accordance with legislation governing personal data and privacy protection within the scope of electronic communications. The providers may be required to give effect to interception warrants issued by Criminal Courts.[130]

The storage of, or access to, information on the terminal equipment of a subscriber or a user is permitted only if the subscriber or user is provided with clear and comprehensive information, notably about the purposes of the processing, and the subscriber or user is offered the right to refuse such processing. [131]

---

127   Art 54 REGICOM.
128   Law No 67/98, of 26 October 1998.
129   Art 4 E-Privacy Law.
130   Art 27(1)(o) REGICOM and arts 187–190 of the Portuguese Criminal Proceedings Code.
131   Art 5 E-Privacy Law.

Data Retention

26.113 Law No 32/2008, of 17 July 2008, implemented the Data Retention Directive. In accordance with this law, providers of public electronic communications service and the providers of public electronic communication networks must retain, for a period of 12 months (or more if the data are used in a judicial procedure), data required:

- to locate and identify the source of the communication;
- to locate and identify the destination of the communication;
- to identify the date, time and duration of a communication;
- to identify the type of communication;
- to identify the user's telecommunications equipment, or what is considered to be its equipment; and
- to locate the mobile communication equipment.

The retention of the content of the communications is strictly forbidden, as well as the retention of data pertaining to calls not completed.

26.114 The retention and transmission of data in accordance with this law is exclusively intended for the investigation, detection and prosecution of serious crimes[132] by competent authorities, and the transmission of data to competent authorities may only be ordered or authorised by reasoned Court order.

The Portuguese Data Protection Authority '*Comissão Nacional de Protecção de Dados*' ('CNPD') is the supervisory body with respect to issues of data retention.

Traffic Data and Location Data

26.115 Law No 32/2008 defines Data as 'Traffic data and location data and the related data necessary to identify the subscriber or user.' The definition of 'traffic data' and 'location data' contained in the E-Privacy Law is coincident with the E-Privacy Directive. The E-Privacy Law regulates traffic data (article 6) and location data (article 7). In accordance with the E-Privacy Law, traffic data relating to users which have been processed and stored by entities providing electronic communication services or networks must be erased or made anonymous when they are no longer needed for the purpose of the transmission of a communication. Such providers may process this data to the extent and for the duration necessary for the purposes of marketing electronic communication services or the provision of value added services provided that the user to whom the data concerns has given prior consent thereto, which may be withdrawn at any time. The processing of traffic data necessary for the purposes of billing and interconnection payments is permitted.[133]

26.116 Prior to obtaining consent from users, the provider must give users accurate and full information on the types of traffic data which are processed, the

---

132   Art 2(1)(g) Law No 32/2008 defines 'serious crime' as 'terrorist crime, violent crime, highly organised crime, illegal restraint, kidnapping and hostage-taking, cultural identity or personal integrity crimes, crimes against national security, counterfeiting currency or equivalent securities, and crimes covered by conventions on safety of air or sea navigation'.

133   In accordance with art 6(2) of the E-Privacy Law, the processing of the following traffic data is allowed for billing and interconnection payments purposes: (i) number or identification, address and type of station of the user; (ii) total number of units to be charged for the accounting period, as well as the type, starting time and duration of the calls made and/or the data volume transmitted; (iii) date of the call or service and called number; and (iv) other information concerning payments such as advance payment, payments by installments, disconnection and notices.

purposes and the duration of such processing, as well as on a possible transmission to a third party for the purpose of providing the value added service. The processing of this data is allowed only until the end of the period during which the bill may lawfully be challenged or the payment completed.

The processing of traffic data must be restricted to workers and employees of the service provider that is responsible for handling billing or traffic management, customer enquiries, fraud detection, marketing electronic communications services or providing a value added service, and shall be restricted to what is necessary for the purposes of such activities.

The overseas transfer of such data is subject to the general provisions of the Portuguese Data Protection Act, which states that the transfer of personal data within EU countries is free, but transfer overseas to non-EU countries it is prohibited unless certain conditions are met.

26.117 Under article 7 E-Privacy Law, the processing of location data is permitted if the data is made anonymous, and also to the extent and for the duration necessary for the provision of a value added service provided the subscriber's or user's consent is obtained. The operators must provide information to subscribers and users regarding the types of location data which are processed, the purposes and the duration of such processing, as well as on a possible transmission to a third party for the purpose of providing the value added service, before obtaining their consent, which they can withdraw at any time or refuse the processing for a specific period of time.

The processing of location data must be restricted to workers and employees of the publicly available communications service provider or the provider of the value added service, and shall be restricted to what is necessary for the purposes of such activities.

Itemised Billing

26.118 Under REGICOM, subscribers have the right to receive itemised bills upon request.[134] In addition, under the E-Privacy Law, undertakings providing electronic communications networks or publicly available services must take appropriate measures to reconcile the rights of subscribers receiving itemised bills with the right to privacy of calling users and called subscribers, notably by submitting proposals to the CNPD regarding means which allow to subscribers anonymous or strictly private access to publicly available electronic communications services.[135]

Presentation and restriction of calling and connected line identification

26.119 Under Portuguese Law, providers of publicly available communication services or networks, where presentation of calling line identification is offered, must offer to users, on a per-line basis and on a per-call basis, the possibility of preventing the presentation of the calling line identification, and offer the called

---

134 Art 39(3)(c) REGICOM.
135 Art 8 E-Privacy Law.

user the possibility of, free of charge, preventing the presentation of the connected line identification to the calling user and rejecting non-identified calls.[136]

Such providers may, under necessity, adequacy and proportionality principles and after consultation of CNPD, override, for a period up to 30 days, the elimination of the presentation of calling line identification, upon written and duly based application from a subscriber that wishes to determine the origin of non-identified calls which upset the peace of the family or its intimacy by means of malicious or nuisance calls. In such a case, in accordance with national law, the data containing the identification of the calling subscriber will be registered and be made available by the provider.[137] In addition, calls to emergency services must be identified and the operators should make available the location data.[138]

Automatic Call Forwarding

26.120   Providers of publicly available electronic communication services or networks must offer, easily and free of charge, to any subscriber the possibility of stopping automatic call forwarding by a third party to the subscriber's own terminal equipment.[139]

Directories of Subscribers

26.121   Before the data is included in printed or electronic directories available to the public or obtainable, subscribers must be informed, free of charge, of the purposes of such directories, and of any further usage possibilities based on search functions embedded in electronic versions of the directories. Subscribers must be given the opportunity to decide whether they wish their personal data to be included in a public directory, and if so, which data, and also to verify, correct, alter or withdraw the data included in the referred directories, free of charge. Additional consent from the subscribers must also be obtained for any purpose of a public directory other than the search of contact details of persons on the basis of their name and, where necessary, a minimum of other identifiers.[140]

26.122   All non-essential communications with direct marketing purposes are subject to a subscriber's prior and express consent, notably if using automatic call and communication systems that are not depending on human intervention. Corporate users, on the contrary, are permitted to receive unsolicited communications, until express refusal and inscription in a list of corporations that do not wish to receive such communications.[141]

However, the provider of goods and services may obtain and use contact data for marketing purposes of its customers, provided that, at the moment of collection, or later at each communication, it grants to its customers (in a simple manner and free of charge) the right to refuse further communications.[142]

26.123   Lists of individuals that wish to receive, or do not oppose the receipt of direct marketing communications, may be kept by the entities promoting such

---

136   Art 9 E- Privacy Law.
137   Art 10(1) E-Privacy Law.
138   Art 10(3) E-Privacy Law.
139   Art 11 E-Privacy Law.
140   Art 13 E-Privacy Law.
141   Art 13° A (1) (2) E-Privacy Law
142   Art 13° A (3) E-Privacy Law.

communications. Lists of corporations that oppose receipt of such communications, however, must be compiled kept current by the Portuguese Consumers General Directorate (*'Direcção-Geral do Consumidor'* ('DGC')).[143]

---

143 Art 13° B E-Privacy Law.

The Romanian Market for Electronic Communications[1]

Horatiu Dumitru and Bogdan-Petru Mihai
Musat & Asociatii, Attorneys-at-law, Bucharest

LEGAL STRUCTURE

Basic Policy

27.1 The Government of Romania recently renewed the legal framework for electronic communications through Government Emergency Ordinance no 111/2011 on electronic communications. This legislation repealed and replaced all past enactments that formed the telecommunication legal framework. This occurred as part of the harmonisation of the national legal framework with the *acquis communautaire*, and considering the liberalisation of the Romanian communications market from 1 January 2003, pursuant to the dissolution of the monopoly held by Romtelecom (the national fixed telephony operator), and given the transposition of Directive 2009/136/EC and Directive 2009/140/EC. The current legal framework is fully compliant with the EU Directives on electronic communications services, and consequently creates more rights for consumers in their relationship with the telecommunication service providers.

27.2 The Romanian telecommunications market is characterised by diverse market segments, such as large corporate customers with integrated data and voice requirements, a number of increasingly demanding data products, and domestic customers seeking inexpensive voice and broadband services. Currently the telecommunication market is very active and competitive, being shared between major players such as Vodafone, Orange, and Cosmote in the mobile telephony market, and Romtelecom and RDS-RCS in the fixed line market.

27.3 The overall policy objectives of the National Authority for Administration and Regulation in Telecommunications ('ANCOM') are to encourage competition in the electronic communications sector, to promote end users' interests and to apply strategies adopted by the government, particularly by issuing secondary regulations in the telecommunications sector that are technology neutral.

Implementation of EU Directives

27.4 Secondary legislation to implement the new enactments was adopted at an accelerated pace, resulting in Romania, by the beginning of 2003, being among the

---

1   Editing of this chapter closed on 6 June 2012.

first countries in Europe that had entirely transposed the new *acquis communautaire* in the electronic communication field. As mentioned above, Romania has recently transposed the 2009 Regulatory Package.

Legislation

27.5   The main regulations adopted by the Romanian government related to the telecommunications market are:

- Government Emergency Ordinance No 111/2011 ('EGO 111/2011')[2]
- Emergency Government Ordinance No 22/2009 on the establishment of the National Authority for Administration and Regulation in Telecommunications ('EGO no 22/2009')[3]
- Government Decision No 12/2009 regarding the organising and functioning of the Ministry of Communications and Information Society ('GD no 12/2009)[4]

27.6   The role of the regulations and decisions issued by ANCOM is to implement and organise the implementation of the agency's statutory obligations, providing the legal basis for the provision of telecommunication services in Romania, while enhancing the competition in the telecommunication market and establishing technology neutral regulation.

REGULATORY PRINCIPLES

Scope of Regulation

27.7   The scope of the new legal framework for 'electronic communications' is broad, governing the rights and obligations of network and service providers, the limited resources legal regime, end users' rights, universal service, and the obligations of network and telecommunication providers with significant market power.[5] The telecommunication services and networks regulated by EGO No 11/2011 are also broad, encompassing signal transport through wire, radio, optic fibres, or other electromagnetic means.[6] While VoIP services are generally comprised in this definition, these services are not specifically regulated under Romanian law.

'Internet Freedom'

27.8   Romanian law does not provide for any sanctions or other such provisions, limiting the end user access to the Internet further to his or her misconduct (eg sanctioning of copyright violations) or otherwise, and we are not aware of any legal initiatives that aim to limit the user access to the Internet, in such a manner. However, the law allows service providers to impose limitations on users' access to the Internet, under the condition that they inform users of such access limitations.

---

2   http://www.ancom.org.ro/comunicatii-electronice-si-servicii-postale_2658
3   http://www.ancom.org.ro/legislatie-organizare-ancom_2657
4   http://www.mcsi.ro/Minister/Despre-MCSI/HG-12-din-16-01-2009
5   Art 1(2) EGO No 111/2011
6   Art 4(1) (6) EGO No 111/2011.

National Regulatory Authorities: Organisation, Regulatory Objectives, Competencies

27.9   EGO No 22/2009, established ANCOM as an autonomous public institution subordinated to the Parliament, entirely financed from its own revenues,[7] and tasked with adopting a national policy in the electronic communications field, audiovisual communications, and postal services, including market and technical regulations.

27.10   ANCOM must maintain its operational and financial independence from network providers, telecommunications services providers, equipment manufacturers, and postal services providers.

27.11   ANCOM's key powers and duties include:[8]

- implementing sector-specific policies and strategies;
- managing limited resources such as radio spectrum and numbering resources;
- drafting and adopting national technical norms and standards (and adopting the technical regulations that make the application of the international standards binding at national level);
- regulating activities within the electronic communication and numbering resources sector, by adopting and implementing general and individual decisions;
- acting as arbitrator and ruling authority in settling disputes between network and service providers, to ensure free competition and protection of users' interests; and
- providing oversight and control over the telecommunication equipment market

27.12   The Ministry of Communications and Information Society ('MCSI'), in its capacity as the specialised body of the central public administration in the field of communications and information technology, has the following main powers:[9]

- defining the strategic and tactical sector objectives, to ensure the planning, elaboration, and implementation of the electronic communication policy, and overseeing the fulfilment of such objectives;
- participating in the process of elaborating enactments and institutional frameworks necessary for the organisation and functioning of the electronic communication sector, and implementation of the normative and methodological frameworks related to the sector policy (including oversight to ensure that such policy is observed);
- representing ensuring representation in the country and abroad; and
- providing oversight to ensure implementation and observance of regulations in the electronic communications sector, as well as the unitary implementing and observance of the legal regulations by the institutions and the entities under its subordination and coordination.

---

7   Art 2 EGO No 22/2009.
8   Art 3 EGO No 22/2009.
9   Art 4 GD No 12/2009.

27.13 ANCOM may request from service providers any information necessary to exercise its powers. In so doing, ANCOM must cite the legal basis and purpose for such solicitation, and may establish terms in which such information must be provided.[10]

ANCOM may also decide to commence an investigation, ex officio, or when it receives a complaint regarding a service provider misconduct or any such request from any person

27.14 In case of disputes between providers of electronic communication networks or services in connection with any obligations imposed by law, one of the providers, being an interested party, must notify ANCOM accordingly, in order to settle such litigation. ANCOM's president, in his position of arbitrator and decision-making body, will settle the dispute through conciliation between the litigation parties.

27.15 Conciliation is an optional procedure with the goal of amicable settlement of a dispute. Therefore, where the parties reach an understanding, conciliation is finalised by a settlement concluded between them. If the parties do not wish to use such a procedure or, notwithstanding that they have chosen this procedure, if the dispute is not settled within 30 days from the date ANCOM was notified, the dispute will be settled through the court process.

27.16 If ANCOM intends to adopt measures for the application of EGO No 111/2011 or special legislation in the field of electronic communications which may have a significant impact on the relevant market, it must utilise the consultation procedure provided by EGO No 111/2011.[11]

27.17 Under the procedural rules, ANCOM must publish on the ANCOM website the matter subject to the consultation process. Any interested person may submit written comments within 30 days or, in the case of measures to be urgently adopted, within 10 days after the date of publication on the Internet.[12]

27.18 A measure subject to the consultation procedure may not be adopted before the expiration of a 10-day period following the deadline for the comments submission. ANCOM must publish a synopsis of the comments gathered no later than the date of publication on ANCOM's website of the decision approving the relevant measure. The published material must also contain ANCOM's position with respect to any comments received on the matter.

Right of Appeal against ANCOM's Decisions

27.19 According to the provisions of article 116 (11) EGO No 111/2011, an affected party, within 30 days of publication or communication of a decision made by the ANCOM, may appeal such decision to the Administrative Division of the Bucharest Court of Appeal, without following the prior administrative procedure set out in Law No 554/2004 on disputes with the public administration.

---

10   Art 138 (2) EGO 111/2011.
11   Art 135 (1) EGO 111/2011.
12   Art 135 (3) EGO 111/2011.

ANCOM'S obligations to cooperate with the Commission

27.20   According to art 6 (1) (d) EGO 22/2009, the ANCOM must cooperate with the European Commission in developing a coherent regulatory policy and unified application of European union legislation.

'Significant Market Power' as a Fundamental Prerequisite of Regulation

Definition of SMP

27.21   The 'Significant Market Power' definition in EGO 111/2011 implements exactly the definition provided in the Framework Directive.[13]

Definition of relevant markets and SMP designation

27.22   ANCOM identifies relevant markets based on the provisions of the Regulation for the performance of market analysis and the determination of significant market power for identification of the relevant markets issued by ANCOM.[14] The Regulation follows the provisions of the Commission Recommendation on relevant markets.

27.23   ANCOM and the Competition Council, following analysis of the relevant product markets, divided the electronic communications sector into the following categories:

- public electronic communications networks, publicly available electronic communications services, and electronic communications services provided for own needs;
- retail markets/wholesale markets;
- provision of electronic communications networks and services/provision of associated facilities;
- provision at fixed locations/provision at non-fixed locations;
- publicly available telephony services/other services; and
- services provided to consumers, and services provided to other end users.

27.24   To date, ANCOM has identified the following specific relevant markets for products:[15]

- the market for access to the fixed public telephone network for call origination, termination, and transit, comprising the access to fixed public telephone networks for origination at fixed locations, termination at fixed locations, and commuted transit of the calls for publicly available telephony services and for dial-up, integrated services digital network ('ISDN') and fax services;
- the market for access to the mobile public telephone network operated by Cosmorom SA for call termination, comprising access to this network for call termination to non-fixed locations for publicly available telephony services originating in other networks;

---

13   Art 94 EGO 111/2011.
14   This Regulation was published in the Official Gazette Part I No 916 of 16 December 2002.
15   ANCOM Decision No 136/2002 modified by ANCOM Decision No 174/2003 modified by ANCOM Decision 1124/2004.

- the market for access to the mobile public telephone network operated by Mobifon SA for call termination, comprising access to this network for call termination to non-fixed locations for publicly available telephony services originating in other networks;
- the market for access to the mobile public telephone network operated by Orange Romania SA for call termination, comprising access to this network for call termination to non-fixed locations for publicly available telephony services originating in other networks;
- the market for access to the mobile public telephone network operated by Telemobil SA for call termination, comprising access to this network for call termination to non-fixed locations for publicly available telephony services originating in other networks;
- the market for the provision of unconditioned full or shared access to the local loop consisting of a pair of twisted metallic wires, for the purpose of provision of broadband electronic communications services and publicly available telephony services at fixed locations;
- the market for the provision of 'bitstream' access to the local loop made of a pair of twisted metallic wires, optical fibre or coaxial cable and to the radio local loop, for the purpose of providing broadband electronic communications services;
- the market for the provision of leased lines-terminal segments services;
- the market for the provision of leased lines-trunk segments services;
- the market for provision of access at fixed location on a public network for individuals;
- the market for provision of access at fixed location on a public network for legal entities;
- the market of local calls at fixed locations for individuals, including the origination of local calls at fixed locations for the telephony services destined to the public, including dial-up and ISDN services, for Internet access and fax services, for individuals;
- the market of local calls at fixed locations for legal entities, including the origination of local calls at fixed locations for the telephony services destined to the public, including dial-up and ISDN services, for Internet access and fax services, for legal entities;
- the market for national calls at fixed locations for individuals, including the origination of national calls at fixed points for telephony services destined to the public, including fax services for individuals;
- the market for national calls at fixed locations for legal entities, including the origination of national calls at fixed points for telephony services destined to the public, including fax services for legal entities;
- the market for international calls at fixed locations for individuals, including the origination of international calls at fixed points for telephony services destined to the public, including fax services for individuals;
- the market for international calls at fixed locations for legal entities, including the origination of international calls at fixed points for telephony services destined to the public, including fax services for legal entities;
- the market for calls at fixed locations by public mobile telephony networks for individuals which includes the origination of calls to fixed locations by the public mobile telephony networks for the telephony services destined to the public including fax services for individuals; and
- the market for calls at fixed locations by public mobile telephony networks for legal entities which includes the origination of calls to fixed locations by the

public mobile telephony networks for the telephony services destined to the public including fax services for legal entities.

27.25   During the past several years, major players such as Vodafone, Orange, Cosmote, Romtelecom, RDS & RCS have been designated as having SMP.

ANCOM's Regulatory Duties concerning Rights of Way, Co-location and Facility Sharing

Rights of way

27.26   Providers of electronic communications networks authorised pursuant to Chapter II of the EGO No 111/2011 must have the right to install, maintain, replace, or move any elements of electronic communications networks, on, above, in, or under the state-owned, or on local administration owned real-estate, to the extent that:

- performing such right of way-related activities does not contravene the specific requirements concerning the town planning, protection of environment, health or public order; and
- the general authorisation granted to a provider of electronic communication does not replace the authorisations issued by the relevant authorities, such as the city authorities or the environment authorities.

27.27   Providers of public electronic communications networks must execute agreements for access or installation of equipment with the owner of the infrastructure. In several Romanian cities, the presence of private underground network infrastructures allows network providers to install their own fibre optics through that infrastructure. Such underground re-wiring of the networks is also imposed by city halls in order for the network providers to remove the aerial cables currently installed, and re-install them using the underground infrastructure.

Co-location and facility sharing

27.28   ANCOM may, in accordance with the provisions of the law, impose obligations on operators to allow access to, and use of, specific elements of the network and of the associated infrastructure, particularly in situations in which it considers that the refusal of access or imposition of terms and conditions with a similar effect would hinder the development of a competitive market at the retail level or be contrary to end users' interests.[16]

27.29   ANCOM may require a provider of electronic communications networks performing rights of way activities under public or private property to allow other providers to use the facilities of the network elements which have been installed (co-location) or share the facility through other means.[17]

---

16   Art 3.4 ANCOM Decision 338/2010 on the general authorisation
17   Art 109 EGO No 111/2011.

REGULATION OF MARKET ENTRY: IMPLEMENTATION OF THE AUTHORISATION DIRECTIVE

General Regulatory Approach

27.30 Prior to providing electronic communications networks or services, the person or entity intending to provide such services must submit a notification of intent to ANCOM, for the purpose of establishing an official record of the provider.[18]

27.31 Pursuant to Article 6 of EGO No 111/2011, ANCOM must establish and update the standard notification form. The form must include the required information which is divided under the following categories:

- data necessary to identify and efficiently communicate with the provider;
- description of the types of networks or services that the relevant person intends to provide; and
- estimated date for starting the activity.

27.32 Any person or entity having submitted a notification form within the term, and in compliance with the conditions, listed above will be authorised automatically to provide the types of networks or services indicated in the notification (having all the rights and obligations under the general authorisation that must be elaborated, updated, modified and repealed).

27.33 If a person's or entity's right to provide electronic communication networks or services has been revoked, such person or entity will not be entitled to provide services under the general authorisation, for the same type of network or service, for a three-year period after such revocation.[19]

Rights of Use for Radio Frequencies

General regulatory approach

27.34 The use of radio frequencies is permitted only upon obtaining a licence, subject to conditions to ensure their efficient use.

27.35 ANCOM may designate certain categories of frequencies that may be used freely, subject to the general authorisation regime concerning the access and the conditions of use, if technically possible and if the risk of harmful interference is low. ANCOM issued a Decision regarding the free use of certain frequencies. [20]

27.36 Where applicable, the granting of the right of use for radio frequencies must comply with the procedure and the conditions harmonised at European level, should such procedures and conditions have been established by international agreements and by observing the provisions under the international agreements to which Romania is a party.

Admissible conditions

27.37 The licence for the use of radio-electric frequencies is an administrative document granted by ANCOM to a provider authorising it to use one or several

---

18   Art 6 (1) EGO No 111/2011.
19   Art 6 (6) EGO No 111/2011.
20   Decision 1722/2011 with respect to the frequencies exempted from the licensing regime.

radio frequencies in order to provide electronic communications networks or services, in compliance with certain technical parameters and for a limited period of time ('use right').

27.38   The licence for the use of radio frequencies establishes the conditions subject to which the holder may exercise the use right.[21] These conditions may target the following:

- the designation of the type of network or service or of the technology for which the right of use has been granted;
- the effective, rational and efficient use of the frequencies, including, where appropriate, territory coverage requirements;
- technical and operational requirements necessary for the avoidance of harmful interference, where such conditions are different from those included in the general authorisation;
- terms for the effective use of the frequencies;
- operational and technical conditions necessary for the avoidance of harmful interference and for the limitation of the effects of electromagnetic fields;
- duration for which the use right is granted;
- possibilities and conditions for the assignment of the use right;
- the tariffs for the spectrum use; and
- other obligations.[22]

Limitation of number of rights of use to be granted

27.39   The number of licences for the use of radio-electric frequencies to be granted may be limited only when necessary to ensure an efficient use of the radio frequency spectrum or for the avoidance of harmful interference.[23]

27.40   A holder of the licence for the use of radio-electric frequencies must pay annually to ANCOM a spectrum usage tariff established by the General Secretariat of the Government at the proposal of ANCOM.

27.41   ANCOM organised bids for the granting of spectrum licenses, the most important being the bid for the 410–415/420–425 MHz spectrum license. Romtelecom won the bid and currently develops a national network based on this license.

Frequency trading

27.42   The licence for use of radio-electric frequencies and the licence for use of numbering resources may be transferred to a third party authorised in accordance with EGO No 111/2011, but only subject to meeting all obligations deriving from these licences, observing the transfer conditions set out therein, and obtaining the approval of ANCOM.[24]

---

21   Art 24 (2) EGO No 111/2011.
22   Art 24 (2) EGO No 111/2011.
23   Art 25 EGO No 111/2011.
24   Art 35 EGO 111/2011.

Rights of Use for Numbers

General regulatory approach

27.43 The National Numbering Plan ('PNN') [25] establishes the structure and the destination of the numbering resources used in Romania for telephony services provided through public fixed electronic communications networks and through public mobile electronic communications networks.

27.44 The licence for the use of numbering resources is an administrative document granted by ANCOM to a provider, authorising it to use certain numbers in order to provide electronic communications services for a limited period of time.

27.45 There are no categories of numbers that can be used freely, subject to the general authorisation regime.

Admissible conditions

27.46 ANCOM may also require holders of licences for the use of numbering resources to pay a fee for the usage of these resources. The licence for the use of numbering resources establishes the conditions by which the holder may exercise their right of use. These conditions must be objectively justified in relation to the service concerned, non-discriminatory, proportionate, and transparent. [26]

They may target the following:

- the designation of the service for which the right of use has been granted, including any requirements related to the provision of that service;
- the effective, rational, and efficient use of numbering resources;
- requirements concerning number portability;
- obligations related to the services for public directories of subscribers;
- the duration for which the license is granted; and
- the tariff for the right of use

27.47 Generally, the ANCOM protects subscribers in the portability process, and may impose on operators obligations that the porting tariffs be linked directly to the costs incurred by the operators. [27]

Limitation of number of rights of use to be granted

27.48 ANCOM must grant licences for the use of numbering resources through an open, transparent, and non-discriminatory procedure, within three weeks after receipt of an application (except for licences that are granted through a competitive or comparative selection procedure, ANCOM must grant within six weeks of receipt of an application).

27.49 The competitive and comparative procedure applies to numbering resources having an important economical value. This procedure entails an auction in which the bidders are evaluated based on the offerings they make as well as on their infrastructure capacity.

---

25   ANCOM's Decision 2895/2007 for the regulation of the National Numbering Plan.
26   Art 41 (3) EGO No 111/2011.
27   Art 75 EGO No 111/2011.

NRA's Enforcement Powers

27.50   ANCOM is empowered to monitor compliance with the provisions of EGO No 111/2011, with specific legislation in the field of electronic communications, with the obligations set out in the general authorisation and licences, and with obligations concerning the use of radio frequencies.

27.51   In case of serious and repeated breaches, or if the respective provider has failed to comply with the measures taken by ANCOM, ANCOM may:

- suspend or revoke the provider's right to provide electronic communications networks or services on the basis of the general authorisation or the licence for the use of numbering resources, as the case may be; or
- suspend or revoke the respective provider's licence for the use of radio frequencies.

27.52   ANCOM has broad control and enforcement powers, allowing it even to seize equipment used by providers operating without the proper authorisation or license.

Administrative Charges and Fees for Rights of Use

27.53   Under the general authorisation, service providers must pay an annual monitoring tariff which is calculated as an equivalent of up to 0.4 per cent of the service provider's annual turnover as calculated according to the law.[28]

27.54   ANCOM sets the tariffs for the use of spectrum frequencies, which cover a broad range of types of use, including use of GSM frequencies and use of various other types of frequencies. The Tables containing the tariffs for spectrum use are contained in Decision No 686/2005 in the list comprising the tariffs for using the frequency spectrum.

27.55   A failure to pay within the due time the monitoring tariff, the spectrum usage tariff, or the numbering resources usage tariff, results in penalties to be applied for each day of delay.

27.56   If the provider fails to pay the tariff and penalties within 60 days from the date when the payment becomes outstanding, ANCOM or the MCSI, depending on the case, may suspend or revoke the provider's right to provide electronic communications networks or services based on the general authorisation, the licence for the use of radio frequencies or the licence for the use of numbering resources.

REGULATION OF NETWORK ACCESS AND INTERCONNECTION: IMPLEMENTATION OF THE ACCESS DIRECTIVE

Objectives and Scope of Access Regulation

27.57   The access regulations of EGO No 111/2011 establish the regulatory framework for the relationships between network operators and service providers, and among network operators with regard to access to public electronic communications networks and associated infrastructure, as well as to their interconnection.

27.58   The objectives of ANCOM and other regulatory bodies established under the legislative framework are to maximise the benefits to end users, ensuring their

---

28   Art 123 EGO No 111/2011.

ability to choose the best offer of electronic communications services in terms of quality, diversity, and price. To promote competition and to ensure service interoperability, ANCOM sets principles and procedures and imposes specific conditions to foster timely and effective implementation of the access and interconnection agreements. The ANCOM approach observes the following principles:

- focusing on the wholesale markets for the provision of fixed telephone networks and services, where the end of monopoly (on 1 January 2003) required prompt intervention from ANCOM;
- prioritising the regulatory measures according to the actual needs of the market; and
- resolving essential issues expediently, within short review periods, and based on the market development.

Basic Regulatory Concepts

27.59 The terms 'access' and 'interconnection' are defined in Romanian legislation according to the definitions provided by the 2002 EU Regulatory Package.[29] More specifically, the extended definition of the terms 'access' and 'interconnection' provided under Article 2(a) and (b) of the Access Directive has been transposed into Romanian law.

27.60 To ensure provision and interoperability of publicly available electronic communications services, any operator of a public communications network has:

- the right to negotiate an interconnection agreement with any other operator of a public communications network for the purpose of providing publicly available electronic communications services, including electronic communications services available to users via another public communications network interconnected with the network of any of the two operators; and
- the obligation, when requested by a third party legally authorised, to negotiate an interconnection agreement with the requesting party, for the purpose of providing publicly available electronic communications services, including electronic communications services available to users via another public communications network interconnected with the network of any of the parties.[30]

Access- and Interconnection-related Obligations with Respect to SMP Undertakings

27.61 If, as a result of a market analysis carried out under the conditions set out by the legal provisions in force, an operator is designated as having SMP in a relevant market, the regulatory authority must impose on that operator one or more of the obligations set out in EGO No 111/2011, as appropriate.

27.62 If, as a result of a market analysis carried out under the conditions set out by the legal provisions in force, the regulatory authority establishes that a relevant market is effectively competitive, it must withdraw or modify, as appropriate, the obligations imposed in accordance with the provisions of EGO No 111/2011. With

---

29 Art 4 EGO No 111/2011.
30 Art 12 EGO No 111/2011.

at least 30 days' notice prior to withdrawal of any obligations imposed on a specific operator, the regulatory authority must inform those having concluded access or interconnection agreements with that operator, in order to allow them to find alternative providers or to renegotiate the agreement concluded.[31]

27.63   ANCOM may impose obligations for transparency in relation to the interconnection of communications networks, to the access to these networks, or to the associated infrastructure. These obligations may consist of making public specified information, such as technical specifications, network characteristics, terms and conditions for supply and use, accounting information, and tariffs.[32]

27.64   In 2012, ANCOM issued nine decisions imposing requirements on SMP operators in their respective markets over the years,[33] such as:[34]

* transparency;
* non-discrimination;
* keeping separate accounting records; and
* justification of tariffs on the basis of cost.

27.65   These above-mentioned obligations are equally mandatory and ANCOM typically imposes them on all operators having SMP in their relevant markets. ANCOM controls the tariffs charged by operators having SMP by imposing such cost-based tariffs, which are calculated using models initially approved by ANCOM.

Regulatory Powers Applicable to All Market Participants

27.66   ANCOM must take all the necessary measures in order to encourage and, where appropriate, ensure, in accordance with the provisions of EGO No 111/2011, access and interconnection under adequate conditions, as well as interoperability of services, in keeping with the principles of economic efficiency, promoting competition, and maximising end-users' benefit.

27.67   In specific cases, ANCOM may impose on operators, regardless of their market position, the obligation to provide access to elements of associated infrastructure on fair, reasonable, and non-discriminatory terms, if necessary to enable end users to access digital radio and television broadcasting services. [35] In addition, in specific cases, the ANCOM may impose on legal persons that are not SMP operators but that control access to end users, the obligation to interconnect their networks, if necessary to ensure end-to-end connectivity. To date, we are unaware of any such legal persons. These obligations are without prejudice to measures that may be taken with regard to SMP undertakings' obligations.

---

31   Art 93 EGO No 111/2011.
32   Art 106 EGO No 111/2011.
33   See para 27.24 above.
34   ANCOM Decisions 101–109/2012.
35   Art 104 EGO No 111/2011.

REGULATION OF UNIVERSAL SERVICES AND USERS' RIGHTS: THE UNIVERSAL SERVICE DIRECTIVE

Regulation of Universal Service Obligations

Scope of universal service obligations

27.68   Pursuant to article 76(1) of EGO No 111/2011, all end users in Romania have the right of access to universal service represents the right of all end-users on the Romanian territory to benefit from the provision of services in the area of universal service, at a specified quality level, regardless of their geographical location, at affordable prices.

27.69   Pursuant to articles 80 and 81 of EGO No 111/2011, universal services include:

- provision of access to the public telephone network, at a fixed point;
- provision of directory enquiry and directories of subscribers services; and
- provision of public pay telephones.

Designation of undertakings obliged to provide universal services

27.70   Based on the policy and strategy established by the MCSI, ANCOM must enable access to universal service throughout Romania. As a starting point, ANCOM designates one or more universal service providers within certain areas, or throughout Romania. Following the provisions of Decision No 7/2011,[36] ANCOM may designate, ex officio, or by auction, the universal service providers for specific areas such as fixed point access or public pay telephones. These designation procedures are complex in nature and are mainly cost-oriented procedures. To award the winning offer, the tender commission must consider the most advantageous financial offer, as regards the volume of the net cost.

27.71   To date, under ANCOM's Decision No 1345/2004, only Orange Romania SA has been designated for a three-year period, following a public tender, as a universal service provider in the electronic communications sector, with a view to providing access to the public telephone network, at a fixed location, by means of telecentres, in five Romanian cities.

Regulation of retail tariffs, users' expenditures and quality of service

27.72   ANCOM must monitor the evolution and level of tariffs of universal service, in particular in relation to the general level of prices and consumer income.[37] ANCOM may require universal service providers to apply common tariffs, possibly by reference to a geographically established average, throughout the national territory, in the light of specific conditions, or to comply with certain tariff ceilings or tariff increase control formulas.[38]

---

36   Decision 7/2011 on the implementation of universal service in the electronic communications sector.

37   Art 83 EGO No 111/2011.

38   ANCOM may impose specific tariffs on all universal service providers in a specific area, by

27.73   ANCOM may require universal service providers to provide tariff options or packages to consumers which depart from those provided under normal commercial conditions, in order to enable individuals with low incomes or special social needs to benefit from publicly available telephone services.[39] The MCSI may establish the categories of persons who will benefit from the tariff options or packages offered.

27.74   ANCOM may impose modifications or withdraw certain tariffs or tariff schemes, but, in so doing, it must follow the consultation procedure.[40]

27.75   ANCOM sets the standards for the quality of universal services, and the methods for evaluation of compliance with such standards. Universal service providers must transmit to ANCOM, and publish adequate and current information regarding compliance with the standards of the quality of universal services they are required to provide.

27.76   ANCOM may require universal service providers to meet certain performance targets regarding the quality of the universal services they are required to provide.[41]

27.77   ANCOM must monitor compliance with the quality of service standards. For this purpose, ANCOM may order verification of data concerning compliance with the performance targets by an independent audit, paid for by the universal service provider concerned, in order to ensure the accuracy and comparability of the data made available by this provider.[42]

Cost calculation and financing of universal services

27.78   If ANCOM estimates that the provision of universal services may unfairly burden universal service providers, it must determine the net cost of the provision of these services.

In determining such cost, ANCOM may:

- calculate the net cost of the obligations to provide universal services; or
- follow the procedure for the designation of the universal service providers under Decision No 7/2011.

27.79   ANCOM must determine the appropriate mechanism to compensate the net cost of the provision of universal services To do so, ANCOM must identify the providers of electronic communications networks, and the providers of electronic communications services, required to contribute to compensation and determine the amount of the contributions due, the manner and deadline for payment, and any other necessary elements. In determining the appropriate compensation mechanism, ANCOM must respect the principles of transparency, minimal competition distortion, non-discrimination, and proportionality.[43] To date, we are unaware of any such compensation.

---

using an average of the tariffs used by all the universal operators in that area. See art 83(3) EGO No 111/2011.

39   Art 83(4) EGO No 111/2011.
40   Art 83(6) EGO No 111/2011.
41   Art 85 (2) EGO No 111/2011.
42   Art 85 (7) EGO No 111/2011.
43   Art 88 EGO No 111/2011.

End User Rights

Contracts

27.80   The contracts between consumers and providers of electronic communications services must be executed in writing and must contain, as a minimum, clauses regarding:[44]

- the identification data of the provider;
- the services provided, the service quality levels offered, and the time for the initial connection;
- in case of contracts for telephony services addressed to the public, the option of the subscriber to include or not its personal data in databases for providing registry services;
- the prices and tariffs for each product or service covered by the contract, the way in which they are applied, and the means by which current information on the tariffs for the provision of the electronic communications services and of the maintenance and repair services may be obtained;
- the duration of the contract, the conditions for renewal and termination of the contract, and the conditions under which service suspension operates;
- the applicable compensations for damages and the procedure for granting them to be applied if the contracted service quality levels or other contractual clauses are not met;
- the method of initiating the procedure for settlement of disputes;[45]and
- categories of measures that providers may take in case of incidents, threats or vulnerabilities with respect to the security of networks.

There is no specific obligation for certain providers to enter into contracts with end users.

Transparency obligations

27.81   Providers of public telephone networks and providers of publicly available telephone services must make available to the public clear, detailed and current information on the applicable prices and tariffs, and on the other conditions concerning the possibility of access to, and use of, publicly available telephone services, to enable end users to make informed choices.[46]

Quality of service: securing 'net neutrality'

27.82   Romanian legislation is actually based on the transparency of certain limitations that may be imposed by service providers with respect to users' access to the Internet, rather than securing net neutrality. More specifically, article 51 of EGO No 111/2011 provides that all information regarding limitations to the access or to the use of certain services, imposed by service providers on users, must be mentioned specifically in consumer contracts, without forbidding such limitations.

Also, ANCOM has established a set of specific quality of service parameters through ANCOM Decision No 1021/2011 on establishing quality indicators for

---

44   Art 51 EGO No 111/2011.
45   An end user may file with ANCOM a complaint alleging a provider's breach of obligations under EGO No 11/2011.
46   Art 60 EGO No 111/2011.

providing Internet access services and the publishing of such parameters. Basically, according to this ANCOM decision, service providers must provide Internet access services while observing certain parameters, and such parameters must be provided in the contracts concluded with consumers.

However, as mentioned above, we do not believe that such provisions are sufficient to secure net neutrality and more regulations are necessary to guarantee such effect.

DATA PROTECTION AND PRIVACY

Confidentiality of Communications[47]

27.83   Law No 506/2004 on the administering of personal data in the electronic communications sector ('Law No 506/2004'), which fully transposes the E-Privacy Directive,[48] regulates data protection in electronic communications.

27.84   Pursuant to this law, providers of publicly available electronic communications services must take appropriate technical and organisational measures to ensure the security of the services they provide. Providers of electronic communications services, together with providers of public network of electronic communications services, must take necessary security measures to ensure the security of their respective network.

27.85   The measures taken must ensure a security level proportional to the actual risk, considering the technological resources and costs to implement such measures.[49]

27.86   If a provider of publically available electronic communications service determines a risk of a breach in network security, the provider must:

● inform subscribers about such risk, as well as any possible consequences;
● inform subscribers about any possible remedies; and
● inform subscribers about the estimate costs for clearing the risk.

27.87   The listening, tapping, storage and any other kinds of interception or surveillance of communications conveyed by means of publicly available electronic communications services and the related traffic data are prohibited, except for the following cases:

● where it is performed by the users concerned;
● where the users concerned have given their prior written consent with regard to the performance of such operations; or
● where it is performed by competent authorities, under legal terms.[50]

27.88   However, the following are permitted:

● the technical storage necessary for conveyance of a communication without prejudice to the principle of confidentiality; and
● the making of authorised recordings of communications and related traffic

---

47   Pursuant to the law, 'communication' means 'any information exchanged or conveyed between a finite number of participants by means of a publicly available electronic communications service'.
48   Published in the Official Gazette Part 1, 25 November 2004.
49   Art 3 Law No 506/2004.
50   Art 4 Law No 506/2004.

data, under legal terms, when carried out in the course of lawful business practice for the purpose of providing evidence of a commercial transaction or of any other business communication.[51]

Data Retention

27.89 Constitutional Court Decision No 1258/2009 found unconstitutional, and therefore repealed, Law No 298/2008 on the retention of data generated or processed by the electronic communication services providers which transposed the Data Retention Directive. On 21 June 2012 a new piece of legislation entered into force, Law No 82/2012 on the Retention of data processed by the networks providers (the 'Data Retention law')[52]

According to the Data Retention Law the service providers must keep databases containing the following categories of data:

● data which is necessary for the tracking and the identification of the source of a communication;
● data wich is necessary for the identification of the destination of a communication;
● data necessary for the identification of the type of communication;
● data necessary for the identification of the user's communication equipment;
● data necessary for the identification of the location of the equipment for mobile communications

Such data are too be retained for a duration of six months from the date of communication

The data can only be accessed by the relevant authorities (penal prosecution authorities, courts of law, other state organs with attributions in the field of national security) under the specific provisions of the law.

Traffic Data and Location Data

27.90 The definitions of 'traffic data' and 'location data' are identical to those in the E-Privacy Directive.[53]

27.91 Traffic data relating to subscribers and users, processed and stored by the providers of publicly available electronic communications services, must be erased or made anonymous when they are no longer needed to conveying a communication.

27.92 A service provider may process traffic data for the purpose of billing a subscriber for no more than three years after the deadline for payment of the relevant bill.

27.93 A provider of publicly available electronic communications service may process traffic data related to subscribers and end users for the purpose of selling or providing value added services,[54] to the extent, and over the duration, necessary for selling and providing such service only if the provider has obtained prior consent

---

51 Art 4 Law No 506/2004
52 Art 3 Law No 82/2012
53 Art 2(b) Law No 506/2004.
54 Pursuant to Law No 506/2004 a 'value added service' means 'any service which requires the

from the subscriber or end user. The user or subscriber may, at any time, withdraw such consent.[55]

27.94   In the cases described above, the provider of the publicly available electronic communications service must inform the subscriber or user of the types of traffic data that are processed, or will be processed, and of the duration of such processing.

27.95   Processing of traffic data must be restricted to persons acting under the authority of providers of publicly available electronic communications services with responsibility for traffic billing or management, customer service, fraud detection, merchandising electronic communications services or providing value added services, and must be restricted to include only traffic data necessary for the purposes of such activities.[56]

27.96   Location data, other than traffic data, relating to users or subscribers of public communications networks or publicly available electronic communications services, may be processed only if:

- such data are made anonymous;
- with the express prior consent of the user or subscriber to which such data refer, to the extent and for the duration necessary for the provision of a value added service; or
- where the value-added service with a location function has as its purpose the uni-directional and undifferentiated transmission of some information to its users.[57]

Itemised Billing

27.97   Service providers must issue itemised bills upon request from a user. While service providers are not required to provide itemised bills free of charge, in practice they do so.

Calling and Connected Line Identification

27.98   Service providers offering calling line identification services must allow users, easily, and free of charge, to withhold their number on a per-call and per-line basis.[58] The police and other authorities may request a service provider to cease the provision of a withholding identity service for specific users.

Automatic Call Forwarding

27.99   Users to whom calls have been automatically forwarded as a result of third party actions may, without charge, request that the provider ceased such call

processing of traffic data or location for other purposes than the transmission of a communication or the billing of the equivalent for such an operation'.

55   Art 5 Law No 506/2004.
56   Art 5 Law No 506/2004.
57   Art 8 Law No 506/2004.
58   Art 7 Law No 506/2004.

forwarding. A provider must cease the call forwarding as soon as practicable after receipt of a request.[59]

Directories of Subscribers

27.100   A universal service provider, and any other person or undertaking making subscribers' data available for inclusion in a directory, must inform all subscribers in advance of the purposes of the directory and any further usage possibilities based on search functions embedded in electronic versions of the directory. Such entities must enable a subscriber, free of charge, to determine whether, and to what extent, the subscriber's personal data is included in the directory, and must provide the subscriber with the opportunity to verify, correct, or withdraw the data.[60]

Unsolicited Communications

27.101   A provider may use automated calling systems without human intervention (ie automatic calling machines), facsimile machines, electronic mail, or any other method using the publicly available electronic communications services, to engage in direct marketing only after having received prior consent from the subscriber.

27.102   Where a natural or legal person, however, obtains from its customers their electronic contact details for electronic mail, in the context of the sale of a product or a service, it may use those details for direct marketing of its own similar products or services, provided that they have given customers, clearly and distinctly, the opportunity to object, free of charge, and in an easy manner, to the such use of electronic contact details when they are collected, and on the occasion of each message where the customer has not initially refused such use.[61]

---

59   Art 10(1) Law No 506/2004.
60   Art 11 Law No 506/2004.
61   Art 12 Law No 506/2004.

The Slovak Market for Electronic Communications[1]

Lubomir Marek
Marek & Partners, Bratislava

LEGAL STRUCTURE

Basic Policy

28.1 In recent years, Slovak telecommunications legislation has undergone significant changes required for harmonisation with applicable EU legislation. In the course of implementing the 2002 Regulatory Package, the Slovak Republic has adopted a new set of legislative acts forming an environment compatible with EU law in the area of electronic communications. Implementation of the 2009 Regulatory Package prompted adoption of new Act No 351/2011 Coll on Electronic Communications ('ECA').[2]

28.2 The overall objectives of the new legislation were to adjust the telecommunications regulatory landscape to changing market conditions, develop effective economic competition, and separate the regulation of operation of electronic communications from the regulation of their content. The new regulatory framework, introduced by transposing the 2002 Regulatory Package, and later amended to transpose the 2009 Regulatory Package, liberalises, and facilitates accessibility of, market entry and promotes information society services and access to the Internet. Furthermore, it strengthens the competencies, and independence, of the Telecommunications Office of the Slovak Republic ('STO').

Implementation of EU Directives

28.3 The Slovak Republic implemented the 2009 Regulatory Package into its legal system through adopting the ECA. The ECA repealed and replaced former Act No 610/2003 Coll on Electronic Communications.

---

1   Editing of this chapter closed on 3 January 2013.
2   The ECA came into effect on 1 November 2011, except for certain provisions coming into effect on 1 January 2012.

Legislation

28.4   The ECA is the main legislative act in the area of electronic communications.[3] Slovak electronic communications legislation also includes implementing regulations issued by the Government of the Slovak Republic (the 'Cabinet') and the Ministry of Transportation, Construction and Regional Development of the Slovak Republic (the 'Ministry'), as follows:

- Decree of the Cabinet setting out details on technical requirements and evaluating procedures in respect of the conformity of radio equipment and terminal telecommunications facilities;[4]
- Decree of the Cabinet setting out technical requirements for operability of terminal facilities designed for receiving digital television signal and operability of analogue television receivers and digital television receivers;[5]
- Decree of the Cabinet on electromagnetic compatibility;[6] and
- Regulation of the Ministry setting out details on organisation of telecommunications services in crisis periods.[7]

28.5   In addition, there have been several measures issued by the STO,[8] which has the power to issue generally binding regulations within the framework of the ECA.

REGULATORY PRINCIPLES: IMPLEMENTATION OF THE FRAMEWORK DIRECTIVE

Scope of Regulation

28.6   The ECA regulates, among other things, conditions for the provision of networks and services, conditions for the use of radio facilities, rights and obligations of undertakings and users of networks and services, protection of networks and services, effective use of frequency spectrum and numbers, protection of privacy and protection of personal data processing in the electronic communications sector, and powers of state authorities in the electronic communications sector.[9] Unless the ECA stipulates otherwise, the ECA does not apply to the content of services provided via networks.[10]

28.7   The ECA's definitions of the terms 'electronic communications network',[11] 'electronic communications service',[12] and 'associated facilities'[13] reflect the definitions of these terms as in the Framework Directive.

---

3   See para 28.1 above.
4   Decree No 443/2001 Coll.
5   Decree No 26/2005 Coll.
6   Decree No 194/2005 Coll.
7   Regulation No 164/2003 Coll.
8   Eg Measure No O-22/2011 setting out details on number portability; Measure No O-24/2011 setting out the tariff of fees for allocated numbers; Measure No O-26/2011 setting out the numbering plan.
9   S 1(1) ECA.
10   S 1(2) ECA.
11   S 2(1) ECA.
12   S 3(1) ECA.
13   S 4(4) ECA.

'Internet Freedom'

28.8   Slovak law does not specifically provide for the imposition of measures that restrict end users' access to the Internet (eg to sanction copyright violations). However, an undertaking may, after prior notice, temporarily suspend, or restrict provision of, a public service due to a subscriber's misuse of the service, until such misuse has been eliminated or until technical measures to prevent such misuse have been implemented, or due to a subscriber's material breach of other contractual terms and conditions.[14]

National Regulatory Authorities: Organisation, Regulatory Objectives, Competencies

28.9   The national regulatory authority in the Slovak Republic is the STO, and it is financed by the state budget.

28.10   The ECA delineates the powers of the STO to transpose Article 8 of the Framework Directive into Slovak legislation.

28.11   The STO may, among other things:[15]

- regulate activities in the field of electronic communications;
- administer the frequency spectrum;
- protect end users' interests with respect to quality and prices of services;
- promote effective competition, efficient investments and innovations, development of the EU common market, adequate access to networks, interconnection of networks and interoperability of services, and protect the freedom of choice of operators;
- conduct out-of-court dispute resolution;
- fulfil tasks relating to ownership right limitations; and
- perform supervision.

28.12   The STO may request, from undertakings or other persons having rights and obligations under the ECA, information necessary to apply the ECA and international treaties.

In addition, the STO may demand from undertakings information which is required to verify compliance with applicable general authorisations, individual authorisations, obligations set out in the ECA, to assess applications for assignment of frequencies, identify characters or numbers, publish comparative studies of quality and price of services, gather statistics, or analyse relevant markets.[16]

28.13   While the STO is the only national regulatory authority in the area of electronic communications, the Ministry has certain competencies, including drafting proposals for the national electronic communications policy and the national frequency spectrum table[17] and submitting them to the Cabinet for approval.

28.14   The STO must cooperate with the Antimonopoly Office of the Slovak Republic ('AMO') in determining and analysing relevant electronic communications

---

14   S 43(1)(d)(3) ECA and s 43(1)(d)(3) ECA.
15   Cf s 6(3) ECA.
16   Cf s 40 ECA.
17   The STO and the Ministry cooperate in drafting proposals of the national frequency spectrum table; cf s 6(3)(c) ECA.

markets and determining undertakings with a significant impact in relevant markets. While exercising their competencies, the STO and the AMO must exchange information and documents.[18]

28.15   Article 3 of the Framework Directive[19] has been sufficiently transposed through the ECA into Slovak legislation to ensure the independence and efficient structural separation of the STO's regulatory powers from activities connected with ownership or control in the area of electronic communications.[20]

28.16   The STO must provide undertakings with the opportunity to comment on proposed measures which may have a significant impact on the relevant market within at least one month following the publication of the draft measure in the STO's bulletin ('Bulletin'). If appropriate, the STO must consider, to the maximum extent possible, the opinion of associations of end users, manufacturers of telecommunications equipment, and undertakings.[21]

28.17   The ECA delegates to the STO the power to resolve disputes regarding end users' complaints[22] and certain cross-border disputes between Slovak undertakings and parties from EU/EEA Member States.[23]

28.18   The STO may also resolve disputes between undertakings or persons that benefit from access or interconnection, on proposal of either party to a dispute arising in connection with fulfilment of obligations under the ECA, or a decision or generally binding legal regulation issued by the STO. The STO must resolve disputes within four months.[24]

Right of Appeal against NRA's Decisions

28.19   Except for certain decisions exempted from the right of appeal,[25] the STO's decisions may be appealed by means of an administrative appeal which must be submitted to the chairman of the STO within 15 days from delivery of the relevant contested decision. The STO's Chairman decides appeals, based on proposals of a special committee established by him. The STO's decisions are further subject to revision by the Supreme Court of the Slovak Republic.

The NRA's Obligations to Cooperate with the Commission

28.20   Sections 10(4) to (8) ECA implement the consolidation procedure.[26] Pursuant to this procedure, if a draft measure of the STO will affect trade between EU/EEA Member States, the STO must consult with the Commission, BEREC,

---

18   S 8(1)(c); s 8(2) ECA.
19   See para 1.39 above.
20   S 6 ECA; s 7 ECA.
21   S 10(1) ECA.
22   S 75 ECA.
23   S 76 ECA.
24   S 77 ECA.
25   Eg decisions relating to general authorisations, determination of relevant markets, determination of cost calculation methods, tenders for frequencies assignment, certificates of special professional qualification and non-judicial dispute resolutions; cf s 74(2) ECA.
26   Art 7 of the Framework Directive; see para 1.53 et seq above.

and EU/EEA Member States' NRAs and take utmost account of their comments.[27] Section 10(6) ECA implements the 'veto procedure' in compliance with Article 7(4) of the Framework Directive.[28]

28.21   Sections 10(9) to (14) ECA implement the co-regulation procedure.[29] Pursuant to this procedure, if a draft measure of the STO seeks to impose, amend, or withdrawing an obligation of an SMP undertaking,[30] and the Commission informs the STO of its reservations, the STO must consult with the Commission and BEREC also taking into account comments of undertakings.[31]

28.22   If the STO decides not to follow a recommendation of the Commission, it must inform the Commission of that and give reasons for its decision.[32]

'Significant Market Power' as a Fundamental Prerequisite of Regulation

Definition of SMP

28.23   The definition of an SMP undertaking contained in sections 17(3) to (5) ECA is based on the provisions of Article 14(2) and (3) of the Framework Directive.[33]

Definition of relevant markets

28.24   The STO determines the relevant markets based on the list of relevant markets recommended by the Commission while taking into account the geographic conditions and other specific national conditions consistent with the principles of competition law.[34] The STO may determine, after consultations under section 10 ECA, a relevant market other than the markets defined in the recommendations and guidelines of the Commission.[35]

28.25   On 20 January 2011, the STO issued a decision[36] providing the list of relevant markets in accordance with the current Market Recommendation.[37] Under this decision, there is only one relevant geographic market covering the entire territory of the Slovak Republic.

28.26   Since 2005, the STO has issued several decisions[38] determining the undertakings listed below as those having SMP in relevant telecommunications markets:

---

27   S 10(4) and (5) ECA.
28   See para 1.55 above.
29   Art 7a Framework Directive; see para 1.58 above.
30   Cf ss 19 to 25 and s 28 ECA.
31   S 10(9) and (10) ECA.
32   S 11(2) ECA.
33   See paras 1.64 and 1.65 above.
34   S 16(1) ECA.
35   S 16(2) ECA.
36   The decision was published in the Bulletin on 1 February 2011.
37   See para 1.73 above.
38   Under s 18(1) ECA, a previous decision expires after the adoption of a new decision.

- Slovak Telekom, a.s. in all seven relevant markets;[39]
- Telefónica Slovakia, s.r.o. in the market for 'Voice call termination on individual mobile networks'[40] and Orange Slovensko, a.s. in the market for 'Call termination on individual public telephone networks provided at a fixed location' and in the market for 'Voice call termination on individual mobile networks';[41] and
- eight smaller undertakings in the market for 'Call termination on individual public telephone networks provided at a fixed location'.

Imposition of remedies

28.27   Under section 18(1) ECA, if the STO determines that a relevant market is not effectively competitive, the STO must impose at least one regulatory obligation on an undertaking identified as having SMP.[42] The STO may not impose these SMP-specific regulatory obligations on undertakings not identified as having SMP.

NRA's Regulatory Duties concerning Rights of Way, Co-location and Facility Sharing

Rights of way

28.28   An undertaking may, if it is in the public interest, and to the extent it is necessary to install and operate a public network, carry its lines over third parties' real property (whether public or private) or to enter upon third parties' real property (whether public or private) for the purposes of installing, operating, repairing and maintaining the lines.[43]

28.29   Rights of way are created by operation of law and registered with the Slovak Real Property Register. An operator must notify the owner or user of real property at least 15 days in advance that the operator's performance of the rights of way will be commencing. The owner or user of the property, who is restricted in a regular use of his property as a consequence of the operator's exercise of the rights of way, is entitled to reasonable compensation.[44]

Co-location and facility sharing

28.30   A public service operator may use third parties' internal distribution systems installed in the buildings or premises where the operator intends to provide its services, provided that the operator compensates the owner of the building or

---

39   Decision No 592/14/2008; Decision No 527/14/2005; Decision No 874/14/2010; Decision No 63/01/2005; Decision No 3/01/2009; Decision No 7/OER/2012; Decision No 07/01/2010.
40   Decision No 6/01/2010.
41   Decision No 07/01/2011; Decision No 08/01/2010.
42   These are regulatory obligations under s 19 to 25 ECA, or, in the case of an undertaking having SMP in a closely related market (Art 14(3) of the Framework Directive), under ss 19 to 21, 23 and 25 ECA.
43   S 66(1) ECA.
44   S 66(2), (3) and (5) ECA.

premises, on a pro-rated basis, for the costs incurred in connection with maintenance and repairs of such systems.[45]

28.31   An operator who is unable to install new lines or facilities, or who can do so only with unreasonable limits to use of third parties' property, because of the need to protect the environment, public health, or public security, or to meet the zone planning objectives, may request another operator to allow it to share or use the existing infrastructure (including buildings, premises, and parts of lines), provided that no significant additional work or and cost is required.[46] Infrastructure sharing is provided under the terms and conditions agreed between the undertakings involved.[47] The agreement may be rejected only if the sharing is technically unfeasible or if there exist significant security issues with respect to the public interest.[48] If the undertakings fail to agree on the terms and conditions, either of them may request the STO to decide on the content of the agreement, including the rules of costs sharing.[49]

REGULATION OF MARKET ENTRY: THE AUTHORISATION DIRECTIVE

The General Authorisation of Electronic Communications

28.32   Consistent with the principles set out by the Authorisation Directive, the provision of networks or services is subject to a general authorisation. However, if it is necessary for the provision of networks or services to obtain an individual right to use numbers or frequencies, an undertaking may request the STO to grant such rights under section 31 or section 32 ECA.[50]

28.33   A general authorisation sets out conditions for the provision of networks or services which may be applied to all, or certain types, of networks or services.[51]

28.34   The STO may only impose on general authorisations those conditions that are listed in section 14(2) ECA; the ECA's list of the admissible conditions corresponds to the list contained in Part A of the Annex to the Authorisation Directive.

28.35   Since the ECA came into effect, the STO has issued a number of general authorisations, of which the General Authorisation No 1/2011 for provision of electronic communications networks or electronic communications services ('General Authorisation No 1/2011') is the most significant one.

28.36   An undertaking is authorised to provide networks or services under the General Authorisation No 1/2011 if the undertaking complies with the conditions set out in the General Authorisation No 1/2011 and has properly fulfilled its obligation to notify the STO.

28.37   An undertaking intending to carry out business in the area of provision of networks or services must notify the STO prior to commencing operations.[52] Upon

---

45   S 67(1) ECA.
46   S 67(2) ECA.
47   The terms and conditions must be non-discriminatory; cf s 67(2) ECA.
48   S 67(3) ECA.
49   S 67(4) ECA.
50   S 13(1) ECA.
51   S 14(1) ECA.
52   S 15(1) ECA.

receipt of sufficient and complete notification, the STO must register the undertaking as a network or service provider and publish such a registration on its website.[53]

Rights of Use for Radio Frequencies

Strategic planning and co-ordination of spectrum policy

28.38 The Ministry must cooperate with the Commission, EU Member States, and EEA Member States in strategic planning, coordination, and harmonisation of frequency spectrum use.[54] Furthermore, in cooperation with the Commission and the EU/EEA Member States, the Ministry must support the coordination of approaches within the frequency spectrum policy in the European Union and, where applicable, harmonised conditions with respect to frequency spectrum availability and its efficient use for the establishment and functioning of the internal market for electronic communications.[55]

Principles of frequency allocation, procedural rules

28.39 Frequencies may be used either only on the basis of a general authorisation for the use of frequencies or an individual authorisation for the use of frequencies.

The STO issues individual authorisations based on an application consistent with the frequency spectrum use plan prepared by the STO, if it is necessary due to reasons which are consistent with those defined in Article 5(1) Authorisation Directive.[56]

28.40 The individual authorisation for the use of frequencies is issued through a decision of the STO on the allocation of frequencies and setting conditions under which the frequencies may be used, a decision of the STO on the allocation of frequencies, or a decision of the STO setting the conditions under which the frequencies may be used.[57]

Transferability and time limitations

28.41 The STO specifies in an individual authorisation whether the rights arising from the allocation of frequencies may be transferred or leased in accordance with the frequency spectrum use plan, and the conditions to which the transfer or lease is subject.[58]

The undertaking must notify the STO of its intention to realise the transfer of rights arising from the allocation of frequencies no later than four weeks before the realisation thereof and the realisation of the transfer within five working days.[59]

---

53   S 15(3) ECA.
54   S 6(2)(c) ECA.
55   S 6(2)(d) ECA.
56   S 32(2) ECA.
57   S 32(1) ECA.
58   S 32(12) ECA.
59   S 32(13) ECA.

The ECA provides for specific situations in which the transfer or lease of the rights may not be carried out.[60]

28.42   An individual authorisation is issued for a period not exceeding 10 years. However, the STO may issue an individual authorisation for a longer period if it is justified by the return on investment period. In terms of frequencies which have not been allocated on the basis of a tender procedure, the STO may extend the individual authorisation on the basis of an application by the holder of the authorisation.[61]

28.43   The STO may refuse to grant an individual authorisation only in limited circumstances stipulated by the ECA (eg if it is necessary to comply with international treaties, assignment is not permitted under the frequency spectrum use plan, or a frequency is not available).[62]

Admissible conditions

28.44   The authorisation granting rights of use for frequencies may be subject only to the conditions listed in section 32(9) ECA, which are consistent with the conditions set out in Part B of the Annex to the Authorisation Directive.[63]

Limitation of number of rights of use to be granted

28.45   Where it is necessary to restrict the number of rights of use of frequencies, or in the case of selected frequencies whose conditions of allocation are determined by the frequency spectrum use plan, the STO will issue the individual authorisation on the basis of the results of a tender procedure, except for the assignment of frequencies for radio analogue terrestrial broadcasting.[64] The STO will issue an individual authorisation for radio analogue terrestrial broadcasting if the person applying for the individual authorisation is a holder of a license for radio analogue terrestrial broadcasting or has concluded an agreement on radio broadcasting transmission with a holder of such a licence.[65]

Rights of Use for Numbers

General authorisations and granting of individual rights

28.46   The STO performs the administration of numbers, prepares and issues the numbering plan, and issues individual authorisations for use of numbers.[66] The STO issued the current numbering plan on 8 December 2011.[67]

28.47   The rights of use of numbers are granted, and the numbers are assigned, based on an individual authorisation for the use of numbers issued by the STO.

---

60   Cf s 32(14) ECA.
61   S 32(11) ECA.
62   Cf s 34(1) ECA.
63   See para 1.112 above.
64   S 33(1) ECA; s 33(18) ECA.
65   S 32(10) ECA.
66   S 29(1) ECA.
67   Measure No O-26/2011 on Numbering Plan.

Individual authorisations are granted to public network or public service operators, upon their request, within three weeks after submission of the complete application.[68] The STO may refuse to grant the authorisation only for one of a limited number of reasons stipulated by the ECA (eg if it is necessary in order to comply with international treaties or the numbering plan does not allow for allocation of the numbers).[69]

Admissible conditions

28.48   The rights of use of numbers may be granted for a limited period of time. An individual authorisation for use of numbers may be subject only to the conditions listed in section 31(4) ECA. Such conditions generally correspond to the conditions set out in Part C of the Annex to the Authorisation Directive.[70]

28.49   Providers of publicly available telephone services must ensure number portability, both in fixed and mobile networks, under the conditions consistent with Article 30 of the Universal Service Directive.[71] The number portability obligation does not apply to the transfer of numbers between fixed and mobile networks.[72]

28.50   The STO may impose on SMP undertakings carrier selection and carrier pre-selection obligations.[73]

Limitation of number of rights of use to be granted

28.51   Unlike Article 5(4) of the Authorisation Directive, the ECA does not provide for the possibility of granting rights of use of numbers of exceptional economic value through a competitive, or comparative, selection procedure.

The NRA's Enforcement Powers

28.52   The ECA empowers the STO to request from undertakings information necessary to verify undertakings' compliance with the conditions set out in the applicable general authorisation, attached to rights for use of frequencies or numbers, or with specific obligations imposed on SMP undertakings under the ECA.[74] The principles that the STO must follow in requesting and gathering such information are consistent with the principles set out in Article 11 of the Authorisation Directive.[75] Where an undertaking fails to provide the STO with the requested information, the STO may impose on such undertaking a penalty of up to €300,000.[76]

28.53   If the STO finds out that an undertaking has not complied with the conditions of the general or individual authorisations, or with the specific obligations imposed on SMP undertakings under the ECA, the STO must notify the

---

68   S 31(2) ECA.
69   S 31(5) ECA.
70   See para 1.117 above.
71   See para 1.209 above.
72   S 48(2) ECA.
73   S 22(1)(a) ECA.
74   S 38(1) ECA.
75   See para 1.120 above.
76   S 73(3)(a) ECA.

undertaking of such findings in writing and give the undertaking an opportunity to comment on the findings within the period determined by the STO. At the same time, the undertaking must remedy the breaches within a reasonable period determined by the STO.[77]

28.54   Where there is a severe or repeated violation of the obligations, or the terms and conditions, defined in the ECA, a general authorisation, a decision of the STO, or a regulation issued on the basis of the ECA, and if the deficiency has not been eliminated although a penalty or a measure imposed by the STO, the STO may prohibit the undertaking to provide networks or services for a maximum period of 24 months, depending on the severity and duration of such violation.[78]

28.55   If the STO discovers that the deficiencies in the activity of an undertaking represent an immediate and serious threat to the public order, public security, public health, or that such deficiencies may result in serious economic or operational problems inflicted on other undertakings, users of networks or services or frequency spectrum users, the STO may order an interim urgent measure.[79]

Administrative Charges and Fees for Rights of Use

28.56   In a general authorisation, the STO may impose on undertakings providing networks or services the obligation to pay administrative fees specified in the authorisation.[80]

28.57   Under section 31(12) ECA, holders of individual authorisations for use of numbers must pay, for each number allocated, an annual fee consistent with the tariff of fees issued by the STO.[81]

Transitional Regulations for Existing Authorisations

28.58   Section 78(4) ECA required the STO, by 19 December 2011, to bring into conformity with the ECA all valid general authorisations and individual authorisations for the use of numbers and individual authorisations for the use of frequencies issued under the previous regulations.

REGULATION OF NETWORK ACCESS AND INTERCONNECTION: THE ACCESS DIRECTIVE

Objectives and Scope of Access Regulation

28.59   In compliance with the objectives set out in the Access Directive,[82] the ECA introduced certain regulatory powers of the STO with the objective of promoting

---

77   S 38(7) ECA.
78   S 73(8) ECA.
79   S 39(2) ECA.
80   Eg under the general authorisation No 1/2011 for provision of electronic communications networks or electronic communications services, the administrative fee is determined as amounting to 0.08 per cent of the annual revenues from the provision of networks or services (but at least € 33.19, even if the undertaking has had no revenues).
81   The current applicable tariff for the use of numbers is set out in Measure No O-24/2011 of 6 December 2011.
82   See para 1.130 above.

effective competition and development of the internal market by preventing SMP undertakings from distorting competition in the end user market, or from acting against the interests of consumers through denying access or interconnection or imposing inappropriate conditions upon undertakings seeking access or interconnection to their networks or associated facilities.

28.60   The access- and interconnection-related provisions of the ECA apply in particular to SMP undertakings and undertakings seeking access or interconnection to their networks. Obligations relating to interconnection of networks apply to undertakings providing public networks, regardless of whether they are SMP undertakings.

Basic Regulatory Concepts

28.61   The ECA established effective, and relatively far-reaching, competencies of the STO. Accordingly, if the STO discovers that there is no effective competition in a relevant market, it has the power to impose on the respective SMP undertakings one or more obligations stipulated by the ECA with the goal of facilitating access and interconnection, promoting the interoperability of networks and services, enhancing competition in the relevant market, and protecting consumer interests. These obligations must, however, be justified and appropriate with respect to the purpose and principles of regulation, ie the promotion of effective competition and internal market development.

28.62   The ECA's definitions of the terms 'access'[83] and 'interconnection'[84] reflect the definitions introduced by the Access Directive.[85]

28.63   The ECA implements the principle of freedom of access.[86] The ECA does not require that undertakings from other EU/EEA Member States seeking access or interconnection obtain an authorisation to operate in the Slovak Republic. Moreover, the ECA permits such undertakings to negotiate with Slovak undertakings agreements on technical and commercial terms of access and interconnection.

28.64   The ECA implements, with respect to network interconnection, the principle of the priority of commercial negotiations.[87] Under the ECA, a public network operator is entitled, and if requested by another undertaking providing a public network, required, to negotiate the interconnection of networks and, if feasible, to interconnect its network with the network of the requesting undertaking on the basis of a contract.[88]

---

83   S 2(7) ECA.
84   S 2(8) ECA.
85   See paras 1.133 and 1.134 above.
86   See para 1.135 above.
87   See para 1.136 above.
88   S 27(1) ECA.

Access- and Interconnection-related Obligations with Respect to SMP Undertakings

Overview

28.65   In compliance with the Access Directive,[89] the STO has the power to impose on SMP undertakings the following obligations:

- transparency;
- non-discrimination;
- accounting separation;
- access to specific network facilities;
- price control and cost accounting; and
- functional separation.

28.66   Once the STO, based on a relevant market analysis, discovers that there is no effective competition in a relevant market, the STO must, after completion of the consultation procedure, determine an SMP undertaking and, at the same time, impose on such an SMP undertaking at least one of the above obligations. These obligations must be justified and appropriate with respect to the purpose and principles of regulation, ie the promotion of effective competition and internal market development.

Transparency obligations

28.67   The STO may, to ensure transparency with regard to access and interconnection, require an SMP to publish specific information, such as accounting information, technical specifications, network characteristics, supply and use terms and conditions, including prices, and conditions limiting the access to services and applications or their use.[90]

28.68   The STO may require an SMP undertaking to publish a reference offer for access and interconnection, in particular if a non-discrimination obligation[91] has been imposed on such SMP undertaking.[92]

Non-discrimination obligations

28.69   The STO, to ensure that the objectives set out in Article 10(2) of the Access Directive are met, may impose on an SMP undertaking the non-discrimination obligation in relation to access or interconnection of networks.[93]

Specific access obligations

28.70   In compliance with Article 12 of the Access Directive, the STO is authorised to require an SMP to meet any reasonable and legitimate request for access, use of certain network elements, and associated facilities and interconnection of

---

89   See paras 1.145–1.166 above.
90   S 19(1) ECA.
91   See para 28.69 below.
92   S 19(2) ECA.
93   S 20 ECA; see para 1.152 above.

networks.[94] The list of the access obligations that may be imposed[95] fully corresponds to that contained in Article 12(1) of the Access Directive. The STO may attach to the access obligations conditions ensuring fairness, reasonableness, and timeliness.[96] When imposing access obligations, the STO considers the factors corresponding to those listed in Article 12(1) of the Access Directive.[97]

Price controls and cost accounting

28.71 If, based on an analysis of a relevant market relating to access or interconnection, the STO discovers a lack of effective competition in that market, and determines that imposing one or more obligations under sections 19 to 22 ECA would be insufficient to prevent an SMP undertaking from charging excessively high or excessively low prices for access or interconnection to the detriment of end users, the STO may apply price control on that SMP undertaking.[98] The STO, in applying such price control, refers to section 12 ECA which sets out the details of price regulation.

Accounting separation

28.72 The scope of the accounting separation obligations the STO may impose under section 21 ECA, and related powers of the STO to request information, are consistent with Article 11 of the Access Directive.[99]

Functional separation

28.73 The STO may impose upon a vertically integrated SMP undertaking functional separation as a 'last-resort' remedy set out in Article 13a of the Framework Directive.[100]

Regulatory Powers with Respect to SMP Undertakings

28.74 The ECA, unlike the legislation that preceded it, does not provide for obligations related to the (mandatory) provision of leased lines.

Regulatory Powers Applicable to All Market Participants

Obligations to ensure end-to-end connectivity

28.75 Section 27(6) ECA grants the STO an option to impose on undertakings controlling access to at least one network termination point the obligation to ensure

---

94 S 22 ECA; see para 1.154 above.
95 S 22(1) ECA.
96 S 22(2) ECA.
97 See para 1.154 above.
98 S 23 ECA.
99 See paras 1.162 and 1.163 above.
100 S 24(1) ECA.

connectivity between network termination points, and in cases where it is reasonably appropriate, to also interconnect their networks or, to the extent necessary, to ensure interoperability of their services.[101]

Regulation of roaming services

28.76   The STO is entitled to impose a penalty of up to €300,000 on undertakings failing to comply with Articles 3 to 4c and 6a(4) of the Roaming Regulation.[102]

Access to digital radio and television broadcasting services

28.77   The ECA empowers the STO to regulate in detail the conditions of conditional access to digital radio and television broadcasting services.[103]

REGULATION OF THE UNIVERSAL SERVICE AND USERS' RIGHTS: THE UNIVERSAL SERVICE DIRECTIVE

Regulation of Universal Service Obligations

Scope of universal service obligations

28.78   The list of the universal service obligations contained in section 50(2) ECA is based on Articles 4–7 of the Universal Service Directive.[104] The ECA specifically includes in the scope of universal service obligations the obligation to provide equivalent access to public telephone services for disabled users. Further, the ECA requires that universal service obligations also include the obligation to meet all reasonable requests for one connection to a public network at a fixed location; this connection must be capable of supporting voice, facsimile, and data communications at a transmission rate that is sufficient to permit functional Internet access, taking into account the technical feasibility and prevailing technologies used by the majority of subscribers.[105] The ECA does not specifically include the provision broadband Internet access in the scope of universal service obligations.

Designation of undertakings obliged to provide universal services

28.79   Section 50(3) ECA sets out the procedure for designating universal service providers, and the fundamental principles and methods of such procedure, consistent with Article 8 of the Universal Service Directive.[106] When designating universal service providers, the STO must consider in particular the financial, technical, and professional conditions of the undertaking and the ability of the undertaking to provide the universal service in a cost effective manner and with the required quality.[107]

---

101   See also para 28.64 above.
102   S 73(1)(c) ECA.
103   S 26(1) ECA.
104   See para 1.175 above.
105   S 50(2)(a) ECA.
106   See para 1.178 above.
107   S 50(5) ECA.

28.80 Currently, Slovak Telekom, a.s. is the only operator designated as being required to provide universal services.

Regulation of retail tariffs, users' expenditures and quality of service

28.81 The STO monitors the evolution and level of prices for services falling within the scope of universal services,[108] and is authorised to impose on universal service providers the obligations corresponding to those described in Article 9(2) and (4) of the Universal Service Directive.[109]

28.82 In a decision designating a universal services provider, the STO determines the quality of service parameters and performance targets of the universal service, and methods of their measurement in line with the applicable technical norms; the STO may also determine the form and means of their publishing. The quality of service parameters may include, among other things, the supply time required for an initial connection, fault rate per access line, or fault repair time. Each universal service provider must submit twice a year to the STO the results of the quality of service parameters, and must publish the results on the provider's website.[110]

Cost calculation and financing of universal services

28.83 A universal service provider is entitled to be compensated for the identified net costs of the universal service, if the provision of such service represents an unfair burden on the provider.[111] If necessary, the STO may establish and maintain a special fund ('special account') for the purpose of compensating net costs. Each public network or service provider whose annual revenue share in the domestic market of public networks or services is at least 0.2 per cent, must contribute to such fund.[112]

Regulation of Retail Markets

Prerequisites for the regulation of retail markets

28.84 In accordance with Article 17 of the Universal Service Directive,[113] the STO may take measures with respect to SMP undertakings in a given retail market if the STO discovers, based on its relevant market analysis, that a given retail market is not effectively competitive and that the regulatory obligations imposed under sections 19 to 23 ECA are not sufficient for the protection of interests of end users.[114]

Regulatory powers

28.85 Within its retail market regulation powers, the STO may, subject to the above prerequisites, impose on SMP undertakings in particular the obligation not

---

108 S 52(4) ECA.
109 See para 1.180 above.
110 S 51 ECA.
111 S 53(1) ECA.
112 S 54 ECA.
113 See para 1.186 above.
114 S 25(1) ECA.

to give preference to a specific group of end users or not to unreasonably bundle services.[115] The STO may also regulate prices in a manner to prohibit SMP undertakings from charging excessive prices, restricting competition, or inhibiting market entry by setting predatory prices.[116]

End User Rights

Contracts

28.86   Any public service provider must enter into a contract with any person requesting provision of the relevant public service,[117] unless there is a basis for the provider to refuse to enter into the contract.[118]

28.87   A subscriber may withdraw without penalty from a contract for the provision of public services if the subscriber does not accept material amendments to the contractual terms and conditions, or if the undertaking, after repeated complaint by the subscriber, does not provide the service according to the contract, does not provide the service in the agreed quality, or does not duly and timely inform the subscriber of the results of examination of the subscriber's complaint.[119]

Transparency obligations

28.88   The STO has determined, in General Authorisation No 1/2011, the scope of information which a public network or service provider must publish in a comprehensible and easily accessible form.[120] The information must be transparent, comparable, adequate, and current.[121]

Quality of service: securing 'net neutrality'

28.89   While the ECA does not specifically address 'net neutrality', the concept is being promoted indirectly through other factors, such as the ability of users to easily switch providers.

European emergency call number

28.90   Under section 41(1)(a) ECA, undertakings providing a public service for establishing domestic calls through a number, or numbers, within the national numbering plan must enable end users, including users of public pay telephones,

---

115   S 25(1) ECA.
116   S 25(2) ECA.
117   S 43(2)(a) ECA.
118   The provider may refuse to enter into a contract on provision of public services only if provision of the requested service is not technically feasible (but this is not applicable to services falling within the universal service or in situations where the provision of public services would be associated with excessive costs), or there is no guarantee that the applicant will comply with the contract, or the applicant does not agree with the terms and conditions of the contract; cf s 43(1)(c) ECA.
119   S 44(6) ECA.
120   Art 4(2) General Authorisation No 1/2011.
121   S 42(2) ECA.

free access to emergency services using the single European emergency call number '112' and other national emergency call numbers.

Other obligations

28.91 An undertaking providing a public telephone service must handle all calls to and from the European telephone numbering system at prices similar to those charged by the undertaking for calls to or from other EU/EEA Member States.[122]

OBLIGATIONS FACILITATING CHANGE OF PROVIDER

28.92 Section 48(4) ECA mandates number portability within one working day. Further details are regulated in STO's Measure No O-22/2011 on details relating to transfer of numbers.

DATA PROTECTION: THE DIRECTIVE ON PRIVACY AND ELECTRONIC COMMUNICATIONS

Confidentiality of Communications

28.93 The ECA recognises a special category of protected data covered by 'telecommunications secrecy'. The telecommunications secrecy encompasses the content of conveyed messages, the related data of the communicating parties, traffic data, and location data.[123]

28.94 Anyone who comes into contact with any information subject to telecommunications secrecy, even if incidentally, must keep it confidential.[124] Information which is subject to telecommunications secrecy may be disclosed only to the STO, the subscriber or user concerned (or the subscriber or user's authorised representatives or legal successors), and to certain categories of public authorities (such as Slovak police authorities).[125]

28.95 Undertakings providing public networks or public services must take appropriate technical and organisational measures to safeguard the security of their networks and services.[126] In case of a particular risk of a breach of network security, the provider of public services must inform the subscribers concerned of such a risk and possible remedies, including cost implications.[127]

28.96 Anyone who wishes to store information on the terminal equipment of a user, or gain access to such information, may do so only if the user concerned has given his or her consent on the basis of clear and complete information about the purpose of the information's processing; for these purposes, using the appropriate settings of the web browser or another computer program will be regarded as consent.

28.97 This obligation will not prevent technical storage of data or access to them, the sole purpose of which is the transmission or facilitation of transmission of a

---

122 S 41(2) ECA.
123 S 63(1) ECA.
124 S 63(2) ECA.
125 S 63(3) ECA.
126 S 64(1) ECA.
127 S 64(5) ECA.

message over a network, or if it is unconditionally necessary in order for the provider of information society services to provide an information society service which is explicitly requested by the user.[128]

The obligation to obtain consent does not apply to police authorities, public prosecutors, or other state authoritics.

Data Retention

28.98   Section 58 ECA fully transposes the Data Retention Directive. This section sets out the scope of data retention and the applicable retention periods. With respect to access to the Internet, Internet e-mail and Internet telephony, the retention period is six months, whereas it is 12 months with respect to other types of communication.

Traffic Data and Location Data

28.99   The ECA defines the term 'traffic data'[129] as data related to a user and to a particular transmission of information in a network, originating upon the transmission and processed for the purposes of the conveyance of a communication (message) in a network or for billing purposes. The ECA defines the term 'location data'[130] consistent with the E-Privacy Directive.

28.100   Traffic data relating to a subscriber or user may not be stored without the consent of the subscriber or user. An undertaking must erase such data, or make the data anonymous immediately after termination of the transmission of a communication (message), unless the ECA provides otherwise.[131]

28.101   An undertaking may process location data other than traffic data relating to a subscriber or a user of a public network or public service only if the data are made anonymous or the subscriber or user has provided consent to the extent, and for the duration, necessary for the provision of a value added service. The subscriber or user may withdraw the consent at any time.[132]

Itemised Billing

28.102   Under Article IV(2)(6) General Authorisation No 1/2011, an undertaking providing a public network or public service must, for services other than pre-paid services, provide, free of charge, a basic level of itemised invoices.

Presentation and Restriction of Calling and Connected Line Identification

28.103   Undertakings offering a calling line identification presentation service must offer the calling party the possibility, to easily, and free of charge, to prevent

---

128   S 55(5) ECA.
129   S 57(1) ECA.
130   S 57(2) ECA.
131   S 57(4) ECA.
132   S 57(2) ECA.

the calling line identification on a per-call or per-line basis.[133] Undertakings offering a connected line identification presentation service must offer the called party the possibility, easily, and free of charge, to prevent the connected line identification to the calling party.[134] Undertakings providing a public network or service may temporarily suspend the presentation of the calling line identification upon application of a subscriber (if technically possible) to trace malicious or threatening calls, and for emergency calls.[135]

Automatic Call Forwarding

28.104   Under section 61 ECA, every subscriber must have the option to easily, and free of charge, stop automatic call forwarding initiated by a third party to the subscriber's terminal.

Directories of Subscribers

28.105   A subscriber who is a natural person has the right to determine whether his or her personal data will be included in a directory of subscribers, and if so, which personal data will be included in the directory, if they are relevant for the purposes of the directory.

A subscriber must not be charged for a request that his or her personal data not be included in the directory, or for a request for verification, correction, or withdrawal of the subscriber's personal data.[136] An undertaking must not publish the subscriber's personal data in its directory of subscribers unless the subscriber has given his or her consent, and must not provide the data to other undertakings, other persons that publish directories of subscribers, or providers of telephone number information services.[137]

---

133   S 60(1)(a) ECA.
134   S 60(1)(d) ECA.
135   S 60(3) ECA.
136   S 59(2) ECA.
137   S 59(3) ECA.

The Slovenian Market for Electronic Communications[1]

Jure Levovnik and Mitja Podpečan
Jadek & Pensa, Ljubljana

LEGAL STRUCTURE

Basic Policy

29.1   Slovenian electronic communications regulation is generally based on the recently adopted Electronic Communications Act ('ZEKom-1').[2] ZEKom-1 encompasses most of the relevant issues dealt with by the relevant EU Directives and forms the basis for a quite extensive executive regulation that regulates certain issues individually and in more detail. Certain specific aspects of electronic communications are dealt with by other laws (such as the Digital Broadcasting Act and the Media Act).

29.2   In terms of objectives to be pursued by the NRA, as well as the secondary objectives and the measures for achieving them, the ZEKom-1 is harmonised with the Framework Directive.[3] In addition, the ZEKom-1 also obliges the NRA to contribute within its competencies to the realisation of policies aimed at the promotion of cultural and linguistic diversity, as well as media pluralism.[4] Since implementation of the 2002 Regulatory Package, the main challenges in the Slovenian market were related to fostering of effective competition and to ensuring appropriate independence of the NRA.

29.3   As at 30 September 2012, 150 electronic communications operators were registered in Slovenia, where the market shares are still relatively concentrated with the incumbent operator (Telekom Slovenije d.d.). Traditional fixed telephony is being replaced by the rapidly developing IP telephony. Telekom Slovenije d.d. still holds a 68 per cent market share in fixed telephony, but its share is constantly decreasing. In mobile telephony, there is some more competition (although Telekom Slovenije d.d. still holds a 49.9 per cent market share which is decreasing); however, the level of penetration of active users in the population has already reached 106.9 per cent. As to fixed broadband internet access, the level of penetration based on population has reached 24.8 per cent. Broadband access at a fixed location is still most commonly provided through xDSL; however, the use of fibre-optic and

---

1   Editing of this chapter closed on 15 January 2013.
2   Official Gazette of the Republic of Slovenia ('OG RS'), no 109/2012, 31 December 2012.
3   Cf Art 8 of the Framework Directive.
4   Art 194(3) ZEKom-1.

wireless technologies (especially mobile ones) are increasingly gaining in popularity. There is also an increased growth in IP TV connections.[5]

Implementation of EU Directives

29.4   ZEKom-1 was enacted primarily with the purpose of implementing those parts of the 2009 Regulatory Package which had not already been implemented with the amendments to its predecessor ZEKom. In general, the ZEKom-1 transposed the 2009 Regulatory Package very consistently. The legislator aimed at transposing the relevant EU Directives into one single act, whereby it partially kept the solutions of its predecessor and at the same time improved the specific national provisions. Only certain specific provisions of the 2009 Regulatory Package have been transposed with the amendments of other acts, such as the Digital Broadcasting Act and the Media Act.

Legislation

29.5   The ZEKom-1 entered into force on 15 January 2013, replacing ZEKom which was adopted in 2004 and subsequently amended several times. Detailed regulation of certain issues is a matter of executive regulation (government regulations and ministers' rules) as well as of general acts of the NRA. The regulation of electronic communications is technology neutral, whereby such neutrality is expressly set as a principle in relation to radio spectrum and measures adopted by the NRA.[6]

29.6   So far, the legislation has managed to enhance competition on the telecommunications market only to a limited extent. Decisions of the NRA (in particular those related to ex ante regulation) have played quite an important role in providing a competitive environment. Nevertheless, Telekom Slovenije d.d. managed to maintain significant advantage in terms of market share in most of the relevant markets, although its market shares are gradually decreasing. In addition, Telekom Slovenije d.d. has been subject to several administrative and court proceedings due to alleged abuses of its dominant position.

REGULATORY PRINCIPLES: THE FRAMEWORK DIRECTIVE

Scope of Regulation

29.7   The ZEKom-1 follows the European model of creating a single legal framework for all transmission networks and electronic communications services provided over those networks and, in that respect, uses the neutral term 'electronic communications'.

The definitions of 'electronic communications network', 'electronic communications service' and 'associated facilities'[7] are identical to those in the Framework Directive. VoIP services are not specifically regulated and are subject to the general

---

5   *APEK*: Report on the Development of Electronic Communications Market for Q3/2012, December 2012, available at: http://www.apek.si

6   Arts 28 and 194(2) ZEKom-1.

7   Art 3(4), (5) and (6) ZEKom-1.

rules applicable to electronic communications services. There is also no specific regulation of complex services, including features of electronic communications services as well as content services.

Internet Freedom

29.8   Based on Article 1(3a) of the Framework Directive, ZEKom-1 introduced a new, relatively rigorous provision on Internet freedom.[8] An individual end user's access to, or use of, services and applications through electronic communications networks can be suppressed or restricted only by the courts in a specific criminal procedure and in accordance with a criminal procedure act, taking into account the principle of proportionality. In principle, reference to the criminal procedure act provides for adequate procedural safeguards set out in the Framework Directive, including the right to be heard and the presumption of innocence. No restrictions can be imposed on an end user whose acts or omissions do not constitute a criminal act.

National Regulatory Authorities: Organisation, Regulatory Objectives, Competencies

29.9   The only NRA in the field of electronic communications in Slovenia is the Communications Networks and Services Agency of the Republic of Slovenia ('AKOMOS'), which is an autonomous legal entity under public law. The NRA is competent to supervise a predominant part of the ZEKom-1 and the corresponding executive regulation, except for certain provisions related to processing of personal data, protection of privacy and data storage, which fall within the competencies of the Information Commissioner.[9] Regulatory objectives for the NRA correspond to the objectives set out in Article 8 of the Framework Directive. Its powers and duties are consistent with the EU Regulatory Framework.

29.10   Whenever other state bodies are also competent for specific areas for which the NRA is competent pursuant to the ZEKom-1, the NRA and such other body shall be obliged to cooperate and consult.[10] The ZEKom-1 establishes specific rules for cooperation between the NRA and the competition authority. They shall provide each other with data and information necessary for the performance of their activities and cooperate in analysing relevant markets and determining SMP, without interference with the NRA's exclusive competence for making decisions in the field of electronic communications.[11]

29.11   ZEKom-1 requires that the NRA be independent and that it performs its duties impartially, transparently and in a timely manner.[12] In general, the provisions aimed at securing NRA's independence fulfil the requirements set out in the Framework Directive.[13]

---

8   Art 140 ZEKom-1.
9   Art 221(1) ZEKom-1.
10   Art 213 ZEKom-1.
11   Art 214 ZEKom-1.
12   Arts 170(2), 171(2) and 217(4) ZEKom-1.
13   Arts 217(4) and 88(1) ZEKom-1.

The lawfulness of the NRA's work is subject to supervision by the ministry competent for individual area of NRA's activity.[14] Such supervision is not mandated by the Slovenian constitution. It does not, however, allow the ministry to interfere with the substance of general or individual legal acts issued by the NRA.

29.12   The NRA has the powers to demand from all persons providing electronic communications networks and services all data, information and documentation it requires for the performance of its tasks.[15] The provisions of ZEKom-1 are in line with Article 5(1) of the Framework Directive.

29.13   The work of the NRA is public. With regard to the provision and publication of information, the ZEKom-1 does not depart from the Framework Directive.

29.14   Public consultation by the NRA and other state bodies is required both before adoption of measures which will significantly affect the electronic communications market as well as in the process of adoption of legislation.[16] The ZEKom-1 does not specify who is to be included among the 'interested public' that may cooperate in the consultation procedure.

29.15   It is explicitly required from the NRA that it take into account recommendations of the Commission and to support and take utmost account of opinions and common positions adopted by BEREC.[17] Several detailed provisions are set out in relation to the cooperation with other regulatory authorities, BEREC and the Commission,[18] as well as with other state bodies and public sector organisations, competition authority, the Information Commissioner and bodies competent for the security and integrity of networks.[19]

29.16   The NRA also has dispute resolution powers, which extend not only to disputes between undertakings providing electronic communications networks or services but also to disputes between such undertakings and consumers.[20] The NRA first attempts to resolve the dispute through a mediation procedure, which is confidential. If any of the parties opposes mediation or the dispute is not resolved through mediation and no court proceedings have been initiated, the NRA issues a binding decision.

The ZEKom-1 also establishes rules for the resolution of cross-border disputes.[21] These rules are in conformity with the Framework Directive.

Right of Appeal against NRA's Decisions

29.17   There is no right to an administrative appeal against the decisions and other individual acts of the NRA, which is why the decisions immediately become final in the administrative procedure. Every decision or other individual act of the NRA issued in administrative procedure may, however, be challenged by filing those

---

14   Art 190(5) ZEKom-1.
15   Art 201 ZEKom-1.
16   Art 204 ZEKom-1.
17   Arts 207 and 208 ZEKom-1.
18   Arts 207–212 ZEKom-1.
19   Arts 213–216 ZEKom-1.
20   Art 217 ZEKom-1.
21   Art 219 ZEKom-1; cf Art 21 of the Framework Directive.

extraordinary legal remedies available under the Administrative Procedure Act for which the NRA itself is competent.[22]

The ZEKom-1 also provides for judicial protection against any final decision or individual act of the NRA.[23] An action may be brought before the Administrative Court in Ljubljana. In spite of the fact that the court procedures shall be speedy and dealt with preferentially, which applies also to the appellate court,[24] this type of judicial protection is not always efficient.

According to the NRA, no interim injunctions or similar preliminary measures have been issued yet by the courts in the proceedings against acts issued by the NRA.

29.18   As the ZEKom-1 does not specify the natural or legal persons who are entitled to file an action before the Administrative Court, the general rules of the Administrative Disputes Act[25] shall apply, according to which an action can be brought only by persons who were either parties or side participants in the proceedings before the NRA.

The NRA's Obligations to Cooperate with the Commission

29.19   The ZEKom-1 has consistently implemented the provisions of the Framework Directive concerning the consolidation procedure.[26] However, the obligation of the NRA to suspend the adoption of the draft measure for a further two months (Article 7(4) of the Framework Directive) is broader than required by the Framework Directive as it is not limited only to measures listed in Article 7(4) of the Framework Directive, but extends to any measures related to market definition and market analysis.

29.20   The provisions of the Framework Directive concerning the co-regulation procedure[27] have also been transposed. The only deviation is that the ZEKom-1 does not explicitly require the NRA to take due account of the views of market participants as provided in Article 7a(2) of the Framework Directive.

29.21   The ZEKom-1 consistently transposes Article 17 of the Framework Directive (Standardisation) as well.[28]

---

22   Arts 191(3) and 191(4) ZEKom-1.
23   Art 192 ZEKom-1. Individual acts of the NRA are not only decisions, but also e g resolutions adopted in individual cases.
24   Art 192(3) ZEKom-1.
25   OG RS, no 105/2006 with subsequent amendments.
26   Cf Art 7 of the Framework Directive and arts 209–210 ZEKom-1.
27   Cf Art 7a of the Framework Directive and art 211 ZEKom-1.
28   Art 202 ZEKom-1.

'Significant Market Power' as a Fundamental Prerequisite of Regulation

Definition of SMP

29.22   The definition of significant market power ('SMP') in the ZEKom-1 fully corresponds to the definition of SMP from the Framework Directive.[29] ZEKom-1 emphasises that two or more operators, operating in a market whose structure is considered to be conducive to coordinated effects, may be treated as operators in a joint dominant position even in the absence of structural or other links between them. Article 14(3) of the Framework Directive has also been implemented in order to facilitate regulation of vertically integrated operators operating in closely related markets.

The criteria, which must, among others, be taken into account when assessing SMP, are in accordance with the Commission Guidelines on market analysis.[30] The ZEKom-1 also explicitly obliges the NRA to act in accordance with EU legislation and to consistently take into account the Commission Guidelines on market analysis when assessing SMP and using the above-mentioned criteria. In so doing, the NRA shall cooperate with the competition authority.[31]

In practice, the NRA has been consistently taking into account these criteria when assessing SMP. It has, however, not yet identified any collective dominance or designated any operator having SMP on a specific market (first market) and as having SMP on a closely related market (second market).

Definition of relevant markets

29.23   Before the ZEKom-1 entered into force, relevant markets were determined by the NRA in the General Act on Determination of Relevant Markets, which in principle took into account the Commission Recommendation on relevant markets, but with some specifics, namely, that the NRA has to a certain extent deviated from the Commission Recommendation by determining seven additional markets which remained subject to ex ante regulation. No sub-national markets have been determined by the NRA.

The ZEKom-1, repealing the General Act on Determination of Relevant Markets, now requires the NRA to determine relevant markets, appropriate to national circumstances, in the analysis of individual relevant markets, and not by adopting a general act.

29.24   Market analysis procedures following the determination of relevant markets must be carried out in cooperation with the national competition authority, taking into account the Commission Guidelines on market analysis.[32] Requirements regarding the frequency of analyses are in line with Article 16(6) of the Framework Directive.

---

29   Cf art 95 ZEKom-1 and Art 14 of the Framework Directive.
30   See arts 96 and 97 ZEKom-1. See also para 1.71 above.
31   Art 98 ZEKom-1.
32   See art 100 ZEKom-1.

Imposition of remedies

29.25   In accordance with the Framework Directive, the NRA does not have any discretion in imposing regulatory obligations upon operators with SMP where it concludes that a certain market either is, or is not, effectively competitive.[33] In other words, the NRA must impose at least one regulatory obligation on an undertaking identified as having SMP. In certain cases, the NRA is allowed to impose certain regulatory obligations (related to access, interconnection and mutual functioning of services) also on undertakings not identified as having SMP, in particular where such undertakings control access to end users and intervention of the NRA is required to ensure end-to-end connectivity.[34]

NRA's Regulatory Duties concerning Rights of Way, Co-location and Facility Sharing

Rights of way

29.26   The ZEKom-1 regulates in detail the rights to install facilities on, over or under public or private property.[35] Such rights encompass both expropriation (in case of private property) and servitudes.

It is underlined that the construction, installation, operation and maintenance of public communications networks and associated infrastructure in accordance with regulations are in the public interest. The same applies to communications networks and associated infrastructure for the purposes of security, police, defence and protection, rescue and assistance and to other communications networks and associated infrastructure if located on real estate owned by bodies governed by public law. Not only operators of PECNs but also operators of ECNs may appear as expropriation or servitude beneficiaries.

29.27   Rights of way shall be granted under the procedure and in the manner set out by the Spatial Planning Act[36] and by the Law of Property Code,[37] unless provided otherwise in the ZEKom-1. The competence for granting rights of way lies with administrative units[38] which shall act pursuant to the rules of administrative procedure. The matters concerning rights of way shall be treated as 'urgent' within the meaning of article 104 Spatial Planning Act, unless the competent administrative unit decides otherwise (such decision shall be reasoned and justified).

In order to establish a servitude, the interested operator must submit to the owner a proposal of a contract, which shall contain certain mandatory provisions (a provision on the permissibility of shared use of facilities of the interested operator by third persons and a provision on monetary compensation).[39] A copy of the

---

33   Cf art 101(1),(2) and (5) ZEKom-1 and art 16(3) and (4) of the Framework Directive.
34   Art 90(4) ZEKom-1.
35   Arts 16–23 ZEKom-1.
36   OG RS, no 110/2002 with subsequent amendments.
37   OG RS, no 87/2002.
38   Administrative units are administrative bodies that perform tasks of the state administration on designated territories within the state.
39   An exception to this rule applies to cases where servitudes are established on public service infrastructure. In such cases, the operator of such infrastructure prepares the proposal for a contract reflecting eventual specific obligations set out in the legislation governing the respective public service infrastructure. An additional exception is that servitudes related to

contract shall be submitted to the NRA, which supervises whether the contract contains all mandatory elements, but has no powers to interfere with the content of the contract.

If the owner fails to agree within 10 days of receipt of the proposed contract, the operator may propose that the competent administrative unit decides on the establishment of a servitude. The parties may appeal against such decision to the competent ministry. After the decision becomes final, no further agreements are required. A copy of the decision shall be submitted to the NRA.

29.28   A servitude encompasses several entitlements,[40] such as construction, installation, operation and maintenance of ECN and associated infrastructure, access to the ECN and associated infrastructure for purposes of operation and maintenance, and removal of natural obstacles during construction, installation, operation and maintenance of the ECN. The servitude may last as long as the ECN and associated infrastructure are operated (this is an exception to the general rule of the Law of Property Code according to which servitudes shall not last more than 30 years).

29.29   An operator intending to construct PECN and associated infrastructure may under certain conditions request that other existing installations are replaced or modified. Costs of such replacement or modification shall be borne by the operator.[41]

Co-location and facility sharing

29.30   The ZEKom-1 encourages co-location and facility sharing in the same manner as mandated by the Framework Directive.[42] The provisions of the ZEKom-1 are designed so as to promote investment into next generation networks.

The NRA has the power to impose the sharing of facilities or property.[43] Where appropriate, it can also impose such obligations ex officio, subject to prior public consultation and consolidation procedures. Where the parties concerned fail to reach an agreement, it can also impose such obligations in favour of persons deprived of access to useful alternatives in order to protect the environment, public health, public security or to meet spatial planning objectives.[44] The powers of the NRA with regard to the sharing of wiring inside buildings are in line with Article 12(3) of the Framework Directive.[45]

Investors or owners of other types of public service infrastructure are obliged to provide to operators and interested state bodies, at cost-oriented prices, shared use of the free facilities of such infrastructure (eg empty ducts, unused optical fibres). In the absence of a voluntary agreement, the NRA may intervene at the request of the interested party.

---

the construction of PECNs on real estate owned by the state or local communities which are financed from public sources shall be granted free of charge (this does not apply to servitudes on highways for which specific rules apply under the Motorway Company of the Republic of Slovenia Act).
40   See art 19 ZEKom-1.
41   Art 12 ZEKom-1.
42   Arts 91–94 ZEKom-1.
43   Cf Art 12 of the Framework Directive and art 91 ZEKom-1.
44   Cf Art 12(2) of the Framework Directive.
45   Art 92 ZEKom-1.

Certain obligations related to co-location and facility sharing are included in other provisions of the ZEKom-1 as well. Such obligations relate to construction of ECNs so as to enable facility sharing (including mandatory installation of an access point) and joint construction.[46]

ZEKom-1 requires owners of ECNs and associated infrastructure to provide the surveying and mapping authority with certain information, including the type, location and availability of networks and objects, so that such information can be entered into the register of property of communications networks and associated infrastructure.[47]

REGULATION OF MARKET ENTRY: THE AUTHORISATION DIRECTIVE

The General Authorisation of Electronic Communications

29.31   Generally, no authorisation is required for the provision of electronic communications networks or services. However, a written notification containing certain operator information is required prior to the commencement of services.[48] Additional authorisation is required for the use of radio spectrum and numbers.

Within seven days of the receipt of a complete notification, the NRA shall record the operator in the official records and send the operator a confirmation. Recording in official records does not form a condition for the exercise of operator's rights and obligations under the ZEKom-1. The confirmation is not an administrative act and does not in itself create rights and obligations under the ZEKom-1.

Notification grants the operator the right to negotiate with other operators for network interconnection and, if appropriate, to obtain operator access, interconnection or a possibility to be designated as the universal service provider.[49]

Rights of Use for Radio Frequencies

Strategic planning and co-ordination of spectrum policy

29.32   Based on the strategic objectives and documents of the Republic of Slovenia and the EU, the international obligations of the Republic of Slovenia and the co-operation with the European Commission and NRAs of other Member States, the NRA shall prepare foundations for adoption of the government regulation on the national radio frequency allocation plan.[50] Based on this regulation, the NRA shall adopt a general act on a plan of radio frequencies usage.[51] Despite the established principles of technology and service neutrality, the general act may limit the use of certain technologies for the reasons of public health, interference prevention, service quality assurance, safeguarding of efficient use of spectrum and other public interests.[52]

---

46   Arts 9(5) and(6) and 10 ZEKom-1.
47   Art 14 ZEKom-1.
48   Art 5 ZEKom-1.
49   Arts 90 and 117 ZEKom-1.
50   Arts 24(3), 25 and 26 ZEKom-1.
51   Art 27 ZEKom-1.
52   For details see arts 28(2) and 29(2) ZEKom-1 and the General act on a plan of radio frequencies usage (OG RS, no 66/2012 and 68/2012) – changes anticipated.

Principles of frequency allocation, procedural rules

29.33   Notwithstanding the principle of general authorisation, the use of radio frequencies is for the reasons provided in the Authorisation Directive subject to the granting of individual rights by the NRA.[53] The NRA shall issue a decision in accordance with the General act on a plan of radio frequency usage, which applies the principles of technology and service neutrality with some limitations.[54]

In order to initiate the procedure, the interested person needs to file an application with the NRA.[55] The NRA shall assign frequencies for broadcasting and public communication services for end users after carrying out a public tender procedure, except in the case of temporary assignment of frequencies for testing purposes and events, for administration of networks which were built with public funds, or when so envisaged by law for the purposes of public interest, or by international treaties or EU legislation.[56] In other cases, the NRA must examine the interest for the frequencies, and in the case of excess interest carry out a public tender procedure.[57] In case of changes to the General act on a plan of radio frequency usage or in order to safeguard efficient use of spectrum, prevent interruption, fulfil obligations of the Republic of Slovenia under international treaties or within EU, meet public demand or for other reasons provided by law, the NRA may ex officio change any previously issued authorisation (decision).[58]

An authorisation is not required when so envisaged by the general act for the purposes of national security, national defence or protection against natural and other disasters.[59] The same applies to frequencies, which are by the General act envisaged for use by authorised radio amateurs.[60]

Transferability and time limitations

29.34   The right to frequency use, which was obtained for a consideration, may be the subject of a transfer or lease, insofar as the acquirer is qualified pursuant to the ZEKom-1 and the trading does not distort competition.[61] The transfer or lease requires approval and authorisation (decision) of the NRA.

The individual right to frequency use is granted for limited period of time, taking into account the appropriate period for investment amortisation, but for not more than 15 years with a possible extension of this period, except regarding public communication services for end users.[62] No time limitations apply to aeronautical and maritime mobile services and different time limitations apply to frequency use for testing purposes and events.

---

53   Art 31 ZEKom-1; see also para 1.109 above.
54   See para 29.32 above.
55   Art 33 ZEKom-1.
56   Arts 33(3)–(6) ZEKom-1. The exemption from the requirement also applies to assignment of respective radio frequencies to certain natural or legal persons, who were granted the right to use in accordance with the international treaties and EU legislation as provided in art 34 ZEKom-1.
57   Art 33(2) ZEKom-1; see also para 29.36 below.
58   Art 57 ZEKom-1.
59   Art 31(2) ZEKom-1.
60   Art 32 ZEKom-1. Foreign radio amateurs with CEPT authorisation may use radio frequencies allocated by rules on radio frequencies that may be used without a decision on the assignment of radio frequencies (OG RS, no 45/2005, 37/2006, 13/2008 and 27/2010) – changes anticipated.
61   Art 55 ZEKom-1.
62   Arts 53 and 54 ZEKom-1.

Admissible conditions

29.35   The decision of the NRA shall, inter alia, determine the conditions that must be fulfilled during the use of the radio frequencies.[63] The set of possible conditions that may be imposed is in complete accordance with Part B of the Annex to the Authorisation Directive and is for respective frequencies not predetermined by national legislation.

Limitation of number of rights of use to be granted

29.36   In cases where a person applies for radio frequencies for broadcasting or public communication services for end users and where it is established that effective use of a certain frequency might be secured only by limiting the number of rights, the NRA shall assign the frequencies based on a public tender.[64]

If the NRA considers that the interest in a particular radio frequency could exceed the availability and thereby prevent the efficient use thereof, it shall publish a public call to acquire the opinions of interested parties regarding the conditions of use of such radio frequencies, particularly regarding the limitation of the number of rights. In cases where the NRA, on the basis of a public consultation, establishes excess interest in certain frequencies, it shall carry out a public tender procedure.[65] If the sole criterion for the selection in the public tender is the bid price, the NRA shall additionally carry out a public auction before granting the right to frequency use.[66] The NRA shall publish a public call for a spectrum auction providing conditions for the auction, including but not limited to deadlines, conditions for success of the auction and detailed auction rules. The President of the Commission, appointed by the NRA for the public tender, shall carry out the spectrum auction orally at the NRA, through writing, certified electronic applications, or in any other appropriate manner. Spectrum auctions are a novelty, first introduced by ZEKom-1.

Rights of Use for Numbers

General authorisations and granting of individual rights

29.37   All numbers to be used as a part of a public communications networks are managed by the NRA, which shall adopt a general act on the numbering plan. Assignment of 'golden' numbers is not regulated.

Numbers are assigned on the basis of a general act by decisions of the NRA in a regular administrative procedure. Only operators (ie persons under general authorisation) and natural or legal persons, who demonstrate the need for numbers in connection with their business, which is pursuant to local laws and EU legislation on public interest, are entitled to apply for numbers. Before granting the right to numbers use, the NRA shall establish if limiting the number of rights is required.[67]

---

63   Art 52 ZEKom-1; see also para 1.112 above.
64   Arts 33(2), (3) and 36 ZEKom-1.
65   The procedure is regulated in detail in arts 37–43 ZEKom-1.
66   For detail see arts 44 and 45 ZEKom-1.
67   See para 29.41 below.

In case limiting is required, the NRA shall carry out a public tender procedure.[68] Only operators, which will distribute the numbers to their users in a non-discriminatory, transparent and cost-based manner, and other natural or legal persons who are entitled to apply for numbers, can take part in the public tender.

The holder of the right to numbers use is indefinitely entitled to assign numbers to end users or service providers and to transfer such a right to another person who is qualified pursuant to the ZEKom-1.[69] The transfer requires approval and authorisation (decision) of the NRA.

Admissible conditions

29.38 The conditions that may be attached to rights of use for numbers correspond to those listed in Part C of the Annex to the Authorisation Directive.[70]

29.39 All operators of publicly accessible telephone services (including mobile operators) must ensure number portability of geographic numbers at a precisely defined location and of non-geographic numbers at any location. This applies also to number transfers from PSTN to VoIP. Number portability between fixed and mobile networks is prohibited. Reasonable costs may be charged for number transfers.[71] An individual decision of the NRA on assigning numbers to the operators may, however, contain additional conditions regarding number portability.[72]

29.40 All operators of public communications networks and providers of publicly available electronic communications services are by law obliged to enable end users to dial any numbers.[73] NRA may only impose specific carrier pre-selection/indirect access obligations to operators with SMP.[74]

Limitation of number of rights of use to be granted

29.41 The number of rights to number use shall be limited if required in order to ensure efficient use of certain numbers. The NRA can limit the number of rights using mutatis mutandis the same principles and comparative and competitive selection procedures, which apply for radio frequencies.[75]

The NRA's Enforcement Powers

29.42 If the NRA establishes an infringement of the ZEKom-1, directly effective EU legislation, the implementation of individual acts and/or measures adopted within the framework of the authorisations it has adopted under the ZEKom-1 and the regulations pursuant thereto, it must notify the operator and request that it provides a statement within reasonable time. After receipt of the statement or after

---

68   Art 65(3) ZEKom-1.
69   Art 70 ZEKom-1.
70   See para 1.117 above.
71   Art 131 ZEKom-1.
72   Art 68 ZEKom-1.
73   Art 76(1) ZEKom-1.
74   Cf arts 101 and 105 ZEKom-1.
75   See para 29.36 above.

the deadline, the NRA may request that the infringement is stopped immediately or in reasonable time and may order proportionate and appropriate measures to stop the infringement.[76] In case of serious and repeated infringements, the NRA may prevent the operator from further provision of networks or services and may suspend for up to three months or withdraw its right to frequency or numbers use if ordered measures are not carried out or are not carried out in a timely manner. Also the NRA may initiate misdemeanour proceedings and impose fines or file criminal complaints.[77]

29.43   Urgent interim measures are permissible in case of violations which represent an immediate and serious threat to public order, public safety and human health and life or cause serious economic or operational problems for other providers or users of networks or services or other users of the radio spectrum.[78] Such measures do not require prior notification of the operator or a final decision of the NRA.

29.44   The NRA may, to the extent proportionate to the purpose of use stated in its request, require the operators and other persons to provide data and information needed for enforcement of rules.[79]

Administrative Charges and Fees for Rights of Use

29.45   The general authorisation requires annual payments to the NRA for administrative charges in amounts which shall be determined by the NRA's decision and depend on the annual revenue of the operator.[80] The operator must, by 31 March, inform the NRA of its revenues from providing public communications networks or publicly available communications services in Slovenia in the previous year. If the operator does not comply, the NRA shall calculate the fees from the operator's cumulative revenue of the previous year.

The level of the additional annual fees for individual rights to frequency use depends on the coverage, population density in the area of coverage, radio frequency, width of the radio frequency band, type of radio communications, or a combination thereof. For the right of use of numbers the level of payments depends on the quantity, length and type of numbers.[81]

Except for the use of radio frequencies for analogue broadcasting, the use of radio frequencies that are assigned on the basis of a public tender is subject to an additional amount for effective use, which is determined in the public tender and is an income of the budget of the Republic of Slovenia.[82] The latter also applies to additional amounts for the use of numbers assigned on the basis of a public tender.

Transitional Regulations for Existing Authorisations

29.46   In general, operators granted authorisations or who have made notifications pursuant to the previously valid law (ZEKom) continue to provide networks

---

76   Art 224 ZEKom-1.
77   Art 228 ZEKom-1.
78   Art 224(7) ZEKom-1.
79   For details see art 201 ZEKom-1.
80   Art 7 ZEKom-1.
81   Art 74 ZEKom-1.
82   Art 60 ZEKom-1.

and services pursuant to the ZEKom-1.[83] However, granted authorisations can be the subject of changes, or can be cancelled or terminated when so provided in the ZEKom-1, and also all open procedures shall be completed under the rules provided in the ZEKom-1.[84] Notwithstanding the general time limitations, granted authorisation for public communications services for end users may in certain circumstances be extended until 26 May 2016.[85]

REGULATION OF NETWORK ACCESS AND INTERCONNECTION: THE ACCESS DIRECTIVE

Objectives and Scope of Access Regulation

29.47 The ZEKom-1 very consistently transposed practically every provision of the Access Directive concerning access and interconnection. The objectives of the access and interconnection regulation are in accordance with those set out in the Access Directive.[86]

29.48 In principle, the access- and interconnection-related provisions apply only to operators of PECNs, regardless of whether they have SMP or not, and to undertakings seeking interconnection and/or access to their networks or associated facilities.[87] Such operators have the rights and obligations to negotiate interconnection and to offer access and interconnection in accordance with Article 4(1) of the 'Access Directive.

Basic Regulatory Concepts

29.49 The definitions of access and interconnection[88] are identical to those established by the Access Directive.

29.50 The role of the NRA is to promote and, where appropriate, ensure adequate access and interconnection and the interoperability of services. Obligations that the NRA may impose are in line with those set out in Article 5 of the Access Directive.

Commercial negotiations have priority. Freedom of access is safeguarded by an explicit provision that operators not performing services or operating networks in Slovenia are not obliged to notify the NRA pursuant to article 5 ZEKom-1 in order to have the right to negotiate access and/or interconnection. In the absence of a voluntary agreement between the parties, the NRA may, upon request of one of the parties, regulate technical and commercial issues of interconnection or access by issuing a binding decision.[89] In justified cases (ZEKom-1 sets no criteria to determine what may be considered as a 'justified case'), it may do so also at its own initiative, subject to procedures referred to in Article 5(3) of the Access Directive.

---

83   Art 237 ZEKom-1.
84   Arts 240 and 241 ZEKom-1.
85   For details see art 243 ZEKom-1.
86   Art 90(4) ZEKom-1. See also Art 5(1) of the Access Directive.
87   See para 1.132 above.
88   See art 3(43) and (32) ZEKom-1.
89   Cf Art 3(1) of the Access Directive and art 90(7) ZEKom-1.

Access- and Interconnection-related Obligations with Respect to SMP Undertakings

29.51   With regard to access and interconnection, the ZEKom-1 obliges the NRA to impose on an SMP operator at least one of the following obligations:

- transparency;
- non-discrimination;
- accounting separation; access to, and use of, specific network facilities;
- price controls and
- cost accounting.[90]

It is completely up to the NRA which obligations to impose, subject to the principle of proportionality. Imposition of obligations is subject to a public consultation procedure, consultation with the Slovenian competition authority, and consolidation procedure. For the imposition of functional separation and any other obligations that are not provided for in the ZEKom-1, prior consent of the European Commission is required.

As regards the above-mentioned access- and interconnection-related obligations, as well as functional separation and voluntary separation, the ZEKom-1 in principle follows the provisions of the Access Directive very consistently, with a small exception: with regard to transparency obligations of operators with obligations to offer wholesale network infrastructure access, the ZEKom-1 failed to transpose the Access Directive consistently as it still refers to unbundled access to local loop only, and does not extend to all forms of wholesale network infrastructure access.[91]

29.52   Currently, several relevant markets are subject to ex ante regulation, one of which is a retail market (market 1 – Access to the public telephone network at a fixed location), while the others are wholesale markets: market 2 (Call origination in the public telephone network provided at a fixed location), market 3 (Call termination in individual public telephone networks provided at a fixed location), market 4 (Access to (physical) network infrastructure (including shared or unbundled access) at a fixed location), market 5 (Broadband access), market 6 (Access segments of leased lines, irrespective of the technology used to provide leased or dedicated capacity), market 7 (Voice call termination on individual mobile networks), market 10 (Transit services in the fixed public telephone network). NRA decisions which are currently in force were issued between 8 June 2007 and 19 April 2011. Obligations have been imposed both on fixed and mobile operators. Telekom Slovenije d.d. was designated as having SMP in all of the aforementioned markets. Being the existing owner of access infrastructure and a designated SMP operator in market 4, Telekom Slovenije d.d. is required to unbundle its facilities (including, but not limited to, fibre-optic infrastructure) and provide co-location.

The current ex ante regulation is quite intensive; in practically all of the regulated markets, the NRA used the entire range of regulatory tools available; it imposed obligations on non-discrimination, transparency, access to, and use of, specific network facilities, price controls and accounting separation.[92] The NRA defined in detail terms and conditions on which SMP operators shall perform the obligations imposed. It applied various methods of price control, depending on the market, service and operator(s) concerned (eg LRIC, LRIC+, FAC HCA, FAC CCA, retail

---

90   See arts 102–106 ZEKom-1. Art 107 ZEKom-1 (regulation of retail prices) is the implementation of Art 17 of the Universal Service Directive. See also paras 1.185 et seq above.
91   Art 102(5) ZEKom-1. See also para 1.151 above.
92   Accounting separation obligations were not imposed only with respect to markets 3 and 7.

price minus, price cap). No functional or legal separation has been imposed by the NRA so far.

Regulatory Powers with Respect to SMP Undertakings

29.53 Apart from the powers related to access and interconnection (see above), no further regulatory powers of the NRA are provided in the ZEKom-1 with respect to SMP undertakings on wholesale markets.

29.54 Following the changes introduced by the 2009 Regulatory Package, the ZEKom-1 no longer provides for obligations related to the mandatory provision of leased lines and carrier (pre-)selection which could be imposed separately from access obligations.

Regulatory Powers Applicable to All Market Participants

29.55 The ZEKom-1 also empowers the NRA to impose certain access and interconnection obligations on operators which have not been designated as having SMP.[93]

29.56 As regards digital radio and television broadcasting, the ZEKom-1 is in complete accordance with the Access Directive.[94]

29.57 The provisions of ZEKom-1 regarding the obligations relating to conditional access systems that may be imposed on an operator, regardless of its market power, and obligations concerning owners of industrial property rights, are also in line with the Access Directive and Annex I, Part I thereto.[95]

REGULATION OF UNIVERSAL SERVICE AND USERS' RIGHTS: THE UNIVERSAL SERVICE DIRECTIVE

Regulation of Universal Service Obligations

Scope of universal service obligations

29.58 The designated universal service provider must provide the minimum universal services provided for in the Universal Service Directive.[96] The catalogue includes a requirement for a functional Internet access with minimum transfer speed of 28.8 kbit/s.[97] Measures for disabled end users shall enable them to use all universal services and grant them a supply of appropriate terminal equipment at reasonable prices.[98]

The government may expand the catalogue and require higher quality of universal services if it finds this to be suitable due to the development of electronic

---

93   See Art 90(4) ZEKom-1 and para 29.25 above.
94   Cf art 112 ZEKom-1 and arts 4(2), 5(1) sentence 2(b) of the Access Directive.
95   See art 113 ZEKom-1.
96   Art 115(2) ZEKom-1.
97   General Act on transfer speed suitable for functional Internet access (OG RS 81/2004 and 111/2006) – changes anticipated.
98   Decree on measures for disabled end users (OG RS 92/2010) – changes anticipated.

communications and the existing supply, development strategy of the country and the interests of end users.[99]

Designation of undertakings obliged to provide universal services

29.59   One or more universal service providers are designated in a public tender procedure for five-year period to cover all of the territory of Slovenia. The rules for public tenders regarding radio frequencies apply mutatis mutandis. If the tender procedure is not successful, the operator with SMP in the market of publicly accessible communications services at a fixed location shall be designated; where there is no such operator, the operator having the greatest number of subscribers to publicly available telephone services at a fixed location shall be designated.[100]

In November 2009, the NRA designated Telekom Slovenije d.d. as the universal service provider for the entire Slovenian market.

Regulation of retail tariffs, users' expenditures and quality of service

29.60   The NRA monitors the evolution and level of retail prices of universal services, which must be the same throughout the whole territory, and may require price adjustments regarding affordability and equality, but also price options or bundled services for low income end users or end users with special needs, if the NRA establishes prohibitive prices compared to the average monthly salary and price increases of more than five per cent over the yearly living costs index.[101] The competent ministry shall determine the categories of end users, which are considered to be low-income end users or end users with special needs. The universal service provider shall offer itemised billing, selective call barring, pre-payment systems for the provision of access to the public telephone network, the use of publicly available telephone services, instalment plans for paying subscriptions to the public telephone network, information on other low cost tariffs and other means of expenditure control (eg free warnings).[102] Prices must be set in such a manner that end users are not required to pay for services, which are not necessary or requested.

29.61   Quality standards for universal services are regulated by a General Act of the NRA.[103] Universal service providers are required to publish data on the quality of universal services at least once a year.[104] If the NRA has a reason to doubt the truthfulness of the data published, it may order an independent audit/review of the data at the expense of the universal service provider concerned. If a universal service provider fails to meet the quality requirements for three consecutive times, the NRA may designate a new provider.[105]

---

99   Art 127 ZEKom-1.
100   Art 118 ZEKom-1.
101   Art 120 ZEKom-1.
102   Art 120(7) ZEKom-1.
103   General Act on the quality of universal services (OG RS, no 79/2007 and 40/2010) – changes anticipated; see also art 123 ZEKom-1.
104   Art 17 of the General Act on the quality of universal services – changes anticipated.
105   Art 123(6) ZEKom-1.

Cost calculation and financing of universal services

29.62   Universal service providers shall be entitled to compensation of net costs as defined by the Universal Service Directive.[106] Net costs shall be compensated from the universal service compensation fund set up and managed by the NRA and financed with contributions of operators acting in the territory of Slovenia which generate revenues exceeding €2 million from public communications networks or services,[107] however, the competent ministry shall compensate net costs for additional universal services. The contributions are determined by a decision of the NRA, taking into account the share of respective operators in the total revenues on the market and must be paid to the compensation fund within 30 days.

Regulation of Retail Markets

Prerequisites for the regulation of retail markets

29.63   Regulation of retail services is permissible only if the relevant market is indicated in the respective recommendation or guideline of the European Commission or if, on the basis of market analyses, the NRA determines that a relevant market has high entry barriers, tends towards ineffective competition and that the competition law is not sufficient for an adequate response, and carries out a public consultation and a consultation with other regulatory authorities, the European Commission and BEREC.[108]

Currently, one retail market is subject to ex ante regulation (market 1 – Access to the public telephone network at a fixed location). Telekom Slovenije d.d. was designated as having SMP in this market by a decision of the NRA dated 8 June 2007.

Regulatory powers

29.64   The list of obligations that may be imposed by the NRA with regard to regulation of retail services corresponds to that set out in the Universal Service Directive and is non-exhaustive.[109] Currently, an obligation to provide cost oriented and non-discriminatory inter-operator lines leases, carrier pre-selection/indirect access obligations, retail tariff regulation and restriction of services bundling have been imposed on Telekom Slovenije d.d. by the decision of the NRA dated 8 June 2007.

End User Rights

Contracts

29.65   Operators are required to provide written or electronic contracts to consumers. Upon request, written or electronic contracts must also be provided to

---

106   Cf art 125(1) ZEKom-1 and arts 12 and 13 of the Universal Service Directive; see also paras 1.183 and 1.184 above. General Act on the net cost calculation method for the universal service (OG RS, no 81/2004) – changes anticipated.
107   Arts 26 and 127(5) ZEKom-1.
108   Art 99(2) and (3) ZEKom-1.
109   Cf art 107(2) ZEKom-1 and Art 17(2) of the Universal Service Directive; see also para 1.189 above.

other (eg business) customers. The contract must contain minimum terms as provided in the Universal Service Directive.[110] End users have to be informed at least 30 days in advance of proposed modifications in contractual obligations and can, unless modifications are necessary to comply with ZEKom-1 or regulations adopted thereunder, withdraw from their contract within another 30 days without notice and without penalties and may choose to return the connected terminal equipment and pay proportional usage fee. The contracts concluded between consumers and operators are subject to limitation of initial commitment period as provided in the Universal Service Directive.[111]

Transparency obligations

29.66 Information on tariffs, prices and payments related to the termination of the contract, access conditions and terms of use of PECS must be transparently published in a clear, comprehensive and easily accessible form. The NRA may by a general act determine which information is to be published to ensure appropriate and quality information.[112]

The NRA may require operators of PECS to publish comparable, adequate and up-to-date information on the quality of their services and on measures ensuring equivalence of end users with disabilities.[113] Upon request, operators must submit this information to the NRA before publishing. The NRA may also by a general act regulate specific issues regarding publishing of such information.

Quality of service: securing 'net neutrality'

29.67 The NRA may, by a decision, determine minimum requirements for the quality of service, which the operators must comply with.[114] The decision must consider the principle of 'net neutrality'.[115] The NRA may also adopt recommendations for compensation of users due to inadequate quality of service.

European emergency call number

29.68 Obligations of operators are regulated in accordance with Article 26 of the Universal Service Directive. Operators must inform users of the existence and importance of the European emergency call number.[116] Misuse of emergency numbers is prohibited.

Other obligations

29.69 Operators must adopt measures for enabling uninterrupted use of specific numbers (112, 113 and 116) and operation of critical parts of networks with

---

110   Cf art 129 ZEKom-1 and Art 20 of the Universal Service Directive.
111   Cf art 130 ZEKom-1 and Art 30(5) of the Universal Service Directive.
112   Art 132(2) ZEKom-1.
113   Arts 133(1) and (2) ZEKom-1.
114   Art 133(3) and (4).
115   For details see paras 1.198–1.120 above and art 203 ZEKom-1.
116   Art 134 ZEKom-1.

priority function for the case of emergency and for rescue, security and defence purposes.[117] Operators must also take steps to limit any interruption of services.

End users are additionally entitled to the following:[118]

- the right to connect own equipment;
- the right to be recorded in the universal directory and to access to directory services;
- the right to at least non-itemised billing for publicly accessible telephone services;
- the right to use all services and applications over the electronic communications network; and
- the right of appeal to a department within the operator against its decision or act regarding access to services or performance thereof.

Obligations Facilitating Change of Provider

29.70
In case of change of providers, the operators have obligations as provided in Article 30 of the Universal Service Directive.[119] The NRA may adopt a detailed regulation regarding the change of provider.

DATA PROTECTION: THE DIRECTIVE ON PRIVACY AND ELECTRONIC COMMUNICATIONS

Confidentiality of Communications

29.71   ZEKom-1 fully transposes the E-Privacy Directive.[120] All forms of surveillance or interception of communications is prohibited, with some exceptions (e g in cases provided in Article 5(2) of the E-Privacy Directive, if required for provision of services, based on user consent or court order, for conveyance of a message, for evidence of a commercial transaction, within organisations receiving emergency calls, security authorities and defence organisations).[121] Unsolicited communications and storing of and accessing information in a user's terminal equipment is regulated in accordance with the E-Privacy Directive.[122]

29.72   The providers shall report to the NRA on every breach of confidentiality and may also inform the respective user.[123] In case of a breach, rectification measures can be ordered and fines can be imposed.

---

117   Art 96 ZEKom-1. See also art 97 et seq ZEKom-1.
118   Art 135 et seq ZEKom-1.
119   Art 131 ZEKom-1.
120   Cf arts 145 and 146 ZEKom-1 and Arts 4 and 5 of the E-Privacy Directive.
121   Cf art 147(5), (7) and (9) ZEKom-1 and Art 5(1) and (2) of the E-Privacy Directive
122   Cf arts 157 and 158 ZEKom-1 and Arts 5(3) and 13 of the E-Privacy Directive.
123   Cf art 159 ZEKom-1 and Art 4 of the E-Privacy Directive.

Data Retention

29.73 Data retention regulation is in complete accordance with the Data Retention Directive and has not yet been challenged. Data shall be retained for 14 months.[124]

Traffic Data and Location Data

29.74 Traffic and location data is defined in accordance with the Data Retention Directive.[125] The processing of traffic and location data and consent requirements are regulated as provided for in the E-Privacy Directive.[126]

Itemised Billing

29.75 Providers of publicly available telephone services, except operators with SMP, may provide itemised billing. In the case of operators with SMP, providing itemised billing is obligatory. Higher levels of itemised billing are not required and shall ensure privacy of natural persons.[127]

Presentation and Restriction of Calling and Connected Line Identification

29.76 The obligations of service providers are regulated in complete accordance with the E-Privacy Directive.[128]

Automatic Call Forwarding

29.77 The obligations of service providers are regulated in complete accordance with the E-Privacy Directive.[129]

Directories of Subscribers

29.78 Rights of subscribers with respect to the inclusion of their personal data in directories are regulated in complete accordance with the E-Privacy Directive.[130] These regulations, to the extent that they are not related to personal data, apply also to legal persons. The subscribers also have the right to request to be excluded from calls that have commercial or research purposes.

---

124 Art 163(5) et seq ZEKom-1.
125 Cf arts 162 and 164 ZEKom-1 and Arts 2 and 5 of the Data Retention Directive.
126 Cf arts 151 and 152 ZEKom-1 and Arts 6 and 9 of the E-Privacy Directive.
127 Art 91 ZEKom-1.
128 Cf art 154 ZEKom-1 and Arts 8 and 10 of the E-Privacy Directive.
129 Cf art 156 ZEKom-1 and Art 11 of the E-Privacy Directive.
130 Cf art 150 ZEKom-1 and Art 12 of the E-Privacy Directive.

The Spanish Market For Electronic Communications[1]

Raul Rubio
Baker & McKenzie, Madrid

LEGAL STRUCTURE

Basic Policy

30.1 The economic recession that Spain is suffering has forced the Spanish legislator to focus on issues other than telecommunications, resulting in a delay in meeting the latest European Telecommunications Directives implementation schedule. Spanish legislators initially sought to enact a new General Telecommunications Act, based on the 2009 Telecoms Package, in order to create a more suitable framework for investments, for effective deployment of next-generation networks, and to promote a more efficient use of the radio-electric spectrum. However, the draft of the new Act was replaced with an amendment to the existing General Telecommunications Act, temporarily implementing the Directives. The creation of a new set of policies further developing the new European framework is, therefore, currently pending. In turn, so too is the comprehensive reform of the telecommunications sector, which is an essential component to the progressive growth the sector has been undergoing, even in this uncertain economic environment.

30.2 In the past, the Spanish Telecommunications Market Commission (*Comisión del Mercado de las Telecomunicaciones* ('CMT')) believed that operators based in Spain were better prepared to benefit from the economic tide than the majority of its EU counterparts. Along these lines, the 2002 legislative package was meant to strengthen these objectives while introducing innovative corrective mechanisms, securing:

- the presence and viability of operators;
- the protection of users' rights;
- minimum State intervention in the sector; and
- the Government's supervision of areas related to public services, the public domain, and the safeguarding of competition.

---

1   Editing of this chapter closed on 5 October 2012.

Implementation of EU Directives

30.3   On 4 November 2003 (ie three months later than the deadline imposed by EU law), the Framework, Authorisation, and Universal Service and Access Directives[2] were transposed into Spanish law by the Spanish Congress through the comprehensive Telecommunications Act 32/2003 ('Telecoms Act').[3] The Telecoms Act superseded the General Telecommunications Act of 1998 ('Old Telecoms Act')[4] with the goal of implementing the new regulatory framework for electronic communications networks and services in Spain. In addition, the latest 2009 EU Telecommunications Regulatory Framework consisting of Directives 2009/136/EC[5] and 2009/140/EC[6] was recently implemented in Spain with Royal Decree-Act 13/2012,[7] an urgent legislative measure, adopted to avoid EU sanctions due to the delay in the application in Spain of a series of Directives. The Royal Decree-Act amends, among others, the Telecoms Act and Electronic Commerce Act.

Legislation

30.4   The Telecoms Act was drafted in very broad terms, with specific rights and obligations of operators described in detail in its implementing regulations, with Royal Decree 2296/2004 approving the regulation on electronic communications markets, access to networks and numbering ('Access and Numbering Regulation'),[8] and Royal Decree 424/2005 approving the requirements to provide electronic communications services and universal services and to protect users ('Universal Service and Users Regulation')[9] arguably being the most significant. The latter was recently updated (not altering the majority of its content) to separately regulate the sections regarding users' rights in a more comprehensive fashion. This amendment was applied through the approval of Royal Decree 899/2009[10] ('Bill of Electronic Communications Services Users' Rights Regulations').

30.5   While the Access and Numbering Regulation deals with, inter alia, numbering resources, the assessment of electronic communications markets, the duties of

---

2   The Telecoms Act also transposed the sections of the E-Privacy Directive which were relevant to electronic communications networks and services.

3   Telecommunications Act 32/2003 of 3 November 2003, Spanish Official Journal No 264 of 4 November 2003.

4   Telecommunications Act 11/1998 of 24 April 1998, Spanish Official Journal No 99 of 25 April 1998.

5   Directive 2009/136/EC amends Directive 2002/22/EC on universal service and users' rights relating to electronic communications networks and services, Directive 2002/58/EC concerning the processing of personal data and the protection of privacy in the electronic communications sector, and Regulation (EC) No 2006/2004 on the cooperation between national authorities responsible for the enforcement of consumer protection laws.

6   Directive 2009/140/EC amends Directives 2002/21/EC on a common regulatory framework for electronic communications networks and services, 2002/19/EC on access to, and interconnection of, electronic communications networks and associated facilities, and 2002/20/EC on the authorisation of electronic communications networks and services.

7   Royal Decree-Act 13/2012 of 30 March 2012, Spanish Official Journal No 78 of 31 March 2012.

8   Royal Decree 2296/2004 of 10 December 2004, Spanish Official Journal No 314 of 30 December 2004.

9   Royal Decree 424/2005 of 15 April 2005, Spanish Official Journal No 102 of 29 April 2005.

10   Royal Decree 899/2009, of 22 May 2009, Spanish Official Journal No 131 of 30 May 2009.

operators with significant market power ('SMP'), and the manner in which inter-connection and access to electronic communications public networks may be obtained,[11] the Universal Service and Users Regulation and the Bill of Electronic Communications Services Users' Rights Regulations focus on, among other things, universal service, the protection of personal data, and the rights of end users of electronic communications services.

30.6   In addition to the Telecoms Act and its implementing regulations, the CMT frequently issues instructions, (*resoluciones*) with respect to matters subject to its control,[12] to operators providing electronic communications services. These instructions, which are binding once they have been issued and, if applicable, published in the Spanish Official Journal, are often an excellent source of background regulatory information.

30.7   In addition to the instructions issued in connection with a particular matter, the CMT also issues guidelines of a general nature (*circulares*),[13] which must always be published in the Spanish Official Journal, for the purposes of ensuring the diversity of operators in the market in accordance with article 1(2)(2)(f) Telecommunications Liberalisation Act.[14]

REGULATORY PRINCIPLES: IMPLEMENTATION OF THE FRAMEWORK DIRECTIVE

Scope of regulation

30.8   The purpose of the Telecoms Act is to set up the principles governing the 'telecommunications'[15] business, which consist of operation of networks and the provision of electronic communications services and their associated resources, in accordance with article 149(1)(21) Spanish Constitution.[16]

30.9   The following areas are excluded from the scope of the Telecoms Act and its implementing regulations:

- the regime applicable to broadcasting through electronic communications networks;
- the legal framework governing media;[17] and
- the following activities already regulated under the 2002 Act on Information

---

11   Art 1 Access and Numbering Regulation.
12   See para 30.14 et seq below. CMT instructions may be accessed online at the following website: www.cmt.es/cmt/decisiones/materia.htm
13   The general guidelines issued by the CMT are publicly available at the following website: www.cmt.es/cmt/circulares/index.htm
14   Act 12/1997 of 24 April 1997 on the Liberalisation of Telecommunications, Spanish Official Journal No 99 of 25 April 1997.
15   The term 'telecommunications' is defined in Annex II (Definitions) of the Telecoms Act as 'any transmission, emission or reception of signs, signals, writing, images, sounds or information of any nature by wire, radio electricity, optical media or other electromagnetic systems'.
16   Art 149(1)(21) Spanish Constitution provides that the national administration (as opposed to the 17 regional administrations into which Spain is divided) has exclusive powers over the general regime of communications, post offices and telecommunications, terrestrial and submarine cables and radio spectrum.
17   Art 149(1)(27) Spanish Constitution vests the Central Administration with exclusive faculties in regulating the basic broadcasting framework (ie press, radio and television and, broadly

Society and Electronic Commerce[18] ('Electronic Commerce Act'), provided they do not entail, entirely or primarily, the transmission of signals through electronic communications:

- information services transmitted through electronic communications networks and services;
- the editorial management of such information; and
- any other 'information society service'.[19]

30.10   Pursuant to the Electronic Commerce Act, the term 'information society service' means 'any service normally provided for remuneration, at a distance, by electronic means and at the individual request of a recipient of services'. For the purposes of this definition:[20]

- 'at a distance' means that the service is provided without the parties being simultaneously present;
- 'by electronic means' means that the service is sent initially and received at its destination by means of electronic equipment for the processing (including digital compression) and storage of data, and entirely transmitted, conveyed and received by wire, by radio, by optical means or by other electromagnetic means; and
- 'at the individual request of a recipient of services' means that the service is provided through the transmission of data on individual request.

30.11   The terms 'electronic communications network', 'electronic communications service' and 'associated facilities', which are defined in Annex II of the Telecoms Act, follow verbatim the definitions under Article 2(a), (c) and (e) of the Framework Directive.[21]

'Internet Freedom'

30.12   Spanish law is ruled by freedom of information principles which benefit Internet users and any communications performed through telecommunications operators. In addition, online contents cannot be blocked unless by a Court Decision. On the other hand, no specific regulations have been passed to ensure Internet freedom, although previous bills and proposed amendments to the Telecoms Act expressly included references to secrecy rights on Internet communications.

---

speaking, any broadcasting media having an impact on Spanish society), notwithstanding the implementation and enforcement powers held by the Autonomous Communities.

18   Act 34/2002 of 11 July 2002 on Information Society and Electronic Commerce, Spanish Official Journal No 166 of 12 July 2002.

19   See para 30.10 below.

20   Cf Directive 98/48/EC of the European Parliament and of the Council of 20 July 1998 amending Directive 98/34/EC laying down a procedure for the provision of information in the field of technical standards and regulations, [1998] OJ L217/18.

21   See para 1.48 et seq above.

National Regulatory Authorities: Organisation, Regulatory Objectives, Competencies

Overview

30.13   The Spanish Regulatory Authorities consist of:[22]

- the Government;
- the CMT;
- the Ministry of Industry, Energy and Tourism (*Ministerio de Industria, Energía y Turismo* (the 'Ministry')), and, in particular, its State Secretariat for Telecommunications and Information Society ('SETSI');[23] and
- the Ministry of Economy.

The Government

30.14   The Government[24] is entitled to delegate, at any time, the powers conferred by the Telecoms Act to the Ministry, the CMT, SETSI,[25] the Ministry of Economy, and also to provide them with the assets, personnel, and financial resources necessary or convenient to achieve their objectives. Among the financial resources, the Government is particularly entitled to allocate fees and taxes in accordance with the terms set out in the Telecoms Act.[26]

The CMT

30.15   The CMT[27] is a 'regulatory agency' (*organismo regulador*),[28] as this term is defined in article 8 Act 2/2011 of 4 March 2011 (the 'Sustainable Economy Act').[29] As such, the CMT has legal personality and full public and private capacity to act.

30.16   The purposes of the CMT are threefold:

1.   to establish and supervise the specific obligations with which operators must comply;
2.   to encourage competition in the markets of electronic communications and broadcasting services (in accordance with their specific regulations); and
3.   to settle disputes between operators, or between operators and other entities which benefit from access and interconnection duties, acting as an arbitration body in disputes between them at the request of any of the interested parties or, alternatively, on its own initiative (when this is justified in order to

---

22   Art 46 Telecoms Act.
23   This State Secretariat directly depends on the Ministry of Industry, Energy and Tourism.
24   The Spanish Government website is the following: www.la-moncloa.es/
25   The General Telecommunications Act and its related provisions initially envisaged the creation of a Regulatory body which was intended to manage spectrum in accordance with guidelines set out by the Ministry: the National Radio Communications Agency ('AER'). However, the Government recently abolished this body and assigned its functions to SETSI, through the Final Provision Six of the Royal Decree-Act 13/2012.
26   See para 30.86 et seq below.
27   The CMT provides updated information on the Spanish telecommunications market: http://www.cmt.es/
28   Art 48 Telecoms Act.
29   Act 2/2011 of 4 March 2011 of Sustainable Economy (Spanish Official Journal No 55 of 5 March 2011).

encourage and, if applicable, guarantee the access, interconnection, and interoperability of the services).[30]

30.17   The CMT reports directly to the Ministry through the Ministry's State Secretariat for Telecommunications and the Information Society, the SETSI serving as a link between the CMT and the Ministry.

30.18   In exercising its powers, the CMT is limited by the provisions of the Telecoms Act and its implementing regulations, the Act 30/1992 of 26 November 1992 (the 'Spanish Administrative Procedural Act')[31] and the Spanish Administration Act.

30.19   The major powers entrusted to the CMT include:

- to arbitrate in disputes arising between operators, when so agreed by the interested parties;[32]
- to allocate numbers to operators;[33]
- to exercise the functions regarding the universal service and its financing;[34]
- to settle conflicts that may arise between operators on matters of network access and interconnection, as well as those matters related to telephone directories, the financing of the universal service and the shared use of infrastructures;
- to adopt measures necessary to safeguard the diversity of service offers, access to electronic communications networks by operators, the interconnection and operation of networks (on the basis of the open network test), and operators' pricing and marketing policies;
- to define the relevant telecommunications markets;[35]
- to initiate inspections at its own initiative in those matters for which it has sanctioning powers; and
- to exercise powers to impose sanctions in accordance with the terms set out in the Telecoms Act.[36]

30.20   The CMT is governed by a council composed of a chairman, a vice-chairman, and seven directors appointed directly by the Government, who must be individuals of recognised professional experience in the telecommunications sector or other regulated markets.

30.21   The positions of chairman, vice-chairman, and directors must be renewed every six years, and those that were originally appointed may be re-elected only once.

---

30   Art 11(4) Telecoms Act.
31   Act 30/1992 of 26 November 1992 on the Legal Regime for Public Authorities and the Common Administrative Procedure, Spanish Official Journal No 285 of 27 November 1992.
32   Once the relevant arbitration proceedings have been initiated, the CMT may, at any time, by the powers vested in it or upon request of the interested parties, adopt the preventative measures it deems appropriate to ensure the effectiveness of the arbitration award or decision made, should there be sufficient legal grounds for such preventive measures.
33   See para 30.62 et seq below.
34   See para 30.124 et seq below.
35   See para 30.32 et seq below.
36   In the proceedings initiated as a result of the complaint made by the Ministry, the CMT (prior to issuing a decision) must submit the case to the Ministry, which will issue a report on the case. The grounds for the CMT decision must be stated if they differ from the Ministry's report.

30.22 The CMT must prepare, and submit to the Spanish Parliament, an annual report on the development of the telecommunications and broadcasting markets.[37]

30.23 The CMT's financial resources are threefold:

(i) the assets and securities constituting its net worth;

(ii) the earnings obtained from the fees collected as payment for the services rendered, as well as those resulting from the exercise of the powers and functions;[38] and

(iii) the transfers of resources made available by the Ministry.

The Ministry

30.24 The Ministry is responsible for proposing to the Government policies which will strengthen the Spanish telecommunications market, and for implementing such policies.[39] Moreover, the Ministry assumes the overall supervision and monitoring powers of the public service obligations (without prejudice to the powers that the Telecoms Act bestows on the CMT with respect to universal service) with which the various electronic communications networks and services operators must comply. Furthermore, the powers which are not assigned to the CMT in accordance with the provisions of the Telecoms Act, and those faculties concerning the assessment of telecommunications equipment and the management of radio spectrum that were not expressly granted to the AER (now attributed to SETSI), are also handled directly by the Ministry.[40]

30.25 The Ministry must also encourage, in order to secure the interoperability of services and increase the freedom of choice of users, the use of the technical standards and specifications identified in the documents drafted by the European Commission in this regards, with the purpose of encouraging the harmonisation of electronic communication network supply, electronic communication services, and related services and resources. In the absence of these regulations, the Ministry must also encourage the application of regulations or international recommendations approved by the International Telecommunications Union (ITU), the European Conference of Postal and Telecommunications Administrations (CEPT), International Organization for Standardization (ISO) and the International Electrotechnical Commission (CEI).[41]

30.26 In order to meet regulatory objectives,[42] the major functions initially entrusted to AER (and now assumed by the Ministry through SETSI) are the following:

- advising on the planning, management, and administration of the Spanish radio spectrum, as well as the processing and granting of 'administrative

---

37 In practice, this annual report reflects all the activities of the CMT, its observations, comments, and suggestions on the performance of the market, compliance with the terms of free competition, and the measures to correct any deficiency detected.

38 See para 30.86 et seq below.

39 Useful information regarding these policies may be found on SETSI's website: http://www.minetur.gob.es/telecomunicaciones/es-ES/SecretariaDeEstado/Paginas/secretaria_estado.aspx

40 Art 46(2) Telecoms Act.

41 Art 15 Telecoms Act.

42 See para 30.23 above.

permits' (*títulos habilitantes*) for its use, except for those cases where the number of administrative permits is limited by the Ministry;[43]
- monitoring and inspecting the telecommunications sector;
- allocating satellite orbit-spectrum resources; and
- managing the radio spectrum reservation fee and certain telecommunications charges.[44]

Right of appeal against NRA's decisions

30.27 All provisions, decisions, and instructions adopted by the CMT or the Ministry in the exercise of their respective public functions bring to a close the administrative proceedings and may be appealed before the Spanish administrative courts (*jurisdicción contencioso-administrativa*).

30.28 Moreover, the arbitration awards passed by the CMT in the exercise of its arbitration functions in accordance with the Arbitration Act 60/2003 (the 'Arbitration Act')[45] may be reviewed, annulled, or enforced by the civil courts (*jurisdicción civil*) in accordance with the provisions established in the Arbitration Act.[46]

The NRA's obligations to cooperate with the Commission

30.29 Pursuant to article 10 Telecoms Act the CMT must take into account the Commission Guidelines on market analysis, as well as the Commission Recommendation on relevant markets.[47]

30.30 In addition to the above, the governmental procedures for fixing tolerable levels of radio emissions (ie levels not triggering public health hazards) must follow the limits and recommendations of the European Commission, which, regardless, must be respected by all other public authorities, at both regional and local levels.[48]

'Significant Market Power' as a fundamental prerequisite of regulation

Definition of SMP

30.31 The Telecoms Act defines the term 'SMP operator' as an 'operator that, individually or jointly with other operators, enjoys a dominant position, ie a position of economic strength allowing it to act, to a notable extent, independently from competitors, clients and, ultimately, individual consumers'.[49]

30.32 Pursuant to Article 3(3) of the Access and Numbering Regulation, the CMT is empowered to determine the existence of a 'collective dominant position'

---

43   See para 30.57 below.
44   The latter are also collected by SETSI (former AER's duty).
45   Arbitration Act 60/2003 of 23 December 2003, Spanish Official Journal No 309 of 26 December 2003.
46   The Telecoms Act actually refers to the Arbitration Act 36/1988 of 5 December 1988 (Spanish Official Journal No 293 of 7 December 1998), but this Act was superseded on 26 December 2003 by the Arbitration Act 60/2003 of 23 December 2003.
47   See para 1.72 above.
48   Art 44(1)(a) Telecoms Act.
49   Cf Annex II Telecoms Act.

where (once it has assessed the specific characteristics of a given market)[50] certain links favouring the market coordination between operators (but not necessarily corporate links) are deemed to exist.

Definition of relevant markets and SMP designation

30.33 The CMT is responsible for defining the relevant electronic communications networks and services markets.[51] The CMT must also assess their geographic scope, which is a key factor in determining the specific obligations (remedies) to be imposed on the relevant operators. The CMT carries out its analysis subsequent to a report prepared by the SDC. The CMT must, in its assessment, take into account in its assessment both the Commission guidelines on market analysis and the Commission Recommendation on relevant markets.[52]

30.34 The purpose of the market analysis is to determine if the various markets are being developed within 'an environment of effective competition'.[53] Should this not be the case in a particular market, the CMT must identify and disclose the SMP operator (or operators) for the market in question. Where the CMT identifies that a specific market lacks an 'environment of effective competition', it may impose, maintain or amend certain specific obligations on SMP operators (eg specific duties of transparency, non-discrimination, access and interconnection, prices, and accounting).[54] When imposing such obligations, the CMT must give preference to measures related to access, interconnection, selection, and pre-selection rather than those with greater impact on free competition. Furthermore, these specific obligations must be based on the nature of the identified issues, and must be proportionate and justifiable (eg they may only remain in effect for the period of time deemed strictly necessary).

30.35 When the CMT imposes specific remedies, it must consider the particular conditions of newly expanding markets. Once effective competition in a given relevant market has been established, the CMT must withdraw those specific obligations it had imposed on SMP operators.

30.36 The CMT is responsible for defining the relevant markets in Spain (which are updated from time to time) and identifying and analysing certain electronic communications markets for the purposes of assessing potential competition issues.

30.37 Prior to the implementation of the 2002 EU Regulatory Package, the CMT adopted Resolution MTZ 2001/4975 of 4 October 2001, in which it identified Telefónica de España (in the fixed telephony, leased lines and interconnection markets, and in the mobile and mobile interconnection markets), Vodafone, and France Telecom (in the mobile and the mobile interconnection markets) as the 'dominant operators' in Spain. To date, they remain the dominant operators.

---

50 Eg market shares of the operators, level of transparency, degree of maturity.
51 Every two years, by means of a decision published in the Spanish Official Journal.
52 See para 1.72 above.
53 Art 10(1) Telecoms Act.
54 The nature and scope of these specific obligations to be imposed on SMP operators are comprehensively described in the Regulation governing, among other things, the electronic communications networks and services, relevant markets and the obligations to be imposed on SMP operators.

NRA's Regulatory Duties Concerning Rights of Way, Co-location and Facility Sharing

Rights of way

RIGHTS OF WAY OVER PRIVATE PROPERTY

30.38   Operators awarded with an 'electronic communications authorisation'[55] enjoy generic rights of way to the extent that such rights are necessary to set up and maintain a public electronic communications network. An operator may only be granted a right of way over private property when the competent authority, assessing the operator's technical proposal,[56] considers that the following two requirements are met:[57]

(i)   necessity (the right of way must be deemed necessary for the installation of the relevant network); and

(ii)   absence of viable economic alternatives.

30.39   In practice, the approval of the relevant 'technical proposal' will include a reference to the right of way granted. Prior to the approval of this 'technical proposal', the operator will request a report from the competent Autonomous Community (ie the regional government where the infrastructure is to be installed), which the competent department of the Autonomous Community must issue for the operator within a maximum period of 15 days following the date it was requested.[58]

30.40   Rights of way over private property will be effected either through:[59]

- the 'compulsory purchase' (*expropiación forzosa*) of such private property or by creating a legal burden on such private property; or
- the declaration of a compulsory 'easement of access' (*servidumbre forzosa de paso*) for the concerned electronic communications networks and services infrastructure.[60]

30.41   In either case the relevant operators will be treated as beneficiaries in the pertinent administrative proceedings.

30.42   In cases of expropriation of private property for the installation of public electronic networks where operators are subject to universal service obligations, a fast-track procedure established under the old Expropriation Act (*Ley de Expropiación Forzosa*)[61] will apply when so stated in the decision of the competent department of the Spanish Administration approving the technical proposal concerned.[62]

---

55   Cf para 30.49 et seq below.

56   Generally the CMT but, in cases where the number of administrative licences has been limited, it will be the Ministry.

57   Art 26(1) Telecoms Act.

58   However, this period may be extended by up to two months at the request of the Autonomous Community concerned when the proposal affects a significant geographic area: art 27(3) Telecoms Act.

59   Art 27(1) Telecoms Act.

60   A declaration which creates a 'legal burden' on the concerned plot of land.

61   Expropriation Act of 16 December 1954, Spanish Official Journal No 351 of 17 December 1954.

62   Art 27(4) Telecoms Act.

RIGHTS OF WAY OVER PUBLIC PROPERTY

30.43   Authorisations granting rights of way over public property must comply with any specific regulations applicable to the management of the public property concerned, and any regulations issued by the title holder on matters relating to the protection and management of such public property (eg local regulations issued by a town hall).

30.44   Once the generic rights of use have been granted, the operator must obtain specific authorisations from the town halls to use public domain resources located within their boundaries. These specific authorisations for using the public domain resources of the municipalities ('Municipality Licences') (which will be granted in accordance with the provisions of Royal Legislative Decree 2/2004 on the Income of Municipalities)[63] must take into account both the aforementioned 'technical proposal' and the applicable regulations of the local zoning plans.

30.45   In practice, the specific terms of these Municipality Licences are negotiated with the town halls, which frequently require ancillary burdens (eg works not strictly necessary). In addition, in the past, Municipality Licences were subject to an annual tax payable to the relevant town hall and subject to a one-time tax on works. However, local taxes imposed to mobile operators by municipalities for the use of networks and antennas have recently been declared null and void.[64]

30.46   Operators benefiting from the rights of way over private or public property must comply with specific administrative regulations passed by the Administration which at any level (national, regional, or local) has powers in the areas of environment, public health, public security, national defence, and/or town and territorial taxation. More particularly, when granting rights to use public or private property, the relevant authorities may impose on the operator conditions relating to:

- compliance with environmental regulations;
- compliance with zoning plans and local zoning regulations;
- the use and maintenance of the public domain; and
- co-location and facility sharing.

Co-location and facility sharing

30.47   When an operator has the right to use public or private property to establish a public electronic communications network, the Ministry may require the operator to share with other operators either:

- the use of the public or private property where the network will be established; or
- the facility and related resources.[65]

30.48   For such purpose, the competent authority (at the national, regional, or local level), subsequent to a hearing with the concerned parties, may require existing operators and/or new entrants to share their infrastructure if such new entrants in the electronic communications networks and services market (being entitled to rights of way over public or private property) are unable to exercise their rights

---

63   Royal Legislative Decree 2/2004 of 5 March 2004 on the Income of Municipalities, Spanish Official Journal No 63 of 13 March 2004.
64   See 12 July 2012 Judgment by the European Court of Justice.
65   Art 30(1) Telecoms Act.

independently due to the lack of alternatives based on justifiable reasons.[66] In this case, the terms and conditions of the facility sharing will be negotiated by the parties concerned. In the absence of an agreement, the terms for the facility sharing will be established by a resolution of the CMT, subsequent to a mandatory report issued by the aforementioned competent authority.[67]

REGULATION OF MARKET ENTRY: IMPLEMENTATION OF THE AUTHORISATION DIRECTIVE

The General Authorisation of Electronic Communications

30.49   The pre-existing regime of individual licences and general and provisional authorisations was replaced by the all-inclusive electronic communications authorisation (the 'Telecoms Authorisation'). The rationale of this framework is to reduce the administrative burden on prospective electronic communications networks and services and lower barriers to facilitate entry into the market.

30.50   Under the authorisation framework, a company intending to provide electronic communications services in Spain needs only to notify the CMT prior to starting its business, and only the CMT can oppose the provision of the services on justified grounds, during a 15-day period following the filing date.[68] Moreover, the restriction contained in the Old Telecoms Act, according to which non-EU companies could not generally have an interest exceeding 25 per cent of the shares of any company holding an 'individual licence',[69] was removed. This means that any operator domiciled in the EU is allowed to provide electronic communications services in Spain regardless of the country of origin of its shareholders.

30.51   Although the amount of bureaucratic intervention was sensibly reduced, applying for a Telecoms Authorisation is still quite an onerous procedure that requires an authorised representative of the new entrant to file a standard application form and include the following documentation:

- articles of incorporation and by-laws/certificate of registration with the Companies' Registry;[70]
- power of attorney in favour of the individual signing the application duly legalised, in the event that the power of attorney is notarised abroad;[71] and
- technical document describing in Spanish the nature and features of the service and/or network to be deployed.

30.52   In addition, the following information must be included in the application:

- corporate name and corporate domicile of the applicant;

---

66   Eg public health, public security or town and territorial planning.
67   If, as a result of the facility sharing set out in article 30 Telecoms Act, the shared use of radio emission stations (*instalaciones radioeléctricas emisoras*) that are part of public electronic communications networks is imposed, and this results in the obligation to reduce the emission power levels, further stations will be authorised, provided that they are deemed necessary to ensure the coverage in the service area.
68   Art 6 Telecoms Act.
69   Art 17(1) Old Telecoms Act.
70   For foreign operators, a sworn-translated version in Spanish of these documents will be required.
71   Again, for foreign operators a Spanish sworn-translated version of this document will be required.

- telephone and fax number of a contact person within the company;[72]
- trade name of the applicant (if different from the corporate name);
- applicant's website; and
- legal representative and contact person, both domiciled in Spain.

30.53 Once the 15-day period has elapsed without the CMT having opposed the provision of the services on justified grounds, the applicant will be deemed to hold off a Telecoms Authorisation and must thereafter submit written confirm to the CMT every three years of its intention to continue the provision of the relevant services.[73] While failure of an operator to provide the CMT with this written confirmation will not result in automatically cancellation of of the Telecoms Authorisation, the CMT will initiate administrative proceedings to terminate the authorisation.[74]

Rights of Use for Radio Frequencies

General authorisations and granting of individual rights

30.54 Except in cases in which the use of spectrum is limited on efficiency grounds[75] or, alternatively, if the requested radio frequencies are free for use pursuant to the national frequency allocation plan (*cuadro nacional de atribución de frecuencias* ('CNAF')),[76] the Ministry grants rights to use radio frequencies by means of an 'administrative concession' (*concesión administrativa*) or, depending on the specific use, an 'administrative authorisation' (*autorización administrativa*).

Admissible conditions

30.55 The Government is entitled to set out non-discriminatory, proportional, and transparent conditions relating to permits for use of radio frequencies, including those conditions guaranteeing the effective and efficient use of the limited frequencies.

30.56 A holder of a right to use radio frequencies, prior to using the frequencies, must undergo inspection or accreditation of the installations to ensure that they comply with any applicable terms and regulations.[77]

Limitation of number of rights of use to be granted

30.57 The Ministry, if it deems it necessary to guarantee 'effective use' of radio frequencies, may, limit the number of rights of use of spectrum to be granted for the operation of electronic communications networks and services, or to extend the duration of existing rights under conditions different from those specified in the initial grant. Prior to doing so, however, it must hold a hearing of 'interested

---

72 This contact person may be domiciled abroad, ie not in Spain.
73 Art 5(2) Universal Service and Users Regulation.
74 Art 6 Universal Service and Users Regulation.
75 See para 30.60 below.
76 Art 45(1) Telecoms Act.
77 This preliminary inspection may be replaced in the future by a technical certificate.

parties' and take into account the requirement of achieving maximum benefits for users and encouraging the development of competition.[78]

In order to limit the number of rights of use, the Ministry must initiate a public tender for the allocation of the relevant frequencies. The Ministry must open such a tender through an order approving the bidding terms and conditions and the call for bids related to the frequencies in question. The Ministry must decide the public tender must be decided within a period of eight months.

Public tenders may not include 'spectrum auctions'. These are viewed sceptically by many who consider the legal nature of these auctions as contrary (or at least foreign) to Spanish administrative law principles.

Charges for rights of use for radio frequencies

30.58   The reservation of the use of frequencies by operators is subject to a specific charge, ie the charge for the reservation of radio spectrum, which takes into consideration the 'fair market value' of the reserved frequency and the income that this may entail for the operator.[79]

30.59   For the purposes of assessing the 'fair market value' and possible returns for the operator arising from the reservation, the following five parameters, among others, must be taken into consideration:[80]

1.   the degree of use and demand of the various frequency bands in different geographic areas;
2.   the type of service for which the reserved frequency is intended, and in particular whether this entails public service obligations;
3.   the spectrum band or sub-band being reserved;
4.   the equipment and technology used; and
5.   the economic value generated by the use of the reserved frequencies.

30.60   These five parameters will be specified on an annual basis in the Spanish Budget Act, which will also include a formula for calculating the number of units reserved for the different radio spectrum services, the different types of radio spectrum services, and the minimum amount payable for reserving radio spectrum.

30.61   The amount of the fee will be paid on an annual basis. It shall initially be payable upon the date on which the right to use the relevant frequencies is granted, and then subsequently on the first day of every year. Non-payment of the fee may result in the suspension or loss of the right to use the relevant frequencies.

Frequency trading

30.62   Although the Telecoms Act does not expressly authorise frequency trading, it does not preclude the possibility of authorising the transfer of certain rights of use of radio spectrum.[81] In such event, the Telecoms Act provides, among other

---

78   Art 44(2) Telecoms Act.
79   This charge must be paid by the individual or company holding the rights over the radio spectrum (as an exception, receiving-only stations that have not reserved radio bands are not forced to pay the charge). The amount levied shall be deposited in the Public Treasury.
80   Annex I Telecoms Act.
81   Art 45(2) Telecoms Act.

things, that transferors of rights over spectrum frequencies (frequency traders) will continue to be liable vis-à-vis the Spanish administration. Moreover, any frequency trading will have to comply with the technical requirements established in the CNAF or set out by the European Union.[82]

Rights of use for numbers

General authorisations and granting of individual rights

30.63 National numbering plans and their implementing provisions identify the services allocated to the number ranges and, if applicable, the corresponding 'addresses' and 'names',[83] including any requirements related to the provision of such services. The content of these 'national numbering, addressing and naming plans' (*planes nacionales de numeración, direccionamiento y denominación* ('Spanish Numbering Plans')) will be proposed by the Ministry and subsequently approved by the Government depending on the specific needs.[84]

30.64 In order to comply with international standards or to guarantee the availability of numbers, addresses, and names, the Ministry may amend the structure or management of national plans or, in the absence of Spanish Numbering Plans or specific plans for each service, adopt measures for the use of numbering resources necessary for the provision of the services. For these purposes, the Ministry must take into account the interests of the affected parties and the costs for operators and users resulting from the adaptation process.[85]

30.65 Pursuant to article 16(1) Telecoms Act, operators providing publicly available electronic communications services (ie undertakings holding a Telecoms Authorisation) are entitled to be awarded 'numbers'[86] and 'addresses'.[87]

30.66 With respect to the allocation of rights of use for numbers, the Access and Numbering Regulation provides that operators managing 'public telephone networks' or providing 'publicly available telephone services'[88] must file a specific application with the CMT including a description in Spanish of certain topics (eg description of the requested numbers, foreseeable use of such numbers, preferred codes, and blocks of numbers).[89] In general terms, once the aforementioned application has been filed, the CMT has a three-week period to allocate and grant the applicant an authorisation to use the requested set of numbers.[90]

---

82 Art 45(2) Telecoms Act.
83 The term 'name' is defined in Annex II to the Telecoms Act as a 'combination of characters (numbers, letters or symbols)'.
84 Arts 26, 27 and 32 of the Access and Numbering Regulation.
85 Art 17 Telecoms Act.
86 The term 'number' is defined in Annex II to the Telecoms Act as a 'series of decimal figures'.
87 The term 'address' is defined in Annex II to the Telecoms Act as a 'series or combination of figures and symbols identifying the specific termination points of a connection, used for routing purposes'.
88 Art 48 of the Access and Numbering Regulation.
89 Art 52(2) of the Access and Numbering Regulation.
90 Art 56 of the Access and Numbering Regulation.

Admissible conditions

30.67   The rights of use for numbers are subject to the following conditions:[91]

- the numbers must be used to provide the services described in the application in accordance with the Spanish Numbering Plan;
- the numbers must be controlled by the holder of the authorisation;[92]
- the holders of the right to use certain numbers must monitor and update a register describing the degree of use of each block of numbers and the transfers made to other operators as a result of the number portability rights of users; and
- the numbers must be used efficiently within 12 months from the authorisation date.

30.68   Operators providing publicly available telephone services or managing public telephone networks must guarantee, upon request made by any means allowing acknowledgement of receipt, the portability of the numbers allocated to their customers within one working day.[93] The costs resulting from updating the elements of the network and systems necessary for enabling a subscriber to retain a given number must be borne by each relevant operator.[94] Other costs associated with the number portability obligation will be jointly borne, on the basis of an appropriate agreement, by the operators concerned.[95]

30.69   Interconnection prices for implementing the number portability obligation must be cost-oriented. Moreover, any direct charges that are imposed by operators on subscribers may not, under any circumstances, deter them from benefiting from their right to number portability.

Limitation of number of rights of use to be granted

30.70   Pursuant to article 17(4) Telecoms Act, the Spanish Numbering Plans may establish competitive or comparative selection procedures for the allocation of numbering resources and names which are deemed to have an exceptional economic value. To date, however, no such numbering selection procedure has been established, but their cost varies based on the number's length.

Charges for rights of use for numbers

30.71   The allocation of numbering blocks or numbers to operators is subject to a specific charge. The telephony numbering charge is payable on 1 January of each year, except for the initial period which is payable upon the allocation of numbering resources to the operator. The amount to be charged must be the result of multiplying the amount of numbers allocated by the value given to each number.[96]

30.72   For the purposes of this charge, most numbers are deemed to consist of nine digits, except in the case of M2M numbering ranges. (If numbers are allocated

---

91   Art 59 of the Access and Numbering Regulation.
92   Sub-allocation of numbers, however, may be authorised by the CMT, provided that the intended use of such numbers was described in the initial application.
93   Arts 18 and 38.2.m Telecoms Act and 44(1) and (3) Access and Numbering Regulation.
94   Article 45(1) of the Access and Numbering Regulation.
95   In the absence of an agreement, the CMT will issue a binding decision.
96   The value of each number, which may be different depending on the number of digits and the different services allocated to it, is set on an annual basis in the Spanish Budget Act.

with fewer digits, the tax authorities, for the purposes of calculating the amount payable, consider that all the nine digits are being used.)

30.73   Notwithstanding the above, in those exceptional cases provided for in the Spanish Numbering Plan and its implementing provisions, and on the basis of the special market value of certain numbers ('golden numbers'), the annual taxable amount may be replaced by the amount resulting from the bidding procedure for the specific golden number.

The NRA's Enforcement Powers

30.74   Although one of the main purposes of the Telecoms Act and implementing regulations is to increase competition in the telecommunications market while minimising the intervention of the Spanish authorities, it is the opinion of many that the NRAs' enforcement powers have increased compared to their pre-existing ex-ante administrative control measures. The rationale for these enhanced ex-post measures is, however, understandable, especially taking into account that the requirements to access the market, and, therefore, the pre-existing ex-ante administrative control measures, were substantially reduced.

30.75   The NRAs holding investigative powers are:[97]

- the CMT, responsible for inspecting those telecommunications activities with respect to which it has specific sanctioning powers under Telecoms Act; and
- the Ministry, which has powers to inspect the telecommunications services and networks (as well as equipment, apparatus, installations, and related civil infrastructure), and competences to control and inspect the use made by operators of the frequencies awarded to them (the former AER's duties).

30.76   To undertake specific technical inspections, both the Ministry and the CMT may request the assistance of SETSI in connection with matters within the scope of their respective powers. The officials of SETSI, the Ministry, and the specifically appointed personnel of the CMT are considered a 'public authority' in the exercise of their inspection functions, and may request necessary support from the national security forces. In this regard, operators must facilitate access of the inspection teams to their installations, documents, and records (regardless of whether these are in electronic or written format) and permit such inspection teams to monitor anything which may affect their services and activities or the networks that they install or operate.[98]

30.77   The inspections may be undertaken by the Ministry and/or the CMT:[99]

- in any office, division or department of the individual or undertaking being inspected or of those individuals representing the latter;[100] and/or
- at the offices of the Ministry or the CMT.

30.78   The Telecoms Act divides infringements into three different categories – very serious infringements, serious infringements, and minor infringements.

---

97   Art 50(1) Telecoms Act.
98   Art 50(5) and (6) Telecoms Act.
99   Art 50(6) Telecoms Act.
100   In this case, the investigated undertaking's working day will be observed, unless otherwise agreed with the inspection team.

30.79   Examples of actions undertaken by operators which are considered 'very serious infringements' include, but are not limited to:[101]

- providing telecommunications services without having the necessary authorisation[102] or using non-authorised technical standards (depending on the merits of the specific case, this may be deemed a 'serious infringement');
- using spectrum frequencies without the necessary authorisation;
- purposely causing damaging interferences;
- installing, deploying, or using non-authorised telecommunications equipment connected to public communications networks, provided that material damage is caused to such networks;[103] and
- not complying with instructions issued by the CMT in connection with the definition of relevant markets and the duties with which SMP operators must comply.

30.80   Examples of 'serious infringements' under the Telecoms Act[104] include, but are not limited to:

- providing telecommunications services without the necessary authorisation or using non-authorised technical standards;[105]
- installing non-authorised radio-electric stations, provided that prior authorisation was mandatory;
- causing damaging interferences without intending to do so;
- installing, deploying or using non-authorised telecommunications equipment connected to public communications networks, provided that material damage is caused to such networks;[106] and
- distributing, selling or showing non-authorised telecommunications equipment.

30.81   Examples of 'minor infringements' under the Telecoms Act include, but are not limited to:[107]

- emitting non-authorised radio-electric signals;
- causing interference; and
- not producing the mandatory tariff or prices information when required by the applicable legislation.

30.82   Sanctions imposed by either the Ministry or the CMT will depend on the gravity of the infringement.[108]

30.83   Failure to comply with instructions issued by the CMT in connection with the definition of relevant markets, with the duties imposed on SMP operators, or with the requirements to provide electronic communications services will generally

---

101   Art 53 Telecoms Act.
102   This in practice would imply starting the provision of the electronic communication services: (i) not having applied for a Telecoms Authorisation at all; (ii) without waiting for the 15-day waiting period to elapse; or (iii) ignoring the formal opposition of the CMT.
103   Depending on the merits of the specific case, this may be considered a 'very serious infringement'.
104   Art 54 Telecoms Act.
105   Depending on the merits of the specific case, this may be considered a 'very serious infringement'.
106   Depending on the merits of the specific case, this may be considered a 'very serious infringement'.
107   Art 55 Telecoms Act.
108   Art 56 Telecoms Act.

trigger a penalty of up to five times the gross benefit connected to the breach. 'Very serious infringements' are sanctioned with a penalty up to five times the gross benefit triggered by the offence, with a limit of €2 million. 'Serious infringements' are sanctioned with a penalty up to twice the gross benefit triggered by the offence, with a limit of €500,000, and 'minor infringements' are sanctioned with a penalty up to €30,000.

30.84   In addition to the above, a fine of up to €60,000 may be imposed on the legal representatives of the infringing undertakings or, alternatively, on their directors.[109] Infringements are subject to a statute of limitations of three years for very serious offences, two years for serious offences, and six months for minor offences. This statute of limitations will be counted as from the date on which the infringement was committed.[110]

30.85   In the event of repeated infringements, the initial date for calculation will be the date on which the offending activity was suspended or, alternatively, the date when the last offending act was perpetrated. However, the infringement will be deemed as still being carried out if the equipment, apparatus, or installations under consideration in the proceedings have not been placed at the disposal of the authorities, or if there is no reliable evid;lence of inability to use them.

Administrative charges and fees for rights of use

30.86   Operators may be subject to four different types of charges;[111]

* general operator charges (*tasa general de operadores*),
* charges for rights of use for numbers (*tasa por numeración telefónica*),[112]
* charges for rights of use for radio frequencies[113] (*tasa por reserva del dominio público radioeléctrico*), and
* administrative management charges (*tasas de telecomunicaciones*).

30.87   The purpose of these telecommunications charges is to cover:[114]

* the administrative costs incurred by the drafting and implementation of resulting EC law and administrative proceedings;
* the costs arising from the management, control, and application of the regime set out in the Telecoms Act;
* the management of notifications addressed to the NRAs; and
* the costs arising from international cooperation, harmonisation/ standardisation, and analysis of the market.

30.88   Without prejudice to the foregoing, the additional purpose of the radio spectrum, numbering and electronic communications networks and services charges is to guarantee the necessary optimum use of these resources, bearing in mind the value and availability of the asset to be used.

---

109   Art 56(4) Telecoms Act.
110   The statute of limitations, however, will be suspended upon the initiation of sanctioning proceedings.
111   Cf Annex I Telecoms Act.
112   See paras 30.70 above.
113   See paras 30.57 above.
114   Art 49(2) Telecoms Act.

30.89   All charges must be non-discriminatory, transparent, justified, and proportional to their purpose.[115]

30.90   Without prejudice to the economic contribution that may be imposed on operators to finance universal service,[116] electronic communications networks and services operators must pay an annual charge that may not exceed 0.2 per cent of their gross operating revenues in Spain to finance the costs associated with the management, control, implementation, and enforcement faculties of the SRAs and, more particularly, the administrative costs generated by the CMT (the actual percentage is set annually in the Spanish Budget Act).

30.91   This annual charge is due on 31 December of each year. However, should an operator lose its authorisation to operate prior to this date, the charge will be due upon the occurrence of such loss of its authorisation.

30.92   The following administrative procedures and management actions undertaken by the Spanish authorities result in the right to levy the administrative management charge to offset the costs incurred:

• issuing registration certificates related to a wide array of different telecommunications regulations (eg certificates for a technical project, installation certificates related to telecommunications infrastructures, or certificates of compliance with technical specifications for telecommunications equipment and apparatus);
• issuing technical reports assessing the conformity of telecommunications equipment and apparatus;
• keeping a register of telecommunication installers;
• undertaking compulsory technical inspections and verifications that are set out in the Telecoms Act and its implementing regulations; and
• processing licences or administrative concessions to use certain frequencies of the radio spectrum on an exclusive basis.

30.93   The individuals or companies subject to the administrative management charge will be those:

• applying for the corresponding technical assessment or entry in the register of telecommunication installers;
• receiving a team of inspectors acting within the scope of their faculties; and
• requesting licences or administrative concessions to use certain frequencies of the radio spectrum on an exclusive basis.

30.94   The specific amount of the administrative management charge will be set on an annual basis in the Spanish Budget Act, and the charge will be payable upon the occurrence of one of the events described above.

30.95   The revenues generated by the administrative management charge will be paid to the Public Treasury (or, if applicable, to the bank accounts authorised for this purpose by the CMT).

---

115   Art 49(3) Telecoms Act.
116   See para 30.123 et seq below.

Transitional Regulations for Existing Authorisations

30.96 Authorisations granted within the framework of the Old Telecoms Act, ie the former administrative concessions, individual licences, and general and provisional authorisations, were subject to a transitional regime characterised as follows:[117]

- existing Authorisations expired upon the entry into force of the Telecoms Act, but their holders were automatically authorised to provide electronic communications networks and services under the Telecoms Act regime (provided they comply with the requirements established in the Telecoms Act),
- the specific requirements applicable to existing Authorisations continued to be enforceable until the Telecoms Act entered into force, and
- existing authorisations granted to a limited number of operators (eg following a public tender procedure), automatically became subject to an administrative concession under the conditions applicable to the expired licence.

REGULATION OF NETWORK ACCESS AND INTERCONNECTION: IMPLEMENTATION OF THE ACCESS DIRECTIVE

Objectives and Scope of Access Regulation

30.97 Pursuant to the Telecoms Act, operators of public electronic communications networks are entitled, and, when requested by other operators of public electronic communications networks, required, to negotiate interconnection agreements in order to provide publicly available electronic communications services and guarantee the provision of services and their interoperability.

30.98 An electronic communications networks and services operator licensed in another EU Member State that requests access or interconnection in Spain will not need to obtain from the CMT authorisation to provide electronic communications networks and services if they are not operating electronic communications networks or rendering electronic communications services within the Spanish territory.

30.99 The CMT, on its own motion, or at the request of an interested party, may intervene in relations between operators in order to encourage and, if applicable, guarantee access and interconnection to the networks and the interoperability of the services, as well as the fulfilment of a number of objectives described in article 3 Telecom Act.[118]

30.100 When an operator wishes to access public electronic communications networks, the CMT may impose on the operator (or those who benefit from the access) certain technical or operational conditions, when deemed necessary to guarantee the normal functioning of the network, in accordance with applicable regulations.

30.101 Any obligations and conditions imposed on operators must be objective, transparent, proportional and non-discriminatory.

---

117 1st Transitional Provision of the Telecoms Act.
118 Art 3 Telecoms Act. Furthermore, the Ministry may act, within the scope of its competencies, to ensure that these objectives are met.

Basic regulatory concepts

30.102   The definitions of 'access' and 'interconnection' in Annex II (Definitions) of the Telecoms Act closely follow their EU counterparts.[119]

30.103   The CMT is empowered to settle disputes concerning the obligations of interconnection and access resulting from the Telecoms Act and its implementing regulations. The CMT, subsequent to a hearing of interested parties, must pass a final resolution on the matters of the dispute within a maximum period of four months from the date on which it intervened, without prejudice to any precautionary measures that it may adopted before passing a final resolution.

30.104   In the event of a cross-border conflict in which one of the interested parties is domiciled in another EU Member State, the CMT, upon request of one an interested party, must coordinate with the other NRA to reach a settlement.

Access and Interconnection-related Obligations with Respect to SMP-undertakings

Overview

30.105   The CMT may impose on SMP wholesale operators obligations regarding:[120]

- transparency, with respect to interconnection and access, whereby operators must make public certain information such as that concerning accounting, technical specifications, network characteristics, terms of supply and use, and prices. In particular, when obligations of non-discrimination are imposed on an operator, they may be required to make public a reference offer;
- non-discrimination, for the purposes of ensuring that they apply equivalent terms in circumstances similar to other operators;
- accounting separation, using the specified format and the technology;
- access to specific network resources and their use; and
- price control to avoid excessively high or low prices which conflict with the interests of end users (eg price/cost comparisons and cost accounting).

Transparency obligations and reference interconnection offers

30.106   Article 7(1) Access and Numbering Regulation requires SMP wholesale operators to disclose access and interconnection-related information regarding accounting, network characteristics, terms of supply and use, and prices. Moreover, when non-discrimination duties have been imposed on the relevant SMP operator, the CMT may oblige require such an operator to publish a reference interconnection offer (*oferta de interconexión de referencia*) including, among other things, a reference to the following topics:[121]

- localisation of the access points, including their associated numbering resources;
- the types of access available, including a comprehensive description of its technical features and capabilities;

---

119   See paras 1.125 and 1.126 above.
120   Art 6 et seq of the Access and Numbering Regulation.
121   Art 7(2) Access and Numbering Regulation.

- technical requirements to be met by the networks or equipments to be interconnected;
- characteristics and requirements of carrier pre-selection, indirect access and number portability;
- service level agreements;
- general requirements to implement and maintain the requested access (eg technical tests and assessments to be performed); and
- tariffs applicable to each section of the reference interconnection offer.

30.107 The CMT is entitled to amend the reference interconnection offer proposed by the relevant wholesale SMP operator.[122]

Non-discrimination obligations

30.108 SMP wholesale operators may be subject to specific obligations for the purposes of ensuring that they apply equivalent terms in circumstances similar to operators rendering equivalent services and provide services and information of the same quality to third parties, which may use them for their own services or for the services of their subsidiaries or associate companies.

30.109 These obligations concern the quality of the services provided, the delivery dates, and the terms of supply.[123]

Specific access obligations

30.110 The CMT may require SMP wholesale operators to satisfy any reasonable requests for access to and use of their specific network and associated resources.

30.111 The CMT may impose obligations to:[124]

- negotiate in good faith with third parties any requests for access to specific network and associated resources, including fully unbundled access to the local loop;
- refrain from denying access to specific network and associated resources previously made available; and
- provide specific wholesale services to be resold by third parties.

Price control obligations

30.112 Where the CMT considers that there is a lack of effective competition in a given wholesale market, it may impose certain price-control obligations on wholesale SMP operators to ensure that their prices are in line with the costs of the relevant services plus a reasonable return on the investments made. If challenged, the SMP operator bears the burden of proof that the relevant prices are, in fact, cost oriented.[125]

---

122 Art 7(3) Access and Numbering Regulation.
123 Art 8 Access and Numbering Regulation.
124 Art 10(1) of the Access and Numbering Regulation.
125 Art 11(1) of the Access and Numbering Regulation.

Accounting separation obligations

30.113 For the purpose of preventing SMP wholesale operators from 'squeezing' the margins of their competitors, they may be subject to separate accounting regarding the access and interconnection markets.[126] Where vertically integrated, the transfer wholesale prices between subsidiaries of the same group may be subject to public disclosure and a specific accounting method to be defined by the CMT.[127]

Related Regulatory Powers with Respect to SMP-undertakings

30.114 Fixed telephony SMP operators must ensure that their subscribers have access to the services of any operator providing publicly available telephone services, either by indirect access or by carrier pre-selection.

30.115 Pursuant to Article 17 of the Access and Numbering Regulation, SMP undertakings operating in the market for the total or partial supply of a minimum number of leased lines, as published in the Official Journal of the European Union in accordance with Article 17 of the Universal Service Directive ('SMP Suppliers of Leased Lines'), will be subject to the principles of transparency, non-discrimination, and cost-orientation of prices.

30.116 SMP Suppliers of Leased Lines must publish on their websites the following information:[128]

- technical characteristics of the leased lines;
- applicable fees (including the initial and subsequent subscription fees and others, if any); and
- conditions of the supply.

30.117 In addition, SMP Suppliers of Leased Lines must apply equivalent terms and conditions to any operators providing similar services.

30.118 If the CMT requires a specific SMP Supplier of Leased Lines to apply cost-oriented retail prices, the supplier must ensure that its fees are cost-oriented by following the accounting requirements set out by the CMT.[129]

Regulatory Powers Applicable to all Market Participants

Obligations to ensure end-to-end connectivity

30.119 The CMT, to the extent necessary to guarantee end-to-end connection, may impose obligations on operators that control access to end users, including, in justifiable cases, the obligation of interconnecting their networks when they have not done so.[130]

30.120 The CMT ensures end-to-end connectivity by requiring operators of public electronic communications networks, at the request of other equivalent operators, to negotiate interconnection agreements in order to provide publicly

---

126　Art 9(1) of the Access and Numbering Regulation.
127　Art 9(2) of the Access and Numbering Regulation.
128　Art 17(1) of the Access and Numbering Regulation.
129　Art 20 of the Access and Numbering Regulation.
130　Art 22 of the Access and Numbering Regulation.

available electronic communications services while securing the provision of services and their interoperability.[131]

30.121   Article 22(2) Access and Numbering Regulation provides that interconnection agreements must be negotiated within four months (unless both parties agree to extend such negotiation period). The CMT may participate in the negotiations, upon request of any of the parties or on its own initiative, where such intervention is considered justified.[132]

Access to digital radio and television broadcasting services

30.122   Although the regime applicable to broadcasting through electronic communications networks is expressly excluded from the Telecoms Act regime (as it was from the pre-existing regulatory framework), Article 24 of the Access and Numbering Regulation sets out the following requirements with which operators intending to provide 'conditional access' services to radio and television digital broadcasters must comply:[133]

- technical capacity to allow total control over the broadcasting services on a national, regional and/or local level;
- supply radio and television digital broadcasters with reasonable and non-discriminatory technical equipment allowing them to enable the reception of their signal by their subscribers; and
- separate accounting.

30.123   In addition to the above, Article 24(d) of the Access and Numbering Regulation provides that set-top boxes must be licensed by the holders of the industrial property rights to manufacturers on equivalent, reasonable, and non-discriminatory terms, taking into account the status of the market and the technology.

REGULATION OF UNIVERSAL SERVICES AND USERS' RIGHTS: THE UNIVERSAL SERVICE DIRECTIVE AND THE BILL OF ELECTRONIC COMMUNICATIONS SERVICES USER'S RIGHTS

Regulation of Universal Service Obligations

Scope of universal service obligations

30.124   The scope of universal services consists of the following obligations:[134]

---

131   Art 22 of the Access and Numbering Regulation.
132   Art 23(3) of the Access and Numbering Regulation.
133   The term 'Conditional Access System' is defined in Annex II to the Telecoms Act as 'any technical measure or mechanism which makes access in an intelligible form to a protected radio or television broadcasting service subject to the payment of a fee or another form of prior individual authorisation'.
134   Art 22 Telecoms Act and Art 27 et seq of the Universal Service and Users Regulation.

- access to fixed public electronic communications network for all end users that 'reasonably'[135] request such access;[136]
- availability to those telephone subscribers of a general directory, in either hard copy, soft copy, or both, which must be updated at least once a year;[137]
- availability of sufficient public pay telephones in the entire national territory to properly meet the needs of end users (in terms of geographic coverage, number of telephones, accessibility of these telephones by users with a disability, and the quality of services);[138] and
- availability of sufficient fixed public telephone lines or other public access points to voice telephony adapted to meet the needs of end-users with disabilities.

Designation of undertakings obliged to provide universal services

30.125   The Ministry periodically will designate one or more operators to provide universal service ('Universal Service Operators'), to ensure that the entire national territory enjoys proper coverage. To date, Telefónica de España, is the only operator designated to provide universal service.

The Ministry, to designate Universal Service Operators, conducts public consultation. If, as a result of such public consultation, existing operators express an interest in being designated as Universal Service Operators in a specific geographic area (exclusively or in competition with other operators), the Ministry will launch public tenders to provide the universal service for a definite duration within the particular geographic area. The following universal services may be subject to such public tender:[139]

- access for all end users to a fixed public electronic communications network;
- provision of telephony services available to the public;
- implementation of a network of public pay telephones;
- commercialisation of a general directory; and
- provision of 'directory inquiry services'.

30.126   Notwithstanding the above, when a competitive procedure is issued in order to appoint an operator with SMP in the fixed public telephony market in a given geographic area, and no applicants express an interest in providing universal services in that area, any operator with significant market power in that area may be appointed Universal Service Operator by the Ministry to guarantee the provision of any service pertaining to the universal service within its relevant geographic area for

---

135 Pursuant to Art 29(2) of the Universal Service and Users Regulation, requests of access for residential use will always be considered 'reasonable'.

136 This connection must offer the end user the possibility of making and receiving telephone communications, and allow fax and data communications at a speed which enables functional use of the Internet. Such use, by definition, has a download speed of 1Mbit per second, pursuant to article 52 of the Sustainable Economy Act (Art of the 28 Universal Service and Users Regulation).

137 At least one general information service on subscriber numbers must be available to telephone end users, including those using public pay telephones. Moreover, all subscribers with access to the public telephone service have the right to be registered in the general directory, without prejudice to those regulations governing data protection and the right to privacy.

138 Users must be able to make emergency calls from public pay telephones free of charge, using the number for emergency calls 112 or other Spanish emergency numbers.

139 Art 37 of the Universal Service and Users Regulation.

a limited period of time.[140] This is the case with Telefónica de España, the Spanish incumbent and current universal service and SMP operator in the fixed telephone market for the entire territory of Spain.

Cost calculation and financing of universal services

30.127 The CMT is responsible for assessing whether the obligation to provide universal service may impose an excessive cost on the relevant Universal Service Operator(s). Should this be the case, the net cost for the provision of the universal service will be calculated periodically in accordance with the Designation Regulation or, alternatively, according to the net savings that a competent Operator would obtain if the obligation to render the universal service did not exist.[141] The Universal Service net cost of Telefónica de España (the Spanish incumbent and current universal service and SMP operator within the fixed telephone market) was valued by the CMT at €43.57 million during the 2010 fiscal year.[142]

30.128 Should the CMT determine the Universal Service net cost is 'excessive', the cost will be financed by all or certain categories of operators (the 'Universal Service Supporters') through a transparent compensation mechanism to be administered by the CMT

30.129 The CMT will determine the contributions to be made by each Universal Service Supporter. These contributions will be deposited in the 'universal service national fund', the purpose of which is to finance the universal service not only though monetary assets originating from Universal Service Supporters but also through contributions made by any individual or legal entity wishing to contribute to the financing of any provision of universal service (eg non-profit organisations). The CMT is responsible for the management of the 'universal service national fund'. The cost of providing the universal service is currently being shared yearly between different operators whose revenues are over the CMT's threshold for each fiscal year.

End User Rights

30.130 In addition to the general rights granted by the Consumers and Users Act 1/2007[143] and other legislation enacted at regional level, consumers and end users of electronic communications networks and services enjoy, among other things, the rights to:[144]

- receive compensation from the operator with respect to any damages sustained;
- receive truthful, efficient, sufficient, transparent, and current information from operators;
- get certain services disconnected at the end user's request;
- receive compensation for interruption of a service;
- enter into contracts with operators facilitating the connection or access to a public telephone network, as well as the minimum contents of these contracts;

---

140 Art 38 of the Universal Service and Users Regulation.
141 Art 24 Telecoms Act.
142 See www.cmt.es/cmt/centro_info/publicaciones/revista/Marzo/Servicio_universal.htm
143 Consumers and Users Act 1/2007 of 16 November 2007, Spanish Official Journal No 287 of 30 November 2007.
144 Art 38 Telecoms Act.

- unilaterally terminate the contract in advance without being subject to any penalties in the event of proposals amending contractual terms;
- choose a method of payment from amongst those commonly used for business transactions in order to pay for the corresponding services;
- keep anonymous or cancel data regarding their transactions when no longer necessary for the purposes of transmitting a communication;[145]
- ensure that the data on their transactions are only used for commercial purposes (or for the provision of value added services in cases for which they have given their consent);
- receive non-itemised bills if they have so requested;
- process anonymous contact data, subject only to the prior consent of the customer (to the extent and for the period of time necessary for the provision, if applicable, of the value added services);[146]
- stop the automatic diversion of a call made at a given terminal by a third party;
- prevent, using a simple process and free of charge, outgoing call line identification;[147]
- prevent, by means of a simple procedure and free of charge, the identification of incoming calls (ensuring the possibility to reject those incoming calls for which the line may not be identified); and
- reject unsolicited automatic calls or faxes made for the purpose of direct sales.

Contracts

30.131   In addition to the above, individual consumers and end users are entitled to enter into contracts with fixed and mobile public telephony operators which must include certain minimum information (eg corporate name and registered and commercial address, client care telephone number, features of the service provided, quality levels, price and other economic terms, duration, termination events, and information regarding personal data protection).[148]

Transparency obligations

30.132   Generally speaking, operators must file with the Ministry, the CMT, the National Consumption Institute, the Spanish Data Protection Agency, and the Consumers and Users Council a copy of the standard terms and conditions to be used, including any amendments and updates, one month prior to the contract's entry into force.[149] The Ministry may then introduce clauses amending such standard terms and conditions to prevent any abusive practices. However, in the event that the standard terms and conditions are intended to be applied to public

---

145 Without prejudice to article 12 of the Electronic Commerce Act, according to which ENCS operators, providers of access to telecommunications networks and data hosting operators may store the traffic and connection data from electronic communications for a maximum 12-month period.

146 This right is not applicable to 112 emergency services.

147 This right is not applicable to 112 emergency services. During a limited period of time, end users may not exercise this right where the recipient of the telephone call has requested the identification of those calls deemed to be malicious or disturbing.

148 Art 8 Royal Decree 899/2009.

149 Art 11.3 Royal Decree 899/2009

service-related communications, the relevant operator must request prior authorisation from the Ministry (specifically, SETSI).[150]

Quality of services: securing 'net neutrality'

30.133 The Telecoms Act includes some provisions stating that net neutrality should be one of the guidelines in the Telecoms Act's implementation, but there are currently no regulations obliging operators to be neutral with respect to their services. It still under discussion whether a net neutrality scheme should be imposed on operators in order to grant an equitable access to the Internet or whether operators should be entitled to interfere, instead, which might promote private investment.

Consumer arbitration

30.134 Operators must have a 'client care service or department' to address customer claims.[151]

30.135 A customer may submit a complaint to the operator, through such service or department, when the event that triggered the complaint was known to the customer. Should the operator fail to respond or resolve the alleged deficiency, the customer is entitled to file a claim with the SETSI, which will issue a final decision within a period of six months. This decision brings to a close the administrative proceedings and may be appealed before the Spanish administrative courts (*jurisdicción contencioso-administrativa*).[152]

DATA PROTECTION: IMPLEMENTATION OF THE E-PRIVACY DIRECTIVE

Confidentiality of Communications

30.136 Operators providing publicly available electronic communications services or networks must guarantee the secrecy of communications pursuant to the Spanish Constitution. They also must take appropriate technical and organisational measures to safeguard the security of their services or networks, with the goal of guaranteeing the levels of protection of personal data required by the Universal Service and Users Regulation. Where there is a risk of security breach, operators must inform subscribers of the risk and possible remedies, as well as cost implications.

30.137 Pursuant to Article 83 of the Universal Service and Users Regulation, an operator may conduct only such interceptions as set out under the Code of Criminal Procedure and the Organic Act governing the prior judicial control of the National Intelligence Centre. The most important features of the Universal Service and Users Regulation are as follows:

- operators subject to obligations: operators providing publicly available electronic communications services or networks;

---

150 Art 11.1 Royal Decree 899/2009.
151 Art 26 Royal Decree 899/2009
152 Art 27 Royal Decree 899/2009.

- affected communications: any kind of electronic communication, including both telephony services and data transmission services;
- procedure: the interception must be allowed by law and requested by a judicial authority;
- interception measure: access to or transmission of the electronic communication and related information to competent authorities;
- information to be provided to the competent authority includes:
  - identification of the party subject to the interception;
  - identification of the other parties involved in the electronic communication;
  - basic services used;
  - supplementary services used;
  - indication of response;
  - cause of termination;
  - location information;
  - information exchanged through the control or signalling channel;
  - regarding its own subscribers: (i) identification of the physical or legal person involved in the communication; and (ii) address to which the provider sends its notifications;
  - regarding both subscribers and non-subscribers, where possible: (i) number of the service contracting party (both the directory number and any electronic communication identification of the subscriber); (ii) terminal identification number; (iii) account number allocated by the Internet service provider; and (iv) email address;
  - where possible, information on the geographic location of the originating or termination terminal; and
  - prior to the interception, the service provider must provide information on the services and characteristics of the telecommunications system, as well as the name and national identification code of the subscribers subject to interception;
- internal measures: the service provider must identify an internal unit entitled to receive interception orders as well as establish internal procedures to facilitate the interception. Additionally, the service provider must configure its equipment so as to facilitate the interception; and
- costs incurred: the service provider is entitled to recoup from the relevant authority any amounts spent or use of communication channels, whether temporary or permanent, specifically established to facilitate the transmission of the intercepted electronic communication and related information. The amounts spent on specific interception equipment do not qualify as cost and cannot be therefore recovered. Regardless, it is not clear what mechanism will be followed to recover the effective costs incurred by the operator.

30.138   As set out in article 22 Electronic Commerce Act, for service providers to use data storage and recovery devices in terminal equipment (e g through the use of cookies), they must obtain the recipient's consent after providing the recipient with clear and comprehensive information regarding the use and purpose. When technically possible, the user consent may be obtained through relevant parameters of a web browser or an application, provided such parameters are set when installing or upgrading the web browser or application. This does not prevent the possible storage or access of data for the purpose of carrying out or facilitating the technical transmission of a communication through an electronic communications network, or insofar as it is necessary to render an information society service expressly requested by the service recipients.

Traffic Data and Location Data

30.139   Article 64 Universal Service and Users Regulation defines 'traffic data' as 'any data processed for the conduction of a communication through an electronic communications network or for billing purposes', and 'location data' as 'any data treated in an electronic communications network which indicates the geographical position of the terminal equipment of a publicly available electronic communications service user'.

30.140   Operators must inform subscribers or users of the types of traffic data processed and the duration of such processing.

30.141   Traffic data related to subscribers and users processed for the purpose of transmitting communications must be erased or anonymised when no longer needed for that purpose. Traffic data necessary for the purpose of billing and interconnection payments may be retained only for the period during which the bill may lawfully be challenged and payment pursued, in accordance with the applicable law. Thereafter, operators must erase or anonymise the personal data.

30.142   Pursuant to Article 65 of the Universal Service and Users Regulation, operators may process traffic data for the purposes of marketing electronic communications services or the provision of value added-services, provided consent is obtained. To that end, operators must inform subscribers with one month before the start of the marketing or the provision of value-added services about the services for which the personal data will be processed, the type of traffic data processed, and the duration of such processing. Such communication must be in a means that ensures the subscriber will receive it. Consent will be deemed to have been obtained for such purposes if no answer is received from the subscribers within such one-month term. Subscribers must be provided, free of charge, with an easy mechanism to opt out from such processing. Regardless, a subscriber may withdraw consent at any time.

30.143   According to Article 70 of the Universal Service and Users Regulation, location data related to users or subscribers of publicly available electronic communications services or networks may only be processed if such data has been made anonymous or the previous and express consent has been obtained from the data subject, to the extent and for the duration necessary for the provision of a value-added service. This consent may be withdrawn at any time.

Data Retention

30.144   The Data Retention Act[153] regulates the data retention obligations for telecommunications operators. In particular, operators must retain the following information of each communication for a period of one year from the communication date:

- originating phone number/user ID;
- name and address of the subscriber;
- IP address and its assignee data, where applicable;
- phone number dialled and trace of any call divert detected;
- name and address or user ID of the destination user, where available;
- date and time of the call/service starting and ending;

---

153   Act 25/2007 of 18 October, on the retention of data relating to electronic communications and public communications networks.

- service description (network and type of call/service used), where available;
- IMSI or IMEI codes, where applicable; and
- cell location, where applicable.

Nevertheless, the content of the communication cannot be lawfully stored.

Itemised billing

30.145   As set out in Article 66 of the Universal Service and Users Regulation, subscribers have the right to request operators not to provide itemised bills, in which case they will receive a bill for the total amount. If such right is not exercised, bills will be provided in an itemised manner. SETSI issues resolutions establishing the different types of presentation of itemised bills which subscribers may request (eg suppression of certain digits of the numbers called or of such numbers used through payment of credit cards).

Calling and Connected Line Identification

30.146   Article 75 of the Universal Service and Users Regulation requires operators offering calling line identification services to allow users to easily, and free of charge, withhold their number on a per-call and per-line basis. Such operators must also enable subscribers to block the numbers of incoming calls and to reject incoming calls automatically in cases where the caller has withheld the caller identification.

Automatic Call Forwarding

30.147   Under Article 82 of the Universal Service and Users Regulation, operators providing public telephony services must offer to their subscribers the ability to easily, and free of charge, stop automatic call forwarding by a third party to its terminal equipment.

Directories of Subscribers

30.148   Pursuant to Article 67 of the Universal Service and Users Regulation, operators must inform their subscribers, in advance and free of charge, about the inclusion of their personal data in a subscribers' directory or communication to a third party for that purpose. Such information must be provided at least one month in advance, and the express consent of the subscriber is required.

Unsolicited Communications

30.149   Based on article 69 Universal Service and Users Regulation, automatic calls (including faxes) without human intervention for selling purposes are only allowed if subscribers have provided their express, prior, and informed consent. Consent for non-requested calls conducted through different means is also required, although in this case it can be provided by an opt-out clause (unless the subscriber has chosen not to be included in subscribers' directories, in which case express consent is mandatory).

30.150   In addition article 21 Electronic Commerce Act prohibits the transmission of publicity or promotional communications via electronic mail (e-mail), or any other equivalent electronic communication means, that has not been previously requested or expressly authorised by the addressees.

30.151   These provisions will not apply where a previous contractual relationship exists, provided that the service provider has obtained the contact data from the recipient by lawful means, and used it to send commercial communications regarding products or services from its own company that is similar to those which were initially the subject matter of the contract with the client.

30.152   In any event, the service provider must offer the recipients of services the possibility of objecting to the processing of their data for promotional purposes by means of a straightforward process and free of charge, both at the time of collecting the data as well as at the moment of each separate commercial communication.

The Swedish Market for Electronic Communications

Stefan Brand and Filip Skoglund
Baker & McKenzie, Stockholm

LEGAL STRUCTURE

Basic Policy

31.1 The basic policy objective for the electronic communications sector in Sweden is to promote efficiency, growth, increased competitiveness, and overall to enhance productivity in society. Further goals are for individuals and authorities to have the greatest possible access to efficient and secure electronic communications with the best possible choice, price and quality, that effective consumer protection is ensured, and that it promotes sustainable development towards a healthy environment.

31.2 Since 1993, when the Swedish government undertook a comprehensive reform of the telecommunications market, competition has increased and new markets have formed.[1] In addition, rapid technological development has resulted in increased convergence of previously separate forms of communications, such as voice and data communications. The high level of IT and mobile maturity, and easy entry into the Swedish market, have attracted a broad spectrum of players, from multinational telecommunications operators to computer companies and systems integrators.

31.3 In the past few years, new legislation has been implemented, fourth generation mobile telephony has acquired its first customers, and Internet services, including IP telephony, are steadily increasing.

Implementation of EU Directives

31.4 The 2009 Regulatory Package has been implemented in Sweden with amendments to the Electronic Communications Act (the 'ECA').[2]

---

1   These include, among others, mobile services, Internet access, Internet services, and IP telephony.
2   Lagen om elektronisk kommunikation (2003:389).

Legislation

31.5 The main legislative acts in Sweden are the ECA and the Electronic Communications Ordinance 'ECO').[3] The ECA is designed to consolidate the previous legislation, adapting it to the converging telecommunications, media, and IT sectors and the harmonised EU rules. It is also intended to make the regulation of the electronic communications market more flexible and includes tools that the national regulatory authority, the Post and Telecom Agency ('PTS'), may use if a market definition and analysis demonstrates that a particular market is not effectively competitive. This system allows for more adaptable regulation, as it is less time-consuming for the PTS to amend regulations or adjust a decision than for the Parliament to amend its legislation. The PTS must have adequate power to be able to amend regulations to adjust to a changing sector, and to tailor obligations it imposes on individual companies on a case-by-case basis.

31.6 In addition, although not strictly legally binding, statements, consultations and guidelines issued by the PTS are in practice very important when identifying rights and obligations in the Swedish telecommunication sector.

REGULATORY PRINCIPLES: THE FRAMEWORK DIRECTIVE

Scope of Regulation

31.7 The ECA covers electronic communications networks, electronic communications services, and associated facilities. It regulates the technical infrastructure, but not the contents of the services. The terms 'electronic communications service' and 'electronic communications network' are, in essence, defined identically[4] to those in the Framework Directive. While the definition of 'associated facilities' is not identical, it has the same meaning as the definition in the Framework Directive.

31.8 Complex services comprising several sub-services where one sub-service includes the conveyance of signals, which is a prerequisite for offering the other sub-services, are regulated as electronic communications services.

31.9 IP telephony services are regulated as electronic communications services in cases where the transfer of the call is implemented in a communications network where the terminal equipment is identified by a telephone number. Conversely, IP telephony services are not deemed electronic communications services where the service only uses the public Internet for the transmission of calls and where the service provider does not control any part of the transfer.

'Internet Freedom'

31.10 Swedish laws do not provide for the imposition of any measures that restrict the end user's access to the Internet, eg to sanction copyright violations. Currently, there are no existing plans to implement such measures.

National Regulatory Authorities: Organisation, Regulatory Objectives, Competencies

31.11 The PTS is the authority responsible for regulating the electronic communications and postal sectors in Sweden. It is responsible, in particular, for the

---

3   Förordning om elektronisk kommunikation (2003:396).
4   Ch 1 s 7 ECA.

definition of relevant markets, identifying operators with significant market power (SMP), and granting authorisations. The PTS is independent, meaning that the Government is not permitted to govern how the PTS should apply an act or decide in a particular matter relating to the exercise of official power.

Although the PTS, among other things, identifies SMP undertakings, etc, the Swedish Competition Authority ('SCA') is the main supervising authority in Sweden for competition law issues and is responsible for the enforcement of competition rules. In accordance with the ECO, the PTS must obtain the SCA's opinion on issues regarding market definitions and identification of undertakings with SMP.

31.12   The PTS has enforcement powers and is, entitled to, among other things, gain access to areas, premises and other spaces and require the provision of information in order to monitor compliance with the ECA.[5]

31.13   In accordance with Article 20 of the Framework Directive, the PTS is empowered under the ECA to resolve disputes between operators.[6] Dispute resolution procedure applies to undertakings that provide electronic communications networks or services, and not to individuals. It is applicable to all obligations that may be issued on the grounds of the ECA, or regulations, authorisations, or decisions regarding obligations that arise on the basis of the ECA. The PTS is required to make a determination within four months from a request to resolve a dispute.

31.14   In addition to the Swedish public court system, the National Board for Consumer Complaints ('ARN')[7] provides consumer dispute resolution. Consumer disputes in relation to electronic communications may, therefore, be tried by the ARN. It is a public authority that functions almost like a court. The ARN's main task is, upon application from consumers, to impartially resolve disputes between consumers and undertakings. Although the decisions of the ARN are non-binding, the majority of undertakings nevertheless comply with them.

Right of Appeal against NRA's Decisions

31.15   A decision by the PTS can be appealed by an entity which is subject to the decision. Moreover, decisions may be appealed by other parties whose rights are affected negatively by the decision.[8] A decision identifying a party as having SMP may only be appealed in connection with the appeal of a decision to implement, cancel, or change SMP obligations.[9]

Appeal is made to the Administrative Court. A leave to appeal is required to appeal to the next level, the Administrative Court of Appeal. A ruling of the Administrative Court of Appeal is final and cannot be appealed.[10]

The NRA's Obligations to Cooperate with the Commission

31.16   The ECA implemented the consolidation and co-regulation procedures by requiring the PTS to follow the procedures set out in Articles 7 and 7a of the

---

5   Ch 7 ss 1–9 ECA.
6   Ch 7 s 10 ECA.
7   SFS (2004:1034), www.arn.se
8   Ch 8 ss 19–19a ECA.
9   Ch 8 s 20 ECA.
10   Ch 8 s 19 ECA.

Framework Directive. The PTS must, among other things, consult with other NRAs and the Commission (and, on certain decisions, also with BEREC), take utmost account of the Commission's recommendations, provide information to the Commission, and notify the Commission of the names of undertakings designated as having universal service obligations.[11]

31.17 The PTS must engage in 'national consolidation' when it intends to take a regulatory measure that will likely have a significant impact on the EU market. The 'veto procedure' (whereby the Commission may veto proposed regulatory measures) has been implemented in accordance with Article 7 Framework Directive.

31.18 The Commission's power to specify and publish standards and specifications is recognised in Chapter 2, Section 3 of the ECA. Undertakings must comply with the Commission's compulsory standards, which are published in the EU Official Journal.

'Significant Market Power' as a Fundamental Prerequisite of Regulation

31.19 SMP has the meaning of 'dominant position' as defined in established EU competition law practice. Specifically, The ECA specifies that:

> 'an undertaking shall be deemed to have significant market power in a relevant market if, either individually or together with others, it has a position of such financial strength that it can to a significant extent act independently of its competitors, its customers and ultimately the consumer'.

SMP may refer to individual or collective dominance. Undertakings with SMP in one market may also be designated to have SMP in closely related markets where links between the two markets allow leveraging of market power.

31.20 The PTS annually determines product and service markets as well as national markets that may require the introduction of SMP obligations under the Act. The PTS makes such decisions following a public consultation and must take into account Commission Recommendations on relevant markets as well as the Commission Guidelines on market analysis. The PTS must define relevant markets and perform market analysis in consultation with the Competition authority.

The PTS must continually monitor and analyse these defined markets to determine whether effective competition exists. If the PTS concludes that a determined market is not effectively competitive, it must identify undertakings with SMP and impose appropriate regulatory obligations.

31.21 In one of the first designations under the ECA, the PTS designated TeliaSonera, the former incumbent, as having SMP in the market for access to the public telephone network at a fixed location for residential customers. The PTS imposed on TeliaSonera, in this market, obligations of, among other things, access, retail-minus pricing, the publishing of a reference offer, transparency, non-discrimination, and accounting separation.

The PTS has also designated TeliaSonera as having SMP in the wholesale broadband access market and the market for wholesale unbundled access. The PTS imposed obligations on TeliaSonera in these markets of, among other things the

---

11   Ch 8 s 11 ECA.

provision of reasonable access, accounting separation, non- discrimination and price control. The PTS has further designated TeliaSonera as having SMP in the market for the minimum set of leased lines, for call origination for public telephone network provided at a fixed location, together with a number of other operators in the market for call termination on individual public telephone networks provided at a fixed location, for wholesale terminating segments of leased lines as well as the market for transit services in the fixed public telephone network.

31.22   The mobile operators TeliaSonera, Tele2, Hi3G, Telenor, Lycamobile, Net1, TDC, and Ventelo have all been designated as having SMP in wholesale voice call termination in their individual markets. Obligations imposed include, among other things, the provision of interconnection, non-discrimination, and cost separation.

31.23   The ECA distinguishes between general regulatory powers and those with respect to SMP undertakings.

31.24   Obligations to be imposed on undertakings with SMP under the ECA mirrors those in the Access Directive and the Universal Service Directive and include requirements regarding transparency, non-discrimination, cost-accounting, interconnection, and other forms of access, price control or accounting separation. At least one obligation must be imposed on undertakings that are found to have SMP in a relevant market.

31.25   The preparatory work of the ECA stipulates a restrictive approach to obligations in markets where competition is satisfactory. Nevertheless, the PTS may, to the extent necessary to ensure end-to-end connectivity, impose obligations on undertakings that control access to end users. Such obligations include, for example, the provision of interconnection to market related prices.

NRA's Regulatory Duties Concerning Rights of Way, Co-location and Facility sharing

31.26   Rights of way and access are regulated in the ECA and in the Right of Way Act.[12] Access to property or rights of way may be granted through individual agreements or in accordance with the ECA or the Right of Way Act. Expropriation issues are dealt with under the Expropriation Act.[13]

Under the Right of Way Act, rights may be granted only to publicly available networks. All undertakings with a general authorisation are eligible to apply for a right of way.

The ECA stipulates that an operator may be required to grant rights or access if necessary to protect the environment, public health, or public security, or in order to attain physical planning objectives.

31.27   In order for the PTS to enforce facility sharing, it should be unambiguous that the building of, among other things, a radio mast is difficult to accomplish due to any of the above stated reasons. In such a situation, the PTS may, upon application from an operator, require another operator to grant co-location to a radio mast if a local authority has denied the operator planning permission to build a mast and there are no alternative options to place the mast. The PTS must consult with the parties involved before making such a decision.

---

12   SFS (1973:1144).
13   SFS (1972:719).

REGULATION OF MARKET ENTRY: THE AUTHORISATION DIRECTIVE

The general authorisation of electronic communications

31.28 In accordance with the Authorisation Directive, the Government of Sweden has abolished the requirement to apply for a licence to provide an electronic communications networks or service. Therefore, under the current regulatory regime, any person or undertaking may provide an electronic communications network or service as long as it complies with the conditions specified in the general authorisation.

31.29 Operators must notify the PTS prior to providing a network or a service. Notification is required;

- for operators who provide public communications networks of the kind that are typically provided for compensation. Typically, if an operator actively recruits customers in the market, and offers connection on determined conditions), this will be considered a public communications network; and
- for service providers who provide publicly available electronic communications services.

Company networks or Virtual Private Networks, and services only offered to a limited and exclusive group of end users are excluded from the notification requirement. Further, providers of Internet telephony (VoIP) services are only required to notify the PTS if the services constitute means to making, and accepting calls, via one or several numbers within the national or international numbering plan. Calls are defined as real-time connections. If the delay in a network that uses Internet protocols is not greater than that the user believes that the communication is in real time, the communication constitutes a call and the service must be notified to the PTS. The PTS has not defined 'delay', and it has been left for the courts and practice to determine the precise meaning of this term.

31.30 The information required by the current notification form is:

- information about the legal entity providing the network or service;
- information as to whether the notified entity will provide communication networks and/or electronic communications services and a short description of the intended business;
- the start date; and
- the annual turnover of the whole group and the turnover of the notified business. If the notified business has not yet commenced, the turnover shall be stated as nil.

The general authorisation is valid until the notified entity's business is terminated. The PTS requires the notified entity to inform it immediately if the business is terminated.

Rights of Use for Radio Frequencies

31.31 The PTS must allocate and assign frequencies on objective, transparent and proportionate conditions. Subject to limited exemptions, the right to use radio transmitters requires application for an individual authorisation. Under the ECA, a licence shall be granted if the intended usage is considered efficient use of frequencies.[14] An application for a frequency authorisation may be rejected if the PTS has reason to believe that a radio transmitter be used in violation of authorisation conditions.

According to the ECA, the grant of frequency rights may be subject to the conditions specified in Part B of the Annex to the Authorisation Directive, including, among other things, network build-out obligations, geographical coverage, and technical specifications. Conditions relating to usage rights may be specified for a limited period of time.

31.32   The number of rights of use for radio frequencies can be limited if it is necessary in order to ensure the efficient use of radio frequencies. The substantive and procedural rules regarding such limitations are set forth in chapter 3 section 7 of the ECA and correspond with the provisions of the Authorisation Directive.

31.33   The PTS may grant frequency usage rights on the basis of competitive or comparative selection procedures (auction or 'beauty contests').

31.34   Spectrum trading is permitted. Authorisations or parts of authorisations to use radio transmitters may be assigned to other undertakings, subject to the consent of the PTS. Consent will not be granted where there is reason to believe that the spectrum transfer will have a negative impact on competition.

Rights of Use for Numbers

31.35   The PTS is responsible for the regulation and use of the national numbering plan. Numbers from the national numbering plan may only be used in accordance with an individual authorisation. Given that numbering capacity is limited, efficient use of these resources is necessary to safeguard access to them. The PTS must make decisions on rights of use of numbers within 21 calendar days after receipt of a completed application.

The PTS must grant numbers on objective, transparent and non-discriminatory terms. Numbers may only be assigned to undertakings that provide or use electronic communications networks or services. An applicant for a number need not be operating under a general authorisation, and therefore, need not file a notification with the PTS.

31.36   Authorisations to use numbers may be subject to conditions regarding, among other things, the type of service for which the number will be used, actual and efficient use of the numbers, authorisation periods, and obligations to adhere to applicable international agreements concerning numbers.

31.37   In Sweden, the assignment of numbers has not previously been viewed as a procedure with economic implications. Numbers have been considered a State-owned public resource that may be utilised according to needs. Through the ECA, however, the PTS may assign numbers of exceptional economic value through a competitive or comparative selection procedure. The ECA does not prescribe procedural rules, but permits the PTS to specify such rules through regulations.

31.38   Number portability was implemented for fixed networks in 1999 and for mobile networks in 2001. The ECA requires undertakings providing public

---

14   Ch 3 s 6 ECA.

telephony services to permit subscribers to keep their telephone number when changing service provider.[15]

31.39   Number trading is permitted. Authorisations or parts of authorisations to use numbers may be assigned, subject to the consent of the PTS.

The NRA's Enforcement Powers

31.40   In order to fulfil its duties as the supervisory authority over the electronic communications market, the PTS may require certain documents to be presented, and gain access to grounds and premises, where activities covered by the ECA are performed. It is also competent to issue such orders, prohibitions and fines as necessary to ensure compliance with the ECA. The PTS may further revoke authorisations, amend conditions, and determine that a business must cease operations, in part or completely.

31.41   The PTS must, as a general rule, before taking action, permit an undertaking that is required to verify compliance with the ECA a reasonable time to respond and state its views or voluntarily remedy any breaches within a certain deadline.

31.42   The PTS may, however, direct immediate compliance in the case of a breach representing an immediate and serious threat to public safety, health and security, or a breach which could, in the PTS's opinion, create serious economic or operational problems for undertakings or end users.

Administrative Charges and Fees for Rights of Use

31.43   The ECA permits the PTS to impose administrative charges on undertakings providing a service or network under the general authorisation or to whom an individual right of use has been granted. The relevant fees are set out in the PTS's Regulation concerning fees according to the Electronic Communications Act.[16] The PTS amends this regulation annually.

31.44   The general authorisation (notification) fees vary, depending on whether the notified undertaking's annual turnover exceeds MSEK 5 (approx €580,000). A notified undertaking with a business turnover below MSEK 5 must pay an official notification fee to the PTS of SEK 1000 (approx €115). Undertakings with a turnover of MSEK 5 or more must pay a yearly fee of 0.165 per cent of such annual turnover. In order for the PTS to charge the correct fee, it will send out at the end of each calendar year a form for operators to complete and return to the PTS. If no such information is provided, the annual turnover will be estimated by the PTS.

REGULATION OF NETWORK ACCESS AND INTERCONNECTION: THE ACCESS DIRECTIVE

Objectives and Scope of Access Regulation

31.45   The Swedish provisions on interconnection and access apply to operators of public communications networks and authorised undertakings seeking interconnection or access to these networks or associated facilities.

---

15   Ch 5 s 9 ECA.
16   PTSFS 2011:6.

Basic Regulatory Concepts

31.46   The ECA constitutes a deregulation of interconnection obligations in comparison to the preceding legislation. The Telecommunications Act which preceded the ECA stipulated a general interconnection obligation for those who provided telecommunications services that were subject to a notification duty, in particular fixed telephony and mobile telecommunications services. The ECA, on the other hand, includes merely a general obligation to negotiate interconnection. Where interconnection and other forms of access cannot be achieved through voluntary agreements concluded on a commercial basis, the ECA provides powers, subject to certain pre-conditions, to introduce special obligations regarding interconnection and other forms of access. Such obligations may include, among other things, making services compatible with other operators' services.[17]

31.47   The ECA defines interconnection as the physical and logical connection of public communications networks to enable users to communicate with each other or to gain access to services that are provided on the network. The preparatory works states that, as the term 'access' is not exhaustively defined in the Access Directive, the inclusion of a specific definition of the term in the ECA would not make the application of the legislation easier. The ECA, therefore, does not define 'access'.

Access- and Interconnection-related Obligations with Respect to SMP Undertakings

31.48   Chapter 4 sections 4–9 of the ECA provides a general framework of obligations the PTS may impose on operators designated as having SMP. The ECA gives the PTS wide discretion to determine how to formulate these obligations and how to adapt them to the circumstances of each individual case.

The primary obligations the PTS may impose on SMP operators in a particular market are obligations to meet reasonable demands for access to and use of networks. These obligations may be paired with an obligation to publish a reference offer or certain specific information. Further, the PTS may require operators to, among other things, offer co-location, apply non-discriminatory terms and conditions, cost separation, price controls, and to observe a particular cost-accounting method.

Regulatory Powers with Respect to SMP-undertakings

31.49   The ECA delegates authority to the PTS to imposed a number of other obligations on SMP operators as remedies in relevant markets which have an impact similar to access obligations, including, among other things, the requirement to provide carrier (pre-)selection. The obligation to provide leased lines on wholesale terms (which was included in the prior legislation) has been revoked.

Regulatory Powers Applicable to All Market Participants

31.50   The ECA delegates to the PTS the authority to impose obligations on non-SMP undertakings controlling access to end users to the extent necessary to

---

17   Ch 4 s 3 ECA.

ensure end-to-end connectivity. Other than interoperability obligations, the ECA does not specify the precise types of obligations the PTS may impose.

31.51   Swedish law is based on the principle of freedom of establishment in relation to radio and television. In order to control the use of frequencies, however, an absolute freedom of establishment is not possible.

31.52   Broadcasts to the public of radio and television programmes will continue to require a licence under the Radio and Television Act (2010:696). The rules concerning retransmission duty, referred to as 'must carry', are specified in said act.

31.53   Electronic Programming Guides ('EPG') and Application Programming Interfaces ('API') are not regulated in the ECA.

REGULATION OF UNIVERSAL SERVICES AND USERS' RIGHTS: THE UNIVERSAL SERVICE DIRECTIVE

Regulation of Universal Service Obligations

31.54   The ECA permits the PTS, if necessary to enable end users to access networks or services at affordable prices, to impose the following universal services obligations on the appropriate undertaking:

- connection to a publicly available communications network in a fixed network termination point;
- access to publicly available telephony services;
- the provision of at least one comprehensive directory to be provided to end users either in printed or electronic form or both and to be updated at least once a year;
- the provision of comprehensive telephone directory enquiry service for end users;
- the provision of public pay telephones or other places with access to voice telephony, including the possibility of making emergency calls from public pay telephones using the single European emergency call number and other national emergency numbers free of charge; and
- the provision of services for disabled users on equal terms as other end users and take suitable measures to manage disabled users' needs for special needs.

31.55   The ECA requires that a fixed connection to a publicly available communications network provided as a universal service enable voice and telefax communication as well as data communication with a minimum data bit rate that allows functional access to the Internet. Such connection must be offered to people with disabilities to the same extent and on the same terms as for other end users.

31.56   Specifying the lowest data bit rate in the statutory text would, with regard to the dynamic developments that characterise the electronic communications sector, risk locking the application of law in an inappropriate manner, ie by specifying a data rate that would appear appropriate, but within a very short period of time would be outdated and considered too low. The ECA does not define the term 'functional access'. The PTS may, therefore determine, on a case-by-case basis, appropriate minimum speed. Currently, the PTS defines 'functional Internet access' as a data rate of at least 1 Mbit/s.

31.57   The ECA is based on the assumption that the market will ensure the provision of universal services. The PTS may intervene only in case of a market failure. The Act specifies that one or more undertakings may be designated to comply with universal service obligations including the provision of access at fixed locations, public pay phones, directory inquiry facilities, and services for disabled users. It also sets out the procedure for designation of undertakings to comply with these obligations.

31.58   In addition to the requirements that may be imposed on operators providing universal services, particular requirements are imposed on operators providing publicly available telephony services. This applies, for example, to sustainability and accessibility in the event of disasters and similar situations and an obligation to cooperate in forwarding emergency calls without interruption and without charge to the end user.

31.59   The PTS may impose obligations on an operator to provide universal services and combine these with conditions concerning the achievement of particular performance goals. An obligation to provide a universal service can also be combined with, for instance, price adjustment in the form of common nationwide tariffs or a particular maximum price. The PTS must monitor compliance with the stipulated performance goals. The relevant operator must make available to the public information concerning the performance of its service. The PTS may, at the expense of the relevant operator, review the information that the operator has made public. If the PTS finds that the performance goals have not been achieved, it may take measures necessary to ensure compliance with such goals.

31.60   There is no universal service funding mechanism in Sweden. However, it is possible for the Government or the PTS to satisfy public and private needs for access to electronic communications services or networks through procurement if the obligation to provide a universal service is considered to impose unreasonable burdens on the operator. This power applies where it is particularly appropriate in view of the costs of providing the service or network.

Regulation of Retail Markets

31.61   The basic principle is that regulation of retail services is permissible only if regulation at wholesale level does not achieve the regulatory objectives. The PTS may impose obligations to apply maximum or minimum prices, or obligations not to take measures that limit competition or not to unreasonably bundle services.[18]

31.62   The PTS has designated TeliaSonera as having SMP in the retail markets 1 and 2 (call origination at a fixed location). The obligations imposed on TeliaSonera are, among other things, to provide access, cost-oriented prices, apply non-discriminatory terms and conditions, accounting separation, reference offers and publication of information. In the fixed and mobile call termination markets (2 and 7), each operator is designated as having SMP within its own network.

31.63   The PTS monitors operators' compliance with the ECA provisions regarding universal service obligations. The procedure for notifying breach and requiring compliance is set out in chapter 7 section 1 of the ECA.

End User Rights

31.64   Operators providing public communications networks or publicly available electronic communications services to consumers must do so in accordance with a

---

18   Ch 5 s 13 ECA.

contract containing a minimum level of information. Such information must include, among other things, the identity and name of the undertaking, details on the services provided, details on prices and tariffs, information on the duration of the contract and the conditions for renewal and information on how to initiate consumer dispute settlement proceedings. The minimum level applies to contracts with other end users, such as business customers, upon request by the end user. The obligation to specify in a contract how a dispute resolution procedure outside the general courts may be initiated, however is limited to consumer matters as ARN's dispute resolution powers are specifically limited to disputes referred by consumers.

31.65   Transparency obligations regarding provisions of price tariffs, terms and quality of services are set out in the ECA. Undertakings providing publicly available electronic communications networks or services must publish transparent, comparable, adequate and up-to-date information on applicable prices, tariffs and general terms and conditions of access to and use of the network or service. Detailed obligations are set out in regulations published by the PTS.[19] Furthermore, the PTS may impose obligations to provide subscribers with information, among other things, on applicable tariffs, changes to emergency call access, and measures implemented to manage traffic. The PTS may also impose an obligation to publish comparable, adequate and current information on quality of services and the measures taken to provide end users with disabilities access to services. The PTS has published regulations setting out quality of services parameters, which include, among other things, emergency calls, customer support, and mobile network coverage. [20]

Quality of service: securing 'net neutrality'

31.66   There are no provisions in the ECA that explicitly deal with 'net neutrality'. According to the PTS, net neutrality means that all Internet traffic shall be treated equally by providers of publicly available electronic communications services and networks. The PTS strives to secure net neutrality mainly by supervising and enforcing the transparency obligations mentioned in the paragraph above.

Other obligations

31.67   Undertakings providing publicly available communications networks or services must take adequate technical and organisational measures to fulfil reasonable requirements of service availability. Operators must also enable end users to call emergency services free of charge and, subject to data protection legislation, must meet all reasonable requests to make available subscriber information. Operators must provide such information on fair, objective, cost-oriented and non-discriminatory terms.

Obligations Facilitating Change of Provider

31.68   Providers of publicly available electronic communications services must facilitate the change of providers by porting numbers to the new provider upon a

---

19   PTSFS 2009:7.
20   PTSFS 2007:1.

subscriber's request.[21] The porting of the number shall be performed by the current provider 'as soon as possible' and the activation of the number with the new provider shall be performed by the new provider at the latest one working day after the porting process has been completed. The PTS has adopted regulations specifying the number portability obligations and requirements.[22] Pursuant to the regulations, a service provider must port numbers so that the service can be provided to the subscriber by the receiving provider at the latest within 10 working days from the time of request by the receiving provider in the case of services at fixed locations to business customers, and within three days from such request in all other cases.

31.69   Geographic numbers need only be ported for the provision of services within the same location. There is no obligation to port numbers between networks providing services at fixed locations and mobile networks. Charges between operators related to the provision of number portability must be cost- oriented and operators are not entitled to any remuneration from the subscriber for the provision of number portability.[23]

DATA PROTECTION: THE DIRECTIVE ON PRIVACY AND ELECTRONIC COMMUNICATIONS

Confidentiality of Communications

31.70   Chapter 6 of the ECA requires operators that provide publicly available electronic communications services to take appropriate measures to ensure the safeguarding of the data they process.[24] To do so, operators providing electronic communications services may need to work with the relevant network operators. Where there are special risks of security breach, the service provider must inform subscribers about such risks. If the service provider is not itself obliged to remedy the risk, it must inform the subscribers of how, and at what approximate cost, the risk can be remedied.[25]

31.71   In the case of a personal data breach, providers of publicly available electronic communications services must, without undue delay, notify the PTS.[26] When the personal data breach is likely to adversely affect the personal data or privacy of a subscriber or user, or if the PTS so requests, the provider must also, without undue delay, notify the subscriber or individual of the breach. Service providers must also maintain an inventory of personal data breaches. The PTS has issued regulations and guidance specifying the obligations and requirements relating to personal data breaches.[27]

31.72   Chapter 6 section 17 of the ECA contains a general prohibition on interception and surveillance of communications. Under chapter 7 section 15 of the ECA, it is an offence to gain access to, or process information from, an electronic communication in a publicly available communications network or service without

---

21   Ch 5 s 9 ECA.
22   PTSFS 2007:7 as amended by PTSFS 2011:5.
23   Ch 5 s 10 ECA.
24   Ch 6 s 3 ECA.
25   Ch 6 s 4 ECA.
26   Ch 6 s 4a ECA.
27   PTSFS 2012:1 and PTS guidance document dated 10 April 2012.

the consent of one of the users of the network or service.[28] This prohibition, however, excludes caching, ie storage solely for the effective transmission of the communication.

31.73 Information, such as cookies, may be stored on or accessed from a subscriber's or user's terminal equipment only if the subscriber or user is provided with information about the purpose of the processing and consents thereto.[29] This must not prevent any storage or access necessary for carrying out the transmission of a communication over an electronic communications network, or as necessary in order to provide a service explicitly requested by the subscriber or user.

Data Retention

31.74 Directive 2006/24/EC (the 'Data Retention Directive') was implemented in the ECA and the ECO on 1 May 2012. Under these rules, providers of publicly available electronic communications networks or services are obliged to retain the categories of data set forth in the ECO for a period of six months from the date of the communication.[30] The data shall be subject to appropriate technical and organisational security measures and may be accessed by specially authorised personnel only.[31]

31.75 Providers of publicly available electronic communications networks and services are entitled to compensation for costs incurred when the data is disclosed. Such compensation must be paid by the competent authority that requested the disclosure.[32] The PTS has produced draft regulations regarding what security measures must be implemented and how the compensation to the service providers must be calculated. To date, the regulations have not yet been adopted.

Traffic Data and Location Data

31.76 Traffic data is defined in the ECA as any data processed for the purpose of the conveyance of a communication on an electronic communications network or for the billing thereof.[33] Location data is defined as data processed in an electronic communications network or by an electronic communications service and which indicates the geographic position of the terminal equipment of a user.[34]

31.77 Service providers must inform subscribers of the type of traffic data that is processed and the duration of the processing.[35]

31.78 Traffic data that is processed and that refers to users that are physical persons or subscribers must be erased or anonymised when the data is no longer needed for the purpose of transmitting the communication.[36] However, this does not apply to data stored in compliance with the data retention obligations described above in Section 6.2. Operators may process data for the purpose of invoicing.

---

28   Ch 6 s 17 ECA.
29   Ch 6 s 18 ECA.
30   Ch 6 s 16a and 16d ECA.
31   S 37 ECO.
32   Ch 6 s 16e ECA.
33   Ch 6 s 1 ECA.
34   Ch 1 s 7 ECA.
35   Ch 6 s 6 ECA.
36   Ch 6 s 5 ECA.

Operators may also, after obtaining consent, process data for the specific services for which the data is required. Users must be permitted to withdraw their consent at any time.

31.79   Traffic data necessary for the purpose of subscriber billing and interconnection payments may be retained only for the period during which the bill may be lawfully challenged and payment pursued.[37]

31.80   Location data that does not constitute traffic data may only be processed if it has been made anonymous or the user or subscriber has provided consent to the processing.[38] Prior to consent being provided, the service provider must inform the user or the subscriber about the type of data that will be processed, the duration and purpose of the processing and whether the data will be forwarded or disclosed to a third party. Consent may be withdrawn by the user at any time.

Itemised Billing

31.81   Providers of publicly available electronic communications networks or telephony services must provide subscribers with itemised bills at no charge, unless the subscriber has requested the bill to be non-itemised.[39] Calls to certain toll-free numbers, such as women's crisis centres, must not be specified on the bill.

31.82   The PTS has issued regulations specifying the obligations and requirements regarding itemised bills.[40] Unless otherwise agreed with the subscriber, the service provider must provide the bill in paper format. The regulations set forth various categories of information that must be included in the itemised bill including, among other things, the number of calls made, cost per unit, and total call duration.

Presentation and Restriction of Calling and Connected Line Identification

31.83   Service providers offering calling line identification services must allow users to easily, and free of charge, withhold their number on a per-call basis).[41] In addition, users must also have the opportunity to block the numbers of incoming calls and to reject incoming calls automatically in cases where the caller has withheld the caller identification.

Automatic Call Forwarding

31.84   Service providers must, at the request of, and at no cost to, the user, cease calls that have been automatically forwarded to the user as soon as practicable after the request.[42]

Directories of Subscribers

31.85   Subscribers must be informed of the purposes of the publicly available subscriber directory or any other directory from which subscriber data can be

---

37   Ch 6 s 6 ECA.
38   Ch 6 s 9 ECA.
39   Ch 5 s 7 ECA.
40   PTSFS 2006:3.
41   Ch 6 s 12 ECA.
42   Ch 6 s 14 ECA.

obtained prior to any data is made available for inclusion in a directory, and without charge.

In order to process personal data concerning subscribers that are physical persons, consent from the subscribers is required. The subscribers must also, free of charge, be able to verify the data, including having erroneous data corrected or withdrawn as soon as practicable.[43]

---

43   Ch 6 s 16 ECA.

The UK Market for Electronic Communications[1]

Peter Strivens, Richard Pike, Ben Slinn and Keith Jones
Baker & McKenzie LLP, London

LEGAL STRUCTURE

Basic Policy

Regulatory approach

32.1   Nearly 30 years since its privatisation British Telecommunications ('BT'), the former monopoly incumbent, still remains the dominant player in many markets, although it faces varying degrees of competition in different areas. Following its formation in 2003 the communications regulator, the Office of Communications[2] ('Ofcom'), undertook a strategic review of the telecommunications sector (the 'Strategic Review') with the aim of reassessing the regulatory framework. Ofcom believed that BT's combination of upstream market power and vertical integration provided it with the ability and incentive to discriminate against its downstream competitors. Its new approach was to require real equality of access to those parts of the fixed telecoms network which BT's competitors cannot fairly replicate. Accordingly it agreed with BT a number of undertakings to address these concerns.[3] These undertakings were given in lieu of a market investigation reference to the Competition Commission.[4] Ofcom has subsequently agreed a number of adjustments and refinements, including exemptions, to these undertakings.[5]

The main elements of the undertakings are:

- BT must supply a range of products in identified wholesale markets (including various wholesale line rental products) to all communications providers on the same timescales, terms and conditions (including price) and by the same systems and processes;

---

1   Editing of this chapter closed on 22 January 2013.
2   Established by Office of Communications Act 2002.
3   Ofcom, 'Final statements on the Strategic Review of Telecommunications, and undertakings in lieu of a reference under the Enterprise Act 2002', 22 September 2005.
4   See para 32.35 below.
5   A consolidated version incorporating all such variations dated 23 March 2010 can be found on Ofcom's website: http://stakeholders.ofcom.org.uk/binaries/telecoms/policy/bt/consolidated.pdf

- BT must maintain a separate division (now known as Openreach), which will control and operate the physical assets making up all of BT's local access and backhaul network. BT must also have an internal compliance board ('Equality of Access Board') to monitor and report to Ofcom on compliance with these undertakings. BT must also comply with a number of other organisational provisions; and
- BT also gave commitments in respect of the design and provision of access to its next generation network.

Failure to comply with the undertakings can be enforced by Ofcom through the UK courts by way of injunction. There is also the potential for third parties affected by a breach to seek damages through the courts for any loss suffered.[6]

32.2 There have also been some significant changes in approach to the use of spectrum since privatisation of the industry. For the first time, in 2000, the government assigned mobile spectrum (the 2100MHz band for 3G use) through an auction and also took the opportunity to introduce more competition through the reservation of one licence for a new entrant. The auction raised billions of pounds for the Exchequer.

32.3 In 2001, the government commissioned an independent review of radio spectrum management issues. The objective of the review was to advise on the principles that should govern spectrum management and the changes required to ensure that all users are focussed on using spectrum in the most efficient way possible. The review made many recommendations but, in summary, concluded that the UK needed to radically change the way in which spectrum is allocated and used.[7]

32.4 Ofcom subsequently undertook its own review of spectrum management and set out its conclusions in its Spectrum Framework Review.[8] It then set out on a process of de-regulation in tandem with developments at the EU level. This has included reducing the number of restrictions both in terms of who can use spectrum and what it can be used for. The new approach has been implemented primarily through measures to authorise:

- spectrum trading;
- spectrum liberalisation; and
- prompt release of unused spectrum into the market allowing maximum flexibility as to subsequent use.

Market conditions

32.5 Despite its continued dominance, BT's share of fixed voice volumes in both the residential and business markets continues to gradually decrease. BT's market share of fixed line services stands at 36 per cent with Virgin Media's share standing at 12 per cent (the share of 'other' operators standing at a combined 52 per cent).

32.6 Broadband take up in the UK had previously been an area of concern, although there are definite signs that this is now improving. As at the end of 2011,

---

6   S 167 of the Enterprise Act.
7   Review of Radio Spectrum Management: An independent review for Department of Trade and Industry and HM Treasury by Professor Martin Cave, March 2002.
8   Ofcom: A Statement on Spectrum Trading – Implementation in 2004 and beyond – 6 August 2004.

the number of fixed broadband connections in the UK stood at 18.8m. As at the first quarter of 2012, the proportion of adults with broadband in the UK (including both fixed and mobile broadband) stood at 76 per cent. The average UK broadband speed in the UK as at November 2011 was 7.6Mbit/s. The UK Government's policy in relation to broadband is to ensure that all UK homes have access to at least 2Mbits/s broadband by 2015, and to promote super-fast broadband in the UK by investing £530 million.[9] At the retail level, BT's market share is slowly eroding. As at the end of 2011, BT's market share of fixed broadband stood at 29.3 per cent, with Virgin Media's share being 20.2 per cent, TalkTalk's share being 18.5 per cent, Sky's share being 17.9 per cent and other providers collectively accounting for the remaining 14.2 per cent.

32.7   There are three GSM operators in the UK: Vodafone, Everything Everywhere (operating also under the legacy Orange and T-Mobile brands)[10] and O_2.[11] There are four 3G operators in the UK, the three GSM operators and Hutchison 3G (UK) Limited (which trades under the '3' brand). Everything Everywhere started operating a 4G LTE service in November 2012 following liberalisation of its 1800MHz licences and others are expected to follow suit in 2013 with licences to be acquired in a forthcoming auction of frequencies in the 800MHz and 2600MHz bands.

32.8   The merger that created Everything Everywhere has left it with the largest market share of all the mobile operators. 3 remains the operator with the smallest market share albeit that it has a larger share of mobile data usage. Ofcom has concluded that the market for mobile call origination is relatively competitive and that no operator has significant market power, save in call termination. (Historically, Vodafone and O_2 had been subject to additional regulatory restrictions.)

Implementation of EU Directives

32.9   The government implemented the 2002 EU Regulatory Framework through the Communications Act 2003. The Act also contained the government's proposals[12] for the reform of the communications industry, notably the transfer of powers to a new single regulatory body for the communications and media industries, Ofcom.

In addition, the government implemented the 2009 EU Regulatory Package (comprising the 'Better Regulation Directive' and the 'Citizens' Rights Directive') through the Electronic Communications and Wireless Telegraphy Regulations 2011[13] which amended the Communications Act 2003 and the Wireless Telegraphy Act 2006, and the Privacy and Electronic Communications (EC Directive) (Amendment) Regulations 2011[14] which amended the Privacy and Electronic Communications Regulations 2003 (the '2011 amendments'). These amendments

---

9   See 'Britain's Superfast Broadband Future' dated December 2010 published by the Department for Culture, Media and Sport.
10   France Télécom and DeutscheTelekom created a joint venture between their UK subsidiaries Orange UK and T-Mobile UK in 2010 under the name Everything Everywhere.
11   In 2005, O_2 was taken over by Telefónica. The operating company has been renamed Telefónica UK Limited but it trades under the O_2 brand.
12   Communications White Paper – A New Future for Communications 12 December 2000 (Cm 5010).
13   SI 2011/1210.
14   SI 2011/1298.

came into force in the UK on 26 May 2011. The general approach of these amendments are to transpose the 2009 EU Regulatory Package into UK law, without going further than what is strictly required by the relevant Directive.

Legislation

32.10 The main pieces of UK legislation applicable to the telecommunications sector are:

- The Communications Act 2003 (the 'Communications Act');
- The Wireless Telegraphy Acts 1967 and 2006 ('WTA');
- The Competition Act 1998 (the 'Competition Act'); and
- The Enterprise Act 2002 (the 'Enterprise Act').

32.11 The Communications Act[15] repealed major parts of the Telecommunications Act 1984 (the 'TAct'), previously the primary source of UK telecommunications law.

32.12 The management and administration of radio spectrum is primarily governed by the WTA (mainly the 2006 Act). It is a criminal offence to establish or use any station for wireless telegraphy except under a licence or in accordance with an exemption.[16]

32.13 In addition to EU law, the main legislative instruments in the UK for dealing with abuse of a dominant position and anti-competitive behaviour are the Competition Act and the Enterprise Act.[17]

REGULATORY PRINCIPLES: IMPLEMENTATION OF THE FRAMEWORK DIRECTIVE

Scope of Regulation

32.14 The Communications Act applies to all providers of electronic communications networks, electronic communications services and associated facilities.

32.15 The definition of an electronic communications network[18] is broad and includes almost any network for the transmission of signals by electrical magnetic or electromagnetic energy. The 2011 Amendments broadened the definition further by including network elements which are not active (however these additional elements do not apply in relation to certain criminal offences under the Communications Act).[19] The person providing the network is the person exercising control of it as opposed to the actual service provider or operator. There is no requirement of ownership or exclusive rights to the network or any element of it. The definition includes private networks.

---

15 It is relatively common for Ofcom to issue guidelines. Sometimes it is required to do so under the Communications Act, for example on the proposed exercise of information gathering powers. It should be emphasised that such guidelines are non-binding. Ofcom is not allowed to fetter its discretion and it therefore must retain the ability to depart from any such guidelines where the circumstances warrant it.

16 S 8 of the WTA 2006.

17 The Enterprise Act came fully into force on 20 June 2003.

18 S 32(1) of the Communications Act.

19 S 32(1)(b)(iv) of the Communications Act.

32.16   An electronic communications service[20] is a service consisting in, or having as its principal feature, the conveyance by means of an electronic communications network of signals, except insofar as it is a content service. The exclusion of content services means that, for example, providers of financial services over the Internet, web hosting, and the provision of an Internet portal do not fall within the definition. Ofcom has said,[21] however, that this definition will be interpreted broadly. Services such as conference calls supported by conference bridges, and voicemail supported by voicemail services will be considered as electronic communications services even though the services involve doing something with the content of a service, as the services consist wholly or mainly in the conveyance of signals rather than the provision of a content service.

32.17   The definition of associated facilities[22] has been updated as a result of the 2011 amendments. These are facilities, elements or services which are available for use, or have the potential to be used, in association with the use of an electronic communications network or electronic communications services (whether or not provided by the person making the facility, element or service available).

32.18   There is an important distinction between private and public electronic communications services and publicly available telephone services. The level of regulation applicable to each is different, with the most onerous obligations being on providers of publicly available telephone services.

32.19   A public electronic communications service is a service that is available to members of the public. The Regulator has said[23] that it will consider that a service is available to the public if it is available to anyone who is willing to pay and to abide by the applicable terms and conditions. A public service is distinguishable from a bespoke service, which is restricted to a limited group of individual and identifiable customers. However, the *number* of customers who receive the service is not an indication of whether or not the service is publicly available. A public service may only have one customer because others have chosen not to take up the service. The important point is that others should not be prevented from taking it up.

32.20   The definition of publicly available telephone services is the same as that in the Universal Services Directive.[24] The main elements of this are:

- a service available to the public;
- for originating and receiving, directly or indirectly, national and international calls;
- through a number or numbers in a national or international telephone numbering plan.[25]

32.21   The current definition of publicly available telephone services described above reflects the amendments contained in the 2009 EU Regulatory Package by removing the reference to 'access to emergency organisations' and to certain specific services (eg directory enquiry facilities, operator assistance etc).

---

20   S 32(2) of the Communications Act.
21   Ofcom: Final Statement: Designation and Relevant Activity Guidelines for the purposes of administrative charging – 31 March 2005.
22   S 32(3) of the Communications Act, as amended by the Electronic Communications and Wireless Telegraphy Regulations 2011 (SI 2011/1210).
23   Guidelines for the interconnection of public electronic communications networks – 23 May 2003. A statement issued by the Director General of Telecommunications.
24   Article 2(c) of the Universal Services Directive.
25   Implemented in General Conditions of Entitlement Part 1.

'Internet Freedom'

32.22   The Digital Economy Act 2010 ('DEA') inserts provisions into the Communications Act[26] regarding obligations on Internet service providers in relation to online infringement of copyright. There are certain 'initial obligations' imposed on Internet service providers which require them to notify subscribers if a copyright owner provides a 'copyright infringement report' to the Internet service provider identifying the subscriber's IP address.[27] There is also an obligation on Internet service providers to provide a 'copyright infringement report' to copyright owners on request.[28] However, both of these initial obligations only apply if there is an 'initial obligations code' in place which also contains these obligations. Ofcom has the power to approve an 'initial obligations code'[29] provided that certain criteria are met,[30] including that the provisions of the code are:

- 'objectively justifiable in relation to the matters to which it relates';
- do not discriminate unduly against particular persons or against particular descriptions of persons;
- proportionate to what they are intended to achieve; and
- transparent in relation to what those provisions are intended to achieve.[31]

Ofcom published a draft initial obligations code on 28 May 2010, and subsequently published a revised version of the code on 26 June 2012,[32] the consultation for which closed on 26 July 2012. The code is expected to be laid before Parliament in early 2013.

In addition, the DEA inserts new provisions into the Communications Act which allow the Secretary of State to impose technical obligations[33] on Internet service providers through additional secondary legislation. However, the Secretary of State cannot impose these obligations until the 'initial obligations code' has been in force for 12 months, and Ofcom has produced (at the direction of the Secretary of State)

---

26   Ss 3 to 16 of the Digital Economy Act 2010 insert the new Ss 124A to 124N of the Communications Act 2003.

27   S 3 of the Digital Economy Act 2010 which inserts the new s 124A of the Communications Act 2003.

28   S 4 of the Digital Economy Act 2010 which inserts the new s 124B of the Communications Act 2003.

29   S 5 of the Digital Economy Act 2010 which inserts the new s 124C of the Communications Act 2003.

30   S 5 of the Digital Economy Act 2010 which inserts the new s 124C(6) of the Communications Act 2003 and s 7 of the Digital Economy Act 2010 which inserts the new s 124E of the Communications Act 2003.

31   S 124E(1)(i) to (l) of the Communications Act 2003.

32   Ofcom: Online Infringement of Copyright and the Digital Economy Act 2010: Notice of Ofcom's proposal to make by order a code for regulating the initial obligations, 26 June 2012.

33   A 'technical obligation' is defined as an obligation for an internet service provider to take a technical measure against some or all relevant subscribers to its service for the purpose of preventing or reducing infringement of copyright by means of the internet (s 124G(2) of the Communications Act 2003). A 'technical measure' is a measure that: (a) limits the speed or other capacity of the service provided to the subscriber; (b) prevents a subscriber from using the service to gain access to particular material, or limits such use; (c) suspends the service provided to the subscriber; or (d) limits the service provided to a subscriber in another way (s 124G(3) of the Communications Act 2003).

a report assessing whether one or more technical obligations should be imposed on Internet service providers.[34]

BT and TalkTalk challenged these provisions of the DEA in judicial review proceedings, arguing that the provisions of the DEA were incompatible with the E-Commerce Directive,[35] the Data Protection Directive,[36] the E-Privacy Directive and the Authorisation Directive. At first instance the High Court dismissed most of BT and TalkTalk's arguments (with the exception of a narrow point regarding allocation of costs for appeals by subscribers).[37] The Court of Appeal dismissed BT and TalkTalk's subsequent appeal.[38]

The DEA grants the Secretary of State the power to make regulations which allow the courts to issue 'blocking injunctions' (an injunction requiring a service provider to prevent its service being used to gain access to a location on the Internet) in respect of a location on the Internet which the court is satisfied has been, is being, or is likely to be used for or in connection with an activity which infringes copyright.[39] However, following a report by Ofcom,[40] the Government announced in 2011[41] that it did not intend to bring forward regulations on site blocking at that time, and subsequently confirmed in 2012[42] that it will seek to repeal ss 17 and 18 of the DEA at an early opportunity.

National Regulatory Authorities: Organisation, Regulatory Objectives, Competencies

Tasks and competencies

32.23   Ofcom has responsibility for the regulation of telecommunications and television and radio broadcasting (including broadcasting standards). It replaced a number of separate regulators which had previously regulated these activities:

- the Broadcasting Standards Commission;
- the Director General of Telecommunications (the 'DG of Telecommunications');
- the Independent Television Commission;
- the Radio Authority;

---

34   Ss 9 and 10 of the Digital Economy Act 2010 which inserts the new ss 124G and 124H of the Communications Act 2003.

35   2000/31/EC.

36   95/46/EEC.

37   *British Telecommunications Plc R (on the application of) v Secretary of State for Business, Innovation and Skills* [2011] EWHC 1021 (Admin).

38   *R (on the application of British Telecommunications Plc) v Secretary of State for Business, Innovation and Skills* [2012] EWCA Civ 232.

39   S 17 of the Digital Economy Act 2010.

40   Ofcom: 'Site Blocking' to reduce online copyright infringement: a review of sections 17 and 18 of the Digital Economy Act.

41   Department for Culture, Media and Sport: Next Steps for Implementation of the Digital Economy Act, August 2011.

42   Department for Culture, Media and Sport Statement: Next Steps to Tackle Internet Piracy, 26 June 2012.

- the Radiocommunications agency[43], and
- the Postcomm.[44]

32.24   Ofcom also has responsibility for the allocation, maintenance and supervision of the UK radio spectrum.[45]

32.25   In addition, PhonepayPlus (formerly the Independent Committee for the Supervision of Standards of Telephone Information Services or 'ICSTIS'), regulates premium rate (or phone paid) services in the UK. Under the Communications Act 2003[46] Ofcom has responsibility for regulating premium rate services in the UK and has confirmed that PhonepayPlus will carry out the day-to-day regulation of premium rate services on Ofcom's behalf.[47] Providers of controlled premium rate services are required to comply with PhonepayPlus' Code of Practice, which has been approved by Ofcom.[48] The 12th edition of the PhonepayPlus Code of Practice, which came into force on 1 September 2011, broadens the applicability of the code to all providers in the premium rate services value chain. Previously the primary obligation to comply with the code of practice rested with the party that entered into the agreement with the network operator.

32.26   Ofcom consists of a chairman, chief executive and various other members, totalling not more than six. It acts collectively through a board.

32.27   Ofcom's principal duties in carrying out its functions are:

- to further the interests of citizens in relation to communications matters; and
- to further the interests of consumers in relevant markets, where appropriate, by promoting competition.[49]

32.28   In addition, the Communications Act sets out a list of objectives which Ofcom is required to secure, including:

- the optimal use for wireless telegraphy of the electromagnetic spectrum; and
- the availability throughout the UK of a wide range of electronic communications services.[50]

32.29   Ofcom has a duty to act in accordance with the six Community requirements as set out in the Framework Directive.[51] Where there is a conflict between the different duties, the duties under the Community requirements will have priority.[52] Ofcom is also required, in certain circumstances, to take due account of all applicable recommendations issued by the European Commission under Article 19(1) of the Framework Directive.[53]

---

43   Office of Communications Act 2002 (Commencement No 3) and Communications Act 2003 (Commencement No 2) Order 2003 No 3142.
44   By virtue of the Postal Services Act 2011.
45   See para 32.12 above.
46   S 120 to 124 of the Communications Act.
47   Formal Framework Agreement between Ofcom and PhonepayPlus, dated December 2007.
48   S 121 of the Communications Act.
49   S 3(1) of the Communications Act.
50   S 3(2) of the Communications Act.
51   S 4(2)–(10) of the Communications Act.
52   S 3(6) of the Communications Act.
53   S 4A of the Communications Act.

Powers

32.30   The government has retained a number of powers, including:

- to give directions to Ofcom in respect of network or spectrum functions for purposes of national security, securing compliance with international obligations or in the interests of public health; and
- changing the level of certain penalties if, for example, it is felt that the level is too low to provide a deterrent effect.

32.31   The Office of Fair Trading ('OFT') is the national competition regulator in the UK. It is an independent statutory body with a board, which consists of a chairman and at least four other members. (Note, the OFT will be replaced shortly by the Competition and Markets Authority (CMA)).

32.32   The OFT and Ofcom have concurrent jurisdiction to enforce both national and EU competition law in respect of commercial activity connected with the communications sector.[54] Subject to a few minor exceptions, Ofcom has the same powers as the OFT for dealing with anti-competitive agreements or abuses of a dominant position. The main powers for dealing with such behaviour are under the Competition Act and EU competition legislation. There are two main prohibitions under the Competition Act:

- Chapter I: a prohibition of anti-competitive agreements; and
- Chapter II: a prohibition on abuse of a dominant position in a market.

32.33   These provisions are more or less identical to Articles 101 and 102,[55] the main difference being that the Competition Act concerns agreements and conduct that may affect trade *within the UK,* whereas Articles 101 and 102 concern agreements and conduct where these may affect trade *between Member States.* The Modernisation Regulation[56] requires conformity when applying national competition law to cases that would be covered by Articles 101 and 102. In any event, the Competition Act[57] provides that there should generally be consistency with EU competition law on substantive issues. The OFT and Ofcom now have concurrent power to enforce Articles 101 and 102 as well as national competition law.

32.34   The penalties for infringing the Chapter I and Chapter II prohibitions are severe and fines may be imposed of up to 10 per cent of turnover for each year of the infringement (up to three years),[58] and disqualification for up to 15 years for directors of offending undertakings. There is also an express right for claims for damages to the Competition Appeal Tribunal ('CAT')[59] if a relevant competition authority concludes that there has been an infringement of UK or EU competition law.[60]

---

54   S 371(8) of the Communications Act.
55   See para 2.1 et seq above.
56   Council Regulation (EC) No 1/2003 of 16 December 2002 on the implementation of the rules of competition laid down in Articles 81 and 82 of the EC Treaty [2003] OJ L1/1.
57   S 60 of the Competition Act.
58   The OFT looks at turnover in the relevant market when setting the fine.
59   The CAT replaced the Competition Commission Appeal Tribunals established as part of the Competition Commission by the Competition Act. It is a specialist independent body for appeals on matters relating to competition law.
60   The right to bring a similar claim in the courts still applies.

32.35 The OFT and Ofcom can both also make market investigation references to the Competition Commission under the Enterprise Act[61] where there are reasonable grounds for suspecting that any feature or combination of features of a market in the UK for goods or services prevents, restricts or distorts competition. Ofcom may also, in certain circumstances, instead of making such a reference, accept undertakings from appropriate persons. As mentioned above, Ofcom accepted undertakings from BT in lieu of such a reference.

32.36 There are regulations in place to co-ordinate regulators' exercise of concurrent jurisdiction[62] and the OFT has issued guidelines on how complaints will be dealt with and how Ofcom, and other regulators with concurrent powers, will work with the OFT.[63] The CAT has also expressed views on how concurrency should operate in practice.

32.37 The guidelines stipulate that the OFT and Ofcom must always inform the other before acting on a case in which they have concurrent powers. Generally, a case should be dealt with by whichever of the OFT or Ofcom is better or best placed to do so. In general, where the dispute concerns the communications sector, this will be Ofcom. If one regulator decides not to take up a case, it should liaise with the other regulator (ie in the present case, Ofcom and the OFT).

32.38 One of the major criticisms of Ofcom is its apparent reluctance to use powers under the Competition Act. After nearly 10 years of operation it is still yet to make a single infringement finding under the Competition Act. Ofcom has produced a number of non-infringement decisions.[64] Ofcom issued two statements of objections in its investigation into BT's residential broadband pricing,[65] but ultimately decided that there was no infringement. There is only one Competition Act investigation currently ongoing, a margin squeeze allegation against BT by Gamma Telecom Limited and Thus plc (now part of Cable & Wireless Worldwide, itself recently taken over by Vodafone). A statement of objections was issued in December 2010 but no further action has been taken since.

32.39 The OFT has taken a number of decisions where it has found a breach of competition law. However, it did not do so in relation to its margin squeeze investigation into BSkyB, the dominant pay-TV operator in the UK (despite issuing

---

61 The Enterprise Act criminalises certain infringements of competition law, under the so-called 'cartel offence'. The current wording is based on 'dishonestly' and relates to price fixing, bid-rigging or market sharing. If convicted, individuals may be jailed and/or disqualified from being a director. This wording is likely to be amended under proposed legislation.

62 Competition Act (Concurrency) Regulations 2004 No 1077.

63 Office of Fair Trading – Concurrent application to regulated industries, 2004.

64 These include: Investigation into BT's residential broadband pricing, 02/11/2010; Complaint from Energis Communications Ltd about BT's charges for NTS call termination (NCCN 500), 01/08/2008; Complaint from Independent Media Support Limited against BBC Broadcast about provision of media access services, 30/05/2007; Complaint against BT about the pricing of cordless fixed-line telephones, 01/08/2006; Reinvestigation of complaint from Floe Telecom Ltd against Vodafone Ltd about an alleged refusal to supply, 28/06/2005; Reinvestigation of complaint from VIP Communications Ltd against T-Mobile Ltd about an alleged refusal to supply, 28/06/2005; Complaint from Gamma Telecom Limited against BT Wholesale about reduced rates for Wholesale Calls from 1 December 2004, 17/06/2005; Pricing of BT Analyst; 28/10/2004; BT 0845 and 0870 retail price change, 20/08/2004; Investigation against BT about potential anti-competitive exclusionary behaviour, 12/07/2004; Suspected margin squeeze by Vodafone, O₂, Orange and T-Mobile, 27/05/2004; available at www.oft.gov.uk/Business/Competition+Act/Decisions/index.htm.

65 On 31 August 2004 and 27 June 2005 – Case CW/613/04/03.

a statement of objections) on the basis that any squeeze was temporary and had no anti-competitive effects.

32.40   Ofcom also has specific information gathering powers under the Communications Act[66] for a wide range of purposes, including ascertaining whether a contravention of a condition has occurred, carrying out a market review and statistical purposes. In addition, Ofcom can now require information for the purposes of assessing the security of a public electronic communications network or service, assessing the availability of a public electronic communications network and identifying electronic communications apparatus that is suitable for shared use.[67] Failure to comply with a request for information can lead to the imposition of a fine of up to £2,000,000[68] and/or criminal proceedings. Ofcom also has information gathering powers under the WTA, which have been widened as a result of the 2011 Amendments and includes information for the purposes of Ofcom's radio spectrum functions.[69] The power to request information is subject to certain limitations. For example, requests must be proportionate to the uses to which the information is to be put; and persons to whom requests are made must be given Ofcom's reasons for requiring the information.[70] In addition, there are certain limitations on Ofcom's ability to require information for the purpose of assessing the security of a public electronic communications network or public electronic communications service[71]. Information that a person may be required to provide to Ofcom under the Communications Act includes:

●   information concerning future developments of an electronic communications network or electronic communications service that could have an impact on the wholesale service made available by the person to competitors; and

●   if a market power determination made in relation to a wholesale market is in force in the person's case, accounting data relating to any retail market associated with the wholesale market.[72]

32.41   Ofcom has issued a policy statement on how it will exercise its information gathering powers.[73] It has said that as a general rule it will seek all the information which it requires to investigate a potential breach of a condition using its statutory powers. It hopes, however, that the information that it requires for other purposes will be provided on a voluntary basis, although it will use its statutory powers if it considers it appropriate to do so. Ofcom confirmed in June 2011 that this policy statement remains applicable in relation to its enhanced information gathering powers under the Communications Act and Wireless Telegraphy Act and it will use such powers in accordance with that policy statement.[74]

---

66   Ss 135 and 136 Communications Act.
67   Ss 135(ie) to 135(ig) Communications Act.
68   S 139(5) of the Communications Act and s 32D of the WTA 2006.
69   S 32A of the WTA 2006.
70   S 137 of the Communications Act.
71   S 137(2A) of the Communications Act.
72   S 135(3A) of the Communications Act.
73   It is required to issue a statement under s 145 of the Communications Act. Ofcom: Information gathering under s 145 Communications Act and s 13B WTA 1949 – 10 March 2005.
74   'Update on policy concerning information gathering for the purposes of section 145 of the Communications Act 2003 and section 32 of the Wireless Telegraphy Act 2006'.

Dispute resolution

32.42   Ofcom has specific duties as regards the resolution of disputes.[75] A dispute is the failure of commercial negotiation about a matter which falls within the scope of section 185 of the Communications Act, the provision of network access and/or other regulatory conditions imposed by Ofcom. In principle there is a distinction between the resolution of disputes and the investigation of complaints alleging, for example, the breach of conditions imposed on dominant providers. In practice, this distinction has been eroded with communications providers successfully relying on dispute resolution to obtain compensation for breach of conditions.[76]

32.43   When a dispute is referred to Ofcom it must first decide whether or not it is appropriate for it to handle the dispute. Until 26 May 2011, Ofcom was obliged to handle any dispute referred to it falling within the scope of section 185 of the Communications Act unless it considered that the dispute could be resolved through alternative means (though Ofcom was obliged to accept the dispute on a second referral if it was not resolved by alternative means within four months).[77] Ofcom received a relatively large number of dispute referrals and the government was eventually persuaded to legislate to give Ofcom more scope to reject referrals, supposedly as a result of amendments to the European Directives. Since 26 May 2011, Ofcom has the ability to refuse to handle a dispute on prioritisation grounds if it is a dispute over network access that does not concern an existing regulatory condition for the benefit of the party referring the dispute.[78] Ofcom has additionally said that it will only accept a dispute where there is:

- clear information submitted by complainants, including information about the scope of the dispute;
- documentary evidence of commercial negotiations on all issues covered by the dispute; and
- a statement by an officer, preferably the Chief Executive Officer, that the company has used its best endeavours to resolve the dispute through commercial negotiation.[79]

32.44   Where Ofcom decides to handle a dispute it must resolve it within four months unless there are exceptional circumstances.[80] In practice, Ofcom has often failed to resolve disputes within four months. It has been accepted that Ofcom has a broad discretion to decide whether or not to extend the period for determining disputes on the basis of exceptional circumstances.[81] Exceptional circumstances most commonly relied on have included the need to conclude other related or relevant proceedings first.

At least in relation to network access disputes, the test that Ofcom must apply in resolving disputes is to decide what is 'fair and reasonable' in the sense of 'fair between the parties and reasonable from the point of view of the relevant

---

75   S 185 of the Communications Act.
76   *British Telecommunications plc v Ofcom (Partial Private Circuits)* [2012] EWCA Civ 1051.
77   S 186 of the Communications Act.
78   Ss 185(1) and 186(2A) of the Communications Act.
79   Dispute Resolution Guidelines – Ofcom's guidelines for the handling of regulatory disputes – 7 June 2011.
80   S 188(5) of the Communications Act.
81   *British Telecommunications plc v Ofcom (NCCN 1007, Ethernet Extension Services)* [2011] CAT 15 at paras [63] to [65].

regulatory objectives'.[82] What exactly this will mean in any given case will depend on the context but a body of case law has developed on a number of related issues including the significance of the presence or absence of regulatory conditions, pre-existing contractual requirements and who must justify an attempt to change or resist changes to existing contractual requirements.

32.45   Ofcom has separate powers to require information in connection with a dispute.[83] Ofcom can impose the same penalties for non-compliance, namely fines of up to £2,000,000, as it can in relation to its other powers to require information. The maximum amount of the fine was substantially increased in 2011 because Ofcom considered that communications providers did not take its requests for information sufficiently seriously, but it has in fact only ever levied a very small number of fines for non-compliance. Until recently, Ofcom has adopted the approach of issuing information requests in draft before issuing them formally so that communications providers could comment on the terms of the request. New guidance indicates that it will no longer issue requests in draft and compliance will therefore be particularly demanding for communications providers.[84]

Right of Appeal against NRA's Decisions

32.46   Prior to the introduction of the Communications Act, the appeals process (including the body) which heard the appeal differed depending upon whether the decision being appealed was taken under the Competition Act or the TAct. Challenges to decisions taken under the TAct were to the normal courts by way of limited judicial review whereas appeals of decisions taken under the Competition Act were to the CAT on the merits.

32.47   The Communications Act made the CAT the appellate body for communications sector matters in general. Decisions by the OFT/Ofcom as to whether there has been an infringement of Chapter I and II prohibitions in the Competition Act (or Articles 101 and 102) are still appealable to the CAT. To this has been added decisions made by Ofcom under Part 2 of the Communications Act (Ofcom's sectoral powers) and most decisions under the WTA.[85] This includes decisions taken pursuant to the exercise of powers to set, modify, revoke and enforce General and Specific Conditions, including access-related conditions. Certain decisions are not appealable to the CAT, including, for example, the decision to designate an undertaking as a provider of a universal service and the making of regulations authorising spectrum trading.[86]

32.48   A peculiar mechanism exists for price control matters (ie matters relating to the imposition of any form of price control on a SMP service). These must be referred by the CAT to the Competition Commission for determination. The CAT

---

82   *Telefonica O2 UK Ltd & Ors v British Telecommunications plc* [2012] EWCA Civ 1002 (*the '08 appeals'*) at para 61 citing general guidance provided by the Competition Appeal Tribunal in *T-Mobile (UK) Ltd v Ofcom* [2008] CAT 12 (the *TRD* Case). The guidance was implicitly approved by the Court of Appeal in its judgment.

83   S 191 of the Communications Act. These powers are in addition to the powers referred to in para 32.40 above.

84   Dispute Resolution Guidelines – Ofcom's guidelines for the handling of regulatory disputes – 7 June 2011.

85   S 192 of the Communications Act.

86   Although it has not been considered as to how this complies with the Framework Directive.

must follow the determination of the Competition Commission[87] unless it decides that, applying judicial review principles, the determination of the Competition Commission would fall to be set aside.

32.49   An appeal to the CAT can be on the grounds that the decision was based on an error of fact, was wrong in law or both or against the exercise of discretion by Ofcom or the government or another person. Appeals from decisions of the CAT are on points of law only and are to the Court of Appeal. Such appeals are only allowed with the permission of the CAT or Court of Appeal.[88]

32.50   It is not possible to appeal a case closure decision where Ofcom genuinely reaches no decision on whether or not there has been an infringement of the Competition Act.[89] The CAT will, however, look at the substance of the regulator's decision. In *Freeserve*, Freeserve challenged the decision by the DG of Telecommunications to close the investigation into its complaint that BT had abused its position through, inter alia, pricing abuses. The DG argued that this decision was not an 'appealable decision' under the Competition Act, because he had decided to close the case rather than take a decision that the Competition Act had not been infringed. In a preliminary hearing,[90] the CAT ruled that the correspondence between the parties was, in effect, a decision that the Competition Act had not been infringed, and therefore that the CAT had jurisdiction to hear the appeal.

32.51   A widely held criticism of the previous appeals system was that the courts were less well equipped than a specialist regulatory body to understand complex technical and economic issues and consequently were often reluctant to overturn the decision of a industry-specific regulator. Under the old appeals system no decision taken by the DG of Telecommunications was ever successfully challenged in the UK courts. Exactly the opposite situation has arisen with appeal to the CAT (and Competition Commission, in the case of price control matters). Ofcom's decisions have been overturned on appeal, in whole or in part, so many times that the UK Government has indicated its intention to narrow the standard of review on appeal,[91] though it may be constrained by the requirements of Article 4 of the Framework Directive.

'Significant Market Power' as a Fundamental Prerequisite of Regulation

Definition of SMP

32.52   The Communications Act provides that a person will have SMP in relation to a market 'if he enjoys a position which amounts to or is equivalent to dominance of the market'.[92] References to dominance must be construed in accordance with the Framework Directive and hence competition law. This can include joint

---

87   S 193 of the Communications Act.

88   S 196(4) of the Communications Act.

89   See, for example, *Independent Media Support Limited v Ofcom* [2007] CAT 29.

90   [2002] CAT 8.

91   Department of Business, Innovation and Skills, 'Implementing the revised EU electronic communications framework: overall approach and consultation on specific issues' (September 2010) and announcement in the Chancellor of the Exchequer's Autumn Statement 2012 reported in 'Government backs reform to regulatory appeals proposes' *The Guardian*, 6 December 2012.

92   S 78 of the Communications Act.

dominance. In determining whether a combination of persons enjoys joint dominance the matters set out in Annex II of the Framework Directive must be taken into
account. To date, there has not been a finding of joint dominance in any of the UK
markets, although Ofcom has considered it specifically in respect of the market for
wholesale access and call origination on mobile telephone networks.

Definition of relevant markets and SMP designation

32.53   Before SMP conditions can be imposed, Ofcom must follow a procedure
which tracks the requirements of the Framework Directive. Ofcom has to identify
the relevant markets and perform a market analysis to determine which operator (if
any) has SMP in that market. It is also required to follow notification and
consultation procedures tracking the equivalent requirements of the Framework
Directive.[93]

32.54   Ofcom (and its predecessor) has conducted detailed reviews of a large
number of markets.[94] They did not follow the Commission Recommendation on
relevant markets precisely but identified a substantially larger number of wholesale
markets. The European Commission has not objected to any of the conclusions
although it has queried Ofcom's reasoning at times. Consultations on market
definitions, SMP and remedies have been carried out simultaneously rather than
taking these in stages as in other countries.

32.55   In certain cases, markets have been defined much more narrowly than was
envisaged by the European Commission. An example of this is for wholesale
services provided over fixed public narrowband networks where the following
markets have been identified. These are:

- residential fixed narrowband analogue access;
- business fixed narrowband analogue access;
- residential fixed narrowband calls;
- business fixed narrowband calls;
- ISDN2 access; and
- ISDN30 access. [95]

32.56   BT has SMP in a number of the fixed line wholesale markets for the whole
of the UK, excluding the City of Kingston-upon-Hull. (KCOM plc, which is the
fixed line incumbent operator within Kingston-upon-Hull, has also been found to
have SMP in relation to a number of fixed line markets in that City.[96]) The
exceptions to this were certain markets for international call services[97] and
wholesale high bandwidth symmetric broadband origination.[98] In 2009, Ofcom

---

93   Ss 79–89 of the Communications Act.
94   The DG of Telecommunications issued market review guidelines setting out the criteria for
use in the assessment of SMP – June 2002.
95   Ofcom Statement: Fixed Narrowband Retail Services Markets – 15 September 2009.
96   The remedies proposed for KCOM plc are broadly similar but not identical to those of BT.
KCOM plc has not been considered further in this chapter.
97   235 different routes had been identified, each as a separate market. BT has SMP in 108, C&W
in 4 and 123 have been found to be competitive. DG Telecommunications Final Statement:
Wholesale International Services markets – 18 November 2003.
98   Ofcom: Final Statement: Review of the retail leased lines, symmetric broadband origination
and wholesale trunk segments markets (Undated).

stated that BT no longer had SMP in the majority of retail fixed telecommunications markets.[99]

32.57 In addition, in the market for fixed geographical call termination[100] all providers of public electronic communications networks listed in the statement have been determined to have SMP in the provision of their own network fixed geographic call termination services. All those providers listed are required to provide network access (ie call termination to all other public electronic communications networks and to set fair and reasonable terms for the provision of call termination services). Additional obligations are imposed on BT.

32.58 In the case of mobile markets, in the market for wholesale voice call termination, Ofcom has determined that each mobile network operator has SMP in the market for the provision of wholesale voice call termination on its own network.[101]

32.59 The analysis of the mobile wholesale voice termination markets reflects the previous decisions made by the DG of Telecommunications and the Competition Commission (to which the DG's decision was referred for review). The rationale is that the relevant market for wholesale mobile call termination is each operator's subscriber base. As each mobile operator controls 100 per cent of the subscriber base it has SMP in that market.

32.60 Controls have also been imposed on the activities of 3, the smaller more recent entrant. The imposition of a price control was hard fought after 3 appealed the finding of SMP. The Court of Appeal upheld the finding of SMP. The current price control, in line with the European Commission's recommendation, imposes wholesale prices at a very low rate, taking into account the network effects of on-net/off-net pricing that the incumbent operators could otherwise engage in.

32.61 Once Ofcom has made a determination of SMP it must set such SMP conditions 'as it thinks appropriate'. This wording differs slightly from that of the Framework Directive: the directive provides that where an NRA identifies that a market is not effectively competitive it shall identify undertakings with SMP and shall impose appropriate obligations on that undertaking. The SMP conditions which Ofcom can impose are set out in the Communications Act and it is for Ofcom to decide which of these are appropriate. In current market conditions this difference is unlikely to be significant.

NRA's Regulatory Duties Concerning Rights of Way, Co-location and Facility Sharing

Rights of way

32.62 The Electronic Communications Code[102] (the 'Code') grants to holders of Code powers certain rights over land, which can override the rights of landowners. The principal benefits are certain exemptions from the Town and Country planning

---

99   Ofcom Statement: Fixed Narrowband Retail Services Markets – 15 September 2009.
100   DG of Telecommunications Final Statement: Review of fixed geographic call termination markets – Identification and analysis of markets, determination of market power and setting of SMP conditions – 28 November 2003 and Ofcom Statement: Fixed Narrowband Retail Services Markets – 15 September 2009.
101   Ofcom: Statement on Whole Mobile Voice Call Termination – 15 March 2011.
102   The Electronic Communications Code is set out in Sched 2 to the Act, as amended by Sched 3

regime as 'Permitted Developments' and the right to a streetworks licence under the New Roads and Street Works Act 1991 in order to carry out works in connection with the installation of electronic communications apparatus in streets. The Law Commission recently published a consultation on proposed reforms of the Code.[103] The Law Commission anticipates that it will publish its report in early 2013 and that the government will have the opportunity to implement reforms to the Code in 2015.

32.63   The Code contains detailed provisions about how those with Code powers should negotiate with owners and occupiers of land (including Crown land) and allows an application for a court order in the event agreement cannot be reached. In practice, most rights are agreed by negotiation, without recourse to the courts.

32.64   Those wishing to benefit from Code powers have to apply on a stand-alone basis. Applications must be made to Ofcom. There is an annual fee[104] which is fixed each year by Ofcom. Successful applicants also have to pay a one-off fee[105] on the granting of Code powers.

32.65   Ofcom can apply the Code to providers of electronic communications networks and providers of conduit systems available for use by providers of electronic communications networks. Conduit providers are entities who make available conduits (eg tunnels, pipes or subways) to electronic communications network providers. Code powers will not normally be granted to persons operating exclusively or mainly private networks.

32.66   Applications for Code powers must contain information on certain matters such as reasons for needing Code powers, description of the electronic communications network or conduit system which the applicant is intending to provide, evidence of willingness and ability to share infrastructure and evidence of an ability to put in place funds for liabilities before the exercise of Code powers.[106] Ofcom has said that for companies applying for Code powers it would expect to see letters from the directors certifying that they will put funds for liabilities in place before exercising their Code powers.

32.67   When considering applications for Code powers, Ofcom must consider certain statutory criteria,[107] including:

- the benefit to the public of the relevant electronic communications network or conduit system; and
- the need to encourage sharing of the use of electronic communications apparatus.

---

to the Communications Act and The Electronic Communications Code (Conditions and Restrictions) Regulations, SI 2003/2553.

103   Law Commission Consultation Paper No 205 'The Electronic Communications Code' published on 28 June 2012.

104   The annual fee for 2012/2013 is £1,000.

105   For 2012/2013 this is £10,000.

106   Under reg 16 of the Electronic Communications Code (Conditions and Restrictions) 2003 (SI 2003/2553), persons benefiting from the Electronic Communications Code must put in place sufficient funds in order to meet certain liabilities. See policy statement on Funds for Liabilities, October 2003.

107   S 107(4) of the Communications Act.

32.68 Ofcom must maintain a register (which is available for public inspection on payment of a fee) of those with Code powers.[108]

32.69 Where a person to whom the Code applies is in contravention of the Code, Ofcom has powers to enforce penalties and suspend application of the Code.[109] Where there is more than one contravention of the Code, Ofcom can impose a separate penalty for each contravention[110] and where there is a continuing contravention Ofcom can impose one penalty for the period of the contravention.[111] For continuing contraventions of the Code, Ofcom can impose a penalty in respect of each day on which the contravention continues in certain circumstances[112] and the amount of such daily penalty can not exceed £100 per day.[113] Any other penalty for contravention of the Code cannot exceed £10,000.[114]

Co-location and facility sharing

32.70 When Ofcom is considering whether or not to grant Code powers it must have regard, inter alia, to the need to encourage sharing of the use of electronic communications apparatus[115] and that restrictions and conditions are objectively justifiable and proportionate to what they are intended to achieve.[116] Ofcom has said that grants of Code powers should be considered more favourably for those network operators which produce evidence of their ability or willingness to share infrastructure. This will particularly be the case where strong representations have been received from third parties against the grant of Code powers on the grounds of highway disruption or because of environmental impact. However, an inability or unwillingness to share should not in itself be regarded as a determining factor.[117]

32.71 Where providers of electronic communications networks and associated facilities with Code powers put up barriers to sharing and there is no viable alternative then Ofcom has the power to impose a condition to secure sharing under the access provisions referred to below.[118]

REGULATION OF MARKET ENTRY: IMPLEMENTATION OF THE AUTHORISATION DIRECTIVE

The General Authorisation of Electronic Communications

32.72 The UK has a system under which operators are generally entitled to provide electronic communications networks and/or electronic communications services without prior approval. Ofcom does have the power to designate certain types of communications networks and services and require that providers of these

---

108 S 108 of the Communications Act.
109 S 110 of the Communications Act.
110 S 110A(2) of the Communications Act.
111 S 110A(3) of the Communications Act.
112 S 110A(4) of the Communications Act.
113 S 110A(5) of the Communications Act .
114 S 110A(6) of the Communications Act .
115 S 109 of the Communications Act.
116 S 109(2)(da) of the Communications Act.
117 The Granting of the Electronic Communications Code – A Statement, issued on 10 October 2003.
118 S 73(3) of the Communications Act.

make a limited notification to Ofcom before commencing service.[119] It has, however, decided not to require any form of notification.

32.73   The terms on which networks or services must be provided are set out in General Conditions of Entitlement[120] and Specific Conditions of Entitlement. General Conditions are applicable to all providers of electronic communications networks and electronic communications services, or to all providers of a particular type. Each of the General Conditions specifies the type of operator to which it applies (public electronic communications networks, publicly available telephone services, etc). Specific Conditions are imposed by Ofcom on individual providers. Obligations imposed on providers who are determined to have SMP take the form of Specific Conditions.

32.74   The Communications Act specifies the matters which can be covered by the General Conditions and by Specific Conditions.[121] The provisions in the Act do not exactly mirror the requirements set out in Annex A to the Authorisation Directive. Instead it sets out several general categories into which General Conditions must fall. For example, conditions can be set making such provision as Ofcom considers appropriate for protecting the interests of the end users of public electronic communications services, for requiring compliance with relevant international standards. As a result of the 2011 amendments Ofcom now has the power to impose General Conditions which:

- specify requirements for provision of services to disabled end users;
- require the provision of specified information to end users free of charge;
- in order to prevent the degradation of service and the hindering or slowing down of traffic over networks, impose minimum requirements for the quality of public electronic communications network;
- require communications providers (in specified circumstances) to block access to telephone numbers or service to prevent fraud or misuse, and enable them to withhold fees payable to another communications provider in these circumstances;
- impose a limit on the duration of a contract between an end user and a communications provider; and
- ensure that conditions and procedures for the termination of a contract do not act as a disincentive to an end user changing communications provider.[122]

Rights of Use for Radio Frequencies

General authorisations and granting of individual rights

32.75   The WTA requires that radio equipment may only be used under the grant of a licence and the installation or use of radio equipment without a valid licence is an offence, except where regulations have been made to exempt specific types of apparatus from needing a licence to use it.[123]

---

119 S 34(1) of the Communications Act.
120 Notification setting general conditions under s 45 of the Communications Act.
121 Ss 51–77 of the Communications Act.
122 Ss51(2)(c)–(h) of the Communications Act.
123 S 8 of the WTA 2006.

32.76   Ofcom is required to exempt, by regulation, apparatus that is not likely to cause undue interference.[124] It has done this through a series of wireless telegraphy exemption regulations.[125]

32.77   Most types of licences are obtained by forwarding an application form to Ofcom. There is an overall time limit of six weeks for granting most licences. Licences will continue to be allocated in accordance with the national frequency plan.

32.78   A licence either authorises the use of particular equipment or authorises the use of a particular block of spectrum. Those licences which authorise equipment may be standard (often referred to as 'pre-packaged') or may be customised to suit the particular need of users. Licences are not normally available for public inspection.

Admissible conditions

32.79   The WTA provides that licences granted by Ofcom may be issued subject to such terms, conditions and limitations as Ofcom thinks fit and these may include particular terms, conditions and limitations as to the strength and type of signal and the times and use and sharing of such frequencies.[126]

32.80   Spectrum for 3G mobile telephony was auctioned in the UK in 2000. The successful bidders, being four existing 2G operators and one new entrant, paid a total of £22,477,400,000 (approx €33.8 billion) for the five licences. The licences included build-out obligations requiring that a telecommunications service be available to 80 per cent of the UK population by the end of 2007. The coverage obligation was duly met by all the operators, albeit that one operator (O_2) was late in achieving full compliance.

32.81   Prior to January 2005, all spectrum licences in the UK were issued with strict restrictions on the technology that could be used. From 2005 onwards, Ofcom has implemented a programme of spectrum liberalisation. New spectrum licences have been auctioned on a 'technology neutral' basis permitting any technology to be used provided it meets technical requirements on, for example, out of band emissions. Restrictions on existing licences have been gradually removed including those restricting 900/1800 MHz frequencies to GSM or earlier mobile technologies and those restricting 2.1 GHz frequencies to UMTS technologies (each removal of restrictions being in line with EU requirements).

32.82   Licences for frequencies in the 800 MHz and 2.6 GHz bands are being auctioned by Ofcom in January 2013 and the auction rules include various conditions and restrictions including the following:

- Spectrum caps consisting in restrictions on the total bandwidth of frequencies that can be held at the conclusion of the auction, including existing holdings, within all bands currently intended for use for mobile communications (ie 800 MHz, 900 MHz, 1800 MHz, 2.1 GHz and 2.6 GHz) and within the most desirable low frequency bands (ie 800 MHz and 900 MHz);[127] and

---

124   S 166 of the Communications Act.
125   See http://stakeholders.ofcom.org.uk/spectrum/information/licence-exempt-radio-use/wireless-telegraphy-regulations/
126   S 9 of the WTA 2006.
127   The Wireless Telegraphy (Licence Award) Regulations 2012 (SI 2012/2817).

- A national roll-out condition applicable to one licence for 10 MHz paired in the 800 MHz band requiring the holder to provide by 31 December 2017 and thereafter maintain an electronic communications network that is capable of providing, with 90 per cent confidence, a mobile telecommunications service with a sustained downlink speed of not less than two megabits per second when that network is lightly loaded, to users in certain indoor locations (ie those without unusually high signal loss) within an area in which at least 98 per cent of the UK population lives and within which 95 per cent of the population of each nation (England, Wales, Scotland and Northern Ireland) lives.[128]

The spectrum caps do not strictly remain in place after the auction has concluded but any transfer of licences in the relevant bands would be subject to a competition assessment by Ofcom in which it could be expected to effectively maintain the caps at least for a reasonable time after the auction.

Limitation of number of rights of use to be granted

32.83   Ofcom can, in order to secure the efficient use of spectrum, impose limitations on the use of particular frequencies. These limitations may be a limit on the number of licences to be granted in a particular frequency[129] or specify uses for which, on particular frequencies, Ofcom will grant licences. Where Ofcom decides to impose such limitations it must set out the criteria that it will apply in determining any limits imposed.[130]

32.84   Ofcom has responsibility for spectrum pricing. The WTA sets out two forms of spectrum pricing:

- Administrative incentive pricing,[131] in which fees are set by regulation on the basis of management criteria. For example, the price may be set to promote efficient use as well as to recover management costs.
- Auctions,[132] in which fees are set directly by the market.

32.85   There have been a number of auctions in the UK, including the auction for 3G spectrum and broadband fixed wireless access in 2000. Ofcom has said that it expects to continue to use market-based methods such as auctions as its preferred mechanism for making primary assignments. These may be complex auctions for large assignments or single round auctions for smaller blocks of spectrum. Where auctions are not suitable other mechanisms such as first come first served will continue to be employed.

Frequency trading

32.86   Frequency trading was introduced in the UK but only in certain licence classes in December 2004.[133] Ofcom has since extended trading to most, but not all,

---

128 See template licence included in 'The award of 800 MHz & 2.6 GHz spectrum: Information Memorandum Update' (Ofcom, 12 November 2012).

129 Wireless Telegraphy (Limitation of Number of Licences) Order 2003 (SI 2003/1902), as amended.

130 S 164 of the Communications Act.

131 S 12 of the WTA 2006.

132 S 14 of the WTA 2006.

133 The Wireless Telegraphy (Spectrum Trading) Regulations 2004 (SI 2004/3154). The 2004

spectrum licences.[134] Licences for the bands currently used for mobile communications (900 MHz, 1800 MHz and 2.1 GHz) were only made tradable in June 2011[135] but the first trade occurred in November 2012 (a trade of 1800 MHz spectrum from EE to 3 to satisfy the requirements of commitments made to the European Commission to get EE's merger cleared).

32.87   Ofcom's consent is required for proposed trades and it can prevent a trade in certain circumstances, for example, if the parties are attempting to escape licence obligations. In the case of frequencies currently used for mobile communications (ie 900 MHz, 1800 MHz and 2.1 GHz), Ofcom is required to conduct a competition assessment before allowing the trade to proceed.[136] This requirement is to be extended to the 800 MHz and 2.6 GHz bands after the auction currently in progress.

32.88   For most spectrum licences, it is possible to transfer the whole or part of the licence or lease the frequencies for a limited period.[137] In parallel with the introduction of frequency trading, Ofcom has said that it will be willing to consider requests from licensees for a change in the use of their licence (assuming usage restrictions have not already been removed).

Recognised spectrum access

32.89   Ofcom has the power to make regulations to facilitate the introduction of a system of recognised spectrum access ('RSA'). This is similar to wireless telegraphy licensing, but it confers certain rights on the holder with respect to transmissions from outside the UK, such as transmissions from a satellite. A holder of RSA is entitled to have their interests in the radio spectrum taken into account by Ofcom in the same way as a licence holder.[138] Ofcom has power to auction RSA rights where appropriate and they will be capable of being traded under the spectrum trading regime.[139] Ofcom has issued RSA for Crown use, radio astronomy and, most recently, for receive only earth stations in certain bands in 2011.[140]

Regulations have been repealed by the Wireless Telegraphy (Spectrum Trading) Regulations (SI 2012/2187).

134   Details on what can and cannot be traded and restrictions on types of trade possible for particular bands are included in 'Trading Guidance Notes' (Ofcom, December 2011).

135   'Statement on proposal to make 900 MHz, 1800 MHz and 2100 MHz public wireless network licences tradable' (Ofcom, 20 June 2011).

136   'Statement on proposal to make 900 MHz, 1800 MHz and 2100 MHz public wireless network licences tradable' (Ofcom, 20 June 2011).

137   'Simplifying Spectrum Trading Spectrum leasing and other market enhancements' (Ofcom, 29 June 2011).

138   For further information see 'Introducing Recognised Spectrum Access', Radiocommunications Agency, July 2002.

139   S 159 of the Communications Act.

140   'Decision to make the Regulations for Recognised Spectrum Access (RSA) for Receive Only Earth Stations in the Bands 1690–1710 MHz, 3600–4200 MHz, and 7750–7850 MHz' (Ofcom, 30 November 2011).

Rights of Use for Numbers

General authorisations and granting of individual rights

32.90   The term 'number' includes data of any description.[141] The government does not, however, feel that it is currently appropriate or necessary for Ofcom to regulate Internet-related providers, such as domain names, Internet addresses or identifiers based on domain names and Internet Protocol addresses. It has therefore specifically excluded Internet-related identifiers from regulation under the Communications Act.[142]

32.91   Ofcom has a duty[143] to publish a Numbering Plan which sets out the numbers which are available for allocation together with the restrictions which apply to their allocation and use and such requirements as Ofcom considers appropriate, for the purpose of protecting consumers, in relation to the tariff principles and maximum prices applicable to numbers adopted or available for allocation. This exists alongside the National Numbering Scheme, which is a record of all numbers allocated, available for allocation or protected.

32.92   Numbers are not owned by communications providers. They are either allocated to them by Ofcom or acquired from a third party by way of a sub-allocation or porting. Providers of both public electronic communications networks and services can be allocated telephone numbers. However, Ofcom has said that normally it would expect service providers to get their allocations from public electronic communications networks. Applicants are required to give information as to their services and the networks over which numbers will be used. If the service provider has not requested a sub-allocation from a network provider and has no arrangements with a network provider to provide a service, Ofcom may determine that the service provider is ineligible in that particular case.

32.93   There were previously no charges or fees for the right to use numbers. However, in 2012 Ofcom introduced a new provision into General Condition 17 as part of a pilot scheme requiring communications providers for certain specific area codes to pay Ofcom an applicable annual number charge within 14 days of receipt of an invoice from Ofcom. The annual number charge will be billed annually in arrears following the end of each charging year (1 April to 31 March), the first charging year being from 1 April 2013 to 31 March 2014. The annual number charge is £0.1/365 for every day within the charging year for which the specific number is allocated to the communications provider, less any reduction calculated in accordance with paragraph 17.17 of General Condition 17.[144]

---

141 S 56(10) of the Communications Act.
142 See the Telephone Number Exclusion (Domain Names and Internet Addresses) Order 2003 No 3281.
143 S 56 of the Communications Act.
144 The amount of any reduction for a charging year is: (a) (the total number of the communication provider's ported numbers) x £0.1 ÷ (the average industry utilisation rate); plus (b) (the total number of the communication provider's wholesale line rental numbers) x £0.1 ÷ (the BT average utilisation rate); plus (c) (the total number of the communication provider's public payphone numbers) x £0.1 ÷ (the communications provider average utilisation rate).

Admissible conditions

32.94 It is Ofcom's duty to secure that what appears to them to be the best use is made of the numbers that are appropriate for use as telephone numbers, and to encourage efficiency and innovation for that purpose.[145]

32.95 The Communications Act sets out admissible conditions for the allocation and adoption of numbers.[146] Ofcom can also set conditions that apply to persons other than non-communications providers which relate to the allocation of numbers to such persons, the transfer of allocations to and from such persons and the use of numbers by such persons.[147]

32.96 The General Conditions of Entitlement also contain a number of provisions as regards the use of numbers including:

- the circumstances under which Ofcom may withdraw an allocation of numbers. For example, where a communications provider has not adopted allocated numbers within six months from the date of allocation; and
- the provision of number portability which must be completed within one business day and must take place as soon as reasonably practicable on reasonable terms. This is currently only required for subscribers of public electronic communications services, for both geographic and non-geographic numbers.[148]

Limitation of number of rights of use to be granted

32.97 The Communications Act contains a right which expressly empowers Ofcom to auction numbers (including individual 'golden numbers') to the highest bidder.[149] It remains to be seen whether Ofcom will take up this option.

The NRA's Enforcement Powers

32.98 The Communications Act creates a broad framework for the enforcement of many of its provisions including new powers for Ofcom to impose penalties for contravention of General Conditions of Entitlement or Specific Conditions.[150] For contravention of a General or Specific Condition, any penalty imposed cannot exceed 10 per cent of the turnover of the offender's relevant business for the relevant period, which is normally one year.[151] Very few penalties have been imposed for breach of a condition but one penalty, imposed on Talk Talk Telecom Limited and Tiscali UK Limited for incorrect billing, was in an amount of £3 million. As set out above, Ofcom has wide powers to request information in connection with an alleged breach of condition.

32.99 The procedure for enforcing a General or Specific Condition[152] is:

- Stage one: Ofcom sends the offender a formal notification and gives the offender the opportunity to remedy the breach.

---

145 S 63 of the Communications Act.
146 S 58 of the Communications Act.
147 S 59 of the Communications Act.
148 General condition 18.
149 S 58(5) of the Communications Act.
150 S 96 of the Communications Act.
151 S 97(1) of the Communications Act.
152 Ss 94–101 of the Communications Act.

- Stage two: If the notification is not complied with, Ofcom can issue an enforcement notification.
- Stage three: As well as or instead of stage two, Ofcom may impose a penalty.
- Stage four: Where there has been a serious and repeated contravention of conditions and the imposition of penalties or notification notices has not succeeded in securing compliance, Ofcom can also give a direction suspending service provision. This direction can include a condition requiring the making of payments by way of compensation for loss and damage suffered by the offending operators' customers or in respect of annoyance, inconvenience or anxiety to which they have been put.[153]
- Stage five: A person who acts in contravention of a prohibition or restriction on service provision is guilty of an offence and will be liable on summary conviction to a fine not exceeding the statutory maximum and on conviction on indictment to a fine.

32.100   Any person who suffers loss or damage as a result of the action in failing to comply with the condition or enforcement notice can bring a separate action for loss.[154] These claims will be dealt with by the courts and not the CAT.

Administrative Charges and Fees for Rights of Use

32.101   Ofcom is required to ensure that its revenues fully cover its costs of regulation. Ofcom has applied an administrative charge based on a revenue measure with a degree of progression so that smaller operators pay a lower proportion of their revenue. The administrative charge applies to all designated providers of electronic communications networks, electronic communications services and associated facilities.[155] A communications provider will be designated if its gross annual turnover from 'relevant activities' provided either to end users or other telecommunications operators exceeds £5 million.

32.102   Providers are divided into bands according to their turnover, and all providers within a band are charged the same administration charge calculated by applying a percentage tariff to the relevant turnover. The percentage tariff for the year 2011/12 is 0.0534 per cent of relevant turnover in the calendar year ended 31 December 2009 and the percentage tariff for the year 2012/2013 is 0.0609 per cent of relevant turnover in the calendar year ended 31 December 2010. Any provider with a turnover over £1 billion pays a set percentage of its actual turnover.

32.103   Fees are normally payable for rights to use spectrum and the amount payable depends on the type of licence granted.

REGULATION OF NETWORK ACCESS AND INTERCONNECTION: IMPLEMENTATION OF THE ACCESS DIRECTIVE

Objectives and Scope of Access Regulation

32.104   Probably the main challenge for regulation in the past decade in the UK was to try to ensure some form of equality of access to BT's network at the

---

153   S 100 of the Communications Act.
154   S 104 of the Communications Act.
155   S 38(2) of the Communications Act.

wholesale level so that other operators and service providers can offer competitive products and services. In 2005, Ofcom acknowledged in the context of the Strategic Review that in the fixed line market, at least, regulatory efforts to secure access at a wholesale level to BT's networks and facilities had a limited effect in opening up the market (BT remained larger than most of its competitors put together) and had also led to a large range of detailed regulatory interventions. Accordingly, in 2005 it proposed certain undertakings to be given by BT under the Enterprise Act, as discussed previously. These undertakings were agreed on 22 September 2005.[156] These supplement the specific obligations imposed under the Communications Act, as discussed below.

32.105   Ofcom also had to deal with the implications for interconnection and access arrangements of BT's next generation network. The undertakings given by BT addressed the competition issues arising from the next generation network by imposing a number of specific requirements on BT as regards its deployment. These included provisions that:

- ensured that other communications providers could purchase unbundled network access products on terms and conditions which allowed those communications providers to 'compete effectively' with end-to-end services that BT provided over its network;
- ensured that BT built its network in a manner to ensure that all other communications providers (including BT) could purchase access on the same terms and conditions (including price) by means of the same systems and processes; and
- prevented BT launching new retail products based on its new network before a suitable upstream wholesale SMP product was available for downstream competitors.

These requirements only apply to the provision of access in markets where BT has SMP. A number of exemptions from these undertakings have been agreed over the years.[157]

Basic Regulatory Concepts

32.106   Under the Communications Act, Ofcom has powers to impose a wide variety of obligations to provide interconnection and access on all communications providers.

32.107   The definition of access in the Communications Act is wide[158] and includes interconnection. Guidelines[159] have set out examples of types of access. The term applies to any wholesale service that enables competitors to deliver their own services to customers. The wholesale product could be a network element, an end-to-end communications service or an interconnection service. Specific examples given include unbundled local loops, interconnection including partial private circuits, reseller products such as calls and access and virtual network services such as mobile virtual network operators.

---

156 Ofcom: Final statements on the Strategic Review of Telecommunications, and undertakings in lieu of a reference under the Enterprise Act 2002 – 22 September 2005.
157 A consolidated version of BT's Undertakings can be found on Ofcom's website: http://stakeholders.ofcom.org.uk/binaries/telecoms/policy/bt/consolidated.pdf.
158 S 151(3) Communications Act.
159 Imposing Access Obligations under the New EU Directives – 13 September 2002.

32.108   Ofcom has said that it is preferable for requests for access to be resolved through commercial negotiation. The Government did not feel that there are any restrictions in the UK that prevent persons from negotiating between themselves on technical and commercial arrangements for network access and as such there is no specific reference to this in the Communications Act.[160]

Access and Interconnection-related Obligations with Respect to SMP Undertakings

Overview

32.109   The Regulator has produced guidelines setting out in general terms in what circumstances and to what extent it will impose access obligations on operators with SMP.[161] The guidelines provide that:

- Before Ofcom imposes an access obligation on an SMP operator it will undertake a regulatory option appraisal. This will take account of matters listed in the Access Directive and other relevant factors.
- The access obligation imposed may be in the form of an obligation to meet all reasonable requests for products within the wholesale market in which the operator has SMP.
- In addition to a general access obligation, Ofcom may also specify that a particular product or minimum set of products should be available within a particular wholesale market.
- If another undertaking requires a new product, it should first submit a request to the SMP operator and both parties should negotiate in good faith. Ofcom's preference is that precise details of new products should first and foremost be refined through commercial negotiation. However, past experience has proved that this does not always work and there may be circumstances when Ofcom needs to get involved by, for example, chairing relevant meetings, specifying terms and timescales on which such products should be offered.
- If the SMP operator can demonstrate that it will incur significant development costs in meeting a request for a new wholesale product, Ofcom may provide that the requesting operator should take on an appropriate level of risk, for example by committing to a level of demand at a price that would justify investment by the SMP operator.
- The SMP operator should be required to supply an equivalent wholesale product when introducing innovative retail services.

32.110   In addition, the Communications Act[162] allows the imposition of obligations relating to transparency, non-discrimination, price control and regulatory accounting. The guidelines make it clear that Ofcom's intention in attaching other obligations to the supply of wholesale products is that those products should be available on terms which are consistent with those which would apply in a competitive market. If an SMP operator supplies a wholesale product but attaches conditions which will have a material adverse effect on competition, Ofcom will view this behaviour as a constructive refusal to supply.

32.111   The additional obligations include:

---

160   As required by Article 3(1) Access Directive.
161   Imposing Access Obligations under the New EU Directives – 13 September 2002.
162   S 87 of the Communications Act.

Transparency obligations These include:

- a requirement to notify prices. This requires a SMP operator to give notice of any price changes typically 28 or 90 days in advance. The period varies in accordance with the perceived risk of abuse by the SMP operator.
- a requirement to notify technical information. This may overlap to some extent with the requirement to publish a reference offer. It is intended to be an additional obligation which in particular imposes a longer 90-day period on the SMP operator for announcing changes in technical specifications.
- an obligation to be transparent as to quality of service. This is a consequence of the fact that the requirement not to discriminate applies also to the quality of service. It imposes an obligation to publish key performance indicators showing that the same level of service applies both to its self-provision and the provision to others.

Non-discrimination obligations Where an access obligation has been imposed Ofcom will generally also impose a non-discrimination obligation. The requirement not to discriminate includes, in particular, a requirement not to discriminate in favour of a service provider's own business.[163] In many cases this is supported by an obligation to maintain cost accounts.

Price control obligations In determining whether a charge control is needed in addition to a non-discrimination obligation, Ofcom has said that it will need to consider the specific conditions of the market.[164] In general, where markets are not competitive but where market power is diminishing it may be sufficient to rely on an imposition of a non-discrimination obligation and require that charges are cost-oriented. In markets which are not competitive and there is little prospect of introducing competition it is generally appropriate to introduce price regulation in the form of cost based prices.

Accounting separation obligations The main purpose of an accounting separation obligation is to ensure compliance with a non-discrimination obligation. The form and content of the accounting information typically provides for separate statements for a number of different activities in respect of a vertically integrated operator.

Reference offers Ofcom has said that it will normally require that information on any new wholesale product is published in the form of a reference offer ('RO'). The requirement to publish a RO specifies in some detail the specific provisions which must be included. These include technical characteristics and standard conditions of access, details of traffic and network management, details of maintenance and quality (including service level commitments) rules of allocation between the parties when supply is limited and standard terms and conditions. Where a RO must be published, service must be provided in accordance with it.

Related Regulatory Powers with Respect to SMP Undertakings

32.112 Previously, Ofcom had a duty to set, as it thinks appropriate, SMP conditions requiring the provision of carrier pre-selection and indirect access and

---

163 On 15 November 2005 Ofcom issued a statement on how it will investigate potential contraventions of requirements not to unduly discriminate: 'Undue discrimination by SMP providers: How Ofcom will investigate potential contraventions on competition grounds of Requirements not to unduly discriminate imposed on SMP providers'.
164 S 3.24, Imposing Access Obligations under the New EU Directives.

the provision of leased lines.[165] However, the provisions containing this duty were removed as a result of the 2011 amendments and therefore no longer apply.[166]

32.113   Ofcom has imposed a number of specific remedies on BT requiring it to provide particular services. These services are generally services which have been the subject of previous disputes and have therefore been scrutinised by either Ofcom or its predecessor. Where there has been detailed regulatory action Ofcom has generally decided to preserve the outcome of the investigations. This has been done in some cases by imposing on BT a specific condition requiring the provision of the relevant service. The principal services dealt with in this way are as:

- *Wholesale Line Rental ('WLR')* This is a service by which BT rents access lines on wholesale terms to competing operators. It means that competitors are able to provide a bundled lines and calls product. It allows competing operators to take on the full retail relationship with the customer and offer a 'single bill' to end-users for all basic communications services. BT's licence was changed in August 2002 to require it to provide WLR and BT has been providing a basic WLR product since September 2002. Ofcom has imposed an additional condition on BT to provide a fit for purpose WLR product in a number of specified markets.

- *ATM Interconnection* This concerns the provision by BT of interconnection products which enable competing operators to interconnect at different points of the BT network, thus enabling them to use more of their own networks to provide broadband services.

- *Flat Rate Internet Access Call Origination ('FRIACO')* FRIACO is the narrowband service by which BT provides to other operators dial up call origination to enable the customer to access the internet on a fixed rate without time based charging. FRIACO has been the subject of intense regulatory scrutiny and the results of this are largely preserved in the condition which sets out BT's obligation to provide the wholesale product. The importance of FRIACO has decreased with the increasing popularity of broadband.

- *Partial Private Circuits ('PPCs')* PPCs are wholesale private circuits provided by a dominant operator (normally BT) connecting the customer's premises to the point of interconnection between BT and another operator. It is intended to allow the competing operator to provide private circuits or other services using in part the BT network and in part its own. The directions reflect previous determinations by the DG of Telecommunications and include requirements on BT as regards migration of services from retail leased lines previously offered to PPCs, ordering procedures, service level agreements and prices.

- *RBS Backhaul and LLU Backhaul* A similar approach has been adopted for RBS Backhaul (which involves the provision of links to mobile phone companies connecting their radio based stations to their networks) and backhaul for local loop unbundling operators. In each case specific directions set out the specific products required, terms and conditions and pricing.

---

165   Ss 90 and 92 of the Communications Act.
166   Electronic Communications and Wireless Telegraphy Regulations 2011 (SI 2011/1210).

Regulatory Powers Applicable to All Market Participants

Obligations to ensure end-to end-connectivity

32.114 The General Conditions[167] provide that all operators providing public electronic communications networks, if requested by an operator of another such network, must negotiate with a view to concluding an interconnection agreement within a reasonable period. This obligation is reciprocal.

32.115 The broad definition of public electronic communications networks means that a wide range of operators are entitled to benefit from, but are also subject to, the interconnection obligations. To qualify as a public electronic communications network, a network must provide publicly available services. To satisfy this test a network must be theoretically available to anyone who is willing to pay for it and abide by the applicable terms and conditions.

32.116 Ofcom has the power to impose certain access related conditions without a prior finding of SMP. Ofcom can impose obligations on operators to provide network access and service interoperability required (in its view) to secure efficiency, sustainable competition, efficient investment and innovation and the greatest possible benefits for end users.[168] This includes requirements relating to facilities sharing and to ensure end-to-end connectivity. Previously the setting of such condition was limited to the situation where there were no viable alternative arrangements. However, as a result of the 2011 amendments, the power of Ofcom to impose such conditions can now be exercised for the purposes of encouraging efficient investment in infrastructure and promoting innovation.[169]

Access to digital radio and television broadcasting services

32.117 Electronic Programme Guides ('EPGs') are specifically regulated. Ofcom has a duty to draw up a code giving guidance to providers of EPGs.[170] Any broadcaster operating an EPG must ensure compliance with the code. The code covers such things as the listing and promotion of the public service channels, with Ofcom having the power to require such a 'degree of prominence' as it considers appropriate for the listing of public service channels on the EPG, and the facilities for accessing those channels.

32.118 There are also specific provisions for conditional access systems. These are defined as any arrangement by means of which access to a programme service requires either subscription or authorisation.[171] In effect, this refers to satellite and to cable systems, the providers of which can charge broadcasters for carriage of content over their networks. The Communications Act contains provisions which allow Ofcom to regulate the price of access to conditional access systems, with the stated intention of maintaining competition between the providers and providing benefit for end users. Ofcom can also set conditions on a 'dominant' provider in relation to network access, use of relevant networks and availability of relevant facilities. Such conditions have been imposed only on Sky Subscriber Services Limited.

---

167 General condition 1.
168 Ss 73–75 of the Communications Act.
169 S 73(3A) of the Communications Act.
170 S 310 of the Communications Act.
171 S 75(3) of the Communications Act.

REGULATION OF UNIVERSAL SERVICES AND USERS' RIGHTS: THE UNIVERSAL SERVICE DIRECTIVE

Regulation of Universal Service Obligation

Scope of universal service obligations

32.119   The Government, and not Ofcom, determines the specific universal service requirements.[172] Ofcom decides how these should be implemented.[173] The services which must be available include:[174]

- a connection to the public telephone network, able to support voice telephony, fax and data at rates sufficient to support functional Internet access.[175] The Government has not set a specific connection speed in the legislation. Guidelines provide that a connection speed of 28.8 Kbit/s is a reasonable benchmark although this may need to be revised over time;
- the provision of at least one comprehensive directory and directory enquiry facility which must be updated once a year;
- the provision of public pay phones to meet the reasonable needs of end users including the ability to use the single European emergency call 112 and the UK emergency call number 999, free of charge;
- billing and payment options to enable subscribers to monitor and control their expenditure and appropriate tariff options for those on low incomes or with special social needs; and
- special measures for end users with disabilities.

32.120   Ofcom can adopt such measures as it considers appropriate to secure compliance with the obligations set out above and designate which communications providers, if any, must provide such services.[176]

Designation of undertakings obliged to provide universal services

32.121   When deciding whether to designate an undertaking to provide universal services, Ofcom will look, inter alia, at the relative size of the undertaking's business, whether it provides service to at least 100,000 served premises, the financial stability of the undertaking and its relative capability to comply with any or all of the specific conditions.[177]

32.122   Ofcom has implemented the above requirements through:

- a number of specific conditions on BT as a universal service provider; and
- a number of General Conditions imposed on all publicly available telephone service providers. For example, General Condition 8 requires the provision of

---

172   S 65 of the Communications Act.
173   As part of its Strategic Review, Ofcom looked at universal service and in particular whether it should be extended to mobile and broadband. Ofcom's conclusion was that currently an extension of the universal service obligation should not be recommended: Review of Universal Service Obligations: Statement and Further Consultation: 14 March 2006.
174   Electronic Communications (Universal Service) Order 2003 No 1904 as amended by the (Universal Service) (Amendment) Order 2011 No 1209.
175   Article 4(2) of the Universal Services Directive.
176   Ss 66–67 of the Communications Act.
177   DG of Telecommunications: Notification of proposals for the designation of universal services providers and setting of conditions – 12 March 2003.

directory information and General Condition 15 requires the provision of certain facilities for end users with disabilities.

Regulation of retail tariffs, users' expenditures and quality of services

32.123 All the components of universal service must be offered at prices that are affordable to end users and uniform throughout the UK, unless Ofcom has determined that there is clear justification for not doing so.[178] Ofcom has a duty to keep under review universal service tariffs and to monitor changes to the tariffs. The conditions imposed on BT provide that where an end user has requested service provided under a universal service obligation, it must not require the end user to pay for any other service that they may not have required, by means for example of bundling.

32.124 The universal service conditions provide that BT must publish information on, among other things, its provision of telephony services on request. This information must be published in accordance with the quality of service parameters, definitions and measurement methods referred to in Annex III to the Universal Service Directive and any other additional standards and/or requirements set by Ofcom. Ofcom has the power to require that such information is independently audited and that the costs of any such auditing are met by the provider.

Cost calculation and financing of universal services

32.125 The Communications Act does provide for the funding of universal services through cost sharing by communications providers.[179] Ofcom does not currently feel that the cost of providing such services represents an unfair burden on BT. It has, however, said that it recognises that in the future consideration may need to be given to its funding.

Regulation of Retail Markets

Prerequisites for the regulation of retail markets

32.126 Ofcom can set SMP conditions[180] in markets for end users of public electronic communications services in certain circumstances. These are where Ofcom has made a determination that a person has SMP in the market and Ofcom considers that it is unable by setting access-related or SMP conditions in wholesale markets to fulfil its obligations under the Act in relation to that market.

32.127

Ofcom has determined that BT has SMP in the retail market of 'access to the public telephone network at a fixed location for residential and non-residential customers'.

---

178 Regulation 4 of the Universal Services Order.
179 S 71 of the Communications Act.
180 S 91 of the Communications Act.

Regulatory powers

32.128   The types of conditions which can be imposed are similar to those mentioned above under wholesale controls.[181] These include:

- price control obligations;
- non-discrimination obligations;
- price publication and notification obligations; and
- cost accounting and accounting separation obligations.

32.129   For fixed narrowband services, previously Ofcom set a safeguard control of RPI-RPI on BT so that BT could not raise its prices in absolute terms.[182] This control lasted until July 2006. Now price controls are aligned with the SMP framework and there is a separate price control for each market (including retail and wholesale markets) in which BT has SMP.

End User Rights

Contracts

32.130   Providers of public electronic communications services to consumers must (on the request of the consumer) offer to enter into a contract or vary an existing contract.[183] A 'consumer' is defined as a natural person who uses or requests the service for purposes outside his or her trade, business or profession. The information which must be contained in the contract mirrors that set out under the Universal Services Directive[184] and the requirements under General Condition 9 have been updated as a result of the 2011 amendments.

32.131   Where the provider intends to modify a condition which is likely to be of material detriment to the consumer, the consumer must be given at least one month's notice of the change and informed of his right to terminate the contract without penalty if the proposed change is not acceptable. This is more limited than the Universal Services Directive,[185] which provides that subscribers have a right to withdraw from their contracts without notice upon notice of proposed modifications in the contractual conditions.

32.132   A provider of a public electronic communications service/public electronic communications network is required to ensure that conditions or procedures for contract termination in contracts with consumers do not act as a disincentive for end users against changing their communications provider.[186] Such providers cannot enter into new agreements with consumers which automatically renew at the end of the initial commitment period.

32.133   Providers of public electronic communications services are also required to provide certain customers with basic codes of practice covering for example how the provider will handle complaints and comply with a Dispute Resolution

---

181   S 91(3) of the Communications Act.
182   An RPI-RPI price cap ensures that prices remain flat.
183   General condition 9.
184   Universal Services Directive, Article 20.
185   Universal Services Directive, Article 20(2).
186   General Condition 9(3).

Scheme.[187] The dispute resolution procedure must be independent, transparent, simple and free of charge.[188]

32.134 Ofcom has approved two schemes. These are:

- The Ombudsman Services: Communications Scheme (formerly known as Otelo); and
- The Communication and Internet Services Adjudication Scheme (generally known as CISAS).

32.135 If a communications provider decides not to join either of the above schemes it is still obliged to have a scheme in place which will need to be approved by Ofcom.

Transparency obligations

32.136 Publicly available telephone service providers only are subject to transparency obligations under the General Conditions.[189] They must ensure, that clear and up-to-date information on matters such as prices and tariffs and standard conditions is published. The list of information which must be published conforms to the list set out in Annex II of the Universal Services Directive.

Quality of service: security 'net neutrality'

32.137 There is currently no legal requirement in the UK specifically requiring 'net neutrality'. However, as a result of the 2011 amendments Ofcom has the power to impose a General Condition imposing certain minimum requirements regarding the quality of public electronic communications networks to 'prevent the degradation of service and the hindering or slowing down of traffic over networks'. However, it appears unlikely that Ofcom will introduce such a General Condition in the near future.

In addition, General Condition 9.2 requires that the following information is provided to consumers by providers of public communications networks and public electronic communications services:

- details of the minimum service quality levels offered, (eg time for initial connection and any other quality of service parameters directed by Ofcom); and
- information on any procedures put in place by the provider to measure and shape traffic so as to avoid filling or overfilling a network link, and information on how those procedures could impact on service quality.

European emergency call number

32.138 Under General Condition 4, a person who provides end users with an electronic communications service, or provides access to such a service by means of a pay telephone, for originating calls to a number or numbers in the national

---

187 General Condition 14.
188 The requirement to comply with a dispute resolution scheme derives from Article 34 of the Universal Service Directive.
189 General condition 10.

telephone numbering plan (excluding click to call services) is required to ensure that end users can access emergency services by using the emergency call numbers '112' and '999' at no charge (and in the case of pay telephones without having to use coins or cards).

Other obligations

32.139   All communications providers who are providers of public electronic communications services are subject to a number of other obligations through the General Conditions. They include the provision of up-to-date, comparable and adequate information on quality of service.

32.140   Providers of public electronic communications networks are required to provide tone dialling and calling line identification.

32.141   Publicly available telephone service providers are subject to an additional level of regulation. Obligations include:

- to provide a basic level of itemised billing;
- additional measures for end users with disabilities;
- requirements as to the approval of metering and billing systems; and
- number portability.

DATA PROTECTION: IMPLEMENTATION OF THE E-PRIVACY DIRECTIVE

Confidentiality of Communications

32.142   The E-Privacy Directive has been implemented by the Privacy and Electronic Communications (EC Directive) Regulations 2003[190] (the 'E-Privacy Regulations').

32.143   There is a prohibition on the use of an electronic communications network to store or gain access to information stored in a user's computer terminal.[191] This includes cookies and other tracking devices. The prohibition does not apply if the user or subscriber:

- is provided with clear and comprehensive information about the purpose and use of the storage of, or access to, that particular information; and
- has given his or her consent.

32.144   These conditions apply whether or not the information relates to personal data.[192] Where the use of a cookie-type device does involve the processing of personal data, service providers will also be required to comply with the provisions of the Data Protection Act.

---

190   SI 2003/2426, as amended by the Privacy and Electronic Communications (EC Directive) (Amendment) Regulations 2004 (SI 2004/1039) and the Privacy and Electronic Communications (EC Directive) (Amendment) Regulations 2011 (SI 2011/1208). The Information Commissioner can impose civil monetary penalties of up to £500,000 (approx €620,000) for serious breaches of the E-Privacy Regulations.

191   Reg 6 of the E-Privacy Regulations, as amended by SI 2011/1208.

192   Personal Data is defined in s 1 of the Data Protection Act. It is defined widely as data relating to living individuals who can be identified from those data, or from those data and other information, which is in the possession of, or is likely to come into the possession of, the data

32.145 Although the E-Privacy Regulations allow for consent to be given by a subscriber[193] setting controls on his or her Internet browser or using another application or programme to signify consent,[194] the Information Commissioner's Office ('ICO') has stated in its Guidance[195] that currently relying on browser settings is not sufficient to establish that the user or subscriber has given their consent to the use of cookies. However, the ICO has stated in its Guidance that the 'implied' consent of the user can be relied upon, especially where express consent is simply not practicable or realistic in context. The ICO's view is that while implied consent is certainly a valid form of consent, in order to be so there must be some action taken by the consenting user, on the basis of a reasonable understanding that such action indicates their agreement to cookies being set.

32.146 There is an exemption to the requirement to obtain the user's consent. Where the use of the cookies is strictly necessary for a service requested by the user, consent is not required. However, the ICO emphasises that this exemption is to be given a narrow interpretation. The prohibition can also be overridden in the interests of national security.[196]

Data Retention

32.147 The UK implemented the Data Retention Directive with the Data Retention (EC Directive) Regulations 2009 (Data Retention Regulations). The Data Retention Regulations place an obligation on public communications providers (that receive a written notice from the Secretary of State[197]) to retain certain communications data for a period of 12 months from the data of the relevant communication. This applies to fixed telephony, mobile telephony and Internet access, Internet email and Internet telephony.

Traffic Data and Location Data[198]

32.148 Location data[199], excluding traffic data, relating to a user or subscriber of a public electronic communications network or service may only be processed:[200]

- where the user/subscriber cannot be identified by that data; or

---

controller. It includes names and addresses but will also include e-mail addresses where the individual can be identified from the address.
193 Defined in reg 2: 'Subscriber' means a person who is a party to a contract with a provider of public electronic communications services for the supply of such services.
194 Reg 6(3A) of the E-Privacy Regulations.
195 Information Commissioner's Office: Guidance on the rules on use of cookies and similar technologies – May 2012.
196 Reg 28 of the E-Privacy Regulations.
197 Reg 10 of the Data Retention Regulations. The Secretary of State must give such a written notice to a public communications provider unless the relevant communications data are retained in the UK by another communications provider in accordance with the Data Retention Regulations.
198 Service providers and operators should also be aware of further obligations concerning the retention of data under the Anti-terrorism, Crime and Security Act 2001 and Data Retention (EC Directive) Regulations 2009 (SI 2009/859).
199 Reg 2 of the E-Privacy Regulations. The definition of location data specifically refers to data relating to the latitude, longitude or altitude of the terminal equipment, the direction of travel of the user and the time the location information was recorded.
200 Reg 14 of the E-Privacy Regulations.

- where necessary for the provision of a 'value added' service *and* the user/ subscriber has consented.

32.149   Prior to obtaining the consent of the user/subscriber, the communications provider must provide certain prescribed information to that user/subscriber set out in the E-Privacy Directive.[201]

32.150   This consent may be withdrawn at any time and the opportunity to withdraw must be given by a simple means and free of charge, at every connection to the public communications network or each transmission of a communication.

32.151   Generally traffic data[202] must be erased or modified so that it no longer constitutes personal data when it is no longer required for the purpose of transmission of the communication.[203] There is an exception for traffic data relating to payment of charges. Traffic data may however be processed and stored for the provision of 'value added' services to that user or subscriber or for the marketing of electronic communications services if the subscriber or user has previously notified the provider that he consents to such processing or storage. The subscriber or user must be given certain prescribed information before he gives his consent.

Itemised Billing

32.152   All communications providers must provide a basic level of itemised billing[204] to all of their subscribers for the provision of publicly available telephone services, on request and at no extra charge or for a reasonable fee.[205]

32.153   In recognition of the fact that such bills may jeopardise the privacy of users, the Regulations state that providers of public electronic communications services shall, at the request of a subscriber, provide subscribers with bills that are not itemised.[206]

Calling and Connected Line Identification

32.154   The provisions of the E-Privacy Directive relating to calling and connected line identification are implemented by the E-Privacy-Regulations.[207] Communications providers must provide information to the public regarding the availability of such facilities.

---

201   Reg 14(3) of the E-Privacy Regulations.
202   Reg 2 of the E-Privacy Regulations. The definition of traffic data specifically includes data relating to the routing, duration or time of a communication.
203   Reg 7 of the E-Privacy Regulations. This also applies to corporate subscribers.
204   General condition 12.
205   This general obligation is subject to a number of limited exceptions for example it does not apply to publicly available telephone services provided on a prepaid basis.
206   Reg 9 of the E-Privacy Regulations.
207   Regs 10–13 of the E-Privacy Regulations.

Automatic Call Forwarding

32.155 A provider of electronic communications services must ensure that on the request of a subscriber any call forwarding is stopped, free of charge, without any avoidable delay.[208]

Directories of Subscribers

32.156 The General Conditions contain a number of provisions which oblige all communications providers to ensure that customers have access to directories, directories enquiries and directory information. These are all subject to the provisions of relevant data protection legislation. The General Conditions include the following provisions:

- All communications providers must ensure that any end user can access operator assistance services and directory enquiry facilities containing directory information on all subscribers in the UK who have been assigned telephone numbers by the communications provider, subject to certain limitations including where a subscriber has exercised his right to have his directory information removed.[209]
- Where a communications provider assigns telephone numbers to subscribers it must ensure that those subscribers are, on request, supplied with a directory containing directory information on all subscribers who have been assigned telephone numbers in the subscriber's local area (or, on request, outside the subscribers' local area). Any directories supplied shall not contain directory information for those subscribers who have exercised their right to have their directory information removed.[210] The directory can be produced by the communications provider or a third party and must be updated on a regular basis, at least once a year.[211]

32.157 Personal data of an individual subscriber must not be included in a directory (whether in printed or electronic form) which is made available to the public, including by means of a directory inquiry service, unless the individual has, free of charge, been:

- informed by the collector of the personal data of the purposes of the directory; and
- given the opportunity to determine whether the personal data should be included in the directory.[212]

32.158 Corporate subscribers also have the right to request that their data will not be included in a directory.[213]

Unsolicited Communications

32.159 The use of personal data for direct marketing purposes is subject to a number of controls under the Data Protection Act. For example, a data subject has

---

208 Reg 17 of the E-Privacy Regulations.
209 General Condition 8.1.
210 General Condition 8.2.
211 General Condition 8.3.
212 Reg 18(2) and (3) of the E-Privacy Regulations.
213 Reg 18(4) of the E-Privacy Regulations.

the right to prevent the processing of his personal data for direct marketing purposes at any time, even if he has previously given his consent.

32.160   The Privacy Regulations extend controls on unsolicited direct marketing to all forms of electronic communications.

32.161   There are different provisions for individuals and corporate subscribers. Individual means a living individual but also includes an unincorporated body of such individuals. This include partnerships. There is also a distinction between those who are subscribers and those who are just users.

32.162   Regarding e-mail – the definition of e-mail[214] is the same as that in the E-Privacy Directive, with a specific clarification that the definition includes SMS.

32.163   The Regulations set out a prior consent requirement for individual subscribers. This prohibition does not apply to corporate subscribers, and the definition of subscriber means that an e-mail to an individual's specific corporate e-mail address will not be caught by the prohibition, as the individual employee will not normally be a party to the contract for the provision of the e-mail service.

32.164   There is an exemption to this in the context of existing customer relationships.[215] This applies where e-mail addresses have been obtained in the course of 'a sale or negotiations for a sale of a product or service'.[216]

32.165   Automated calling or communication systems – for both individuals and corporate subscribers there is a prohibition unless the subscriber has specifically consented.[217]

32.166   Unsolicited faxes[218]– There is a prohibition for individuals and for corporate subscribers who have specifically notified the caller that they do not want to receive such communications.[219]

32.167   Unsolicited calls – here there is a prohibition for corporate subscribers or individuals who have previously notified the caller that such calls should not be made on that line.[220]

32.168   Those involved in direct marketing should also be aware of the British Code of Advertising, Sales Promotion and Direct Marketing.

---

214   Reg 2 of the E-Privacy Regulations. See Chapter 3 on the E-Privacy Directive.
215   As required by Art 13 of the E-Privacy Directive.
216   Reg 22(3) of the E-Privacy Regulations. Art 13 of the Directive refers to in the context of a sale only.
217   Reg 19 of the E-Privacy Regulations.
218   For both faxes and calls, Ofcom must keep a register of numbers where the subscriber has registered a general objection to receiving unsolicited marketing calls and faxes on that number; both corporate and individual subscribers can register: regs 25 and 26 of the E-Privacy Regulations, as amended.
219   Reg 20 of the E-Privacy Regulations.
220   Reg 21 of the E-Privacy Regulations.

Part 4
Telecommunication Laws in Non-EU Member States

The Croatian Market for Electronic Communications

Iskra Bubaš and Igor Mucalo,
Veršić Marušić Law Office, Zagreb

LEGAL STRUCTURE

Basic Policy

33.1   The Croatian market for electronic communications services has been rapidly changing due to the fast advancement of technology and introduction of new services. Market indicators at the end of 2011 show that the majority of profit has been acquired from telephony services. However, there has been an increasing demand for broadband Internet access in fixed networks (858,020 extensions at the end of 2011). Croatian Telecom (Hrvatski telekom d.d. ('HT')) is a leading fixed network operator. Other operators, including HT's subsidiary Iskon Internet d.d. ('Iskon'), hold 39.9 per cent of users of the telephony services in fixed public communications network and their market shares are increasing. Efficient market competition in both mobile and fixed communications has been reflected, among others, in the growing number portability (33.9 per cent more number portability in fixed networks and 4.4 per cent in mobile networks in 2011). The number of Internet Protocol Television ('IPTV') services users is also rising. Currently 40 per cent of 1.5 million Croatian households with a TV set use the services of cable, IPTV or satellite operators.

The national regulatory body is the Croatian Post and Electronic Communications Agency (Hrvatska agencija za poštu i elektroničke komunikacije ('HAKOM')). After a public consultation and with the prior consent of the Croatian Government, HAKOM adopts its annual work programmes, setting out its objectives and tasks with respect to regulatory and other activities in the area of electronic communications. HAKOM's objectives in 2012 have been focused primarily on promotion of efficient competition, as a prerequisite for increasing investments in the electronic communications market, and ensuring good service quality and a high level of user protection.[1]

---

1   HAKOM's Annual Work Plan for 2012, p 3, Official Gazette ('OG'), 121/11.

Implementation of EU Directives

33.2　During the EU accession negotiations, Croatia adopted the Electronic Communications Act,[2] which entered into force on 1 July 2008, harmonising Croatian legislation with the 2002 Regulatory Package. As a part of the accession preparations, Croatia was further required to transpose in its national legislation the 2009 Regulatory Package by the middle of 2011. In this respect, the Amendments to the Act ('Amendments')[3] were adopted on 2 August 2011. The extensive Amendments aim, among others, to further strengthen HAKOM's independence, ensure protection of users, improve market analysis, simplify procedures for allocation of radio frequencies, and provide for more efficient mechanisms for protection of personal data.[4] The majority of provisions introduced by the Amendments entered into force on 10 August 2011. However, the Amendments' provisions such as those governing HAKOM's notification obligations towards the Commission, NRAs and BEREC, the consolidation and co-regulation procedures, additional requirements in relation to market analysis and a new legal regime regarding safety and integrity of electronic communications and protection of personal data, enter into force on the day of Croatia's accession to the EU.[5] Thus, although the relevant Croatian electronic communications regulations have been harmonised with the EU legal framework to a large extent, they will be fully in force upon Croatia's accession to the EU.[6]

Legislation

33.3　The Electronic Communications Act as amended by the Amendments ('ECA')[7] is the main legislative act governing electronic communications. On the basis of the ECA, a number of ordinances and other bylaws have been adopted. The Amendments provide for adoption of further bylaws at the latest by 10 August 2012,[8]which will complete the electronic communications legal framework.

REGULATORY PRINCIPLES: THE FRAMEWORK DIRECTIVE

Scope of Regulation

33.4　The ECA governs electronic communications in a comprehensive manner. It includes provisions on use of electronic communication networks, electronic communications services, universal services, protection of users' rights, electronic communication infrastructure, regulation of the electronic communications market, management of radiofrequencies, and organisation, tasks and powers of HAKOM. Particular aspects of use of electronic communications for provision of commercial

---

2　Published in the OG 73/08.
3　Published in the OG 90/11.
4　The Croatian Government Amendments Proposal, 7 July 2011.
5　See art 125 Amendments.
6　Croatia signed the Accession Treaty on 9 November 2011. The estimated date of Croatia's accession to the EU is 1 July 2013, provided that all Parties have ratified the Accession Treaty by then.
7　Published in the OG 73/08, 90/11.
8　See art 122(2) the Amendments.

activities, provision of content services through electronic media as well as protection of consumers are governed by special regulations.[9] There are no legal provisions specifically regulating Voice over Internet Protocol ('VoIP') services and thus they fall under the general electronic communications legal regime as set forth in the ECA.

The ECA's definitions of 'electronic communications network', 'electronic communications service' and 'associated facilities' correspond to the respective definitions of these terms set out in Articles 2(a), (c) and (e) of the Framework Directive.[10]

Internet Freedom

33.5   The ECA does not provide for any specific rules in relation to access to the Internet. The Internet falls under the ECA's definition of electronic communications networks and thus the respective legal regime as to the access to and use of services through electronic communications networks applies to the Internet as well. Some aspects of services provided via Internet, such as electronic commerce, Internet marketing and e-mail advertising communications to consumers, are dealt with in special regulations.[11]

Croatian laws do not provide for the imposition of measures in relation to the online copyright infringement that restricts an end user's access to the Internet. HAKOM recently opened informal public consultations on the possible impact of the Anti Counterfeiting Trade Agreement ('ACTA') on the Croatian electronic communications market, particularly with respect to ACTA's provisions on protection of copyrights on the Internet. The consultations will be closed on 28 May 2012[12] and their results remain to be seen.

National Regulatory Authorities: Organization, Regulatory Objectives, Competencies

33.6   HAKOM is the national regulatory agency entrusted with regulatory and other activities in the area of electronic communications. It is also entrusted with regulatory tasks related to postal services pursuant to a special regulation.[13] With respect to participation in the European and international organisations and institutions in the electronic communications sector, Croatia is represented by the Ministry of Maritime Affairs, Transport and Infrastructure ('Ministry'). HAKOM participates in work of administrative and working bodies of these organisations and institutions, jointly with the Ministry.

Similar to Article 8 of the Framework Directive, HAKOM's regulatory principles and objectives may be classified in three categories:

---

9   These include the Electronic Signature Act, OG 10/02, 80/08, the Electronic Trade Act, OG 173/03, 67/08, 36/09, 130/11, the Consumer Protection Act, OG 79/07, 125/07, 79/09 and The Electronic Media Act, OG 153/09, 84/11.
10   See legal definitions of these terms set out in art 2(1) (7), (10) and (43) ECA.
11   These include the Electronic Signature Act, OG 10/02, 80/08, the Electronic Trade Act, OG 173/03, 67/08, 36/09, 130/11 and the Consumer Protection Act, OG 79/07, 125/07, 79/09.
12   See HAKOM's website http://www.hakom.hr/default.aspx?id=116&subid=946 (accessed on 22 January 2012).
13   The Postal Services Act, OG 88/09, 61/11.

- promotion of competition;
- promotion of interests of users; and
- contribution to the development of the EU internal market.[14]

With respect to its regulatory activities, HAKOM is required to cooperate with the Croatian Competition Agency ('AZTN'), the general competition regulator.[15] The ECA expressly prescribes that its application shall not affect AZTN's tasks and powers, thus ensuring that HAKOM's regulatory activities do not overlap with AZTN's. HAKOM may request opinions from AZTN, propose that AZTN initiates proceedings in all cases of prevention, restriction or distortion of competition, and provide AZTN with its expert and technical support.

As required by the Framework Directive, the ECA's provisions assure that HAKOM is an independent authority with sufficient human and financial resources to implement the assigned tasks impartially and transparently. HAKOM is established as an independent nonprofit legal entity with public authorities, seated in Zagreb. It is governed by a Council of seven members, appointed and resolved by the Croatian Parliament upon the proposal of the Croatian Government. The ECA prescribes the professional qualifications required for the Council's members and also excludes certain categories of persons from the appointment due to potential conflict of interest (such as, for example, civil servants, political party officials, and individuals employed with legal entities falling under the scope of the ECA).[16] Internal organisation and functioning of HAKOM is regulated by its Statute.[17] HAKOM's Administrative Service, managed by the Executive Director appointed by HAKOM's Council, performs expert, administrative and technical activities. Any form of influence that may endanger HAKOM's independence and autonomy is prohibited. HAKOM may not seek or take instructions from any other body and is accountable for its work to the Croatian Parliament. The Ministry may provide HAKOM with guidelines for enforcement of the Government's electronic communications policy. However, such guidelines must be made public and may not influence HAKOM's decisions. Financial resources for HAKOM's activities are covered from special fees on the basis of its annual financial plan.[18]

HAKOM's tasks[19] are consistent with the EU Regulatory Framework and include control and regulation of tariffs and general conditions of operators, market analysis and imposition of regulatory obligations on SMP operators, as well as designation of operators of universal services. Further, HAKOM is entrusted with the control of general authorisations and granting individual licences for use of radio frequencies. Its activities include efficient management of radio frequency spectrum, adoption of the Addressing and Numbering Plans, and plans for allocation of radio frequencies.

HAKOM keeps, and regularly updates, the prescribed registries and databases in relation to electronic communications infrastructure and radio frequencies, among other things. It is entrusted with inspection control and adoption of bylaws for the implementation of the ECA. HAKOM is authorised to request from operators of electronic communications networks or services, delivery of all necessary data and

---

14   See art 5(3), (4) and (5) ECA.
15   Established and operating pursuant to the Competition Act, OG 48/95, 52/97, 89/98 and its bylaws.
16   See art 8(6) and (7) ECA.
17   HAKOM's Statute, OG 116/08, 115/10, 152/11.
18   See para 33.23 below.
19   HAKOM's tasks are governed by art 12 ECA.

information, including financial and confidential data, as well as to carry inspection of business premises, respective infrastructure and equipment, and to review business books, records and other documents.[20]

HAKOM's decisions and other administrative acts are regularly published on its website.[21] Particular acts and documents, such as bylaws for enforcement of the ECA, decisions having significant impact on the relevant market and those adopted in the administrative disputes against HAKOM, must be published both in the Official Gazette and on HAKOM's website. HAKOM's registries and data bases must be publicly available, free of charge, in electronic form, on its website, offering the possibility of comprehensive data browsing. Prior to adoption of measures having a significant impact on the relevant market, HAKOM is required to carry out public consultations. In order to ensure the harmonised application of the 'acquis communautaire' when imposing regulatory obligations, HAKOM must cooperate with the Commission and the NRAs.[22]

HAKOM is entrusted with the resolution of disputes between operators of electronic communications networks or services or disputes between operators and other legal entities using access or interconnection services.[23] HAKOM is required to issue a decision on dispute in the shortest period of time, no later than four months as of the day of initiating the procedure. Dispute resolution procedures set out by the ECA do not preclude either party's right from bringing an action before the competent court.

Rights of Appeal against NRA's Decisions

33.7 No appeals are permitted against HAKOM's decisions and other administrative acts. However, they may be challenged in administrative disputes before the High Administrative Court.[24] Administrative disputes may be initiated by a party who considers that the disputed HAKOM decision or other administrative act affects its rights or legal interests. If the court finds that a claim is grounded, it will annul the disputed decision.

HAKOM's Obligations to Cooperate with the Commission

33.8 In order to ensure harmonised application of the EU law when carrying regulatory activities, HAKOM is required to take into account the relevant 'acquis communautaire' and the Commission's recommendations and guidelines, as well as opinions and common positions adopted by BEREC.[25] The consolidation and co-regulation procedures, set out in Articles 7 and 7a of the Framework Directive,

---

20   See art 15(1) ECA.
21   HAKOM's official website: www.hakom.hr
22   See art 23 ECA. The said provision shall be entirely replaced by the consolidation and co-regulation procedures set out in art 22 Amendments, which shall enter into force on the day of Croatia's accession to the EU. See para 33.8 below.
23   See art 20(1) ECA.
24   Administrative disputes were subject to a significant legal reform introduced by the Administrative Disputes Act, OG 20/10, in force as of 1 January 2012.
25   See art 5(7) ECA.

were introduced by the Amendments.[26] However, the respective provisions governing these procedures will start to apply upon Croatia's accession to the EU. The ECA's provisions currently in force provide for HAKOM's obligation to cooperate with the NRAs and the Commission when imposing regulatory measures.[27] Further, when intending to adopt measures that may have impact on trade between the EU Member States, HAKOM must, simultaneously with carrying out a public consultation, notify the Commission and the NRAs. HAKOM shall take into account their remarks and suggestions when adopting such measures. If required so by the Commission, HAKOM must suspend the adoption of a measure for two months and amend the draft measure pursuant to the Commission's requirements.

The ECA provides for the application of standards and specifications published in the Official Journal of the European Union. In the absence of such standards and specifications, international standards and specifications of the competent European and international standards organisations apply.[28]

'Significant Market Power' as a Fundamental Prerequisite of Regulation

Definition of SMP

33.9   The ECA defines SMP in line with Article 14 para 2 of the Framework Directive, stating that an operator will be deemed to have significant market power if it (i) individually, (ii) as an operator controlled by another operator, or (iii) jointly with other operators, enjoys a position equivalent to dominance, ie a position of economic strength affording it the power to behave to an appreciable extent independently of competitors, users and consumers.[29]

Definition of relevant markets and SMP designation

33.10   The ECA's rules on the procedure for identifying relevant markets and SMP designation are essentially identical to those provided in Articles 15 and 16 of the Framework Directive.[30] Provisions on cooperation with BEREC and obligatory notifications to the Commission will enter into force upon Croatia entering the EU.[31]

HAKOM defines the relevant markets, conducts a market analysis and determines the markets which are not effectively competitive and are therefore subject to sector-specific regulation. These procedures must be conducted regularly, at least in three-year intervals. HAKOM must take account of the Commission's Guidelines in market analysis and Market Recommendation, but is free to identify additional relevant markets if they meet the three criteria laid down in the Market Recommendation.

Currently, HAKOM has regulated all of the markets identified in the Market Recommendation, and in addition the following markets based on the fulfillment of the three criteria:

---

26   Art 22 Amendments introduced the entirely new wording of the current art 23 ECA, which shall enter into force on the day of Croatia's accession to the EU.
27   See art 23 ECA in force until Croatia's accession to the EU.
28   See art 24(2) ECA.
29   See art 55(1) ECA.
30   See art 52–54 ECA.
31   See art 52(3) and (4) ECA.

- publicly available local and national telephone services provided at a fixed location for residential customers;
- publicly available local and national telephone services provided at a fixed location for non-residential customers;
- retail broadband access; and
- wholesale trunk segments of leased lines (non-competitive relations).

Each market is defined as national in its geographic scope, and for each market HAKOM has identified the SMP operator and imposed one or more remedies. HT was identified as having SMP in markets 2 and 4–6 from the Market Recommendation (call origination on public fixed network, wholesale network infrastructure access at a fixed location, wholesale broadband access, wholesale terminating segments of leased lines) and in market 4 above (wholesale trunk segments of leased lines). In market 1 from the Market Recommendation (public telephone network access at a fixed location) and markets 1–3 above (telephone services provided at a fixed location for residential and non-residential customers, retail broadband access) HT was found to have SMP together with its subsidiary Iskon. In markets 3 and 7 from the Market Recommendation (call termination on individual fixed networks, call termination on individual mobile networks) all of the operators were identified as SMP for their own networks.

The ECA requires HAKOM to impose at least one remedy on SMP enterprises. Such remedies must be appropriate and proportional, and must take into account the investments of the SMP operator, especially those in the development of emerging markets.[32] Additionally, HAKOM may, in justified cases, impose obligations on network operators which do not have SMP but control access to end users, with the purpose of assuring 'end-to-end connectivity'.[33]

NRA's Regulatory Duties Concerning Rights of Way, Co-location and Facility Sharing

Rights of way

33.11 Operators of public communications networks have infrastructure operators' rights in the entire Croatian territory, which includes the right to build, maintain, develop and use the electronic communications infrastructure and associated facilities on public property, on state and local government owned property and on property owned by other legal entities and natural persons, in line with the ECA and other special regulations.[34]

With respect to private property, such rights may be acquired by the agreement between the infrastructure operator and the private owner. Additionally, if the construction is in the interest of the State, private real estate may be expropriated by the State pursuant to special regulations.[35]

Public property managers, state and local government, and all state owned legal persons, must abide by the principle of non-discrimination when granting the right of use of property for the purpose of building electronic communications infrastructure and associated facilities or access to that infrastructure and facilities they

---

32   See art 56(2) and (3) ECA.
33   See art 66(5) ECA.
34   See art 27(1) ECA.
35   Expropriation Act, OG 9/94, 35/94, 112/00, 114/01, 79/06, 45/11, 34/12.

manage. If their consent is necessary in the process of granting building permits and other construction related licences they must give it within 30 days. The request may only be denied if it is established that construction is not technically feasible, or if the construction would be contrary to the requirements concerning the protection of human health, environment, space or cultural goods.[36]

The legal status of previously built electronic communications infrastructure and facilities is resolved through the institute of 'right of way'.[37] An infrastructure operator is entitled to the right of way if it has acquired the use permit for the infrastructure or the facilities in question, or has been using it for a minimum of three years without a court dispute with the real estate owner. If one of these conditions is met, HAKOM will, upon request, issue to the infrastructure operator a right of way certificate. The infrastructure operator pays a fee for the right of way to the land owner. HAKOM's Ordinance provides detailed provisions on the procedure of granting the right of way certificate and the calculation of the amount of the land owner's fees.[38]

Co-location and facility sharing

33.12   The ECA implements the concepts established in Article 12 of the Framework Directive.[39] HAKOM must encourage shared use of infrastructure and facilities, in particular with the aim of protecting human health, environment, space, cultural goods and national security. If the legal conditions for infrastructure access and shared use are met,[40] the infrastructure operator must allow the beneficiary operator access to and shared use of its infrastructure and associated facilities. Access and shared use is given pursuant to the agreement between the infrastructure operator and the beneficiary, and in exchange for an agreed fee.

If the beneficiary operator is unable to achieve access to infrastructure and facilities as a result of the requirements related to the protection of human health, environment, space, cultural goods and national security, HAKOM may, upon prior public consultation, order the infrastructure operator to allow access and shared use of its infrastructure to the beneficiary operator. HAKOM may additionally impose on the infrastructure operator the obligation to apply the principles of non-discrimination and cost-orientation when granting access, the obligation to draft and publish the reference offer for access and the obligation to negotiate access with beneficiary operators. If the infrastructure operator refuses to grant access, HAKOM will, upon request, investigate whether the legal conditions for granting access are met, and if it determines that they are, pass a decision replacing the access agreement.

---

36   See art 27(2)–(4) ECA.
37   See art 28 ECA.
38   Ordinance on the Certificate and the Fee for the Right of Way, OG 152/11.
39   See art 30 ECA.
40   Prescribed by the Ordinance on the Manner and Conditions of Access and Shared Use of Electronic Communications Infrastructure and Associated Facilities, OG 136/11, 44/12.

REGULATION OF MARKET ENTRY: IMPLEMENTATION OF THE AUTHORISATION DIRECTIVE

The General Authorisation of Electronic Communications

33.13   In line with the Authorisation Directive, the ECA provides for the regime of general authorisation for operators entitling them to:[41]

- provide electronic communications networks and services;
- build, install, and use electronic communications infrastructure;
- nationally and internationally negotiate and agree on access and interconnection; and
- be designated an operator of one or more universal services.

The general authorisation regime obliges each operator to perform its activities in line with the provisions of the ECA and the relevant bylaws. Operators must notify HAKOM in advance about their beginning, changes to and termination of the provision of electronic communications networks and services. Within eight days from notification HAKOM issues to the operator a certificate confirming that the notification was dully submitted. However, the operator may start providing its services before receiving the certificate. HAKOM keeps and regularly updates the publicly available list of operators which have been issued the certificate.[42]

Rights of Use for Radio Frequencies

Strategic planning and co-ordination of spectrum policy

33.14   The management and use of the radio frequency spectrum, as a scarce natural resource, is of special state interest. HAKOM is entrusted with the management of radio frequencies and is required to cooperate with the NRAs of the EU Member States and the Commission in promoting the harmonised approach to the radio frequency management policy. The manner of management of radio frequencies and their efficient use is subject to HAKOM's regular review through public consultations.

The switchover from analogue to digital broadcasting in Croatia was completed on 31 December 2010. Frequencies from the Croatian Digital TV Plan, based on the Geneva 2006 Frequency Plan (GE06), shall be fully available after 2015. HAKOM's recently adopted frequency allocation plan[43] opens the 900 MHz frequency band for GSM and UMTS systems following the EU's approach of more flexible usage of the 900 MHz frequency band.

Principles of frequency allocation, procedural rules

33.15   Frequency allocation is based on the Table on Allocation of the Radio Frequency Spectrum[44] ('Table') and frequency allocation plans. HAKOM adopts

---

41   See art 31 ECA.
42   See art 32 ECA.
43   Published in the OG 35/12, in force as of 23 March 2012.
44   Table on Allocation of the Radio Frequency Spectrum is a constituent part of the Ordinance

the plans specifying the conditions of allocation and use of radio frequencies within individual radio frequency bands as determined by the Table.[45]

Principal conditions of allocation and use of radio frequencies and procedural rules of granting licences for use of radio frequencies are prescribed by HAKOM Ordinance.[46] A prior licence granted by HAKOM is required for the use of radio frequencies, except in rare cases provided by the ECA.[47] General licences are granted to any legal and natural persons for the use of the radio frequency bands which, pursuant to the Table, may be used on the basis of such licences.[48] Individual licences are granted upon application for the radio frequency bands for which the Ordinance on Allocation of the Radio Frequency Spectrum provides the granting of such licences.[49] Pursuant to the ECA and the said Ordinance, due to the limitation of the available radio frequency spectrum, in certain cases HAKOM is required to initiate procedures for granting individual licences on the basis of a public invitation, public tender or public auction.[50] Temporary licences for use of radio frequencies may be granted upon application for the purpose of market or technical inspection, research or design, or for events of temporary character.[51]

Applications for individual licences are filed with HAKOM on the prescribed publicly available form[52] and are processed in order as they were filed. When it is not possible to accept all filed applications for individual licences granted on the basis of a public invitations, given the availability of a radio frequency band, HAKOM must carry out a public tender or a public auction.

Licences for the use of radio frequency spectrum intended for digital radio diffusion may be granted only to operators of a public communications network. Further, licences for the use of radio frequency spectrum intended for analogue radio diffusion shall be granted to publishers of electronic media, who carry out their activities pursuant to the special regulations governing electronic media.

Radio frequencies allocated exclusively for military use are not subject to licensing.[53] Further, Croatian Armed Forces, police, intelligence agencies, and the administration body competent for protection and rescue and emergency services do not require a licence for the use of radio frequency bands allocated for civil or military use; rather they require only HAKOM's prior approval.[54] The armed forces must deliver to HAKOM a written report on the use of such frequencies, at HAKOM's request.

---

on Allocation of the Radio Frequency Spectrum, adopted by the Ministry upon the proposal of HAKOM's Council, OG 136/08, 17/10, 118/10, 119/10, 87/11.

45   See art 82 ECA.
46   Ordinance on Conditions of Allocation and Use of the Radio Frequency Spectrum, OG 45/12, enters into force on 15 May 2012, revoking the earlier Ordinance, OG 136/07, 70/10, 39/11.
47   See art 82a ECA. The exceptional cases are described below.
48   See art 87 ECA.
49   See art 88 ECA.
50   See art 88a, 89 and 90 ECA.
51   See art 91(2) ECA.
52   See art 12 Ordinance on Conditions of Allocation and Use of the Radio Frequency Spectrum.
53   See art 86(1) ECA.
54   See art 86(2) ECA.

Transferability and time limitations

33.16 Holders of individual licences may transfer or lease the entire or a particular part of the assigned radio frequency band to another person with HAKOM's prior consent.[55] When deciding on an application for granting such consent, HAKOM considers principles of objectivity, transparency, proportionality, and non-discrimination, and determines if the person to whom the radio frequency band is transferred or leased meets the conditions set out in the relevant individual licence, ie such transfer or lease implies the entire assignment of rights and obligations arising from the respective individual licence, including the conditions of allocation and use. The radio frequency bands which may be transferred or leased are specified in the Ordinance on the Allocation of Radio Frequency Spectrum.

General licences are granted for an indefinite period of time.[56] Duration of individual licences is determined by HAKOM depending on their type, but may not exceed 20 years.[57] Temporary licences may not be granted for a period longer than one year. Holders of individual licences may apply for the prolongation of the right to use radio frequency spectrum at the latest sixth months prior to the expiry of their validity.[58] Upon receipt of the application for prolongation, HAKOM conducts a public consultation, and must grant the application unless an additional interest for the respective radio frequency spectrum has been expressed. Should there be such additional interest, HAKOM must initiate a procedure for granting an individual licence on the basis of a public invitation, public tender, or public auction.

Admissible conditions

33.17 Individual licences are granted within 30 days, provided that the application complies with conditions of allocation and use of the respective radio frequencies as determined by the Table, and that the requested radio frequencies are available.[59] Individual licences issued on the basis of a public invitation, public tender or public auction will be granted to a legal or natural person fulfilling the prescribed technical, financial, space and personnel conditions.

Limitation of Number of Rights of Use to be Granted

33.18 HAKOM may limit the number of individual licences only in cases prescribed by the ECA[60] or when, due to availability of a certain radio frequency band, it is not possible to accept all applications.

---

55   See art 92 ECA.
56   See art 4(6) Ordinance on Conditions of Allocation and Use of the Radio Frequency Spectrum.
57   See art 4(1) Ordinance on Conditions of Allocation and Use of the Radio Frequency Spectrum.
58   See art 91a(3) ECA.
59   See art 88(2) ECA.
60   The exceptions are provided for in art 82a(6) and (7) ECA and include limitations of use of radio frequencies necessary to avoid harmful interferences, protect human health from the activity of electromagnetic field and ensure technical quality of service, among other things.

For the use of radio frequency spectrum on the basis of individual and temporary licences, fees are paid in favour of the state budget and HAKOM.[61]

Public auctions for granting individual licences are conducted when:

- HAKOM has received several applications for granting individual licences on the basis of a public invitation which may not be accepted given the availability of the respective radio frequency band; or
- such procedure of granting individual licences is prescribed by the Ordinance on Allocation of the Radio Frequency Spectrum, considering the limitation or economic value of the available radio frequency spectrum.[62]

Selection criteria and applicable forms of public auction are specified in the respective auction documents prepared by HAKOM. The decision on selection of the most favourable participants includes granting one or several licences. Such decision must be elaborated and delivered to all participants.

Rights of Use for Numbers

General authorisations and granting of individual rights

33.19   Allocation of numbers is specified by the Numbering Plan[63] adopted by HAKOM, allowing equal availability of the respective number of addresses and numbers to all operators and users. Prior to adoption of the Numbering Plan, HAKOM is required to conduct a public consultation and assign numbers in a manner that is transparent, objective, equal, and impartial with respect to the needs of operators and users.

The ECA differs between primary and secondary assignments of numbers.[64] Any operator may apply to HAKOM for a primary assignment of numbers. Numbers assigned on the basis of a primary assignment may be further assigned to other operators and end users on the basis of a secondary assignment. While primary assignments are based on HAKOM's decision, secondary assignments are subject to contractual arrangements. However, operators are not permitted to trade the assigned numbers in any way and the stipulated fee for a secondary assignment to an end user may not exceed the costs incurred to an operator in relation to a primary assignment.[65]

Operators may transfer their rights to use numbers to other operators with HAKOM's prior consent. HAKOM must issue such consent if the operator to whom the right to use numbers will be transferred fulfills all prescribed conditions for a primary assignment of numbers.

Admissible conditions

33.20   HAKOM must grant a primary assignment if the purpose of the use of numbers stated in the application complies with the Numbering Plan and the

---

61   Calculation, amount and manner of payment of fees are prescribed by the Ordinance on Payment of Fees for Right of Use of Addresses, Numbers and Radio Frequency Spectrum, adopted by the Ministry, OG 154/08, 28/09, 97/10, and HAKOM's Ordinance on Payment of Fees for Performance of HAKOM's Activities, OG 133/11.

62   See art 90 ECA.

63   Published in the OG 154/09, 41/12.

64   See art 70(1) ECA.

65   See art 7(2) Ordinance on Allocation of Addresses and Numbers, OG 154/08.

numbers are available. The use of numbers assigned to operators by a primary assignment is subject to the payment of fees.[66] Further, operators who were granted a primary assignment are required to comply with the following conditions of use:[67]

- they must use the assigned numbers in accordance with the Numbering Plan;
- they may use the assigned numbers only for the purposes stated in the application for a primary assignment;
- they must commence use of the assigned numbers within six months from the date of receipt of HAKOM's decision on the assignment of those numbers;
- they must keep an up-to-date list of the numbers assigned by a primary assignment;
- they must keep an up-to-date list of numbers they were further assigned by a secondary assignment and deliver it to HAKOM upon request; and
- they must make accessible from all electronic communications networks in Croatia the numbers assigned to other operators and end users by a secondary assignment.

HAKOM may completely or partially revoke its decision on the primary assignment of numbers upon fulfillment of any of the conditions prescribed by the ECA.[68] Such decision must be elaborated and based on the principle on proportionality, taking into account the public interest and economic effect.

Operators of publicly available telephone services, including mobile electronic communications network services, are required to enable the end users of their services, upon their request, to keep the assigned numbers independently of the change of the operator.[69]

Limitation of number of rights of use to be granted

33.21   HAKOM is required to process applications for primary assignments in the order they are filed and to adopt its decision within 30 days as of filing of the application. The manner and procedure of assignment of numbers is further specified in the Ordinance on Assignment of Numbers.[70] Croatian regulations do not provide for competitive or comparative selection procedures.

The NRA's Enforcement Powers

33.22   The ECA assigns broad enforcement powers to HAKOM. In this respect, HAKOM is authorised to control and regulate tariffs and general terms and conditions, impose regulatory obligations on SMPs, monitor whether obligations

---

66   Calculation, amount and manner of payment of fees are prescribed by the Ordinance on Payment of Fees for the Right of Use of Addresses, Numbers and Radio Frequency Spectrum, adopted by the Ministry, OG 154/08, 28/09, 97/10 and HAKOM's Ordinance on Payment of Fees for Performance of HAKOM's Activities, OG 133/11.
67   See art 73 ECA.
68   See art 75(1) ECA. The decision on a primary assignment may be revoked in cases, for example, when an earlier decision was adopted on the basis of inaccurate data or documents, the operator has not commenced the use of the assigned numbers within six months of the receipt of the decision on a primary assignment or has failed to pay the required fee within an additional period determined in the notice, among other things.
69   See art 76 of the ECA and para 33.30 below.
70   Published in the OG 154/08.

arising from general conditions have been fulfilled, prohibit performance of activities of electronic communications networks and services, and grant and revoke individual licences. Its enforcement powers include requesting information from operators.[71] Operators must comply with HAKOM's requests within the appropriate deadline set by HAKOM which may not be shorter than eight days, or be held liable for a misdemeanour offence.

HAKOM's powers include conducting inspections.[72] As a result of such inspections, HAKOM may either initiate misdemeanor procedures, in which case it may temporarily seize the documents and objects, including the electronic communications equipment that may be used as evidence, or, in cases prescribed by law, issue misdemeanor orders imposing fines and ordering measures.[73] The ECA differs between:

- especially serious breaches of law subject to fines ranging from 1 per cent to 5 per cent of the annual gross turnover of electronic communications networks and services, achieved in the last year for which the financial reports have been completed;[74]
- serious breaches of law with fines ranging from HRK 100,000 to HRK 1,000,000;[75] and
- other breaches of law with fines between HRK 20,000 to HRK 500,000.[76]

Administrative charges and fees for rights of use

33.23   Costs of HAKOM's regulatory and other activities are covered from fees for:

- management of address and numbering space;
- management of radio frequencies; and
- other activities in relation to electronic communications services, paid in a prescribed proportion from the operator's total annual gross turnover in the previous calendar year achieved from the provision of electronic communications networks and services.

On the basis of its annual financial plan, HAKOM determines the calculation, amount and manner of payment of respective fees.[77] Amounts of fees are determined in accordance with the principles of objectivity, transparency, proportionality and non-discrimination, particularly taking into account HAKOM's regulatory principles and objectives set out in the ECA.[78]

Further, additional fees are paid for rights of use of numbers and radio frequencies in favour of the state budget in accordance with the Ministry's Ordinance.[79]

---

71   See para 33.6 above.
72   See art 12(1)(1–27) ECA.
73   See art 112(4) and (7) ECA. Conditions for issuing misdemeanour orders are further prescibed by the Misdemeanour Act, OG 107/07.
74   See art 118(1)(1–4) ECA.
75   See art 119(1)(1–60) ECA.
76   See art 120(1)(1–37), art 121(1)(1–5).
77   See art 16(2) and (4) ECA and Ordinance on Payment of Fees for Performance of HAKOM's Activities, OG 133/2011.
78   See art 16(5) ECA.
79   Ordinance on Payment of Fees for Right of Use of Addresses, Numbers and Radio Frequency Spectrum, OG 154/08, 28/09, 97/10.

Transitional Regulations for Existing Authorisations

33.24 The ECA provides for the obligation of legal entities and natural persons performing activities of electronic communications networks and services on the basis of general licences to adjust their activities with the amended ECA by 08 November 2011.[80] HAKOM must adjust conditions of allocation and use of radio frequencies set out in licences granted before the Amendments, and, if necessary, grant new licences until the day of Croatia's accession to the EU.

REGULATION OF NETWORK ACCESS AND INTERCONNECTION: IMPLEMENTATION OF THE ACCESS DIRECTIVE

Objectives and Scope of Access Regulation

33.25 The ECA implements Access Directive concepts in its section VIII 'Competition'. The provisions respectively address both access and interconnection, empowering HAKOM to impose regulatory obligations on network operators with and without SMP.

Basic Regulatory Concepts

33.26 The ECA's definitions of 'access' and 'interconnection' are practically identical to those in Article 2 of the Access Directive.[81] Operators may negotiate and agree on technical and commercial solutions for access and interconnection at the national or international level. However, operators of public communications networks, when requested by other operators of public communications networks, must negotiate interconnection with each other, to ensure the provision and interoperability of services. Additionally, HAKOM, in order to achieve the necessary access and interconnection, may impose regulatory obligations both on SMP operators and other operators controlling access to their end users. [82]

Access- and Interconnection-related Obligations with Respect to SMP Undertakings

Overview

33.27 HAKOM generally imposes access- and interconnection-related obligations on SMP operators on the basis of regulatory orders following market analysis. In addition, HAKOM may exceptionally use individual access orders and may also impose obligations when an SMP operator and another operator fail to conclude an access agreement.

Transparency obligation

33.28 HAKOM may impose on operators transparency obligations, ordering them to make public certain access- and interconnection-related information, such as:

---

80   See art 118(1) ECA.
81   See art 2(1) ECA.
82   See art 66 ECA.

- accounting information;
- technical specifications;
- network characteristics;
- terms and conditions for supply; and
- use and prices.[83]

If an operator is also under the obligation of non-discrimination, HAKOM may request from the operator to publish a reference offer. There are detailed requirements for the content and manner of publishing of such a reference offer,[84] requiring the operator to include the data determined by the Access Directive. HAKOM may amend such published reference offer yearly and exceptionally in shorter intervals.

Non-discrimination obligations

33.29   HAKOM may impose on operators the obligation of non-discrimination in relation to interconnection or access.[85] Such operator must ensure identical conditions to other operators providing identical services, and provide services and information to other operators under the same conditions and quality level as provided for its own needs and the needs of its subsidiaries.

Specific access obligations

33.30   HAKOM may impose obligations on operators to meet reasonable requirements for access to and use of specific network elements and the associated infrastructure and facilities, in particular where denial of access would hinder competition at the retail level, or would not be in the end users' interest.[86]

HAKOM may, in particular, require from the operator the following:

- to grant access to specified network elements and equipment, including access to non-active network components or unbundled local loop access in order to enable, inter alia, carrier selection or pre-selection or the offer for further sale of subscriber extensions;
- to negotiate in good faith with operators requesting access;
- not to withdraw access to facilities already granted;
- to provide specified services on a wholesale basis for resale by third parties;
- to grant open access to technical interfaces, protocols or other key technologies that are indispensable for the interoperability of services or virtual network services;
- to provide co-location or other forms of shared use of electronic communications infrastructure and associated facilities;
- to provide special services necessary for ensuring interaction of services for the end users, including the facilities for intelligent networks services or roaming services in mobile networks;
- to provide access to operational support systems or similar software systems necessary to ensure fair competition in the provision of services;
- to interconnect networks or network facilities; and

---

83   See art 58 ECA.
84   Ordinance on Reference Offers (OG 37/09).
85   See art 59 ECA.
86   See art 61 ECA.

- to ensure access to related services, such as identification and location services and presence services.

In imposing specific access obligations, HAKOM must consider the following factors:

- the technical and economic viability of using or installing competing facilities, in the light of the rate of market development, taking into account the nature and type of interconnection and access involved, including the viability of other wholesale access services, such as the access to cable facilities;
- the feasibility of providing the access proposed, in relation to the capacity available;
- the initial investment by the facility owner, bearing in mind the risks involved in making the investment;
- the need to safeguard competition in the long term;
- where appropriate, any relevant intellectual property rights; and
- the provision of pan-European services.

Price control and cost accounting obligations

33.31   Where market analysis indicates the risk that the SMP operator might charge excessive prices or apply a price squeeze, HAKOM may impose on it obligations relating to cost recovery and price controls, including cost orientation of prices and the use of cost accounting systems.[87] The cost recovery mechanism or pricing methodology should promote efficiency, competition and maximise consumer benefits, while taking into account the prices available in comparable competitive markets. In order to promote investments, especially those into new generation networks, HAKOM must allow the operators a reasonable rate of return on capital, taking into account all the risk of such investments.

The burden of proof that charges are derived from costs including a reasonable rate of return on investment lies with the SMP operator. For the purpose of calculating the cost of efficient provision of services, HAKOM may use cost accounting methods independent of those used by the operator, or the reference value method. It may also require the operator to provide full justification for its prices, and where appropriate, require those prices to be adjusted.

Accounting separation obligations

33.32   HAKOM may impose on operators the obligation of accounting separation of certain activities related to interconnection or network access.[88] This includes requesting a vertically integrated operator to render visible its wholesale prices and internal price transfers so as to ensure non-discrimination and prevent unfair cross-subsidising. HAKOM may also request inspection of the operator's accounting records to verify compliance with the imposed obligations.

---

87   See art 62 ECA.
88   See art 60 ECA.

Functional separation of vertically integrated operators

33.33   The provision of the ECA empowering HAKOM to order the functional separation of vertically integrated operators will enter into force upon Croatia's accession to the EU.[89] The concept is practically identical to the one from Article 13a of the Access Directive.

Regulatory Powers with Respect to SMP Undertakings

33.34   Article 128 of the ECA provides that regulatory obligations imposed on SMP operators pursuant to the preceding Telecommunications Act[90] ('TA') remain in force until they are replaced by HAKOM's new decisions taken in accordance with the ECA.

The Amendments to the ECA have abolished the former provisions stipulating separately the obligations of SMP operators regarding the connection and use of public telephone network at fixed locations to allow for carrier selection on a call-by-call basis as well as carrier pre-selection. The provision of the ECA stipulating the obligations regime in the market of the minimum set of leased lines will cease to apply upon Croatia's accession to the EU.[91] To date, HAKOM has not analysed this market pursuant to the new ECA rules. However, certain regulatory obligations in this respect, which were imposed on HT as the SMP operator pursuant to the old TA regime, are still in force.

Regulatory Powers Applicable to All Market Participants

Obligations to ensure end-to-end connectivity

33.35   In ensuring end-to-end connectivity, HAKOM may oblige SMP operators and those non-SMP operators controlling access to end users to interconnect their networks with those of other operators. HAKOM may also determine the technical or implementing conditions assuring the regular operation of the network pursuant to applicable standards or technical specifications.[92]

Access to digital radio and television broadcasting services

33.36   Public communications networks intended for the provision of digital television services must be appropriate for digital television services and programmes with widescreen format (16:9). HAKOM may also impose the following obligations on television services operators:

- to ensure access to application programme interfaces or electronic programme guides under fair, reasonable and non-discriminating conditions;
- to apply the standards for the transmission of the digital radio and television signal which have been determined as obligatory by the Commission; and

---

89   See new art 64 ECA.
90   OG 122/03, 158/03, 177/03, 60/04, 70/05.
91   See current art 64 ECA.
92   See art 66(5) ECA.

- in cooperation with equipment manufacturers, to ensure the provision of interconnected digital television services to end users with disability.[93]

Conditional access systems for digital radio and television services must have the necessary technical arrangements enabling operators, at the national, regional or other levels, to have complete control over services using such conditional access systems. Operators of conditional access services, who provide access to digital radio and television services for electronic media broadcasters, must offer all electronic media broadcasters, under fair, reasonable and non-discriminating terms, technical services which allow their subscribers service access by means of conditional access devices.[94]

Holders of industrial property rights to conditional access devices and systems must grant licences to manufacturers of consumer equipment under fair, reasonable and non-discriminatory terms. Those manufacturers may not be prevented from including in the same product a common interface allowing connection with other access systems or components specific to another access system, provided that such common interfaces comply with the relevant and reasonable conditions ensuring transaction security of conditional access system operator.[95]

REGULATION OF THE UNIVERSAL SERVICE AND USERS' RIGHTS: THE UNIVERSAL SERVICE DIRECTIVE

Regulation of universal service obligations

Scope of universal service obligations

33.37 Universal services comprise one or more of the following services:

- access to public telephone network and publicly available telephone services at a fixed location allowing end users to make and receive local, national and international telephone calls, facsimile communications and data communications at data rates that are sufficient to permit functional Internet access, taking into account prevailing technologies used by the majority of subscribers, as well as their technological feasibility;
- access of end users to at least one comprehensive directory of all subscribers of publicly available telephone services;
- access of end users, including users of public-pay telephones, to a telephone directory enquiry service;
- installation of public-pay telephones at public and always accessible places pursuant to reasonable needs of end users in terms of the geographical coverage, quality of service, number of public-pay telephones and their accessibility to disabled users;
- special measures for disabled users; and
- special tariff systems adjusted to the groups of end users with special social needs.[96]

In order to ensure equal access to universal services to disabled persons, operators of universal services must, among other things:

---

93 See art 96 ECA.
94 See art 98(1) and (2) ECA.
95 See art 98(5) ECA.
96 See art 35(2)(1–6) ECA.

- ensure an adequate number and distribution of public-pay telephones adjusted to the needs of disabled users, where every settlement with over 500 inhabitants must obtain one such public-pay telephone;[97]
- enable disabled users to have access to emergency services in the same way as other users;[98] and
- ensure that disabled users have access to directory enquiry services and the directory of all subscribers in the same way as other users.[99]

Designation of undertakings obliged to provide universal services

33.38 HAKOM must determine, at least once every two years, whether universal services have been provided in an appropriate manner and at adequate quality level, as well as which operators are interested in the provision of one or more universal services or coverage of different geographical areas of the state territory, allowing all interested parties to participate in this procedure.[100]

Should HAKOM determine that particular universal services are not being appropriately provided, it will either designate one or more operators to provide those universal services, or carry out a public tender.[101] In case no offers are submitted, HAKOM will designate one or more operators for provision of particular universal services, taking into account the significant market power of operators. A decision on designation of universal services providers includes conditions of provision of universal services and quality of service parameters. When designating operators for provision of universal services HAKOM is prohibited from distorting competition and must take into account the principles of objectivity, transparency and non-discrimination. Once Croatia becomes an EU Member State, HAKOM must notify the Commission of the adoption of decisions designating universal services operators.[102]

After a public consultation in 2010, HAKOM determined that universal services would not be appropriately provided and accessible to all end users, so no operator was designated as a universal services provider and it carried out a public tender. On the basis of submitted offers, HAKOM designated Imenik d.o.o. as the operator for provision of the universal service of access to a comprehensive directory of all subscribers of publicly available telephone services for the period of five years.[103] As no offers were submitted for the provision of other universal services, HAKOM designated HT as the SMP operator, to provide all other universal services for the period of five years.[104]

---

97   See art 23(2) HAKOM's Ordinance on Universal Services in Electronic Communications, OG 23/09.
98   See art 24(4) HAKOM's Ordinance on Universal Services in Electronic Communications, OG 23/09.
99   See art 25(5) HAKOM's Ordinance on Universal Services in Electronic Communications, OG 23/09.
100 See art 36(1) ECA.
101 See art 36(4) ECA. The manner of conduct of public tender is further prescribed by HAKOM's Ordinance on Universal Services of Electronic Communications, OG 23/09.
102 See art 36(9) ECA.
103 Decision of HAKOM's Council of 01 October 2010, Class: 344–01/10–01/990, reference no: 376-12-10-1.
104 Decision of HAKOM's Council of 27 October 2010, Class: 344–01/10–01/989, reference no: 376-12-10-1.

Regulation of retail tariffs, users' expenditures and quality of service

33.39 Operators of universal services must obtain HAKOM's prior approval for the retail prices of universal services. They must ensure special price tariffs adjusted to the group of end users with special social needs.[105] HAKOM may request that universal services operators ensure pre-paid systems for access to public communications network and use of publicly available telephone services and repayment of connection fees by installments.[106] Operators of universal services are required to publish recent notices and information on the conditions of provision of universal services and regularly deliver them to HAKOM. The conditions of provision and price of a certain type of universal services must be the same for the entire area where the services are being provided.[107]

Operators of universal services must enable their subscribers, free of charge, to inspect and control the costs of the provided universal services. This includes the limitation of outgoing calls, when the costs exceed the previously set amount and restriction on certain types of outgoing calls.[108] Further, they are required to provide to subscribers, free of charge, a detailed itemised bill, where the costs of provided universal services must be clearly separated from other costs.

Quality of universal service parameters are set out in HAKOM's Ordinance on Universal Services in Electronic Communications.[109] Operators of universal services are required to submit to HAKOM their reports on the values of the prescribed quality parameters. Such reports are filed annually or in shorter intervals if requested by HAKOM. HAKOM may check the authenticity of the reported data. In case the operator of universal services does not meet the quality of universal service parameters, HAKOM issues a written warning. Within 30 days the operator must submit to HAKOM a written statement committing to the provision of universal services in the prescribed manner and proposing measures to eliminate the shortcomings.[110] Otherwise, HAKOM must publish the list of relevant markets where universal services are not being provided in a prescribed manner and follow the procedure for designation of universal services provider.

Cost calculation and financing of universal services

33.40 Operators of universal services may request from HAKOM compensation for the costs of providing such services. HAKOM calculates the net costs of provision of universal services in order to decide if such costs impose an unfair burden on the operators. Net costs are calculated as a difference between net costs incurred by the operators of universal services when doing business with and

---

105 See art 17(1) of HAKOM's Ordinance on Universal Services in Electronic Communications, OG 23/09.
106 See art 35(5) of ECA.
107 See art 21(3) of HAKOM's Ordinance on Universal Services in Electronic Communications, OG 23/09.
108 See art 22 of HAKOM's Ordinance on Universal Services in Electronic Communications, OG 23/09.
109 See arts 7–16 HAKOM's Ordinance on Universal Services in Electronic Communications, OG 23/09. Quality of universal services parameters include supply time for initial connection, faults rate per access line, dialing tone delay time, unsuccessful call ratio, bill correctness complaints, among other things.
110 See art 6(2) HAKOM's Ordinance on Universal Services in Electronic Communications, OG 23/09.

without the obligation to provide universal services. Funds for recovery of net costs are acquired from the contributions paid by all operators of public communications services whose turnover exceeds 2 per cent of the total annual turnover on national retail markets of these services.[111] Contributions are set in proportion to the share of each operator's annual turnover in the total annual turnover of all operators. An operator of universal services whose portion in the annual turnover in the market of universal services exceeds 70   per cent may not request compensation for net costs.[112]

Regulation of Retail Markets

Prerequisites for the regulation of retail markets

33.41   Where market analysis shows that a given retail market is not effectively competitive and that access regulatory obligations would not be sufficient, HAKOM must impose appropriate regulatory obligations on SMP operators on the given retail market.[113]

Regulatory powers

33.42   HAKOM's regulatory obligations may, in particular, include the prohib-ition to charge excessive prices, hinder market entry or restrict competition by setting predatory prices, the prohibition to show undue preference to specific end users or unreasonably bundle certain types of services. Available measures include introducing retail price caps, controlling individual tariffs, cost-orientation of prices and setting of prices according to those on comparable markets.[114]

SMP operators must notify HAKOM of their retail prices 45 days before publica-tion. HAKOM may, before or after price publication, amend or revoke retail prices, or determine the principles of the accounting system, if such prices are contrary to the imposed regulatory obligations or the legislation regulating consumer protec-tion.[115]

HAKOM, in ensuring that the necessary and appropriate cost accounting systems are implemented, may specify the format and accounting methodology to be used. Operator's compliance with the cost accounting system is subject to yearly independent audits, the results of which are published by HAKOM.[116]

In exceptional cases HAKOM may regulate retail prices in the relevant markets where competition is effective in order to ensure the availability of special pricing systems adjusted to end users with special social needs or the possibility for end users of universal services not to pay additional unnecessary costs for the provision of these services.[117]

---

111   See art 40(3) ECA.
112   See art 40(8) ECA.
113   See art 63(1) ECA.
114   See art 63(3) and (4) ECA.
115   See art 63(5) ECA.
116   See art 63(6) and (7) ECA.
117   See art 63(8) ECA.

End User rights

Contracts

33.43   End users are entitled to enter into contracts with operators for the subscription of their services on the basis of the published general business terms and conditions and tariffs, which represent an integral part of those contracts. General business terms and conditions must be clear and comprehensive and include the following:

- name and seat of the operator;
- details on the provided services;
- manner and conditions of entering into subscription contracts, duration, transfer, renewal and termination of contracts, including fees for termination of contracts prior to the expiry of binding period;
- provisions on prices and refunds applicable in cases when the agreed levels of service quality have not been fulfilled or when the use of services has been disabled due to the operator's fault;
- provisions on the manner for initiating procedures for deciding on end users' complaints, including the dispute settlement procedures; and
- provisions on procedures in case of non-payment of the provided services.[118]

Contracts must also include provisions mandated by other regulations, such as those on consumer protection.

The binding duration of subscription contracts may not exceed two years. Operators of public communications services are required to offer one-year subscription contracts and allow their end users to set in advance the day of entry into the contract and the termination date. Subscribers may terminate subscription contracts at any time. Contracts may stipulate that, when a subscriber terminates the contract prior to the expiry of the binding duration, it must pay a month's tariff for the remaining period or, if more favourable, compensation in the amount of a discount for the acquired products and services.[119] Subscribers are entitled to terminate contracts without paying any penalty if:

- the operator of public communications services is not able to fulfill any of its obligations pursuant to the general terms and conditions (in which case subscribers need only pay the due amount for the provided services);[120] or
- the proposed modifications of the general terms and conditions are less favourable for subscribers in comparison to those valid at the time at which it entered into the subscription contract (in which case subscribers may terminate their contracts within 30 days as of the publication of the proposed modifications).[121]

Transparency obligations

33.44   Operators of public communications services are required to deliver their general terms and conditions and tariffs, as well as their modifications to HAKOM for its inspection at least eight days before publication. Modifications may not be

---

118   See art 42(1)(1–6) ECA.
119   See art 41(5) ECA.
120   See art 41(6) ECA.
121   See art 42(7) ECA.

applied to existing end users before the expiry of the 30-day period from the day they were published, unless they are exclusively in favour of end users, in which case they are applicable from the day they were published. Operators of public communications services are required to notify end users, in written or electronic form, on the intended modifications and their right to terminate subscription contracts, at the latest by the day of their publication. In case of the intended modification or cancellation of a package of services or other additional services, operators must notify end users, at least 30 days in advance, and offer them different package of services or other additional services. Operators of public communications services must ensure the single information point through which end users may request information on tariffs, packages of services and other additional services, thus enabling end users to choose the most favourable tariffs.[122]

HAKOM is required to publish links on its website to the general terms and conditions and tariffs of all operators.[123] HAKOM ensures that end users are able to make an independent estimation of costs arising from the tariffs of public communications services. Operators of public communications services must regularly publish transparent, comparable and up-to-date information on their tariffs, packages of services and other additional services. Such information must be published in a clear and integral manner and form which is easily accessible to end users.

Operators of public communications services must notify their users, free of charge, on any information of public interest, delivered to them by the competent public authorities, in relation to the following:

- the most frequent manners of use of electronic communications services for illegal activities or for distribution of harmful content;
- the legal consequences of such illegal activities or distribution of harmful content (such as copyright infringement); and
- the manner and means of protection from risks for personal safety, privacy and personal data when using electronic communications services.[124]

Quality of service: securing 'net neutrality'

33.45   Standards for quality of electronic communications networks and services are set out in HAKOM's Ordinance on the Manner and Conditions for the Provision of Electronic Communications Networks and Services.[125] Operators with turnovers exceeding 2 per cent of total turnover on the relevant market of electronic communications services and those from which HAKOM requests so, must, at their own expense, at lest every six months, or exceptionally in a shorter interval, assure assessment and inspection of their billing systems, carry out measurement of quality of service and make necessary improvements pursuant to HAKOM's requests.[126] HAKOM must check the information on quality of service delivered by operators and publish the information at least every six months to the extent necessary to notify users on quality of service.

---

122   See art 43(8) ECA.
123   See art 42(2) and 42a(5) ECA.
124   See art 43(7) ECA.
125   Published in the OG 154/11.
126   See art 61(1) of the Ordinance on the Manner and Conditions for the Provision of Electronic Communications Networks and Services, OG 154/11.

European emergency call number

33.46   Users of public communications networks and publicly available telephone services are entitled to make calls to the single European emergency call number 112, as well as to other call numbers for access to other emergency services in Croatia, free of charge, from any telephone device, including all public pay phones. Operators of public communications networks and publicly available telephone services must deliver to the central authority, competent for taking emergency services calls, all available data on calls made to the number 112. Equal access to all call numbers to emergency services must be ensured to disabled persons. The Ordinance on the Single European Emergency Call Number[127] specifies the manner and conditions of using the emergency call number 112, technical requirements for operators and quality parameters.

Other obligations

33.47   Subscribers of publicly available telephone services have the right to have their personal information entered in the public directory. Prior to entering sub-scribers' personal data in the public directory, operators must inform subscribers, free of charge, of the purpose of the directory and all other possible uses of their personal data resulting from browsing the electronic edition of the directory.[128] Further, subscribers must be informed of their right to be entered in the public directory and to check, amend, or delete, free of charge, their personal data from the public directory. Natural persons are entitled to request, free of charge, that their personal data not be entered in the directory. On the other hand, legal entities may not request any limitations regarding the entry of their personal data necessary for identification and communication. Any purpose of the public directory, other than browsing of personal data on the basis of name and surname or legal entity's name and if necessary, other indicators, is subject to a subscriber's prior consent. Operators of publicly available telephone services shall ensure that their subscribers have access to the public directory inquiry service. Once Croatia becomes an EU Member State, end users will be entitled to have direct access, either through voice call or text message, to directory inquiry services in other EU countries.[129] The ECA provides for setting up of at least one comprehensive public directory of all subscribers, in printed and electronic form, and of at least one directory enquiry service. The manner and conditions of setting up of directories and directories inquiry services are further prescribed by HAKOM's Ordinance on Directories and Directory Enquiry Services.[130]

Operators of publicly available telephone services are required to support the international access code '00' when establishing international calls to public com-munications networks outside Croatia. After Croatia's accession to the EU, opera-tors will be further required, when technically and economically feasible and unless subscribers have limited access to calls from certain geographical areas, to ensure access to non-geographical numbers in the EU, all numbers used in the EU, including the numbers from the EU Member States numbering plans and UIFNs,[131]

---

127   Published in the OG 82/09.
128   See art 47(3) ECA.
129   See art 47(8) second sentence ECA. The said provision shall enter into force on the day of Croatia's accession to the EU.
130   Published in the OG 23/09.
131   Universal International Freephone Number (UIFN).

access to directory inquiry services, and establishment of all calls to numbers from the ETNS.[132]

After Croatia enters the EU, HAKOM will be required to ensure that all operators of publicly available telephone services enable establishment of calls to numbers from the 116 range (intended for services with special social sensitivity), and, in particular, to the number 116000 (the missing children hotline).[133] Access to numbers from the 116 range must be ensured for disabled users, particularly when traveling to other EU States.

Obligations facilitating change of provider

33.48   The ECA allows subscribers, if they so request, to retain their assigned numbers independently of the change of the operator. In the case of geographic numbers, the numbers can be retained at a specific location and in the case of non-geographic numbers the numbers can be retained at any location.[134] This does not apply in case of change of geographical location of users or in case of number portability between fixed and mobile electronic communications networks. Number portability and its activation on the other operator's network must be completed in the shortest period of time possible. The duration of disconnection and activation of numbers, regardless, may exceed one working day. Fees connected to number portability must be cost-oriented. Provisions on compulsory duration of subscription contracts may not cause any limitation or present an obstacle to number portability.

DATA PROTECTION: THE DIRECTIVE ON PRIVACY AND ELECTRONIC COMMUNICATIONS

Confidentiality of Communications

33.49   Operators of public communications services and public communications networks are required to undertake respective measures to protect the safety of electronic communications networks and services. The Amendments introduced further requirements with respect to protection of personal data and entrusted HAKOM with the respective enforcement powers and notifying obligations. These new provisions entirely correspond to the E-Privacy Directive rules and will be applicable after Croatia's accession to the EU.[135]

In order to ensure confidentiality of electronic communications, the ECA prohibits listening, tapping, storing and any form of interception or surveillance of electronic communications, except in special cases prescribed by regulations governing national security.[136] The described prohibition does not refer to technical storage of

---

132   European Telephony Numbering Space (ETNS). See art 78(2) ECA. The said provision shall enter into force on the day of Croatia's accession to the EU.

133   See art 78 ECA. The said provision shall enter into force on the day of Croatia's accession to the EU.

134   Number portability is governed by art 76 ECA and HAKOM's Ordinance on Number Portability, OG 42/09, 62/11.

135   See art 99(4)–(10) ECA, introduced by art 95 Amendments, which shall enter into force on the day of Croatia's accession to the EU.

136   See art 100(1) and 108 ECA.

data necessary for a transfer of a communication or legally authorised recording of communications and related traffic data during legal business activities for the purpose of providing proof on commercial transactions or other business communications. Operators of public communications networks and publicly available electronic communications services must ensure and maintain, at their own expense, a function of secret surveillance of electronic communications and services.[137] The operational and technical authority[138] competent for the activation and management of electronic communications surveillance sets out the measures and norms of information safety which operators are required to comply with. The obligations of operators with respect to secret surveillance of electronic communications networks and services are prescribed in detail by special regulations governing national security and criminal procedure.[139]

The Amendments provide for special provisions governing information requirements, notification procedures, and respective enforcement powers of HAKOM and the competent authority for protection of personal data in relation to a breach of such data; these provisions are consistent with articles 4(3), 4(4) and 15a of the E-Privacy Directive. These provisions will apply upon Croatia's accession to the EU.[140] Among other, the provisions prescribe that HAKOM and the authority competent for protection of personal data may order cessation of the infringements and adopt respective measures in case of failure of operators of publicly available electronic communications services to comply with the information requirements.[141]

Data retention

33.50   The ECA is fully complaint with the Data Retention Directive with respect to the obligations of operators of publicly available electronic communications services or public communications networks to retain certain data, in order to enable the conduct of investigation, detection and prosecution of crime as well as for the purpose of protection of defence and national security.[142] Operators must retain data for a period of 12 months from the date of the communication. The security principles which the operators must follow in relation to retained data prescribed by the ECA[143] are identical to those set out in Article 7 of the Data Retention Directive.

The following categories of data may be retained:

- data necessary to trace and identify the source of a communication;
- data necessary to identify the destination of a communication;
- data necessary to identify the date, time and duration of a communication;
- data necessary to identify the type of a communication;
- data necessary to identify users' communication equipment or what is considered to be their equipment; and

---

137   See art 108(1) ECA.
138   The Operational and Technical Center for Telecommunications Surveillance established pursuant to the Security and Intelligence System Act, OG 79/06, 105/06.
139   These special regulations include Security and Intelligence System Act, OG 79/06, 105/06, and Criminal Procedure Act, OG 152/08, 76/09, 80/11, 121/11.
140   See art 99(a) ECA introduced by art 96 Amendments and art 107(a) ECA introduced by art 102 Amendments.
141   See art 107(a)(1) ECA.
142   See art 109 ECA.
143   See art 109(5) ECA.

- data necessary to identify the location of mobile communication equipment.[144]

Retained data include information on unsuccessful calls, while it is not required to retain data on unconnected calls. Retention of data revealing the content of the communication is prohibited.

Traffic Data and Location Data

33.51   The ECA defines traffic data as any data processed for the purpose of transfer of a communication through an electronic communications network or for the purpose of calculation and payment of costs.[145] Location data is defined as any data processed in the electronic communications network or through the electronic communication service, indicating geographical location of the terminal equipment of the user of publicly available electronic communications service.[146]

Traffic data in relation to subscribers or users, processed and stored by operators of public communications networks or publicly available electronic communications services, must be deleted or made anonymous when no longer needed for transfer of a communication, except in special cases prescribed by the ECA.[147] These exceptions include:

- processing of traffic data necessary for calculation of costs of services and interconnection;
- processing of traffic data for commercial purposes (subject to a subscriber's or user's prior consent); and
- retaining of data for the purpose of conducting investigations, discovery and criminal prosecution of criminal offences as well as protection of defense and national security, subject to special regulations.

Prior to obtaining their consent, operators must notify subscribers or users on types of traffic data which are being processed and the duration of data processing.

Location data relating to subscribers or users of public communications networks or publicly available electronic communications services may be processed only if made anonymous or on the basis of a prior subscriber's or user's consent, in the manner, and during the period, necessary for provision of value-added services.[148] Prior to obtaining this consent, operators must inform subscribers or users of the type of location data, purpose and duration of their processing and whether the location data will be delivered to third parties for provision of value-added services. Subscribers and users may withdraw their consent at any time. Further, they retain the right, free of charge and in a simple manner, to temporarily refuse processing of location data for each connection to an electronic communications network or each transfer of a communication. Processing of location data is permitted only to authorised persons and must be limited to the essential activities in relation to provision of value-added services.

---

144   See art 110(1) ECA.
145   See art 2(1)(55) ECA.
146   See art 2(1)(41) ECA.
147   See art 102(1) ECA.
148   See art 104(1) ECA.

Itemised Billing

33.52 Itemized bills must be provided to subscribers of public communications services at their request, and free of charge.[149] Itemized bills must include all necessary information enabling subscribers easily to check the costs of provided services. This information does not include information on calls to emergency numbers or information incompatible with the special regulation governing protection of personal data. Itemized billing must protect the subscribers' right to privacy.

Presentation and Restriction of Calling and Connected Line Identification

33.53 Operators of public communications services offering the possibility of presentation of calling line identifications must enable users, (free of charge and in a simple manner), when making calls, to prevent the identification of their calling line identification for every individual call or all calls.[150] They must also enable subscribers (also free of charge and in a simple manner), when receiving calls, to prevent presentation of calling line identification of incoming calls. When the calling line identification is presented prior to connection, operators must enable subscribers receiving a call to refuse incoming calls when the calling line identification has been prevented by the subscriber making a call. Operators offering the possibility of connected line identification must enable their subscribers, when receiving calls, to prevent presentation of connected line identification in a simple manner and free of charge. Operators of publicly available electronic communications services, offering the possibility of presentation of calling or connected line identification, are required to inform the public of their services and possibility of presentation and restriction of calling and connected line identification in an appropriate and publicly available manner.[151]

Automatic Call Forwarding

33.54 Subscribers are entitled to a simple, and free of charge, method of barring automatic call forwarding towards a subscriber's terminal device made by a third party.[152]

Directories of Subscribers

33.55 Directories of subscribers must include the following subscriber data:

- name and surname or name of the legal entity;
- telephone number or numbers;
- address; and
- for natural persons, their consent or prohibition for publishing their names and telephone numbers in the printed or electronic directory or to be available through directory enquiry services.[153]

---

149 See art 44(1) (3) ECA.
150 See art 103(1) ECA.
151 See art 103(6) ECA.
152 See art 46 ECA.
153 See art 4(3) Ordinance on Directories and Directory Enquiry Services, OG 23/09 in relation to art 47 ECA.

They may also include: information on type of business or category, type of offered services, the subscriber's consent relating to searching for the name connected to an identified number, or other use of information.

The Macedonian Market for Electronic Communications[1]

Metodija Velkov,
Polenak Law Firm, Skopje

LEGAL STRUCTURE

Basic Policy

34.1 The Macedonian market for electronic communication services has undergone a liberalisation process which has created increased competition. The latest report prepared by the national regulatory body in the Republic of Macedonia, the Agency for Electronic Communications ('AEC'), which refers to Q1 of 2012,[2] gives a detailed account of the supply side structure of the various relevant markets. The report shows that, in this period:

- out of 44 notified entities, 36 entities provide publicly available telephone services at a fixed location for national and /or international traffic (including Makedonski Telekom, ONE and Blizoo);
- out of seven notified entities, three entities provide publicly available telephone services in a public mobile communication network for national and /or international traffic (T-Mobile Skopje, ONE and VIP);
- out of 122 notified entities, 106 entities provide Internet access services; and
- out of 84 notified entities, 77 entities provide broadcasting related services, such as transmission of terrestrial radio or television programme services, rebroadcasting radio, or television programme services, among others.

The report also lists the main indicators for the development of the market for electronic communication in Q1 of 2012, which concern the demand side of the various relevant markets. Specifically), the total number of fixed lines (of all technologies) has decreased from 422,053 in Q4 of 2011 to 415,341 in Q1 of 2012 and the total number of fixed lines by 100[3] of population has also decreased from 20.56 in Q4 of 2011 to 20.23 in Q1 of 2012. The total number of active subscribers of mobile telephony services has decreased from 2,213,223 in Q4 2011 to 2,197,148

---

1   Editing of this chapter closed on 1 September 2012.
2   Report on the development of the market for electronic communications in the first quarter of 2012, issued by the AEC, available in Macedonian at: http://www.aek.mk/index.php?option=com_content&view=category&id=54&Itemid=123&lang=mk
3   The value of such indicator has been calculated on the basis of the estimated population of the Republic of Macedonia which, pursuant to official data, was 2,052,722 on 31 December 2009, as a reference date.

in Q1 of 2012 and the number of active subscribers in the mobile telephony by 100 of population has decreased from 107.82 in Q4 of 2011 to 107.03 in Q1 of 2012. On the other hand, there is an increase in the total number of Internet access subscribers; the total number of broadband Internet access subscribers (excluding subscribers through mobile networks) has increased by 3.89 per cent from 282,370 in Q4 of 2011 to 293,344 in Q4 of 2012. Also, the total number of broadband Internet access subscribers through mobile networks (2G/3G) has increased by 2.77 per cent from 373,288 in Q4 of 2011 to 383,610 in Q1 of 2012. The total number of narrowband Internet access subscribers through mobile networks (2G) has increased by 1.86 per cent from 158,295 in Q4 of 2011 to 161,337 in Q1 of 2012. Finally, the total number of TV subscribers has increased only by 0.22 per cent from 251,584 in Q4 of 2011 to 252,145 in Q1 of 2012.

The Assembly of the Republic of Macedonia recently amended the Law on Electronic Communications ('LEC')[4] (the main legislative act in the Macedonian legal system governing electronic communications). These amendments reflect an important policy decision with respect to electronic communications in broadcasting. Specifically, the amendment set 1 June 2013 as the date by which analogue television terrestrial broadcasting is to be replaced by digital television terrestrial broadcasting in Macedonia.

Also, the AEC, as the national regulatory body for the market for electronic communication services, has recently prepared a five-year regulatory strategy for the period from 2012 to 2016, whose stated overall goal is:

'by appropriate regulation and other activities, to support the provision of electronic communication services, in particular broadband services, at the highest possible bandwidth, in the shortest possible time, at feasible prices, and to as many people as possible'.[5]

The AEC also prepares annual programs for its work and publishes such programs on its website (www.aec.mk).

Implementation of EU Directives

34.2   As a candidate country for accession to the European Union, the Republic of Macedonia has undertaken extensive efforts to harmonise its legislation with the Community acquis, including in the domain of electronic communications. In this vein, Macedonia has adopted the EU 2003 Regulatory Framework, while work on transposition of the EU 2009 Regulatory Framework into Macedonian legislation is underway.

Legislation

34.3   In the Macedonian legal system, electronic communications are governed by the LEC and policy documents and bylaws adopted by the AEC to implement the LEC.

---

4   Law on Electronic Communications ('Official Gazette of the Republic of Macedonia' no. 13/2005; 14/2007; 55/2007; 98/2008; 83/2010; 13/2012 and 59/2012)

5   Recommendations for a Five year strategy of the AEC (2012–2016), available at: http://www. aec.mk/index.php?option=com_content&view=article&id=537%3A-2012–2016-&catid=44% 3Anastani&Itemid=151&lang=mk

REGULATORY PRINCIPLES

Scope of Regulation

34.4 The LEC regulates the conditions and the manner of performing activities in the field of electronic communications in the Republic of Macedonia, the establishment and jurisdiction of the AEC, and other issues relating to electronic communications.[6]

For the purposes of the LEC, 'electronic communication network' is a:

> transmission systems and, where applicable, switching or routing equipment and other assets which permit the transmission of signals by wire, by radio, by optical or by other electromagnetic means, including satellite networks, fixed (circuit and packet switched, including Internet) and mobile terrestrial networks, electricity cable systems, in case if used for the transmission of communications signals, broadcasting networks and cable television networks, regardless of the type of information transmitted.'[7]

Furthermore, 'electronic communications service' is defined as 'a service normally provided for compensation which consists wholly or mainly of transmission of signals via electronic communications networks, including telecommunications services and transmission services in networks intended for broadcasting or cable television, but excluding the services that enable or perform editing control over the content transmitted via electronic communications networks or services, as well as the information society services.'[8]

However, Article 3 LEC expressly provides that the provisions of this law do not apply to electronic communications networks and equipment used for the needs of the defence of the country and the military forces, the police and the national security service and in the field of international exchange of classified information and to the radio and/or television programme services broadcasted regardless of the technical means of broadcasting, in coded or not coded form, intended for receipt by the public.

'Internet Freedom'

34.5 The LEC, as well as other regulations currently in force in Macedonia, do not expressly create a special right to access the internet, nor do they specifically regulate measures restricting end-users' access to or use of 'services and applications through electronic communications networks', within the meaning of the 'internet freedom' provision of the EU 2009 Regulatory Framework.

National Regulatory Authority: Organisation, Regulatory Objectives, Competencies

Overview

34.6 The LEC provides for two bodies to regulate matters concerning electronic communications and sets out their different competences:

---

6   Art 1 LEC
7   Art 4 item 2 LEC
8   Art 4 item 2 LEC

- the Ministry of Information Society and Administration,[9] and
- the AEC.

Article 6 paragraph (2) LEC, however, sets out separate competences for the Minister of Information Society and Administration, as well.

The competences of the Ministry of Information Society and Administration are expressly enumerated in the LEC. Namely, the Ministry is in charge of the following:

implementing the policies of the Government of the Republic in the field of electronic communications;
initiating adoption or amendment of the existing regulations and preparing regulations in the field of electronic communications in cooperation with AEC, with other state bodies and other institutions;
performing activities in relation to the development of electronic communications and information technology and creation and development of the information society;
ensuring harmonisation with other regulations that also cover matters related to the electronic communications development;
supervising the lawfulness of AEC's work; and
giving opinion upon the Plan for Radio Frequency Bands Allocation.[10]

The LEC also provides that the Minister of Information Society and Administration must, among other things:

- prepare the National Strategy for development of electronic communications and information technology, taking into account the strategy for development of the information society in the Republic of Macedonia, and organise public debate prior to its submission for adoption by the Assembly of the Republic of Macedonia;
- approve a tender procedure for selecting a universal service provider and for closing a contract with the universal service provider;
- submit proposals to the Government of the Republic of Macedonia for the use and period of implementation of the European 'E-112' single emergency call number in the Republic of Macedonia;
- represent the Republic of Macedonia in international organisations in the field of communications and information society; and
- negotiate and sign bilateral and international treaties in this field on behalf of the Government of the Republic of Macedonia.[11]

The AEC is established by the Assembly of the Republic of Macedonia as an independent regulatory body and a not-for-profit legal entity with public authorisations determined by law. The AEC, in its work, including the decision-making processes within the scope of its authorisations, must be independent from, and impartial to any other state body or other public legal entity or trade company performing activities in the field of electronic communications.

---

9   The Ministry of Information Society and Administration is the competent ministry in this field as of 1 January 2012. The competent ministry prior to this date was the Ministry of Transport and Communications.
10   Art 6 para (1) LEC.
11   Art 6 para (2) LEC.

The AEC has two bodies:

- the Commission; and
- the Director.

The Commission consists of five members appointed (and which may be dismissed) by the Assembly of the Republic of Macedonia. Members are appointed for a five-year term and can be re-appointed for one additional consecutive term (but cannot be appointed for more than two consecutive terms). The Commission's competences include, among other things, appointing and dismissing the Director and monitoring the implementation of the AEC's annual work programme.

The Director is appointed by the Commission, through a public competition, for a five-year term, and can be re-appointed for one more consecutive term (but cannot be re-appointed for more than one additional consecutive term). The Director has the right to attend and participate in the Commission's meetings, without the right to vote. The Director manages the AEC's work, is responsible for the lawful work of the AEC, represents the AEC, adopts decisions on issues which the Commission does not decide, adopts decisions in administrative matters on issues within AEC's competences, adopts by-laws and other acts for implementing LEC, and has other competences under the LEC.

The AEC's scope of work

34.7   The AEC, within the scope of its work, must promote efficient competition in the provision of electronic communications networks and services, associated facilities, and other services by:

- enabling users, including end users with special needs, to benefit from choice, price, and quality of access to electronic communications services;
- protecting users from distortion or restriction of competition in the electronic communications market;
- stimulating efficient investment in infrastructure, and supporting innovations;
- promoting efficient use of radio frequencies and number space; and
- ensuring that, in similar circumstances, there is no discrimination in the treatment of network operators and service providers.[12]

The AEC's competences

34.8   The AEC's tasks and competences are enumerated in Article 9 LEC. These competences include, among other things:

- supervising, controlling, and monitoring the work and activities of operators of electronic communications networks and service providers;
- registering notifications of operators of electronic communications networks and electronic communications services providers;
- taking measures to prevent network operators and service providers from engaging in anti-competitive activities;
- issuing approvals for use of radio frequencies approvals;
- assigning numbers and series of numbers to such network operators and service providers;

---

12   Art 8 para (3) LEC.

- maintaining an electronic register of constructed public electronic communications networks; and
- adopting and implementing of by-laws and technical regulations necessary for implementation LEC.

The AEC's powers

34.9   The AEC has broad power to perform its tasks and competences under the LEC. For example, the AEC may request from electronic communications network operators and electronic communications service providers any data or information necessary to carrying out AEC's activities stipulated in Article 8 paragraph (3) LEC.

The AEC's powers (and duties) also include inspecting and supervising the implementation of the LEC, the secondary regulations, and the obligations or measures imposed by the AEC, through its inspectors for electronic communications.

AEC's cooperation with other state authorities

34.10   In the performance of its functions, the AEC must cooperate with other state agencies and bodies on issues related to the electronic communications. Specifically, the AEC must cooperate with the Commission for Protection of Competition of the Republic of Macedonia ('CPC') (in the implementation of relevant market analysis and determination of operators with significant market power) and the Broadcasting Council of the Republic of Macedonia (in the procedure for assignment of radio frequencies for the purposes of broadcasting). The AEC, the CPC, the other state agencies and bodies must exchange data and information necessary for exercising their competences, but the scope of such exchange of information is limited to the data and information relevant and proportionate to the purpose for which they are exchanged.[13]

The AEC may also exchange available information with other regulatory bodies on their request, provided that the exchanged information is relevant to the competence of the other regulatory bodies and that the scope of exchange of information is limited to the data and information relevant and proportionate to the purpose for which they are exchanged.[14]

Dispute resolution function

34.11   The AEC has competence to resolve disputes related to obligations under the LEC between:

- operators of electronic communications networks and service providers concerning interconnection and/or access, upon proposal by either party in the dispute or upon personal initiative, in accordance with the LEC;
- operators of electronic communications networks and service providers under the LEC provisions and related secondary regulation; and

---

13   Art 21 para (2) LEC.
14   Art 31 para (4) LEC.

- users and operators of electronic communications network and service providers under the LEC provisions and related secondary regulation.[15]

Such disputes may be resolved through a mediation process or an arbitration process, as described further below. AEC's role in such processes is governed by the rules on general administrative procedure and the LEC.

In cases prescribed by the LEC where the AEC resolves disputes, AEC must initiate a procedure for resolving a dispute ex officio or upon a request of a party to the dispute. The AEC must resolve the dispute within 42 days of receipt of a proposal for initiation of such a dispute resolution procedure. The deadline for resolution of the dispute may be extended if necessary due to the complexity of the procedure, but cannot exceed four months.

Network operators and service providers may agree in writing to resolve the dispute by means of mediation in the manner and procedure set forth in the LEC. A mediation procedure is initiated by a written proposal of the party or parties to AEC. The parties to the dispute appoint the mediator by agreement, as an impartial third party, but if they fail to reach an agreement within seven days, any party can request AEC to appoint a mediator. The AEC must appoint a mediator within seven days of receipt of the request. The mediator prepares a written proposal for a decision for resolving the dispute and delivers it to the parties. If the parties accept the decision, its content is entered in a protocol signed by the parties and the mediator. If they do not accept the decision, the mediation procedure is considered to have failed.

In addition, operators of electronic communications networks and providers of electronic communication service may agree in writing to resolve the dispute by means of arbitration, in accordance with the LEC. However, the AEC may instruct the parties to resolve the dispute through mediation if it believes that this may better bring about a timely resolution of the dispute. The arbitration procedure is initiated when one or both parties to the dispute submits a written proposal to the AEC by, which, in turn, forwards the proposal to an Arbitration Council that administers the arbitration process.

The Arbitration Council is established in such way that each party to the dispute elects one arbitrator from AEC's list of arbitrators within a period of seven days of submitting the proposal for arbitration procedure. This list is comprised of at least ten qualified persons in the field of law, economics, or technical sciences appointed by the AEC's Commission, the Minister of Information Society and Administration, and other interested parties. Such arbitrators are appointed for a term of five years (with the potential to be re-appointed for another term) and they must be impartial and independent of the parties in the procedure

Both arbitrators elected by the parties to the dispute, within seven days of their appointment, must, by agreement, elect a third arbitrator chosen from the list of arbitrators, who must be the Chairperson of the Arbitration Council. If no Chairperson or any other arbitrator has been appointed in the set period, the AEC Director must appoint these persons within five days from expiry of that period. The deadline for appointment of arbitrators may be extended by agreement between the parties, who must notify the AEC of such agreement.

The parties to a dispute may, by agreement, select the rules of procedure for the Arbitration Council. In the absence of such an agreement, the Arbitration Council

---

15   Art 9 para (1) line 21 LEC.

must determine the rules of procedure to conduct the arbitration. The Arbitration Council must hear the parties' arguments, examine the claims and complaints, and make proposals to the parties to reach an amicable settlement of the dispute. If an amicable settlement of the dispute cannot be reached, the Arbitration Council must resolve the dispute. The arbitration decision is made publicly available pursuant to the LEC, but the record of the arbitration itself remains confidential.[16]

Arbitrations end with the adoption of an arbitration decision by a majority of votes of the Arbitration Council. The arbitration decision is served on the parties and deposited with AEC. The arbitration decision, including any conclusions stated therein regarding the facts or legal issues is binding on the parties to the dispute and will be enforced through the courts. There is no right of appeal against the decision of the arbitration council.[17]

Legal Remedies against AEC's Decisions

34.12   The AEC Director's decisions adopted pursuant to the LEC are final, and, therefore, may not be appealed. However, a party unsatisfied with a decision of the Director may file a lawsuit against it before the Administrative Court, as a legal remedy to ensure judicial review of such decisions.[18]

The AEC's Obligations to Cooperate with EU institutions

34.13   The LEC expressly provides that the AEC, in conducting its operations, must consider the recommendations and standards of the European Commission and European Union and worldwide best practices, for the purpose of promoting and developing the electronic communications market in the Republic of Macedonia.[19]

The Concept of 'Significant Market Power' Under the LEC

Definition of significant market power

34.14   The LEC provides that an operator of a public communications network or a provider of a public communications service will be deemed to have significant power in a relevant market for public communications networks or services, in a given geographical area, if it has the power and capacity individually or jointly with other operators or service providers to act independently from the competitors and users in that market with respect to prices or services offered.[20]

Moreover, if two or more operators provide services in a relevant market the structure of which enables coordinated effects or parallel activities, they can be treated as operators that jointly have significant market power on a relevant market, even in the absence of structural or other links between or among them.[21]

---

16   Art 131 LEC.
17   Art 131 LEC.
18   Art 137 LEC.
19   Art 22 LEC.
20   Art 40 para 1 LEC.
21   Art 40 para 2 LEC.

If one operator or service provider has significant market power in a relevant market, it will also be deemed to have significant market power in a market closely related to it if the links between the two markets are such as to allow the market power held in one market to be transferred to the other market.[22]

Article 40 LEC also provides that when assessing whether an operator has significant market power in a relevant market, the AEC must consider the following criteria:

- the operator' market share in the relevant market and changes in the market share over time;
- entry barriers in the relevant market and their effect on competition;
- the effect on the operator of purchasing power of large users;
- demand elasticity;
- the development stage of the relevant market;
- technological advantages;
- development of sales and distribution networks;
- economies of scale or economies of integration;
- the degree of vertical integration;
- the degree of product differentiation; or
- access to financial resources.

Furthermore, when assessing whether two or more operators jointly possess significant market power in a relevant market, the AEC must take into account the following criteria:

- the level of market concentration, distribution of market shares and their changes over time;
- entry barriers in the relevant market and their effects on competition;
- the effect on the operators of purchasing power of large users;
- transparency in the relevant market;
- the development stage of the relevant market;
- homogeneity of products;
- demand elasticity;
- the amount of technical innovations and development of technology;
- the existence of available (unused) assets;
- the existence of formal or informal links between operators;
- punitive mechanisms employed by the operators; or
- the existence of price competition.

When assessing the market power of operators and service providers, the AEC must cooperate with the CPC.

Definition of relevant markets and SMP designation

34.15   The AEC determines effective competition in relevant product or service markets in the electronic communications sector, as well as the relevant geographic market, in accordance with the Law on Protection of Competition[23] and in cooperation with the CPC. The AEC must take into consideration the recommendations and standards of the European Commission. The AEC must, together with

---

22   Art 40 para 3 LEC.
23   Law on Protection of Competition ('Official Gazette of the Republic of Macedonia' no.145/2010 and 136/2011).

the CPC, regularly review the existence of effective competition in a particular relevant market.

If the relevant market analysis conducted by the AEC shows that the market lacks sufficiently effective competition, the AEC will determine the operator (or operators) with significant market power in that market, after obtaining an opinion from the CPC, and will determine the appropriate remedies to impose on such operator (or operators).

Pursuant to its latest decisions (in 2010 and 2011),[24] the AEC has determined, in accordance with EC recommendations, a total of 14 relevant product and services market in the electronic communications sector in the Republic of Macedonia that are susceptible to ex ante regulation. These are:

- Relevant markets for retail sale of products and services:
    1   access to the public telephone network at a fixed location for residential and business customers;
    2   publicly available telephone services provided at a fixed location for residential and business customers; and
    3   minimum set of leased lines.
- Relevant markets for the wholesale of products and services:
    4   call origination on a public telephone network provided at a fixed location;
    5   call termination on a public telephone networks provided at a fixed location;
    6   transit services in the fixed public telephone network;
    7   wholesale (physical) network infrastructure access (including shared or fully unbundled access) at a fixed location;
    8   wholesale broadband access;
    9   wholesale terminating segments of leased lines;
    10 wholesale trunk segments of leased lines;
    11 access to public mobile communication networks and call origination on public mobile communication networks;
    12 call termination on public mobile communication networks;
    13 broadcasting transmission services, to deliver broadcast content to end users; and
    14 SMS termination on public mobile communication networks.

Also, pursuant to these AEC decisions, the relevant geographic market for the electronic communications market is the entire territory of the Republic of Macedonia.

The AEC, to date, has concluded and published market analysis of the relevant markets 3, 9, 10 and 14, as defined in its latest decisions. Prior to this, the AEC had concluded and published market analysis of all the relevant markets (18 in total) as they were defined in its previous decision that is no longer in force (and, therefore, these prior market analyses are also no longer relevant pursuant to the currently applicable AEC decisions).

---

24 Decision to determine the relevant markets susceptible to ex ante regulation, adopted by the Director of the AEC on 17 September 2010 and published in the 'Official Gazette of the Republic of Macedonia' no 133/2010; Decision to supplement the Decision to determine the relevant markets susceptible to ex ante regulation, adopted by the Director of the AEC on 15 April 2011 and published in the 'Official Gazette of the Republic of Macedonia' no 59/2011.

With respect to relevant markets 3, 9 and 10, the AEC has identified Makedonski Telekom AD Skopje as a SMP operator in all three markets and imposed obligations upon this operator in such markets (including, in market 3, regulation of retail prices).[25]

With respect to relevant market 14, the AEC has identified *three* operators as having SMP – T-Mobile Macedonia Joint Stock Company for Mobile Communications Skopje, ONE Telecommunication Services DOOEL Skopje, and Company for communication services VIP OPERATOR DOOEL Skopje.

These operators must provide interconnection and access under transparent and non-discriminatory conditions and keep separate accounting records for activities related to interconnection and access, and they are also subject to price control and an obligation for cost based accounting with respect to interconnection and access.[26]

The AEC has administrative discretion to impose on SMP enterprises one or more obligations set out in the LEC, under the conditions and for the purposes expressly stipulated therein.

However, for the purpose of ensuring connection to network end points, the AEC may, to the extent necessary, choose to impose additional obligations on operators that do not have significant market control but control access to end users. Such additional obligations may include an obligation for interconnection or access, if such interconnection or access has not been established. Such additional obligations and conditions determined by the AEC must be objective, transparent, proportional, and non-discriminatory.[27]

The AEC's Regulatory Duties Concerning Rights of Way, Co-location and Facility Sharing

Rights of way

34.16 Under the Law on Construction Land,[28] construction land owned by the Republic of Macedonia may be granted by the competent authorities under a long-term lease, or awarded for permanent use for the construction of infrastructure facilities (such as electronic communication networks) based on an infrastructure project, in a procedure stipulated in this law. Furthermore, construction land located in the buffer zone of roads may be granted under a long-term lease, with a limited right for installation of underground infrastructure facilities for joint economical use, on the basis of an infrastructure project. The Republic of Macedonia reserves its right to install other systems on such land. In addition, rights of way may be established on construction land owned by the Republic of Macedonia or by municipalities by an administrative decision or an agreement concluded with the relevant competent authorities.

---

25 See Second analysis of relevant market 3 – Minimum set of leased lines, 9 – Wholesale terminating segments of leased lines, and 10 – Wholesale trunk segments of leased lines, issued by the AEC in March 2011 and published on its website.
26 See Final Document on the analysis of the market for services of SMS termination in public mobile communication networks, issued by AEC in September 2011 and published on its website.
27 Art 44 para 11 LEC.
28 Law on Construction Land ('Official Gazette of the Republic of Macedonia' no 17/2011 and 53/2011).

To establish the right of use and easement on a plot of land in private property, an operator must submit a draft contract to the owner of the real estate. Such contract must contain the amount of the compensation for the right of use and easement of the real estate, which must correspond to the market value, without taking into account unusual or personal circumstances and interest. If the owner of the real estate does not agree to sign the draft contract within ten days of receiving it, the operator may initiate an expropriation procedure, in accordance with the Law on Expropriation,[29] to establish the right of use and easement in such real estate.[30]

A right of use and easement in the expropriated real estate in private property consists of the right of:

- construction, installation and maintenance of electronic communications networks and associated facilities;
- entry onto real estate to access the electronic communications network and associated facilities for operation and maintenance purposes; and
- removal of natural barriers during the construction, installation, and maintenance of the electronic communications network.[31]

The operator must take necessary measures to avoid causing damages to the real estate, and if such damage is caused, the operator must compensate the owner of the real estate for the damages.

The operator and the owner of the real estate must agree on the period and date of cessation of the right of use and easement. However, the right of use can also cease pursuant to an act of the body competent for expropriation if either:

- either party so requests and the competent body determines that the right of use is no longer required, or
- the owner of the real estate so requests and the competent body determines that the operator has not commenced to use the real estate within two years after obtaining the right of use of the real estate, except where there were justified reasons for such delay.[32]

Co-location and facility sharing

34.17 Operators of public communications networks that have the right to construct and install facilities on public or private property, must construct or install such facilities in such a manner so as to enable their joint use and conclude agreements for their joint use, where the economic use of space, urban planning, and protection of the environment requires so. However, the operator of public communication network may reject a request for joint use of its communications facilities/assets if either:

- the joint use is technically impossible or would cause damage to the integrity and safety of the network; or
- the party requesting joint use does not agree to pay the fee for joint use.[33]

The AEC is responsible for encouraging operators to reach an agreement for the joint use of the facilities/assets and to do so must publicly announce on its website

---

29   Law on Expropriation ('Official Gazette of the Republic of Macedonia' no 95/2012).
30   Art 91 LEC.
31   Art 90 LEC.
32   Art 92 LEC.
33   Art 30 LEC.

the intent for construction of a public communication network, or a significant part of a network. If the operators cannot reach agreement for such joint use, AEC must initiate a dispute resolution procedure in accordance with the provision LEC. In cases where operators cannot reach an agreement on the amount of the fee for joint use of the facilities, the AEC must, within a period of 30 days from the date of submitting the request by either party, decide the amount of the fee, based on the actual costs.

REGULATION OF MARKET ENTRY

The General Authorisation of Electronic Communications

34.18   To construct or use electronic communications networks or provide electronic communications services, network operators and service providers are required to submit a notification on a prescribed form to the AEC prior to the commencement of such construction, use, or service.[34] Within seven days of receipt of a complete notification, the AEC will register the network operator or service provider it in its official records and issue a written confirmation of such registration. The AEC must publish on its official website data on the notified operators and service providers.

Registration in the AEC's records is, however, not a sufficient condition for exercising the rights and obligations of network operators or service providers in accordance with the LEC and the confirmation for registration issued by the AEC does not on its own create rights and obligations in accordance with the LEC, unless the other requirements provided for in the LEC or other laws are also met (such as, among other things, obtaining approval for use of radio frequencies).

Network operators and service providers are also required to notify the AEC in case of change or cessation of the provision of public communications networks or services. Failure to submit a notification for the commencement, change, or cessation of provision of public communications networks and services in a timely manner, or the submission of a false notification, constitutes a misdemeanour subject to a fine. Network operators and service providers must also, within 30 days of any change in their name or registered office address or in the name, address, contact number or unique citizen's number of their legal representatives, notify the AEC of such change.

The LEC provides for a system of requirements and obligations that apply to network operators and service providers, including those that apply to specific categories of operators. For example, all operators of public telephone networks must ensure that users of publicly available telephone services, including users of public pay phones, are able to call emergency call numbers free of charge. In addition, all operators of public telephone networks or publicly available telephone services must enable, free of charge, emergency call services identification of the calling number, as well as caller location information.[35] Furthermore, network operators or providers of public mobile communications services must, upon receipt of a written request from a competent state body for promotion and support of the tourism in the Republic of Macedonia, ensure that SMS messages and notifications regarding the protection, improvement, and promotion of the national

---

34   Art 28 LEC.
35   Art 86 LEC.

and cultural wealth and the tourism of the Republic of Macedonia, are sent in a manner prescribed by the AEC.[36] Network operators and providers of public mobile communications services also must enable the sending, free of charge, of SMS messages that contain information from the Electronic class register (E-class register)[37] provided by the Ministry of Education and Science.[38]

Rights of Use for Radio Frequencies

Overview

34.19   The AEC plans, manages, supervises and controls the efficient and continuous use of the radio frequency spectrum in accordance with the LEC and applicable international regulations. In this respect, the AEC prepares and adopts, upon previous approval from the Government of the Republic of Macedonia, the Plan for Radio Frequency Bands Allocation.[39]

The AEC also prepares and adopts the Plan for Assignment and Use of Radio Frequencies in accordance with the Plan for Radio Frequency Bands Allocation. This plan determines in detail the conditions and the manner of using the radio frequencies in certain radio frequency bands, the availability of radio frequencies, and the manner of issuing approvals for using the radio frequencies.[40] The AEC maintains a Register of Assigned Radio Frequencies being used in the Republic of Macedonia and of the users of such radio frequencies.

In preparing the Plan for Assignment and Use of Radio Frequencies, the AEC coordinates its activities with the state bodies and institutions competent for civil aviation, the state bodies competent for defence and national security, and the Broadcasting Council of the Republic of Macedonia, with respect to that part of the plan which falls within the competences of these intuitions.

General authorisation and granting of individual rights

34.20   Legal entities and individuals may utilise radio frequencies without an approval from the AEC where such radio frequencies are utilised in accordance with the Plan for Radio Frequency Bands Allocation for the needs of the national security and defence, as well as in cases where such use is provided for in relevant bylaws and in international treaties ratified by the Republic of Macedonia.

In other cases, radio frequencies may be utilised on the basis of a general approval or an individual approval issued by the AEC, in accordance with the Plan for Assignment and Use of Radio Frequencies.

Every legal entity and individual is entitled to utilise radio frequencies that in accordance with the Plan for Radio Frequency Bands Allocation may be utilised on

---

36   Art 29-a para (7) LEC.
37   The E-class register is a project of the Ministry of Education and Science realised as a web-based application which aims to improve communication between teachers and parents, to enable quick and easy inspection of information in class registers by the teachers in the school, and to enable centralised and fast statistical analysis. Its website address is: http://ednevnik.edu.mk/
38   Art 29-a para (8) LEC.
39   Art 55 LEC.
40   Art 56 LEC.

the basis of a general approval for use of radio frequencies, in line with the conditions for assignment and use defined in the Plan for Assignment and Use of Radio Frequencies. The AEC issues such general approval in case of minor risk of harmful interference or in harmonised radio frequency bands, and, in particular, for the purpose of implementing the decisions and recommendations of the CEPT and its bodies.[41]

AEC issues individual approvals for use of radio frequencies in accordance with the Plan for Assignment and Use of Radio Frequencies in one of four prescribed procedures in the LEC, specifically:

- based on an individual application (Article 60);
- based on an open call procedure (Article 61);
- based on a public tender (Article 62); and
- based on a public tender with a public bidding (Article 66-a).

Approval for use of radio frequencies allocated for digital radio broadcasting by a public communication network operator for broadcasting of programme services of radio broadcasters through its digital terrestrial multiplex must be issued based on an open call procedure or a public tender.[42]

Furthermore, approval for use of radio frequencies allocated for digital radio broadcasting by a radio broadcaster which is the sole broadcaster in a certain local service zone must be issued on the basis of a decision for awarding a licence for carrying out a radio broadcasting activity adopted by the Broadcasting Council and published in the 'Official Gazette of the Republic of Macedonia'.[43] Also, the AEC shall issue to a radio broadcaster an approval for use of radio frequencies for analogue radio broadcasting, provided that such radio broadcaster has previously obtained a decision by the Broadcasting Council for awarding it a licence for carrying out a radio broadcasting activity and such decision has been published in the 'Official Gazette of the Republic of Macedonia'.[44]

The AEC must issue an approval for use of radio frequencies based on an individual application if such manner of issuing an approval for radio frequencies is determined in the Plan for Assignment and Use of Radio Frequencies, and if the following conditions are met:

- the application is in the prescribed form, includes the prescribed content, and encloses the necessary documentation;
- the application is in accordance with the requirements for assignment and use for which the appropriate radio frequencies are determined by the Plan for Assignment and Use of Radio Frequencies; and
- the requested radio frequencies are available.

The AEC must issue such approvals in the order in which the applications were submitted and must issue the approval within 42 days of receipt of the application. However, the AEC must, through an administrative decision, reject an application if it determines that:

- a previously issued approval for use of radio frequencies to the applicant has been revoked in the last five years due to the fault of the applicant;

---

41   Art 59-a LEC.
42   Art 58 para (2) LEC.
43   Art 58 para (3) LEC.
44   Art 58 para (4) LEC.

- the assignment of radio frequencies does not enable the efficient use of the radio frequency bands; or
- the operation of the applicant's radio devices would cause harmful interference in the operation of other radio devices and equipment, receivers or electrical, or electronic systems.

The AEC must issue an individual approval for use of radio frequencies based on a previously implemented open call procedure for radio frequencies for which such particular manner of issuance of approvals has been determined by the Plan for Assignment and Use of Radio Frequencies due to limited availability of the radio frequency band.

The AEC must announce an open call for submission of applications for issuance of an approval for use of radio frequencies at least once per year. The AEC must publish such open call in the 'Official Gazette of the Republic of Macedonia', in an international journal, and on the AEC's website. A one-time fee is payable to the AEC for the granting of the approval for use of radio frequencies. The AEC determines the amount and terms for such payment, with the consent of the Government of the Republic of Macedonia. Applications must be submitted in the prescribed form and with the prescribed content and necessary documentation within 30 days of the announcement of the open call.

If the AEC determines, based on the applications received, that the particular radio frequencies are sufficient to cover all applicants within the deadline specified in the open call, the AEC will issue such approvals under the procedural rules applicable when approvals are issued based on an individual application. If, however, the AEC determines within the specified deadline that, based on the applications received, there is not sufficient availability of the particular radio frequencies, the AEC must adopt a decision announcing a public tender, or a decision announcing a public tender with a public bidding procedure, within 30 days of the expiry of the specified deadline.[45]

The AEC issues an individual approval for use of radio frequencies based on a public tender procedure also when such procedure has been determined in the Plan for Assignment and Use of Radio Frequencies due to the scarcity of radio frequency bands.

The public tender procedure is initiated upon a decision of, and carried out by a special commission formed by, the AEC Director from among AEC employees. A one-time fee is payable for the granting of the approval for use of radio frequencies, and the amount and terms for its payment is determined by the AEC, with the Government of the Republic of Macedonia approving the amount of the fee. The selection criteria for the most favourable bidder are also determined in this decision, based on the principles of objectivity, transparency, proportionality, and non-discrimination.

The decision to initiate the public tender procedure is published in the 'Official Gazette of the Republic of Macedonia'. The deadline for submitting bids cannot be shorter than 30 days or longer than 90 days from the date of publication of such decision. The opening of the bids is public and minutes are kept of such opening. The public tender is considered successful if at least one timely and correct bid that meets the requirements from the tender documentation has been received. The AEC, however, may, in the decision to initiate the public tender procedure, set some

---

45   Art 61 para (5) LEC.

other minimum number of bids necessary for the procedure to be considered successful. The Commission reviews and assesses the bids received and prepares a rank list of bids and a report of the procedure. The AEC Director adopts a decision for selection of the most favourable bidder and issues one or more approvals for use of radio frequencies no later than 60 days as of the expiry of the deadline for submission of bids.

The AEC issues individual approvals for use of radio frequencies based on a public tender procedure with public bidding when the single criterion for selection of the most favourable bidder is the offered price and if such procedure has been determined by the Plan for Assignment and Use of Radio Frequencies due to the scarcity or the economic value of the radio frequency band.

The public tender procedure is initiated upon a decision of the AEC Director and is carried out by a special commission formed by the AEC Director from among AEC employees. The AEC determines the amount of the market value of the radio frequencies as a one-time fee for the granting of the approval for use of the radio frequencies and the Government of the Republic of Macedonia approves such amount.

The decision to initiate the public tender procedure is published in the 'Official Gazette of the Republic of Macedonia'. The public tender with public bidding is deemed successful if the number of bidders that have qualified is greater by at least one than the number of approvals for use of radio frequencies determined in the decision which are to be granted.

The public bidding is held on the premises of the AEC by means of an oral bidding, but it can also be carried out under different terms set out by the AEC in the decision for initiation of this procedure. At the start of the bidding, the president or vice president of the AEC Commission announces the initial amount of the market value of the radio frequencies as determined by the AEC and invites the bidders to start offering higher bids. During each bid, the bidders may not offer an increase of the bid that is lower than three per cent of such initial amount of the market value of the radio frequencies. Before establishing the highest bid, the president or the vice president of the AEC Commission must invite three times the bidders to submit a higher offer. If, after the third invitation to submit a higher offer, no offer higher than the current is submitted, the president or the vice president of the AEC Commission will announce that the current offer is the highest and no new offers may be submitted.

Transferability and time limitations

34.21 Approvals for use of radio frequencies are issued for a period not exceeding 20 years. By exemption, such approvals for use on aircrafts and vessels are valid until such aircrafts and vessels are commissioned out of use. For special events approvals may be issued for a period not exceeding 60 days. For purposes of research, measurement, and attestation of radio communication equipment for a restricted area of coverage, approvals may be issued for a period not exceeding 90 days.

The validity of the approval may be extended by submitting a request to the AEC in a period not shorter than 30 or longer than 90 days before the validity expires. The new approval may be issued for a period not exceeding 20 years. However, the validity of the approval for use of radio frequencies intended for the purposes of research, measurement, and attestation of radio communication equipment and of the approval for use of radio frequencies intended for special events may not be extended.

The right to use radio frequencies may be transferred or assigned to another entity only based on prior approval of the AEC. If such frequencies are used for broadcasting, prior consent of the Broadcasting Council of the Republic of Macedonia will also be required.

The request for approving such transfer or assignment must be submitted in writing to AEC, and the AEC will verify whether the proposed transferee or assignee meets all statutory requirements and that such transfer will not distort competition or impair the safe, secure, and efficient use of the radio frequency spectrum.

Admissible conditions

34.22   The approvals for use of radio frequencies contain data on the holder, the radio frequencies assigned, the location and area of coverage, period of validity, as well as specific conditions to be met. Specifically, the AEC may specify measures to be taken in order to ensure the efficient use of radio frequencies, including, where appropriate, requirements regarding coverage or signal strength, and technical and operational conditions necessary for the avoidance of harmful interference and limitation of public exposure to electromagnetic fields. The approval contains conditions for the transfer of rights to use radio frequencies, conditions for payment of fees, additional obligations undertaken by the selected bidder during participation in the public tender, and obligations under international law.

- The AEC will revoke an issued approval for use of radio frequencies ex officio if it determines that:
- the application for the granting of the approval for use of radio frequencies contained false data;
- the conditions set out in the LEC or in the approval have been violated;
- the deficiencies established by the AEC have not been remedied within the set deadline;
- the fees for use of radio frequencies were not paid following; or
- there is no other way to avoid harmful interference of the signals of radio communications devices to other devices, receiver, or electrical or electronic systems.

The AEC may also revoke an approval upon the proposal of the holder, but only if such holder has met all of his obligations under the LEC and the approval.

Rights of Use for Numbers

Overview

34.23   The AEC adopts a Numbering Plan which determines the structure, length, and allocation of the numbers for access to public communications networks and public communications services. In this regard, the AEC is responsible for ensuring efficient structuring and use of numbers and series of numbers to meet the needs of operators eligible for the allocation of numbers and to ensuring that the assignment and use of numbers is fair and non-discriminatory.

General authorisations and granting of individual rights

34.24   The numbers and series of numbers of the Numbering Plan may be used by operators of public communications networks, public communications service providers, or providers of universal service only subject to obtaining a decision issued by the AEC for the allocation of such numbers or series of numbers.[46] Such a decision is issued only based on an application submitted to the AEC in the prescribed form and content. The AEC Director must issue such a decision within 15 days of receipt of a complete application. However, the AEC may reject such application if it determines that:

- the application contains false data;
- the applicant is not eligible for such allocation;
- a decision on allocation of numbers and series of numbers issued to the applicant was revoked ex officio in the last five years; or
- the intended use does not justify the allocation of the requested quantity or type of numbers.

The holder of the right to use numbers and series of numbers may not transfer or lease the allocated numbers and series of numbers without a prior approval from AEC and unless all fees due under the LEC have been paid.[47] Moreover, the holder of such right may assign the allocated numbers and series of numbers provided that the holder has paid all fees due under the LEC and provided that the new holder meets the requirements for use of such numbers and series of numbers in accordance with a decision issued by the AEC.[48]

Admissible conditions

34.25   Article 80 LEC provides, among other things, that the holder of the right to use numbers and series of numbers of the Numbering Plan may reserve numbers and series of numbers for a period of one year, with a possibility to extend the period for at most an additional year. The holder is obliged to use the allocated numbers and series of numbers solely for the purpose for which they are allocated and to return the allocated numbers and series of numbers when they are no longer in use. The holder is also required to meet its obligations set out in international treaties and regulations applicable in the Republic of Macedonia.

The AEC may revoke ex officio the right to use the allocated numbers and series of numbers, if it finds that the holder of such right no longer meets the requirements under the LEC, if the annual fees for the user of such numbers have not been paid, or if the holder has not commenced using the allocated numbers and series of numbers within one year of the date of the allocation. Prior to revoking such right, the AEC must submit to the holder a notification stating the reasons for the same.

All operators of public communications networks and providers of public telephone service (fixed or mobile) must provide their subscribers the option of number portability ie ensure that their subscribers may retain the number regardless of the operator or service provider, in the event of geographic numbers, to a specific location and in the event of non-geographic numbers, to any specific location.

For such number portability, the operator may charge the other operators and subscribers or operators a one-time amount to cover the expenses associated with of number portability. Such one-time amount must be included in the interconnection agreements, whereas any direct (administrative) costs that are charged to subscribers may not act as a disincentive to use the service. The AEC may issue a decision

---

46   Art 78 LEC.
47   Art 80 item (d) LEC.
48   Art 80 item (e) LEC.

determining the one-time amount that should be included in the interconnection agreements. Operators will be required to bear the costs for adapting their networks to enable number portability and to bear the maintenance costs for such facilities. In 2011, the AEC adopted a regulation prescribing in detail the manner and timing of implementation of number portability.[49]

The NRA's Enforcement Powers

34.26 The AEC exercises its duties and authorisations to supervise the implementation LEC and the relevant secondary regulations through its inspectors.

Network operators, service providers, or other legal entities or individuals that perform activities in the field of electronic communications must allow such inspector to conduct supervision and to enter a premise, vehicle, ship, vessel, or aircraft where the electronic communications equipment and technical infrastructure are located and must provide at the request of the inspector the necessary data and documentation. If the inspector has not been granted entrance in such premises, the inspector may enter such premises with a warrant issued by a competent court.[50]

If network operators, service providers, or other legal entities or individuals that perform activities in the field of electronic communications cause harmful interruptions in the work and use of other communications networks and facilities or fail to act according to secondary regulations, the inspector will seal the working premises or communications equipment that is not compliant with the LEC. To remedy the determined irregularities and deficiencies, the inspector will unseal the working premises or electronic communications equipment upon a written request by the affected party.[51]

If violations of the LEC, its secondary regulations, or the obligations and measures imposed by the AEC are discovered, the AEC Director may issue a decision:

- ordering the party committing the violation to undertake measures within a given time limit to remedy the determined irregularities and deficiencies;
- prohibiting further activities that violate the provisions LEC, the secondary regulations, or the obligations and measures imposed by the AEC;; and
- initiating a procedure under the Law on Misdemeanours or the Criminal Procedure Code.[52]

Prior to adopting such decision, however, the Director must send a warning notice to the network operator or service provider specifically stating the nature of the violation, as well as the measure that can be imposed, and setting a deadline for remedying the established violation, which cannot be shorter than 30 days.[53] The Director must adopt the decision within seven days as of the expiry of the deadline set in the warning notice.[54]

---

49 Rulebook on number portability ('Official Gazette of the Republic of Macedonia' no 59/2011).
50 Art 135 paras (4) and (5) LEC.
51 Art 135 paras (6), (7) and (8) LEC.
52 Art 136 para (1) LEC.
53 Art 136 para (2) LEC.
54 Art 136 para (3) LEC.

Administrative Charges and Fees for Rights of Use

34.27   The LEC provides for a number of fees and charges that are payable by network operators and service providers.

- Users of radio frequencies must pay to the AEC an annual radio frequencies usage fee, the amount of which is regulated in detail in secondary regulations adopted by the AEC and which is used for supervise, monitor, and measure the radio frequency spectrum and to cover the AEC's administrative costs arising from performing its competences regarding the radio frequency spectrum.[55]
- Holders of allocated numbers and series of numbers must pay to the AEC an annual fee for the use of allocated numbers and series of numbers. The amount of such fee is calculated based on the type, use, and length of the numbers and is regulated in detail in secondary regulations adopted by the AEC, and such fee is used to cover the AEC's administrative costs for managing, monitoring and implementing the Numbering Plan.[56]
- Operators of public communications networks and public communications services providers must pay to the AEC an annual fee for its supervision of the market for electronic communications. Such fee must not exceed 0.5 per cent of the total annual gross revenue of the operator or service provider generated from the use of public communications networks and provision of public communications services in the previous calendar year, or for a shorter period in the year in which the operator or the service provider commenced its operations, but, regardless, must not exceed the amount of €250,000 in Denar equivalent. The amount of the fee is regulated in secondary regulations adopted by the AEC.

Network operators and services providers must submit a report to AEC on their total revenue in the previous year at latest by 15 March of the current year, and must pay the annual fee for supervision of the market for electronic communication by 15 April based on such report.[57]

REGULATION OF NETWORK ACCESS AND INTERCONNECTION: IMPLEMENTATION OF THE ACCESS DIRECTIVE

Objectives and Scope of Access Regulation

34.28   The LEC contains provisions regulating interconnection and access obligations which have been transposed from the Access Directive. Such provisions grant the AEC authorisation to impose measures and obligations on all network operators, regardless of whether they have significant market power, to ensure access and interconnection between them.

Basic regulatory concepts

34.29   The LEC prescribes definitions of the terms 'access' and 'interconnection' which are the same as those set out in the Access Directive.

---

55   Art 75 LEC.
56   Art 83 LEC.
57   Art 32 LEC.

All operators of public communication networks are entitled, and upon request of another operator required, to negotiate on interconnection of and access to their networks and facilities in order to provide public communications services and ensure interoperability of services. Network operators must provide other operators access or interconnection in accordance with the LEC and the obligations imposed by the AEC.

An operator of public communications network must respond to a request for access or interconnection to its network with that of other operators within ten working days of receipt of a request. The interconnection or access agreement must be concluded within 45 days of receipt of the interconnection or access request.[58] If the parties cannot reach an agreement, the AEC must, upon request from one of the parties, resolve the dispute in accordance with the provisions of the LEC. In such procedure, the AEC decides only those issues on interconnection or access on which the parties cannot agree. The obligations and conditions set by the AEC in such a case must be objective, transparent, proportional and non-discriminatory. The network operator or service provider requesting interconnection or access bears the costs for establishing the interconnection or the access, unless the parties agree otherwise.

Access- and Interconnection-related Obligations with Respect to SMP Undertakings

Overview

34.30   In order to ensure provision of proper access and interconnection and functioning of the services and to enable efficiency, sustainable competition, and maximum benefits for end users, the AEC may impose access and interconnection related obligations on SMP operators under the conditions and in a procedure as prescribed in the LEC.

Transparency obligation

34.31   To ensure transparency in the conditions for interconnection and access, the AEC may impose on an SMP operator the obligation to publish specific information relating to accounting, technical specifications, network characteristics, conditions for use, prices, and other information relating to interconnection and/or access.

SMP operators must submit to the AEC, within 30 days as of the date of a decision determining that they are SMP operators, a draft reference offer for interconnection and/or access and a draft reference offer for unbundled access to the local loop, which must be sufficiently detailed. Such draft reference offers are subject to obtaining approval from the AEC within a period of 30 days of their submission and the operator must publish the reference offers on its website within five days of receipt of the AEC's approval. The operator must apply the prices in the approved reference offers starting from the first day of the month following the month when it obtained AEC approval. An SMP operator must not deviate from the terms and conditions of the approved reference offer when concluding agreements on inter-connection and/or access. The AEC may request SMP operators to make changes in

58   Art 44 para (4) LEC.

the approved reference offer and submit to it updated reference offers reflecting the market conditions and the regulatory environment (operators may also do this on their own initiative).[59]

Non-discrimination obligations

34.32   The AEC may impose obligations on an SMP operator to ensure equal treatment in relation to interconnection and/or access. In such a case, the particular operator must apply equal conditions in equal circumstances for other operators providing the same services and must provide services and information to other operators under the same conditions and with the same quality as those for its personal services or for its subsidiaries or partners.[60]

Specific access obligations

34.33   The AEC may also impose obligations on an SMP operator to meet all reasonable requests for access to, and use of, specific network elements and associated facilities.[61] The AEC must impose such obligations where it finds that the rejection of access or unreasonable terms and conditions with a similar effect would hinder the creation of a sufficiently competitive market at the retail level, or where it would be contrary to the end user's interest.

As part of such obligations, AEC may impose additional obligations to ensure fair, reasonable, and timely compliance with other obligations, including, without limitation, an obligation to:

- provide access to specified network elements or facilities, including unbundled access to the local subscription lines;
- negotiate in good faith with operators requesting access;
- maintain, and not deny access to facilities the access to which has already been granted;
- provide specified services wholesale for resale by third parties;
- grant open access to technical interfaces, protocols, or other technologies that are indispensable for the interoperability of services or for virtual network services;
- allow joint use on the same location or other forms of sharing means, including facilities, cable ducts, and mast sharing (electronic communications infrastructure and associated infrastructure capacities and means);
- provide services necessary to ensure interoperability of end-to-end services to users, including facilities for intelligent networks or roaming in mobile networks;
- interconnection of networks or network capacities; and
- provide access to an operative support system or similar software systems necessary for ensuring a fair competition in service provision.

When determining such additional obligations and assessing whether they are proportional to the expected benefits, AEC must take into account:

---

59   Art 45 LEC.
60   Art 46 LEC.
61   Art 51 LEC.

- the technical and economic viability of use or installation of competitive equipment in connection with the degree of market development and the nature and type of interconnection and access proposed;
- the technical and economic feasibility of providing the proposed access, with respect to the available capacities;
- the initial investment by the operator, taking into account the risks involved in such investment;
- the need to protect competition on a long-term basis; and
- where appropriate, any relevant intellectual property rights.

In 2011, the AEC has adopted a bylaw regulating the specific access obligations in greater detail.[62]

Price control obligations

34.34   The AEC may impose obligations on an SMP operator to base its prices for service on actual costs and price controls, including obligations that prices for specific types of interconnection and access be cost-based and determined on the basis of the features and capabilities that will be included in the cost accounting systems.[63] The AEC must impose such obligations if it finds, based on previously conducted market analysis, that there is a lack of effective competition in a particular market. Nevertheless, the AEC must allow the operator a reasonable rate of return of its invested assets, taking into account also the risks that are part of the investment.

The AEC may, on the basis of market analysis, impose additional price obligations on an SMP operator in a particular retail market which is intended for users which the AEC determines to be insufficiently competitive. Specifically, the AEC must determine that the regulated wholesale market, as well as the services related to selection and/or pre-selection of an operator, does not achieve the goals of the LEC and the conditions determined in the agreement for universal service provision (if such an agreement has been concluded with the SMP operator).

Such obligations may include prohibitions on:

- charging excessive prices;
- obstruction of market entry;
- restriction of competition by setting excessively high or low prices;
- giving unfair advantages to particular end users; and
- unreasonable linking of particular services in a package offer.

The AEC may prescribe one of the following methods of retail price regulation, which must be proportional and justified in accordance with the objectives of the LEC:

- retail price capping (price cap regime);
- regulation of individual prices;
- cost-orientated prices; and
- determination of prices according to prices on comparable markets.[64]

---

62   Rulebook on the access and use of specific network elements ('Official Gazette of the Republic of Macedonia' no 31/2011).
63   Art 48 LEC.
64   Art 49 LEC.

Accounting separation obligations

34.35   The AEC, after conducting a market analysis, may impose on an SMP operator an obligation to keep separate accounting for activities related to interconnection and/or access. In particular, the AEC may impose on a vertically integrated SMP operator obligations of transparency in wholesale and internal transfer for the purpose of complying with the non-discrimination obligation and preventing unlawful cross-subsidisation.[65]

Related Regulatory Powers with Respect to SMP Undertakings

34.36   In order to enable the subscribers of an SMP operator in the relevant market for access to and use of the public telephone network at a fixed location to access the services of any operator or public telephone service provider interconnected to such SMP operator, the AEC must require the operator to provide:

- a service for selecting an operator by dialling the code of the selected operator for each phone call; and
- a service for pre-selection of the operator, with an option to change the pre-selection in the same manner as selecting an operator.

The prices for provision of these services must be set out in the agreements for interconnection or access and must be cost-based, and the direct (administrative) costs, if any, charged to the subscribers, may not deter subscribers for using these services.[66]

If the AEC determines, based on a market analysis, that there is not sufficiently effective competition in the market for providing part of the minimum set or the whole package of leased lines, the AEC may impose on an SMP operator in the relevant market for leased lines the obligation to provide the full minimum set of leased lines or only part thereof under equal and transparent conditions and at cost-oriented prices.[67]

Regulatory Powers Applicable to All Market Participants

Obligations to ensure end-to-end connectivity

34.37   In addition to obligations imposed to SMP operators under the LEC, the AEC may also, to the extent necessary to ensure connection to network end points, impose obligations also on non-SMP operators with control of the access to end users. Such obligations may include, among other things, a requirement for interconnection or access, if such has not been established; such obligations must be objective, transparent, proportional and non-discriminatory.[68]

Access to digital radio and television broadcasting services

34.38   Public communications networks designated for the distribution of digital television services must be planned so as to be appropriate for the distribution of

---

65   Art 47 LEC.
66   Art 52 LEC.
67   Art 50 LEC.
68   Art 44 para (11) LEC.

television services and wide-screen format programs. Operators of public communications networks must, upon receipt and redistribution of television services or widescreen programmes, maintain their format. Operators of public communications networks, at the AEC's request, must provide access to application programme interfaces or to electronic programme guides under fair, reasonable, and non-discriminatory conditions.[69] The AEC prescribes the conditions for the operation of digital television equipment that is used by the customers.

An operator of a digital terrestrial multiplex that has received approval from the AEC to use radio frequencies for broadcasting programme services to broadcasters licensed by the Broadcasting Council of the Republic of Macedonia to broadcast through the operator's digital terrestrial multiplex, must apply the principles of objectivity, transparency, proportionality, and non-discrimination equally towards all such broadcasters.[70] Such operator must conduct its business in accordance with the LEC, its secondary regulations, and the Plan for Radio Frequency Bands Allocation of transmission capacities to a digital terrestrial multiplex, adopted by the Broadcasting Council.

Conditional access systems for digital television or radio services must have the technical features to allow the possibility for full control by public communications network operators. Operators that offer conditional access services which provide access to digital television and radio services must offer to all broadcasters, under fair, reasonable and non-discriminatory conditions, technical assistance that enables their subscribers to access their services by means of decoders. Such operators must keep accounting records for the provision of conditional access services separate from the accounting records of their other activities.[71]

REGULATION OF UNIVERSAL SERVICES AND USERS' RIGHTS: THE UNIVERSAL SERVICE DIRECTIVE

Regulation of Universal Service Obligations

Scope of universal service obligations

34.39 Under Article 33 LEC, the universal service must include one or more of the following services:

- connection of the end user to the public telephone network at his or her reasonable request by ensuring access to public telephone services at a specified fixed geographical location, enabling incoming and outgoing calls in the local, national and international telephone traffic, facsimile communications and data transfer at a minimum speed of 9600 bit/s and at an acceptable price;
- ensuring access to information in the single telephone directory and directory assistance services;
- providing a reasonable number of public pay phones from which one can make, free of charge, emergency calls in order to meet the needs of end users considering the geographical coverage with sufficient number of public pay phones, including the possibility for access of users with special needs and the corresponding quality of services; and

---

69   Art 120 LEC.
70   Art 120-a LEC.
71   Art 121 LEC.

- ensuring conditions for equal access to and use of public phone services by end users with special needs, including access to emergency calls services, the single telephone directory and directory assistance service under equal conditions as other end users in the Republic of Macedonia.

Designation of undertakings obliged to provide universal services

34.40   The AEC may designate one or more universal service providers to ensure that these services are available in the whole territory of the Republic of Macedonia. Universal service providers may provide different services or cover different parts of the territory of the Republic of Macedonia.

Under Article 35 LEC, universal service providers are designated in a public tender procedure organised by the AEC. Before initiating this procedure, the AEC publishes an open call for expression of interest in providing one or more services included in the universal service. The AEC must allow at least 30 days from the date it publishes the open call for expression of such interest. In designating universal service providers, the AEC must apply the principles of objectivity, transparency, effectiveness, and non-discrimination, and it may not exclude any legal entity or individual performing a business activity from the universal service provider selection procedure.

If a universal service provider is not selected in the public tender procedure, the AEC may decide to designate one or more universal service providers, in accordance with the principles of effectiveness, objectivity, and transparency. The AEC may designate as the universal service provider the SMP operator in the market of public telephone services at a specified fixed location or the operator with the highest number of subscribers to public telephone services at a specified fixed location. The AEC concludes an agreement with the universal service provider for a period of five years, but must first obtain prior approval from the Minister of Information Society and Administration.

The AEC monitors the work of the universal service provider, and organises a public debate once every two years regarding such work of the provider. The universal service provider is obliged to submit data about its work to AEC at least once a year.

Regulation of retail tariffs, users' expenditures and quality of service

34.41   The AEC is responsible for monitoring the levels and changes of the prices of the services included in the universal service. In this role, the AEC may demand that the prices of individual services forming part of the universal service are equal in the whole territory of the Republic of Macedonia. The AEC may also require that the universal service provider use one of the following models for formation of the prices of individual services included in the universal service:

- limitation of the retail prices (price cap model);
- price formation based on the geographic average; or
- other similar model for price formation.[72]

Universal service providers must determine prices and general terms and conditions for providing universal service so that subscribers of specific services provided as

---

72   Art 36 paras (1), (3) and (5) LEC.

part of the universal service are not required to pay for services which are not necessary or not required for the provisions of the services in question. The universal service provider must also enable its subscribers to limit the use of services, by providing the option for selective call barring for outgoing calls, provide them, free of charge, with itemised bills for the services, and provide them with the option of pre-paid access and use of the service.

The AEC prescribes the quality requirements for the services included in the universal service, the quality parameters and their measurement, in accordance with the standards applicable in the European Union. The AEC also monitors the quality of the universal service and, when necessary, undertakes corresponding measures within its authorisations under the LEC. If the universal service providers fail to comply with the determined quality parameters three times consecutively, the AEC may initiate a procedure to cancel the agreement with the designated universal service provider and to designate a new universal service provider.[73]

Cost calculation and financing of universal services

34.42   The universal service provider is entitled to compensation if the AEC determines that the provision of the individual services forming part of the universal service is unduly burdensome. In such a case, the AEC will calculate the compensation as net costs for providing the particular universal service. However, such compensation cannot exceed the actual costs for providing the universal service. The actual costs are calculated as the difference between the actual costs for providing the universal service and the costs that the universal service provider would have incurred if he were not a universal service provider, taking also into account any benefit to the universal service provider arising from the provision of the universal service, including any non-material benefits. The AEC prescribes the method of calculating actual costs and such non-material benefits, taking into account the recommendations on universal service of the European Union. The AEC Director adopts a decision determining the level of compensation or determining that, based on the calculations, the universal service provider has no right to compensation or is entitled to a lower amount of compensation for the actual costs than the amount of compensation suggested by the universal service provider. [74]

The funds for compensating the actual costs for the provision of the universal service are provided by operators that own public communications networks or provide public communications services in the whole territory of the Republic of Macedonia and earn a minimum gross revenue, as determined by the AEC. Such funds cannot exceed 1 per cent of the total revenues generated by all operators subject to the payment obligation in performing activities with public communications networks and providing communications services. The operators must deposit the funds in a separate account of the AEC within a time period and in the amount as determined in a decision of the AEC, at the latest by 30 April of the current year for activities of the preceding year. The AEC makes the payment on an annual basis to each universal service provider from such account in the amount of the confirmed actual costs for the provision of the universal service.[75]

---

73   Art 37 paras (1), (3) and (7) LEC.
74   Art 38 LEC.
75   Art 39 LEC.

End User Rights

Contracts

34.43 Article 96 LEC requires operators to provide connection or access to the public communications networks on the basis of contracts with subscribers, which must contain, at a minimum:

- the name and address of the operator;
- the services being provided, offered service quality, and the time for the initial connection;
- the type and manner of maintenance of the services;
- detailed information on prices and tariffs, and the time periods for notifying any changes of the same;
- information on the entry into force, duration, the conditions for extension and termination of the subscriber contract, as well as the provision of the services;
- any compensation and the refund arrangements which apply if agreed service quality levels are not met;
- instructions on how to initiate dispute settlement procedures;
- an obligation to notify subscribers of intended changes to the conditions in the subscriber contract and instructions on how to accept the new conditions for extension or termination of the contract;
- the option to have the subscriber data not be publicly accessible in the subscriber registry service and the telephone directory; and
- procedures that will be followed in the event of non-payment or untimely payment of fees for the services.

An operator must inform a subscriber with whom it has a contract, within a period of not less than 30 days, of all proposed changes to the terms and conditions of the contract, as well as of the subscriber's right that, within the same period, the subscribers may terminate the contract without notice or consequences, if the subscriber disagrees with the proposed changes.[76]

Transparency obligations

34.44 Operators and providers of public communications service must publish detailed and transparent information on applicable prices and tariffs and on the general conditions for access to and use of public communications services. Details concerning such obligations are regulated in the 'Rulebook on the type and contents of information that operators of public communications networks and/or public communications service providers are required to publish in connection with the general terms and conditions for access to and use of public communications services, their prices, tariffs and quality parameters'.[77]

Article 99 LEC provides that subscribers to publicly available telephone services must have the right to an entry in the single telephone directory. Network operators and service providers that allocate telephone numbers to subscribers must approve all reasonable requests of the subscribers for entry in the directory assistance services and telephone directories, with all the relevant data, in a manner and at

---

76   Art 96 para (3) LEC.
77   This Rulebook was published in 'Official Gazette of the Republic of Macedonia' no 35/2011 with subsequent amendments.

prices available to the public. The subscriber must have the right, upon a previously submitted request to the operator, to choose the data that will not be included in publicly available directory assistance services or telephone directories. Operators must ensure confidentiality of subscribers' data, including its storage, disclosure, and usage. All end users of publicly available telephone services must have access to universal directory assistance services.

It is also important to note in this regard that the AEC, prior to adopting or amending decisions or other bylaws within its competence that could significantly affect the relevant market of electronic communications, must publish the proposed decision or bylaw on its website and request public comment. The AEC must allow for a minimum of 30 days for such public comment. Following the expiry of the period for public comment, and before adopting the decision or bylaw, the AEC must publish on its website the comments received and the AEC's views on them. If the AEC finds it necessary, it may hold a public hearing on such proposed decisions or bylaws, and invite representatives of all interested parties.[78]

Quality of services: securing 'net neutrality'

34.45   The LEC does not contain provisions specifically directed at securing 'net neutrality'. However, the LEC does authorise the AEC to prescribe the requirements for the quality of services included in the universal service, the parameters and how they are to be measured, which must be in accordance with the standards applicable in the European Union.[79]

The AEC monitors the quality of the universal service and when necessary shall undertake proper measures within its statutory authorisations. Universal service providers must at least once a year submit to the AEC data on the quality of the provided universal service on the basis of the quality parameters and measurement methods and to publish them in an available, detailed and comprehensible manner. If the AEC has a reasonable doubt as regards the truthfulness of this information, it may ex officio order an audit to be carried out by an independent audit company at the expense of the universal service provider. If the universal service providers fail to achieve the determined quality parameters three times in succession, the AEC may initiate a procedure to cancel the agreement with the designated universal service provider and designate a new universal service provider.

DATA PROTECTION: IMPLEMENTATION OF THE E-PRIVACY-DIRECTIVE

Confidentiality of Communications

34.46   The LEC requires operators of public communications networks and providers of public communications services to maintain the secrecy and confidentiality of communications, and, for this purpose, to adopt the appropriate technical and organisational measures for the protection of their networks and/or services and notify their subscribers on any risks and risk mitigation methods. This confidentiality obligation refers to:

---

78   Art 105 LEC.
79   Art 37 LEC.

- the content of the communications;
- traffic data and location data relating to communications; and
- unsuccessful call attempts.[80]

The LEC prohibits all forms of interception, interruption, recording, storage, transfer, and diverting of such communications and data, except in cases where necessary for conveyance of a message as a facsimile message, electronic mail, electronic mailbox, voicemail, SMS message, and others, or for achieving compliance with the provisions of the LEC.[81]

If operators of public communications networks and providers of public communications services need to obtain information on the content of communications, or copy or store communications and related traffic data, they must inform subscribers when concluding the subscriber's contract or before the commencement of the provision of public communication services, and must delete data on the contents of the communication as soon as technically feasible and no longer necessary to provide a specific public communication service.[82] However, recording of communications and the associated traffic data is permitted for the purpose of securing evidence for market transactions or any other business communications, or within organisations receiving emergency calls, for their registration, identification, and resolution.[83]

Furthermore, the use of electronic communications networks to store data or gain access to data stored in the terminal equipment of subscribers or users for further processing is only permitted in cases where the operator of public communications networks and the provider of public communications services:

- previously informs the subscriber or user of the purposes of processing such data;
- gives the subscriber or user the right the opportunity to refuse such processing; and
- provides the subscriber or user with a designated contact person to whom such refusal can be submitted.[84]

In addition, storage of or access to data is permitted for the sole purpose of faster transfer of a message over an electronic communications network, or if essential for the provision of an information society service explicitly requested by the subscriber.[85]

Communications may be intercepted in a procedure determined by the Law on Interception of Communications[86] and in a manner that does not infringe upon fundamental rights and freedoms guaranteed under the Constitution of the Republic of Macedonia and under international conventions to which Macedonia is a party. Operators of public communications networks and providers of public communications services must enable the competent state authority for interception of communications to intercept and monitor such communications in real time.

---

80 Art 111 para (1) LEC.
81 Art 111 para (2) LEC.
82 Art 111 para (5) LEC.
83 Art 111 para (7) LEC.
84 Art 111 para (8) LEC.
85 Art 111 para (9) LEC.
86 Law on Interception of Communications ('Official Gazette of the Republic of Macedonia' no 121/2006 and subsequent amendments)

Traffic Data and Location Data

34.47   Operators of public communications networks and providers of public communications service must store the traffic data of the last 24 months unprocessed and they must store such data in the Republic of Macedonia.[87]

Such network operators and service providers may store and process traffic data required for billing and interconnection payments until payment is completed. They must stipulate in the subscriber's contract the manner of storage, duration of storage and manner or processing of traffic data, and must declare that they will treat such data in accordance with the LEC.

Providers of public communications services may, only after obtaining a subscriber's or user's prior consent, process traffic data for the purposes of marketing electronic communications services or for the provision of value-added services. Subscribers or users must be informed of the types and duration of traffic data processed prior to giving consent and they have the right to withdraw their consent at any time.[88]

Traffic data may only be processed by the responsible persons with the operator of public communications networks or provider of public communications services who are responsible for billing or traffic management, customer relations, fraud detection, electronic communications services marketing, or provision of value added services, and the processing must be restricted to the extent that is necessary for conducting the activities.[89]

Location data other than traffic data relating to users or subscribers may be processed only in anonymised form or on the basis of prior consent by the user or subscriber, but only to the extent and for the duration necessary to provide a value-added service. Prior to giving their consent, users or subscribers must be informed about:

- the type of data to be processed;
- the purpose and duration of such processing; and
- the possibility that location data may be transmitted to third parties for the purpose of providing the value-added service.

Subscribers or users may withdraw consent at any time. In addition, subscribers or users who have consented to the processing of such data must have the option to easily, and free of charge, temporarily reject the location data processing for every network connection of transmission of communication.[90]

Data Retention

34.48   Macedonia has still not transposed EU Directive 2006/24/EC (Data Retention Directive) into the LEC, although, as a candidate country for EU membership, it has undertaken to harmonise its legislation with EU regulations, including in the field of electronic communications.

---

87   Art 112 paras (1) and (6) LEC.
88   Art 112 para (3) LEC.
89   Art 112 para (5) LEC.
90   Article 114 paras (1), (2), (3) and (4) LEC.

Itemised Billing

34.49 Operators must provide its subscribers of public telephone services access to itemised bills enabling them to control the charged amount. Such itemised bills must not include data on calls to free of charge phone numbers and emergency call numbers.

The LEC requires operators to provide subscribers upon their request, free of charge, itemised bills for all types of telephone services used by the subscriber within five working days of receipt of the request. Such itemised bills do not contain individual data for all types of telephone services, but upon request from the subscriber, itemised bills containing such individual data shall be provided.[91]

Calling and Connected Line Identification

34.50 Pursuant to Article 113 LEC, operators of public communications networks or providers of public communications service who offer calling line identification must:

- enable the calling party, before each call, to easily, and free of charge, block the calling line identification; and
- to enable the called party, before each call, to easily, and free of charge, prevent the display of the calling line identification.

Providers of public communications services must enable their subscribers automatically, and free of charge, to prevent the identification for all calls from their lines.

Operators of public communications networks or providers of public communications service who offer called line identification must:

- if the identification is possible prior to connecting the call, allow the called party to easily reject incoming calls where the calling line identification has been prevented by the called subscriber or user; and
- enable the called party to easily, and free of charge, prevent the connected line identification to the calling user.

However, network operators and service providers must disable the prevention of calling line identification for emergency calls.

Automatic Call Forwarding

34.51 Article 116 LEC provides that subscribers must have the option, by using simple means and free of charge, to stop automatic call forwarding by a third party to their terminal equipment. However, this is applicable only if the implementation is technically feasible and would not cause disproportionate costs to the operator.

Directories of Subscribers

34.52 Article 119 LEC requires a publisher of telephone directories to inform subscribers, free of charge, of the purposes of the telephone directories and of the

---

91   Article 101 para (3) LEC.

use of such data before including the subscribers' information in printed or electronic telephone directories available to the public. Subscribers must also be permitted to determine if any of their personal data will be included in a telephone directory and to verify their personal data or request that the data be corrected or deleted. Refusal to include personal data in a public telephone directory, their verification, confirmation, alteration or deletion must be free of charge.

Unsolicited Communications

34.53   Article 117 LEC provides that using automated calling systems for making calls to subscribers' telephone numbers without human intervention, such as through facsimile machines or electronic mail, for the purposes of direct marketing, is only permitted with subscribers' prior consent. In this regard, the LEC prohibits sending electronic mail for the purposes of direct marketing where the identity of the sender on whose behalf the message is sent is disguised or concealed, or where there is no valid address to which the recipient may send a request that such communications be terminated.

The Norwegian Market for Electronic Telecommunications[1]

Espen Sandvik and Nicolai Stenersen
Arntzen de Besche Advokatfirma AS, Oslo

LEGAL STRUCTURE

Basic Policy

35.1   The overall market conditions in Norway are characterised by full liberalisation, mainly through the implementation of EU legislation. However, the former incumbent telecommunications operator, Telenor, still has a large share of the various telecommunications markets.

35.2   The main objective of Norwegian telecommunications law, as stated in the Electronic Communications Act ('E-Com Act') of 4 July 2003, as amended,[2] is:

> 'to secure good, reasonably priced and future-oriented electronic communications services for the users throughout the country through efficient use of society's resources by facilitating sustainable competition, as well as stimulating industrial development and innovation'.[3]

Implementation of EU Directives

35.3   Norway is not a member of the European Union ('EU'). As a member of the European Free Trade Association ('EFTA'),[4] however, Norway is a contracting party to the European Economic Area ('EEA') Treaty.

35.4   The EEA Treaty imposed an obligation on the contacting parties to implement the then existing EC legislation by 1 January 1993. In addition, Article 102 of the EEA Treaty provides a system for the implementation of all subsequent EC directives covered by the EEA Treaty. In practice, all EC Directives will be implemented.

---

1   Editing of this chapter closed on 24 October 2012.
2   LOV-2003-07-04-83.
3   § 1-1 E-Com Act.
4   European Free Trade Association, currently consisting of Iceland, Liechtenstein, Switzerland and Norway.

Legislation

35.5 The E-Com Act is the main statutory instrument governing the telecommunications sector in Norway, and it is supplemented by various regulations, the most significant of which is the Regulation on Electronic Communication Networks and Electronic Communications Services of 16 February 2004 ('E-Com Regulation').[5]

REGULATORY PRINCIPLES: THE FRAMEWORK DIRECTIVE

Scope of regulation

35.6 The E-Com Act applies to a variety of activities connected to the transmission of electronic communications (transmission of sound, text, pictures or other data using electromagnetic signals in free space or by cable in a system for signal transmission) and associated infrastructure, services, equipment and installations.[6] It also covers management and use of the electromagnetic frequency spectrum, and use of numbers, names and addresses. The same applies to all radiation of electromagnetic waves from electronic communications and all inadvertent radiation of electromagnetic waves that may interfere with electronic communications. The E-Com Act does not, however, regulate content.

35.7 An 'electronic communications network' is defined as an 'electronic communications system that includes radio equipment, switches, other connection and routing equipment, associated equipment or functions'.[7] 'Electronic communications service' is defined as a 'service that wholly or primarily comprises arrangement of electronic communications and that is normally provided for a fee'.[8] The E-Com Act does not define 'associated facilities'.

35.8 The Norwegian Post and Telecommunications Authority ('NPT') considers VoIP to be covered by the definition of electronic communication service, provided that the VoIP service offers all-to-all communication (rendering it possible both to originate and terminate calls in other networks).[9] Therefore, all regulations applicable to electronic communication services are also applicable to VoIP services.

Internet Freedom

35.9 To date, Norwegian law has not implemented the 'Internet freedom' principle of Article 1(3a) of the Framework Directive. The Ministry of Communications, however, published on 23 June 2010 a Green Paper with a proposal to implement this principle.[10] It has been distributed for hearing. The proposal, if enacted, will lead to changes in the E-Com Act and the E-Com Regulation.

National Regulatory Authorities: Organisation, Regulatory Objectives, Competencies

35.10 The NPT is an autonomous administrative agency, subordinate to the Norwegian Ministry of Transport and Communications. The NPT is responsible

---

5   FOR-2004–02–16–401.
6   § 1–2 E-Com Act.
7   § 1–5 No 2 E-Com Act.
8   § 1–5 No 4 E-Com Act.
9   NPT Guidelines, 14 June 2006.
10 'Draft changes in the E-Com Act, E-Com Regulations and Number Regulations – Green Paper' (23 June 2010).

for the monitoring of the postal and telecommunication markets in Norway. Further, the NPT has been empowered to pass subordinate legislation supplementing the E-Com-Act. The NPT also manages spectrum and national numbering resources and regulates the placing on the market of radio and communications equipment.

35.11   The NPT cooperates with the Norwegian Competition Authority with respect to issues governed by the Norwegian Competition Act.[11] This cooperation is regulated in an agreement between the two administrative bodies.[12]

35.12   The Ministry, or other governmental bodies, may not instruct the NPT or the Competition Authority on how to handle individual cases.[13]

35.13   Both the NPT and the Competition Authority may demand certain information from the telecommunications operators. The NPT has extensive powers to demand information regarding, among other things, the quality of services, terms and conditions, contingency plans in the event of bankruptcy, and specifications for interfaces.[14] The Competition Authority may demand any information that it believes is significant in relation to the enforcement of the Competition Act.[15]

35.14   The Civil Services Act[16] applies to any decision adopted by the NPT. Before the NPT makes individual decisions regarding issues that may affect the telecommunications market, all interested parties must be heard.[17] Before deciding on issues that may affect trade among EEA countries[18] the NPT must consult with the EFTA Surveillance Authority ('ESA').

35.15   In disputes between telecommunications providers, the NPT may act as a mediator,[19] and in certain cases also adjudicate.[20]

Right of Appeal against NRA's Decisions

35.16   Decisions made by the NPT may be appealed to the Ministry of Transport and Communications.[21] Decisions made by either the NPT or the Ministry may also be tried by the courts of law.[22] Discretionary elements of the decisions, however, are not subject to the court's review. The Ombudsman for Public Administration[23] may also consider decisions of the NPT, but is only empowered to make non-binding statements.

---

11   LOV-2004–03–05–12.
12   Agreement of 28 February 2005, revised 17 December 2008.
13   § 10–2 (2) E-Com Act.
14   § 10–3 E-Com Act.
15   § 24 Competition Act.
16   LOV-1967–02–10.
17   § 9–2 E-Com Act.
18   Including all EU Member States.
19   § 11–1 E-Com Act.
20   § 11–2 E-Com Act.
21   § 11–6 E-Com Act.
22   § 11–1 (2) E-Com Act.
23   The Parliamentary Ombudsman is appointed by the Parliament and investigates complaints from citizens concerning injustice or maladministration on the part of public administration

The NRA's Obligations to Cooperate with the Commission

35.17   While the NPT must cooperate with ESA rather than the Commission, as Norway is a member of the EEA rather than the EU, the ESA and the Commission communicate and cooperate closely.

35.18   The NPT must consult with ESA before deciding any matter that may have a cross-border effect between EEA countries.[24]

35.19   If the ESA concludes that a draft decision of the NPT regarding definitions of new markets or appointment or withdrawal of a SMP position may affect trade among EEA nations or establish trade barriers violating the EEA agreement, or if the ESA is in serious doubt as to whether the draft decision complies with EEA law, it may instruct the NPT to withdraw the draft decision.[25]

35.20   In matters relating to the definition of relevant product and service markets and geographical markets, and in matters regarding analysis and assessment of significant market power,[26] NPT's decisions must comply with ESA recommendations.[27]

'Significant Market Power' as a Fundamental Prerequisite to Regulation

Definition of SMP

35.21   The Norwegian law definition of Significant Market Power (SMP) is the same as in Article 14(2) of the Framework Directive.[28] SMP in one market is relevant when considering possible SMP in a closely related market.[29]

Definition of relevant markets

35.22   The NPT is responsible for defining relevant product and services markets.[30] In so doing, the NPT must consider the ESA's recommendations.[31]

35.23   To date, the NPT has identified seven product markets, none of which deviate from the Commission Recommendation.[32]

35.24   The NPT is also responsible for identifying providers having SMP. This identification must be conducted in cooperation with the ESA, and according to ESA's recommendations.[33] To date, several providers have been identified as having SMP.

---

24   See fn 18 above, and § 9–3 E-Com Act.
25   § 9–3 (2) E-Com Act.
26   See paras 35.21 et seq below.
27   § 3–2 E-Com Act.
28   § 3–1(1) E-Com Act.
29   § 3–1(2) E-Com Act.
30   § 3–2 E-Com Act.
31   ESA recommendation 5 November 2008 (No 688/08/COL).
32   See para 1.73 above.
33   § 3–2 E-Com Act.

Imposition of remedies

35.25 The NPT is not required to impose obligations on SMP undertakings. Rather it is given discretion to impose a wide range of obligations on such undertakings. Some such obligations, however, may not be imposed without consultation with the ESA.[34] The NPT may also impose obligations on undertakings not having SMP, but only with respect to interconnection[35] co-location obligations.[36]

NRA's Regulatory Duties Concerning Rights of Way, Co-location and Facility Sharing

Rights of way

35.26 As a starting point, rights of way must be obtained by means of voluntary agreements with the landowners. If it is not possible to reach an agreement with a landowner, the E-Com Act and the Compulsory Acquisition Act[37] may, in certain cases, entitle the telecommunications provider to be granted a right of way for telecommunications purposes.[38] Compulsory acquisition requires payment of compensation to the landowner.[39] The Ministry of Transport and Communications is empowered to grant the right to undertake a compulsory acquisition.[40]

35.27 If the construction of telecommunication facilities falls within the scope of the Norwegian Planning and Construction Act,[41] notification or application must be filed with the local planning authorities in advance.

Co-location and facility sharing

35.28 The NPT may impose obligations on providers of electronic communication networks in relation to facility sharing, if considerations of effective use of resources, of health, environment, safety, or other social considerations suggest that duplication of infrastructure should be avoided.[42]

35.29 The NPT may impose facility sharing requirements on providers that have been granted rights of way through compulsory acquisition.[43] Further, the NPT may impose on providers with SMP an obligation to accept reasonable requests for co-location or other shared utilisation of infrastructure within the market where the provider has SMP. The NPT may only impose such facility sharing or co-location requirements if necessary to promote sustainable competition.[44]

---

34   § 9–3 E-Com Act and § 3–4(3) E-Com Act.
35   § 4–2(2) E-Com Act.
36   § 4–4 E-Com Act.
37   LOV-1959–10–23–3.
38   § 12–3 E-Com Act and § 2(9) Compulsory Acquisition Act.
39   § 2(9) Compulsory Acquisition Act.
40   § 5 Compulsory Acquisition Act.
41   LOV-2008-06-27.
42   § 4–4 E-Com Act.
43   See para 35.26 above.
44   § 4–4 (3) E-Com Act.

REGULATION OF MARKET ENTRY: THE AUTHORISATION DIRECTIVE

The General Authorisation of Electronic Communications

35.30   Prior to adoption of the E-Com Act (adopting a general authorisation regime), SMP providers of public telecommunications networks and services were subject to individual licensing. Currently, individual licences are required only for the use of numbers and certain radio frequencies.

35.31   The general authorisation regime is subject to various conditions,[45] which reflect most of those admissible according to Annex A of the Access Directive.[46]

35.32   Notification is required for:[47]

'the establishment, operation and provision of access to electronic communication networks which are being used for provision of public electronic communication services, public telephony services and public transmission capacity'.

The notification procedure involves the filing of a notification and interface forms with the NPT. The activities subject to notification may begin once notification has been filed.[48] Confirmation of registration is not given unless requested, but operators that have been registered are listed on the NPT website.[49]

Rights of Use for Radio Frequencies

Strategic planning and co-ordination of spectrum policy

35.33   The NPT may regulate the transfer of spectrum licences.[50] To date, however, the NPT has not issued such regulations. Currently, therefore, a spectrum licence may not be transferred unless a right of transfer follows from either the licence itself[51] or from a subsequent decision by the NPT.[52] Transfers must be notified to the NPT.[53]

Principles of frequency allocation, procedural rules

35.34   The NPT established a national frequency plan forming the basis for awards of both general authorisations and individual licences.[54]

---

45   Ch 2 E-Com Act.
46   See paras 1.98 et seq above.
47   § 2–1 E-Com Act and §1–2 E-Com Regulation.
48   § 1–2 E-Com Regulation.
49   www.pt.no
50   § 6–5(4) E-Com Act.
51   § 6–3(6) E-Com Act.
52   § 6–5 E-Com Act.
53   § 6–5 E-Com Act.
54   § 6–1 E-Com Act (frequency plan published on www.npt.no).

35.35   The Regulation on Allowed Use of Frequencies of 19 January 2012 ('Frequency Regulation')[55] establishes a general authorisation for the use of frequencies below 9 kHz and above 400 GHz.[56] Certain frequencies between 9 kHz and 400 GHz are also covered by the general authorisation, but only for designated types of use (ie use for remote controls and radio controls for toys), and on conditions relating to technical requirements.

35.36   Frequencies not covered by the general authorisation may not be used without an individual licence, which may be granted by either the Ministry or the NPT.[57] An application may be declined if this is justified in light of objectives such as efficient use of resources through sustainable competition, free movement of services, and harmonised use of frequencies.[58]

Admissible conditions

35.37   The conditions that may be attached to a licence[59] reflect the conditions allowed for in Part B of the Annex to the Authorisation Directive.[60] The conditions must be objectively justified, non-discriminatory, proportionate, and transparent.[61]

Limitation of number of rights of use to be granted

35.38   The NPT may limit the number of individual licences for use of the spectrum, but only if necessary to protect the interests of users and to ensure sustainable competition.[62] Before the NPT may limit the number of such licences, it must hold a public hearing.[63] A decision to limit the number of licenses must be in writing, and include the reasons for the decision. Interested parties must be permitted to apply for the licences, and awards must be based on criteria that are objective, transparent, non- discriminatory, and proportionate.

To date, the NPT has awarded such licenses based on both beauty contests and auctions. The NPT decides on a case-by-case basis the appropriate process for awarding a particular licence.

Rights of Use for Numbers

General authorisations and granting of individual rights

35.39   The NPT is authorised to establish numbering plans.[64]

---

55   FOR-2012-01-19-77.
56   § 4 Frequency Regulation.
57   § 6–2(1) E-Com Act and § 3 Regulation F04.07.2003 No 881.
58   § 6–2 E-Com Act.
59   § 6–3 E-Com Act.
60   See para 1.112 above.
61   Ot.prp no 58 2002–2003, item 9.4.2.
62   § 6–4 E-Com Act.
63   § 9–2 E-Com Act.
64   § 7–1 E-Com Act and § 4 Number Regulation (FOR-2004–02–16–426).

35.40   It is not possible to obtain ownership of numbers. Rights of use for numbers are awarded through individual licences from the NPT.[65]

35.41   When considering applications for rights to use numbers, the NPT must consider certain factors such as availability, future needs, the needs of the applicant, and the applicant's exploitation ratio for previously awarded numbers.[66]

Admissible conditions

35.42   The Number Regulation lists the conditions that may attach to the right of use. These conditions reflect those listed in Part C of the Annex to the Authorisation Directive, items 1, 2, 3, 5 and 9. [67]

35.43   The NPT assigns the right to use a number from the number plan.[68]

35.44   Most five- and eight-digit telephone numbers are covered by obligations relating to number portability in the form of provider portability at cost-oriented prices.[69] These obligations do not include an obligation to offer geographic portability (portability of fixed line numbers between different geographical locations) or portability between service types (ie between fixed line and mobile operators).

35.45   Undertakings with SMP in the market for access to public telephony in fixed networks must offer call-by-call carrier pre-selection by use of a prefix.[70] Such undertakings must also offer fixed carrier pre-selection.[71]

Limitation of number of rights of use to be granted

35.46   The E-Com Act does not include procedures for limiting the number of rights of use of numbers to be granted. It is, therefore, left to the NPT's discretion to determine the best means for determining such limitations. In determining whether to adopt such limitations, the NPT must consider the factors listed in section 8 of the Number Regulation, including future needs for numbering resources.

The NRA's enforcement powers

35.47   The NPT is charged with supervision to ensure that providers comply with the conditions attached to general authorisations and individual licences.[72]

35.48   Undertakings' obligations to either make public, or submit to the NPT, information regarding quality of service form the factual basis for the NPT to exercise its supervisory powers.[73] In addition, the NPT gathers information from

---

65   § 7–1(2) E-Com Act and § 5 Number Regulation.
66   § 8 Number Regulation.
67   § 9 Number Regulation.
68   § 10 Number Regulation.
69   § 7–3 E-Com Act and § 3–5 to 3–7 E-Com Regulation.
70   § 3–1 E-Com Regulation.
71   § 3–2 E-Com Regulation.
72   § 10–1 E-Com Act.
73   § 10–3 E-Com Act.

sample surveys, the taking of measurements, and other control activities.[74] The NPT may access premises without advance warning if necessary to gather relevant documentation.[75]

35.49   If the NPT discovers that an operator has not met the conditions applicable to its licence, the NPT must notify the operator in question. The operator has one month to correct the breach, after which the NPT may issue instructions to remedy the defect.[76] No deadline to correct the breach has to be set in relation to undertakings that have previously been in breach of their obligations, nor in relation to technical deficiencies concerning equipment and installations.[77] Prior to the one-month deadline, the NPT may impose sanctions if it believes there is an immediate and serious threat to security or health.[78]

35.50   Continued breach gives rise to sanctions such as financial penalties,[79] revocation of licence,[80] and closing down of networks.[81]

Administrative charges and fees for rights of use

35.51   Annual fees for operators registered in accordance with the notification procedure are calculated in accordance with provisions of the fee regulation.[82]

35.52   The fees are calculated and collected by the NPT. The total annual fees to be collected by the NPT are fixed by Parliament in the state budget.[83] This total is divided among the respective types of operators and licences according to a distribution key found in the Fee Regulation, which allocates percentages of the total fee to the various registrations and licences. For instance, 49 per cent of the total fees must be taken from spectrum licence holders.[84] The fees for use of numbers are, however, fixed.

REGULATION OF NETWORK ACCESS AND INTERCONNECTION: THE ACCESS DIRECTIVE

Objectives and Scope of Access

35.53   The objective of the E-Com Act's access-specific regulations is to promote sustainable competition, and facilitate national and international competition in the market.[85]

35.54   Access obligations are mainly placed on SMP operators, but apply to some extent also to other providers of electronic communication networks and services. The obligations are not in all cases limited to public networks, but it is assumed that

---

74   § 10–1 E-Com Act.
75   § 10–1 E-Com Act.
76   § 10–6(4)E-Com Act.
77   § 10–6(4)E-Com Act.
78   § 10–9 E-Com Act.
79   § 10–7 E-Com Act.
80   § 10–8 E-Com Act.
81   § 10–9 E-Com Act.
82   FOR 2005–02–21 no 168.
83   § 1(1) Fee Regulation.
84   § 1(2) Fee Regulation.
85   § 3–4(3) E-Com Act.

they will have a very limited application on private networks. The access regulations do not regulate content requirements.

Basic Regulatory Concepts

35.55   The access-related powers vested in the NPT lie in its ability to enact regulations supplementing the E-Com Act, as well as its ability to impose obligations on operators in individual cases. The E-Com Act does not include an express obligation for the NPT to use these powers, except for the obligation to supervise the market.[86] General principles of administrative law, however, require agencies such as the NPT to use powers as necessary to meet statutory objectives (in the case of the NPT, statutory objectives of the E-Com Act).

35.56   The NPT must exercise its powers consistent with requirements of transparency, proportionality, non-discrimination, and objectivity.[87] Further, the NPT must observe requirements imposed by administrative law concerning decision-making procedures,[88] and apply the reasonableness test attached to most access obligations.[89] The NPT must follow consolidation and consultation procedures before it may take certain actions.[90]

35.57   'Access' is not defined, but must be understood in light of the definition of article 2(b) Access Directive.[91] In addition, certain statutory provisions clarify the scope of the obligations related to the notion of access.[92]

'Interconnection' is defined as a 'function that provides for handling traffic between providers so that end users may communicate with each other and have access to public electronic communication services independent of the provider connection'.[93]

35.58   Interconnection is dealt with separately from access in the E-Com Act, notwithstanding that it is considered to be a specific type of access.

35.59   While the E-Com Act does not specifically refer to the principle of freedom of access,[94] it does not include any obstacles to voluntary interconnection negotiations, and no authorisation is required to request access or interconnection. The E-Com Act also does not clearly express the priority of commercial negotiations principle.[95]Given the requirement of the Access Directive, however, it is assumed this principle must be observed as a guideline.[96]

Access- and Interconnection-related Obligations with Respect to SMP Undertakings

35.60   Some obligations incumbent on SMP undertakings apply by law, whereas others are imposed by the NPT on a case-by-case basis. Both types of obligations

---

86   § 10–1 E-Com Act.
87   Ot.prp No 58, 2002–2003, items 6.4 and 9.2.
88   § 9–1 E-Com Act.
89   Eg § 4–1(1) E-Com Act.
90   § 9–2 and § 9–3 E-Com Act.
91   See para 1.133 above.
92   § 2–2 E-Com Regulation.
93   § 1–5 E-Com Act.
94   Cf para 1.135 above.
95   Cf para 1.136 above.
96   Cf the comments to § 4–2 in the preparatory works, Ot.prp nr 58, 2002–2003.

have their legal basis in the E-Com Act and the E-Com Regulation. In addition, the NPT may in 'special cases' impose obligations in addition to those explicitly described in the E-Com Act.[97] The Act does not in itself place any limitations on the type of measures that can be imposed on SMP undertakings in such 'special cases'. This does not, however, mean that the NPT has unlimited discretion to impose obligations, as it must observe general principles of proportionality and objectivity. The NPT also must follow consultation procedures when deciding to impose obligations.[98]

35.61   The NPT may impose on SMP operators the requirement of the publication of 'specified information'.[99] Such information includes, but is not limited to, accountancy data, technical specifications, and prices. Obligations to prepare and publish standard terms and conditions for offers on electronic communication networks and services may also be imposed. Such standard offers must always be prepared in relation to access to the local loop.[100]

35.62   The NPT may, in individual cases, impose non-discrimination obligations in relation to access and interconnection.[101] Such obligations also apply automatically by application of law in certain cases.[102] These obligations are subject to a reasonableness test.

35.63   The NPT may impose on SMP operators an obligation to accept all reasonable requests for entering into or amending agreements for access to electronic communication networks and services.[103] A non-exhaustive list of the relevant types of access encompasses bitstream access, access to the mobile network for virtual operators and for operators with limited coverage, and re-sale of subscriptions.[104] The NPT may also, subject to certain conditions, impose co-location obligations[105] and access obligations in relation to information and support systems.

35.64   These obligations are in addition to the interconnection obligations that apply also to non-SMP operators.[106]

35.65   Rights of access apply also to virtual mobile operators.[107]

35.66   The NPT may regulate prices for access and interconnection if necessary to prevent operators from exploiting their market position to the detriment of end users by keeping a disproportionately high price level or by establishing a price squeeze on competing operators.[108] The NTC may impose specific methods for price regulation and accountancy.

---

97   § 3–4(2) E-Com Act.
98   § 9–3 E-Com Act.
99   § 4–6 E-Com Act.
100   The transparency requirements are further elaborated in § 2–5 and § 2–6 E-Com Act, see also § 4–8(4) and § 4–12(2) E-Com Act.
101   § 4–7 E-Com Act.
102   Chapter 2 E-Com Regulation.
103   § 4–1 E-Com Act.
104   § 2–2 E-Com Regulation.
105   § 4–4 E-Com Act.
106   See paras 35.70–35.72 below.
107   Ot.prp no 58, 2002–2003 item 7.2.
108   § 4–9 E-Com Act.

35.67   The NPT may impose accounting separation between the respective business sectors of a telecommunications company or between specific activities connected to access and interconnection.[109]

Regulatory Powers with Respect to SMP Undertakings

35.68   In addition to the access and interconnection obligations described above, SMP operators in the market for access to public telephony services in the fixed network that control access to end users must offer their customers call-by-call carrier selection and carrier pre-selection at cost oriented prices.[110]

35.69   Further, undertakings with SMP in the leased lines market must offer such leased lines to other operators.[111] Such offers must be on non-discriminatory terms and at cost-oriented prices.

Regulatory Powers Applicable to All Market Participants

Obligations to ensure end-to-end connectivity

35.70   All operators may be subject to access and interconnection obligations regardless of their market position, if necessary to ensure end-to-end communication.[112] Such obligations may be imposed without following hearing and consultation procedures.[113]

35.71   Providers of access to electronic communication networks must conduct interconnection negotiations with other operators, if requested.[114] This is a statutory obligation that applies without specific imposition by the NPT.

35.72   The NPT may order undertakings given a right to expropriation[115] to grant co-location to other operators without similar rights.[116] The NPT may also impose obligations concerning the joint use of infrastructure even if not requested by any undertaking, when justifiable on grounds of efficient use, health, environment, security, or other reasons.[117] The NPT must conduct a public hearing prior to imposing such obligations.[118]

Regulation on roaming services

35.73   The Roaming Regulation is implemented in Norwegian law through the E-Com Regulation.[119]

---

109   § 4–8 E-Com Act.
110   § 4–11 E-Com Act.
111   § 4–12 E-Com Act and § 2–3 E-Com Regulation.
112   § 4–1(4) and § 4–2(2) E-Com Act.
113   § 9–2 and § 9–3 E-Com Act.
114   § 4–2(1) E-Com Act.
115   § 13–3 E-Com Act.
116   § 4–4 (1) E-Com Act, and Regulation F04.07.2003 No 881 § 2.
117   § 4–4 (2) E-Com Act.
118   §9–2 E-Com Act.
119   §2–7 E-Com Regulation.

Access to digital radio and television broadcasting services

35.74 Providers of access control services for radio and television broadcasting services must accept all reasonable requests for access from content suppliers. The criteria for access must be objective, reasonable, non-discriminatory, and publicly available.[120] The NPT may grant exemptions from such obligations for operators that do not have SMP, but only if the general access to such services is not reduced from such exemption.

REGULATION OF THE UNIVERSAL SERVICE AND USER'S RIGHTS: THE UNIVERSAL SERVICE DIRECTIVE

Regulation of Universal Service Obligations

Scope of universal service obligations

35.75 In order to secure the provision of universal service obligations, the NPT may either enter into a contract with, or impose an obligation through an administrative decision on one or more providers of electronic communications networks and services.[121]

35.76 The services covered are:

- provision of public telephone services and digital electronic communications networks;
- provision of public pay telephones;
- provision of number information services;
- provision of telephone directories and
- provision of special services for disabled persons and other end users with special needs.

Designation of undertakings obliged to provide universal services

35.77 To date, these universal service obligations have been imposed through a licence granted to Telenor ASA.

Regulation of retail tariffs, users' expenditures and quality of service

35.78 Providers required to provide universal services may not charge customers for extra costs incurred in connection with providing network access. The obligation to provide customers with access to public telephony services applies to all places with permanent all-year residences or business activity.[122]

35.79 In order to monitor the provision of universal services, the NPT may request that a provider issue a yearly report regarding the services offered and the quality of the services.[123]

---

120 § 4–3 (1) and § 4–8 (2) E-Com Act and Chapter 4 E-Com Regulation.
121 § 5–1 E-Com Act.
122 § 5–1 E-Com Regulation.
123 § 5–9 E-Com Regulation.

35.80   Breach of the universal service obligations may result in fines, and, in theory even imprisonment up to six months. The size of the fines is decided by the NPT.[124]

Cost calculation and financing of universal services

35.81   Providers of universal services may request that their extra costs be covered through a financing fund, if these costs constitute an unreasonable burden.

35.82   The NPT may decide whether such costs should be regarded as an unreasonable burden and to impose duties on all providers to contribute to such financing.[125]

Regulation of Retail Markets

Prerequisites for the regulation of retail markets

35.83   The NPT may regulate end user services[126] only if regulation of access and interconnection[127] does not achieve the desired objectives.[128]

35.84   The NPT determined that Telenor has SMP in the end user market for fixed line subscription and has imposed obligations on Telenor's wholesale offers. The NPT withdrew its previous decision stating that Telenor has SMP in the end user markets for fixed line traffic.

Regulatory powers

35.85   The NPT may regulate the retail markets by prohibiting SMP operators from, among other things, excessive pricing, predatory pricing, price discrimination, and unreasonable product bundling.[129] The types of obligations the NPT may impose include, for example, maximum prices, cost orientated prices, and geographical levelling. While the E-Com Act does not specifically limit the scope of these measures, it is assumed that they are subject to the requirements of objectivity and proportionality.[130]

35.86   Operators with SMP in all, or parts of,[131] the leased lines market, must offer leased lines to end users on non-discriminatory terms.[132] The terms and conditions for such offers must be made public, unless the NPT determines that it would be unreasonable to require an operator to make such information public[133] The NPT may require an operator to offer prices that are cost-oriented. [134]

---

124   § 12–4 E-Com Act.
125   § 5–2 E-Com Act and § 5–7 and § 5–8 E-Com Regulation.
126   § 4–10 E-Com Act.
127   § 4–9 E-Com Act.
128   See paras 35.62–35.67 above.
129   § 4–10 E-Com Act
130   Ot.prp No 58, 2002–2003, item 6.4.
131   § 2–3 E-Com Regulation.
132   § 4–12(1) E-Com Act.
133   § 4–12(2) E-Com Act and § 2–5 E-Com Regulation.
134   § 4–12(1) E-com Act.

End User Rights

Contracts

35.87 Providers of electronic communication networks used for public communication services and providers of public communication services must offer end users the option of entering into subscription agreements.[135] The minimum contents for such offers include, among other things, price and duration, procedures for complaint, and remedies in the case of defective services.[136] Changes in subscription agreements that are believed to be of significance to the customer must be notified the customer with at least one months' notice.[137]

Transparency obligations

35.88 The NPT may impose on providers of electronic communication services to end users obligations to publish the terms and conditions for such services.[138] This obligation includes information on prices.[139]

Quality of service: securing 'net neutrality'

35.89 Providers of electronic communication networks used for public communication services must measure and publish information on their quality of service levels.[140] Further, the NPT may impose requirements on electronic communications networks, services, associated equipment, installation and use of standards to ensure the interaction between network and service quality, efficient utilisation of capacity in the network that is used by several providers, secure life and health, or to avoid harmful interference.[141]

European emergency call number

35.90 The number 112 has been implemented in Norway as an emergency number. This is supplemented by the numbers 110 (fire) and 113 (medical). All calls to Norwegian emergency services must be free of charge.[142]

---

135 § 1–8 E-Com Regulation.
136 § 1–8 E-Com Regulation.
137 § 2–4 E-Com Act and § 1–8 E-Com Regulation.
138 § 2–5 E-Com Act.
139 § 2–5 E-Com Act.
140 § 2–2 E-Com Act cf. § 1–6 E-Com Regulation
141 § 2–3 E-Com Act.
142 § 2–6 E-Com Act.

DATA PROTECTION AND PRIVACY

Confidentiality of Communications

35.91   Norway recently proposed modifying sections of the E-Com Act to implement the EU Data Storage Directive. To date, the proposed modification has not
been adopted. [143]

Under the proposed modifications, to ensure the confidentiality of traffic and
localisation data and other necessary data used to identify the subscriber or user,
operators must erase or anonymise such data as soon as they are no longer
necessary for communication or invoicing purposes. The same applies when there is
a duty to store data and where necessary to fulfil other requirements under law. A
user's consent must be obtained for other means of managing the data.[144]

35.92   Operators providing an electronic communication network for public electronic services, or providing public electronic communication service themselves,
must store data on traffic and localisation, and data necessary to identify the
subscriber or user, for a period of up to six months. The NPT may allow exceptions
from the storage obligations, or impose such storage obligations on others than the
said providers.[145] The data stored must only be used for investigations and criminal
proceedings of serious criminal offences. The duty is limited to data generated or
processed in the provider's communication network by the use of fixed-line, mobile
telephone, Internet- line or access and e-mail.

The NPT may adopt regulations, issue individual decisions, or enter into agreements on measures to maintain the confidentiality, integrity, and availability of
such. Further, the NPT may, by regulation, permit providers to request a certificate
of good conduct from persons who are to process the data on behalf of the
provider.

35.93   Notwithstanding applicable principles of confidentiality, the prosecuting
authority and the police may receive information about unlisted telephone numbers
or other information concerning a subscriber, as well as information about electronic communication addresses. Such information may also be disclosed as part of
a testimony in a court of law. It may also be disclosed to other authorities to the
extent basis for this is found in other legislation than the E Com Act. [146]

Breaches of confidentiality concerning personal data must on certain conditions be
reported to the Data Inspectorate.[147]

Traffic Data and Location Data

35.94   'Traffic data' is defined as any data necessary in to transfer communication
in an electronic communications network or for the billing of such transfer.[148]
'Localisation data' is defined as data processed in an electronic communications

---

143 §§ 2–7 and 2–9 E-Com Act.
144 § 2–7 proposed E-Com Act.
145 § 2–7a) proposed E-Com Act.
146 § 2–9 under proposed E-Com Act.
147 § 2–6 Data Privacy Regulations
148 § 7–1 E-Com Regulations.

network and which indicate the geographical placing of the terminal equipment employed by the user of a public electronic communications service.[149]

35.95 Service providers may process traffic data only for the purpose of transmitting the communication, for invoicing, for fulfilling the duty to store information, or fulfilling requirements of the law under the proposed Act.[150] Any other processing of traffic data, such as processing for marketing purposes, requires the consent of the subscriber to whom the traffic data relate.[151] The consent must be freely given, specific and informed, and the service provider must inform subscribers of the types of data processed, the duration and purpose of such processing, and whether the data is intended to be transferred to a provider of a additional service beyond public telephone service. A user must be able to withdraw the consent at any time.[152]

35.96 Under the proposed modifications to the E-com Act, traffic data processed for the purpose of transmitting communications or invoicing must be erased or anonymised when it is no longer necessary for that purpose. The same applies for traffic data no longer needed under the duty to store information or to fulfil requirements of the law.[153]

35.97 Location data other than traffic data (ie not included in the definition of 'traffic data') may be processed under the same conditions as for traffic data. [154]

Itemised Billing

35.98 Service providers must, unless otherwise agreed, provide subscribers with non-itemised bills. At the request of a subscriber, a service must provide itemised bills.[155]

Calling and Connected Line Identification

35.99 Service providers offering calling line identification services must allow calling end users to withhold the display of their own number on a per-call and per-line basis. End users must also be able to reject incoming calls where the caller has withheld the caller identification. The services must be offered free of charge. The service may be temporarily eliminated at the request of an end user who believes they have been exposed to insulting telephone calls. The service also does not apply for calls to emergency services. The service provider must store the identification details of the calling end user and present these to the police for the purpose of investigations.[156]

---

149 § 7–2 E-Com Regulations.
150 § 2–7 E-Com Act.
151 § 2–7 E-Com Act.
152 § 7–4 E-Com Regulations, cf Personal Data Act.
153 § 2–7 under proposed E-Com Act.
154 § 2–7 under proposed E-Com Act.
155 § 1–9 E-Com Regulations.
156 § 6–1 E-Com Regulations.

Automatic Call Forwarding

35.100   A provider of a public telephone service must, free of charge, give the user or subscriber the possibility to request that third parties' calls are not automatically forwarded to the user's or subscriber's terminal equipment.[157]

Directories of Subscribers

35.101   The provider of a public telephone service making a subscriber's data available for inclusion in a publicly available printed or electronic directory must inform the subscriber in advance, and free of charge, of the purposes of the directory and the possible use of the data based on search functions in the electronic directory. The subscriber must have the opportunity, free of charge, to verify, correct or withdraw the data. The subscriber also has the right to refuse that his or her data be made available.[158]

---

157   § 6–4 E-Com Regulations.
158   § 6–2 E-Com Regulations.

The Russian Market for Electronic Communications

Edward Bekeschenko
Baker & McKenzie, Moscow

LEGAL STRUCTURE

Basic Policy

36.1 In recent years the telecommunications market in Russia has undergone significant changes and has become one of the most rapidly growing markets in the world. This is a result of liberalisation, development of the infrastructure in the telecommunications industry, and the continuous growth of the Russian economy in general. The liberalisation of the Russian telecommunications market started in 1995 after the adoption of the first consolidated law regulating telecommunications in Russia.[1] The liberalisation process is not finished yet. Currently the Russian telecommunications market is competitive and includes a large number of alternative providers at the level of networks and services and expands from year to year.

36.2 According to the Monitoring of the Results of Social and Economic Development of Russia for 2011,[2] in 2011 the volume of telecommunications services provided in Russia increased by 9.1 per cent (by 4.5 per cent in 2010). The volume of telecommunications services provided in Russia in 2011 was worth €36,450m. Based on the 2011 results, telecommunications services comprise 19.2 per cent of the total volume of services provided for a fee in Russia. The increase in the volume of telecommunications services is influenced by further development of telecommunications networks, implementation of new types of services, tariff policy of telecommunications providers, population income level, and corporate activity.

36.3 The mobile telecommunications service is the fastest developing and expanding telecommunications service in Russia. As of 1 October 2011, there were 250 million mobile facilities/telephones in Russia, an increase of 7.4 per cent compared to 1 October 2010.

36.4 Based on the results of the first nine months of 2011, mobile services comprise 44.4 per cent of the total volume of telecommunications services provided in Russia, local telephone services and public pay telephone services comprise

---

1   Federal Law No 15-FZ 'On Communications' dated 16 February 1995, as amended.
2   http://www.economy.gov.ru/minec/activity/sections/macro/monitoring/doc20120202_05

11 per cent, postal special communications services comprise 8 per cent, and international and long distance local telephone services comprise 6.7 per cent.[3]

Implementation of EU Directives

36.5   Russia is not a member of the EU and is very unlikely to become an EU member in the near future. Russian telecommunications legislation will not need to be adapted to the laws of the EU, and there are doubts as to whether the EU telecommunications legislation would be appropriate for Russia's current stage of development.

36.6   The current Russian telecommunications legislation differs significantly from EU legislation, as it is more complicated and less liberalised.

Legislation

36.7   Russian telecommunications legislation consists of a number of laws and regulations covering different features of the provision of telecommunications services. The Law on Communications (the 'Communications Law')[4] establishes the general telecommunications regulatory principles and sets out general requirements for the provision of telecommunications services, licensing, numbering, radio frequency spectrum allocation, and execution of state control, among other things. To implement the Communications Law, between 2005 and 2007, the Government adopted a number of resolutions regulating different types of telecommunications services. These resolutions set out requirements for, among other things, conclusion, fulfilment, and termination of agreements for provision of particular types of telecommunications services and procedures for considering claims and issuing bills.

36.8   Decisions of the State Commission for Radio Frequencies (the 'SCRF') set out the procedures for use of radio frequency spectrum in Russia.

36.9   Various Russian state bodies regulate different aspects of the provision of telecommunications services, such as encryption, equipment commissioning, and allocation of number resources, among others.

36.10   The main objectives of Russian telecommunications legislation are to ensure:

- the effective operation of telecommunications providers;
- development of competition in the telecommunications market;
- equal rights to all telecommunications providers;
- development of new technologies; and
- integration of the Russian telecommunications infrastructure with that of other countries.

36.11   Russia has recently acceded to the WTO. As a WTO member Russia is obliged to amend its legislation, including the telecommunications legislation, in compliance with WTO principles. Therefore, in the near future Russian telecommunications laws and regulations will be adjusted to WTO requirements.

---

3   'Communications' section of the monitoring referred to in fn 2.
4   Federal Law No 126-FZ 'On Communications' dated 7 July 2003, as amended.

REGULATORY PRINCIPLES

Scope of Regulation

36.12 The Communications Law has adopted a wide, and technology-neutral approach.[5] It regulates the establishment and operation of all telecommunications networks and facilities, radio frequency spectrum use, and provision of telecommunications and postal services in Russia and in territories under Russian jurisdiction. The Communications Law also provides definitions of basic telecommunications terms. Thus, a telecommunications network is understood as a technological system including telecommunications facilities and lines and designated for telecommunications and postal communications.[6] A telecommunications service means activities for the receipt, processing, storage, transfer and delivery of telecommunications messages and mail.[7] The government has announced that further changes to the law will be forthcoming.

36.13 There are separate secondary laws (including those relating to licensing requirements) with respect to data transfer (with or without VoIP), telematic, mobile, local, intra-zone, long distance local and international telephone telecommunications services, telecommunications services for the purposes of television and (or) radio broadcasting, and telegraph telecommunications services.

36.14 Additionally, Russian telecommunications regulation includes separate secondary laws relating to use of the radio-frequency spectrum, requirements for telecommunications networks, their construction and operation, certification of telecommunications equipment, and allocation of number resources, among other things.

'Internet Freedom'

36.15 There are no laws limiting access to the Internet and attempts to introduce such regulations have been rejected by legislators (State Duma).

36.16 On 28 July 2012 the Federal Law amending Russian legislation on the protection of children from information (the 'Child Protection Law')[8] was adopted. The Child Protection Law provides for formation of a unified register of domain names, indicators of Internet site pages and network addresses, containing information prohibited for distribution in Russia (the 'Register'). A site may be included in the Register by a court order. In some cases an authorised state body may add a site to the Register without a court order if the site contains:

- materials with pornographic images of minors and (or) seeking to involve minors in pornography;
- information on methods of development, production and use of drugs, psychotropic substances and their precursors, on places for the acquisition of such drugs, psychotropic substances and their precursors, on methods and locations of cultivation of drug-containing plants;

---

5   Arts 1 and 3 Communications Law.
6   See Art 2(24) Communications Law.
7   See Art 2(32) Communications Law.
8   Federal Law No 139-FZ 'On the Introduction of Amendments into the Federal Law on protection of children from information damaging their health and development and other Russian legislation' dated 28 July 2012.

- information on methods of committing suicide as well as calls to commit suicide.

36.17   If an Internet site contains other information prohibited for distribution in Russia, it may be added to the Register by a court decision.

36.18   If a site is added to the Register, the owner of the site must remove the site or page containing information which is prohibited for distribution in Russia. If the owner fails to remove the site or page, the hosting provider must restrict access to the site.

36.19   These rules with respect to maintenance of the Register and inclusion of information in it came into force on 1 November 2012.

National Regulatory Authorities (NRA): Organisation, Regulatory Objectives, Competencies

36.20   State regulations on the provision of services and other telecommunication activities are drafted by the President, the Government, and the Ministry of Telecommunications and Mass Communications (the 'MTMC'), which is the federal governmental authority for telecommunications. The MTMC is the state body responsible for the preparation of draft federal laws, presidential decrees, and government resolutions in the area of telecommunications and information technology. The MTMC is also entitled to issue its own regulations, such as setting out requirements for the use of numbering resources, regulations on the use of radio frequencies, and rules for the provision of telecommunications services to customers, among other things.

36.21   The other state agencies overseeing the telecommunications sector are the Federal Service for Supervision in the Sphere of Telecommunications, Information Technology and Mass Communications ('Roskomnadzor'), and Rossvyaz – the Federal Communications Agency (the 'FCA').

36.22   Roskomnadzor is responsible for exercising day-to-day control in the area of telecommunications and mass media, monitoring the use of the frequency spectrum, registering frequency assignments, registering mass media, issuing licenses in the area of telecommunications and mass media, and protecting of personal data.

36.23   The FCA is responsible for coordination of international and federal programmes in the area of information technology and communications, the numbering resources of providers, certifying the compliance of equipment, and organising the operation, development and modernisation of the federal communications and national information and telecommunications infrastructure.

36.24   The MTMC also organises the work of the SCRF. The SCRF is made up of representatives of various ministries and state bodies. The main tasks of the SCRF are to coordinate the use of radio frequency spectrum by different state bodies and to allocate frequency spectrum. The SCRF is responsible for the allocation and use of the frequency spectrum, scientific and technical research in the area of use of the frequency spectrum, frequency spectrum demilitarisation/ conversion, technical policy for use of the frequency spectrum and electromagnetic compatibility.

36.25   The MTMC and its subordinate state agencies interact with the Federal Antimonopoly Service (the 'FAS'), a competition regulator acting directly under the Government. The FAS is entitled to prohibit the MTMC and its subordinate state agencies from adopting acts or performing actions which may result in the restriction of competition. The FAS is also entitled to provide the MTMC with recommendations aimed at ensuring competition. State agencies are usually independent, but they all interact with one other. State agencies act under a particular ministry (such as Roskomnadzor and the FAC) or the Government (such as the FAS).

Right of Appeal against NRA's Decisions

36.26 Any decision of the MTMC, Roskomnadzor, or FAC may be appealed in court. If a decision violates a right of a legal entity or a private entrepreneur, a claim may be filed with an Arbitrazh (state commercial) ourt. If a decision violates the rights of an individual who is not an entrepreneur, a claim may be filed with a court of general jurisdiction (general court), but these cases are very rare. In both cases, a claim must be filed within three months of the claimant having learned of the decision violating the claimant's rights.[9]

36.27 A judgment should be rendered by an Arbitrazh court within three months after the filing of the claim.[10] This term may be extended up to six months.

36.28 While judges typically adhere to these deadlines, in rare situations they resolve cases in protracted timeframes.

36.29 A court judgment may be appealed to the court of appeal within one month.[11]

36.30 A claimant must prove to the court that the NRA's decision violates the claimant's rights. The respective regulatory authority must prove that the decision was issued in compliance with the law.

36.31 Sub-laws adopted by the MTMC may also be challenged by legal entities in an Arbitrazh court and by individuals in a general court. After filing a claim, judgment should be rendered within one month in a general court and within three months in an Arbitrazh court. There is no statute of limitations for challenging a regulation.

'Significant Market Power' as a Fundamental Prerequisite of Regulation

36.32 While Russian legislation does not contain a definition of 'significant market power', it defines 'dominant position' as 'the position of a business entity (group of persons) or several business entities (groups of persons) is considered as dominant in a particular product market if such position enables such entities (groups of persons) to significantly influence the general conditions of product circulation on the particular market and (or) eliminate other business entities from such market and (or) impede their access to the market.'[12] The Competition Law

---

9   Art 256(1) Code of Civil Procedure; Art 198(4) Code of Arbitrazh Procedure.
10   Art 200(1) Code of Arbitrazh Procedure.
11   Art 259(1) Code of Arbitrazh Procedure.
12   Art 5(1) Federal Law No 135-FZ 'On Protection of Competition' dated 26 July 2006 (the 'Competition Law').

sets out several criteria to determine whether an entity holds a 'dominant position' (eg market share, possibility of access of competitors to the market, among others.).[13]

36.33   A commodity market is understood as the sphere of circulation of goods (including goods manufactured in a foreign country) which may not be replaced with other goods or replaceable goods, within the borders of which (including geographical borders) based on economic, technical or other possibilities or advisability an acquirer may acquire goods and outside which such possibility does not exist.[14] In the sphere of communications a commodity market will mean a market in which the telecommunications services may be acquired.

36.34   The Communications Law, and by-laws promulgated thereunder, seek to ensure effective and fair competition in the telecommunications services market.

NRA's Regulatory Duties concerning Rights of Way, Co-location and Facility Sharing

Rights of way

36.35   The RF Land Code (the 'Land Code') provides for a specific category of land designated for communications purposes.[15] In order to carry out activities in the areas of communications (except for space communications), radio and television broadcasting, rights to land plots may be granted for the location of infrastructure facilities, including radio relay, aerial, and underground cable communications lines and relevant restricted zones, amplification stations, land-based satellite communications facilities and infrastructure.[16]

36.36   Such land is provided for telecommunications needs for permanent use or fixed-time use on a free-of-charge basis, lease or easement for construction and use of telecommunications infrastructure. Such titles and rights are subject to state registration. Lease and fixed-time use on a free-of-charge basis agreements signed for a term of less than one year do not require state registration.

36.37   Ownership, other property rights, and restrictions (encumbrances) to real estate such as buildings, masts, and other constructions must be registered in the Unified State Register of Rights to Immovable Property and Transactions Therewith. Aerials and underground communication cables and related equipment are also subject to registration as immovable property.[17]

Co-location and facility sharing

36.38   Telecommunications organisations, on the basis of an agreement with the owner or other possessor of buildings, power transmission line supports, railway networks, pillar supports, bridges, collectors, tunnels, roads and other engineering

---

13   See, eg Art 5(1) and (3) Competition Law.
14   Art 4(4) Competition Law.
15   Art 87 Land Code.
16   Art 91 Land Code.
17   Art 1 'Regulations on the Specifics of State Registration of Ownership and Other Property Rights to Cable and Line Telecommunications Facilities' approved by Government Resolution No 68 dated 11 February 2005.

facilities and technological sites, and rights of way are entitled to perform construction and use of telecommunications equipment and facilities on such property.[18] An owner or other possessor of the property may require the telecommunications organisation to pay a reasonable fee for use of the property unless otherwise is provided by the applicable legislation.

36.39   Telecommunications providers are entitled, for a fee, to locate telecommunications cables in line and cable telecommunications facilities regardless of the ownership of such facilities.[19]

REGULATION OF MARKET ENTRY

Licensing of Electronic Communications

36.40   Telecommunications services may only be provided on the basis of a licence. The list of telecommunications services subject to licensing and the licensing conditions are provided for in the Resolution on Licensing (the 'Resolution on Licensing').[20] Roskomnadzor is the federal authority currently responsible for the issuance of licences for the following telecommunications services subject to mandatory licensing:

- local telephone services, except for local telephone services with use of public telephones and public access facilities;
- long distance local and international telephone call services;
- telephone services in the allocated telecommunications network;
- intra-zone telephone services;
- local telephone services with use of public telephones;
- local telephone services with use of public access facilities;
- telegraph telecommunication services;
- personal radio-calling services;
- mobile radio communication services in the public use telecommunications network;
- mobile radio communication services in the allocated telecommunications network;
- mobile radio telephone communication services;
- mobile satellite communication services;
- telecommunication services on provision of telecommunications channels;
- telecommunication services on data transfer, except for VoIP;
- VoIP services;
- telematic services;
- telecommunication services for cable broadcasting purposes;
- telecommunication services for air broadcasting purposes;
- telecommunication services for wired radio broadcasting purposes; and
- postal services.

36.41   A licence may be obtained upon application. If the telecommunications service requires the use of a radio frequency, number resources or other limited

---

18   Art 6(3) Communications Law.
19   Art 6(5) Communications Law.
20   Government Resolution No 87 'On Approval of the List of Communications Services Subject to Licensing and the Lists of Licensing Conditions' dated 18 February 2005.

resources, the licence may be obtained only through a competitive procedure (auction or tender).[21]

36.42   The application form must contain basic information about the applicant, the term, and the territory where the licensee intends to provide telecommunications services. A copy of the company charter, certificate of registration as a legal entity or private entrepreneur, certificate of registration as a taxpayer, network configuration chart, a short description of the services to be provided, and confirmation of payment of the state fee (RUB 2,600, approximately €65) for issuance of the licence must be submitted to Roskomnadzor.

36.43   If an undertaking, in providing telecommunications services. intends to use radio frequency spectrum, perform cable television broadcasting and wired broadcasting, provide VoIP services, services on the provision of telecommunications channels that go beyond the territory of the Russian Federation or a single constituent territory of the Russian Federation, postal services, the undertaking, in its licence application must also submit to Roskomnadzor a description of the telecommunications networks and facilities that will be used for provision of the services as well as a plan and economic justification of the telecommunications network development.

36.44   If an application is made for a licence to provide telecommunications services requiring the use of a radio frequency, the decision of the SCRF on frequency allocation must be attached to the licence application.

36.45   The Roskomnadzor must decide whether to issue the licence within 30 days after the application is filed. In cases requiring submission of a description of telecommunications networks and facilities and a plan and economic justification of the telecommunications network development, Roskomnadzor considers license applications within 75 days after filing the application.

36.46   The territory for which the licence is valid is specified in the licence. There are no restrictions on the number or type of telecommunications licences that a single licensee may hold.

36.47   Licences are issued for a term of up to 25 years. An application to extend the term of a licence must be submitted no less than two months, and no earlier than six months, prior to its expiry. The licence may be prolonged for the term of its issuance or for another term, but not for more than 25 years.

36.48   The Communications Law does not permit the transfer to another person or entity, of a licence, or any rights that are based on the licence. The licence may be re-issued by Roskomnadzor only to a legal successor of the licensee, for which purpose the legal successor must provide documents evidencing transfer of the relevant telecommunications networks and devices for provision of telecommunications services to it. If the licence was for the use of a radio frequency, the radio frequency use permit needs to be re-issued prior to re-issuing the licence.[22]

36.49   The grounds for refusal to issue a licence to provide telecommunications services are limited to the following: [23]

- non-compliance of the documents attached to the application form with the requirements of the Communications Law;

---

21   Art 31(1) Communications Law.
22   Art 35(1) Communications Law.
23   Art 34 Communications Law.

- failure to provide a document required by the Communications Law;
- providing documents that contain incorrect information;
- non-compliance of the activity for which the licence is requested with the applicable standards and regulations;
- failure to win an auction/tender for issuance of a telecommunications licence;
- termination of the SCRF decision on allocation of a radio frequency band; or
- technical impossibility of implementing the telecommunications service for which the licence is requested.

36.50   The refusal of Roskomnadzor to issue a licence may be challenged by the applicant in court.

36.51   The licence may be suspended by Roskomnadzor in the following cases:[24]

- indication of violations that may result in damaging rights, legal interests, human life and health as well as the provision of the needs of state authorities, national defence, state safety and provision of law enforcement;
- termination of a decision of the SCRF on use by the licence holder of radio frequencies, if such termination makes it impossible to provide the services; and
- failure by the licence holder to fulfil an order of the licensing authority that obliged the licence holder to eliminate a violation.

36.52   Roskomnadzor also may terminate a licence without applying to the courts if the provider is liquidated or ceased its activities as a result of reorganisation or has applied for termination of the licence.

The license may also be terminated in court in case of: [25]

- indication of incorrect information in documents being the grounds for passing a resolution on issuance of the licence;
- failure to eliminate circumstances on the basis of which the licence was suspended within a prescribed term; or
- failure by the licensee to perform obligations imposed on it during an auction/tender.

Rights of Use for Radio Frequencies

Strategic planning and co-ordination of spectrum policy

36.53   The Communications Law[26] requires that the procedures for frequency allocation and for national frequency allocation and use have to be transparent. Allocation of the frequency spectrum must comply with the Frequency Allocation Table, which must be reviewed by the Russian state frequency commission at least once every four years. A new Frequency Allocation Table shall be approved by Russian Government.

36.54   A telecommunications provider intending to use radio frequencies for provision of telecommunication services, must comply with the requirements for allocation of radio frequency bands and assignment of radio frequencies and radio frequency channels prior to obtaining the relevant telecommunications license.

---

24   Art 37 Communications Law.
25   Art 39 Communications Law.
26   Art 22(4) Communications Law.

Principles of frequency allocation, procedural rules

36.55   The SCRF allocates radio frequency bands and Roskomadzor subsequently assigns radio frequencies and radio frequency channels.

36.56   To obtain a decision of the SCRF allocating frequency bands, an applicant must file an application with the SCRF including:

- a letter with a request to allocate frequencies;
- special forms on the technical data related to radio electronic facilities or a list of the significant technical information on high frequency facilities; and
- an explanatory note.

36.57   A decision on frequency band allocation may be suspended for up to 90 days in case of a violation of the conditions of frequency band use.

36.58   A decision of the SCRF may be terminated in the following cases:

- upon a written application of the radio frequency spectrum user;
- upon cancellation of a telecommunications licence, if telecommunications activities are connected with the use of the radio frequency spectrum;
- upon the user of the radio frequency spectrum failing to fulfil the conditions stipulated by the decision of the SCRF on frequency allocation;
- upon liquidation of the legal entity granted the radio frequency spectrum allocation;
- upon failure to eliminate a violation being the grounds for suspension of the SCRF decision on frequency allocation;
- upon a court decision; or
- upon other grounds as provided by applicable legislation.

36.59   Radio frequencies and radio frequency channels are assigned upon an application filed with Roskomnadzor.

36.60   A Roskomnadzor decision on radio frequency and frequency channel assignment may be suspended for up to 90 days or terminated in case of a violation of the conditions for the use of radio frequency and frequency channels.

36.61   In practice, issuance of a decision of the SCRF on radio frequency band allocation and a decision of Roskomnadzor on the assignment of radio frequencies and radio frequency channels takes approximately six months.

Transferability and time limitations

36.62   The Communications Law does not provide for the transfer of the right to use a radio frequency to another entity without a separate decision of a competent authority.[27]

36.63   Radio frequencies, radio frequency bands and channels are allocated/ assigned for a term of up to ten years.

Admissible conditions

36.64   Generally, allocation of rights to use frequencies is subject to the following conditions:

---

27   Art 24(2) Communications Law.

- the frequency band should correspond to the Frequency Allocation Table;
- the parameters of the electronic equipment must correspond to the national electromagnetic compatibility standards and regulations;
- the applicant must submit all the necessary documents and certificates for the electronic equipment;
- the activity in the area of telecommunications for which the frequency spectrum allocation was requested complies with the applicable standards and regulations, and
- the results of the international procedure for coordination of radio frequency use need to be positive.

Limitation of number of rights of use to be granted

36.65 In practice, the competent Russian state authorities may limit rights to use the radio frequency spectrum on a case-by-case basis. This may be caused by the technical characteristics of equipment or a particular frequency, force majeure events, performance of work of great importance, special and socially significant events, international coordination of frequency allocations, etc.

36.66 Under the Communications Law,[28] a tender or auction is necessary to issue licences to telecommunications providers if the SCRF determines that the radio frequency spectrum available for the provision of telecommunications services limits the number of telecommunications providers in the territory. In such a case, the winner of the tender or auction obtains a licence and a decision on frequency allocation. Auctions and tenders are organised by Roskomnadzor.[29]

36.67 There is no separate procedure for allocation of radio frequencies on the basis of a tender or auction.

36.68 The use of a radio frequency spectrum is subject to a one-time fee and annual fees.[30] However, the amount of such fees is determined on a case-by-case basis, depending on the allocated frequency bands and channels and technologies used by a telecommunications provider.

Rights of Use for Numbers

General authorisations and granting of individual rights

36.69 Under the Communications Law, allocation of numbering resources is within the exclusive jurisdiction of the State.[31] The FAC allocates numbering resources upon application of a provider, within 60 days of the application being filed.[32]

36.70 Providers must pay a state fee for allocation of numbering resources, the amount of which is set in the Russian Tax Code.

---

28 Art 31(1)(1) Communications Law.
29 Art 5.3.3 'Regulations on the Federal Service for Supervision in the Sphere of Telecommunications, Information Technology and Mass Communications' approved by Government Resolution No 228 of 16 March 2009.
30 Art 23(4) Communications Law.
31 Art 26(1) Communications Law.
32 Art 26(5) Communications Law.

36.71   Rights to use numbers already granted may be withdrawn in the following cases:

- a provider files an application for the withdrawal of numbering resources;
- the telecommunications licence issued to a provider has been terminated;
- the numbering resources have been used by a provider in violation of the numbering system and plan;
- the allocated numbering resources have not been used by a provider in whole or in part for two years since allocation; or
- a provider fails to fulfil the obligations undertaken during the tender procedure.

36.72   The provider must be notified of the impending withdrawal of the right to use numbers, and about the reasons for the withdrawal, 30 days prior to the date of such withdrawal.[33]

36.73   A provider having obtained numbering resources must:

- approve the numbering plan determining the distribution of the obtained numbering resources throughout the respective territory;
- file a copy of the numbering plan with the FCA for its inclusion into the register of the Russian numbering system and plan;
- prevent the use of the numbering resources allocated to the provider for provision of telephone services by other providers;
- submit information on the use of the numbering resources to the FCA prior to 30 June and 31 December; and
- inform the FCA on the change of its location not later than within 30 days from the date of the change.

Admissible conditions

36.74   Providers must begin using the allocated numbering resources in full, or in part, within two years after allocation.[34] Providers must bear all expenses associated with allocation or changes of numbering resources.

36.75   Information about the allocation of the numbering resources to a particular provider is not considered confidential.

36.76   Numbering resources may not be transferred from one provider to another without the prior permission of the FAC.[35]

36.77   Telecommunications providers must notify a customer of a change of number and the new number 60 days prior to the date of change, unless the change is caused by emergency events.[36] In the case of a mass change of customers' numbers, customers must be notified through mass media sources and the telecommunications providers' equipment.

---

33   Art 26(2) Communications Law.
34   Art 16 'Rules on Distribution and Use of Number resources of the Unified Telecommunications Network of the Russian Federation' approved by Government Resolution No 350 dated 13 July 2004.
35   Art 26(7) Communications Law.
36   Art 45(2) Communications Law.

36.78 At the request of a customer, a telecommunications provider may (in the case of local telephone services),[37] and must (in the case of mobile services)[38] change a customer's number. Thus in case of local telephone services the provider may refuse the request to change the customer's number.

Limitation of number of rights of use to be granted

36.79 If the total number of allocated numbers in a particular region is more than 90 per cent of the available numbering resources, further allocation shall be made through a tender.[39]

The NRA's Enforcement Powers

36.80 The Roskomnadzor has the right to suspend the operation of a licence, to terminate a licence in some cases without applying to a court, and to apply to a court for termination of the licence if the provider fails to comply with the terms and conditions of the licence.[40]

36.81 Prior to suspending a license, the Roskomnadzor may send the provider a notification of the license termination in the following cases:

- indication by the competent state authorities of a violation connected with failure to comply with the statutory norms;
- indication by the competent state authorities of a violation by a licence holder of the licence conditions;
- failure to provide telecommunications services for more than three months, including failure to provide the services from the date stipulated in the licence.

36.82 The Roskomnadzor has the right to inspect the work of providers, but scheduled inspections of the same entity or person may not be conducted more than once every two years (for entities providing telecommunications services in a single constituent territory of Russia). With respect to entities providing telecommunications services and having a network and facilities in several constituent territories of Russia, such inspections must be held so as to conduct control measures in all branches of the legal entity within two years. An inspection should take no more than one month. However, Roskomnadzor has the right to make an unscheduled inspection if it receives information on a violation of the law, licensing conditions, or technological process by the provider, or in case of emergency.[41]

36.83 The Chief State Inspector for Telecommunications and Information, his deputies, senior inspectors and inspectors have the right to issue written protocols on administrative offences with regard to violations of communications law, to undertake investigations, assessments, calculations and measurements, to suspend the operation of telecommunications equipment and networks, and to request the

---

37 Art 64 'Rules on Provision of Local, Intra-Zone, Long-Distance Local and International Telephone Services' approved by Government Resolution No 310 dated 18 May 2005.
38 Art 48 'Rules on Provision of Mobile Services' approved by Government Resolution No 328 dated 25 May 2005.
39 Art 26(5) Communications Law.
40 See paras 36.51 and 36.52 above.
41 Arts 10–16 'Rules on State Supervision Over Activity in the Sphere of Telecommunications' approved by Government Resolution No 110 of 2 March 2005 (the 'Rules on Supervision').

necessary documents and information.[42] The Chief State Inspector, his deputies and senior inspectors may also impose administrative penalties for violation of the law and issue compulsory orders to eliminate violations.[43]

Administrative Charges and Fees for Rights of Use

36.84   Telecommunications providers rendering services within the public use telecommunications network must pay deductions to the universal service reserve. These obligatory payments are calculated on the basis of the profits a provider received within the relevant quarter from provision of telecommunications services to customers within the public use telecommunications network, except for amounts of taxes to be paid by customers. Such payments must be made at the rate of 1.2 per cent of a provider's profits.[44]

36.85   State fees for allocation of numbering resources are set in Article 333.33 of the Tax Code. For example, the payment for allocation of a single phone number is RUB 20 (approximately €0.50).

36.86   A telecommunications provider must pay a one-time fee and annual fees, the amounts of which are determined on a case-by-case basis depending on the allocated frequency bands and channels and technologies used by the provider.

REGULATION OF NETWORK ACCESS AND INTERCONNECTION

Objectives and Scope of Access Regulation

36.87   The purpose of the regulation of access and interconnection is to ensure adequate access to telecommunications services throughout the Russian Federation, to promote sustainable competition, to ensure growth of the telecommunications infrastructure, and to protect the rights of end users.

Basic Regulatory Concepts

36.88   The Communications Law uses a single term for access and interconnection: 'interconnection service';[45] defined as 'the activity aimed at satisfaction of telecommunications providers' needs with respect to organisation and interaction of telecommunications networks enabling connections and transmission of information between users of interconnected telecommunications networks.'[46]

36.89   Each provider has the right to interconnect its network to the public use telecommunications network, subject to certain conditions. Interconnection of the telecommunications networks and their interaction are governed by interconnection agreements between the providers. The prices for interconnection and transit of traffic must be set by the connecting providers reasonably and in good faith. Disputes between providers regarding interconnection agreements are resolved by the courts.

---

42   Art 7 Rules on Supervision.
43   Art 8 Rules on Supervision.
44   Arts 60(1) and 60(2) Communications Law.
45   Art 18 Communications Law.
46   Art 2(33) Communications Law.

General interconnection agreements must include technical, economic, and informational conditions.[47] Interconnection agreements for interaction of telecommunications networks for broadcasting television and (or) radio programmes must include technical and economic conditions only.[48]

Technical conditions include:

- interconnection levels (not applicable to telecommunications broadcasting services);
- location of interconnection hubs with respect to each interconnection level; and
- technical characteristics of interconnection hubs,
- scope of, procedures and terms for performance of interconnection works and distribution thereof among telecommunications providers;
- procedures for transmission of traffic/broadcasting programmes/signals;
- procedures for cooperation regarding systems of management of telecommunications networks;
- procedures for operational and technical support for telecommunications lines and facilities;
- procedures for the adoption of measures on the stable functioning of telecommunications networks (including emergency situations); and
- technical parameters of broadcasting programmes' signals (applicable to telecommunications broadcasting services only).

Economic conditions include:

- a list of interconnection services and traffic (broadcasting programmes' signals transmission) services, and prices for such services; and
- procedures for payment for interconnection services and traffic (broadcasting programmes' signals transmission) services.

Informational conditions include:

- information on customers, required by a telecommunications provider for performance of payments, consideration of claims, as well as procedures for transfer of such information,
- requirement for compliance with the confidentiality of transferred information.

36.90   The Communications Law for the first time provides a definition of a provider holding a key position in the public use telecommunications network (the 'Incumbent Provider), and also establishes special conditions for connecting telecommunications networks of other providers to the networks of such Incumbent Providers.

Access- and Interconnection-related Obligations with Respect to Incumbent Providers

36.91   The Communications Law defines an Incumbent Provider as a telecommunications provider that, together with its affiliates, holds not less than 25 per cent of

---

47   Art 38 'Rules on Interconnection of Telecommunications Networks and Their Interaction' approved by Government Resolution No 161 dated 28 March 2005 (the 'Interconnection Rules').

48   Art 24 'Rules for Interconnection and Interaction of Telecommunications Networks for Broadcasting Television and (or) Radio Programmes' approved by Government Resolution No 760 dated 13 December 2006 (the 'Interconnection Broadcasting Rules').

the installed capacity in a geographically determined numeration zone, or in the whole territory of the Russian Federation, or has the possibility of performing transmission of not less than 25 per cent of total traffic.[49]

36.92   Roskomnadzor manages the Register of Incumbent Providers.

36.93   Incumbent Providers must establish equal terms for connection to the public use telecommunications network for other providers rendering similar services, as well as for transit of their traffic.[50] Furthermore, Incumbent Providers must provide such other providers with connection services and transit of traffic services under the same terms and at the same level of quality as they do for their own divisions or affiliates. No Incumbent Provider may refuse to enter into interconnection agreements with other providers, unless providing the interconnection would contradict the terms of a specific provider's licence or the law regulating the formation and functioning of the Russian unified telecommunications network.

36.94   The procedure for interconnection of the telecommunication networks of providers with the telecommunication network of the Incumbent Provider is determined by Section III Interconnection Rules and Section III Interconnection Broadcasting Rules.

36.95   The prices of the Incumbent Provider for interconnection and traffic transit are subject to state regulation. Incumbent Providers must maintain separate records of income and expenditures with respect to performed activities, rendered services, and parts of the telecommunications network used for the provision of services.

36.96   Incumbent Providers must adopt rules of interconnection and publish them within seven days of adoption. Should the MTMC notify an Incumbent Provider that its terms and conditions for interconnection do not comply with the applicable legislation, the Incumbent Provider must rectify such violation within 30 days after such notification.

Regulatory Powers Applicable to All Market Participants

Obligations to ensure end-to-end connectivity

36.97   The Resolution on Licensing lists the licensing requirements for separate types of telecommunications services that may be provided in Russia. One such requirement that the majority of providers of telecommunications services must fulfil is the provision of connectivity within the provider's network.

Regulation of roaming services

36.98   The customer should not have to pay for a telephone connection established as a result of a call by another customer, except, among other things, for cases where a telephone connection has been established with a customer located outside the constituent territory of Russia indicated in the decision on the assignment to a telecommunications provider of numbering capacity including a customer's number assigned to the given customer, unless otherwise established by a telecommunications services agreement. The fee for the services shall be paid by the customer to the telecommunications provider having the agreement with such customer (even in the case of roaming).

---

49   Art 2(11) Communications Law.
50   Art 19(1) Communications Law.

Access to digital radio and television broadcasting services

36.99   There are no specific rules with respect to the access to digital radio and television broadcasting services.

REGULATION OF UNIVERSAL SERVICES AND USERS' RIGHTS

Regulation of Universal Service Obligations

Scope of universal services obligations

36.100   The concept of universal telecommunications services was first introduced by the Communications Law to target those categories of the population that presently have difficulty in taking advantage of telecommunications resources. Universal services under the Communications Law include public pay telephone services and services for data transmission and Internet access through public access facilities.[51]

36.101   Public pay telephones must be located in such a manner that individuals may reach a phone by foot in a maximum of one hour. Each populated locality must have at least one such public pay telephone offering free access to emergency medical and other related services. Localities with 500 or more inhabitants should have at least one public access Internet station.[52]

36.102   Pursuant to the Communications Law, universal service undertakings must provide such services to any user of telecommunications services in Russia within a determined period, at a standard level of quality, and at affordable prices.[53]

Designation of undertakings obliged to provide universal services

36.103   Regional authorities arrange tenders among telecommunications providers rendering services within a public use telecommunications network for the right to provide universal services in certain geographical areas. The company that offers the best terms of service will be awarded the contract. If a tender fails for any reason, the obligation to provide universal services in a particular geographical area will be imposed by the Government (at the recommendation of the MTMC) on the Incumbent Provider, which may not decline such obligation.[54]

Regulation of retail tariffs, users' expenditures and quality of service

36.104   Rates for universal services are subject to state regulation.[55] Tariffs for universal services are calculated by the FAC upon the passing of a resolution on

---

51   Art 57(1) Communications Law.
52   Art 57(2) Communications Law.
53   Art 2(30) Communications Law.
54   Art 58 Communications Law.
55   Government Resolution No 242 'On Approval of the Rules for the State Regulation of Tariffs for Universal Telecommunication Services' dated 21 April 2005 (the 'Universal Services Resolution').

conducting a tender for provision of universal services and are included in the agreement on conditions for provision of universal services.[56]

The tariff unit for provision of universal services is:

- one minute of telephone connection, for telephone services with the use of public pay telephones; and
- one MB of information, for data transfer services and the provision of access to the Internet through points of public access.[57]

Cost calculation and financing of universal services

36.105 Within six months of conclusion of a universal services agreement, the universal service provider must submit to the FAC an estimated amount of the maximum loss to be compensated. Universal service providers are reimbursed out of a universal services reserve to which all providers of public use telecommunications network are required to make contributions of 1.2 per cent of the profits a provider received within the relevant quarter from provision of telecommunications services to customers within the public use telecommunications network, except for amounts of taxes to be paid by customers.[58]

36.106 The maximum amount of compensation for losses from universal services is determined as the balance between the income and the economically justified expenses of the provider resulting from providing universal services, and the income and expenses of the provider which the provider would have absent such an obligation.

Regulation of Retail Markets

36.107 Under the Communications Law customers have the option of choosing between two schemes of charging for local connections: either subscription based or time-based billing.

36.108 The Communications Law preserves telecommunications service discounts for selected categories of individuals, who must, however, pay initially for the use of such services in full and only then claim reimbursement from the respective government budget account. Under the old legislation, such citizens enjoyed access to services at privileged rates, while the providers were compensated later from the government budget and often incurred substantial losses as a result. Under the current legislation, users obtain their own refunds on a case-by-case basis.[59]

End User Rights

Contracts

36.109 The principal legal acts regulating the rights of telecommunications service users include:

---

56   Art 6 Universal Services Resolution.
57   Art 7 Universal Services Resolution.
58   See para 36.84 above.
59   Art 47 Communications Law.

the Russian Civil Code, the Communications Law and, with respect to consumer rights, additionally the Law 'On Consumer Rights Protection' (the 'Consumer Rights Protection Law'),[60] and the rules on provision of different types of telecommunications services approved by the Government with respect to a particular type of service (the 'Rules').

36.110 The contract between a provider of telecommunications services and an individual is a public contract.[61] Therefore, for telecommunication services rendered to individuals, a provider may not give preference to individual over another with respect to entering into the contract, and may not refuse to enter into the contract if the provider is capable of providing the required service or services.[62]

36.111 The Rules contain a list of terms and conditions that must be included in a contract for the provision of services to individual. Additionally, the Rules provide material terms and conditions that must be included in the contract. Such material terms vary subject to the service type. However, if any of the material terms is not included in the contract, the contract is deemed invalid.

Transparency obligations

36.112 At a customer's request, the telecommunications provider must provide information to the customer on the provider, its working hours, and relevant services (including information on the applicable tariffs, customer's account, and technical defects affecting the services). The Communications Law provides individuals with certain guarantees, including the right of a customer to retain its number whenever the customer changes its address, the right to receive at least sixty days prior notice if its number is to be replaced, compulsory conclusion of the contract with a new owner of the premises to which telephone services are provided, and access twenty four hours per day, free of charge, to emergency telephone numbers.[63]

36.113 Tariffs payable for publicly available telecommunications services are subject to government regulation.[64] The tariffs of a provider must be the same for all users.[65]

Quality of service: securing 'Net Neutrality'

36.114 Telecommunications undertakings must provide users with services of such quality as may be required by legislation and rules, and in accordance with the quality requirements established in the contract.[66]

36.115 A provider is liable for the quality of its services. Whenever the rights of a consumer are breached, the consumer is entitled to certain remedies such as, among other things, the right to reduce the cost of a particular service, to refuse to perform the contract, or to claim a penalty and request compensation for damage.

36.116 A breach of a telecommunications services contract initiates the obligatory procedure for pre-trial settlement of a dispute the user must first send the

---

60   Law No 2300–1 'On Consumer Rights Protection' dated 7 February 1992.
61   Art 45(1) Communications Law.
62   Art 426 Russian Civil Code.
63   Art 45 Communications Law.
64   Art 28(2) Communications Law.
65   Art 426(2) Civil Code.
66   Art 4 Consumer Rights Protection Law.

provider a claim before applying to a court, and may only take the matter to court if such claim is rejected or ignored.

Emergency call number

36.117   The unified telephone number for the emergency services in Russia is 112.

Obligations Facilitating Change of Provider

36.118   Russian legislation does not provide any specific obligations connected with the change of provider. However under the Rules, a customer may unilaterally terminate an agreement with the provider subject to payment for rendered services.

DATA PROTECTION

Confidentiality of Communications

36.119   The Constitution guarantees the right to privacy of correspondence, telephone conversations, and postal, telegraph and other messages.[67] This guarantee is restated in the Communications Law, specifically, the guarantee of the confidentiality of correspondence, telephone conversations, telegraph and other communications transmitted via telecommunications networks.[68]

36.120   The Communications Law also imposes an obligation on providers to ensure the privacy of communications.[69] Providers rendering electronic communications services must take measures necessary to secure the privacy of telecommunications.

36.121   Information on messages, postal messages, and postal transfer of funds and messages, postal messages and funds transferred through telecommunications and postal networks may be issued only to the senders, addressees and their authorised representatives.[70] Inspection of postal messages by persons who are not authorised employees of a telecommunications provider, opening postal messages, inspection of enclosures, examination of information and documentary correspondence, transferred through telecommunications and postal networks may be performed only under a court order.[71]

Data Retention

36.122   Special state organisations may be granted with the right to intercept and review information sent by means of electronic communications and to intercept telephone communications for the purpose of investigation. Such interception or review may be conducted only after obtaining a court order.

---

67   Art 23(2) Constitution of the Russian Federation dated 12 December 1993.
68   Art 63(1) Communications Law.
69   Art 63(2) Communications Law.
70   Art 63(4) Communications Law.
71   Art 63(3) Communications Law.

36.123 In cases prescribed by federal law, telecommunications providers must supply to criminal investigation authorities information on the users of telecommunications services or services rendered, as well as other information necessary for the performance of their investigatory functions.[72]

Traffic Data and Location Data

36.124 'Traffic' is defined as 'a loading created by the stream of calls, messages, signals transmitted to telecommunications facilities'.[73]

36.125 Location data is not defined in Russian legislation. The Navigation Activities Law (the *'Navigation Activities Law'*)[74] contains a definition of 'navigation activities': 'activities connected with the determination and use of the coordinate and timing parameters of facilities.' Navigation activities may be conducted in Russia without limitation of the accuracy of determination of navigation facilities' coordinates, except for territories and facilities with a special operating regime, a list of which is approved by the Government.[75]

Itemised Billing

36.126 The Rules list the information that must be included on bills issued to a customer. However, at the request of a customer, the telecommunications provider must provide the customer with an itemised bill at the customer's expense. With respect to local, intra-zone, long distance and international telephone services such additional expenses may not exceed 10 per cent of the monthly subscription fee.[76]

Presentation and Restriction of Calling and Connected Line Identification

36.127 No obligations are imposed on telecommunications service providers in relation to calling line identification and connected line identification.

Automatic Call Forwarding

36.128 If a customer has an additional customer number in the local telephone network such number may be used for call forwarding to the customer's device.[77]

Directories of Subscribers

36.129 Information about customers, and information relating to telecommunications services provided to them in the possession of any telecommunications

---

72   Art 64(1) Communications Law.
73   Art 2(29) Communications Law.
74   Federal Law No 22-FZ 'On Navigation Activities' dated 14 February 2009.
75   Art 8 the Navigation Activities Law.
76   Art 116 'Rules on Provision of Local, Intra-Zone, Long-Distance Local and International Telephone Services' approved by Government Resolution No 310 dated 18 May 2005.
77   Art 8.1 'Rules on Provision of Mobile Services', approved by Government Resolution No 328 dated 25 May 2005.

provider, is deemed to be confidential information and subject to protection. The following information is confidential and is subject to legal protection:

- the name or nickname of individuals;
- the firm name of legal entities, the names of their head officers or employees;
- the address of a customer or the address of the installation of the end equipment;
- the customer's numbers and other data allowing identification of a customer or his or her equipment; and
- information on charges for the services rendered, including on the customer's connections, traffic and payments.[78]

36.130   Telecommunications providers are entitled to use databases on their customers for performance of informational and service support. The following data may be used for the following purposes:

- name of a customer that is an individual and his or her customer number;
- the firm name of a customer that is a legal entity;
- the customer's numbers indicated by it; and
- the address of equipment installation.

Information on customers that are individuals may not be used for informational and service support without their written consent and may be submitted to third parties only subject to the written consent of the customers, unless otherwise provided in federal laws.[79]

36.131   Telecommunications providers must update the information contained in databases of their customers, and the services provided to them, in a timely manner, and must keep such information for three years.[80]

---

78   Art 53(1) Communications Law.
79   Art 53(2) Communications Law.
80   Art 12 'Rules for Cooperation of Telecommunications Providers with Competent State Investigation Authorities' approved by Government Resolution No 538 dated 27 August 2005.

The Swiss Market for Electronic Communications[1]

Markus Berni and Kathleen Weislehner
Baker & McKenzie, Zurich

LEGAL STRUCTURE

Basic Policy

37.1　On 1 January 1998 the Swiss telecommunications market was liberalised. As a result of the opening of the market, consumers have been enjoying a wider range of services; prices, especially in the area of fixed line telephony, have been decreasing. Mobile telephony and broadband services have been boosted as well. At the end of 2009, the penetration rate for mobile telephony subscriptions in Switzerland was 112.4 per cent.[2] With this penetration rate, Switzerland ranks in the last third of the classification compared to EU countries. Prices for mobile telephony have remained relatively high.

37.2　Notwithstanding that in 2003, the Federal Government decided to open access to local loops,[3] Swisscom has retained total control of local loops. Due to the opening of access, however, alternative providers are no longer dependent on the former monopolist, and consumers benefit from a wider range of services. Despite the high number of telecommunications providers,[4] however, the former monopolist, Swisscom, today still dominates many markets, mainly those linked to the provision of fixed line services, but also mobile telephony.[5]

37.3　From the beginning, the regulatory regime of the Swiss telecommunications legislation was less interventionist than in many EU Member States in that the provision of telecommunications services generally required merely a notice to the regulator and no licence. As of April 2007, the telecommunications legislation was further liberalised: a licence is now only required for operators that use radio

---

1　Editing of this chapter closed on 30 September 2012.
2　Cf the Swiss Federal Council's report on the evaluation of the telecommunication market dated 17 September 2010 ('Evaluation Report 2010'), p 31.
3　This was done by means of amendment to the ordinance before the Federal Telecommunications Act itself has been amended, which was politically controversial.
4　In 2010, there were 580 registered telecommunications services providers, cf Official Telecommunication Statistics 2010 dated 3 April 2012 ('Official Statistics 2010'), p 12.
5　Eg Swisscom's market share in the area of fixed line services based on the number of client contracts amounts to 70 per cent compared to approximately 68 per cent in 2007, cf Official Statistics 2010.

frequencies and for operators providing services under the universal service obligation. Moreover, the interconnection regime was based from the beginning on the paradigm of self-regulation through negotiations. In March 2012, the Swiss Federal Government announced that it intends to draft a consultation paper on a partial revision of the Telecommunications Act. According to the Swiss Federal Council, the Telecommunications Act in its current wording is challenged by rapid technological developments in the telecommunications industry which it may not be able to tackle. For example, the current Act was tailored to copper networks, which will, in the long run, be replaced by fibre and cable networks and mobile radio systems. The Swiss Federal Council has stressed that provision of technology-neutral, open and fair access to networks, provision of universal services, protection of users, and a functioning Internet are at the centre of telecommunications policy.[6]

Implementation of EU Directives

37.4   Switzerland is not a member of the EU and is not a contracting party to the EEA Treaty. Initially, the liberalisation of services was intended to be part of the second package of bilateral agreements between Switzerland and the EU. However, due to the complexity of the matter, the parties agreed to suspend negotiations on the services dossier. Therefore, the Federal Telecommunications Act of 30 April 1997 ('LTC')[7] does not include all of the principles set out in the 2002 and 2009 EU Regulatory Packages, although the intention of the legislator on the occasion of the 2007 revision clearly was to adapt Swiss legislation to the EU regulatory framework. In particular, the Swiss drafters did not introduce ex-ante provisions which allow the regulatory authority to define the relevant markets and the providers which have a dominant position ex officio and to impose certain obligations on these providers. Under the LTC, relations between the telecommunications services providers are governed by the parties themselves, and the regulatory authority may only impose conditions for interconnection where the parties cannot reach an agreement.

Legislation

37.5   The 2007 amendments to the 1997 LTC took effect in April 2007. Major points of amendment included, among other things, abolition of the licence regime for telecommunications services providers (as mentioned above, a licence is now only required for operators that use radio frequencies and for operators providing services under the universal service obligation) and adopting obligations of dominant providers and means for their enforcement. As noted above, the Swiss Federal Council is already considering working on another revision of the LTC in order to tackle future challenges.

37.6   The transmission of radio and television programmes is covered by the Federal Act regarding Radio and Television of 24 March 2006 ('LRTV').

37.7   The Federal Government has adopted several ordinances based on the LTC.[8] A new version of the Ordinance on Telecommunications Services came into effect

---

6   Cf media information of the Swiss Federal Council dated 28 March 2012 (http://www.admin.ch/aktuell/00089/index.html?lang=en&msg-id=43935).

7   RS (Systematic Compilation of Swiss Law (an official source), available at: www.admin.ch) 784.10.

8   Such as, among others, 'Ordinance on Frequency Management' (RS 784.102.1), 'Ordinance

on 1 April 2007.[9] This Ordinance regulates in greater detail the unbundling of the local loops (full access), bitstream access, and shared line access.

REGULATORY PRINCIPLES

Scope of Regulation

37.8   The LTC applies to the transmission of 'information' by means of telecommunications techniques, including the transmission of radio and television programme services, provided the LRTV does not prescribe otherwise. This rule stipulates the priority of the telecommunications law. The LRTV only applies to 'programme services' (as defined in article 2(a) LRTV).[10] 'Information', for the purposes of the LTC, includes signs, signals, characters, images, sounds and any other form of representation addressed to human or other living beings or to machines. 'Transmission by means of telecommunications techniques' means sending or receiving of information, by wire, cable or radio, by means of electrical, magnetic or optical signals or other electromagnetic signals.

37.9   Although the concepts and terminology of the LTC are in the spirit of the EU legislation, the terms 'electronic communications network', 'electronic communications service', and 'associated facilities' as such are not defined in Swiss law. The LTC uses the term 'telecommunication service' which is defined as 'transmission of information for third parties by means of telecommunications techniques'.[11] The LRTV does not prevent the increasing harmonisation of telecommunication and broadcast (convergence), and thus, the scope of application of the LTC is deemed to be in accordance with that of the 2002 EU Regulatory Package.[12]

37.10   The provisions in the LTC are technology-neutral and, consequently, apply to all telecommunications services, irrespective of the technical means with which they are rendered. As VoIP falls under the definition of 'telecommunication service', the LTC applies to VoIP services. Swiss legislation relating to telecommunications does not include any specific definitions of VoIP, and, therefore, regulation of VoIP services is based on general telecommunications legislation.

'Internet Freedom'

37.11   There are various provisions based upon which federal authorities or courts may recommend or even order Internet pages to be blocked. The Federal Council may order the surveillance, restriction, or interruption of telecommunications in extraordinary circumstances or when vital national interests require it.[13] In case propaganda material (calling for violence against human beings or destruction of

---

on Address Elements in Telecommunications' (RS 784.104), 'Ordinance on Telecommunications Facilities' (RS 784.101.2), 'Ordinance regarding Telecommunications Fees' (RS 784.106).

9   RS 784.101.1; RO (Official Compilation of Swiss Law, available at: www.admin.ch) 2003 544.

10   Art 2 LTC with further specifications in Art 94 et seq Ordinance on Telecommunications Services.

11   Art 3(b) LTC.

12   Message (explanations from the Federal Government) of 12 November 2003 to the revision of the LTC, published in the Federal Gazette No 49 of 16 December 2003, p 7951 et seq, p 7967; message of 18 December 2002 to the revision of the LRTV, published in the Federal Gazette No 8 of 4 March 2003, p 1569 et seq, p 1659.

13   Art 48 LTC.

things) has been spread through the Internet, the Federal Police Department is, after consultation with the Swiss Intelligence Service, entitled to:

- order the deletion of a website provided that the propaganda material is on a Swiss computer; or
- issue a blocking recommendation to Swiss providers if the propaganda material is not on Swiss computers.[14]

Furthermore, access to Internet pages may be ordered to be blocked where the content available on the respective pages violates certain provisions of the penal code (eg child pornography). In addition, blocking orders may serve as one means of enforcement in proceedings on violation of intellectual property rights. For example, a person whose copyrights have been infringed upon may claim that the infringer stops the infringement. Where the infringement took place online, this may be enforced by a blocking order with respect to the Internet page in question.

National Regulatory Authorities: Organisation, Regulatory Objectives, Competencies

37.12   In comparison to the NRAs within the EU, the Swiss regulatory authorities only possess a few, clearly defined regulatory instruments with little administrative discretion. The regulatory objectives result from the aim of the LTC, which is to ensure that a range of cost-effective, high-quality, and nationally and inter-nationally competitive telecommunications services are available to private indi-viduals and the business community.[15]

37.13   The Federal Communications Commission ('ComCom') is an independent regulatory authority which consists of five to seven members nominated by the Federal Government. The members must be independent specialists. They inform the public of their activities, and each year produce a report for the Federal Government.[16] At the request of one party and based on a proposal made by the Federal Office of Communication ('OFCOM'), ComCom decides on disputes between telecommunications services providers regarding access.[17] Furthermore, ComCom grants the licences for the provision of the universal service and the licence to use the radio-communication frequency spectrum.[18] It approves national numbering plans[19] and adopts detailed rules for the implementation of number portability and the free choice of service providers.[20]

37.14   OFCOM is the supervisory and administrative authority responsible for all telecommunication, radio and television broadcasting matters. It prepares decisions of the Swiss Government, the Federal Department of Environment, Transporta-tion, Energy and Communication ('DETEC'), and ComCom. OFCOM is respon-sible for the registration of telecommunications services providers[21] and supervision of all legal provisions and licences. Furthermore, it publishes the names and addresses of the licensees as well as further information in relation to such

---

14   Art 13e(5) Swiss Act on Measures to Maintain Internal Security.
15   Art 1(1) LTC.
16   Arts 56 and 57 LTC.
17   Art 11a(1) LTC.
18   Art 14(1) and 24a(1) LTC.
19   Art 28(3) LTC.
20   Art 28(4) LTC.
21   Art 4(1) LTC.

licences.[22] In addition, OFCOM manages and monitors the frequency spectrum and the Swiss utilisation rights and orbital positions of satellites.[23] The national frequency allocation plan is subject to approval of the Federal Government.[24]

37.15 If ComCom is asked to intervene in relations between service providers and the issue of market dominance is raised, OFCOM must consult with the Swiss Competition Commission (an independent federal authority tasked with protecting competition using instruments provided by the Federal Act on Cartels and other Restraints of Competition ('Act on Cartels') to determine whether a provider has a dominant position in the market. The Competition Commission may publish its opinion.[25]

37.16 Moreover, in the area of licences for radio frequencies, ComCom must consult with the Competition Commission if there is doubt whether the granting of a licence eliminates or constitutes a serious obstacle to effective competition.[26]

37.17 All persons subject to the LTC must provide the competent authorities with the necessary information to implement the LTC.[27]

37.18 Both ComCom and OFCOM have specific dispute resolution powers. If telecommunications services providers cannot reach an agreement on the access conditions (eg to local loops, bitstream access, interconnection, and leased lines) within three months, ComCom, upon request of one of the parties and based on the proposal made by OFCOM, determines the conditions of access. ComCom may also grant interim legal protection.[28]

37.19 OFCOM and ComCom have no dispute resolution powers relating to disputes involving customers. The LTC provides for a conciliation procedure for the settlement of disputes between customers and providers of telecommunications services. In the event of such disputes, either party may invoke a conciliation committee (*Schlichtungsstelle Telekommunikation*) for the settlement of such disputes.[29] The parties, however, are not bound by the committee's decision.[30]

Right of Appeal against the NRA's Decisions

37.20 Administrative orders issued by ComCom or OFCOM are open to administrative appeal before the Federal Administrative Court.[31] The appellate procedure is governed by the Law on Administrative Procedure unless otherwise provided by the Law on the Federal Administrative Court.[32] With certain exceptions,[33] decisions of the Federal Administrative Court may be appealed to the Federal Supreme Court.

37.21 The right of appeal is given to anyone:

---

22   Arts 19b and 24f LTC.
23   Arts 25(1) and 26(1) LTC.
24   Art 25(2) LTC.
25   Art 11a (2) LTC; see also para 37.57 below.
26   Art 23(4) LTC; see also para 37.39 below.
27   Art 59(1) LTC.
28   Art 11a (1) LTC.
29   The conciliation committee's website is www.ombudscom.ch
30   Art 12c LTC; see also para 37.74 below.
31   Arts 31 and 33 Law on the Federal Administrative Court, RS 173.32.
32   Art 37 Law on the Federal Administrative Court.
33   Art 83(p) Law on the Federal Supreme Court.

- who participated in the proceedings before the lower instance or was not given the opportunity to participate;
- who is particularly affected by the order or decision in question; and
- whose interest in the annulment or modification of the order or decision is worthy of protection.[34]

DETEC also has the right to appeal the decision to the Federal Supreme Court.[35]

37.22   Civil courts have jurisdiction over disputes between operators arising from a negotiated agreement or from decisions concerning access.[36]

'Dominant Position in the Market' as a Fundamental Prerequisite of Regulation

Definition of 'dominant position in the market'

37.23   The term 'significant market power' as such is not mentioned in the LTC and is not defined in the Act on Cartels.[37] The latter distinguishes between the concepts of 'market power'[38] and 'dominant position in the market',[39] and the LTC refers to 'dominant position in the market'.[40] Nonetheless, the definition of 'dominant position in the market' under Swiss law is very similar to the EU definition of SMP in Article 14(2) of the Framework Directive.

37.24   Under Swiss competition law, 'enterprises having a dominant position in the market' means:

'one or more enterprises in a specific market being able, as regards supply or demand, to behave in a substantially independent manner with regard to the other participants (competitors, suppliers or customers) in the market'.[41]

37.25   Under the LTC, providers of telecommunications services holding a dominant position must provide access to their installations and services (such as unbundled access to local loops, bitstream access, interconnection, and leased lines) to other providers without discrimination, according to the principle of transparency, and at cost-oriented prices.[42]

Definition of relevant markets

37.26   Under Swiss law the definition of 'relevant market' is the same as under Community law. The relevant factual market consists of all telecommunication services and installations which the demand side of the market (provider desiring access to local loops, etc) considers to be interchangeable. The geographic market consists of the area in which the demand side of the market requests these services

---

34   Art 89(1) Law on the Federal Supreme Court, Art 48(1) Law on Administrative Procedure.
35   Art 89(2) Law on the Federal Supreme Court.
36   Art 11b LTC.
37   RS 251.
38   Art 2(1) Act on Cartels.
39   Art 4(2) Act on Cartels.
40   Art 11(1) LTC.
41   Art 4(2) Act on Cartels.
42   Art 11(1) LTC; see para 37.60 below for more details.

and installations.[43] According to the Competition Commission, the broadcasting of TV programmes via satellite is no substitute for reception via cable.[44]

37.27 Swisscom is still the market leader in both fixed line and mobile telephony. With respect to mobile telephony, its market share in 2010 (based on the amounts of customers) amounted to approximately 59 per cent.[45] According to the Federal Government's additional report to the Evaluation Report, the liberalisation has had positive effects on the fixed line market insofar as customers may now choose among a wide range of telecommunications services providers and prices have decreased.[46] Providers who cannot reach an agreement with Swisscom regarding access to Swisscom's installations and services have enhanced possibilities of applying to ComCom for a decision on the conditions of access. In recent years, ComCom has issued numerous orders and the Federal Administrative Court has rendered a good number of decisions with respect to conditions of interconnection and access.[47]

NRA's Regulatory Duties concerning Rights of Way, Co-location and Facility Sharing

Rights of way

37.28 Owners of land in public use[48] must permit providers of telecommunications services to use this land for installation and operation of lines and public call boxes, provided such installation does not interfere with the public use of the land. In return, providers must consider the owner's use of the land up to the moment they wish to use the land for the placement of any infrastructure. Moreover, providers must remove their lines if the landowner decides to use his or her land in a manner which conflicts with the position of a line. In order to minimise disruption, providers must coordinate the necessary work. Provided public use is not disrupted, no compensation is payable for the use of land by a telecommunications services provider, except that the owner of public land may levy a cost-covering fee. All costs relating to the construction of infrastructure are to be paid by the network owner.[49]

37.29 Furthermore, in order to ensure that private land, and land owned by a State or Municipality but which is not in public use, is also available for telecommunication purposes, DETEC may grant a telecommunications services provider the right to expropriate the land. In such cases, full compensation for the total value of the expropriated land must be paid.[50]

---

43   This definition can be found on the OFCOM website (http://www.bakom.admin.ch/), e g on the access application form and in the evaluation report on the telecommunication market, p 60 et seq, where reference is made to the definition foreseen in the Ordinance of 17 June 1996 on the Control of Concentrations of Undertakings.

44   RPW 1999/2, p 210 et seq, available at www.weko.admin.ch

45   Cf Official Statistics 2010, p 44.

46   Evaluation of the telecommunication market – additional report of the Federal Council dated 28 March 2012 ('Additional Report 2012 to the Evaluation Report 2010'), p 8.

47   Cf, e g ComCom website, http://www.comcom.admin.ch/themen/00500/00782/index.html?lang=en

48   Such as roads, footpaths, squares, waterways, lakes and banks.

49   Art 35 LTC and Art 75 Ordinance on Telecommunications Services.

50   Art 36(1) LTC and Federal Law on Expropriation (RS 711).

Co-location and facility sharing

37.30 In addition, in order to protect public interests such as zone planning concerns, protection of landmarks and the environment in general, and to prevent technical difficulties, OFCOM may require telecommunications services providers to allow third persons co-use of their telecommunication facilities in return for fair compensation, unless the facility lacks sufficient capacity. 'Fair compensation' means the relevant pro rata share of the full costs.[51] For the same reasons, OFCOM may require providers to install and use telecommunication installations and other facilities jointly.[52]

37.31 Ownership of telecommunication lines remains with the provider who built or acquired the lines, even if they are located on land owned by others. Land owners are liable for any damage they cause to telecommunication lines on their land, but only to the extent that such damage is caused wilfully or as a result of gross negligence.[53]

REGULATION OF MARKET ENTRY

General Regulatory Approach

37.32 With the entry into effect of the amended LTC, the system for licences for telecommunications services was abolished. The former licences are replaced by a general obligation of notification[54] which corresponds to the European system of 'general authorisation'. However, licences are still required for the provision of universal services[55] and the use of radio frequencies.[56]

37.33 All providers of telecommunications services must notify OFCOM for registration.[57] Furthermore, they must:

- have the necessary technical capacities;
- undertake to comply with the applicable legislation, in particular the LTC and its implementing provisions;
- comply with employment legislation and guarantee the working conditions customary in the sector; and
- offer an appropriate number of apprenticeships.[58]

Subject to any international obligations to the contrary, ComCom may prohibit the provision of telecommunications services in Switzerland to undertakings incorporated under foreign law, unless a reciprocal right is granted.[59]

37.34 OFCOM may levy an administrative charge to cover its expenses for the registration and supervision of the telecommunications services providers.[60]

---

51   Art 36(2) LTC and Art 79 Ordinance on Telecommunications Services.
52   Art 36(3) LTC.
53   Art 37 LTC.
54   Art 4(1) LTC.
55   See para 37.63 below.
56   See para 37.38 below.
57   Art 4(1) LTC.
58   Art 6 LTC.
59   Art 5 LTC.
60   Art 40(1)(a) LTC; cf also para 37.53 below.

37.35 The Federal Government may require telecommunications services providers to publish information on the quality of their services[61] and may adopt regulations to prevent misuse of value-added services.[62]

37.36 Moreover, providers of telecommunications services still must submit a request for the allocation of address elements.[63]

37.37 With respect to the universal service obligation, the system of granting individual licences is maintained.[64]

Rights of Use for Radio Frequencies

37.38 A special regime, distinct from the notification procedure, applies to the use of radio frequencies. Anyone intending to use the radio frequency spectrum up to 3000 GHz must obtain a licence.[65] A licence is granted only if, having regard to the national plan for their allocation, enough frequencies are available.[66] The national frequency allocation plan is the most important instrument for planning the radio frequencies resource. It is based on the CEPT and ITU guidelines and consists of several sections: first, the actual plan itself (radio services classified according to frequency ranges) and, secondly, the requirements for radio interfaces plus the other rules and restrictions on use of the corresponding frequency range. The plan distinguishes between civil, non-civil (eg military) or shared, as well as between primary and secondary band allocations.[67] Pursuant to the Ordinance on Frequency Management and Radio Licences, there are two different classes of frequency:

(i)   frequencies to be allocated to a limited number of licence holders per application territory (class A); and

(ii)   frequencies to be allocated to an indefinite number of licence holders per application territory (class B).[68]

OFCOM formulates the frequency allocation plan which is approved by the Federal Government.[69] ComCom grants the individual licences for rights to use frequencies.[70]

37.39 Additionally, the granting of a licence is subject to the condition that it does not eliminate or constitute a serious obstacle to effective competition, unless an exception can be justified on grounds of economic efficiency. In the case of doubt, ComCom must consult with the Competition Commission.[71] The applicant, furthermore, must have the necessary technical capacities and undertake to comply

---

61   Art 12a(2) LTC.
62   Art 12b LTC.
63   Art 4 Ordinance on Address Elements in the Telecommunications Area (RS 784.104); cf also para 37.43 below.
64   Art 14(1) LTC; see para 37.63 below for more details.
65   Art 22(1) LTC, Art 7(1) Ordinance on Frequency Management and Radio Licences (RS 784.102.1).
66   Art 23(3) LTC.
67   The plan can be consulted on the OFCOM website: http://www.bakom.admin.ch/
68   Art 6 Ordinance on Frequency Management and Radio Licences.
69   Art 3(2) Ordinance on Frequency Management and Radio Licences, Art 25 LTC.
70   Art 24a LTC.
71   Art 23(4) LTC.

with the applicable legislation, its implementing provisions, and the licence conditions. Again, ComCom may refuse to grant a licence to undertakings incorporated under foreign law if no reciprocal rights are granted.[72]

37.40   Radio-communications licences are granted on the basis of an open invitation to tender if the frequencies are requested to provide telecommunications services and there are not enough frequencies available to meet all applicants' present and future needs.[73] OFCOM is responsible for frequency management and granting of radio-communications licences.[74] It must do so in accordance with the principles of objectivity, non-discrimination, and transparency and must guarantee the confidential character of all information provided by applicants.[75] OFCOM charges a licence fee for radio-communications licences (except for radio-communications licences intended for the broadcasting of radio and television programme services in accordance with the provisions of the RTVA).[76]

37.41   The Swiss regulatory regime does not permit spectrum trading.

Rights of Use for Numbers

37.42   The administration and allocation of numbers and address elements is the responsibility of OFCOM; however, the national numbering plans must be approved by ComCom.[77] In January 2010 a new numbering plan[78] took effect.

37.43   OFCOM grants number blocks to providers of telecommunications services. The providers, therefore, must submit a request to OFCOM stating their range of services, the geographical extent of their network and their plan to use these numbers for a minimum period of three years.[79] There is no competitive or comparative selection procedure for the use of numbers. Providers, after being granted numbers, pass them on to their clients. The grant of individual numbers to natural and legal persons is possible if they intend to use the numbers for the identification of a certain specified service.[80]

37.44   The LTC contains obligations for telecommunications services providers relating to number portability and carrier selection.[81] Number portability with respect to fixed line telephony and mobile telephony was implemented by all providers in March 2000; however, number portability between fixed line and mobile telephony has not yet been introduced.[82] As to carrier selection, operators providing fixed line telephone services are required to allow any subscriber to choose another carrier (call-by-call and pre-selection) for national and international calls. In the area of mobile telephony, to date only call-by-call selection is possible

---

72   Art 23(1) and (2) LTC.
73   Art 24(1) LTC. Other principles govern the granting of radio-communications licences which are entirely or partially intended for the broadcasting of radio and television programme services, cf Art 24(1bis) LTC.
74   Art 25(1) LTC.
75   Art 24(2) LTC.
76   Art 39 LTC; cf also para 37.52 below.
77   Art 28(1) and (3) LTC.
78   RS 784.101.113/2.2 Numbering Plan E.164.
79   Arts 20 and 21 Ordinance on Address Elements in the Telecommunications Area (RS 784.104).
80   Art 24b et seq Ordinance on Address Elements in the Telecommunications Area.
81   Art 28(4) LTC.
82   RS 784.101.112, Art 3.

until the technology allows the safe introduction of carrier pre-selection on the mobile network.[83]

37.45   The management, allocation and revocation of numbers and address elements are subject to an administrative charge.[84]

37.46   The LTC allows for introduction by the Federal Government of a mandatory alternative dispute resolution procedure between the holders of address elements and third parties.[85]

The NRA's Enforcement Powers

37.47   OFCOM and ComCom are vested with extensive powers to monitor and enforce compliance with the applicable legal provisions. Several penal provisions contained within the LTC itself add to these enforcement powers.

37.48   All persons subject to the LTC must disclose to the competent authority information required for the implementation of the law.[86] In particular, OFCOM, as the supervisory body, ensures compliance with international telecommunications law, the LTC, its implementing provisions, and the licence conditions.[87]

37.49   Where OFCOM detects a breach of law, it can pronounce sanctions and may:

- call on the responsible person to remedy the infringement or take measures to prevent any repetition of the infringement (and the responsible person must inform OFCOM of the measures taken);
- require the responsible person to surrender to the Confederation any revenue generated during the infringement;
- make the licence subject to conditions;
- restrict, suspend, revoke or withdraw the licence; or
- restrict, suspend or prohibit the activity of the responsible person.[88]

If ComCom granted the licence, ComCom will take the corresponding measures at the request of OFCOM. The competent authority may order interim measures.[89] Moreover, OFCOM may impose administrative sanctions (fine of up to 10 per cent of the average turnover generated in Switzerland during the last three business years) if an undertaking contravenes the applicable law, the licence conditions or a decision having the force of law.[90]

37.50   The LTC also contains a number of penalties for illegal conduct, such as falsification or misuse of information, interference in telecommunications or broadcasting, violation of the notification requirement for telecommunications services providers, use of frequency spectrum without licence, acting contrary to the licence conditions, putting into service addressing resources not assigned to the respective

---

83   RS 784.101.112, Art 9; cf also RS 784.101.112/2, technical and administrative provisions re free carrier selection, prepared by ComCom, entered into force in January 2010, available on the OFCOM website: http://www.bakom.admin.ch/
84   Art 40(1)(f) LTC; see para 37.53 below.
85   Art 28(2bis) LTC.
86   Art 59(1) LTC.
87   Art 58(1) LTC.
88   Art 58(2) and (3) LTC.
89   Art 58(4) and (5) LTC.
90   Art 60 LTC.

person, supply of telecommunications installations which do not comply with the regulations in force, or intentional or negligent infringement of the law or of any decision taken thereunder and notified to the person with an indication of penalties available under the LTC, etc.[91] Such offences are prosecuted and heard by the Department in accordance with the provisions of the Federal Law on Administrative Penalty Rules.[92] The Department may delegate these tasks to OFCOM.[93]

Administrative Charges and Fees for Rights of Use

37.51   Providers of telecommunications services are charged a fee which is exclusively used to finance uncovered costs of the universal service and the costs for administering the financing mechanism.[94] Providers whose turnover resulting from telecommunications services offered does not reach CHF 5 million are exempted from the payment.[95]

37.52   Radio licences are subject to a fee whose amount is calculated on the basis of:

- the frequency range allocated, the class of frequency and the value of the frequencies;
- the bandwidth allocated;
- the territorial scope; and
- the timescale.

If the radio licence is granted by tender, the licence fee will correspond to the amount of the bid, less administrative expenses for the invitation to tender and the allocation of the radio licence. ComCom may set a minimum bid. Authorities, public bodies, public transport undertakings, diplomatic authorities and private bodies performing duties of public interest may be exempted from payment of the licence fee, provided that they do not supply telecommunications services and that they make rational use of frequencies.[96]

37.53   In addition, the competent authority levies an administrative charge to cover its expenses, for, among other things:

- the registration and supervision of telecommunications services providers;
- the management, allocation and revocation of address elements (including numbers);
- the allocation, supervision, modification and revocation of universal service licences and radio-communications licences; and
- the decision on access, the provision of directory data, interoperability, leased lines and facility sharing.[97]

DETEC sets the exact amount of the administrative charges to be paid by the telecommunications services providers.[98]

---

91   Art 49 et seq LTC.
92   RS 313.0, cf Art 55(1) LTC.
93   Art 55(2) LTC.
94   See para 37.69 below.
95   Art 38 LTC and Art 25 Ordinance on Telecommunications Services.
96   Art 39 LTC.
97   Art 40 LTC; see paras 37.34 and 37.45 above and para 37.67 below.
98   Art 41(2) LTC.

REGULATION OF NETWORK ACCESS AND INTERCONNECTION

Objectives and Scope of Access Regulation

37.54 Following the EU terminology, the LTC uses the general term of 'access', whereas 'interconnection' is a particular case of access. Furthermore, the obligations of providers with a dominant position in the market are precisely stated. Notwithstanding this, the LTC does not contain ex-ante provisions[99] in order to avoid a regime which would be seen as excessively interventionist.

37.55 Access obligations only apply to telecommunications services providers with a dominant position in the market. Article 11 LTC addresses issues relating to the access to installations and services of such providers.

37.56 Access can be granted in various forms, in particular in the form of 'fully unbundled access to the local loop' which means 'provision of access to the local loop for another telecommunications services provider for utilisation of the entire frequency spectrum of the twisted pair metallic line', or in form of 'fast bitstream access' which is defined as 'the establishment of a high-speed connection to the subscriber from the exchange to the building connection on the twisted pair metallic line by a telecommunications services provider and making this connection available to another provider for the provision of broadband services'.[100] 'Interconnection' means 'setting up access through connection of the facilities and services of two telecommunications services providers in order to enable a logical interaction of the connected parts and services by means of telecommunications as well as the access to services of third parties'.[101]

Basic Regulatory Concepts

37.57 Under the LTC, commercial negotiations between parties prevail over regulatory intervention. Regulators may only intervene if the providers themselves cannot reach an agreement on a particular issue. If the providers fail to do so within three months, ComCom must set the access conditions upon request of one of the parties and based on a proposal from OFCOM. If, at this point, it is unclear whether a provider has a dominant position in the market, OFCOM must consult with the Federal Competition Commission.[102] To enable the Federal Competition Commission to respond within the required four weeks,[103] the two authorities have devised a questionnaire to be submitted by the parties having requested a decision on the conditions of access. The questionnaire gathers information on the affected providers, markets, and services. It includes questions about turnovers, market shares, conditions of demand, and market entry requirements, among other things.[104]

37.58 Additionally, ComCom sets details regarding the accounting and financing information to be furnished by the dominant telecommunications services provider

---

99   See para 37.4 above.
100   Art 3(d^bis) and (d^ter) and Art 11 LTC.
101   Art 3(e) LTC.
102   Art 11a(1) and Art 11a(2) LTC.
103   Art 72 Ordinance on Telecommunications Services.
104   The questionnaire can be found on the OFCOM website: http://www.bakom.admin.ch/ under 'Topics', 'Telecommunication', 'Network Access', 'Access Applications'. It is available in German, French and Italian only.

(in the framework of the procedure described above).[105] OFCOM, on the other hand, is entitled to a copy of all access agreements executed between telecommunications services providers.[106]

37.59   Although the principle of freedom of access is not explicitly stated in the LTC, there are no obstacles for registered providers wishing to conclude access agreements.[107]

Access- and Interconnection-related Obligations with Respect to Undertakings with a Dominant Position

37.60   Under the LTC, undertakings deemed to have a dominant position in the market have a clearly defined legal obligation to provide access to their facilities and services to other providers. The provision of access includes the fully unbundled access to local loops, bitstream access for four years, rebilling for fixed network local loops, interconnection, leased lines, and access to cable ducts (provided these ducts have sufficient capacity). Details regarding these specific access obligations are set out in the Ordinance on Telecommunications Services.[108] Access must be provided according to the principles of non-discrimination and transparency and at cost-oriented prices. Therefore, no applicant may be disadvantaged compared to other business units, subsidiaries and partners of the undertaking with a dominant position in the market.[109] Conditions and prices for each of the access services must be stated separately and unbundled from all other services.[110] Prices for access services are to be determined according to the relevant costs of access, the long run incremental costs (LRIC), a constant mark-up,[111] and a return on investment customary in the industry.[112]

37.61   Besides the obligation to provide access without discrimination, in a transparent manner and at cost-based prices, no other specific obligations can be imposed on undertakings with a dominant position in the market.

Regulatory Powers Applicable to All Market Participants

37.62   End-to-end connectivity is guaranteed based on the fact that providers of universal services must ensure that all users of these services can communicate with one another (ie interoperability). Such providers also have a duty to interconnect, even if they do not have a dominant position in the market.[113] The Federal Government may extend the obligation of interoperability to other telecommunications services which are accessible to the public and satisfy a common need.[114]

---

105   Art 11a(4) LTC, cf Ordinance of the ComCom on the Telecommunications Law (RS784.101.112), Art 13a.
106   Art 11(4) LTC.
107   Cf Art 51 Ordinance on Telecommunications Services.
108   Art 58 et seq Ordinance on Telecommunication Services.
109   Art 52(2) Ordinance on Telecommunications Services.
110   Art 11(2) LTC.
111   Constant surcharge based on a fair proportion of the relevant joint and common costs.
112   Art 54 Ordinance on Telecommunications Services.
113   Art 21a LTC.
114   Art 21a(2) LTC.

REGULATION OF UNIVERSAL SERVICES AND USERS' RIGHTS

Regulation of Universal Service Obligations

Scope of universal service obligations

37.63   The holder of a licence to provide a universal service must provide the following services at a level which corresponds to the technological 'state of the art':

- a public telephone service, ie transmission of speech in real time by means of telecommunications techniques, including transmission of data employing transfer rates compatible with the channels for transmitting speech, as well as access to the network and additional services;
- access to emergency call services;
- public call boxes in sufficient numbers; and
- access to the Swiss directories of subscribers to the public telephone service.[115]

Moreover, these services must be ensured nationwide in such a way that they are offered to disabled persons at terms and conditions with respect to quality, quantity and prices which are comparable to those offered to persons without disabilities.[116]

Designation of undertakings obliged to provide universal services

37.64   ComCom periodically grants one or several licences to provide a universal service. These licences are granted on the basis of an open invitation to tender. The procedure is conducted in accordance with the principles of objectivity, non-discrimination, and transparency. If it is clear from the start that the invitation to tender cannot take place under competitive conditions, or if there are no suitable applicants, ComCom may require one or several providers to provide universal services.[117]

37.65   Applicants wishing to obtain a licence to provide universal services must:

- have the necessary technical capacities;
- furnish convincing evidence that the service, in particular with respect to finances, can be offered and operated for the entire duration of the licence, and state what financial compensation will be required;
- undertake to comply with the applicable legislation, in particular the LTC and its implementing provisions and the licence conditions; and
- undertake to comply with employment legislation and guarantee the working conditions that are customary in the sector.[118]

37.66   To date, Swisscom has been granted the only licence to provide the universal service for the whole country. The last public invitation to tender took place in 2007. Swisscom, being the only applicant, was again granted the only licence to provide the universal service. The licence will expire at the end of 2017.

---

115   The Federal Government may require a universal service licensee to set up a directory of all customers which have access to the universal service.
116   Art 16 LTC.
117   Art 14 LTC.
118   Art 15 LTC.

37.67   ComCom may levy an administrative charge for its oversight of universal service licensing, including, among other things, licence allocation.[119]

Regulation of retail tariffs, users' expenditures and quality of service

37.68   The legislation provides for certain quality standards and price caps to be established by the Federal Government. In particular, the universal service must be available nationwide at a certain quality, and prices must not depend upon distance.[120] The Federal Government has clarified these objectives in the Ordinance on Telecommunications Services. Price caps have been set for the following services:

- connection to the network;
- domestic traffic to fixed line terminals;
- surcharge for the use of public call boxes; and
- use of the transcription service for hearing impaired people, including round-the-clock emergency call service.[121]

Within the licence territory, quality is examined based on various criteria, including, among other things, the waiting period for installation of a station, voice transmission quality, repair time, time for connection build-up, billing accuracy, reaction time for operator assistance and number of public call boxes ready for use.[122]

Cost calculation and financing of universal services

37.69   If it is clear before the granting of the licence that, even with cost-effective management, it will be impossible to cover the costs for the provision of a universal service in a given area, the licence holder will be entitled to financial compensation.[123] The financing of this compensation can be ascertained through contributions by all telecommunications services providers.[124] To date, however, such contribution duty, however, has not been introduced.

Regulation of Retail Markets

37.70   Swisscom still dominates the retail market, especially with respect to fixed line telephone services.[125] However, with the introduction of more precise obligations regarding the granting of access imposed on providers with a dominant position in the market,[126] the end users are in a position to choose from a new, wider, and more advantageous range of services.

37.71   Retail services as such are not directly regulated under Swiss Telecommunications Law. These services are only indirectly regulated within the fields of

---

119   Art 40(1)(d) LTC; see also para 37.53 above.
120   Art 17 LTC.
121   Art 22 Ordinance on Telecommunications Services.
122   Art 21 Ordinance on Telecommunications Services.
123   Art 19(1) LTC.
124   Art 38 LTC; see para 37.51 above.
125   See para 37.2 above.
126   Art 11 LTC; see para 37.60 above.

access,[127] universal service,[128] address elements,[129] and through OFCOM's supervision of individual telecommunications services providers.[130]

37.72   In addition, anti-competitive behaviour may be sanctioned under the Act on Cartels.[131]

End User Rights

Contracts

37.73   Contracts between providers and end users are governed by general contract law. The LTC does not regulate such contracts except for the content of contracts between universal service licensees and end users (requiring that these licensees provide a certain range of services to end users).[132] The general tort law applies in the case of civil liability.

37.74   The LTC establishes a conciliation procedure for the settlement of disputes between end users and providers of telecommunications services. The costs of the proceedings are borne by the telecommunications service provider, and the final decision does not bind the parties.[133]

Transparency obligations

37.75   Through the telecommunication statistics gathered and published by OFCOM every year, the end user has access to information on the terms and price tariffs of the services offered by telecommunications services providers.[134] Moreover, the LTC authorises the Federal Government to require providers of telecommunications services to publish information on the quality of their services.[135]

DATA PROTECTION

Confidentiality of Communications

37.76   Protection of the secrecy of telecommunication is a constitutional right.[136] Consequently, the LTC imposes a duty on all telecommunications services providers not to disclose to third parties any information relating to subscribers' communications or give anyone else an opportunity to do so.[137] Providers of

---

127   See para 37.60 above.
128   See para 37.63 above.
129   See para 37.42 above.
130   See para 37.48 above.
131   RS 251.
132   See para 37.63 above.
133   Art 12c LTC; further details are contained in Arts 42 et seq Ordinance on Telecommunications Services.
134   Arts 97 et seq Ordinance on Telecommunications Services.
135   Art 12a LTC.
136   Art 13 Federal Constitution (RS 101).
137   Art 43 LTC.

telecommunications services must inform their clients about the risks involved in using their services and must provide requisite means to eliminate these risks.[138]

37.77   The interception and surveillance of communications are dealt with in the Federal Act concerning the surveillance of post and telecommunication communication[139] and in the Swiss Criminal Procedure Code.[140] A special federal authority is entrusted with the surveillance of communications in the post and telecommunications sector. For an order of surveillance, the following conditions must be met:

- certain facts lead to the strong suspicion that one of the criminal offences listed in the Criminal Procedure Code has been committed;
- the surveillance is justified by the severity of the criminal offence; and
- other means of investigation have been unsuccessful, or the investigation would be unpromising or unreasonably complicated if there was no surveillance.[141]

Any order of surveillance must be approved by the competent judicial (as the case may be, federal or cantonal) authority.[142]

37.78   The processing of data on terminal equipment of third persons (eg the installation and use of cookies, web-bugs, and hidden identifiers, among other things) by means of transmission using telecommunications techniques is only permitted for the provision of telecommunications services and their billing, or if the users have been informed about the processing and its purpose as well as about the fact that they may subject to the processing.[143]

Traffic Data and Location Data

37.79   The terms 'traffic data' and 'location data' are not defined in Swiss telecommunications legislation. However, there are a few provisions dealing with the protection of such data.

37.80   ComCom and OFCOM are permitted, if necessary for the fulfilment of their obligations under telecommunications legislation, to process personal data and personality profiles. In so doing, they are required to take measures necessary to ensure the protection and security of the data being processed and transferred.[144] Moreover, both OFCOM and ComCom may transfer to other Swiss authorities data, including sensitive data and personality profiles obtained in administrative procedures, needed by these authorities for the execution of their legal obligations. Subject to any international obligations to the contrary, the transfer of such data to foreign surveillance authorities is restricted to cases where the requested data is used exclusively for the surveillance of providers of telecommunications services and for market surveillance.[145]

37.81   Data on the location of mobile telephone users may only be processed by the telecommunications services providers for the purpose of:

---

138   Art 87 Ordinance on Telecommunications Services.
139   RS 780.1.
140   RS 312.0.
141   Art 269 Swiss Criminal Procedure Code.
142   Art 272 Swiss Criminal Procedure Code.
143   Art 45c LTC.
144   Art 13a LTC.
145   Art 13b LTC.

- the provision of telecommunications services and their billing; or
- the provision of other services, if the clients have given their consent, or in anonymous form.[146]

Itemised Billing

37.82 Customers are entitled to receive all relevant data relating to a particular invoice, including the numbers called, date, time and duration of connection, and the relevant charge.[147] Customers may request to receive itemised invoices. There is, however, no duty to provide this information free of charge.

Calling and Connected Line Identification

37.83 Where technically feasible, providers of telecommunication services must offer their clients the possibility, easily and free of charge, of having their number supressed on the equipment of the person called, on a per-call or permanent basis.

37.84 A customer who can establish that he or she is the target of abusive calls is entitled to be informed of the number, name, and address of the customer (or customers) from whose equipment such calls were made.[148]

Automatic Call Forwarding

37.85 Where technically feasible, providers of telecommunications services must offer their subscribers the possibility of stopping automatic call forwarding to their terminal by third persons. This service must be offered free of charge.[149]

Directories of Subscribers

37.86 All telecommunications services providers providing access to the public telephone service must keep a directory of their customers.[150] Moreover, a universal service licensee may be obliged to keep a universal directory of all customers benefiting from universal services.[151] However, customers have the right to refuse to have their address elements entered in such a directory. The directories are published (in paper and online). The provider of an electronic directory must take measures necessary to prevent the copying of directories to countries which have a lower level of data protection than Switzerland. The provider of the electronic directory must also ascertain, by technical and organisational measures, that the directory entries cannot be changed or deleted by unauthorised persons.[152]

---

146 Art 45b LTC.
147 Art 45(1) LTC and Art 81 Ordinance on Telecommunications Services.
148 Art 45(2) LTC and Art 82 Ordinance on Telecommunications Services.
149 Art 86 Ordinance on Telecommunications Services.
150 Art 21 FMG and Art 31 Ordinance on Telecommunications Services.
151 Art 16(1)(d) LTC.
152 Art 88(3) and (4) Ordinance on Telecommunications Services.

37.87   The Federal Government determines the minimum content of an entry.[153] In particular, the name and surname (or company name), the complete address and subscriber's phone number must be published.[154]

Unsolicited Communications

37.88   The customer's directory entry may contain a sign showing that he or she would not like to receive advertising material from third parties, and that his or her data must not be passed on for advertising purposes.[155] Furthermore, all providers are obliged to combat unfair mass advertising as defined in the Federal Act on Unfair Competition.[156]

---

153 Art 12d(2) LTC.
154 Art 11 Ordinance on Telecommunications Services.
155 Arts 11(e) and 88(1) Ordinance on Telecommunications Services.
156 Art 45a LTC and Art 83 Ordinance on Telecommunications Services; Art 3(o) Act on Unfair Competition, RS 241.

The Turkish Market for Electronic Communications

Birturk Aydin and Hakki Can Yildiz
Esin Attorney Partnership, Istanbul

LEGAL STRUCTURE

Basic Policy

38.1   The Turkish electronic communications sector has undergone significant developments in the recent years. Most importantly, a new legal framework has been established with the enactment in November 2008 of the Electronic Communications Act No 5809 ('ECA') which was followed by the adoption of a number of secondary regulations.

Previously, Turkey achieved full liberalisation of the sector by opening its markets with effect from 1 January 2004, which brought an end to the monopoly of the state-owned incumbent operator in the public electronic communications network, Türk Telekomunikasyon A.S. ('TT'). In 2005, within the scope of the liberalisation process, the majority shareholding of TT was privatised. Following the liberalisation of the telecommunications market, numerous operators have obtained authorisation and licences to provide electronic communications services.

Another important driver for development in the electronic communications sector is Turkey's ongoing membership negotiations with the European Union ('EU'). In order to become an EU Member, Turkey must harmonise its national laws and regulatory system in several areas with that of EU, including the requirement of full alignment with the EU *acquis communautaire* in the area of information society and media. To this end, the negotiation chapter on Information Society and Media was opened on 18 December 2008 following the adoption of the ECA.[1]

At the national level, the highest policy making body in Turkey concerning electronic communications is the Ministry of Transport, Maritime Affairs and Communications ('Ministry'). Ensuring free and effective competition, aligning national laws with those of EU, promoting broadband Internet access, expanding

---

1   2012 Progress Report on progress made by Turkey in preparing for EU membership can be reached at http://ec.europa.eu/enlargement/pdf/key_documents/2012/package/tr_rapport_2012_en.pdf

the universal service, and reducing retail prices for communications services are the priority policy areas in the Turkish communications sector.[2]

Despite attempts toward a liberalised and competitive sector, it is difficult to argue that effective competition has been achieved in the sector. As of the end of June 2012, TT has a 83.89 per cent market share in fixed line services which has been decreased from a 91 per cent market share as of the end of 2011.[3] With respect to the provision of broadband services, TTNET, a subsidiary of TT, holds a market share of 82.93 per cent. However, competition has been much more effective in mobile markets in comparison to fixed line and broadband service provision. Moreover, Turkey still lags behind the EU in broadband penetration, with an average Internet speed of 2.7 Mbps across the country.[4] This also means there is a large room for growth and further technological development in the sector. This is also evidenced by the fact that the total number of subscribers who are provided with Internet services from fibre networks have increased from around 190,000 subscribers as of June 2011 to around 470,000 subscribers as of June 2012 which amounts to an increase of 147.7 per cent.[5]

Implementation of EU Directives

38.2   Alignment with the EU electronic communications regulatory framework is a key element in Turkey's accession process. Related to this, one of the most important objectives of the ECA is the harmonisation of Turkey's electronic communications regulatory framework of with that of the EU. As a result, a significant part of the 2002 Regulatory Framework has been transposed into Turkish law with the adoption of the ECA and the secondary legislation.

The 2012 Progress Report on Accession ('Progress Report') notes that further efforts are needed to bring the legislation into line with the EU framework, in particular regarding the provisions on market access and interconnection, regulation of retail tariffs, spectrum management and universal service obligations.[6] However, significant progress has been made on introducing competitive safeguards. But, enforcement of the rights of new entrants to the fixed voice and broadband markets is proving to be difficult in practice, resulting in limited competition.

In summary, it can be argued that, although the legislation is mostly consistent, with the 2002 Regulatory Package in particular, there are problems in practice regarding implementation and enforcement of the legislation. Therefore, effective future implementation and enforcement of the legislation will be crucial for

---

2   These priority policy areas are declared in the website of the Ministry which can be reached at http://www.ubak.gov.tr/ – in the English version of the website go to the Communication section.
3   Market Report for Three Months Issued by the ITCA/Second Quarter of 2012, April – May – June.
4   State of the Internet Report, Vol 4, No 4, Fourth Quarter, 2012, Akamai.
5   Market Report for Three Months Issued by the ITCA/Second Quarter of 2012, April – May – June.
6   2012 Progress Report on progress made by Turkey in preparing for EU membership can be reached at http://ec.europa.eu/enlargement/pdf/key_documents/2012/package/tr_rapport_2012_en.pdf

progress in the development of competition, particularly in fixed line and broadband Internet provision.[7]

Legislation

38.3 The Turkish regulatory framework consists of several pieces of legislation. The principal legislation is the ECA, which is essentially based on the principles introduced by the 2002 Regulatory Framework. Similar to the 2002 Regulatory Framework, the ECA relies on competition law concepts and declares the enhancement of competition one of its main objectives.[8]

The ECA amends the previous legislation, but not in its entirety. The provisions of older laws (eg Law No 4502 which amended the previous Telecom and Telegraph Law No 406, Universal Service Law No 5369 ('USO Law'), Wireless Act No 2813, Law on the Establishment of Information Technologies and Communication Authority No 2813), are still applicable to the extent they do not contradict the provisions of the ECA.[9] The Information Technologies and Communication Authority ('ITCA') is empowered to issue secondary legislation to provide clarity on the application and implementation of the ECA. The ITCA has issued numerous regulations and communiqués regulating different aspects of the sector since the enactment of the ECA.[10]

With respect to television ('TV') and radio broadcasting, activities are mainly regulated by the Radio and Television Supreme Council ('RTSC'), under the Law on the Radio and Television Supreme Council No 6112 ('Law on RTSC'). The Law on RTSC deals with matters relating to radio and TV broadcasts transmitted by any and all techniques, methods or means, and by electromagnetic waves or other means for reception domestically or abroad.[11]

The ECA does not provide a consolidated and simplified regulatory framework which is required at EU level, and there are overlaps with previous laws and secondary legislation.[12] While it can be argued that the ECA and the secondary legislation are in line with the 2002 Regulatory Package, full alignment with the EU regulatory framework, a condition for Turkey to accede as an EU Member, is yet to be achieved, in particular, with respect to the adoption of the 2009 Regulatory Package.

---

7   İzak Atiyas, 'Regulation and competition in the Turkish telecommunications industry', in Tamer, Çetin and Fuat, Oguz (eds) *The Political Economy of Regulation In Turkey*, (New York, Springer, 2011), pp 177–192.

8   Art 2 ECA.

9   Art 65(2) ECA.

10   These regulations and communiqués regulate different aspects of the electronic communications sector including authorisation, access and interconnection, imposition of obligations on operators with significant market power, and numbering. A list of the regulations and communiques can be found at http://www.tk.gov.tr/mevzuat/yonetmelikler/index.php and http://www.tk.gov.tr/mevzuat/tebligler/index.php

11   Art 2 Law on RTSC.

12   EU-Turkey Accession Negotiations, Impact Assessment of Chapter 10 on Information Society and Media, *Andrea Renda, Selen Guerin, Emrah Arbak*, CEPS Special Report, 3 July 2009, p 2.

REGULATORY PRINCIPLES: THE FRAMEWORK DIRECTIVE

Scope of Regulation

38.4   According to Article 2 of the ECA, the following are subject to the provisions of the ECA: regulation, authorisation, supervision, and activities relating to the construction and operation of electronic communications networks and their associated facilities, provision of electronic communications services, manufacture, importation, installation, sale, and operation of electronic communications equipment, and planning and allocation of scarce electronic communications resources, including the allocation of frequency spectrum.

As part of the process to harmonise the electronic communications regulatory framework with the EU Regulatory Package, two key terms, 'electronic communications network' and 'electronic communications service', are defined in the ECA identical to the definitions provided in the Framework Directive. Therefore, the ECA adopted an approach which resembles the 2002 EU Regulatory Package, whereby it recasts terminology from telecommunications to electronic communications to establish a technology neutral regulatory regime. In particular, the ECA defines electronic communications networks and services in a way to cover all forms of infrastructure, services, and equipment supplied for the transmission of all kinds of signals, symbols, sounds, images, and data which could be converted into electrical signals. As a result, services such as VoIP, whereby electrical signals are conveyed over IP-based electronic communications networks, in principle, fall under the regulatory regime established by the ECA.

On the other hand, some features of the electronic communications sector are subject to the jurisdiction of the RTSC. The Law on RTSC provides certain provisions that are applicable for electronic communications network providers such as cable operators, satellite operators, and digital platform operators. Infrastructure and platform operators which provide networks for TV and radio broadcasts must obtain a broadcast transmission authorisation from the RTSC.[13] It has been widely reported that the Ministry has plans to merge the ITCA and RTSC to create a technology neutral regulatory framework which takes into account the technological developments in the communications sector, including the convergence of communications services and broadcasting.

Internet Freedom

38.5   Online content is monitored by the Telecommunication Communication Presidency ('TCP') which operates under the ITCA, under Law No 5651 on the Regulation of Publishing on the Internet and Prevention of Crimes Committed through the Internet.[14] Pursuant to Article 1 of Law No 5651, the purpose and the scope of this Law is to regulate the principles and the procedures on:

- the liabilities and responsibilities of content providers, hosting providers, access providers, and public use providers; and
- the prevention of crimes committed through the Internet by means of the agency of hosting and access providers.

---

13   Art 14(1) Regulation on the Administrative and Financial Conditions regarding the Media Service Providers as well as Platform and Infrastructure Operators, which was issued by RTSC and published on the Official Gazette dated 15 June 2011 no 27965.

14   Law No 5651 on the Regulation of Publishing on the Internet and Prevention of Crimes Committed Through the Internet.

In accordance with a frequently applied provision in Turkey, Article 8 of Law No 5651, access to online content may be blocked by means of a court order in the event that there is reasonable indication that any such online content constitutes one of the crimes listed in the said law. These crimes include sexual exploitation and abuse of children, facilitation of drug use, obscenity, gambling, and crimes committed against the founder of the Turkish Republic, Atatürk. In addition, under Article 9 of Law No 5651, any third party has the right to seek removal of content which infringes their rights, including but not limited to copyrights.

In practice, blocking of access is applied to the whole Internet site, and not only to the relevant content provided on the Internet site. Since May 2009, the TCP has not published any statistics on banned websites, and as a result, concerns have arisen regarding the transparency of the sanctions imposed by the TCP. The Progress Report issued by the Commission also indicated that the laws on the Internet limit freedom of expression and restrict citizens' right to access to information, and that they need to be revised.

National Regulatory Authorities: Organisation, Regulatory Objectives, Competencies

38.6   As the policy-making body for the electronic communications sector, the Ministry is assigned with certain powers and duties under Article 5 of the ECA. These powers, in general, relate to the designation of policies and priorities, promotion of research and development projects in the fields of communication, and taking necessary measures against the risk of interruption of communications in the case of natural disasters and extraordinary situations.

The ITCA, given that it was formerly the Telecommunications Authority, on the other hand, is the national regulatory authority within the meaning of the Framework Directive. It was established in 2000, and renamed the ECA in 2008, as a part of the process of alignment with EU regulations. The decision-making body of the ITCA is its Board which is composed of seven members. The President and the members of the Board are appointed by the Council of Ministers for a term of five years.[15]

The ECA and the Law on the Establishment of the ITCA determine the administrative independence, the duties, and the powers of the ITCA. In practice, however, there are still some areas where certain aspects of its independence from the Ministry and other State bodies must be further ensured in order to achieve full compliance with the EU regulatory framework. Areas in need of improvement include, among others, appointment and dismissal rules of the Board and transparency in the decision-making process of the Board.[16]

The powers and duties of the ITCA are set out in Article 6 of the ECA. The policy objectives and principles which are binding on the ITCA derive from the legal reasoning behind these powers and duties. The powers and duties of the ITCA include, among others:

- issuing regulations to foster competition and to eliminate practices which hinder competition;
- imposing obligations on operators with significant market power ('SMP');

---

15   Art 8 Law on the Establishment of ITCA No 2813.
16   Progress Report.

- inspecting the infringements of competition rules in the electronic communications sector and imposing sanctions where necessary;
- protecting the rights of end users;
- granting rights of use for scarce electronic communications resources;
- managing spectrum frequency and allocating frequencies; and imposing retail and wholesale tariffs.

The ITCA also must cooperate with different regulatory bodies. Pursuant to Article 7 of the ECA, the ITCA may review and investigate behaviour which infringes competition in the electronic communications sector and impose necessary remedies. Article 7(b) of the ECA also stipulates that the Competition Authority ('CA') should take into account the opinion and the ex ante measures of the ITCA in cases related to the sector. In 2011, the ITCA and the CA executed a protocol to enhance cooperation, clarify overlapping responsibilities, and prevent disputes (which have arisen in the past) regarding the jurisdiction of these two bodies.[17] Moreover, during the market analysis process, the ITCA is required to consult with the CA in a consultation period lasting for at least one month.[18]

Right of Appeal against NRA's Decisions

38.7 Interested parties may appeal the administrative acts or decisions of the ITCA before the administrative courts.[19] Interested parties are those whose interests are violated by a decision or act of the NRA.[20] The appeal process is, in essence, subject to the general administration laws of Turkey. Consequently, interested parties should file an appeal before the administrative courts within 60 days of announcement date, or the date the parties are notified, of the administrative act concerned. The administrative courts have the authority to decide to stay the execution of the decision of the NRA if the concerned party specifically requests it from the court and if implementation of that decision would result in damages which are difficult or impossible to compensate in the future.[21]

Decisions of the NRA are not subject to judicial review of expediency in the administrative inspection.[22] In other words, administrative courts may not decide whether the subject matter of the NRA decision is fit for the intended purpose. The decision of the administrative courts must be based on whether the decision of the NRA was taken in compliance with relevant legislation. Decisions of the administrative courts may be appealed before the Council of State of Turkey (the appeal court for the decisions of the administrative courts).

The NRA's Obligations to Cooperate with the Commission

38.8 Turkey has committed to implement the relevant EU Regulatory Framework as part of the accession negotiations which are currently being carried out with the EU. In this regard, implementation of the electronic communications regulatory framework is carried out in coordination with the Commission and its relevant

---

17   Cooperation Protocol between ITCA and CA dated 02 November 2011.
18   Art 5 Market Analysis Regulation.
19   Art 62 ECA.
20   Art 2(1)(a) Act on the Procedure of Administrative Justice No 2577 and dated 20 January 1982.
21   Art 27(2) Act on the Procedure of Administrative Justice No 2577 and dated 20 January 1982.
22   Art 62 ECA.

departments.[23] Turkey is also an observer member of the Body of European Regulators for Electronic Communications ('BEREC')[24] and a member of the Independent Regulators Group ('IRG').

Significant Market Power' as a Fundamental Prerequisite of Regulation

Definition of SMP

38.9 The ECA and the Market Analysis Regulation ('Market Analysis Regulation') which is enacted in November 2012, set forth the principles and procedures to determine SMP undertakings in a relevant electronic communications product or service market.[25] The ECA's definition of SMP is almost identical to the definition provided in the Framework Directive.[26] Pursuant to Article 6(1)(ö) of the ECA, the ITCA is assigned the task of defining relevant markets, undertaking market analysis, and identifying operators with SMP in the relevant markets.

Definition of relevant markets

38.10 The Market Analysis Regulation sets out the rules and principles governing the process for market analysis and for identification of individual operators having SMP in the relevant markets. Pursuant to Article 5 of the Market Analysis Regulation, the first step of the market analysis process is the definition of the relevant market. Other steps of the market analysis process are, respectively: determination of whether the relevant market requires ex ante regulation, analysis of the level of competition in the relevant market; identification of the operators with SMP; and, finally, imposition of obligation(s) on operators with SMP. Each of these steps is governed by rules and principles parallel to those of the Framework Directive.

Imposition of remedies

38.11 There are, however, some divergences between the Market Analysis Regulation and the EU Regulatory Framework. For example neither ECA nor the Market Analysis Regulation entitle the ITCA to impose functional separation on operators with SMP.[27] Although Article 10 of the Market Analysis Regulation allows the ITCA to impose different remedies than those which are set forth in the Market Analysis Regulation, this provision in itself is not very clear. Moreover, it is not very likely that ITCA, by relying solely on this provision, would have the ability to extend the scope of its jurisdiction to impose a remedy as stringent as functional

---

23 Art 30(1) Regulation on the Organisation of Information Technologies and Communication published in the Official Gazette dated 8 July 2011 No 27958.
24 http://berec.europa.eu/files/document_register/2012/8/MC%20(12)%2033%20List%20of%20BEREC%20Office%20MC%20Members-Observers_24.07.12.pdf
25 Regulation on Identifying the Operators with Significant Market Power and the Obligations to be Imposed which was published in the Official Gazette dated 1 September 2009 No 27336.
26 Art 3(r) ECA.
27 Please see the sub-section below on 'Access and interconnection-related obligations with respect to SMP undertakings' for more detail on the comparison of ECA and the Regulatory Framework in respect of imposition of additional remedies to SMP undertakings.

separation. On the other hand, similar to the EU Regulatory Framework, the ITCA must impose at least one of ex ante obligation on reaching the conclusion that there is an SMP operator in the relevant market.[28]

NRA's Regulatory Duties Concerning Rights of Way, Co-location and Facility Sharing

Rights of way

38.12   The provisions of the Framework Directive concerning rights of way have been transposed into the national law in the ECA. However, although the ECA attributes a great deal of importance to rights of way, Progress Report for 2012 notes that operators face difficulties in acquiring rights of way to deploy mobile/ wireless networks.[29] The ECA does not distinguish between public electronic communications networks ('PECN') and electronic communications networks ('ECNs') and extends the scope of the right of way to include all network operators.

The ECA provides that as a general rule, save for reasonable and just grounds, technically feasible right of way requests must be accepted by the relevant operator, if such right of way would not consistently hinder the use of rights of property owners and should not result in economically disproportionate costs. Furthermore, public bodies and institutions must assess the right of way requests without delay and finalise them within 60 days. Their decisions should be non-discriminatory and transparent.

With respect to the arrangements to be made with private parties, the ECA states that the principle of freedom of contract applies and that the parties must mutually agree on the terms and conditions as well as the fees to be charged.

If the operator and the owner of private property cannot reach an agreement for the granting of a right of way, the ECA further provides that if the provision of electronic communication network and/or services require a right of way, private properties may also be expropriated subject to procedures set out in the Expropriation Act No 2942 of 4 November 1983. In such a case, ownership of the expropriated property remains with the State, and the operator is granted a right to use the relevant property for the purpose of constructing an electronic communications network.

Co-location and facility sharing

38.13   With respect to co-location and facility sharing, the ECA and regulations issued by the ITCA provide parallel provisions to the corresponding provisions of the Framework Directive. The ECA empowers the ITCA to impose co-location and facility sharing obligations on operators on the condition that the ITCA, in so doing, should take into account certain factors such as the competition related implications of imposing such obligations.[30] For example, the reference offer of TT,

---

28   Art 10 Market Analysis Regulation
29   Progress Report 2012, p 54.
30   Art 12(2)(ç) ECA. The procedures and principles regarding co-location and facility sharing are further regulated under Regulation on the Procedures and Principles regarding

which is approved by the ITCA, includes terms and conditions on co-location and facility sharing.[31]

Furthermore, pursuant to Article 24 of the ECA, if there is a request of right of way regarding a property on or under which an electronic communications network has already been constructed, and if the operators of such network have already been imposed with co-location or facility sharing obligations, co-location and facility sharing options will be given priority over the option of granting a right of way.

In addition to the ECA and the ITCA regulations, a number of regulations issued by other entities also govern the granting of rights of way, co-location and facility sharing.[32]

The ITCA does not provide any specific provisions aimed at promoting infrastructure-based competition over service-based competition. Secondary legislation provides that co-location and facility sharing obligations must be imposed by the ITCA while taking into account several objectives, including, among others, the promotion of an effective and sustainable competition environment and the promotion of new investments and technology development.[33] However, neither the ECA nor its secondary legislation singles out one objective as to be given priority among others. In this respect, it can be argued that it holds a neutral view with respect to the subject which is similar to that of the EU electronic communications regulatory framework.[34] Finally it should be noted, however, that ITCA has excluded in 2011 next generation access networks from market analysis until 2016 or until the percentage of next generation access networks based on subscriptions reaches 25 per cent of all fixed broadband subscriptions.[35]

REGULATION OF MARKET ENTRY: THE AUTHORISATION DIRECTIVE

The General Authorisation of Electronic Communications

38.14   Turkey has adopted a very similar authorisation and licensing system to that of the EU. The ECA provides that, if no allocation of resources is needed, a company seeking authorisation will be deemed authorised upon notifying the ITCA of its intention to provide an electronic communications network or service. In

---

Co-location and Facility Sharing which was published on the Official Gazette dated 2 December 2010 No 27773.

31   http://www.btk.gov.tr/elektronik_haberlesme_sektoru/tarifeler_ve_erisim/
referans_arabaglanti_teklifleri/ROYTEPT_15Agustos2012.pdf (In Turkish).

32   Eg 'Regulation on Rights of Way and Constructing Telecommunication Infrastructure Facilities, Sharing of these Facilities and Determination of Fees for Contributing to these Facilities as well as the Maintenance Fees' which is issued by the Metropolitan Municipality of Istanbul is a very significant piece of regulation which is applicable for constructing all kinds of electronic communications networks, in particular the fibre roll-out projects carried out within the city of Istanbul.

33   Art 5 Regulation on the Procedures and Principles regarding Co-location and Facility Sharing which was published on the Official Gazette dated 2 December 2010 No 27773.

34   From a general policy perspective, the Government has declared its intent to foster competition in electronic communications sector through the promotion of alternative infrastructures. cf Genişbant ve Fiber: İktisadi Düzenleyici İncelemeler, Deneyimler ve Öneriler, *Doğ Dr. Ertuğrul Karağuha* and others, a report issued by ETCA, April 2010, Ankara.

35   Decision of the ITCA dated 03 October 2011 No 2011/DK-10/511.

other words, it is envisaged by the ECA that all companies willing to provide electronic communications services must notify the ITCA in advance, regardless of the type of activity they intend to carry out. Nonetheless, the companies which do not need allocation of resources will be deemed as authorised upon their notification, without any further requirement of obtaining a licence or confirmation from the ITCA. On the other hand, operators who need allocation of scarce resources (eg numbers, frequency, or satellite positions), will be deemed as authorised upon obtaining a right of use from the ITCA after completion of the relevant procedures.

Under general authorisation, authorised companies must carry out their activities in accordance with the applicable legislation. The conditions are provided in different provisions of the legislation, and are applicable to all operators, regardless of whether they have SMP. If the ITCA comes to the conclusion that authorised operators are not complying with these general conditions, their authorisation may be revoked.

Rights of use for radio frequencies

Strategic planning and co-ordination of spectrum policy

38.15   The ITCA is the primary body responsible for frequency spectrum management in Turkey. In this regard, the ITCA carries out national frequency planning, international frequency coordination, frequency allocations, and registration procedures in order to ensure the efficient and effective use of, and to prevent harmful interference on, the frequency spectrum. While the Ministry is responsible for determining the authorisation policy with respect to electronic communications services that must be carried out at the national level by a limited number of operators,[36] the ITCA grants rights of use. Furthermore, the ITCA determines the procedures for the provision of services and networks which do not involve usage of frequency bands, but which must be carried out by a limited number of operators.

The resolutions of international organisations, such as the International Telecommunication Union ('ITU'), the EU, and the European Conference of Postal and Telecommunications Administrations ('CEPT'), are taken into account in the allocation of the frequency spectrum. The ITCA carries out the international frequency registrations maintained by the ITU.

The ITCA is entitled to limit the number of rights of use that can be granted to operators if such limitation is necessary to ensure efficient use of resources. Rights of use which are limited in number are allocated through auctions; other rights of use are granted to the applicants within 30 days

With respect to terrestrial TV and radio broadcasts, the RTSC is the body responsible for frequency spectrum planning of the frequency bands, which are to be allocated by the ITCA. Digital switchover is due to be realised in Turkey in 2014, and the RTSC will be the competent body to carry out the procedures for the auctions for the allocation to broadcasters of the necessary frequency bands.[37]

Principles of frequency allocation, procedural rules

38.16   As a general rule, those who wish to use frequency spectrum must apply to the ITCA for frequency allocation, and register themselves with the relevant

---

36   Art 16(7) Authorisation Regulation.
37   Art 26 Law on RTSC.

registry maintained by the ITCA. However, the ITCA may determine that certain wireless equipment, systems, and frequency bands do not require frequency allocation and registration. Users of such frequency spectrum may not interfere with the frequency bands allocated to, and registered in the name of third parties.

Transferability, limitation of number of rights of use to be granted

38.17   The ECA established a legal framework for the auction and trade of spectrum. Specifically, the Auction Regulation sets out procedures and principles applicable to the auctions to be carried out by the ITCA for granting rights of use which are limited in number.[38] With respect to spectrum trading, pursuant to the Authorisation Regulation, approval of the ITCA is required for the transfer of a right of use of a frequency for which the ITCA has not limited the number of rights of uses to be granted.[39]

Rights of Use for Numbers

38.18   Pursuant to Article 31 of the ECA, the ITCA has the power and the duty to allocate numbers and to prepare the national numbering plan in accordance with the policies of the Ministry.[40] The Numbering Regulation sets out the provisions for granting individual rights of use for numbers as well as the rights and obligations of the operators to whom the rights of use for numbers are granted.[41] Operators can apply for the right of use for numbers during their authorisation, notification or at a later stage. The Numbering Regulation states that if the numbers are to be allocated through auctions, the relevant process set out in the legislation will be applied.[42] However, no further detail is provided with respect to the auctions for allocation of numbers. The allocated numbers are not the property of the operators, but they rather have a have a right of use in these numbers. These numbers cannot be transferred without the approval of the ITCA.

The NRA's Enforcement Powers

38.19   The ITCA is authorised to take necessary measures to ensure compliance with legislation, authorisations and licences, and to impose administrative fines on operators in the event that an operator's activities are in breach of the relevant legislation including the breaches of authorisations and licences. Pursuant to Article 60(1) of the ECA, the ITCA is entitled to charge administrative fines on operators with an amount of up to 3 per cent of the net sales generated in the preceding calendar year. The ITCA is also entitled to take necessary measures for the proper performance of national security, public order and public services, and

---

38   Auction Regulation regarding Authorisation in the Electronic Communications Sector which was published in the Official Gazette dated 15 January 2010 and No 27463.

39   Authorisation Regulation, which was published in the Official Gazette and came into force on 28 May 2009

40   National Numbering Plan defines the system of numbers for providing information on routing, addressing, pricing and service type. ITCA is entitled to modify the National Numbering Plan.

41   Numbering Regulation which was published on the Official Gazette dated 27 June 2009 No 27271.

42   Ie the Auction Regulation

for the implementation of provisions enacted by laws. The ITCA is, in principle, entitled to revoke authorisation in cases of gross negligence or non-performance of payment in due time.

On the other hand, a fine for a term of 5,000 to 15,000 days, the maximum limit of which is TRY 1,500,000 will be imposed on the operators and/or officers of the operators providing electronic communications services and networks and/or constructing and/or operating associated facilities without due authorisation.[43] Furthermore, if the relevant authorisation is be made through the grant of a right of use (ie if allocation of resources is involved), imprisonment up to six months can also be imposed on the officials of the operator providing such services without having obtained the right of use.[44]

Administrative Charges and Fees for Rights of Use

38.20   Pursuant to Article 11 of the ECA, authorisation fees consist of administrative fees and fees for right of use. Administrative fees are collected by the ITCA from all operators and these fees cannot exceed 0.5 per cent of the net sales generated by the respective operator. On the other hand, the ITCA determines the fees for right of use for which the number of licences to be granted by ITCA is not limited. These fees for right of use cannot be less than a minimum amount set by the Council of Ministers. Finally, fees for rights of use, for which only a limited number of licences are to be granted by ITCA, will be determined through auctions.

REGULATION OF NETWORK ACCESS AND INTERCONNECTION: THE ACCESS DIRECTIVE

Objectives and Scope of Access Regulation

38.21   The ECA provides a general framework for access and interconnection obligations, whereas the Access Regulation and the Market Analysis Regulation set out detailed rules and principles including provisions on the imposition of access related obligations to undertakings with SMP.[45]

In general, the electronic communications legislation provides general conditions that are applicable to all operators, regardless of whether they have SMP in the relevant market, and specific obligations which can be imposed only on the operators having SMP. With the enactment of the Access Regulation, and in particular, the recent enactment of the Market Analysis Regulation both of which clarify many of the uncertainties arising form the ECA, the system of imposing remedies on operators with SMP has become closer to that of the Access Directive. The Market Analysis Regulation which entered into force in November 2012 provides a clear set of rules for the procedure of carrying out the market analysis and impose obligations on the operators with SMP whereas the Access Regulation, which has been in force since September 2009, provides similar rules but its scope its

---

43   If a law or a regulation stipulates that the calculation of an administrative or judicial fine is based on days (eg a penalty of 100 days' judicial fine), the amount of the daily fine can vary from a minimum of TRY 20 to a maximum of TRY 100.

44   Art 63 of the ECA.

45   Access and Interconnection Regulation which was published on the Official Gazette dated 8 September 2009 No 27343.

limited to access-related matters. As a result of the enactment of the Market Analysis Regulation, there are now two different pieces of secondary legislation regulating, wholly, or in the case of the Access Regulation, partially, the same issue. Nevertheless, it can be argued that these two regulations do not conflict with each other, at least in terms of the principles they uphold.

Basic Regulatory Concepts

38.22   Pursuant to Article 2 of the ECA, 'access' means provision of electronic communications network, infrastructure and/or associated services by an operator to other operators. Article 15 of the ECA defines the scope of access-related obligations by providing a list consisting of types of access. These types of access include:

- interconnection between two networks;
- wholesale provision of services for the purposes of resale;
- access to relevant software systems and physical infrastructure; and
- access to the components of networks, including unbundled access to the local loop.

The ITCA is entitled to impose one or more of these types of access obligations on operators with SMP under the conditions set forth in the ECA, the Access Regulation and the Market Analysis Regulation.

Article 17 of the Access Regulation sets out the principle of freedom to contract, which provides that the operators are entitled to freely negotiate access agreements subject to the general conditions of their authorisations and other restrictions imposed by the ITCA.

Access and Interconnection-related Obligations with Respect to SMP Undertakings

38.23   Most of the remedies that can be imposed on operators with SMP under the ECA, Access Regulation and the Market Analysis Regulation are very similar to those envisaged in the EU Regulatory Framework. Similar to the EU Regulatory Framework, an additional obligation other than the general conditions can only be imposed on an operator which is found, following market analysis, to have SMP.

One of the most important divergences from the 2009 Regulatory Package is that there is no remedy which the ITCA can use to impose functional separation on an operator. In practice, however, structural and functional separation was imposed by an ex post measure taken by the Competition Authority in 2005, during the privatisation of the incumbent fixed line operator, TT. Accordingly, the Competition Authority, acting alone, prohibited the privatised incumbent operator from providing Internet and cable TV services at the retail level.[46] It imposed a structural separation of the cable TV network, and as a result, TT was forced to transfer its control over the cable TV assets. It also imposed an obligation on the privatised TT to restructure its Internet service providing arm as a separate legal entity.[47]

---

46   Decision of the Competition Board dated 21 July 2005 No 05–48/681–175 regarding the privatisation of 55 per cent of the share capital of Turk Telekom.

47   This separation was not a typical functional separation since the access network was not separated from the provision of access services as a whole, but rather, TT was forced to carry

A list of the remedies that can be imposed on operators with SMP is provided below.

Non-Discrimination: the ITCA is empowered to impose non-discrimination obligations on undertakings with SMP. Furthermore, the ITCA is entitled to impose non-discrimination obligations within the context of other obligations, such as imposing an obligation to allow access in a non-discriminatory manner within the context of access-related obligations.[48]

Transparency and reference offers: The ITCA may impose transparency obligations on operators with SMP, including the obligation to submit reference offers. The ITCA is entitled to request operators to make amendments to their reference offers.[49]

Account separation and cost accounting: The ITCA may impose on operators with SMP an obligation to keep their accounts in accordance with the rules and principles to be determined by ITCA for account separation and cost accounting.[50]

Access to, and use of specific network elements: The ITCA is entitled to impose on the undertakings with SMP obligations to allow access to third parties.[51] The ITCA can impose the necessary access obligations if it decides that the refusal of the types of access listed in Article 15 of the ECA, or imposition of unreasonable terms and conditions for such access would hinder competition.

Price controls: The ITCA may impose on the undertakings with SMP obligations to set cost oriented prices in their access tariffs.[52]

In addition to the specific remedy related to access-related price controls the ITCA is also entitled to regulate tariffs of the undertakings with SMP which are related to other types of wholesale activities and retail activities of those undertakings.[53] In this respect, the Tariff Regulation provides the rules and principles for the regulation of retail tariffs and lists certain methods for the determination of retail tariffs. These methods are listed in Article 6 of the Tariff Regulation as cost based tariffs, price cap regulation, and simply imposing minimum or maximum prices for services.

Carrier selection and carrier pre-selection: Article 33(1) of the ECA suggests that the ITCA is entitled to impose obligations to provide carrier selection and pre-selection on any operator regardless of whether or not that operator is designated as having SMP. However, Article 16 of the Access Regulation specifically states that these obligations can be imposed only on the operators having SMP.

---

out its internet service providing activities under a separate legal entity, named TTNet, so as to ensure non-discrimination and transparency related to the provision of access. In early 2012, TT had attempted to provide retail Internet access services after obtaining consent from the ITCA. The Council of State, however, rendered a stay of execution for this consent of the ITCA as a result of which TT was forced to cease its retail internet access activities. The lawsuit for the annulment of the consent of ITCA is still pending before the Council of State as of May 2012.

48   Art 10 Access Regulation and Art 10 Market Analysis Regulation
49   Art 19 ECA, Art 11 Access Regulation and Art 10 Market Analysis Regulation
50   Art 21 ECA, Art 13 Access Regulation and Art 10 Market Analysis Regulation
51   Art 16 ECA, Art 7 Access Regulation and Art 10 Market Analysis Regulation
52   Art 20 ECA, Art 12 Access Regulation and Art 10 Market Analysis Regulation
53   Art 13(2)(b) and (c) ECA,

Regulatory Powers Applicable to All Market Participants

38.24   The ITCA is entitled to impose facility sharing obligations, in return for a reasonable charge, on operators who have constructed their facilities on or under public or private property, or who are authorised to use such properties. Similarly, co-location obligations can also be imposed on operators to provide co-location within their own facilities in return for a cost-based charge.[54]

Pursuant to Article 17(3) of the ECA, the ITCA also regulates facility sharing and co-location of shared antenna systems and broadcasters' facilities in order to ensure radio and TV broadcasts from specified emission points.

Finally, all operators are obliged to negotiate interconnection with each other upon request. In the event that the parties fail to agree on interconnecting with one another, the ITCA may impose interconnection so as to ensure end-to-end connectivity.[55]

REGULATION OF THE UNIVERSAL SERVICE AND USERS' RIGHTS: THE UNIVERSAL SERVICE DIRECTIVE

Regulation of Universal Service Obligations

Scope of universal service obligations

38.25   Universal services in Turkey are mainly regulated by the USO Law No 5369. Article 5 of the USO Law defines the scope of the universal services, which include fixed lines, payphones, directories, emergency calls, communication for maritime safety, and Internet access.[56] The scope of Internet services covered under the USO Law is not limited to narrowband Internet access; rather it extends to any type of purchase of infrastructure equipment and facility provision. That said, there is no clarity in the USO Law as to what type of broadband services are covered by the term 'Internet service' as part of universal service obligation.

Moreover, the ECA has introduced another significant change which is related to the provision of electronic communications network services and digital broadcasting to the entire country over the terrestrial network. Accordingly, operators which provide network and digital broadcasting will be able to benefit from the universal service fund even if they are not determined as a universal service provider.

Designation of undertakings obliged to provide universal services

38.26   In accordance with the USO Law, universal service providers are designated by the Ministry by way of auctions among the operators who submitted their

---

54   Art 17 ECA.
55   Art 16(2) ECA and Art 9 Access Regulation.
56   The Council of Ministers is entitled to re-evaluate the scope of universal service obligation periodically. Council of Ministers has used its authority to extend the scope of the universal service in the past. For example, provision of services for the purpose of extending the use of information technologies, purchase of communication equipment by public bodies for the free of charge use of disabled persons, and wireless mobile networks in certain rural areas have been defined as universal service (Decisions dated, respectively, 13 February 2006, 29 June 2010 and 13 May 2011).

interest for such designation. Prior to the USO Law, only the incumbent fixed line operator could have been designated as a universal service provider. However, under the application of the USO Law, only TT, the incumbent operator, has been designated as a universal service provider to date.

Regulation of retail tariffs, users' expenditures and quality of service

38.27   Pursuant to Article 6 of the Tariff Regulation,[57] the ITCA is empowered to impose obligations on undertakings with SMP to set their tariffs in accordance with tariffs that should be approved by the ITCA. Furthermore, the ITCA can require that a tariff be based on one or more of the methods listed in Article 6 of the Tariff Regulation (cost based tariffs, price cap regulation, or simply imposing minimum or maximum prices for services).

TT's fixed line retail tariffs are subject to regulatory oversight and the approval of the ITCA in accordance with the relevant provisions of the Tariff Regulation. On the other hand, mobile operators are free to determine their retail prices provided that such retail prices not exceed a maximum cap, which is updated twice in every year in line with the inflation rates and other developments in the sector. Mobile operators are under the scrutiny of the ITCA which (by occasionally imposing fines) prevents them from charging a fee for calls to other mobile networks above the cap. Finally, the retail prices for Internet service provision are currently not subject to the approval of the ITCA. However, at the wholesale level, TT's prices that can be charged to Internet service providers operating at the retail level (including TT's own subsidiary, TTNET), are subject to the approval of the ITCA within the scope of price controls related to access tariffs.

Cost calculation and financing universal service

38.28   The financing of universal services is mainly regulated under the USO Regulation.[58] The costs arising from provision of universal services are financed by a fund to be established by the Ministry. In the determination of costs, Article 7 of the USO Law stipulates that the benefits arising in connection with providing universal services must be taken into account.

With respect to the financing of universal service, Article 5 of the USO Regulation stipulates that 2 per cent of the authorisation and licence fees, 1 per cent of the annual turnover of all operators, including TT, but excluding mobile operators, 10 per cent of the amount to be paid by the mobile operators to the Treasury on a monthly basis,[59] and 20 per cent of the administrative penalties must be transferred to an account of the Ministry. Although in practice this account is referred to as the universal service fund, it is argued by several players in the sector that this account is not operated as a fund, since the political nature of this fund poses the risk that it may be used for purposes other than the provision of universal services in the

---

57   Tariff Regulation which was published on the Official Gazette dated 12 November 2009 No 27404.

58   Regulation on the Procedures and Principles regarding the Collection of Universal Service Incomes and Expenditures which was published in the Official Gazette dated 29 June 2006 No 26213.

59   Pursuant to Law No 5793, the total amount which must be paid by each mobile operator to the Treasury, on a monthly basis, is equal to 15 per cent of the gross sales of the respective mobile operator generated in the relevant month.

electronic communications sector.[60] According to the Progress Report, the scope and implementation of universal service obligations are not in line with those of the EU.

Regulation of Retail Markets

Prerequisites for the regulation of retail markets

38.29 Pursuant to Article 4 of the USO Law, the operators which are designated as universal service providers are obliged to provide universal service in accordance with the USO Law. Article 4 further states that universal service providers must comply with the principles set out in Article 3 while they provide universal service. Accordingly, ITCA can impose certain conditions to the undertakings which are designated as universal service providers.

Pursuant to Article 3 of the USO Law, any person living in the Turkey, without any discrimination on the basis of region and place of residence, must be provided with universal services. The universal services must be offered taking into account the gross domestic product per capita at affordable and reasonable prices. Furthermore, universal services must be offered at predefined service quality standards and continuity must be essential in the provision of, and access to, the universal services.

Article 3 also entitles ITCA to impose obligations on the universal service providers to take specific measures regarding reasonable pricing and the technology used in the provision of the universal services in order to ensure that low income households and disabled persons are provided with universal services.

Finally, Article 13 of the ECA allows ITCA to impose retail tariff controls on the retail operators including the operators designated as universal service providers.

End User Rights

Contracts

38.30 The Regulation on Consumer Rights in the Electronic Communications Sector which was published in the Official Gazette No 27655 on 28 July 2010 ('Regulation on Consumer Rights') sets out mandatory terms of contracts signed between subscribers and operators. Pursuant to Article 14 thereof, a contract must include, at least, the following information:

- subject, date, place, and term of the contract;
- liabilities, names, titles, and full addresses of the parties;
- conditions relating to termination or renewal of the contract;
- definition of the services to be provided, and quality of service level;
- indication of the time when the first connection is to be made;
- kinds of maintenance and repair services to be provided;
- applicable tariffs and procedures to obtain information on tariff changes;
- compensation and/or pay-back procedures if the service level under the contract cannot be achieved due to the fault of the operator;
- legal consequences of default by the subscriber;

---

60 cf 'The Concept of Universal Service in Telecommunications Sector', *Bülent Kent*, Gazi Üniversitesi Hukuk Fakültesi Dergisi C. XVI, Y. 2012, Sa. 2.

- tariff and subscription package chosen by the subscriber at the date of the contract;
- dispute resolution procedures;
- information on the technical equipment, devices and hardware required for the services benefited by the subscriber;
- measures to be taken by the subscriber or the operator against circumstances which may occur while utilising the services and which threaten security; and
- date of approval by the ITCA, if any.

Transparency Obligations

38.31 Pursuant to Article 6 of the Regulation on Consumer Rights, the operators are obligated to provide, at a minimum, without request, and in a means that is easily accessible to all consumers, the following information in relation to access to the electronic communication services and utilisation of such:

- name, title, and address of the operator;
- standard conditions of contracts between consumer and the operator; and
- dispute resolution mechanisms concerning consumer complaints.

Quality of service: securing 'net neutrality'

38.32 The operators are obligated to provide electronic communication services to consumers and end users in similar positions, under equal terms, and without discrimination[61].

The ITCA is entitled to set the parameters related to the quality of services, and to determine the content and type of information to be published by the operators and other issues related to the quality of services, for the purpose of enabling consumers and end users to reach comprehensive, sufficient, and clear information on the quality of service levels.[62]

In this respect, the ITCA enacted the Regulation on the Service Quality within the Telecommunications Sector,[63] providing procedures for, and principals on, the provision of services at both national and international levels.

Obligations Facilitating Change of Provider

38.33 Article 32 of the ECA stipulates that operators must provide number portability between providers and implement the necessary arrangements in accordance with the regulations of the ITCA. The Number Portability Regulation sets out the detailed provisions including the obligations of operators with respect to number portability.

Article 6(2) of the Number Portability Regulation provides that number portability should be available between the fixed networks as well as mobile networks. Accordingly, number portability on fixed networks has been operational in 2012.[64]

---

61   Art 47 Electronic Communications Law No 5809.
62   Art 52 Electronic Communications Law No 5809.
63   Published in the Official Gazette No 27697 on 12 September 2010 .
64   Progress Report 2012 p 53.

However, the time limits for the transfer of numbers are not in line with the 2009 Regulatory Framework and each number transfer process can take up to seven days.[65]

DATA PROTECTION: THE DIRECTIVE ON PRIVACY AND ELECTRONIC COMMUNICATIONS

Confidentiality of Communications

38.34   Article 26 of the Constitution of Turkey provides the right to freedom of communications. This provision also secures the confidentiality of communications as a fundamental right which can only be limited under certain circumstances and subject to the conditions provided in Article 26 and the Criminal Procedural Code. Any violation of confidentiality of communications not based on legal grounds is a crime under the Turkish Criminal Code.[66]

The confidentiality of communications in the electronic communications sector is regulated under the Regulation on Processing of Personal Data and Protection of Privacy in the Electronic Communications Sector ('Regulation on Personal Data and Privacy')[67] which was issued in June 2012, repealing an earlier regulation and introducing more stringent measures. It sets out the procedures and principles regarding the processing and retention of personal data as well as protection of privacy, all of which are binding on the operators active in the electronic communications sector. This regulation is due to enter into force on 24 January 2013.

This regulation is partially based on the EU's E-Privacy Directive (Directive 2002/58/EC) and Data Retention Directive (Directive 2006/24/EC), but it fails to reflect subsequent amendments made in the EU Electronic Communications Regulatory Framework including those introduced in 2009 with the Citizens' Rights Directive (Directive 2009/136/EC) and the Cookies Directive (Directive 2009/136/EC).

The Regulation places special focus on the retention of personal data, establishing categories of data which must be retained by operators for one year from the date of communication. The list of categories of data and other provisions on data retention are in large part based on the corresponding provisions of the Data Retention Directive (Directive 2006/24/EC).

Furthermore, a detailed set of rules is provided on the measures against the illegal processing of, and access to, personal data. Accordingly, operators will be required to have a security policy concerning their processing of personal data and take the necessary managerial and technical measures to secure personal data appropriate to the risk. In contrast to the previous regulation, minimum requirements for these measures are listed, including measures for the prevention of unrequested, illegal

---

65   Cf (in Turkish): http://www.nts.gov.tr/#/surecler/

66   From the perspective of Turkish criminal law, it should be emphasised that interception, recording, retention, disconnection or surveillance of the telecommunications would be considered within the scope of the crimes committed against private life, which are provided for under Article 132 to Article 138 of the Turkish Criminal Code. Indicated actions, however, would not constitute any crime, if the prosecutor decides upon performance of such in order to ascertain the existence of a crime or in order for the prevention of crimes pursuant to Article 135 of the Criminal Procedure Code.

67   Published in the Official Gazette No 28363 on 24 July 2012.

and unauthorised destruction, loss, modification, storage, recording, processing, disclosure and access.

The new Regulation also introduces a five-year retention requirement on operators for records of access to personal data. Additionally, the ITCA may require submission of information and documents on security measures and modifications to them.

Where a risk threatening personal data security arises, the operator must inform the ITCA and its subscribers and users of the risk in an effective and prompt manner. If the risk is not within the scope of the operator's preventive measures, the operator also must inform the subscribers and users how to prevent the risk and the approximate cost of prevention.

In the event of a breach of personal data security, the operator must notify the ITCA on the measures taken to protect against the risk and the information provided to subscribers and users on the type and effect of the risk.

If the subscribers/users may be negatively affected by the risk, the operator must notify the subscribers and users of the type of risk, where more information on the risk may be found and the measures available to reduce its negative effects. Operators must record the cause and effect of the breach of personal data security as well as the remedial measures taken.

In light of the above, it can be stated that the provisions on risk management, security, traffic data, location data and subscriber directories are regulated under detailed provisions which are more consistent with the corresponding EU Directives in comparison to the previous regulations. Moreover, significant changes as well as more onerous responsibilities are imposed on operators. At the same time, the enactment of the Regulation on Personal Data and Privacy is definitely a step toward ensuring regulatory certainty in the sector and the provisions it introduces will also help Turkey bring its data protection and privacy regulations in the electronic communications sector closer to the standards of the international community and in particular to those of the EU.

Traffic Data and Location Data

38.35   Pursuant to Article 8 of the Regulation on Personal Data and Privacy, traffic data may be processed for the purpose of: resolving disputes arising in connection with billing and consumer complaints; billing traffic management; or interconnection. Traffic data which is to be processed to provide value-added communication services or marketing of electronic communications services may be processed only after obtaining the consent of the data subject. Furthermore, such consent will be valid only if the data subject has first been informed of the type and period of the data processing. A data subject may withdraw consent at any time in the same way as consent was initially granted or by a 'simple method'; however, there is no definition of 'simple method'. The authorisation to process traffic data may only be provided to those persons who are authorised to carry out traffic management, interconnection, and billing activities, to evaluate consumer complaints, and to market electronic communications services. After completion of the necessary activities carried out for processing and retaining the traffic data, such processed and retained data must be either deleted or anonymised. Competent public authorities are also entitled to request in writing traffic data from operators in order to carry out inspection duties, to evaluate consumer complaints, and to resolve disputes in connection with interconnection and billing.[68]

As with traffic data, location data may only be processed to provide value-added communication services, and then only with the consent of the data subject or after the data have been anonymised. Consent is valid only if the data subject has first been informed of the type, purpose, and period of the data processing. As with traffic data, a data subject may withdraw consent at any time in the manner which the data subject initially granted the consent or by a 'simple method' (which, as noted above, is not defined). Location data may, however, be processed without the data subject's consent where required by law, court order or in cases of emergency assistance calls.

The international transfer of the traffic data, retained data and location data by operators is prohibited. The violation of this prohibition may result in a monetary fine of up to 3 per cent of the operator's annual turnover, and repetition of the violation may result in revocation of the operator's licence.

Itemised Billing

38.36   Subscribers may reserve the right to receive itemised and non-itemised bills, based on their request. Visually handicapped persons, additionally, are entitled to request their bills to be issued in a manner that they can utilise.[69]

While operators are obliged to send bills via post, bills may be sent through an electronic environment at a subscriber's request. Subscribers may reserve the right to revoke such request at any time.

Lastly, operators must enable their subscribers to obtain billing information (with at least three months' usage details) on the Internet, without demanding any additional charge. Moreover, operators must, upon a subscriber's request, send such information to the subscriber via post.[70]

Presentation and Restriction of Calling and Connecting Line Identification

38.37   According to Article 17 of the Regulation on Personal Data and Privacy, operators must enable their subscribers, free of charge, to prevent his or her identity from being revealed, when making a call. Operators must inform their subscribers of this option.

If the calling subscriber hides his or her identity, the subscriber who receives the phone calls may request the operator to block these calls.

The operator must inform its subscribers of these options free of charge and through text messages, media, broadcasters, post or Internet.

Automatic Call Forwarding

38.38   Operators must provide to subscribers, free of charge and in simple methods but within technical limits, the ability to terminate automatic calls

---

68   Art 10 Regulation on Personal Data and Privacy
69   Art 5 Regulation on Consumer Rights
70   Art 20 Regulation on Consumer Rights

forwarded by third persons via telephone or other similar electronic communications equipment.[71]

Directories of Subscribers

38.39   Directories of subscribers are regulated under Article 19 of the Regulation on Personal Data and Privacy. Accordingly, operators must inform subscribers in advance, and free of charge, of the publication purposes of the written or electronic directory, before they are recorded. They must also informed subscribers of the types of data to be published in the directory. Personal data to be published in a directory must be determined by taking into account the purpose and scope of the directory service.

Subscribers may, at any time, and free of charge, request that their information in the directories be amended, verified, or removed.

---

71   Art 18 Regulation on Personal Data and Privacy

The Ukrainian Market for Electronic Communications[1]

Vyacheslav Yakymchuk, Olena Kuchynska
Baker & McKenzie, Kyiv

LEGAL STRUCTURE

Basic Policy

39.1 Since Ukraine's independence in 1991, significant changes have been incorporated into the regulatory framework of the Ukrainian telecommunications sector. Those changes initiated, to a large extent, the process of adjusting domestic legislation to the fundamental principles adopted by the European Union.

39.2 The former Ministry of Communications of Ukraine created several umbrella organisations to take over its previous operational functions. Consequently, all organisations involved in planning, building, and operating public telecommunications networks in Ukraine were merged into Open Joint Stock Company Ukrtelecom (now Public Joint Stock Company Ukrtelecom ('Ukrtelecom')), which became the major operator of fixed-line telephone communications, owner of up to 90 per cent of cable ducts, and later, the only telecommunications operator holding a 3G license (UMTS/WCDMA standard). In 2011, 92.79 per cent of the shares of Ukrtelecom were privatised by Ukrainian-registered ESU, a cellular network builder and subsidiary of EPIC Invest, an Austrian investment company.

39.3 Following the adoption of the Telecommunications Law,[2] most regulatory functions were transferred from the former Ministry of Communications of Ukraine to an independent authority, the National Commission for Communications Regulation, established on 19 April 2005,[3] which in 2011 was reorganised into the National Commission for the State Regulation of Communications and Informatization (the 'NCCIR')[4].

---

1   Editing of this chapter closed on 4 January 2013.
2   Law of Ukraine No 1280-IV 'On Telecommunications', dated 18 November 2003.
3   Presidential Decree No 664/2005 'On Composition of the National Commission for Communications Regulation', dated 19 April 2005.
4   Presidential Decree No 1067/2011 'On the National Commission for for the State Regulation of Communications and Informatization', dated 23 November 2011.

39.4   Ukraine's telecommunications market is highly diversified. Under the Telecommunications Law,[5] only undertakings registered in Ukraine may provide telecommunications services in Ukraine. Telecommunications companies in Ukraine are privately held entities, some of which have foreign investment. Since 2000, foreign investors have been authorised to establish telecommunications companies in Ukraine, and hold up to 100 per cent equity interest in Ukrainian telecommunication companies (the previous limit was 49 per cent). A foreign undertaking, however, may not establish radio broadcasting or television companies, but may hold equity interest in such companies without any restriction as to the amount.[6]

39.5   Pursuant to the Law on Main Principles of Information Society Development in Ukraine in 2007–2015,[7] the development of Ukrainian communications legislation and its harmonisation with international law, implementation of communications into all sectors of life, expansion, development, and accessibility of telecommunications services and resources are declared to be among the most crucial issues for the promotion of the information society in Ukraine.

Implementation of EU Directives

39.6   The Partnership and Co-operation Agreement between the European Communities and their Member States, and Ukraine[8] predetermined the implementation of the EU regulatory framework into Ukrainian legislation.[9] The EU Adaptation Law,[10] with the goal of adoption of the *acquis communautaire*, prescribes the approximation of Ukrainian legislation with that of the EU in certain priority areas, including competition, the information society, technical rules, and standards.

The Coordination Council for the Adaptation of the Legislation of Ukraine to the Legislation of the European Union, the government agency responsible for the approximation, examines proposed legislation that is within the scope of EU legislation, to ensure its conformity with EU law. Proposed laws or regulations that are found to contradict EU law may be adopted for a fixed term only, provided there are compelling reasons for such adoption. The Cabinet of Ministers of Ukraine adopts, on an annual basis, a plan for implementation of the Nationwide Programme of Adaptation of the Legislation of Ukraine to the Legislation of the European Union (the 'Step Plan').[11]

39.7   Ukraine has implemented a number of the rules contained in the 2009 EU Regulatory Package. For example, the registration principle for telecommunications

---

5   Art 6.
6   Until 2006, foreign investors were limited to holding no more than 30 per cent equity interest in Ukraine radio broadcasting or television companies.
7   Law of Ukraine On Main Principles of Information Society Development in Ukraine in 2007–2015 No 537-V dated 9 January 2007.
8   Signed on 14 June 1994.
9   Presidential Decree No 1072/2000 'Program of Ukraine's Integration into the European Union', dated 14 September 2000; Law of Ukraine No 1629-IV 'On the Nationwide Program of Adaptation of the Legislation of Ukraine to the Legislation of the European Union', dated 18 March 2004.
10   Law of Ukraine No 1629-IV 'On the Nationwide Program of Adaptation of the Legislation of Ukraine to the Legislation of the European Union', dated 18 March 2004.
11   Eg Resolution of the Cabinet of Ministers of Ukraine dated 28 March 2012 No 156-p On Adoption of the Step Plan for Implementation in 2012 of the Nationwide Program of Adaptation of the Legislation of Ukraine to the Legislation of the European Union.

activities, extending authorities of the NCCIR to market definition and market analysis, facilitating access to the market and universal services, were incorporated into the Telecommunications Law. Further, the 2012 Step Plan includes plans to amend the Telecommunications Law to improve regulations with respect to the NCCIR's market definition and market analysis, to conform with the Framework Directive.

Legislation

39.8   Ukrainian telecommunications legislation consists of laws adopted by the Parliament and implementing regulations of the NCCIR. The Cabinet of Ministers of Ukraine, within its authorities of general policy-making and coordination in the telecommunications sector, may also adopt some implementing legislation.[12] The Telecommunications Law establishes the competence of state authorities in regulating telecommunications activities, and determines the legal status of telecommunications network operators (operators), telecommunications service providers (providers) and consumers of telecommunications services. The Telecommunications Law also regulates access to telecommunications markets, interconnection of telecommunications networks, rights of way, privacy issues, authorisations, pricing policy, and dispute settlement. The Radio Frequencies Law[13] provides comprehensive rules for the allocation, assignment, interrelation, and use of radio frequencies in Ukraine. The NCCIR adopts, among other things, licensing conditions for different types of services in the telecommunications market and rules for allocation and use of numbering resources.

39.9   Since its adoption in 2003, the Telecommunications Law has undergone (and continues to undergo) significant changes, which the goal of conforming the law with EU directives and regulations and further liberalising telecommunications markets.

39.10   Decisions of the NCCIR in individual cases, provided they are adopted within its competence, are binding on those to whom they are addressed. In addition, the NCCIR may impose sanctions on market players. The NCCIR also submits proposals to other governmental authorities with respect to draft laws, other regulations, and standards in the telecommunications sector.[14]

REGULATORY PRINCIPLES

Scope of Regulation

39.11   The scope of the Telecommunications Law extends to fixed-line and mobile telephone communications, maintenance and operation of on-air and cable radio broadcasting and television networks, leasing of electronic communications channels, and communication services based on the Internet protocol telephony (IP telephony).[15] The Telecommunications Law does not apply to telecommunications

---

12   Eg Rules of accepting and rendering telecommunications services, adopted by the Regulation of the Cabinet of Ministers of Ukraine dated 11 April 2012 No 295.
13   Law of Ukraine No 1770-III 'On Radio Frequency Resource of Ukraine', dated 1 June 2000.
14   Art. 18 Telecommunications Law.
15   Arts. 1, 42(7), 56 Telecommunications Law.

networks which do not interact with publicly available networks, except for the use of such networks under a state of emergency or in the event of war.[16]

39.12   The terms 'telecommunications' and 'electronic communications' are used interchangeably throughout the Telecommunications Law. 'Telecommunications network' is defined as:

> 'a complex of technical means of telecommunications and structures designed for routing, commuting, transmitting and/or receiving symbols, signals, written text, images and sounds or communications of any kind by radio, wire, optical or other electromagnetic systems between terminal equipment'.[17]

'Telecommunications service' is defined as 'a product of activities of a telecommunications operator and/or provider aimed at the satisfaction of consumer needs in the area of telecommunications'. VoIP services are fully covered by the definition of 'electronic communications'. There is no definition of 'associated facilities'. Rather, article 1 of the Telecommunications Law defines 'technical means of telecommunications' to be 'equipment, stations and linear structures designed for the formation of telecommunications networks'.

'Internet Freedom'

39.13   Currently there is no specific legislation governing Internet freedom in Ukraine. General regulations, in particular relating to freedom of speech, protection of public morals, and data protection apply to communications over the Internet. Recently, there have been a few initiatives from law enforcement agencies to restrict access to some information on the Internet and to limit anonymity of users on the Internet.

National Regulatory Authorities: Organisation, Regulatory Objectives, Competencies

39.14   The NCCIR is the state agency responsible for the regulation of the Ukrainian telecommunications sector. In this capacity, the NCCIR is responsible for:

- maintaining the Register of Operators and Providers of Telecommunications ('Telecommunications Register');
- addressing licensing issues;
- allocating numbering resources;
- regulating tariffs;
- regulating interconnection agreements;
- controlling quality of telecommunications services;
- defining and analysing markets; and
- resolving certain disputes between market players.

39.15   The NCCIR's regulatory objectives, as pursuant to article 16 Telecommunications Law, are:

---

16   Art 5(2) Telecommunications Law.
17   Art 1 Telecommunications Law.

- satisfaction of consumer demand for telecommunications services;
- creation of favourable organisational and economic conditions for attracting investment;
- increase in the volume and quality of services; and
- development and modernisation of telecommunications networks, considering national security interests.

39.16   The NCCIR is authorised to make filings with the Anti-Monopoly Committee of Ukraine ('AMC') with respect to competition law infringements.[18] Once a filing is made, the AMC will proceed with the case in accordance with the Competition Law.[19]

39.17   Telecommunications companies must submit to the NCCIR certain information and reports about their activities,[20] including periodic statistical reports.

39.18   The NCCIR must co-operate with Ukrainian governmental authorities and with the NRAs of other countries.[21]

39.19   The NCCIR has the power to resolve disputes between telecommunications undertakings which relate to interconnection, national roaming services, number portability, and use of personal numbers,[22] without prejudice to the right of either party to bring an action before the courts.

Right of appeal against NRA's decisions

39.20   Any foreign or Ukrainian undertaking affected by a particular administrative act of the NCCIR may bring a court action seeking annulment of such administrative act, recovery of damages, or both.[23] According to applicable rules governing jurisdiction, disputes with central governmental authorities (such as the NCCIR) are heard by the Kiev District Administrative Court or, in the case of individual acts, at the discretion of the claimant, by the administrative court having jurisdiction in the place of residence of the claimant.[24]

Generally, there are no legal restrictions on enforcement of court decisions against state authorities. If a court decision renders a particular administrative act void, such administrative act will be annulled within the prescribed period of time. However, an undertaking seeking to recover damages from a state authority may find it difficult due to possible unavailability of state budget funds for such recovery.

---

18   As prescribed by art 18(14) Telecommunications Law.
19   Law of Ukraine No 2210-III 'On the Protection of Economic Competition', dated 11 January 2001.
20   Art 39 Telecommunications Law.
21   Art 18(22) Telecommunications Law.
22   Art 18(19) Telecommunications Law.
23   Explanation No 02–5/35 of the Presidium of the Supreme Commercial Court of Ukraine 'On Certain Practical Issues of Resolving Disputes Related to the Recognition of Acts of State or Other Authorities Ineffective', dated 26 January 2000.
24   Art 19 Code of Administrative Procedure, dated 6 July 2005.

'Significant Market Power' as a Fundamental Prerequisite of Regulation

Definition of SMP

39.21   The Telecommunications Law defines SMP only with respect to the market for traffic transmission. Specifically, an SMP operator is defined as a telecommunications operator, whose share of net income for the preceding 12 months originating from traffic transmission in the fixed-line or mobile networks exceeds 25 per cent of the total net income of all telecommunications operators for the same period.[25] This SMP definition was introduced into the Telecommunications Law in 2010. Previously, the concept of SMP had been expressed through the concept of a monopolistic operator, defined as an operator who occupies the monopolistic (dominant)[26] position on the market of specific telecommunications services on a nationwide or regional basis.[27] While these two concepts exist concurrently in the Telecommunications Law, under the proposed amendments to the Telecommunications Law, only the SMP concept will be used and it will be extended to all telecommunications markets as defined by the NCCIR.

39.22   Pursuant to the Competition Law, an undertaking is deemed to occupy a monopolistic position if it is the sole market-player in a relevant market, or it is not subject to significant competition due to the limited access available to other entities to the procurement of raw materials or sale of goods or services, existing barriers to access in to the market by other entities, privileges enjoyed by such undertaking, or other circumstances.[28]

39.23   An undertaking is presumed to enjoy a monopolistic position in a relevant market if its market share exceeds 35 per cent of the relevant market, unless such undertaking proves that it is subject to significant competition. An undertaking may be deemed to enjoy a monopolistic market position if its market share is equal to or less than 35 per cent but it is not subject to significant competition, in particular, due to a comparatively insignificant market share of its competitors.

39.24   Each of two or more entities is deemed to enjoy a monopolistic position in a respective market if there is no significant competition between them with respect to a particular product and they, jointly, are not subject to significant competition from other market players. Finally, each of several business entities is deemed to occupy a monopolistic position if the following conditions apply:

- the combined market share of no more than three business entities, to which the largest market shares in a relevant market belong, exceeds 50 per cent of the relevant market; or
- the combined market share of no more than five business entities, to which the largest market shares in a relevant market belong, exceeds 70 per cent of the relevant market:

provided that such business entities are unable to prove that there is significant competition between them with respect to a specific product or they are subject to significant competition by the other market players.

---

25   Art 1 Telecommunications Law.
26   The terms 'monopolistic' and 'dominant' are used synonymously in Ukrainian law. For convenience, the term 'monopolistic' will be used throughout the rest of this chapter.
27   Art 1 Telecommunications Law.
28   Art 12(1) Competition Law.

39.25 The determination of whether a specific undertaking or group of entities has a monopolistic position in a relevant market falls within the authority of the AMC.[29]

Definition of relevant markets

39.26 The 2010 amendments to the Telecommunications Law delegated to the NCCIR the authority to define relevant markets for the purpose of improving regulation of such markets, enhancing competition, and defining the SMP operators. According to the Procedure for Market Analysis of Traffic Transmission Markets and Defining SMP Operators, adopted by the NCCIR,[30] the following markets are defined as traffic transmission markets:

- markets of services of traffic termination in the fixed-line networks;
- markets of services of traffic termination in the mobile networks; and
- markets of services of traffic transit in the fixed-line and mobile networks.

39.27 In 2011 the NCCIR conducted an analysis of services of traffic termination in the fixed-line and mobile networks. The NCCIR based its conclusions on the assumption that a telecommunications operator, providing services of traffic termination on its own telecommunications network, is the only entity which can provide such services on its network and it, therefore, has 100 per cent market share. Consequently, each telecommunications operator providing services of traffic termination is identified as an SMP operator in the market of traffic termination on the fixed-line or mobile networks respectively.

39.28 As a result, 433 undertakings were identified as SMP operators in the market of traffic termination in fixed-line networks and eight undertakings were identified as SMP operators in the market of traffic termination in mobile networks.

39.29 The Competition Law imposes general restrictions and obligations on a monopolistic undertaking. In addition, SMP and monopolistic operators are required to comply with certain telecommunications-specific restrictions and obligations. In particular, a SMP and monopolistic operator may not refuse interconnection with another telecommunications operator.[31] Furthermore, an SMP and monopolistic operator is required to provide the NCCIR with detailed information regarding the technical and commercial conditions for interconnection with its network, to be published by the NCCIR, on an annual basis, in a catalogue of interconnection offers.

39.30 The NCCIR regulates the following matters with respect to SMP and monopolistic operators:

- technical, organisational and commercial conditions for interconnection;
- interconnection fees charged (capped or fixed tariffs are established both for SMP and monopolistic operators); and
- tariffs for the lease of communications channels charged (capped or fixed tariffs are established for monopolistic operators only).

---

29 Art 37(4) Telecommunications Law.
30 Decision of the NCCIR No 444 dated 25 August 2011.
31 Art 60(5) Telecommunications Law.

39.31 The NCCIR may also impose obligations on SMP and monopolistic operators to develop and provide universal services in certain areas of Ukraine with low penetration of telecommunications services.

NRA's Regulatory Duties concerning Rights of Way, Co-location and Facility Sharing

39.32 Article 10(6) Telecommunications Law provides that telecommunications operators have rights of way over the 'lands reserved for communications purposes'[32] for laying out underground telecommunications networks or their repair. Cabinet of Ministers of Ukraine determines the tariffs for exercising such rights of way.

39.33 Rights of way over particular property, regardless of its ownership, may be granted on the basis of an agreement with the property owner, law, testament, or on the basis of a court decision.[33] As most land in Ukraine is publically owned (whether national or municipal), in practice, rights of way are granted by decisions of the relevant local councils allocating particular land plots for specific purposes, eg for laying out telecommunications lines or installing masts.

39.34 Current Ukrainian laws and regulations do not address co-location and facility sharing. However, to enhance development of next generation networks, the NCCIR is preparing a draft law permitting joint use of telecommunications equipment and networks by operators.

REGULATION OF MARKET ENTRY

The General Authorisation of Electronic Communications

39.35 An undertaking wishing to provide telecommunications services must apply to the NCCIR at least a month in advance of the commencement of the services for inclusion into the Telecommunications Register.[34] The NCCIR must decide whether to include the undertaking in the Telecommunications Register within ten business days after receipt of the application and must notify the undertaking within the following three business days. If the NCCIR rejects the application, it must notify the undertaking within ten business days after receipt of the application, and include in the notice the reasons for such rejection. In such a case, the undertaking may submit a new application once it has remedied the deficiencies in the rejected application.

39.36 If an undertaking wishes to provide telecommunications services that are subject to licensing, it must, together with the application for inclusion in the Telecommunications Register, submit an application for a licence, including required supplementary documents such as, eg copies of statutory documents, title

---

32   Land plots allocated for air and cable telephone and telegraph lines and satellite means of communications, art 75 Land Code of the Ukraine, dated 25 October 2001. Such land may be held in state, municipal, or private property.

33   Art 100 Land Code. Since easements/servitudes, including rights of way, are a relatively new concept in the Ukraine, there is as yet little guidance as to how a court should exercise such powers.

34   Art 42(1) Telecommunications Law.

documents to production facilities, plans of establishment and use of telecommunications networks, documents confirming availability of financial and human resources.

39.37 The following telecommunications services are subject to licensing by the NCCIR:

- local, inter-city, and international fixed line telecommunications services (including with use of wireless technologies) with the right to engage in maintenance and operation of telecommunications networks and to lease communications channels;
- mobile telecommunications services with the right to engage in technical maintenance and operation of telecommunications networks and to lease communications channels; and
- technical maintenance and operation of telecommunications networks, television and radio air broadcasting networks, wire broadcasting networks, and television networks.

39.38 The NCCIR must decide whether to issue a licence within 30 business days from the date of receipt of the application.[35] The NCCIR must notify the applicant of its decision within three business days.[36]

39.39 If the NCCIR decides to issue a licence, it must inform the applicant of the amount of the official fees the applicant must pay for issuance of the licence, and the procedure for payment and receipt of the licence.[37]

39.40 An applicant may appeal to the courts a decision refusing to issue a licence.

39.41 A licence grants the right to an undertaking to provide particular telecommunications services, within a certain territory and on certain licensing terms and conditions. In addition to the standard licensing terms and conditions set by the NCCIR (applicable to all undertakings providing a particular type of telecommunications services), a licence may provide for special terms and conditions established by the NCCIR on a case-by-case basis. The NCCIR may amend such special licensing terms and conditions on renewal of the licence.[38]

39.42 The duration of a licence is determined by the NCCIR on a case-by-case basis, but may not be shorter than five years.[39] A licence may be renewed by filing an application with the NCCIR at least four months before its expiration. The NCCIR may not refuse the renewal of a licence if the licensee has complied with the licensing terms and conditions, or if the failure to comply with the licensing terms and conditions was caused by events or circumstances beyond the licensee's control.[40]

39.43 The NCCIR performs state oversight over the telecommunications market via regular and extraordinary audits and other measures targeted at prevention and revealing and remedying breaches by market players. If an audit uncovers a violation of telecommunications laws and regulations, the NCCIR issues an order requiring the licensee to remedy the violation. The undertaking issued such an order must remedy the violation within the designated time and must report to the

---

35   Art 46(1) Telecommunications Law.
36   Art 46(2) Telecommunications Law.
37   Art 46(4) Telecommunications Law.
38   Art 49(5) Telecommunications Law.
39   Art 48(5) Telecommunications Law.
40   Art 49(2) Telecommunications Law.

NCCIR accordingly.[41] Failure to remedy the violation or a repeated breach is a ground for revocation of the licence.[42]

39.44   The NCCIR may decide to limit the number of licences and make a 'competition announcement' if it is necessary to ensure the efficient use of networks and limited resources.[43] The NCCIR must issue licences on a competitive basis within four months after the competition announcement. The results of a competition may be appealed to the courts.

39.45   The NCCIR may revoke a licence on the following grounds:[44]

- application for revocation by the licensee;
- submission by a licensee of false information when applying for a licence;
- transfer of a licence to another undertaking or individual for the purpose of providing telecommunications services;
- failure of an operator or provider to remedy a violation of the licensing terms and conditions;
- an operator's or provider's repeated prevention of NCCIR officials from conducting an audit of the operator or provider;
- repeated violation of the licensing terms and conditions; and
- winding up of a corporate operator or provider or death of an individual operator or provider.

Rights of Use for Radio Frequencies

General regulatory approach

39.46   The Radio Frequencies Law governs the use of radio frequencies. An undertaking intending to use radio frequencies must apply to the NCCIR for a licence. The NCCIR must decide whether to issue a licence within 60 business days from the date of the application. A licensee must pay official fees for the grant of a licence. In addition, a licensee must make monthly payments for the use of radio frequency resource.[45]

39.47   A licence is issued for the use of specific bands and channels of radio frequencies in specific regions or cities, for the purpose of providing certain telecommunications services. A licence is issued for a minimum period of five years and may be renewed by filing a renewal application at least four months prior to the expiration of the licence.[46]

39.48   The issue of a licence for the use of radio frequency resource is dependent, among other things, on whether there are frequencies available in the respective radio frequency resource that are not in use by other operators or by the military. The technical issues involved in the licensing procedure, falls within the competence of the Ukrainian State Centre for Radio Frequencies', a state enterprise that is subordinate to the NCCIR.

---

41   Art 19–1 Telecommunications Law.
42   Art 55(1) Telecommunications Law.
43   Art 47(1) Telecommunications Law.
44   Art 55 Telecommunications Law.
45   Arts 32 and 49 Radio Frequencies Law, Chapter XV of the Tax Code, dated 2 December 2010.
46   Arts 31(4) and 37(1) Radio Frequencies Law.

Admissible conditions

39.49   A number of special conditions are attached to a licence for the use of radio frequency resource:

- receipt by the licensee of a permit for the use of the respective radio emission device(s);
- use of certified equipment;
- the licensee's compliance with the health standards and requirements for the protection of the population from electromagnetic radiation; and
- a schedule for the commencement of the use of radio frequencies throughout different regions.[47]

Limitation of number of rights of use to be granted

39.50   A licence for the use of radio frequency resource shall be granted via tender if there is limited availability of radio frequencies.[48] The NCCIR defines the procedure for the tenders, results of which maybe appealed in court.

Frequency trading

39.51   Frequency trading is not permitted in Ukraine.[49]

Rights of Use for Numbers

General authorisations and granting of individual rights

39.52   An operator may obtain rights of use for numbers by filing an application with the NCCIR. The NCCIR must issue or refuse a permit for the use of numbers within one month from the application.[50] The permit is issued within three days of payment of the prescribed fee by the operator. The right of use for numbers is valid for the term of the licence, or for not less than five years in case the activity is not subject to licensing. While the right of use for numbers may not be assigned to a third party, the numbers assigned to an operator may be used by a provider holding a copy of the operator's license.

39.53   The NCCIR may withdraw all or some numbers if:

- the use of such numbers is not commenced within the timeframe specified in the relevant permit;
- the numbers are being misused (e g are transferred to a third party); or
- the relevant licence has expired, been revoked, or been invalidated.[51]

Admissible conditions

39.54   Conditions may be attached to a permit for the use of numbers, for example:

---

47   Art 36(2) Radio Frequencies Law.
48   Art 30(3) Radio Frequencies Law.
49   If the frequency license holder transfers the licence to another undertaking, through sale or otherwise, the licence will be revoked pursuant to art 38(1)(3) Radio Frequencies Law.
50   Art 70(2) Telecommunications Law.
51   Art 70(4) Telecommunications Law.

- conditions relating to the efficient and targeted use of the numbers in accordance with the requirements set out in the permit; or
- information about a client ordering short numbers. [52]

An operator must submit to the NCCIR annual information on its use of the numbers for which it has received a permit.

39.55 The Telecommunications Law[53] grants to subscribers the right of number portability and establishes the corresponding obligation of telecommunications operators and providers. To date, the NCCIR has not adopted a procedure for providing number portability.[54]

Limitation of number of rights of use to be granted

39.56 According to the Telecommunications Law, numbers are deemed to be a scarce resource. In case there are no numbers available in a particular territory, the NCCIR must arrange for creation of reserve numbers and, in the interim, may temporarily terminate consideration of applications for allocation of numbers in the territory.[55]

The NRA's Enforcement Powers

39.57 The NCCIR is vested with the regulatory powers of enforcing licensing conditions in accordance with the Telecommunications Law.[56] To that end, the NCCIR is authorised to conduct regular and extraordinary audits of the undertakings included in the Telecommunications Register.

39.58 Under the Telecommunications Law, to the extent required to conduct state oversight over the telecommunications market, the NCCIR is permitted unrestricted access to the property and facilities of telecommunications operators and providers and to obtain, free of charge, any information, clarifications, and other materials from business entities in the telecommunications market.[57]

39.59 If the NCCIR finds that an undertaking does not comply with the telecommunications laws and regulations, it must issue an order to remedy any breaches within a prescribed time limit.[58] An undertaking's failure to remedy such breaches within the prescribed time may result in the revocation of the relevant telecommunications licence.[59]

---

52 Order No 769 of the Nation Commission on Regulation of Communications 'On the Approval of the State Regulations of the Numbering Resource of the Public Communications Networks of Ukraine', dated 1 June 2007.
53 Art 32 (1)(16–1) Telecommunications Law.
54 Art 39 (1)(4–1) Telecommunications Law.
55 Chapter 1, cl 3.6, Order No 769 of the Nation Commission on Regulation of Communications 'On the Approval of the State Regulations of the Numbering Resource of the Public Communications Networks of Ukraine', dated 1 June 2007.
56 Art 19(3) Telecommunications Law.
57 Art 19(3) Telecommunications Law.
58 Art 19–1 (5) Telecommunications Law.
59 Art 55(1)(4) Telecommunications Law.

Administrative Charges and Fees for Rights of Use

39.60   The Cabinet of Ministers of Ukraine has established the following administrative fees for the right of use:[60]

- one-time fees for the issue of telecommunications services licences, which vary from €30 to €900,000 per licence;[61]
- one-time charges for the allocation of numbers, number blocks or codes, which vary from €0.05 to €1,000 per item;[62]
- one-time fees for the issue of licences for radio frequencies use, which vary from €17 to €136,000 per MHz in each region;[63] and
- monthly fees for radio frequencies use, which vary from €0.04 to €1,500 per MHz in each region.[64]

REGULATION OF NETWORK ACCESS AND INTERCONNECTION

Objectives and Scope of Access Regulation

39.61   The objectives of the NCCIR in regulating interconnection are:

- regulating technical, organisational, pricing, and commercial conditions of interconnection with SMP and monopolistic telecommunications operators; and
- ensuring effective competition, non-discrimination and fair conditions which are acceptable to the parties to interconnection agreements and are beneficial for end users.[65]

39.62   Interconnection-related provisions of Ukrainian telecommunications laws generally apply to network providers regardless of their market position,[66] although SMP and monopolistic operators have stricter obligations regarding interconnection.[67]

Basic Regulatory Concepts

39.63   The NCCIR regulates the manner of submission, consideration, and approval of proposals of operators in relation to interconnection of telecommunications networks, sets requirements applicable to agreements on interconnection of telecommunications networks, and regulates the relations of operations with respect to interconnection. In so doing, the NCCIR may adopt binding decisions on the merits of a dispute, which may be cancelled only in court.[68]

39.64   There is no definition of 'access' in Ukrainian law. 'Interconnection of telecommunications networks' is defined as 'the installation of physical and/or

---

60   The fees are paid in Ukrainian hryvnia, the amounts in euro provided in this chapter are approximate.
61   Resolution No 773 of the Cabinet of Ministers of Ukraine, dated 16 June 2004.
62   Resolution No 1147 of the Cabinet of Ministers of Ukraine, dated 27 December 2008.
63   Resolution No 200 of the Cabinet of Ministers of Ukraine, dated 22 February 2006.
64   Art 320 Tax Code.
65   Art 57 Telecommunications Law.
66   Chapter IX Telecommunications Law.
67   See para 39.64 below.
68   Arts 57(2), (3) Telecommunications Law.

logical connection between different telecommunications networks enabling users to exchange information directly or indirectly'.[69]

Access- and Interconnection-related Obligations with Respect to SMP Undertakings

39.65   Telecommunications operators having SMP or holding a monopolistic position may not reject interconnection with a telecommunications network of another operator at points which are indicated in the catalogue of interconnection offers, except where the interconnecting telecommunications network does not comply with the standards prescribed by the Telecommunications Law.[70] Moreover, the NCCIR fixes tariffs for access to telecommunications networks of operators which have SMP or hold a monopolistic position.[71] The NCCIR may also impose on operators which have SMP or hold a monopolistic position, obligations of price control, transparency, and non-discrimination.[72]

Regulatory Powers Applicable to All Market Participants

39.66   The following Telecommunications Law provisions (both obligations and rights) apply to all network operators regardless of their market position:

● obligation for material terms of interconnection agreements, such as technical conditions of interconnection and interconnection charges, to be the product of free negotiations between network operators;[73]
● obligation for interconnection charges to be based on the economic costs of providing interconnection;[74]
● right for interconnection disputes between operators to be resolved by the NCCIR on a timely basis and in a transparent manner,[75] and
● right to appeal to the court's rulings of the NCCIR on interconnection agreements.[76]

39.67   Telecommunications operators must, among other things, comply with technical requirements applicable to networks, provide other operators with information required for the preparation of interconnection agreements, ensure timely settlement under such agreements, avoid creating obstacles to interconnection, and exchange data on telecommunications services provided through interconnected networks.[77]

39.68   The Telecommunications Law provides for the settlement of disputes arising in connection with entry into, amendments to, and termination of interconnection agreements, national roaming services, number portability and use of personal numbers by the NCCIR upon an application from a party to such an

---

69   Art 1 Telecommunications Law.
70   Art 60(5) Telecommunications Law.
71   Art 57(4) Telecommunications Law.
72   Art 57(1)(4), 58 Telecommunications Law.
73   Art 57(1)(1) Telecommunications Law.
74   Art 57(1)(2) Telecommunications Law.
75   Art 57(2) Telecommunications Law.
76   Art 57(3) Telecommunications Law.
77   Art 58 Telecommunications Law.

agreement.[78] Any party who is not satisfied with an NCCIR decision may appeal such decision to a competent court.

REGULATION OF UNIVERSAL SERVICES AND USERS' RIGHTS

Regulation of Universal Service Obligations

39.69 'Public (universal) telecommunications services' are defined as a minimum of telecommunications services, identified by the Telecommunications Law, that are available for all customers throughout Ukraine.[79] Universal services include:

- connection of terminating equipment to fixed-line public telecommunications networks ('public (universal) access');
- local fixed-line voice telephony service;
- free access to emergency services; and
- access to operator services via public payphones.[80]

In 2011, the technological neutrality principle was introduced in relation to the public (universal) services, ensuring that such services may be provided via both wired and wireless access technologies.

39.70 The NCCIR may impose obligations to provide a universal service on SMP or monopolistic operators and on regional fixed-line operators in certain areas of Ukraine with low telecommunications services penetration.[81]

Quality of service: securing 'net neutrality'

39.71 Net neutrality is not directly regulated in Ukraine. However, the Rules of accepting and rendering telecommunications services, adopted by the Regulation of the Cabinet of Ministers of Ukraine, dated 11 April 2012 No 295, directly or indirectly establish some rules of net neutrality, mostly through spelling out the rights of consumers and the obligations of service providers.

DATA PROTECTION

Confidentiality of Communications

39.72 Telecommunications network providers and service providers are required to take technical and organisational measures to ensure protection of telecommunications facilities, telecommunications networks, and information which is transmitted via these networks.[82]

Exceptions from the confidentiality of communications principle may be made exclusively by a court in accordance with the law, with the purpose of preventing

---

78   Art 18(19), 61(1) Telecommunications Law.
79   Art 1 Telecommunications Law.
80   Art 62(1) Telecommunications Law.
81   Art 64(5) Telecommunications Law.
82   Art 9(3) Telecommunications Law.

crime or ascertaining the truth in the course of a criminal investigation, provided it is not possible to obtain information by any other means.[83]

39.73   As a general rule, the collection, storage, use, and dissemination of confidential information about an individual without his or her consent is not permitted, except in cases determined by law, and only in the interest of national security, economic welfare, or human rights.[84] Network operators and service providers must ensure, and are liable for, the confidentiality of user information.[85]

Traffic Data and Location Data

39.74   Current Ukrainian laws do not define traffic data or location. However, operators (network providers) are required to keep records on telecommunications services actually provided and may disclose information on users and services in certain limited cases determined by law.[86]

Data Retention

39.75   Under the Telecommunications Law,[87] telecommunications operators and providers must ensure, and are liable for, the safekeeping of consumers' data, including information about the nature and time of services provided, and contents of correspondence. Public telephone directories may contain information about names and last names of persons (names of an entity), and their addresses and telephone numbers, provided that the consumers agreed in the service agreement to disclose such information. The consumer may request, with no charge, to have the consumer's information removed from the electronic directories, partially or in full. The consumers' information and the information about services provided to the consumer may be disclosed only in case and according to the procedures provided by law. In practice, those cases are limited to access to information for law enforcement purposes, which requires permission to be granted by court. In other cases a written consent of the consumer is required.

Itemised Billing

39.76   Itemised billing is not currently regulated in Ukraine.

Presentation and Restriction of Calling and Connected line identification

39.77   Calling and connected line identification is not currently regulated in Ukraine. Operators typically provide calling line and connected line identification services by default and free of charge. In practice, subscribers can order calling line identification restriction services.

Automatic Call Forwarding

39.78   Automatic call forwarding is not currently regulated in Ukraine.

---

83   Art 31 Constitution of Ukraine, dated 28 June 1996.
84   Art 32 Constitution of Ukraine.
85   Art 34(1) Telecommunications Law.
86   Eg as requested by competent Ukrainian authorities.
87   Art 34 Telecommunications Law.

Directories of Subscribers

39.79 Telephone directories, and their electronic versions and databases of referral and information services, may contain the family name, first name, middle name, title, address, and telephone number of a subscriber only if the subscriber has agreed, in the relevant telecommunications services contract, that such information may be made publicly available. A subscriber has the right to have his complete or partial information withdrawn, free of charge, from electronic databases.[88]

Unsolicited Communications

39.80 Dissemination of unsolicited communications ('spam') both by operators and providers of telecommunications and by subscribers is prohibited by the Rules of Receiving and Rendering Telecommunications Services adopted by the Cabinet of Ministers of Ukraine on 11 April 2012.[89] Dissemination of spam by a subscriber is a ground for temporary suspension of provision of telecommunications services. Moreover, the Criminal Code[90] has been amended to protect Internet users from spam resulting in malfunction or breaking down of computers, automated systems, computer networks, or networks of electronic communications.[91]

39.81 The only way in which unsolicited communications are permitted is upon obtaining prior consent of the addressee. Ukrainian law does not include the concept of, or rules on, opt-in and opt-out systems.

---

88 Art 34(2) Telecommunications Law.
89 Decision No 295.
90 Criminal Code of Ukraine, dated 5 April 2001.
91 Art 363–1 Criminal Code.

Index

All references are to paragraph number.

Latvia – *contd*
portability of numbers, 20.32
price control, 20.40
privacy
    automatic call forwarding, 20.78
    calling line identification, 20.77
    confidentiality of
        communications, 20.64–20.71
    connected line identification, 20.77
    data retention, 20.72
    directories of subscribers, 20.79
    itemised billing, 20.76
    location data, 20.73–20.75
    subscribers directory, 20.79
    traffic data, 20.73–20.75
quality of services
    end user rights, 20.59–20.62
    universal service obligations,
        20.49–20.51
regulatory principles
    appeal against NRA's decisions, 20.15
    co-location, 20.21–20.22
    co-operation by NRA with
        Commission, 20.16
    facility sharing, 20.21–20.22
    'Internet freedom', 20.8
    national regulatory authorities,
        20.9–20.14
    rights of way, 20.21–20.22
    scope of regulation, 20.7
    significant market power, 20.17–20.20
retail markets regulation, 20.54–20.55
retail tariffs, 20.49–20.51
rights of use for numbers
    fees, 20.34
    general authorisations, 20.30–20.32
    portability of numbers, 20.32
rights of use for radio frequencies
    conditions, 20.27–20.28
    fees, 20.34
    general authorisations, 20.26
    granting individual rights, 20.26
    limitation of number to be
        granted, 20.29
rights of way, 20.21–20.22
significant market power
    definition, 20.17
    imposition of remedies, 20.20
    relevant markets, 20.18–20.19
specific access obligations, 20.40
subscribers directory, 20.79
traffic data, 20.73–20.75
transparency obligations, 20.40
Universal Service Directive
    end user rights, 20.56–20.62
    facilitating change of provider, 20.63
    retail markets, 20.54–20.55
    universal service obligations,
        20.47–20.53
universal service obligations
    cost calculation, 20.52–20.53
    designation of undertakings
        obliged to provide, 20.48
    financing of services, 20.52–20.53
    quality of services, 20.49–20.51

Latvia – *contd*
universal service obligations – *contd*
    retail tariffs, 20.49–20.51
    scope, 20.47
    users' expenditures, 20.49–20.51
Leased Lines Directive (92/44/EEC)
generally, 1.3
Licensing Directive (97/13/EC)
generally, 1.4
Lithuania
access and interconnection powers
    applicable to all market
        participants
    digital radio and television
        broadcasting services,
        21.70–21.72
    end-to-end connectivity, 21.68
    roaming services, 21.69
access and interconnection powers
    applicable to SMP
        undertakings
    accounting separation, 21.64
    cost accounting, 21.63
    functional separation, 21.65
    imposition of obligations in
        practice, 21.66
    introduction, 21.59
    non-discrimination obligations, 21.61
    price control, 21.63
    regulatory powers, 21.67
    specific access obligations, 21.62
    transparency obligations, 21.60
Access Directive
    basic concepts, 21.57–21.58
    objective of regulation, 21.56
    powers applicable to all market
        participants, 21.68–21.72
    powers applicable to market
        participants designated as
        having SMP, 21.59–21.67
    scope of regulation, 21.56
accounting separation, 21.64
administrative charges, 21.54
allocation of frequencies, 21.44
appeal against NRA's decisions,
    21.25–21.26
Authorisation Directive
    administrative charges, 21.54
    enforcement by NRA, 21.53
    fees for rights of use, 21.54
    general authorisation, 21.41–21.42
    rights of use for numbers, 21.48–21.52
    rights of use for radio
        frequencies, 21.43–21.47
    transitional regulations, 21.55
automatic call forwarding, 21.104
basic policy, 21.1–21.5
calling line identification, 21.103
co-location, 21.38–21.40
confidentiality of communications,
    21.92–21.97
connected line identification, 21.103
co-operation by NRA with
    Commission, 21.27–21.29
cost accounting, 21.63